reelin' & rockin'

✧ Rock & Roll Reference Series ✧

1. **ALL TOGETHER NOW**
   The First Complete Beatles
   Discography, 1961-1975
   by Harry Castleman & Walter J. Podrazik

2. **THE BEATLES AGAIN**
   (Sequel to *All Together Now*)
   by Harry Castleman & Walter J. Podrazik

3. **A DAY IN THE LIFE**
   The Beatles Day-By-Day, 1960-1970
   by Tom Schultheiss

4. **THINGS WE SAID TODAY**
   The Complete Lyrics and a Concordance
   to The Beatles Songs, 1962-1970
   by Colin Campbell & Allan Murphy

5. **YOU CAN'T DO THAT**
   Beatles Bootlegs
   & Novelty Records, 1963-1980
   by Charles Reinhart

6. **SURF'S UP!**
   The Beach Boys On Record, 1961-1981
   by Brad Elliott

7. **COLLECTING THE BEATLES**
   An Introduction & Price Guide to Fab Four
   Collectibles, Records & Memorabilia
   by Barbara Fenick

8. **JAILHOUSE ROCK**
   The Bootleg Records of Elvis Presley, 1970-1983
   by Lee Cotten & Howard DeWitt

9. **THE LITERARY LENNON:
   A COMEDY OF LETTERS**
   The First Study of All the Major and Minor
   Writings of John Lennon
   by Dr. James Sauceda

10. **THE END OF THE BEATLES?**
    (Sequel to *The Beatles Again* and
    All Together Now)
    by Harry Castleman & Walter J. Podrazik

11. **HERE, THERE & EVERYWHERE**
    The First International Beatles
    Bibliography, 1962-1982
    by Carol D. Terry

12. **CHUCK BERRY—ROCK 'N' ROLL MUSIC**
    Second Edition, Revised
    by Howard A. DeWitt

13. **ALL SHOOK UP**
    Elvis Day-By-Day, 1954-1977
    by Lee Cotten

14. **WHO'S NEW WAVE IN MUSIC**
    An Illustrated Encyclopedia, 1976-1982
    by David Bianco

15. **THE ILLUSTRATED DISCOGRAPHY
    OF SURF MUSIC, 1961-1965**
    Third Edition
    by John Blair

16. **COLLECTING THE BEATLES, VOLUME 2**
    An Introduction & Price Guide to Fab Four
    Collectibles, Records & Memorabilia
    by Barbara Fenick

17. **HEART OF STONE**
    The Definitive Rolling Stones
    Discography, 1962-1983
    by Felix Aeppli

18. **BEATLEFAN**
    The Authoritative Publication of Record
    For Fans of the Beatles, Volumes 1 & 2
    Reprint Edition, With Additions

19. **YESTERDAY'S PAPERS**
    The Rolling Stones In Print, 1963-1984
    by Jessica MacPhail

20. **EVERY LITTLE THING**
    The Definitive Guide To Beatles
    Recording Variations, Rare Mixes &
    Other Musical Oddities, 1958-1986
    by William McCoy & Mitchell McGeary

21. **STRANGE DAYS**
    The Music Of John, Paul, George & Ringo
    Twenty Years On
    by Walter J. Podrazik

22. **SEQUINS & SHADES**
    The Michael Jackson Reference Guide
    by Carol D. Terry

23. **WILD & INNOCENT**
    The Recordings of
    Bruce Springsteen, 1973-1985
    by Brad Elliott

24. **TIME IS ON MY SIDE**
    The Rolling Stones
    Day-By-Day, 1962-1986
    by Alan Stewart & Cathy Sanford

25. **HEAT WAVE**
    The Motown Fact Book
    by David Bianco

26. **BEATLEFAN**
    The Authoritative Publication of Record
    For Fans of the Beatles, Volumes 3 & 4
    Reprint Edition, With Additions

27. **RECONSIDER BABY**
    The Definitive Elvis
    Sessionography, 1954-1977
    by Ernst Jorgensen, Erik Rasmussen &
    Johnny Mikkelsen

Available only through Popular Culture, Ink., P.O. Box 1839, Ann Arbor, Michigan 48106
Phone: 1-800-678-8828

28 **THE MONKEES:**
A MANUFACTURED IMAGE
The Ultimate Reference Guide to Monkee Memories & Memorabilia
by Ed Reilly, Maggie McManus & Bill Chadwick

29 **RETURN TO SENDER**
The First Complete Discography Of Elvis Tribute & Novelty Records, 1956-1986
by Howard Banney

30 **THE CHILDREN OF NUGGETS**
The Definitive Guide To "Psychedelic Sixties" Punk Rock On Compilation Albums
by David Walters

31 **SHAKE, RATTLE & ROLL**
The Golden Age Of American Rock 'N' Roll, Volume 1: 1952-1955
by Lee Cotten

32 **THE ILLUSTRATED DISCOGRAPHY OF HOT ROD MUSIC, 1961-1965**
by John Blair & Stephen McParland

33 **POSITIVELY BOB DYLAN**
A Thirty-Year Discography, Concert & Recording Session Guide, 1960-1991
by Michael Krogsgaard

34 **OFF THE RECORD**
Motown By Master Number, 1959-1989 Volume 1: Singles
by Reginald J. Bartlette

35 **LISTENING TO THE BEATLES**
An Audiophile's Guide to the Sound of the Fab Four, Volume 1: Singles
by David Schwartz

36 **ELVIS—THE SUN YEARS**
The Story Of Elvis Presley In The Fifties
by Howard A. DeWitt

37 **HEADBANGERS**
The Worldwide MegaBook Of Heavy Metal Bands
by Mark Hale

38 **THAT'S ALL**
Bobby Darin On Record, Stage & Screen
by Jeff Bleiel

39 **REELIN' & ROCKIN'**
The Golden Age Of American Rock 'N' Roll, Volume 2: 1956-1959
by Lee Cotten

✧ Rock & Roll Remembrances Series ✧

1 **AS I WRITE THIS LETTER**
An American Generation Remembers The Beatles
Edited by Marc A. Catone

2 **THE LONGEST COCKTAIL PARTY**
An Insider's Diary of The Beatles, Their Million-Dollar Apple Empire and Its Wild Rise and Fall
Reprint Edition, With Additions
by Richard DiLello

3 **AS TIME GOES BY**
Living In The Sixties
Reprint Edition, With Additions
by Derek Taylor

4 **A CELLARFUL OF NOISE**
Reprint Edition, With Additions
by Brian Epstein

5 **THE BEATLES AT THE BEEB**
The Story Of Their Radio Career, 1962-1965
Reprint Edition, With Additions
by Kevin Howlett

6 **THE BEATLES READER**
A Selection Of Contemporary Views, News, & Reviews Of The Beatles In Their Heyday
Edited by Charles P. Neises

7 **THE BEATLES DOWN UNDER**
The 1964 Australia & New Zealand Tour
Reprint Edition, With Additions
by Glenn A. Baker

8 **LONG LONELY HIGHWAY**
A 1950's Elvis Scrapbook
Reprint Edition, With Additions
by Ger Rijff

9 **IKE'S BOYS**
The Story Of The Everly Brothers
by Phyllis Karpp

10 **ELVIS—FROM MEMPHIS TO HOLLYWOOD**
Memories From My Twelve Years With Elvis Presley
by Alan Fortas

11 **SAVE THE LAST DANCE FOR ME**
The Musical Legacy Of The Drifters, 1953-1993
by Tony Allan with Faye Treadwell

12 **TURN ME ON, DEAD MAN**
The Complete Story of the Paul McCartney Death Hoax
by Andru J. Reeve

Available only through Popular Culture, Ink., P.O. Box 1839, Ann Arbor, Michigan 48106
Phone: 1-800-678-8828

This book is dedicated to the memories of

Buddy Holly
1936-1959

Ritchie Valens
1941-1959

Jay P. Richardson
(The Big Bopper)
1930-1959

Eddie Cochran
1938-1960

Jesse Belvin
1932-1960

Sam Cooke
1931-1964

Johnny Burnette
1934-1964

Little Willie John
1937-1966

Frankie Lymon
1942-1968

Jim Drake
(Nervous Norvous)
d. 1968

Tommy Edwards
1922-1969

Gene Vincent
1935-1970

James Shepherd
(The Heartbeats;
Shep and The
Limelights)
d. 1970

King Curtis
(Ousley)
1934-1971

Thomas Wayne
1940-1971

David Seville
1911-1972

Billy Williams
1916-1972

Clyde McPhatter
1932-1972

Bobby Darin
1936-1973

Ivory Joe Hunter
1914-1974

Jimmy Reed
1925-1976

Elvis Presley
1935-1977

Bob Luman
1937-1978

Ray Smith
1934-1979

Larry Williams
1935-1980

Warren Smith
1932-1980

Janey Vogel
(The Skyliners)
d. 1980

David Lynch
(The Platters)
d. 1981

Ronnie Self
1938-1981

Roy Brown
1925-1981

Bill Justis
1926-1982

Joe Tex
1933-1982

Danny Rapp
(Danny and
The Juniors)
1941-1983

**Little Esther
Phillips**
1935-1984

Ricky Nelson
1940-1985

Bobby Nunn
(The Coasters)
1927-1986

Eskew Reeder
(Esquirita)
d. 1986

O'Kelly Isley
(The Isley Brothers)
1937-1986

Roy Orbison
1936-1988

**Johnnie Sanders
Richardson**
(Johnnie and Joe)
d. 1988

Paul Robi
(The Platters)
d. 1989

Patti McCabe
(The Poni-Tails)
d. 1989

Bobby Day
1932-1990

Kripp Johnson
(The Dell-Vikings)
d. 1990

Thurston Harris
1931-1990

Dee Clark
1938-1990

Margo Lopez
(The Tune Weavers)
d. 1991

Tony Williams
(The Platters)
1928-1992

Jimmy Weston
(The Danleers)
d. 1993

Marv Johnson
1938-1993

Conway Twitty
1933-1993

Each of them,
done too soon....

reelin' & rockin'

THE GOLDEN AGE OF AMERICAN ROCK 'N ROLL, VOLUME II: 1956-1959

by
Lee Cotten

Popular Culture, Ink.
1995

Copyright © 1995 by Lee Cotten.
All Rights Reserved.

No part of this data may be may be reproduced, stored in a retrieval system, or transmitted in any form or by any means, electronic, mechanical, photocopying, recording, or otherwise, without prior written permission of the copyright proprietor thereof.

Cover art is copyright © 1995 by
Popular Culture, Ink.
All Rights Reserved.

Book design and layout by
by Tom Schultheiss.

ISBN 1-56075-039-1
LC 87-63455

Published by
Popular Culture, Ink.
P.O. Box 1839
Ann Arbor, MI 48106

PCI Collector Editions
are published especially for discerning collectors and libraries.
Each Collector Edition title is released in limited quantities
identified by edition, printing number, and number of copies.
Unlike trade editions, they are not generally available in bookstores.

10 9 8 7 6 5 4 3 2 1
(First edition, first printing: 1000 copies)

Printed in the United States of America

"The best rock-and-roll books in the world!"

Contents

Preface xv

The Golden Age of American Rock 'n Roll, 1956-1959

1956 1
1957 101
1958 217
1959 335

MONTH-BY-MONTH GUIDE TO EVENTS

	1956	1957	1958	1959
A Look Ahead	3	103	219	337
January	8	107	222	341
February	17	115	231	350
March	27	124	239	359
April	35	133	249	369
May	44	141	258	379
June	53	151	268	389
July	60	160	278	399
August	67	169	287	408
September	74	178	296	417
October	81	189	305	428
November	88	198	315	438
December	94	207	325	449

TOP RECORDS OF THE MONTH

	1956	1957	1958	1959
January	12	110	225	345
February	22	119	234	354
March	30	127	243	363
April	39	137	253	373
May	47	145	262	383
June	57	155	272	394
July	62	163	281	402
August	70	173	291	413
September	77	183	299	422
October	84	193	309	432
November	90	202	319	444
December	96	211	328	452

ARTISTS OF THE MONTH

Paul Anka 434	Carl Dobkins, Jr. 414	Mickey & Sylvia 120
Frankie Avalon 374	Bill Doggett 84	Ricky Nelson 283
Chuck Berry 263	Fats Domino 57	Carl Perkins 48
Jimmy Bowen 128	The Everly Brothers 156	The Platters 254
Buchanan & Goodman 70	Fabian 403	Elvis Presley 40
The Champs 244	The Fleetwoods 445	Lloyd Price 364
Jimmy Clanton 301	Connie Francis 346	Jimmie Rodgers 194
Dick Clark 13	George Hamilton IV . 91	The Royal Teens 235
Sanford Clark 78	Buddy Holly &	Bobby Rydell 454
The Coasters 165	The Crickets 184	Santo & Johnny 424
Sam Cooke 203	Ivory Joe Hunter 97	Jack Scott 292
Dave "Baby" Cortez .. 384	Sonny James 111	David Seville 273
Danny &	Johnny &	The Teddy Bears 329
The Juniors 227	The Hurricanes 424	Conway Twitty 320
Bobby Darin 395	Buddy Knox 128	Ritchie Valens 355
Bobby Day & The	Jerry Lee Lewis 212	Gene Vincent 63
Hollywood Flames . 310	Little Richard 22	Larry Williams 174
The Dell-Vikings 146	Frankie Lymon &	Sheb Wooley 273
The Diamonds 138	The Teenagers 31	

SIDEBAR MINI-BIOGRAPHIES

Lee Allen 287	The Cadillacs 169	The Dells 271
Annette 360	Jo Ann Campbell 108	Mark Dinning 440
The Applejacks 242	Johnny Carroll 370	Dicky Doo &
The Aquatones 239	Johnny Cash 172	The Dont's 210
The Bell-Notes 362	The Channels 68	Don & Dewey 126
Tony Bellus 353	The Chantels 201	Harold Dorman 452
Jesse Belvin 182	Bobby Charles 28	The Dubs 198
Joe Bennett &	Clifton Chenier 47	Huelyn Duvall 250
The Sparkletones .. 162	Eugene Church 391	Tommy Edwards 307
Bob Bernard 350	Dee Clark 190	Donnie Elbert 233
The Big Bopper 278	Joe Clay 44	The Eldorados 9
Bobby "Blue" Bland .. 96	The Cleftones 61	The Elegants 280
Eddie Bo 351	Eddie Cochran .. 141, 439	Esquirita 298
The Bobbettes 155	Jackie Lee Cochran .. 268	Paul Evans 359
Eddie Bond 38	Cozy Cole 316	Tommy Facenda 451
Clarence Brown 152	The Collins Kids 81	The Falcons 88
James Brown 199	The Cookies 11	Narvel Felts 281
Roy Brown 135	Billy Craddock 369	The Fiestas 344
Johnny Burdette	The Crescendos 223	The Fireballs 402
Trio 36	The Crests 342	The Fireflies 429
Sonny Burgess 270	Pat Cupp 76	The Five Keys 170
Solomon Burke 107	Mac Curtis 37	The Five Satins 125
The Cadets 54	The Danleers 288	The Flamingos 154

Artist	Page
Eddie Fontaine	180
Frankie Ford	296
The Four Lovers	74
The Four Preps	241
John Fred & The Playboys	325
Bobby Freeman	305
Ernie Freeman	289
Lowell Fulson	18
The Gladiolas	115
Charlie Gracie	209
Larry Hall	432
Thurston Harris	181
Wilbert Harrison	393
Dale Hawkins	136
Ronnie Hawkins	372
Screamin' Jay Hawkins	89
The Heartbeats	260
Bobby Helms	171
Bobby Hendricks	290
Clarence Henry	82
Ersel Hickey	232
Joe Houston	55
Ferlin Huskey	134
The Impalas	341
The Islanders	418
The Isley Brothers	410
Wanda Jackson	90
Jan & Arnie	253
The Jodimars	222
Little Willie John	27
Johnny & Joe	124
Buddy Johnson	77
Marv Johnson	352
Bill Justis	258
The Kalin Twins	225
Jerry Keller	438
Carole King	400
King Curtis	60
Sonny Knight	67
The Kodaks	269
Kathy Linden	261
Little Anthony & The Imperials	308
Little Bill	389
Little Esther	46
Little Joe & The Thrillers	224
Trini Lopez	343
Robin Luke	299
Bob Luman	192
Lewis Lymon & The Teenchords	116
Carl Mann	401
Janis Martin	19
Jimmy McCracklin	249
Clyde McPhatter	95
The Meadowlarks	189
The Mello-Kings	309
Sal Mineo	319
The Monotones	231
The Mystics	381
Sandy Nelson	442
Nervous Norvous	45
The Olympics	315
Junior Parker	142
Bill Parsons	318
The Passions	431
Paul Peek	240
Ray Peterson	208
Phil Phillips	382
The Playmates	161
The Poni-Tails	178
"Groovy" Joe Poovey	200
Johnny Preston	392
Arthur Prysock	419
The Rainbows	69
Marvin Rainwater	109
The Ravens	17
Jimmy Reed	8
Della Reese	160
Jody Reynolds	259
Cliff Richard	408
Jay P. Richardson	278
Billy Lee Riley	117
Johnny Rivers	412
The Rivieras	449
Marty Robbins	443
Floyd Robinson	380
The Rock-A-Teens	421
Doug Sahm	399
Tommy Sands	144
Jimmy Scott	306
Ronnie Self	133
The Sensations	29
Ray Sharpe	430
The Shepherd Sisters	191
The Six Teens	62
Skip & Flip	379
The Skyliners	326
Huey Smith & The Clowns	75
Ray Smith	411
Warren Smith	53
Joe Smith	279
The Solitaires	143
Dodie Stevens	428
Billy Storm & The Valiants	383
Nolan Strong & The Diablos	35
The Teen Queens	20
Joe Tex	441
Irma Thomas	450
The Three Chuckles	94
Johnny Tillotson	297
Nick Todd	173
Allen Toussaint	252
Ed Townsend	234
The Tune Weavers	151
Jesse Lee Turner	420
Sammy Turner	422
The Virtues	409
The Wailers	390
Jerry Wallace	10
Baby Washington	327
Johnny "Guitar" Watson	417
Thomas Wayne	317
Billy Williams	83
The Willows	56
Link Wray	361

APPENDIXES & BIBLIOGRAPHY

Appendix A: Record Company Addresses, 1956-1959 461
Appendix B: Selected New York City Record Labels by Listed by Address 473
Bibliography 475

INDEXES

Performer Index 479
Song Index 491

About the Author 507

**"I DON'T CARE WHAT PEOPLE SAY
ROCK AND ROLL IS HERE TO STAY...."**

Danny and The Juniors, 1958

Preface

In this volume, the reader will be confronted by an almost schizophrenic use of the term "rock 'n roll." How can both Jerry Lee Lewis and Tommy Edwards be considered rock 'n rollers in the same breath? Or, Little Richard and Ferlin Huskey? Or, for that mater Carl Perkins and Jimmy Reed?

Just thinking along these lines entices the reader into a morass from which there is no easy extrication. In a work such as this, which artists are to be included? Which should be excluded?

Is Fats Domino a rocker? Certainly. Ray Charles? Usually. Nat King Cole? Rarely.

What about Johnny Cash? Frequently. Marty Robbins? Sometimes. Jim Reeves? Seldom.

The Platters are certainly considered to be a rock 'n roll group, but what about the Diamonds (infrequently) and the Crew Cuts (no way)?

If Janis Martin and Wanda Jackson sing rock 'n roll, what about Connie Francis or Annette?

If David Seville's "Witch Doctor" is rock 'n roll why isn't "The Chipmunk Song" by Seville and the Chipmunks?

No one would exclude Elvis from a list of rockers. But, is "Love Me Tender" a rock 'n roll song?

And, Buddy Holly's 1957 hit, "That'll Be The Day," is unquestionably rock, but what about his "Raining In My Heart" from 1959?

In fact, it is this very diversity over time that is at the heart of rock 'n roll. It is rock's finest attribute. Rock music doesn't have an inflexible definition. It continually absorbs its future direction from a myriad of past influences. At one moment, it can encompass the frenzied rockabilly twang, the Louisiana backbeat shuffle, and the joyful sadness of the blues. Where it will lead in the future only makes for wonderful speculation in the present.

About This Series

It has taken more than five years to complete this volume in the series on the Golden Age of American Rock 'n Roll. That's a year longer than the period encompassed by the book. Part of the reason was my employment with a major West Coast chain of record stores. After fourteen years as owner of Golden Oldies in Sacramento, it looked like the perfect job opportunity. Three-and-a-half years later, in January 1993, I was more than happy to leave. As I wrote on my resignation form, I felt that I had to get on with my life. As a result of this decision, Volume Three, covering the years 1960-1963, should be ready in about half the time it took to complete *REELIN' AND ROCKIN'*.

In the original preface to this series, I wrote that there would also be a fourth volume, covering the years from 1964 to 1969. Prior to the publication of *SHAKE, RATTLE & ROLL*, I had already decided to close the series in 1963. Unfortunately, by that time it was too late to make any changes to the manuscript. There are two reasons for stopping at the end of 1963. First, this has always been meant to be a series on American rock 'n roll. The period following 1963 was the golden age of British rock 'n roll. The second reason for not continuing is the time involved. As I told my previous employer, "I have to get on with my life." By the time I finish Volume Three, I will have coexisted with this series for about a dozen years.

Change in Format

There is one significant change in the layout of this volume when compared with *SHAKE, RATTLE & ROLL*. The brief sidebars—those tidbits of information in the book's margins—have now been incorporated into the text; in their place, nearly each page of the day-by-day sections of the book contains a brief biography of an artist or group mentioned on that page. This change is the result of suggestions received from readers. I agree that having two or three pieces of information on a performer scattered through the book makes researching more difficult. And, in the end, the function of this book is as a research tool.

Rock and Roll Hall of Fame Update

In the preface to *SHAKE, RATTLE & ROLL*, I discussed the beginnings of the Rock and Roll Hall of Fame Foundation, an organization that had inducted four sets of performers by March 1989, the date of that volume's publication. At that time, the foundation had not yet broken ground for a "hall" to house the Hall of Fame. Part of the problem was the existence of two separate factions within the Foundation: those who wanted the facility in New York City and those who were pulling for Cleveland. In the late summer of 1989, the Foundation received a major setback when their request for a grant of $6.9 million from the federal Office of Housing and Urban Development was rejected. Facing a deadline from the New York group, the Cleveland backers of the Hall of Fame raised $40 million in pledges to keep the project alive. The Cleveland group held a ground breaking ceremony on June 6, 1993. A gala dedication ceremony and concert was held Labor Day weekend, 1995.

In the meantime, each January has seen a new slate of inductees into the Rock and Roll Hall of Fame:

1990 Performers
Hank Ballard
Bobby Darin
The Four Seasons
The Four Tops
The Kinks
The Platters
Simon and Garfunkel
The Who

1991 Performers
LaVern Baker
The Byrds
John Lee Hooker
Curtis Mayfield
Wilson Pickett
Ike and Tina Turner

1992 Performers
Bobby "Blue" Bland
Booker T and the M.G.'s
Johnny Cash
The Jimi Hendrix Experience
The Isley Brothers
Sam and Dave
The Yardbirds

1993 Performers
Ruth Brown
Cream
Creedence Clearwater Revival
The Doors
Etta James
Frankie Lymon and the Teenagers
Van Morrison
Sly (of the Family Stone)

1994 Performers
The Animals
The Band
Duane Eddy
The Grateful Dead
Elton John
John Lennon
Bob Marley
Rod Stewart

1990 Non-Performers
Gerry Goffin and Carole King (songwriters)
Holland-Dozier-Holland (songwriters)

1990 Forefathers
Louis Armstrong
Charlie Christian
Ma Rainey

1991 Non-Performers
Dave Bartholomew (producer, songwriter)
Ralph Bass (producer)

1991 Early Influences
Howlin' Wolf

1992 Non-Performers
Leo Fender (guitar manufacturer)
Doc Pomus (songwriter)

1992 Forefathers
Elmore James
Professor Longhair

1993 Non-Performers
Dick Clark
Milt Gabler (producer)

1995 Performers
The Allman Brothers Band
Al Green
Janis Joplin
Led Zeppelin
Martha and the Vandellas
Neil Young
Frank Zappa

1995 Early Influences
The Orioles

1995 Non-Performers
Paul Ackerman (*Billboard* Music Editor)

Even the most casual observer can see that by 1994 the musical styles encompassed in the term rock 'n roll have changed drastically insofar as the Rock and Roll Hall of Fame Foundation is concerned. Most recently, critics of the Foundation were quick to bemoan the inclusion of Bob Marley, a reggae artist, and Rod Stewart, who some feel is a hustler from the less serious side of rock 'n roll. After all, there are still many rockers from pre-1964 who have not been inducted. These include Gene Vincent, Brenda Lee, Del Shannon, the Shirelles, the Moonglows, Jimmie Rodgers, the Flamingos, Martha Reeves and the Vandellas, and Brook Benton.

Finally, there is no Introduction to REELIN' & ROCKIN.' That's what SHAKE, RATTLE & ROLL was all about!

Now, it's time to begin what may be the most exciting period in American rock 'n roll, the four years starting on New Years Day, 1956.

LEE COTTEN
Sacramento, California

reelin' & rockin'

The Golden Age of American Rock 'n Roll

1956

1956
A Look Ahead

"Well, all my friends are boppin' the blues; it must be goin' 'round."
Carl Perkins, 1956

In 1956, it looks like Carl Perkins is right. Almost everyone seems to be "boppin' the blues." Rock 'n roll gains a toehold on the American music scene by the end of 1955. Less than a year later, it explodes across many areas of American culture. Led by the unprecedented success of Elvis Presley, rock 'n roll is most definitely here to stay.

As might be expected, it is those most closely involved in rock 'n roll who are the last to realize its staying power. Even the most successful recording artists and record company executives are convinced that rock 'n roll is a passing fad—just like Davy Crockett coonskin caps or Captain Midnight decoder rings. To the American public, rock 'n roll is a flash in the pan—quicksilver—swamp gas—moonbeams.

Through the halls of New York's Tin Pan Alley and Nashville's Music Row, the chorus is the same: "Rock 'n roll might be big today, but it will be long forgotten by Christmas. You can take my word for it."

At the same time that funeral arrangements are being made for rock 'n roll, record sales grow at a pace that literally outruns the industry's ability to press new product. In 1956, the sales of phonograph records top $320 million. 1956 is the first year of rock 'n roll merchandising, again led by Elvis Presley, who has a line of products on the shelves for Christmas... total take in three months: $20 million.

Record companies will spend most of 1956 searching for the "new Elvis." Sun Records, Elvis' old label, has better luck than most, coming up with Carl Perkins ("Blue Suede Shoes"), Johnny Cash ("Get Rhythm"), Warren Smith ("Rock 'n' Roll Ruby"), Roy Orbison ("Ooby Dooby"), and Jerry Lee Lewis ("End of the Road"). Mercury releases singles by Eddie Bond ("Rock 'Em Daddy") and Ray Moss ("Corrine Corrina"). M-G-M turns to Marvin Rainwater ("Mr. Blues") and Andy Starr ("Rockin' Rollin' Stone"). Decca dabbles in rock 'n roll with Buddy Holly ("Love Me"). Columbia issues rocking singles by Sid King and His 5 Strings ("Booger Red") and Joe Maphis ("Guitar Rock"). Starday has Link Davis ("Sixteen Chicks"). King finds Mac Curtis ("If I Had A Woman"). Even Elvis' current label, RCA Victor, tries to replace him with Janis Martin ("Will You Willyum?").

One change within the industry that is dictated by teenagers is the rapid elimination of 78 r.p.m. records in favor of the newer 45 r.p.m. singles. By 1958, virtually all singles will be available only in the new format. Coupled with the elimination of the "78" is the growth in sales of the long-play album. The biggest jump in the availability of rock 'n roll albums comes just before Christmas 1956, when the number leaps from twelve to fifty. Included in the new releases is are the first albums from Fats Domino (ROCK AND ROLLIN'), Frankie Lymon and the Teenagers (MEET THE TEENAGERS) and Little Richard (LITTLE RICHARD on Camden). By the end of the year, Elvis Presley has two albums in the Top Ten, including ELVIS at Number One.

Speaking of Frankie Lymon and the Teenagers, their success leads to an influx of vocal groups composed of high school students with little or no professional experience. The music trade papers are quick to take note when M-G-M signs the Cubs, featuring a fourteen-year old lead vocalist, while RCA Victor inks the Three Jays, aged ten, eleven and thirteen. In turn, this trend will be followed by untrained teenagers as solo singing idols.

Another peculiarity of rock 'n roll is the two-sided hit record. Elvis has them in droves. So do Fats Domino and Little Richard. This is an outward manifestation of the hunger of teenagers for more music from their favorite stars. And, this is during a time when recording artists churn out four or five singles and two or three albums each year.

This is the year that rock 'n roll begins to make itself heard on television. It is an uphill struggle, as evidenced by Ed Sullivan's vow to keep Elvis off his show. Sullivan caves in after Steve Allen presents Elvis on July 1st, and beats Sullivan's show in the ratings for the first time that season.

There are also two distinctly opposite views of rock 'n roll from the C&W and R&B camps:

Throughout 1956, opposition to rock 'n roll from within the country music community gathers momentum. The popularity of traditional C&W music has been hit especially hard by the success of rock 'n roll, which is jokingly referred to as "back-shack" music in country field. Record sales for established country stars falter. Rock 'n roll acts take away slots on the weekly, national radio shows such as the "Big D Jamboree," the "Ozark Jubilee," and the "Louisiana Hayride." Younger country artists, among them Sonny James and Marty Robbins, switch to a rock 'n roll style. In May 1956, *Billboard* reports that country deejays are spinning rock 'n roll disks, "not because they like rock, but because they feel it is necessary to go along with listener's preferences."

In the R&B community, record executives quickly capitalize on the increased appeal of their music for white teenagers, while noting that the traditional R&B buyers are no longer the primary consumer of their product. By mid-1956, promotion of R&B singles is being directed at both audiences. Some R&B executives drop the term "rhythm and blues" altogether. Herman Lubinsky of Savoy Records even goes so far as to say, "We don't make rhythm and blues records." Insiders argue whether R&B should be tailored to appeal to white consumers by adding together the elements of "pop" and R&B into a new, "synthesized" medium. On the other hand, Little Richard, Fats Domino, Chuck Berry, and Ray Charles hold on to a significant teen audience without altering their style.

The R&B charts are also quicker to note the rise of rock 'n roll than are the "pop" charts. At the time that "In the Still of the Night" (the Five Satins) is at Number 5 on the R&B charts, it is not even in the Top 30 on the "pop" charts. "Fever" (Little Willie John) is a top R&B song long before it reaches the "pop" audience. "It's Too Late" (Chuck Willis) is another Top 5 R&B single, yet it never enters the "pop" charts. And, finally, "Roll Over Beethoven" (Chuck Berry) is Number 29 on *Billboard*'s Top 100 the first week it is on that chart (June 20, 1956), yet it drops to bottom of the "pop" chart for 4 weeks while at the same time it is climbing rapidly up the R&B charts.

As early as February 1956, *Billboard* notes that rock 'n roll deejays are becoming a major force in booking R&B acts. They achieve this power by promoting stage shows via their own radio programs. Alan Freed, at WINS radio, and later WNEW-TV, in New York City, is the most visible, but he is not alone. Also in New York, Tommy "Dr. Jive" Smalls, of WWRL, had been promoting R&B dances and shows long before Freed moved to New York from Cleveland. However, it is Freed's shows that first break the $100,000-a-week mark at the Brooklyn Paramount. By 1958, Freed's week-long events will bring in more than $200,000 a week in ticket sales. In Los Angeles, Gene Norman and Dick "Huggie Boy" Hugg team up to produce shows at the downtown Paramount Theater. George "Hound Dog" Lorenz, of WKBW, promotes dances in Buffalo. In Detroit, rival shows are presented by deejays Robin Seymour, of WKMH, and Mickey Shore, of WJBK. Talent agents complain that disk jockeys put pressure on them by threatening not to play an artists' record unless that artist performs on the jock's stage show. In addition, deejays claim the right to pay less for the talent than normal on the assertion that the broadcast publicity for the show will generate increased record sales. (These stage shows, whether they are at the Paramount in Los Angeles, the Fox in Atlanta, or the Apollo in Harlem, are held in movie theaters and almost invariably feature a bill that alternates between a movie and a hour's worth of live entertainment.)

It is apparent that deejays have become the most powerful players in an industry that is operating without guidelines as to what would, could, or should be a hit record. On June 30, 1956, Alan Freed launches his nationwide radio show aimed directly at teenagers who want to hear only rhythm and blues and rock 'n roll music. The show, sponsored by Camel cigarettes, airs on CBS radio from 9:00 to 9:30 p.m. (EST) nightly. The trade journals soon report that CBS-TV is making overtures for Freed to produce a half-hour of rock 'n roll on the "Stage Show" program one Saturday night. Freed has been New York City's hottest deejay for a couple of years with his show on WINS, Monday through Saturday from 6:30-9:00 p.m. (EST). Other radio networks soon put plans into action: the Dumont network wants to put Al "Jazzbo" Collins on daily with a half hour of rock music, and NBC plans an hour-long Saturday afternoon show to be aired from 5:00-6:00 p.m.

But, everything is not roses inside the world of rock 'n roll. The first real sign of trouble comes on March 23, 1956, when eleven teens are arrested during a "riot" at a three-day engagement of an Alan Freed stage show in Hartford, Connecticut. This is followed by altercations in Washington and Minneapolis. In early April, the New York *Daily News* runs an anti-rock 'n roll series of stories about the riots. That same month, Freed is interviewed on CBS-TV. In Boston, WBZ radio, in an hour-long documentary about rock 'n roll, expresses pro and con views on rock 'n roll. In Boston, the religious community pressures city administrators to ban rock 'n roll altogether. This is just the type of news needed to start a crusade by people opposed to rock 'n roll. During the summer of 1956, the press fuels the furor by reporting that rock 'n roll riots are breaking out across the country. The climax comes in California in July, when 2,500 people tear apart the Palomar Garden Ballroom in San Jose following a Fats Domino show. The conservative press drives home the formula: rock music + riots = juvenile delinquency. It is a simple, and simplistic, view.

Through all of this turmoil, in 1956 rock 'n roll becomes a tidal wave, sweeping across the country. It is a fluid life-form, and it's ability to change keeps it alive. It seems to thrive on negative publicity. Lacking a rigid musical tradition or the formulas imposed on other styles of music, it is free to become what its listeners demand. At the very heart of rock 'n roll lies the concept that there are no rules as to what does, or doesn't, qualify.

NATIONAL NEWS

Of primary national importance across the country in 1956 is the resurgence of miniature golf, a fad from the 1930s... this is also the year of the gas-powered lawnmower and the disposable diaper... Massachusetts' Senator John Kennedy fails to gain his party's nod as Vice Presidential candidate, and in November, Ike once again defeats Stevenson for President in a landslide... John Kennedy does win a Pulitzer Prize for PROFILES IN COURAGE, while the Hugo Award (science fiction) goes to Robert Heinlein's DOUBLE STAR and a best seller is Jackie Collins' JAMES DEAN RETURNS, reportedly dictated by Dean... the Cold War is in full swing: Russian Premier Krushchev tells the world, "We will bury you," and a bid for freedom in Hungary is defeated by Soviet troops at the cost of 50,000 lives... in November, Alabama's segregationist busing laws are stricken down by the U.S. Supreme Court... the Dow Jones average hovers around 500... the average working woman earns $2,500 a year—if she works... it is estimated that teens spend $4 billion a year... advertising endorsements by movie and sports stars tops $1 million a year—total... the Salk polio vaccine is marketed... "As the World Turns" premiers... "Requiem for a Heavyweight" takes the Emmy for Best Single Program, its star, Jack Palance, wins for Best Single Performance, and Rod Serling wins for Best Teleplay... "Caesar's Hour" takes Emmys for best hour-long series and best male and female performers (Sid Caesar and Nanette Fabray) and best supporting performers (Carl Reiner and Pat Carroll)... the top rated show is "I Love Lucy"... TV quiz shows dominate the evening hours; on NBC, Mike Wallace hosts "The $100,000 Big Surprise," the first show to offer a prize that large... the number of drive-in theaters tops 7,000, while the cost of a ticket rises above $1.00... the Academy Award for Best Picture goes to "Around the World in 80 Days"; Yul Brenner is Best Actor for "The King and I," and Ingrid Bergman wins for "Anastasia"... on Broadway, Tonys go to "The Diary of Anne Frank" (drama) and "Damn Yankees" (musical)... the fashion trend in haircuts for young men is the flattop (for weenies) or ducktail (for greasers); for women, it is the Dior's "sack" dress.

January 1956

JIMMY REED
Remarkably, Jimmy Reed was the bestselling pure blues recording artist from 1955 into the early 1960s. His biggest hits, "Baby What You Want Me To Do," "Ain't That Lovin' You Baby," "You Got Me Dizzy," "Honest I Do," and "Bright Lights, Big City" defined the rolling, amplified, boogie-based blues. He was born James Mathis Reed, September 6, 1925 or 1926. He was the youngest of the ten children born to Joseph and Virginia Reed of Dunleith, Mississippi. Reed was taught to play harmonica by his father, and he learned guitar technique from a childhood friend, Eddie Taylor. Taylor was Reed's accompanist for many years, and he also played with John Lee Hooker, Elmore James, and Sunnyland Slim. There were many performers who were personally influenced by Reed. One was Albert King who was Reed's drummer in the 1950s. Stevie Wonder learned to play harmonica by listening to Reed's records. Another was Delbert McClinton, the legendary Texas roadhouse performer and acclaimed harmonica player in the Reed tradition, whose band, the Straitjackets, often backed Reed in Fort Worth. Reed moved from Mississippi to Chicago about 1947. He worked in a steel mill for two years before beginning to entertain part-time in Chicago and nearby Gary, Indiana. At first he accompanied himself only on guitar, but by the early 1950s, he had fashioned a harmonica rack allowing him to play both instruments at once. His first record was "Roll and Rhumba" released in 1953 by Vee-Jay and also leased to Chance Records. After that, he recorded exclusively for Vee-Jay until 1967. In the mid-1960s, his health declined as a combined result of alcoholism and epileptic seizures. Jimmy Reed died August 29, 1976 following a performance at the Savoy Club in San Francisco. There is no truth to the legend that his coffin was shaped like a whiskey bottle.

JAN 1   In Los Angeles, Louis Jordan and His Tympany Five rock the patrons at the Savoy Ballroom for the third straight night.

The Howard Theater in Washington, DC, welcomes Lloyd Price, Bubber Johnson, the Turbans, and the Cardinals through Thursday.

New Releases for the first week of January include two from Vee-Jay: the classic "Ain't That Loving You Baby" by **Jimmy Reed** and "I'll Be Forever Loving You" by the El Dorados. Also new this week: an early cut by the Platters, "Tell the World" on Federal; "I'll Be Home" by the Flamingos on Checker; "Devil or Angel" by the Clovers on Atlantic; "Eddie My Love" by the Teen Queens on R.P.M.; The Pastels' "Put Your Arms Around Me" on United; Lin Records' "Busy Body Rock" by The Mints; "Dem Low-Down Blues" by Marvin Rainwater on M-G-M; Pat Boone's cover of Little Richard's "Tutti Frutti" on Dot; and "So Lonely," a posthumous release from Johnny Ace on Duke.

JAN 3   Chuck Berry is booked for the week into Mandy's Lounge in Buffalo, New York.

JAN 6   The Apollo Theater in New York City offers Joe Williams with the Count Basie band in a week-long engagement. Also on the bill are the Colts and comedian George Kirby.

Ray Charles and his orchestra start a three-day engagement at the 5-4 Ballroom in Los Angeles, after which he will appear at various locations on the West Coast for a week. Across town, Gene and Eunice are at the Savoy Ballroom for the weekend.

In Detroit, the Flame Show Bar welcomes Bubber Johnson and his orchestra for a week.

JAN 7   At Columbia Pictures in Hollywood, production starts on the film "Rock Around the Clock," featuring the hit song of the same title as well as the rock 'n roll style of Bill Haley and His Comets. Noted radio deejay Alan Freed is also featured in the film and will act as technical consultant. Freed has taken a month off from his daily radio show on WINS in New York City to complete the picture. As Freed was preparing for the movie it was announced that he had struck a deal with Columbia Records and WINS to take packaged rock 'n roll shows cross-country for appearances in local movie theaters.

EARLY JANUARY

Eddie Cochran and Hank Cochran, billed as the Cochran Brothers although they are not related, take a regular job on the "California Hayride" broadcast for two hours every Saturday beginning at 8:00 p.m. over KOVR-TV, Stockton, California.

New Releases for the second week in January are the Midnighters' "Sweet Mama, Do Right" on Federal; "That's The Way the Big Ball Bounces" by Frankie Starr on Decca; "Maybe It's All For The Best" by the Hurricanes on King; B. B. King's "Jump With You Baby" on R.P.M.; "Squeeze Box Boogie" by Clifton Chenier on Specialty; "Lover Boy" by the Paris Sisters on Decca; and a two-sided hit for Fats Domino on Imperial, "Don't Blame It on Me" b/w "Bo Weevil." Also new this week is "Rock-a-bye Baby" on RCA Victor by Skeeter Bonn, a new member of the "WWVA Jamboree" in Wheeling, West Virginia.

JAN 10   Elvis Presley has his first recording session for RCA Victor Records at their studio in Nashville. He departed Sun Records the previous November after sixteen months on the label. The first song recorded for RCA is "I Got A Woman," a staple of his live act. Other songs taped during the two-day session include "Heartbreak Hotel" and "I Was The One."

JAN 11   Al Hibbler fronts the "All New Rock 'N' Roll Show" at the downtown Paramount Theater in Los Angeles. Appearing on the bill are Shirley and Lee, LaVern Baker, the Robins, and the **El Dorados**. There are daily performances through January 18.

JAN 13   Ruth Brown headlines the week-long revue at the Apollo Theater in New York. Appearing with Miss Brown are the Roy Milton combo, Charlie and Ray, and the Five Keys.

In Los Angeles, the Midnighters perform for the crowd at the Savoy Ballroom for the weekend.

Lillian Briggs opens at the Flame Show Bar in Detroit for the week.

In Washington, the Howard Theater presents Pearl Bailey for the week.

JAN 14   The Charms and Chuck Willis headline a weekend tour of Virginia-area theaters, starting tonight with a show in Richmond. The troupe moves on nightly to Portsmouth, Norfolk, and Newport.

Elvis Presley performs on "The Louisiana Hayride" radio broadcast in Shreveport. Presley has been a regular on the show since November 1954, appearing almost every Saturday evening while squeezing in a week-long tour in between "Hayride" dates. This coming week he tours Texas, starting in San Antonio (15) and ending in Ft. Worth (20) before returning to the "Louisiana Hayride" (21).

In New Orleans, the Spiders open a three-day, weekend run

THE EL DORADOS
The El Dorados are remembered today only for "At My Front Door." Unknown to many casual listeners, the group had a recording career that spanned four years and produced a wealth of enjoyable music. The original members of the El Dorados were Pirkle Lee Moses, Jr., lead tenor; Jewel Jones, first tenor; Louis Bradley, second tenor; James Maddox, baritone; and Robert Glasper, bass. They began as the Five Stars in 1952 while all were students at Englewood High in Chicago. In 1954, Glasper and Moses were replaced by Richard Nickens, bass, and Arthur Bassett, tenor. When Moses returned, the group became a sextet. Winning an amateur show led to a contract with Vee-Jay Records of Gary, Indiana, a label already hot with the Spaniels. At the same time the group was renamed the El Dorados, after a model of Cadillac. Their first release was "My Lovin' Baby." The group then backed Hazel McCollum on "Annie's Answer," one of many records to hop on the Midnighter's "Annie" craze. In early 1955, the group became a quintet again when Bassett left and was not replaced. "At My Front Door" was released nationally in September 1955, and by October, it was a hit across the country. Unfortunately for the El Dorados, Pat Boone covered the song which drastically diluted their appeal in the "pop" market. The El Dorados were unable to come up with another major hit, however they were able to maintain a full schedule of personal appearances long after their days as a viable recording act were over. It was long rumored that the El Dorados had left behind many unissued tracks. In 1992, Vee-Jay finally released a collection of the El Dorados songs including many which were available for the first time.

at the Dew Drop Cafe and Hotel at 2846 LaSalle. Regular entertainment in the hotel's lounge is offered Friday through Sunday nights.

MID-JANUARY

Fats Domino plays a short engagement at the Orchid Room in Kansas City. He has recently been joined by longtime band member Herb Hardesty on sax. Hardesty had previously left the Fat Man to start his own group.

B. B. King is touring in Florida for a month.

Johnny Otis is working steadily with his band of performers in the Los Angeles area. Each Monday they play the Harlem Hot Spot; Tuesdays it's the Oasis Club; and Wednesday finds the troupe at the Rutland Inn. Every Friday, Otis hosts his local television show on KCOP, Channel 13, at 8:00 p.m.

Clyde McPhatter and Ruth Brown are linked romantically in the music press after stories that Miss Brown and longtime husband Willis "Gatortail" Jackson have split. Reached at his home in Buffalo, McPhatter denied everything. It seems that the rumors were fueled by a September 1955 Atlantic Records' release from the duo, "Love Has Joined Us Together."

New releases for the third week in January include "No Money Down" by Chuck Berry on Chess; "Right Around the Corner" by Boyd Bennett and His Rockets on King; "She Knocks Me Out" by Piano Red on Groove; "The Greatest Magic of All" by **Jerry Wallace** on Mercury; "Our Love" by Ernie Freeman's Combo (featuring Bobby Relf) on Cash; Sonny Boy Williamson's "Boppin' With Sonny" on Ace; and Johnny Lee Hooker's "Mambo Chillun" on Vee-Jay.

JAN 16   Ray Charles takes his combo on a one-week tour of Texas. Accompanying Charles are Etta James, Joe Turner, Floyd Dixon, and the Clovers.

JAN 18   Following the closing of their successful stint at the Flamingo Hotel in Las Vegas, the Platters hit the road for 15 one-nighters.

JAN 19   Al Hibbler and his rock 'n roll revue move up the coast to the San Francisco Paramount Theater. Performances continue daily through January 26.

JAN 20   Following her appearance at the Apollo, Ruth Brown takes off on a week-long trek through Virginia. Meanwhile, the Apollo offers Dinah Washington with the Clifford Brown orchestra for this week.

This week, the Howard Theater in Washington plays host to the rhythm and blues style of the Charms, the Heartbeats, Nolan Lewis, Donna Hightower, and Choker Campbell's combo.

In Detroit, the Turbans, the Moonglows, and Faye Adams start five days in four different theaters belonging to the Korman The-

---

JERRY WALLACE
Throughout his lengthy recording career, Jerry Wallace wavered between country music and straight "pop." In between, he found time to wax a few records that appealed to the rock 'n rollers. He was born December 15, 1930, and he has claimed Kansas City as his hometown. His father, who was in the grocery business, traded a crate of eggs for Jerry's first guitar as a fourteenth birthday present. In high school, Jerry excelled in baseball and was the region's pole vault champion. After high school, Jerry joined the Navy. On his discharge, he began pursuing a recording career in earnest. An obscure 1952 effort for Vogue Records pointed toward the future. "There'll Be Some Changes Made" was a rousing, country-tinged song that tried to appeal to the "pop" audience. He sharpened his recording career by working for the Tops budget label churning out covers of current hit records for those with only forty-nine cents to spend. In 1953, one of his efforts for Tops covered the Hilltoppers' "P.S. I Love You." In 1954, Allied Records issued his long-forgotten "Gee, But I Hate To Go Home." These efforts brought him to the attention of Mercury Records, which recorded Wallace in a strictly "pop" vein. Although he had a fine baritone voice, he lacked emotion. As a result, "Autumn Has Come and Gone" in 1955 and "Gloria" in 1956 failed to attract an audience. In 1957, he cut his first record for Challenge of Los Angeles. "Blue-Jean Baby" was a medium-tempo, soft rock number. Two records later, in 1958 Wallace hit pay dirt with "How the Time Flies," a chunky, pop-rock number. His biggest hit was "Primrose Lane" in 1959. He remained with Challenge until 1963, issuing 24 singles. For the next dozen years, he recorded country for Mercury, Liberty, Decca (MCA), United Artists. Glenolden and M-G-M.

ater Chain. Tonight, they're at the National Theater. Tomorrow, it's the Duke Theater, and Sunday, the troupe is at the Castle Theater. On January 25-26, the performers find themselves at the Booker. T. Theater.

In Los Angeles, the 5-4 Club welcomes Smiley Lewis for three days. At the Savoy Ballroom, the "Lucky Seven Revue" features Little Willie John, Earl King, Champion Jack Dupree, Otis Williams and His Charms and several lesser known performers. The "Lucky Seven" had been on the road since late October 1955.

JAN 23   Ray Charles and Joe Turner continue to tour in Louisiana, but co-stars Etta James and the Clovers take off for the West Coast where they will team with band leader Joe Morris.

In Washington, the Casino Royal at 14th and H Streets, offers the talents of Steve Gibson and His Red Caps for a week.

New Releases for the fourth week in January include four from Atlantic: "Drown In My Own Tears" by Ray Charles, "Get Up, Get Up" by LaVern Baker, "In Paradise" by the **Cookies,** and "A Tear Fell" by Ivory Joe Hunter. Also new this week is "Heartbreak Hotel" by Elvis Presley on RCA Victor; two from the Five Keys: "The Story of Love" on Aladdin and "What Goes On?" on Capitol; two from Jubilee Records: "Rock 'N Roll Call" by the Four Tunes and "Don't Go To Strangers" by the Orioles; Brook Benton's "Bring Me Love" on Okeh; Marvin and Johnny's "Wonderful, Wonderful One" on Modern; and the Empires' "Tell Me Pretty Baby" on Wing, a subsidiary of Mercury Records.

JAN 26   Buddy Holly has his first professional recording session in Nashville at Bradley's Barn, a studio owned and operated by Owen Bradley. Holly's first single will be released in April.

JAN 27   In Detroit, the three-day "Rock 'N Rollarama" is a complete sellout. The Fox Theater show features Bobby Charles, the Cadillacs, the Cleftones, the Four Tunes, the Royal Jokers, Bob Crewe, the Three Chuckles, and Della Reese. The run is produced by Mickey Shorr, WJBK deejay, and brings in 42,000 fans who pay $57,000 at the gate.

Also in Detroit, the Korman theater chain plays host to a week-long show by Sonny Til "and His New Orioles," the Charms, the Flamingos, the Sweethearts, Nolan Strong, and Dakota Staton. The acts will appear in a different venue in the area each night starting at the National Theater tonight.

The Howard Theater in Washington features Dinah Washington and jazz/R&B saxophonist Illinois Jacquet and his orchestra.

Bill Haley and His Comets rake in $23,000 for two shows at the Syria Mosque Theater in Pittsburgh.

In Los Angeles, the Clovers "wow" the patrons at the 5-4 Ballroom, while at the Melodie Room, Joe Houston knocks 'em dead with his wild sax riffs.

THE COOKIES
The Cookies began their somewhat obscure recording career on Lamp Records in 1954 with "Don't Let Go." After Lamp folded, the group's manager, Jesse Stone, brought them to the attention of Atlantic Records. In early 1955, their first Atlantic single was "Precious Love." Their second release, "In Paradise," was their best seller as the Cookies. The group was composed of Marjorie "Margie" Hendricks, Ethel McCrea, and Doretta Jones. When their third Atlantic single, "Down By the River," didn't do as well, the Cookies turned to singing backing vocals on numerous Atlantic releases. There was one release by a group called the Cookies on Josie in 1957, "Hippy-Dippy-Daddy." They were hired by Ray Charles in 1958 to back him on his tours, thereby giving his live performances more of a gospel feel. By the end of the year, the name of the Cookies had been changed to the Raelettes. As such, the group (with numerous personnel changes, including Mabel John of Stax Records, reported to be the older sister of Little Willie John) became a mainstay of Charles' recordings and tours for more than thirty years. The Raelettes had a handful of single releases on Ray Charles' Tangerine label in the 1960s, and "One Hurt Deserves Another" briefly made the "pop" and R&B charts in 1967. The group did even better in 1968 in the R&B field with "I'm Gettin' 'Long Alright," and the classic "Bad Water," which was a big seller in the both fields during the summer of 1970. (Note: This group was apparently related to the group of the same name that had several hits, including "Chains," on Dimension Records in 1962-63; the Dimension group reportedly sang backing vocals for Atlantic Records, and one of the members was named Dorothy Jones.)

JAN 28 Elvis Presley makes his national television debut as a guest on "Stage Show" on the CBS-TV network. He will return for the next three consecutive Saturday nights. The show is produced by comedian Jackie Gleason (who does not appear) and "stars" big band leaders Tommy and Jimmy Dorsey.

Carl Perkins appears on "The Big D Jamboree" radio show broadcast nationwide from Dallas.

LATE JANUARY

Departing Kansas City, Fats Domino continues to tour throughout the Midwest before returning to his hometown of New Orleans, where, in early February, he will entertain during the Mardi gras celebration.

THE TOP ROCK 'N ROLL RECORDS FOR JANUARY 1956

1. The Great Pretender - The Platters
2. Only You - The Platters
3. Burn That Candle/Rock A-Beatin' Boogie - Bill Haley and His Comets
4. See You Later, Alligator - Bill Haley and His Comets
5. When You Dance - The Turbans
6. Speedo - The Cadillacs
7. Tutti Frutti - Little Richard
8. Seven Days - Clyde McPhatter
9. At My Front Door - The El Dorados
10. Mystery Train - Elvis Presley
11. Hands Off - Jay McShann and Priscilla Bowman
12. Poor Me - Fats Domino
13. Witchcraft - The Spiders
14. Feel So Good - Shirley and Lee
15. Adorable - The Drifters
16. Jivin' Around (part 1-2) - Ernie Freeman's Combo
17. Need Your Love So Bad - Little Willie John
18. Come Home - Bubber Johnson
19. All Around the World - Little Willie John
20. That's Your Mistake - Otis Williams and His Charms

Also on the "pop" charts:
Sixteen Tons - Tennessee Ernie Ford
Memories Are Made of This - Dean Martin
Moments to Remember - The Four Lads
I Hear You Knockin' - Gale Storm
Love and Marriage - Frank Sinatra

January 1956
SPECIAL RECOGNITION

DICK CLARK

The first volume of THE GOLDEN AGE OF ROCK 'N ROLL closed with a "special recognition" piece on Ahmet Ertegun, the owner of Atlantic Records. That biography focused on the role he and his company had played in shaping the future of rock 'n roll from 1952 through 1955. It is fitting, therefore, that the second volume should open with another such look at the man who will exert the most influence in shaping the future of rock 'n roll from 1956 through 1959.

Considering that he would wield such an enormous influence over the course of popular music, Dick Clark knew very little about rock 'n roll in 1956.

Richard Wagstaff Clark was born November 30, 1929. He grew up in the small community of Mount Vernon on the New York shore of Lake Erie. He was an indifferent school student until he reached the tenth grade and discovered the magic of radio. Later he wrote, "I loved the fantasy world radio created." His life changed forever when his parents took him New York City to see a live broadcast of the "Jimmy Durante-Garry Moore Show." As though struck by lightning, he realized that working in radio was to be his future.

Dick Clark

The summer after high school, Clark was given a job at WRUN-AM radio, a Rome, New York. The station was owned by his uncle and managed by Clark's father. For weeks, he was only an office-boy, but one day the station manager invited him to fill in for a vacationing weather forecaster on WRUN's fledgling FM rural broadcast. By the end of the summer, Clark had advanced to station breaks.

Clark attended Syracuse University where he majored in advertising with a minor in radio. In his senior year he landed a job with WOLF, a country music station in Syracuse. Then he came back to WRUN for a short time where he broadcast using the name "Dick Clay." This led to his first television job, as newscaster at WKTV in Utica. In early 1952, as "Dick Clark" once again, he went to work for WFIL radio and television in Philadelphia. That summer, WFIL radio decided to junk its network shows in order to follow the new trend of having announcers play records over the air. A few months later, WFIL became one of the first to try a similar format on television. Bob Horn, a WFIL radio deejay, aired an early form of music video in a show called "Bandstand." Within a month, in order to add spice to the TV broadcast, teenagers were invited to come to the studio to dance while Horn spun records over the air. The show was immediately successful among high school students in the Philadelphia area.

While Horn was working his magic on TV, Clark was successfully hosting a similar version of the show on WFIL radio. In 1955, when Horn went on vacation, Clark filled in on "Bandstand." A year later, on July 9, 1956, after Horn's much-publicized arrest for drunken driving, Clark took over "Bandstand" full time.

By his own admission, Dick Clark knew almost none of the songs on that first day's playlist. He did have the insight to work with the kids in the studio, asking them about their favorite songs, checking on the popular trends in clothes, and watching for the latest dance fads. Clark was young enough, at age 26, to become a "buddy" to the dancers in the studio, and he projected a wholesome, nonthreatening image.

After several years of local success for "Bandstand"—as well as Clark's personal crusade to get the show a spot on national TV—"Bandstand" finally got the "go-ahead" from the network heads in New York. On August 5, 1957, Dick Clark hosted the first national broadcast of "American Bandstand" over ABC-TV from 3:00 to 4:30 p.m. This was the perfect time-slot to reach teenagers coming home from school. In the beginning, the show broadcast live every weekday afternoon from the WFIL's Studio "B" in Philadelphia. The teens who flooded to the studio were a fresh-scrubbed crowd. Girls were forbidden from wearing slacks or tight sweaters while boys had to wear a jacket and tie. No one was allowed to smoke or chew gum. Eventually, the studio audience was built around a regular group of Philadelphia high school students who had their own national following.

On February 15, 1958, Clark parlayed his afternoon success into a regular spot on ABC-TV's Saturday night lineup. "The Dick Clark Show" was a rock 'n roll variety revue, broadcast live from New York. Meanwhile, "American Bandstand" continued to appear coast-to-coast during the week. On October 4, 1959, Clark launched yet another ABC television venture, a panel show titled "World of Talent."

The major difference between the original local broadcast and the revamped "American Bandstand" was the size of the audience. Every afternoon, there were 20 million fans watching the show. By that first October, "American Bandstand" was killing the competition on both CBS (by 20 percent) and NBC (by a whopping 48 percent). By the end of the year, the show was being carried by sixty-five stations across the country.

With the increase in the number of viewers, the influence of "American Bandstand" and Dick Clark increased exponentially. Playing a new record in the "spotlight" portion of the show virtually guaranteed the sale of thousands of copies within a week. Any record played daily as part of some ongoing dance contest was almost certain to be a national Top Ten contender. Agents scrambled and cajoled for a chance for their acts to appear as one of the two or three "live" spots on every show. It wasn't long before the power of the show and its host became a matter of concern within the music business.

It appeared to many people inside the music business that Clark wielded this power with more concern for the local music companies than for the desires of the national audience. Philadelphia-based record companies seemed to have little trouble placing their records on the daily play list at "American Bandstand." Artists who recorded for Chancellor Records (Frankie Avalon, Fabian and Jodie Sands), Jamie Records (Duane Eddy), Swan Records (Freddy Cannon, Billy and Lillie, and Dickey Doo and the Don'ts), and Cameo/Parkway Records (Bobby Rydell, Chubby Checker, Dee Dee Sharp, and the Dovells) were frequent guests on the show. In addition, competitors were quick to note that Clark had personally invested in local record pressing plants and the records manufactured in these plants were played on "Bandstand" with more frequency than those pressed elsewhere.

In 1959, the foundation of Clark's musical empire became the focus of the U.S. Senate subcommittee that was investigating pay-for-play ("payola") charges within the music business. Clark blamed election year politics for the scrutiny he received. Still, investigators were able to show that Clark held partial copyrights to one-hundred and fifty songs, many of which were played on his show. He also had financial ties to thirty-three music-related businesses, including publishers, recording companies, and pressing plants, most of which were located in Philadelphia. At the end of the investigation, the Senators could find nothing specifically illegal about such activities. However, in mid-October 1959, Clark received an ultimatum from ABC-TV: give up his outside music business activities or leave the network. Without a second thought, Clark divested himself of his music holdings. As a result, he sidestepped the career-ending fate of his New York rival, Alan Freed.

After starring in "Because They're Young" (1960) and co-starring behind Fredrick March in "Young Doctors In Love" (1961), Clark moved his headquarters to Los Angeles in the 1960s. In 1965, he produced the daily "Where the Action Is" for ABC-TV. "Action" was a "Bandstand"-type show featuring Paul Revere and the Raiders as hosts that was broadcast from the beaches near Los Angeles. Clark remained as host of "American Bandstand" after it left ABC-TV in 1987 and went into syndication. When he finally gave up his spot as host in 1989 the show had become the longest running television variety show of all time.

Clark was far from idle. He was working on a number of musical-related events and programs. He began producing the annual "American Music Awards" show in 1973. This production was conceived to offset a bias felt by many of the younger entertainment executives on the part of the Grammy awards in favor of "adult contemporary" music. By the 1990s, it seemed that even "The American Music Awards" had lost its cutting edge. Clark also became a popular television host on the "$10,000 Pyramid," "TV's Bloopers and Practical Jokes," and most recently, "Scattergories."

In 1987, shares in Dick Clark Productions were traded publicly. By the 1990s, Clark was producing made-for-tv films as well as theatrical movies. In 1992, the firm posted a net profit of $1 million, although there were reports that revenues were slipping late in the year. A 1990 *Forbes* magazine article placed his personal fortune at $180 million.

Clark's personal taste in music was set in the 1940s when he was a teenager and college student. Evidence of this can be seen in the theme music used for "American Bandstand." With all the rock 'n roll tunes he could have chosen, Clark picked "Bandstand Boogie" by Les Elgart's Orchestra. On "The Dick Clark Show," with its prime Saturday night time-slot, the emphasis soon shifted away from rockers like Jerry Lee Lewis, who appeared on the first show. By 1959, "pop" performers such as Gordon McRae, Joni James, Mitch Miller, Jaye P. Morgan, Jane Morgan, and Vic Damone were making frequent appearances. That same year, on "World of Talent," the regular guests were such notables as comedians Jack E. Leonard and Sam Levinson, actresses Zsa Zsa Gabor and Joan Fontaine, and vocalists Abbe Lane and Julius LaRosa.

There is no doubt that Clark tried to get a "feel" for the music he was spinning. It was also obvious that he personally liked the teenagers and performers as individuals. Nevertheless, as Clark has publicly stated, the sole basis for his relationship with rock 'n roll was monetary.

As with many famous individuals, Dick Clark's public persona seems to differ from his private side. In his autobiography, Clark summarized his personality by stating, "I'm afraid sometimes I'm not a thoughtful person; I want to be thoughtful, but sometimes I'm off the mark."

However, for every individual who carried a grudge for Clark there are many more who would come to his defense. He was genuinely liked by many of the artists that he helped, among them Bobby Darin, Connie Francis, Frankie Avalon, and Fabian.

When asked what he feels is his main contribution to popular music has been, Dick Clark invariably replies that he is proud to have presented more artists on television than any other person. There is little doubt that this is true. On the other hand, Clark must also accept a large share of the responsibility for changing rock 'n roll from the vital, energized music form that it was in 1956 into the homogenized, "teen-pop" that it became by 1959.

At the same time that Clark was presenting all those music acts, his own name was becoming better known than most of the artists. As Hank Ballard put it in a 1987 interview, "The man was big. He was the biggest thing in America at that time. He was bigger than the President!"

February 1956

FEB 1   Ray Charles winds up his coast-to-coast tour with shows in Florida.

Having completed production on the movie "Rock Around the Clock," which had a two-week shooting schedule, Bill Haley and His Comets headline the "Biggest Rock 'n Roll Show of '56" tour as it begins a week along the East Coast. The revue features Roy Hamilton, the Platters, LaVern Baker, the Five Keys, Bo Diddley, the Drifters, Shirley and Lee, Joe Turner, and Red Prysock's band. (See also FEB 5.)

Rock 'n roll joins a professional ice skating show with the production of "Rock 'n' Roll Revue" at the Roxy Theater in New York.

Screamin' Jay Hawkins begins a week at the Royal Theater in Baltimore.

Chuck Berry is booked into the Casa Loma Ballroom in St. Louis. This was Berry's first engagement in his hometown since "Maybellene" became a hit in 1955.

FEB 3   Leaving Washington's Howard Theater, Illinois Jacquet opens for a week at the Royal Theater in Baltimore. After he closes this date, Jacquet will join Ella Fitzgerald for a tour of Europe as a featured member of Norman Grantz' "Jazz at the Philharmonic."

Despite a raging snowstorm, Carl Perkins, Johnny Cash and members of the "Big D Jamboree" had a sellout crowd of 1,600 in San Antonio. The next night, they will do just as well at the Field House in Odessa.

The Apollo Theater presents a week-long engagement by Jay McShann's combo with Priscilla Bowman, Joe Tex, Danny Overbea, and the **Ravens**.

In Detroit, the National Theater hosts a three-day revue headlined by Big Maybelle. Also appearing are Nappy Brown, the Harptones and the Colts.

In Los Angeles, the 5-4 Ballroom offers Oscar McLollie, while the Savoy Ballroom presents T-Bone Walker and Charles Brown for the dance crowd.

FEB 5   Between his Saturday night television appearances on "Stage Show," Elvis Presley undertakes a short tour along the Eastern seaboard with a show tonight in Norfolk. During the week he performs nightly in the Carolinas and Virginia.

Buddy Johnson, his sister Ella, and their orchestra entertain in New Orleans at the Coliseum Arena.

THE RAVENS
The popularity of the Ravens spanned more than two decades—by any standard, a long life in the music business. Led by Jimmy Ricks' expansive bass voice, the original members of the Ravens were Leonard Puzey, second tenor; Warren Suttles, first tenor; and Ollie Jones, baritone. The group began playing clubs in Harlem, and they found early acceptance for their novel bass-lead sound. They began their lengthy recording career in 1946 with the release of "Honey" on Hub Records. At the time, few vocal groups appealed directly to the blues side of music. The Ravens issued a total three singles on Hub, including "My Sugar Is So Refined," one of their best-loved standards. After their brief stay with Hub, Jones was replaced by Maithe Marshall, who possessed a soaring falsetto. In 1948, the Ravens signed with King Records and set about rerecording their best material, including "Honey," "My Sugar Is So Refined," "Out of a Dream" and "Bye Bye Baby Blues." After a year and four King releases, the group moved on the National Records, a subsidiary of Savoy, where they recorded their first major hit, "Old Man River." This was followed by "Write Me a Letter," another big seller. The group issued more than twenty singles on National before signing with Columbia Records in 1950. Suttles was replaced by Louis Heyward before the Ravens left National, but Heyward stayed only briefly before his place was taken by Louis Frazier. Success eluded the recordings by the Ravens on Columbia and its subsidiary Okeh. Shortly after leaving Okeh in 1952, Marshall left and was replaced by Joe Van Loan. By 1954, the Ravens were Ricks with Van Loan, Frazier and Jimmy Stewart. This is the group, with Suttles filling in for Frazier, that recorded for Mercury and Jubilee.

The "Biggest Rock 'n Roll Show of '56" stops for a performance at the National Guard Armory in Washington.

New Releases for the first week of February include "Blue Suede Shoes" by Carl Perkins on Sun; "Why Do Fools Fall In Love" by Frankie Lymon and the Teenagers on Gee; "How Soon?" by the Jacks on R.P.M.; Jimmy McCracklin's "It's All Right" on Hollywood; "To Our Love" by the Counts on Dot; "Come On Home" by Chuck Willis on Okeh; the Dells' "Dreams of Contentment" on Vee-Jay; the Turbans' "Sister Sookey" on Herald; and Shirley and Lee's "That's What I'll Do" on Aladdin.

FEB 6 The Orchid Room in Kansas City plays host to the Diablos for a lengthy engagement.

LaVern Baker opens at the Showboat in Philadelphia for a week.

EARLY FEBRUARY

The Coasters sign with Atlantic Records' subsidiary, Atco. The group is led by Bobby Nunn and Carl Gardiner, two former members of the Robins. Rounding out the quartet are Billy Guy and Leon Hughes.

The Harptones embark on a six-month European tour to promote their hits, including the smash 1953 release, "Sunday Kind of Love."

Gleason's Bar of Music Club in Cleveland announces their bookings during the month of February include Little Walter, Joe Turner, **Lowell Fulson**, and the Moonglows.

A new picture, "Rhythm and Blues Review," the follow-up to the successful "Rock & Roll Review," opens in 1,000 movie houses.

FEB 10 Chuck Berry makes his West Coast debut with a three-day run at the Savoy Ballroom in Los Angeles. Across town, Smiley Lewis is at the 5-4 Ballroom for the weekend. (See also FEB 12.)

Screamin' Jay Hawkins begins a three-day stand at the Bronx Opera house. Working with Hawkins are the Cadillacs, the Heartbeats, Ann Cole, and the Valentines. There are five shows Friday, and six shows each Saturday and Sunday.

Roy Hamilton headlines a thirteen-day tour though the Midwest. Also on the bill are Shirley and Lee, Joe Jones and the Erskine Hawkins' combo.

At the Apollo Theater in New York City, Lloyd Price headlines the revue which features the Drifters, Mickey and Sylvia, the Spiders, and Bubber Johnson. Price brings in $30,000 in ticket sales during the week.

Detroit's Flame Show Bar welcomes Bill Doggett and Earl Bostic for a two-week run.

Jay McShann and his orchestra headline this week's revue at the Howard Theater in Washington. Also on stage are Priscilla Bowman, the Ravens, Danny Overbea, Joe Tex, and the Flamingos.

LOWELL FULSON

Lowell Fulson, born March 31, 1921, continues to work his magic into the 1990s. A man of immaculate taste, both artistically and privately, he personifies the very word "gentleman." Fulson's recording career began on Gild Edge Records, a small Oakland, California, company. His first record, issued in 1946, was "Cryin' Blues (Street Walkin' Woman)." At that time, he was newly arrived on the West Coast from his birthplace in Tulsa, Oklahoma. He began performing in Oklahoma and Texas when he was still a teenager. In the late 1930s, Fulson played in a string band and toured with an obscure performer who billed himself as Texas Alexander. Fulson's relocation to Oakland came compliments of the U.S. Navy, when he was assigned to nearby Alameda Naval Air Station. When he was discharged, he returned briefly to Tulsa before moving permanently to Oakland where he became an integral part of the Bay Area's up-and-coming blues community. Fulson's first recordings were released simultaneously on Gild Edge, Big Town and Downbeat, all issued during 1946. Fulson had a hit in 1949 with "Come Back Baby" on Downbeat. In 1950 when he reworked a Memphis Slim song into "Every Day I Have The Blues," a hit on Swing Time. This was followed by three more hits on the label including "Lonesome Christmas." "Reconsider Baby," released in 1954 on Checker was his last hit in the 1950s, but by this time he was a mainstay in nightclubs from Oakland to Texas. In the mid-1960s, he was recording for Kent Records, and he was rediscovered by the music buyers. His recording of "Black Night" became a classic. In 1967, his original version of "Tramp" preceded that of "Otis & Carla" (Otis Redding and Carla Thomas) and was almost as big a hit. Today he resides in Palmdale in Southern California.

FEB 11   Ray Charles starts a three-week tour of New York state that will run to the end of February.

The Platters appear on "The Perry Como Show" on NBC-TV singing "The Great Pretender."

FEB 12   As part of his stay at the Savoy Ballroom in Los Angeles, Chuck Berry appears on the Savoy-sponsored television show broadcast on KCOP-TV from 8:00 to 8:30 p.m. Berry's tour will continue with shows in San Jose and at the Filmore Auditorium in San Francisco.

FEB 13   A package rhythm and blues tour featuring the Heartbeats, the El Dorados, Jesse Powell, Gloria Mann, and Sam "The Man" Taylor opens for a week in theaters in the "New Jersey chain" operated jointly by Stanley and Warner Brothers. Dates include the Capitol Theater in Passaic tonight, the Embassy in Orange (14); the Ritz in Elizabeth (15); the Regent in Patterson (16); the DeWitt in Bayonne (17); and the Fabian in Hoboken (18).

New Releases for the second week of February include "Smokestack Lightning" by Howlin' Wolf on Chess; two from Imperial: Smiley Lewis' "One Night" and "Try Rock and Roll" by Bobby Mitchell; "Diddy Wah Diddy" by Bo Diddley on Checker; two versions of "Sweet Sixteen:" from the Colts on Vita and the Sounds on Modern; "She's Gone, Gone" by the Penguins on Mercury; "Woo Ho Ho" by Lloyd Price on Specialty; and "(Shimmy, Shimmy) Ko Ko Wop" by the El Capris on Bullseye. Also new this week are singles by artists who will be heard from in the near future: the Everly Brothers' "Keep A-Lovin' Me" on Columbia and Chris Kenner's "Don't Let Her Pin That Charge on Me" on Baton.

FEB 14   Mandy's Club in Buffalo, NY, brings Screamin' Jay Hawkins to its stage for ten days.

MID-FEBRUARY

RCA Victor signs sixteen-year old **Janis Martin** to a recording contract. Miss Martin is described as "the female Elvis Presley."

It is announced that negotiations are almost complete for Bill Haley and His Comets to make their first overseas tour starting in June with shows at the London Palladium. Other engagements would include Liverpool, Edinburgh, Glasgow, and Newcastle. However, complications arise and the booking is postponed until the summer of 1957.

Several heretofore "pop" labels announced plans to enter the rhythm and blues/rock 'n roll market in a big way. Mercury will use its jazz subsidiary, Wing Records, to try to gain ground lost during the past year. Mercury execs announced that Wing would record "anything with a beat." Acts reassigned from Mercury to Wing include the Penguins, Buddy and Ella Johnson, Red Prysock and Joe Liggins. "Pop" artists previously on Wing will now record for the parent company. RCA Victor will act in a similar fashion with

JANIS MARTIN
Janis Martin was the original "Female Elvis Presley." There were other young women who claimed the title, including Alis Lesley, who toured Australia with Little Richard, Gene Vincent and Eddie Cochran. Janis Darlene Martin was born March 27, 1940, in Sutherland, Virginia. She began practicing guitar at age four, entered her first talent contest at age eight, and placed first in a state-wide competition at age ten. She was a regular performer on the "WDVA Barn Dance" broadcast from Danville, Virginia. She had her own radio program on WHEE in Martinsville. In 1953, she joined the cast of the "Old Dominion Barn Dance" broadcast nationally over CBS radio from Richmond. With the coming of rock 'n roll, Janis was naturally drawn to the new musical form. Her contacts had little difficulty gaining an audition with RCA Victor Records, a label with strong country ties. Her first release was "Will You, Willyum?" b/w "Drugstore Rock and Roll." The single reportedly sold nearly a million copies. Her billing as the "Female Elvis Presley" brought congratulations and a dozen roses from Elvis, an RCA Victor recording star, himself. Janis responded by recording "My Boy Elvis," the song for which she is best remembered. In all, she issued more than twenty RCA Victor singles, including a rousing version of "Ooby Dooby." Janis' popularity, coupled with her professionalism, brought her prolonged success on tours as well as television. In 1957, she was a regular member of Jim Reeves touring act when it went to Europe to entertain American troops. While riding this wave of popularity, she retired at age eighteen to raise a family (she had married at age fifteen). She was back briefly in 1959 on Palette Records. In 1960, she retreated from show business, remaining with her family in Baltimore. By the late 1970s she was making local appearances, and in 1987, she toured England, again.

THE TEEN QUEENS
The Teen Queens were a Los Angeles duo composed of sisters Betty and Rosie Collins. Their brother, Aaron, was a member of the Cadets/Jacks. Aaron and Maxwell Davis, the music arranger for Modern Records, the company releasing singles by the Cadets/Jacks, co-wrote "Eddie My Love." As the song was written from a female point of view, it was necessary to audition a new group to record the song. Enter Betty and Rose. After an audition, in October 1955, they signed a recording contract with R.P.M. Records, a Modern subsidiary. "Eddie My Love" was released in late 1955. The record began to sell slowly in the Los Angeles area, finally achieving national attention in early January 1956. As was the common practice at the time, "Eddie My Love" was covered by several other "pop" vocal groups, including the Chordettes and the Fontane Sisters. All three acts had a hit with the song in the "pop field" although only the Teen Queens' record sold well in the R&B market. Although the version by the Teen Queens has certainly sold more than a million copies since 1956, none of the three groups received a gold record for "Eddie My Love" at the time. The Teen Queens followed with "Baby Mine" in April 1956, but sales were minimal. The same was true of their next three R.P.M. singles, "Billy Boy," "Red Top," "Rock Everybody," and "I Miss You." In 1958, unable to come up with a second hit on R.P.M., the duo moved on to RCA Victor Records where their lone release, "Dear Tommy" failed to draw much attention. Two years later, they were on Antler Records. Their first Antler single was an answer to "There Is Something On Your Mind," redone as "There Is Nothing On Your Mind." One more Antler single, "I Heard Violins," and the recording career of the Teen Queens was over.

Groove Records, and Columbia is putting new life into Okeh Records.

Johnny Lee Hooker is currently performing nightly at the Club Basin Street in Detroit where he remains the headliner for a month.

Pee Wee Crayton is booked to play a month-long gig at the Melodie Room in Los Angeles.

FEB 17 Little Richard headlines the revue at the Apollo Theater in New York. Also appearing on the bill are the Flamingos, Guitar Slim, and Linda Hopkins. Richard performs "Tutti Frutti," "Get Out of That Bed," and "Don't You Wish You Had a Man Like Me?"

Bobby Charles opens for three days at the Ebony Club in Houston. He is riding the popularity of "See You Later, Alligator" by Bill Haley and His Comets, which Charles wrote and released on Chess as "Later, Alligator."

Vocalist Arthur Prysock and his brother, saxophonist Red Prysock, join forces for a rare duet appearance at the Crossing Inn, Trenton, New Jersey.

It's a blues weekend at the Los Angeles-area clubs as the Savoy welcomes B. B. King for the first of two weekends and the 5-4 offers the duo of T-Bone Walker and Charles Brown.

The Moonglows, the Charms, the Colts, Dinah Hightower, and Choker Campbell's band entertain patrons this week at the Howard Theater in Washington.

FEB 18 The State Theater in Hartford welcomes LaVern Baker for a two-day engagement.

Carl Perkins performs in Dallas on the "Big D Jamboree." After the show, he is signed to a long-term contract with the nationwide radio show.

FEB 20 Squeezing in another week-long tour between his fourth "Stage Show" on February 18 and a "Louisiana Hayride" broadcast on February 25, Elvis Presley invades Florida. Concert locations include Sarasota, Tampa and Jacksonville.

The Rivera Theater in Detroit hosts its first rock 'n roll revue featuring Frankie Lymon and the Teenagers, the Jewels, the **Teen Queens**, the Five Keys, Ivory Joe Hunter, Bob Crewe, and the Ernie Freeman Combo. The same troupe returns to the Riviera for another one-nighter on February 27 after appearing in Cleveland (see below, FEB 24).

The Platters open an lengthy engagement at Miami's Club Calvert.

New Releases for the third week in February include the first release from the Coasters, "Down In Mexico" on Atco; a re-release of an earlier side from Little Richard, "Directly From My Heart" on Peacock; "Church Bells Are Ringing" by the Willows on Melba; "W-P-L-J" by the 4 Deuces on Music City; LaVern Baker's "My Happiness Forever" on Atlantic; "Tell Me" by the Three Chuckles on Vik; "I Love You Darling" by the Valentines on Rama; "Song of the Dreamer" by Billy Brooks on Duke; "Chicken" by the Cheers on Capitol; and Champion Jack Dupree's "Me and My Mule" on King.

FEB 24   The Frankie Lymon show from the Riviera Theater on February 20 travels to Cleveland for a two day engagement at the 105th Street Theater. The show is produced by WERE, reportedly making it the first of its kind in Cleveland sponsored by a "pop" deejay.

    Roy Hamilton and his revue open for the week at the Flame Show Bar in Detroit. (See above FEB 10)

    New York's Apollo Theater offers a program of dance acts this week.

    The 5-4 Ballroom in Los Angeles presents the Clovers for three days.

FEB 25   Deejay Alan Freed is chairman of the Teenagers March for Childhood Nephrosis fund drive. In New York, 11,000 rock 'n roll fans turned out to distribute half a million pledge cards for the cause in spite of a drenching downpour.

New Releases for the fourth week of February include a cover version of "Blue Suede Shoes" by Boyd Bennett and His Rockets on King; "Please, Please, Please" by James Brown and the Famous Flames on Federal; "My Biggest Mistake" by Joe Tex on King; the Heartbeats' "Darling, How Long" on Hull; "False Love" by the Spaniels on Vee-Jay; "I'm a Fool" by the Turks on Money; Little Walter's "Who?" on Checker; B. B. King's "Let's Do the Boogie" on R.P.M.; "Number One" by Etta James on Modern; "Down and Out" by the Daps on Marterry; Gloria Lynne's "Affection" on Ember; Johnny Fuller's "Sister Jenny" on Imperial; and "16 Teens" by the Rover Boys on ABC-Paramount.

LATE FEBRUARY

    The Cavalcade of Rock 'n' Roll, a touring caravan dominated by Vee-Jay Records artists, arrives on the West Coast after successful engagements in Chicago, Milwaukee, Dallas, Tucson, and Phoenix. Featured performers include the Spaniels, the El Dorados and Jimmy Reed. (See MAR 9.)

    RCA Victor announces that Elvis Presley has six singles among the company's top 25 selling records. This would include his hit "Heartbreak Hotel" as well as the five singles previously available on Sun Records that RCA has re-released.

    As the Willow's "Church Bells Are Ringing" begins to pick up airplay, the title on the label is changed to "Church Bells May Ring" to fit the actual words of the song.

TOP ROCK 'N ROLL RECORDS FOR FEBRUARY 1956

1. The Great Pretender - The Platters
2. See You Later, Alligator - Bill Haley and His Comets
3. Tutti Frutti - Little Richard
4. Speedo - The Cadillacs
5. Only You - The Platters
6. Why Do Fools Fall In Love - Frankie Lymon and the Teenagers
7. Burn That Candle - Bill Haley and His Comets
8. When You Dance - The Turbans
9. Mystery Train - Elvis Presley
10. Seven Days - Clyde McPhatter
11. Devil Or Angel - The Clovers
12. Bo Weevil - Fats Domino
13. Ain't That Lovin' You Baby - Jimmy Reed
14. Jivin' Around (Pt. 1-2) - Ernie Freeman Combo
15. Eddie My Love - The Teen Queens
16. Need Your Love So Bad - Little Willie John
17. Hands Off - Jay McShann and Priscilla Bowman
18. Drown In My Own Tears - Ray Charles
19. Blue Suede Shoes - Carl Perkins
20. I'll Be Home - The Flamingos

Also on the "pop" charts:
Rock and Roll Waltz - Kay Starr
Lisbon Antigua - Nelson Riddle
Band of Gold - Don Cherry
Dungaree Doll - Eddie Fisher
No, Not Much - The Four Lads

February 1956
ARTIST OF THE MONTH

LITTLE RICHARD

"A-Wop-Bop-A-Lu-Bop-A-Lop-Bop-Bop!"

Many people heard Little Richard for the very first time when he was wailing away about his "Tutti Frutti." The novelty aspect of the record caught Middle America completely by surprise. What forces could came together to create such a hyperactive sensation? And, what in the world was all this fuss about tutti-frutti ice cream?

Four months later, Little Richard was singing about "Long Tall Sally." This time there was no mistaking his intent. Hidden underneath barely intelligible lyrics was something about jumping back in the alley.

Teens everywhere had a field day trying to shoehorn the song's lyrics into sexual innuendoes.

His contemporaries in rock 'n roll music, especially Chuck Berry and Fats Domino, skirted around sexual issues. They barely hinted at the ideas presented by Little Richard in "She's Got It," "Oh, My Soul," "Rip It Up," "Ready Teddy," "The Girl Can't Help It," "Lucille," and "Keep A Knockin'."

Richard Penniman was a fully formed talent when he leapt into the social consciousness of America. Most people didn't realize that "Tutti Frutti" wasn't his first record. He'd been recording since 1951, first for RCA Victor then for Peacock, but these records tended toward the blues side of R&B. Even his uptempo songs such as "Little Richard's Boogie" or "Get Rich Quick" barely hinted at his transformation when he reached Specialty Records in the fall of 1955.

Born December 5, 1932*, Richard Wayne Penniman grew up in Macon, Georgia, one of twelve children born to Charles "Bud" Penniman, a man sometimes described as a Seventh Day Adventist preacher and sometimes as a moonshiner. The family performed gospel as the Penniman Singers, and Richard also appeared with the Tiny Tots Quartet. As a teenager, he gave in to the lure of one Dr. Hudson. Hudson was the last of a breed, a touring charlatan who offered a hodgepodge of musicians, including a buck-dancing Richard Penniman, to lure customers to his snake oil concession at county fairs. By the time Richard was fifteen he was traveling as a regular with Sugarfoot Sam's Minstrel Show. He returned to Macon to perform the blues nightly at the Tick Tock Club owned by a lady named Miss Ann. During the day he washed dishes at the cafeteria in the bus station.

Little Richard

In 1951, at age eighteen, he won talent contest in Atlanta. This led to the recording contract with RCA Victor. Victor released four singles from two sessions, but each met with indifference. "Get Rich Quick" (March 1952) and "Ain't Nothin' Happenin'" (July 1952) came the closest to his later style, although both were restrained by comparison. The remaining cuts were typical blues numbers from the period, and even "Thinkin' 'Bout My Mother" couldn't rise above its maudlin sentiment.

The RCA Victor material provided him with two years of one-night stands. In 1954, without a contract, he found himself in Houston. He cut two singles for Don Roby's Peacock Records, initially listed as by the Tempo-Toppers. These records fared little better than those from RCA Victor, although "Rice, Red Beans, and Turnip Greens" sounds like a precursor to "She's Got It." In early 1955, he recorded two final singles for Peacock backed by the Johnny Otis combo. One song, "Little Richard's Boogie," offers a glimmer of the style to come. There is a pounding, insistent, back beat from the drums and piano, and Richard's vocal almost breaks free at several points in the song. Unfortunately, Otis' ever-present xylophone is too close to jazz and distracts from the overall effect.

Back in Macon in early 1955, Richard was once again working as a dishwasher when he recorded a demonstration tape at a local radio station using musicians from his touring ensemble. At Lloyd Price's sug-

---

(*For many years Little Richard gave his date of birth as Christmas Day, 1935.)

gestion, he mailed the demo off to Specialty Records in Los Angeles. Specialty was the record label for Price, as well as Percy Mayfield, Joe Liggins, and Roy Milton, as well as several of Little Richard's favorite gospel groups. Listening to the demo songs today, one is immediately struck by the intensity in his delivery. This is evident in the swinging "Baby" as well as in the more traditional blues number, "All Night Long." For the first time in a recording studio, Richard allowed his voice to soar and swoop while urging the band to play with abandon.

Art Rupe, head of Specialty, had heard of Little Richard before he listened to the tape. Still, he must have been impressed with the changes in Richard's style. However, he was a busy man, and it was almost six months before Rupe gave Richard "the call."

Richard has stated that his strongest influences were two of gospel's greatest voices, Marion Williams, of the Clara Ward Singers, and Mahalia Jackson. Other influences included a host of gospel groups including the Swan Silvertones and the Five Blind Boys From Alabama. He has also given credit to Clyde McPhatter's pure tenor voice on the singles he cut with the Dominoes. However, the most influential performer in Richard's life may have been Billy Wright, a little known blues singer from Atlanta who was very popular in New Orleans. Richard met Wright in 1952. He was immediately taken by Wright's flashy wardrobe. Wright's hair glistened with pomade and was piled high on his head. The affectation that really caught Richard's eye was Wright's stage makeup. Seeing a man wearing eye-liner and face powder was a first for Richard Penniman from Macon, Georgia.

On September 13, 1955, Richard was at J & M Studios in New Orleans for his first Specialty session. Backing him were the cream of local session musicians: Lee Allen and Red Tyler, saxophones; Huey Smith (augmenting Richard), piano; Frank Fields, bass; Justin Adams, guitar; and Earl Palmer, drums. Over the next two years, Little Richard would record more than fifty songs, including alternate takes, for Specialty. From this wealth of material, Specialty would release nine singles and two albums during the same period.

And, the sound of these records... Wow! Envision a freight train roaring out of control—the whistle screaming, the brakes screeching—down a narrow canyon, the sound all full of energy and echo. In Richard's music there was always an underpinning of pile-driving boogie as the drums, bass, guitar and piano played off each other. The horn section, always heavy on saxophones, was blasting away on top. In between there was Little Richard's voice, an odd mixture of screaming banshee and tormented soul, who introduced each saxophone break with a bloodcurdling "Ow-wooooo." Each record was mixed so tight you couldn't squeeze another note in between the grooves. Double Wow!

Richard's live performance had to be seen to be believed. His band, appropriately nicknamed the Upsetters, would take to the stage in matching white suits, sometimes with their lapels decorated in velvet or fur. There would be as many as nine musicians wailing away when the curtain opened: five saxophones, two guitars, bass, and drums. During their thirty-minute set as the show's opening act, it was the mission of the band to work the crowd into a dancing frenzy. And, while they were playing, they performed intricate step routines choreographed by Grady Gaines, the lead tenor sax man. At the height of this turmoil, the band would kick into something repetitious, such as the riff that opens "The Girl Can't Help It." The crowd, sensing that Little Richard was about to appear would become completely hysterical. The front of the stage would be packed with squirming bodies to a depth of thirty or forty feet. At just the right moment, out would come the show's star, wearing a turban two feet tall. Carefully, the turban was removed to reveal Richard's gleaming black hair, rising in wave after ebony wave, piled up six or eight inches high. After all this setup, the remainder of the show could have easily been anti-climatic. Not so. Richard worked the crowd with all the fury he could muster, driving through his repertoire at breakneck speed. Less than an hour later the show was over. As the Upsetters roared through the closing number, Richard slowly left the stage, drenched with sweat. His bare chest was heaving, the shirt having been ripped off his back before the beginning of the second number. It was an act that defied an encore.

For eighteen months, from early 1956 to the middle of 1957, everything Little Richard recorded became a hit. His club dates were all triumphant sellouts. He was picked to be in several early movies about rock 'n roll, including the best of the lot, "The Girl Can't Help It," for which he cut the title track. Then, on October 12, 1957, as he was touring Australia with Gene Vincent and Eddie Cochran, his world came crashing to a halt. Legend has it that he was frightened when an engine on his airplane caught fire. Whatever the reason, he refound religion and renounced rock 'n roll. He hadn't been in a recording studio since the previous January, and Specialty refused to allow him out of his contract without one last session. On October 18, 1957, he walked into a Hollywood studio for what many thought would be the last time.

He entered Oakwood Seminary in Huntsville, Alabama, where he studied to become a Seventh Day Adventist preacher. Specialty had enough songs "in the can" to keep singles and albums coming for another year. Sensing that he was being cheated, in August 1959, Richard hired a lawyer to collect back royalties from Specialty Records that he estimated at $25,000.

By this time, he was also being approached by record companies to sing gospel. In January 1959, he signed with a Los Angeles agency to set up a gospel tour, and in June it was announced that he had signed with Gone Records. His Los Angeles recording sessions would be supervised by Billy Ward. Eventually Richard also accepted invitations from Mercury and Atlantic Records to return to the studio to sing religious material.

Three years of less than spectacular success as a gospel performer appear to have created problems in Richard's resolve to remain true to his religious beliefs. By October 1962, he was touring England, singing rock 'n roll once again. He relished in his new-found influence on younger musicians who were forming bands named the Beatles, Gerry and the Pacemakers, the Searchers, and the Rolling Stones. A year later, he toured Europe and the Beatles and the Rolling Stones were his opening acts.

His overseas success brought him again to the attention of stateside record companies. First, Vee-Jay, then Specialty, and finally Modern, Okeh, and Brunswick took him back into the studio. Vee-Jay, Modern, and Okeh were more interested in having him rerecord his old hits. Specialty, in five sessions, tried to rekindle the magic from 1957. None of the resulting records were very successful. Of note from the Vee-Jay sessions was an unknown left-handed guitarist from Richard's tour band named Jimi Hendrix.

Through the remainder of the 1960s, Little Richard made his living one night at a time, working his magic on each crowd the same way he did in the 1950s. In Las Vegas in 1968, he was the hit of the Strip, packing in the crowds while he sang contemporary soul as well as his older hits. Then, in 1969, lightning struck once again in the form of a worldwide rock 'n roll revival. There was ample work for Little Richard, as well as Jerry Lee Lewis, Chuck Berry, Bill Haley, and all the others who had struggled through the "British Invasion."

Reprise Records offered Little Richard a contract that, for once, did not include a greatest hits package. He was the special added attraction on a Canned Heat album. He sang another movie's title song in "$" (also called "Dollars"), and made a few guest appearances on television.

In 1976, religion—and a positive attempt to shake a $10,000-a-month cocaine habit—once again brought Little Richard back to the church. This time, the conversion lasted almost ten years during which time he coauthored his autobiography. In 1984 he was back in show business, making the round of late night television talk shows. He sued Specialty Records for back royalties estimated at $115 million, but the suit was dismissed after it was learned that he had settled the earlier suit against Specialty in 1959 for $11,000.

Richard made a cameo appearance in the 1985 film "Down and Out in Beverly Hills" as well as singing "Good Gosh A' Mighty" for the soundtrack. A year later, he was one of the first inductees into the Rock and Roll Hall of Fame. Little Richard was back in the limelight to stay.

Little Richard was always unpredictable off, as well as on, stage. He personified the out-of-control lifestyle many people assume all rock 'n rollers live. His outrageous guest appearances on television talk shows were legendary. Only in the 1990s does he seem to have mellowed even a little. In 1990, he was finally awarded his star on Hollywood's Walk of Fame. He received a Grammy Award, his first, for Lifetime Achievement in 1993. The same year he was invited to perform for President Clinton's inaugural festivities.

Richard has been active on the recording scene, too. In 1990, his version of the childrens' song, "Itsy Bitsy Spider" was part of FOR OUR CHILDREN, an album released by Walt Disney Records. In late 1992, he had his own album on Walt Disney Records, SHAKE IT ALL ABOUT, full of similar material including "The Hokey Pokey," "Old MacDonald," and, for old time sake, "Keep A-Knockin'."

How ironic. Here was Little Richard entertaining the children—and the grandchildren—of the same teenagers he had teased with exotic visions of what might happen if they "jump back in the alley."

"A-Wop-Bop-A-Lu-Bop-A-Lop-Bam-Boom!"

Indeed!

March 1956

MAR 2   The only rhythm and blues group on this week's bill at the Apollo Theater in New York is the Leaders.

In Los Angeles, Ruth Brown plays to a packed house each of her three nights at the 5-4 Ballroom. At the Savoy, Charles Brown plays his third weekend date in a month at the club.

New Releases for the first week of March include "The Magic Touch" by the Platters on Mercury; "Dancing the Bop" by the Jodimars on Capitol; an instrumental version of "Blue Suede Shoes" by Sam "The Man" Taylor on M-G-M; "Are You Ever Coming Back?" by **Little Willie John** and "Raining in My Heart" by the Hurricanes, both on King; "Little Fool" by Charlie and Ray on Herald; and "Mumbles Blues" by Bobby Lewis on Spotlight. In a tie-in with the eminent release of the movie "Rock Around The Clock," Decca issues a 12-inch album by Bill Haley and His Comets under the same name featuring five songs from the picture.

EARLY MARCH

Gleason's Bar of Music in Cleveland announces that guest artists for the month will include Chuck Willis, Muddy Waters and Charles Brown.

MAR 9   The Los Angeles-area clubs offer a diverse group of acts this weekend. The 5-4 Ballroom presents Amos Milburn and Etta James while the Savoy Ballroom introduces the "Vee-Jay Revue" with Jimmy Reed and the El Dorados.

Patrons at Detroit's Flame Show Bar welcome the Ravens for the week. Also in Detroit, the Club Basin Street presents the Drifters, and the Charms for three days.

"Slippin' and Slidin'," the flip side of Little Richard's "Long Tall Sally," is picked as the number one new record on NBC radio's "National Juke Box Fan Club."

MAR 10   Eddie Cochran, one-half of the Cochran Brothers act, is made a regular member of "Hollywood Jubilee," a weekly show at Los Angeles' American Legion Stadium. Also appearing on the "Jubilee" are country/rockabilly artists Terry Fell, Tom T. Hall, and Jerry Capehart, who will soon become a songwriting partner with Cochran.

Louis Jordan and his Tympany Five guest on NBC-TV's "The Perry Como Show."

LITTLE WILLIE JOHN
He was born William Edward John although many accounts list his name as William John Wood. One source lists him as Mertis John—his father's name—and one even states that his real name was John Davenport, a pseudonym used by Otis Blackwell, one of the composers of "Fever." His birth took place near Camden, Arkansas, on November 15, 1937, although November 17 is frequently, and erroneously, given. When "Little Willie" was a youngster, his family moved to Detroit, which he named as his hometown for the rest of his life. A natural performer, he attracted the attention of band leader Paul Williams before he turned twelve, although other accounts have him joining Williams at a later date. With Williams, he reportedly recorded "The Hucklebuck," a major R&B hit for Savoy Records, in early 1949. In 1952, billed only as "Little Willie," Federal Records released "Last Laugh Blues," a duet with Little Esther Phillips. Around this time he was also a featured vocalist with Duke Ellington and Count Basie. His association with Federal led to his signing with the parent company, King Records, in June 1955. He had an immediate R&B hit with "All Around The World," followed by "Fever," his first gold record. He continued to have success as a recording artist through the 1950s, with "Talk To Me, Talk To Me" also selling a million copies. In 1960, "Sleep" and "Heartbreak, (It's Hurtin' Me)" sold well. Little Willie John continued to be a big draw in concert after his recording career slowed. In 1966, he was convicted of manslaughter after knifing a man in a Seattle bar, and was sentenced to Washington State Prison. There, on May 26, 1968, he died. The official cause was listed as "classic acute myocardial infarction" (a massive heart attack), although most sources maintain that he died of pneumonia. Many of Willie's supporters continue believe that he died from injuries suffered in a beating.

MAR 11   The "Rhythm and Blues Revue" opens a three-day run at the Ritz Theater in New Orleans. Scheduled to appear are Joe Turner, Amos Milburn, Nat King Cole, Sarah Vaughan, Lionel Hampton, Count Basie, Faye Adams, the Larks, and Ruth Brown, among others.

In Albuquerque, Marvin and Johnny start a tour of the Southwest covering New Mexico, Arizona, Texas and Oklahoma.

MAR 12   At Detroit's Greystone Ballroom it's a battle between jazz and blues as Dinah Washington, Little Willie John, T-Bone Walker, and the Clovers are pitted against a variety of contemporary jazz artists. Little Willie John is currently booked locally at the Club Vogue.

New Releases for the second week of March include "Long Tall Sally" by Little Richard on Specialty; "Ivory Tower" by Otis Williams and His Charms on DeLuxe; "Cherry Lips" by the Robins on Whippet; "My First Real Love" by Connie Francis on M-G-M; the Midnighters' "Open Up the Back Door" on Federal; "Seven Nights to Rock" by Moon Mullican and "Little Miss Bobby Sox" by Bonnie Lou, both on King; "Please Don't Drive Me Away" by Charles Brown on Aladdin; and two on Chess, "We Go Together" by the Moonglows and "Don't You Know I Love You" by **Bobby Charles**.

MAR 14   The motion picture "Rock Around the Clock," is released to theaters. The picture features Bill Haley and His Comets, Alan Freed, the Platters (backed by Ernie Freeman's combo), and Freddy Bell and the Bellboys. Eighty percent of the film's running time is taken up with music as seventeen songs are featured.

Elvis Presley starts six sold out shows over a two-day period at the Fox Theater in Atlanta.

MID-MARCH

Andre Williams and the Five Dollars are at the Detroit's Twenty Grand Recreation Club for the month.

MAR 16   Heading the revue at the Apollo Theater in New York are the Four Aces. Other acts include Diahann Carroll and Lucky Millinder's orchestra.

"The Battle of the Blues" at Los Angeles' Savoy Ballroom features Johnny "Guitar" Watson and Jimmy Witherspoon for the weekend. Charles Brown returns to the 5-4 Ballroom for three days.

Also in the Los Angeles area, Amos Milburn and Etta James start three days at three different locations. Tonight's show is at the Valley Gardens Club in North Hollywood. On Saturday they're at the Long Beach Auditorium, followed on Sunday by a show at the Casino Gardens in Santa Monica.

The Drifters headline the Howard Theater's revue this week in Washington. Also appearing are Bo Diddley, Mickey and Sylvia, and the Heartbeats.

The Flame Lounge in Detroit is visited by the Orioles and Della Reese.

BOBBY CHARLES
Bobby Charles' claim to fame lies with his composition "Later Alligator," which Bill Haley released as "See You Later, Alligator" in December 1955. Charles' real name is Robert Charles Guidry, and he was born in Abbeville, Louisiana, on February 21, 1938, although his date of birth is also listed as August 12, 1940, which would make him just sixteen when his original version was released on Chess Records in November 1955. Charles has been called the first white R&B artist, and he was certainly one of the first white artists on Chess, outside of the company's small contingent of country performers. Growing up the Louisiana bayou country imbued Charles with the same rhythms as Smiley Lewis, Huey Smith, and Fats Domino. He was working in local bands at age fourteen and was discovered by a local record store owner who arranged for his recording session in New Orleans and sent the master tape to Chess Records. It is part of the Charles legend that Leonard Chess, the record company owner, did not know that Charles was white until after the record's release. Bobby Charles recording career failed to ignite and after seven singles with Chess he moved on to Imperial in 1958. In the 1960s, he recorded for several small companies, including Farie, Hub City, Jewel, and Paula. He attempted a comeback engineered by Paul Butterfield in the early 1970s, but his fame has never spread far beyond south Louisiana. As a songwriter, Charles has had some success, penning "But I Do" for Clarence Henry and "Walking To New Orleans" for Fats Domino.

MAR 17   After an absence of one month, Elvis Presley returns to "Stage Show" on CBS-TV for a guest shot. He will make one last appearance on "Stage Show" next Saturday, March 24.

On ABC-TV, Carl Perkins makes his first national guest shot on Red Foley's "Ozark Jubilee."

New Releases for the third week of March include Elvis Presley's first long play album, ELVIS PRESLEY, from RCA Victor. Also out this week are "I'm in Love Again" b/w "My Blue Heaven" from Fats Domino on Imperial; "R-O-C-K" by Bill Haley and His Comets on Decca; "Corrine Corrina" by Joe Turner on Atlantic; "Ding Dong" by Freddie Bell and the Bellboys on Wing; "Ain't He Sweet" by the **Sensations** on Atco; Tommy Leonetti's "Wrong" on Capitol; and two cover versions of "Long Tall Sally" by Marty Robbins on Columbia and Pat Boone on Dot, as well as Boone's "I Need Someone" on Republic.

MAR 21   Carl Perkins headlines the show at the Norfolk, VA, Auditorium. Attendance is pegged at more than 2,000. Following the show, and en route to New York for a March 24 appearance on Perry Como's NBC-TV show, Perkins is seriously injured in an auto accident in Dover, Delaware, suffering a fractured skull and broken shoulder. More seriously injured with a broken neck was his brother and rhythm guitarist, Jay. Carl will remain in the hospital until April 10, and his recuperation will take another month. Jay will never fully recover.

MAR 23   Alan Freed stages a three-day "Rock 'n' Roll Stage Show" at the State Theater, Hartford. Although Freed denied that there was a riot, eleven teens were arrested over the weekend. After the melee, Dr. Francis J. Braceland of the Institute of Living in Hartford referred to rock 'n' roll as a "communicable disease with music appealing to adolescent insecurity and driving teenagers to do outlandish things... It's cannibalistic and tribalistic." Dr. Braceland's remarks prompted a published defense of both rock 'n' roll and Freed by three well-known band leaders of another generation, Sammy Kaye, Benny Goodman, and Paul Whiteman.

In Harlem, the Apollo Theater offers a gospel and spiritual caravan.

At the 5-4 Ballroom in Los Angeles, Ruth Brown entertains the crowd for three days.

Ivory Joe Hunter brings his smooth delivery to Detroit's Flame Show Bar for the week.

New Releases for the fourth week of March include two from Atlantic: "Ruby Baby" by the Drifters and "Off Shore" from the Cardinals. Also new this week are "Little Girl of Mine" by the Cleftones on Gee; "Girl In My Dreams" by the Cliques (featuring Jesse Belvin) on Modern; "Baby" by the Premiers on Dig; "Fruit Boots" from saxophonist Red Prysock on Wing; and "Rock Island Line" by Bobby Darin and the Jaybirds on Decca.

THE SENSATIONS

The Sensations were one of the few R&B vocal groups with a female lead. The group originally formed in Philadelphia in 1954, appearing in amateur shows as the Cavaliers. At that time, the lead singer for the group was Yvonne Mills and Alphonso Howell sang bass. The unique makeup of the group caught the attention of Atlantic Records, and the Sensations (as they were now dubbed) began a three-year association with Atlantic's Atco subsidiary. The first two singles released by the Sensations were old standards that had been given a major musical overhaul. Both "Yes, Sir That's My Baby" and "Ain't He Sweet" received a major push from Atco but failed to catch on. These were followed by "My Heart Cries For You," "Little Wallflower," and "My Debut To Love." When the Atco contract expired, Yvonne retired from show business to marry and raise a family. In the early 1960s, the now Yvonne Baker was approached by Howell who wanted to reform the group. They were joined by Sam Armstrong of the Rays and Richie Curtin of the Hideaways. The group signed with Chess Records, which released another old standard, "Music, Music, Music" in 1961 on the Argo label. The record sold fairly well, and it was followed in early 1962 by the Top Ten smash, "Let Me In," the record for which the group is best remembered.

MAR 30   During Easter vacation, Alan Freed kicks off another ten-day run at the Paramount movie house in Brooklyn. Heading the show are the Platters. Also on the bill are the Royaltones, the Rover Boys, the Willows, Frankie Lymon and the Teenagers, the Cleftones, the Jodimars, and Sam "The Man" Taylor's band. The six-shows-a-day revue, with ticket prices ranging up to $2.50, will gross $204,000.

T-Bone Walker and Arthur Prysock share the spotlight at the Flame in Detroit for the next week.

Al Hibbler headlines the review at the Regal Theater in Chicago. Others on the bill include the Orioles and Della Reese.

This Easter weekend also finds the Medallions, Jimmy Witherspoon and Chuck Higgins playing various clubs in the San Francisco area.

In Los Angeles, Amos Milburn and Etta James play the 5-4 Ballroom.

Louis Jordan brings his Tympany Five to Washington's Howard Theater this week.

LATE MARCH

The White Citizen's Council of Birmingham, Alabama, starts a campaign to rid all local jukeboxes of rock 'n roll records.

TOP ROCK 'N ROLL RECORDS FOR MARCH 1956

1. The Great Pretender - The Platters
2. See You Later, Alligator - Bill Haley and His Comets
3. Why Do Fools Fall In Love - Frankie Lymon and the Teenagers
4. Blue Suede Shoes - Carl Perkins
5. Heartbreak Hotel/I Was The One - Elvis Presley
6. Eddie My Love - The Teen Queens
7. Tutti Frutti - Little Richard
8. Bo Weevil - Fats Domino
9. Speedo - The Cadillacs
10. The Magic Touch - The Platters
11. Mystery Train - Elvis Presley
12. Drown In My Own Tears - Ray Charles
13. Devil Or Angel - The Clovers
14. Ivory Tower - Otis Williams and His Charms
15. Long Tall Sally - Little Richard
16. I'll Be Home - The Flamingos
17. Ain't That Lovin' You Baby - Jimmy Reed
18. Need Your Love So Bad - Little Willie John
19. Down in Mexico - The Coasters
20. Church Bells May Ring - The Willows

Also on the "pop" charts:
Poor People of Paris - Les Baxter
I'll Be Home - Pat Boone
Theme From "The Three Penny Opera" - Dick Hyman

Hot Diggity - Perry Como
A Tear Fell - Teresa Brewer

March 1956
ARTIST OF THE MONTH

FRANKIE LYMON AND THE TEENAGERS

Frankie Lymon & The Teenagers

The clarity of the upper range of Frankie Lymon's voice was the pure, natural high tenor that a professional singer could strive a lifetime to achieve—and a rhythm and blues vocal group could hang a career on. Lymon came by his honestly enough. In late 1955, he had just turned thirteen, and his voice hadn't "changed" yet.

Lymon was born on September 30, 1942, in the Washington Heights section of New York City. He was raised by his grandmother in her home on West 165th Street. In the same neighborhood, there was a quartet of Stitt Junior High students calling themselves the Ermines, then the Coupe de Villes, and eventually the Premiers. The boys had joined to rehearse on street corners and in the school auditorium, and to dream of making a record. The group, a combination of blacks and Puerto Ricans, consisted of fifteen-year-olds Sherman Garnes, who had an incredible bass range for someone so young; Jimmy Merchant, tenor; and Joe Negroni, baritone—along with fourteen-year old Herman Santiago, tenor.

Meanwhile, Lymon was already a veteran performer, having sung with his father's gospel quartet, the Harlemaires. Later Santiago would remember him as "talented, bright, and very cocky." Even at this young age, he was a precocious, natural-born showman.

The Premiers were working on a self-penned number they called "Why Do Birds Sing So Gay" and needed a high tenor to pull it off. Their plight reached the ears of Richard Barrett, a member of the Valentines, the most successful vocal group from the neighborhood. Barrett knew of Lymon—he lived above the grocery where Lymon worked part-time—and through him, eventually they all got together. It was Lymon's suggestion to change the focus of the song as well as its title. Together, they came up with "Why Do Fools Fall In Love."

The Valentines were under contract to Rama Records, a 42nd Street company owned by George Goldner. He would soon control several independent labels including Gee, Gone, End, Goldisc, and Tico. Barrett acted as a talent scout for Goldner, and he was able to arrange for an audition for the Premiers with Goldner who was immediately impressed. At the subsequent recording session, band leader Jimmy Wright suggested the group change its name to the Teenagers to reflect the ages of its members.

Gee released the single of "Why Do Fools Fall in Love" in early February, 1956, it was an instant smash. Overnight, the Teenagers found themselves swamped with offers to perform. In less than three weeks, the group made its professional debut at the Rivera Theater in Detroit.

By the end of the month, the single had rocketed up the charts. The Teenagers were on their way to becoming a show business phenomenon of the highest magnitude.

The instant appeal of the Teenagers lay with their youth, something Jimmy Wright had seen at the beginning. Lymon exuded a cherublike innocence while singing sweet love songs. Their early records were polished pieces of "pop" fluff driven by the power of Garnes' bass line—which was accentuated by an electric bass. All of this worked to support Lymon's childlike delivery of the lyric. The group, especially Lymon, was also very energetic on stage, something that is only hinted at in the few filmed performances of the group that remain. Choreography was always a big part of the Teenagers' act. They were trained by Cholly Atkins who went on to even bigger fame working with the Temptations. Finally, Gee Records packaged the Teenagers so they would not be upsetting to middle class American parents. They even began appearing in letter-sweaters, the epitome of high school fashion.

In March 1956, Alan Freed booked the group to perform in one of his rock 'n roll reviews at the Brooklyn Paramount. They were on the same stage with such acknowledged stars as the Platters and Bill Haley and His Comets. In April a second single, "I Want You To Be My Girl," was released. A week later the group made its television debut on CBS-TV's "Shower of Stars." By the end of the month, the boys found themselves part of a full-blown tour, "The Biggest Rock 'n' Show of 1956," again featuring Bill Haley and the Platters. The Teenagers debuted at the Apollo in June, and two weeks later, they were at Detroit's Fox Theater. The end of June saw the release of their third single, "I Promise To Remember." They worked shows with Carl Perkins and Chuck Berry from the Carolinas to Detroit during July.

In August, production began in Hollywood on the movie "Rock, Rock, Rock" with the Teenagers making a cameo singing appearance. Then they were back in New York for Alan Freed's week-long Labor Day revue at the Brooklyn Paramount. In early September, the Teenagers appeared on Freed's radio show on CBS. They also appeared at the Apollo where they headlined during a week that saw the release of their next single "ABC's Of Love." After that, they went back to Hollywood to film another cameo for "Don't Knock The Rock." In late September, they embarked on another tour with Bill Haley and Chuck Berry that lasted until late November, a month that saw the release of their fifth single "Baby, Baby." In December, their first long play album, "Meet The Teenagers," was released.

The pace of their career had to slow after such a demanding year as 1956. The boys were all still students, having enrolled in the School for Professionals. On the road, they took correspondence courses and had traveling tutors. Nevertheless, their education was falling behind. For the first two months in 1957, the group remained at home, with only the release of "Paper Castles" to keep their spirits up. However, this was just a temporary respite. The Siren of fame was calling and 1957 promised to be bigger than 1956.

On March 1, the group received $7,500 for a week's engagement in Panama for the annual carnival. Then came a three-month tour of Britain, starting at the London Palladium. While in London, the Teenagers recorded a second long play album for Gee records. Unknown to the fans, "Frankie Lymon and the Teenagers at the London Palladium" was actually recorded at the EMI studios. The Teenagers played dates in Glasgow and Dublin, as well as around England through June. While they were away from the states, Gee released another single, "Out In The Cold Again."

The Teenagers returned to the States in time to star on Alan Freed's nine-day Fourth of July revue at the New York Paramount Theater, but there were changes in the wind.

For some time George Goldner had been trying to convince Lymon to go solo. After his success in Great Britain, Lymon finally agreed to split with the group. In July, 1957, he appeared without the Teenagers as a guest on the debut of Freed's weekly television show. That same month saw the release of "Goody Goody," the last single credited to Frankie Lymon and the Teenagers although it sounded more like a solo effort by Lymon.

In September, Lymon started an eighty-day marathon tour with the "Biggest Show of Stars for 1957" as a solo act. The same month, Goldner's Roulette Records released his first solo single, "My Girl." In the theaters, "Mister Rock and Roll" was also a hit. In November, Lymon's "Little Girl" appeared on Roulette while the Teenagers had "Flip-Flop" on Gee.

January 1958 brought another release from Lymon, "Thumb, Thumb." He and the Teenagers reunited briefly to perform "Goody, Goody" on Dick Clark's "American Bandstand" on ABC-TV. In late March, Lymon appeared solo again on Alan Freed's annual Easter production at the New York Paramount Theater and joined the troupe when it hit the road for a month. In June, he was at the Apollo Theater with the Coasters. A month later, his latest single, "The Only Way To Love You," was released by Roulette. Then, for eight months, Lymon dropped out of sight.

Two years as an entertainer had taken their toll on Lymon, who was now all of fifteen. After the heady success of the Teenager's first two singles, record sales had slipped with each new release. "Goody Goody" briefly claimed a spot on the music charts in the summer of 1957, but it was the last record by Lymon or the group to have any significant sales until 1960. The decline of his recording career was temporarily offset by his acclaim as a stage performer. Now, as he began to mature, even that was in jeopardy.

January 1959 brought "Up Jumped a Rabbit" from Lymon. In March, he was traveling with "The Biggest Show of Stars for 1959." A month later, while he was still playing one night stands, "What a Little Moonlight Can Do" became his last release on Roulette.

Then, just as quickly as he had become a star, Frankie Lymon was a star no longer.

Lymon's years in the adult world of entertainment had introduced him to drugs, and he was firmly in the grip of a heroin addiction. In 1961 he tried to come clean. His rehabilitation lasted a few years. However, he made the news when he was arrested on June 21, 1966, on a narcotics charge. In a magazine article in 1967, he was quoted as saying he had been a pimp when he was twelve, a marijuana-smoking student in junior high, and womanizer by the time he was fifteen. He entered the Army in 1967, apparently in lieu of a jail sentence; but a short time later he received a less than honorable discharge at Fort Gordon, Georgia. He had recently married Emira Eagle, a local school teacher. He stayed in the Augusta area, appearing at a local lounge. Things were looking up. In mid-February, 1968, he told Emira he had a weekend gig in New York. On February 27, 1968, he died in the same house on 165th Street where he had grown up. An empty syringe was by his side.

As with most young performers of the era, the Teenagers quickly lost the rights to their own material. First off, Goldner's publishing firm handled the song, taking fifty percent of the royalties off the top. Original copies of the single of "Why Do Fools Fall In Love" listed Frankie Lymon, Herman Santiago, and George Goldner as the song's composers. Santiago's name was soon dropped. By the mid-1960s, both Goldner and Lymon had sold off their rights to the song. Goldner was reportedly in debt from gambling losses, and Lymon always needed money for drugs.

In 1984, on behalf of Emira Lymon, a lawyer and an artist's agent joined forces to try to wrest the copyright away from the current owner. The case became much more confused when it started to look like Lymon had left a second, and possibly a third widow. First, Elizabeth Waters claimed to have married Frankie in 1964 in Virginia. However, it turned out that she had been married to someone else at the time. As Miss Waters' claim went to court, Zola Taylor, ex-member of the Platters, came forth with the startling news that she had been sexually active with Lymon as early as the "Biggest Rock 'n' Roll Show of 1956" tour. She also claimed to have married Lymon in Las Vegas, or maybe it was Tijuana, about 1965, although she could not produce a marriage certificate. The first hearing, held in Philadelphia, was decided in favor of Miss Waters as Lymon's first wife. Emira appealed and won a reversal based on her claim that she was Lymon's last wife.

Herman Santiago and Jimmy Merchant also pursued their claim to the song's publishing rights through the federal court system. In December 1992, the two singers and Emira Lymon, received complete rights to the song.

By 1980, Sherman Garnes and Joe Negroni had both died when the two remaining Teenagers decided to rebuild the group. Santiago and Merchant performed with Garnes' brother, while the high tenor parts were handled by Pearl McKinnon of the Kodaks, and later by Frankie's brother, Lewis Lymon. The group appeared briefly off Broadway in a musical tribute to the Teenagers. In 1993, Frankie Lymon and the Teenagers were inducted into the Rock and Roll Hall of Fame.

Frankie Lymon has been called the "father" of the girl group sound. He was a direct influence on Arlene Smith of the Chantels who, as a young teenage recording star herself, idolized him. Others who fell heir to Lymon's style were Little Anthony and the Imperials and the Isley Brothers. It is interesting that the Chantels, the Imperials and the Isley Brothers all recorded for George Goldner's labels and were produced by Richard Barrett.

April 1956

APR 1 The first big caravan of the spring hits the road with an Easter Sunday performance in Richmond, Virginia. "The Rhythm and Blues of 1956" features Fats Domino, the Clovers, the Cadillacs, Little Richard, Ruth Brown, the Turbans, Ann Cole, and Little Willie John. In its first four days on the road the show nets $52,000 against a set performance fee of $3,500 a night or 60 percent of the gate. Booking has been so extensive that the artists will perform for five weeks straight without a day off. During the first two weeks, performances will be confined to the East Coast, including Charlotte (2), Winston-Salem (3), and Philadelphia (4). Also scheduled are shows in Baltimore, Pittsburgh, Buffalo, and Newark. New York City is obvious by its omission. (See also APR 8 and APR 20. This revue should not be confused with "The Rhythm and Blues Revue.")

In Hollywood, Elvis Presley has a screen test with producer Hal Wallis of Paramount Pictures. As a result, Presley signs a three-picture deal with Wallis.

APR 2 Chuck Berry heads the lineup at the Greystone Ballroom's rhythm and blues revue in Detroit. Also on the bill are Big Maybelle, Andre Williams and the Don Juans, Bobby "Mumbles" Lewis, **Nolan Strong and the Diablos**, Arthur Prysock, and Otis Williams and His Charms.

New Releases for the first week of April include "I Want You to Be My Girl" by Frankie Lymon and the Teenagers on Gee; "Strange Love" by the Native Boys on Combo; "Tough Mama" by the Nitecaps on Groove; the Five Keys' "I Dreamt I Dwelt in Heaven" on Capitol; "Now That You're Gone" by the El Dorados on Vee-Jay; and "The Rock and Roll Story" by Dave Appell and the Applejacks on President.

APR 3 Elvis Presley guests on "The Milton Berle Show" telecast over NBC-TV from the aircraft carrier U.S.S. Hancock which is docked at the San Diego Naval Station. He will also perform a pair of shows at the San Diego Arena on April 4-5.

APR 4 The Three Chuckles and the Penguins headline "Rock-A-Rama" in Albany, New York.

APR 6 In Los Angeles, the Savoy features Roy Milton for the weekend and the 5-4 Ballroom welcomes Richard Berry and the Ernie Freeman Combo for three days.

NOLAN STRONG & THE DIABLOS

Nolan Strong's beautifully controlled falsetto was a major influence on Smokey Robinson of the Miracles. In fact, Nolan Strong and the Diablos were among the very first R&B groups from Detroit to receive a major, national following. In turn, Strong was most influenced by the very early recordings of Clyde McPhatter, when McPhatter was lead tenor with the Dominoes, and by Sonny Til, lead singer with the Orioles. While the Diablos were still in high school, they were discovered by Jack and Devora Brown of Fortune Records when the boys came to his fledgling record company to make a demonstration record. In April 1954, "Adios, My Desert Love" was their first Fortune release. While the single failed to capture national attention, it was a solid-seller in many areas of the country. The group followed with their most significant record, "The Wind." This record sold considerably better than "Adios, My Desert Love," however, it also failed to make the national charts. When Berry Gordy was starting to build his Motown recording empire, he offered Strong $1000.00 to sign, but Strong remained with Fortune into 1964. In 1956, the other members of the Diablos were Willie Hunter, baritone; Jimmy Strong—Nolan's brother, tenor; George Scott, bass; and Bob "Chico" Edwards, guitar. Nolan Strong died February 21, 1977, at the age of forty-three.

APR 7   The Platters make their first national television appearance, on CBS-TV's "Stage Show."

EARLY APRIL
> Chuck Willis, a big name in r&b music during the early 1950s on Okeh Records, but more recently in a slump so far as record sales, signs with Atlantic Records in a move destined to rejuvenate his flagging career. Going against the obvious bad-luck connotations, Willis' first Atlantic session was held in New York on Friday the 13th.
>
> Gleason's Bar of Music in Cleveland announces that it has booked the Five Keys, Bo Diddley, and Guitar Slim for appearances during the month.
>
> Pee Wee Crayton starts a month of nightly appearances at Mike's Waikiki Club in Los Angeles.
>
> In Kansas City, the Orchid Room reports booking Ray Charles, Charles Brown, Ruth Brown, Fats Domino, the Turbans, and the Cadillacs for appearances during the month.
>
> Also during the month, the **Johnny Burnette Trio** from Memphis appears on three consecutive Sunday nights on "The Ted Mack Amateur Hour" on ABC-TV. Their rockabilly performance wins each weekly competition and places them on the roster for the show's annual final competition to be broadcast in September.

APR 8   Elvis Presley undertakes his first major tour of the year, beginning tonight in Denver. Other dates include El Paso, Wichita Falls, Lubbock, El Paso, San Antonio, Corpus Christi, Waco, Tulsa, Amarillo, Ft. Worth, and Houston.

The "Rhythm and Blues Revue" is back in New Orleans for a three-day, weekend run at two theaters simultaneously as the performers are shuttled between the Palace and Gem Theaters. (See also MAR 11 for a list of performers.)

The "Rhythm and Blues of 1956" tour featuring Fats Domino plays the National Guard Armory in Washington, DC. (See also APR 1 and APR 20.)

New Releases for the second week of April include "Love Me" b/w "Blue Days, Black Nights" by Buddy Holly on Decca; "Rock 'n' Roll Ruby" by Warren Smith on Sun; "My Heart's Desire" by the Wheels on Premium; "What Is Your Decision?" by the Harptones on Andrea; "Why Did I Fall In Love" by the Jacks on R.P.M.; "Fine Little Girl" by the Solitaires and "Train To Paradise" by Robert and Johnny, both on Old Town; "Right Now, Right Now" by the Alan Freed Band on Coral; "She's Mine" by Joe Tex on King; "Hey, Baby, Baby" by Jimmy Swan on M-G-M; and Arthur Lee Maye and the Crowns' "Gloria" on Specialty. Also out this week is a record featuring half-a-dozen Sacramento teenagers, including thirteen-year old Trudy Williams: "A Casual Look" by the Six Teens on Flip.

APR 10   "The Rhythm and Blues of 1956" troupe performs at the Mutual Arena in Toronto. This is the first time such an aggregation

---

JOHNNY BURNETTE TRIO
Johnny Burnette (born March 25, 1934) and his brother, Dorsey (born December 28, 1932), were from Memphis, and they loved boxing almost as much as they loved singing. When they were unable to make a financial career of their pugilistic skills, they enlisted Paul Burlison (born February 4, 1929, Brownsville, Tennessee) to form a trio. Hard work led them to the Hideaway Club where they became regular performers. Their first record, "You're Undecided," was a country effort released on the minuscule Von label from Booneville, Mississippi, in 1953, almost a year before the first single by Elvis Presley. Along with Elvis, the Rock 'n' Roll Trio (as Burnette's group was first known) turned Memphis music on its ear. After Elvis appeared on national television in January 1956, the Rock 'n' Roll Trio wrangled an invitation to perform on "The Ted Mack Amateur Hour." As a result of their popularity on the show, they were signed by Coral Records and their first Coral single, "Tear It Up," was released in May 1956. They had six more releases on Coral over the next eighteen months, and while none received much national attention, they were remained a big draw from Tennessee to Texas. In 1956 and again in 1958, Johnny Black, the brother of Elvis' bass player Bill Black, replaced Dorsey on tour. In fact, it was Black who appeared with the group in their only film appearance in "Rock, Rock, Rock!" Both Johnny and Dorsey Burnette had success as singer/songwriters in the 1960s.

has performed in Ottawa's capitol city. (See also APR 1.)

APR 11   Eddie Fontaine and Shirley Gunter and the Queens play Utica, New York, as part of a twenty-one-day tour.

APR 12   CBS-TV airs "Shower of Stars," a preview of a possible entry in the network's fall lineup. Representing the rock 'n roll side of music are Frankie Lymon and the Teenagers.
   Earl Bostic starts a week-long engagement at Zardi's Jazzland in Hollywood.

APR 13   In Los Angeles, Lloyd Price visits the Savoy Ballroom for three days. At the 5-4 Ballroom across town, Bill Doggett and Faye Adams are the featured entertainers for the next two weekends.
   Roy Hamilton and the Sensations appear at the Howard Theater in Washington for the week.

APR 14   Alan Freed brings his rock 'n roll package show to Baltimore for the evening.

APR 15   Amid increasing news reports of a darker side to rock 'n roll, Alan Freed guests on CBS-TV to state his views on the subject. Eric Sevareid, CBS commentator, hosts the discussion which also includes interviews with teenagers and newsreel footage of a Freed-sponsored show at a theater in Camden, New Jersey.
   The rock 'n roll show at the University of Detroit's Memorial Hall features the Four Aces, Cathy Carr, Bobby Darin, and Otis Williams and His Charms.

MID-APRIL
   Connie Francis graces the stage for two weeks at the White Elephant Club in Pittsburgh.
   The Royal Peacock Club in Atlanta plays host to Screamin' Jay Hawkins for two nights.
   Mac Curtis, the pride of Weatherford, Texas, signs with King Records and cuts his first session in Dallas at Jim Beck's Studios. King plans a mid-May release for Curtis' first disc.

APR 16   ABC Radio debuts "Rhythm on Parade," a rock 'n roll show broadcast nationally from the Flame Show Bar in Detroit.

New Releases for the third week of April include two on Atlantic: "Treasure of Love" by Clyde McPhatter and "Fee-Fee-Fi-Fo-Fum" by LaVern Baker; "Baby Mine" by the Teen Queens on R.P.M.; "Graduation Day" by the Rover Boys on ABC-Paramount; Smiley Lewis' "She's Got Me Hook, Line and Sinker" on Imperial; "You're the Apple of My Eye" by the Four Lovers on RCA Victor; and a cover version of "Corrine Corrina" by Roy Moss on Mercury.

APR 19   After serving a two-year hitch in the U. S. Army, Clyde

MAC CURTIS
Wally Erwin "Mac" Curtis, Jr. was born on January 16, 1939, in Fort Worth, Texas. He spent his early childhood with his grandparents in the nearby small town of Olney. According to Curtis, his earliest rock 'n roll influence was the Marty Robbins version of "That's All Right," purchased by mistake from a local record store when Curtis wanted the version by Elvis Presley. By age sixteen, Curtis was a seasoned performer and was already recording demonstration tapes at the Clifford Herring Studio in Fort Worth. He auditioned for King Records and was signed in early 1956. His first release was "If I Had Me a Woman," and its sales were marginal. Curtis followed with "Grandaddy's Rockin'," a rompin', stompin' Texas rockabilly number. His third single, "You Ain't Treatin' Me Right," led to appearances on Alan Freed's Christmas stage show at the Brooklyn Paramount in December of 1956. Just as his musical career seemed poised to take off, he was drafted into the U.S. Army. There were more releases on King through 1957. Then, he returned to Fort Worth and through Major Bill Smith's intervention was able to place his music on to a succession of labels including Felsted and Dot as well as Smith's local labels Brownfield, Shalimar, LeCam and Maridene. Curtis was rediscovered in the 1970s by Rollin' Rock Records, which released several long-forgotten demo tapes as well as contemporary material. Curtis also recorded for Tower, Epic, and GRT.

EDDIE BOND
Edward James Bond quit school in his junior year to go to work in a furniture factory. He joined the Navy at age eighteen (he was born July 1, 1933, in Memphis). When he returned to Memphis, he formed the Stompers, with a featured vocalist named Johnny "Ace" Cannon. Eddie and his father put up the financial backing for Johnny Burnette's first single with the Rock 'n' Roll Trio on Von Records. In September 1955, Eddie toured through several southern states with Elvis. That same year, he auditioned for Sun Records, but was turned down. His first singles, "Double Duty Lovin'" and "Love Makes a Fool (Every Day)" were released on Ekko, the same label that released the first singles by the Cochran Brothers. Bond's move to Mercury in 1956 produced three fine rockabilly singles before he signed with Mercury's subsidiary, Starday. In 1957, he became a regular member of the "Louisiana Hayride." He returned to Sun Records for a session in 1957, but the material was not released at the time. Undaunted, Bond continued to see his records released on a seemingly endless list of local and regional labels including Stomper Time, Spa, United Southern Artists, Pen, Diplomat, Goldwax, Memphis, Millionaire, Tagg, and XL. With limited resources for distribution, virtually every single disappeared without impact. Even scattered country singles on Coral and Decca received little notice. Only "The Legend of Buford Pussar" on his own Tab label created much in the way of sales, and this led to his writing an unused score for "Walking Tall," the movie based on Pussar's life. While maintaining an unsteady career as a performer and recording artist, Bond was more successful as a radio announcer in Memphis and a record store owner in his current home of Hernando, Mississippi.

McPhatter is a civilian once again. He has continued to record during his enlistment, and his recent "Seven Days" on Atlantic is popular in both the rhythm and blues and "pop" markets.

APR 20   Not to be outdone by the success of "The Rhythm and Blues of 1956" tour, the second unit of "The Biggest Rock 'n Roll Show of '56" rakes in more than $100,000 in its first five days, starting with a performance tonight at the auditorium in Hershey, Pennsylvania. Headlining again are Bill Haley and His Comets. The tour also features Frankie Lymon and the Teenagers, the Platters, Clyde McPhatter, LaVern Baker, Joe Turner, the Drifters, the Cleftones, the Teen Queens, Bo Diddley, the Colts, the Flamingos, and Red Prysock's combo. Additional performances include the Warner Theater, Atlantic City (21); the Mosque, Richmond (22); Norfolk (23); Scranton (24); the Arena, Philadelphia (25); and the White Plains County Center, White Plains, NY (26). The tour is booked solid for 45 days, through June 3, and the projected gross is expected to top $1 million. (See also APR 28.)

The Apollo Theater in New York offers the sweet vocal style of Della Reese paired with the honking sax of Illinois Jacquet for patrons this week.

The "Rhythm and Blues of 1956" revue plays the Sportatorium in Dallas.

Across the Lone Star state, Gatemouth Brown and Earl King are at the Austin Sports Center.

In Chicago, Mickey and Sylvia and the Coasters headline a week-long revue at the Palace that also features Ella Johnson with the Buddy Johnson combo.

The Savoy Ballroom in Los Angeles spotlights the Medallions, Young Jesse, Richard Berry, and Vernon Green for the weekend.

APR 21   Recovered from the injuries sustained in an auto accident the previous month, Carl Perkins headlines a police benefit show at the Stuart Auditorium in Beaumont, Texas. Also on the bill are Johnny Cash and other stars of the "Big D Jamboree" as they start a short tour of Texas. Succeeding nights have the group playing Galveston (22), San Antonio (23), and Wichita Falls (24).

APR 22   Fats Domino brings "The Rhythm and Blues of 1956" revue to the Loyola Field House in New Orleans. Sharing the spotlight are Ruth Brown, the Clovers, Little Willie John, Little Richard, the Turbans, and the Cadillacs.

New Releases for the fourth week of April include "Fever" by Little Willie John on King; "Rock 'Em Daddy" by **Eddie Bond** on Mercury; "Will You, William?" by Janis Martin on RCA Victor; "She Loves to Rock" by the Flairs on ABC-Paramount; "Breath of Air" by the Squires on Vita; Gene Allison's "Good-bye My Love" on Calvert; and "You Gotta Rock and Roll" by Bob Oakes and his Sultans on Regent.

APR 23   Elvis Presley opens for two weeks at the New Frontier Hotel in Las Vegas. The pairing of Presley's brand of uninhibited rock 'n roll and the sweet serenading of headliner Freddy Martin and his orchestra is less than successful but Presley doggedly completes the contract, "The Legend" to the contrary.

APR 27   Roy Milton brings his brand of swinging rhythm and blues to the 5-4 Ballroom in Los Angeles. Also in town, the new show at the Savoy Ballroom features Earl Bostic and Sarah Vaughan.

Joe Houston rocks the Rock and Roll Club in Pittsburgh. Houston is on a major tour of the East Coast and Midwest which will take him to Buffalo, Providence, New York, Chicago, Philadelphia, St. Louis, Kansas City, and Baltimore.

The Apollo Theater in New York welcomes the Willows, T-Bone Walker, Big Maybelle, and Willis Jackson's combo.

APR 28   Brenda Lee (born Brenda Mae Tarpley) debuts on the "Junior Ozark Jamboree," a spin-off of the popular "Ozark Jamboree" broadcast from Springfield, Missouri. At this time, Miss Lee is eleven and has her own deejay show that originates from her parents' record shop in Augusta, Georgia. (Brenda Lee will be the subject of an end-of-month biography in the next volume of THE GOLDEN AGE OF ROCK 'N ROLL.)

APR 29   "The Biggest Rock 'n Roll Show of '56" takes in $129,000 during the seven-day period beginning today in Montreal. Tomorrow, the revue is in Toronto. (See also MAY 1.)

APR 30   The Rover Boys open a week-long run at Washington's Casino Royal.

LATE APRIL
After auditioning more than 200 applicants for a spot on their roster as "the next Elvis Presley," Capitol Records signs twenty-one-year-old Gene Vincent from Norfolk, Virginia.

TOP ROCK 'N ROLL RECORDS FOR APRIL 1956

1. Heartbreak Hotel/I Was the One - Elvis Presley
2. Blue Suede Shoes - Carl Perkins
3. The Magic Touch/Winner Takes All - The Platters
4. Why Do Fools Fall In Love - Frankie Lymon and the Teenagers
5. Long Tall Sally/Slippin' and Slidin' - Little Richard
6. Ivory Tower - Otis Williams and His Charms
7. The Great Pretender - The Platters
8. Eddie My Love - The Teen Queens
9. R-O-C-K/Saint's Rock and Roll - Bill Haley and His Comets
10. Blue Suede Shoes - Elvis Presley
11. I'm In Love Again/My Blue Heaven - Fats Domino

12. Church Bells May Ring - The Willows
13. Drown In My Own Tears - Ray Charles
14. Bo Weevil - Fats Domino
15. Please, Please, Please - James Brown and the Famous Flames
16. Winner Take All - The Platters
17. Down In Mexico - The Coasters
18. I Want You To Be My Girl - Frankie Lymon and the Teenagers
19. Little Girl of Mine - The Cleftones
20. Corrine, Corrina - Joe Turner

Also on the "pop" charts:
Eddie, My Love - The Fontane Sisters
Rock Island Line - Lonnie Donegan
Themes from "Man With The Golden Arm" - Richard Maltby
Why Do Fools Fall In Love - Gale Storm
Why Do Fools Fall In Love - The Diamonds

April 1956
ARTIST OF THE MONTH

ELVIS PRESLEY

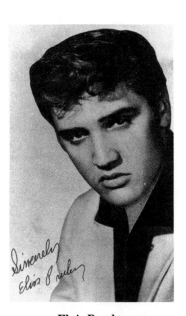

Elvis Presley

He was being referred to as "The King" as early as May 1956. And no one disputed the title—except Elvis. At the time, it was impossible to realize the overwhelming change he was leading, not just in music, but in the very fabric of American life.

He didn't invent rock 'n roll, but he was its premier interpreter. He didn't create the flamboyant stage antics, but he brought them to a new level of excitement. He didn't write the songs he sang, but he molded each one until it became uniquely his own creation.

The heart of the success of Elvis Presley was his ability to take the material he was offered, submerge himself in its meaning, and come up with his own point of view. At the same time, he was able to draw the listener into the music by lifting the song to a higher plane. It was an astounding feat of musicianship, and he continued to work his magic for twenty-three years.

Joe Turner and Bill Haley sang "Shake, Rattle and Roll" before Elvis, but spend two minutes with Elvis' record and the other versions pale by comparison. The same can be said for Carl Perkins' "Blue Suede Shoes," Lloyd Price's "Lawdy Miss Clawdy," and Ray Charles' "I Got a Woman." After Elvis sang "Hound Dog," Big Mama Thornton considered herself lucky to find work. The only singer who could sing Little Richard's material with as much verve as Little Richard was Elvis. The list could go on for pages.

His life story is required litany for every student of American popular music. He was born on January 8, 1935, in the small, Mississippi Delta town of Tupelo. Born to hard working parents, Elvis Aron was the surviving son of twins, the other being named Jesse Garron. He was surrounded by cousins, aunts and uncles from both sides of his family. The Presleys found solace from their near-poverty in the Assembly of God Church. At an early age, Elvis was already impressed by the musical style of the revival preachers. As a birthday present, Elvis received an inexpensive guitar instead the bicycle he really wanted.

In 1948, the family moved to Memphis in search of better-paying jobs. Here in the confluence of delta blues and riverboat jazz, Elvis heard music that appealed to him at gut-level. For a year, the family moved from one apartment to another before finally settling in Lauderdale Courts, a government housing project where one of the Presley's neighbors was Ruby Black. Mrs. Black's oldest son, Bill, had married and moved away. Bill worked days on the loading dock at the Railway Express Agency, but he spent his nights playing stand-up bass in a floundering country band. Mrs. Black's younger son, Johnny, became close with Elvis. The two sat for hours in the evening singing songs of every description. There were other young musicians in the area, including the Burnette brothers, Johnny and Dorsey. And, there was a teen recreational hall at Lauderdale Courts where these would-be performers could try out the songs on a live audience.

Elvis plugged away at high school, receiving passing grades but little other recognition. That is, until he performed at the spring talent show during his senior year. The printed program listed him as "Elvis Prestley, guitarist," sixteenth out of twenty-one performers in a minstrel revue. Legend has it that he was invited back at the end of the show for the evening's only encore. Encouraged by his new-found popularity, he stopped by the Memphis Recording Service a few months later to make an acetate of two of his favorite songs, "My Happiness" and "That's When Your Heartaches Begin." The recently discovered acetate, found in the possession of one of Elvis' boyhood friends, clearly shows that his vocal style was already mature and self-confident.

Elvis left his name with the studio's secretary, but nothing came of it. Six months later, in January 1954, he was back to record another couple of songs. This time, Sam Phillips, the owner of the studio, was behind the controls. Phillips liked what he heard enough to make a note of this young man with the truck-driver's sideburns and flamboyant clothes. Still, as before, there was no immediate callback.

In late June 1954, Phillips received in the mail a demonstration record of a new song, "Without You." He wanted to issue the song, but he was unable to locate the disc's singer. Phillips placed a call to the Presley home for Elvis to drop by the studio. Elvis was unable to sing "Without You" to Phillips' satisfaction. However, Phillips did put the young singer in touch with Bill Black and Black's band member, guitarist Scotty Moore. A weekend of rehearsals followed.

On July 5, 1954, the trio arrived at Sun Records for an 8:00 p.m. session. Three hours later, they had recorded a minor miracle in the form of "That's All Right," a blues piece written and recorded in the late 1940s by Arthur Crudup. Elvis took the material, wound it up tight and breathed life into it at the speed of light. The result was little short of phenomenal. The next night, against all the odds, lightning struck a second time. Elvis turned "Blue Moon of Kentucky," Bill Monroe's hillbilly anthem, into a rompin', stompin' rockabilly record. A week later, Memphis radio stations were playing the two-sided single, and the rest, as they say, was history.

Not everything Elvis touched became gold. He did not impress either the crowd or the management of the "Grand Ole Opry" on October 2, 1954. However disappointed he must have been, Elvis put this setback behind him. His second single was already out. "Good Rockin' Tonight" took the musical themes explored in "That's All Right" and improved greatly on the formula.

Two weeks after his "Grand Ole Opry" experience, Elvis easily won over the crowd at Shreveport's "Louisiana Hayride," a venue which had nurtured Hank Williams, among others. Elvis was a hit throughout Texas and Louisiana and on up to Missouri and Ohio. In fact, he was a sensation everywhere he appeared.

While his records were gaining in popularity, his stage show was splitting the very fabric of small southern towns into two camps. You either liked him—or you hated him.

Following the example of the Assembly of God revivalists, Elvis's performance was full of flash and motion. He bumped and boogied with the music. He bopped across stage. He thrust his pelvis with the beat. It was as close to male burlesque as most people had ever seen. Teens loved it—their parents worried; women screamed—men felt threatened.

As Elvis was reaching the first plateau of his popularity, he met Colonel Tom Parker. Parker was an ex-carny barker who now managed country artists including Hank Snow and Eddy Arnold. Parker's charm worked its magic with Elvis' mother, and the Colonel began adding young Presley to the bottom of the bill on Hank Snow tours.

In only eighteen months, Elvis had outgrown Sun Records. Any number of companies wanted his services. In the end, his contract went to the highest bidder, a consortium of RCA Victor Records and Hill and Range Publishing. Sam Phillips received $35,000. Elvis settled for $5,000 in back royalties owed to him by Phillips.

A January 1956 session produced "Heartbreak Hotel," and the record sold a million copies in two months. By mid-summer, Elvis was the hottest phenomenon the music business had ever seen. Every record went gold. Million-dollar deals were cut with Hollywood producers and merchandise hawkers. His personal appearances could sell out the largest coliseum in hours. His cameo performance on a television show automatically guaranteed a ratings bonanza for the night.

His first movie was "Love Me Tender," an offbeat western in which he sang four silly songs. The movie broke box office records. Six months later, he appeared in the semi-autobiographical "Loving You," singing a half-dozen ballads and soft rock 'n roll tunes. There were turn-away crowds wherever it played. In "Jailhouse Rock" and "King Creole" he portrayed juvenile delinquents and he sang hot rock 'n roll—songs like "Hard Headed Woman" and "(You're So Square) Baby I Don't Care." The crowds couldn't be contained.

It looked as though nothing could go wrong.

Then Uncle Sam sent him his draft notice, and he entered the Army in March 1958. His mother died suddenly that August. In September, the Army shipped him off to Germany for eighteen months. It was a one-two-three punch from which many people, Elvis included, thought he might not recover.

They were all wrong.

(Elvis' story will continue in the third volume of THE GOLDEN AGE OF AMERICAN ROCK 'N ROLL.)

May 1956

JOE CLAY

Joe Clay released two of the hottest rockabilly singles ever—then disappeared with hardly a trace. Clairborne Joseph Cheramie was born in Harvey, Louisiana, on September 9, 1938. C.J., as he was know to his friends, began his brief musical career at an early age, learning the guitar, bass and drums by the time he was a teenager and living in New Orleans. The C.J. Cheramie Trio soon had their own local fifteen-minute, country-music radio show on WWEZ. This led to a spot on the "Louisiana Hayride" in 1955, at the same time Elvis Presley was a regular on the show. Encouraged by his quick success and by WWEZ deejay Charlie "Jolly Cholly" Stokeley, C.J. sent a demonstration tape to RCA Victor, which led to a recording session at the Starday Studios in Houston. C.J. was renamed Joe Clay for his initial release on Vik Records, RCA's subsidiary. His first release featured two new songs he had covered from other obscure rockabilly artists: "Ducktail" by Rudy Grayzell and "Sixteen Chicks" by Link Davis. In fact, Davis had played guitar on Clay's session. The record sold well enough for RCA to set up a New York session for Clay's second release. "Get On The Right Track" featured Mickey "Guitar" Baker, who would soon find himself recording for Vik as part of Mickey and Sylvia. After neither of Clay's releases reached a national audience, his brief contract with RCA was allowed to expire. He returned to New Orleans, picked up his old name and continued to perform as C.J. Cheramie for a couple of years. Then, he gave up entertainment for a steady job as a school bus driver. He was rediscovered by the British in the 1980s which, in turn, led to more gigs for him in New Orleans. He still drives the bus during weekdays, but at night and on weekends, he's Joe Clay—Rocker.

MAY 1 "The Biggest Rock 'n Roll Show of '56" continues to play to packed houses with a show tonight in Rochester. This week the troupe will play Buffalo (2), Pittsburgh (3), and Columbus, Ohio (4). (See also MAY 6.)

MAY 4 Dinah Washington and the Charms are featured at the Apollo Theater in New York for the week.
Lowell Fulson and the Moonglows heat up the action at the 5-4 Ballroom in Los Angeles for the next three days. Also in town, Oscar McLollie and the Cliques are at the Savoy.
At Detroit's Flame Show Bar, Roy Hamilton and Gloria Lynne bring their blend of "pop blues" to a week-long engagement.

MAY 5 After six-weeks of recuperation, Carl Perkins returns to the "Big D Jamboree" where he is a regular member.

MAY 6 Fats Domino's "Rhythm and Blues of 1956" tour winds up with a show in Birmingham, Alabama. After leaving Toronto on April 10, the package made dates in the Midwest and Texas before swinging through the Southeast, eventually dropping as far south as New Orleans for two shows at Loyola University's Field House. (See APR 1 and 8.)
The Olympia Theater in Detroit hosts "The Biggest Rock 'n Roll Show of '56."

New Releases for the first week in May include several hot rockabilly entries: "Sixteen Chicks" by Link Davis on Starday; "Ducktail" by **Joe Clay** on Vik; "If I Had Me a Woman" by Mac Curtis on King; and "Ooby Dooby" b/w "Booger Red" by Sid King and the Five Strings on Columbia. Other releases include "I Want You, I Need You, I Love You" by Elvis Presley on RCA Victor; "Dear Heart" by the Spaniels on Vee-Jay; "I'm Nobody's Angel" by the Turbans on Herald; the Flamingos' "A Kiss From Your Lips" on Checker; "Every Night About This Time" by the Sophomores on Dawn; "Dark Is the Night," an instrumental from B.B. King on R.P.M.; and "Dealer of Dreams" by the Penguins on Wing. This week also sees the re-release of Joe Turner's original 1941 version of "Corrine Corrina" on Decca, which features guitar by Billy Mure, who recently had a minor hit with "Cosmic Guitar" on Cosmic, and who would achieve fame as leader of the Supersonic Guitars in the 1960s.

EARLY MAY

The Cochran Brothers (Eddie and Hank) start a week-long tour of Hawaii as the opening act for country star Lefty Frizzell.

Big Jay McNeeley is on the West Coast playing dates in San Diego, Oceanside, Las Vegas, Stockton, Phoenix, San Jose, and Sacramento.

MAY 11 Al Hibbler, Mickey and Sylvia, and the Coasters star for the week at New York's Apollo Theater.

Little Richard brings his outrageous brand of rock 'n roll to the Shrine Auditorium in Los Angeles as he headlines a show featuring the Turks, the Robins, and Marvin and Johnny. In days to come, Little Richard will appear at the Green Mill Ballroom in Ventura; Sweet's Ballroom in Oakland; and the Filmore Auditorium in San Francisco before returning to Los Angeles for a movie screen test. Soon thereafter, he is forced to return to his home in Macon, Georgia, for a brother's funeral.

Also in Los Angeles this weekend, the Savoy offers Lloyd Price for three days while the 5-4 Ballroom presents Roy Milton and his combo.

The Flame Show Bar in Detroit welcomes Billie Holiday for the week.

The Clovers, Ivory Joe Hunter, and the Isley Brothers entertain the crowd this week at Washington's Howard Theater.

MAY 12 Alan Freed's "Rock 'n' Roll Dance Party" on CBS-radio features the Robins, Kitty White, and Count Basie's orchestra.

MAY 13 Elvis Presley begins another lengthy tour today with an afternoon concert in St. Paul and an evening performance across the Mississippi River in Minneapolis. Other dates include La Crosse, WI (14); Memphis (15); Little Rock (16); Springfield, MO (17); Des Moines (18); Lincoln, NE (19); Omaha (20); Topeka (21); Kansas City (24); Detroit (25); Columbus, OH (26); and Dayton (27).

New Releases for the second week in May include several from Atlantic: "Hallelujah, I Love Her So" by Ray Charles; "Love, Love, Love" by the Clovers; and "It's Too Late" by Chuck Willis. Other releases include two from Federal: "Tore Up Over You" by the Midnighters and "How Long, How Long Blues" from Billy Ward and his Dominoes; two novelties: "Stranded in the Jungle" by the Jayhawks on Flash and "Transfusion" by **Nervous Norvous** on Dot; "Up on the Mountain" by the Magnificents on Vee-Jay; and two from Chess: "Roll Over Beethoven" by Chuck Berry and "Kiss Me Baby" by the Four Tops, of which more would be heard in the 1960s.

MID-MAY

Sun Records signs Wink, Texas rockabilly artists Roy Orbison and the Teen Kings. Orbison and the band had previously released "Ooby Dooby" on the small Jew-El label, and it had recently

NERVOUS NORVOUS

Two of the most incredible records in rock 'n roll history have to be "Transfusion" and "Ape Call" b/w "Wild Dogs of Kentucky." Words fail to adequately describe the lunacy in the grooves. "Nervous Norvous" was none other than Jimmie Drake, a truck driver living in Oakland who was forty-four in 1956. At that time he also performed with the Four Jokers, a night club singing group that incorporated large amounts of comedy in their routine. He wrote a novelty song titled "Transfusion," which the Four Jokers recorded for the Diamond label. The record failed to catch on, due as much to the lead vocalist's feeble delivery as to the macabre lyrics. "Transfusion" was about the results of a car crash, told in a black-humor vein. Undaunted, Drake contacted a local deejay, Red Blanchard, and between them they rerecorded Drake's version of the song, complete with the sounds of an auto accident: screeching brakes and the shrieking of twisting metal. After shopping the demonstration tape, "Transfusion" caught the ear of Randy Wood, owner of Dot Records, a man not particularly known for his sense of humor, black or otherwise. "Transfusion" was an instant success. Teenagers loved the morbid take on a serious subject while parents were repulsed by the whole idea. Nervous Norvous followed with "Ape Call," a somewhat gentler song, about a Tarzan-like man, with each lyric punctuated by a shrill "Tarzan" yell. "Ape Call" was backed by "Wild Dogs of Kentucky," a song almost as bizarre as "Transfusion." The last Dot single for "Norvous" was "The Fang." By 1957, Drake had returned to truck driving and part time radio announcing in Oakland. There was a single in the 1960s on Embee and another on Big Ben. Neither caused must of a stir. Drake died in relative obscurity in 1968.

started picking up some West Texas action. Sam Phillips decides to have Orbison rerecord the number for Sun, and this is the version that is released on the Sun label.

Pee Wee Crayton leaves Los Angeles for a Midwest tour, stopping in Coffeyville and Wichita, Kansas; Chicago; Detroit; and Buffalo.

MAY 18 Attesting to the rising popularity of rock 'n roll, the first national convention of the National Association of Jazz and Rhythm and Blues Disc Jockeys convenes in Chicago and will run through May 20. Membership is pegged at one thousand.

Appearing this weekend at the 5-4 Ballroom in Los Angeles, Lowell Fulson and the Moonglows make a return engagement. Marvin and Johnny, the Chimes, and Wynona Carr are also at the Savoy.

In New York, the Midnighters share the spotlight with Cab Calloway at the Apollo Theater.

Dinah Washington opens a two-week stand at the Flame Show Bar in Detroit.

MAY 19 The "Big D Jamboree" is headlined by Carl Perkins and Ferlin Huskey.

The Loyola University Field House in New Orleans plays host to the traveling troupe of Bill Haley and His Comets, the Platters, Clyde McPhatter, Joe Turner, the Teenagers, the Teen Queens, Bo Diddley, the Flamingos, the Colts, the Drifters, and Red Prysock's band. In Birmingham, Alabama, at another show on this tour, members of the White Citizens Council picket the Municipal Auditorium to protest the combination of white and black performers.

MAY 20 Big Jay McNeeley performs at the Sirocco Club in Los Angeles.

MAY 21 Little Willie John entertains the crowd at the Motor City Arena in Detroit.

New Releases for the third week in May include "Tear It Up" by the Johnny Burnette Trio on Coral; "I Don't Know" by James Brown on Federal; "I Love My Baby" by the Tokens on Melba; "Never No More" by the Colts on Vita; "Blue Eyed Mermaid" by Bobby Darin on Decca; Lloyd Price's "Country Boy Rock" on Specialty; and "Pink Cadillac" by Sammy Masters on Starday. Two female rhythm and blues artists with fine track records also release singles this week on Savoy: Big Maybelle's "Candy" and **Little Esther**'s "You Can Bet Your Life."

MAY 22 Joe Houston entertains the crowd at the American Legion Stadium in Los Angeles.

MAY 25 The Howard Theater in Washington offers the talents of Ruth Brown, the Cadillacs, the Turbans, and Choker Campbell's band for fans this week.

In New York, the Apollo Theater plays host to the Clovers,

LITTLE ESTHER
Esther Mae Jones could sing in just about any style she desired. She was born in Galveston, Texas, on December 23, 1935, and she began singing gospel in church as a young child. Her family moved to Los Angeles in the early 1940s, and her family entered her in various local amateur shows. Her stage presence even then was so great that at the age of thirteen she came to the attention of Johnny Otis, local R&B music entrepreneur and owner of the Barrelhouse Club. As Little Esther, she teamed with various other artists under the supervision of Otis for a string of hit records on Savoy, including "Double Crossing Blues," "Mistrustin' Blues," "Deceivin' Blues," "Cupid's Boogie," "Wedding Boogie," and "Far Away Christmas Blues," all released in 1950. In 1952, she went solo and moved on to Federal Records where she had another hit with "Ring-A-Ding-Doo." By 1954, with no further hits to her credit, she was semiretired from show business at the age of eighteen. Over the next six years, she performed only occasionally in her new hometown of Detroit. Then, in 1962, she had a crossover hit with "Release Me" on Lennox Records. She also recorded successfully for Atlantic beginning in 1965. It was at this time that she altered her vocal style slightly and became a popular attraction at the Newport and Monterey Jazz Festivals. In 1972, she was recording for Kudo records, and in 1975, where she had her last hit single, "What a Diff'rence a Day Makes." Esther Phillips passed away on August 7, 1984, in California.

Pee Wee Crayton, and the Paul Williams band.

The Five Keys and **Clifton Chenier**, the king of zydeco music, perform for the crowd at the 5-4 Ballroom in Los Angeles this weekend.

MAY 26   Carl Perkins makes a guest appearance on "The Perry Como Show" on NBC-TV. He had been en route to New York the previous March to appear on Como's show when he was involved in the auto accident that sidelined his career.

MAY 28   The Greystone Ballroom in Detroit features a "Jazz vs Rock and Roll" show with B. B. King, the Royal Jokers, and the Count Basie orchestra with Joe Williams.

Carl Perkins and Johnny Cash begin a one-week tour of the Memphis area. Also appearing are Warren Smith, Eddy Bond, and Roy Orbison and the Teen Kings.

New Releases for the fourth week in May include Bill Haley and His Comets' latest, "Hot Dog, Buddy, Buddy" on Decca; "Rattle My Bones" by the Jodimars on Capitol; "Be-Bop-A-Lulu" by Gene Vincent and His Blue Caps on Capitol; Billy Bland's "Chicken Hop" on Old Town; "One Night Only" by Otis Williams and His Charms; Gene and Eunice's "Let's Get Together" on Aladdin; Lee Andrews and the Hearts' "Bluebird of Happiness" on Gotham; and the Five Satins' "I'll Remember (In the Still of the Night)" on Ember.

MAY 30   Louis Jordan plays a one-night stand at the Savoy Ballroom in Los Angeles.

THE TOP ROCK 'N ROLL RECORDS FOR MAY 1956

1. Heartbreak Hotel/I Was the One - Elvis Presley
2. Blue Suede Shoes - Carl Perkins
3. The Magic Touch/Winner Take All - The Platters
4. Long Tall Sally/Slippin' and Slidin' - Little Richard
5. Ivory Tower - Otis Williams and His Charms
6. I'm In Love Again/My Blue Heaven - Fats Domino
7. Why Do Fools Fall In Love - Frankie Lymon and the Teenagers
8. I Want You To Be My Girl - Frankie Lymon and the Teenagers
9. R-O-C-K/Saint's Rock and Roll - Bill Haley and His Comets
10. Blue Suede Shoes - Elvis Presley
11. Corrine Corrina - Joe Turner
12. Little Girl of Mine - The Cleftones
13. Graduation Day - The Rover Boys
14. I Want You, I Need You, I Love You/My Baby Left Me - Elvis Presley
15. Please, Please, Please - James Brown and the Famous Flames
16. Fever - Little Willie John
17. The Great Pretender - The Platters
18. Church Bells May Ring - The Willows

CLIFTON CHENIER
Clifton Chenier was the "King of Zydeco." Born June 25, 1925, in Appaloosas, Louisiana, Chenier effortlessly integrated the various musical styles from his melting-pot birthplace. As a result, his music, while maintaining its roots deeply embedded in Zydeco, contains generous helpings of rock 'n roll and rhythm and blues. Chenier began issuing records in 1954 with singles coming out on three labels simultaneously: "Rockin' the Bop" on Post, and "Louisiana Stomp," which was issued first on Elko and reissued immediately on Imperial. (Original releases of both records list Chenier's first name as "Cliston.") Imperial, by far the largest of the three record companies, chose not to follow up on Chenier, but another Los Angeles company, Specialty, issued three of Chenier's hottest recordings in 1955: "Boppin' the Rock," "Think It Over" and "The Cat's Dreamin'." He moved on to the Chess labels where, in 1957-58, he had two singles for Argo, followed in 1960 with "Bayou Drive" on Checker. In 1959-60, "Big Chenier" had a pair of singles on Goldband, a label championing many forms of Louisiana music. Through the 1960s, Bayou Records, another local label, came out with nineteen straight Chenier singles in the 1960s. Jin, another local Louisiana company, recorded Chenier with Rod Bernard (of "This Should Go On Forever"), but only one single, "Shake, Rattle and Roll" b/w "Rockin' Pneumonia" was issued. Arhoolie, dedicated to "roots music" also issued fifteen singles by Chenier from 1964 to 1976. In 1969, "Black Owl" was a lone release from Bell, probably the biggest record company to release Chenier material. Chenier passed away on December 12, 1987. His legacy is carried on by his son, C. J. Chenier, who fronts his dad's Red Hot Louisiana Band.

19. Ruby Baby - The Drifters
20. Treasure of Love - Clyde McPhatter

Also on the "pop" charts:
Ivory Tower - Cathy Carr
Moonglow and Theme from "Picnic" - George Cates
Moonglow and Theme from "Picnic" - Morris Stoloff
The Happy Whistler - Don Robertson
Ivory Tower - Gale Storm

May 1956
ARTIST OF THE MONTH

CARL PERKINS

Carl Perkins

Carl Lee Perkins has lived his entire professional life in the shadow of two performers. All three men started with the same small record company. All came from the same area of the South. And, in the early days, all three frequently shared the same stage.

First, it was Elvis.

Perkins was born April 9, 1932, on a cotton farm in Lake County, Tennessee, between Ridgely and Tiptonville. He might have stayed on the farm if Elvis hadn't cut his first record for the Sun label in Memphis in July 1954. At the time, Carl had formed a band with his brothers Jay, on rhythm guitar, and Clayton, on stand-up bass. Their strongest influences were Bill Monroe and Hank Williams. They had been playing around the local area for a few years as the Perkins Brothers with little success. Times were tough. Perkins was married and his wife took in laundry while he worked menial farm jobs during the day and picked guitar at night.

Carl sent numerous demonstration tapes off to the record companies with offices in New York and Nashville. More often than not, the packages were returned unopened. However, he had the encouragement of his family and friends who believed that if Elvis could make a record sounding "like that" then so could Carl. So, he decided to travel to Memphis with his brothers and audition for Sam Phillips of Sun Records.

In October, 1954, three months after Elvis recorded "That's All Right," the Perkins boys loaded their 1941 Plymouth and tied Clayton's bass on top. Along with their new drummer, W. S. Holland, they eventually arrived on the doorstep at 706 Union Avenue in Memphis asking if they could cut a record. Sam Phillips was reluctant to grant an audition, but he was eventually persuaded. He was impressed by what he heard, but he still felt that the boys didn't have enough original material to put them under contract. Discouraged, the band returned to Lake County to write some more songs.

Then on January 25, 1955, they were back. Carl was signed to a two-year contract. The resulting "Movie Magg" came out on Phillips' newest label, Flip Records, to a less than enthusiastic reception. However, it enabled the band was to get bookings. They played the bottom half of a bill with Elvis as he toured Mississippi and Arkansas playing school gymnasiums and National Guard Armories.

Enter Johnny Cash, the second of Carl's shadows.

Carl Perkins was well aware of Johnny Cash before Cash came to Memphis. Cash brought his unique brand of country-rock to Sun Records in June 1955, and "Cry, Cry, Cry" was immediately successful. In October, Perkins' had his second release with "Gone, Gone, Gone," this time on the Sun label. As before, the record did little business. Cash and Perkins became immediate friends. Cash extended an open invitation for Perkins to tour with him whenever possible. (Luther Perkins was Cash's lead guitarist, but, according to Carl, the two are not related.)

That fall, the music world was heating up with bids for Presley's recording contract. Phillips decided he could make a rockabilly star out of just about any guitar-slinger, even Carl Perkins. All that was needed was the right song. With this encouragement, Carl set off on a tour with Presley and Cash. According to Perkins, it was in Parkin, Arkansas, after a show that he wrote down the words to a song about someone he had seen on the dance floor warning his date to stay away from his new blue suede shoes. Carl recorded the song on December 19, 1955.

Christmas came and went. Carl and his growing family were living in a government housing project where they paid thirty-two dollars a month for a small apartment, including utilities.

At first it looked like he would be snake-bit for a third time as the record languished on dealers shelves. In reality, all it needed was a little luck. On January 28, 1956, Elvis was in New York making his first national television broadcast and plugging "Heartbreak Hotel." Perkins was relegated to an appearance in Dallas on radio's "Big D Jamboree." Perkins did get asked back to the "Big D" as a regular, and he pushed "Blue Suede Shoes" each Saturday night for a month. Slowly, it began to catch on—first in the country market, then with teenagers, and finally with rhythm and blues fans.

On March 17, 1956, Perkins had his own television debut on Red Foley's "Ozark Jubilee" on ABC-TV. Five days later, following a show in Norfolk, VA, the band was en route to New York for a March 24 appearance on Perry Como's NBC-TV show. Perkins' driver, Dave Stewart, fell asleep at the wheel and their car plowed into a pickup truck near Dover, Delaware. Stewart died, and Carl suffered a fractured skull and a broken shoulder. He remained hospitalized until April 10. His brother, Jay, had a broken neck and never fully recovered. Jay's spot in the band was eventually filled by Eddie Starr.

Unable to capitalize personally on the success of "Blue Suede Shoes," Perkins' career went into a tail spin. "Blue Suede Shoes" sold a million copies while he was recuperating. Then, Elvis covered it for RCA Victor with a supercharged arrangement that stole much of Perkins' thunder. Elvis' version eventually outsold Perkins around the world.

As a follow-up to "Blue Suede Shoes," Perkins next recorded "Boppin' The Blues," a song that looked like "a natural" for him. However, the very thing that caused teenagers to pick up on Elvis' version of "Blue

Suede Shoes" over that of Perkins was also a hindrance to "Boppin' the Blues." Perkins' style of rock 'n roll was too hesitant and too ponderous by comparison.

To make a point: Perkins' version of "Blue Suede Shoes" has that familiar instrumental "ba-dum-bump" and a pause between the lines of the opening verse:

> "Well, it's one for the money...(ba-dum-bump, pause),
> Two for the show...(ba-dum-bump, pause)..."

Elvis barely took a breath at the same points, while the band tore along at breakneck speed. Both artists sang the same song. Both records had two similar instrumental breaks. However, Elvis clipped fifteen seconds off his version, creating a sense of urgency and excitement. Exactly what was missing in Perkins' style. Where "Blue Suede Shoes" had approached the top of the record charts in pop, country, and blues, "Boppin' The Blues" was dead in the water after only a month.

Perkins' continued to record, and on December 4, 1956, he was in the Sun studio, involved in a session in which he was recording "Matchbox." For this session, he was utilizing Jerry Lee Lewis—at that time an unknown piano player from Ferriday, Louisiana. Also in the studio as an observer was Johnny Cash. Suddenly, through the door came Elvis. The long standing comradeship between Elvis, Perkins and Cash—coupled with the boldness of the young Lewis—resulted in a loose-knit, off-the-wall songfest. The session is most often referred to as "The Million Dollar Quartet."

After this, the high points of Perkins' career were fewer and further apart. He had a cameo singing part in the movie "Jamboree" in 1957. He later recalled that he was offered his choice between two songs that he would sing in the film. Perkins chose "Glad All Over." The other song, "Great Balls Of Fire," went by default to Jerry Lee Lewis. Was this Perkins' bad luck raising its head again?

When the hits stopped coming, Perkins found steady work touring behind Johnny Cash. In 1958, Columbia Records picked up Perkins' contract from Sun Records right before it did the same for Cash. Perkins' first two Columbia releases were "Pink Pedal Pushers" and "Pointed Toe Shoes." Both were obvious attempts to capitalize on the "cat clothes" song-style that had launched his career, but neither single was very successful. To Columbia's credit, they did not cancel Perkins' contract. A fine long-play album, WHOLE LOTTA SHAKIN', was released, and a total of twelve singles came out during Perkins' five-year stay.

In 1963, he quietly moved on to Decca Records. That same year he toured Europe for the first time and found that his overseas fans had not forgotten him. Among the most ardent were the Beatles who had adopted his rockabilly guitar style to their own vision of pop music. In May 1964, he returned to England to share the spotlight with Chuck Berry. The tour that also featured two English bands, the Animals and the Nashville Teens. Legend has it that he visited Abbey Road studios during his off-hours, and played guitar on the Beatles' version of his own "Matchbox."

In October 1964, the Beatles' version of "Matchbox" was a smash hit in the states. At the same time, Carl was back in England performing with Gene Vincent. He was invited by the Beatles to visit a couple of their recording sessions as they recorded "Honey Don't" and "Everybody's Trying To Be My Baby." Perkins also recalled that they recorded "Blue Suede Shoes" and "Your True Love" at this session, but these songs have not been "officially" released.

In 1966, Perkins signed with the small Dollie label. His records were well received by the critics—"Country Boy's Dream" was a "turntable hit," as Carl put it. However, they failed to attract much attention with the public.

A year later, Johnny Cash came to Perkins' rescue again, taking him on tour as part of his own band—an association that lasted nine years. In 1969, Cash landed a summer-replacement ABC-TV show. He offered Perkins a regular solo spot. The show was picked up the next two years as part of ABC-TV's regular schedule. Also in 1969, Cash had a hit with Perkins' song, "Daddy Sang Bass." During this time, the two friends worked together to shake off their long-time addiction to "pep pills" and whiskey while they were becoming born-again Christians.

Perkins returned to Columbia in 1970, and he recorded his most critically acclaimed album, BOPPIN' THE BLUES, featuring the country-blues group NRBQ. A year later, he dented the country music charts with "Me Without You." In 1972, he did the same with "Cotton Top" and "High on Love."

Carl Perkins was briefly under contract with Mercury Records in 1974. Wanting to experience some freedom from the larger recording corporations, he formed Suede Records in 1976. The label was set up to promote his own band, the C. P. Express, which featured his two sons, Greg on bass and Stan on drums (both remain in his band in the 1990s). Elvis' death in 1977 brought the re-release of "The E. P. Express," Perkins' 1975 tribute on Mercury. For a moment it looked as though there might be some good out to come out of his friend's tragedy. As before, it didn't happen. In 1978, Perkins signed with Jet Records in England, and his album OL' BLUE SUEDE IS BACK was a minor hit overseas.

In the early 1980s, he came under Elvis' shadow again as a regular performer at Memphis' annual memorial concert each August held to commemorate the anniversary of Elvis' death.

The 1980s found Perkins' career taking many divergent paths. He appeared in a movie ("Into the Night," 1985, starring David Bowie) and a music video (for Elvis' version of "Blue Suede Shoes," 1987). He worked on Paul McCartney's TUG OF WAR album (1982), and he was the subject of a television special taped in England marking the 30th anniversary of "Blue Suede Shoes" that featured George Harrison, Ringo Starr, and Eric Clapton ("Blue Suede Shoes: A Rockabilly Session with Carl Perkins and Friends," 1986). He recorded an album in Stuttgart, Germany, with his old Sun-mates Jerry Lee Lewis and Johnny Cash (THE SURVIVORS, 1981), and the same trio, along with Roy Orbison, got together to record an album at the old Sun Records studio (CLASS OF '55, 1985). His 1985 album CARL PERKINS on Dot/MCA featured new versions of vintage Perkins classics interspersed with some fine new country songs. In 1989, he had an album, BORN TO ROCK, on Universal, a label owned by 1950s rocker Jimmy Bowen.

The year 1987 proved to be Carl Perkins' biggest in so far as recognition from his peers. In January, he was inducted into the Rock and Roll Hall of Fame in its second year. On April 6, during an NBC-TV broadcast, he received the Career Achievement Award by the Academy of Country Music.

He was back in 1992 with a new album, FAMILY, FRIENDS AND LEGENDS on Platinum Records featuring Carl working with some new faces—Travis Tritt and Joan Jett—as well as a couple of older faces—Charlie Daniels and Chet Atkins. In 1993, three albums were released simultaneously by RCA/BMG Records: "CARL PERKINS AND SONS," "TAKE ME BACK," and "DISCIPLE IN BLUE SUEDE SHOES." That same year, he joined the Kentucky Headhunters on a rousing version of "Dixie Fried," a cut from their album RAVE ON. Perkins also appeared on the music video for the song.

Carl lives today in Jackson, Tennessee. He has been married to Valda since 1952, and besides Gerg and Stan, the couple have two more children, Debbie and Steve.

It's obvious to all who come to his concerts that he is enjoying his status as a living legend. He has always been down-to-earth, and he wears his humility well. As he progressed through his fifties, Perkins has become an elder statesman for the early days of rock 'n roll. He had always been an intelligent spokesman, but now the writers and critics were listening.

June 1956

JUN 1   The Cadillacs headline the show at the Apollo Theater in New York. Sharing the bill are Screamin' Jay Hawkins, Shirley Gunter and the Queens, the Cookies, and the Flairs (featuring Cornell Gunter, brother of Shirley Gunter).

Louis Jordan and His Tympany Five tear up the house during their stay at Zardi's Jazzland in Los Angeles. Also in town and opening tonight for the weekend are Sonny Thompson with Lulu Reed and the Champions at the Savoy and Amos Milburn and Eddie Bo at the 5-4 Ballroom.

JUN 2   Carl Perkins and Johnny Cash, along with **Warren Smith**, Eddy Bond, and Roy Orbison perform at 8:00 p.m. at Overton Park Shell in Memphis.

JUN 3   Bill Haley and "The Biggest Rock 'n Roll Show of '56" stop at Washington's National Guard Armory for two shows.

JUN 4   Gene Vincent and His Blue Caps play their first live gig in Myrtle Beach, North Carolina.

New Releases for the first week in June include "My Prayer" from the Platters on Mercury and "St. Theresa of the Roses" by Billy Ward and His Dominoes (featuring Jackie Wilson) on Decca. There's also plenty of rockabilly action this week: "Boppin' The Blues" by Carl Perkins on Sun; Janis Martin's cover version of "Ooby Dooby" on RCA Victor; "Pink and Black" by Sonny Fisher on Starday; "Tennessee Rock 'n' Roll" by Bobby Helms on Decca; and "Tired and Sleepy" by the Cochran Brothers on Ekko. Rounding out the week's releases are "Mixed Up Rhythm and Blues" by Johnny Taylor on Fire; "Shattered Dreams" by the Youngsters on Empire; "Woe Is Me" by the Cadillacs on Josie; and "Peace and Love" by the Five Keys on Capitol.

JUN 5   Bill Haley and His Comets end a tour with a show in Charleston, West Virginia.

Elvis Presley returns to ABC-TV's "Milton Berle Show," broadcast this time from the network's studios in Los Angeles. His performance, including a bump-and-grind rendition of "Hound Dog," which he will not record until July 2, is viewed by an estimated twenty-five-percent of the American population and brings a howl of protest from the critics. The next night, Presley starts a brief three-day swing through Southern California with a show in San Diego followed by Long Beach (7) and Los Angeles (8).

WARREN SMITH

Johnny Cash had written a rock 'n roll number in early 1956, and he had even gone so far as to record a demo tape of the number. But, Johnny was already walking a fine line between his country roots and his rock 'n roll leanings. He decided to pass the song along to another singer. Enter Warren Smith. Born February 7, 1932 (or 1933), in Louise, Mississippi, Smith was fresh out of the Air Force and working with a country band at Memphis' Cotton Club. Cash and Sun Records' owner, Sam Phillips, dropped by the club one night and approached Smith during the band's intermission. Smith thought he was dreaming. He was being offered the chance to make his first record with a song written by Johnny Cash! Using Clyde Leonard's band, Smith cut "Rock 'n' Roll Ruby" in February 1956 and was released by Sun in late March 1956. "Rock 'n' Roll Ruby" sold reasonably well in the South, and was followed by "Ubangi Stomp" b/w "Black Jack David." Smith's only national hit was "So Long, I'm Gone," recorded in January 1957 with Jerry Lee Lewis on piano. The record was released in May and broke nationally a month later. Smith remained with Sun for only one more release. He recorded for Warner Brothers in 1959 and, in 1960, he became the first country artist signed by Liberty Records, and he had immediate success. His first Liberty single, "I Don't Believe I'll Fall in Love Today" has a national hit. He joined the "Grand Ole Opry" and was a member until an automobile accident in 1967 almost ended his career. There were still singles here and there, on Skill, Mercury, and Jubal, and albums on Lake County and Harvest, both in 1977. However, his time in the limelight was over. Warren Smith died of a heart attack in 1980.

THE CADETS
It was difficult enough for a vocal group to have a successful R&B career. To have a pair of careers running parallel was almost unheard of. The Cadets, who had a big hit during the summer of 1956 with "Stranded in the Jungle" were the same group that had a big seller a year earlier with "Why Don't You Write Me" as the Jacks. The singles were released on Modern and R.P.M., respectively, with R.P.M. being a subsidiary of Modern. The group was composed of Willie Davis, first tenor; Ted Taylor, first tenor; Aaron Collins (the brother of Betty and Rosie, the Teen Queens), second tenor; Lloyd McGraw, baritone and the group's manager; William "Dub" Jones, bass. The group started releasing singles as both the Cadets and Jacks beginning in early 1955. As the Jacks, they concentrated on ballads; and as the Cadets, they sang uptempo dance numbers and novelty tunes. Ted Taylor was the first to leave the group. He went on to have success singing urban blues beginning in the late 1960s. Taylor was replaced by Prentice Moreland. There were no more new singles from the Jacks after July 1956, but an album was released by the group in March 1957, although several of the songs on the LP had been released as by the Cadets, and two were by an unrelated group, the Rockets. The final single from the Cadets on Modern came in December 1957. McGraw, Jones, and Collins launched the MJC label and recorded one single as the Rockateers with little success. Most of the group also were the Peppers on Ensign and the Cadets on Sherwood and Jan-Lar. Collins and Davis joined the Flairs (later referred to as the Flares of "Foot Stompin'" fame). Jones found fame when joined the Coasters, replacing Bobby Nunn in time to sing on "Yakety Yak."

JUN 6   Roy Hamilton cancels his upcoming engagement at the Savoy Ballroom in Los Angeles. He is hospitalized in New York after being diagnosed with a lung ailment which the press lists variously as either tuberculosis, pneumonia, or exhaustion. First reports state that Hamilton will quit show business and devote his time to painting. In fact, his "retirement" is only temporarily.

JUN 7   Smiley Lewis entertains the midway throng at New Orleans' Lincoln Beach.

JUN 8   This week, the Apollo Theater in New York City plays host to Clyde McPhatter. Also appearing on the bill are Frankie Lymon and the Teenagers, the Pretenders, the Valentines, the Cleftones, and the Sil Austin combo.
The Cadillacs start a three-night stint at the Motorama, Detroit's premier automotive convention.
Amos Milburn and Eddie Bo are held over for a second weekend at the 5-4 Ballroom in Los Angeles. Added to the bill are the Teen Queens.

JUN 9   "Stage Show," CBS-TV's Saturday night variety showcase, features the Colts in their premier television appearance. The Colts are managed by Buck Ram, who also manages the Platters, the Flairs, the Penguins, and Shirley Gunter and the Queens.

New Releases for the second week in June include "Rip It Up" b/w "Ready Teddy" from Little Richard on Specialty; "Stranded in the Jungle" by the **Cadets** on Modern; "Billy's Blues" by Billy Stewart on Chess; "A-1 In My Heart" by the Spiders on Imperial; "Please Love a Fool" by the Meadowlarks on Dootone; Modern's "Have Mercy, Mr. Percy" by Long Tall Marvin (Marvin Phillips formerly of Marvin and Johnny); "Key to the Kingdom" from the Nutmegs on Herald; and three on Atco: "Down Through the Years" by Guitar Slim, "One Kiss Led To Another" by the Coasters, and "Happy and Gay" by the Castelles. Also out this week is the original version of "Transfusion," by the Four Jokers on Diamond.

JUN 11 Shirley and Lee and the Joe Jones combo wrap up a series of East Coast one-nighters with a show in Rocky Mount, North Carolina.

JUN 15 This week, New York's Apollo Theater offers a gospel and spiritual caravan.
Fats Domino rips through a weekend engagement at the 5-4 Ballroom in Los Angeles.

JUN 16 Connie Francis guests on "Stage Show" on CBS-TV.
Bill Haley and His Comets are booked to play a week in Canada, starting with tonight's show in Winnipeg. Other dates include Melville, Saskatchewan (18), Regina (19), Saskatoon (20), Edmonton (21), Calgary (22), Lethbridge, Alberta (23). Following

the Winnipeg show, Haley left the tour to attend his father's funeral in Pennsylvania. He was scheduled to return for the Calgary show; but he was delayed by weather, finally arriving at the theater at 2 a.m. while other acts filled the time. To compensate the many disappointed fans, Haley and His Comets gave a free show in Calgary on June 23 at 11 a.m.

JUN 18   **Joe Houston** and his orchestra perform at the Hollywood Paladium for the Temple Dance League.

Chuck Berry is booked into the Rock and Roll Club in Pittsburgh for the week.

The Platters open at Washington's Casino Royal for the week.

New Releases for the third week in June include several records from groups hoping for another hit: "Let the Good Times Roll" from Shirley and Lee on Aladdin; "Until the Day I Die" by the Teen Queens on Flip; "Can't We Be Sweethearts" by the Cleftones on Gee; "Merry-Go-Rock" by the Robins on Whippet; and "I Just Got Lucky" by Sonny Til and the Orioles on Vee-Jay. Also new this week are "This Is The Night" by the Kool Gents on Vee-Jay; "See You Soon, Baboon" by Dale Hawkins on Checker; "Take It Easy, Greasy" by Bobby Charles on Chess; "Pretty Bad Blues" by Ronnie Self and "Respectfully, Miss Brooks" by Marty Robbins, both on Columbia; and the Empires' "Don't Touch My Gal" on Wing. This weeks' release of "I've Got to Have You Baby" by the Pretenders on Rama features Jimmy Jones who would have hits with "Good Timin'" and "Handy Man" in 1960.

JUN 21   Clarence "Gatemouth" Brown entertains the crowd at New Orleans' Lincoln Beach midway.

In Detroit, the Fox Theater presents a revue headlined by LaVern Baker. Also performing are Frankie Lymon and the Teenagers, the Rover Boys, the Cleftones, Lonnie Donegan, the Royal Jokers, the Johnny Burnette Trio, the Nitecaps, Johnny "Guitar" Watson, the Pretenders, and Bobby "Mumbles" Lewis.

JUN 22   The Heartbreakers and the Moonglows, backed by the Dizzy Gillespie combo, are the week's fare at the Apollo Theater in New York City.

Elvis Presley begins a week-long tour of the Southeast with a three-day stand at the Paramount Theater in Atlanta, followed by concerts in Savannah (25); Charlotte (26); Augusta (27); Charlotte, again (28); and Richmond (30).

Washington's Howard Theater offers a gospel revue headlined by the Five Blind Boys of Mississippi for patrons this week.

JUN 24   In New Orleans, the Platters, Little Willie John, the Orioles, and James Brown and the Famous Flames entertain at a dance at the Labor Union Hall.

JUN 25   In Florida, Bo Diddley opens for a week at the Palms Club in Hallendale.

JOE HOUSTON

Joe Houston was a one-man whirlwind on sax. Born in Austin, Texas, about 1925, he first played "be-bop" on alto in the style of Charlie Parker. As a teenager, he was literally "picked off the street" for a two-year run with the King Kolax jazz band, which also featured Gene Ammons and John Coltrane. In the 1940s, after hearing Jay McShann, he switched to tenor sax and played on "Chicken Shack" by Amos Milburn. This led to a long association with Joe Turner beginning in 1949. Turner was helpful in getting Houston a recording contract with the Combo label in Los Angeles. Beginning in 1951 and over the remainder of the decade, Houston issued eighteen singles on the label, starting with "Forest Fire." At the same time, he also recorded for Modern (five singles in 1951-53), Imperial ("Atom Bomb" in 1953), Lucky ("Go, Joe Go" in 1954) and Recorded In Hollywood ("Cornbread and Cabbage" in 1953). By this time, his style was invariably a stomping blast of rhythm. In 1955, he issued his masterpiece, "All Nite Long" on Money. The single was a best seller all along the West Coast and led to ten years of rock 'n roll tours with artists such as Buddy Holly, the Platters, Jerry Lee Lewis and the Everly Brothers. Other memorable recordings included "Blow, Joe, Blow" and "Worry, Worry, Worry." When rock 'n roll waned in the States, Houston took his act to Europe, where he was hailed as a hero. Art Laboe, of the "Oldies But Goodies" album series, was especially helpful in keeping Houston's career going during the 1960s and 1970s. Joe Houston maintained his jazz contacts which allowed him to play blues revival shows one weekend and jazz festivals the next.

New Releases for the fourth week in June include "Who Do You Love" by Bo Diddley on Checker; "I Promise To Remember" by Frankie Lymon and the Teenagers on Gee; "The Fool" by Sanford Clark on Dot; Champion Jack Dupree's "Big Leg Emma" on King; "I'll Never Let You Go" by the Valentines on Rama; the **Willows**' "My Angel" on Melba; "Angel of My Life" by Richard Berry on R.P.M.; and Brad Suggs' "Bop, Baby Bop" on Meteor.

THE WILLOWS
Released in February 1956, the Willows' single of "Church Bells Are Ringing" soon received a name-change to the more familiar "Church Bells May Ring." Today, original copies of the "Church Bells Are Ringing" record fetch collector's prices ten times higher than the more common release. The Willows began their long career as the Five Willows on the Pee Dee label in 1952 with "Love Bells." The next year, they were on Allen Records for "My Dear Dearest Darling." There were two additional singles on Allen and two more on Herald, all by the Five Willows, before "Church Bells May Ring" was released on Melba as by the Willows. The group consisted originally of twin brothers Joe and Ralph Martin, baritone and second tenor; John Thomas Steele, bass; Richie Davis, first tenor; and Tony Middleton, lead tenor. By the time they arrived on Melba, Steele had been replaced by Freddie Donovan. On "Church Bells May Ring," the bridge ("Hello, hello, hello again; my friends I hope that we can meet again") is sung by Richard Simon, a friend of the group. After three more singles on Melba, the group recorded one single each for Club, Eldorado, and Gone. In 1964, Williams left the Willows and he recorded as a solo artist on more than a half-dozen labels, including Phillips and A&M. After Middleton departed, the group continued to perform as a quartet on Heidi, Warwick, Mercury, and Mala Records. Their lone Mercury release, "Lazy Daisy" was reportedly backed by Fats Domino and his band.

JUN 27   In New Orleans, Otis Williams and the Charms are the special guests at Lincoln Beach.

JUN 28   The midway crowd at Lincoln Beach in New Orleans welcomes Big Boy Myles and the Upsetters.

JUN 29   The Cadillacs and LaVern Baker headline this week's show at the Apollo Theater in New York. Filling out the bill are the Jayhawks, the Schoolboys, the Bop-Chords, Robert and Johnny, Billy Bland, the Cookies, the Sensations, and the Mickey Baker orchestra.
   Little Willie John begins a three-day engagement at New Orleans' Dew Drop Cafe.
   In Los Angeles, the midnight-to-dawn "Rhythm and Blues Revue" at the Hill Street Theater features Nat King Cole, Joe Turner, Ruth Brown, Cab Calloway, Faye Adams, Count Basie, Sarah Vaughan, Lionel Hampton, Amos Milburn, the Delta Rhythm Boys as well as ten lesser acts.

JUN 30   The Platters make an appearance on CBS-TV's "Stage Show."
   On CBS-radio, LaVern Baker and the Cadillacs guest on Alan Freed's "Rock 'n' Roll Dance Party" broadcast coast-to-coast from 9:00 to 9:30 EDT.
   Roy Orbison and the Teen Kings appear on "The Ed Sullivan Show" on CBS-TV.
   At Lake Tahoe, California, Chuck Higgins plays the area's first rock 'n roll dance, held at the American Legion Hall.
   Ray Charles appears at the Masonic Temple in Algiers, Louisiana.

LATE JUNE
   The summer beach season in Wildwood, New Jersey, will feature several rock 'n rollers at the local clubs. The Riptide has booked the Jodimars and Doc Starkes and the Nite Riders. The Treniers will play six weeks at the Beachcomber, and the Ravens are set for Club Esquire.
   As the new single by the Five Satins begins to sell, the title is changed from "I'll Remember (In the Still of the Night)" to the more concise "In the Still of the Night." Some pressings of the record also list the group simply as the Satins.

THE TOP ROCK 'N ROLL RECORDS FOR JUNE 1956

1. Heartbreak Hotel/I Was The One - Elvis Presley
2. I'm In Love Again/My Blue Heaven - Fats Domino
3. I Want You, I Need You, I Love You/My Baby Left Me - Elvis Presley
4. Transfusion - Nervous Norvous
5. I Want You To Be My Girl - Frankie Lymon and the Teenagers
6. The Magic Touch - The Platters
7. Blue Suede Shoes - Carl Perkins
8. Ivory Tower - Otis Williams and His Charms
9. Long Tall Sally/Slippin' and Slidin' - Little Richard
10. Treasure Of Love - Clyde McPhatter
11. Be-Bop-A-Lulu - Gene Vincent and His Blue Caps
12. Corrine Corrina - Joe Turner
13. Ooby Dooby - Roy Orbison and the Teen Kings
14. Fever - Little Willie John
15. Love, Love, Love - The Clovers
16. Hallelujah, I Love Her So - Ray Charles
17. Stranded In The Jungle - The Jayhawks
18. Rip It Up/Ready Teddy - Little Richard
19. Little Girl Of Mine - The Cleftones
20. Why Do Fools Fall In Love - Frankie Lymon and the Teenagers

Also on the "pop" charts:
The Wayward Wind - Gogi Grant
Standing On The Corner - The Four Lads
I Almost Lost My Mind - Pat Boone
Picnic - The McGuire Sisters

June 1956
ARTIST OF THE MONTH

FATS DOMINO

(Continued from the first volume of THE GOLDEN AGE OF AMERICAN ROCK 'N ROLL.)

Fats Domino

In the period covered in this volume of The Golden Age of Rock 'n Roll, Fats Domino came into his own as an entertainer, rolling off hit after hit in a continuous stream that would eventually place him just below Elvis as the all-time hit-maker among solo performers.

During the years 1956 through 1959, he released nineteen singles and every one was a best seller. On the "pop" music charts, eight songs made the Top Ten. Thirteen of the singles were two-sided "pop" hits as both sides were strong enough to make the charts. On the rhythm and blues side, Domino had five Number One singles, and another six that reached the Top Ten. In the same four years, he released three albums, each of which went into the national Top Twenty.

Eventually someone tabulated his record sales, marking it at 65 million with twenty-three singles selling more than a million copies each. The numbers are certainly higher than that today.

His longevity can be attributed to his style of "good-time music." Each record was up-tempo, bouncy, and tightly-produced—a two-minute slice of teenage life meant for dancing. He would start with a common phrase, such as "ain't that a shame" or "sick and tired" or "I'm gonna be a wheel some day." Then he would toss in a few suitable phrases to flesh out the title. Stir in a whirlwind instrumental backing with one or two sax breaks, and faster than you could say "boogie with a back beat," he'd sell another million records.

A classic example is the romping "You Done Me Wrong" from 1954. The single features a two-chorus, pounding-piano introduction, followed by two verses of Fats singing nothing more than "oh, oh, oh, oh." After this comes the song, all eight-lines of it, followed by two more verses of "oh-oh-oh-oh" with a fade-out at 1:58 minutes.

In the beginning, Domino recorded using the same combo he and his producer, Dave Bartholomew, put together to play club dates. Eventually, the duo handpicked the cream of New Orleans musicians to play on Domino's records. Among them were Roy Montrell on guitar, who recorded the smashing "(Every Time I Hear) That Mellow Saxophone" for Specialty in 1956. Tenor saxophone duties fell to Herb Hardesty, Lee Allen, and Alvin "Red" Tyler. Hardesty was with Domino from "The Fat Man" in 1949 through the hit and the miss years until 1972. Allen had a string of hit instrumentals, the biggest of which was "Walking With Mr. Lee" in 1958 on Ember Records. The drum assignment was split between Earl Palmer and Cornelius Coleman. Palmer later moved to Los Angeles where he became a highly respected session musician. Finally, there was Bartholomew on trumpet. Bartholomew had fronted one of the hottest combos in New Orleans in the 1940s and 1950s. He also co-wrote many of Domino's hits. With Domino performing somewhere every night for three-hundred days each year, just getting him into the studio proved to be a real problem. By the end of the decade, the instrumental tracks were all prerecorded before Domino came into a session. Even Fats' unique piano style was on tape, having been aped by Allen Toussaint or James Booker.

Most of the songs for which Fats Domino is best remembered came from the period 1956 through 1959. His earlier releases, while doing very well in the rhythm and blues community, were not played on enough radio stations nationally to break into the mainstream. That began to change in 1955 with "Ain't That A Shame," his first crossover record. From then on, it was one success followed by another. Songs like "I'm In Love Again," "Blueberry Hill," "Blue Monday," "I'm Walkin'," "Valley of Tears," "Whole Lotta Loving," "I Want To Walk You Home," and "Be My Guest" capsulized the period, marking specific moments in time for teenagers. All across the country, his music was played on jukeboxes, heard on radio stations, bought in record stores. When Hollywood came calling, Domino was fortunate enough to be available. He had cameo singing roles in "Shake Rattle and Rock" (1956), "The Girl Can't Help It" (1956), "The Big Beat" (1957), and "Jamboree" (1957).

His last Top Ten hit came in 1960, although he stayed with Imperial until 1963 before moving on the ABC-Paramount, the company that had offered Ray Charles the chance to sing country and western music in 1962. Fats decided not to follow Ray Charles' lead. Instead, for his first ABC-Paramount release, he recorded "There Goes (My Heart Again)" in his usual rollicking style. Unfortunately, in an attempt to appeal to the "pop" record-buyers of the early 1960s, the songs he recorded for ABC-Paramount featured a variety of vocal groups composed of either bothersome females voices or Ray Conniff sound-alikes. Try as he might, he could not regain the musical direction of his hit days, eventually churning out a truly horrible rendition of "Red Sails In The Sunset." Only "Heartbreak Hill," the last of the ABC-Paramount singles, dropped most of the "pop" trappings, but by this time it was too late. For Fats Domino, the hits stopped coming altogether in 1964.

In 1965, he signed with Mercury Records, which released his first live album, recorded in Las Vegas. His final fling at record success was "Lady Madonna" for Reprise in 1968. The song had been released earlier in the year by the Beatles with Paul McCartney copying Domino's piano style. The Beatles' version was a multi-million seller—Domino's version barely peeked into the bottom of the music charts.

By this time, he didn't really need more hit records. His royalty checks each year ran into the millions, and he was a star on the nightclub circuit. As a result, his recording projects became fewer and fewer. There was another live album for Atlantic Records in 1973, followed by an album for Sonet in 1979. In 1990, he recorded another live album in New Orleans for Tomato Records.

In 1973, he made an appearance in "Let The Good Times Roll," a nostalgia-laden documentary filmed at a rock 'n roll revival concert. In 1985, when Rick Nelson and Fats Domino teamed up to play the Universal Amphitheater in Los Angeles, the show proved to be so popular that they took the act on the road for a very successful tour. Unfortunately, Nelson's untimely death on December 31 of that year put and end to any further plans. The Universal show was also videotaped and later shown on television. In 1986, Fats hosted a cable television special on HBO that brought together Little Richard, Jerry Lee Lewis, and Ray Charles—along with Fats—all four playing piano on stage at the same time in New Orleans' Storyville Jazz Hall. It was something to behold.

Fats Domino was among the first set of performers inducted into the Rock and Roll Hall of Fame in January 1986. A year later, at the 29th Grammy Awards ceremony, he received a Lifetime Achievement award from the National Academy of Recording Arts and Sciences.

Today, he performs only when it pleases him, and he is always paid top dollar. His shows both in the United States and abroad are still sellouts although the act has changed little from the 1950s. The old formula still holds true. Keep it upbeat—keep it simple—and keep it under two minutes.

Like his hit song says, Fats Domino stayed long enough to "be a wheel someday."

July 1956

KING CURTIS
Curtis Ousley (born February 7, 1934, in Ft. Worth, Texas) was a child prodigy on saxophone. Reportedly, he made his first records in Texas in 1952. He went straight from high school into Lionel Hampton's band. By the 1950s he was a free-lance studio musician in New York, playing under the pseudonym, King Curtis. Known primarily through his distinctive work with the Coasters, he is credited with bringing the saxophone solo to prominence in rock 'n roll records. This may be too broad an accolade, however, it is certain that Curtis became more well known than any of his R&B contemporaries on sax. While at Atco/Atlantic, he worked with most of the company's stars including Joe Turner and Chuck Willis. He also found time to moonlight for dozens of artists outside of the Atlantic stable, including one session with Buddy Holly. King Curtis' first album, HAVE TENOR SAX, WILL BLOW, was released in 1959 on Atco. From 1960 to 1962, he recorded albums for Tru-Sound, New Jazz, Prestige and Everest. In 1962, He had his biggest selling instrumental hit with "Soul Twist" on Enjoy Records. Shortly thereafter, he began a two-year association with Capitol Records that placed three singles on the charts and produced three albums. Then he returned to Atco where he remained until the early 1970s. During this period, many of his singles made both the R&B and the "pop" charts, and he also recorded ten more albums for Atco. He worked sessions with artists as diverse as Roberta Flack, Eric Clapton, the Rascals and Champion Jack Dupree. In 1971, he became Aretha Franklin's musical director. Shortly after, on August 13, 1971, King Curtis was stabbed to death while trying to break up an argument in front of his New York apartment.

JUL 1   Elvis Presley makes a onetime guest appearance on "The Steve Allen Show" on NBC-TV. Allen, well aware of the controversy created by Elvis' spot on the Milton Berle television show in June, drapes Elvis in a tuxedo and has him sing "Hound Dog" to a woeful basset hound.

JUL 2   Carl Perkins headlines the "Top Record Tour" as it opens a five-week road trip in Columbia, South Carolina. Also featured are Frankie Lymon and the Teenagers, Chuck Berry, Cathy Carr, Shirley and Lee, Bobby Charles, the Cleftones, the Spaniels, Al Hibbler, Della Reese, and Illinois Jacquet's combo.

At the RCA Victor studio in New York, Elvis records "Hound Dog" and "Don't Be Cruel." The coupling of these two songs into a single 45 r.p.m. release will result in Elvis' biggest hit record, selling an estimated five million copies in the United States upon its initial release.

New Releases for the first week of July include "So Long" b/w "When My Dreamboat Comes Home" by Fats Domino in Imperial; "Rompin' and Stompin'" by Freddy Bell and the Bell Boys on Wing; "The Elvis Blues" by Otto Bash on RCA Victor; "Sam" by George Hamilton IV on Colonial; and "Movin' On" by **King Curtis** on Groove.

JUL 6   In New York, Little Richard starts a frantic week at the Zanzibar Club in Buffalo. Nightly he will break all-time attendance figures, drawing many patrons from Canada.

The Apollo Theater in New York offers another rhythm and blues bill this week, with Big John Greer's combo backing Little Jimmy Scott, the Wheels, and the Hamilton Sisters.

In New Orleans, at the legendary Dew Drop Hotel and Cafe, Bobby Marchan entertains the crowd for two nights. Marchan will achieve fame as a member of Huey Smith and the Clowns as well as for his solo recordings in the 1960s.

JUL 7   At 11:15 p.m., following a concert by Fats Domino at the Palomar Garden Ballroom in San Jose, California, pandemonium breaks out and a riot ensues. The promoter of the show claims that the ruckus was not the result of over exuberance by the show's 2,500 patrons but of teenage toughs who threw beer bottles into the throng. The nights total: nine dancers and three police officers were hospitalized, one thousand beer bottles were smashed, and $3,000 in damages was done to the hall. (See JUL 20 and 29.)

Johnny Cash makes his first appearance on "The Grand Ole Opry" broadcast nationally over radio from Nashville's Ryman Auditorium.

JUL 9   In Florida, Larry Birdsong opens for a week in Hallendale at the Palms Club.

New Releases for the second week of July include "Hound Dog" b/w "Don't Be Cruel" from Elvis Presley on RCA Victor; "Tonight You Belong to Me" by Patience and Prudence on Liberty; "Honky Tonk" (parts 1-2) by Bill Doggett on King; and two from Vee-Jay: "Baby Come Along With Me" by the Spaniels and "A Fallen Tear" by the El Dorados. Also out this week is "Flying Saucer" (parts 1-2) by Buchanan and Goodman on Luniverse, the record that would start the fad of "cut-in" novelty singles.

JUL 13   The Five Keys are the only R&B group on the bill this week at the Apollo Theater in New York, as the house also offers "the "Rhythm on Ice" package.
This week Bill Doggett and his combo entertain the crowd at the Flame Show Bar in Detroit.

JUL 16   Toronto's Maple Leaf Gardens hosts its largest crowd up to this time when Little Richard joins the "Top Record Stars" package. Attendance is pegged at more than 13,000.

New Releases for the third week of July include "Ape Call" by Nervous Norvous on Dot; "Lipstick, Powder and Paint" by Joe Turner and "I Gotta Get Myself a Woman" b/w "Soldier of Fortune" by the Drifters, both on Atlantic; "Get on the Right Track" by Joe Clay on Vik; "See-Saw" by the Moonglows on Chess; "Rip It Up" by Bill Haley and His Comets on Decca; "I'm Sending an S.O.S." by the Avons on Hull; "I Love You, Baby" by Jimmy Reed on Vee-Jay; and the final posthumous release from Johnny Ace, "Still I Love You So" on Duke.

JUL 17   The "Top Record Stars" package, without the benefit of Little Richard tonight, rocks Canton, Ohio, pulling in almost 4,000 fans.

JUL 19   Jimmy Beasley plays Club Harlem in Los Angeles.

JUL 20   As an aftereffect of the riot that followed his show in San Jose on July 8, Fats Domino finds his scheduled show in Stockton, California, canceled. Hurriedly, the promoter moves the show to nearby Tracy without further incident.
The Flame Show Bar in Detroit offers the blues guitar duo of T-Bone Walker and Pee Wee Crayton for patrons this week.

JUL 22   In Detroit, the Hollywood Theater offers the "Top Record Show" featuring Carl Perkins, Frankie Lymon and the Teenagers, Al Hibbler, Cathy Carr, Chuck Berry, Shirley and Lee, Bobby Charles, Della Reese, the **Cleftones**, and the Spaniels.

THE CLEFTONES
Not many R&B vocal groups remained together for nine years. Even fewer had hits over that long a span. The Cleftones succeeded on both counts. The group formed in 1955, when members of the Clefs and the Silvertones joined together to form a single unit. The original Cleftones were high school students in the Jamaica suburb of New York City: Charlie James, first tenor; Herbie Cox, second tenor; Berman Patterson, second tenor; William "Buzzy" McClain, baritone; and Warren Corbin, bass. After months of practice the group was granted an audition with George Goldner of Tico/Rama Records. The result was "You Baby You," the first release on the Gee label, and a single that reportedly sold 150,000 copies in early 1956. Their second single, "Little Girl of Mine" did even better. The next single, "Can't We Be Sweethearts" also sold well. Unfortunately, Goldner showed little inclination to develop his artists. After five more singles, the group found themselves on Roulette, another label with ties to Goldner. Three years and three singles later, they were back on Gee. By this time, Buzzy McClain had left, and he was replaced by Gene Pearson of the Rivileers. Berman Patterson also departed, and his place was taken by Patricia Span. In 1961, the Cleftones released "Heart and Soul," the single for which they are best remembered. The record might have been even bigger if Jan and Dean hadn't covered the Cleftones' version. After a second flirtation with success, the group found their next five records being released with little promotion. In 1964, there was one single on the Ware label, another Goldner subsidiary, and the Cleftones disbanded until the 1970 oldies revival brought them out of their self-imposed retirement. The Cleftones are still together, entertaining fans into the 1990s.

THE SIX TEENS

In rock 'n roll music, quartets were the norm; quintets were rare; and as for sextets—there may have been only one. They called themselves what they were, the Six Teens. Well, it beats their first name, the Sweet Teens. The group was the brainchild of Ed Wells, a senior member of the aggregation at sixteen. Lead vocals were handled by Trudy Williams. She was only thirteen when "Forever More," the Sweet Teens only single, was issued by Flip Records, a new Los Angeles label. The record disappeared without a trace, and lesser acts might have been discouraged. Not these teens. This was the year of Frankie Lymon and the Teenagers, an act that proved that teens could have their own hit records. The changed their name to the Six Teens and rebounded with "A Casual Look," one of the biggest rock 'n roll records of the summer of 1956. Featuring Trudy's slightly off-key, nasal delivery, the record was built upon a dirge-like rhythm, with the three female voices soaring above the harmony of the three male voices. "A Casual Look" cracked the Top Ten on the R&B charts and did almost as well in the "pop" side of the house. However, their next two singles, "Send Me No Flowers" and "Only Jim," failed to attract enough airplay or sales break into the national market. The group rebounded a year later with "Arrow of Love." There were seven more singles issued into 1960, but none did well outside of the Los Angeles area. By this time, the various members had mostly drifted on to other endeavors. Richard Owens joined the group after "A Casual Look." He later had a long career with the Jayhawks/Vibrations, beginning with "Johnny's House Party" on Aladdin. Another member of the Six Teens, tenor Kenny Sinclair, joined the revival of the Olympics in 1970.

New Releases for the fourth week of July include the Johnny Burnette Trio's "Midnight Train" on Coral; Brook Benton's "Love Made Me Your Fool" on Epic; "You've Sinned" by the Solitaires and "Tonight" by the Supremes, both on Old Town; "Bad Luck" by B.B. King and "Out of this World with Flying Saucers" by Dave Barry, both on R.P.M.; and "Don't Feel Sorry For Me" by Jimmy Beasley on Modern.

JUL 25   Roy Orbison and the Teen Kings along with Warren Smith are currently touring through Arkansas, Tennessee and Mississippi. Tonight, they play a date in Grenada, Mississippi.

JUL 26   The Hawkettes entertain their fans at the annual Russell Ice Cream Company's "Rock and Roll Night" in New Orleans. The group was comprised of several local brothers named Neville.

              Joe Turner celebrates twenty-five years in show business with a performance at the Little Harlem Club in Los Angeles.

JUL 28   Norman Grantz presents his seventh annual rhythm and blues jubilee at the Shrine Auditorium in Los Angeles. Among those appearing are B. B. King, Ernie Freeman, the Medallions, the Dreamers, and Shirley Gunter.

              Gene Vincent and His Blue Caps make their national television debut performing "Be-Bop-A-Lulu" during their appearance on the "Perry Como Show" on NBC-TV.

              In Los Angeles, the "Blues Jubilee" plays the Shrine Auditorium. Spotlighted are Fats Domino, the Coasters, Clyde McPhatter, the **Six Teens**, the Teen Queens, the Turks, and Oscar McLollie.

JUL 29   In an effort to show that the fans are not at the root of the recent rash of riots connected with rock 'n roll shows, Fats Domino is re-booked into the Palomar Gardens in San Jose. Attendance was limited to those over 18 years of age and there wasn't even a hint of trouble this time.

              Little Richard and his band perform at the dance at the Labor Union Hall in New Orleans.

JUL 30   At the Casino Royal in Washington, DC, a rhythm and blues revue is offered for the first time. Acts appearing three times nightly for the week are Clyde McPhatter, LaVern Baker, the Jayhawks, and the Rainbows with Don Covay. The Penguins were also originally booked for this date but they did not appear.

TOP ROCK 'N ROLL RECORDS FOR JULY 1956

1. I Want You, I Need You, I Love You/My Baby Left Me - Elvis Presley
2. I'm In Love Again/My Blue Heaven - Fats Domino
3. My Prayer/Heaven On Earth - The Platters
4. Be-Bop-A-Lulu - Gene Vincent and His Blue Caps
5. Transfusion - Nervous Norvous

6. Treasure of Love - Clyde McPhatter
7. Heartbreak Hotel - Elvis Presley
8. Stranded in the Jungle - The Cadets
9. Fever - Little Willie John
10. Rip It Up/Ready Teddy - Little Richard
11. Stranded in the Jungle - The Jayhawks
12. Love, Love, Love - The Clovers
13. I Want You To Be My Girl - Frankie Lymon and the Teenagers
14. Ivory Tower - Otis Williams and His Charms
15. The Magic Touch - The Platters
16. Long Tall Sally - Little Richard
17. The Fool - Sanford Clark
18. It's Too Late - Chuck Willis
19. A Casual look - The Six Teens
20. Please, Please, Please - James Brown and the Famous Flames

Also on the "pop" charts:
Born To Be With You - The Chordettes
On The Street Where You Live - Vic Damone
More - Perry Como
Allegheny Moon - Patti Page
Sweet Old-Fashioned Girl - Teresa Brewer

July 1956
ARTIST OF THE MONTH

GENE VINCENT

Gene Vincent was rock's tragic hero.

Born in the seaport city of Norfolk, Virginia, on February 11, 1935, Eugene Vincent Craddock joined the Navy at age seventeen. In May 1955, while in the service, he was involved in a motorcycle accident that left him with a shattered left shinbone. The injury did not heal properly, and he spent the remainder of the year in a cast. While recuperating in a Veteran's Hospital in Portsmouth, Virginia, Vincent practiced playing guitar. He eventually paid Don Graves, another patient, twenty-five dollars for a song titled "Be-Bop-A-Lulu" that he had written about a local stripper.

Gene Vincent

Back in Norfolk, Gene Vincent, as he now referred to himself, tried to catch on as a country singer. He spent his spare time hanging out at the local country radio station, WCMS. He auditioned for "Country Showtime," the station's popular live show hosted by "Sheriff" Tex Davis. At this time, Capitol Records was sponsoring a national contest to find a singer who could compete with Elvis Presley. Capitol received two-hundred entries, including one from Gene Vincent. Tex Davis made certain that Ken Nelson, Capitol's A&R man, was aware of Vincent's demo tape. In April, 1956, Capitol offered Vincent a recording contract.

The first session was held in Nashville in early May, 1956, using the same "Country Showtime" band Vincent had used to make the demo he sent to Capitol: "Galloping" Cliff Gallup, a plumber for the local school system, lead guitar; "Jumping" Jack Neal, bass; "Wee" Willie Williams, a part-time deejay at WCMS, rhythm guitar; and Dickie "Be-Bop" Harrell, the WCMS house drummer. The resulting session yielded four completed songs: "Be-Bop-A-Lulu," "Race With The Devil," "Woman Love," and "I Sure Miss You."

His first single was credited to Gene Vincent and His Blue Caps. The band's name reportedly referred to President Eisenhower's baby blue golf cap. Originally "Woman Love" was the A-side, but critics complained about the song's suggestive lyrics and impassioned delivery, and Great Britain's BBC radio actually banned the song. A few enterprising deejays flipped the disk over and tried "Be-Bop-A-Lulu." The song featured Vincent's slithering tenor vocal over an understated rhythm backing. "Be-Bop-A-Lulu" was an immediate hit.

Within a month, Vincent and his band had become more than just local celebrities. In July, as sales of "Be-Bop-A-Lulu" peaked, they made their national television debut on Perry Como's NBC-TV show. They were playing bookings up and down the eastern seaboard, and the schedule became more than Willie Williams' marriage could endure. In mid-September, during a week-long stay at the Casino Royal in Washington, DC, Williams turned in his resignation. He was quickly replaced by Paul Peek, a guitarist who, although barely nineteen, was already a seasoned country performer.

Vincent's second single was "Race With The Devil." With a title like that, it also met with immediate and overwhelming radio rejection. "Race With The Devil" was quickly replaced by "Bluejean Bop" as Vincent's latest release.

Long nights of standing on stage eventually caused Vincent's injured leg to bother him again. He was back in a full-leg cast just as he was invited to make a cameo appearance in the first big-budget rock 'n roll movie, "The Girl Can't Help It." The scene with Vincent and the Blue Caps performing "Woman Love" came off without a hitch after the wardrobe department hid the cast under his jeans and painted the toe of the cast black to resemble a shoe.

In December 1956, Gene Vincent was booked for a month at the Sands Hotel in Las Vegas. After barely a week, the pain in his leg forced him to cancel the remainder of the engagement, and he reentered the Veteran's Hospital in Portsmouth for treatment. He remained in the hospital for three weeks and recuperated at home for an additional three months. During this time guitarist Cliff Gallup resigned and returned to WCMS full-time.

When Vincent resumed touring in 1957 he was fitted with a metal brace in place of the cumbersome plaster cast. He would wear the brace for the rest of his life. There were changes within the band, also. Russell Wilaford replaced Gallup on guitar. Other new faces appeared in the band throughout the year: Johnny Meeks, Scotty McKay, Jerry Merritt, and Juvey Gomez, on guitar; Bobby Lee Jones, bass; and Tommy Facenda, backing vocals and guitar. By June, 1957, only "Be Bop" Harrell remained from the original lineup. For recording sessions, the lead guitar was usually played by a studio pro such as Grady Martin, James Burton, Glen Campbell, or Buck Owens.

In the summer of 1957, Vincent had gone eight months without a major release as the two singles after "Bluejean Bop" did not garner any attention. However, with his hushed vocal wrapped around the insistent rhythm of "Lotta Lovin'" it looked like he was finally back on track. He was invited to appear on Dick Clark's "American Bandstand" as well as the "Big D Jamboree" in Dallas. This led to an October tour of Australia with Little Richard. Also on this tour was Eddie Cochran, a new face on the rock 'n roll scene but a polished performer who had been around since 1954. Vincent and Cochran became fast friends, and Cochran sang backing vocals on Vincent's RECORD DATE album.

In November, 1957, Vincent and the Blue Caps received what finally amounted to show business acceptance when they appeared on Ed Sullivan's CBS-TV show. Early the next year, "Dance To The Bop" became Vincent's final hit single in the United States. He was still a popular draw, and he made a second movie appearance in "Hot Rod Gang" in which he sang four songs. Throughout the spring of 1958 as Vincent crisscrossed the country there were increasing rumors about his unruly behavior on and off stage. He was drinking heavily to keep up his energy level and taking two bottles of aspirin a day to lessen his various pains.

By the end of 1958, Vincent had lost his new home in Dallas to back taxes. He moved to Los Angeles where he was reduced to playing an occasional low-paying gig. Finally, the remaining Blue Caps quit in disgust. The band's roster had been changing almost monthly as members left to pursue their own careers. Several ex-Blue Jeans briefly outperformed the master. Paul Peek had a regional hit with "Sweet Skinny Jenny" on NRC in 1958. Tommy "Bubba" Facenda blanketed the country with the various versions of his novelty single "High School, U.S.A." on Atlantic in late 1959. Scotty McKay recorded "Brown Eyed Handsome Man" for Ace in 1960, then signed with Dot Records using his real name Max K. Lipscomb, and eventually became a respected session guitarist who worked with "Sir Doug" Sahm and an early ZZ Top lineup, among many others.

In 1959, it looked as though Gene Vincent was about to put his demons behind him. He started by working small venues in the Pacific Northwest with pickup bands. This led to a tour of Japan in June where ten thousand fans welcomed him at the airport. The first five days in Japan, he played to 286,000 ticket holders, but after a few weeks Vincent reportedly became paranoid. He fled back to Los Angeles, leaving guitarist Jerry Merritt to impersonate Vincent during the remaining tour dates.

In December, Vincent finally traveled to England where he was hailed as a conquering hero. His appearance in head-to-toe black leather on "Boy Meets Girls," a British television rock 'n roll show, led to a permanent spot on the show's lineup. What had been originally scheduled to be a month-long stay in England was extended indefinitely.

Vincent soon convinced his buddy, Eddie Cochran, to come share the wealth. Cochran, whose career was also stalled in America, arrived in England in January 1960. The duo immediately embarked on a twelve-week tour. Tragically, that April, Cochran was killed in a taxi accident as he and Vincent were rushing to make an airline connection. Vincent also re-injured his leg as well as breaking his collar bone and several ribs. For Vincent, however, the psychological damage was even worse. He tried to continue with the tour, using Jerry Keller to fill Cochran's slot, but Keller only lasted a week before he returned to the states to report to the Army. Freddy Cannon was invited to fill in, but he turned Vincent down. Unable to book tour dates as a headliner, Vincent resigned himself to performing in the provincial theaters as another act on the evening's bill.

In 1961, he toured South Africa where he found renewed energy. The next year he performed in England almost exclusively, teaming with Brenda Lee as well as headlining his own shows. In Liverpool, where the Beatles were just another supporting act, he received a hero's welcome. Vincent remained in England for most of the next four years, performing when asked and making records that did not sell. His contract with Capitol Records expired in 1963, and no one in his homeland much cared.

In 1966, he briefly made the entertainment news when he signed with Challenge Records. Then he dropped from sight again for another three years. In 1969, he was asked to perform at the Toronto Peace Festival, featuring such high-powered acts as John Lennon and the Doors, as well as such older luminaries as Chuck Berry and Jerry Lee Lewis. In the shuffle, Gene Vincent was lost. He returned to the England vowing never to leave.

His life was now in a tailspin as he came to rely more and more on alcohol and pills. For two years he barely scraped by. There were still occasional stateside albums: I'M BACK AND I'M PROUD on Dandelion and THE DAY THE WORLD TURNED BLUE on Kama Sutra, both issued in 1970. That same year he tried a comeback show at the Felt Forum in Los Angeles, but there was virtually no demand for Gene Vincent or his new records.

In failing health in 1971, he returned to America in an unsuccessful attempt to put together yet another record deal. His appearance at the San Francisco Folk Festival, where he was backed by Commander Cody, failed to draw much attention. He returned to his home in the Los Angeles area, and a few days later he was admitted to the Inter-Valley Hospital in Newhall, California, suffering from an acute bleeding stomach ulcer. He died quietly on October 12 at the age of thirty-six.

Gene Vincent's influence can best be seen in the brief career of the Stray Cats, a rock trio that tried in 1982 to build a career on Vincent's stinging sound. Even the Stray Cats could not maintain their momentum for long, even with strong material.

At the beginning of his career, Gene Vincent was too close to Elvis in style. By the end, he was too far away.

August 1956

AUG 3   Elvis Presley roars through Florida on a ten-day swing, beginning tonight in Miami where he will perform six shows in two days. Other concerts on this short tour include Tampa (5); Lakeland (6); St. Petersburg (7); Orlando (8); Daytona Beach (9); Jacksonville (10-11); and New Orleans (12).

"The Steve Allen Show" on NBC-TV welcomes Louis Jordan and His Tympany Five who perform live from San Francisco.

The Howard Theater in Washington presents the Platters and the Blockbusters for the week.

AUG 6   Clyde McPhatter plays the Palms Club in Hallendale, Florida, for the week.

Production begins on "Rock, Rock, Rock," yet another rock 'n roll movie starring Alan Freed and Bill Haley and His Comets. Also appearing in the picture are Frankie Lymon and the Teenagers, Chuck Berry, the Moonglows, the Flamingos, and LaVern Baker. The Johnny Burnette Trio also appear in the film, but Dorsey Burnette (bass) is replaced by Johnny Black, brother of Bill Black of Elvis' combo.

New Releases for the first week of August include several from rhythm and blues groups looking for that elusive second hit: the Cliques' "I'm In Love With a Girl" on Modern; the Four Fellows' "I Sit In My Window" on Glory; "Kneel and Pray" by the Ravens on Argo; and the Cardinals' "I Won't Make You Cry Anymore" on Atlantic. Also new this week are "Confidential" by **Sonny Knight** on Vita; "Ina-Dell" by Ravon Darnell on Tampa; the catchy instrumental "Congo Mambo" by Guitar Gable on Excello; Muddy Waters' "Don't Go No Further" on Chess; and "Lindy Lou" by Little Butchie Saunders and the Buddies on Herald.

EARLY AUGUST
Little Richard wins the *Cash Box* magazine deejay poll as the Most Outstanding Up and Coming Male Artist.
In Detroit, the Royal Jokers are currently at the Rendevou Club.

AUG 9   Shirley and Lee bring their show to New Orleans' Lincoln Beach as the evening's entertainment.

AUG 10   The Ernie Freeman Combo entertains at the Backstage Club in Los Angeles for the next few weeks.

SONNY KNIGHT
Today, Sonny Knight lives comfortably in Hawaii, where he continues to perform his hits, as well as more "tropical" songs for tourists. His voice still retains the controlled vibrato that he used to make "Confidential" such a unique hit. He was born Joseph C. Smith, in 1934 in Maywood, Illinois. At one time, he considered becoming an author. His family moved to Los Angeles in the early 1950s, and he gravitated to the flourishing R&B scene. He broke into show business by performing at amateur night shows put on by local clubs. In 1953, with his confidence pumped up, he auditioned for Aladdin Records. He was dubbed Sonny Knight (his own play on words) for his two Aladdin releases. In 1955, there was a long-forgotten single on Cal-West under his real name, and another for Specialty as Sonny Knight. In 1956, when there were no more releases by Specialty, Knight recorded "Confidential" for an independent producer-songwriter who placed the song with Vita Records. Just as the single began to sell locally, it was leased to Dot; and "Confidential" became a hit in the "pop" market, eventually selling about a half-million records. In 1957, both Aladdin and Specialty reissued Knight's earlier material. After "Confidential," Knight virtually disappeared, only to resurface in 1964 with "If You Want This Love" a minor hit on the Aura label. Then he dropped out of sight again. By 1981, he had finished his novel. The author of "The Day The Music Died" was listed as Joseph C. Smith.

AUG 12   The Platters have a guest spot on "The Ed Sullivan Show" on CBS-TV.
   Johnny Cash, Johnny Horton, Faron Young, and Roy Orbison start a short jaunt through West Texas that kicks off tonight with a show in El Paso.
   Still in New Orleans, Shirley and Lee perform at the Blue Eagle Club.

New Releases for the second week of August include "Oh What a Nite" by the Dells on Vee-Jay; "Walking in the Rain" by Mickey and Sylvia on Groove; "Hold My Baby's Hand" by James Brown and the Famous Flames on Federal; Jimmy McCracklin's "You're the One" on Irma; "Rock and Roll Party" by Red Prysock on Mercury; "Answer to the Flying Saucer—U.F.O" (parts 1-2) by Syd Lawrence on Cosmic; and a reissue of the original 1953 version of "Hound Dog" by Willie Mae "Big Mama" Thornton on Peacock.

AUG 13   In Florida, Joe Turner starts a week's engagement at the Palms Club in Hallendale.

MID-AUGUST

The Penguins rerecord "Earth Angel" for Mercury in an attempt to cash in on renewed attention for the song generated by Buchanan and Goodman's "Flying Saucer." Release of the new version will come during the third week of August. Dootone Records is also rushing the original version of "Earth Angel" into re-release.

Carl Perkins plays a delayed engagement in Pittsburgh at the Copa. Perkins' injuries suffered in his March auto accident necessitated the rebooking. As per the original contract, Perkins receives $750 a night instead of his current salary.

AUG 17   The Apollo Theater in New York City reopens after a month's renovation with Clyde McPhatter and the El Dorados sharing the bill for the week.
   Louis Jordan starts the first of two weekend stands at the Savoy Ballroom in Los Angeles.

AUG 18   The Roy Orbison-Johnny Cash-Johnny Horton-Faron Young aggregation opens a six-day tour of Ontario, Canada.

AUG 19   The Johnny Otis Show plays an afternoon show at the Oasis Waitress Club in Los Angeles.

AUG 20   The Palms Club in Hallendale hosts the Cadillacs for a week.
   Sonny Burgess and the Pacers appear at the Newport High School Auditorium.

New Releases for the third week of August include "The Closer You Are" by the **Channels** on Whirlin' Disc; "Out of Sight, Out of Mind" by the Five Keys on Capitol; Smiley Lewis' "Down Yonder We Go Ballin'" on

---

THE CHANNELS
The Channels were Earl Lewis, lead tenor (born February 11, 1941); Lawrence Hampden, first tenor; William Morris, second tenor; Edward Doulphin, baritone; and Clifton Wright, bass. As students at Machine and Metals Trade High School in Harlem, Lewis and Wright were singing street corner harmony when they were asked to join a trio calling themselves the Channels. A successful debut at an amateur show led to an unreleased session for the Brownstone label. The group then approached Bobby Robinson, a local record shop owner head of the Red Robin label. As luck would have it, Robinson was ready to begin a new recording company. The Channels' first session produced "The Closer You Are," which featured Lewis' self-assured tenor and intricate harmonizing from the group—a Channels trademark. It was the first release on Whirlin Disc Records, and although it was a strong contender during late 1956, "The Closer You Are" didn't chart nationally. The group followed with "The Gleam in Your Eyes" and two more singles before they left Robinson in a dispute over royalties and writing credit. They landed with Gone Records in 1957 and released "That's My Desire" and "The Altar of Love" before they returned to Bobby Robinson's Fury and Fire labels for a total of three singles in 1958, including "My Love Will Never Die," reportedly their best selling record. By this time, disillusionment had caused several members to quit; and the Channels disbanded in 1960. Lawrence Hampden formed his own group of Channels with one single each on Enjoy and Hit Records. There was also a copycat group on the Times Square label. Earl Lewis recorded a single for Rare Bird in 1971; and a year later, "Earl Lewis and the Channels" released an album on Memories of the Past Records that had been recorded about 1969 when Earl was appearing with the Earl-Jades.

Imperial; "Cool It Baby" by Eddie Fontaine on Decca; "Love the Life I Live" by the Pipes on Dootone; and "Blue Mood" by Julie Stevens and the Premiers on Dig. Also new this week are several novelty records: another cut-in, "Marty on Planet Mars" by Marty on Novelty; "Green Door" by Jim Lowe on Dot; and "We Want a Rock and Roll President" by the Coney Island Kids on Josie. Also out this week is "You Must Be Falling In Love" on Winley by the Duponts, featuring lead vocalist Anthony Gourdine, soon to lead the Imperials as Little Anthony.

AUG 21 Dinah Washington is booked into Zardi's Jazzland in Los Angeles for an extended engagement.

AUG 22 Elvis Presley begins filming "The Reno Brothers" for 20th-Century Pictures. Although he is contracted to Hal Wallis and Paramount Pictures (see APR 1, 1956). Wallis did not have a suitable project and loaned Presley to 20th-Century. After reworking the script to allow Presley to sing four songs, the title of the picture is changed to "Love Me Tender" on the basis of the strength of one of them. (See NOV 16, 1956.)

AUG 24 Tommy "Dr. Jive" Smalls, New York deejay, produces this weeks Apollo Theater revue featuring the Clovers, Bo Diddley, the Valentines, the Five Satins, Charlie and Ray, Big Maybelle, and the Channels.

Big Jay McNeeley is the guest artist at the Flame Show Bar in Detroit for the week.

In Washington, the Howard Theater offers the Five Keys, Faye Adams, Guitar Slim, and the **Rainbows** for patrons this week.

AUG 25 Bill Haley and His Comets wind up a record-breaking engagement at the Steel Pier in Atlantic City.

AUG 26 The dance crowd at the Blue Eagle Club in New Orleans welcomes Little Junior Parker and Bobby "Blue" Bland.

In Detroit, Roy Orbison, Johnny Cash, Johnny Horton, and Faron Young play a one night stand.

AUG 27 Ruth Brown visits Hallendale's Palms Club in for the week.

New Releases for the fourth week of August include "Whirlwind" by Otis Williams and His Charms on DeLuxe; "Do Something for Me" by Little Willie John on King; "That's The Way It Goes" by the Harptones on Rama; "I Can't Love You Enough" by LaVern Baker on Atlantic; "Tough Lover" by Etta "Miss Peaches" James on Modern; "Red Top" by the Teen Queens on R.P.M.; the Falcon's "This Day" on Mercury; "He Drives Me Crazy" by the Hearts on Baton; "If You Only Knew" by Little Jimmy Scott on Savoy; and Phil Flowers' "Honey Chile" on Hollywood. Also new this week is "Confessin' My Dream" on Savoy by Wilbert Harrison, whose "Kansas City" will sell a million copies in 1959.

THE RAINBOWS
The Rainbows were R&B's first supergroup. Except in reverse. The members weren't brought together because they were famous; they went on to fame after leaving the Rainbows. The Rainbows began in Washington, DC, as a street corner group called the Serenaders. This group did not record professionally, but a practice tape was issued in the 1970s. The Rainbows came into being when Henry Womble (1st tenor) and Frank Hardy (bass) joined with Ronald Myles (lead/2nd tenor), John Berry (lead/2nd tenor), and James Nolan (baritone). This group, plus Donald Watts (piano), went to New York and auditioned for Bobby Robinson, "the man to see" in R&B at the time. Robinson sent the young men back home to practice. A year later, in June 1955, they were back, and they recorded "Mary Lee," a song composed on the spur of the moment. The record was issued on Robinson's Red Robin label and the group had a minor—although locally well-received—hit. The group was signed—and "Mary Lee" was reissued—by Pilgrim Records, a slightly larger concern. Their second record was "Shirley," another local-only hit. By this time, two of the original members of the Rainbows were replaced by Don Covay (of "Mercy, Mercy, Mercy" fame) and Chester Simmons (a future promo man in records). In December 1956, this group recorded "They Say" for Rama Records, a George Goldner label. The group had no more records released, but they continued to perform. From time to time, future stars Marvin Gaye (who was with the Marquees at this time) and Billy Stewart (from Bo Diddley's band) would fill in for a missing Rainbow. In 1958, Harvey Fuqua of the Moonglows held auditions to fill vacancies in his group, and he hired the Marquees on the spot.

AUG 29   Alan Freed presents his "Second Anniversary Rock and Roll" show at the Brooklyn Paramount Theater, celebrating his move to New York from Cleveland in 1954. Headlining the production are Fats Domino, Frankie Lymon and the Teenagers, the Harptones, Joe Turner, the Cleftones, and the Penguins. In its nine-day run, the multiple-show-per-day revue will see a gross of $220,000.

AUG 31   Clyde McPhatter, LaVern Baker, and the Drifters appear at the Howard Theater in Washington for the week.

TOP ROCK 'N ROLL RECORDS FOR AUGUST 1956

1. My Prayer/Heaven On Earth - The Platters
2. Hound Dog/Don't Be Cruel - Elvis Presley
3. I Want You, I Need You, I Love You/My Baby Left Me - Elvis Presley
4. The Flying Saucer (parts 1-2) - Buchanan and Goodman
5. Be-Bop-A-Lulu - Gene Vincent and His Blue Caps
6. The Fool - Sanford Clark
7. I'm In Love Again/My Blue Heaven - Fats Domino
8. When My Dream Boat Comes Home/So Long - Fats Domino
9. Stranded in the Jungle - The Cadets
10. Ape Call - Nervous Norvous
11. Fever - Little Willie John
12. Rip It Up/Ready Teddy - Little Richard
13. Honky Tonk (parts 1-2) - Bill Doggett
14. Treasure of Love - Clyde McPhatter
15. Love, Love, Love - The Clovers
16. Rip It Up - Bill Haley and His Comets
17. Stranded in the Jungle - The Jayhawks
18. Let the Good Times Roll - Shirley and Lee
19. A Casual look - The Six Teens
20. Transfusion - Nervous Norvous

Also on the "pop" charts:
Whatever Will Be, Will Be (Que Sera, Sera) - Doris Day
Canadian Sunset - Hugo Winterhalter
Song for a Summer Night - Mitch Miller

August 1956
ARTISTS OF THE MONTH

BUCHANAN AND GOODMAN

In early 1956, Richard Goodman (b. April 19, 1934) was studying law at Columbia University. In high school, he had hung around the stage doors of New York's up-and-coming rock 'n roll music business.

This resulted in his becoming a part-time songwriter. The Nutmegs' "Keys to the Kingdom" was as close as he had come to having a hit. He even produced an early Jimmy Castor session with "I Promise To Remember" issued as a single on Wing before it was covered by Frankie Lymon and the Teenagers.

Goodman was peddling his songs when he met Bill Buchanan, an employee at Monument Publishing in New York. The two hit it off, and Goodman even sold some of his songs to Monument. As their friendship grew, they came up with the idea of doing a record parody of Orson Welles' infamous 1939 radio broadcast, "War of the Worlds." Their interest in rock 'n roll radio predetermined that music and disc jockeys would play important part in this endeavor.

The result was "The Flying Saucer." Buchanan and Goodman used musical snips from more than a dozen rock 'n roll and rhythm and blues records that they interjected into a manic dialog about outer space aliens invading the earth. Performed as though part of a regular radio show, the "deejay" constantly interrupted the opening song after a few seconds to announce breathlessly the advance of the aliens upon some unnamed metropolis. "Flying Saucer" had an interesting release pattern. It first came out on Buchanan and Goodman's Luniverse label as "Back to Earth." Then the name was changed to "Flying Saucer" and it appeared briefly on Radioactive before reverting to Luniverse again.

Buchanan & Goodman

Goodman brought a copy of "Flying Saucer" to Alan Freed at WINS radio. Freed was enthusiastic and promised to play it on that evening's show. Almost immediately, "The Flying Saucer" became a hit, eventually becoming the biggest novelty record of the year, spawning "Flying Saucer the 2nd." Meanwhile, Buchanan and Goodman became the hottest comedy act on vinyl since Andy Griffith's homespun humor and Stan Freberg's lunacy peaked in 1954. All through this time, Buchanan and Goodman continued to use the pay-phone in the back of the neighborhood drug store as their office.

"The Flying Saucer" quickly ran into legal problems. Buchanan and Goodman had taken the various pieces of music without asking permission from the legal copyright holders. In October 1956, Buchanan and Goodman, as well as their Luniverse Records, were sued for copyright infringement, record piracy, and "unfair competition" by Arc Music (a division of Chess/Checker Records representing "Maybelline" and "See You Later, Alligator") and by Commodore Music (a division of Imperial Records representing "Ain't That A Shame," "Poor Me" and "I Hear You Knocking"). Each publisher wanted payment of royalties of two cents per record sold for the use of each song. Two-cents was the normal royalty at the time for the sale of one record of a complete song. Two weeks after they filed suit, Arc and Commodore were joined by Fats Domino and Smiley Lewis who asked for personal damages of $20,000 and $10,000 respectively.

Meanwhile, Buchanan and Goodman completely disregarded their legal problems and assembled "Buchanan and Goodman On Trial," undoubtedly the finest "cut-in" record ever released. Using a court setting as a background, the record ripped along at a breakneck pace. The juxtaposition of the dialog and the musical highlights bordered on true comedic genius. Unfortunately, in light of their continuing legal problems, many radio stations were afraid to air the single, resulting in very poor sales.

In mid-November, the trial against Buchanan and Goodman began in New York. The trial centered on their use of snips of songs in "The Flying Saucer" as well as "Flying Saucer the 2nd." Plaintiffs now totaled seventeen including Modern Records. Modern became involved because a portion of the song "Stranded in the Jungle" was included on "Flying Saucer the 2nd." Buchanan and Goodman contended in court that this version was not sung by the Cadets but had been recorded by Buchanan and Goodman using an imitation group.

Buchanan and Goodman offered a unique defense: rather than hurting the sales of the litigates' records, "The Flying Saucer" had actually created a broader market for their records. At first, the other record companies balked. When Buchanan and Goodman showed that the Penguins' "Earth Angel"—a rhythm and blues hit in early 1955—had begun to sell again in the teen market after "The Flying Saucer," the defendants settled their various lawsuits for about a quarter-cent per record, or, in some cases, for nothing.

After the trial was over, the duo returned to more familiar territory. "Flying Saucer The 2nd" was re-released in the summer of 1957, followed that Christmas by the holiday-themed "Santa and the Satellite."

Aside from being the label for their cut-in singles, Luniverse Records issued only one album, an oddity by the Dell Vikings. In 1956, before the group became famous, they had recorded an acappella session in the basement of Barry Kaye, a Pittsburgh disc jockey. After "Come Go With Me" became a hit in 1957, Kaye approached Goodman with his tape. The songs were remastered and instruments were dubbed over the vocal tracks. The resulting album sold very well in the Northeast.

After the first handful of cut-in singles, the comedic form of Buchanan and Goodman settled into a familiar style. More often than not, the brief record passages that were used came as the answer to some inane question asked by a fictional journalist.

Buchanan and Goodman parted after working together a little more than a year during which they released a half-dozen singles. In late 1957, Bill Buchanan was working as public relations director of WKIT radio in Garden Grove, New York. He joined with Bob Ancell, formerly a deejay in Akron, as Buchanan and Ancell for a mildly successful single, "The Creature." Buchanan and Howard Greenfield (who later co-wrote many hit songs with Neil Sedaka) also released "The Invasion" as by Buchanan and Greenfield. Buchanan also had solo efforts with "The Thing" and "Beware." Bill Buchanan eventually left music altogether, moving to Mexico where he was reported to be making a handsome living as an exporter of jewelry.

After splitting with Buchanan, Dickie Goodman quit the duo route altogether, preferring to work alone. Starting in 1961, he issued a series of parodies on television shows and movies with "The Touchables," "The Touchables in Brooklyn," "Santa and the Touchables," "Horror Movies," "Berlin Top Ten," "Ben Crazy," and "James Bomb."

In 1969, "On Campus" and "Luna Trip" offered a slight change of pace in subject matter for Goodman. "On Campus" actually sold well enough to stay on the record charts two months. In the 1970s, Goodman's parodies covered more topical subjects with "Senate Hearing," "Watergrate," "Energy Crisis," and "Mr. President." In 1975, he had his biggest hit since "The Flying Saucer" with another movie parody, "Mr. Jaws." This single eventually outsold all of his other records combined.

Goodman continued issuing his cut-in singles through the mid-1980s, with his humor more often than not directed at the latest movie release. "Kong" and "Star Warts" in 1977 were the last most people heard from him. Topical humor is a difficult business, and cut-in records simply went out of style. In 1986, he was living in Fort Myers, Florida.

After careers that opened with such frenzy and controversy, Bill Buchanan and Dickie Goodman faded into obscurity with uncharacteristic quietness.

For those who wonder, here are the songs used in "The Flying Saucer" in order of their appearance:

Nappy Brown, "Open Up That Door" (sax intro)
The Platters, "The Great Pretender" ("real...")
The Teenagers, "I Want You To Be My Girl" ("come on baby...")
Little Richard, "Long Tall Sally" ("jump back in the alley")
Fats Domino, "Poor Me" ("What I'm gonna do")
Elvis Presley, "Heartbreak Hotel" ("let's take a walk...")
Penguins, "Earth Angel" ("earth angel")
Smiley Lewis, "I Hear You Knocking" ("I hear you knocking")
Little Richard, "Tutti Frutti" ("a-wop-bop-a-lu-bop...")
Platters, "The Magic Touch" ("here I go reeling...")
Platters, "The Magic Touch" ("still around")
Don Cherry, "Band of Gold" (intro, part 2)
Fats Domino, "Ain't That A Shame" ("ain't that a shame")
Don Cherry, "Band of Gold" ("don't want the world...")
Nappy Brown, "Don't Be Angry" ("don't-a be angry...")
Carl Perkins, "Blue Suede Shoes" ("you can do anything...")
Chuck Berry, "Maybelline" ("motor cooled down...")
Bill Haley, "See You Later, Alligator" ("see you later...")
Platters, "My Prayer" ("always be there")

September 1956

THE FOUR LOVERS

In Newark, New Jersey, in 1952, the Variety Trio featured Nick Massi (bass) and brothers Nick and Tommy DeVito (guitarists). They frequently played the Bellbrook Club, singing and doing a little comedy. One night, Francis Stephen Castelluccio, a friend of the trio from the neighborhood, asked if he could join them for a song. Apparently as a joke, he sang in a nasal falsetto—with the nightclub crowd, he was a hit. In 1951, the trio were on radio twice a week with a fifteen-minute broadcast from the El Morocco Club, and Frankie performed as a special guest. In 1952, the act broke up, and Tommy DeVito took a job with the band at the Strand Bar. Frankie joined him and was discovered by a country artist, Texas Jean Valley, who passed him off as her brother under the name Frankie Valley. Using her influence, he wrangled a contract with Mercury Records in 1953, and he recorded several songs with Texas Jean's band backing him. The first release, "My Mother's Eyes" was on Corona, a Mercury subsidiary, as by Frankie Valley and the Travelers. That record, and the follow-up, "Somebody Else Took Her Home," issued in May 1954 on Mercury, went nowhere. In 1954, Frankie, Tommy and Nick DeVito, and Hank Majewski formed the Variatones. For two years, they worked night clubs, including the Branch Room, a cocktail lounge in the Four Seasons Bowling Alley on Chestnut St. in Union, New Jersey. The hard work brought them to the attention of RCA Victor Records. For their first release, "Apple of My Eye," the Variatones changed their name to the Four Lovers. The group recorded a total of five singles for RCA before jumping to Epic for a single. In 1959, Nick Massi returned to replace Majewski, and Nick DeVito was succeeded by Bob Gaudio of the Royal Teens. By 1961, Frankie Valley had become Frankie Valli, and the Four Lovers were the Four Seasons.

SEP 1   The Hacienda Hotel chain offers an exclusive performance contract to Billy Ward and His Dominoes based on their four-week, sold-out engagement at the Hacienda in Fresno, California. Ward, currently starring at Harrah's Club in Lake Tahoe, is noncommittal.

SEP 2   Charles Brown brings his smooth brand of blues to the Labor Union Hall in New Orleans.

Fats Domino guests on "The Steve Allen Show" on NBC-TV. The show originates from Washington, DC, for the evening.

Little Richard plays and afternoon concert at Los Angeles' Wrigley Field.

SEP 3   The Penguins open for a week at Brooklyn's Paramount Theater.

New Releases for the first week of September include "Dixie Fried" by Carl Perkins on Sun; "Brown-eyed Handsome Man" b/w "Too Much Monkey Business" by Chuck Berry on Chess; "Be Lovey Dovey" by the **Four Lovers** on RCA Victor; "Walkin' in a Dream" by Solomon Burke on Apollo; "Chicken Shack" by Amos Milburn on Aladdin; and "Send Me Flowers" by the Six Teens on Flip.

SEP 7   New York City's Coliseum is the site for a ten-day run of "The Happy Music Show" to coincide with the record industry's "Diamond Jubilee" exposition. Headlining the show are Bill Haley and His Comets.

In Los Angeles, the Savoy Ballroom offers Dinah Washington for patrons this weekend.

EARLY SEPTEMBER

Gene Vincent starts his first professional tour with bookings in Pennsylvania, New York and New England.

SEP 8   The Diamonds perform on "The Perry Como Show" on NBC-TV.

SEP 9   Elvis Presley makes the first of three historic appearances on CBS-TV's "The Ed Sullivan Show." Sullivan, recuperating from a recent auto accident, is absent, and his place is taken by British actor Charles Laughton. The show is broadcast from New York, but Elvis' portion emanates from the CBS studios in Los Angeles.

On ABC-TV, The Johnny Burnette Trio wins second place in the finals of "The Ted Mack Amateur Hour."

On CBS-radio, the "Rock 'n' Roll Dance Party" is visited by Frankie Lymon and the Teenagers, LaVern Baker and Sam "The Man" Taylor.

In Texas, Faron Young, Johnny Cash, Sonny James, Johnny Horton, Charlene Arthur, and Roy Orbison begin an extended tour which will take them to Colorado, Florida and Tennessee. (See OCT 14.)

SEP 10   In Florida, Little Walter blows the roof off the Palms Club in Hallendale during his week long engagement.

New Releases for the second week of September include three on Atlantic: "Thirty Days" by Clyde McPhatter, "From the Bottom of My Heart" by the Clovers, and "Lonely Avenue" b/w "Leave My Woman Alone" by Ray Charles. Also new this week are "You'll Never Know" by the Platters on Mercury; the Jayhawks' "Don't Mind Dying" on Flash; "Everybody's Wailin'" by **Huey Smith and the Clowns** on Ace; and "Hit, Git and Split" by Young Jesse on Modern. Another new single, "The Convention" by the Delegates on Vee-Jay, features Dee Clark of the Hambone Kids and soon to be a major solo artist.

SEP 12   Bill Haley and His Comets start a three-day engagement at the North Carolina State Fair in Castonia.

SEP 14   The Teenagers headline an all-group bill at New York's Apollo Theater this week. Also appearing are Harptones, the Cleftones, and the Valentines.

For the next three nights, Little Richard brings down the house at the Savoy Ballroom in Los Angeles.

In Detroit, Louis Jordan performs at the Flame Show Bar for the coming week.

Lloyd Price headlines this week's show at the Howard Theater in Washington. Also on the bill are Mickey and Sylvia and comedian George Kirby.

MID-SEPTEMBER

In Rhode Island, Fats Domino's concert at the Enlisted Men's Club at the Newport Naval Station is marred by a riot following the show as a thousand men wreck the club after the lights are suddenly doused. Domino blames the altercation on the fact that beer was served in quart bottles and not paper cups. No performer was injured although Domino lost a suitcase with four hundred dollars worth of stage clothes.

The Falcons are currently in the middle of an extended engagement at Lee's Club Sensation in Detroit.

SEP 17   The Palms Club in Hallendale greets Ray Charles for a week-long stay.

HUEY SMITH & CLOWNS

Huey Smith's recording career was successfully schizophrenic. He was a studio pianist and led a vocal group. His barrel house, rolling piano can be heard in the opening strains of Smiley Lewis' "I Hear You Knockin'." It is also behind Guitar Slim's "Things I Used To Do" and Little Richard's "Tutti Frutti." He played behind Shirley and Lee, Earl King, Fats Domino, and many other R&B artists who recorded in New Orleans in the 1950s. Smith was born January 26, 1934, in the Crescent City. He learned blues piano from his uncle, and his style was influenced by Professor Longhair (Roy Byrd). In 1948, he formed his first band, the Honeyjumpers. A year later he met Eddie Jones ("Guitar Slim") and the two formed a lasting friendship. With Willie Nettles on drums, they became a trio, playing local clubs. In 1951, Smith dropped out of school when Slim signed with Imperial Records. Smith recorded under his own name on Savoy in 1952. After Slim signed with Specialty in 1954, Huey Smith found it more lucrative to stay in New Orleans and work sessions than to tour. His first release on Ace Records, "My Love Is Strong," was actually the B-side of an Eddie Bo single. His second single on Ace, "Little Liza Jane," credited Huey "Piano" Smith and the Clowns. Membership in the Clowns varied frequently. Bobby Marchan was the best known, but he also had a successful career in New Orleans as a female impersonator at the Dew Drop Lounge, and so he rarely toured with the group. Others in the Clowns were Curley Moore, Roosevelt Wright, James Rivers, Raymond Lewis, Gerri Hall, and John "Scarface" Williams. Occasional members were Robert Parker, Jesse Hill and James Booker. The Clowns struck pay dirt in 1957 with "Don't You Just Know It" b/w "High Blood Pressure."

PAT CUPP

Pat Cupp was Texarkana's best known rock 'n roller. He was also a member of Texarkana's best known country group. He was born in nearby Nashville, Arkansas, on January 21, 1938. In the 1940s, his parents were members of the Musical Cupps, a family aggregation of pickers and singers with a large regional following. He joined the act at an early age, and was content to sing country until Elvis began making frequent Friday night stopovers in Texarkana in 1954-55. Pat joined with schoolmate Carl "Cheesie" Nelson to form an act built around Nelson's uncanny imitation of young Elvis. Backstage at one of Elvis' Texarkana gigs, Elvis was so impressed with the duo that he brought them out as part of the show. Another time, when Elvis was delayed because of a car accident, Cupp and Nelson filled in with Scotty Moore and Bill Black, Elvis' regular musicians, until Elvis could make the show. Cupp's big break came in early 1956, when he was asked to fill in for Elvis on the "Louisiana Hayride" radio show in Shreveport while Elvis made a TV appearance in New York. Pat was signed by R.P.M. Records of Los Angeles, though his only session was at the studios of KWKH radio in Shreveport. Pat Cupp and the Flying Saucers had only one single released by R.P.M., "Long Gone Daddy," although he recalls waxing eight songs during his session. Every singer with a guitar was issuing rock 'n roll records at the time, and Cupp's fine effort got lost in the shuffle. He soon joined the Air Force, but he kept his talent honed by playing occasional club dates. In the 1970s, several of his songs were issued by Rollin' Rock Records. Cupp still performs around Texarkana, while "Cheesie" is the president of Texarkana College.

Gene Vincent and His Blue Caps open for a week's stay at the Casino Royal in Washington.

New Releases for the third week of September include two on R.P.M.: Paul Anka's "I Confess" and "Long Gone Daddy" by **Pat Cupp**. Also new this week are "Blueberry Hill" by Fats Domino on Imperial; Little Brenda Lee's "Jambalya" on Decca; "The ABC's of Love" by Frankie Lymon and the Teenagers on Gee; "I Got Loaded" by the Cadets on Modern; "Priscilla" by Eddie Cooley and the Dimples on Roost; "Aladdin's Lamp" by the Flairs on ABC-Paramount; "Sweet Dreams" by the Crescendos on Atlantic; "Juke Box Rock N' Roll" by Johnny Bragg and the Marigolds on Excello; and "Lee Allen's "Shimmy" on Aladdin.

SEP 21 At New York's Apollo Theater, The Platters headline a bill that also includes Young Jesse.

Dinah Washington brings her polished style to the Flame Show Bar in Detroit for the week.

Chuck Berry shares the spotlight with Buddy and Ella Johnson, Shirley and Lee, and the G-Clefs this week at the Howard Theater in Washington.

SEP 24 Guitar Slim brings his outrageous act to the Palms club in Hallendale for the week.

Following his altercations in Newport, this week Fats Domino is booked for three shows a night at the Casino Royal in Washington, DC.

Billy Ward and His Dominoes open a week-long engagement at Zardi's Jazzland in Los Angeles.

At Detroit's Greystone, Dinah Washington makes an appearance on a show featuring Little Willie John, Joe Turner, Big Jay McNeeley, and the Five Keys.

New Releases for the fourth week of September include "Bluejean Bop" by Gene Vincent and His Blue Caps on Capitol; "The Greatest Builder" from Bobby Darin on Decca; "Everyone Needs Someone" by Connie Francis on M-G-M; "Long, Lonely Nights" by Little Julian Herrera on Dig; the Gum Drops' "Natural Born Lover" on King; "He Loves You Baby" by Luther Bond and the Emeralds on Federal; and "Fine Girl" by the Calvaes on Cobra. Also new this week are two from Atco: "She's Mine, All Mine" by the Royal Jokers and Glenn Reeves' "Rockin' Country Style." Finally, from Specialty comes "Every Time I Hear That Mellow Saxophone" by Roy Montrell, guitarist in Fats Domino's combo.

SEP 25 Continuing on the fair circuit, Bill Haley and His Comets are booked for three days at the New Jersey State Fair in Trenton.

SEP 26 The Leona Theater in Pittsburgh presents a spectacular one-day show featuring LaVern Baker, Carl Perkins, the Shepherd Sisters, the Turbans, Joe Turner, and the Moonglows.

Elvis Presley performs two concerts in his birthplace of Tupelo, Mississippi. The grandstand at the Mississippi-Alabama Dairy Show and Fair holds 7,500 but an estimated 50,000 fans try to attend.

SEP 27   In Detroit, the Diablos and the Serenaders entertain at the Linwood Theater.

SEP 28   Having completed their summer tour of fair grounds, Bill Haley and His Comets are off on yet another string of theater one-nighters, this one lasting until December 2. Sharing the spotlight with Haley's band are the Platters, Frankie Lymon and the Teenagers, Clyde McPhatter, the Clovers, Chuck Berry, Shirley and Lee, the Flairs, Shirley Gunter and the Queens, and the **Buddy Johnson** orchestra. Tonight's show is in Hershey, Pennsylvania. Other venues this month include Toronto (29), and Montreal (30). The Haley troupe are currently scheduled to make their first overseas tour early in 1957, with scheduled stops in the Philippines and Australia.

Ruth Brown headlines this week's revue at the Apollo Theater. Also on the bill are the Cadets, the Magnificents, and Johnny "Guitar" Watson.

Detroit's Flame Show Bar welcomes Roy Milton and his band for the week.

In Hollywood, Gene Vincent headlines a show that also features the Coasters, and Alis Lesley, who bills herself as the "Female Elvis Presley."

SEP 29   Carl Perkins cancels his regular appearance on the "Big D Jamboree"
to fulfill an engagement in California.

LATE SEPTEMBER

Della Reese is currently performing nightly at the Club Rendevou in Detroit.

THE TOP ROCK 'N ROLL RECORDS FOR SEPTEMBER 1956

1. Don't Be Cruel/Hound Dog - Elvis Presley
2. My Prayer/Heaven on Earth - The Platters
3. The Flying Saucer (part 1-2) - Buchanan and Goodman
4. Honky Tonk (part 1-2) - Bill Doggett
5. The Fool - Sanford Clark
6. I Want You, I Need You I Love You - Elvis Presley
7. Let the Good Times Roll - Shirley and Lee
8. Be-Bop-A-Lulu - Gene Vincent and His Blue Caps
9. When My Dreamboat Comes Home/So Long - Fats Domino
10. St. Theresa of the Roses - Billy Ward and His Dominos
11. Rip It Up - Little Richard
12. Out of Sight, Out of Mind - The Five Keys

BUDDY JOHNSON
In the 1950s, Buddy Johnson was one of the most successful R&B band leaders. Today, few people remember him. Buddy was born Woodrow Wilson Johnson, January 10, 1915, in Darlington, South Carolina. His earliest musical training came in school and church; but, when he felt a career in music calling him, he left home and went to New York City. The year was 1938, and jazz was riding a wave of national popularity. Johnson had little difficulty in finding work as a pianist, and in 1939, he traveled to Europe with the Cotton Club Revue. Back in the States, he was approached by Decca Records, and his first release, "Stop Pretending," was very successful in early 1940. His sister, Ella, followed him to New York and was the vocalist on Buddy's "Please Mr. Johnson," another hit in 1940. During the War, Buddy and Ella formed a series of first big bands to play their unique style of dance music, featuring an uptempo delivery with jazz overtones. Arthur Prysock joined the troupe in 1943, and he was featured on "They Say I'm the Biggest Fool" in 1944. Buddy Johnson's orchestra was in great demand for the next fifteen years, crisscrossing the country, constantly booked to play one-night stands as well as longer engagements. Many of their records pointed the way toward the R&B explosion in the 1950s, including "That's The Stuff You Gotta Watch" (1944) and "Fine Brown Frame" (1947). Others appealed to the ballroom crowd: "Because" (1950), "My Reverie" (1951) and "Stormy Weather" (1951). When their long-term contract expired, Buddy and Ella left Decca and signed with Mercury in 1953, where they continued to have success with their first release, "Hittin' On Me." By the mid-1950s, their style of music produced no more hit records, but the band was still in great demand backing other acts touring with the various rock 'n roll caravans.

13. In The Still of the Night - The Five Satins
14. Rip It Up - Bill Haley and His Comets
15. Fever - Little Willie John
16. See-Saw - The Moonglows
17. Ka Ding Dong - The G-Clefs
18. A Casual Look - The Six Teens
19. You'll Never Know/It Isn't Right - The Platters
20. I'm In Love Again - Fats Domino

Also on the "pop" charts:
Tonight You Belong To Me - Patience and Prudence
Soft Summer Breeze - Eddie Heywood
Just Walking In The Rain - Johnnie Ray

September 1956
ARTIST OF THE MONTH

SANFORD CLARK

Sanford Clark

Sanford Clark's star burned brightly for only the briefest of musical moments. However, his career extended, although with much less fire, for a long time afterward, and his legacy has illuminated music for years.

Today, Sanford Clark is known almost exclusively for the rock-a-ballad "The Fool" although he released more than two-dozen singles over a span of a dozen years.

Clark moved from Tulsa, Oklahoma, where he was born in 1935, to Phoenix as a teenager. He had shown an interest in music from his earliest childhood and was trying to find work at a radio station or singing in a band when he met Lee Hazlewood.

Hazlewood was an Army veteran who had also moved from his home in Oklahoma. He settled in Arizona in the early 1950s. He soon landed a job with a Tucson radio station. Eventually, he tried his hand at starting a record label with the strange name of EB. X Preston. As one of his productions, Hazlewood recorded Duane Eddy, at this time just another unknown guitarist, in a country duet with Jimmy Delbridge. The result was "Soda Fountain Girl" by Jimmy and Duane with Buddy Long and the Western Melody Boys. The record was an immediate flop.

Hazlewood moved to Phoenix to work at KTYL. There, he renewed the acquaintance of Al Casey, another guitarist he had known in Tucson. It was through Casey that Hazlewood eventually met Sanford Clark. In April 1956, Clark joined the cast of "Arizona Hayride" with Jimmy and Duane. It was a fortuitous occasion. Hazlewood was ready to try his hand at another record label, and he had a song written by his wife that was waiting for the right singer. Hazlewood, Clark, and Casey joined to form MCI Records, and their first session produced "The Fool."

Using his position as a deejay, Hazlewood had no trouble in breaking "The Fool" in Phoenix. Local reaction was immediate, but the men had little money left with which to promote their record nationally. Dot Records of Gallatin, Tennessee, soon came to the rescue, asking the trio if they could distribute the song on their label. A deal was struck, and MCI Records closed shop.

This was during the early months of 1956, and the record industry was frantically scrambling to catch up with the lead of Elvis Presley. In that frenzied atmosphere, "The Fool" immediately caught on with teenagers.

"The Fool" broke all sorts of musical conventions. It opens with a repetitive, jangling guitar motif attributed to Al Casey. This leads to Clark's understated vocal. The record then goes through an unexpected change in tempo before returning to the basic pattern. Clark's voice is hushed, almost a whisper, and it creates a tension-filled atmosphere by barely changing intonation through all this. It was an effective ploy meant to draw the listener into the lyrics which relate the tale of one who was foolish enough to tell his baby good-bye. As such, they expressed a universal feeling to which all listeners could relate. There is no true guitar break in the middle of the song, only a prolonged playing of the opening riff. The overall sound is a mixture of ambient echo and spaciousness, yet the musical result is sparse, as well. It was also bouncy enough to entice teens onto the dance floor. This was a heady combination during that first, full summer of rock 'n roll.

It was impossible to pigeonhole Clark's style. It had strong elements of rock 'n roll, country and western, "pop," and rockabilly. And, at 2:42 minutes, the "The Fool" was almost a third longer than the average single record of the day.

"The Fool" quickly went on to sell a million copies. "A Cheat," the follow-up on Dot, did not fare as well. Patterned loosely on "The Fool," it opened with Clark singing in the same quiet style. Behind the vocal, Casey's guitar played a single-note pattern that was at best repetitive and at worst distracting. This time, there was not one, but two identical instrumental breaks that were completely out of place within the framework of the song, sounding as though they had been lifted from another record altogether.

In rock 'n roll's early days, few artists received a second chance at success. So it was with Sanford Clark.

In an attempt to come up with another hit, Clark tried just about every musical style of the day. He had already attempted rockabilly. The flip sides of "The Fool" and "A Cheat" were both passable attempts at the style, but it was the rock-ballad side that sold.

By late 1956, as the sound of rock 'n roll started to change, Clark issued "9 LB. Hammer," an obvious attempt to cash in on the craze created by "Rock Island Line." A remake of "The Glory of Love" came next. It was sung with a syrupy, "pop" feel and accompanied by a completely unnecessary choral group. Then there was "Love Charms," a less-than-successful attempt at a novelty approach. Finally, Clark tried to go back to his rock 'n roll roots with "Swanee River Rock" backed with "Modern Romance." The A-side was a cover of the Ray Charles hit, while "Modern Romance" was a rocker despite the title. Nothing clicked.

Hazlewood continued to produce records in Phoenix, hooking up in 1957 with Duane Eddy again. This time the pairing produced twenty "twangy guitar" hits on Jamie Records over the next four years. It also opened the door for Sanford Clark, as he was included in the deal that brought Eddy to Jamie. Eddy even played those haunting guitar accompaniments on a few of Clark's sessions. However, while Clark watched Eddy having hit after hit, his own career sputtered to a halt. There were five singles on Jamie, and each was less in touch with the music-buying public than the last. To his credit, through them all, Clark gamely kept working at his craft.

Al Casey tried to capitalize on Clark's fleeting success by issuing "Fool's Blues" as a guitar instrumental on Dot. He stuck with that idea and eventually had a minor hit on Stacy Records in 1963 with "Surfin' Hootenanny," done in a style he copied from Duane Eddy.

Sanford Clark joined the Air Force in 1960. When he returned to Phoenix a few years later, he found that Hazlewood had left Jamie Records and was working as an independent producer in Los Angeles. Hazlewood took Clark under his wing again, and placed "Guess It's Love" with Trey Records, a subsidiary of Atlantic, that Hazlewood co-owned. There were also singles by Clark on Project and Warner Brothers. However, as before, no one was listening. Hazlewood teamed with Donnie Owens, another Phoenix singer who had a minor hit in 1958 with "Need You" on Guyden Records. Together, they produced most of Clark's final eight singles. There were five on Ramco, including a 1966 remake of "The Fool" co-produced by Waylon Jennings. In three singles on LHI, they tried to update Clark's image through a variety of country-flavored styles. Again, the singles met with little reaction from the fans. Even a well-produced album on LHI, "Return of the Fool," found no market. It was Clark's only American long-play release.

Hazlewood moved on to new projects. His greatest success came as producer on a string of hits with Nancy Sinatra starting in 1966 with "These Boots Are Made For Walking."

Without a producer or record company, Sanford Clark seemed to have vanished after his days with LHI Records. He was last heard from working in Nevada as a professional gambler and croupier. This is fitting somehow. After all, in 1956, he had placed his money, resources, and talent on "The Fool." And, for the next dozen years, he had let that bet ride through the good times and the lean.

If a man follows his dream to success, can he be The Fool after all?

October 1956

OCT 1   In Florida, Shirley and Lee open for a week at the Palms Club in Hallendale.

Steve Gibson and His Red Caps, featuring Damita Jo, open for a week at the Casino Royal in Washington.

New Releases for the first week of October include "She's Got It" b/w "Heebie Jeebies" from Little Richard on Specialty; Billy Ward and His Dominos' "Will You Remember?" on Decca; "Cops and Robbers" by Bo Diddley on Checker; "My Story of Love" by the Valentines on Rama; "Love Me Tender" by the Sparrows on Davis; "The Vow" by the Flamingos on Checker; and the rockabilly number "Ubangi Stomp" by Warren Smith on Sun. Out this week is "You Done Me Wrong" on Herald by Joe Jones, a New Orleans artists who will have a major hit with "You Talk Too Much" in 1960.

OCT 5   The Turbans represent the only rhythm and blues act at the Apollo Theater in New York this week as the house offers a Latin revue.

In Washington, the Howard Theater presents the Cardinals, the Cleftones, Al Jackson, and Erskine Hawkins' orchestra for the week.

OCT 7   Bobby "Blue" Bland, Little Junior Parker and Buddy Ace perform at the Blue Eagle Hall in New Orleans.

EARLY OCTOBER

After enjoying an unprecedented hit with their unique cut-in novelty record
"The Flying Saucer," Bill Buchanan and Dickie Goodman are sued by two music publishers representing five different songs heard on the disk. The publishers ask the court for an accounting of profits and $100,000 in damages.

New Releases for the second week of October include "Rudy's Rock" by Bill Haley and His Comets on Decca; "Fallen Out of Love" from the Three Chuckles on Vik; "A Thousand Miles Away" by the Heartbeats on Hull; "Rubber Biscuit" from the Chips on Josie; "A Teenager Sings the Blues" by Johnny Nash on ABC-Paramount; and the novelty song "Elvis Presley for President" by Lou Monte on RCA Victor. Six new rockabilly entries this week are "Rock and Roll Polka" from the **Collins Kids** on Columbia; "Train Kept A-Rollin'" by the Johnny Burnette Trio on Coral; Werly Fairburn's "I'm A Fool About Your Love" on Savoy; "Rock House" from

THE COLLINS KIDS
Larry and Lorrie Collins were indeed "kids" when they caught the public's fancy in 1956. Lawrence Albert Collins was born October 4, 1944, in Tulsa, and Lawrencine "Lorrie" May Collins was born May 7, 1942, in Tahlequah, Oklahoma. In the early 1950s, the Collins family lived in Sapulpa, Oklahoma. By 1953, both Larry and Lorrie were already accomplished singers and musicians, and they auditioned and won a spot on Tex Ritter's "Town Hall Party," a television show broadcast across Los Angeles from studios in Compton, California. The family commuted between Oklahoma and California for a year before settling permanently in southern California. The professionalism of the Collins Kids brought them appearances on the "Grand Ole Opry" and the "Ozark Jubilee." In 1955, they signed with Columbia Records just as rockabilly was becoming widespread. Their first record, "Beetle-Bug Bop" was released that November. Larry was featured on a double-neck electric guitar, and he had been coached by Joe Maphis, the reigning country guitarist of the area and a regular on "Town Hall Party." Their singles for Columbia in 1956-57 were almost all in a style that combined rock 'n roll and country while playing up their childhood innocence: "Rock and Roll Polka," "Don't Bother Me," "Hop, Skip and Jump," "Rock Boppin' Baby," and "Party." The duo appeared frequently on television variety shows. They became friends with Ricky Nelson and were invited to perform on the Nelson's weekly TV show. Lorrie even dated Ricky for a time. They continued as an act until 1962 when Lorrie decided to marry and settle down. Today, both of the Collins Kids continue in the music business. Larry is a successful songwriter ("Delta Dawn"). Lorrie still makes occasional appearances in the Las Vegas casinos.

Roy Orbison and Barbara Pittman's "I Need a Man," both on Sun; and "Rough House Blues" by Al Terry on Hickory.

OCT 11   Following a ten-day hiatus, the Bill Haley-Platters tour rolls on through December 2.

Elvis Presley rips through Texas on a five-day jaunt, opening tonight in Dallas, and continuing in Waco, Houston, San Antonio, and Corpus Christi on succeeding nights.

OCT 12   Fats Domino opens for a week at the Twin Coaches Club in Belle Vernon, Pennsylvania, near Pittsburgh.

The Apollo Theater in New York presents a week-long revue heavy on rhythm and blues, featuring the Dells, the Channels, Robert and Johnny, the Solitaires, the Flamingos, the Pearls, Ruth McFadden, Titus Turner, and the Velours.

Steve Gibson and the Red Caps start a two-week gig at the Flame Show Bar in Detroit.

OCT 13   Carl Perkins makes a regularly scheduled appearance on the "Big D Jamboree" in Dallas.

OCT 14   A country revue featuring Johnny Cash and Roy Orbison plays a show in Memphis. The troupe has just visited cities throughout Florida and will remain in Tennessee through October 23 before moving on to New Mexico and West Texas through early November.

Johnny Otis brings his revue to the Sunday matinee at the Club Oasis in Los Angeles.

Bill Haley and His Comets perform at the Fair Park Auditorium in Lubbock, Texas.

New Releases for the third week of October include "Ain't Got No Home" by **Clarence "Frogman" Henry** on Argo; "Laura Lee" by Bobby Charles on Chess; "Wonderful Girl" from the Five Satins on Ember; "I Won't Plead No More" by James Brown on Federal; "The Glory of Love" by the Angels on Gee; "All Alone" by the Charmers and "Confidential" by Charles Brown, both on Aladdin; and "Suffering with the Blues" by Little Willie John and "Rockin' Up a Storm" by Boyd Bennett and His Rockets, both on King.

MID-OCTOBER

The "Top Ten Revue of 1956" is playing Texas, with stops in San Antonio, Houston and Austin. Performers scheduled to appear include Little Richard, Joe Turner, Bill Doggett, the Moonglows, the Five Keys, Faye Adams, Etta James, the Robins, and Big Jay McNeeley's orchestra.

The Mello-Tones are currently booked into Lee's Club Sensation in Detroit.

OCT 19   The Apollo Theater premiers the rhythm and blues movie,

CLARENCE HENRY
In the 1990s, it took Rush Limbaugh to rediscover Clarence Henry. Not that Henry was forgotten—or even hard to find. Far from it. Henry was born March 19, 1937, in New Orleans. He began to learn piano at age five, and switched to trombone by the time he was twelve. This musical expertise came in handy in 1954 when he joined the band backing Bobby Mitchell's Toppers. When the Toppers started touring, Henry soon returned home, got married, and formed his own combo. He was discovered by Chess Records in 1955. His first single was "Troubles, Troubles" b/w the novelty "Ain't Got No Home." Deejays soon flipped the record over, and "Ain't Got No Home" caught the music buyer's ear. The song featured Henry singing in a variety of styles, including that of a gravel-voiced frog. The nickname of "Frogman" stuck. Henry took to the road for a year to promote his record. However, when he was unable to come up with a second hit, he returned to New Orleans. In 1960, Chess Records once again brought him into the studio to record "I Don't Know Why I Love You." The song was released on Argo, a Chess subsidiary, where it received a name change to "But I Do." It was a Top Ten hit in early 1961. "You Always Hurt the One You Love" did almost as well, and there were three more medium-sized singles into 1962 before Henry's recording career slowed again. And he went back home to his family. As other members of the New Orleans music scene became famous and moved away to places like Los Angeles and Las Vegas, Henry remained behind to entertain the multitude of fans who arrived looking for some real R&B music. He was living happily and performing frequently when Limbaugh began playing "Ain't Got No Home" on his national radio show to make a point of the homeless in America.

"Rockin' the Blues." The picture has vocal spots featuring the Harptones, the Wanderers, and the Hurricanes. Accompanying the movie, as was the regular custom, the Apollo presents a stage show with the Wheels, whose "Teasin' Heart" had been released two weeks previously by Premium Records. Also appearing are Marie Knight and Jimmy Cavello's House Rockers.

Bo Diddley rocks the house for the week at the Howard Theater in Washington. Sharing the spotlight are the Cadets and Roy Milton and his band.

OCT 20   The "Biggest Show of '56" plays the Olympia Theater in Detroit. Featured performers are Bill Haley and His Comets, the Platters, Frankie Lymon and the Teenagers, Clyde McPhatter, the Clovers, Chuck Berry, Shirley and Lee, Shirley Gunter, the Flairs, and Ella and Buddy Johnson.

OCT 21   B. B. King plays the Sunday dance party at New Orleans' Blue Eagle Hall.

New Releases for the fourth week of October include the frantic "I Put A Spell On You" by Screamin' Jay Hawkins on Okeh; "Goodnight My Love" by Jesse Belvin on Modern; "Blanche" by the Three Friends on Lido; "I Feel Good" by Shirley and Lee on Aladdin; "Juanita" by Chuck Willis on Atlantic; "Bim Bam Boom" by the El Dorados on Vee-Jay; The Midnighters' "Come On and Get It" on Federal; "Pneumonia" by Joe Tex on King; the new distribution for "Confidential" by Sonny Knight on Dot; "On My Word of Honor" by B. B. King on R.P.M.; and "I'm Gonna Shake this Shack Tonight" by Sid King and the Five Strings on Columbia.

OCT 26   Pearl Bailey, fronting husband Louis Bellson's orchestra, starts a week at New York's Apollo Theater.
The offering at Detroit's Flame Show Bar for the next two weeks is the **Billy Williams** Quartet.

OCT 27   Carl Perkins starts a series of engagements in the Toronto area. Tonights show at the Uptown Theater features the very mixed bag of the Cleftones, the Drifters, and the G-Clefs, along with Eileen Rodgers, Otis Rush, and Cathy Carr.
Pee Wee Crayton begins an extended engagement at Lee's Club Sensation in Detroit.

OCT 28   Elvis Presley appears on "The Ed Sullivan Show" on CBS-TV for a second time.

OCT 29   This week, brothers Red and Arthur Prysock stop by the Palms Club in Hallendale, Florida.
The Greystone Ballroom in Detroit offers the talents of Bo Diddley, the Cadets, Joe Williams and Count Basie's orchestra.

BILLY WILLIAMS
In the mid-1930s, Wilfred "Billy" Williams (born December 28, 1916, in Texas) was a student at Wilberforce College in Ohio when a professor took notice of his fine singing voice. The professor was so impressed that he drafted several other students and put together the Harmony Four. Their name was soon changed to the Charioteers in recognition of their show-stopping version of "Swing Low, Sweet Chariot." After a brief period of local success, the group found themselves with a fifteen minute program on WLW radio in Cincinnati in early 1938. During their stay at WLW, their style became more and more secularized. By the time they moved on to a New York City station, gospel numbers made up a small part of their performance. In New York, they were heard by executives of Columbia Records. Beginning with "I'm Getting Sentimental Over You," the group turned out a series of finely crafted singles over the next ten years. A few of their bigger selling records were "I Miss You So," "A Kiss and a Rose," and a 1947 version of "Open the Door, Richard." In 1949, Williams left the Charioteers to form his own group, The Billy Williams Quartet. They were immediately popular and about 1952 became a mainstay for five seasons on CBS-TV's "Your Show of Shows" featuring Sid Caesar. Besides Williams, the quartet was comprised of Gene Dixon, Johnny Ball and Claude Riddick. Following their million-selling "I'm Gonna Sit Right Down and Write Myself a Letter" in 1957, the group maintained a full schedule of nightclub appearances until the early 1960s when Williams lost his voice to diabetes. For a time, Williams lived in Teaneck, New Jersey, and then in Chicago where he was working as a social worker when he died on October 17, 1972.

THE TOP ROCK 'N ROLL RECORDS FOR SEPTEMBER 1956

1. Hound Dog/Don't Be Cruel - Elvis Presley
2. Honky Tonk (part 1-2) - Bill Doggett
3. My Prayer - The Platters
4. Blueberry Hill - Fats Domino
5. You'll Never Know/It Isn't Right - The Platters
6. The Fool - Sanford Clark
7. Love Me Tender/Any Way You Want Me - Elvis Presley
8. Let the Good Times Roll - Shirley and Lee
9. In the Still of the Night - The Five Satins
10. I Can't Love You Enough/Still - LaVern Baker
11. St. Theresa of the Roses - Billy Ward and His Dominos
12. Out of Sight, Out of Mind - The Five Keys
13. See-Saw - The Moonglows
14. The Flying Saucer (part 1-2) - Buchanan and Goodman
15. Blue Moon (EP) - Elvis Presley
16. Rip It Up - Bill Haley and His Comets
17. Rip It Up - Little Richard
18. Be-Bop-A-Lulu - Gene Vincent and His Blue Caps
19. I Don't Care If the Sun Don't Shine (EP) - Elvis Presley
20. Priscilla - Eddie Cooley and the Dimples

Also on the "pop" charts:
Green Door - Jim Lowe
Friendly Persuasion - Pat Boone
True Love - Bing Crosby and Grace Kelly
Tonight You Belong To Me - The Lennon Sisters

October 1956
ARTIST OF THE MONTH

BILL DOGGETT

Bill Doggett

To many fans of rock 'n roll Bill Doggett's claim to fame rests solely on the instrumental riff that is the very backbone of "Honky Tonk." The guitar figure opening this classic song is arguably the most familiar in all rock music. Without doubt, it definitely ranks right alongside the opening lines of Jimmy Reed's "Baby What You Want Me To Do" or Chuck Berry's "Sweet Little Sixteen."

In 1956, as teenagers scrambled to purchase the year's hottest instrumental, few realized that Doggett's contribution within the framework of the recording was obscured by the guitar and saxophone. Doggett didn't even play the bass or drums, the two other instruments that can be clearly discerned by the ear. Doggett contented himself with augmenting the shuffling bass line on his Hammond organ.

In a field dominated by performers whose age hovered around twenty, Doggett was twice that when he and his combo came up with the bouncy tune for which he would be remembered.

William Ballard Doggett was born February 16, 1916*, in the north side of Philadelphia. Philadelphia was a town well known for its jazz organists—Wild Bill Davis and Jimmy Smith both claim Philly as their home town. However, Doggett did not take up the organ at the start of his musical training. At age nine, he was attracted to the trumpet, but the family's finances could not afford one. Bill's mother, Wynona, was a church pianist and his inspiration. Within a few years he switched to piano and was hailed as a child prodigy by the time he was thirteen. At fifteen he formed his first combo, the Five Majors. While attending Central High School, he found work playing in the pit orchestra at the Nixon Grand theater with the Jimmy Gorman Band.

Eventually, he inherited Gorman's fifteen-piece orchestra. His career as band leader was short-lived as he came to the conclusion that the field was overcrowded. In financial distress, he sold his orchestra to Lucky Millinder and joined Millinder himself. In 1939, Doggett teamed with Jimmy Mundy, the arranger for Benny Goodman, in forming another orchestra. Late that year, Doggett made his first recordings as part of Mundy's band. Two Mundy singles with Doggett were released on Varsity: "Little Old Lady From Baltimore" and "All Aboard."

Doggett returned to Millinder's orchestra as pianist in 1941. He appeared on the next eight of Millinder's recordings, all but one of which were issued by Decca Records. In late 1942, he joined the Ink Spots, the most popular vocal group of the era. Doggett became the group's arranger and pianist. He stayed with the group for two years. During this time, he recorded five singles with the quartet, including "I'll Get By" and "A Lovely Way To Spend an Evening."

During the next ten years, Doggett toured and recorded with several of the nation's top singers and bands including Johnny Otis, Wynonie Harris, Illinois Jacquet, Louis Jordan, Ella Fitzgerald, Coleman Hawkins, Lionel Hampton, Eddie "Lockjaw" Davis, Oran "Hot Lips" Page, Willis "Gatortail" Jackson, and Paul Gayten, as well as such lesser luminaries as Helen Humes, the King George Octet, Buddy Tate's orchestra, Jesse Powell, Vic Dickenson, and Bill Jennings.

When he joined Jordan in 1949, he was hired as a pianist to replace Wild Bill Davis when Davis left to devote his career to bringing the organ into jazz circles. Doggett remained on piano, being a featured performer on many of Jordan's classic Decca recordings including "Saturday Night Fish Fry" and "Blue Light Boogie." Doggett credits his time with Jordan for educating him to the finer points of pleasing the audience.

With this vast experience under his belt, it is little wonder that he decided to organize another combo of his own. The only question is why did he wait so long? The answer lies with the psychological difficulties he met in his own conversion to the organ. He had first toyed with the idea of playing an organ in a "pop" music setting when he worked for

---

(* Date of birth also given as February 6.)

Louis Jordan. However, like most other musicians at that time, Doggett felt that the sound of an organ much too sacred and should be reserved for a church setting. When he was finally on his own, he decided that he needed a new, fresh sound so he would stand apart from a field crowded with other piano combos. It was an agonizing decision, but he felt he was right in switching to the organ. The ensuing trio, originally formed in late 1951, was led by Doggett on the Hammond. It also included Jimmy Canady on guitar and Berisford "Shep" Shepherd on drums. Doggett quickly landed a recording contract with King Records of Cincinnati; and the combo's third release, "Moondust," was a minor hit single.

The next three years saw the personnel in Doggett's group change and expand. Canady left to be eventually replaced by guitarist Billy Butler. Butler had doubled as lead vocalist while with the Harlemaires on Atlantic Records. The final additions to the combo came with the acquisition of Clifford Scott on saxophone and Carl Pruitt on bass.

Over the course of his early association with King - from his first sessions in 1952 through early 1956—more than two dozen singles had been released. Many were moderately successful within the rhythm and blues community and a small number had caught on with the jazz fans. Most of the tunes were delivered in a mildly swinging groove reflecting his years with Louis Jordan and Lucky Millinder. He also recorded in a slow blues style perfected during Doggett's tenure with the Ink Spots and Ella Fitzgerald. None of his prior releases hinted at the explosion he would unleash with "Honky Tonk." In fact, the single just prior to "Honky Tonk" was a coupling of two old standards: "Stella By Starlight" and "What a Difference a Day Makes."

"Honky Tonk" came together in February 1956 during the many one-night stands the group played from coast to coast. It was one of those easy "grooves" that a combo invents to fill a little time on stage. At first hearing, there was really nothing fancy about it. However, Doggett knew he had a potential dance hit on his hands as night after night he received a positive response from the crowd. Finally, on June 16, 1956, the tune was recorded for King Records in a New York studio.

"Honky Tonk, Part 1," as mentioned earlier, opens with one of the most recognizable guitar figures in rock 'n roll music. After twelve bars, the swinging tempo remains "medium cool" as the sax enters to duet with the guitar on a note-for-note repeat of the opening chorus. The first solo, lasting three verses, is taken by Butler on guitar, playing in the upper musical register. When Scott, on saxophone, jumps in for his own solo, he virtually repeats the previous guitar solo, throwing in some jazz intonations for good measure. This lasts a brief verse and a half as Part One fades out.

The saxophone completely carries Part 2. The side opens with Scott picking up the tune just beyond the point where the record faded in Part One. The second sax verse is punctuated by a brief, joyous "yelp" from a band member. Verse three is reminiscent of the inventive solos of Red Prysock, although Scott's work is somewhat more restrained. For his fourth verse, Scott features a growling motif, followed by a modified version of the opening theme played in a descending notation. "Honky Tonk, Part 2" reaches its climax with a brief guitar solo, before sax and guitar, with Doggett's organ finally playing near the forefront, close out the number.

The success of "Honky Tonk" was a two-edged sword. The combo received more offers for bookings than they could fill in ten years. However, most of the requests were to appear in rock 'n roll settings, and none of the musicians considered themselves to be in a rock 'n roll vein. They were jazz performers, first and foremost. Doggett once commented on "Honky Tonk," saying, "It was something that's rare in jazz, a group playing something the same way twice." To the group's everlasting credit, they were able to pull off a shaky marriage between the two musical camps.

His follow-up records, as expected, bordered more on the rhythm side of rhythm and blues than on the blues side. Doggett's "Slow Walk," featuring Scott on a fine saxophone treatment, rivaled Sil Austin's original version, and both were hits in late 1956. On the other hand, "Leaps and Bounds," an original tune and a driving piece of music, received a lighter, jazz feeling in the combo's two-part treatment.

In 1957, Doggett went back to his own roots for "Ram-Bunk-Shush," a tune that had been a hit for Lucky Millinder. On Doggett's version, he allowed Scott and Butler free-rein with the format. Doggett's version of Tiny Bradshaw's "Soft" provided as close to a change-of-pace as one can find during Doggett's recordings in this period. Led by a flute, the piece foresaw the coming of "The Swinging Shepherd Blues" a year later.

Doggett remained with King Records until 1960. By then, he was reduced to covering "Smokie" by Bill Black's Combo. Over the next few years he recorded with Warner Brothers, where he was talked into a series of vain attempts to catch the latest dance craze, such as "(Let's Do) The Hully Gully Twist." Then he was off to Columbia, ABC-Paramount, and Sue for sporadic singles and albums. His drawing power in the early 1960s was still strong enough to afford him regular work at jazz festivals both in America and in Europe. By the mid 1960s, rock 'n roll had long since changed its form and left him behind. At the same time, his status within the jazz community had declined. As he found it increasingly difficult to get regular bookings, he turned his efforts toward the passage of civil rights legislation, using his concerts to promote public awareness.

By the 1970s, Doggett had reestablished his credentials with the jazz community, and regular offers for bookings started coming in. He arranged his schedule to allow longer stays at the regional jazz clubs in New Orleans, Cleveland, and New York State.

Doggett always pointed to Wild Bill Davis as his inspiration. Before Davis, virtually no other performer used the organ in the jazz setting. Fats Waller and Count Basie had done a few blues numbers on organ, but, as Doggett said, "Davis gave it life." In return, Doggett offered hope to other jazz organists looking toward the "pop" market, notably Jimmy Smith and Jimmy McGriff who each had hits in the 1960s.

Today, Bill Doggett is semiretired at his home in Islip, Long Island. However, when the promoters call with lists of new dates, he still likes to perform occasionally in America and Europe.

November 1956

THE FALCONS

The Falcons were an influential group in their hometown of Detroit. They represented the transition between 1950s R&B and Motown's soul music of the 1960s. Eddie Floyd (born June 25, 1935, in Montgomery, Alabama) had an uncle who was one of Detroit's early music entrepreneurs. This uncle owned a variety of small record labels including LuPine and Kudo. The Falcons were formed when Eddie and Bob Manardo were working together in Detroit. Finding a mutual interest in music, they enlisted Arnett Robinson, second tenor; Tom Shetler, baritone; and Willie Schofield, bass. Eddie's uncle was able to obtain local bookings for the group early in 1956; and that August, the group saw their first single, "This Day," released on Mercury. The record sold poorly, and it wasn't until November 1957, that their second release, "Now That It's Over," would be released on Falcon, a small Chicago label. As with most groups, there were numerous personnel changes over the years. By 1959, the group featured Floyd and Schofield; Joe Stubbs, tenor, and brother of Levi Stubbs who sang with the Four Tops; Bonny Rice, baritone; and Lance Finnie on guitar. That year, the group had it's biggest hit with "You're So Fine," a rough-hewn, undisciplined ballad released by UnArt, a subsidiary of United Artists Records. Stubbs and Finnie departed the group soon thereafter, and their places were filled by Wilson Pickett (born March 18, 1941, Prattville, Alabama) and Robert Ward. Featuring Picket's lead vocal, the Falcons had their only other hit in 1962 with "I Found a Love" on LuPine. Floyd and Pickett went on to strong solo careers during the 1960s, and Bonny Rice became known as Sir Mack Rice, songwriter of Pickett's "Mustang Sally." Ward was a founding member of the Ohio Untouchables which later became the Ohio Players, a major force in soul music beginning in 1971.

NOV 2   "Dr. Jive's All Star Rhythm and Blues Caravan" opens a week-long run at Washington's Howard Theater. Appearing are the Dells, the El Dorados, the Debutantes, the Solitaires, Screamin' Jay Hawkins, Robert and Johnny, and Eddie Cooley and the Dimples.

NOV 3   The **Falcons** open at the Club Rendevou in Detroit for the week.

New Releases for the first week of November include a nice variety of couplings, starting with two from Atlantic's top female singers: "Jim Dandy" by LaVern Baker and "Smooth Operator" by Ruth Brown. Also new this week are three instrumentals: "Tricky" by Gus Jenkins and his orchestra on Flash, "Slow Walk" by Bill Doggett on King; and "Teenage Rock" by sax-wizard Red Prysock on Mercury. There are two versions of "I'll Be Spinning," by the Cadets on Modern and by Johnnie and Joe on Chess. Rounding out the week's releases are "You're Mine" by Robert and Johnny on Old Town; Rudy Tutti Grazell's "Jig-Ga-Lee-Ga" on Starday; and the little-known Christmas ditty, "I'm Gonna Lasso Santa Claus" by Little Brenda Lee on Decca.

NOV 8   Gatemouth Brown brings his own brand of boogie-blues to the Blue Eagle Hall in New Orleans for a Thursday night.

NOV 9   The headliners at the Apollo Theater this week in New York are the Coasters. Sharing the spotlight are the Cardinals, Gloria Lynne, Della Reese, and Erskine Hawkins and his orchestra.

NOV 10   In Dallas, Carl Perkins headlines KRLD's "Big D Jamboree." In Detroit, Andre Williams and the Diablos start a week-long stand at the Club Rendevou.

New Releases for the second week of November include Jimmy Reed's "You've Got Me Dizzy" on Vee-Jay; "Hot Dog! That Made Him Mad" by Wanda Jackson on Capitol; Terry Fell's "Caveman" on RCA Victor; Connie Francis' "I Never Had a Sweetheart" on M-G-M; "'Cause You're Mine" by the G-Clefs on Pilgrim; and "Movin' and Groovin'" by the David Clowney Band on Ember. New this week is "Shame, Shame, Shame" by Smiley Lewis on Imperial. The song is featured in the dramatic movie "Baby Doll," and a rousing version with Lewis backed by the Warner Brothers orchestra also appears on the soundtrack.

NOV 13   The case against Buchanan and Goodman goes to trial in New York City. The duo is being sued over their use of snips of other record companies' songs in "The Flying Saucer" and "Flying Saucer the 2nd." In addition, their company, Luniverse Records, is being sued for "unfair competition."

NOV 15   The top stars of Memphis' own Sun Records, Carl Perkins, Roy Orbison, and Warren Smith, open a five day run at the hometown Malco Theater.

MID-NOVEMBER

Despite a blinding eight-hour snow storm, it is Standing Room Only when Bill Haley and His Comets play Denver. Supporting acts are Frankie Lymon and the Teenagers, Chuck Berry, the Platters, Shirley and Lee, the Clovers, and the Flairs.

Fats Domino begins a lengthy stay at the Neapolitan City showroom in New York City.

NOV 16   "Dr. Jive's Rhythm and Blues Caravan" fills the bill at New York City's Apollo Theater. The show features the Dells, Robert and Johnny, the Chips, the Heartbreakers, **Screamin' Jay Hawkins**, the Schoolboys, Ann Cole, Bo Diddley, and the Cadillacs. "Dr. Jive" is Tommy Smalls, a deejay at WWRL radio in New York.

Downtown at the Times Square Paramount Theater in New York, Elvis Presley's first picture, "Love Me Tender," has its premiere. The national release comes on November 21.

The Flame Show Bar in Detroit presents Gene and Eunice for the coming week.

Pearl Bailey and Louis Bellson's orchestra entertain at the Howard Theater in Washington.

NOV 17   Promoting her new release, "Hot Dog! That Made Him Mad," **Wanda Jackson** (page 90 ➤) starts a week's tour of the Midwest with a rockin' show in Kansas City. On succeeding nights she will appear in St. Joseph, Topeka, Omaha, Independence, Wichita, and Hutchinson, Kansas.

In New Jersey, Ray Charles romps through a concert at the Laurel Springs Auditorium.

NBC-TV welcomes Brenda Lee to "The Perry Como Show."

NOV 18   Della Reese and Otis William and His Charms perform for the Sunday dance at Detroit's Greystone Ballroom.

CBS-TV's "The Ed Sullivan Show" brings Fats Domino to the show to sing "Blueberry Hill."

NOV 19   The Esquires open for a week at Washington's Casino Royal.

New Releases for the third week of November include "The Girl Can't Help It" by Little Richard on Specialty; "A Cheat" by Sanford Clark on Dot; "Baby, Baby" by Frankie Lymon and the Teenagers on Gee; "Love

SCREAMIN' JAY HAWKINS
He had the strangest stageshow in the land. His own record company called him a "wild weirdie." His antics preceded those of Alice Cooper and Ozzy Osbourne by many years. Jalacy "Jay" Hawkins was born in Cleveland on July 18, 1929. When he was fifteen, he joined the Army during World War II. He became proficient on saxophone and piano and was assigned to the Special Services. When Jay left military service in 1952, he worked with the Tiny Grimes combo as a combination valet and blues shouter. Grimes got recording sessions for Hawkins with Gotham Records ("Carnation Blues") and Atlantic ("Screamin' Blues"—unreleased). With no immediate success, Hawkins took a summer job singing in Atlantic City where he met Wynonie Harris who was in the middle of a long string of hits. Harris took Hawkins with him on tour, which eventually led to Hawkins recording two singles on Timely, a subsidiary of Apollo Records, in 1953. In 1954, Hawkins had records on Mercury, Wing (a Mercury label), and Grand. On Grand, he recorded a love song titled "I Put a Spell On You." In 1955, Hawkins' recording contract ended up with Okeh Records, a Columbia subsidiary, and he was talked into rerecording "Spell" as a novelty. In order to get the desired results, everyone working the session was roaring drunk. Needless to say, "I Put a Spell On You" possessed the right ingredients to make it stand out from the crowd. At Alan Freed's suggestion, Hawkins developed a stage act using a coffin and a flaming skull named "Henry." When funeral parlors refused to rent him a coffin, he bought one. He also purchased a hearse that he had painted with zebra stripes. In the 1960s, Hawkins was semiretired in Honolulu. He returned to performing in the 1970s and continues to be a crazy as ever.

Is Strange" by Mickey and Sylvia on Groove; "I Wanna Holler" by Little Butchie Saunders on Herald; and "The Midnight Creeper" by the Johnny Otis Orchestra on Dig.

NOV 22 This Thanksgiving finds Elvis Presley in Toledo for a concert. He will also play Cleveland (24) and Louisville (26) while in the area.

NOV 23 Guitar Slim brings his antics to Detroit's Flame Show Bar for a week.

Joe Turner, the Five Satins, Etta James, and Ann Cole entertain patrons at the Howard Theater in Washington this week.

New Releases for the fourth week of November include several selections from the picture "Don't Knock The Rock" including the title tune by Bill Haley and His Comets on Decca; "You Can't Catch Me" by Chuck Berry and "Over and Over Again" by the Moonglows, both on Chess; "Ever Since I Can Remember" by the Bowties on Royal Roost; and the Flamingos' "Would I Be Crying?" on Checker. Also new this week are "One in a Million" b/w "On My Word of Honor" by the Platters on Mercury; "The Way You Look Tonight" by the Jaguars on R-Dell; "Midnight" by the Jodimars and "Wisdom of a Fool" by the Five Keys, both on Capitol; "Shirley" by the Schoolboys on Okeh; "Little By Little" by Nappy Brown on Savoy; "I'm Not Afraid" by Bobby Relf on Dot; "29 Ways" by Willie Dixon on Checker; and "Dreamy Eyes" by the Youngsters on Empire.

NOV 30 At the Apollo this week are the G-Clefs, the Five Satins, Frankie Brunson, Jo Ann Campbell, and the El Dorados.

At Detroit's Flame Show Bar, B. B. King performs for the next ten days.

WANDA JACKSON
Wanda Lavonne Jackson was born October 20, 1937, in Maud, Oklahoma. Her father, Tom, played guitar, fiddle and piano and had been a professional musician until he married. In 1941, the family left Oklahoma for Bakersfield, California, where Wanda was exposed to the new country sounds of Rose Maddox. She was impressed enough to acquire her first guitar. The Jacksons returned to Oklahoma when Wanda was twelve. A year later, she had her own fifteen-minute radio show, and by the time she was sixteen, she was fronting the Merle Lindsey Band's half-hour program. This exposure brought Wanda to the attention of Hank Thompson, a country superstar of the early 1950s. She was invited to perform with him at Oklahoma City's Trianon Ballroom, and then to tour with him. Thompson wanted her to sign with Capitol Records, his label, but Capitol wouldn't take a chance on Wanda because of her age. Thompson did help her get a contract with Decca Records. Her first session, in March 1954, was cut while she was still sixteen. She recorded straight country for Decca and had hits with "You Can't Have My Love" (a duet with Billy Grey of Thompson's band) and "Lovin' Country Style." She became a regular on the "Ozark Jubilee;" and, in late 1955, she toured with Elvis Presley and saw the excitement in rockabilly music. She was an instant convert. She finally signed with Capitol in the summer of 1956, and her first session produced "I Gotta Know." This was followed by "Hot Dog! That Made Him Mad," "Cool Love," "Fujiyama Mama," "Honey Bop," and "Mean Mean Man," all done in a torrid style. One of her last rockers was "Let's Have a Party" in 1960, featuring her band's new guitarist, Roy Clark. Shortly thereafter, she switched back to country music and had a best selling record with "Right or Wrong."

THE TOP ROCK N' ROLL RECORDS FOR NOVEMBER 1956

1. Love Me Tender/Any Way You Want Me - Elvis Presley
2. Don't Be Cruel/Hound Dog - Elvis Presley
3. Blueberry Hill - Fats Domino
4. Honky Tonk (part 1-2) - Bill Doggett
5. You'll Never Know/It Isn't Right - The Platters
6. A Rose and a Baby Ruth - George Hamilton IV
7. Confidential - Sonny Knight
8. Slow Walk - Sil Austin
9. Priscilla - Eddie Cooley and the Dimples
10. Love Me (EP) - Elvis Presley
11. Rudy's Rock - Bill Haley and His Comets
12. Out of Sight, Out of Mind - The Five Keys
13. In the Still of the Night - The Five Satins
14. Since I Met You Baby - Ivory Joe Hunter
15. The Fool - Sanford Clark

16. My Prayer - The Platters
17. Let the Good Times Roll - Shirley and Lee
18. Oh, What A Night - The Dells
19. I Feel Good - Shirley and Lee
20. Brown Eyed Handsome Man/Too Much Monkey Business
    - Chuck Berry

Also on the "pop" charts:
Singing the Blues - Guy Mitchell
Cindy, Oh Cindy - Eddie Fisher
Cindy, Oh Cindy - Vince Martin and the Tarriers
Hey, Jealous Lover - Frank Sinatra

November 1956
ARTIST OF THE MONTH

GEORGE HAMILTON IV

George Hamilton IV

George Hamilton IV was the first artist who came out of a true country and western background to have a major impact on the teenage rock 'n roll audience. The reason was simple: he was one of them. He was not yet twenty when he sang "A Rose And a Baby Ruth." Hamilton loaded the song with enough sweet anxiety to make every teenage girl take notice.

Hamilton was born on July 19, 1937 in Matthews, North Carolina. With his family being middle-class and Southern, George was brought up to believe in the Bible, the value of a good education, and country music. Unlike many other young aspiring performers, George received generous amounts of encouragement from his parents as soon as he showed an aptitude toward music. His father, George III, had been an amateur musician during his own high school days. He welcomed the idea that his son might follow the old man's lead. According to reports, both parents were also big fans of the "Grand Ole Opry."

By the time George reached high school, he was already composing songs on his new guitar. Unlike most teens of the era, his musical interest lay with country music. However, he would occasionally throw in a little rock 'n roll while performing with local bands during high school. When he entered the University of North Carolina at Chapel Hill in 1955, the last thing he saw in his future was a recording career.

Nevertheless, performing was in his blood. He soon formed another combo to play fraternity parties and school dances. When he began his sophomore year in the fall of 1956, he was already making plans to cut his first record. The only recording company located in Chapel Hill was Colonial, a small concern that had released just two singles before Hamilton showed up. For his inaugural release, Hamilton chose a number that he had first heard when its composer performed it on a television show broadcast from nearby Durham.

That composer was John D. Loudermilk. Loudermilk would go on to write "Sittin' In The Balcony" for Eddie Cochran (which Loudermilk also recorded on Colonial under the name Johnny Dee), "Norman" and "Paper Tiger" for Sue Thompson, "Ebony Eyes" for the Everly Brothers, and "Indian Reservation" for Paul Revere and the Raiders among many other hits. He also had a moderately successful recording career of his own beginning in 1960 with "Language of Love." The song George Hamilton IV chose to record was "A Rose and a Baby Ruth."

The record became an immediate success in the Carolinas, overwhelming Colonial's ability to keep up with orders. This good news quickly reached New York. In short order Hamilton and Colonial Records found themselves being courted by the record executives from ABC-Paramount. A deal was struck providing Hamilton with overdue royalties and Colonial with a small lump sum payment for Hamilton's recording contract. ABC-Paramount re-released "A Rose and a Baby Ruth" in October 1956, and in just four weeks it zoomed into the Top Ten across the nation.

The recording was simplicity personified. The instrumental backing was virtually nonexistent: brushes on the snare drum, a light stroke on the bass to keep time, a muted guitar, a restrained vocal group—along with Hamilton's hushed delivery—and that's it. The lyrics tell the story of an admirer's gift to his sweetheart after they quarrel: "Dear, I believe you won't laugh when you receive, this rose and a Baby Ruth." It may well have been the first of the teeny-bopper hits. It certainly helped boost the acceptability of artists like Frankie Avalon, Jerry Wallace, Dodie Stevens, and the Fleetwoods, all yet to come.

Hamilton's collegiate good looks and southern charm appealed to the national television audience. He was booked on many of the weekly variety shows, including those of Arthur Godfrey, Patti Page, and Steve Allen. He also made the obligatory pilgrimage to Philadelphia to lip-sync his song on "American Bandstand."

It didn't take long before Hamilton discovered just how fickle the music-buying public could be. As a follow-up to his hit, he recorded "Only One Love" and "High School Romance," but it was nearly a year before he cracked the Top Ten again, this time it with "Why Don't They Understand," a rolling piece of country-flavored schmaltz overproduced by Don Costa and complete with violins and a chorus singing "woo-ooo" and "doo-wa." It was no wonder that his popularity went into a nose-dive for the next few years.

However, his good fortune didn't desert him completely. As his career in popular music waned, he returned to his country roots. Jimmy Dean invited him to appear on WMAL-TV in Washington, DC, and soon Hamilton had his own regular program at the station. Later, he had a daily show on ABC-TV. Rather than give up on his college education, he transferred his credits to American University in Washington. He graduated from A.U. in 1960.

In 1959, the "Grand Ole Opry" inducted him into the fold. He started having country hits while still with ABC-Paramount. In 1960, he scored with "Why I'm Walkin'" and "Before This Day Ends," the latter staying on the country charts for nearly half a year. In 1961, his last hit for ABC-Paramount was "A Walk on the Wild Side." His transition to country music became complete early that same year when he signed with RCA Victor, one of the strongest labels with offices in Nashville. He had an immediate country hit with "Three Steps to a Phone" followed by "To You and Yours." In 1962, he had success with "China Doll" and "If You Don't Know I Ain't Gonna Tell You." With "Abilene" in 1963, he topped the country charts while crossing over into the popular field for the last time.

His easygoing vocal style was an asset when he combined folk with country in the mid-1960s. He continued to have big country hits into early 1970s with "Truck Drivin' Man," "Break My Mind," "Early Morning Rain," and "She's A Little Bit Country." In 1969, he made his first trip overseas, playing the Wembley Music Festival in England. He was asked to star in a syndicated Canadian television show that ran from 1971 to 1978 and was eventually broadcast worldwide.

It's no wonder George Hamilton IV became known by the unofficial title of International Ambassador of County Music.

December 1956

THE THREE CHUCKLES
The Three Chuckles merit the briefest of footnotes in the history of rock 'n roll. Mainly, they acted as the launching pad for Teddy Randazzo, himself only another footnote. The Three Chuckles began life in Brooklyn as a typical night club act of Italian heritage: Tom Romaro (guitar) and Russ Gilberto (bass) behind Randazzo on accordion. They were doing well, working the New Jersey resorts and clubs in the Catskills. In 1953, while playing the lounge of a Detroit bowling alley, they fell into a one-shot deal with the local Boulevard Records. "Run Around" did attract the attention of an executive at RCA Victor, which led to a recording contract with "X" Records, a subsidiary. The spelling was altered to "Runaround" as it was immediately reissued and the group had a Top Twenty hit centered on the East Coast. In person, the boys were a knockout—very professional, as might be imagined, and with those sharp Italian looks, the girls were attracted in droves. Their sophomore single was "Foolishly" in the same vein as "Runaround," and it sold fewer copies. Two records later, they again caught on with "Times Two, I Love You." The "X" label was soon closed and the Three Chuckles were transferred to Vik. Here they had five singles through late 1956, including "And the Angels Sing," a minor hit. This led to the group's appearance in the best of the early rock 'n roll movies, "Rock, Rock, Rock" and "The Girl Can't Help It." In 1957, Randazzo went solo with a starring role in the film "Mister Rock and Roll." He also recorded for Vik ("Little Serenade" was a minor hit in 1958), before going on to ABC-Paramount where he issued sixteen singles between 1959-62. Randazzo also composed "Goin' Out of My Head" and "Outside Looking In" for Little Anthony and the Imperials.

DEC 1   Johnny Lee Hooker appears at the Apex Bar in Detroit.

DEC 2   Clarence "Gatemouth" Brown returns to the Blue Eagle in New Orleans.

New Releases for the first week of December include "Blue Monday" b/w "What's the Reason I'm Not Pleasin' You" by Fats Domino on Imperial; "Young Love" by Sonny James on Capitol; "Guided Missiles" by the Cuff Links on Dootone; Mac Curtis' "That Ain't Nothin' But Right" on King; and "Rock and Roll Guitar" by the New Blockbusters on Antler.

DEC 4   At the Paramount Theater in Los Angeles, "The Greatest Stage Show of '56" features the Platters, the Penguins, the Teen Queens, and the Blockbusters.
   At Sun Studios in Memphis, Carl Perkins is finishing up a session with Jerry Lee Lewis on piano and Johnny Cash in attendance when Elvis Presley stops by to visit. The foursome join together to sing a variety of songs ranging from gospel to hillbilly to "pop" over the next two hours. Portions of the impromptu jam session are tape recorded by Sun's owner, Sam Phillips, and it will become legendary as the "Million Dollar Quartet."

DEC 5   The motion picture "Rock, Rock, Rock" opens across the country. In New York City alone, it is on seventy screens this week. The film "stars" Alan Freed and Teddy Randazzo as well as introducing Tuesday Weld. Both Randazzo, of the **Three Chuckles**, and Miss Weld are given musical numbers, but Miss Weld's singing voice is actually dubbed by Connie Francis. On this date, Alan Freed appears at the Lowe's Victoria Theater in New York with Chuck Berry and Connie Francis. Trade reports give Alan Freed 10% of the film's profits and Freed's Snapper Music is publishing thirteen of the twenty-one tunes in the picture, including "Tra La La" (LaVern Baker) and "You Can't Catch Me" (Chuck Berry). A special "deejay only" album package featuring songs from the film by Chuck Berry, the Johnny Burnette Trio, LaVern Baker, Frankie Lymon and the Teenagers, and the Three Chuckles is being mailed to 600 radio stations nationwide.

DEC 7   "Rhythm and Blues Week" is initiated at the Apollo Theater in New York. Featured performers the Clovers, Big Maybelle, Etta James and the Peaches with the James Moody Band. The live acts alternate with showings of the picture "Rhythm and Blues Review."

At the Baby Grand Club in New York, the show is headlined by Gene and Eunice.

New York's new rock 'n roll nightspot, Neapolitan City, hosts **Clyde McPhatter**, the Heartbeats, Della Reese, and Jimmy Cavello and the House Rockers.

EARLY DECEMBER

In Memphis, B. B. King forms his own record label, Blues Boy Kingdom. Because King is under contract with R.P.M. records, the label will seek out new talent for its roster.

Gene Vincent cancels a month-long engagement at the Sands Hotel in Las Vegas after the first week because he is suffering pains in his leg. He injured his shinbone in a motorcycle accident in 1955 while serving as a dispatch rider in the Navy. He enters the Veteran's Hospital in Portsmouth, Virginia, for treatment. It is reported in the music press that he will remain in the hospital for three months.

New Releases for the second week of December include the album ROCK, ROCK, ROCK from Chess which features Chuck Berry, the Moonglows, and the Flamingos performing songs from the film as well as other hits. Also out this week are "End of the Road" b/w "Crazy Arms" by Jerry Lee Lewis on Sun; "Bottles To The Baby" by Charlie Feathers on King; "Juice," an instrumental from Al Casey and "Eternally" by the Twilighters," both on Dot; "Bad Boy" by the Jive Bombers on Savoy; "I Wanted To Be Free" by the Jay Netts on J&S; and "You Gave Me Peace of Mind" by the Spaniels on Vee-Jay.

DEC 14   Jerry Lee Lewis, Carl Perkins, and Warren Smith play a show in Huntsville, Alabama. The next evening finds them in nearby Sheffield.

DEC 15   The Blue Eagle Hall in New Orleans welcomes the blues package of **Bobby "Blue" Bland** (page 96 ➤) Little Junior Parker and Buddy Ace back for the second time in two months.

New Releases for the third week of December include "Modern Don Juan" by Buddy Holly and "Evermore" by Billy Ward and His Dominos, both on Decca; "Party Doll" by Buddy Knox b/w "I'm Stickin' With You" by Jimmy Bowen on Triple-D; "Happy Am I" by the Four Lovers on RCA Victor; "Young Love" by Tab Hunter" on Dot; Little Willie John's "A Little Bit of Loving" on King; and "Feelin' Happy" by Joe Turner on Atlantic.

DEC 21   Alan Freed's now-annual Christmas-week show at the Brooklyn Paramount Theater again sets box office records. Among the artists appearing are Shirley and Lee, Screamin' Jay Hawkins, Jesse Belvin, the Moonglows, the Heartbeats, Mac Curtis, the Dells, George Hamilton IV, the G-Clefs, Eddie Cooley and the Dimples, Teddy Randazzo, the Three Friends, and Freddie Mitchell's orchestra.

CLYDE MCPHATTER

Clyde McPhatter did not rejoin the Drifters after he returned from the Army. Instead, he began a solo career with his old label, Atlantic Records. In 1955, McPhatter's first two singles, "Everyone's Laughing" and "Love Has Joined Us Together" (a duet with Ruth Brown) failed to catch the public's fancy. However, his next two singles, "Seven Days" and "Treasure of Love," were both hits. Then came "Thirty Days," another dud, before he had a string of four hits in a row. His career was now swinging wildly between the peaks and valleys. In 1958, "A Lover's Question" was his only hit single, but it sold a million copies. When he was unable to follow with a single that sold even reasonably well, it was clear that something was wrong between McPhatter and Atlantic. McPhatter felt obvious concern that Atlantic was not supporting his releases, so late in 1959, he jumped ship, joining M-G-M Records. A year with M-G-M did little for his future, and he jumped once again, landing with Mercury in 1960. Here he found someone he could trust in Clyde Otis, the reigning king of R&B artist and repertoire men. More to the point, Otis had been able to take Brook Benton and Dinah Washington and turn their lackluster careers around. For a while, Otis was able to work his magic with McPhatter, starting with "Ta-Ta" and following with "Lover Please," that reached the Top Ten. But, McPhatter's days with Mercury were numbered. His long-running R&B stardom was now gone. During the 1960s, he recorded for Amy and Decca with no success. His live performances became positively strange. He blamed his personal troubles on an ex-wife, but by this time McPhatter was his own worst enemy. On June 13, 1972, he died in a Bronx hotel room of the effects of long term alcoholism. He was just thirty-eight.

The Apollo Theater's Christmas-week show has a gospel flavor as it headlines the Golden Gate Quartet.

DEC 22   In New Orleans, Little Walter romps through an evening at the Blue Eagle Hall.

DEC 23   Ray Charles and his orchestra entertain at the Labor Union Hall in New Orleans.
Little Richard performs at the Elks Auditorium in Los Angeles.

New Releases for the fourth week of December are always scarce, but they do include "Ooh, Baby, Baby" by the Midnighters on Federal; Art Neville's "Oooo-Whee, Baby" on Specialty; and "Lonesome Train" by the Johnny Burnette Trio on Coral.

DEC 25   Christmas Day in Detroit brings the opening of a week-long run of a rock 'n roll show and film package at the Fox Theater. Among those performing on the bill are Ivory Joe Hunter, Bo Diddley, the Royal Jokers, Guy Mitchell, Della Reese, Bunny Paul, Bobby "Mumbles" Lewis, the Nitecaps, and the Three Chuckles. On the screen is the magnificent, full-color, Cinemascope rock 'n roll epic, "The Girl Can't Help It," which has musical cameos by Little Richard, Fats Domino, Eddie Cochran, Gene Vincent and the Blue Caps, Johnny Olenn's Band, and the Platters.
Also in Detroit, the Christmas dance at the Greystone Ballroom also features Della Reese, the Nitecaps and the Royal Jokers as well as Little Willie John and Arthur Prysock.

DEC 28   Set at the Apollo this New Year's week are Al Hibbler with Illinois Jacquet's orchestra.
Bo Diddley is booked into the Flame Show Bar in Detroit for a week-long New Years' celebration.
In Washington, the Howard Theater offers Ruth Brown, the Clovers, and the Rainbows this week.

LATE DECEMBER

Randy Wood, founder of Dot Records, opens negotiations with ABC-Paramount to sell his company. What appears as an open-and-shut deal in the beginning runs into various stumbling blocks and will not be complete until April 1957.

Jerry Gold, artist and repertoire director for Pilgrim Records, jumps ship to start his own record company, Paris Records, taking with him Pilgrim's two bestselling acts, the G-Clefs and the Esquires.

THE TOP ROCK 'N ROLL RECORDS FOR DECEMBER 1956

1. Blueberry Hill - Fats Domino
2. Love Me Tender/Any Way You Want Me - Elvis Presley

BOBBY "BLUE" BLAND
Bobby Bland's vocal style combines the smooth, uptown blues that was all the rage beginning in the 1940s with an earthy, gospel-tinged delivery. He was born Robert Calvin Bland (or Brooks), in Rosemark, Tennessee, on June 27, 1930. By the time he was in his teens, his family had moved to Memphis. Here he became enamored with the music he heard. In the late 1940s, he joined the Beale Streeters, a loose-knit combo that included several young men who would become prominent in Memphis blues: Johnny Ace, B. B. King, Rosco Gordon, Herman "Little Junior" Parker, and Earl Forrest. The local talent scout for Modern/R.P.M. Records of Los Angeles was bandleader Ike Turner. With the success of King's "Three O'Clock Blues" on R.P.M. in 1951, Turner was able to get Bobby Bland and Junior Parker signed to Modern Records. Beginning in 1951, Modern released two singles by "Robert Bland," "Crying All Night Long" and "Good Lovin." These records brought him to the attention of Duke Records, a Memphis label. Bland had only one release on Duke, "Army Blues," before he was drafted. Duke was purchased by Peacock Records of Houston in July 1952, and that November, Bland's "Lovin' Blues" was released. Bland continued to record during his four years in the Army, His first real taste of success came with "It's My Life Baby," released in May 1955. His first national hit came with "Farther Up the Road," released in July 1957, a record that sold equally well in "pop" and blues markets. For the next four years, he continued to have blues hits, with the best sellers being "I'll Take Care of You" (1959), "Lead Me On" (1960) and "Cry, Cry Cry" (1960). In 1961, his popularity in the "pop" field was solidified with "I Pity the Fool" and "Turn On Your Lovelight. "Until 1974 there was hardly a time that Bland didn't have a record on the "pop" and blues charts.

3. Love Me (EP) - Elvis Presley
4. A Rose and a Baby Ruth - George Hamilton IV
5. Honky Tonk (part 1-2) - Bill Doggett
6. Since I Met You Baby - Ivory Joe Hunter
7. Don't Be Cruel/Hound Dog - Elvis Presley
8. Confidential - Sonny Knight
9. When My Blue Moon Turns to Gold Again (EP) - Elvis Presley
10. Slow Walk - Sil Austin
11. Priscilla - Eddie Cooley and the Dimples
12. Slow Walk - Bill Doggett
13. You'll Never Know/It Isn't Right - The Platters
14. I Feel Good - Shirley and Lee
15. Ain't Got No Home - Clarence "Frogman" Henry
16. Wisdom of a Fool - The Five Keys
17. In the Still of the Night - The Five Satins
18. Young Love - Sonny James
19. Jim Dandy - LaVern Baker
20. Poor Boy (EP) - Elvis Presley

Also on the "pop" charts:
Gonna Get Along Without You Now - Patience and Prudence
Garden of Eden - Joe Valino
Moonlight Gambler - Frankie Laine
Rock-a-bye Your Baby - Jerry Lewis

December 1956
ARTIST OF THE MONTH

IVORY JOE HUNTER

Ivory Joe Hunter (yes, that was his given name) had two hit records that came six years apart with songs that were very similar. And, just before Hunter released the second song, crooner Pat Boone sold a million copies of the first. This is as it should be, for Ivory Joe Hunter was a songwriter of prodigious output.

As befits life in Kirbyville, a rural town in East Texas, Ivory Joe was raised in a religious environment. He was born on November 10, 1914*, one of sixteen in a family where it seemed everyone wanted to be a musician. His father was a preacher who played blues guitar, and his mother played piano and sang spirituals. Ivory Joe was encouraged to take up the piano at an early age. He was also active in the church choir, and sang with several spiritual quartets as a teenager. However, like his father, and like many other teens maturing between the two World Wars, his musical taste was swayed by the rhythms of blues, swing, and hot jazz.

Ivory Joe Hunter

(*Hunter's date and place of birth are also given as October 10, 1911, Monroe, Louisiana.)

At age sixteen, Ivory Joe became a proficient enough performer to attract the attention of music historian Alan Lomax. Lomax recorded the teenager for the Library of Congress as he accompanied himself on vocal with a pounding version of "Stagolee" in the family living room.

Hunter fronted his first combo just after graduating from high school. He soon moved to nearby Port Arthur where his exuberant style of barrel-house piano made him instantly popular with the local music fans. In 1931, he formed a second band in Port Arthur's sister city of Beaumont where he secured a radio program on KFDM. Five years later he had moved ninety miles inland to Houston where he remained until 1942. It was in Houston that he first played "whites only" clubs, singing the popular ballads of the day.

When he sensed that he gotten as far as he could in Texas, he transferred his base of operations to Oakland, California. Here, and in Los Angeles, he worked with musicians, many of them also ex-Texans, who were playing a style of jazz mixed with rhythm and blues that he found very appealing.

Hunter realized that to be successful in music he had to concentrate on the business side. He knew the music would take care of itself. With this in mind, he envisioned himself as the proud owner of his own record company. In 1945, he founded Ivory Records; and his first release was "Blues at Sunrise," featuring Johnny Moore's Three Blazers. The Three Blazers was a trio that included Charles Brown on piano and would later feature a variety of lead singers including Brown and Floyd Dixon. Later sides by the group also featured Hunter on piano and vocal. In 1946, Hunter formed Pacific Records. On Pacific, he issued such locally popular sides as "Pretty Mama Blues" and "Jumpin' at the Dew Drop" under his own name.

Hunter's smooth vocal styling and successful track record attracted the larger record companies. In 1947, he signed with King Records of Cincinnati, a leader in the rhythm and blues field. His singles on King reached a much wider audience, and most were successful. In late 1949, he had a hit with "Waitin' In Vain," followed by "Guess Who" b/w "Landlord Blues." Hunter's rendition of "Guess Who" revealed the direct influence of Billy Eckstine, the master of the sweet, romantic ballad style in the 1940s. The instrumental backing opened with a saxophone, xylophone, and single violin squeezing every bit of sentiment possible out of the opening twelve bars. The remainder of the song was heavy-laden, featuring a trombone's mournful answer to Hunter's high baritone vocal, piano triplets, and a heavy bass. Songwriting credits went to Mrs. I. J. Hunter.

"Jealous Heart" was also a minor hit for King in late 1949. A few months later, in January 1950, "I Quit My Pretty Mama" was selling very well when Ivory Joe jumped to M-G-M Records. His first release for M-G-M was also his biggest success on the label. "I Almost Lost My Mind" was also the best selling rhythm and blues record during the first few months of 1950.

He had other rhythm and blues hits on M-G-M in 1950, including "S. P. Blues" and "I Need You So," before his winning streak ended abruptly. For the next three years he continued to issue records and crisscross the country as a popular performer. He knew that his career was stymied, and he felt that he needed another change of scenery.

In 1954, he signed a contract with Atlantic Records. Atlantic was in the midst of a major expansion fueled by its nonstop string of rockin' rhythm hits by Ruth Brown, the Clovers, LaVern Baker, the Drifters, Joe Turner, and Ray Charles. Hunter's first Atlantic release, "It May Sound Silly" sold moderately. In early 1956, Hunter recorded another of his own compositions, "A Tear Fell." With this song, he got a firsthand taste of the business of cover records as he watched Teresa Brewer's version race up the "pop" charts while his own record languished in the rhythm and blues field. He could take consolation in the royalties that Miss Brewer's version of "A Tear Fell" generated, as well those from Pat Boone's rendition of "I Almost Lost My Mind," which sat atop the "pop" charts in the fall of 1956.

The success of Boone's record brought the suggestion that Hunter might be able to issue his own follow-up in a similar style. Thus was born "Since I Met You Baby." Hunter recorded his song on September 5, 1956, while Boone's version of "I Almost Lost My Mind" was high on the charts. Upon its release, "Since I Met You Baby" became an instant hit with both the rhythm and blues and the "pop" crowd, and it sold strongly for the next four months.

"Since I Met You Baby" and "I Almost Lost My Mind" were so close to being the same song it was eerie. The two melodies were similar, built on the standard twelve-bar blues format with the first line sung twice and the verse closed by a third line. The lyrics ran parallel to each other. In the first song Hunter sang, "When I lost my baby, I almost lost my mind." In the second, it went, "Since I met you baby, my whole life has changed." The second verses of the two songs mirror each other: "I went to see the Gypsy and had my fortune read"—"I don't need nobody to tell my troubles to." "Since I Met You Baby" was sung at a faster tempo, allowing enough time for a vocal chorus bridge. "I Almost Lost My Mind" moved more slowly as befitted its subject matter.

In 1956, Hunter's second taste of success came as he was entering his mid-forties; not exactly the age to be playing rock 'n roll. And, unlike some others, Hunter never tried to be something that he wasn't. Deep down he was a ballad singer with a song writer's knack for good material, and he stuck with his strong points.

In early 1957, Atlantic issued "Empty Arms," which was once again covered and outsold by Teresa Brewer. Hunter's version was backed by "Love's A Hurting Game," a song that appealed to enough rhythm and blues buyers to enter the charts on its own. A year later, "Yes I Want You" did almost as well with rhythm and blues buyers, but it failed to find a market with "pop" fans. By this time, Hunter's time in the spotlight was nearing an end.

His contract with Atlantic expired in 1958, and he signed with Dot Records, ironically the company for which Pat Boone had recorded "I Almost Lost My Mind." Hunter had been experimenting with a combination of rhythm and blues and country music beginning with his days at M-G-M. He convinced the executives at Dot to record "City Lights," a country song that had been a hit for Pay Price in 1958. Unlike Price's original, Hunter's version relied on a strong bass line, a blues piano break, and his own soulful vocal. The record was reminiscent of, and a direct precursor to, the country-tinged hits that Ray Charles would have in the 1960s. Unfortunately, while "City Lights" was a juke box favorite, its sales appeal was limited.

"City Lights" did open the doors of Nashville's "Grand Ole Opry" for Hunter, and he became a member in the 1960s. He never again had a hit record as a performer though he recorded for Goldisc, Capitol, Smash, Vee-Jay, Stax, and a half-dozen other companies. Nevertheless, he remained a strong draw in clubs across the country. In 1970, he was invited to appear at the Monterey Jazz Festival. Shortly afterward, he recorded an album of blues for Epic, followed by a country effort for Paramount in 1973. He kept up a rigorous schedule until he was felled by lung cancer. He passed away in Memphis November 8, 1974, just two days shy of his sixtieth birthday. As a measure of the respect he had earned in both country and soul music, the benefit concert held in his memory featured legendary performers from both fields, including George Jones and Isaac Hayes.

At the time of his death, it was reported that he had published more than 2,500 songs, including "My Wish Came True" and "Ain't That Loving You Baby" which had both been hits for Elvis Presley.

reelin' & rockin'

THE GOLDEN AGE OF AMERICAN ROCK 'N ROLL

1957

1957
A Look Ahead

"I want to holler but the joint's too small."
Huey Smith and the Clowns, 1957.

The biggest rock 'n roll news in 1957 is the debut of "American Bandstand" on ABC-TV in August. Every afternoon, across the country, teens (and quite a few mothers, too) park themselves in front of the television set to watch Philadelphia teenagers dance to the latest rock 'n roll records. The show is an immediate success, completely winning the afternoon time slot which has previously been the sole domain of soap operas. According to the Trendex ratings, during its ninety-minute time period (3:00-4:30 p.m.), "American Bandstand" averages a 32.7 share in September and a 33.2 share in October, beating CBS by 20% and NBC by 48%. The show is carried by sixty-five stations across country. Soon, other televised deejay shows spring up in Baltimore, Washington, Chicago, New York, and Cleveland.

In the United States in 1957, the music industry falls in step behind the beat of rock 'n roll. For many, there is a collective sigh of relief when Christmas 1956 comes and goes and rock 'n roll is still here. Music's business side concentrates on entrenching itself with American fans.

Overseas, rock music is just beginning to gather momentum. Although England and Australia have a few rock artists of their own, it is American rockers the fans clamor to see. Great Britain plays host to the Teenagers and Bill Haley and His Comets. Buddy Holly and the Crickets, Little Richard, Gene Vincent, Eddie Cochran, and Paul Anka travel in the opposite direction, captivating the fans in Australia and the Far East. Meanwhile, the Platters conquer the rest of the world with successful tours of Latin America and Europe.

The traveling caravans of stars almost become a thing of the past. There are fewer booking agencies willing to undertake such a massive endeavor required to put an eighty-day tour on the road with fifty performers. This is especially true following the riots at rock concerts in 1956. The Shaw Agency and Universal Attractions continue the tradition, with "The Biggest Rock and Roll Show of '57" rolling across the land in various forms throughout most of the year. By November 1957, there are reports that even the biggest and best package shows are losing money. By the end of 1957, television guest appearances are the prime means of exposure for recording acts. The performer usually makes little money, if any, from his televised performance and must rely on the wide exposure to increase his record sales and boost his personal appearance fees.

The new trend in live entertainment is toward teenage "hops," which require a smaller guarantee but offer a bigger percentage of the gate for the artist. Most of these "sock hops" are sponsored by local deejays who can guarantee massive free radio advertising.

One beneficiary of rock 'n roll's success in 1957 is the blues. As fans look back to the roots of rock 'n roll, they discover artists like Little Junior Parker, Bobby "Blue" Bland and Jimmy Reed, all of whom have "pop" hits in 1957. More traditional blues artists, such as Muddy Waters, Howlin' Wolf, and Little Walter, also benefit from the increased attention.

The death of the 78 r.p.m. record is eminent. Dealers report that sales of 78's account for about 6% of their volume as compared with 10% in mid-1956. The largest buyer of 78s, the juke box vendors, are rapidly converting their older model boxes to accommodate the 45 r.p.m. singles. In a move seen by many as the death knell of the "78," RCA Victor increases the price of a 78 r.p.m. single to $1.15 while 45s remain at ninety-eight cents. In addition, the record companies, who are also among the largest manufacturers of record players, are pushing the 45 r.p.m. format by decreasing the list price of their 45 r.p.m. players.

For the record business in general, 1957 is a boom year. It is not uncommon for a company to post an increase in sales of 25% over 1956. Capitol Records, a major producer, reports sales of $12 million for the first quarter of 1957. Even the relatively smaller Dot Records announces sales of $2.8 million for the same period.

In a May 27, 1957, article, *Billboard* notes that radio stations are "galloping, herdlike toward a policy of playing the 40 bestselling records almost exclusively." In radio, "Top 40" becomes the byword in most major markets. As the number of new records increases weekly, it becomes impossible for the staff at a radio station to wade through stacks of singles trying to pick those that will be hits. Consequently, the stations begin concentrating on a play-list of current hits, interspersed with a few new entries, usually from artists with a proven track record. The immediate result of this policy is reduced exposure for new artists. As an adjustment to this development, record companies begin offering deejays inducements to play their new records. This "pay for play" tactic isn't new. It has existed, in one form or another, for years in the music business. However, when powerful record companies begin dealing with equally powerful deejays, the ante increases almost exponentially.

The music industry is seen as "slave to the teenage girl who dominates the purchase of pop singles," according to *Billboard*. Contrary to popular opinion, radio listeners are not mainly teenagers. In the 4:00-6:00 p.m. hours, when teen listening is at its highest, they make up only 12% of the audience. During the same period, 51% are housewives, with adult men accounting for 31% and children 6% of the audience. Insiders are beginning to wonder why radio should be controlled by a product picked by only 12% of the listeners.

Rock 'n roll music is almost unseated in 1957 as the favorite music of teenagers, not by "pop" music, but by calypso, a music formed of rhythmic melodies and styles based on traditional songs of Jamaica. This new wave of music is led by Harry Belafonte, a part-time New York actor who took up singing in 1949 to pay the rent. In 1956, his third album, CALYPSO, rises to Number One on the charts, and the calypso craze is ignited. After a brief flare-up, calypso fades due to a lack of major talent. Only Belafonte is able to transcend the fad.

Rock 'n roll, and especially its rockabilly segment, becomes stronger in 1957 with the addition of several exciting artists: the Everly Brothers, Buddy Holly and the Crickets, Buddy Knox and Jimmy Bowen, and Jerry Lee Lewis. This "music with a beat" pumps life into rock 'n roll, keeping it fresh and animated.

Country music continues to have problems coping with rock 'n roll. However, there is a change of heart as the rise of rockabilly leads to wider acceptance of country artists in the "pop" field. This trend of country artists crossing over into "pop" music includes Ferlin Huskey, Sonny James, Bobby Helms, Marty Robbins, Marvin Rainwater, Don Gibson, and Jim Reeves.

One casualty of the increase in rock 'n roll's acceptance is the female vocalist. Few women will ever be accepted into the ranks of the rock 'n roll performer. One reason lies in the fact that a major appeal of rock 'n roll is the idolatry of the performer, and young, handsome male stars hold an appeal to the young women who buy most of the records. In addition, there is an acceptance by male teens of male rockers over female rockers. Add to this the fact that the music business has always been a male-dominated industry. On a societal level, in the 1950s, less than 20% of all women are employed full-time. Americans believe that the place for women is in the home, raising children and taking care of the husband. Thus. it is easy to see that even those women who might want to make a career of rock 'n roll music were faced with huge obstacles.

On the technical side of music, Stereo is just beginning to be introduced into the market place. At February's High Fidelity Show in Hollywood, the hit with the 40,000 industry personnel in attendance is the sound of a bouncing Ping-Pong ball emanating from a pair of speakers.

In 1957, there are still concentrated attacks on rock 'n roll for being morally degenerating. "Wake Up Little Susie" is banned in Boston. For five days in June, the *Chicago Daily News* charges that record companies, disk jockeys, and radio stations are responsible for the "vulgar, cheap junk" on pop records. The stories are written by Don Henahan, the new music critic at the *Daily News*. According to later published reports, Henahan only did a week's worth of interviews in preparation for the story, and many of his observations were superficial observations. Henahan maintained that pop music is the product of "manipulation by money-hungry adults of the half-felt cravings of teenagers."

NATIONAL NEWS

Sputnik I and II, the first space satellites, are launched by Russia... the U.S. tests the first Thor ICBM... there are more than 400 UFO sightings during the year... a Massachusetts high school bans the ducktail haircut... elsewhere, the new teen fad is "cramming," seeing how many can fit in a telephone booth—or a Volkswagen, the recent import from Germany... Congress passes the voting rights bill, protecting the right to vote for all Americans... the National Guard is called out in Little Rock to enforce the Supreme Court's order to desegregate the city's schools... everyone is talking about Brigitte Bardot's nude scenes in "And God Created Woman," however "The Bridge Over The River Kwai" wins Oscars for Best Picture and Best Actor (Alec Guinness), while Joanne Woodword wins as Best Actress for "The Three Faces of Eve"... Humphrey Bogart dies... the average annual salary is $4,200... Paul Getty, a real estate tycoon, is said to be worth $1 billion... TV's Grammy goes to the top-rated "Gunsmoke" as Best Dramatic Series, and "The Phil Silvers Show" as Best Comedy Series (the show's third win in a row)... videotape is perfected, allowing immediate replays... there are rumors of "fixing" in television's big-money quiz shows... the best selling work of fiction is James Gould Cozzens' BY LOVE POSSESSED"... "The Fly," by George Langelaan, wins the Playboy Writing Award for short story... in baseball, Mickey Mantle is voted the Most Valuable Player in the American League as well as receiving the Cy Young Award as A.L. Rookie of the Year, both for the second straight year... after the season, the Brooklyn Dodgers and the New York Giants relocate to California... a student at the University of California at Berkeley begins publishing *Rolling Stone* magazine... the new toy this year is the Frisbee... Ford Motor Company introduces the Edsel... by the end of the year, most American believe the country is in a financial recession.

January 1957

JAN 3   LaVern Baker departs the States en route to Australia. In her wake, she leaves a $125,000 life insurance policy naming Georgia Gibbs as the sole beneficiary. In a letter to Miss Gibbs, Miss Baker writes that the policy is to provide for Miss Gibbs should she deprived by Miss Baker's untimely death "of the opportunity of copying my songs and arrangements in the future." The letter closes with "Tra La La and Tweedle Dee, LaVern Baker."

JAN 4   In New York City, Clyde McPhatter headlines the revue at the Apollo Theater. Also appearing are Mickey and Sylvia, Clarence "Frogman" Henry, Jesse Belvin, and the Heartbeats. Emcee for the show is "Jocko" Henderson, deejay on New York's WOV radio.

JAN 5   Brenda Lee makes her second appearance on NBC-TV's "The Perry Como Show."

JAN 6   Elvis Presley makes his final appearance on "The Ed Sullivan Show" on CBS-TV. It is only during this show that Elvis is photographed "from the waist up" as he performed one of his more torrid musical numbers.

Solomon Burke makes a television appearance on "The Steve Allen Show" on NBC-TV. Burke was introduced by boxer-turned-performer Joe Louis who wrote the song that Burke performed, "You Can Run, But You Can't Hide."

In New Orleans, Shirley and Lee take the occasion of their return to their hometown for tonight's engagement at the Labor Union Hall to announce that their agent, the Gale booking agency, is seeking punitive damages from a number of imposters posing as Shirley and Lee from Florida to Texas. The duo claim to have lost $15,000 in bookings recently.

New Releases for the first week of January are, as usual, few in number, but they do include "Playing For Keeps" b/w "Too Much" by Elvis Presley on RCA Victor; "Let's Make It" by James Brown and the Famous Flames on Federal; and "Drive In" by Sonny Thompson and his orchestra on Chart.

EARLY JANUARY

RCA Victor eliminates its subsidiary, Groove Records, combining the operation under Vik, another in-house label. This is an interesting move because Groove is having its biggest success with "Love Is Strange" by Mickey and Sylvia while Vik has never had a major

SOLOMON BURKE
Solomon Burke was nicknamed the "Bishop of Soul" in the 1960s, an apt description of a man with roots firmly established in the church. He was born in Philadelphia, in 1936. His family was active in the locally popular House of God For All People. As young as age four, he was already attracting attention with his radio ministry. By the time he was nine, he was a soloist with the church choir din their frequent radio shows. His broadcast audience spread from Pennsylvania to the Carolinas. Billed as the "Boy Wonder Preacher," he traveled throughout the area with his Godfather, a popular revivalist named Daddy Grace. By this time, he had become the spiritual head of his own church, Solomon's Temple. By all accounts, young Burke was a frantic sermonizer, spellbinding in his delivery. It was this training which would eventually come to the fore when he switched to secular music. With his astounding stage presence and built-in popularity, it was only a matter of time before he would be making records. A local Philadelphia deejay brought Burke to the attention of Apollo Records, a New York company with strong ties to both the gospel and blues markets. Burke's first single, released the third week in 1955, was "Christmas Presents." According to Burke, he composed the song for his grandmother. In appreciation, she gave him a guitar for his Christmas. Apollo's attempt to divert Burke from religious to secular music was virtually complete by the time "You Can Run, But You Can't Hide" was released. In the process, he had lost much of the individuality and verve that had marked his childhood success as a minister. After seven singles and little success, Burke moved on to Philadelphia's Singular Records by 1959. It would remain for Atlantic Records to bring Burke's gospel background to material such as "Just Out of Reach of My Two Empty Arms," a major hit in 1961.

release. Groove was originally spun off by RCA Victor in January 1954 specifically to handle the rhythm and blues artists signed to the parent company. At one time or another, the label's roster included Piano Red, Champion Jack Dupree, Frankie Brunson, the El Vinos, and the Nitecaps.

As the new year opens, record companies are busy signing older artists. Imperial inks longtime blues-shouter Roy Brown, and Ember signs Rudy Green who has been on the scene since the mid-1940s.

JAN 8   Bill Haley and His Comets start their first overseas tour with shows in Newcastle, Australia. This is followed by a twenty-day romp through the southern continent. Appearing on stage with the Comets are Big Joe Turner and LaVern Baker. The package had originally been scheduled to start the tour with three days worth of appearances in Manila, Philippine Islands, with a ten-day tour of Australia, but demand for tickets in Australia forced a cancellation of the Manilla shows and the extension of the Australian leg of the tour.

JAN 11   Opening at the Apollo for a week's run are Ocie Smith, the Valentines, and Dinah Washington with Cannonball Adderly's band.

Little Richard headlines the revue at Washington's Howard Theater. Also appearing are the Cadillacs, the Cookies, and Charlie and Ray.

New Releases for the second week of January continue to be slim but include "Ain't That Love" by Ray Charles on Atlantic; **Jo Ann Campbell**'s "Come On Baby" on Eldorado; "Next Time You See Me" by Little Junior Parker on Duke; "Only Jim" by the Six Teens on Flip; "Put Your Arms Around Me Honey" by Bobby Charles on Chess; "Message of Love" by the Orbits on Flair-X; and "Come Go With Me" by the Dell-Vikings on Fee-Bee.

MID-JANUARY

The Five Satins are in the middle of a tour that has taken them to the West Coast. While driving across Utah en route to shows in Denver, all three of their cars are involved in accidents at various locations forcing the Denver promoter to send a chartered airplane to fetch the group from Ogden.

JAN 17   The Lotus Club in Washington, DC, presents the Diamonds for the next five days.

JAN 18   Clyde McPhatter, Clarence "Frogman" Henry, Jesse Belvin, the Heartbeats, and Screamin' Jay Hawkins entertain patrons this week at the Howard Theater in Washington.

JAN 19   Following the lead of Elvis Presley, who a year earlier had appeared on Jackie Gleason's "Stage Show" on CBS-TV, Johnny

---

JO ANN CAMPBELL
Jo Ann Campbell was 4'-8" of pure showbiz. With her blazing blue eyes and pile of blonde hair, it's no wonder Alan Freed nicknamed her "The Blonde Bombshell." In her hometown of Jacksonville, Florida, as a high school majorette, she was the state champion baton twirler in 1952. In 1954, she joined a U.S.O. tour of Europe as a dancer. Back in the states, she moved to New York to study modern dance. She soon joined the Johnny Conrad Dancers, a troupe that appeared frequently on television variety shows. At the time "Come On Baby" was released, she was eighteen (born July 20, 1938), although press releases claimed she was just fourteen. Few females could sustain a rockabilly act over a long period, but this didn't bother Jo Ann. She released a series of torrid rockers with titles like "Rock and Roll Love," "Wassa Matter With You," "Nervous," "Crazy Daisy," and "Motorcycle Michael." Her natural beauty brought her a cameo roles in "Go, Johnny Go!" (1959), in which she sang "Motorcycle Michael," and "Hey, Let's Twist" (1961) which starred Joey Dee. Even though she had two releases on Eldorado and seven on Gone, she remained hitless until 1960, when her novelty number "Kookie Little Paradise" on ABC-Paramount bounced around the upper echelons of the pop charts for two months. She did even better two years later with "(I'm The Girl On) Wolverton Mountain" an answer to Claude King's big hit. The follow-up Cameo single, "Mother, Please!" also appeared briefly on the charts. In 1964, she and her husband, producer/songwriter Troy Seals, recorded under the name Jo Ann and Troy, having a minor on Atlantic with "I Found a Love Oh What a Love." Today, they live in Henderson, Tennessee.

Cash makes a rare TV appearance on "The Jackie Gleason Show" broadcast over the CBS network. Cash is such a hit that Gleason inks him to an option for nine more appearances during the remainder of 1957.

JAN 20 The Clovers, Larry Birdsong and Roy Milton and his orchestra play the Sunday dance at the Labor Union Hall in New Orleans.

"The Ed Sullivan Show" on CBS-TV welcomes Sonny James to sing "Young Love."

New Releases for the third week of January include three from Atlantic: "Fools Fall In Love" by the Drifters, "Lucky Lips" by Ruth Brown, and "Near You" by the Cardinals. Other releases for this week include "Ram Bunk Shush" by Bill Doggett on King; "Ding Dong" by the Echoes on Gee; Brenda Lee's "One Step At a Time" on Decca; "Butterfly" by Charlie Gracie on Cameo; "Ooo Baby" by Sanford Clark on Dot; "Your Wild Heart" by the Poni-Tails on Point; "It Hurts To Be In Love" by Annie Laurie on DeLuxe; and "Go Away, Don't Bother Me" by the Collins Kids on Columbia.

JAN 24 Alis Lesley, billed as "The Female Elvis," packs the house at Washington's Lotus Club through the weekend.

JAN 25 Little Richard and his ten-piece band pack the house for a week at the Apollo Theater in New York. Sharing the boards are Charlie and Ray, the Schoolboys, and Andre Williams.

JAN 28 The Greystone Ballroom in Detroit hosts the "Big Show of 1957," featuring Dinah Washington, the Platters, Little Willie John, Ray Charles, and Sill Austin's combo.

New Releases for the fourth week of January include "Just Because" by Lloyd Price on K.R.C.; "Gonna Find Me A Bluebird" by **Marvin Rainwater** on M-G-M; "The Wall" by Brook Benton on Epic; "Will You Be Mine" by the Penguins on Mercury; "Valley of Love" by the Turbans on Herald; "Why Do You Love Me Like You Do?" by the Cleftones on Gee; "Walking Along" by the Solitaries on Old Town; and two from Whirlin' Disc: the Empires' "Linda" and the Channels' "The Gleam in Your Eyes."

JAN 29 The Platters, just back from a tour of the Far East, start at two-week engagement at the Town and Country Club in Brooklyn.

JAN 31 Bill Haley and His Comets, wasting little time after their Australian tour, leave the States for Great Britain. (See FEB 6.)

LATE JANUARY

George Goldner of Gee/Rama/Tico Records launches a new label, Roulette Records. Roulette issues as its two premier releases, "Party Doll" by Buddy Knox and "I'm Stickin With You" by Jimmie

MARVIN RAINWATER

For a man who became a very popular entertainer, Marvin Rainwater tried many other occupations first. He was born Marvin Perry in Wichita, Kansas, July 2, 1925. He planned to become a veterinarian, and had begun studies at Washington State University when World War II intervened. After serving in the Navy, he became part-owner of an Oregon sawmill. In the late 1940s, he and his brother, Ray, owned an excavating business in Virginia. Marvin had first sung in public during his Navy days, and he and Ray formed a country band. In 1952, they sold their business to finance Marvin's dream of becoming a singing star. For his stage name, Marvin took his mother's maiden name, Rainwater, and soon he was billed as the "Singing Cherokee." The act caught the attention of local record producers, and Marvin recorded a large number of songs that were eventually released on such labels as Crown, Spin-O-Rama and Premier. Red Foley offered Marvin a regular spot on his weekly radio show, the "Ozark Jubilee." Marvin signed with M-G-M Records, but his recording career was almost immediately sidelined when "I Gotta Go Get My Baby," a 1955 release that verged on rockabilly, was beaten handily in the marketplace by Teresa Brewer. Rainwater appeared on "Arthur Godfrey's Talent Scouts," a national TV show, as well as Godfrey's daily radio program. Marvin's career rebounded, and in 1957 he had two million-selling singles, "Gonna Find Me a Bluebird" and "Majesty of Love," the later a duet with Connie Francis. His only other major hits were "Half-Breed" and "Whole Lotta Woman." He also recorded for Warwick, Warner Brothers, and United Artists. When his popularity waned in the States, he found new fans in England who were eager to welcome him.

Bowen. Previously, both songs had been available on one single as by the Rhythm Orchids, issued by Texas-based Triple D Records.

Fats Domino's name is being bandied around Hollywood as a possibility to star in an upcoming film biography of Fats Waller. (Domino never appeared in a dramatic film role.)

THE TOP RECORDS FOR JANUARY 1957

1. Blueberry Hill - Fats Domino
2. Love Me Tender - Elvis Presley
3. Young Love - Sonny James
4. Love Me (EP) - Elvis Presley
5. A Rose And A Baby Ruth.- George Hamilton IV
6. Blue Monday/What's The Reason I'm Not Pleasing You - Fats Domino
7. Since I Met You Baby - Ivory Joe Hunter
8. Love Is Strange - Mickey and Sylvia
9. Jim Dandy - LaVern Baker
10. On My Word Of Honor/One In a Million - The Platters
11. When My Blue Moon Turns to Gold (EP) - Elvis Presley
12. Too Much/Playing For Keeps - Elvis Presley
13. Honky Tonk (part 1-2) - Bill Doggett
14. Ain't Got No Home - Clarence "Frogman" Henry
15. Poor Boy (EP) - Elvis Presley
16. Wisdom of a Fool - The Five Keys
17. Don't Be Cruel/Hound Dog - Elvis Presley
18. Slow Walk - Bill Doggett
19. Slow Walk - Sil Austin
20. Confidential - Sonny Knight
21. Paralyzed (EP) - Elvis Presley
22. Priscilla - Eddie Cooley and the Dimples
23. A Thousand Miles Away - The Heartbeats
24. Without Love - Clyde McPhatter
25. You Got Me Dizzy - Jimmy Reed
26. The Girl Can't Help It - Little Richard
27. Little By Little - Nappy Brown
28. Rudy's Rock - Bill Haley and His Comets
29. Bad Boy - The Jive Bombers
30. On My Word of Honor - B. B. King

Also on the "pop" charts:
Hey! Jealous Lover - Frank Sinatra
Don't Forbid Me - Pat Boone
Banana Boat (Day-O) - Harry Belafonte
The Banana Boat Song - The Tarriers
Young Love - Tab Hunter

January 1957
ARTIST OF THE MONTH

SONNY JAMES

The biggest hit in Sonny James' career began as a plaintive ballad by an unknown songwriter. From the original version, James borrowed most of the arrangement, specifically the repetitive guitar figure. Although Sonny James had a few minor country hits in the early 1950s, his career wasn't exactly causing a stir before "Young Love." With this song, he crossed over from traditional country into the rarefied air of "pop" music. In the process, he found two audiences that welcomed him for more than a dozen years.

Sonny James

Sonny was born James Loden on May 1, 1929, in Hackleburg, Alabama. The Loden family performed throughout the South. "Sonny," as his family referred to him, joined them on stage at an early age. By the time he was a teenager, he had logged experience on radio and on stage that belied his youth. However, as he began to make a major career move, his National Guard unit was called to active duty for fifteen months during the Korean War. Like many other aspiring performers in a similar situation, he continued to perform wherever he could gather an audience, be it at an orphan's home or the NCO Club. He also spent time in Korea composing a sheaf of songs that would eventually come in handy.

Back in the states, he returned to the county fairs and small clubs he had toured with his family. As he honed his skills, the name of "Sonny" James Loden quickly reached the halls of the influential country music men in Nashville. Chet Atkins became an early convert. He brought Sonny to the attention of Ken Nelson, Chief of Artists and Repertoire at Capitol Records. Nelson would achieve a degree of notoriety on his own in April, 1956, when he dreamed up the nationwide talent contest that eventually discovered Gene Vincent. It was Nelson who suggested Loden should drop his last his name.

Sonny James began recording for Capitol in 1952, and during the four years prior to "Young Love," he issued seventeen singles. His earliest releases from 1952 through 1954—"Shortcut," "That's Me Without You," "Somebody's Heartache," "I Forgot More Than You'll Ever Know," "My Greatest Thrill," "That's How I Need You," "The Table Next To Mine," and "She Done Gave Her Heart To Me"—failed to gather much attention outside the South.

("I Forgot More Than You'll Ever Know" was rerecorded by James in 1960 at which time it became a major country hit.)

His records relied heavily on the country styles popular at the time. Most dripped with steel guitar runs, and featured a two-step or waltz-time beat with James' crystal-clear voice rising and dropping octaves at a time. Occasionally, a vocal group was added to smooth the mix. However, there was little in James' style or delivery to separate him from the rest of the country singers in the early 1950s.

Undaunted, he continued to record and tour. During November 1956, on a one-night stand in Atlanta, he was approached by Bill Lowrey, a local music entrepreneur. Lowrey held publishing rights to a song composed by a couple of Atlanta teenagers, Carole Joyner and Ric Cartey. James listened to the demo with enthusiasm and assured Lowery that he would record it as soon as he returned to Nashville. True to his word, "Young Love" became his next release.

"Young Love" became a hit single virtually overnight. Rushed into release by Capitol in late November, the record was being played coast-to-coast on country radio stations within a week. By mid-December, "pop" music stations had clambered aboard the Sonny James bandwagon. This type of activity brought a rash of cover versions, including one by movie star Tab Hunter that Dot Records released the third week in December. Another version was by the Crew-Cuts on Mercury Records. In December, Sonny James was elated when "Young Love" jumped into popular music charts. Four weeks later it was number 3 where it held steady for three weeks while right behind it was Tab Hunter's version. On February 6, the James version peaked at number 2. A week later it slipped back a notch as Hunter's "Young Love" went on to top the charts.

James' slightly off-key vocal style added to, rather than detracted from, the overall effect of the record. As mentioned, James borrowed the guitar lick from the demo—a simple, single-string playing of the notes of the four chords upon which the song was built. His version added a vocal group singing "Ooo-oo" and "Aah-aah." He changed a word or two—"the heavenly rapture of your embrace" became "the heavenly touch of your embrace." The main contribution from James came when he rushed the tempo, imparting a sense of urgency, while singing the lyrics with deliberate passion.

(The demo by Ric Cartey and the Jiva-Tones, featuring Jerry Reed playing guitar, was soon released by Bill Lowrey on his own Stars, Inc. label. It was soon picked up and reissued by RCA Victor.)

Sonny James' taste of success in the "pop" field created the musical equivalent of Frankenstein's monster. Executives at Capitol wanted James to concentrate almost exclusively on teen-oriented material. James obliged, starting with "First Date, First Kiss, First Love," a reliable facsimile of "Young Love" that even included the line, "Now, we know the bliss that only young love can yield." This single was followed by "A Mighty Lovable Man," backed with "(Love Came, Love Saw) Love Conquered." Both sides suffered from overproduction by Capitol's recording staff and were too "pop" to appeal to fans of either rock 'n roll or country music.

On the other hand, the next single, "Uh-Huh-mm," was a song one could easily imagine Elvis recording. Featuring a double-quick tempo, the song also used a dead-air hesitation by the combo at the end of each verse so James could breathlessly sing "uh-huh-mm" in his best lip-curled imitation of Elvis. The flip side, "Why Can't They Remember?" was a typical teen-oriented tune. Co-written by James, the song featured a pianist playing triplets, a choral group sing "bum-bum" and "hold me darling," and another of James' dramatic readings.

For the next few years, James continued to put out similar records in an unsuccessful attempt to appeal to teenagers. "Let's Play Love" had a boogie-beat on piano but the vocal group again derailed the effort. "I Can't Stay Away From You" was a slow fox-trot with a heavy echo that was a change of pace for James. The flip side, "Let Me Be The One To Love You," sounded as though it might have been written with Ricky Nelson in mind. "Yo-Yo," another single from this period, is a confused combination of the deep, echoed voice from Eddie Cochran's "Summertime Blues" with jangling guitars in the style of the Everly Brothers.

None of the singles after "Young Love" did very well in either the "pop" or country markets. It was 1960 before James rerecorded "I Forgot More Than You'll Ever Know" in an attempt to bring his flagging country career back on track. While this song was his most successful since 1957, he had already decided to leave Capitol Records for a smaller company where he would have more control over the direction of his career.

His first move was to the National Record Company (NRC) in Atlanta, Bill Lowrey's latest recording venture and a label with a better-than-average track record when it came to discovering raw talent. NRC had already released early singles by Ray Stevens, Jerry Reed, and Joe South. Sonny James only recorded one single for the label, a pop-country ballad titled "Jenny Lou." Then, he moved on to brief association with Dot Records, the company that had issued Tab Hunter's version of "Young Love." On Dot, he approached the style that would become his trademark. Issued in 1962, "Just One More Lie" was a pleasing combination of folk and country delivered in a confident voice by James and with only a hint of that distracting vocal chorus.

Also in 1962, James rerecorded "Young Love" for Groove Records, RCA Victor's subsidiary. It came complete with a sweet "do you remember the song that made us fall in love" intro. By this time, James must have sung the song thousands of times in his live performances. Nevertheless, he still gave this version a credible reading.

Sonny James returned to Capitol in 1963. A year later, he had a major hit with "You're The Only World I Know." Over the next few years, he was one of the top rated country artists in every poll. His career took another odd twist in 1967 when he had a best seller with "I'll Never Find Another You," a song made popular two years earlier by the Seekers. This seemed to set off a chain reaction, as many of his hit records for the next few years were remakes of previous "pop" hits: "Born To Be With You" (Chordettes); "Only The Lonely" (Roy Orbison); "Running Bear" (Johnny Preston); "Since I Met You Baby" and "Empty Arms" (Ivory Joe Hunter); "It's Just a Matter of Time" and "Endlessly" (Brook Benton); "Only Love Can Break a Heart" (Gene Pitney); and "Bright Lights, Big City" (Jimmy Reed). Most of these records also sold well in the "pop" market, insuring that more would follow.

In 1974, James left Capitol for Columbia Records, but he continued having hits with other artists' songs: "What In The World's Come Over You" (Jack Scott); "In the Jailhouse Now" (Jimmie Rodgers and Webb Pierce); and "Caribbean" (Mitchell Torok). At Columbia, he also had best selling singles in "Is It Wrong (For Loving You)," "A Little Bit South of Saskatoon" and "Something Is Wrong With My Baby." He moved on to Monument Records in 1979. By this time, his career as a top-selling country singer had passed as the style of country music had changed. It now featured glitz and glamour as Kenny Rogers and Dolly

Parton crisscrossed back and forth between country and "pop." At the same time, Waylon and Willie were leading the "outlaw" movement back to its roots while Jimmy Buffett had invited everyone down to Margaritaville. There wasn't much room left in country music for an artist who just sang from the heart.

Sonny James' professional life is a microcosm of the difficulties an artist can encounter when his popularity too quickly outdistances his own expectations. In the case of Sonny James, he lost sight of the direction he had plotted for his career. James just wanted to sing country in the style of Ernest Tubb and Hank Snow. However, he "lucked" onto a piece of material that took his career in the opposite direction. Enormous pressure was exerted on him by his management and the executives of his record company to conform to the rules of "pop" hit-making. While the fame and money might have been worth the effort for a while, one can't help wonder if Sonny James might have traded those four years chasing "pop" hits for a chance to sing his songs his own way.

February 1957

FEB 1 The Apollo Theater offers up a fine show featuring the Buddy Johnson orchestra with sister Ella Johnson. Also on the bill are the Spaniels, the Cleftones and Chuck Berry.

In Detroit this week, the Flame Show Bar welcomes "Gatemouth" Brown. Also in town, the Club Vogue plays host to Little Willie John, and the Four Tops are at the Old Frolic Club.

Jazz is the offering this week at Washington's Howard Theater, as the bill is filled by Lionel Hampton, Sarah Vaughan and Nat King Cole.

FEB 2 Carl Perkins guests on the "Ozark Jubilee" a weekly live show broadcast from Springfield, Missouri. Brenda Lee is a regular act on the "Jubilee."

Fats Domino makes a rare television appearance on "The Perry Como Show" on NBC-TV, singing "Blueberry Hill" and "Blue Monday."

The Police Athletic League, in conjunction with "Negro History Week," hosts a rock 'n roll revue at the Savoy Ballroom in New York. The show features the Channels, the Bop Chords, the Hearts, the Chips, the Fi Tones, and Johnnie and Joe.

FEB 3 Jimmy Reed entertains tonight at the Blue Eagle Ballroom in New Orleans.

FEB 4 The Royal Jokers, the Velvets and the Capris perform between movies at the Linwood Theater in Detroit.

New Releases for the first week in February include Dot Records' reissue of the original Fee-Bee single, "Come Go With Me" by the Dell-Vikings. Also new this week are "That's What I Wanna Do" by Shirley and Lee on Aladdin; "Sittin' in the Balcony" by Johnny Dee on Colonial; "Shake a Hand" by the Four Lovers on RCA Victor; "Little Darlin'" by the **Gladiolas** on Excello; "One More Time" by Andy Starr on M-G-M; "Ruby Pearl" by Jackie Lee Cochran on Decca; and two blues singles from Chess/Checker: Floyd Dixon's "I'm Ashamed of Myself" (Checker) and Howlin' Wolf's "My Life" (Chess).

FEB 5 Fats Domino embarks on a short series of one-nighters with a show in Raleigh, North Carolina. On succeeding nights, he is booked to play Forestville, North Carolina; Newport News and Blacksburg, Virginia; Wilmington, Deleware; Lynn and Springfield,

THE GLADIOLAS
Many R&B performers watched helplessly as their best material was usurped by white artists. The Gladiolas were no exception. Members of the Gladiolas attended Barr Street High in Lancaster, South Carolina. Maurice Williams and Earl Gainey, both tenors, had sung together in a gospel group, the Junior Harmonizers before they formed the Royal Charms (also referred to as the Royal Charmers) with William Massey, tenor-baritone; William Jones, baritone; and Norman Wade, bass. The nearest record companies willing to take on unknown R&B vocal groups were in New Orleans, Memphis and Nashville. Since Nashville was the closest, the group piled into one car and drove straight through to Ernie's Record Shop, home of Excello Records. Ernie Young granted them an audition. He was pleased by what he heard, and set them up with an instant session. Among the songs taped that day was "Little Darlin." Thinking the name Royal Charms could be confusing to music buyers because there were groups named the Royals and the Charms, the name was changed to the Gladiolas. Excello had recently had a hit by another flower group, the Marigolds, and it might be lucky to follow suit. Young knew that with an inexperienced group like the Gladiolas, who could predict how the record would fare. So, he made sure that the Diamonds, a well-known "pop" group would cover the song. The Diamond's version caught on quickly, helped along by the group's appearances on television variety shows. The Gladiolas also did well, considering their record received little airplay except on strictly R&B radio stations. They never had another hit—as the Gladiolas, that is. Several members continued under yet another name, Maurice Williams and the Zodiacs; and, as such, the group sold a million copies of "Stay" in 1960-61.

LEWIS LYMON & TEENCHORDS

Following in the shadow of a famous brother is difficult at best. For Lewis Lymon, it gave him the drive to succeed. Lewis grew up in the same New York neighborhood as Frankie. He sang on street corners—everybody did. He joined a vocal group—so did all his friends. And, according to Bobby Robinson, owner of Fury Records, when the time was right for him to make a name for himself, Lewis Lymon and three friends walked into Robinson's record shop unannounced. Lewis was about eleven at the time. Robinson quickly arranged an impromptu audition, and the group had a recording session in short order. The first Fury release for the Teenchords, with Lewis Lymon's name prominent on the label, was "I'm So Happy (Tra-La-La-La)." The original members of the Teenchords were Lymon, lead tenor; Ralph Vaughan, first tenor; Rossilio Rocca, second tenor; Lyndon Harold, baritone; and David Little, bass. Most of the members were students at George Washington High. According to one story, they were "discovered" backstage at the Apollo Theater during one of Frankie's appearances. The Teenchords released only three singles on Fury. None of them reached the public's attention, and the group's disgust at Robinson's business practices forced them to look for another label. According to Lymon, Robinson owed the group money in back fees for personal appearances, as well as royalties from record sales and song writing. The Teenchords recorded one single for Juanita Records ("Dance Girl") before signing with George Goldner's End Records. There were only two singles released on End before the group disbanded. In the 1980s, joined Frankie's old group, the Teenagers, during that group's revival.

Massachusetts; closing with a performance in Allentown, Pennsylvania on February 12.

FEB 6   Bill Haley and His Comets become the first American rock 'n roll act to tour the United Kingdom as they begin their fourteen-day tour of the British Isles with shows at London's Dominion Theater. The group also plays dates in Birmingham, Manchester, Leeds, Glasgow, Liverpool, Cardiff, Plymouth, and Southampton performing a total of seventeen shows during their stay. Haley's reception in London is marred by public outcry over the exorbitant price of tickets to his shows. This "beef" turns even more sour when payees are treated to only twenty minutes of Bill Haley and His Comets on stage after sitting through an hour and a half of unknown British talent.

FEB 7   Tommy Leonetti is booked for a week at the Lotus Club in Washington.

EARLY FEBRUARY

ABC-Paramount Records purchases and reissues the Kent Record Company (K.R.C.) master of Lloyd Price's "Just Because."

FEB 8   The Empire Theater in New York is the latest to offer rock 'n roll revues as well as motion pictures. Tonight's inaugural show features the Heartbeats, the Channels, the Valentines, and **Lewis Lymon and the Teenchords**. Artists will appear on stage at the Empire from Friday through Tuesday.

Johnny Cash headlines the show at Cincinnati's Music Hall. Other performers on the mostly country bill include Marty Robbins and Johnny Horton.

Chuck Berry takes the spotlight this week at the Howard Theater in Washington. He is ably assisted by the Spaniels, the Cleftones, and Buddy Johnson's orchestra featuring Ella Johnson.

In Detroit, the Falcons heat up the week at the Rondevoo Club. Nappy Brown also opens for a week at the Flame Show Bar.

FEB 9   Carl Perkins guests on the "Big D Jamboree" broadcast from Dallas.

New Releases for the second week in February include "Paper Castles" by Frankie Lymon and the Teenagers on Gee; "Your True Love" b/w "Matchbox" by Carl Perkins on Sun; "Baby Loves Him" by Wanda Jackson and "Cloud 99" by the Jodimars, both on Capitol; "Sugar Sugar" by the Cadillacs on Josie; "Party Doll" by Roy Brown on Imperial; "Feelin' Low" by Ernie Chaffin on Sun; and "Why Do You Have To Go" by the Dells on Vee-Jay.

FEB 14   Alis Lesley returns to the Lotus Club in Washington with her Elvis impersonation. Sharing the bill is Jackie Lee.

FEB 15   With a total of thirty-one performers traveling on two converted buses, the "Greatest Show of 1957" package kicks off on a cross-country tour with a pair of sold-out shows in Pittsburgh. There will be seventy-two one night stands over the next ninety two days. Headlining of the tour are Fats Domino, Chuck Berry, LaVern Baker, Clyde McPhatter, and Bill Doggett. Others appearing include the Five Keys, the Moonglows, the Five Satins, Eddie Cooley and the Dimples, Charles Brown, Ann Cole, and the Schoolboys. The ages of the members of this last group caused a problem in that the New York Board of Education refused to allow them to skip school. The matter was resolved at the last minute by enrolling them in the Professional Children's School, which assigned a tutor to accompany the lads. After leaving Pittsburgh, the caravan heads for Detroit's Olympia Stadium (16), Youngstown (17), Toledo (18), and Indianapolis (19) before crossing Canada for a show in Toronto on the February 20. The tour is then scheduled to wind its way down the western seaboard before wig-wagging across the States. (See also FEB 26.)

Jackie Wilson performs for the week at Lee's Club Sensation in Detroit.

At the Apollo this week, the Tarriers headline a calypso revue.

MID-FEBRUARY

It is reported that Jesse Belvin has been signed for a role in an upcoming film bio of jazz great Billie Holiday.

Fats Domino turns thumbs-down on a European tour scheduled for late May. It seems he likes to stick closer to New Orleans. Nonetheless, plans are still being made for an overseas trip for The Fat Man, possibly as early as the fall of 1957.

FEB 16   In New Orleans, the Dew Drop Cafe presents Billy Wright for the first of two weekend stands.

"The Perry Como Show" on NBC-TV showcases the talents of Mickey and Sylvia singing "Love Is Strange."

FEB 17   Shirley and Lee return to New Orleans to perform at the Labor Union Hall's Sunday night dance.

FEB 18   Dinah Washington opens for the week at the Casino Royal in Washington.

New Releases for the third week in February include a three cover versions of recent rock 'n roll records: "Little Darlin'" by the Diamonds on Mercury, "Just Because" by Larry Williams on Specialty, and "Sittin' In The Balcony" by Eddie Cochran on Liberty. Also new this week are "I'm Walkin'" by Fats Domino on Imperial; "Symbol of Love" by the G-Clefs on Paris; "So Rare" by the Jimmy Dorsey Orchestra on Fraternity; Buchanan and Goodman's latest cut-in, "The Banana Boat Story," on Luniverse; "Flying Saucers Rock and Roll" by **Billy Lee Riley** and the

BILLY LEE RILEY
Billy Lee Riley was the "work horse" of Sun Records. Born in Pocahontas, Arkansas, October 5, 1933, he was several years older than most of the "stars" on Sun Records. He joined the Army at age fifteen, and upon return, started his first combo in Jonesboro, Arkansas, which was successful enough to have a local radio program. In 1955, after hearing Elvis' Sun recordings, Billy moved to Memphis. To make a living, he owned a restaurant then gave that up to drive a truck. In his off hours, he started another band with Jack Clement, owner of the local Fernwood studio. Riley cut a demo of "Trouble Bound" with in 1956. Clement, who also was an engineer at Sun, took the tape to Sun's owner, Sam Phillips, who was impressed enough to release the demo and then grant Riley studio time. Riley's first Sun session produced "Flyin' Saucers Rock and Roll." In recognition of the song title, his band was christened the "Little Green Men." At this time, the members were Roland Janes, guitar; Jimmy Wilson, piano; Pat O'Neil, bass; and James Van Eaton, drums; and this single featured Jerry Lee Lewis on piano. Lewis repaid Riley by taking Janes and Van Eaton to form his own combo. Riley's second session for Sun produced "Red Hot," which was covered by Bob Luman on Imperial Records. Riley never had a national hit, but his virtuosity on various instruments (piano, guitar, bass, and drums) meant he was always in demand around the studio. He played on sessions for Barbara Pittman, Jerry Lee Lewis, Bill Justis and Charlie Rich, among others. He also recorded under various pseudonyms, including Lightnin' Leon, Prince Albert, the Rockin' Stockings, Sandy and the Sandstones, and Darron Lee. Riley moved to Los Angeles in the early 1960s and backed the Beach Boys, Dean Martin, Sammy Davis, Jr. Rick Nelson, and Johnny Rivers.

Little Green Men on Sun; "The Letter" by the Medallions on Dooto; "Jungle Magic" by Dorsey Burnette on Abbott; and "Don't Say Goodbye" by the Moonglows on Chess. This final record was one of the first to use a violin section on a R&B release.

FEB 22   Working the long holiday weekend celebrating Washington's Birthday, Alan Freed produces another stage show. The venue has changed from past events and takes place at the Times Square Paramount Theater instead of the Brooklyn Paramount. Alternating with screenings of "Don't Knock the Rock," Freed's latest rock 'n roll flick, are live performances by the Platters, Frankie Lymon and the Teenagers, Buddy Knox and Jimmy Bowen with the Rhythm Orchids, Ruth Brown, the Cleftones, Nappy Brown, the Cadillacs, the Duponts, and Bobby Charles. Gross receipts top $125,000 for the week.
     In an unprecedented move, the Apollo Theater books "Dr. Jive's Rhythm and Blues Revue" for two solid weeks. Headliners are Mickey and Sylvia. Also on stage are the Teenchords, Little Joe and the Thrillers, Big Maybelle, Solomon Burke, and the Drifters.
     In Chicago, the Regal Theater hosts a rock 'n roll show featuring Joe Turner, Gene and Eunice, the Spaniels, the El Dorados, Jimmy Reed, and Screamin' Jay Hawkins. It was also advertised that Bobby Charles would appear (see above).

FEB 23   Jerry Lee Lewis makes a guest appearance on the "Big D Jamboree" broadcast from Dallas' Sportatorium.

FEB 24   Brenda Lee makes her first national television appearance on "The Steve Allen Show" on NBC-TV.
     At the Labor Union Hall in New Orleans, Joe Turner is offered as tonight's entertainment.

New Releases for the fourth week in February include "I'm Sorry" by the Platters and "Head Snappin'" by Red Prysock, both on Mercury; "Lucille" by Little Richard on Specialty; "I'm A Country Boy" by Clarence "Frogman" Henry on Argo; "Honey, Where You Going?" by Jimmy Reed on Vee-Jay; "Dirty Woman" by Champion Jack Dupree on Vik; "40 Cups of Coffee" by Bill Haley and His Comets on Decca; "Caterpillar" by Ray Campi on TNT; "I'll Always Be In Love With You" by the Hurricanes on King; and "No Other One" by Connie Francis on M-G-M.

FEB 26   Fats Domino and the "Greatest Show of 1957" continues across the western half of the United States and Canada, leaving behind a string of ten sold-out concerts. Tonight's show is in Denver, followed nightly by performances in Salt Lake, Butte, Calgary, Edmonton, Spokane, Tacoma, Portland, Vancouver, and Seattle. The tour runs through mid-March. To facilitate the movement of the many performers over such a vast area, two Convair airplanes have been chartered—a first for a rock 'n roll caravan.

FEB 28   Jimmy Reed kicks off a seventeen-day outing through Texas and Oklahoma with a show in Waco.

LATE FEBRUARY

Bill Haley and His Comets, just back from their tour of the British Isles, depart for a tour of Australia, returning to America on March 18.

Atlantic Records signs the Bobbettes, a female quartet who's ages range from ten to twelve.

On the tour circuit, Lloyd Price is currently in the middle of a two-week stand in Miami.

THE TOP ROCK 'N ROLL RECORDS FOR FEBRUARY 1957

1. Too Much/Playing For Keeps - Elvis Presley
2. Young Love - Sonny James
3. Blue Monday/What's The Reason I'm Not Pleasing You
         - Fats Domino
4. Love Is Strange - Mickey and Sylvia
5. Blueberry Hill - Fats Domino
6. Jim Dandy - LaVern Baker
7. Since I Met You Baby - Ivory Joe Hunter
8. Butterfly - Charlie Gracie
9. Love Me (EP) - Elvis Presley
10. Ain't Got No Home - Clarence "Frogman" Henry
11. Love Me Tender - Elvis Presley
12. Teenage Crush - Tommy Sands
13. Without Love - Clyde McPhatter
14. On My Word Of Honor/One In A Million - The Platters
15. Lucky Lips - Ruth Brown
16. Party Doll - Buddy Knox
17. The Girl Can't Help It - Little Richard
18. A Rose And A Baby Ruth - George Hamilton IV
19. Bad Boy - The Jive Bombers
20. I'm Stickin' With You - Jimmy Bowen
21. Gone - Ferlin Huskey
22. Poor Boy (EP) - Elvis Presley
23. Little By Little - Nappy Brown
24. Ram-Bunk-Shush - Bill Doggett
25. Come Go With Me - The Dell-Vikings
26. When My Blue Moon Turns To Gold (EP) - Elvis Presley
27. I'm Walkin' - Fats Domino
28. Honky Tonk (part 1-2) - Bill Doggett
29. A Thousand Miles Away - The Heartbeats
30. Ain't That Love - Ray Charles

Also on the "pop" charts:
You Don't Owe Me A Thing - Johnnie Ray
I Dreamed - Betty Johnson

Marianne - Terry Gilkyson and the Easy Riders
Marianne - The Hilltoppers
So Rare - Jimmy Dorsey and his orchestra and chorus

February 1957
ARTIST OF THE MONTH

MICKEY AND SYLVIA

Mickey & Sylvia

Young Sylvia Vanderpool (born March 6, 1936) enjoyed growing up in New York City. She was right in the middle of the exciting world of popular music. By age fourteen, she was spending her time daydreaming of a recording career like that of "Little" Esther Phillips, who had been discovered by Johnny Otis a year earlier when she was just thirteen. To make her dream come true, Sylvia entered every talent contest in the neighborhood. At one such event, a talent scout for Columbia Records was impressed by her jubilant style, charming personality, and wholesome beauty. The scout introduced her to Oran T. "Hot Lips" Page, who had just had a hit duet with Pearl Bailey, "Baby, It's Cold Outside."

In 1952, Page and Sylvia recorded a fine blues single for Columbia Records, "Pacifying Blues" b/w "Chocolate Candy Blues." Shortly after, she had a release with Nelson Clark's orchestra, "I Was Under The Impression" b/w "Sharp Little Sister." A year later, as "Little Sylvia," she continued recording on her own, beginning on Savoy Records, Little Esther's former label. Then Sylvia went to Jubilee Records where she recorded "I Went To Your Wedding" and "A Million Tears." None of her recordings came close to commercial acceptance, and she returned to Washington Irving High a disappointed young lady.

In April 1954, just before her high school graduation, she landed a session with Cat Records, the new subsidiary of Atlantic. Her lone release, the second in the Cat series, was "Fine Love" b/w "Speedy Life" under the listing "'Little' Sylvia Vanderpool with Mickey Baker." The addition of Baker's name was a sign of things to come.

Miss Vanderpool was once again disappointed when her lone Cat release failed to gather even minuscule air play. However, she was fascinated by Baker's guitar technique. Learning the guitar had been a lifelong ambition, and in Baker's friendship she found a teacher. She proved to be a fine student, picking up the basic intricacies of the instrument in near-record time.

McHouston Baker was born October 15, 1925, in Louisville, Kentucky. He never knew his father, and his mother was an alcohol-driven kleptomaniac who spent as much time in jail as at home. By the early 1950s, he had escaped his environment. By this time he was billed as Mickey "Guitar" Baker, a tribute to his work in studios from New Orleans to New York. He had provided instrumental backing for records on several labels including King and Savoy. On Okeh Records, he played the guitar accompaniment on Big Maybelle's 1954 version of "Whole Lot of Shakin' Going On." He also had a few singles under his own name, notably "Mambola" and "Oh, Happy Day" on Savoy in 1952. In 1955, he released "Shake Walkin'" on the Rainbow label. That same year, Baker became a regular addition to Alan Freed's "Rock 'n' Roll Band" during the week-long runs at the Brooklyn Paramount Theater.

Just who suggested that the couple should become a recording act is not known, although it was Miss Vanderpool who most wanted the spotlight. Billed as Mickey and Sylvia, the duo's first release came in July, 1955, with "I'm So Glad" on Rainbow, the label that had Baker under contract. That October, they shared the bill at the Philadelphia Academy of Music with Al Hibbler, Red Prysock, and the Moonglows. In December, they had their second release on Rainbow, "Forever and a Day." In February 1956, the act made its debut at the Apollo Theater in New York. They performed at the Palace in Chicago in April and returned to the Apollo in May. By this time Rainbow had another record out by the duo, "Where Is My Honey."

After three releases, their contract with Rainbow expired, although they were gaining a strong reputation through their many personal appearances. It was several months before they signed with Groove Records, an RCA Victor subsidiary. In August 1956, their first release on Groove was "Walking in the Rain," a song that had also been released by Johnnie Ray. Three months later, Groove issued "Love Is Strange," the song for which Mickey and Sylvia are instantly recognized.

"Love Is Strange" had an infectious rhythm. Nicknamed "cha-lypso," it was a combination of Caribbean calypso, a Latin dance step, and the blues. Baker's shimmering guitar figure opens the record, and the guitar work throughout is one of the record's strong points. Vocally, the two play off each other in a flirtatious style not unlike the earlier "Baby, It's Cold Outside" by Pearl Bailey and "Hot Lips" Page. In the middle of the winter of 1957, "Love Is Strange" was like a bright ray of sunshine.

To plug "Love Is Strange," Mickey and Sylvia appeared at New York's Apollo, Philadelphia's Uptown, and Washington's Howard Theaters for a full week each during three consecutive months, beginning in January, 1957. The nine bookings were unprecedented, but the ploy worked. The single caught the public's ear and sold 800,000 copies in its initial release. It has easily surpassed the one million mark in the time since. The composers of the tune, listed as Baker and Ethel Smith, were sued for copyright infringement by the writers of "Billy's Blues," a song by Billy Stewart. However, the plaintiffs lost their case in the early 1960s in a rare jury trial instead of the usual judge's decision.

As "Love Is Strange" was riding high on the charts, RCA Victor decided to close its Groove subsidiary and place most of the affected artists on its other rock 'n roll label, Vik. So, in March 1957, the duo's next single, the two-sided hit "There Oughta Be A Law" b/w "Dearest," came out on the new label.

Mickey and Sylvia appeared in Jocko's "Rocketship Show" at the New York Lowe's State Theater during Easter week of 1957. This show played opposite the Freed revue at the Brooklyn Paramount. Freed never forgave Baker for playing a rival show, and Baker never again appeared on one of Freed's revues.

May 1957, Vik released "Love Will Make You Fail in School," followed in August by "Love Is a Treasure." Neither song was up to the standards laid out by "Love Is Strange" or "There Oughta Be A Law." As a result, it was almost a year between hits for the duo.

In the meantime, they toured with Ray Charles and Joe Turner in October 1957. By this time, their personal relationship had begun to sour due to the strain of constant performing. As he watched each record sell less than the last, Baker knew he could be making more money playing sessions back in New York. In November, they mutually agreed to take some time off to pursue other interests.

The plan worked, and in May 1958, they returned with a fine new single, "Bewildered," followed in July by "It's You I Love." RCA Victor closed down the Vik label, so Mickey and Sylvia's November release, "Oh, Yeah! Uh-Huh," came out on RCA. It was the last of the Mickey and Sylvia singles for more than a year. Sylvia decided to retire from the act for a while to start a family.

Mickey continued on. In April, 1959, Atlantic released a single by Mickey and Kitty, "Ooh-Sha-Lala," featuring Baker and Kitty Noble. The record did not catch on. The same fate befell their second and third releases, "St. Louis Blues" and "My Reverie." Meanwhile, Baker had an instrumental, "Third Man Theme," issued under his own name on Atlantic. By the end of the year, both the duo and Baker as a solo artist were off the label.

Mickey and Sylvia returned on RCA Victor in July 1960 with "Sweeter as the Day Goes By." The record featured Sylvia's voice with little evidence of Mickey either vocally or, what's worse, instrumentally. The instrumentation was lush with violins, pianos and a vocal chorus. However, this couldn't make up for the loss of Mickey's playfulness. The duo's next single was "What Would I Do," an old Shirley and Lee song, backed by "This Is My Story" for release in November 1960. The single, especially the A-side, was more energetic than anything the duo had recorded in years, and as a result it sold moderately well. The B-side featured an orchestra conducted by Mickey Baker. This was a step in the right direction, although Baker's guitar continued to be placed in the background. There was one more single released in 1960, but it made little difference. RCA Victor allowed their contract with Mickey and Sylvia to expire.

In August 1961, "Lovedrops" was the first of four singles issued by Mickey and Sylvia on the Willow label. The final Willow release was a rerecording of "Love Is Strange." It was clear to both artists that the magic had gone out of their relationship. Once again they parted, and this time the break was final.

Mickey tired of the American music scene and moved to Paris in 1962. Sylvia started using her married name, Sylvia Robinson. Under this name, she issued a few singles on Sue Records, as well as on her old label, Jubilee, before dropping from sight to raise her family.

In the summer of 1964, RCA dug through its vaults and released a single made up of an old Mickey and Sylvia side, "Gipsy" b/w "Let's Shake Some More." This was followed almost a year later by "From the Beginning of Time." By this time, rock 'n roll music had changed dramatically and the singles disappeared under a flood of hits from British acts.

Nothing was heard from either Mickey or Sylvia for a few years, until Sylvia and her husband emerged as cofounders of All Platinum Records, and its subsidiary labels Stang, Vibration and Sugar Hill. In 1970, Sylvia's composition, "Love On A Two-Way Street," became a top hit for the Moments on Stang.

On Vibration, Sylvia again tasted success as a recording artist when she issued her highly suggestive single "Pillow Talk" in early 1973. A year later, All Platinum re-released "Lovedrops," the Mickey and Sylvia single from 1960, followed shortly thereafter by the final single release from Mickey and Sylvia, "Anytime You Want Me."

In 1975, Vibration also had a hit with a female artist who's time in the spotlight appeared to have passed. Shirley Alston, former lead vocalist with the Shirelles, issued "Shame, Shame, Shame" under the name Shirley (And Company).

The biggest hit for Sugar Hill Records came in 1977 with the disco smash, "Raper's Delight" by the Sugar Hill Gang. In the early 1980s, Sugar Hill bought the large Chess Records catalog and began a program of reissues before selling the catalog to MCA Records.

Mickey Baker remained in France, playing jazz and blues, the music he loved best. He occasionally returned to America for session work for artists with which he shared a common vision. These included Sunnyland Slim, Willie Mabon and Champion Jack Dupree. He also found time to write "Jazz Guitar," a best selling textbook on jazz guitar technique. When last heard from, he was working on his autobiography, which was scheduled to be published in 1994.

During their heyday, Mickey and Sylvia issued a string of finely crafted singles. Going against the trend at the time, they refused to record songs that only mimicked "Love Is Strange." Relying on Mickey's extensive recording background, as well as Sylvia's drive for recognition, they composed and recorded individual songs with loving care and professionalism. True, none of the singles after "Love Is Strange" came close to the top of the record charts. However, the duo had a longer than usual rock 'n roll career. Afterward, they were able to turn their experience into a larger gain—Sylvia as a record company executive and sometime recording artist and Mickey as a respected guitarist and instructor.

March 1957

JOHNNIE & JOE

Joe Rivers was from Charleston, South Carolina. His family moved to New York City when he was nine, and he attended the Artist Guild of America's school for talented children. This led to Sunday morning appearances on a local television show similar to the "Little Rascals." Joe Rivers was greatly influenced by his neighbor, Clyde McPhatter. When Rivers was fourteen, he teamed with Rex Garvin, age ten, who was already an accomplished pianist. Johnnie Sanders Richardson was also one of Joe's neighbors. Her mother, Zell Sanders, was owner of J&S Records, a small company with minor hits by Baby Washington and the Hearts. It was Mrs. Sanders who first suggested that Johnnie and Joe would make a good vocal duo, with Garvin's piano accompaniment. Their first single was "I'll Be Spinning." The record sold very well in New York and Pittsburgh. J&S Records had limited funds and could not press enough singles to meet the demand, so the song was leased to Chess Records. It was followed by "Over the Mountain, Across the Sea." The duo had three releases more singles on Chess, "I Was So Lonely," "Why, Oh Why" and "Darling," yet never had another hit. They also released "I Adore You" on ABC-Paramount, as well as singles on Blue Rock, Gone, and several other labels. "Over the Mountain" began selling again in 1960, opening the way for more personal appearances. However, Johnnie was married, and, when Joe took a bride, the act broke up. Zell Sanders discovered the Jaynettes, and their only hit, "Sally, Go 'Round the Roses," was written by Johnnie. Johnnie and Joe reunited in 1973 for the Madison Square Garden revival shows, but Johnnie chose not to continue as a performer. By this time, Joe found a new "Johnnie" in Carol Sylven. Johnnie died in 1988.

MAR 1   Frankie Lymon and the Teenagers are booked for a weeklong engagement in Panama for the annual carnival. It is reported that the group will be paid $7,500 for the week's worth of work. A single performance in Colon draws an overflow crowd of 13,000.

Etta James begins a lengthy tour with a show in Columbus, Georgia. She will travel through Florida and Texas then up to Colorado. Usually appearing with her vocal group, the Peaches, this is her first solo outing. Her recent legal troubles resulting from her smash 1955 hit, "The Wallflower" (better known as "Dance With Me Henry"), have been resolved. Miss James sued Georgia Gibbs and Mercury Records for borrowing her song and arrangement virtually note for note.

As Mickey and Sylvia start their second week at the Apollo Theater, a change in the lineup of supporting acts takes place. Added to the roster are the G-Clefs and the Channels.

MAR 2   In Chicago, the Central Park Theater hosts a "midnight rhythm and blues show" featuring Otis Rush, the Magnificents, Sunnyland Slim, Andre Williams, Jimmy Rogers, and the Calvaes.

MAR 3   In Chicago, the Catholic Diocese bans rock 'n roll records from all school functions because of the music's "tribal rhythms" and its "encouragement to act in a hedonistic manner." Within a matter of days, sales of rock 'n roll singles in the Chicago area go through the roof.

New Releases for the first week in March include "A White Sport Coat (And a Pink Carnation)" by Marty Robbins on Columbia; "Over The Mountain, Across the Sea" by **Johnnie and Joe** and Chess; "Come Seven" by Bobby Day on Class; and The Jivers' "Ray Pearl" on Aladdin. Also out this week is "Lovable" on Specialty with the artist listed as Dale Cook. Those familiar with the Sour Stirrers weren't fooled for a minute. They knew it was Sam Cooke.

EARLY MARCH

The Platters leave the United States for a twelve-week tour of England.

Fats Domino is on tour in Texas and Oklahoma with his "Big Show," featuring Ann Cole.

Also on the tour circuit is a package billed as "The Big Three," headlined by Little Junior Parker, Bobby "Blue" Bland, and Chuck Edwards. All three artists record for Duke Records of Houston.

In New Orleans, the Hawkettes and Bobby Mitchell are currently at the San Jacinto Club.

MAR 8   Lloyd Price and Amos Milburn share the spotlight at the Apollo Theater in New York this week. Also on the bill are the Clovers.

The Cardinals, Big Maybelle, the Solitaires, the Harptones, Ocie Smith, and Nappy Brown entertain this week at the Howard Theater in Washington.

MAR 10   On CBS-TV's "The Ed Sullivan Show," Charlie Gracie makes an appearance to plug "Butterfly."

New Releases for the second week in March include two from Chess Records: "School Day" by Chuck Berry and "Got My Mojo Working" by Muddy Waters. Other new releases this week include "Red Sails in the Sunset" by Joe Turner on Atlantic; "I Smell Trouble" by Bobby "Blue" Bland on Duke; "How Do I Love You" by B. B. King on R.P.M.; "Everybody Loves Me" by the Sophomores on Dawn; "Nobody's Woman" by Charlie Feathers on King; "Baby Come Home" by Robert and Johnny on Old Town; and "Oh Happy Day" by the **Five Satins** on Ember. Also new this week is as re-release of "Chickee Wah-Wah" by Bobby Marchan on Gale. The single had originally be on Ace Records, but when it began to garner local air play, it was issued by the Gale Agency on its own label.

MAR 13   Bo Diddley headlines a revue at the Uptown Theater in Philadelphia. Also in the spotlight are Faye Adams, and the Turbans.

MAR 14   Gene Vincent, Sonny James, Sanford Clark, George Hamilton IV, and Carl Perkins perform together in Cleveland.

MAR 15   A three-day show kicks off in Detroit's Michigan Theater with headliners Al Hibbler, Buddy Knox and Jimmy Bowen with the Rhythm Orchids, Ruth Brown, Cathy Carr, Nappy Brown, Annie Laurie, the Dell-Vikings, Otis Williams and His Charms, George Hamilton IV, Sam "The Man" Taylor, and Sil Austin.

Also in Detroit tonight, Louis Jordan and His Tympany Five start a wild week at the Flame Show Bar.

In New York, the Apollo Theater offers up the Cadillacs, Joe Tex and Linda Hopklns as the week's entertainment.

Roy Brown, the Spiders, Art Neville, Bobby Mitchell, and Dave Bartholomew's orchestra rock the Granada Theater in New Orleans.

MAR 17   Fifteen-year old Aretha Franklin, billed as "America's Youngest National Gospel Singer," performs with her father, Reverend C. L. Franklin, in a gospel marathon at New Orleans' Municipal Auditorium.

Also in New Orleans, "Gatemouth" Brown entertains at the Blue Eagle Ballroom, located on the corner of Saratoga and Felicity.

THE FIVE SATINS
Fred Parris was the lead vocalist of the Scarlets, a popular group signed to Bobby Robinson's Red Robin label in 1954. Under the military's "buddy system," the group joined the Army, only to find each member being shipped to a different base. On weekends, Parris returned to his home in New Haven, Connecticut. He joined another group of amateur singers, and they came to the attention of the owner of Standord Records. Their first session was almost cancelled when the band failed to show up. Undaunted, the group recorded "All Mine" acappella. For their second single, Parris and his friends, Al Denby, Eddie Martin, and Jim Freeman, with Jesse Murphy on piano, used the basement of St. Bernadette's Church Hall to record "I Remember," a song Parris wrote while on guard duty. When "I Remember" started to sell in the northeast, the name was changed to "In the Still of the Nite." The recording was then leased to Ember Records, and it sold close to a million copies. "In the Still of the Night" has become one of the most famous "oldies" of all time. Because Parris could not perform with the Five Satins, his place was taken by Bill Baker. For the next Five Satins session, Tommy Kilebrew replaced Al Denby. With Baker's lead, the group recorded "Wonderful Girl," "Oh Happy Day," "To the Aisle" and "Our Anniversary." Parris was discharged from the Army in time to wax "She's Gone (With the Wind)," released as Fred Parris and the Scarlets on Kilk Records. With the Five Satins, Parris was lead vocalist beginning with "A Night Like This." The group had become dissatisfied with Ember's accounting practices and lack of promotion. Over the next few years, they recorded for Cub, Chancellor, Warner Brothers, United Artists, Roulette, and a half-dozen other labels. Parris recorded solo and with various groups including the Restless Hearts, New Yorkers, and Cherokees.

DON & DEWEY

Don and Dewey are remembered as an early inspiration for the Righteous Brothers. Don "Sugarcane" Harris and Dewey Terry were born in 1938 and grew up in Pasadena. They joined the Squires, a group of high school friends who had local hits in 1955 with "Lucy Lou" on Kicks and "Sindy" on Mambo (later Vita). In 1956, Don and Dewey left to record for Johnny Otis' Dig Records, and they also appeared on the Spot and Shade labels. From 1957 to 1959, Don and Dewey recorded for Specialty. Beginning with "Jungle Hop," their singles showed all the exuberance of their labelmates Little Richard and Larry Williams. Don and Dewey recorded the original versions of "Big Boy Pete" (a 1960 hit for the Olympics), "Leaving It All Up To You" (a 1964 hit for Dale and Grace), "Farmer John" (a hit for the Premiers in 1964), as well as "KoKo Joe" and "Justine" (early recordings by the Righteous Brothers). Don played guitar and experimented with the amplified violin while Dewey accompanied on piano. They developed an exciting stage act and were regulars with the Johnny Otis revues into the 1960s. Their 1962 recording of "Don't Ever Leave Me" on Rush Records featured Jackie DeShannon and Johnny "Guitar" Watson. In 1964, when the Righteous Brothers were just beginning, Don and Dewey played on Little Richard's comeback Specialty sessions. They also toured England and France with Richard. A year later, they were appearing in Las Vegas lounges as the cabaret act, Rudy Hunter and the Fabulous Tones. In the late 1960s, Dewey was living in Denver playing jazz. Don joined Frank Zappa's Mothers of Invention as electric violinist, and recorded with John Mayall's Bluesbreakers in 1970. He reunited with Dewey to play an oldies show at Radio City Music Hall in the early 1970s. They remained together into the 1980s.

MAR 18   Mickey and Sylvia entertain patrons at the Casino Royal in Washington this week.

New Releases for the third week in March include "Searchin'" b/w "Young Blood" by the Coasters on Atco; "All Shook Up" by Elvis Presley on RCA Victor; "There Oughta Be a Law" by Mickey and Sylvia and "Come On" by the Sharps, both on Vik; "If You Can't Rock Me" by the Strikes on Imperial; "C. C. Rider" by Chuck Willis and "Empty Arms" by Ivory Joe Hunter, both on Atlantic; "Florence" by the Paragons on Winley; and "Close Your Eyes" by the Pretenders on Whirlin' Disc.

MAR 19   In Memphis, Elvis Presley purchases an eighteen-room, $100,000 home at 3764 South Bellvue Boulevard. The home, already known locally as Graceland, will become his permanent residence for the next twenty years. Eventually Graceland will become one of the most-visited private homes in the world.

MAR 22   Bo Diddley headlines the revue at the Apollo Theater this week. Talent also includes Screamin' Jay Hawkins, Andre Williams and Larry Birdsong.
   In Philadelphia, the Uptown Theater offers Mickey and Sylvia, Bullmoose Jackson, and the Jive Bombers for the week.
   Lloyd Price shares the spotlight with the Clovers, Amos Milburn and Edna McGriff at the Howard Theater in Washington this week.

MAR 23   Janis Martin and Sanford Clark make guest appearances on Red Foley's "Ozark Jubilee," broadcast on ABC-TV from 10:00 to 11:00 p.m.

MAR 24   Billy Riley and His Little Green Men make an appearance at the Blue Moon Club in Tulsa.
   Johnny Cash and Jerry Lee Lewis headline a country show in Kansas City.

MAR 25   Charlie Gracie opens for a week at the Casino Royal in Washington.

New Releases for the fourth week in March include "Ring-A-Ding" by Tommy Sands on Capitol; "Hey Bo Diddley" by Bo Diddley on Checker; "Barefoot Girl" by the Playmates on Roulette; Sanford Clark's "Glory of Love" on Dot; "B-I-Bickey-Bi, Bo Bo Go" by Gene Vincent and His Blue Caps on Capitol; "Just To Hold My Hand" by Clyde McPhatter on Atlantic; "I Need Your Lovin'" by Conway Twitty on Mercury; "Thirty-Second Lover" by the "5" Royales on King; the Robins' "All of a Sudden My Heart Sings" on Whippet; "Rockin' Love" by Carl Mann on Jaxon; "You Are My Sunshine" by Smiley Lewis on Imperial; "Jungle Hop" by **Don and Dewey** on Specialty; and "Pretty Girl" by Nappy Brown on Savoy. There are also two instrumentals in this week's offerings: "Wild Fire" by Piano Red on RCA Victor and "King's Rock" by King Curtis on Apollo.

MAR 26   In the United Kingdom, the Platters begin a two-week engagement at the Empire Theater in Glasgow, Scotland.

MAR 28   Fats Domino fails to appear at the Memphis Auditorium due to illness. The rest of the troupe, including Chuck Berry and LaVern Baker, carry on without him.

Elvis Presley starts a record-breaking nine-day tour of the Midwest and Northeast with a concert in Chicago's International Amphitheater. Other dates through the end of the month are St. Louis (29); Ft. Wayne (30); and Detroit (31). (See also APR 1.)

MAR 30   Brenda Lee makes an appearance on the CBS-TV's "Ozark Jamboree."

Jerry Lee Lewis repeats as a guest of the "Big D Jamboree" broadcast from 8:30-10:30 from the Sportatorium in Dallas.

MAR 31   Sun Records stablemates Jerry Lee Lewis, Johnny Cash and Carl Perkins start a southern tour with a show in Little Rock. Other dates include Monroe, Louisiana, April 1; Sheffield, Alabama (2); Jackson, Mississippi (3); Memphis (4); and Odessa, Texas (5).

LATE MARCH

Newly formed Roulette Records, in the midst of a phenomenal string of hits, suffers a minor setback when it is sued by Monte Carlo Records which contends that Roulette's use of the roulette wheel logo infringes on Monte Carlo's label style.

THE TOP ROCK 'N ROLL RECORDS FOR MARCH 1957

1. Party Doll - Buddy Knox
2. Too Much/Playing For Keeps - Elvis Presley
3. Teenage Crush - Tommy Sands
4. Young Love - Sonny James
5. Butterfly - Charlie Gracie
6. I'm Walkin' - Fats Domino
7. Gone - Ferlin Huskey
8. Love Is Strange - Mickey and Sylvia
9. Come Go With Me - The Dell-Vikings
10. Blue Monday - Fats Domino
11. I'm Stickin' With You/Ever-Lovin' Fingers - Jimmy Bowen
12. Jim Dandy - LaVern Baker
13. Little Darlin' - The Diamonds
14. Lucky Lips - Ruth Brown
15. Just Because - Lloyd Price
16. Bad Boy - The Jive Bombers
17. I'm Sorry/He's Mine - The Platters
18. One Step At A Time - Brenda Lee
19. Sittin' In The Balcony - Eddie Cochran
20. Sittin' In The Balcony - Johnny Dee

21. Lucille/Send Me Some Lovin' - Little Richard
22. Blueberry Hill - Fats Domino
23. Since I Met You Baby - Ivory Joe Hunter
24. A Thousand Miles Away - The Heartbeats
25. It Hurts To Be In Love - Annie Laurie
26. The Girl Can't Help It - Little Richard
27. All Shook Up - Elvis Presley
28. Your True Love - Carl Perkins
29. Fools Fall In Love - The Drifters
30. Next Time You See Me - Little Junior Parker

Also on the "pop" charts:
Butterfly - Andy Williams
Party Doll - Steve Lawrence
Round and Round - Perry Como

March 1957
ARTISTS OF THE MONTH

BUDDY KNOX AND JIMMY BOWEN

Buddy Knox

Wayne Knox was nicknamed "Buddy" by his parents on the day he was born, July 20, 1933*. Growing up on the family's wheat farm in Happy, Texas, he had a normal childhood. Happy was a sleepy, Panhandle town—a wide spot on highway 87 on the flat plains south of Amarillo. By the time he was in high school, Knox was an accomplished guitarist and songwriter. About the age of sixteen, he penned two of his future hits, "Party Doll" and "Hula Love." His small combo was a featured attraction in the teen canteens and armories around Amarillo. Following high school graduation in 1951, he entered West Texas State in nearby Canyon on an athletic scholarship.

Several years later, while doing graduate study at West Texas State, Buddy became acquainted with two younger athletes, Jimmy Bowen and Don Lanier, who shared his love for music. They soon formed a vocal trio calling themselves the Serenaders with Knox and Lanier playing accompaniment on guitar while Bowen plucked a stand-up bass. Their stated ambition at this time was simply to follow the age-old tradition of singing on moonlit nights beneath the windows of the women's dormitory. The boys quickly found acceptance performing at college dances, fraternity and sorority parties, and local teen clubs.

Also working the same territory was Roy Orbison and his band the Teen Kings. At the time, Orbison was a student at North Texas State in Denton, near Fort Worth. By the spring of 1956, he had already done some recording in Clovis, New Mexico, at a small studio owned and operated by Norman Petty. One rock 'n roll number, "Ooby Dooby," had

---

(* Knox's birth date is also given as April 14, 1933.)

subsequently been issued by the Teen Kings on the small Je-Wel label of Clovis. It had done well enough to bring the band to the attention of Sun Records in Memphis which, in the summer of 1956, recorded and released a second version of the song that sold well enough to make the national record charts.

That fall, Knox was close to receiving his Master's Degree, but Bowen was contemplating leaving college. The boys decided it would be nice to have a souvenir recording of their time together, and Orbison suggested that they give Petty a try. The trio loaded up their instruments and drove to Clovis.

Petty was impressed enough with the young men to grant them three days of recording time for a flat fee of sixty dollars. Petty had an ulterior motive. In return for his generosity, he was to have first crack at the publishing rights of any song recorded. To augment the sound of the trio, David Aldred, from Clovis, played drums and an unknown young lady brought along her cymbals from the high school band. Finally, a female vocal group composed of Knox's sister and two of her friends sang in the background. After the first day, Bowen, who really could not play bass very well, was replaced by a local musician.

During their sessions, the combo completed only four songs, "Party Doll," sung by Knox and "I'm Stickin' With You," "Ever Lovin' Fingers," and "My Baby's Gone," all sung by Bowen. The end result of three day's work was a small handful of acetates to take back to college.

Knox had resigned himself to the coming breakup of the group. Bowen, on the other hand, was convinced that the recordings showed potential.

Jimmy Bowen was born November 30, 1937, in Santa Rita, New Mexico, but he grew up in Dumas, Texas. In high school he was a part-time deejay at KDDD radio as well as being a top athlete. Bowen took his copies of the acetates to a Dumas business acquaintance, Chester Oliver, who advanced Bowen enough money to have five-hundred copies of a single pressed using two of the songs, "Party Doll" and "I'm Stickin' With You."

Initially, the record came out on the Blue Moon label. However, Bowen ran into problems because there was another company in Santa Clara, California, using the Blue Moon name. Nevertheless, the record was on the local market long enough to attract the attention of Dumas teenagers. As the record gained in popularity, the combo was also forced to change its name, as there was already a rhythm and blues quartet called the Serenaders. As a result, the trio came up with the name the Orchids, reportedly from the flowered shirts favored by Knox. By mid-December 1956, "Party Doll" b/w "I'm Stickin' With You" was out again, this time on Triple D Records, named after KDDD radio.

In late December, Don Lanier mailed a copy of the new single to his sister who was a New York fashion model. Miss Lanier was acquainted with a few people in the music business, including publishers Phil Kahl and Howie Richmond. These two men, in turn, knew Morris Levy, an entrepreneur in the music business, and George Goldner, owner of a series of labels including Tico, Gee, and Rama. Levy and Goldner were impressed enough with the Knox-Bowen record that they decided to be-

Jimmy Bowen

come partners and form a new company, Roulette Records, to handle its release. It was their decision to split the two songs, putting out a separate single under each artist's name. As a result, "I'm Stickin' With You" b/w "Ever Lovin' Fingers" by Jimmy Bowen became Roulette #4001, while "Party Doll" by Buddy Knox became Roulette #4002. As there was no second song by Knox available, "My Baby's Gone," featuring Bowen, was issued as the flip side of "Party Doll" under Knox' name. One last change was in order: the combo became known as the Rhythm Orchids, adding a little pizzazz to an otherwise wilting designation.

Both "Party Doll" and "I'm Stickin' With You" were issued the last week in January 1957, and Levy and Goldner called on all their promotional expertise. They pushed the record with deejays up and down the East Coast while Kahl's publishing business made certain that both songs were covered by enough artists to insure that each tune would be a hit—by somebody. In the end, everyone did well. Knox's version of "Party Doll" outsold those by Steve Lawrence, Roy Brown and Wingy Manone. Bowen's cut of "I'm Stickin' With You" far outdistanced the cover by the Fontane Sisters.

"Party Doll" was a bright, bouncy tune that owed more to the heritage of country music, especially Hank Williams and Jimmie Rodgers, than it did to rock 'n rollers like Elvis or Carl Perkins. Knox delivered the song in an unabashedly naive manner considering that the lyrics openly express the yearning for a woman "to be with him when he's feelin' wild" so she can "run her fingers through my hair." Teens quickly caught on to such lines as, "Baby, I want to have a party with you." The song's topper was the repetitive phrase, "I'll make love to you." In 1957, this was more than enough to bring out the standard-bearers for decency, and many of the nation's radio stations initially banned the record.

"I'm Stickin' With You" was different from the get-go. Opening with an interesting lick on guitar, the rest of the song is almost nonchalant in its delivery. Bowen sang what should be a paean to lifetime fidelity in a decidedly unhurried voice, even humming part of a verse in the middle. With repetitious lines such as "be-bop, I love you baby," the song defies comprehension, much less close inspection.

The Rhythm Orchids capitalized on their success by appearing at the Paramount Theater in Times Square with the Alan Freed revue in February 1957. In March, they did a three-day show at Detroit's Michigan Theater as "Party Doll" topped the music charts. "I'm Stickin' With You" did not trail far behind.

Just as things seemed to be going smoothly, the combo received a blow from which it never fully recovered. Knox was called to six-months active duty in the Army Reserves. Roulette issued a perfunctory statement that Knox had twenty songs "in the can." However, there was no mistaking that without a full agenda of personal appearances, a major part of their promotional effort would be lost. In mid-April, "Lieutenant" Buddy Knox released "Rock Your Little Baby To Sleep," while Bowen issued "Warm Up To Me Baby."

In June, both Knox and Bowen had self-titled albums out on Roulette. A month later, they spent Knox's first weekend pass filming a cameo appearance for the rock 'n roll movie, "Jamboree." Knox sang "Hula

Love" and Bowen performed "Cross Over," while assigned to strumming a guitar on camera rather than playing his stand-up bass.

True to their word, Roulette continued to issue records by each artist. By the end of the year, they each had two more singles. Bowen's "Ever Since That Night" and "Cross Over." were both lightweight efforts, and neither sold appreciably. Knox fared a little better with "Hula Love" and "Swingin' Daddy."

Knox was able to get enough time off from his duties in the Army Reserve so that he and Bowen could fill dates with "The Biggest Show of Stars for '57" during September and October 1957. Then it was back into uniform for a few more months.

In April 1958, Knox and Bowen appeared together at a benefit for the police department of Beaumont, Texas. They would not perform together on stage for another thirty years.

As the fathers of what has come to be called the Tex-Mex sound, Knox and Bowen saw their thunder stolen by Buddy Holly and the Crickets during the fall of 1957. Holly based much of his musical style on the Rhythm Orchids and even used Norman Petty's studio in Clovis to record many of his hits. What Holly brought to the music was youthful exuberance, something that Knox and Bowen seemed to lack.

Not surprisingly, the two Buddys, Knox and Holly, lived up to their name and remained friendly toward each other. According to Knox, he and Bowen were originally offered two of Holly's compositions including "That'll Be The Day." However, before they had a chance to record them, Holly secured his own recording contract with Brunswick Records. Knox was not one to hold a grudge, and even named his daughter Holly. There were other ties between the two artists. Bob Montgomery, Holly's first singing partner, played guitar on Knox's "I Think I'm Gonna Kill Myself" and also wrote "A Taste of the Blues," which Knox recorded. Jerry Allison, drummer with the Crickets, played on Knox' "Swingin' Daddy" and "Lovey Dovey." Allison and Sonny Curtis—another Cricket—composed a later Knox effort, "This Time Tomorrow." Curtis also co-wrote "Lovey Dovey" and penned Knox' "Gypsy Man," which was produced by Montgomery.

For Bowen, the hits stopped altogether after "By The Light of the Silvery Moon" in the summer of 1958. He had a few more singles on Roulette, including "My Kind of Love," an early song writing effort by Neil Sedaka that fails to show Sedaka's future promise.

Bowen moved on to Crest Records in Hollywood. Here, he got lost between musical styles, with "Somebody to Love" reaching out for the "pop" crowd while the flip side, "Don't Drop It," was aimed at the country audience. This was followed by sporadic releases on Decca and Capehart. By the time he recorded for Reprise, in the 1963, his heart was no longer into performing. It was the production side of the business that appealed to him most. In that capacity, Jimmy Bowen became one of the most respected men in the music business, with his name appearing on hundreds of records by artists as diverse as Glen Campbell to Frank Sinatra. In 1977, he transferred his homebase to Nashville to pursue his love of country music. Here he held top-management positions with Warner Brothers and MCA Records. In 1989, he issued Carl

Perkins' BORN TO ROCK album on his own Universal label, with distribution by MCA. In the 1990s, Bowen was head of Capitol Records' Nashville division.

By 1958, Dave Aldred had quit the band, and he turned up in Philadelphia as the drummer for Dickey Doo and the Don'ts.

Buddy Knox worked hard to overcome the six months he lost while on active duty, and his records through 1958 did fare better than those by Bowen. By the time he issued "I Think I'm Gonna Kill Myself," in March 1959, barely a month after Buddy Holly's tragic death, it was obvious to Knox that his brand of rock 'n roll music was no longer in vogue.

A year later, Knox was dropped by Roulette; he signed with Liberty Records on the West Coast. On Liberty, Knox had a few mid-sized hits including "Lovey Dovey" in 1960 and "Ling-Ting-Tong" in 1961. However, as remakes of the R&B classics by the Drifters and the Charms, Knox' versions lacked originality.

Like Bowen, Knox also issued singles on several labels through the 1960s. In early 1965, "Joann" appeared on Ruff Records, and Buddy plugged the song on "American Bandstand" and "Shindig" that March. He was reunited with Bowen for a brief time at Reprise, with Knox as artist and Bowen as producer. On United Artists, Knox even had a minor country hit with "Gypsy Man" in 1968. He remained with the label until late 1970. It was to be his final long-term recording contract.

By this time, Knox had moved to Vancouver, where he became a Canadian citizen. Co-owner of a nightclub, he performed to his heart's content. He also discovered that his British fans had not forgotten him, and he made several trips to England. During a very successful 1977 tour of England, along with veteran rockers Jack Scott, Warren Smith, and Charlie Feathers, one show was recorded and subsequently released on EMI under the title "Our Rock 'n' Roll Legends."

In 1989, Knox and Bowen and the other Rhythm Orchids performed one final time, back where it all began, on the campus at West Texas State.

April 1957

APR 1   Frankie Lymon and the Teenagers open a three-month British tour with the first concert of a two-week stand at the London Palladium. At age thirteen, Lymon becomes the youngest performer to headline a show at the Palladium. Opening-night reviews in the British press were less than kind, noting that the pit orchestra drowned out the singing and the Teenagers' dance routines were "adding little to the presentation." Within a day, the blaring orchestra had been replaced by a small combo and strenuous rehearsals had sharpened the Teenagers' dance steps. While in London, the Teenagers will record a long-play album for Gee records at the EMI studios titled FRANKIE LYMON AND THE TEENAGERS AT THE LONDON PALLADIUM although it is not recorded at the Palladium before an audience. Following the sold-out Palladium shows, the group is booked for a ten-week romp through the British Isles.

Elvis Presley continues to build up mounting revenues on his tour as he plays Buffalo tonight. Remaining shows include Toronto (2); Ottawa (3); and Philadelphia (5-6). Total gross revenues from this brief jaunt are more than $300,000.

New Releases for the first week in April include two on Okeh: "I Am Old Enough" by the Schoolboys and "Darling Please Forgive Me" by Screamin' Jay Hawkins. Also new this week are "Out In The Cold Again" by Frankie Lymon and the Teenagers on Gee; "Rang Tang Ding Dong (I'm a Japanese Sandman)" by the Cellos on Apollo; "Big Fool" by **Ronnie Self** on Columbia; "Pledge of Love" by the Penguins on Atlantic; "Louie Louie" by Richard Berry and the Pharaohs on Flip; the Midnighters' "In The Doorway Crying" on Federal; Donnie Elbert's "What Can I Do" on DeLuxe; and "Teenage Cutie" by Lucky Wray with Link and Doug on Starday.

APR 6   In New York, Alan Freed, acting as national spokesman for the Arthritis Foundation, hosts a nineteen-hour telethon over WABD-TV that features various rock 'n roll talent.

In Pittsburgh, following a teen dance at the White Oak Youth Center, five hundred people engage in a riotous free-for-all. Eighteen are arrested.

Carl Perkins makes a guest appearance on the "Louisiana Hayride" in Shreveport.

In Dallas, Johnny Cash is the headliner at the "Big D Jamboree."

RONNIE SELF

He was nicknamed "Mr. Frantic," and the title fit both the artist and the man. He was born Ronald Sprague, July 5, 1938, in rural southwestern Missouri. He grew up in nearby Springfield. Ronnie learned to play guitar at an early age, and he began performing as a youngster. He was soon appearing on KWTO radio's "Ozark Jubilee," broadcast nationwide each Saturday night from Springfield. This exposure brought him to the attention of ABC-Paramount Records, and in 1956, "Pretty Bad Blues" was released. His eccentricities became apparent when he doomed any further ABC releases by barging into the corporate headquarters and berating company executives. At the time, a second single, "Sweet Love" was scheduled for release. Mysteriously, the session tapes disappeared. He bounced back and signed with the Phillip Morris Caravan of country stars in early 1957, and he remained with this touring company until mid-1958, when he left without giving notice. During this time, he recorded with Columbia Records, and his first session produced "Big Fool." He followed with a series of romping rockers, including "Ain't I'm a Dog" "Bop-A-Lena," and "Date Bait." Bucking the trend of cute teen idols, "Bop-A-Lena" became a minor hit in the spring of 1958. From 1959 to 1962, he recorded for Decca, but his success now lay with songwriting, including "Sweet Nothin's" and "I'm Sorry" for Brenda Lee. He had a lone single for Kapp in 1963, then moved on to Amy and Scratch. By this time, he had a reputation from being more than a little unreliable. He was also a raving alcoholic. Ronnie died August 28, 1981, at his home in Springfield. Less than six months later, Diana Ross had a Top Ten hit with "Mirror, Mirror" which had her version of "I'm Sorry" on the B-side.

FERLIN HUSKEY

He wasn't content to be well-known country performer, he also regularly exorcised the two other personalities who were his alter egos. Ferlin Huskey (he changed his name to the more familiar "Husky" in the late 1950s) was born December 3, 1927, in Flat River, Missouri, although his birthplace is variously given as nearby Hickory Grove or Cantrell. His interest in music came naturally, as this was one of the few diversions available to farm people at the time. Huskey entered show business as a radio personality, eventually working his way to Bakersfield, California. Even then, Bakersfield was a hot bed of country talent, and it attracted the attention of newly formed Capitol Records. In 1951, Huskey began his lengthy association with Capitol by issuing "China Doll." However, for a year, he dismissed his real name in favor of the name "Terry Preston." As Ferlin Huskey, he relegated himself to being part of a duo with Jean Shepherd. Their biggest hit at the time was "Dear John Letter." By 1953, Huskey was issuing records under his own name, that of Preston, and as part of the duo. After having a major hit in 1953 with "Hank's Song," an ode to Hank Williams, he decided to retire Terry Preston. All of this recording activity led to a great demand for Huskey/Preston on the one-night stand circuit that was every country performer's bread-and-butter. To relieve the boredom, he invented another character, Simon Crum, a hay-seed comedian. His characterization was so complete that many people thought they were two separate people. Crum also had a successful recording career on Capitol, beginning with "Cuzz Yore So Sweet" in 1955. Huskey is best known for his lilting rock-a-ballad, "Gone," a song he had recorded years earlier under the Terry Preston name. Under each of his various names, Huskey remained with Capitol until 1972.

APR 7   Johnny Cash, Carl Perkins and Jerry Lee Lewis and Billy Lee Riley and His Little Green Men resume their tour of the Southwest with a show in Abilene, Texas. Tomorrow, the troupe is in Little Rock at the Robinson Auditorium, followed by a show in Winfield, Louisiana (9). (See MAR 31)

On "The Ed Sullivan Show" on CBS-TV, Buddy Knox and Jimmy Bowen, along with the Rhythm Orchids, make an appearance singing "Party Doll" and "I'm Stickin' With You." Also on the show, **Ferlin Huskey** sings "Gone."

EARLY APRIL

Billy Ward requests, and receives, a release from a contract requiring him to bring his Dominos to Zardi's Jazzland nightclub in Hollywood. According to Ward, the place "rocks too much." Ward added that the style of music the Dominos have been singing for the past year has changed. "We aren't a rock and roll group anymore," Ward stated.

New Releases for the second week in April include a cover of the Fats Domino hit—"I'm Walking"—by adolescent television star Ricky Nelson on Verve Records, a company with only jazz experience heretofore. Other releases this week include "Bye, Bye Love" by the Everly Brothers on Cadence; "A Fool In Love" by the Robins on Whippet; Roy Orbison's "Devil Doll" on Sun; and "The Glory of Love" by the Velvetones on Aladdin.

APR 10   Fats Domino, Chuck Berry, and LaVern Baker play the Syria Mosque in Pittsburgh. While on this tour, the same troupe plays the Boston Gardens (13).

Ricky Nelson premiers "I'm Walking" on the weekly ABC-TV show "The Adventures of Ozzie and Harriet," in an episode titled "Ricky the Drummer." Ricky co-stars on the show with his parents and his brother David.

APR 12   Dot Records, a leading independent record company founded by Randy Wood in the back room of his record store in Gallatin, Tennessee, is formally sold to ABC-Paramount. Negotiations had been in the works for six months with numerous rumors that the sale had either been consummated or had fallen through.

In Detroit, Little Esther opens a one-week stand at the Flame Show Bar.

Tommy Ridgely's band plays the Dew Drop Lounge in New Orleans for the next three days.

APR 13   Sanford Clark guests on the "Big D Jamboree" in Dallas.
The Diamonds appear on NBC-TV's "The Perry Como Show."

APR 14   Johnny Cash performs on a Hank Snow revue in Syracuse, New York.

APR 15   Little Richard and his band "rip it up" at the Madison Ballroom in Detroit. Tickets are priced at 75 cents.

Ruth Brown opens a week-long engagement at Washington's Casino Royal.

New Releases for the third week in April include two from Roulette: "Rock Your Little Baby to Sleep" by Buddy Knox and "Warm Up To Me Baby" by Jimmy Bowen. Also new this week are "Jim Dandy Got Married" by LaVern Baker on Atlantic; "Let The Four Winds Blow" by **Roy Brown** on Imperial; "Fabulous" by Charlie Gracie on Cameo; "Baby She's Gone" by Jack Scott on ABC-Paramount; B. B. King's "Troubles, Troubles, Troubles" on Modern; "Looby Doo" by Bobby Byrd on Zephyr; "It Hurts the One You Loves You" by Ray Doggett on Decca; "It's a Groove" by the Five Keys on Capitol; and two versions of "Rosie Lee," by the Mello-Tones on Gee and by the Tunedrops on Gone.

MID-APRIL

Gene Vincent and Eddie Cochran rock the rafters at the Mastbaum Theater in Philadelphia for a week.

APR 17   The Orioles are included on the bill with veteran showman Cab Calloway as he starts a two-month engagement at the Royal Nevada Hotel in Las Vegas.

APR 18   In the midst of savoring what will be the peak of his recording career, Buddy Knox is notified that he has been called to six-months active duty as a Second Lieutenant in the Army Reserves. Roulette Records, Knox's label, reports that there is enough material to keep Knox's voice before the public with a succession of singles and a long-play album.

APR 19   In New York, the Apollo Theater offers a revue featuring Louis Jordan and Little Willie John.

At the Brooklyn Paramount, Alan Freed produces another all-star lineup for Easter Week featuring more than a dozen rock 'n roll acts packed into a sixty-minute show. Included on the bill are the Harptones, Bobby Marchan, the Heartbreakers, Bo Diddley, the Dell-Vikings, Buddy Knox and Jimmy Bowen with the Rhythm Orchids, the Solitaires, the Cellos, Charlie Gracie, the Pearls, and the G-Clefs. The week-long run nets $150,000.

Also in New York City, Lowe's State Theater hosts the week-long "Jocko's Rocketship Show," a rival rock 'n roll festival featuring Mickey and Sylvia, the Clovers, the Diamonds, the Heartbeats, the Paragons, Lewis Lymon and the Teenchords, the Jive Bombers, Jo Ann Campbell, and Ella Johnson with the Buddy Johnson Orchestra.

Big Maybelle, Annie Laurie, and Bubber Johnson's combo are booked into the Dew Drop Hotel and Cafe for the three-day weekend.

Della Reese starts a two-week gig at the Club Rondevoo in Detroit.

ROY BROWN

Roy Brown is acknowledged as a major influence on the early pioneers of rock 'n roll. He was the composer and original singer of "Good Rockin' Tonight." Roy Brown was born September 10, 1925, in New Orleans. He was a child of the church, and was singing in a gospel quartet as a teenager. He moved to Los Angeles after high school and sought a career as a boxer. His plans were thwarted when he turned twenty and won an amateur contest by impersonating Bing Crosby. His initial entry into the entertainment profession was as a ballad singer. He moved to Texas and was working in Galveston when he wrote "Good Rockin' Tonight." At this time, his first records were being issued on Gold Star, apparently without his approval. He was forced to flee Galveston in a hurry, and he arrived in New Orleans with only the clothes on his back—and his composition of "Good Rockin' Tonight." He took the song to Wynonie Harris, who was appearing at the Dew Drop Inn, in hopes of earning a few dollars. Harris was unreceptive, but Brown talked the club into allowing him to do the song as a guest artist. He was an immediate hit. Brown contacted Cecil Gant, a local band leader, who called the owner of DeLuxe Records in New Jersey. Brown ended up singing his song over the telephone. The owner was impressed enough to travel to new Orleans immediately. Brown's recording of "Good Rockin' Tonight" was a hit, and Wynonie Harris soon had his own version in the marketplace. Brown's career ran at full steam for the next dozen years. His hit records on DeLuxe included "Boogie At Midnight" (1949); "Hard Luck Blues" and "Love Don't Love Nobody" (1950); and "Big Town" (1951). By the late 1950s, he was recording for Imperial and having his first "pop" hits with "Party Doll" and "Let the Four Winds Blow." Roy Brown died May 24, 1981, in Los Angeles of a heart attack.

DALE HAWKINS
Dale Hawkins had a knack for picking superlative guitarists. He was born August 22, 1936, in Goldmine, Louisiana. His family soon moved to Bossier City, which lay across the Red River from Shreveport. Dale quit high school at age fifteen to join the Navy at the beginning of the Korean War. When he returned home, he began studies at a local business college but left to work in a record store. In 1956, he recorded a demonstration tape and took it to KWKH radio in Shreveport. Deejays at the station were impressed enough to bring Hawkins and his band to the studio to rerecord the songs. Dale's combo was led by James Burton on guitar. Burton, born August 20, 1942, was staff guitarist on Shreveport's "Louisiana Hayride" broadcast at age fourteen. At KWKH that day, Hawkins and his band recorded "See You Soon, Baboon." The demo was mailed to Chess Records which released it "as is" on their Checker subsidiary. Hawkins followed with his biggest hit, "Susie-Q," featuring Burton's instantly recognizable opening guitar figure. Burton left Hawkins to join Bob Luman's rockabilly band and later became lead guitarist for Ricky Nelson and Elvis Presley. His replacement was Roy Buchanan. Hawkins released a total of fifteen singles on Checker Records through 1961, among the best of which are "My Babe," "La-Do-Da-Da" and "Lonely Nights." He also recorded for Tilt, Zonk, Atlantic, ABC, and Bell. He produced hit records for Dean and Marc on Bullseye and the Five Americans on Abnak. In the late 1970s, it was reported that he was a Baptist minister, but in the 1980s, he was playing rock 'n roll in Little Rock. He was very well received during his 1989 tour of England.

Billed as a "For Lovers Only" rhythm revue, the Dells, Jimmy Reed, Screamin' Jay Hawkins, the Nutmegs, Margie Day, and Andre Williams perform at Washington's Howard Theater for the week.

APR 20   Sun Records' stablemates Carl Perkins, Jerry Lee Lewis and Johnny Cash set off on a tour of western Canada and the northern United States. Appearing with the Sun trio for the first week is Sonny James. Thereafter, Wanda Jackson completes the foursome. Tonight's inaugural show is in Minneapolis, followed by dates in Ontario including Sault Ste. Marie (21), Sudbury (22), Pembroke (23); Ottawa (24), and Fort Francis (26). Back in the States, the troupe performs in Duluth, Minnesota (27); Des Moines, (28); Aberdeen, South Dakota (29); and Moorhead, Minneapolis (30). (See May 1, below.)

On NBC-TV, Pat Boone pays "The Perry Como Show" a visit.

APR 21   Howlin' Wolf brings his exciting brand of blues to the Blue Eagle Ballroom in New Orleans.

Lloyd Price and his R&B orchestra play the Greystone Ballroom in Detroit. Also, sharing the spotlight are Sil Austin, the Diablos, the Don Juans, and the Five Dollars.

APR 22   Little Junior Parker and Bobby "Blue" Bland split the headlining chores as they open for a week at the Melody Ballroom in Detroit.

New Releases for the fourth week in April include "Valley of Tears" by Fats Domino on Imperial; "What Made Maggie Run" by the Dell-Vikings on Dot; "Susie-Q" by **Dale Hawkins** on Checker; "Love Letters In The Sand" by Pat Boone; "Goin' Steady" by Tommy Sands on Capitol; "Start Movin'" by Sal Mineo on Epic; "Guitar Man" by Al Casey on Dot; "Arrow of Love" by the Six Teens on Flip; "Everyone's Laughing" by the Spaniels on Vee-Jay; "Don't Ask Me To Be Lonely" by the Dubs on Gone; "Darling It's Wonderful" by the Lovers on Lamp; Dean Beard's "Rakin' and Scrapin'" on Atlantic; and "Butterfingers" by Tommy Steele, England's top rock 'n roller, on London. The week also sees a pair of reissues of older material: Little Richard's "Maybe I'm Right" on Peacock and "Baby Please Come Home" by Lloyd Price on Specialty.

APR 26   Frankie Lymon and the Teenagers open for two weeks at the Empire Theater in Glasgow, Scotland.

Bill Haley and His Comets are booked for two days in East Liberty, Pennsylvania.

At the Broadway Capitol Theater in Detroit, Faye Adams headlines a show that features the Coasters, Jack Scott, Johnnie and Joe, Amos Milburn, Johnny Janis, and Red Prysock's combo. The show runs through April 28.

Louis Jordan and Little Willie John entertain patrons at the Howard Theater in Washington this week.

APR 28   Bill Haley and His Comets make a guest appearance on "The Ed Sullivan Show" on CBS-TV.
           In New Orleans, the Blue Eagle offers the talented Larry Birdsong for tonight's patrons.

APR 29   The Platters begin a two-weeks at the Palladium in London.

LATE APRIL
Gene Autry, famous motion picture cowboy star, launches Challenge Records. Among the first artists signed to the label are Jerry Wallace, formerly with Mercury, and Dave Burgess, formerly with Tops.

Academy Award winning Hollywood producer Dino DeLaurentiis announces that he has hired Alan Freed to star in a big-budget documentary about the rock 'n roll phenomenon. (No such picture was ever made by DeLaurentiis, and Freed never made a documentary.)

TOP ROCK 'N ROLL RECORDS FOR APRIL 1957

1. All Shook Up/That's When Your Heartaches Begin - Elvis Presley
2. Little Darlin' - The Diamonds
3. I'm Walkin' - Fats Domino
4. Party Doll - Buddy Knox
5. Gone - Ferlin Huskey
6. Butterfly - Charlie Gracie
7. Come Go With Me - The Dell-Vikings
8. Teen-Age Crush - Tommy Sands
9. Gone - Ferlin Huskey
10. I'm Stickin' With You/Ever-Lovin' Fingers - Jimmy Bowen
11. Sittin' in the Balcony - Eddie Cochran
12. School Day - Chuck Berry
13. I'm Sorry/He's Mine - The Platters
14. Young Love - Sonny James
15. Lucille/Send Me Some Lovin' - Little Richard
16. Too Much - Elvis Presley
17. Just Because - Lloyd Price
18. A White Sport Coat - Marty Robbins
19. Love Is Strange - Mickey and Sylvia
20. Little Darlin' - The Gladiolas
21. Sittin' in the Balcony - Johnny Dee
22. Peace in the Valley (EP) - Elvis Presley
23. Empty Arms - Ivory Joe Hunter
24. There Oughta Be A Law - Mickey and Sylvia
25. Jim Dandy - LaVern Baker
26. Bad Boy - The Jive Bombers
27. Lucky Lips - Ruth Brown
28. C. C. Rider - Chuck Willis
29. Next Time You See Me - Little Junior Parker

30. One Step at a Time - Brenda Lee

Also on the "pop" charts:
Why, Baby, Why - Pat Boone
Ninety-Nine Ways - Tab Hunter

The Diamonds

April 1957
ARTISTS OF THE MONTH

THE DIAMONDS

Most books attempting to deal objectively with the history of rock 'n roll would dismiss the Diamonds with little notice, preferring to concentrate only on artists who could be considered true rock 'n rollers. Fans of the Diamonds might have a point when they claim that their group "don't get no respect."

The quartet is usually considered to be of Canadian origin. When they first got together during their high school days in Toronto in the early 1950s, this was true. However, by the time the group began recording, they were equally divided between Canadians and Californians. Dave Sommerville, Mike Douglas, Ted Kowalski, and Bill Reed formed the original group. When Kowalski and Reed left, Californians John Felton and Evan Fisher replaced them.

In the beginning the group practiced several different vocal group styles, including four-part "barbershop" harmony, as well the phrasing made popular by the Four Lads. One of the major recording acts at the time was the Four Aces led by Al Alberts. Dave Sommerville, as the Diamond's lead vocalist, decided against copying Alberts' bombastic delivery, and the Diamonds remained more relaxed in their musical production. The Diamonds followed the usual path in their infancy as a group, performing in local clubs, school functions, church socials, and anywhere they could find an audience.

Along the way, they came to the attention of Coral Records, a subsidiary of Decca. This resulted in two cover records, including "Black Denim Trousers and Motorcycle Boots" (a hit for the Cheers) b/w "Nip Sip" (a Clovers' tune) during the summer of 1955. Neither single sold well enough to convince Coral to retain the group. However, Bill Randle, an influential deejay from Cleveland, liked the group enough to mention their name to an executive at Mercury. The Diamonds soon signed with one of the labels that helped develop the market for "cover" records and knew how to exploit it.

Along with other "pop" acts working during this period, the Diamonds' decision to cover the records of rhythm and blues artists was the result of economic reality: cover records sold very well in many markets where the original versions would not have been acceptable. Among the bigger hits for the Diamonds in 1956 were "Why Do Fools Fall In Love," "Church Bells May Ring," "Love, Love, Love" and "Ka-Ding-Dong," originally recorded by the Teenagers, the Willows, the Clovers, and the G-Clefs, respectively.

Their biggest hit came with a cover of the Gladiolas' "Little Darlin'." The original version came out during the first week in February, 1957. In less than two weeks, the Diamonds had their version on the street. Legend has it that prior to the recording session the group rehearsed the song all night in their hotel room, eventually becoming so fed up that they exaggerated the bass and falsetto parts in an attempt to turn the song into a satire of itself. A quick spin of the Gladiolas' record proves this to be at least partially false. The Gladiolas lead singer, Maurice Williams, invented all the vocal trills and hiccups used by Sommerville. On the other hand, the spoken bridge is not performed by the Gladiolas' bass singer; so, here the Diamonds' John Felton did bring something new to the session. The Diamonds continued covering other artists' records after "Little Darlin'." "Words of Love," a hit for the group in the summer of 1957 actually brought the first royalties of any significance to its writer, Buddy Holly, who's own version sank without a trace. The Diamonds' version of "Silhouettes" by the Rays did very well, but could not outsell the original. By late 1957, the music industry finally began to accept a truth that had been well known to teenagers on the street for two years: original rock 'n roll singles could not be copied by just anyone. Rock n' roll was a form of expression that relied as much on delivery as on lyrics or musical notation. Rock 'n roll singers would soon learn this lesson for themselves. As many of them switched from small independent companies to major labels, their first session usually included an attempt to rerecord their earlier hits by copying the original style.

Foreseeing the future, the Diamonds sought out an original song of their own to record. In the spring of 1957, Chuck Willis' "C. C. Rider" had become the first of a string of rhythm and blues songs based on a dance named the stroll. The Diamonds were approached by veteran songsmith Clyde Otis, who had composed a song based on the new dance with fourteen-year old Nancy Lee. Released in December 1957, "The Stroll" became a huge hit partly as a result of repeated airings on "American Bandstand," ABC-TV's nationally broadcast afternoon show. "The Stroll" was perfect for television because the dance was exuberant and photogenic.

The Diamonds' popularity waned after "The Stroll." They continued issuing singles, some of which were cover tunes. However, by mid-1959, after "She Say (Oom Dooby Doom)," the group's popularity had run its course, and they no longer appealed to teenage record buyers. Two years passed during which time the Diamonds became a popular attraction on the dinner club circuit and in Las Vegas, New York, and Chicago. There was one minor hit single in 1961, a version of the Danleer's 1958 hit, "One Summer Night." Shortly thereafter, the group disbanded.

The members remained in touch, and in 1973, the Diamonds reunited to appear on a television special saluting rock 'n roll pioneers. The success of the show led to sporadic nightclub and casino bookings. In May 1982, the group was playing the Nuggett Casino in Sparks, Nevada, when John Fenton was killed in a private plane crash. Obituaries stated the group was working on their first album in twenty years, although no album was released at this time. In 1989, the Diamonds reformed to join a rock 'n roll tour, of all things, appearing across America with Dion and the Belmonts, the Flamingos, and the Silhouettes.

The Diamonds have taken their share of the blame heaped upon white artists of the 1950s who made their living covering the records of black singers. In retrospect, the group only did what they felt was necessary to succeed in a very difficult business. They didn't invent cover records. In fact, they didn't record as many covers as many other "pop" artists who found greater success.

If the cover records were a scandal, the roots of the practice lay the disparity between the races that was an everyday part of life in many parts of the United States at the time. Segregation within the music business had been around since the advent of recorded sound. By the 1950s, "race" or "sepia" records were forbidden fruit to many white teens, especially those living in areas where a major Negro presence was either lacking or repressed. Like all such temptations, it was only the true fruit itself, not some imitation, that could satisfy the craving. That is why teenagers across the South listened in the middle of the night to clear-channel WLAC from Nashville. The same was true in Texas, where Wolfman Jack broadcast from Del Rio. And, in Los Angeles, it was Art Laboe on XPRS with its transmitter located in Tijuana. Ultimately, rock 'n roll survived cover records to become a stronger music form.

The Diamonds survived, too. In 1987, the group released DIAMONDS ARE FOREVER, an album aimed at the country market. Two singles, "Just A Little Bit" and "Two Kinds of Women" did well enough to be listed on various country charts. Over the years, the original members of the group retired for one reason or another. By the 1990s, the Diamonds consisted of Gary Owens, a member since 1975; Bob Duncan, with the group since 1989; Jerry Siggins, who joined in 1991; and Bill New, who became a Diamond in 1993. They remain a popular draw in casino lounges and nightclubs.

May 1957

MAY 1   The tour featuring Carl Perkins, Jerry Lee Lewis, Wanda Jackson, and Johnny Cash continues across Canada with a performance in Winnipeg. On following nights, the caravan will perform in Saskatoon, Manitoba (2); Calgary (3) and Camrose, Alberta (5); Trail (6) and Cranbrook, British Columbia (7); Lethbridge (8), LaCombe (9) and Edmonton, Alberta (10); Regina, Saskatchewan (11); before returning to the States to play Billings, Montana (12). (See APR 20 and MAY 13.)

MAY 3   The Royal Peacock Cafe in Atlanta books Eddie "Cleanhead" Vinson, Gene and Eunice, and the Cootie Williams combo for the next four days. The entertainers are performing throughout the South, including stops in Tampa, St. Petersburg, and Mobile.

MAY 4   Alan Freed hosts "Rock 'N Roll Revue," his first nationally televised show. Airing from 7:30 - 8:00 p.m., EDT, over the ABC network, the program is devoted to exposing new, as well as established, rock 'n roll and "pop" acts. Featured on each show is Freed's Rock and Roll Orchestra led by Sam "The Man" Taylor. Guests for this inaugural show are Guy Mitchell, Sal Mineo, June Valli, Martha Carson, the Dell-Vikings, the Clovers, and Screamin' Jay Hawkins. The format will be repeated on May 11 as ABC-TV looks to see if there is enough audience appeal to offer the show weekly.

MAY 5   Freddy Bell and the Bell Boys arrive in England. They are booked for twenty-eight shows in thirty-one days. Earlier in the year, the group successfully toured the Philippines and Australia. They were such a hit that offers for a return trip insured they will repeat the tour in the near future.

    Tonight, Lloyd Price makes his first appearance in five years in his hometown of New Orleans with a show at the Labor Union Hall.

MAY 6   Frankie Lymon and the Teenagers start a week-long run at the Globe Theater in Stockton, England.

New Releases for the first week in May include three from Mercury: "My Dream" by the Platters, "Rockin' Is My Business" by Freddy Bell and the Bellboys, and "Ellie Mae" by Louis Jordan. Also new this week are **Eddie Cochran**'s "Mean When I'm Mad" on Liberty; "Hop, Skip and Jump" by the Collins Kids on Columbia; "I Drempt I Was Elvis" by Sonny Cole on Excel; "My Steady Girl" by the Rays on XYZ; "Chicken

EDDIE COCHRAN
Eddie Cochran's influence was far greater than his record sales would indicate. He seemed to always be on the perimeter of someone else's success. He also produced a prodigious output as a session guitarist. Edward Ray Cochran was born October 3, 1938, in Albert Lea, Minnesota. In 1953, Eddie was already an accomplished guitarist when the Cochran family moved to Bell Gardens, a small town southeast of Los Angeles. Here, Eddie met others who shared his passion for music including Conrad "Guybo" Smith, proficient on steel guitar and soon to change to the bass. Smith would back most of Cochran's recordings. In 1954, Eddie met Hank Cochran. The two were not related, but still called themselves the Cochran Brothers. Eddie decided to devote his life to music, and he left school in early 1955 at age sixteen. He and Hank were playing various country barn dances when they met Jerry Capehart, another guitarist, who placed them with Ekko Records. Their first single, "Two Blue Singing Stars," was a tribute to country legends Hank Williams and Jimmie Rodgers. This was followed by two more releases on Ekko. In January 1956, the Cochran Brothers secured a regular spot on the "California Hayride" broadcast from Stockton, but soon Eddie lost interest and returned to Los Angeles, ending the Cochran Brothers team. In 1956, Eddie issued "Skinny Jim," a lone single on Crest Records. It went nowhere, but Cochran was offered a cameo singing part in "The Girl Can't Help It," a big-budget rock 'n roll movie, in which he sang "Twenty Flight Rock," a song without a record label. In 1957, he signed with Liberty Records. His first release, was a cover of Johnny Dee's "Sittin' In The Balcony." (Continued in Nov. 1959.)

Baby Chicken" by Tony Harris on Ebb; "United" by the Lovenotes on Holiday; and Jo Ann Campbell's "Funny Thing" on ElDorado. Also new this week is "The Rock-A-Billy Walk" by Hank and Frank on XYZ. Hank (Bob Crewe) and Frank (Frank Slay), record producers and owners of the XYZ label, would soon work with Danny and the Juniors and the Four Seasons.

EARLY MAY

The Dell-Vikings sign with Mercury Records. Originally, they had recorded for Pittsburgh's Fee-Bee label, with the masters having been leased by Dot Records for national distribution. In a possible attempt to avoid future lawsuits, Mercury alters the group's name to read Del Vikings.

It is reported in the music press that sales of 45 r.p.m. records to juke box operators account for 50-60% of all 45 r.p.m. record sales (both singles and extended plays). Consequently, a juke box hit is virtually guaranteed a top ten slot on the record sales charts.

MAY 9   Bill Haley and His Comets make a nationally televised appearance on "Ray Bolger's Washington Square Show" on NBC at 9:00p.m.

MAY 10   At the Club Rondevou in Detroit, Otis Williams and his Charms open for a week.
The Apollo Theater in New York welcomes the Pearls, the Cellos, Little Jimmy Scott, the Cleftones, Lewis Lymon and the Teenchords, and Clarence "Frogman" Henry.

MAY 11   Bill Haley and His Comets start a three-week string of one-nighters with a show in Mahoney, Pennsylvania.
Alan Freed's second "Rock 'N Roll Revue" airs tonight. The ABC-TV show features Ivory Joe Hunter, LaVern Baker, and Charlie Gracie. (See JUL 12.)

MAY 12   **Junior Parker** and the Buddy Ace orchestra entertain at New Orleans' Blue Eagle tonight.

MAY 13   Johnny Cash, Jerry Lee Lewis and Wanda Jackson join a Sonny James tour running through May 22.
Frankie Lymon and the Teenagers begin a series of one-night stands in and around London.
The Casino Royal in Washington, DC, presents Ivory Joe Hunter for a week.

New Releases for the second week in May include "You Hit the Wrong Note Billy Goat" by Bill Haley and His Comets and "Dynamite" by Brenda Lee, both on Decca; Warren Smith's "So Long, I'm Gone" on Sun; "Get on the Right Track" by Ray Charles and "Hypnotized" by the Drifters, both on Atlantic; "Rock All Nite" by Shirley and Lee on Aladdin; "100 Years From Today" by Alice Jean and the Mondellos on Rhythm; "Any Little

JUNIOR PARKER
"Little" Junior Parker is best known for the rousing blues he recorded for Duke Records beginning in the late 1950s. He is less well known for the rustic songs issued by Sun Records a few years earlier. Herman Parker was born in West Memphis, Arkansas, on March 27, 1933 (also given as March 3, 1927). He idolized Sonny Boy Williamson, and to that end was self-taught on the harmonica. He joined Sonny Boy on tour, and was such a shadow that people thought he was Williamson's son—thus the "Junior" moniker. In Memphis, Parker worked gigs with Bobby Bland, Johnny Ace and B. B. King in a loose-knit group called the Beale Streeters. In 1952, Sam Phillips of Sun Records issued Parker's "Feelin' Good," the first R&B hit for the label. Parker followed with "Mystery Train," the song Elvis jived two years later, by adding elements of Parker's B-side, "Love My Baby." In 1953, Parker toured under Johnny Ace, a Duke Records star, and Parker was wooed by Duke. The move was fortuitous. Sun, once Elvis began recording, virtually closed its blues operation in favor of rockabilly. Duke, on the other hand, was nurturing a stable of blues artists, Ace and Bland included. In 1954, Parker's first Duke record was "Dirty Blues." Five singles and three years later, he released "Next Time Your See Me," his masterpiece. He followed with "Sweet Home Chicago," "Five Long Years," and "Drivin' Wheel," each a classic. In 1962, Duke changed Parker's style, releasing "Annie Get Your Yo-Yo," a shuffle-dance number. Unfortunately for the lovers of the blues, it became Parker's biggest hit. When the dance craze faded, his days as a viable blues man were numbered. He moved on to a succession of labels, Mercury, Blue Rock, Minit, Capitol, having minor hits along the way. Parker passed away November 18, 1971, during surgery in Chicago.

Thing" by Paul Evans on RCA Victor; "Eager Beaver Baby" by Johnny Burnette and "I'm Gonna Sit Right Down and Write Myself a Letter" by Billy Williams, both on Coral; "Run, Run, Little Joe" by the Gladiolas on Excello; Charlie and Ray's "I Love You Madly" on Herald; and two versions of "Johnny's House Party," the original by Johnny Heartsman and the Gaylarks on Music City and a cover by Earl Palmer's Party Rockers with the Jayhawks on Aladdin.

MID-MAY

Featured acts at the Denver convention of the Music Operator's of America includes Mickey and Sylvia and Ivory Joe Hunter.

MAY 16   Tommy Sands begins a two-week engagement at the Roxy Theater in New York City.

MAY 17   Clyde McPhatter fronts the Buddy Johnson band for a week at New York's Apollo Theater. Also on the bill are Ella Johnson, the **Solitaires** and the G-Clefs.

The Coasters, Shirley and Lee, the Cleftones, Bobby Marchan, and Huey Smith star at the Howard Theater in Washington for a week.

In a show heavy on the blues, the Greystone Ballroom in Detroit welcomes Nappy Brown, Big John Greer, Little Willie John, Jimmy Reed, Sil Austin, Big Maybelle, Little Esther, and Annie Laurie.

Also in Detroit, the Queen of the Blues, Miss Billie Holiday, begins a week-long engagement at the Flame Show Bar. Also on the bill as a supporting act is Jackie Wilson.

MAY 18   The "Grand Ole Opry" in Nashville features Johnny Cash. The next night, Cash plays Valdosta, Georgia.

Fats Domino plays a benefit for St. David's Catholic School at the Rosenwald Gymnasium in New Orleans. The show, running from 10:00 p.m. to 2:00 a.m. would appear to be a little too late in the evening for most of the students.

MAY 19   The Dublin Theater Royale welcomes the visiting American act Frankie Lymon and the Teenagers for a week-long stay.

B. B. King brings his show to the Blue Eagle Ballroom in New Orleans.

Tommy Sands (page 144 ➤) sings "Teenage Crush" and "Goin' Steady" on "The Ed Sullivan Show" on CBS-TV.

MAY 20   Joe Turner goes into the Casino Royal in Washington for a week.

New Releases for the third week in May include "Jenny, Jenny" by Little Richard and "Short Fat Fanny" by Larry Williams, both on Specialty; "Whole Lot of Shakin' Going On" by Jerry Lee Lewis on Sun; "Stardust" by Billy Ward and His Dominos on Liberty; "Think" by the

THE SOLITAIRES
The Solitaires rivaled the Dell-Vikings and the Drifters for the number of singers who passed through their ranks. Each of the original Solitaires was in high school when they formed in Harlem in 1953. Winston "Buzzy" Willis, second tenor, joined forces with Bobby Baylor, lead tenor; Nick Anderson, first tenor; Rudy Morgan, baritone; and Pat Gaston, bass. Willis worked part time for a radio station; and, through this connection, the Solitaires were introduced to the owner of Old Town Records. Before it came time to cut their first record, the group was already undergoing personnel changes. Herman Curtis, who had previously recorded with the Vocaleers on Red Robin under the name Curtis Dunham, was brought in to flesh out the group's sound. Also, Bobby Williams and Monte Owens replaced Morgan and Anderson. Their first single, "Wonder Why" b/w "Blue Valentine," was released in February 1954. There were four more singles on Old Town into 1955 before Curtis joined the Air Force. His replacement was Milton Love, who shared lead vocal with Baylor on "The Wedding," the biggest hit for the Solitaires. In 1956, Freddy Barksdale took the place of Gaston, who also joined the Air Force. Williams left about 1956, and he died in 1961. Curtis was back in 1957, but he sang with the group only briefly before choosing to rejoin the Vocaleers. Willis and Baylor went into the Army, and their spots were taken by ex-members of the Fi-Tones, Cecil Holmes and Reggie Barnes. When Milton Love entered the Army in 1961, the Solitaires went into semi-retirement until 1963. At that time, the group consisted of Love, Baylor, Barksdale, and Cathy Miller. For the next two years, the group recorded sporadically under several names with "Fool That I Am" on M-G-M being the only single issued as by the Solitaires.

143

"5" Royales on King; a cover version of "United" by Otis Williams and His Charms on DeLuxe; "Love Charms" by Sanford Clark on Dot; "Rockin' in Baghdad" by Jerry Reed on Capitol; and "What Do You Do?" by the Channels on Whirlin' Disc.

MAY 21   Meridian, Mississippi, presents its annual "Jimmie Rodgers Day" celebration. During the two-day event, Johnny Cash makes an appearance tonight. Carl Perkins and Ronnie Self appear as part of the entertainment tomorrow.

Bill Doggett and his combo open an eight-week tour with a show in Newport News, Virginia.

Gene Vincent appears on the "Ozark Jubilee" broadcast from Springfield, Missouri.

MAY 23   Sonny James, Johnny Cash, Gene Vincent, Jerry Lee Lewis and Wanda Jackson play a two-day benefit for the Police Department in Beaumont, Texas. Shows this day are at 2:30, 7:00 and 9:00. On the 24th, shows are at 7:00 and 9:00. Tickets both days are $.50 and $1.00.

MAY 24   The Howard Theater in Washington presents LaVern Baker, the Heartbeats, Johnnie and Joe, and Red Prysock's band for the week.

MAY 25   Fats Domino makes an appearance on "The Perry Como" show on NBC-TV.

Jerry Lee Lewis, Johnny Cash and Wanda Jackson share headliner duties on the "Big D Jamboree" in Dallas.

Gene Vincent joins Sonny James, Ferlin Husky, Bobby Helms, and Bobby Lord for a show at the Topeka Municipal Hall. (See MAY 30.)

MAY 26   Chuck Willis "strolls" in to the Labor Union Hall in New Orleans.

MAY 27   The Drifters open a week-long run at the Casino Royal in Washington.

A 10% federal tax on reels of blank tape is proposed in the United States House Ways and Means Committee. This tax would seek to curb the rise in home tape-recording of records. (See JUN 20.)

New Releases for the fourth week in May include "To the Aisle" by the Five Satins on Ember; "Mr. Lee" by the Bobbettes on Atlantic; "Diana" by Paul Anka on ABC-Paramount; "Words of Love" by the Diamonds on Mercury; "Eighteen" by Connie Francis on M-G-M; Johnny Dee's "Teenage Queen" on Colonial; "Cupid" by Frankie Avalon on Chancellor; "Angels Cried" by the Isley Brothers on Teenage; "High Voltage" by Bobby Lord on Columbia; "Is Your Love For Real" by the Midnighters on Federal; "My Girl Friend" by the Cadillacs on Josie; and "Old Time Rock and

TOMMY SANDS

Tommy Sands seemed driven to be a star. While he succeeded on various levels, he was always one step away from obscurity. He was born August 27, 1937, in Chicago. His parents were both professional musicians, so it came naturally for Tommy to lean toward performing. By age nine, he was working on WBKB radio's "Barn Dance." When his family moved to Houston, Tommy landed a local radio show. Then he discovered acting. When he was sixteen, he joined a musical production that ended up on Broadway in New York. After high school, he moved to Hollywood where he hoped to break into movies. To augment his income, he auditioned for "Hometown Jamboree," a Los Angeles TV show. This led to an RCA Victor recording contract and guest appearances on Tennessee Ernie Ford's national TV show. For a time, he was managed by Colonel Tom Parker, until Parker spotted Elvis Presley. Sands was not convincing as a country act, and he might have faded into obscurity if Colonel Parker had not suggested Sands for the role in an NBC-TV teleplay titled "The Singing Idol" which Elvis had passed on. The show was telecast January 30, 1957, and Sands' career as a "pop-rock" singer was launched. He signed with Capitol Records, and "Teenage Crush" sold a quick million copies by riding on Sands' TV coat tails. However, his next two singles, "Ring-A-Ding-A-Ding" and "Goin' Steady," reflect Capitol's lack of understanding of rock 'n roll. Sands' next two releases failed to chart, and it looked like his recording career was doomed again. Then came the movie version of "The Singing Idol," titled "Sing, Boy, Sing." The film's wide exposure generated new record sales; and, more important, it opened the door for Sands' brief movie career. In 1967, he left show business and moved to Hawaii where he opened a nightclub.

Roll" by Champion Jack Dupree on Vik.

MAY 29   The Royal Jokers start a week at the Club Rondevoo in Detroit.

MAY 30   Johnny Cash opens a tour of western states with a show in Clovis, New Mexico. The next night he plays San Diego. (See JUN 1.)

Gene Vincent, Sonny James, Ferlin Husky, and Bobby Lord appear for "Decoration Day" activities in Kansas City.

MAY 31   Joe Turner, the Moonglows, Do Diddley, and Choker Campbell's band entertain the crowd at Washington's Howard Theater this week.

THE TOP ROCK 'N ROLL RECORDS FOR MAY 1957

1. All Shook Up/That's When Your Heartaches Begin - Elvis Presley
2. Little Darlin' - The Diamonds
3. Gone - Ferlin Huskey
4. School Day - Chuck Berry
5. Come Go With Me - The Dell-Vikings
6. A White Sport Coat - Marty Robbins
7. Party Doll - Buddy Knox
8. I'm Walkin' - Fats Domino
9. I'm Sorry/He's Mine - The Platters
10. I'm Stickin' With You - Jimmy Bowen
11. Butterfly - Charlie Gracie
12. Searchin'/Young Blood - The Coasters
13. A Teenager's Romance/I'm Walking - Ricky Nelson
14. C. C. Rider - Chuck Willis
15. Lucille/ Send Me Some Lovin' - Little Richard
16. Fabulous - Charlie Gracie
17. Ring-A-Ding-Ding/My Love Song - Tommy Sands
18. Empty Arms - Ivory Joe Hunter
19. Sittin' In The Balcony - Eddie Cochran
20. Goin' Steady - Tommy Sands
21. Just Because - Lloyd Price
22. Teen-Age Crush - Tommy Sands
23. Start Movin' - Sal Mineo
24. Bye Bye Love - The Everly Brothers
25. Peace In The Valley (EP) - Elvis Presley
26. Valley of Tears/It's You I Love - Fats Domino
27. Over The Mountain, Across the Sea - Johnnie and Joe
28. Little Darlin' - The Gladiolas
29. Rock Your Little Baby to Sleep - Buddy Knox
30. Rosie Lee - The Mello-Tones
31. Sittin' In The Balcony - Johnny Dee

32. There Oughta Be a Law - Mickey and Sylvia
33. Just To Hold My Hand - Clyde McPhatter
34. Young Love - Sonny James
35. Next Time You See Me - Little Junior Parker

Also on the "pop" charts:
Love Letters In The Sand - Pat Boone
Four Walls - Jim Reeves
Freight Train - Charles McDevitt Skiffle Group

May 1957
ARTIST OF THE MONTH

THE DELL-VIKINGS

The Dell-Vikings were one of the first rhythm and blues vocal groups to completely grasp the style of rock 'n roll. In doing so, they incorporated and homogenized both musical forms without diluting either.

The original group members were joined by a strong bond: the United States Air Force. In 1955, the five men, who shared a love for R&B group harmony, were stationed at the Air Force installation at the Pittsburgh airport in nearby Carapolis. They sang together in every spare moment, and with their practice came the desire to hear for themselves what they sounded like.

In October 1956, the quintet consisted of Norman Wright (born October 21, 1937), lead tenor ; Corinthian "Kripp" Johnson, first tenor; Don Jackson, second tenor; Clarence Quick, bass; and Dave Lerchey, baritone. During a rehearsal, this group recorded nine acappella songs in the basement of a local deejay and music entrepreneur, Barry Kaye. Listening to the playback, they agreed that the sound was "close." Their style was "coming around." All they needed was "a little more work." At this time no one thought that anything more would come of the tape.

Three months later, the group was in downtown Pittsburgh's Sheraton Hotel in a makeshift studio set up by Fee-Bee Records, a small local label owned by Joe Auerbach. They had recruited a pickup band of Air Force buddies featuring Joe Lopes on guitar, Gene Upshaw on sax, and someone, remembered only by the name Peoples, on drums. From this session, they were able to successfully record "Baby, Let Me Know," "Come Go With Me," "True Love" "When I Come Home," "Don't Be a Fool" and "Watching the Moon." Their first Fee-Bee release came in the fall of 1956 as "True Love" and "Baby, Let Me Know" were pared as the second record released by Fee-Bee. "True Love" was a typical R&B ballad of the day and clearly shows that the Dell-Vikings had worked hard during their rehearsals.

In early December, "True Love" began to receive local airplay, prompting Auerbach to re-release the song with a stronger B-side. During the second week of January 1957, the retitled "How Can I Find True

Love?" was issued back-to-back with "Come Go With Me." It took almost no time before deejays flipped the single and discovered a snappy number that caught their attention. Popularity for "Come Go With Me" began to spread. First in Pittsburgh, then in Youngstown, then in Cleveland.

Facing orders for records that he could not afford to have pressed, Auerbach went looking for a distributor of his hit-in-the-making. Within three weeks, a deal with Dot Records had been struck. Auerbach was allowed to release small quantities of subsequent releases on the Fee-Bee label for local distribution while national sales of records by the Dell-Vikings would be on the Dot label. The Dot release of "Come Go With Me" came during the first week in February. Demand for the record by this time was so strong that it jumped onto the music charts across the nation within a week.

"Come Go With Me" is a classic "feel good" rock n' roll song. A close listen reveals that there's a lot going on between the grooves. Norman Wright's opening "Dom dom dom" is sharply delivered. The vocal group crackles with verve. Clarence Quick's bass vocal rolls along while the rest of the group glides easily in the middle of the mix. The delivery by the entire group is energetic and the feeling is spontaneous. Upshaw's sax solo in the middle of the record is exciting, actually bordering on hysteria as the group cheers the player on with shouts and hand claps. This is one finger-snapping, dance-to-the-music, good-time record.

There was always a sense of urgency surrounding the Dell-Vikings due to the transitory nature of their employment. As if to underscore this aspect of the group, Don Jackson was shipped off to Germany prior to the group's second Fee-Bee session, and he was replaced by Donald Edgar "Gus" Backus. Backus (born September 12, 1937) may have worked with the group for a short time prior to their first Fee-Bee session, and he later claimed to have sung lead on "Come Go With Me." One source lists him as a cofounder of the group in 1955.

In March, Fee-Bee rushed the group into a full-sized studio in Ohio where they recorded about a dozen songs. Fee-Bee released "Maggie," which featured a fine lead by Joey Briscoe, a Pittsburgh country singer who would later become a permanent part of the group. The flip side, "Down in Bermuda" seems to have been lost in the shuffle between Fee-Bee and Dot as it never appeared on a Dot single.

In Mid-April, Alan Freed invited the Dell-Vikings to appear at his annual Easter-week revue at the Brooklyn Paramount. A week later, the retitled "What Made Maggie Run?" was issued as the group's second single on Dot. For unknown reasons, it failed to attract airplay or sales.

From this point on, the personnel connected with the Dell-Vikings underwent such a variety of transitions that only the dedicated will be able to follow.

First, Mercury Records made a play for the group. Mercury had discovered that when the group signed their exclusive recording contract with Fee-Bee, only Kripp Johnson was over twenty-one; the others were under age. This meant that when Fee-Bee negotiated its contract with Dot, only Johnson was legally bound to the contract. The remaining members were under no obligation, to either Fee-Bee or Dot. Jumping at the chance for more money, the younger Dell-Vikings signed with Mercury in May. It took until October before Mercury and Dot settled their legal disputes with Fee Bee. Under the final agreement, Fee Bee retained management rights to the group through December 1, 1957, after which Mercury gained all legal rights to the group's name.

Mercury didn't wait until December before altering their group's name to read "Del Vikings." On Mercury, the group initially consisted of Norman Wright, Dave Lerchey, Clarence Quick, Billy Blakeley (who replaced Johnson), and Gus Backus. As a result of this maneuvering, Mercury's Del Vikings and Dot's Dell-Vikings had singles released the same week in June. "Cool Shake," on Mercury, featured Gus Backus singing over a rhythmic instrumental and vocal backing. The single sold moderately well and encouraged Mercury to record a full album of Del Vikings' material. "Whispering Bells," the group's latest release on Fee-Bee, became their third on Dot. Like "Come Go With Me," "Whispering Bells" was something wildly exciting.

"Whispering Bells" takes off like a rocket. There is a growling sax intro for one chorus. Then the sax is joined by Lopes' stinging guitar and those slapping hand-claps again for the second chorus. Quick's fine bass voice jumps in with "Ding, da-da-da-Ding" while the group answers back. By the time the record gets to Kripp Johnson's lead vocal, he is even more wound up than Norman Wright was on "Come Go With Me." The sax break and the hand claps return for a brief interlude before the whole thing careens off into the night. It was a song that could raise goose-bumps if you listened too close. It was that good!

Back at Fee-Bee, Johnson recorded "I'm Spinning" with a studio vocal group. The record came out on Dot in October listing Kripp Johnson and the Dell-Vikings as the artists. Mercury sued and won exclusive rights to the name of the group, no matter how it was spelled. There were no further singles by the Dell-Vikings on Dot. Fee-Bee churned out a few more singles, including "Willette," but none left a mark. (Interestingly, the studio group recording behind Johnson at this time went on to minor R&B fame as the Versatiles.)

During these various personnel changes, Chuck Jackson sang with the group, replacing Dan Lerchey who was transferred to Germany. Jackson would go on to become a soul star in the 1960s. Jackson has stated variously that he was the baritone on "Come Go With Me" (which he wasn't), that he joined the group on stage before "Whispering Blues" (which he might have), and that his first session was his duet with Johnson on "Willette" (which is likely). Jackson remained with the group for two years. Kripp Johnson recalled Jackson as a member of the group he used on tours during the time of the Dot-Mercury split.

In July 1957, it was reported that ElDorado Records was set to release an album of nine songs by the Dell-Vikings that were outside the Fee-Bee/Dot agreement. The basement tapes had surfaced! What became of ElDorado's album is just one of the unanswered questions concerning the Dell-Vikings. The material was eventually overdubbed with instruments and released by Buchanan and Goodman on their Luniverse label using some of their profits from "The Flying Saucer" and that single's various offspring. Luniverse also released two singles in 1957 including

"Somewhere Over The Rainbow." In short order, Luniverse was sued by Dot and all their product was pulled off the market.

Maybe the public had become saturated. After all, there were records being issued on four labels by three groups of Dell-Vikings. They did have three hit singles on the charts in August 1957. No singer before Elvis had ever done that. No one would do it again until the Beatles in 1964. However, there would be no more hits for either group of Dell-Vikings after that. The group made another appearance with Alan Freed's week-long Labor Day revue at the Brooklyn Paramount in September. Shortly thereafter they filmed a cameo performance in the movie "The Big Beat," which was released in February 1958.

By November, the Air Force had shipped Backus to Germany and his place in the Del Vikings was taken by Joey Briscoe. That same month saw another release by Kripp Johnson on Dot, "Woke Up This Morning." This time the record listed no backing vocal group.

On Mercury, the Del Vikings recorded a fine, up-tempo version of "Sunday Kind of Love" featuring Norman Wright. In June 1958, after his contract with Fee-Bee and Dot expired, Kripp Johnson joined his friends on Mercury. Together, they covered "You Cheated" in the fall of 1958. Unfortunately, the Shields' version was racing up the charts, battling the original by the Slades for the public's attention. The Shields won, and the Slades came in second. The Del Vikings didn't get out of the gate. Johnson appeared on several later Mercury singles, including "Flat Tire," a novelty which was the group's final release on Mercury in November 1958. But by this time, as Norman Wright said recently in an interview, "the whole thing (with Mercury) was becoming a circus."

After a total of eight singles and two albums, the group left Mercury. They resurfaced more than a year later on the small Alpine label. The association was short lived and only one single, "Pistol Packin' Mama," was released. The last remaining members of the original Pittsburgh quintet quietly dispersed shortly thereafter.

Kripp Johnson remained on Mercury as a solo artist, issuing several singles including "A Door Is Open," released in July 1959. However, the production staff was used to working with Brook Benton at this time, and Johnson's singles are layered with heavenly choirs, brass bands and fiddle sections. Each quickly went on to "record heaven" without so much as a whimper.

Finally departing Mercury himself, Johnson gathered some acquaintances to form a new set of Dell-Vikings, and they recorded five singles for ABC-Paramount between 1961 and 1963. One of these, "Bring Back Your Heart," did well enough to get the group an invitation to appear on "American Bandstand." Times were rapidly changing, and the group found itself relegated to appearances at college fraternity parties in the South. One final single, "I've Got To Know," was issued in 1964 by the otherwise obscure Gateway Records. After that, Johnson threw in the towel.

One other single of otherwise unknown origin appeared during the 1960s. "Understand" b/w "It's Too Late" was issued on the Eedee label by a group listed as Buddy Carle and the Del Vikings.

Gus Backus enjoyed his tour of duty in Germany so much that he remained in Europe afterward where he fronted several sets using the Dell-Vikings' name. Norman Wright and Clarence Quick got together as the Del Vikings for an oldies revival concert in New York in the early 1970s, then Quick tried for a time to keep the group's name alive on the night club circuit. This was apparently the group that issued one single on Sceptor Records in 1972.

Then, for eighteen years, the Dell-Vikings remained close to their various homes. There were families to raise and jobs to work. Gus Backus spent the time working in the oil fields of Mexico. Several weekends each year, other members of the Dell-Vikings got together to perform in small clubs just like they did back in 1956. In the 1980s, Backus surfaced in Germany where he was attempting to restart his career.

In early 1990, Kripp Johnson and Norman Wright were appearing as the Del Vikings with Ritzy Lee (who said he had been with the group since 1958) and John Bias, who joined in 1965.

The two most recent releases from groups calling themselves the Del Vikings are an album of rerecorded songs titled THE DEL VIKINGS GREATEST HITS that appeared on Jango about 1990. In 1991, ROCK AND ROLL REMEMBERED was issued by the group on BVM Records.

Kripp Johnson passed away at his home in Pontiac, Michigan, in June 1990, after losing a nine-month fight with cancer. At the time of his death, he was performing with a group of Dell-Vikings. His final appearance had come that April before the South Florida Group Harmony Association. Johnson and the group received a standing ovation.

So far, this biography has not mentioned the fact that the Dell-Vikings were widely regarded as the first racially integrated vocal group. Maybe that's just as well. The Dell-Vikings never thought too much about it. They were having too much fun to involve themselves in that political tree-shaker.

June 1957

JUN 1   Fats Domino starts a week-long tour through the Rocky Mountain States with a show in Amarillo. Consecutive nights find the Fat Man in Pueblo, Denver, Albuquerque, Tucson, and Phoenix. Since the "Greatest Show of 1957" tour wound up in May, he has vacationed in his home of New Orleans where he appeared for a week at the Safari Room.

Johnny Cash continues his tour of California with a show in Los Angeles. Succeeding days find him performing in Ventura (2), Tulare (3), Porterville (4), San Jose (5), Pomona (6), Salinas (7), and Oakland (8).

NBC-TV broadcasts a special, "Five Stars for Springtime." Ricky Nelson is one of the stars highlighted.

JUN 2   Bill Haley and His Comets complete their three-week tour with a show tonight in Angola, Indiana.

On television tonight, NBC's "The Steve Allen Show" welcomes the Diamonds.

JUN 3   The Eddie Vinson, Gene and Eunice, Cootie Williams troupe winds up their southern tour with a week at the Palm Club in Hallendale, Florida.

New Releases for the first week in June include three from Decca's subsidiary, Brunswick: "That'll Be The Day" by the Crickets, "Ten Little Women" by Terry Noland, and "Watch Your Step" by Chuck and Bill. Other releases this week include "Happy, Happy Birthday, Baby" by the **Tune Weavers** on Casa Grande; "I'm the One" by Jimmy McCracklin on Irma; "Uh-Uh Honey" by the Lane Brothers on RCA Victor; "Blue Jean Baby" by Jerry Wallace on Challenge; "Love Roller Coaster" by Joe Turner on Atlantic; and "The Sun Is Shining" by Jimmy Reed on Vee-Jay. Also out this week is Elvis Presley's latest single, "Loving You" b/w "Teddy Bear" from RCA Victor.

JUN 3   Dinah Washington opens a week-long engagement at Pep's in Philadelphia.

JUN 6   Frankie Lymon and the Teenagers start another week's engagement on their tour of the British Isles. This week, they play Coventry, England.

JUN 7   LaVern Baker headlines the rhythm and blues revue at New York's Apollo theater for a week. Also in the spotlight are the Heart-

THE TUNE WEAVERS
The Tune Weavers were one of the rare brother-sister acts in rock 'n roll. Margo and Gilbert Lopez, from Boston, decided to form a vocal group with the help of Margo's husband, John Sylvia, and a cousin, Charlotte Davis. Originally they called themselves the Tone Weavers, but changed their name after an emcee mistakenly introduced them as the Tune Weavers. Their first recording session yielded "Happy, Happy Birthday Baby," a song composed by Margo and Gilbert. It was released first on the small Casa Grande label, but when it began to break in Philadelphia, the song was leased to Chess Records, which issued it on its Checker subsidiary. "Happy, Happy Birthday Baby" featured Margo's pleading soprano and was tailor-made for the teen audience. For reasons which are unclear, Checker took "Ol Man River," the B-side of the hit, and released it as the Tune Weaver's next single by adding an unrelated instrumental on the flip side. This ploy infuriated the Tune Weavers and the owners of Casa Grande. Consequently, none of the remaining Casa Grande singles appeared on Checker. "I Remember Dear" b/w "Pamela Jean," their second Casa Grande release, was a fine recording, but the lack of national distribution caused the single to disappear with barely a trace. The same was true of "I'm Cold" the final Casa Grande single. The group soon returned to less glamorous pursuits in Boston. In 1962, Checker did release one final single by the group, "Your Skies of Blue" b/w "Congratulations on Your Wedding." Just why they waited five years is unknown. Margo continued as a solo performer, but with limited success. She was living in San Diego in 1991 when she died of a heart attack at age fifty-five. At the time of her death, she was booked to perform on a tour billed as "The Golden Voices of Rock and Roll."

CLARENCE BROWN
Clarence "Gatemouth" Brown, the legendary Texas bluesman was born in Vinton, Louisiana, April 18, 1924. "Gate," as he is affectionately known—the nickname coming from the gaps between his front teeth—was a major influence on blues guitarists from his earliest recording, 1947's "Gatemouth Boogie" on Aladdin. His Texas roots began when he was only a week old, and his family left Vinton and moved twelve miles west, to the town of Orange, Texas. He was taught to play guitar and violin by his father, Clarence, Sr. As young Clarence matured, he was inundated with the musical styles of the area, especially Cajun and western swing. He served in the Army Air Corps during World War II, and upon returning to Orange, decided to earn his living in music. He started his first band in 1945. Two years later, he was discovered by Don Robey, owner of the Bronze Peacock Club in nearby Houston. Through Robey, Brown was signed to Aladdin Records. His two Aladdin releases failed to attract widespread attention, and he returned to Houston disappointed. By early 1949, Robey had started his own record company, Peacock, and he put Brown on the roster. Gate's third Peacock release, "Mary Is Fine," became his biggest selling record. Over the next fifteen years, dozens of singles by Brown were issued on Peacock and other labels owned by Robey. Brown never earned royalties from his records and supported himself by constantly touring through Texas, Oklahoma and Louisiana. His legendary status began to spread after he left Peacock and was able to perform something other than the blues. His later recordings are an eclectic mixture of country, jazz, and bossa nova, as well as the blues, and he often combined his unique guitar and fiddle styles. Today, "Gate" is a mainstay on the Blues Festival circuit.

beats, Johnnie and Joe, Johnny Mathis, the Coasters, and Red Prysock's band.

Chuck Berry plays Schenectady, New York, with Jo Ann Campbell and Louis Lymon and the Teenchords.

Ruth Brown, the Five Keys, the Pearls, and Johnny Heartsman headline the Howard Theater revue in Washington this week.

B. B. King romps through the first night of a week-long stay at the Flame Show Bar in Detroit.

EARLY JUNE

Johnny Moore, lead vocalist of the Drifters, is drafted into the Army. His place in the group is taken over by Bobby Hendricks, formerly lead vocalist of the Flyers.

JUN 8   Louis Jordan guests on Jackie Gleason's CBS-TV show seen on the East Coast from 8:00 to 9:00 p.m.

JUN 9   Fats Domino arrives on the West Coast for a series of one-nighters. He is scheduled to stay on the West Coast through mid-July.

Johnny Cash makes a special appearance in St. Louis to open Ryon's Park.

In New Orleans, Clarence "Gatemouth" Brown with Tommy Ridgely's orchestra plays the grand opening of the San Souci Ballroom at 2832 LaSalle, next door to the Dew Drop Hotel and Cafe. Both establishments are owned by Frank Painia.

Also in New Orleans, Huey Smith and the Clowns with Professor Longhair entertain at the Labor Union Hall.

JUN 10 The Platters play a sold-out show in California's Oakland Auditorium.

Connie Francis co-stars behind the Kirby Stone Four this week at Washington's Casino Royal.

New Releases for the second week in June include two from the Dell-Vikings: "Whispering Bells" on Dot and "Cool Shake" b/w "Jitterbug Mary" on Mercury. Also new this week are "I Found a Million Dollar Baby," Bobby Darin's first single on Atco; "Everybody's Been Rockin' My Baby" by Rod Willis on Chic; "Please Send Me Someone to Love" by the Moonglows on Chess; "Rockin' Pneumonia and the Boogie Woogie Flu" by Huey Smith and His Clowns on Ace; and "Gloria" by Dee Clark on Falcon. Also out this week is Ray Vernon's "Evil Angel" on Cameo. His real name is Vernon Wray and he is the brother of Link Wray.

JUN 11 On tour in Canada, Gene Vincent and His Blue Caps play the Trianon Ballroom in Regina, Saskatchewan. Other performers include Sonny James, Bobby Lord, and Bobby Helms. In two shows, the troupe brings in 1,445 fans for a net of $2,900.

Clarence "Gatemouth" Brown starts the first of two weekend stands at the lounge of the Dew Drop Hotel.

JUN 12   Chuck Berry and LaVern Baker share the bill for the week at Wildwood-by-the-Sea, New Jersey.

The Tomato Festival in Warren, Arkansas, plays host to Jerry Lee Lewis, Onie Wheeler, and Johnny Cash.

Bandleader Jimmy Dorsey dies after a two-month illness. He was 53. At the time of his death, his recording of "So Rare" was near the top of all the "pop" record charts.

JUN 14   The "Fantabulous Rock and Roll Show of 1957" takes to the road for five weeks. The headliner is Ruth Brown. Also on the bill are the Coasters, Bo Diddley, the Five Satins, the Drifters, the Schoolboys, and Smiley Lewis. Opening night finds the troupe in Charlotte, North Carolina. Other cities already set include Knoxville, Birmingham, Louisville, Chattanooga, Greenville and Kinston, North Carolina.

Jackie Wilson is back at the Flame Show Bar in Detroit. He will appear for two weeks as a supporting act.

At the Apollo Theater for a week are Faye Adams, the Jive Bombers and the Heartbreakers.

JUN 15   Johnny Cash and Carl Perkins return to the "Big D Jamboree" in Dallas. The following week, Perkins and Roy Orbison are reported to be playing dates in the New Mexico area.

The Platters top a long list of entertainers at a Los Angeles benefit for teens at the Moroccan Theater. Others on the show are Roy Brown, the Velvetones, and the Planets.

MID-JUNE

It is announced that Otis Blackwell, composer of such rock 'n roll hits as "All Shook Up," and "Don't Be Cruel" has signed as musical director for a new motion picture, "The Hit Record." Production is slated to begin in Hollywood on July 22. Talent signed at this time includes Fats Domino, Little Richard, Carl Perkins, Charlie Gracie, Buddy Knox, Jimmy Bowen, Jodie Sands, and Lewis Lymon and the Teenchords. By the time of its release, later in 1957, the title of the film had been changed to "Jamboree" (and was also known as "Disc Jockey Jamboree"). Jerry Lee Lewis is added to the roster of entertainers at the last minute. Also, originally scheduled to have a cameo, but not appearing in the final cut of the film, is Jackie Lee.

JUN 16   Tonight is one of the busiest for rock 'n roll fans in New Orleans in recent memory. Huey Smith and the Clowns tear it up at the new San Souci Ballroom in New Orleans while Howlin' Wolf wails at the moon at the Blue Eagle Ballroom and Shirley and Lee rock the crowd at the Labor Union Hall.

JUN 17   Bill Haley and His Comets take their act to the heart of calypso country, Kingston, Jamaica, as they start a short tour.

In California, Fats Domino starts a tour that will lead from

THE FLAMINGOS
One of the best-loved "oldies" from the 1950s is "I Only Have Eyes For You" by the Flamingos. Zeke Carey (born in Bloomfield, West Virginia) was living in Gary, Indiana, and he often visited his cousin Jacob Carey in nearby Chicago. Through his local church Zeke also met Johnny Carter and Paul Wilson. The four young men shared an enthusiasm for other R&B vocal groups, especially Sonny Til of the Orioles. Soon after the boys began to practice, Sollie McElroy joined to sing lead. In 1953, the Flamingos signed with Chicago's Chance Records. Their first single, "If I Can't Have You," released in March 1953, did well in the Great Lakes area; and it was followed by "That's My Desire" and "Golden Teardrops." In 1955, after six singles on Chance, the group switched to Parrot Records, another small Chicago label, where they released three singles. In 1955, Nate Nelson joined, replacing McElroy. After suffering through the lack of national distribution by Chance and Parrot, the group signed with Checker Records, yet another Chicago label, but one able to promote records coast to coast. Their third Checker single, "I'll Be Home" became their first national R&B hit. Shortly thereafter, Zeke Carey and Johnny Carter were drafted and Tommy Hunt was added as the group became a quartet. When Zeke returned from the Army in 1958, he found the Flamingos' business dealings in a shambles. He was able to get the group released from its Checker contract, and they signed with George Goildner's End label. Their first release under the new contract was "Lovers Never Say Goodbye," their biggest selling single to date. Two singles followed before "I Only Have Eyes For You" was released in April 1959. It was a major hit in the R&B and "pop" markets through the summer of 1959. Over the next three years, the Flamingos had seven more hit singles and two best selling albums.

Bakersfield (tonight) to San Francisco. On the way, he will play Anderson (17), Tulare (18), Fresno (19), San Jose (20), Oakland (21), Sacramento (22), and the New Filmore Auditorium in San Francisco (23). The biggest night on this leg of the tour is in Sacramento where a single performance at the Memorial Auditorium brings in $8,175. The show in Fresno grosses $7,775, breaking the old house record. Other dates on the Domino schedule include Salem and Coquille, Oregon. In thirty days, Fats Domino rakes in $104,000.

Steve Gibson and His Red Caps open a week-long run at Washington's Casino Royal.

New Releases for the third week in June include "Love Will Make You Fail In School" by Mickey and Sylvia on Vik; "Silver Bracelet" by Ray Stevens on Prep; "Words of Love" by Buddy Holly on Coral; "Sick and Tired" by Chris Kenner on Imperial; the Charts' "Deserie" on Everlast; "This I Promise You" by the Five Keys on Capitol; "Let's Get Wild" by Rudy "Tutti" Grazell on Mercury; and Dion and the Timberlanes' "The Chosen Few" on Mohawk.

JUN 19   Tommy Leonetti opens a weekend engagement at Pittsburgh's Club Copa. He remains there until June 23.

JUN 20   The House of Representatives passes a bill levying a 10% tax on tape and wire recorders, players, and recorder-players. Previously, phonographs had been subject to the same tax.

JUN 21   Chicago's Opera House hosts a two-day rock 'n roll show that brings in $16,000. Headlining is Tab Hunter, who is making his stage singing debut. Reportedly, Hunter is so nervous that he is forced to deliver "Young Love" while seated in a chair. Show-stoppers include Charlie Gracie, Chuck Berry, and Eddie Cochran, but the night is stolen by the Everly Brothers, displaying an ease and professionalism that prompts one reviewer to write that they "strolled out to the mike so casually, like they had their shoes off."

Della Reese is at the Club Rondevoo in Detroit for the week.

In Washington, Solomon Burke, the Sensations, the **Flamingos**, and the Spaniels are featured at the Howard Theater for a week.

JUN 22   Jerry Lee Lewis makes an appearance on the "Big D Jamboree" in Dallas.

New Releases for the fourth week in June include a bevy of frantic rhythm singles: "Say So" by Mac Curtis on King; Dickie Lee's "Stay True Baby" on Tampa; "Drag Strip Baby" by Little Norman on Decca; "Kiss-a Me Baby" by Narvel Felts on Mercury; Marvin Rainwater's "My Brand of Blues" on M-G-M; "King Kong" by Big "T" Tyler on Aladdin; and "Hot Rod Queen" by Roy Tan on Dot. Other releases new this week include "Cherry" by Clarence "Bad Boy" Palmer on Savoy; "What'cha Gonna

Do?" by Tommy Ridgely on Herald; "Quit My Baby" by B. B. King on Modern; Sonny Knight's "Lovesick Blues" on Dot; and "Oh, Baby Doll" by Chuck Berry on Chess. Finally, certain to bring another round of lawsuits, comes "Flying Saucer, the 2nd" by Buchanan and Goodman on Luniverse, featuring snips of current hits by Elvis, the Everly Brothers, Marty Robbins, the Dell-Vikings, the Coasters, and others.

JUN 27 Bill Haley and his Comets appear in Baltimore at the Coliseum.

JUN 28 "Dr. Jive's Rhythm and Blues Revue" opens at the Apollo Theater in New York for the week. Headliners are newcomers Donnie Elbert, Ann Cole, the **Bobbettes**, and the Velours, as well as the Sensations, Charlie and Ray, the Jesters, the Heartbeats, and the Charts. Accompaniment is provided by Roy Brown and his combo.
Faye Adams is welcomed by this week's patrons at Detroit's Flame Show Bar.

JUN 29 Bill Haley and his Comets play an outdoor show in Bridgeport, Connecticut, sharing the bill with jazz great Lionel Hampton.

JUN 30 "The Ed Sullivan Show" welcomes the Everly Brothers. Also on tonight's bill is the Charles McDevitt Skiffle Group performing "Freight Train." The group is composed of McDevitt on guitar, Nancy Whiskey on vocals, and Mark Sharatt on washboard. Skiffle is a form of English folk music with a pronounced shuffle beat.

LATE JUNE
The summer season on the shores of Wildwood, New Jersey, bring a few rock 'n rollers into the clubs. Featured performers include Charlie Gracie, Sarah Vaughan, and George Hamilton IV at the Sea Isle Casino and Gloria Mann at the Shelter Haven Hotel.

THE TOP ROCK 'N ROLL HITS FOR JUNE 1957

1. All Shook Up - Elvis Presley
2. Bye Bye Love - The Everly Brothers
3. White Sport Coat - Marty Robbins
4. Searchin'/Young Blood - The Coasters
5. Little Darlin' - The Diamonds
6. A Teenager's Romance/I'm Walking - Ricky Nelson
7. School Day - Chuck Berry
8. Start Movin' - Sal Mineo
9. Valley of Tears/It's You I Love - Fats Domino
10. Come Go With Me - The Dell-Vikings
11. Over the Mountain, Across the Sea   Johnnie and Joe
12. Gone - Ferlin Huskey
13. Goin' Steady - Tommy Sands

THE BOBBETTES
The Bobbettes sold two million copies of a bouncy little ditty that they composed to make fun of a fifth grade teacher. The group was formed in 1955 by two sisters, Jannie and Emma Pought, who joined with six other girls, including Reather Dixon, Helen Gathers, and Laura Webb, as the Harlem Queens. At this time they were between the ages of nine and thirteen. Not only were they all students at P.S. 109 in New York City, most also lived in the same apartment building near 99th Street and Second Avenue. The Harlem Queens appeared on various amateur shows including the regular Wednesday night affair at the Apollo Theater. By early 1957, the size of the group had been reduced to a quintet. After composing "Mr. Lee," the group's manager decided to let their youth and naivete work in their favor. They journeyed downtown to the offices of Atlantic Records where the girls boldly asked for an audition. It's a wonder the young ladies weren't thrown out on their collective ears. But, times and the music business were different then, and the brazenness of the quintet not only brought smiles from the front office staff, it brought Ahmet Ertegun and Jerry Wexler out of the back offices to listen. The two Atlantic executives set up a session on February 13, 1957, and "Mr. Lee" was waxed. The single was released in May, but it languished for two months before catching the public's ear. The Bobbettes released a total of six singles on Atlantic, but none of the others created much of a stir. Their last Atlantic release was 1960's "I Shot Mr. Lee." The Bobbettes released a second version of the song at the same time on Triple-X Records, and it became a moderate hit. The group's second Triple-X single, "Have Mercy Baby" also did well. The Bobbettes also recorded for Gallant, King, End, Gone, Jubilee, Diamond, RCA Victor, Mayhew, and QIT into the 1980s.

14. C. C. Rider - Chuck Willis
15. Rock Your Little Baby To Sleep - Buddy Knox
16. My Dream - The Platters
17. With All My Heart - Jodie Sands
18. Fabulous - Charlie Gracie
19. Gonna Find Me a Bluebird - Marvin Rainwater
20. I'm Gonna Sit Right Down and Write Myself a Letter - Billy Williams
21. Susie-Q - Dale Hawkins
22. Jenny Jenny/Miss Ann - Little Richard
23. He's Mine/I'm Sorry - The Platters
24. Teddy Bear/Loving You - Elvis Presley
25. I'm Walkin' - Fats Domino
26. Party Doll - Buddy Knox
27. Just To Hold My Hand - Clyde McPhatter
28. Lucille/Send Me Some Lovin' - Little Richard
29. (You Hit the Wrong Note) Billy Goat - Bill Haley and His Comets
30. Short Fat Fannie - Larry Williams
31. Empty Arms - Ivory Joe Hunter
32. Whole Lot of Shakin' Going On - Jerry Lee Lewis
33. Let the Four Winds Blow - Roy Brown
34. Stardust - Billy Ward and His Dominoes
35. Warm Up To Me Baby - Jimmy Bowen

Also on the "pop" charts:
Dark Moon - Bonnie Guitar
It's Not For Me To Say - Johnny Mathis
I Like Your Kind Of Love - Andy Williams

June 1957
ARTIST OF THE MONTH

THE EVERLY BROTHERS

The term "rockabilly" comes from the combination of two words describing two musical forms, rock 'n roll and hillbilly. Nowhere was this musical marriage made so well as it was with the Everly Brothers.

The two years in age that separated Don and Phil must have seemed like an insurmountable gap when they were young. Youth has a way of looking at age like that. Certainly, the two brothers were as different as night from day. At one time, Don liked to write songs and paint in oils while Phil liked fast cars and faster women. Later, it was Phil who just wanted to sit by the fire and play with his children while Don played with fast cars and faster women.

Only when they sang did they come together to form a whole, their voices intertwining in sugarcoated harmony.

Two sons were born to Margaret and Isaac "Ike" Everly of Brownie, in western Kentucky. Isaac Donald was born February 1, 1937; and

Phillip was born January 19, 1939. They were exposed to music from birth. Early in his own life, Ike turned his back on coal mining, the traditional occupation in the Kentucky hill country. He decided to be a musician. He and his two brothers, Charlie and Leonard, became one of the most popular musical groups in Muhlenberg County. At one time, they even composed an instrumental tune combining bluegrass and ragtime they called "That's the Mood I'm In." Due to their lack of knowledge of the business side of music, they never copyrighted the tune. It was later altered a little, and it became a hit for Glenn Miller as "In The Mood" under another writer's name.

Ike and his brothers played everywhere the music would take them. And eventually, the music led them to Chicago for a four-year stay before the act broke up. Ike and Margaret and their sons (Don was born in Brownie before they left, and Phil was born in Chicago) moved on to Iowa for another seven years. By 1945, the family had settled in Shenandoah, and Ike was making three appearances each day on a local radio station. Over time, Margaret and the boys joined Ike on the air. By 1950, The Everly Family Show was the most popular in the region. Eventually, they moved from Shenandoah to Evansville, Indiana. As the demand for live radio performers declined, the family took to the road again to supplement their income. They traveled from one small backwoods town to the next, singing bluegrass for any event where music was welcome: county fairs, political meetings, and revivals.

Don & Phil Everly

They finally settled in Knoxville, where they appeared on radio again from 1953 to 1955. One performer with which Ike had maintained a long correspondence, was Chet Atkins. When they finally got together, Atkins was rapidly becoming a success in Nashville as both a session guitarist and recording artist for RCA Victor. When Atkins was introduced to Don and Phil, he immediately liked what he saw—and what he heard. Through his contacts in Nashville, Atkins secured a six-month contract for Ike's boys with Columbia Records.

Their only recording session for Columbia came in November 1955, during which they were backed by members of Carl Smith's band. Columbia issued one single, "The Sun Keeps Shining" b/w "Keep A' Lovin' Me," while two additional songs from this session remained unreleased: "If Her Love Isn't True" and "That's The Life I Have To Live." The recording offered nothing to distinguish it from any other country single by artists from Appalachia. The boys sang both songs in a dragging, waltz tempo. A fiddle wavered mournfully, and a steel guitar offered a short instrumental punctuation. Only the vocal, harmonious and showing strength, offered any promise. The record received a little airplay from deejays who knew of the Everly family, but mostly it was just filed and forgotten.

Lack of immediate success was nothing new to the Everlys. However, Don was asked to sign on as a songwriter with Hill and Range, a major Nashville music publishing house. Meanwhile the duo worked the few singing jobs they could land. Still nothing much happened, so Don switched over to Acuff-Rose, another music publisher. Here, he was able to place his song, "Thou Shalt Not Steal," with Kitty Wells, one of the reigning queens of country music. His first royalty check was for

$600.00. The Everlys were impressed.

So was Wesley Rose, the son of Fred Rose of Acuff-Rose. Wesley was aware that Archie Bleyer was looking for country talent for his recently formed Cadence Records. Up to that point, Bleyer had concentrated on middle-of-the-road "pop," and he had been very successful with the Chordettes and Andy Williams. Rose persuaded Bleyer to give the Everlys a chance. In March 1957, the Everly Brothers had their first session for Cadence. In the studio, overseeing the music and playing guitar was their old friend, Chet Atkins. Two songs were recorded, both of them published by Acuff-Rose: "I Wonder If I Care As Much," written by Don and Phil, and "Bye Bye Love," composed by the husband-wife team of Boudeleaux and Felice Bryant. The teaming of the Everlys and the Bryants was to be one of those odd pairings that produce sparks at every juncture.

"Bye Bye Love" was the obvious choice for the A-side. Chunky, full-chord strumming by the Everlys on their Gibsons introduced their voices, as high and pure as a mountain stream. Throw in a driving rhythm, tie a ribbon around it, and call it rockabilly.

Teens who flipped the single over and listened to the B-side must have been caught completely off guard. The vocals snarled and twisted and slid around each other on the chorus. Don's solo on the verse was from a place so far back in the hills the sun only broke through once a week—on Mondays to dry the wash. This wasn't rock 'n roll. Not even close! This was hillbilly music!

It's difficult to comprehend or appreciate at this late date the breakthrough that the Everly Brothers achieved when they recorded "Bye Bye Love." In the three years since Elvis recorded "Blue Moon of Kentucky" for Sun Records, Southern musicians had been working diligently to merge country and blues into a musical style that was at once completely different and at the same time instantly recognizable. The Everlys did it in 2:20 minutes of their first Cadence single. And, the next time, they did it even better.

For many acts, the second release is more important than the first. The first time around, they have the advantage of being fresh and different. The second time, they can upset listeners by being too close to the original. And, they can do just as much harm if they are too far afield.

"Wake Up Little Susie" hit this difficult path square in the center. The opening guitar figure—by now an established part of each record—was even more thrilling than that used on "Bye Bye Love." The vocals were more urgent. The song, again by the Bryants, had the advantage of being on the risque side. It dealt with a teenage couple who fell asleep at a drive-in movie and got caught while sneaking the girl home at dawn's early light.

The quartet of Everlys and Bryants worked their magic for the next three years, and the records couldn't come off the presses fast enough: "All I Have To Do Is Dream," "Bird Dog," "Devoted to You," "Problems," "Take a Message to Mary," "Poor Jenny." Each was composed by the Bryants and sung to perfection by the Everlys.

And, there was still enough wax to go around for Don to have his own songs here and there: "'Til I Kissed You," "Oh What A Feeling," and

"Since You Broke My Heart." Phil even contributed "When Will I Be Loved." Their new friend, Roy Orbison, gave them "Claudette," which he had written for his wife. As the saying goes, the boys were rolling in high cotton.

There were only a few times when they stumbled. "This Little Girl of Mine," a Ray Charles tune, with it's bouncy stop-and-go rhythm, didn't really suit the Everlys' style. As this was their third Cadence release, it could have been disastrous. Never mind! Cadence quickly released "All I Have To Do Is Dream" b/w "Claudette," and their fourth single became their biggest selling record of the 1950s.

In 1958, riding a yearlong string of hits and widespread popularity, the Everly Brothers switched gears for their second album. To their everlasting credit, and to the consternation of the critics of the day, the Everlys chose to record songs that they had grown up loving and playing with their family. SONGS OUR DADDY TAUGHT US featured the brothers harmonizing in an unabashedly rural style. Included were such gems as "Rocking Alone in an Old Rockin' Chair," "Roving Gambler," "That Silver Haired Daddy of Mine," and "Who's Gonna Shoe Your Pretty Little Feet." A lesser act might have seen their career go up in flames. Not the Everlys.

What they did was change record labels, signing the most lucrative recording contract up to that time.

(Look for more on the Everly Brothers in the next volume of THE GOLDEN AGE OF AMERICAN ROCK 'N ROLL.)

July 1957

DELLA REESE
She sang gospel for years. Then she decided to make some money. Born in Detroit on July 6, 1931 (or 1932), Delloreese Patricia Early (her last name is also given as Tellafaro) began her lengthy professional career in 1945 with the Mahalia Jackson choir before joining the Clara Ward Singers in 1949. In college at Wayne University, she formed her own group, the Meditation Singers. In 1955, she left gospel music and began accepting bookings in nightclubs. Her trained voice and specific enunciation caught the ear of a scout for Jubilee Records and Miss Reese found herself in the studio recording material that ranged from straight "pop" to jazz. On Jubilee, she issued records (her first was "In the Still of the Night") for two years. In 1957, she had a "pop" hit with "And That Reminds Me," a jazz number that played upon that enunciation as well as the range of her voice. Unfortunately, her singing style required limited her choice of acceptable material. It took five singles before "Sermonette" approached the hit charts again in late 1958. By then, she was negotiating to switch to RCA Victor. Her biggest hit, by far, was "Don't You Know" in 1959. This million-selling ballad showcased Reese's style perfectly. The song was simplicity personified. Ten lines of verse written by Bobby Worth were set to the tune of "Musetta's Waltz" by Puccini. On the strength of "Don't You Know," she built a career as a top-notch draw in the best clubs across the country. She moved from Detroit to a Hollywood penthouse. In 1965, she signed with ABC-Paramount Records where had a few minor hits. For the next fifteen years, she appeared frequently on television and in nightclubs. She also studied acting, finding success with this career move when she landed a recurring role on "The Jeffersons."

JUL 1 Frankie Lymon and the Teenagers, fresh from their successful tour of Britain, open at the Paramount Theater in New York City as headliners of yet another Alan Freed production. Also booked for the Fourth of July week are the Cadillacs, Paul Anka, Lewis Lymon and the Teenchords, the Moonglows, Teddy Randazzo, Johnnie and Joe, Clyde McPhatter, the Everly Brothers, Chuck Berry, LaVern Baker, Joe Turner, Screamin' Jay Hawkins, and Jodie Sands. Appearing tonight and tomorrow only is Jackie Dee. The nine-day run grosses $120,000.

Della Reese starts a week-long stand at the Oklahoma State Fair.

New Releases for the first week of July include three versions of "Long, Lonely Nights": by Lee Andrews and the Hearts on Chess; by Clyde McPhatter on Atlantic; and by the Kings on Baton. Also new this week are "Goody, Goody" by Frankie Lymon and the Teenagers on Gee; Lloyd Price's "Lonely Chair" on K.R.C.; "Drive-In Show" by Eddie Cochran on Liberty; "Lotta Lovin'" by Gene Vincent and the Blue Caps on Capitol; "Juke Box Man" by Mel Tillis on Columbia; Don Deal's "Unfaithful Diane" on Era; and Melvin Endsley's "Keep A-Movin' Me Baby" on RCA Victor.

JUL 3 The female rockabilly sensation, Jackie Dee, headlines at the revue at the Uptown Theater in Philadelphia. Miss Dee is a sixteen-year old country singer from Batavia, Illinois. Her real name is Sherry Lee Myers, and she will go on to fame and fortune as Jackie DeShannon.

JUL 4 For the Independence Day weekend, the Apex Bar in Detroit offers the boogie sounds of John Lee Hooker through July 7.

JUL 5 Bill Haley and his Comets play a one-nighter at the Convention Hall in Wildwood, New Jersey.

T-Bone Walker, known among his peers as "Mister Guitar," opens for a week at the Flame in Detroit.

Roy Brown, Faye Adams, the Ravens, the Channels, and the Cellos take over at the Howard Theater in Washington this week.

JUL 7 For the next two weeks, the Diamonds are touring the Midwest, starting tonight in Milwaukee and ending in Chicago on July 23.

EARLY JULY

Following the success of Elvis Presley Enterprises, Little Richard enters the perfume market with an aroma labeled "Princess Cheri."

The **Playmates**, continuing their reputation as one the of the great lounge acts of the era, start their summer engagement in Atlantic City's Bamboo Club.

JUL 8   For the next three nights at Washington's Carter Baron Amphitheater, Brenda Lee, Sonny James and George Hamilton IV co-star behind Red Foley in an "Ozark Jubilee" package.

New Releases for the second week in July include "Wanderin' Eyes" by Charlie Gracie on Cameo; "Shake It Up" by Conway Twitty on Mercury; "You're Mine, You're Mine" by James Brown and the Famous Flames on Federal; "I'm a King Bee" by Slim Harpo on Excello; "Bermuda Shorts" by the Delroys featuring Milton Sparks on Apollo; and "Peanuts" by Little Joe and the Thrillers on Okeh.

JUL 9   "Loving You," Elvis Presley's second motion picture, premiers at the Strand Theater in Memphis. Presley and his current girlfriend, Anita Wood, attend a sneak preview the previous night. The movie opens nationally on July 30.

JUL 10   The "Fantabulous Rock 'N Roll Show for '57" arrives in New Orleans for a show at the Municipal Auditorium. Performers include Ruth Brown, Smiley Lewis, the Coasters, the Schoolboys, Bo Diddley, the Five Satins, the Drifters, Robert Parker, Johnny Hartman, and Dave Bartholomew's orchestra.

JUL 12   After the two trial runs in May, Alan Freed kicks off a thirteen-week, national television show devoted to rock 'n roll. The show will be broadcast from 10:00 to 10:30 p.m. (EDT) every Friday over the ABC-TV network. Tonight's show features performances by the Everly Brothers, Johnnie and Joe, Buddy Knox, Ferlin Huskey, Frankie Lymon, Billy Williams, the Charles McDevitt Skiffle Group featuring Nancy Whiskey, and Connie Francis.

In Detroit, John Lee Hooker moves into the Club Basin Street for a week. Across town, the Royal Jokers start their week at Lee's Club Sensation.

JUL 13   Charlie Feathers headlines the "Big D Jamboree" in Dallas. Also adding a little rockabilly flavor to tonight's stageshow and broadcast are "Groovy" Joe Poovey and Gene Rambo.

JUL 14   Marvin Rainwater makes a rare television appearance, singing "Gonna Find Me A Bluebird" on "The Ed Sullivan Show" on CBS-TV.

THE PLAYMATES

More than a few lounge acts worked their way into the ranks of rock 'n roll stars. Included among these were Freddy Bell and the Bell Boys, The Treniers, the Four Lovers, Charlie Gracie, Steve Gibson and the Red Caps... and the Playmates. They were a trio of professionals from Waterbury, Connecticut: Danny Conn (born March 29, 1930), Morey Carr (born Morey Cohen, July 31, 1932) and Chic Hetti (born February 26, 1930). As college students in Connecticut, they met in 1952 and formed the Nitwits, the type of instrumental-comedy-singing group that was popular on the "borscht circuit." They were young and energetic, and their stage show brought them continuous bookings. In early 1957, they approached the newly formed Roulette Records and bluffed their way into a recording contract by pretending they were a calypso group. Roulette took the bait, and the Playmates found themselves promoting their first two singles, "Barefoot Girl" and "Island Girl." They sold a quarter of a million copies of their cover version of the Twin Tones' "Jo-Ann," a teen ballad that became their first national hit. Their next three singles, released in 1958, also sold moderately well. Late in the year, the Playmates spent fifteen minutes at the end of a recording session laying down a novelty number about a race between a Cadillac and a Nash Rambler. "Beep Beep" sold a million copies almost overnight. In 1959, the Playmates had a minor hit with "Star Love" before selling close to a million copies of "What Is Love?" The Playmates, now nearing thirty years of age, played all the rock 'n roll gigs. They toured on busses filled with teen idols and appeared on "American Bandstand," and they continued to have minor hits until 1962. When music passed them by, Chic became a teacher, Donny worked as salesman, and Morey sold real estate.

JOE BENNETT & THE SPARKLETONES

By 1957, rock 'n roll was geared to the teenage audience, so it was logical that record companies would seek out rock 'n roll acts composed entirely of teenagers. The Sparkletones certainly filled that requirement. During 1957, they were aged fourteen to seventeen. The group's members were all from Spartanburg, South Carolina, and by all accounts, they were religious, churchgoing youngsters. However, when they strapped on their guitars, they possessed an absolutely wild streak. Their first release, "Black Slacks," paid tribute to a the teen fad of wearing black slacks, especially the ones with a buckle across the back, an action that was perceived as rebellious by Southern school authorities. The Sparkletones reveled in the association. Led by Joe Bennett on Fender guitar, the Sparkletones were comprised of Howard Childress, guitar; Jimmy Denton, drums; and Wayne Arthur, stand-up bass. The freshness of "Black Slacks" caught the music buyer's ear in the summer of 1957, and it remained a major hit for four months. The Sparkletones followed with "Penny Loafers and Bobby Sox," an ode to footwear. It did about half the business of "Black Slacks," but that was still a hit by anyone's accounting. After two hits, the bottom dropped out. The Sparkletones were caught in the record companies drive for something newer, fresher. In early 1958, ABC Paramount, the group's label, was promoting Danny and the Juniors and the Royal Teens. The Sparkletones continued to produce excellent rockabilly records based on Gene Vincent's style. There were three more singles on ABC in 1958, the best of which was "Cotton Pickin' Rocker." In 1959, the group released three singles on Paris Records. In early 1960, Top Rank Records issued "The King Is Coming Back" by Eddie and Billy. This record welcoming Elvis home from the Army was the group's last gasp.

JUL 15   NBC-TV's "Studio One" airs an original farce by Romeo Muller about rock 'n roll titled "The Hit."

New Releases for the third week in July include "When I See You" by Fats Domino on Imperial; "Black Slacks" by the **Sparkletones** on ABC-Paramount; "Lasting Love" by Sal Mineo on Epic; "And That Reminds Me" by Della Reese on Jubilee; and "Let's Start All Over Again" on Mercury by Tony Williams, former lead singer with the Platters. Hot numbers this week include "All Night Long" by Bob Luman on Imperial; "Teenage Dream" by Marty Robbins on Columbia; and "Later Baby" by Johnny Janis on ABC-Paramount In an interesting move, "Flat-Foot Sam" by the Oscar Wills combo with vocal by T. V. Slim is issued by two subsidiaries of Chess Records: on Argo as by Oscar Wills, and on Checker as by T.V. Slim. Also new is "Double Date" on Republic by Randy Starr, who formed the New Christy Minstrels in the 1960s.

MID-JULY

The Platters, in the middle of a tour of Latin America, headline a gala musical show at the Opera Theater in Buenos Aires. Originally only scheduled for a twelve-week tour, the group has been extended an additional six weeks.

Gene Vincent and his Blue Caps are booked through the end of July along the East Coast.

JUL 19   The Flame Show Bar in Detroit opens its doors wide for the Bill Doggett combo this week.

Chuck Willis, Ann Cole, Charlie and Ray, the Cookies, the Velours, and Ocie Smith hold forth at Washington's Howard Theater for a week.

JUL 21   "The Fantabulous Rock 'N Roll Show of '57" winds up its month-long tour from Texas to the Midwest with a show in St. Louis. It is reported that the gate for each show averaged from $5,000 to $12,000 per night.

Big Maybelle, Wynonie Harris, and Noble "Thin Man" Watts share the spotlight at the Labor Union Hall in New Orleans.

New Releases for the fourth week in July include "Humpty Dumpty Heart" by LaVern Baker and "That Train Has Gone" by Chuck Willis, both on Atlantic; "You're Long Gone" by Joe Therrien, Jr. on Brunswick; "Miss You" by Bill Haley and His Comets on Decca; Jimmy Bowen's "Ever Since That Night" on Roulette; "Cool Love" by Wanda Jackson on Capitol; "Farther Up the Road" by Bobby "Blue" Bland on Duke; "Greenback Dollar, Watch and Chain" by Ray Harris on Sun; "The Living End" by Bobby Bare on Capitol; and Ricky Shaw's "Teen Age Marriage" on Golden Crest. This is also the week for male-female duo releases with Gene and Eunice's "Don't Treat Me This Way" and Shirley and Lee's "The Flirt," both on Aladdin; and Johnnie and Joe's "There Goes My Heart" on J & S.

JUL 23   Fats Domino plays the Dallas Sportatorium. As 6,000 fans leave the building, there are knife attacks and gunfire in what is thought to be a racially motivated riot.

JUL 25   Bobby Darin begins a five-day stand at the Lotus Club in Washington.

JUL 26   Milwaukee is the jumping-off point for a caravan of stars headlined by the Coasters, the Five Satins, the Cellos, Gene and Eunice, Lulu Reed and Sonny Thompson's orchestra. Plans call for the tour to last six to ten weeks while appearing from the Midwest to California. The troupe will stop in Denver on July 31.
  Connie Francis plays a one-nighter in Washington, DC.
  Fats Domino guests on Alan Freed's weekly ABC-TV show.

JUL 28   Jerry Lee Lewis belts out "Whole Lot of Shakin' Going On" as he makes his national television debut on NBC-TV's "The Steve Allen Show." It is one of the wildest musical performances seen on television since Johnnie Ray was at the height of his popularity in the early 1950s.
  Nappy Brown, Annie Laurie and Big John Greer entertain patrons at New Orleans' Labor Union Hall.

LATE JULY

The music industry is jumping with rumors of Little Richard's religious leanings. In attempt to downplay this story, a spokesman for his promoter, the Gale Agency, reports that there are more than enough bookings to keep Richard on the road for months to come. At this time, the Wild Man of Rock 'n Roll is performing in Des Moines' Veterans Auditorium. The show is a sellout even though it is not advertised on local radio or in newspapers.

Fats Domino reportedly took in $100,000 during a thirty-day tour of the East Coast. Back on the West Coast, Hollywood insiders still consider him to be the front-runner for the lead in the film biography of Fats Waller.

Agents for Brenda Lee announce that she is leaving her longtime association with Springfield's "Ozark Jubilee." In the future, she will be based out of Nashville.

TOP ROCK 'N ROLL RECORD FOR JULY 1957

1. Teddy Bear/Loving You - Elvis Presley
2. Bye Bye Love - The Everly Brothers
3. Searchin'/Young Blood - The Coasters
4. Short Fat Fannie - Larry Williams
5. Over the Mountain, Across the Sea - Johnnie and Joe
6. I'm Gonna Sit Right Down and Write Myself a Letter
  - Billy Williams
7. A White Sport Coat - Marty Robbins
8. Jenny, Jenny/Miss Ann - Little Richard

9. C. C. Rider - Chuck Willis
10. All Shook Up - Elvis Presley
11. Whispering Bells - The Dell-Vikings
12. Valley of Tears/It's You I Love - Fats Domino
13. A Teenager's Romance/I'm Walking - Ricky Nelson
14. Stardust - Billy Ward and His Dominos
15. Little Darlin' - The Diamonds
16. Start Movin' - Sal Mineo
17. Come Go With Me - The Dell-Vikings
18. Gonna Find Me a Bluebird - Marvin Rainwater
19. My Dream/He's Mine - The Platters
20. Susie-Q - Dale Hawkins
21. Whole Lot of Shakin' Going On - Jerry Lee Lewis
22. With All My Heart - Jodie Sands
23. School Day - Chuck Berry
24. Just to Hold My Hand - Clyde McPhatter
25. Let the Four Winds Blow - Roy Brown
26. Rock Your Little Baby to Sleep - Buddy Knox
27. Diana - Paul Anka
28. Flying Saucer, the 2nd - Buchanan and Goodman
29. To the Aisle - The Five Satins
30. Gone - Ferlin Huskey
31. Goin' Steady - Tommy Sands
32. Fabulous - Charlie Gracie
33. Empty Arms - Ivory Joe Hunter
34. What Can I Do - Donnie Elbert
35. Goody Goody - Frankie Lymon and the Teenagers
36. Just Because - Lloyd Price
37. It Hurts To Be In Love - Annie Laurie
38. Don't Ask Me - The Dubs
39. The Sun is Shining - Jimmy Reed
41. Rang Tang Ding Dong - The Cellos
42. Lucille/Send Me Some Lovin' - Little Richard
43. Cool Shake - The Del Vikings
44. Please Send Me Someone to Love - The Moonglows
45. Next Time You See Me - Little Junior Parker
46. Oh, Baby Doll - Chuck Berry
47. I'm Walkin' - Fats Domino
48. Mr. Lee - The Bobbettes
49. Dynamite - Brenda Lee
50. Miss You So - Lillian Offitt

Also on the "pop" charts:
Tammy - Debbie Reynolds
Rainbow - Russ Hamilton
Send For Me - Nat King Cole
Old Cape Cod - Patti Page

July 1957
ARTIST OF THE MONTH

THE COASTERS

If one accepts as a basic premise that rock 'n roll should be fun, then the Coasters can honestly lay claim to being rock 'n roll's Court Jesters. The sang of good times, and their songs were jubilant expressions of freedom. They had a string of hits and a longevity unmatched by any other rock 'n roll vocal group in the 1950s, except for the Platters. Unlike the Platters, who played fancy supper clubs and toured the major cities of the world, the Coasters bounced around the states doing one night stands in small clubs catering to the working class.

The Coasters

The driving force behind the Coasters was the songwriting team of Jerry Leiber and Mike Stoller. Leiber and Stoller had their first hit in 1952 with Charles Brown's "Hard Times." They went on to compose "Hound Dog," a rhythm and blues smash for Willie Mae "Big Mama" Thornton in 1953, three full years before Elvis. They also composed "K. C. Lovin'" released by Little Willie Littlefield in 1953. This song would make an important contribution to the legacy of rock 'n roll in 1959 as "Kansas City" by Wilbert Harrison.

Up to 1954, the team had been happy just to write the songs. However, they were soon active in the production of recording sessions. This led to the ownership of their own Spark label early in the year. Their first two releases met with overwhelming apathy on the part of deejays and the music-buying public. Then came "Riot In Cell Block #9" by the Robins.

The Robins' story began in Alameda, a seaport on the Oakland side of the Bay. In 1945, two brothers, William and Roy Richards, joined with their high school chum, Ty Terrell, to form a trio. A year later, the three teenagers traveled to Los Angeles hoping to break into the music business. At this time, the young men were receiving most of their influence from the secular music of the day, as opposed to many rhythm and blues artists who came directly from religious backgrounds. The A Sharp Trio, as they called themselves, found that landing a singing job was difficult. They soon drifted to the Barrelhouse Club, the Watts hangout for aspiring R&B artists, owned by Johnny Otis. Otis took an interest in the young men, and a date for a recording session was set. By this time, the trio had become the Four Bluebirds with the addition of Bobby Nunn on bass. The two Richards brothers sang baritone and Terrell was lead tenor. Their only session at this time produced "My Baby Done Told Me" b/w "Courtroom Blues" on Excelsior. The group's plumage changed soon after, and they became the Robins.

The Robins recorded for Aladdin, and it's subsidiary, Score, in 1949. At the same time, the group was becoming a featured attraction with the Johnny Otis Show. In 1949 and 1950, they often backed artists such as Little Esther or Mel Walker on sessions produced by Otis for Savoy Records. In 1950, the Robins also had a hit on Savoy under their own name with "If It's So Baby." Through 1952, they issued a few singles on R.P.M., Modern and Recorded In Hollywood. The next year they were on

RCA Victor before recording for Crown in 1954.

During 1954, two important changes took place for the Robins. First, they became a quintet with the addition of tenor Carl Gardner. And, second, they came under the watchful eye of Leiber and Stoller, proud owners of their new Spark Record Company.

During this time, Los Angeles had become a hotbed of musical activity when it came to rhythm and blues vocal groups. The Penguins, Medallions, and Meadowlarks were selling records by the truckload for Dootone. The Platters were working for King and soon would be on Mercury. Marvin and Johnny were recording for Specialty. The Flairs, Crowns, and Cadets/Jacks were recording for the Modern/R.P.M./Flair record group.

From the Flairs, Leiber and Stoller borrowed Richard Berry to sing the bass lead on the Robins' first Spark release, "Riot In Cell Block #9." Berry was chosen over Bobby Nunn for this piece, because they felt the lead vocal required a hard edge, something Nunn's resonant bass lacked. "Riot" is the perfect introduction to the music that this group would continue to make for the next eight years. The song is a musical "playlet" told from the perspective of a prison inmate involved in a cell block riot. This was certainly not the subject matter expected of a song with intentions of appealing to a mass audience. Nevertheless, the total musical production unites the single and captures the listener's attention—from the opening siren and tommy-gun, to the saxophone blaring over the vocal group's choral interjections, to Berry's snarling recitation. While it was not a national hit, "Riot In Cell Block #9" sold nearly 100,000 copies in Los Angeles and the Bay area. As the follow-up to "Riot," Leiber and Stoller penned "Framed," another opus about legal entanglements. This time Nunn sang the lead part. In the next year, there were three more singles by the group, each showing part of the promise that would soon be fulfilled: the swinging "Whaddya Want;" the driving "One Kiss," and the frantic "I Must Be Dreamin'."

In August 1955, the Robins finally released the single that would enable their popularity to cross the California state line. "Smokey Joe's Cafe" is another first-person account, this time of a budding romance gone very wrong. The saxophone solo by Gil Bernal has just the right amount of rhythmic slurring to produce a feeling that is at odds with the song's message of frolicsome fun. As the song began selling in Los Angeles, Atlantic Records approached Leiber and Stoller, asking to distribute "Smokey Joe's Cafe" as well as handle all of the Robins' future releases on Atlantic's subsidiary label, Atco. As part of the deal, Leiber and Stoller would become independent producers for other Atlantic acts. Remarkably, the original members of the Robins balked at the deal. They had apparently been having second thoughts for sometime at the direction their music was taking. Leiber and Stoller worked with the Robins' management and came up with a solution: the three original members of the Robins would continue to keep the group's name, but Bobby Nunn and Carl Gardner would be free to record for Atco as long as they called themselves something else.

"Smokey Joe's Cafe" appeared on Atco as by the Robins, but all later releases were under the group's new name, the Coasters. To augment Gardner and Nunn, two singers and a guitarist were hired: Leon Hughes was a tenor of distinction, and Billy Guy was a comedic singer with unlimited vocal inflections. As guitarist, Adolph Jacobs provided technique as well as humor. In the spring of 1956, the group followed "Smokey Joe's Cafe" with "Down In Mexico." This single did well in the R&B market, but the next one, "One Kiss Led to Another," didn't. After their first Atco session, Leon Hughes quit the group, and his place was filled by "Young" Jesse Obe who had a solo hit with "Mary Lou" in 1955.

The Coasters struck gold with their third single for Atco, the two-sided smash "Searchin'" b/w "Young Blood." Both are raw, bare-boned recordings. Billy Guy scatters his voice all over the map on "Searchin'" while Carl Gardner's "Young Blood" is a lip-smacking, lascivious romp. The record quickly sold two million copies as first one side, then the other, was played on radio stations across the nation during the summer of 1957. Then, the bottom dropped out. The group's infectious clowning about sexual subjects quickly brought the wrath of the national guardians of the country's moral health.

For a year, the group could barely sell a copy of their latest release. "Idol With the Golden Head," "What Is The Secret of Your Success," and "Gee Golly" each attracted increasingly less attention. There was really nothing wrong with the material or the delivery. The Coasters just got caught in a general backlash directed against rock 'n roll.

This was a trying time for the Coasters, and there was plenty of finger-pointing between the members of the group, Leiber and Stoller, and Atco. The result was a revamping of the group's personnel in 1958. Cornell Gunter, who had sung in the Flairs, replaced Jesse Obe. Bobby Nunn got fed up, and Will "Dub" Jones, formerly with the Cadets/Jacks, took his spot.

Their base of operations was also moved from Los Angeles to New York so Leiber and Stoller could be closer to Atlantic's headquarters. A secondary advantage, but one that became immediately apparent with their next single release, was the availability of New York's premier tenor sax man, Curtis Ousley, better know as King Curtis. The instantly recognizable sound of King Curtis' solos led to his status as the sixth Coaster. This, then, was the lineup for most of the Coasters' hits: Dub Jones, bass; Carl Gardner, lead; Cornell Gunter, tenor; and Billy Guy, baritone; with Adolph Jacobs on guitar and King Curtis on sax.

The first single by this aggregation was "Yakety Yak," released in early May 1958. In June it topped the R&B charts, and in another month it was the best selling record throughout country. The most important difference between "Yakety Yak" and its predecessors was the song's point of view. "Yakety Yak" was aimed directly at teenagers, talking to them about problems within their own realm of experience.

Then, just as quickly as "Yakety Yak" had climbed the charts, the next release, "The Shadow Knows," plummeted out of sight without a trace. One reason may be that "The Shadow Knows" reverted to their earlier style of delivery. Billy Guy's infectious humor, when it was backed by a swampy, ghoulish musical mix, just didn't catch on.

The Coasters quickly rebounded with their next recording, "Charlie Brown." The song hit the airwaves like lightning, zipping back and forth across America. As with "Yakety Yak," "Charlie Brown" was specifically planned to appeal to teenagers. The story of a budding juvenile delinquent is couched in comedic terms and punctuated by Dub Jones' searing bass line, "Why's everybody always pickin' on me?" Record sales quickly topped the million mark.

By this time, the Coasters and Leiber/Stoller had learned to follow the proven formula. "Along Came Jones" took on America's preoccupation with TV westerns, and "Poison Ivy" preached the lesson of "look but don't touch." Both were instant hits with "Poison Ivy" also going gold. However, rock 'n roll music thrives on originality, and after "Poison Ivy" the smash hits stopped coming. Singles by the group still sold well enough to keep the group working the club and tour circuits. Nevertheless, it was not until 1961, and "Little Egypt," that the Coasters again had a record that really fired the public's attention. After that, the group's popularity as a viable recording act was over.

As the 1960s progressed, the cohesive unit that had been the Coasters began to fall apart. The first change was the addition of Earl Carroll of the Cadets, who joined the group in 1961 for "Little Egypt." Shortly thereafter, Cornell Gunter left. The Coasters quit Atco for King Records in 1966, and a year later were recording for Date, a subsidiary of Columbia Records. In 1968, Dub Jones was replaced by Ronnie Bright, the bass voice on Johnny Cymbal's "Mr. Bass Man." Bright had also sung with the Valentines. In 1972, Billy Guy dropped out of the group, and Jimmy Norman filled his spot.

After he left the group, Bobby Nunn toured with his own version of the Coasters made up of Billy Wilson, Grady Chapman (who had recorded with the Robins on RCA Victor, the Suedes on Money, and under his own name on several Los Angeles labels), and Bobby Sheen (of Bob B. Soxx and the Blue Jeans). Later Nunn's group, called the Coasters Mark II, contained Chapman, Randy Jones, and Billy Richards, Jr. (son of the original member of the Robins). Nunn died in Los Angeles, November 5, 1986, following a heart attack.

In the 1970s, Cornell Gunter formed his own group of Coasters with Teddy Harper and Nathaniel "Buster" Wilson, who had sung bass with the Hollywood Saxons and the Shields. Wilson was shot to death in Las Vegas in 1980 in a gruesome, gang-styled execution. Ten years later, Gunter was shot to death in North Las Vegas by an unknown assailant following an argument. At the time, "Cornell Gunter and His Coasters" was appearing at the Lady Luck Hotel and Casino.

In the 1980s, the Coasters were manned by Carl Gardner (who claims to be the only person with the rights to the group's name), Billy Guy, Earl Carroll, and Ronald Bright.

Throughout their career, the Coasters released some of the finest music of any rock 'n roll group, and it is surprising how so much of it received so little attention. On the group's B-sides and lost singles were hidden such little gems as "Zing Went the String of My Heart," "I'm A Hog For You," "Three Cool Cats," "Bad Blood," "What Is The Secret of Your Success?" "Sorry But I'm Gonna Have To Pass," "Shoppin' For Clothes," "Run Red Run," "Hongry," and "Bad Detective."

Now, as the song says, "That is rock and roll."

August 1957

AUG 2 Buddy Holly and the Crickets begin their first bookings on the East Coast R&B theater circuit with a week at the Howard Theater in Washington. The revue is headlined by Clyde McPhatter. Also appearing are the **Cadillacs**, Edna McGriff, the Hearts, and Otis Rush.

Bill Haley and His Comets, along with the Moonglows, open for two days at Artillery Ball Park in Kingston, Pennsylvania.

In New York, "Alan Freed's Big Beat Party" welcomes Jerry Lee Lewis to the airwaves.

AUG 4 The Everly Brothers guest on "The Ed Sullivan Show" on CBS-TV.

Roy Hamilton and the Clovers share top billing at the Municipal Auditorium in New Orleans. Also appearing are Annie Laurie, the Spaniels, Donnie Elbert, Huey Smith and the Clowns, Johnnie and Joe, Screamin' Jay Hawkins, Bobby Marchan, and Buddy and Ella Johnson.

AUG 5 The ABC-TV network premiers an afternoon dance party show, "American Bandstand," hosted by Dick Clark. Musical guests on the show almost always pantomime (or "lip-sync") to their hit records. On this opening show, performers were Billy Williams and the Chordettes.

Charlie Gracie embarks on a tour of England with a rave-up at London's Hippodrome. The demand for the American rocker so overwhelms the promoter that the tour is extended two weeks.

Jerry Lee Lewis and Carl Perkins rock the crowd 'til 2 a.m. in Knoxville's Chilhowee Park.

New Releases for the first week in August include a re-release on Checker of "Happy, Happy Birthday Baby" by the Tune Weavers; two from Roulette: "Honeycomb" by Jimmie Rodgers and "Hula Love" by Buddy Knox; Ricky Nelson's "You're My One and Only Love" on Verve; "Face of an Angel" by the **Five Keys** (page 170 ➤) on Capitol; "Caught" by Paul Evans on RCA; Clarence "Frogman" Henry's "I Found a Love" on Argo; and "Jailbait" by Andre Williams on Fortune.

AUG 6 The Lane Brothers, Chet Atkins and the Rhythm Rockers join other RCA Victor artists for a concert at Milwaukee's Temple of Music.

THE CADILLACS
Four young men singing in the night under the street light near their apartment. In 1953, Manhattan was full of such sights. Earl Carroll was a student attending P.S. 139 at 140th Street and 7th Avenue. He and three friends formed the Carnations to sing at school functions and amateur shows. When the young men thought they were polished enough, they auditioned for Esther Navarro, a local talent scout. Miss Navarro was impressed with their harmony and attitude, and soon the young men were in the studio. At this time, joining Carroll, were Laverne Drake; Robert Phillips; James "Poppa" Clark, a former member of the Five Crowns on Rainbow; and probably Gus Willingham. The resulting tapes were taken to Jubilee/Josie Records, and a deal was struck in early 1954. The group's name was changed to the Cadillacs, and their first release on Josie (spelled "Joz" at that time) was "Gloria" b/w "I Wonder Why." Both sides caught on, with "Gloria" becoming a standard group song. Over the next few months, Clark and Willingham left to be replaced by Earl Wade (formerly with the Crystals and Opals) and Charles Brooks. There were three more singles before "Speedo" was released in October 1955 to become a major hit across the country. The follow-up, "Zoom," also did well. In early 1957, the group split into two units. Carroll took Brooks, Phillips, and Wade and formed the Original Cadillacs. Laverne Drake, and new members Bobby Spencer (formerly with the Crickets on Jay Dee, Chords, Pearls, and Harptones), Jimmy Bailey, and Roland Martinez continued to record as the Cadillacs. This situation was resolved within a year, as Carroll, Spencer, Martinez, Bailey, and Drake became the sole Cadillacs group. This group had a minor hit with "Peek-A-Boo" in 1958. The Cadillacs also recorded for Smash, Capitol, Arctic, and Mercury/Polydor.

AUG 7   The musical guest on today's "American Bandstand" is Dale Hawkins singing "Susie-Q."

EARLY AUGUST
Imperial Records signs Ricky Nelson to an exclusive, long-term recording contract. Ricky's second single has just been released by Verve Records, but he and his parents never formally signed with the label.

The Platters' manager, Buck Ram, visits Hollywood in an attempt to drum up support for a movie deal, tentatively titled "The Flying Platters." Ram's idea is to have a camera team follow the troupe during their upcoming visit to Brazil or Argentina. Eventually, an album titled "The Flying Platters" is released, but there is no movie.

"The Singing Cowboy" Gene Autry shares the spotlight at Wilkes-Barre, Pennsylvania, with Bill Haley and His Comets and the Moonglows.

Art Rupe of Specialty Records announces the hiring of a new Hollywood artist and repertoire man, Sonny Bono.

AUG 8   Paul Anka makes an appearance on "American Bandstand."

AUG 9   Fats Domino starts a week-long stand at the Club Bolero in the New Jersey resort, Wildwood-by-the-Sea. His fee for the week is reported to be $10,000.

Clyde McPhatter, the Cadillacs, Otis Rush, and Buddy Holly and the Crickets open for a week at the Royal Theater in Baltimore.

On "American Bandstand" the guests include Lee Andrews and the Hearts singing "Long Lonely Nights."

AUG 11 Jerry Lee Lewis has a second guest shot on "The Steve Allen Show." This is the only time that the Allen show ever beat out "The Ed Sullivan Show" for supremacy of the Sunday night television ratings.

As part of its 4th Annual Army Talent Show, "The Ed Sullivan Show" on CBS-TV presents Lt. Buddy Knox performing with Jimmy Bowen and the Rhythm Orchids.

New Releases for the second week in August include two on Decca: Buddy Holly's "Rock Around With Ollie Vee" b/w the original version of "That'll Be the Day" and Brenda Lee's "Ain't That Love." Also out this week are "Deep Purple" by Billy Ward and His Dominoes on Liberty; "Idol with the Golden Head" by the Coasters on Atco; "It Ain't Me" by Ray Campi on Dot; "Dumplin's" by Ernie Freeman on Imperial; Little Walter's "Boom Boom Out Goes the Light" on Checker; Noble "Thin Man" Watts' "Easy Going" on Baton; and Sonny Knight's "Short Walk" on Starla.

AUG 12 Gene Vincent makes a rare television appearance on this

THE FIVE KEYS
The Five Keys were among the most respected of the early R&B vocal groups. The group was formed in Newport News, Virginia, in 1946 when two sets of brothers got together to vocalize. Rudy and Bernie West, and Raphael and Ripley Ingram called themselves the Sentimental Four. When they added Dickie Smith, they changed their name to the Five Keys. Raphael was drafted in 1950, and his place was permanently filled by Maryland Pierce. In early 1951, the Five Keys signed with Aladdin Records, and their second release was the million-selling "The Glory of Love" with Rudy West on lead and Dickie Smith on the bridge. Both Rudy and Dickie joined the Army in 1952, and they were replaced by Ulysses Hicks and Raymond Loper, although West continued to record with the group until he was released from the Army in 1956. The group remained with Aladdin until late 1953, issuing a total of nineteen singles. Lead vocals on most of the Aladdin singles was handled by Rudy West, Dickey Smith, or Maryland Pierce. The group signed with Capitol Records in September 1954, and their first Capitol release was another the million-seller, "Ling, Ting, Tong." Over the next two years, the Five Keys had hits with "Close Your Eyes," "The Verdict," "Out of Sight, Out of Mind," and "Wisdom of a Fool." The Five Keys remained on Capitol through 1958, with a total of nineteen singles, before moving on the King Records in 1959. With King, they released two of their eight singles on the label before Rudy West broke away from the group for three solo releases. At that time, his place in the group was filled by Thomas Threat. The Five Keys had one last single on Seg-Way, a remake of "Out of Sight, Out of Mind." In 1964, the group was still active in clubs. In the early 1970s, members of the Five Keys included Rudy and Bernie West, Dickie Smith, Raymond Loper, and Ripley Ingram.

afternoon's "American Bandstand." He performs "Be-Bop-A-Lulu."

MID-AUGUST

Chuck Berry and Lloyd Price share top billing as they begin a tour of the Pacific Northwest and West Coast.

ABC-Paramount Records announces the signing of a trio of eighteen-year old women, the Poni-Tails.

It is reported that Alan Freed and an all-star troupe leave for a three-week tour of England, but there is no further confirmation.

AUG 16 At the Apollo Theater, Buddy Holly and the Crickets play New York City for the first time. Also opening this week's booking are Clyde McPhatter, Otis Rush and the Cadillacs.

Mickey and Sylvia begin a week-long engagement at New Orleans' Safari Club.

The Shubert Theater in Detroit offers a smorgasbord of talent during a week-long run. Featured are Fats Domino, the Billy Williams Quartet, Paul Anka, Ann Cole, the Velours, Jo Ann Campbell, Lee Andrews and the Hearts, the Delroys, the Schoolboys, and the Bobbettes.

Also playing Detroit for a week, Otis Williams and His Charms are at the Flame Show Bar.

AUG 17 Wanda Jackson, female rockabilly star, opens a two-day engagement at Cleveland's Circle Star Theater.

AUG 18 The Blue Eagle Ballroom in New Orleans presents Little Junior Parker for the dance crowd tonight.

AUG 19 Jerry Lee Lewis appears on "American Bandstand." He was one of the few performers who only performed "live" on the show. Also on guesting on today's show are Jimmy Bowen and the Rhythm Orchids.

New Releases for the third week in August include "Love Is A Treasure" by Mickey and Sylvia on Vik; "To Each His Own" by Billy Ward and His Dominoes on Decca; "My Special Angel" by **Bobby Helms** on Decca; "Little Bitty Pretty One" by Bobby Day on Class; "Tell Me Why" by the Rob-Roys on Back Beat; "Carol" by the Schoolboys on Okeh; and "Leaving It up To You" by Don and Dewey on Specialty.

AUG 22 Jerry Lee Lewis embarks on a summer tour of the South with a show in Nashville. The following night, he performs in Philadelphia, Mississippi. Thereafter, he plays from one small burg to the next—through Georgia and Florida.

AUG 23 Buddy Holly and the Crickets guest on Alan Freed's ABC-TV show.

At the Apollo Theater, "Dr. Jive and his Top Ten Rhythm and Blues Revue" holds down this week's spot. Featured acts include

BOBBY HELMS
Bobby Helms was a seasoned performer by the time he was ten. He grew up in Bloomington, Indiana, the same town in which he was born, August 15, 1993. The owner of W9XZ radio (later WTTS) liked the boy and befriended him with a radio show. When television came to Bloomington, Helms hosted the "Hayloft" program. He and his country band played the area and built a loyal following. On a friend's advice, he sent a demo tape to Ernest Tubb, a country star who had a broadcast every Saturday at midnight on Nashville's WLAC radio, a clear-channel station. Helms was invited to appear on Tubb's show, which led to a contract with Decca Records. His first single, released in June 1956, was "Tennessee Rock and Roll," an up-tempo country tune. Decca waited almost a year before issuing his second single, "Fraulein," which became a smash hit that remained on the country charts for fifty-two weeks and had a respectable showing in the "pop" market. "Fraulein" was followed by "My Special Angel" and "Jingle Bell Rock," the two songs Helms is associated with today. Helms had minor hits with his next four singles, "Just a Little Lonesome," "Jacqueline," "Borrowed Dreams" and "The Fool and the Angel." In 1957-58, he was a television guest on "The Ed Sullivan Show," "American Bandstand" and Dick Clark's Saturday night show. Decca tried to convert Helms' country style to compete with crossover artists like Jim Reeves; but, by the end of 1958, his recording career had dried up. He still made frequent appearances on the "Grand Ole Opry" and continued to record for Decca until 1962. He moved on to Columbia, Kapp, Little Darlin, Ashley, Certron, American National Sound, Million, Larrick, Gusto and Stardom. Today, Helms lives in Martinsville, Indiana, and he continues to perform locally.

the Shells, the G-Clefs, Jo Ann Campbell, the Dells, the Paragons, Johnnie and Joe, the Cleftones, and the Cadillacs.

On television, "Showtime At The Apollo" welcomes Amos Milburn and the Clovers.

Ray Charles, the Turbans, Nappy Brown, and Jimmy Witherspoon entertain patrons for a week at Washington's Howard Theater.

AUG 25   Jimmie Rodgers makes his national prime time TV debut on "The Ed Sullivan Show" on CBS. Also on the program is Miss LaVern Baker.

AUG 26   Buddy Holly and the Crickets appear on "American Bandstand."

New Releases for the fourth week in August include "Wake Up Little Susie" by the Everly Brothers on Cadence; Johnny Burnette's "Drinking Wine Spo-Dee-O-Dee" on Coral; "Ain't I'm a Dog" by Ronnie Self on Columbia; "The Mystery of You" by the Platters on Mercury; and "I Found My Love" by the Velvetones on Aladdin.

AUG 30   Bill Haley and His Comets are booked for a four-day stand at the Michigan State Fair.

Running through the Labor Day weekend, Alan Freed's ten-day "Holiday Rock 'N Roll Stage Show," with Little Richard headlining, kicks off at the Brooklyn Paramount Theater. This event also features Buddy Holly and the Crickets, Mickey and Sylvia, the Del Vikings, the Diamonds, the Moonglows, the Five Satins, the Five Keys, the Tune Weavers, Larry Williams, Jo Ann Campbell, Ocie Smith, the Cleftones, Jimmie Rodgers, and Shaye Cogan.

This week's show at the Apollo Theater in New York headlines Fats Domino and his seven-man band. Also offered are Bo Diddley, the Harptones, Lee Andrews and the Hearts, Little Joe and the Thrillers, and Big Maybelle. The gross ticket sales for the Sunday (SEP 1) show is the largest in the theater's history up to this time.

Carl Perkins begins a two-day layover in the Los Angeles area.

Della Reese opens a two-week run at Detroit's Fiesta Club.

Buddy and Ella Johnson headline this week's revue at the Howard Theater in Washington. Also on hand are the Charts, the Dubs, and Huey Smith and the Clowns.

Elvis Presley's five-day tour of the Pacific Northwest begins with a bang as tonight's concert in Spokane's Memorial Stadium grosses $22,000. Tomorrow, two shows in Vancouver's Empire Stadium will bring in $44,000. (See also SEP 1.)

AUG 31   **Johnny Cash** makes a Napa, California, appearance at the Dream Bowl.

In Dallas, the "Big D Jamboree" presents three up-and-coming rockers, Gene Rambo, Joe Poovey and Johnny Carroll.

JOHNNY CASH
Johnny Cash walked a fine line. He could be pure country one minute, and cross over into the musical mainstream the next. He was born in Kingsland, in rural, south-central Arkansas, on February 26, 1932, although his early press releases claimed 1933. His family moved to Dyess, Arkansas, just up river from Memphis, when he was three. His father, Ray Cash, was an itinerant farmer, hobo, and odd-job laborer. He was also part-Cherokee, and the pride of his heritage burned within him. The move to Dyess meant hope for the poverty-stricken Cash family. Ray and his oldest son, Roy, worked hard developing their government-subsidized farm. When he was a little older, Johnny joined them. He would work the fields by day, and listen to the family's radio at night, picking out the Memphis stations with their mix of country and blues songs. Johnny began composing songs, unknowingly combining the best of both styles. His family, especially his mother, Reba, encouraged him. When he was older, he left home to work in Pontiac, Michigan. The job lasted two weeks before Johnny fled back to Arkansas. In 1950, he enlisted in the Air Force and was stationed in Germany, where he bought his first guitar to relieve the boredom. He started setting his songs to music, and one of the first he finished was "Folsom Prison Blues." In 1954, he moved to Memphis where he met two would-be musicians, Luther Perkins and Marshall Grant, who were mechanics working with Roy. The three decided to have a try at being professional entertainers. They approached Sun Records, but owner Sam Phillips was busy promoting Elvis Presley's first records and wasn't interested in country music. It took a year to get Phillips to grant an audition. Their first Sun single was "Hey Porter" b/w "Cry! Cry! Cry!" Their second release was "Folsom Prison Blues."

LATE AUGUST

Following an engagement at Lakewood Park in Mahoney, Pennsylvania, Bill Haley and His Comets open an extended engagement at the Casino Cafe in Sea Isle City, New Jersey. Afterward, the group will tour from the Midwest to the West Coast where they are supposed to start production on a third movie co-starring Alan Freed. However, a last-minute change in Freed's schedule initially delays the starting date on the movie by two months allowing the Comets to extend their West Coast bookings. Eventually, as the public's taste shifted away from Haley's music, the movie deal was cancelled altogether.

Also on the West Coast, Faye Adams begins a six-week trek.

Clarence "Frogman" Henry, Bullmoose Jackson, and Lewis Lymon and the Teenchords are touring the British West Indies for two weeks.

Liberty Records sends its new recording artist, Eddie Cochran, out to visit with disc jockeys in Cleveland, Detroit, Chicago, and St. Louis.

Dot Records announces the signing of Pat Boone's brother, Nick Boone. So as not to confuse the record-buying public, a name change is in order, and the new artist comes up with **Nick Todd** (that's "Dot" spelled backward, sort of).

Noble "Thin Man" Watts and the Orioles start a tour of the South.

Jackie Wilson, recent lead tenor with Billy Ward and His Dominoes, gives his solo career a boost with an engagement at New York's Baby Grand Club.

Universal International Pictures announces the signing of Fats Domino, the Del Vikings, and the Diamonds. All are set to start shooting cameos for the new rock 'n roll picture, "The Big Beat."

THE TOP ROCK 'N ROLL RECORDS FOR AUGUST 1957

1. Teddy Bear/Loving You - Elvis Presley
2. Bye Bye Love - The Everly Brothers
3. Searchin'/Young Blood - The Coasters
4. Diana - Paul Anka
5. Short Fat Fannie - Larry Williams
6. Whispering Bells - The Dell-Vikings
7. I'm Gonna Sit Right Down and Write Myself a Letter - Billy Williams
8. Whole Lot of Shakin' Going On - Jerry Lee Lewis
9. Stardust - Billy Ward and His Dominoes
10. The Flying Saucer, the 2nd - Buchanan and Goodman
11. Jenny Jenny/Miss Ann - Little Richard
12. That'll Be The Day - The Crickets
13. To The Aisle - The Five Satins
14. Over The Mountain, Across the Sea - Johnnie and Joe
15. Mr. Lee - The Bobbettes
16. Gonna Find Me A Bluebird - Marvin Rainwater

NICK TODD

Being the brother of one of the hottest singers in the land is a two-edge sword. Nick's older brother was Pat Boone. Nick was born on June 1, 1935, in Jacksonville, Florida, almost exactly a year after Pat. When Pat started his recording career in Nashville with Republic Records in 1954, Nick was attending David Lipscomb College, also in Nashville. In 1956, he was surprised when he won a Nashville talent show that he entered "because I was expected to." This led to work with a college quartet and an eventual single on Deb Records, "High School Baby" by Nicky Dean and the Sports. While the record was "tame" according to Nick, there was enough innuendo to upset the Church of Christ leaders of the college. The end result was that he lost his position as editor of the yearbook. Dot Records, Pat's label at the time and a company with their headquarters in nearby Gallatin, took notice. Nick was signed, and in a reverse campaign, his new name (Nick Todd) was bandied about "because he didn't want to capitalize on Pat's name." In the meantime, Nick graduated from Lipscomb in May 1957 and began acting classes in New York at Columbia University, which Pat was also attending at the time. His first Dot single was "Plaything." It featured Nick's passably pleasant vocal, along with a "cute" female vocal group and a "swinging" bastardization of rock 'n roll instrumental backing. That said, it sold enough copies to just miss the Top Forty in the fall of 1957. It was followed that winter by the less successful cover of "At the Hop." Even with nine singles on Dot, Todd never planned on a singing career. He did make the usual TV appearances, the shows of Ed Sullivan and Patti Page, as well as the Pat Boone Chevy Showroom. He tried to break into Broadway with little success and after a few years moved to Florida where he became a social worker.

17. A White Sport Coat - Marty Robbins
18. A Teenager's Romance/I'm Walking - Ricky Nelson
19. Goody Goody - Frankie Lymon and the Teenagers
20. Honeycomb - Jimmie Rodgers
21. All Shook Up - Elvis Presley
22. Valley of Tears/It's You I Love - Fats Domino
23. Start Movin' - Sal Mineo
24. Susie-Q - Dale Hawkins
25. Let The Four Winds Blow - Roy Brown
26. Cool Shake - The Del Vikings
27. What Will I Tell My Heart/When I See You - Fats Domino
28. C. C. Rider - Chuck Willis
29. Long, Lonely Nights - Lee Andrews and the Hearts
30. Long, Lonely Nights - Clyde McPhatter
31. School Day - Chuck Berry
32. Oh, Baby Doll - Chuck Berry
33. Rockin' Pneumonia and the Boogie Woogie Flu - Huey Smith and the Clowns
34. Darling, It's Wonderful - The Lovers
35. Lotta Lovin' - Gene Vincent
36. Little Darlin' - The Diamonds
37. With All My Heart - Jodie Sands
38. Come Go With Me - The Dell-Vikings
39. You're My One and Only Love - Ricky Nelson
40. Rock Your Little Baby To Sleep - Buddy Knox
41. Hula Love - Buddy Knox
42. My Dream - The Platters
43. He's Mine - The Platters
44. Black Slacks - Joe Bennett and the Sparkletones
45. Farther Up the Road - Bobby "Blue" Bland
46. Rang-Tang-Ding-Dong - The Cellos
47. High School Romance - George Hamilton IV
48. I Love You So Much It Hurts - Charlie Gracie
49. Dynamite - Brenda Lee
50. Miss You So - Lillian Offitt

Also on the "pop" charts:
White Silver Sands - Don Rondo

August 1957
ARTIST OF THE MONTH

LARRY WILLIAMS

In the beginning, all Larry Williams wanted out of life was to be a rock 'n roll star. He got his wish. In the end, he also got a whole lot more than he bargained for.

Williams was born on May 10, 1935, in New Orleans. His family moved west to Oakland at the end of World War II. Although he would receive his start in New Orleans and his sound would be a direct descendent of the Crescent City, he always considered the Oakland area to be his home.

Larry Williams

In high school, Williams was pianist and part time vocalist with the Lemon Drops, an up-and-coming Oakland club band. Soon after graduation, probably during the summer of 1953, he moved back to New Orleans. At that time, the two hottest acts in town were Fats Domino and Lloyd Price. Domino was unapproachable, but Price took an immediate liking to Williams' brash countenance and offered him a job as his personal valet and chauffeur. Williams toured with Price until early 1954, when Price was drafted into the Army. Williams returned to Oakland, gathered the Lemon Drops together and traveled to Los Angeles to audition the band with Art Rupe, owner of Specialty Records, Price's label. Rupe wasn't impressed, and Williams and the band returned to Oakland to work the club scene for the next two years.

Price received his discharge in late 1955. He had served in the Army's Special Services Division, where he worked with a big band touring the Far East. It was this sound that he most wanted to put on wax. Rupe was adamant that Price should return to the R&B style that had brought his first hit records. The situation could not be resolved, and Price left the label. Price moved to Washington, DC, and formed the Kent Record Company (K.R.C.). In January 1957, he issued "Just Because" and it's immediate success brought a distribution offer from ABC-Paramount. In early February, 1957, ABC-Paramount leased and reissued Price's "Just Because," and the record swept the country.

In Los Angeles, Art Rupe couldn't believe his ears. The sound of Price's big band R&B was catching on. Well, if Price could do it, so could Specialty. Rupe contacted Larry Williams and asked him to come immediately to Los Angeles for a session. Under Rupe's guidance, Williams copied the Price version of "Just Because" note for note, using an identical piano-triplet, three-horn instrumental arrangement, as well as Price's vocal inflection. The two records were as alike as was humanly possible. The only advantage Price had was that his was on the market first. However, in the record business, the winner is often determined on the basis of timing. In sales, Price's "Just Because" far outsold that of Larry Williams.

Williams returned to the studio in April, this time using members of Little Richard's Upsetters to give his sound a distinctly New Orleans feel. Among the songs he recorded were the traditional children's tune, "Iko, Iko (Jockomo);" a teen-oriented ballad, "High School Dance;" and

175

an off-the-cuff novelty, "Short Fat Fannie." Of course, it was the novelty that sold a million copies.

The song defies analysis or accurate description. Williams opens by whistling the melody line. The lyrics tie together the song titles of more than a dozen rock n' roll hits, including four from Little Richard: "Slippin' and Slidin'," "Long Tall Sally," "Rip It Up," and "Tutti Frutti." Williams was also able to work in "Hound Dog," "Heartbreak Hotel," "Fever," "Blue Suede Shoes," "Mary Lou," "Honky Tonk," "Jim Dandy," "Blue Monday," and Blueberry Hill."

In September, Williams was in New Orleans to try a recording session at J&M Studios, the home of all those hits by Fats Domino, Huey Smith, and Lloyd Price. For unknown reasons, only one song was completed, and Williams retreated to Los Angeles. He would not return to the Crescent City to record for another year, and even that session also would end poorly.

After singing about "Short Fat Fannie," Williams followed with a song about "Bony Moronie," who was "as skinny as a stick of macaroni." As crazy as it might sound, this record also sold a million copies. In 1957, the New Orleans sound was riding high. Fats Domino was in the seventh year of his string of hits. Huey Smith and the Clowns had a hit with "Rocking Pneumonia and the Boogie Woogie Flu." Larry Williams had even recorded a duplicate version of the song two months before Smith's single was released, but it was not issued at the time.

The songs that Williams may be most recognized for today are "Dizzy, Miss Lizzy" and "Slow Down," issued back-to-back as his fourth single. The Beatles recorded both songs in 1964, and their version of "Slow Down" was a hit single. Williams' originals are classic New Orleans-style rock 'n roll, although his delivery on "Dizzy, Miss Lizzy" shows less intensity than "Slow Down." It may have been that he was put off by the simplicity of his own song, which included lyrics such as the opening lines, "You make me dizzy, Miss Lizzy, when we rock and roll; you make me dizzy, Miss Lizzy, when we do the stroll." "Slow Down" opens with an extended instrumental riff featuring a romping piano, a slamming drum, and a tick-tight rhythm section. Williams belts out the lyrics with an anxiety worthy of Little Richard himself.

In February, 1958, when "Dizzy, Miss Lizzy" was released, it was the heyday of Frankie Avalon, Ricky Nelson, and Paul Anka. Even Little Richard had given up on rock 'n roll for religion, and teenagers didn't want a copycat. Williams didn't help his own cause when his next single was "Hootchy Koo." This was the type of grinding dance song that Hank Ballard would take to perfection with "Finger Poppin' Time" two years later. "Hootchy Koo" was followed by "Bad Boy," a song so similar to "Dizzy, Miss Lizzy" that it might have brought a lawsuit for plagiarism if it hadn't also been composed by Williams.

With two gold records, Larry Williams had enough credibility to remain a viable touring act for several years, even without another hit. In 1959, he was arrested for possession of narcotics and Specialty dropped him from the company roster. Williams soon signed with Chess Records and had a minor hit with "My Baby's Got Soul." There were three more singles by Williams on Chess but none broke the ice. In the meantime,

Specialty continued to issue his remaining sides, but they were overdubbed with female vocalists in an attempt to capture the teen audience again.

In 1967, Williams went on to work as a producer for Epic and Okeh, subsidiaries of Columbia Records. His 1967 production of "(Why) Am I Treated So Bad" by the Staple Singers was their first crossover hit. He teamed vocally with Johnny "Guitar" Watson, as well as producing their album TWO FOR THE PRICE OF ONE and the single "Mercy, Mercy, Mercy." He also produced Little Richard's sessions for Okeh. In the 1950s, the two men had been on friendly terms, even sharing the same band from time to time. Now, both men were heavily into cocaine, and they fought constantly over the most trivial events. It was reported that at one point, Williams took after Richard with a pistol, claiming nonpayment for drugs.

Even in the late 1960s, at the pinnacle of the era of hallucinogens, Williams' behavior was his own worst enemy. He tried to operate his own musical revue starring Johnny "Guitar" Watson, but he was not up to the long-term, logistical nightmare such an endeavor could create. On the other hand, he wrote the title song for the Michael Caine-Jane Fonda movie, "Hurry Sundown," which one critic described as "the best thing about the movie." After that, Larry Williams retired to his homes in Oakland and Los Angeles.

There were enough royalties coming from his songwriting to keep him high all the time. However, Larry Williams was an opportunist and a manipulator, and he needed to nurture that side of his life. He had always been a fine-looking man, one who found it easy to meet attractive women. Put this with the fact that he was dealing heavily in drugs, and you come up with Larry Williams, Super-Pimp.

In 1978, he was asked to join the musical cast of "American Hot Wax." After a few days on the set he was let go, for "extravagant behavior, including drug use." A year later, he recorded THAT LARRY WILLIAMS, a disco-funk album for Fantasy Records. The front cover presented Williams all decked out in a full-length fur coat and hat, pouring champagne into the radiator of his Rolls Royce. Even with all that to promote it, nothing came of the album.

On January 2, 1980, his lifestyle finally caught up with him. His body was discovered inside his luxury home in the hills above Los Angeles. He had been shot once in the head. All the doors to the house were locked. The police ruled it was suicide—those close to him weren't so sure. At the funeral, Little Richard sang a gospel song in tribute. At last, all of Larry Williams' sins were forgiven.

Larry Williams' story shouldn't have ended this way. He had talent and ego enough for a whole platoon of rock 'n rollers. He also had business sense, personality and drive. At another time, he might have ended up owning the record company, like his mentor, Lloyd Price. Instead he always worked for "the man." However, he liked the good life that came with being a famous recording star. At the height of his popularity, the size his retinue was legendary, even by Hollywood standards. Larry Williams was a case of extreme overindulgence. Just like his finest records.

September 1957

THE PONI-TAILS
The Poni-Tails were three young ladies from Lyndhurst, Ohio. Antoinette "Toni" Cistone, Karen Topinka, and LaVerne Novak attended the same small high school and dreamed of a singing career patterned after the Chordettes or the Fontane Sisters. Before that happened, Karen left the group and was replaced by Patricia "Patti" McCabe, another student. Influenced by Toni's Italian ancestry, they composed a song titled "Que La Bozena." During a benefit performance, they were approached by a local music entrepreneur who promised to get them a recording contract. "Que La Bozena" was released in January 1957 as the flip side of "Your Wild Heart" on Point Records, a division of R-K-O motion pictures. "Your Wild Heart," a syrup-sweet teen ditty, was covered by Joy Layne on Mercury Records, a company with wide-reaching distribution, and Miss Layne's record flirted around the Top Forty for the better part of two months while the Poni-Tails' version disappeared without a trace. Disappointed, the Poni-Tails turned their attention to their studies. Before long ABC-Paramount Records showed some interest. "It's Just My Luck To Be 15" was their first ABC release. It didn't catch on, and it was nine months before their second ABC single. "Born Too Late" easily cracked the Top Ten in the "pop" field and did well in the R&B market as well. The Poni-Tails had a moderate hit with "Seven Seconds in Heaven," patterned after "Born Too Late." Then, "Early to Bed," flopped. "I'll Be Seeing You," their fourth ABC single, sold slowly following its September 1959 release. "Before We Say Goodnight" was their final single before being released from their ABC contract. It was 1960, and other interests lay in their future. Toni and LaVerne married and moved to Ohio. Patti passed away on January 17, 1989, after a bout with cancer.

SEP 1   Carl Perkins performs in San Diego, part of his current West Coast tour.

Elvis Presley's tour of the Pacific Northwest continues with a performance at Tacoma's Lincoln Bowl Stadium. The remaining dates on this short run include Seattle's Ranier Ball Park (2) and Multnomah Stadium in Portland (3). Total revenue from the tour approaches $150,000.

In Washington, Jodie Sands opens a two-day stand entertaining on the nightly S.S. Mount Vernon cruise on the Potomac River.

SEP 2   The Bobbettes perform "Mr. Lee" on "American Bandstand."

New Releases for the first week in September include the original version of "Plaything" by Ted Newman on Rev. Also new are "Keep A Knockin'" by Little Richard on Specialty; The Dell-Vikings' "I'm Spinning" on Dot; "Reet Petite" by Jackie Wilson on Brunswick; "You Send Me" by Sam Cooke on Keen; "Teacher's Pet" by Frankie Avalon on Chancellor; two from Atlantic: "Swanee River Rock" by Ray Charles and "I Need a Girl" by Joe Turner; the **Poni-Tails**' "It's Just My Luck to be 15" on ABC-Paramount; "Hey Babe" by the Cleftones on Gee; "It Was There" by Johnnie and Joe on J & S. Also out this week is "Dearest One" on Onyx by Dean Barlow, formerly with the R&B group the Crickets on M-G-M.

SEP 3   The Mello-Kings make an appearance on ABC-TV's "American Bandstand."

SEP 4   Charlie Gracie opens at the Hippodrome Theater in London.

SEP 6   Commencing his solo career, Frankie Lymon joins the package tour put together by Super Attractions. Opening at the Syria Mosque in Pittsburgh, the "Biggest Show of Stars for '57" hits the road for eighty days. The acts in the revue will change several times during the tour. In the beginning, in addition to Lymon, headliners include Fats Domino, LaVern Baker, Chuck Berry, Paul Anka, Clyde McPhatter, the Spaniels, the Drifters, Johnnie and Joe, and the Bobbettes. Along the way, Johnnie and Joe, the Bobbettes, and the Spaniels will leave, to be replaced by the Clovers, Buddy Holly and the Crickets, Buddy Knox and Jimmy Bowen with the Rhythm Orchids, and the Everly Brothers. Succeeding nights will see the troupe in Richmond (7); Washington's Griffith Stadium (8); Norfolk (9); Akron (10); Cincinnati (11); and Columbus (12). Salary for the Crickets was reported to be $1,000 per week for the foursome. (See also SEP 13.)

A gospel and spiritual revue fills the bill at the Apollo Theater for the week.

A special two-week run at the Flame in Detroit features Della Reese, T-Bone Walker, and the Four Tops. Also in town, John Lee Hooker returns to the Apex Bar for the weekend.

SEP 7   Gene Vincent and His Blue Caps are guests of the "Big D Jamboree" in Dallas.

EARLY SEPTEMBER

Bill Haley and His Comets play the Casa Loma Ballroom in St. Louis. They are starting a tour through the West Coast states, ending in Washington on October 16.

The Jive Bombers are set for a four-week run at the French Quarter in Union City, New Jersey.

It is reported in the music press that Rosco Gordon is scheduled for an upcoming tour of South America in the immediate future.

Johnny Cash is hospitalized in Memphis with a throat ailment that ultimately requires minor surgery. He is told by his doctors to refrain from touring for at least a month.

SEP 8   Louis Jordan and his Tympany Five and B. B. King and his combo share the spotlight for a show at the Municipal Auditorium in New Orleans.

Jimmie Rodgers returns to the "Ed Sullivan Show" on CBS-TV to plug "Honeycomb."

New Releases for the second week in September include "Be-Bop Baby" by Ricky Nelson on Imperial; "Cross Over" by Jimmy Bowen on Roulette; Kathy Linden's "The Touch of Love" on National; "Plaything" by Nick Todd on Dot; "The Majesty of Love" by Marvin Rainwater and Connie Francis on M-G-M; "Honest I Do" by Jimmy Reed on Vee-Jay; "The Beating of My Heart" by the Moonglows on Chess; and two from Atlantic Records: "Down in the Alley" by the Clovers and Ruth Brown's "Show Me." Also out this week is "Hey Little School Girl" on Okeh by the Marquees, featuring a young Marvin Gaye.

SEP 10   Jimmie Rodgers stops by "American Bandstand" to sing "Honeycomb" for the teen audience.

SEP 12   On "American Bandstand," the Tune Weavers sing "Happy, Happy Birthday Baby."

SEP 13   Continuing to travel north, the "Biggest Show of Stars for '57" tour plays Hershey, Pennsylvania, tonight and the Maple Leaf Gardens in Toronto tomorrow. As they move through Canada and the Northeast, succeeding nights find the entertainers in Montreal (15), Syracuse (16), and Rochester (17). The two shows in Montreal

EDDIE FONTAINE
Being mistaken as the younger brother of a successful female vocal group has its perks—and its drawbacks. So it was with Eddie Fontaine and the Fontane Sisters. Eddie Reardon was born in 1938, in Queens, a borough of New York City. As a young boy, he prepared for a show business career by becoming a proficient guitarist. In 1947, when he returned to New York after two years in the Navy, he began a successful night club career. In 1954, he auditioned for RCA Victor, and his cover of Sonny Thompson's "Rock Love" was released in early 1955 on RCA's Vik subsidiary. "Rock Love" was also covered by the Fontane Sisters (that was their real last name). Eddie had a spot on Alan Freed's Easter week Paramount show. Fontaine had six more singles on RCA subsidiaries Vik and "X." Upset at the "pop" material he was being offered, Eddie left RCA and recorded one single, "It Ain't Gonna Happen No More," for the small Jalo label before signing with Decca in early 1957. He appeared in the movie "The Girl Can't Help It," promoting "Cool It," his first Decca release. A total of nine singles later (including two as Eddie Reardon on Brunswick, a Decca subsidiary), and he signed with Sunbeam. His first release was "Nothin' Shakin'," a rompin' rocker. Unknown to Fontaine, the song's publisher leased an early demo version of "Nothin' Shakin'" to Argo Records, one of the Chess labels. The Argo version sold moderately in the fall of 1958 and was Fontaine's only charted single. Eddie's Hollywood experience taught him that acting was where his future lay. From 1961-63, he appeared in the TV series "The Gallant Men." In the 1970s, he had a recurring role as Fonzie's father on "Happy Days." He also had guest roles on "Rockford Files," "Police Woman," and "The Six Million Dollar Man." He continued to sing in clubs, although his act consisted on mostly Italian love songs.

brings in 30,000 fans, which is a one-day record for the Forum. (See also SEP 18.)

The Everly Brothers perform "Wake Up Little Susie" on "American Bandstand."

At the Apollo Theater, the week's revue features Dinah Washington, the Charts, and Ocie Smith.

Mickey and Sylvia, Otis Williams and His Charms, Sonny Til and the Orioles, and Jackie Wilson hit the boards at Washington's Howard Theater for a week.

SEP 14   **Eddie Fontaine** guests on "Stage Show" on CBS-TV.

SEP 15   "The Ed Sullivan Show" is visited by Billy Ward and His Dominoes who sing "Stardust" and their latest release, "Deep Purple."

MID-SEPTEMBER

Based on their faith in the Westrex StereoDisk system, RCA Victor announces that stereophonic records will become a commercial reality by 1958. Experimental stereo records date from the 1930s.

Capitol Records signs the entire Johnny Otis Revue to recording contracts. Otis and his troupe, including the Three Tons of Joy, Mel Williams, Marie Adams, and the Moonbeams, had previously recorded for Otis' Dig Records, which is currently inactive. Otis is one of the most widely respected rhythm and blues band leaders, having backed early sides by a long list of artists including Little Richard and Big Mama Thornton.

The Coasters, the Five Satins, and the Cellos play the Mammoth Gardens in Denver.

Mercury/Starday Records signs song writer J. P. "Jape" Richardson, a disk jockey at KTRM, Beaumont, Texas. Richardson has recorded a couple of sides for D Records and has had several songs recorded by other artists on Starday and Hickory Records.

The Nelsons, everyone's favorite TV family, are embroiled in a lawsuit over Ricky's recording contract. Verve Records, the company issuing the first two singles sues for breach of contract when Ricky jumps ship to Imperial Records. The Nelsons countersue, asking for $42,000 in unpaid royalties. In turn, Verve countersues, asking for one million dollars in damages. Stay tuned.

Ruth Brown and her husband, Earl Swan, tenor sax session musician with Atlantic Records, announce the birth of their first child. Miss Brown's maternity leave will last only two weeks, as she is has bookings scheduled in mid-October.

SEP 16   "American Bandstand" hosts Gene Vincent and His Blue Caps and the Diamonds on ABC-TV.

New Releases for the third week in September include "Jailhouse Rock" by Elvis Presley on RCA Victor; "Come Along With Me" by the Del Vikings on Mercury; Paul Anka's "I Love You Baby" on ABC-Paramount; "Have I Sinned" by Donnie Elbert on DeLuxe; **Thurston Harris**' version of "Little Bitty Pretty One" on Aladdin; "My Surprise" by the Six Teens featuring Trudy Williams on Flip; "Ma, He's Making Eyes At Me" by Marie Adams and the Three Tons of Joy on Capitol; Narvel Felts' "Cry Baby Cry" on Mercury; and Jay Holliday's "Wang Dang Do" on East-West.

SEP 18   "The Biggest Show of Stars for '57" is set for a run through the Deep South, and to avoid local segregation laws, several acts including Paul Anka, Jimmy Bowen and Buddy Knox with the Rhythm Orchids and Buddy Holly the Crickets, depart while Johnnie and Joe, the Spaniels, and the Bobbettes are added to the southern leg. Starting along the East Coast, "The Biggest Show of Stars for '57" plays a one-nighter at the Coliseum in Baltimore tonight. Continuing through the South, the tour plays Raleigh (19), Winston-Salem (20), Charlotte (21), Atlanta (22), Columbus, Georgia (23), Chattanooga (24), Birmingham (25), New Orleans (26), and Memphis (27). The Everly Brothers leave the tour following the show in Winston-Salem. (See also SEP 26 and 28.)

On "American Bandstand," Frankie Avalon, a local Philadelphia teenager best known at this time for his trumpet stylings, makes a non-performing appearance.

CBS-TV premiers "The Big Record," a weekly variety program hosted by Patti Page. Tonight's guests are Sal Mineo and Billy Ward and His Dominoes.

SEP 20   Art Neville and the Hawkettes play a "back to school" dance for teenagers at the Labor Union Hall in New Orleans.

Joe Bennett and the Sparkletones begin an "indefinite" engagement at the Royal Nevada Hotel in Las Vegas. They continue at the hotel well into October.

The Howard Theater in Washington offers a New Orleans-flavored revue this week. Featured are Larry Williams, Clarence "Frogman" Henry, Huey Smith and the Clowns, Bobby Marchan, Screamin' Jay Hawkins, the Lovers, and the Mello-Kings.

SEP 21   In New York, Johnny Mathis and the Flamingos share this week's billing at the Apollo Theater.

The two musicians who had been with Elvis Presley throughout his professional career quit the act in a dispute over wages. Scotty Moore, electric guitar, and Bill Black, bass, have been an integral part of Presley's success, playing on virtually every recording session and performing with Presley on tour and even appearing in several of his movies. Moore will continue to record with Presley until 1969 while Black will form Bill Black's Combo, a successful instrumental group beginning in late 1959. Moore will become a successful record producer, beginning with "Tragedy" by Thomas Wayne in 1959. He will continue to play on Elvis' recording sessions until 1969.

New Releases for the fourth week in September include Frankie Lymon's

THURSTON HARRIS
In 1957-58, Thurston Harris and Bobby Day battled each other up and down the music charts. Harris was born in Indianapolis, July 11, 1931. He was a popular local blues singer when he took an offer to tour with Joe Liggins, a famed Los Angeles band leader. Once back in Los Angeles, Harris fell in with Al Frazier, a singer with great aspirations. Frazier had been a member of the hectic LA vocal group scene since 1948. In 1953, he was looking for singers for the Lamplighters, his latest group. Harris was one of the first to join. The Lamplighters recorded thirteen singles on Federal over the next three years, most of which featured Harris on lead vocal. Members of the Lamplighters also recorded as the Tenderfoots on Federal, but Harris is not featured on these sides. Harris, tired of the constant touring, returned to Indianapolis as soon as the Lamplighters broke up. Based on his experience with the Lamplighters, he had little trouble in signing a solo contract with Aladdin Records, a Los Angeles company. For his first session, Harris used the Lamplighters as his backing group. The song he chose was a version of Bobby Day's "Little Bitty Pretty One." During the late months of 1957, the two singles raced each other up the "pop" and R&B charts, with the Harris version winning in both markets. In June 1958, Harris and Day were at it again, this time recording versions of "Over and Over." Day won handily this time as his version was the flip side of "Rock-In Robin." Harris had more than a dozen singles on Aladdin through 1960. He continued with Imperial after it absorbed Aladdin. He also recorded for Dot, Cub and Reprise into 1964. After all his success, Harris retired to Indianapolis for several years before moving to the Los Angeles area, where he drove a bus. Thurston Harris died on April 14, 1990, of a heart attack.

first solo single, "My Girl" on Roulette; "Wait and See" by Fats Domino on Imperial; "Peggy Sue" by Buddy Holly on Coral; "School Fool" by Mark Dinning on M-G-M; **Jesse Belvin**'s version of "You Send Me" on Modern; "That's My Desire" by Bob and Earl on Class; and "You're Gonna Cry" by the Spaniels on Vee-Jay.

SEP 26   The Rays lip-sync "Silhouettes" on "American Bandstand" today.
   LaVern Baker headlines the "Biggest Show of Stars for '57" show at New Orleans' Municipal Auditorium. Sharing tonight's bill are Chuck Berry, Frankie Lymon, Clyde McPhatter, the Spaniels, Johnnie and Joe, the Drifters, and the Bobbettes. Fats Domino, originally advertised for the New Orleans show, is dropped before the show date. (See Sep 17 and 18.)

SEP 27   Jerry Lee Lewis headlines this week's show at New York's Apollo Theater. A review of his portion of the show reveals that during the nine minutes he was actually on stage he whipped through four songs. Also on the bill are the Quails, Margie Day, and Titus Turner.
   Elvis Presley plays the Mississippi-Alabama Dairy Show and Fair in his birthplace of Tupelo, Mississippi. The show is a benefit to raise money to build the Elvis Presley Youth Recreation Center that is to be built near the house in which he was born.
   Roy Hamilton is welcomed to the Flame Show Bar in Detroit for the week.

SEP 28   The "Biggest Show of Stars for '57" tour heads west with a show at the Municipal Auditorium in Tulsa. Other shows through the end of this month include Oklahoma City (29) and Wichita Falls (30). (See also OCT 1.)

SEP 29   Carl Perkins plays a concert in Kansas City.

SEP 30   Bill Haley and His Comets begin a major tour of Europe that will cover France, Germany, Switzerland, Italy, Belgium, and Greece.
   The Clabon Theater in New Orleans offers a rock 'n roll stage show this week featuring Professor Longhair, Bobby Mitchell, Big Boy Myles, and the "Original" Clowns.

LATE SEPTEMBER
   "Mister Rock and Roll" is released to theaters. Featuring Alan Freed, the nonstop parade of performers includes Frankie Lymon and the Teenagers, Little Richard, LaVern Baker, Clyde McPhatter, the Moonglows, Brook Benton, Teddy Randazzo, and Ferlin Huskey. Although listed as a performer, Chuck Berry's "Oh, Baby Doll" was edited from many prints of the movie.

JESSE BELVIN
Jesse Belvin is called the "Godfather of Los Angeles Doo-Wop." His given name was Jessie Lorenzo Belvin, and he was born in Texarkana or San Antonio, on December 15, 1932 (often given as 1933). When he was four, his family moved to the northern California coast. By 1940, following his father Jack's death, the family was living in Los Angeles. His early vocal training came from his mother, the director of the Mount Olivet Baptist Church. Jesse made his first records in 1951 as vocalist with the Big Jay McNeely band on Imperial Records. That same year, Jesse recorded "Confusin' Blues" under his own name for Specialty. Almost a year passed before he teamed with Marvin Phillips (later of Marvin and Johnny) as Jesse and Marvin on Specialty. "Dream Girl," the duo's only single, was a major R&B hit in early 1953. Belvin's Specialty career resumed in 1955 with two additional singles. Dissatisfied with Specialty, in 1955, he, Mel Williams and a young Eugene Church as the Sheiks, with one single, "So Fine," issued by Federal. Belvin's first Modern release, "Goodnight My Love," issued in late 1956 was his biggest hit. He also joined with Eugene Church again as the duo the Cliques (two singles on Modern: "The Girl in My Dreams" and "My Desire"). While under contract to Modern, Belvin recorded one single for Class, "I'm Confessin'" using the same producer and backing vocalist (Ricki Page) who had worked on "Goodnight My Love." (The record was released in 1960.) In 1958, Belvin was a member of the Shields, a group put he hurriedly put together to cover the Slades' "You Cheated" for Tender Records. Those who have claimed participation include Mel Williams, Johnny "Guitar" Watson, Charles Wright (of the Watts 103rd Street Rhythm Band), Buzzy Smith, and Nathaniel "Buster" Wilson. Frankie Ervin is generally agreed to be the lead vocalist.

THE TOP ROCK 'N ROLL RECORDS FOR SEPTEMBER 1957

1. Diana - Paul Anka
2. That'll Be The Day - The Crickets
3. Whole Lot of Shakin' Going On - Jerry Lee Lewis
4. Honeycomb - Jimmie Rodgers
5. Mr. Lee - The Bobbettes
6. Teddy Bear/Loving You - Elvis Presley
7. Bye Bye Love - The Everly Brothers
8. Searchin'/Young Blood - The Coasters
9. Stardust - Billy Ward and His Dominoes
10. Short Fat Fannie - Larry Williams
11. Whispering Bells - The Dell-Vikings
12. You're My One And Only Love - Ricky Nelson
13. Hula Love - Buddy Knox
14. I'm Gonna Sit Right Down and Write Myself a Letter
    - Billy Williams
15. Lotta Lovin' - Gene Vincent and His Blue Caps
16. Goody Goody - Frankie Lymon and the Teenagers
17. Happy, Happy Birthday Baby - The Tune Weavers
18. Black Slacks - Joe Bennett and the Sparkletones
19. To The Aisle - The Five Satins
20. Lasting Love - Sal Mineo
21. Farther Up the Road - Bobby "Blue" Bland
22. The Flying Saucer the 2nd - Buchanan and Goodman
23. Zip Zip - The Diamonds
24. Jenny Jenny - Little Richard
25. When I See You - Fats Domino
26. Rebel - Carol Jarvis
27. Long, Lonely Nights - Clyde McPhatter
28. Long, Lonely Nights - Lee Andrews and the Hearts
29. Rocking Pneumonia and the Boogie Woogie Flu - Huey Smith
    and the Clowns
30. Cool Shake - The Del Vikings
31. Susie-Q - Dale Hawkins
32. Wake Up Little Susie - The Everly Brothers
33. All Shook Up - Elvis Presley
34. Gonna Find Me A Bluebird - Marvin Rainwater
35. Keep A Knockin' - Little Richard
36. Deep Purple - Billy Ward and His Dominoes
37. Peanuts - Little Joe and the Thrillers
38. Over The Mountain - Johnnie and Joe
39. Humpty Dumpty Heart - LaVern Baker
40. A Teenager's Romance - Ricky Nelson
41. A White Sport Coat - Marty Robbins
42. Plaything - Ted Newman
43. With All My Heart - Jodie Sands
44. Alone - The Shepherd Sisters
45. Be-Bop Baby - Ricky Nelson

46. Drive-In Show - Eddie Cochran
47. Let the Four Winds Blow - Roy Brown
48. Darling It's Wonderful - The Lovers
49. Think - The "5" Royales
50. School Day - Chuck Berry

Also on the "pop" charts:
Love Letters in the Sand/Bernadine - Pat Boone
Remember You're Mine - Pat Boone
Just Between You and Me - The Chordettes
And That Reminds Me - Della Reese
June Night - Jimmy Dorsey

September 1957
ARTIST OF THE MONTH

BUDDY HOLLY (AND THE CRICKETS)

Buddy Holly

Charles Hardin Holley was born on September 7, 1935, in the Lubbock, a small town situated in the middle of West Texas. This is a land that's frying-pan flat as far as the eye can see in all directions. Lubbock is a hundred miles south of Amarillo and three hundred miles west of Dallas. The area has always exuded a sense of independence born from its isolation.

Locked into Lubbock, teenagers had few choices for an evening's entertainment on the town: a movie at the theater, swing by at the roller rink, a burger and shake at the drive-in, or making out in their parent's car in the groves of cottonwood trees along the Brazos River.

And, there was music. Occasionally, there would be a dance for teens at the high school gym, the National Guard Armory or the fair grounds. Less frequently, troupes of country performers would play the Cotton Club, Lubbock's favorite nightspot. Occasionally, the Cotton Club admitted teens for Saturday afternoon performances. Between times, if a teenager wanted music, there was always the radio. Lubbock's two most popular stations aired mostly country and western tunes. If a teenage boy wanted any other type of music, he had to play it himself.

Charles was the fourth of four children born to Lawrence and Ella Holley. In West Texas, nearly everyone has a nickname, and the family always called him "Buddy." The Holleys enjoyed a rich musical tradition. The older brothers, Larry and Travis, had taught themselves to play guitar. Their sister, Pat, joined her mother in the evening as they sang duets at the living room the piano. Every Sunday found the family attending services at the Baptist Church, singing hymns of praise and joy to God.

At age eleven, Buddy started taking piano lessons from a local music teacher. He was an inquisitive pupil with some natural ability. He was also impatient. He switched from piano to steel guitar to acoustic guitar in a matter of months. With the guitar, he found an instrument that would allow him to more fully express his feelings.

In 1951, Buddy met Bob Montgomery, another young guitarist, who had been born in Lampasas and had come with his family to Lubbock in 1949. Both boys were students at J.C. Hutchinson Junior High School. Montgomery's personal taste in music ran to country, especially Hank Williams, and Montgomery had a major influence over Buddy's choice in music. The boys soon added a younger member, Larry Welborn, to fill out their sound playing bass. Eventually, the trio, still calling itself Buddy and Bob, landed a regular spot on KDAV radio's "Sunday Party." About this time, Buddy also appeared a few times on KDAV with Jack Neal, another Lubbock teenager, as Buddy and Jack.

In high school, Buddy was consumed with his music. His school work suffered as a result. So did his love life. In fact, the only diversion from his music was cruising through the streets of Lubbock in his brother's pickup truck.

Buddy graduated from high school in 1954. In hopes of landing a contract with a record company, the boys traveled to Wichita Falls, the nearest Texas town with a recording studio. Here they made a demonstration tape of a handful of their songs. They also used the studios at KDAV as well as professional studios in Dallas and New Mexico to record their material. During this time, Montgomery usually handled the lead vocals and wrote most of the songs. Other local musicians were added from time to time, including Sonny Curtis, on guitar and fiddle, and Don Guess, on bass. A demonstration tape was eventually given to a Columbia Records promotion man who was visiting KDAV. He never called back.

In 1954, Bill Haley and His Comets were breaking new ground with "Shake, Rattle and Roll" and "Dim, Dim The Lights." It was also the year Elvis Presley released his first two singles on Sun Records. Elvis was an immediate sensation in Texas, and he crisscrossed the state frequently over the next two years. One of his first appearances in Lubbock, at the Fair Park Coliseum on June 3, 1955, drew a crowd estimated at 6,000. An hour before the start of this concert, Buddy and Bob opened for Elvis at Connelly's Pontiac Showroom in a free show to attract customers to the auto dealership. It was the catalyst that would forever alter Buddy's life. Gone was the country music, replaced by pure rock 'n roll.

By that October, Buddy and Bob expanded again to include Jerry Allison on drums. The group opened for Bill Haley and His Comets at Fair Park Coliseum. That night the show's promoter, Eddie Crandall from Nashville, took enough of an interest in Buddy and Bob to indicate that he would try to get them a contract with a record company. It took a two months, but, in December, Decca Records took the bait. There was just one hitch—Decca only wanted Buddy. Bob Montgomery was magnanimous, insisting Buddy go on alone. Larry Welborn also remained in Lubbock, presumably to finish high school.

Buddy's first session in Nashville took place at Owen Bradley's studio on January 26, 1956. To back him, Buddy brought along Don Guess to play bass and Sonny Curtis on lead guitar. This group was augmented by professional guitarist Grady Martin. Bradley would not allow Buddy to play guitar as this made recording the vocals too difficult. Buddy completed four songs, including "Love Me" and "Blue Days, Black Nights" which became his first single. On the record label, his name was spelled for the first time "Buddy Holly." Listening to the songs recorded that day, Buddy's voice sounds tentative. He is trying hard to copy Elvis' vocal inflections, but he must have been intimidated by the strange environment and the "hurry up" attitude of Bradley and his staff. The single received some airplay in Washington, DC, and in Missouri, but otherwise it was quickly forgotten.

A year earlier, Holly had used Norman Petty's NorVaJak studio, located in Clovis, New Mexico, a hundred miles west of Lubbock. Over the next few months Holly drove that distance frequently to record more tapes as practice before returning to Nashville for another session in July. This time, along with Guess and Curtis, he brought Jerry Allison to play drums. Buddy had been working on a new song, "That'll Be The Day," and he recorded a version during this session. He also laid down "Rock Around With Ollie Vee," a Curtis-penned, rompin,' stompin' rock 'n roll number, and a fine version of "Ting-A-Ling," a rhythm and blues hit for the Clovers. None of these songs were issued as singles at the time.

Buddy's third and final Decca session took place on November 15, 1956. This time, none of Holly's band was permitted to record with him. Grady Martin played lead guitar while Boots Randolph's sax was a new addition to the sound. Buddy tried another version of "Rock Around With Ollie Vee," but it lacked the snap of the first version. Two other songs, the least commercial of the three recorded that day, "Modern Don Juan" and "You Are My One Desire," were issued as a single in January 1957. The record never had a chance for success. Neither did Holly's Decca recording contract when it came up for renewal.

Holly returned to Lubbock, and for two months he submerged himself in making demonstration tapes. He recorded day and night, with and without other accompaniment, in an attempt to discover exactly what had gone wrong in Nashville. If he ever got the chance to record again, he wasn't going to make any mistakes. And, he wasn't going to have any producer telling him how to record his own music.

By this time Don Guess and Sonny Curtis had dropped out of Buddy's band. The reason may have centered on that third Nashville session when they weren't invited to record. In any case, Holly and Allison continued alone.

In early 1957, Holly decided to return to NorVaJak Studios in Clovis. A year earlier, Roy Orbison had used the studio to record the original version of "Ooby Dooby," released on Je-Wel Records. Buddy Knox and Jimmy Bowen had also recorded "Party Doll" and "I'm Stickin' With You" at NorVaJak. As one of their first sessions, Holly and Allison accompanied a local Clovis singer, Gary Tollett. In return, Tollett promised to send his cousin any demo tapes made by Holly. Tollett's cousin was an employee of Roulette Records, the New York label that had signed Knox and Bowen. Also working the Tollett session was rhythm guitarist, Niki Sullivan, who had recently rehearsed with Holly and who had tagged along to work Holly's first session. Larry Welborn was also on hand for the gig. On February 25, 1957, two tracks were recorded by Holly and his group, "I'm Looking For Someone To Love," a straight-ahead rhythm piece, and a second version of "That'll Be The Day."

Larry Welborn could not devote his full attention to Holly's music, so it was necessary to find someone to play bass. As a replacement, Holly sought out Joe B. Mauldin, a sixteen-year old high school student. On March 12, Holly, Allison, Mauldin, and Sullivan returned to Clovis and recorded two more songs, "Last Night" and an early version of "Maybe Baby."

Holly's contract with Decca did not allow him to rerecord any of the songs he had performed for the Decca. To skirt this barrier, it was necessary to come up with a pseudonym for the group. The name chosen was the Crickets, apparently to reverse the popular trend of naming vocal groups after birds. The four-song demo tape was mailed to Tollett's cousin at Roulette. The company executives contacted Holly, stating that they were impressed with his songwriting but not the performance. They suggested that Buddy Knox record "That'll Be The Day," and Jimmy Bowen take "I'm Looking For Someone To Love." Norman Petty asked Buddy to hold off on giving his final consent until he had a chance to market the demo tape himself. Petty sent the tape to Peer-Southern Music Publishing in New York, and eventually, an executive at Coral-Brunswick Records called back. Coral and Brunswick were both subsidiaries of Decca, although on an autonomous basis insofar as talent acquisition was concerned.

As part of their deal, Norman Petty became manager of the group. He was aware that Holly's notebook was full of songs. At Petty's insistence, the Crickets signed with Brunswick as a group, while Holly had a solo arrangement with Coral. In June, 1957, Brunswick Records released "That'll Be The Day" by the Crickets while "Words of Love" came out on Coral by Buddy Holly. Only "That'll Be The Day" caught the public's ear. "Words of Love" was covered by the Diamonds who beat Holly's version on the streets by three weeks.

At first, sales of "That'll Be The Day" were slow, but at least there were sales. Through the summer of 1957, the popularity of "That'll Be The Day" inched its way from the Southwest to the West Coast and back to the Northeast. By early August, there were sustained sales and the record began to appear on the national charts. Four weeks later, "That'll Be The Day" was one of the top selling records across the country in both the rock 'n roll and R&B markets.

It was the crossover into rhythm and blues that first hinted at the size of the success that awaited the Crickets. In August, the group started playing the East Coast theater circuit of the Howard in Washington, the Royal in Baltimore, and Apollo in New York City. For one week at each venue, the Crickets won over the predominantly black audiences with their energetic stage show. Buddy Holly and the Crickets were on their way!

Holly's career quickly went into overdrive. Every other month seemed to bring a new release from either the Crickets or Buddy Holly. September 1957: two from Holly, "Peggy Sue," on Coral and "Rock Around

With Ollie Vee" on Decca. October 1957: "Oh Boy" by the Crickets. January 1958: three releases: "Maybe Baby" by the Crickets, "You Are my One Desire" by Holly on Decca, and "Listen To Me" by Holly on Coral. April 1958: "Rave On" by Holly on Coral. June 1958: "Think It Over" by the Crickets and "Girl On My Mind" by Holly on Decca. July 1958: "Early in the Morning" by Holly on Coral. September 1958: "It's So Easy" by the Crickets and "Real Wild Child" by Ivan on Coral. October 1958: "Heartbeat" by Buddy Holly on Coral.

At the same time, the Crickets were touring almost nonstop. August-September 1957: Alan Freed's ten-day Labor Day show at the Brooklyn Paramount. September-November 1957: eighty days with "The Biggest Show of Stars for 1957." December 1957: Alan Freed's Brooklyn Paramount revue for ten days and a television debut on "The Ed Sullivan Show." January 1958: a seventeen-day tour with the Everly Brothers. January-February 1958: a ten-day tour of Hawaii and Australia with Paul Anka. February 1958: a week-long swing through Florida with the Everly Brothers. March 1958: a four-week tour of England. March-May 1958, six weeks with Alan Freed's "Big Beat" tour. July 1958: a tour of the Midwest. October-November 1958: "The Biggest Show of Stars for '58."

In November 1958, the Crickets staggered back to Lubbock exhausted. Record sales had fallen off as Holly's musical style became lighter, with less of the hard driving rock 'n roll he had performed in the beginning. There was dissension among the Crickets as to just which direction their music should be taking. Holly was convinced he was on the right track, and he was determined to continue. The other Crickets wanted their freedom, and Holly granted it. He returned to New York with the wife he had married the previous August. Through the winter, Buddy Holly recorded copiously, using stings and orchestral arrangements. As if to solidify his new approach to music, in January 1959, Holly's "It Doesn't Matter Anymore" was released on Coral.

On January 23, Buddy Holly, with two new Crickets, headlined "The Winter Dance Party" tour with the Big Bopper and Ritchie Valens. Eleven days into the tour, Holly displayed the impatience that was the driving force throughout his life. The tour had been plagued by foul weather and mechanical problems with the chartered bus. Following the show at the Surf Ballroom in Clear Lake, Iowa, Holly booked a private plane to fly to the next day's show, leaving the rest of the troupe to travel by bus. He offered to take along his new Crickets, Tommy Allsup and Waylon Jennings. However, they were talked out of their seats by the Big Bopper and Ritchie Valens. Just after midnight, the plane lifted off from the airport in nearby Cedar Rapids as a light snow fell. The next morning, February 3, the wreckage of their light plane was discovered scattered across a snow-covered field barely a mile from the airport. There were no survivors.

In recognition of the breadth of his achievements during the short span of his popularity, Buddy Holly was inducted into the Rock And Roll Hall of Fame in its first year, 1986. Later that same year, Buddy Holly was admitted into the Songwriters' Hall of Fame.

October 1957

OCT 1   Swinging back through Texas, "The Biggest Show of Stars for '57" continues with a performance at the new Dallas Auditorium. On succeeding nights, shows are held in Fort Worth (2); Waco (3); San Antonio (4); Corpus Christi (5); Houston (6); Austin (7); El Paso (8); and the Municipal Auditorium in Albuquerque (9). (See OCT 10.)

Little Richard's tour of New South Wales and Australia begins with a show in Wollongong, NSW. Along with Richard are Gene Vincent, Eddie Cochran, and Alis Lesley, a female Elvis impersonator. Other shows by the troupe are Newcastle (2); Brisbane (3); Sydney (4-5); Broken Hill (7, afternoon); Wayville (7, evening); West Melbourne (8-10); and Sydney (11-12) where 71,000 fans see the last two day's performances. (See also OCT 13.)

OCT 4   Jackie Wilson stops by the "American Bandstand" show to perform his first solo recording, "Reet Petite."

The Del Vikings headline the show at the Apollo Theater this week. Also sharing the spotlight are the Tunedrops, Varetta Dillard, the Mello-Kings, Slim Gailard, and Earl Bostic's combo.

OCT 5   Joe Poovey and Gene Rambo bring their style of Texas rockabilly to the "Big D Jamboree" in Dallas tonight.

OCT 6   Jimmy Reed plays the Sunday ball at the Blue Eagle in New Orleans.

On CBS-TV, "The Ed Sullivan Show" welcomes the Everly Brothers.

New Releases for the first week in October include two on Dot: "April Love" by Pat Boone and a reissue of "A Cheat" by Sanford Clark; two from Ember: "Our Anniversary" by the Five Satins and "The Joker" by Billy Myles; two from Specialty: "Bony Moronie" by Larry Williams and "Leavin' It All Up to You" by Don and Dewey; two from Dooto: "Blue Moon" by Don Julian and the **Meadowlarks** and "A Lover's Prayer" by Vernon Green and the Medallions; and two from Columbia: Marty Robbins' "The Story of My Life" and "Party" by the Collins Kids. Additional releases this week include "Love Me Forever" by the Four Esquires on Paris; "Buzz, Buzz, Buzz" by the Hollywood Flames on Ebb; Sal Mineo's "Party Time" on Epic; "Fools Rush In" by Malcom Dodds and the Tunedrops on End; and "Say It" by the "5" Royales on King.

THE MEADOWLARKS
The Meadowlarks were another in the seemingly endless tapestry of R&B vocal groups inhabiting the Los Angeles basin in the 1950s. Don Julian was a member of the high school choir, but he wanted to sing more than the normal glee club offerings. His ideas on group harmony found receptive listeners in Earl and Randy Jones and Ronnie Barrett. Their practice sessions brought the Meadowlarks to the attention of Modern Records, and resulted in two singles on Modern's R.P.M. subsidiary. "Love Only You" was released in January 1954, with "L.S.M.F.T. Blues" following two months later. ("L.S.M.F.T." was the abbreviation for the popular cigarette slogan, "Lucky Strike Means Fine Tobacco.") Both singles sold a few copies in the local area, but R.P.M. dropped the Meadowlarks from its roster after the second release. It was a year before the group had another record. In the spring of 1955, Dootone Records was having a run of hits with the Penguins ("Earth Angel") and the Medallions ("The Letter b/w "Buick 59"), and they were ready for another group. The Meadowlarks obliged with their strongest effort, "Heaven and Paradise." Their next two singles were in a similar style: "Always and Always" and "This Must Be Paradise." There were three additional Dootone releases with "Blue Moon" being the last. None approached the popularity of "Heaven and Paradise." For most R&B vocal groups, this would be the end of the story. However, Don Julian had bigger plans. Through numerous personnel changes, kept the group together playing clubs, dance halls, and bars on the strength of their local hits. In 1964, he was fronting a group he called the Larks. The 1960s were the time of the weekly dance craze, and the Larks had their moment in the spotlight with "The Jerk," a Top Ten hit in early 1965.

DEE CLARK
Delectus (Dee) Clark, Jr. was born November 7, 1938, in Blytheville, Arkansas. The Clark family moved to Chicago when Dee was three. When he was thirteen, he was a member of the Hambone Kids with Roland Strong and Samuel McGrier. In 1952, the Hambone Kids had three singles on Okeh fronting the Red Saunders Orchestra. Their first release, "Hambone," was a "pop" hit. It was also the inspiration for "Bo Diddley." In 1955, Clark was a member of the Goldentones that had one single, "Run Pretty Baby" on Jay-Dee. In 1956, he formed the Kool Gents, which may have included at various times Cicero Blake, Doug Brown, John and Teddy Carter, John McCall, and Howard McCain. In 1955, they released "Come To Me" on Bethlehem, a King Records company, followed by two singles on Vee-Jay: "This Is the Night" (1955) and "I Just Can't Help Myself" (1956). Working as the Delegates, Vee-Jay released "The Convention" (1956) and "Mother's Son" (1957). Then, Clark went solo on Falcon Records, a Vee-Jay subsidiary. He still occasionally used the Kool Gents/Delegates as his backing group, and several Kool Gents sides found their way into Clark's first album YOU'RE LOOKING GOOD. Clark's first Falcon release was "Gloria" followed by "24 Boy Friends." He inherited Little Richard's backing band, the Upsetters, when Richard entered seminary in 1958, and they are featured on his third Falcon single, "Wondering." Clark's next releases were on Abner, another Vee-Jay label, and they were all nationally successful: "Nobody by You," "Just Keep It Up," "Hey Little Girl," "How About That," and "At My Front Door." Beginning in 1960, he was back with Vee-Jay for "You're Looking Good," and "Your Friends" (the latter featuring the Dells). This unbroken string of bestselling singles peaked in 1961 with "Raindrops," his biggest hit.

OCT 10   Buddy Holly and the Crickets rejoin "The Biggest Show of Stars for '57" for its final six-week push. The troupe, now headlined by Chuck Berry, is currently composed of Buddy Knox and Jimmy Bowen with the Rhythm Orchids, Fats Domino, the Everly Brothers, the Drifters, Clyde McPhatter, LaVern Baker, Frankie Lymon, Paul Anka, and Paul Williams' orchestra. As the troupe heads to the West Coast, the schedule through the end of the month looks like this: Tucson (tonight); Phoenix (11); San Diego (12); Fresno (13); Los Angeles (14-16); San Jose (17); Sacramento's Memorial Auditorium (18); San Francisco's Civic Auditorium (19); the Oakland Auditorium (20); Portland (22); Vancouver (23); Tacoma (24); Seattle (25-26); Spokane (27); Moscow, Idaho (28); Calgary (29); Edmonton (30); and Regina, Saskatchewan (31). (See also OCT 31 and NOV 1.)

On "American Bandstand," Thurston Harris sings "Little Bitty Pretty One."

OCT 11   In a rare move for "American Bandstand," the Del Vikings perform all three of their hits, "Come Go With Me," "Whispering Bells," and "Cool Shake," instead of the usual one or two songs allowed most guests.

Jerry Lee Lewis begins a week-long stand at the Casino Royal in Washington.

Also in Washington, Earl Bostic, Dale Hawkins, Little Joe and the Thrillers, Lee Andrews and the Hearts, and Eddie "Cleanhead" Vinson entertain this week at the Howard Theater.

Roy Hamilton headlines this week's show at the Apollo Theater. Performing along with Mr. Hamilton are the Tune Weavers, the Lovers, Billy Barnes, and Ann Cole.

OCT 13   Following last night's show in Sydney, Little Richard announces that he is quitting show business. He plans to fly back to Los Angeles where he will be baptized into the Seventh Day Adventist Church. After his proclamation, and at the urging of his saxman Clifford Burks, he throws four diamond rings valued at $8,000 into Sydney's Hunter River, "to prove his faith in God."

New Releases for the second week in October include "Raunchy" by Bill Justis on Phillips International; "Rock and Roll Music" by Chuck Berry on Chess; two from Ace: "I Trusted You" by Jimmy Clanton and "Just a Lonely Clown" by Huey Smith and the Clowns; "Rock the Joint" by Bill Haley and His Comets on Decca; "Baby, Baby" by Dale Hawkins on Checker; "Hello Little Girl" by Lloyd Price on K.R.C.; "24 Boy Friends" by **Dee Clark** on Falcon; and two rockabilly entries from Argo: Ray Stanley's "I Can't Wait" and the Silva-Tones' "Roses Are Blooming."

MID-OCTOBER
Johnny Nash is awarded an every-other-week spot on Arthur Godfrey's morning radio show

OCT 16   Recovered from his recent throat surgery, Johnny Cash takes to the road with a show in Valdosta, Georgia.

OCT 17   Elvis Presley's third motion picture, "Jailhouse Rock," premiers in Memphis at the Lowe's State Theater. As a high school student, Elvis Presley had worked in this same theater as an usher. Although Presley is at home at Graceland, he does not attend. The picture opens in theaters across the country on November 8.

OCT 18   The Coasters headline a traveling revue opening tonight in Oklahoma City. Also on the bill are Lowell Fulson, Lillian Offitt, the Cadillacs, Johnny "Guitar" Watson and Ernie Freeman's combo. Subsequent dates will take the troupe to the West Coast.

Jerry Lee Lewis is top-billed on a show in Miami that features Johnny Cash and other country performers. In succeeding nights, they will appear in Charlotte (19), Tampa (20), Orlando (21), Jacksonville (22), and Pensacola (23). Following this tour, Jerry Lee travels north to appear on the first three dates of George "Hound Dog" Lorenz' Eighth Anniversary Show of Stars Tour which is booked into Buffalo, Rochester, Scranton, Providence, and Hartford. Lorenz is the top deejay in Buffalo. Other talent on the second tour include the Billy Williams Quartet, Roy Hamilton, the Bobbettes, the Tune Weavers, the Mello-Kings, the Clovers, the Lovers, Screamin' Jay Hawkins, Thurston Harris, and Doc Bagby's combo.

Billy Ward and His Dominoes appear at the Apollo Theater this week. Also spending time in the spotlight are Little Joe and the Thrillers, the Chantels, Charlie and Ray, the Five Satins, and Bobby Darin.

The Clovers, Sil Austin and his combo, Thurston Harris, and the Dubs headline this week's Howard Theater revue in Washington.

Also appearing in Washington, the **Shepherd Sisters** open for a week at the Casino Royal.

The saga of Little Richard's religious conversion continues as he attempts to remain true to his beliefs while fulfilling his commitment to his recording contract with Specialty Records: in Los Angeles, Richard decides to acquiesce on behalf of his recording agreement by waxing half a dozen songs in one three-hour session at Master Recorders. This will be his final rock 'n roll recording date for the next six years.

OCT 19   Billy Williams opens a two-day engagement at Philadelphia's Erie Social Club.

OCT 20   A star-studded revue produced by Alan Freed takes England by storm. Little Richard was originally scheduled to be headliner. The actual package features Jo Ann Campbell, the Moonglows, and Teddy Randazzo, formerly with the Three Chuckles. The troupe will remain in England though November 14.

THE SHEPHERD SISTERS
If you wanted to start a new record company in the 1950s, and you wanted to have a hit right off the bat, but you didn't have enough cash on hand to play the payola game, what better ploy to get airplay than to name the company after Alan Freed's son? Enter Lance Records and the Shepherd Sisters. The Shepherds really were sisters—four of them, Martha, Mary, Judy and Gayle. And they really could sing. In fact they had been singing for quite some time before they came to the attention of New York's music hustler Morty Craft. The sisters had sung for U.S.O. clubs and for less-than-wholesome nightclubs. They were veterans Arthur Godfrey's Talent Scouts. In 1954, they cut "Gone With the Wind" (no relation to the movie score) for Capitol, but the record faded at the post. At this point, Craft came along and had them redo "Gone With the Wind" for his Melba label, but even with a Louis Prima rhythm it couldn't attract attention. Their follow-up on Melba was "Remember That Crazy Rock 'N Roll Tune?"—the less said the better. Finally, they hit with "Alone," one of only two singles issued by Lance Records. And, as predicted, Alan Freed played the grooves off the thing. As rock records go, this one was just plain weird—not to mention that the women were well beyond the teenagers they appeared to be in the song. "Alone" did have a beat—in fact the drum was one of the few instruments you could hear behind the la-la's and yeah-yeah's of the foursome. Mercury records snatched up the group for one release, "Getting Ready for Freddy." It sounded like the Andrews Sisters attempting rock 'n roll. They went through record labels like a dose of salts: M-G-M, Warwick, Big Top, United Artists, York, and 20th Century. Finally, on Atlantic in 1963, in the midst of the heyday for girl-groups, they had a minor hit with the sweet "Don't Mention My Name." It was their last hurrah.

BOB LUMAN

Bob Luman is better known today as a country performer, a career change he made in 1960. Prior to that, he was one of the hottest rock 'n roll acts around. Robert Glynn Luman was born April 15, 1937, in the east Texas town of Nacogdoches. His father taught him to play fiddle and guitar and gave him an appreciation for country music. In 1955, Luman was finishing high school as a promising athlete, with an offer to join the Pittsburgh Pirates rookie camp. At the same time, he was trying to start a country band. Before he was to report to baseball camp, Luman fell under the spell of rockabilly music. Elvis Presley frequently played east Texas between his weekly appearances on Shreveport's "Louisiana Hayride," and Luman was mesmerized by the crowd's reaction to Presley. Luman immediately changed musical direction, as well as his plans for the future. He named his band the Shadows, and they won a Texas talent contest, defeating the up-and-coming Mac Curtis. Luman was invited to cut a few records for a Dallas music entrepreneur, but none of the material was released at the time. For two years, Luman made personal appearances in the Texas-Louisiana area, including the "Louisiana Hayride." At the "Hayride," he met Dale Hawkins and James Burton. Hawkins was just beginning his successful recording career, and Burton was his lead guitarist. When Imperial Records "discovered" Luman in 1957, he asked Burton to join him in Los Angeles for the sessions that produced three Imperial releases: "All Night Long," "Red Hot," and "Make Up Your Mind Baby." That same year, Luman and Burton the band had an extended appearance in the movie "Carnival Rock." In 1958, Burton joined Ricky Nelson's band, and Luman had a lone single on Capitol before signing with Warner Brothers Records in mid-1959. His first releases were "Class of '59" and "Buttercup."

OCT 21   On American Bandstand," the Five Satins sing "To The Aisle." The show's other performing guest is the Rover Boys.

New Releases for the third week in October include two additional versions of "Raunchy:" by Ernie Freeman on Imperial and by Billy Vaughn on Dot. Other releases this week include "Dance to the Bop" by Gene Vincent and His Blue Caps on Capitol; and "Kisses Sweeter Than Wine" by Jimmie Rodgers on Roulette; "Red Hot" by **Bob Luman** on Imperial; "Cool Baby" by Charlie Gracie on Cameo; Buchanan and Ancel's "The Creature" on Flying Saucer; "Rock-A-Chicka" by Warner Mack on Decca; and the Teen Queens' "I Miss You" on R.P.M. Also out this week is "Hey! Little Girl" by the Techniques on Roulette. The recording, by four seniors from Georgia Tech, had originally been issued on the Stars label, owned by Atlanta entrepreneur Bill Lowrey.

OCT 23   Chuck Willis makes a one-night stand at the Mammoth Gardens in Denver.

OCT 25   Bill Haley and His Comets begin a month-long tour of South America. They will play one-week stands in Buenos Aires, Montevideo, and Rio de Janeiro.
   At Washington's Howard Theater, headliners this week are the Five Satins, the Five Keys, and the Moonglows.

OCT 26   Gene Vincent guests on "The Dick Clark Show" on ABC-TV.
   Elvis Presley starts a brief four-day, three-city tour of California with two shows at the San Francisco Civic Auditorium. The other dates are the Oakland Auditorium (27) and the Pan Pacific Auditorium in Los Angeles (28-29).

OCT 27   Joe Bennett and the Sparkletones are guest on CBS-TV's "The Ed Sullivan Show."

OCT 28   The Shepherd Sisters open for a week at Pittsburgh's Copa Club.
   During his two-day appearance (28-29) at the Pan Pacific Ballroom in Los Angeles, Elvis Presley is ordered by local police to "clean up" his act.
   One of the biggest shows to hit New Orleans this year features Joe Turner, Ray Charles, Mickey and Sylvia, Roy Brown, Larry Williams, Bo Diddley, Nappy Brown, the Velours, and Annie Laurie.
   Bill Doggett's combo plays a one night stand at the Greystone Ballroom in Detroit.

New Releases for the fourth week in October include two from ABC-Paramount: "Why Don't They Understand" by George Hamilton IV and "Two Timin' Woman" by Jack Scott; "Did We Have A Party" by Billy Brown on Columbia; two from Chess: "Teardrops" by Lee Andrews and the Hearts and "I Just Go Wild Over Rock and Roll" by Bobby Dean; two from Mercury, "Love Bug Crawl" by Jimmy Edwards and "Beggar to a

King" by Jape Richardson (soon to be better known as the Big Bopper); and two from Atlantic: "Party Party" by Dean Beard and "St. Louis Blues" by LaVern Baker. Other releases include "Oh Boy!" by the Crickets on Brunswick; "Hard Times (The Slop)" by Noble "Thin Man" Watts on Baton; The Dells' "Time Makes You Change" on Vee-Jay; and "Five More Steps" by Ray Stevens on Prep. Also out on Columbia is "Moondreams" by the Norman Petty Trio. Petty is the owner of the studio in Clovis, New Mexico, where Buddy Holly records, and this recording features Holly on guitar. Holly later issued his own version of the Petty tune.

OCT 31   In Regina, "The Biggest Show of Stars for '57" adds the Diamonds to its roster.

Jimmie Rodgers guests on the CBS-TV show "Shower of Stars."

LATE OCTOBER

The Platters wind up their eight-week tour of Latin America and fly to Paris where they open at the Olympia Theater.

THE TOP ROCK 'N ROLL RECORDS FOR OCTOBER 1957

1. Wake Up Little Susie - The Everly Brothers
2. Honeycomb - Jimmie Rodgers
3. Jailhouse Rock/Treat Me Nice - Elvis Presley
4. That'll Be the Day - The Crickets
5. Diana - Paul Anka
6. Happy, Happy Birthday Baby - The Tune Weavers
7. Whole Lot of Shakin' Going On - Jerry Lee Lewis
8. Mr. Lee - The Bobbettes
9. Keep A Knockin' - Little Richard
10. Hula Love - Buddy Knox
11. Be-Bop Baby/Have I Told You Lately - Ricky Nelson
12. Lotta Lovin' - Gene Vincent and the Blue Caps
13. Black Slacks - Joe Bennett and the Sparkletones
14. Peanuts - Little Joe and the Thrillers
15. Stardust - Billy Ward and His Dominoes
16. Teddy Bear/Loving You - Elvis Presley
17. Deep Purple - Billy Ward and His Dominoes
18. My Special Angel - Bobby Helms
19. You're My One and Only Love - Ricky Nelson
20. Silhouettes - The Rays
21. Bye Bye Love - The Everly Brothers
22. Short Fat Fannie - Larry Williams
23. Back to School - Timmie Rodgers
24. I'm Gonna Sit Right Down and Write Myself a Letter
      - Billy Williams
25. Alone - The Shepherd Sisters
26. Honest I Do - Jimmy Reed
27. Little Bitty Pretty One - Thurston Harris

28. You Send Me - Sam Cooke
29. Rebel - Carol Jarvis
30. Searchin' - The Coasters
31. Whispering Bells - The Dell-Vikings
32. Plaything - Ted Newman
33. To the Aisle - The Five Satins
34. Plaything - Nick Todd
35. Farther Up the Road - Bobby "Blue" Bland
36. Long, Lonely Nights - Clyde McPhatter
37. Goody, Goody - The Teenagers
38. Think - The "5" Royales
39. Wait and See - Fats Domino
40. Lasting Love - Sal Mineo
41. Swanee River Rock - Ray Charles
42. Dumplins - Ernie Freeman
43. Silhouettes - Steve Gibson and the Red Caps
44. Dumplins - Doc Bagby
45. Idol With the Golden Head - The Coasters
46. He's Gone - The Chantels
47. Cool Shake - The Del Vikings
48. Long Lonely Nights - Lee Andrews and the Hearts
49. Rockin' Pneumonia and the Boogie Woogie Flu - Huey Smith and the Clowns
50. Jenny Jenny - Little Richard

Also on the "pop" charts:
Chances Are - Johnny Mathis
Fascination - Jane Morgan

October 1957
ARTIST OF THE MONTH

JIMMIE RODGERS

Jimmie Rodgers

Camas, Washington, Jimmie Rodgers' home town, was a very small timber processing town on the Columbia River. It was about twenty miles east of Portland—far enough away to develop its own distinct personality, yet near enough to feel as though it was in the mainstream.

James Fredrick Rodgers was born in Camas on September 18, 1933, and he did not leave town until after he had graduated from high school. During all that time, he is remembered in his hometown only for becoming a proficient pianist under his mother's tutelage.

He enrolled in nearby Clark College with aspirations to become a music teacher like his mother, but the Korean War soon interrupted his plans. In a patriotic mood, he enlisted in the Air Force and was shipped to Korea. To pass the time, he formed a combo called the Rhythm Kings. The group found the nearby military bases eager for live entertainment.

In 1955, he transferred to an Air Force installation near Nashville. He soon gravitated to Printer's Alley, the unofficial hub of Music City. Printer's Alley was a short street behind Ryman Auditorium, at that time of the permanent home of the "Grand Ole Opry." From the outset, he knew that if he wanted to work the clubs in this area, he would have to play guitar. So, he bought one and had the strings set for open-tuning, meaning he could play a chord by placing his thumb across all six strings at one fret. A short time later, he was booked into the Club Unique as a folk singer. One of the songs he performed regularly was "Honeycomb," a tune previously recorded by Georgie Shaw.

In 1955, the most popular folk singers in the nation were the Weavers, a quartet formed by Pete Seger in 1948, that featuring Lee Hays, Fred Hellerman and Miss Ronnie Gilbert. They had major hit records in the early 1950s with such standards as "On Top of Old Smokey" and "Goodnight, Irene." In their repertoire were such lesser known pieces as "Kisses Sweeter Than Wine," and it was this type of music that appealed to Rodgers.

After his discharge, Rodgers returned to Camas, but he found small town life no longer held any appeal for him. He liked entertaining, and he decided to try to earn a living as a singer. He formed a combo with hopes of playing the small clubs and dances between Camas and Portland. Eventually, he appeared at the Fort Cafe in Vancouver, Washington. Here, the crowd's reaction to this new singer with the pure tenor voice was immediate. He remained at the Fort Club for three months.

Encouraged by this success, he took to the road alone, traveling to Los Angeles to audition for Art Linkletter's television program. When he didn't receive a call back, he worked his way to New York. Here, he tried out for one of television's most popular amateur shows, "Arthur Godfrey's Talent Scouts." Rodgers was accepted and eventually won one of the weekly contests hands down.

While he was in New York, he took time to visit the record companies to see if he could capitalize on his television success. One of his first stops was newly formed Roulette Records, which was in the middle of a two-record hot streak with its first two releases: "Party Doll" and "I'm Stickin' With You." Rodgers had a brief audition for an executive but departed without leaving a forwarding address. With money to spend, Roulette was ready to offer Rodgers a recording contract, but he could not be located. It was six months before Roulette tracked him back to Camas. Roulette rushed him to New York for a recording session. His first release was "Honeycomb." When Rodgers had first sung the song in Nashville in 1955, he found that it received little audience reaction. Over time he discovered that people responded more positively if he jumped up the musical scale a half-note at the end of each chorus, thereby increasing the tension within the song.

"Honeycomb" caught the American record-buying public completely off guard. Even today, it is difficult to point to one specific reason this song was such a success. Maybe it's because "Honeycomb" is just so darn happy. Not to mention that stepping up the musical key added to the listener's enjoyment. Then there are the hand claps in the third verse. Nothing sells a record faster than enthusiastic hand claps, and "Honeycomb" sold a million copies.

Rodgers' second single was that old Weaver's tune, "Kisses Sweeter Than Wine." The Weavers had sung the song almost like a dirge. Rodgers had tried that approach in various clubs, and he couldn't bring it off. On the other hand, when he threw in those changes in key, more hand claps, and sped the whole thing up about four times faster than the original...

"Kisses Sweeter Than Wine" quickly sold a million copies.

His third single, "Oh-Oh, I'm Falling In Love Again," offered Rodgers a chance to let the purity of his voice really shine. There's the usual change in key in the middle of the song, about the time the hand claps take charge, just in case a shining vocal wasn't enough. "Oh-Oh, I'm Falling In Love Again" also went gold.

For his next single, Jimmie Rodgers changed direction completely. "Secretly" was a bouncy little ballad with lyrics guaranteed to drive a teenage girl into a tizzy: "Wish we didn't have to meet—secretly; wish we didn't have to kiss—secretly..." By this time, it was clear that someone other than Jimmie Rodgers was behind all this wholesomeness. The names of Hugo and Luigi appeared on some of the records, but they seemed to be producers or some such. Truth be known, Hugo Peretti and Luigi Creatore were the masterminds behind Rodgers' success. It had been their influence that secured Rodgers' recording contract in the first place. "Oh, Oh, I'm Falling in Love," "Secretly," and "Are You Really Mine" were all composed by Hugo and Luigi using the pseudonym "Al Hoffman, Dick Manning, and Mark Markwell." They arranged the songs and used Peretti's orchestra on Rodgers' sessions. Rodgers' main contribution was his wonderfully naive voice.

Over night, Jimmie Rodgers became the most frequent guest on prime-time television variety shows. He appeared on Ed Sullivan numerous times. He also showed up regularly on the Dinah Shore show and the Perry Como show. He even made it to "American Bandstand!" On March 31, 1959, he launched his own weekly NBC-TV variety show.

After "Are You Really Mine" and "Bimbombay" in 1958, Rodgers' recording career began a slow decline. One reason may have been the departure of Hugo and Luigi, They moved on to produce most of Sam Cooke's hits on RCA Victor in the 1960s. In 1962, Rodgers signed with Dot Records, which placed him in the newly created post of Director of Folk Music. As a producer, he worked with Debbie Reynolds and Pat Boone. He had only moderate success as a recording artist at Dot, with "It's Over" in 1966 being as close as he came to a hit. A year later he switched to A&M Records and issued the critically acclaimed album CHILD OF CLAY, which contained the song "Turnaround," a favored song at weddings for many years.

On December 2, 1967, under mysterious circumstances, he suffered a fractured skull alongside a Los Angeles freeway. According to an interview with Rodgers published in 1987, he and his music conductor, Eddie Samuels, had attended a social gathering. Rodgers left about two a.m. and was en route home when he noticed that he was being followed by another car that was blinking its lights. Thinking that it was Samuels, who was supposed to be following him home, Rodgers pulled off the freeway and stopped. Someone got out of the second car. When Rodgers lowered his window, he was hit by an object he later described as similar to a tire iron. He remembered lying on the ground with three people around him. Meanwhile, Samuels had gone on to Rodgers home. After waiting about an hour, he decided to back track. He saw Rodgers' car alongside the off-ramp. As he stopped, he noticed a police car pulling away with its lights off. It was alleged that Rodgers had been assaulted by members of the Los Angeles Police Department. The official police report stated that Rodgers had been pulled over by an off-duty policeman for erratic driving, and had accidentally fallen, striking his head. At the very least, it appeared that police officers had left a seriously injured person at the scene. According to Rodgers, three police officers were dismissed as a result of this incident for falsification of police reports.

Recovery for Rodgers was very slow and painful. He remained hospitalized for almost a year, during which time he underwent three brain surgeries. He finally had a steel plate placed in his skull. His weight dropped to 118 pounds. He tried a comeback in 1969 on Joey Bishop's television show, but decided that his unsteady appearance that night precluded any attempts at live performing for a while.

He moved from Los Angeles to San Diego to concentrate on writing music. He composed the music for the popular television special, "The Christmas Mouse." He composed the music used by the United States sky diving team during the 1988 Olympics. He eventually returned to Los Angeles, where he currently lives with his second wife, Trudy, a performer with the American Folk Ballet. One of his four children, Michelle Rodgers, records Christian music.

Jimmie Rodgers' career began as rock 'n roll was losing its harder edge. As such, his timing couldn't have been better. He sang songs that were not threatening to teens or parents, yet appealed to both. By the time his career came to its untimely end in 1967, he had sold more than 30 million records. He often referred to himself simply as a folk singer. In reality, his contribution to music was that he was among the first to sing "soft rock."

November 1957

THE DUBS

Many might consider the Dubs to be a one-hit wonder. While it is true that the group only had one real hit record, the group produced some fine music over the course of eight years. The most famous lineup of the Dubs included Richard Blandon, lead tenor; Cleveland Still, first tenor; Cordell Brown, second tenor; James "Jake" Miller, baritone; and Tommy Grate, bass. Each man was originally from the South and had moved to New York City by the mid-1950s. Blandon and Grate had sung with the Five Wings while Still and Miller were in the Scale-Tones. These four, along with Tommy Gardener of the Scale-Tones formed a group they called the Dubs, but their first release, "I Won't Have You Breaking My Heart" on ABC-Paramount (1956), came out as by the Marvels. The first Dubs record was "Don't Ask Me (To Be Lonely)" on Johnson Records. When the record began to garner airplay, the song, along with the Dubs contract, was sold to Gone Records. It did well enough to crack the "pop" charts for a month in the summer of 1957. "Could This Be Magic" followed. Frequent spins on "American Bandstand" coupled with appearances by the group, and "Could This Be Magic" soon approached a million copies in sales. After "Could This Be Magic," the next two Dubs' records failed to catch on. Then, in 1959, "Chapel of Dreams" was issued. While it didn't sell nearly as many copies as "Could This Be Magic," it did feature the same high standards by the group. The Dubs had no more hits. After leaving Gone, they returned to ABC-Paramount for five singles into 1962. There was a release on Gone in 1962 as well as a release on End, which was part of the same company. 1963 saw one record on Wilshire followed a year later by another on Josie. The Dubs remained active over the years, and in the late 1980s, they were still working in the New York area.

NOV 1   "The Biggest Show of Stars for '57" winds down in its final month of dates, playing the Arena Auditorium in Denver tonight. With the troupe at this time are Fats Domino, Frankie Lymon, LaVern Baker, Chuck Berry, Clyde McPhatter, the Everly Brothers, the Diamonds, Buddy Knox and Jimmy Bowen with the Rhythm Orchids, Paul Anka, Buddy Holly and the Crickets, Eddie Cochran, and the Drifters. On succeeding nights for the next few weeks the group entertains in Wichita, Kansas (2); Kansas City (3); Omaha (4); Topeka (5); St. Louis (6); Indianapolis (7); Ft. Wayne (8); Louisville (9); Detroit's Fox Theater (10); Toledo (11); Pittsburgh (12); Erie, Pennsylvania (13); Troy, New York (14); Boston (15); Hartford (16); the Forum in Montreal (17); Ottawa (18); Buffalo (19); Philadelphia (20); Norfolk (22); Charlotte (23). The tour closes in Richmond on November 24.

       The Apollo Theater in New York welcomes Little Willie John, the Heartbeats, Donnie Elbert, the **Dubs**, the Channels, Linda Hopkins, and Arnett Cobb's combo for the week.

NOV 3   Little Richard was scheduled to rip it up at the Municipal Auditorium in New Orleans from 8:00 p.m. to midnight. Unfortunately for his fans, his conversion to religion took precedence.

       Paul Anka and Jimmie Rodgers appear on "The Ed Sullivan Show" on CBS-TV.

       Also on television this Sunday night, Jerry Lee Lewis makes his third appearance on NBC-TV's "The Steve Allen Show."

       The "Fall Fantabulous Rock and Roll Show" tour, originally scheduled to wind up its jaunt this evening is now booked to continue for two more weeks, visiting cities in Texas, Arizona and New Mexico as well as Denver, Kansas City, Evansville, Columbus, Flint, and St. Louis.

       The Platters return to the United States from their lengthy tour of Latin America and Paris.

NOV 4   In the afternoon, Jerry Lee Lewis makes a return engagement on "American Bandstand" to plug his latest release, "Great Balls of Fire."

       In the evening, Paul Anka appears on CBS-TV's "The Big Record Show."

New Releases for the first week in November include "Great Balls of Fire" by Jerry Lee Lewis on Sun; "Speedy" by the Bobbettes on Atlantic; "Sweet Georgia Brown" by the Coasters on Atco; "This Is the Nite" by the Valiants on Keen; two from ABC-Paramount: "At The Hop" by Danny and the Juniors and "Penny Loafers and Bobby Socks" by Joe Bennett and the Sparkletones; "Henrietta" by Jimmy Dee on Dot; "Teenage Riot" by Portugese Joe on Surf; "Do Anything" by the Five Keys on Capitol; "When I Get You Back" by Tony Harris on Ebb; and "The Echoes Keep Calling Me" by Little Joe and the Thrillers on Okeh.

NOV 5   On ABC-TV this afternoon, Joe Bennett and the Sparkletones appear on "American Bandstand."

EARLY NOVEMBER
With Little Richard off to seminary, leadership of his band, the Upsetters, has been taken over by vocalist Dee Clark.

NOV 8   Chicago's Regal Theater hosts Screamin' Jay Hawkins, the Dells, and Big Maybelle for the week.
Little Willie John, Linda Hopkins, the Channels, and Bobby Day and the Satellites begin a week-long run at Washington's Howard Theater.
After three years in show business, Chuck Berry makes his debut on television lipsyncing to his recording of "Rock and Roll Music" on "American Bandstand."
B. B. King opens a week-long stand at the Flame in Detroit.

NOV 9   Elvis Presley performs for fifteen thousand fans at the Honolulu Stadium. The next night, he plays for the troops at Schofield Barracks in Pearl Harbor.

New Releases for the second week in November include "Oh Julie" by the Crescendos on Nasco; Frankie Lymon's "Little Girl" on Roulette; "Pretty Baby" by Bobby Darin on Atco; "Patty Baby" by Terry Noland on Brunswick; "The Way I Love You" by Jodie Sands on Chancellor; "Sugar Doll" by Johnny Jay on Mercury; "That Dood It" by **James Brown** and the Famous Flames on Federal; "Shake, Baby, Shake" by Champion Jack Dupree on Vik; and "Bad Luck Blues" by Smiley Lewis on Imperial. Also new this week is "Charm Bracelet" by Bob Crewe on Vik. Crewe recorded numerous singles under his own name. However, he achieved his greatest success as a producer (the Four Seasons and Mitch Ryder and the Detroit Wheels) and with his own 1967 instrumental, "Music to Watch Girls By." On "Charm Bracelet," Crewe is backed by the Rays.

NOV 12   "Jamboree," the latest motion picture with a rock 'n roll theme, opens nationwide. Featured performers are Jerry Lee Lewis, Fats Domino, Buddy Knox, Carl Perkins, Jimmy Bowen, Lewis Lymon and the Teenchords, Charlie Gracie, and newcomers Jodie Sands and Frankie Avalon. The movie also featured the voice of Connie Francis dubbing for co-star Freda Holloway.

NOV 15   The Five Satins begin a tour of Hawaii with a show in Honolulu. (See NOV 29.)

JAMES BROWN
James Brown has been nicknamed Butane Brown, Mr. Dynamite, Soul Brother Number One, and the Godfather of Soul. The name that most perfectly fits is The Hardest Working Man in Show Business. At one time, he held the house record in every R&B club and theater in America. His greatest influence was his friend Hank Ballard. In turn, Brown was a model for Mick Jagger, Michael Jackson, and Prince. Brown was born May 3, 1933, in Barnswell, South Carolina. He has called Augusta, Georgia, home for most of his life. At age thirteen, he was a member of the Cremora Trio, a group of local sidewalk entertainers. He wanted to become a professional boxer or a semipro baseball player, but a leg injury ended his sports career. In 1949, he was arrested for armed robbery, and he served four years in a Georgia reformatory. When he was released, he had redirected his energy into music. He formed the Famous Flames, patterned after Ballard's Midnighters. They were discovered while performing in Macon, Georgia. In February 1956, they recorded "Please, Please, Please," a sweat-soaked, gospel-tinged ballad. The song was released on Federal Records, part of the King label. It was a major hit in the R&B market for four months in the summer of 1956. The Famous Flames included Bobby Byrd, Fred Pulliam, and Sylvester Keels. For the next few years, Brown and his group turned out a series of emotional tear-jerkers and foot-stompin' dance tunes. He put together an instrumental combo to back him on tour and in the studio that was second to none. In his quest for perfection, he would stand beside each player and harass them until they could play the sounds he heard inside his mind. In 1958, Brown released "Try Me." It went to Number One in the R&B market; and, equally as important, it cracked the "pop" field, where it sold well for three months during the winter of 1958-59.

Washington's Howard Theater presents the Coasters, Ernie Freeman's combo, and the Hollywood Flames for a week.

Bill Haley and His Comets make a rare television appearance on "The Big Record" on CBS-TV.

Jackie Wilson, the Five Keys, and Ruth Brown fill out this week's revue at the Apollo Theater in New York.

MID-NOVEMBER

Gene Vincent and the Blue Caps are scaling down their tours, appearing at local teen dances across the country. The act sells out the house at the Prom Ballroom, Minneapolis; the Armory in Moorehead, North Dakota; the Riverside Ballroom in Green Bay; the Crystal Ballroom in Fargo, North Dakota; and the Castle Rock Ballroom in Trenton, New Jersey.

NOV 17   On CBS-TV, Gene Vincent and His Blue Caps perform "Lotta Lovin'" and "Dance to the Bop" during an appearance on "The Ed Sullivan Show."

New Releases for the third week in November include "Who's Sorry Now" by Connie Francis on M-G-M; "I'll Come Running Back to You" by Sam Cooke on Specialty; "My Blind Date" by Don Deal on Era; "Walking with Mr. Lee" by Lee Allen on Ember; "26 Miles" by the Four Preps on Capitol; "You're the Greatest" by Billy Scott on Cameo; Dickie Lee's "Good Lovin'" on Sun; and Bill Craddock's "Bird Doggin'" on Colonial. Also out this week is "Hey, Schoolgirl" by Tom and Jerry on Big. "Tom Graph" and "Jerry Landis," students at New York's Forest Hill High and clerking in a shoe store and grocery market, were future superstars using their real last names, Simon and Garfunkel.

NOV 19   Carl Perkins embarks on a two-week tour of the West Coast. (See NOV 26.)

The Mammoth Gardens in Denver hosts Bill Doggett's combo for the evening.

NOV 22   Plugging their recently released "Hey, Schoolgirl," Tom and Jerry perform on "American Bandstand."

The Flame Show Bar in Detroit welcomes the Billy Williams Quartet as this week's entertainment.

Ruth Brown, the Del Vikings with Kripp Johnson, and Jackie Wilson entertain this week's patrons at the Howard Theater in Washington.

NOV 23   The "Big D Jamboree" in Dallas welcomes **"Groovy" Joe Poovey** and Gene Rambo to the roster tonight.

New Releases for the fourth week in November include "(I Love You) For Sentimental Reasons" by Sam Cooke on Keen; the Casuals' "So Tough" on Back-Beat; "I Want You to Know" b/w "The Big Beat" by Fats Domino on Imperial; "Say! Boss Man" by Bo Diddley on Checker; two

---

"GROOVY" JOE POOVEY
With a moniker like that, he should have been a shoo-in. He began his career in show business in his hometown of Fort Worth where he was a radio disc jockey as a teenage. In 1955, he joined the "Big D Jamboree" in Dallas. The Big D was an every-Saturday-night show broadcast from the Sportatorium to radio stations all across the South and Southwest. For a time, Poovey was the Big D's token rock 'n roller in much the same vein as Elvis was the token rocker on the "Louisiana Hayride," another Saturday night radio show broadcast across the region from Shreveport. For three years, Groovy Joe Poovey played the taverns and roadhouses across Texas and the surrounding states while keeping his Saturday evenings open for Dallas. In 1958, he shifted his base back to Fort Worth when he became a regular on "Cowtown Hoedown." He still found time to make appearances on the Big D as well as the "Red River Roundup" in Paris, Texas. In Fort Worth, he also did some guest shots on the local television shows "Top Ten Dance Party" and "Teenage Downbeat." It is interesting to note that with all of this performing, he didn't begin recording until 1958 on the small Dixie label out of Madison, Tennessee. He is best known for "Ten Long Fingers," which was issued with "Thrill of Love" as the B-side. He had two other singles on Dixie, "Move Around" and "Eight to the Bar." In late 1960, he had one release on Azalea Records, "I Dreamed About the Blues." This was followed in 1962 by a single on Sims. He is rumored to have recorded for Eagle and Cimmaron, but a thorough search of discographies for both companies does not reveal any records by Groovy Joe. By the mid-1960s, Poovey had slipped back into obscurity.

from Atlantic: "Teen Age Letter" by Joe Turner and "Betty and Dupree" by Chuck Willis; "Flip-Flop" by the Teenagers on Gee; "Showtime" by Neil Sedaka on Decca; "Twenty Flight Rock" by Eddie Cochran on Liberty; two from the Tune Weavers: "Ol Man River" on Checker and "I Remember Dear" on Casa Grande; the Falcon's "Now That It's Over" on Falcon; Wanda Jackson's "Fujiyama Mama" on Capitol; two from Gone: "Wait a Minute" by Jo Ann Campbell and the Gone All-Stars' "7-11;" "Maybe" by the **Chantels** on End; "Beep-Beep-Beep" by Bobby Day on Class; "Been So Long" by the Pastels on Mascot; and "Woke Up This Morning" by Kripp Johnson on Dot. This week also saw the release of two versions of "Bertha Lou," by Clint Miller on ABC-Paramount and by Johnny Faire on Surf. The song had originally been released by Dorsey Burnette on Cee-Jam, but he was signed to another label. Dorseny's vocal was erased and Johnny Faire used Burnette's music track for his version.

NOV 26   Carl Perkins with Johnny Cash and the Tennessee Two play Eureka, California. They travel through Oregon entertaining in Medford (27), Klamath Falls (28), Coquille (29), and Portland (30). (See DEC 1.)

NOV 27   Ricky Nelson, currently on a brief Southern California tour, plays Long Beach. He is set for San Diego on the 29th.
On "American Bandstand," Bill Haley and His Comets perform "(You Hit the Wrong Note) Billy Goat."
Ray Charles and Billie Holiday play a benefit show at New York City's Carnegie Hall.

NOV 28   The Diamonds open a week-long gig at the Lotus Club in Washington.

NOV 29   Remaining in New York, Ray Charles headlines this week's show at the Apollo Theater, which also features Screamin' Jay Hawkins.
Roy Hamilton headlines a week-long stand at the Howard Theater in Washington. Also appearing on the bill are the Tune Weavers, the Spaniels and Wynona Carr.
At Philadelphia's Uptown Theater, Frankie Lymon headlines this week's revue which also features the Rays, Thurston Harris, Billy Myles and Lee Andrews and the Hearts.
In Honolulu, a capacity crowd welcomes the Five Satins, Don and Dewey, and Sonny Knight to the Civic Auditorium.
Jackie Wilson headlines this week's revue at the Flame Show Bar in Detroit. During the past year, he appeared frequently at the Flame as a supporting act.

NOV 30   Wanda Jackson rocks the "Big D Jamboree" in Dallas tonight.

LATE NOVEMBER
Della Reese is currently playing an extended engagement at

THE CHANTELS
The Chantels are credited with starting the succession of girl groups that dominated rock 'n roll from 1957 into the early 1960s. At the time of their first release, the Chantels were age fourteen to seventeen. Led by Arlene Smith, the other members included Lois Harris, Sonia Goring, Jackie Landry, and Rene Minus. They attended the same Catholic high school in the Bronx; and, like their male counterparts, the girls received their musical training by vocalizing in places with a natural echo. Legend has it that they cornered Alan Freed backstage for an impromptu audition. More likely, they came to the attention of Richard Barrett, leader of the Valentines and a local record producer. Barrett had ties to George Goldner through his own group and his discovery of the Teenagers, whom the Chantels openly idolized. Barrett introduced the Chantels to Goldner, who placed them on his new End label. Their first release featured two of Arlene's compositions, "He's Gone" b/w "The Plea." The record sold well in the Northeast during the last quarter of 1957. To follow, the group recorded another of Arlene's tunes, "Maybe." Featuring her impassioned delivery, "Maybe" became a major hit in both the R&B and "pop" fields. The group's next two records, "Every Night (I Pray)" and "I Love You So," were also hits. Then, as happened so often in rock's early days, the Chantels' career stalled. Singles were released every few months for the next two years on both End and Gone, and none sold well. The group left Goldner and signed with Carlton Records in 1961. Their first Carlton single, "Look In My Eyes" was as big a hit as "Maybe." "Well, I Told You," also did well. Then it was another two years before their final hit, "Eternally," on the small Ludix label. The group moved on to 20th Century-Fox and Verve, before ending their recording career with one single on RCA Victor in 1970.

Blinstrub's Club in Boston.

Gale Garnett, vocalist on "Art Ford's Greenwich Village Party," a local television show in New York, is signed to record an album for Emgee Records.

THE TOP ROCK 'N ROLL RECORDS FOR NOVEMBER 1957

1. Jailhouse Rock/Treat Me Nice - Elvis Presley
2. Wake Up Little Susie - The Everly Brothers
3. You Send Me - Sam Cooke
4. Silhouettes - The Rays
5. Be-Bop Baby/Have I Told You Lately That I Love You - Ricky Nelson
6. Little Bitty Pretty One - Thurston Harris
7. My Special Angel - Bobby Helms
8. Honeycomb - Jimmie Rodgers
9. Keep A Knockin' - Little Richard
10. Happy, Happy Birthday Baby - The Tune Weavers
11. Mr. Lee - The Bobbettes
12. Hula Love - Buddy Knox
13. Rock and Roll Music - Chuck Berry
14. Diana - Paul Anka
15. Alone - The Shepherd Sisters
16. Lotta Lovin' - Gene Vincent and the Blue Caps
17. Could This Be Magic - The Dubs
18. Peggy Sue - Buddy Holly
19. Raunchy - Bill Justis
20. That'll Be The Day - The Crickets
21. Whole Lot of Shakin' Going On - Jerry Lee Lewis
22. Peanuts - Little Joe and the Thrillers
23. Wait and See - Fats Domino
24. Back To School - Timmie Rodgers
25. Deep Purple - Billy Ward and His Dominoes
26. Honest I Do - Jimmy Reed
27. Bony Moronie/You Bug Me Baby - Larry Williams
28. Black Slacks - Joe Bennett and the Sparkletones
29. Raunchy - Ernie Freeman
30. Swanee River Rock (Talking 'Bout That River) - Ray Charles
31. Plaything - Nick Todd
32. Kisses Sweeter Than Wine - Jimmie Rodgers
33. The Joker - Billy Myles
34. Send For Me - Nat King Cole
35. The Story of My Life - Marty Robbins
36. Reet Petite - Jackie Wilson
37. Party Time - Sal Mineo
38. Rebel - Carol Jarvis
39. Hey! Little Girl - The Techniques
40. Farther Up The Road - Bobby "Blue" Bland
41. Love Me Forever - The Four Esquires

42. Stardust - Billy Ward and His Dominoes
43. Great Balls Of Fire - Jerry Lee Lewis
44. Little Bitty Pretty One - Bobby Day
45. Teardrops - Lee Andrews and the Hearts
46. Oh Boy! - The Crickets
47. Only Because - The Platters
48. Buzz, Buzz, Buzz - The Hollywood Flames
49. Why Don't They Understand - George Hamilton IV
50. At the Hop - Danny and the Juniors

Also on the "pop" charts:
Melodie D'Amour - The Ames Brothers
I'm Available - Margie Rayburn

November 1957
ARTIST OF THE MONTH

SAM COOKE

Sam Cooke is the father of the modern soul ballad. His legacy is most clearly seen in the work of Smokey Robinson and Marvin Gaye, although his influence on soul and rock vocalists through the 1960s and into the 1970s spanned such diverse personalities as Aretha Franklin and Rod Stewart.

But before he became a singer with soul, he was a singer who saved souls.

The Cook family of Chicago was deeply religious, helmed as it was by the Reverend Charles Cook, a popular Baptist preacher in the city. Sam was born into this family on January 22, 1931*. By age nine, young Sam had joined with two of his sisters to form a gospel trio named the Singing Children. As a teenager, Sam was a member of the nationally famous Highway Q. C.'s with his younger brother, L. C. Cook. When he was nineteen he was chosen as lead vocalist with the Soul Stirrers, replacing the legendary R. H. Harris. The Soul Stirrers were one of the top acts on the all night gospel circuit. The group had recorded for Aladdin in the 1940s. In 1948, they signed with Specialty Records.

Sam Cooke

Specialty was founded in 1946 by Art Rupe; and during Specialty's first two years, Rupe issued only up-tempo blues recordings. Then, in 1948, he discovered the wide-open field of gospel records. For the next few years, Specialty concentrated on gospel and boogie-based blues to the exclusion of most other types of music.

In 1950, Cooke's debut recording session with the group produced one of his most moving performances, "Jesus Gave Me Water." With Cooke's soaring vocal leading them, the Soul Stirrers were something to behold. Their arrangements were brilliant, shining examples of close

---

(*Date and place of birth also given as January 2 in Mississippi.)

gospel harmony. Cooke brought "style" to the gospel format. Unlike many other gospel groups of the time—including his Specialty label-mates the Swan Silvertones, the Gospel Harmonettes, and the Chosen Gospel Singers—Cooke seldom resorted to gravel-voiced exhortations. On those occasions, such as "Were You There," when he did become overly exuberant, Cooke had no problem bringing down his share of fire and brimstone.

Cooke always expressed admiration for the other lead vocalists in the gospel field. Dorothy Love Coates of the Gospel Harmonettes was a close friend of the Cooks. Alex Bradford and Clarence Fountain of the Original Five Blind Boys of Alabama were inspirations to Cooke. However, he also found that he could relate to the recordings of Billy Eckstine and Billie Holiday, and, beginning in 1955, Tony Williams of the Platters.

By early 1957, Cooke was a gospel superstar of the highest magnitude, and he was being pressured by Specialty to issue records in the popular field. The constraints against gospel performers recording secular material were incredibly strong and deeply interwoven into the fabric of black society. Still, the monetary and worldly rewards for singing gospel could never approach those for singing for the masses. So Cooke gave in and recorded the pleasant little song, "Loveable" which was released in March under the pseudonym Dale Cook. (Although his birth name is spelled Cook, Sam always referred to himself professionally as Cooke). This ploy fooled no one. Sam Cooke's voice was too unique to hide behind a slight change in name. It also didn't help that "Loveable" was a reworking of "Wonderful," a gospel song previously released by the Soul Stirrers. The Soul Stirrers even provided the backing chorus on "Loveable." All that Cooke needed to complete the change was to switch a couple of words—"girl" in place of "Jesus" for example.

"Loveable" set up a howl from Cooke's gospel fans. He was booed off stage wherever the Soul Stirrers made a personal appearance. His experiment in "pop" forever closed the door on his gospel career. He was released from the Soul Stirrers, with his place being taken by another future soul star, Johnnie Taylor. However, during the next five months, there were no more releases by "Dale Cook" or even "Sam Cooke" by Specialty. The company was busy having hits with Little Richard's "Jenny, Jenny" and "Keep A Knockin'" and Larry Williams' "Short Fat Fannie" and "Bony Moronie." It looked as though Specialty was ready to sweep Cooke under the carpet.

At this time, Specialty's chief artist and repertoire man, Bumps Blackwell, asked for a release from his own contract. There were royalties due to Blackwell which the company chose not to pay in cash, so Blackwell was offered Cooke's exclusive recording contract, in lieu of money. Blackwell knew a gem in the rough when he saw it and accepted. Blackwell and Cooke approached Rex Productions which placed Cooke with Keen Records, a new label recently started by Bob Keane.

In September 1957, Cooke released "You Send Me" on Keen, and the result was immediate and overwhelming. He may have burned his gospel bridges, but he was accepted with open arms by teens and adults looking for a stylized ballad singer.

Cooke sang his new songs with the same conviction he had brought to gospel music. His beautifully controlled tenor soared with all the grace of a butterfly. It reached up to the heavens and swooped down in a free-fall of incredible proportions. He could swirl around a single word in a song, twisting it inside out. The emotion Cooke injected into his singing wasn't as raw as Otis Redding's would be, but it was many steps above that of Johnny Mathis, whose career was just getting underway.

As soon as "You Send Me" started to make waves, there were the expected allegations from Specialty. A February 1958 lawsuit claimed that Cooke had actually written and recorded "You Send Me" while under contract to Specialty, then rerecorded it for Keen. As such, rights to the song would have belonged to Specialty. Cooke claimed that the song had actually been written by his brother, Charles L. Cook (L. C. Cook), who was under no such restraints with Specialty.

Specialty countered by issuing two "Sam Cooke" releases of its own, "I'll Come Running Back To You" "and "That's All I Need To Know." However, during the time that his career was up for grabs, Cooke had only recorded a few nonreligious songs for Specialty, so their stockpile was quickly depleted.

The musical pattern laid down in "You Send Me" was the basis for most of Cooke's hit records during his first year with Keen. "(I Love You) For Sentimental Reasons," "Lonely Island," and "Love You Most of All" were love songs, all tied up in pretty arrangements and sung with a rolling, medium-tempo. These were songs meant for dancing in the dark, with syrupy lyrics and a romantic mood perfect for snuggling with your steady date.

In early 1959, Cooke released "Everybody Likes to Cha Cha Cha" which represented a change in dance-style before he returned to the two-step with "Only Sixteen."

For two years, Cooke was unable to come close to the success he had with "You Send Me." That single sold 2-1/2 million copies in six months. His records with Keen were all big enough hits to ride high on the record charts. However, "Everybody Likes to Cha Cha Cha" and "Only Sixteen," which should have topped out near Number One, sputtered long before reaching that plateau.

If Sam Cooke's reputation was based only upon the sweet dance tunes he recorded for Keen, his career would have been a pleasant interlude in the ongoing course of rock 'n roll. But, Cooke was a multifaceted singer of depth and style. The first indication of the breadth of his talent came with the release of his self-titled album. Only the inclusion of "You Send Me" kept it from being a total homage to Tin Pan Alley's finest songwriters. "That Lucky Old Sun, "The Bells of St. Marys," "Around the World," and "Summertime" were a few of the fine tunes given the "Cooke's tour." His second album, ENCORE, continued in the same vein, and included "It's the Talk of the Town," "Accentuate the Positive," and "I Cover the Waterfront."

The crowning achievement of Cooke's years with Keen Records came in the form of the album TRIBUTE TO THE LADY, his public recognition of one of his early and strongest influences, blues veteran Billie Holiday. "She's Funny That Way," "I've Got A Right to Sing the Blues," and "They Can't Take That Away From Me" have enough swing to impress Sinatra. Cooke shows no hesitation in taking on difficult pieces such as "Crazy In Love" and "God Bless The Child." However, the highlight of the album is "Lover Girl," a minor-key blues that gives Cooke a chance to stretch his remarkable talent.

Cooke recorded more than sixty songs while at Keen. When he tackled standards such as "Stealing Kisses" and "Accentuate The Positive," he gave each a surprisingly fresh and energetic reading. He even recorded a few semireligious songs such as "I Thank God" and "That's Heaven To Me."

By 1959, Cooke's recording contract was on the auction block, eventually being sold to RCA Victor. Interestingly, just after he joined RCA Victor, Keen issued his second biggest hit up to that time, the million-selling "Wonderful World."

(Look for more on the life and career of Sam Cooke in the next volume of THE GOLDEN AGE OF AMERICAN ROCK 'N ROLL.)

December 1957

DEC 1 Buddy Holly and the Crickets make their television debut as guests on CBS-TV's "The Ed Sullivan Show" singing "That'll Be The Day" and "Peggy Sue." Also on tonight's show, The Rays perform "Silhouettes," Bobby Helms sings "My Special Angel," and Sam Cooke is awarded a gold record for "You Send Me" during his appearance.

    The Carl Perkins-Johnny Cash tour continues with a show in Redmond, Oregon. Other dates include Boise (2); Salt Lake City (3); and Grand Junction, Colorado (4).

DEC 2 Danny and the Juniors guest on "American Bandstand" singing "At the Hop." On the same program, Jimmy Dee sings "Henrietta."

New Releases for the first week in December include Ricky Nelson's "Stood Up" b/w "Waitin' In School" on Imperial; two from Mercury: "The Stroll" by the Diamonds and "Your Book of Life" by the Del Vikings; "Don't Let Go" by Roy Hamilton on Epic; "Lonesome Love" by Wes Bryan on United Artists; "Do What You Did" by Thurston Harris on Aladdin; "Jo-Ann" by the Playmates on Roulette; and Carl McVoy's "You Are My Sunshine" on Hi.

DEC 5 On ABC-TV's "American Bandstand," the Diamonds debut a record promoting a new dance hyped as "rock 'n roll's answer to the minuet." Kids form two lines facing each other while a couple "strolls" down the middle.

DEC 6 The Chicago Civic Opera House hosts a rock 'n roll show featuring Jerry Lee Lewis, Sam Cooke, the Rays, the Del Vikings, Nick Todd, Bonnie Guitar, and the Four Lads.

    In New York, this week's revue at the Apollo Theater features Clyde McPhatter with the Spaniels and the Bobbettes.

DEC 7 The Everly Brothers appear on Perry Como's NBC-TV show.

    In Los Angeles, Gene Vincent guests on "Hometown Jamboree" on KTLA-TV, channel 5.

    The "Big D Jamboree" in Dallas welcomes Johnny Carroll, Gene Rambo, and Joe Poovey tonight.

    Bill Haley and His Comets play a gig in Pottstown, Pennsylvania.

    Inaugurating the first of his many trip abroad, Paul Anka plays the Trocadero Theater in London.

EARLY DECEMBER

Ronnie Self, who is contracted to appear on "The Phillip Morris Country Music Show," a goodwill unit giving free shows throughout the South and Midwest, takes a brief leave of absence to tour the Midwest plugging his Columbia release, "Ain't I'm a Dog."

DEC 8 The Platters make a guest appearance on "The Ed Sullivan Show" on CBS-TV. They previewed their latest release, "You're Making a Mistake." On the same show, **Ray Peterson** sings his latest release, "Fever."

Sal Mineo performs on NBC-TV's "The Steve Allen Show."

DEC 9 Mickey and Sylvia open for a week at Sciolla's Club in Philadelphia. Also in town are the Applejacks, playing a week-long engagement at the 19th Hole Tavern.

New Releases for the second week in December include two from Specialty: "Twitchy" by Rene Hall and "Just a Little Lovin'" by Don and Dewey; "Fire Engine Baby" by the Jive-A-Tones on Felsted; "You're My Baby" by the Night Hawks on Stars; "September Song" by Billy Ward and His Dominoes on Decca; Johnny Burnette's "Rock Billy Boogie" on Coral; The Sophomore's "Charades" on Epic; "I'm Gonna Be A Wheel Someday" by Bobby Mitchell on Imperial; and two from Liberty: "Baby" by the Slades and "Willa Mae" by Al Casey. While not a commercial release, this week, the soundtrack to the movie "Jamboree," pressed in long-play form, is mailed to 1,500 deejays across the country.

DEC 11 The Four Esquires make a guest appearance on "The Big Record" on CBS-TV.

DEC 12 In a small wedding chapel in Hernando, Mississippi, Jerry Lee Lewis, 22, marries Myra Gale Brown. Within six months the perceived disparity in their ages, the fact that she was his second cousin, the revelation that he was married to another woman when he married Myra, and the disclosure that Myra was Lewis' third wife will cause the couple extensive grief.

With the pending release of "Dede Dinah," Frankie Avalon is asked back to "American Bandstand" to perform.

Sam Cooke headlines the show at the Casino Royal in Washington for a week.

DEC 13 Brenda Lee is making the rounds of radio and television stations in Chicago before appearing tomorrow in Columbus, Indiana, for employees of Hamilton Manufacturing Company.

Charlie Gracie (➤) opens at Andy's Log Cabin in Philadelphia.

DEC 14 Gene Vincent and His Blue Caps perform in Dallas on the "Big D Jamboree."

RAY PETERSON

As a child, Ray Peterson suffered through a bout with polio. To relieve the boredom of his hospitalization, he sang, both for his own enjoyment and to entertain the other patients. By the time he turned professional he boasted a hour-and-a-half octave range. Ray was born in Denton, Texas, April 23, 1939, and he spent his childhood in San Antonio. He began performing in amateur shows while still in school. Unlike many of the other young male singers from Texas, Peterson did not follow the lead of Elvis Presley and opt for a rockabilly style. Instead, he relied on his vocal power and control to win over listeners. After graduation, he moved to Los Angeles in an attempt to further his singing career. He had little trouble finding a job in a night club and soon was noticed by an executive of the Hollywood branch of RCA Victor Records. At the time, Elvis was serving a two-year hitch in the Army, and it was a priority with RCA to find new, young, talented singers. RCA's search would also turn up Rod Lauren and Johnny Restivo, but neither would have the success of Ray Peterson. Ray's first RCA single was a version of "Fever," a song which was popular in his club act. "Fever" had been a hit for Little Willie John in 1956. While Peterson's version was fine by the standards of the day, it sold poorly. (Six months later, Peggy Lee would sell a million copies of her torrid version of "Fever.") In May 1959, Ray released "The Wonder of You," a dramatic ballad in the style of Jackie Wilson. The manner in which "The Wonder of You" builds to its exciting climax could be considered a model for the hits by the Righteous Brothers. After a four-month run with "The Wonder of You," Peterson's follow-up was a mellow version of "Goodnight My Love," which had been a 1956 hit for Jesse Belvin. Issued in October 1959, Peterson's version sold moderately for six weeks late in the year.

MID-DECEMBER

A story currently circulating through the music industry points to the speed with which an independent label's "hot" record can be picked up and released by a major company. In Cleveland, there is some local action over "I Can't Help It" by Burt Taylor recorded for the Marc label. Atlantic becomes interested and makes a quick deal. An overnight letter is sent to influential disc jockeys as Marc ships the last 200 copies of the original pressing to New York where they are overprinted with Atlantic's label and shipped off to the same deejays. The next day, the metal pressing "mother" is received at Atlantic's pressing plant, and singles start coming off the line. In the meantime, Taylor is booked for an appearance January 3 on "American Bandstand." For all of this flurry of activity, the record, as well as Burt Taylor, quickly disappeared, leaving barely a trace.

DEC 16 Bobby Helms and Gene Vincent are the guests on "American Bandstand" on ABC-TV.

New Releases for the third week in December include "You Are My Destiny" by Paul Anka on ABC-Paramount; "La Dee Dah" by Billy and Lillie on Swan; "Mary, Mary Lou" by Bill Haley and His Comets on Decca; "Swingin' Daddy" by Buddy Knox on Roulette; "Dede Dinah" by Frankie Avalon on Chancellor; "Dedicated to the One I Love" by the "5" Royales on King; and the Quarternotes' "Like You Bug Me" on Dot.

DEC 17 Bobby Darin, still hoping for his first hit, stops by "American Bandstand" to be interviewed by Dick Clark.
In Scotland, Paul Anka is mobbed by adoring fans during his appearance at Glasgow's Odeon Theater where he is backed by the John Barry Seven. Barry would become famous for his film music, including most of the James Bond thrillers, as well as the stirring music for such diverse movies as "Lion in Winter," "Out of Africa" and "Dances With Wolves."

DEC 19 Elvis Presley receives his draft notice to report for two years service in the U. S. Army on January 20, 1958. He asks for, and receives, a two-month extension because he is under contract to film "King Creole" in February. (See MAR 24, 1958.)

DEC 20 The Cadillacs headline the revue at the Apollo Theater in New York through Christmas Eve.

DEC 21 Freddy Bell and the Bell Boys start an extended engagement at the Cafe de Paris in Miami Beach.

DEC 22 Frankie Lymon and the Teenagers perform on the "Ed Sullivan Show" on CBS-TV.

DEC 23 ABC-TV's "American Bandstand" welcomes the Four Esquires.

CHARLIE GRACIE
In 1957, Charlie Gracie's hit singles were part of a move toward a "softer" rock 'n roll sound. Few people know that he was recording a form of rockabilly six years earlier. Charlie Anthony Bernard Graci was born January 12, (or May 6) 1936, in Philadelphia. He began studying the guitar at age ten, and soon was making guest appearances on Paul Whiteman's TV show. He was a seasoned performer at age fifteen when he recorded six songs for Cadillac Records of New York City. Three singles were released in 1951-52, including his first, "Boogie Boogie Blues." Young Charlie became a nightclub sensation in the summer beach resort of Wildwood, New Jersey, and "Wildwood Boogie," released in 1954 on the 20th Century label, paid tribute to the area. Gracie signed with Cameo Records, a Philly label, in 1956, and had a million-seller with "Butterfly" b/w "Ninety-Nine Ways" early the next year. Gracie followed with "Fabulous," "Wanderin' Eyes," and "Cool Baby." Most of his Cameo singles were overproduced by early rock 'n roll standards, but this seemed to appeal to teenage girls who found him nonthreatening. In 1957, he appeared in the film "Jamboree" and made his first successful tour of England. Gracie never had another success to match "Butterfly," and, in 1959, he began a three-single association with Coral Records before moving on to Roulette for two singles. From 1961 to 1965, he recorded briefly for Felsted, President and Diamond. For years, he remained a mainstay in the Wildwood area. In the early 1970s, he released one single on the Sock & Soul label. In 1979, he returned to England and found the crowds undiminished. By the mid-1980s, he was touring the lounge circuit from Texas to New England, with his annual stay in Wildwood now expanded to eighteen weeks each summer. Gracie continues to live in Philadelphia.

New Releases for the fourth week in December include two from RCA Victor: "Don't" b/w "I Beg of You" by Elvis Presley and "Oh Lonesome Me" by Don Gibson; "Lend Me Your Comb" by Bernie Nee on Columbia; "So Tough" by the Kuf-Linx on Challenge; "Sing, Boy Sing" by Tommy Sands on Capitol; and "Be My Lovin' Baby" by the Penguins on Dooto; "Click-Clack" by **Dickey Doo and the Don'ts** on Swan.

DEC 25   Alan Freed's annual Christmas-week show at the Brooklyn Paramount opens for a ten-day run, grossing $193,000 to break the house record which has stood since Frank Sinatra's heydays in the 1940s. Headliners for the Freed revue are Fats Domino and Jerry Lee Lewis. Other acts include the Everly Brothers, Thurston Harris, the Twin Tones, Little Joe and the Thrillers, Paul Anka, the Rays, Terry Noland, Lee Andrews and the Hearts, Buddy Holly and the Crickets, Danny and the Juniors, the Dubs, Jo Ann Campbell, the Teenagers, and the Shepherd Sisters. Industry sources report that, due to the large, star-studded roster, the shows needed to generate $148,000 just to break even.

Also tonight, Paul Anka and Danny and the Juniors make an appearance on CBS-TV's "The Big Record."

The Four Esquires guest on "The Ed Sullivan Show" on CBS-TV.

In Detroit, the Greystone Ballroom's holiday show features the Clovers, Pee Wee Crayton, and "local boy made good," Jackie Wilson.

Chuck Berry entertains the hometown holiday revelers at the Dugout Club in St. Louis.

Chuck Willis, Charlie and Ray, the Heartbeats, Ocie Smith, and the Velours entertain the holiday crowd at Washington's Howard Theater through January 2.

DEC 28   Carl Perkins and Sanford Clark blow the lid off the State Theater in Niagara Falls as the only rockers on an otherwise country show.

DEC 30   Jimmie Rodgers starts a six-day run at the Frontier Room in Vancouver, Washington.

LATE DECEMBER

RCA Victor announces a retail price hike for 45 r.p.m. singles from 89 to 98 cents. Over the next few weeks RCA is followed first by Mercury and Imperial, then eventually by all record companies.

The 98 cent price for single 45 r.p.m. records will hold steady for the next twenty-five years which must be some sort of "record" in itself.

DICKY DOO & THE DON'TS

Their name was ludicrous—it was also catchy. Their music was a combination of driving rock 'n roll—and lounge-act lunacy. In fact, the group known as Dicky Doo and the Don'ts might not have existed at all if it hadn't had a hit record first. The idea behind the group came from Gerry Granahan, a Pennsylvania singer/songwriter. Granahan, born June 17, 1939, had tried his hand at being a radio deejay on WPTS in his hometown of Pittston. In 1956, he moved to New York to seek his fortune. He found work singing on demonstration records. In his off time, he put together a novelty song titled "Click Clack." By his own account, he sang all the parts and played all the instruments on the recording. Through the contacts he had made, he was able to land "Click Clack" with Swan Records of Philadelphia. Dick Clark played the record on "American Bandstand" and it took off, staying a hit for almost four months. This success brought Granahan one little problem. He was besieged with offers for the group to make personal appearances—but there was no group! He hired four singers: Harvey Davis; Al Ways; Ray Gangi; and Dave Aldred, from Lubbock, Texas, who had played drums with Buddy Knox and the Rhythm Orchids. In April 1958, Granahan had two singles issued. "No Chemise, Please" was issued under his own name on the Sunbeam label. As Dicky Doo, Swan released "Nee Nee Na Na Na Na Nu Nu" b/w "Flip Top Box." Both records did reasonably well, with "Chemise" becoming a perennial favorite in the Northeast. Granahan put his solo career on hold, preferring to concentrate on the success of Dickey Doo. The group had minor hits with "Leave Me Alone" and "Teardrops Will Fall" into early 1959. In 1960, they were recording for United Artists, with four singles issued over the next seven years before disappearing.

THE TOP ROCK 'N ROLL RECORDS FOR DECEMBER 1957

1. You Send Me - Sam Cooke
2. Raunchy - Bill Justis
3. Jailhouse Rock - Elvis Presley
4. Peggy Sue - Buddy Holly
5. At the Hop - Danny and the Juniors
6. Great Balls of Fire - Jerry Lee Lewis
7. Silhouettes - The Rays
8. Wake Up Little Susie - The Everly Brothers
9. Rock and Roll Music - Chuck Berry
10. Kisses Sweeter Than Wine - Jimmie Rodgers
11. Be-Bop Baby - Ricky Nelson
12. My Special Angel - Bobby Helms
13. Raunchy - Ernie Freeman
14. Oh Boy! - The Crickets
15. Little Bitty Pretty One - Thurston Harris
16. Bony Moronie/You Bug Me Baby - Larry Williams
17. Why Don't They Understand - George Hamilton IV
18. Honeycomb - Jimmie Rodgers
19. Buzz, Buzz, Buzz - The Hollywood Flames
20. Teardrops - Lee Andrews and the Hearts
21. The Joker - Billy Myles
22. The Story of My Life - Marty Robbins
23. Could This Be Magic - The Dubs
24. Keep A' Knocking - Little Richard
25. Jingle Bell Rock - Bobby Helms
26. I'll Come Running/Forever - Sam Cooke
27. Hula Love - Buddy Knox
28. Alone - The Shepherd Sisters
29. Happy, Happy Birthday Baby - The Tune Weavers
30. The Big Beat/I Want You to Know - Fats Domino
31. Santa and the Satellite - Buchanan and Goodman
32. Peanuts - Little Joe and the Thrillers
33. Stood Up/Waiting In School - Ricky Nelson
34. Dance to the Bop - Gene Vincent and the Blue Caps
35. Wait and See - Fats Domino
36. Love Me Forever - The Four Esquires
37. Black Slacks - Joe Bennett and the Sparkletones
38. That'll Be the Day - The Crickets
39. Back To School - Timmie Rodgers
40. Swanee River Rock - Ray Charles
41. Diana - Paul Anka
42. Little Bitty Pretty One - Bobby Day
43. Penny Loafers and Bobby Sox - Joe Bennett and the Sparkletones
44. Reet Petite - Jackie Wilson
45. Hey! Little Girl - The Techniques
46. Honest I Do - Jimmy Reed
47. Hard Times (The Slop) - Noble "Thin Man" Watts

48. You Can Make It If You Try - Gene Allison
49. Whole Lot of Shakin' Going On - Jerry Lee Lewis
50. Oh Julie - The Crescendos

Also on the "pop" charts:
Raunchy - Billy Vaughn
All the Way - Frank Sinatra

December 1957
ARTIST OF THE MONTH

JERRY LEE LEWIS

Jerry Lee Lewis

"I'm a rompin', stompin', piano-playing son of a bitch. A mean son of a bitch. But a great son of a bitch." (Jerry Lee Lewis, quoted in TIME, March 14, 1983.)

He offered no compromise. He offered no excuses. He has lived most of his life under the microscope of professional stardom. And, if you asked him, he'd tell you that he wouldn't have had it any other way.

Born on September 29, 1935, Jerry Lee was brought up in a religious family in Ferriday, Louisiana. Throughout his life, he was never able to fully escape either his southern upbringing or his Assembly of God beliefs. His family taught him that music made for dancing came from the Devil; that playing in honky-tonks was sinful; that drinking and carousing with women would send him straight to hell. "You've got to walk and talk with God to go to heaven... I have the devil in me! If I didn't have, I'd be a Christian!" (Jerry Lee Lewis, 1957 recording session.)

Even at an early age, Jerry Lee was incorrigible. At fifteen, the family sent him off to study at the Assembly of God's Institute Bible School in Waxahatchie, Texas. His parents hoped he would learn theology and music. His wayward attitude soon got him expelled. In 1952, Jerry Lee married his preacher's daughter, but he soon abandoned her in favor of playing boogie piano at Haney's Big House. Eighteen months later, and a month before his divorce from wife number one was official, he married wife number two. A month later, his new wife bore him a son, Jerry Lee, Junior.

By this time, Jerry Lee eas already pursuing a professional career in music. In 1954, he went to Shreveport and auditioned (unsuccessfuly) for the "Louisiana Hayride." At the same time, he recorded two songs at the Hayride's studios at KWKH Radio, "I Don't Hurt Anymore" and "If I Ever Needed You." The music remained unreleased for forty years.

In 1956, rock 'n roll was in full swing, and Jerry Lee ached to become a part of the movement. The family raised a small amount of money to finance a trip to Memphis so Jerry Lee could audition for Sun Records, the closest record company with the biggest clout. Lewis showed up unannounced only to discover that Sam Phillips, the owner, was out of town. Jerry Lee refused to leave, and a makeshift audition was allowed by the studio's engineer, Jack Clement. Jerry Lee was told to come back in a month.

In late November 1956, when Jerry Lee returned to Sun Studios, he found that Phillips had been impressed with his audition tape. Phillips even arranged for Lewis to team up with guitarist Roland Janes and drummer James Van Eaton. Both Janes and Van Eaton have stated that the only reason they were chosen was because they happened to be available. During his first session, Jerry Lee recorded a self-penned number, "End of the Road," and "Crazy Arms," a hit at the time for Ray Price. He sang both songs with fervor and zeal. According to Janes, even at this early date it was obvious that Lewis "wanted to set the world on fire." The opening line from "End of the Road" proved prophetic: "The way is dark, the night is long, I don't care if I never get home!"

Jerry Lee remained in Memphis for a few weeks, waiting for the release of his record. He had an open invitation to drop by Sun Studios whenever he wanted. Looking back at the volume of music he recorded at this time, he must have stayed at Sun Records day and night. His piano style, which would soon be nicknamed "pumping," proved attractive to Phillips and other Sun artists. Lewis can be heard on Billy Lee Riley's "Flying Saucer Rock and Roll" recorded during this period.

On December 4, Jerry Lee was working an afternoon session behind Carl Perkins. Johnny Cash was also hanging around, giving Perkins support, when Elvis Presley dropped by his former studio. Part of the resulting jam session, nicknamed the Million Dollar Quartet, was taped for posterity. One of the most interesting aspects of that afternoon's frivolity was the assuredness of Jerry Lee. He more than held his own with three of the top performers of 1956.

A week later, "End of the Road" was on the street. The single sold moderately well in Memphis, New Orleans, East Texas, and Arkansas. Not enough to bring national attention, but more than enough to send Jerry Lee to Dallas for a February shot on "The Big D Jamboree" and out on the road with Perkins and Cash in March.

When not on tour, Lewis returned frequently to the studio where he continued to record virtually every song in his large repertoire. Cash, Perkins, and Lewis set off to conquer western Canada and the northern United States in April. While he was playing one-night stands across the nation in May, Sun Records released Jerry Lee's second single.

For years, "Whole Lot Of Shakin' Going On" was thought to have been a one-take performance. Not so. The song had gone through at least four revisions in January before the final, "one" take, probably from a session in February. Even then, Jerry Lee was a perfectionist when it came to his recordings. To Jerry Lee's credit, it is remarkable how well "Whole Lot Of Shakin' Going On" has withstood the passage of time, remaining fresh and new, and retaining its infectious, lascivious humor. It was his masterpiece.

"Whole Lot Of Shakin' Going On" turned the Bible Belt on its collective ear. The song was suggestive enough to cause the pulpit to forget for a while about that hip-shaker, Elvis the Pelvis. The opening couple of verses are nothing more than barrel-house boogie with a thumping backbeat. Then Jerry Lee hunkers down with the vocal, talking sweet talk to his "dancing" partner, "All you gotta do, honey, is kinda stand in one spot, and wiggle around just a little bit." It set up a religious howl guaranteed to turn the single into a million seller.

As "Whole Lot Of Shakin'" was creating havoc, Jerry Lee made his first national television appearance, on "The Steve Allen Show" on July 28, 1957. Much has been written of the power of television to make or break a new performer. Jerry Lee was very much aware that his three minutes on camera might be his last, and he was prepared to make an impression. He tore into "Whole Lot Of Shakin'" with a ferocity only hinted at in the single. As he brought the song to its climax, he kicked his piano stool backwards, out of his way. Allen, caught up in the moment, sent the stool careening back across the stage. For 99 percent of the Americans watching that Sunday night, this was their first taste of the real fury behind rock 'n roll. The incident was told and retold so many times in the following weeks that it became a basic part of the legend for both Lewis and Allen, as well as an integral part of the history of rock 'n roll.

"Whole Lot Of Shakin'" had caught America off balance. Lewis followed it by recording a song that really tore the roof off. In its importance to the artist, "Great Balls of Fire" can be compared to Elvis' second single, "Good Rockin' Tonight." By November, when Sun Records released "Great Balls of Fire," Lewis' critics were ready for just about anything. What they got, by the second line of the song, was "too much love drives a man insane." Well, at least there wasn't any "wiggling." The recording was much more energetic than "Whole Lot Of Shakin'," more out of control, if that was possible. It lacks the rolling, left hand piano of "Whole Lot Of Shakin'," but, this works in the song's favor, creating a heightened sense of delirium. The single sold its first million copies in ten days.

"Great Balls of Fire" was released to coincide with the premiere of the movie "Jamboree" in which it was performed. In December, Jerry Lee celebrated by taking his third wife, Myra Brown, the thirteen-year old daughter of the bass player in his touring band, Jay Brown. Jay just happened to be Jerry Lee's first cousin. At this point it should come as no surprise that Jerry Lee was still married to wife number two.

For Jerry Lee, things couldn't have been better. He had two million-selling singles. He was on tour throughout the States. In 1958, he went on a tour of Australia. He was booked to perform on almost every television variety show—especially the ones in need of a ratings boost. In February, "Breathless" became his third straight gold single as he was finally getting officially divorced from his second wife.

In May 1958, Sun released "High School Confidential," the title song from another movie that featured Lewis in a musical cameo. In anticipation of a third successful single, a million copies were shipped to dealers. On May 22, Jerry Lee arrived in England for a month of sold-out concerts. In celebration, Lewis' English record company, Decca, threw a cocktail party in his honor. Jerry Lee thought it would be a fine idea to bring along Myra for support. Unfortunately, most of the guests were from the British press. One comment led to another, and before anyone could "put a spin on it," British newspapers were having a field day castigating this American rock 'n roller for taking a child bride who just happened to be a very close relative.

It was a nightmare of his own creation, but one from which he could not awake. As the news reached the States, Jerry Lee's record sales plummeted as deejays across the country refused to play his songs. On June 9, Jerry Lee published a remarkable letter of contrition in *Billboard* that said in part, "I hope that if I am washed up as an entertainer, it won't be because of this bad publicity..." Jerry Lee wasn't just washed up, he was exiled as though he had the Plague.

Jerry Lee suffered through six years of rejection by both the industry and most of his fans. However, he never gave up. He played any backwater dive that paid enough to cover his expenses. He continued to lay down copious numbers of tracks at Sun studios in Memphis, and Sun continued issuing singles.

The largest enclave of Jerry Lee Lewis fans existed in the very shadow of the site of his debacle. In 1962, he was booked to play England, and once again he appeared before full houses. Over the next few years, he would return often to appear in the United Kingdom, as well as to perform in Europe.

By this time, he had signed a recording contract with Smash, a Mercury Records subsidiary. He was beginning to see his singles and albums on the American sales charts again.

In 1968, Jerry Lee turned away from rock 'n roll altogether. Insofar as his recordings went, he became a full-fledged country performer. He had always expressed a fondness for country music, and he had recorded as much country as rock 'n roll. The only difference was that now he was actively promoting his country side. "Another Time, Another Place," sung by Lewis with deep emotion, topped the country charts in 1968. This was followed by "What Made Milwaukee Famous (Has Made a Loser Out of Me)," another hit in the country market. For the next ten years, he continued to turn out one bestselling single after the next, totaling more than two dozen in all.

However, he still played rock 'n roll on tours. In 1969, he was invited to join John Lennon's "Rock 'N' Revival Concert" in Toronto. In 1970, he signed with Mercury Records proper. That same year, Myra filed for divorce. Without her at the helm of his life, he relied on alcohol and pep pills to keep going.

Throughout 1972, Jerry Lee was honing his talent on a crossbreed of rock and country. Jerry Lee's version of "Me and Bobby McGee" was a raucous paean to hitchhiking. It expressed a completely different feeling from the versions by composer Kris Kristofferson or blues-belter Janis Joplin. Jerry Lee's "Chantilly Lace" outdid the Big Bopper's original in it's lip-smacking, wild-eyed lustfulness. He took the Bobby "Blue" Bland standard, "Turn on Your Lovelight," and wound up the velocity until the song became airborne. In 1973, Mercury released THE SESSION, a double album by Jerry Lee that featured top British rockers. It became his best selling album ever. In 1978, he signed with Elektra Records, but after two albums, the contract ended up in court. He was without a major recording contract for years; then, in 1995, Sire Records released YOUNG BLOOD, an album filled with Jerry Lee's usual fire and flair.

Over the years, the path of his career has been marked by heart-rending tragedies. His first two sons died accidentally, and two of his six wives also died. He has been sued for back taxes since 1975, and he has lost most of his personal property and wealth to the Internal Revenue Service. In 1981, he was hospitalized near death with a perforated stomach. In 1988, he filed for bankruptcy, claiming debts of $3 million and an income near zero. In the 1990s, the Internal Revenue Service continued to make periodic visits to Lewis' various properties, taking cash and valuables to meet his debt.

There have also been incredible successes along the way. In 1986, he teamed with Ray Charles, Fats Domino, and Little Richard for a supercharged cable television special taped in New Orleans. He and his latest wife, Kerrie, welcomed the birth of Jerry Lee's third son in 1988. That same year he acted as consultant on "Great Balls of Fire," a major motion picture depicting his early life.

In March 1993, he opened his own nightclub in Memphis, Jerry Lee Lewis' Spot. Located on the east end of the historically-restored section of Memphis' Beale Street, the new club was a few blocks from 706 Union Avenue, the original home of Sun Records. At the time, he said that he only wanted a place where he could go and play his own type of music when he felt like it.

Maybe he just wanted to feel like he had come back home to stay.

reelin' & rockin'

THE GOLDEN AGE OF AMERICAN ROCK 'N ROLL

1958

1958
A Look Ahead

"If you don't like rock 'n roll, think what you been missin'."
Danny and the Juniors, 1958.

"Rock and Roll is an economic thing," says "pop" singer Jo Stafford, quoted in *Billboard*, October 13, 1958. "Today's nine-to-fourteen year old group is the first generation with enough money given to them by their parents to buy records in sufficient quantities to influence the market. In my youth if I asked my father for 45-cents to buy a record, he'd have thought seriously about having me committed."

According to record industry reports, during 1958, 5,249 singles are issued by some six hundred labels. This is an 11% increase over 1957. Of this number, fewer than 6% of the singles make the Top Fifty.

Still, rock 'n roll singles make up less than half of the ten best sellers: Elvis' "Hard Headed Woman," the Platters' "Twilight Time," Connie Francis' "Who's Sorry Now," and Johnny Cash's "Ballad of a Teenage Queen." "Pop" music is represented by Perry Como's "Catch a Falling Star," Laurie London's "He's Got the Whole World in His Hands," the Chordettes' "Lollipop," Tommy Dorsey's "Tea for Two Cha Cha," and Peggy Lee's "Fever." The National Academy of Recorded Arts and Sciences announces the first Grammys, with "Nel Blu Dipinto Di Blu" winning for Best Record and Best Song. Oddly, the only rock 'n roll winner is "Tequila" for Best Rhythm and Blues Performance.

After Elvis is inducted into the Army in March, his female fans are soon courted by a legion of new performers eager to take his place. Thus, 1958 is the year of the teen idol, as young, handsome teenage male vocalists come to the forefront of rock 'n roll. Led by Ricky Nelson, Paul Anka, Frankie Avalon, Bobby Darin, Jimmie Rodgers, the Everly Brothers, and Jimmy Clanton, these new singers steal most of the thunder away from artists, such as such as Buddy Holly, Jerry Lee Lewis, Eddie Cochran, Dale Hawkins, Gene Vincent, and Buddy Knox, whose style leans more toward hot rockabilly. The "doo-wop" sound of the vocal group is already equated with older rock 'n roll, and it appears as though the rockers will soon follow. However, as if to prove that good ol' rock 'n roll isn't dead yet, 1958 is also the year that Jack Scott begins his rise to fame.

For a time in 1958, it seems as though rock 'n roll (and "pop" music in general) has run out of fresh ideas. In their search for new material, recording artists turn their attention to songs from earlier decades, coming up with hits from such standards as "Who's Sorry Now" (1923), "Twilight Time" (1944), "Smoke Gets In Your Eyes' (1939), "Jingle Bell Rock" (based on the 1857 traditional song), and "It's All in the Game" (melody 1912, lyrics 1951). The most immediate result from rock's apparent lack of direction and motivation is the decline in sales of phonograph records for the first time in years, back to an annual figure of $300 million.

With the big tours reduced to only one or two major packages a year, many rock 'n roll artists turn to the state fair circuit. The fair route is an uncertain one for young performers, and the success of various rock 'n rollers—Frankie Avalon, the Everly Brothers, and Ricky Nelson—can be matched equally against the failures of others.

The ladies are still absent from the rosters of rock 'n roll hits in 1958 with one notable exception. Connie Francis begins the longest and strongest streak of hits by a female vocalist from 1955 to 1965. During the year, she is joined by a small sorority of other female vocalists including Kathy Linden, the Chantels, the Poni-Tails, the Shirelles, the Storey Sisters, Ruth Brown, and the Quin-Tones. There are still many females singing "pop," including Peggy Lee, Patti Page, Joni James, Toni Arden, Betty Johnson, Doris Day, the McGuire Sisters, the Fontane Sisters, and the Chordettes. By the end of the year, the trade papers note a new trend: female teens begin buying records sung by females.

In early March 1958, the press begins to concentrate on the strangle hold by union-controlled rackets over the juke box industry. In St. Louis, state authorities move to clean up what is termed a "hoodlum infiltration" in the pinball, juke box, and cigarette vending industry. Robert Kennedy, staff counsel for the Senate Rackets Committee, announces that Chicago, Detroit, and Cleveland will be spotlighted in the committee's investigation into the nationwide relationship between the coin machine industry and labor unions. The Senate Commerce Communication Subcommittee branches out to probe ties between radio broadcasters and the record business.

Not satisfied with becoming a major force in the booking of rock 'n roll talent, *Billboard* reports that many deejays are moving into the field of producing and selling master recordings. For some time deejays have acted as artists, music publishers, and talent managers. One of the most active is Bill Randle of WERE radio in Cleveland. Randle has cut and sold many masters. Randle says he records mostly in Cleveland with local musicians at sessions that cost an average of $500. Some of Randle's masters were cover records: "Corrido Rock" by Johnny Church, which he sold to Verve; "Yeah, Yeah (Class Cutter)" by Bill Farrell, sold to Date, a Columbia subsidiary; and "Tequila" by Eddie Platt, sold to ABC-Paramount. Others were originals: "Mexican Rock and Roll" and "Blues Stay Away From Me" by Carl Carter, sold to Dot; "Chemise" by George Peters, sold to Mercury; "I Can't Help It" by Bert Taylor, sold to East-West, an Atlantic subsidiary; and "Don't Wake Up" by Laura Lee Perkins and

"Shape Up" by Ernie Freeman, both sold to Imperial.

Riots at rock 'n roll concerts continue, with those in Boston in May getting most of the publicity. Once again, the incident takes place during an Alan Freed tour, which collapses within days following a melee that injures 15 people. This time, Freed is indicted by Boston authorities for creating a civil disturbance. The repercussions severely weaken Freed's career, setting up his final fall a year later.

Reflecting on the increasing power of television to promote rock 'n roll singers, Marvin Rainwater has an astute observation: "While records play an important part in the continuing exploitation of an act, the insurance of regular television exposure is equally important." (*Billboard*, September 15, 1958.) Television's influence over the recording industry reaches an all time high, with Dick Clark's "American Bandstand" leading the way. Television now plays an enormous role in America's daily quota of entertainment.

NATIONAL NEWS

Two California entrepreneurs form Wham-O Toys to introduce the hula-hoop; in six months, they sell 30 million... the United States launches its first space satellite, Explorer I, and NASA is created to handle the country's space program... civil war breaks out in Vietnam... the portable radio is made possible by the introduction of the transistor... there are 1,000 computers in the United States... DeGaulle becomes Premier of France... Stan Musial gets his 3,000th hit... Arnie Palmer wins $40,000 on the PGA circuit... the New York Yankees win the World Series, beating Milwaukee 4 games to 3... "Black Orpheus" creates quite a stir, but the Academy of Motion Picture Arts and Sciences honors "Gigi" for Best Picture and Best Director (Vincent Minnelli)... Phil Silvers finally loses the Best Comedy Show Emmy to Jack Benny... "Maverick" gets an Emmy as Best Western (yup, that's a category in 1958, as 6 of the top 10 shows are westerns)... Boris S. Pasternak of Russia refuses to accept the Nobel Prize for DOCTOR ZHIVAGO, which is the best selling work of fiction this year... "The Music Man" wins a Tony for Best Musical and "Sunrise at Campobello" is the Best Dramatic Play... Ford's Edsel is declared a flop... the tuition at Harvard is $1,250 a year... women are wearing the chemise dress... ex-President Truman declares that the nation is definitely in the middle of a recession.

January 1958

THE JODIMARS
In June 1955, after being refused a $50.00-a-week raise, three of Bill Haley's Comets hired their own manager and began setting bookings in secrecy. Taking the first letters from their given names, Joe Ambrose, Dick Richards and Marshall Lytel called themselves the Jodimars. Ambrose (real last name D'Ambrosia), sax, was a Philadelphia high school student when he was hired by Haley. Richards (real last name Bocelli), drums, was half of a Philadelphia lounge act in 1953 when Haley offered to take him on tour. Lytel, bass, joined the Comets in 1951 when he was seventeen. He had been a child star on Paul Whiteman's national TV show, originating from Philadelphia. He is also credited with bringing the "slap-bass" technique to rock 'n roll. In forming the Jodimars, they enlisted Charlie Hess, guitar; Bob Simpson, piano; and Jim Buffington, drums. By September 1955, they were ready for a formal break, and they signed with Capital Records, issuing a total of six singles through 1957 with no hits. Constant bickering between the original Jodimars and the newer replacements meant frequent personnel changes. By the late 1950s, they were a popular act on the Nevada casino circuit. Lytel left the Jodimars in 1958 and joined the Buddy Mars Band, working the Nevada scene. He recorded "Click Clacking Heels" for Cameo (as Marshall Lytell) and "One Little Grain of Sand" on Milestone (as Marshall and Wes). Moving to Los Angeles, he changed his name to Tommy Page and worked the state with the Page Boys before moving to Florida to sell real estate. Ambrose and Richards continued on as the Jodimars for a few years. Richards later worked as a phys-ed teacher in Springfield, Pennsylvania, before becoming a Broadway and film actor. Ambrosia took a "day job" while continuing to perform on weekends. By the 1970s, he was a pit boss at Caesar's in Las Vegas.

JAN 3   Al Hibbler, Bo Diddley, and the Chantels are this week's performers at Washington's Howard Theater.

JAN 5   The Everly Brothers appear on CBS-TV's "Ed Sullivan Show."

New Releases for the first week in January include "Get a Job" by the Silhouettes on Ember; "Short Shorts" by the Royal Teens on Power; "Helpless" by the Platters on Mercury; "Altar of Love" by the Channels on Gone; "Little Pigeon" by Sal Mineo on Epic; "Hoy Hoy" by the Collins Kids on Columbia; a re-release of "Been So Long" by the Pastels on Argo; "You Are My One Desire" by Buddy Holly on Decca; "Talkin' 'Bout You" by Ray Charles on Atlantic; "You're Something Else" by Jimmy Reed on Vee-Jay.; and two from Sun: "Ballad of a Teenage Queen" by Johnny Cash and "Glad All Over" by Carl Perkins.

JAN 7   Buddy Knox is the headline guest on "American Bandstand" on ABC-TV. Also appearing on this afternoon's show are the Hollywood Flames singing "Buzz-Buzz-Buzz."

EARLY JANUARY
  Gene Vincent and the Blue Caps are on the road in Wisconsin.
  Bo Diddley takes receipt his custom-built, square guitar from the Gretsch Company. The guitar was designed by Diddley and built to his specifications.
  The **Jodimars**, a band made up of several former members of the Bill Haley outfit, sign with Imperial Records. They have had several minor hits for Capitol in 1955-56. Their new lead singer is Audrey Wyatt, a former Miss Canada.

JAN 8   The Everly Brothers take to the road for a seventeen-day tour. Accompanying the duo are Jimmie Rodgers, Buddy Holly and the Crickets, the Rays, the Shepherd Sisters, Paul Anka, Danny and the Juniors, the Tune Weavers, the Hollywood Flames, Jimmy Edwards, Billy Brown, the Mello-Kings, and Eddie Cochran. Midway through the tour, Rodgers drops out due to illness.
        Jerry Lee Lewis rocks the television studio audience on CBS-TV's "The Big Record."

JAN 10 Roy Hamilton, the Dubs, Thurston Harris, the Chantels, the Five Satins, and Jo Ann Campbell appear in New York at the St. Nicholas Sports Center.
        LaVern Baker, Little Joe and the Thrillers, Donnie Elbert,

and the Silhouettes perform for a week at the Howard Theater in Washington.

JAN 11   Fats Domino performs a benefit at the Labor Union Hall in New Orleans on behalf of the Caffin Recreational Center.

JAN 13   On the crossover strength of his new release, "Ballad of a Teenage Queen," Johnny Cash visits with local rock 'n roll deejays in Windsor, Ontario, and Detroit.

The aggregation known as Dickey Doo and the Don'ts makes an appearance on "American Bandstand."

New Releases for the second week in January include "Oh-Oh, I'm Falling In Love Again" by Jimmie Rodgers on Roulette; "This Little Girl of Mine" by the Everly Brothers on Cadence; "Good Golly, Miss Molly" by Little Richard on Specialty; "Jeannie, Jeannie, Jeannie" by Eddie Cochran on Liberty; Bobby Lee Trammell's "Shirley Lee" on Fabor; "I Got a Baby" by Gene Vincent and His Blue Caps" on Capitol; "500 Miles To Go" by the Heartbeats on Gee; two from Cameo: "Crazy Girl" by Charlie Gracie and "Bad Motorcycle" by the Storey Sisters; "Make Up Your Mind Baby" by Bob Luman on Imperial; and "Just For You and Me" by Joe Tex on Ace. This week also sees the release of the Picks' "Moonbeams" on Columbia. The Picks is the vocal group that backs Buddy Holly and the Crickets.

JAN 14   The **Crescendos** perform "Oh Julie" on ABC-TV's "American Bandstand." On the same show, Sam Cooke sings "You Send Me."

Braving a winter cold snap, Johnny Cash starts a tour with a show in Battle Creek, Michigan. The following dates are already set: Saginaw (15); Kalamazoo (16); Sault Ste. Marie, Ontario (17); Niagara Falls (18); and Toledo (19).

JAN 15   The Del Vikings appear on CBS-TV's "The Big Record.

Carl Perkins and his band set off on ten days of one-nighters swinging through Idaho, Utah, and Nevada through January 25. Tonight's opening show is in Pocatello.

MID-JANUARY

RCA Victor announces that tests conducted at its pressing facility in Indianapolis have determined that stereo records are incompatible with the monaural hi-fi players currently in use.

JAN 16   The Lane Brothers being a five-day engagement at the Lotus Club in Washington, DC.

JAN 17   Sam Cooke opens for a five-day run at the Club Elegante in Brooklyn.

At the Apollo Theater in New York, this week's fare includes the Silhouettes, **Little Joe and the Thrillers**, Donnie Elbert,

THE CRESCENDOS
"Oh Julie" shot up the charts in early 1958, peaking in the Top Ten in March. The Crescendos consisted of cousins George and Jimmy Lanius; Tommy Fortner, Jim Hall, and Kenny Brigham. In 1957, all were students at Nashville's Cumberland High. They formed a vocal group and began a successful run of talent shows. In the fall, they were noticed by a local deejay who wrangled an introduction with Ernie Young, the owner of Excello Records. Excello was one of the few Nashville labels, large or small, that was recording something other than country music. Although the Crescendos had fine-tuned a number of songs, they were given a new number, "Oh Julie," to record during their first session. The single was released on Nashboro Records, a subsidiary of Excello. The primitive sound of "Oh Julie" was the key to its appeal. Instrumental backing was kept to a minimum: piano triplets, muted guitar, and a snare drum. The echo was restrained, with the Crescendos' voices, especially George Lanius' lead, right up front. Finally, an unidentified female vocalist sang mysteriously in the background. "Oh Julie" was covered by Sammy Salvo for RCA Victor, but teens couldn't be persuaded to buy the Salvo version over that of the Crescendos. The boys found themselves in constant demand; and, within a year, they had succumbed to the pressure and broken up. Various groups labeled as the Crescendos were used to fill tour and record contracts. The two follow-up singles on Nashboro, "Crazy Hop" and "Young and In Love," as well as their lone Scarlet release "Strange Love," featured none of the original members. Among those who worked in these pseudo groups were future record producers Buzz Cason and Larry Butler, as well as Dale Ward who had a minor hit with "Letter to Sherry." One set of Crescendos became the Casuals who backed Brenda Lee on tour.

Lewis Lymon and the Teenchords, and LaVern Baker.

JAN 19   The Casuals perform "So Tough" on American Bandstand."

JAN 20   Former radio deejay Douglas "Jocko" Henderson begins telecasting a daily afternoon teen dance party over WATV in New York. His opening show features the impressive lineup of Sam Cooke, Roy Hamilton, LaVern Baker, the Dubs, Little Joe and the Thrillers, and Thurston Harris.

Dale Wright is a guest on "American Bandstand."

Sarah Vaughan begins a week-long stay at the Casino Royal in Washington.

New Releases for the third week in January include "To Be Loved" by Jackie Wilson on Brunswick; "The Walk" by Jimmy McCracklin on Checker; "Thumb Thumb" by Frankie Lymon on Roulette; "High Blood Pressure" by Huey Smith and the Clowns on Ace; "Zoom, Zoom, Zoom" by the Collegiates on Winley; "Don't Tell Anybody" by the Paris Sisters on Decca; "Maybelle" by Dave Burgess on Challenge; "Rocket Ride" by Narvel Felts on Mercury; Billy Brown's "Meet Me in the Alley, Sally" on Columbia; "What You Want" by Mac Curtis on King; and "The Big Guitar" by the Owen Bradley Quintet on Decca.

JAN 21   On "American Bandstand," Johnny Cash, known primarily as a country performer, sings his pop entry, "Ballad of a Teenage Queen."

JAN 23   Fats Domino, currently working a tour that will take him from Texas to the West Coast, plays a one-nighter in El Paso. He is set for dates in Tucson, Phoenix, Albuquerque, Cheyenne, Denver, Colorado Springs, and Pueblo.

After years of struggling, Connie Francis finally hits pay dirt with "Who's Sorry Now," the song she is asked to perform on this afternoon's "American Bandstand."

JAN 24   In Baltimore, the Crescendos make an appearance on the locally televised "Buddy Deane Show."

In Philadelphia, Frankie Lymon and the Teenagers perform "Goody Goody" on "American Bandstand."

George Hamilton IV starts a two-day gig at the Twin Coaches Lounge in Pittsburgh.

JAN 25   Jerry Lee Lewis is booked into the Riverside Rancho Club in Los Angeles. This is his first appearance in the City of Angels.

JAN 26   Billy Myles performs "The Joker" on "The Ed Sullivan Show" on CBS-TV. Also on the show, making their second appearance, are Buddy Holly and the Crickets.

JAN 27   Stopping in Hawaii while en route to Australia, Paul Anka,

---

LITTLE JOE AND THE THRILLERS

Little Joe Cook preceded the Newbeats in using falsetto. In 1957, Cook had mid-sized hit with his attempt—in 1966, the Newbeats sold a million copies of "Bread and Butter." Cook began in gospel and was a member of the acappella Evening Star Quartet in his home of Philadelphia. The group included three of Cook's cousins, Sam, Leonard and Amos Bell, and Jimmy Coleman, a friend. The Evening Stars began recording for Apex Records in 1949. In 1951, while two of the cousins were in the Army, the group recorded for Gotham, with two singles released: "Say a Prayer for the Boys in Korea" and "Jesus, I'll Never Forget." In addition to recording, the quartet toured extensively, especially in the South, and they had a popular gospel radio show on WHAT in Philadelphia. In the mid-1950s, Cook formed the Thrillers with himself on lead tenor, Ferris (or Farris) Hill (lead), Richard Frazier (tenor), Donald Burnett (baritone) and Harry Pascle (bass). The group auditioned as a gospel group for Columbia Records, but was signed to the R&B subsidiary, Okeh. Their first single was "Let's Do the Slop," based on a current dance craze. The record was a minor Philly hit. As they were preparing for their second release, "Peanuts," the group disbanded, believing there would never be any real success. "Peanuts," featuring Cook's wavering falsetto, was plugged relentlessly by "American Bandstand" and the group was booked to play several engagements at the Apollo Theater in New York. Interesting to note, while "Peanuts" reached into the Top Twenties on the "pop" charts, it didn't rank at all in R&B. There were a half-dozen more singles on Okeh into 1961, but none fared well. Cook went on to other labels, while his daughters had a 1962 hit with "Pop-Pop Pop-Pie" as the Sherrys.

Jerry Lee Lewis, Buddy Holly and the Crickets, and Jodie Sands perform at Honolulu's Civic Auditorium. (See JAN 30.)

(Little) Richard Penniman enrolls at Oakwood College in Huntsville, Alabama. Oakwood is an all-Negro theological school operated by the Seventh Day Adventist Church. Using some of his rock 'n roll money, Richard paid cash-in-advance for his four-year tuition.

New Releases for the fourth week in January include "Sweet Little Sixteen" by Chuck Berry on Chess; "Rock and Roll Is Here to Stay" by Danny and the Juniors on ABC-Paramount; "Maybe Baby" by the Crickets on Brunswick; "Listen to Me" by Buddy Holly on Coral; "Walkin' To School" by the **Kalin Twins** on Decca; "Blast Off" by Noble "Thin Man" Watts on Baton; "I've Got Love If You Want It" by Warren Smith on Sun; "Bop-A-Lena" by Ronnie Self on Columbia; "Always and Forever" by the Four Esquires on Paris; Jo Ann Campbell's "You're Driving Me Mad" on Gone; two versions of "Tequila:" by the Champs on Challenge and by Eddie Platt on ABC-Paramount. Also new this week is Little Willie John's latest King release "Talk To Me, Talk To Me," a song written by Joe Seneca, who would portray a legendary blues singer in the movie "Crossroads."

JAN 29   Sam Cooke appears on "The Big Record" on CBS-TV.
Eddie Cochran makes a rare television appearance on "American Bandstand."

JAN 30   In Australia, Paul Anka, Jerry Lee Lewis, Buddy Holly and the Crickets, and Jodie Sands begin their six-day tour of the continent with a pair of shows at Sydney's Stadium. (See also FEB 1.)

JAN 31   Clyde McPhatter, the Rays, the Hollywood Flames, and Screamin' Jay Hawkins raise the roof at the Howard Theater this week in Washington.

LATE JANUARY

T-Bone Walker is begins a series of weekend dates at Oakland's 53 Club.

THE TOP ROCK 'N ROLL RECORDS FOR JANUARY 1958

1. At the Hop - Danny and the Juniors
2. Peggy Sue - Buddy Holly
3. Great Balls of Fire - Jerry Lee Lewis
4. Stood Up/Waitin' In School - Ricky Nelson
5. Kisses Sweeter Than Wine - Jimmie Rodgers
6. Raunchy - Bill Justis
7. You Send Me - Sam Cooke
8. The Stroll - The Diamonds
9. Jailhouse Rock - Elvis Presley

THE KALIN TWINS
Herb and Hal really were twins named Kalin. They were born February 16, 1939 (occasionally listed as 1934), in Port Jarvis, New York. In their early childhood, the Kalin family moved to Washington, DC. The boys' singing career began when they were age five, and they remained inseparable for the next two decades except for the brief period Hal was serving in the Air Force. They got their professional start playing Washington night clubs. After some success, they cut a demonstration tape and tried to peddle their songs in New York, but with no takers. A songwriter named Clint Ballard came to their aid and was able to get an A&R man at Decca Records to listen to the demo. Decca was a label with a series of country-based "pop" hits, and the sound that the Kalin Twins had developed fit right in. The first Kalin Twins single, "Jumping Jack" b/w "Walk to School," was a flop. Not so, their second release, "When." The song was co-written by Paul Evans, who would shortly have his own hits, and it sold a million copies during the late summer of 1958. The twins followed with "Forget Me Not" (which almost cracked the Top Ten), "It's Only The Beginning" (which almost made the Top Forty) and "Sweet, Sugar Lips" (which disappeared after a brief week's popularity). Remarkably, the Kalin Twins were able to turn their year in the limelight into an elongated career. To supplement their income from performing, they took jobs in the federal government's bureaucracy. In 1989, the Kalin Twins appeared in London in the production of "Oh, Boy!" a Broadway-type show that paid tribute to Buddy Holly and the 1950s. Today, they still live in the Washington area, and they are still performing occasionally to very receptive crowds.

10. Oh Boy! - The Crickets
11. Silhouettes - The Rays
12. La Dee Dah - Billy and Lillie
13. Raunchy - Ernie Freeman
14. Buzz, Buzz, Buzz - The Hollywood Flames
15. Bony Moronie/You Bug Me Baby - Larry Williams
16. Why Don't They Understand - George Hamilton IV
17. Wake Up Little Susie - The Everly Brothers
18. Rock and Roll Music - Chuck Berry
19. Be-Bop Baby - Ricky Nelson
20. My Special Angel - Bobby Helms
21. Teardrops - Lee Andrews and the Hearts
22. Oh Julie - The Crescendos
23. The Story of My Life - Marty Robbins
24. Get a Job - The Silhouettes
25. I'll Come Running Back to You - Sam Cooke
26. Honeycomb - Jimmie Rodgers
27. Don't Let Go - Roy Hamilton
28. Little Bitty Pretty One - Thurston Harris
29. (I Love You) For Sentimental Reasons/Desire Me - Sam Cooke
30. The Big Beat/I Want You to Know - Fats Domino
32. Jingle Bell Rock - Bobby Helms
33. Maybe - The Chantels
34. Jo Ann - The Playmates
35. Dede Dinah - Frankie Avalon
36. The Joker - Billy Myles
37. You Are My Destiny - Lee Allen
38. Could This Be Magic - The Dubs
39. Hey! Little Girl - The Techniques
40. Henrietta - Jimmy Dee
41. Hey, Schoolgirl - Tom and Jerry
42. Dance to the Bop - Gene Vincent and His Blue Caps
43. Don't/I Beg of You - Elvis Presley
44. Short Shorts - The Royal Teens
45. You Can Make It If You Try - Gene Allison
46. Do What You Did - Thurston Harris
47. She's Neat - Dale Wright
48. Hard Times (The Slop) - Noble "Thin Man" Watts
49. Penny Loafers and Bobby Sox - Joe Bennett and the Sparkletones
50. Bertha Lou - Clint Miller

Also on the "pop" charts:

Sugartime - The McGuire Sisters
Sail Along Silvery Moon - Billy Vaughn

January 1958
ARTISTS OF THE MONTH

DANNY AND THE JUNIORS

In Philadelphia in 1957 there was a wildfire sweeping the South Side. With "American Bandstand" on national television every afternoon, hundreds of Philly teenagers were anxiously waiting for their chance. For most, this "chance" meant a minute in the "American Bandstand" dance spotlight.

There were a few South Side teenagers who were waiting for another type of chance. They were using the school restrooms as echo chambers to practice vocal harmony. These teens were waiting for a chance to make their own record. In their dreaming, the record would be dropped off at WFIL-TV's Studio "B." It would be heard by the show's producers or, maybe, by Dick Clark, himself. Their record would get a spin on the air and then, hopefully, they would be given their minute in the spotlight. South Philly kids knew they had an inside track—a real chance.

Danny & The Juniors

And, a remarkable number of these teenagers succeeded. Among the first were four high school students who had begun putting in their time in the restrooms as early as 1955. They called themselves the Juvenaires, hinting that they were all fourteen or fifteen years old. The group consisted of Dave White Tricker (aka Dave White), tenor; Joseph Terranova (aka Joe Terry), baritone/bass; Frank Maffei, second tenor; and Danny Rapp, lead tenor. Rapp also acted as the group's choreographer, teaching the others steps and routines to use on stage to make their act more exciting.

One night in late 1957, they were working a record hop as the intermission entertainment. They were spotted by Johnny Madera, a local man who dabbled in the music business. He was impressed enough with the Juvenaires to mention them to Artie Singer, a songwriter and vocal tutor. Singer had a side-business with his own label, Singular Records. Eventually, Singer invited the group to audition. They ran through a few of the standard vocal group songs that they had been rehearsing, and Singer asked if they had any original material. It turned out that David White had composed a piece he called "Do the Bop." Singer liked the tune and had the group record a demo version so he could test it with some local deejays.

Of course, one of the first people to receive a copy of the tape was Dick Clark. Clark, like Singer, was impressed. He also had two suggestions. First, the name of the group needed to be shortened from Juvenaires to Juniors. Next, since the term "bop" was currently out of fashion, the song's title needed a revision. If the song had a change of title... Well, who knows? And, no promises.

The title was quickly changed to "At The Hop," and the group was rushed to Reco-art Studios in Philadelphia to rerecord the song. It took thirteen takes to get it right, and a completed acetate was sent to the studios of "American Bandstand." Dick Clark loved it! But, he didn't have any immediate openings for the group. Then, lady luck smiled on Danny and the Juniors. At the last minute, Little Anthony and the Imperials cancelled an appearance on "American Bandstand." Clark immediately thought of the Juniors as a replacement. Overnight, "At the Hop" took off like it had a life of its own. In a week, the single sold 7,000 copies in Philadelphia alone. Financially strapped, Singular Records couldn't handle the massive orders and quickly leased the record to ABC-Paramount for $5,000.

"At The Hop" was dynamic, fresh, exuberant—a wonderful exhortation to dancers everywhere to come to the dance. Opening with a ripping four-chord piano figure by Walter Gates, the boys followed, working their wordless, four-part harmony through one complete cycle. The lyrics were aimed squarely at the fifteen-year old dance crowd, inviting them to "do the dance sensations that are sweeping the nation."

The first week in November, ABC-Paramount had their version of "At The Hop" on the street. On December 2, the group had another guest appearance on "American Bandstand." The record made the national charts a week later, and quickly sold well in excess of a million copies. "At The Hop" remained a very popular record for the next six months.

The group appeared on Alan Freed's ten-day Christmas bash at the Brooklyn Paramount. In January, they joined the Everly Brothers on a seventeen-day tour. That same month, their second single, "Rock and Roll Is Here To Stay," was released by ABC-Paramount.

Considered the anthem of the era, "Rock and Roll Is Here To Stay" was as close to a duplicate of "At The Hop" as was legally possible. A similar four-chord piano intro was followed by a similar one-word vocal effort to loosen up the group's vocal cords, and then there were the lyrics every teen was waiting to hear someone say: "Rock and roll will always be, it'll go down in history!"

Next came "Dottie," a song that almost ruined the group's budding reputation. Barely changing the course of the previous two singles, "Dottie" opened with a guitar playing the four-chord intro previously allotted to the piano. The song then became bogged down with mindless lyrics such as "Dottie you're the most, Dottie hold me close" and "D O double-T I E, Dottie, you are the one I love." The record peaked into the Top 40 in the fall of 1958.

There were four more singles but no more hits on ABC-Paramount during the eighteen months following "Dottie." The novelty "Crazy Cave" quickly lost the listener's interest when, for no apparent reason, the Juniors used various harmonic tactics while the tune went up and down the scale. The closest any of their later recordings came to capturing the spirit of "At The Hop" was "I Feel So Lonely." With "Somehow I Can't Forget" they paid tribute to the tight harmony made popular four years before by the Four Aces. Their final ABC-Paramount release was "Playing Hard to Get" one more attempt to make the "Hop" formula work again.

Even with their record sales faltering, the Juniors did not despair. This was a Philadelphia group. They had any number of local labels to approach, all of which were fat with royalties from records being played on "American Bandstand."

Swan Records, a company that at this time boasted Dick Clark's partnership, took Danny and the Juniors and turned them into another new-dance-of-the-week unit. Their first Swan release, "Twistin' U.S.A.," was issued in the fall of 1960 during the height of Chubby Checker's first go-round with "The Twist." In fact, the instrumental backing on the Juniors' version of "Twistin' U.S.A." had originally been used when the same song appeared on Checker's first album. "Twistin' U.S.A." had little else to recommend it, other than its timing. It came when discotheques needed a hot, new dance number every few weeks. "Twistin' U.S.A." happily obliged, rocketing right up the national charts and rocketing right back down again in a brief two months.

The same fate met most of Danny and the Junior's releases in 1961 and 1962. With only a few exceptions, each new single was based on a popular dance step of the day: "Pony Express," "Doin' the Continental Walk," and "Cha Cha Go Go." The best that can be said of these singles is that many featured the soon-to-be legendary Roy Buchanan on guitar. In December 1960, they tried a Christmas song, "Candy Cane, Sugary Plum," that fared poorly. They even tried to bring a little levity to the situation on "Twistin' All Night Long," a song built around imitations of other rock 'n rollers singing about the twist. On "Twistin' All Night Long" the Juniors received help from Freddy Cannon and an otherwise unknown vocal group, the Four Seasons. Even "Back to the Hop" couldn't recapture those heady days of 1958. Their final single for Swan was "We Got Soul," which, of course, was something they didn't have.

After Swan, Danny and the Juniors could land only one-shot record deals so they jumped from one label to the next. In 1962, the group recorded "Twisting England" for Top Rank followed by "Oh La La Limbo" for Guyden Records, another Philadelphia Label. For two weeks in early 1963, it looked like the Guyden single might attract national attention, then it faded. Later that year, they were on Mercury for "Let's Go Skiing," followed over the next few years by "I Can't See Nobody" on Ronn (1968, as by Danny and Jerry), a rerecording of "Rock & Roll Is Here To Stay" on Luv (1968), and a rerecording of "At the Hop" on Crunch Records (1973).

Dave White was the first to leave the group, shortly after "Ooh La La Limbo." White went on to co-write "1-2-3," a 1965 hit for Len Barry, the former lead singer with the Dovells, another Philly group.

After a few years working clubs as a trio, the group's vacancy was filled by Bill Carlucci, formerly of Billy and the Essentials. In 1967, Danny and the Juniors disbanded. However, in 1969, as America was swept up in the rock 'n roll revival, the group reformed, with Jimmy Testa of the Four J's filling in for White. They performed "At The Hop" in the film documentary "Let The Good Times Roll" in 1974. A year later, the group appeared on Shirley Alston's WITH A LITTLE HELP FROM MY FRIENDS album on Prodigal. Alston was the former lead singer with the Shirelles.

In December 1976, the group consisted of Joe Terry (Terranova), Bill Carlucci and Frank Maffei. They recorded "Here Comes Fonzi!" a takeoff on television's "Happy Days" show, with the single issued on Sit On It Records of Philadelphia. In 1978, Terranova left the group for a few years. Soon thereafter, Danny Rapp moved to the West Coast and formed his own edition of Danny and the Juniors. Unfortunately, he was unable to find success in his professional as well as his personal life. On April 5, 1983, Rapp committed suicide in a motel room in Parker, Arizona.

In the meantime, Dave White recorded "Pastel, Paint, Pencil, and Ink," a solo album for Bell Records issued under his full name, David White Tricker. Today, he lives in Southern California where he scores music and writes songs for movies and cartoons.

In the 1980s, Danny and the Juniors continued to perform as an oldies act with Terry, Maffei and Carlucci. They found waiting audiences across the country as they worked state and county fairs as part of Dick Clark's traveling revue. To flesh out their sound, they added saxophonist Lonnie Baker from Sha Na Na Na. While playing club dates in 1986, the group was selling copies of a live album they had privately recorded. In 1987, Joe Terry led the group in their first studio recording in a decade, a new rendition of "Some Kind of Wonderful" on Topaz Records. In 1993, Terry and the group issued "Together You and I" on Downtown.

Danny and the Juniors had a much longer career than might have been imagined from their meager beginnings. They are often thought of as a one-"hop" wonder, but they had a few other medium-sized hits over a span of four years. However, they continue to be labeled as a group that could only perform dance songs. This is a pity. Those long afternoons in the school rest room, listening to their close harmonies bounce back and forth across the tiled walls and floor, produced vocal arrangements not that far removed from those of Dion and the Belmonts, who would soon follow the lead of Danny and the Juniors.

February 1958

FEB 1   In Australia, Paul Anka, Jerry Lee Lewis, Jodie Sands, and Buddy Holly and the Crickets perform again at Sydney's Stadium doing three shows during the day. Other stops during their stay in Australia include Brisbane (3); Melbourne (4); and then Brisbane again (6 and 8).

Back in the States, George Hamilton IV appears on "The Perry Como Show" on NBC-TV.

New Releases for the first week in February include "Don't You Know I Love You So" by Fats Domino on Imperial; "We Belong Together" by Robert and Johnny on Old Town; "Look At Me" by Terry Noland on Brunswick; "Book of Love" by the **Monotones** on Mascot; "A Little Bird" by the Hollywood Flames on Ebb; "Cotton Pickin' Rocker" by Joe Bennett and the Sparkletones on ABC-Paramount; "I Met Him on a Sunday" by the Shirelles on Tiara; "Billy" by Kathy Linden on Felsted; James Brown's "Begging, Begging" on Federal; Laurie London's "He's Got the Whole World in His Hands" on Capitol; and two from Atco: "Gee, Golly" by the Coasters and "Just In Case You Change Your Mind" by Bobby Darin.

FEB 4   Four guys and a gal, known collectively as the Royal Teens, are guests on "American Bandstand."

FEB 6   Bob Hope's NBC-TV special, "Hope in Hollywood," features Nick Todd.

Pat Boone's self-titled television show debuts on ABC-TV at 9:00 p.m.

FEB 7   Upon completion of a short stay at the Orpheum Theater in New York, Sam Cooke begins a seventeen-day tour of the South and Midwest with a show in Columbus, Ohio. At Pittsburgh's Syria Mosque he pulls in $18,000 for two shows. He will wind up on February 23 in Richmond. Other acts accompanying Cooke are the Drifters, Thurston Harris, the Silhouettes, the Dubs, and Ernie Freeman's combo. (See also FEB 19.)

Gene Vincent guests on "American Bandstand" on ABC-TV.

The week-long revue at the Howard Theater in Washington features Lee Allen, the Pastels, the Dells, Robert and Johnny, the Playmates, Varetta Dillard, and Choker Campbell.

FEB 9   Paul Anka appears on "The Ed Sullivan Show" on CBS-TV.

FEB 10 The Platters are at Sciola's nightclub in Pittsburgh.

THE MONOTONES

The Monotones' biggest hit was a love song. It wasn't a syrupy ballad like most other love songs. Rather, it was a driving, get-up-and-dance number. Today, most listeners only remember the "thump" in the middle of the opening line. The Monotones were a sextet from Newark, New Jersey, that consisted of Charles Patrick, George Malone, Warren Davis, Frank Smith, and John and Warren Raynes. Charles Patrick's brother, James, was a member of the Kodaks, a moderately successful group. The members of the Monotones grew up in the same neighborhood and belonged to the same choir. Wanting to test their talent outside of the church, they imitated the style of the Heartbeats, famous for "A Thousand Miles Away." However, when they began writing their own songs, they used the bouncy rhythm of a popular toothpaste commercial for their opening line. "You'll wonder where the yellow went, when you brush your teeth with Pepsodent" became "I wonder, wonder who, (thump) who wrote the Book of Love?" When the Kodaks showed an interest in their new song, the Monotones knew that "Book of Love" had the potential to be successful. After a disappointing audition with Atlantic Records, in late 1957, they were accepted by Hull, the New York label that was home to the Heartbeats. "Book of Love" was released on Hull's Mascot subsidiary, and it began to sell on the East Coast. Hull leased the song to Chess Records, which immediately put it out on its Argo label. During the spring of 1958, "Book of Love" sold over a million copies. The Monotones continued to record under contract to Hull, although their next three singles, including "Legend of Sleepy Hollow," were released on Argo. Their final two singles came out on Hull. In the early 1980s, Charles Patrick, John Smith, Warren Raynes, and George Malone were continuing the Monotones' tradition.

ERSEL HICKEY
Ersel Hickey's life is one for the books. He was one of seven children in a family of vaudeville performers. Following the lead of his sister, who became an "exotic dancer," Ersel left home at age fifteen to join a carnival. Tiring of the constant travel, he settled in Buffalo and became a locksmith. He also started writing songs. He composed "Bluebirds Over the Mountain" and recorded a demonstration tape of the song and gave it to George "Hound Dog" Lorenz, the reigning deejay in the Buffalo area. Lorenz liked the song. More important, he liked the singer. Lorenz began playing the demo over the air. The result was electric. People called in wanting to know the name of the singer with the unique voice. Hickey was quickly signed to Epic Records, a division of Columbia, and he rerecorded "Bluebirds Over The Mountain" in one take—for which he received a $50.00 artist's fee. According to Hickey, the record sold more than two million copies, although it appeared only briefly on the "pop" charts during the early summer of 1958. Nevertheless, record sales did bring him offers for personal appearances, beginning with a guest shot on "American Bandstand" a week before the record was officially released. He issued four more singles on Epic. All fared poorly. To its credit, Epic did not pull the plug on Hickey's contract earlier. Hickey's personal appearances also dried up. His final Epic single was "What Do You Want" in the fall of 1959. He moved to New York and began a calculated assault on the Brill Building, the working home of many of rock's best songwriters. His songs started to sell, and he began to receive regular royalty payments. After leaving Epic, he cut one single each for Kapp, Laurie, Apollo, Janus, and Toot through 1971. In 1979, he was trying for a break as a country-disco singer.

New Releases for the second week in February include "Breathless" by Jerry Lee Lewis on Sun, "Lonely Island" by Sam Cooke on Keen; "Lollipop" by the Chordettes" on Cadence; "Yeah, Yeah" by Billy Farrell on Date; "Can't Wait" by the Del Vikings on Mercury; "Rave On!" by Sonny West on Atlantic; Donnie Elbert's "My Confession of Love" on DeLuxe; The Teen Tones' "Gypsy Boogie" on Nu-Clear; "The Voice" by Fred Paris and the Scarlets on Klic; and "Steady With Betty" by Benny Joy on Dixie. Another release this week is "Everybody's Movin'" by Glenn Glenn on Era. Glenn's real name was Glenn Trout. He was from San Dimas, California, and he had just finished his basic training at Fort Ord.

FEB 14   Ersel Hickey, who's recording of "Bluebirds Over the Mountain" will be officially released in a few days, makes a guest appearance on ABC-TV's "American Bandstand." Hickey is in the midst of a whirlwind promotional tour taking him to radio and television stations in Baltimore, Washington, New York, Hartford and Newark, as well as Philadelphia.
   Lee Andrews and the Hearts along with Billy Williams hold forth for a week at the Apollo Theater in New York.

FEB 15   "The Dick Clark Show" is ABC-TV's latest Saturday night entry. Tonight's premier stars Jerry Lee Lewis, Pat Boone, the Royal Teens, Chuck Willis, Johnnie Ray, and Connie Francis. The show is broadcast from the Little Theater in New York from 7:30 to 8:00 p.m. (EST). Only Jerry Lee actually performs "live," singing "Breathless." The rest lip-sync to their records.
   Danny and the Juniors are booked into the Erie Social Club in Philadelphia for two days.

MID-FEBRUARY
   Della Reese is performing at Mr. Kelly's in Chicago.
   At the New York studios of Columbia Pictures, filming is underway on the movie, "Let's Rock," also issued with the title "Keep It Cool." Appearing in the film are Paul Anka, Danny and the Juniors, the Royal Teens, Della Reese, and Roy Hamilton.
   Carl Perkins jumps from the Sun label to Columbia Records.

New Releases for the third week in February include a third version of "So Tough," by the Cuff Links on Dooto. Other new records this week are "I Found a Job" by the Heartbeats on Roulette; "Dinner with Drac" by John Zacherle on Cameo; "Bluebirds Over the Mountain" by **Ersel Hickey** on Epic; "Substitute" by LaVern Baker on Atlantic; and two rockers from Mercury: "Drop Top" by Roy Perkins and "My Honey" by Jimmy Edwards. Finally, Mickey Gilley's "Call Me Shorty" on Dot is released this week. Gilley had a sting of hard-driving piano rockers similar to those of his cousin, Jerry Lee Lewis, before he toned down his act and became a country superstar in the 1970s.

FEB 19   The Casuals stop by ABC-TV's "American Bandstand" to plug "So Tough."

The Sam Cooke revue performs two shows at the New Orleans Municipal Auditorium. Appearing with Cooke are Thurston Harris, the Silhouettes, the Dubs, the Drifters, and Ernie Freeman and his combo. (See also FEB 20.)

FEB 20   The Everly Brothers, Bill Haley and His Comets, Jimmie Rodgers, Buddy Holly and the Crickets, and Jerry Lee Lewis set off on a one-week tour of Florida with a show at the Peabody Auditorium in Daytona Beach. Other dates include Tampa (21), Jacksonville (22), West Palm Beach (23), and Miami (24). (See also FEB 25.)

The Four Esquires start an extended engagement at Philadelphia's Celebrity Room.

Sam Cooke brings his revue to New Orleans' Labor Union Hall.

FEB 21   Chuck Berry, the Chantels, **Donnie Elbert**, the Dells, Little Joe and the Thrillers, the Pastels, and the Heartbeats share the bill at the Uptown Theater this week in Philadelphia.

At the Apollo Theater in New York City, the bill is a gospel and spiritual revue.

Patrons at the Howard Theater in Washington are entertained by Noble "Thin Man" Watts, Gene Allison, the Turbans, Lee Andrews and the Hearts, and Dee Clark.

FEB 22   "The Big Beat," a full-color entry in the rock 'n roll motion picture sweepstakes, premiers in Detroit. The lineup of stars includes Fats Domino (who's version of the title tune is already a hit), the Del Vikings, and the Diamonds. The remaining musical roster is filled by pop and jazz luminaries. This week, to plug the movie, the Del Vikings stop by several local radio stations with copies of their latest single "Can't Wait," which is featured in "The Big Beat."

The second "Dick Clark Show" on ABC-TV features Chuck Berry, Billy and Lillie, the Chordettes, the Mark IV, and Bill Justis.

FEB 24   The Diamonds begin a week's stay at the Casino Royal in Washington, DC.

New Releases for the fourth week in February include "Dizzy, Miss Lizzy" b/w "Slow Down" by Larry Williams on Specialty; "How Many Times" by Lloyd Price on K.R.C.; "Every Night (I Pray)" by the Chantels on End; "Movin' and Groovin'" by Duane Eddy on Jamie; "The Things I Love" by the Fidelities on Baton; Gene Summers' "School of Rock and Roll" on Jan; "Sunglasses After Dark" by Dwight Pullen on Carolton; "Skinny Minnie" by Bill Haley and His Comets on Decca; Doc Starkes and the Nite Riders' "Apple Cider" on Swan; "Good and Bad" by Jerry Wallace on Challenge; "Ponitail Partner" by Bing Day on King; "For Your Love" by **Ed Townsend** on Capitol; and Dave Clowney's "Hoot Owl" on Paris. Finally, this week saw the release of "Got a Job" by the

DONNIE ELBERT
Donnie Elbert had complete mastery over his voice. He could make it swoop like an eagle or float like a butterfly. It had a range of multi-octaves (just how many is a matter of conjecture). On top of this, he was a songwriter possessed with creative zeal and intuition. Yet, for all of his talent, he always remained an elusive figure—a shadow in the world of rock 'n roll. The exact date and place of birth are obscure, although he calls Buffalo, New York, his home. In the spring of 1957, he began his long recording career on DeLuxe Records, a subsidiary of mighty King Records of Cincinnati. His first release is his best known, a stirring take on "What Can I Do." The single made the national "pop" charts but failed to do as well in the R&B field. Two singles later, he issued another stunning piece of work in "Have I Sinned." This was followed by "Do The Stroll," Elbert's attempt to break into the dance-song-of-the-week club. He rebounded with another soaring ballad, "My Confession of Love." There were a few more singles on DeLuxe, but none fared well and by the end of 1958, his contract was not renewed. In 1959, he sang lead on "Night After Night" by the Derbys lone single on Mercury although he wasn't really a member. In 1960, he moved on to Vee-Jay, recording four singles with no sales. Brief stops with Jalynne, Gateway and Rare Bullet Records also proved to be futile. On All Platinum Records in the early 1970s, he recorded a series of previous Motown hits like "Where Did Our Love Go, "I Can't Help Myself (Sugar Pie, Honey Bunch)," and "Ooo Baby, Baby," but sales were limited. One single, "Can't Get Over Losing You," which he composed, did capture the magic of his earlier recordings. By the 1980s, he had virtually disappeared, remaining reclusive in Buffalo.

Miracles on End. The answer to "Get a Job" was a minor hit, and in 1959, the group issued "Bad Girl" on Chess before signing with Berry Gordy and becoming a Motown success story.

FEB 25   The Everly Brothers, Jimmie Rodgers, Buddy Holly and the Crickets, Jerry Lee Lewis, the Royal Teens, and Bill Haley and His Comets play the War Memorial Auditorium in Ft. Lauderdale as they close down their short tour of Florida. During the second show, Jerry Lee, decked out in a leopard skin vest, demolishes the piano bringing a premature end to his portion of the show.

The Jodimars open for a five-week run at Harold's Casino in Reno.

Mr. Kelly's in Chicago welcomes Sarah Vaughan for an extended engagement.

FEB 26   "American Bandstand" welcomes the return of the Hollywood Flames singing "Buzz, Buzz, Buzz." On the same show, Jackie Wilson plugs his latest release, "To Be Loved."

FEB 27   As advance publicity for their upcoming tour of England, Buddy Holly and the Crickets appear over Britain's ITV network on Jack Hylton's "See You, Soho."

FEB 28   LaVern Baker opens a two-week engagement at the Blackhawk in San Francisco.

THE TOP ROCK 'N ROLL RECORDS FOR FEBRUARY 1958

1. At the Hop - Danny and the Juniors
2. Short Shorts - The Royal Teens
3. Don't/I Beg Of You - Elvis Presley
4. The Stroll - The Diamonds
5. Oh Julie - The Crescendos
6. Dede Dinah - Frankie Avalon
7. You Are My Destiny - Paul Anka
8. Stood Up/Waitin' In School - Ricky Nelson
9. La Dee Dah - Billy and Lillie
10. Don't Let Go - Roy Hamilton
11. Peggy Sue - Buddy Holly
12. Maybe - The Chantels
13. 26 Miles - The Four Preps
14. Great Balls of Fire - Jerry Lee Lewis
15. Jo-Ann - The Playmates
16. Ballad of a Teenage Queen - Johnny Cash
17. Oh Boy! - The Crickets
18. Why Don't They Understand - George Hamilton IV
19. I'll Come Running Back To You - Sam Cooke
20. Click Clack - Dicky Doo and the Don'ts
21. Kisses Sweeter Than Wine - Jimmie Rodgers

ED TOWNSEND

Ed Townsend was born April 16, 1929, in Fayetteville, Tennessee. His family soon moved to nearby Memphis where his father was a minister. While attending Manassas High, Ed was elected to the International American Methodist Episcopal Youth Council, a position that included a world tour with other young leaders. He taught school for a year after graduating from Arkansas State. In 1951, he joined the Marines during the Korean conflict. In Korea, he was noticed by bandleader Horace Heidt. He joined Heidt after his military duty, and performed in countries in the Far East, as well as cities in the States. Townsend settled in Los Angeles where he had his own TV show and music publishing business. As a composer, he was in demand by such luminaries as Nat King Cole, Etta James, and Bull Moose Jackson. He also recorded one single, "A Bordertown Cathedral," for Calvert Records. This activity did not go unnoticed by the Los Angeles record labels. In June 1956, Apollo Records issued "Give Me One More Chance," followed, in April 1957, by "Every Night." Neither sold well, and in early 1958, he moved to Capitol Records. His first Capitol release was "For Your Love," a soaring ballad in the style of Brook Benton, but with a gospel feel. He followed with "When I Grow Too Old To Dream," which sold moderately. There were releases on Capitol through 1959, including "Hold On," "Don't Ever Leave Me," and "I'm In Love," but none caught the public's ear. He moved on to Warner Brothers Records, but his popularity as a recording artist was over. As a songwriter, however, many other artists performed his material, including the Impressions, who had a hit in 1974 with "Finally Got Myself Together." Ed Townsend co-produced Marvin Gaye's classic 1973 album "Let's Get It On," as well as co-writing half the songs including the title tune.

22. Sweet Little Sixteen - Chuck Berry
23. Bony Moronie - Larry Williams
24. Buzz, Buzz, Buzz - The Hollywood Flames
25. You Send Me - Sam Cooke
26. She's Neat - Dale Wright
27. Raunchy - Bill Justis
28. Oh, Oh, I'm Falling In Love - Jimmie Rodgers
29. Teardrops - Lee Andrews and the Hearts
30. The Story of My Life - Marty Robbins
31. This Little Girl of Mine - The Everly Brothers
32. Jailhouse Rock - Elvis Presley
33. Good Golly, Miss Molly - Little Richard
34. You Can Make It If You Try - Gene Allison
35. Walking With Mr. Lee - Lee Allen
36. Raunchy - Ernie Freeman
37. Desire Me/(I Love You) For Sentimental Reasons - Sam Cooke
38. Rock and Roll Music - Chuck Berry
39. Wake up Little Susie - The Everly Brothers
40. Silhouettes - The Rays
41. My Special Angel - Bobby Helms
42. Who's Sorry Now - Connie Francis
43. Little Pigeon - Sal Mineo
44. Tequila - The Champs
45. The Walk - Jimmy McCracklin
46. Sing, Boy, Sing - Tommy Sands
47. I Want You To Know/The Big Beat - Fats Domino
48. Henrietta - Jimmy Dee
49. 7-11 - The Gone All-Stars
50. We Belong Together - Robert and Johnny

Also on the "pop" chart:
A Wonderful Time Up There/It's Too Soon To Know - Pat Boone
Catch a Falling Star - Perry Como

February 1958
ARTISTS OF THE MONTH

THE ROYAL TEENS

Ft. Lee, New Jersey, lies just over the George Washington Bridge from New York, a city that is home to hundreds of record labels, big and small. For a musically talented teenager growing up in Ft. Lee, the thought of that golden opportunity waiting across the Hudson River must have been a driving inspiration. And so a group of Ft. Lee teenagers, all students at Bergenfield High, formed a rock 'n roll band in 1957 with high hopes and a generous helping of talent. This was going to be quite an odyssey.

The Royal Teens

Tom Austin, leader of the group, played drums. Bill Dalton was on guitar. Thirteen-year old Billy Crandall blew the sax. And handsome Bob Gaudio tinkled the ivories. In the beginning, they concentrated on rock n' roll instrumentals. None of the boys actually had the courage to stand behind a microphone and sing. In an attempt to add some glamor to the group, they called themselves the Royal Tones.

They started by working dances at the Catholic Youth Organization hall, sock hops at the high school gymnasium, and deejay appearances at the National Guard Armory. At one of these dances, the group was noticed by a New York talent scout for Power Records who was looking for a band to back a vocalist on a session for the label.

In the studio, with some time remaining after the initial vocal session, the band asked if they could use the time to record a tune they'd written. Austin and Gaudio had composed a semi-instrumental in honor of a new fashion fad that had teenage girls cutting their dungarees off just below the inseam to make them very short. As the group ran through the song in the studio, it occurred to someone to add a chorus of female voices singing the call-and-response lyrics, such as they were.

With a leering wolf-whistle from one of the guys, echoed by the same sliding notes on the guitar, "Short Shorts" was off and running. The boys all shouted "Who likes short shorts?" and an anonymous set of girls answered "We like short shorts!" One chorus of this and the sax kicked in for a verse. The second vocal chorus was the same as the first, followed by a break for the guitar. The third vocal chorus was exactly the same as the first two. And, the sax led the way as the song faded out at two minutes, twelve seconds. Of such simplicity are legends made.

It's entirely conceivable that "Short Shorts" was only meant to be a throwaway song, something mindless to fill the flip side of "Planet Rock," a rousing sax-and-guitar instrumental that gave the group a chance to really show off their musical talent. However, at this late date, no one is going to admit to the possibility that the wrong side of the record sold a million copies.

After a name change to avoid a conflict with another band called the Royaltones, Power Records released the single by the newly dubbed Royal Teens during the first week of 1958. Action on "Short Shorts" was hot from the start. Alan Freed played the song every night on WINS radio in New York, and Dick Clark played it every afternoon on "American Bandstand." Overwhelmed with orders it could not afford to fill, Power Records quickly leased all rights to "Short Shorts" to ABC-Paramount, the label having a major hit with "At The Hop." In early February, the group, now sporting a female vocalist, was the guest on television's "American Bandstand." On February 15, the Royal Teens were among those performing on the premier of "The Dick Clark Show," ABC-TV's new Saturday night entry. A few days later, the group was off on a short tour of Florida, sharing the spotlight with the Everly Brothers, Jerry Lee Lewis, the Crickets, and Bill Haley. By then, Billy Crandall had dropped out of the group because of his youth. His replacement was Larry Qualiano.

Early in April, the Royal Teens set off on an eighty-day, cross-country tour called "The Biggest Show of Stars for '58," featuring Sam Cooke,

Paul Anka and the Everly Brothers. Later in the month, their second single was released. "Big Name Button" was another novelty about a piece of wearing apparel. This time, professional songwriters composed the tune. Unfortunately, name buttons were not as inherently taboo a subject as short shorts. In an attempt to add a new twist, this time a bass voice was used to punctuate the "vocals" by the group. As with "Short Shorts," the instrumental breaks were more interesting than the verse. The B-side was "Sham Rock," a clone of "Short Shorts." The tune, composed by the combo, used the same back-and-forth vocal between the boys and girls. The record failed to attract any attention.

In the late summer of 1958, the Royal Teens appeared on Alan Freed's Labor Day extravaganza. ABC-Paramount issued their third single, "Harvey's Got a Girlfriend." "Harvey" was another attempt to make the "Short Shorts" formula pay off. It did only marginally better than "Big Name Button." The flip side, a ballad titled "Hangin' Around," painfully pointed to the reason the boys had been so reluctant to trade in their status as an all-instrumental band.

The Royal Teens added a new member in late 1958, Joe Frankavilla (aka Joey Villa) from Brooklyn. Villa had been lead vocalist with the Three Friends on their hit record, "Blanche." He met the Royal Teens at the studios of ABC-Paramount while he was recording as a solo artist with little success. After Villa joined the group, there was one final single from ABC-Paramount, "Open the Door (Forgot the Key)." It was another novelty, but without the format of "Short Shorts," and it might have been a hit if it had been released by the Coasters. Again, the flip side featured a ballad, and this time the boys showed that they had been practicing on their close harmony. However, most deejays had given up on the Royal Teens. The record faded without a whimper.

For a few months, the Royal Teens retreated to Ft. Lee. Bill Dalton decided to give up his aspirations for a career in music to attend college, and Al Kooper filled his place in the group. They returned to Power Records for one single, "Sittin' With My Baby." The flip side, "Mad Gass" was "Sham Rock" without the vocals. Not an auspicious way to rekindle a career.

Deciding that novelty songs were a dead issue, the group became serious in its attempt to become a vocal harmony unit. In the spring of 1959, they auditioned for Capitol Records and were awarded a contract. Their first single, "Believe Me," used the style of up-tempo ballad made popular by Dion and the Belmonts. The song was successful enough to remain on the charts almost four months although it never really became a major hit.

The second Capitol release, "The Moon's Not Meant For Lovers (Anymore)" b/w "Was It A Dream," continued in the same vein, but neither had the emotional impact of "Believe Me." "It's The Talk of the Town" was an attempt to revive an older tune, just as Dion and the Belmonts had done with "Where or When." This time, though, it was too little too late. Their contract with Capitol was not renewed. Joey Villa continued with Capitol for a short time as a solo artist, issuing "(She's My) All-American Girl" in late 1960.

So, after eighteen months and three singles with Capitol, it was back to Ft. Lee again. Kooper left to pursue other musical interests and was replaced by Frank Cappola. The group had little trouble landing a recording deal with Power Record's subsidiary Mighty—another small company with huge aspirations. The Royal Teens' first single on Mighty was "Leotards," a blatant, lackluster knock-off on "Short Shorts." Even the B-side, "Royal Blue," their first instrumental since "Planet Rock," sounded as though it had been thrown together in a hurry. Two more singles were issued by Mighty in 1960, "Cave Man" and "Little Trixie." Nothing much happened with any of these records. Finally, the Royal Teens disbanded.

Bob Gaudio soon joined the Four Lovers just as they changed their name to the Four Seasons. He arrived in time for "Sherry" and "Big Girls Don't Cry." He remained with the group until 1972, co-writing many of their hits while also becoming a respected producer who worked with many top performers including Frank Sinatra.

In 1961, Tom Austin joined the Army. Later he worked in real estate in Ramsey, New Jersey. He has written a film treatment of his days in rock 'n roll. In 1993, he was hopeful that a movie based on his memoirs would be produced by Frankie Avalon.

Bill Crandall stayed with the music business, joining a group that became the Knickerbockers, which had a hit with "Lies" in 1965.

Al Kooper wrote "This Diamond Ring," the first and biggest hit for Gary Lewis and the Playboys in 1965. In 1966, he formed the Blues Project, a short-lived, but highly respected blues-fusion combo. This led to his formation, in 1968, of Blood, Sweat and Tears, the most popular of the combos combining blues in a big band setting. Kooper left the group before it recorded so he could work with Steven Stills and Mike Bloomfield on SUPER SESSION album. For a time, Kooper remained in demand as a producer and session guitarist, working with such luminaries as Bob Dylan, the Rolling Stones, and B. B. King.

In 1965, the Royal Teens surfaced again, comprised of Larry Qualiano, Joey Villa and Frank Cappola from the group's heyday. They issued one single on Swan Records, "I'll Love You (Til the End of Time)," another Dion-sounding ballad.

Joe Villa lives in New York and still performs as a comedian/lounge singer. He occasionally appears as a member of the Three Friends.

In 1970, a group calling itself the Royal Teens recorded an album for Musicor Records of Hollywood. The album, NEWIES BUT OLDIES, featured hits from 1969, such as the "Honky Tonk Woman," recorded as though they were from the 1950s. "Hey Jude" was issued as a single.

Like the Royal Teens, "Short Shorts" also had a second career. In the 1970s, the song was used in television commercials by the Nair hair removal product. The point being that if a lady was going to wear short shorts, she also needed to use Nair. And, of course, the song has appeared on many compilation albums and in many movies about the 1950s. "Short Shorts" is like a cheap horror movie: "The Nonsense Lyric That Refused To Die."

March 1958

MAR 1   Buddy Holly and the Crickets start a month-long tour of England with a show in London at the Trocadero Theater, Elephant and Castle. Other dates on this tour include London's Gaumont Theater, Kilburn (2); South Hampton (3); Sheffield,, (4); Stockton (5); New Castle (6); Wolverhampton (7); Nottingham (8); Bradford (9); Birmingham (10); Worcester (11); three venues in London (12-14); Ipswich (15); Leicester (16); Don Caster (17); Blackburn (18); Hull (19); Liverpool (20); Walthamstow (21); Salisbury (22); Bristol (23); Cardiff (24); and finally, London's Gaumont Theater, Hammersmith, on March 25. Other acts appearing on the bill with the Crickets were British music hall performers. (See also MAR 2.)

Also in Great Britain, for the second time, Paul Anka begins a twenty-three-day tour. Tonight he plays the Arthur Matthews Music Hall in Aberdeen, Scotland. Succeeding nights find him at Chaird Hall, Dundee (2); and Usher Hall, Edinburgh (3). He is also set to play Newcastle, Sheffield, Leicester, Brighton, Bristol, Plymouth, Bournemouth, York, Hull, Manchester, Liverpool, and Croydon.

In Washington, DC, the Diamonds open for a week at the Casino Royal.

On ABC-TV's "Dick Clark Show," guest artists are Teresa Brewer, Eddie Platt, John Zacherle, the Chantels, and the Four Dates.

MAR 2   Buddy Holly and the Crickets appear live on "Sunday Night at the London Palladium" on Britain's ATV network.

In New Orleans, Buddy and Ella Johnson perform at the Labor Union Hall.

Sam Cooke guests on "The Steve Allen Show" on NBC-TV.

MAR 3   The Crescendos begin a brief stay at the Latin Casino in Philadelphia.

New Releases for the first week of March include "Believe What You Say" b/w "My Bucket's Got a Hole in It" by Ricky Nelson on Imperial; "You Excite Me" by Frankie Avalon on Chancellor; "Solitude" by Billy Ward and His Dominos on Liberty; "You" by the **Aquatones** on Fargo; "Corrido Rock" by "Handsome" Jim Bascomb on Dot; Mac Curtis' "Missy Ann" on King; "Our Song" by Tom and Jerry on Big; Glenn Reeves' "Rock-A-Boogie Lou" on Decca; "Everybody Rock & Roll" by the Isley Brothers on Gone; and Little Joe and the Thrillers' "What's Happened to Your Halo!" on Okeh.

THE AQUATONES
The Aquatones were high school students from Valley Stream, a town on Long Island, near New York City. Unlike most other vocal groups at this time, the Aquatones were also accomplished musicians. Lead vocalist of the group was Larry Vannata, who doubled on piano. The Aquatones featured Barbara Lee, who also played bass. The group's professionalism brought them a recording contract with the new Fargo label. Their first release was "You," a plaintive teen-oriented ballad. In April, as the record began to gather momentum, the group made a national appearance on Dick Clark's Saturday night TV show. Benefiting from this exposure, "You" became a mid-sized hit over the next three months. The group toured and appeared on various national TV shows during the year. In 1958, Fargo issued "Say You'll Be Mine" and "Our First Kiss." Neither sold well enough to make the national charts. There were five more unsuccessful singles on Fargo. With college and careers lying just ahead, the Aquatones disbanded in 1960. Vannata continued as a musician, playing on Pete Antel's small hit, "Night Time" on Cameo in 1962. Vannata also backed various groups on tour, including the Fireflies and Four Jacks and a Jill. He returned to Long Island, became a music producer and teacher, and married Barbara Lee. Together, they played society dances and debutante balls. In 1972, they reformed the Aquatones to play the local club scene. Besides Vannata and Lee, the Aquatones now included Mike Roma, vocals and trumpet, who had toured with Jimmy Dorsey; Tom Vivona, sax, holding a Masters Degree from Manhattan School of Music; Vic Kastel, vocals and guitar, who appeared with Joey Dee and the Starliters and played sessions behind Gary Bonds, the Exciters, and Shirley Ellis; and Russ Nagy, drums, a member of the Bell Notes.

PAUL PEEK
Paul Edward Peek was born June 23, 1937, in High Point, South Carolina. His family soon moved to Greenville. Paul's first taste of show business came from his sisters (Margie, Jackie and Elizabeth), who were country performers on WFBC as the Peek Sisters. Paul played drums in the school band and sang in the glee club until he got his first guitar. He quickly became proficient and joined a series of local bands including the Green Valley Boys and the Circle E Ranch Boys. About 1954, he moved to Asheville where, for the next eighteen months, he was on afternoon radio five times a week with Cousin Wilbur and the Country Store Gang. By the summer of 1956, he had moved to Washington, DC, where he was working in Red Redding's band. That September, Gene Vincent played Washington's Casino Royal Lounge when Wee Willie Williams quit the Blue Caps. Peek auditioned and was hired, just as the group left for Hollywood to film their cameo for "The Girl Can't Help It." In early 1958, Peek signed with the new NRC label of Atlanta. For his first session, he used a guitar lick he had picked up from Eddie Cochran to open "Sweet Skinny Jenny." The session reportedly featured Esquirita and Ray Stevens on piano; Joe South and Jerry Reed on guitar; and Bill Mack, an ex-Blue Cap, on bass. The sound they achieved was rip-roaring rock 'n roll. However, the sound that was selling was teen "pop." Still, Peek's record was moderately successful in the South. Peek rejoined Vincent for the RECORD DATE album sessions in 1958. He also appeared with Vincent in another movie, "Hot Rod Gang." NRC released four more singles through 1960. In 1961, Peek had a minor hit with "Brother-In-Law (He's a Moocher)" on Fairlane. Columbia released two singles by Peek in 1966, including another sleeper, "Pin the Tail on the Donkey."

MAR 6 Sam Cooke starts his historic three-week run at the Copacabana in New York City.

MAR 7 Chuck Berry headlines this week's rhythm and blues show at New York's Apollo Theater. He shares billing with the Heartbeats, the Velvets, Big Maybelle, and a new act, the Shirelles.
   Pearl Bailey, the Billy Williams Quartet, the Pastels, and Malcom Dodds and the Tunedrops entertain this week at the Howard Theater in Washington.

MAR 8 Jerry Lee Lewis guests again on "The Dick Clark Show," performing "Breathless" and "You Win Again." Also on tonight's bill are the Silhouettes (singing "Get a Job"), Johnny Cash, the Mark IV, and the Platters.
   Ray Charles is at the Club Bel Air in Chester, Pennsylvania.
   Frankie Avalon guests on NBC-TV's "Perry Como Show."

MAR 9 The Everly Brothers and Joe Bennett and the Sparkletones appear on the "Ed Sullivan Show" on CBS-TV.

MAR 10 The Paris Sisters start a twelve-day run at the Cave Supper Club in Vancouver, Washington.

New Releases for the second week of March include "Heading for the Poorhouse" by the Silhouettes on Ember; "Pink Peddle Pushers" by Carl Perkins on Columbia; the Crescendos' "School Girl" on Nasco; "Sweet Skinny Jenny" by **Paul Peek** on NRC; Solomon Burke's "Don't Cry" on Apollo; the Chanticleers' "To Keep Your Love" on Lyric; "Everybody Stroll" by the O. C. Allstars on Savoy; and "Baby Doll" by Joe Allison on Dot.

MAR 14 Little Richard's eleven-man touring band, the Upsetters, headlines this week's show at the Apollo Theater in New York City. Also appearing are the Bill Doggett combo, Little Willie John, and the Pastels.
   The Platters start a nine-day engagement at the Twin Coaches Club in Pittsburgh.
   Johnny Cash and Carl Perkins, currently touring Canada, play a one-nighter at the Exhibition Hall in Regina, Saskatchewan. The two shows break the one-day house record with a gross of $6,700.
   In New Orleans, Bobby Mitchell and the Toppers entertain a Mardi Gras "crew" party at the Shipwreck Dance held at the F&M Patio.
   In Washington, DC, the Howard Theater welcomes Lloyd Price, the Spaniels, and the Dubs for the week.

MAR 15 Ricky Nelson and Wanda Jackson perform at the State Fair Music Hall in Dallas.
   Charlie Gracie starts a two-day stand at the Erie Social Club in Philadelphia.

At Russwood Baseball Park, Elvis Presley gives two sold-out shows in his hometown of Memphis. This will be his final concert appearance for three years.

This week's "Dick Clark Show" offers Andy Williams, Frankie Avalon, Dickey Doo and the Don'ts, and Huey Smith and the Clowns.

MID-MARCH
Gene Vincent wraps up filming his appearance in the movie "Hot Rod Rock."
Capitol Records announces that an extended play release of Vincent's songs in the film will soon be forthcoming.

MAR 16 Clyde McPhatter does double duty in New Orleans with a concert at 7:00 p.m. followed by a dance at 9:00 p.m. at the Booker T. Auditorium. Appearing with McPhatter are the Silhouettes and Lee Allen's combo.

New Releases for the third week in March include three classic rock 'n roll songs: "Endless Sleep" by Jody Reynolds on Demon; "Do You Wanna Dance" by Bobby Freeman on Josie; and "Witch Doctor" by David Seville on Liberty. In addition, there are two releases from ABC-Paramount: "Crazy Love" by Paul Anka and the Larktones' "The Letter;" Bobby Day's "Little Turtle Dove" on Ebb; and three from RCA: "Cool It Baby" by Jimmy Dell, "Groovy" by Joe Dodo, and A. Tousan's "Happy Baby." Another new release this week is "Never Let You Go" on Ebb by the Ambers, a group featuring Ralph Mathis, Johnny's brother.

MAR 18 Jerry Lee Lewis appears on "American Bandstand." He performs an unprecedented three songs: "You Win Again," Whole Lotta Shakin' Goin' On" and "Breathless."

MAR 22 Arthur Prysock begins a two-day engagement at the Dew Drop in New Orleans.
Connie Francis appears on "The Steve Allen Show" on NBC-TV.
On ABC-TV's "The Dick Clark Show," the entertainment is Betty Johnson, the Diamonds (singing "High Sign"), and Bill Haley and His Comets.

MAR 23 The Rays appear for the second time on television's "The Ed Sullivan Show." The **Four Preps** also perform "26 Miles.

MAR 24 In Memphis, Elvis Presley in inducted into the U. S. Army and is bussed to Fort Chaffee, Arkansas. Over the next three days, he will have his I. Q. tested, receive his inoculations, be issued his uniform, and have his famous haircut.
This afternoon, Billy and Lillie sing "La Dee Dah" on ABC-TV's "American Bandstand."

THE FOUR PREPS
The Four Preps were "Hollywood" through and through. Bruce Belland began singing in the local church choir. He came naturally to his musical talent through his mother, who was a piano instructor. The four singers, Belland, Glen Larson, Marvin Ingram (real name Inabett), and Ed Cobb met while attending Hollywood High. They enrolled in UCLA and joined forces to entertain at campus functions. During one event, they recorded their performance. Belland and Larson took the tape to local record labels with little encouragement until they approached the manager of the popular duo Les Paul and Mary Ford. Within days, the Four Preps were invited to record for Capitol Records. In November 1956, their first release was "Dreamy Eyes," a smooth ballad that appealed to teen listeners. The group's first break came as guests on the popular Tennessee Ernie Ford TV show. "Dreamy Eyes" was followed by four singles that failed to catch on, including such "dreamy" titles as "Moonstruck in Madrid," "Falling Star." During this period, Ingram was replaced by Don Clarke. Belland recalled a brief musical passage he had composed in junior high. Larson worked with him, and they put together "26 Miles." The record, released exactly a year after "Dreamy Eyes," was an ode to the Southern California lifestyle. They followed with "Big Man" and "Lazy Summer Night." By 1959, record sales were off, but the group was now an established club act. 1960's "Down By The Station," a musical treatment of a children's rhyme, sold well. A year later, "More Money For You And Me" was the first of two mid-sized hits utilizing the group's ability to mimic other acts. "Letter to the Beatles" had just been released in 1964 when lawyers representing the Beatles forced Capitol to pull the record. Three years later, and still recording for Capitol, the Four Preps disbanded.

New Releases for the fourth week of March include "Happiness" by Billy and Lillie on Swan; "Honey Bop" by Wanda Jackson on Capitol; Ray Charles' "Yes, Indeed" on Atlantic; Thurston Harris' "I'm Out to Getcha" on Aladdin; "You Got Me Cryin'" by Jimmy Reed on Vee-Jay; "Stack-a-Records" by Tom Tall and the Tom Cats on Crest; and Johnny Rivers' "Baby Come Back" on Gone.

MAR 27 In a previously recorded performance, Buddy Holly and the Crickets guest on "Off the Record" over Britain's BBC-TV network. At this time, the Crickets were already back in the States.

MAR 28 Alan Freed's annual Easter vacation package, billed as "The Big Beat Show," opens for an unusually brief two-day run at the New York City Paramount Theater. Headliner this go-round is Jerry Lee Lewis. Also on the bill are Chuck Berry, Buddy Holly and the Crickets, Frankie Lymon, Billy and Lillie, Larry Williams, Jo Ann Campbell, the Twin Tones, the Chantels, Dicky Doo and the Don'ts, the Casuals, Screamin' Jay Hawkins, the Velours, the Bell Notes, Ed Townsend, and the Pastels. This is the first of Freed's extravaganzas actually setup as a full concert, running two-and-a-half hours. Previously, the shows at the New York and Brooklyn Paramount Theaters ran about an hour with a movie screened between the multiple daily performances. The reason behind the new format is that "The Big Beat Show" is set for a road trip immediately following the Paramount stay.

To commemorate the Easter season (and possibly not wanting to compete against Freed) the Apollo offers a gospel and spiritual revue for their fans this week.

On "American Bandstand," Frankie Avalon is invited back to sing "You Excite Me."

The Applejacks are booked into Andy's Log Cabin in Philadelphia.

Pvt. Elvis Presley leaves Ft. Chaffee en route to Ft. Hood, Texas, where he will receive his eight-week basic training.

MAR 29 Johnny Cash and Gene Vincent and His Blue Caps are guests on "Country America," broadcast from Los Angeles on KABC-TV.

The Four Esquires are booked into the Townhouse in Pittsburgh for the week.

This week's "Dick Clark Show" offers Joni James, Fats Domino, the Four Lads, Don Gibson, and the Voxpoppers.

MAR 30 Following the Paramount Theater dates, Alan Freed and his "Big Beat Show" hit the road for a six-week tour. Tonight's show is in New Haven followed by the Bronx (31). (See also APR 1.)

"The Ed Sullivan Show" is visited by Della Reese.

LATE MARCH

Recently signed to M-G-M records, Morton Downey, Jr. opens for an extended engagement at the Living Room in New York City.

THE APPLEJACKS

They were a Philly bar band, pure and simple. Dave Appell, leader of the group, went on to become a mainstay with one of the most successful of the rock-oriented record labels. In the early 1950s, the band played the bar circuit in Philadelphia, sharpening their skills at the Bamboo Club, the Lindenwold Inn and the 19th Hole. In 1954, they had a brief stay with Decca Records, issuing only two singles, "My Heart Will Wait For You" and "Sweet Patootie." Not much happened. A lone release on Tone Craft Records in 1955, "Ring Around My Baby," fared even worse. By 1956, the guys were trying their hand at rock 'n roll with New York's President label: "Teenage Girl" and "The Rock And Roll Story." Late in the year, when Cameo Records was founded in Philly, Appell and the combo were the logical choice for the label's house band, alternating with Bernie Lowe's orchestra. In addition, they got to record a few singles—still under the name Dave Appell and the Applejacks: "Love In the Jungle," "No Name Theme" and "Walk On." For their fourth Cameo single, in September 1958, the band's name was shortened to the Applejacks. This was the year of "Tequila," thus the song chosen was a revived Latin folk tune, issued as "Mexican Hat Rock." Pushed by "American Bandstand," the song took off. As a Philly band, they were easily added to Bandstand's revolving roster of acts as well as appearing in New York on the Saturday evening version of "The Dick Clark Show." They played Atlanta with Dick Clark and Sam Cooke in October, and toured with Jerry Lee Lewis later that same month. The Applejacks had two more minor dance hits, "Rock-A-Conga" "Bunny Hop." Their music can be heard on numerous Cameo-Parkway releases by Chubby Checker, Bobby Rydell, Dee Dee Sharpe, and the Dovells, to name a few. Appel went on to produce Tony Orlando and Dawn.

THE TOP ROCK 'N ROLL HITS FOR MARCH 1958

1. Tequila - The Champs
2. Sweet Little 16 - Chuck Berry
3. Who's Sorry Now - Connie Francis
4. 26 Miles - The Four Preps
5. Oh, Julie - The Crescendos
6. Don't/I Beg Of You - Elvis Presley
7. The Walk - Jimmy McCracklin
8. Breathless - Jerry Lee Lewis
9. Get a Job - The Silhouettes
10. Short Shorts - The Royal Teens
11. Good Golly, Miss Molly - Little Richard
12. Ballad of a Teen-Age Queen - Johnny Cash
13. The Stroll - The Diamonds
14. Maybe Baby - The Crickets
15. Maybe - The Chantels
16. Oh-Oh, I'm Falling In Love - Jimmie Rodgers
17. Rock and Roll Is Here to Stay - Danny and the Juniors
18. At The Hop - Danny and the Juniors
19. Dinner With Drac - Zacherle
20. You Are My Destiny - Paul Anka
21. Dede Dinah - Frankie Avalon
22. Don't Let Go - Roy Hamilton
23. Tequila - Eddie Pratt
24. Stood Up/Waitin' in School - Ricky Nelson
25. Click Clack - Dicky Doo and the Don'ts
26. Been So Long - The Pastels
27. Oh, Lonesome Me - Don Gibson
28. Betty and Dupree - Chuck Willis
29. So Tough - The Casuals
30. We Belong Together - Robert and Johnny
31. Sing, Boy, Sing - Tommy Sands
32. College Man - Bill Justis
33. Jo-Ann - The Playmates
34. La Dee Dah - Billy and Lillie
35. Great Balls Of Fire - Jerry Lee Lewis
36. Billy - Kathy Linden
37. Lollipop - Ronald and Ruby
38. She's Neat - Dale Wright
39. Don't You Just Know It - Huey Smith and the Clowns
40. You Can Make It If You Try - Gene Allison
41. 7-11 - The Gone All-Stars
42. Lonely Island/You Were Made For Me - Sam Cooke
43. This Little Girl of Mine - The Everly Brothers
44. Kisses Sweeter Than Wine - Jimmie Rodgers
45. Book of Love - The Monotones

46. Bad Motorcycle - The Storey Sisters
47. Every Night - The Chantels
48. Now and For Always - George Hamilton IV
49. Whole Lotta Woman - Marvin Rainwater
50. Twilight Time - The Platters

Also on the "pop" charts:
Lollipop - The Chordettes
Sugartime - The McGuire Sisters
He's Got the Whole World in His Hands - Laurie London

March 1958
ARTIST OF THE MONTH

THE CHAMPS

The Champs

The year 1958 saw a dramatic increase in a short-lived rock 'n roll fad, instrumental combos. Not that rock 'n roll instrumentals hadn't been on the scene before. Or that there wouldn't be rock 'n roll instrumentals later. It was that the flood gates opened wide in 1958.

A year earlier, the biggest-selling instrumental was "Raunchy." As recorded by the tune's co-composer Bill Justis, it was a swinging tune that sounded exactly like what it was: professional studio musicians playing rock 'n roll. Justis never had another song that sounded remotely like "Raunchy." "College Man," the follow-up single was a failure—even with Billy Lee Riley's brief vocal at the end. When Ernie Freeman recorded "Raunchy," he almost stole Justis' thunder with another group of studio musicians from Los Angeles. Freeman simply emphasized the backbeat, where Justis had employed a shuffle. Such was the state of the rock 'n roll instrumental in 1957.

By the end of 1959, the field would be awash with Santo and Johnny, Johnny and the Hurricanes, Dave "Baby" Cortez, Duane Eddy, the Fireballs, the Virtues, the Wailers, Link Wray and His Ray Men, the Royaltones, the Rock-A-Teens, Sandy Nelson, and such non sequiturs as Cozy Cole and Preston Epps. However, the group that really created the demand was the Champs.

The story of the Champs begins with Dave Burgess, who was born on December 13, 1934, in Beverly Hills, California. Burgess first recorded in 1953 for Okeh Records, the subsidiary of Columbia that was devoted to issuing country, blues and jazz records. Burgess was about eighteen when Okeh released his two singles: "Don't Put a Dent in My Heart" and "Too Late For Tears." In 1955, he had two singles on the small Tampa label: "Don't Turn Your Back on Love" and "Five Foot Two, Eyes of Blue." All four singles were aimed at the country market, and all four missed their mark.

In 1956, Burgess was on Tops Records, a major player in the line of budget singles. Tops would take unknown but otherwise talented performers, have them copy the latest hits of the day as closely as possible to the original version, then issue them four-to-a-disc for forty-nine cents. Tops' slogan was "twice the music at half the cost," and it was a bargain until the unsuspecting shopper got home and played the record. Burgess appeared on an unknown number of these records in 1956-57, but at least ten came out with his name in the credits. For Tops, Burgess recorded versions of Elvis' "Love Me" and "Love Me Tender," Harry Belafonte's "Banana Boat Song (Day-O)," and Marty Robbins "Singing the Blues," among others. Burgess's version of "Love Me Tender" was also issued by another budget label, Gilmer, from Van Nuys, California.

The ethics of the budget-record business aside, Burgess was getting a firsthand education in recording and performing. In 1957 he was working as a disc jockey in the Mojave Desert town of Lancaster. To pass the long hours, he composed songs and sent them off to music houses. Two of his tunes became very successful that year: "I'm Available," by Margie Rayburn in the "pop" field, and "I'll Be There," sung by Ray Price in the country market.

His songwriting brought him in contact with Challenge Records, a Los Angeles company founded in April 1957 by Gene Autry, cowboy movie star and soon-to-be professional baseball team owner. Under the pseudonym of Dave Dupree as well as his own name, Burgess recorded four of the first eight singles issued by Challenge, three of which (by "Dupree") had less than promising titles: "Don't Cry, For You I Love," "Well, It Isn't Fair," and "A Job Well Done."

Burgess also became a regular session guitarist for Challenge. Also playing on the Challenge sessions with Burgess was Daniel Carlos Flores (aka Chuck Rio), a popular club entertainer who was proficient on several instruments including piano and saxophone. Other musicians on these dates included Buddy Bruce, guitar; Cliff Hils, bass; and Gene Alden, drums.

One afternoon in 1957, Burgess and the other musicians were working on a Jerry Wallace session. With some studio time remaining, Burgess asked the musicians to stay and help him come up with a tune for the B-side of "Train To Nowhere," a piece he and Rio had previously recorded. Rio volunteered a Tex-Mex sax line that he had found successful in his club work, and the others thought it might work. Bruce opened the tune with a snappy guitar rhythm. Hils worked a little magic on the bass. Alden followed, playing the backbeat on the bell of his large cymbal. Burgess plucked the muted strings of his electric guitar. Finally, Rio jumped in on saxophone. Rio called the number "Tequila," and the title was spoken after each bridge. In ten minutes, they had a "take."

Everyone who heard the tune liked it, and Challenge decided to release the single immediately. First, however, the group needed a name, and someone came up with the Champions, after Autry's famed horse. The Champions soon became the Champs, and demo copies were sent out to the major deejays across the country in late December 1957.

One of the disc jockeys receiving "Tequila" was Bill Randle in Cincinnati. From the feedback Randle got each time he played "Tequila" on his radio show, he knew the song was going to be a hit. He also knew enough about the record business to realize that Challenge might have trouble coming up with several hundred thousand singles at a moment's notice. He figured Challenge might be willing to take on a partner. When contacted, a company spokesperson simply stated that Gene Autry had no money problems.

Through Randle's contacts, Eddie Platt, an otherwise unknown band leader, cut a version of "Tequila" that copied all the licks from the original disc. The Platt version was set for release on Decor Records when it hit the airwaves in Cleveland. Both Roulette and ABC-Paramount bid on the rights to the Platt record, and both thought they had a deal. On January 29, 1958, both companies sent out telegrams to deejays, distributors and the press to be on the lookout for Eddie Platt's "Tequila" on their respective labels. ABC-Paramount won the rights by offering to pay session costs (less than $2,000) with royalties to follow. Roulette had bid on a straight buy-out in the "five figure" range.

"Tequila" by the Champs and by Eddie Platt were in the stores by the end of January. In most markets, it was neck-and-neck race between the two, with little initial concern as to which was the winner. By March, as America had a chance to hear both versions, the Champs had pulled ahead, topping both the "pop" and R&B charts. "Tequila" went on to sell more than a million copies. It also won the 1958 Grammy for Best Rhythm and Blues Performance.

As requests for personal appearances poured in, the Champs realized that their first obstacle was to come up with an actual, working combo. Burgess, Rio, and Alden were joined by Dale Norris, the guitarist with Rio's nightclub band, and Joe Burnas on bass. The group hit the road with little rehearsal or preparation, and it showed during their first weeks as they worked with more seasoned performers. Rio was an old hand at live performing; and, by June 1958, he had grown upset with the lack of professionalism within the group. By this time, bassist Burnas had already been replaced by Van Norman. Soon, Rio and Alden quit the group in the middle of the tour to return to Los Angeles. They would soon be recording as Chuck Rio and the Originals on Jackpot, playing in a style similar to that of the Champs. As a replacement, Dean Beard was contacted. Beard had a minor rockabilly hit with "Rakin' and Scrapin'" on Atlantic in 1957. As a pianist, Beard was added to the Champs lineup in a package deal that brought along his band's saxophonist, Jimmy Seals, and drummer, Dash Crofts.

While the Champs were struggling with personnel problems on the road, their second single, "El Rancho Rock," was released in April. It followed in the Tex-Mex footsteps of "Tequila" with a tune based on the traditional Mexican number "El Rancho Grande." The B-side, "Midnighter" was even better, a rocking tune that featured Rio's distinctive "dirty" sax on top of a driving beat. "El Rancho Rock" sold about half a million copies in two and a half months. The group's third single, "Chariot Rock," was issued in July. It also sold moderately well, insuring that the group would continue to be a major draw on the club and theater circuits.

The constant touring continued to wreck havoc on the group. When Dean Beard left the Champs in late 1958, Seals and Crofts remained. At this point, there was little loyalty between the members of the Champs, and performing had become a "job," something most professional musicians hate to consider. The faces within the group were changing constantly. Bobby Morris, one of the top C&W bass players in the nation, worked with the Champs in the fall of 1958. Johnny Meeks, formerly with Gene Vincent and a Los Angeles session guitarist at this time, joined the group in 1959. Glen Campbell, an up-and-coming guitarist, took Burgess' place on tour in 1960 so that Burgess could remain in Los Angeles and work sessions. There were many, many other changes in personnel over the years.

After "Chariot Rock," the Champs lost their stronghold on the rock n' roll instrumental field. However, the singles kept coming at the rate of four a year. Mostly, they were uninspired. "Rockin' Mary" was a perfunctory remake of "Mary Had a Little Lamb." "Gone Train" slogged along at a pace that sounded like a musical quagmire. Not until "Too Much Tequila" in early 1960 did the Champs again spark the public's interest. Using a twin-sax lead and a romantic, mariachi-based tune, the single sold well enough to keep the band on the road for several more years.

It was almost exactly two years between "Too Much Tequila" and "Limbo Rock" with no hits. Separating the two were six singles, including "Red Eye," an instrumental similar to Dale Hawkins' "Susie Q;" "Tough Train," which continued Burgess' fixation with railroading; and "Jumping Bean," another entry in the Tex-Mex field. "Sombrero" was noteworthy only in that it was a virtual remake of "Tequila" with a slightly different approach by the sax. The tune even had a spoken phrase like "Tequila."

By this time, the country was being swept by a new dance craze every week. Meanwhile, the Champs were repeatedly recording variations of "Tequila." When the group finally realized what was happening, they were able to turn out a fine song named after a current dance fad, the limbo. "Limbo Rock" remained popular through the summer of 1962 before the Champs saw their thunder stolen by Chubby Checker's vocal version of the tune. There would be no more hit records from the Champs. However, with the success of "Limbo Rock," the Champs were again rejuvenated as a performing act. Through a myriad of face changes, the group continued until 1965.

Danny Flores (Chuck Rio) and Gene Alden continued performing in the Los Angeles area, with Flores billing himself from time to time as "Mr. Tequila" or "Chuck Flores with the Champs" as well as "Chuck Rio and the Originals."

Dean Beard recorded on Challenge after leaving the group, and continued to have singles issued by half a dozen companies over the next ten years.

Jimmy Seals and Dash Crofts stayed together, forming the soft-rock duo, Seals and Crofts. As such, in the mid-1970s, they had a six-year span of hits that included "Summer Breeze" and "Diamond Girl."

Glen Campbell became the biggest star in country music for a time, with his own TV show and everything. He started having hits on Capitol Records almost as soon as he left the Champs in 1961, and continued to top the country charts, as well as placing records in the upper reaches of the "pop" charts, into the early 1980s. His biggest hits were "Wichita Lineman" (1968), "Galveston" (1969), "Rhinestone Cowboy" (1975), and "Southern Nights" (1977).

And, what about Dave Burgess? After his long association with the Champs, he received substantial royalties only from "Too Much Tequila." Flores (writing as Chuck Rio) was credited with writing "Tequila." The basic tune for "El Rancho Rock" was written by two composers named Ramos and Uranga. "Limbo Rock" came from Billy Strange. Burgess had written about half of all the other songs recorded by the group. Burgess continued songwriting and had a hit with "Everlovin'" for Ricky Nelson in 1961. Eventually, he went into the music publishing business full-time.

April 1958

APR 1   Continuing to play the East Coast, Alan Freed's "Big Beat Show" stops in Philadelphia. On succeeding nights, the tour stops at the New York Coliseum (2); Dayton (4); Grand Rapids (5); Other venues during the month include Syracuse, Buffalo, and Troy, New York; Cleveland, Canton, Columbus, and Toledo, Ohio; Windsor and London, Ontario; Flint; Cincinnati; St. Louis; Tulsa; Oklahoma City; Wichita; Kansas City; and Omaha. (See APR 25.)

APR 4   Fats Domino is the star this week in the Apollo Theater's entertainment package. Sharing the vocal chores are the Dells, the Spaniels, and the Flamingos.

Mickey and Sylvia headline the week-long revue at the Howard Theater in Washington. On the bill are the Drifters and the Quin-Tones.

APR 5   Paul Anka headlines "The Dick Clark Show" on ABC-TV. Also appearing are the Everly Brothers, **Jimmy McCracklin**, and the Shirelles, singing "I Met Him On a Sunday."

APR 6   Bill Haley and His Comets depart the states on a tour of South America. (SEE APR 9.)

Johnny Otis's troupe of performers begins a four-week tour of Britain. Accompanying Otis are Mel Williams, the Three Tons of Fun, the Moonbeams, and Marie Adams.

In Norfolk, VA, "The Biggest Show of Stars for '58," another multi-act troupe or rock 'n rollers, is launched by the Irving Feld Agency on a coast-to-coast jaunt. Originally named "The Big Rock and Roll Show" and also billed along the way as the "Greatest Show of Stars," the tour was originally laid out for ten weeks, but it soon expanded to eighty days, through June 8. Booked to appear are Sam Cooke, the Everly Brothers (for the last half of the tour), the Royal Teens, the Silhouettes, Paul Anka, Jimmy Reed, Jimmie Rodgers (for the Canadian portion), Roy Hamilton, LaVern Baker, the Crescendos, the Monotones, the Playmates, the Storey Sisters, Huey Smith and the Clowns, and Clyde McPhatter. Early sites for the tour include Richmond; Charlotte; Winston-Salem; Raleigh; Hershey, Pennsylvania; Rochester; Pittsburgh (14); Scranton; Quebec; Montreal; Toronto; Kitchener, Ontario; Erie; Columbus, Ohio; Louisville; Youngstown; Indianapolis; Chicago; Minneapolis; Grand Forks; Winnipeg, Manitoba; Regina, Saskatchewan; Edmonton and Calgary, Alberta; Spokane; Seattle; Portland; Eugene, Oregon; San Jose; San Francisco; Los Angeles; and San Diego. This leg will be

JIMMY McCRACKLIN
If Jimmy McCracklin hadn't become a singer and composer of the blues, most likely he would have been a professional boxer. He still brought the dynamics of pugilism to his performances. He was born James David Walker, August 13, 1921, in Helena, Arkansas. During World War II, he joined the Navy and was awarded the military's All-American Light-Heavyweight title. Following his discharge, an auto accident ended his boxing career. At the time, he was living in the San Francisco Bay area, which was becoming a the West Coast Mecca for the blues. McCracklin (as he now called himself), began playing piano in small club bands. In 1945, as his popularity grew, he recorded for small labels located in Oakland and Los Angeles. In 1952, he was on Peacock Records of Houston, with singles released over the next three years, including "My Days Are Limited" and "Blues Blasters Boogie." In February 1955, he released "It's All Right" on Hollywood Records followed, in 1956, by a couple of singles on the small Irma label. In December 1957, McCracklin and his band, the Blues Blasters, were stranded in Chicago during a tour. McCracklin rented a studio and cut several songs including "The Walk." He sold the masters to Checker Records for cash to continue the tour. "The Walk" became his first national hit. In 1959, he signed with Mercury and released "The Wobble" and "The Georgia Slop." Over the years he founded several labels himself, including Art-Tone, which had a Top Ten R&B hit in 1961 with "Just Got To Know." His association with Imperial Records, beginning in 1965, produced more hits in the R&B market, including "Think" and "My Answer." He also wrote songs for others, including "Tramp," recorded by Lowell Fulson and by Otis and Carla; and "The Thrill Is Gone," B. B. King's best selling single.

followed by a week in Texas as the tour swings back through the South.

New Releases for the first week in April include the prophetic "Hang Up My Rock and Roll Shoes" b/w "What Am I Living For" by Chuck Willis on Atlantic. Other releases on Atlantic this week include Clyde McPhatter's "Come What May" and Joe Turner's "Jump for Joy." Rounding out the biggest release week in some time are "Rumble" by Link Wray and His Ray Men on Cadence; "Wear My Ring Around Your Neck" b/w "Doncha' Think It's Time" by Elvis Presley on RCA; "You're the One That Done It" by Thomas Wayne on Mercury; "You Mostest Girl" by Bobby Lee Trammell on Radio; "All I Have To Do Is Dream" b/w "Claudette" by the Everly Brothers on Cadence; "Johnny B. Goode" by Chuck Berry on Chess; "Try The Impossible" by Lee Andrews and the Hearts on United Artists; **Huelyn Duvall**'s "Humdinger" on Challenge; "Sick and Tired" by Fats Domino on Imperial; "Little Pig" by Dale Hawkins on Checker; "Valerie" by the Mello-Kings on Herald; "Rags to Riches" by the Rays on Cameo; and "Nee Nee Na Na Na Na Nu Nu" by Dicky Doo and the Don'ts on Swan. Also out is "Hey Little Nell" by the Four Mints on NRC. One of the Four Mints is Ray Stevens.

EARLY APRIL

Billboard magazine notes that "Leroy" b/w "My True Love" by Jack Scott is purchased by Carlton Records from Brill Records. (This news item is incorrect. See the Jack Scott biography, August 1958.)

Marvin Rainwater, whose "Whole Lotta Woman" is in the Top Ten in England, leaves on a six-week tour of the British Isles.

Carl Perkins cancels a tour of Canada to remain bedside with his brother, Jay Perkins, who is in critical condition in Memphis. Carl was scheduled to appear with Sonny James and Buddy Knox.

Charlie Gracie plays several shows in London in a return engagement.

APR 8   Tommy Edwards is booked for five days at Robert's Show Club in Chicago.

APR 9   Bill Haley and His Comets begin their lengthy tour of Latin America with a concert in Buenos Aires. Cities on their itinerary include Caracas, Venezuela (17); Rio de Janeiro; Sao Paulo; Porte Allegre, Brazil; and Montevideo.

APR 10   Chuck Willis, age thirty, dies at Hugh Spalding Hospital in Atlanta. He had a perforated stomach ulcer and had undergone surgery a week earlier. He had suffered from ulcers for two years, and a couple of weeks ago a plate of barbeque set off this final round of problems.

APR 11   In New York, the Apollo Theater offers the talents of Sammy Davis, Jr. and the Will Maston Trio.

The Dallas Sportatorium is the scene of a show featuring Roy

HUELYN DUVALL

Huelyn Duvall was another rocker from that hotbed of rock 'n roll activity, Dallas/Ft. Worth. Among others, this area gave us Delbert McClinton, Bruce Channel, Mac Curtis, Ronnie Dee (Dawson), "Groovy" Joe Poovey, and Major Bill Smith (producer of "Hey, Baby!" "Hey Paula," "Last Kiss," and hundreds more.) Duvall was introduced to music at an early age. He was a fan of country music, especially Hank Snow, Marty Robbins and Johnny Horton, each of whom was recording in the early 1950s. However, it was at an Elvis show that Duvall's musical direction took focus. He formed the Tight Strings and began booking himself into every venue that would have him. On stage, Duvall was dynamic. Couple that with his rugged good looks, and he looked like a rising star. Along the way, he met Danny Wolfe, a composer of great rock numbers. Wolfe had already placed several songs with Gene Vincent and had a three-single career on Dot in 1957-58. Wolfe brought Duvall to the attention of Challenge Records of Hollywood. Beginning in 1957 with "Comin' or Goin'" b/w "Teen Queen," Duvall issued five serious rock singles for the label into 1960, including "Three Months to Kill" and "Friday Night on a Dollar Bill." The most treasured of his singles was "Pucker Paint," a Wolfe composition and a song that Wolfe had previously issued on Dot. Duvall traveled to San Diego for several sessions, which led to shows in California. National sales eluded him, but he remained popular in Texas. In the 1960-70s, Duvall appeared on Starfire and Twinkle (a Major Bill label). When he felt it was time to leave music behind and get a real job, he became a successful manager with a computer firm. In the 1980s, he discovered that he was well known in England, so he put together an act for a successful European tour.

Hamilton, the Clovers and Thurston Harris.

APR 12 Dale Hawkins, the Four Preps, Lou Monte, Robert and Johnny, and David Seville are this week's talent on "The Dick Clark Show."

APR 13 The "Big Rhythm & Blues Show of '58" plays a concert and dance at the Booker T. Auditorium in New Orleans. The revue is headlined by the Midnighters. Also appearing are the "5" Royales, Little Willie John, Bo Diddley, the Cadillacs and the Upsetters.

APR 14 Connie Francis opens at the Casino Royal in Washington for a week's run.

New Releases for the second week in April include "Leroy" b/w "My True Love" by Jack Scott on Carlton; Connie Francis' "I'm Sorry I Made You Cry" on M-G-M; "Susie's House" by John D. Loudermilk on Columbia; "Dance with Me" by Dale Wright on Fraternity; Jo Ann Campbell's "You-oo" on Gone; "Go On To School" by Jimmy Reed on Vee-Jay; Joe Jones' "A-Tisket A-Tasket" on Roulette; and three odes to the latest fashion statement, the sack dress: "Boppin' in a Sack" by the Lane Brothers on RCA, "Sack Dresses" by the Sad Sacks on Imperial, and "Sack Dress" by the Beavers on Capitol.

MID-APRIL

The Kingston Trio, three California college students who sing folk songs, have their first New York City engagement, joining Stan Getz at the Village Vanguard.

In Portland, the Paris Sisters are playing Amato's Supper Club.

Bobby Day, fronting the Googie Rene big band, is touring the Northwest for twenty-one days.

A new "dance" imported from England is making the rounds. Called "hand jive," it features complicated hand movements and little actual dancing. Records titled "Hand Jive" have already been released by the Betty Smith Group on London (apparently the original version) and the Show Brothers on Robin.

While Bill Haley is currently on tour in Latin America, a press release states that he will be visiting art galleries in the hope of purchasing a masterpiece or two for an art gallery in Booth Corners, Pennsylvania, of which he is co-owner.

APR 16 Dion and the Belmonts perform "I Wonder Why" on "American Bandstand."

On CBS-TV's "The Big Record," Jimmie Rodgers makes a guest appearance.

APR 18 That New Orleans wild man and his vocal group, Huey Smith and the Clowns, make their television debut performing "Don't You Just Know It" on "American Bandstand."

Johnny Cash plays a date at Fort Smith, Arkansas. The next

night he plays Sulphur Springs, Texas, before traveling to Nashville for appearances on "The Grand Ole Opry."

In New Orleans, Eddie Bo performs at the new High Hat Club for the next three days. He remains a weekend fixture at the club for the next four weekends.

Buddy Knox, Sonny James, Jimmy Bowen, Jerry Reed, and the Casuals play the annual police benefit show in Beaumont, Texas.

Louis Jordan and His Tympany Five bring down the house at the Apollo Theater in New York for a week.

APR 19   In Paris, the Platters start a five-month tour of Europe and North Africa. They are guaranteed $10,000 to $15,000 a week in bookings. Venues will include the Brussels' World Fair and the Olympia in Paris.

Allen Toussaint (mistakenly billed as "Alvin") co-stars on the bill at the Dew Drop Cafe in New Orleans for two days.

On ABC-TV, "The Dick Clark Show" presents Carl Perkins, David Seville, the Four Aces, and the Aquatones.

APR 20   Marvin Rainwater plays the London Coliseum.

On CBS-TV, Freddy Bell and the Bellboys perform on "The Ed Sullivan Show."

New Releases for the third week in April include "Rave On" by Buddy Holly on Coral; "Secretly" by Jimmie Rodgers on Roulette; "Big Man" by the Four Preps and "Baby Blue" by Gene Vincent, both on Capitol; and "Everybody Rock" by Jimmy McCracklin on Checker. Also new this week is a release by ex-Cricket Niki Sullivan, "It's All Over" on Dot Records.

APR 23   Dallas' Sportatorium hosts a rock 'n roll night headlined by former country artist Tommy Sands.

APR 25   On the basis of the popularity of their recently released single, "I Met Him On a Sunday," the Shirelles are booked to appear at the Howard Theater revue in Washington. This week's headliner is Louis Jordan.

Alan Freed's "Big Beat Show" stops in Minneapolis. Other nights this month include the Chicago Opera House (26) and Ft. Wayne (27).

APR 26   "The Dick Clark Show" presents Connie Francis, Somethin' Smith and the Redheads, and actor Tony Randall.

APR 27   Carl Perkins and Roy Orbison begin a tour of the Midwest with a show in St. Louis. Other cities on their itinerary include Topeka, Sioux City, Omaha, Lincoln, and Wichita.

The Everly Brothers and Sal Mineo are guests on "The Ed Sullivan Show" on CBS-TV.

APR 28   Johnny Cash begins a swing through Canada's Maritime Provinces with a show in Campbelton, New Brunswick.

ALLEN TOUSSAINT

Without Allen Toussaint the sound of New Orleans rhythm and blues would have been considerably different. Born January 14, 1938, he came under the spell of the legendary Professor Longhair as a youth. He put together his own combo when he was fourteen, playing talent shows at the Dew Drop Cafe. In the late 1950s, he was a sought-after session pianist, often playing piano on Fats Domino's recordings. He frequently replaced Huey Smith when the Clowns went on tour. Eventually, he gave up touring for the demanding, and lucrative, studio work. In 1958, RCA issued his first album, THE WILD SOUND OF NEW ORLEANS (as by Al Tousan), which featured the tune "Java," a 1964 hit for Al Hirt. In the early 1960s he worked for the Minit label, producing and writing hits for Ernie K-Doe ("Mother In Law"), Irma Thomas ("Ruler of my Heart" and "Its' Raining"), and Benny Spellman ("Lipstick Traces" and "Fortune Teller"). He also produced Chris Kenner ("I Like It Like That") and Jesse Hill ("Ooh Pooh Pah Doo") for Minit. He wrote and produced Lee Dorsey's "Ya-Ya" on Fury and "Workin' In The Coal Mine" on Amy. He produced Clarence Henry's "But I Do" on Argo. Toussaint recorded the original version of "Whipped Cream," a 1965 hit for Herb Alpert and the Tijuana Brass. In the late 1960s, he and Marshall Seahorn teamed to form a number of New Orleans labels, culminating with the opening of Seasaint Studio in 1973. Here he worked with the Neville Brothers (who were recording as the Meters). Toussaint was one of those most responsible for the rediscovery of New Orleans' R&B heritage in the 1970s. He has worked with Paul Simon, Paul McCartney, the Pointer Sisters, and The Band. In 1977, his album SOUTHERN NIGHTS featured the title cut which became a hit for Glen Campbell.

In Chicago, Eddie Cochran and Gene Vincent headline the Youth Rally at the Chicago Stadium. The duo are in the middle of a forty-date tour which began in California and will include a swing through Canada.

New Releases for the fourth week in April include two versions of "Jennie Lee:" the original by **Jan and Arnie** on Arwin and a cover by Billy Ward and His Dominoes on Liberty. Also new this week are the Champs' "El Rancho Rock" on Challenge; "Big Name Button" by the Royal Teens on ABC-Paramount; "Wrong Again" by Sonny Curtis on Dot; and "Wondering" by Little Junior Parker on Duke. Also out is "No Chemise, Please" by Gerry Granahan on Sunbeam. Granahan also records as Dickey Doo and Jerry Grant. Finally, catching up with the previously mentioned English trend is "Willie and the Hand Jive" by Johnny Otis on Capitol.

THE TOP ROCK 'N ROLL HITS FOR APRIL 1958

1. Twilight Time - The Platters
2. Tequila - The Champs
3. Book of Love - The Monotones
4. Who's Sorry Now - Connie Francis
5. Witch Doctor - David Seville
6. Oh, Lonesome Me - Don Gibson
7. Don't You Just Know It - Huey Smith and the Clowns
8. Believe What You Say/My Bucket's Got A Hole In It - Ricky Nelson
9. Billy - Kathy Linden
10. Sweet Little Sixteen - Chuck Berry
11. Breathless - Jerry Lee Lewis
12. 26 Miles - The Four Preps
13. Wear My Ring Around Your Neck/Doncha' Think It's Time - Elvis Presley
14. Don't - Elvis Presley
15. Maybe Baby - The Crickets
16. The Walk - Jimmy McCracklin
17. Ballad of a Teenage Queen - Johnny Cash
18. All I Have To Do Is Dream - The Everly Brothers
19. Dinner with Drac - Zacherle
20. To Be Loved - Jackie Wilson
21. Good Golly, Miss Molly - Little Richard
22. Oh, Julie - The Crescendos
23. We Belong Together - Robert and Johnny
24. Talk To Me, Talk To Me - Little Willie John
25. Rock and Roll Is Here To Stay - Danny and the Juniors
26. Every Night (I Pray) - The Chantels
27. Skinny Minnie - Bill Haley and His Comets
28. Short Shorts - The Royal Teens
29. For Your Love - Ed Townsend
33. Oh-Oh, I'm Falling In Love Again - Jimmy Rodgers
31. Lonely Island/You Were Made For Me - Sam Cooke

JAN AND ARNIE

If the name sounds familiar, it's because this duo soon "morphed" into the hugely Jan and Dean. One would never guess this after listening to the few recordings by Jan and Arnie. Instead of trying to musically capture the crescendos of the ocean, or the roar of racing in the street, Jan and Arnie were interested in layering their voices on recording tape to the point where it was difficult to tell if it was two or two-hundred singers on the record. Jan Berry and Arnie Ginsberg attended University High, one of the secondary schools catering to elite Bel Air. One evening, so the story goes, after slipping in to see a local striptease artist who billed herself as Jennie Lee, Jan and Arnie composed a song built around her bump-and-grind routine. The song began "Bomp ba-ba-bomp, ba-ba umm-dap umm-dap, umm-wa-wa-wa..." In Berry's garage they used a pair of home reel-to-reel tape recorders and overlaid various sounds, including a simplistic vocal line, on top of each other until they had created a catchy tune titled "Jennie Lee." For backing instrumentation, Jan played piano and Arnie kept time by beating on a box. Their efforts came to the attention of Arwin Records and they overdubbed even more parts at a local studio using Ernie Freeman's combo. The record caught on immediately in L.A., abut soon after, Jan and Arnie began having problems with their friendship. They were able to put together two more singles, "Gas Money" and "I Love Linda," each in the same vein as "Jennie Lee," before the partnership dissolved. Arnie remained briefly with Arwin, putting together a group called the Rituals for one single, "Girl from Zanzibar." After that, he gave up the musical side of show business for a career in commercial art. Jan joined with Dean Torrance to form Jan and Dean. In the beginning, they continued to issue singles on Challenge similar to "Jennie Lee."

32. You Excite Me - Frankie Avalon
33. The Stroll - The Diamonds
34. Been So Long - The Pastels
35. Crazy Love/Let the Bells Keep Ringing - Paul Anka
36. Get a Job - The Silhouettes
37. Just Married - Marty Robbins
38. You Are My Destiny - Paul Anka
39. So Tough - The Casuals
40. Click Clack - Dicky Doo and the Don'ts
41. Maybe - The Chantels
42. Dede Dinah - Frankie Avalon
43. I Met Him on a Sunday - The Shirelles
44. Don't Let Go - Roy Hamilton
45. Sing, Boy, Sing - Tommy Sands
46. Tequila - Eddie Platt
47. Yes, My Darling - Fats Domino
48. At The Hop - Danny and the Juniors
49. Rumble - Link Wray and His Ray Men
50. You - The Aquatones

Also:
Are You Sincere - Andy Williams
Chanson D'Amour - Art and Dotty Todd
Lazy Mary - Lou Monte
Looking Back - Nat King Cole
Catch a Falling Star - Perry Como

April 1958
ARTIST OF THE MONTH

THE PLATTERS

(This biography is a continuation of the information presented in the first volume of THE GOLDEN AGE OF AMERICAN ROCK 'N ROLL.)

During the period covered in this volume, 1956 through 1959, the Platters became the most popular vocal group in the world. The size of this accomplishment must be weighed against the sheer number of other vocal groups working the fine line between "pop" and rock and roll. Only two other groups, the Four Aces and the Kingston Trio approached such lofty heights.

After half-dozen quickly forgotten releases on Federal Records, from 1953 to 1955, the Platters established their popularity "overnight" with "Only You," their first release on Mercury Records. "Only You" eventually sold more than a million copies. Refusing to acknowledge the possibility of a sophomore slump, their second Mercury single, "The Great Pretender," did even better, topping the R&B and "pop" music charts in early 1956. "(You've Got) The Magic Touch" came close to the top spot later that spring, while "My Prayer" peaked at Number One in late summer. That made four million-selling singles in a row, a mark unequaled up to that time by any other vocal group, and a statistic that would stand until 1964 and the Beatles.

After "My Prayer," the Platters concentrated on personal appearances, and sales of their singles declined slightly. On the other hand, the next four singles, "You'll Never Know," "On My Word of Honor," "I'm Sorry," and "My Dream" each featured such strong material on the B-side that the second song was almost as popular as the hit side.

Demand for concerts by the group came from all over the world. The Platters happily obliged their fans in Europe, South America, Latin America, and the Far East to such an extent that their nickname became "the Flying Platters." They played the world's largest concert halls, including the Olympia in Paris and the Palladium in London, as well as huge stadiums from Buenos Aires to Tokyo. Most of these engagements ran a week or more, and a month-long layover in one city was not out of the ordinary for the Platters.

Hollywood beckoned early and often. The Platters appeared in many of the rock 'n roll films of the 1950s. Beginning with the best of the bunch, "The Girl Can't Help It," the group also put in cameo appearances in "Carnival Rock," "Girl's Town," and "Rock Around the Clock." In 1959, the group even appeared in the overseas film, "Europe At Night."

The Platters

The Platters were the first rock 'n roll "super group." The fans knew each member by name and face: Tony Williams, the soaring lead tenor; Herb Reed, the resonant bass; Paul Robi, who lent strength to the baritone spot; David Lynch, the fine second tenor; and Zola Taylor, a very attractive performer who could hold her own vocally with the fellows while adding sparkle to their stage act. While each of the Platters boasted a specific skill, the group's strength lay in the smooth texture of their unique vocal blend.

The Platters also had the singular ability to sing newly-written songs and make them sound like old standards while breathing freshness into older material. The force behind this "yin and yang" was Buck Ram. Ram prided himself on being a songwriter, claiming solo composer's credit for "The Great Pretender," "My Prayer," "(You've Got) The Magic Touch," "Enchanted," "My Dream," "Heaven in Earth," and "Helpless," as well as co-songwriting credit for "Only You," "Twilight Time," "I Wish," "Remember When," "I'm Sorry," and "It's Raining Outside." Over the years, there has been some criticism of Ram in this area, and, in a 1989 interview, Tony Williams stated "The Great Pretender" was probably written by "Run Joe" Taylor, who sold the song to Ram for twenty-five dollars. Williams also claimed credit for changing "(You've Got) The Midas Touch" to "(You've Got) The Magic Touch," a significant move that undoubtedly increased the song's popularity.

In the summer of 1958, after more than a year of medium-sized hits, the Platters topped the charts with "Twilight Time," the first of their hits using previously recorded material. "Twilight Time" had been composed by Buck Ram in 1944; and it became the trademark of the Three Suns, who recorded a version on Majestic in 1946 and had a hit with the tune on RCA Victor in 1950. The Platters repeated the feat by the end of 1958 with "Smoke Gets In Your Eyes," a perfect example of the group's ability to bring a new approach to an older song. "Smoke Gets In Your Eyes" was composed in 1933, about the same time most of the group was born.

The first era for the Platters ended on April 6, 1960, when Tony Williams announced to a stunned world that he was leaving the group to pursue a solo career. His position within the structure of the Platter's sound was considered by many to be impossible to fill. Acting as the group's manager, Buck Ram first hired Sonny Barnes, who lasted less than a year in a thankless situation. Barnes was replaced by Charles Edward "Sonny" Turner who stayed with the group through most of the 1960s.

Williams recorded solo for Mercury and Reprise but could not approach the success he had with the Platters. He continued to perform extensively through the 1980s in a group that also featured his wife Helen.

Zola Taylor left the group in 1962, begging off because of personal reasons. Her place was filled by Sandra Dawn. By all accounts, Zola Taylor led a colorful life after her time with the Platters. However, nothing prepared the world for her confession in 1984 that she had an affair with fifteen-year old Frankie Lymon beginning in 1956 while the Platters and the Teenagers were on tour together. She also claimed to have married Lymon in Tijuana in 1965, but no marriage certificate was produced.

After Miss Taylor's departure, Paul Robi was the next to leave the group. In 1964, his spot was taken by Nate Nelson, a former member of the Flamingos. Nelson was still with the Platters when he died of coronary artery disease in 1984. Robi died of cancer in 1989.

The next to leave was David Lynch. An admitted alcoholic, Lynch was on the road to recovery when he died on January 2, 1981.

After Tony Williams left, the Platters continued on, although Mercury Records at first balked at issuing any material that did not feature Williams on lead vocal. Buck Ram, a lawyer by trade, effectively convinced Mercury Records of the error of their decision. Nevertheless, the ties between the group's manager and their record company were strained, and there were no more hits by the group on Mercury after 1962.

In 1966, the Platters signed with Musicor Records. Ten years after "Only You" and "The Great Pretender," a new group of Platters, relying on a sound reminiscent of the Four Tops, staked out their claim in the world of soul music. Over a two-year period, they had hits with "I Love You 1000 Times," "With This Ring" and "Washed Ashore."

At the time the Platters were originally formed, each member, including Buck Ram, owned a percentage of the group's success. As the individual members left, Ram bought out each of their shares. Eventually, Ram gained complete control the Platter's name. This did not stop the various members from forming their own versions of "The Platters." However, one by one, Ram successfully sued each one. In 1974, "The Buck Ram Platters" were recording once again for Mercury. This time, there was nothing approaching a hit record, but there was money to be made touring. The Buck Ram Platters also recorded "My Ship Is Coming In" for Ram's own Ram Records in the late 1970s and "I Do It All The Time" as the Platters for Ram's Antler Records in 1980. By this time, their sound resembled that of the Chi-Lites. Neither single was successful.

In the mid-1980s, control of the Platters' name was wrested from Ram by Jean Bennett. Williams was coaxed out of semi-retirement as was Miss Taylor. Herb Reed, who had continued with most of the previous incarnations of the Platters, also joined this group. By the late 1980s, Williams and his wife, Helen, were working as the Platters. This group contained Bobby Rivers, Ted E. Fame, and Rocky "Shad" Williams, a relative of Tony's.

In January 1990, the Platters were inducted into the Rock and Roll Hall of Fame. At that time, the group was composed of Tony Williams, Zola Taylor, Martha Robi (Paul's widow), Herb Reed, and Rosylin Atkins.

"The voice of the Platters" was hushed August 14, 1992, when Tony Williams succumbed to emphysema which was compounded by diabetes.

Lately, "Herb Reed and the Platters" have been appearing at various Nevada casinos, a favorite showcase for the group as far back as 1956.

May 1958

BILL JUSTIS

He is best known for an exciting instrumental with a bouncy beat. He never recorded another tune quite like it. Justis was born October 14, 1926, in Birmingham. His family relocated to Memphis in 1931, in the middle of the Great Depression. He was taught piano by his mother, although he opted for the saxophone in high school. By 1954, he had directed musicals for Tulane University. He returned to Memphis and ingratiated himself into the inner circle of Sun Records, whose owner, Sam Phillips, later said that he thought Justis was a "joke." Justis persevered, and after directing several Sun sessions, he was granted studio time of his own. Working on a sax riff he had originally titled "Backwoods," Justis joined with guitarist Sid Manker to put together "Raunchy." The record opens with Manker's guitar figure, accompanied by Roland Janes' jangling rhythm guitar, before Justis chimes in on sax. Justis' version of "Raunchy" sold a million copies, while cover versions by Ernie Freeman and Billy Vaughn also did well. To realize what a stretch "Raunchy" was for Justis, one needs only to flip the single over and listen to "Midnight Man." It features an off-key vocal (Justis?) fronting an offending vocal group. Justis' second single was "College Man," combining the best and worst of the previous tunes. After opening with a cheerleader yell, the song was so structured that the instruments couldn't "soar" until the bridge—which featured a raw, full-chord guitar jam worthy of today's heavy metal bands. By contrast, Justis' sax sounds over-rehearsed. After several years with Sun, in 1963 Justis overproduced Fats Domino's sessions for ABC-Paramount, contributing to Domino's decline in popularity. With Smash Records, Justis had a chance in the 1960s to record what he wanted, and it was all overblown and instantly forgettable. Justis passed away in Nashville, on July 15, 1982.

MAY 1 Playing tonight at Pittsburgh's Syria Mosque, Alan Freed's "Big Beat Show" tour thunders on amid a growing controversy concerning incidents involving unruly crowds.

On "American Bandstand," veteran performer Roy Hamilton sings his latest hit, "Don't Let Go."

On a world tour, the Platters draw a reported crowd of 21,000 to the 14,000-seat stadium in Oran, North Africa.

MAY 2 Della Reese plays a week at the Howard Theater in Washington. Along with Miss Reese are Thurston Harris, the Tune Weavers, and Little Joe and the Thrillers.

MAY 3 Ersel Hickey makes a rare television appearance on "The Dick Clark Show." Also appearing are Jimmie Rodgers, singing "Honeycomb," and the Champs, performing "Tequila."

Carl Perkins winds up a tour with a show in Wichita, Kansas.

Alan Freed's "Big Beat" tour reaches a tumultuous climax in Boston tonight, where a riot by "berserk gangs of teenagers" is reported. Fifteen people are hurt or stabbed following the show. As the tour moves on to other cities, reaction varies. The crowd is well-behaved in Montreal (4); Lewiston, Maine (5); Providence, Rhode Island (7); and at the Arena in Hershey, Pennsylvania. A May 6 show, scheduled as a benefit for the Catholic Youth Organization in Troy, New York, is cancelled by the Albany Diocese of the Catholic Church. A performance in New Haven on May 8 is cancelled by city government, and a May 9 show in New Britain, Connecticut, is cancelled by the chief of police. (See also MAY 10 and MAY 16.)

New Releases for the first week in May include "Yakety Yak" by the Coasters on Atco; Sam Cooke's "All of My Life" on Keen; "Why, Oh Why" by Kathy Linden on Felsted; "I Wonder Why" by Dion and the Belmonts on Laurie; Ronnie Self's "Big Blon' Baby" on Columbia; Ray Vernon's "Window Shopping" on Cameo; "Cha-Hua-Hua" by the Pets on Arwin; Carole King's "The Right Girl" on ABC-Paramount; and two from Phillips International: "Scroungie" by **Bill Justis** and "After the Hop" by ex-Drifter Bill Pinckney. Finally, there are two versions of the same song: "Little Chick-ee-Wah-Wah" by Huey and Jerry on Vin and "Chickie-Chickie Wah Wah" by Ray Stevens on Capitol. Huey and Jerry were Huey Smith and Gerri Hall, of the Clowns.

MAY 6 Carl Perkins' show in La Puente, California, kicks off his West Coast tour. Other stops in the state include San Diego, Riverside, Los Angeles, San Francisco and Eureka, followed by Portland, Oregon, and Seattle, Washington (18).

The Jordanaires, most famous as the backing vocal group on most of Elvis Presley's hits, preview their new release "Little Miss Ruby" on "American Bandstand."

MAY 7   The Champs guest on "American Bandstand" performing "Tequila" and "El Rancho Rock."

The Four Preps are booked to play Sciola's Club in Philadelphia for four days.

EARLY MAY

Johnny Cash is on tour of the Maritime Provinces of Canada. (See also MAY 10.)

MAY 8   Jimmie Rodgers, Mickey and Sylvia, Roy Hamilton, Lee Andrews and the Hearts, and the Champs appear as a special guest performers at the Music Operators of America convention in Chicago.

MAY 9   **Jody Reynolds** debuts "Endless Sleep" on "American Bandstand."

Huey Smith and the Clowns headline the week-long stand at the Apollo Theater in New York. Also on the bill are the Bobbettes, the Isley Brothers, and the Red Prysock combo.

Cutting across Canada, "The Biggest Show of Stars for '58" plays Regina, Saskatchewan.

The legendary Professor Longhair entertains the crowd at the High Hat Club in New Orleans for the next three days.

In Italy, the Platters begin filming a movie.

Count Basie's orchestra featuring Joe Williams headlines the revue at the Howard Theater in Washington for the week.

MAY 10   After forty shows in forty-five days, Alan Freed's lengthy tour winds up on a sour note as the final performance, scheduled for Trenton, New Jersey, is cancelled by a Major in the National Guard, who cites concerns for public safety.

Johnny Cash closes his tour through Canada with a show at St. Johns, New Brunswick. The next day he is back in the States for a performance in Utica, New York.

"The Dick Clark Show" offers Dicky Doo and the Don'ts, Link Wray, Jan and Arnie, and Pat Suzuki.

MAY 11   Connie Francis is a guest on "The Ed Sullivan Show." Also on the bill are Art and Dotty Todd and Al Hibbler.

MAY 12   "American Bandstand" plays host to Mickey and Sylvia.

The latest rock 'n roll motion picture, "Let's Rock" featuring Danny and the Juniors, Paul Anka, and the Royal Teens, opens in theaters across the country.

JODY REYNOLDS

Jody Reynolds' "Endless Sleep" has been tagged the first "swamp rock" record. In fact, it was the forerunner of "death rock." Jody was born in Denver, December 3, 1938. Soon thereafter, his family moved to Oklahoma, before settling in Southern California in the early 1950s. In high school, Jody formed his first band. After graduation, he and the band toured through the Southwest. In Phoenix, he was introduced to Al Casey, a hot local guitarist. By 1958, he had logged thousands of miles and hundreds of shows. His acquaintances in the music business led to Demon Records, a subsidiary of Liberty. For his first session, Reynolds asked Casey to play lead guitar, and his style is very evident in the shimmering chords of "Endless Sleep." The song seemed to promote suicide ("Come with me baby in my Endless Sleep"), and right-minded adults created an uproar. Nevertheless, "Endless Sleep" came close to selling a million copies, and began a trend that spawned "Teen Angel," "Tell Laura I Love Her," "Patches," and "Last Kiss." Reynolds second single, "Fire of Love," was a mid-sized hit in the fall of 1958. Demon was busy promoting the Olympics, who were hot with "Western Movies," and Reynolds was shuffled aside. Demon released five more singles through 1959, but Reynolds never had another hit. In 1959, he produced the Strangers' "Caterpillar Crawl," a popular instrumental with a "swamp" feel. In 1961, Reynolds and Casey recorded "Thunder" as the Storms on Sundown. It was their own version of "Caterpillar Crawl." A year later, there was one single on Emmy, followed in 1963 by one single each on Smash and Brent. He recorded a duet on Titan with Bobbie Gentry in 1967 just before her "Ode to Billy Joe." By the end of the 1970s, he had rerecorded "Endless Sleep" for Pulsar, Gusto and Hollywood. Today, he lives in Yuma, Arizona.

In Vancouver, "The Biggest Show of Stars for '58" tour plays to a half-filled house, grossing only $8,000 in two shows.

New Releases for the second week in May include "Purple People Eater" by Sheb Wooley on M-G-M; "Dottie" by Danny and the Juniors on ABC-Paramount; the Chantels' "I Love You So" on End; "Love Bird" by Charlie Gracie on Cameo; "Real Wild Child" by Johnny O'Keefe on Brunswick; and "Better You Should Whip-a-me" by Dean Storey on Surf.

MAY 14   Johnny Cash headlines the country and western portion of Memphis' Cotton Carnival show.

MID-MAY

In Rome, the Platters, who are continuing their five-month overseas tour, have an audience with Pope Pius XII. In addition, while in Italy, they film a musical short to be shown at a later date on "The Ed Sullivan Show."

MAY 16   Fats Domino performs for the Spring Formal at Vanderbilt University in Nashville.

On "American Bandstand," Jack Scott sings "Leroy" and "My True Love."

Johnny Cash takes his tour to Texas with an opening show in Amarillo. Also on the bill are Danny and the Juniors, Roy Orbison, Don Gibson, and Sonny Burgess. Other dates already set for the two-show-a-day tour include Lubbock (17) and Austin (18). Cities that are planned for this tour include Austin, Corpus Christi, San Antonio, Tucson, Albuquerque, Oklahoma City.

Dinah Washington takes the spotlight at the Apollo Theater in New York for the week. She is accompanied by the Tune Weavers and Willis Jackson's combo.

Ray Charles is the star at the Howard Theater in Washington this week. Also appearing are the Cookies, the Turbans, the **Heartbeats**, and Robert and Johnny.

Also in Washington, Steve Gibson and His Red Caps open at the Showcase Lounge for the weekend.

In Boston, Alan Freed is indicted on charges stemming from the incident on May 3. He is charged with anarchy and inciting a riot. He pleads innocent and is released on $3,000 bail. The case will slowly work its way through the local court system for nearly a year. Freed will quit his job at WINS radio after the station refuses to back him in his hour of need. (See also MAR 4, 1959.)

MAY 17   Marty Robbins appears on "Jubilee U.S.A." broadcast nationally on ABC-TV from Springfield, Missouri. This is his third stint on the show in the past four months.

Also tonight, ABC-TV's "Dick Clark Show" welcomes Chuck Berry, Billy and Lillie, Art and Dotty Todd, Betty Johnson, Frankie Lymon, and Phillips International recording artist, Carl McVoy.

THE HEARTBEATS

The Heartbeats were formed in 1955 by a group of high school friends in the Queens suburb of New York City. The original members of the group were Albert Crump, first tenor; Robert Brown, second tenor; Vernon Seavers, baritone; and Wallace Roker, bass. In 1956, James "Shep" Shepherd, a student at Food Trades High School, joined the group as lead singer. A popular R&B group, the Miller Sisters, lived in the neighborhood, and through their assistance, the Heartbeats signed with Gotham Records of Philadelphia. Their first release, "Tormented," was released on the Network label, a subsidiary of Gotham. The father of the Miller Sisters was A&R man with Hull Records, and he arranged for the next single by the Heartbeats, "Crazy For You," to be released on Hull. The record sold well on the East Coast, and was followed by "Darling How Long" and "Your Way." Their fourth Hull single was "A Thousand Miles Away." When the recording began to sell nationally, it was re-released on Rama, one of George Goldner's labels. For four months through the winter of 1956-57, "A Thousand Miles Away" was a runaway R&B hit. There were two more singles on Rama, including "Everybody's Somebody's Fool," and two on Gee into 1957, but none created much furor. By this time, Shepherd and the other Heartbeats were arguing constantly. When the split came, Shepherd opened a restaurant in a New York suburb while working as a solo act. The remaining Heartbeats returned to school and jobs. The Heartbeats had recorded enough material for two singles on Roulette in 1958. In 1960, "A Thousand Miles Away" was reissued, and it sold in moderate numbers. As a result, two more singles were issued on Gee, followed by one on Guyden. In 1961, Shepherd returned to Hull with his new group, the Limelites, and a new song, "Daddy's Home."

MAY 18   In New Orleans, Guitar Slim has a two-day stand at the Blue Eagle Club.

New Releases for the third week in May include two on Sun Records: "High School Confidential" by Jerry Lee Lewis and "Guess Things Happen That Way" by Johnny Cash. Other releases this week include "Ooh! My Soul" by Little Richard on Specialty; "As Long As I Live" by Jackie Wilson on Brunswick; "For Your Precious Love" by the Impressions featuring Jerry Butler on Falcon; "You Know (I Can't Live Without You)" by Ronnie and the Rockin' Kings on RCA; and "Crash the Party" by Bennie Joy on Antler.

MAY 22   Jerry Lee Lewis arrives in England for what promises to be a whirlwind, sold-out tour of the British Isles. He is scheduled for thirty-seven concerts during the next month. Anticipating an overwhelming response from the fans for Jerry Lee's first tour of Britain, his English label, Decca Records, throws a party tonight in his honor. Invited guests include a large contingent of the British Press. Jerry Lee attends the celebration, accompanied by his wife Myra. It is soon broadcast worldwide that his new bride is his fourteen-year old second-cousin.

MAY 23   The Dew Drop in New Orleans welcomes Faye Adams for a three-day engagement.

MAY 24   Dick Clark's Saturday night ABC-TV show features Dion and the Belmonts, singing "I Wonder Why." Also on the show are Johnny Nash, **Kathy Linden**, the Playmates, and Bobby Helms, who sings "Jacqueline."

MAY 25   Frankie Lymon and the Teenagers get together to perform on the "Ed Sullivan Show" on CBS-TV.
   In New Orleans, Little Junior Parker and Bobby "Blue" Bland perform for the Sunday ball at the Blue Eagle Club.

New Releases the fourth week in May include "You're Making a Mistake" by the Platters on Mercury; "The Thing," a novelty cut-in by Bill Buchanan on Gone; "Rebel Rouser" by Duane Eddy on Jamie; Rudy Grazell's "I Think of You" on Sun; "Tail Light" by Ray Peterson on RCA; "Hot Rock" by the Ram Rocks on Antler; "We've Had It" by Joe Bennett and the Sparkletones on ABC-Paramount; "Crazy Dream" by Terry Noland on Brunswick; Lloyd Price's "Such a Mess" on K.R.C.; "Next" by Billy Brown on Columbia; the Swallows' "We Want to Rock" on Federal; and "Love Is Everything" by Carl Dobkins, Jr. on Decca. Also new this week is "Ooh-Marie" by Dick Dale on Del-Tone. The sound of Dale's Fender guitar would become synonymous with "surf music."

MAY 28   Back in the States after struggling through only three performances in England, Jerry Lee greets the press with wide-eyed wonderment at their self-righteous questions about his marriage.

KATHY LINDEN
In the 1950s world of rock 'n roll, female vocalists were a rarity. Kathy Linden, born about 1937 in Moorestown, New Jersey, made her first public appearance at the tender age of five—not as a singer, but as a dancer. Her first single, "It's Just My Luck to be Fifteen" came out on National (when she was about 17). When it failed to generate interest, she continued her musical training at the Philadelphia Conservatory of Music where she studied piano and violin. Of course, being young and in Philadelphia, she naturally gravitated to the booming rock 'n roll scene brought on by the huge success of locally-produced "American Bandstand." Her natural musical talent brought her to Felsted Records, a New York label with strong ties to Philly. In early 1958, her first Felsted single, "Billy," became a hit, peaking near the Top Ten. It was preteen fluff, a cute song wrapped up in a bright package. "You'd Be Surprised," her second single, didn't do quite as well. Felsted decided that the success of her first record came as a result of being tied to a specific boy's name. This brought several less successful follow-ups: "Oh, Johnny, Oh," "Georgie," and "Just a Sandy Haired Boy Named Sandy." Each was a futile attempt to capture the magic of her first single. It was her sixth record, "Goodbye, Jimmy, Goodbye," that became next big hit, also peaking near the Top Ten. "You Don't Know Girls," the single after "Goodbye, Jimmy, Goodbye," was her last charted single. Her eighth, and final, Felsted release once again tried the name game with "Mary Lou Wilson and Johnny Brown." Nothing came of it. In 1962, she slipped over to Capitol Records but she was still trying to knock on the same old door. Her first release was "Remember Me (To Jimmy)." After three more singles, including another "Jimmy," she retired from show biz to devote her life to personal pursuits.

MAY 30 Dick Clark's rock 'n roll tour, scheduled to open with a two-day stand at Brooklyn's Ebbet's Field (former home of the Brooklyn Dodgers), is cancelled in the wake of the repercussions from the Boston riot of May 3. The Clark trek was scheduled for eight weeks.

Billy Wright performs for two days at the Dew Drop Cafe in New Orleans. He will return for the next weekend.

MAY 31 The "Biggest Show of 1958" tour stops at Atlantic City's Steel Pier.

LATE MAY
Chuck Berry is booked to play Topeka, Kansas, through June 1.

THE TOP ROCK 'N ROLL RECORDS FOR MAY 1958

1. All I Have To Do Is Dream/Claudette - The Everly Brothers
2. Witch Doctor - David Seville
3. Wear My Ring Around Your Neck/Doncha' Think It's Time - Elvis Presley
4. Twilight Time - The Platters
5. Johnny B. Goode - Chuck Berry
6. Book of Love - The Monotones
7. Big Man - The Four Preps
8. Oh Lonesome Me - Don Gibson
9. For Your Love - Ed Townsend
10. Tequila - The Champs
11. Secretly/Make Me a Miracle - Jimmie Rodgers
12. Rumble - Link Wray and His Ray Men
13. You - The Aquatones
14. Talk To Me, Talk To Me - Little Willie John
15. To Be Loved - Jackie Wilson
16. What Am I Living For/Hang Up My Rock and Roll Shoes - Chuck Willis
17. Billy - Kathy Linden
18. Who's Sorry Now - Connie Francis
19. Believe What You Say/My Bucket's Got a Hole In It - Ricky Nelson
20. Do You Wanna Dance - Bobby Freeman
21. Don't You Just Know It - Huey Smith and the Clowns
22. Sick and Tired/No, No - Fats Domino
23. Crazy Love/Let the Bells Keep Ringing - Paul Anka
24. Skinny Minnie - Bill Haley and His Comets
25. Just Married - Marty Robbins
26. Jennie Lee - Jan and Arnie
27. The Walk - Jimmy McCracklin
28. Nee Nee Na Na Na Na Nu Nu - Dicky Doo and the Don'ts
29. We Belong Together - Robert and Johnny
30. I Wonder Why - Dion and the Belmonts
31. Endless Sleep - Jody Reynolds

32. I'm Sorry I Made You Cry - Connie Francis
33. I Met Him on a Sunday - The Shirelles
34. You Excite Me - Frankie Avalon
35. Pretty Baby - Ronald and Ruby
36. 26 Miles - The Four Preps
37. Don't - Elvis Presley
38. Breathless - Jerry Lee Lewis
39. Sweet Little Sixteen - Chuck Berry
40. Maybe Baby - The Crickets
41. Every Night (I Pray) - The Chantels
42. Ballad of a Teenage Queen - Johnny Cash
43. Lonely Island - Sam Cooke
44. Come What May - Clyde McPhatter
45. El Rancho Rock - The Champs
46. Rave On - Buddy Holly
47. High School Confidential - Jerry Lee Lewis
48. Yakety Yak - The Coasters
49. Guess Things Happen That Way - Johnny Cash
50. Jennie Lee - Billy Ward and His Dominoes

Also on the "pop" charts:
Padre - Toni Arden
Sugar Moon - Pat Boone
Return to Me - Dean Martin
Kewpie Doll - Perry Como

May 1958
ARTIST OF THE MONTH

CHUCK BERRY

(This biography is a continuation of the one begun in
volume one of THE GOLDEN AGE OF AMERICAN ROCK 'N ROLL.)

The clown prince of rock 'n roll defied all the odds during the late 1950s by continuing to issue hit records as though he were a one-man music machine. "School Day" and "Rock & Roll Music," in 1957, and "Sweet Little Sixteen" and "Johnny B. Goode," in 1958, were his biggest records during the period. He also recorded many other songs aimed directly at the teenage audience.

After the success of "Maybellene" in 1955, Berry immediately recorded two more songs with "car" themes, "No Money Down" and "You Can't Catch Me." Neither approached the stratospheric level of "Maybellene," but this did not slow his songwriting for a moment.

He wrote songs that spoke of the joy and innocence of young women: "Sweet Little Sixteen," "Sweet Little Rock And Roll," "Oh Baby Doll," "Carol," "Little Queenie," and "Beautiful Delilah."

There were even occasional songs about the fellows: "Johnny B. Goode," "Bye Bye Johnny," "Let It Rock," and "Anthony Boy."

Other songs took on the issues of importance to those under the age of twenty: "Almost Grown," "School Day" and "Come On."

Berry also composed songs that, at first glance, would appear to be far outside his ability. "Havana Moon" was a soft number with a Caribbean flavor. "Wee Wee Hours" was blues in the classic sense. He even did a Mexican turn on "Hey Pedro."

On rare occasions, he would also sing the compositions of others. He recorded two numbers by blues master Charles Brown, "Drifting Blues" and "Merry Christmas Baby." Berry's version of the latter tune became a standard rock 'n roll Christmas song, vying with Brown's original and the remake by Elvis Presley for airtime during the holiday season. His version of the standard "That's My Desire" offered a rare glimpse into the ballad side of Chuck Berry, just as his romp down "Route 66" showcased Berry's inventive knack as a vocalist.

He waxed quite a few instrumentals that showcase the wide variety of his expertise on guitar: "Deep Feeling," "Roly Poly," "Guitar Boogie," "Blues For Hawaiians," "Blue Feeling," "Rock at the Philharmonic," "Mad Lad," and "Blue on Blue."

He wrote songs that paid tribute to the sheer frolic of a rock 'n roll dance: "Around and Around," "Oh Carol," "Rock and Roll Music," and "Reelin' and Rockin'."

And, he issued songs which were meant to be just plain fun, like "Jo Jo Gunne" and "Run Rudolph Run,"

Occasionally, there was a song with a message. "Memphis (Tennessee)" was a father's anguished cry in the night. "Back in the U.S.A." and "Promised Land" used humor to tell of the breakneck speed at which life is lived "on the road."

In the 1960s, Berry's songwriting appeared to mellow. His songs dealt with teenage marriage ("You Never Can Tell"), the aimlessness of puberty ("No Particular Place To Go"), and lost love ("Nadine").

The change in Berry's point of view was not without cause. Throughout his brief career, he had run afoul of the law many times. Usually a woman was at the center of the turmoil. In December 1959, following an appearance in El Paso, Chuck and his band visited nearby Juarez, Mexico. A fourteen-year old Apache waitress was invited to return to St. Louis to work in Berry's Club Bandstand, a nitery Berry had recently opened. According to Berry's autobiography, when he refused her amorous advances she left in a fit of anger. On December 21, following the arrest of the young woman for solicitation, the St. Louis police apprehended Berry for violation of the Mann Act. This federal statute strictly forbade transporting a minor across state lines for the purpose of prostitution. Whether or not Chuck fully realized the consequence of his action was lost in the circus atmosphere of his court appearance. He was convicted and sentenced to five years in prison and fined $5,000.00. He appealed the verdict based on racial comments made by the presiding judge, and the case went to trial again in October 1961. Most of the original verdict was upheld. Chuck Berry received a sentence of three years at the Indiana Federal Prison and a fine of $10,000. Two months into his sentence he was transferred to Leavenworth Federal Prison in Kansas. He completed his time at the Federal Medical Center in Springfield, Missouri.

Chuck Berry

Chuck Berry was never the same again. He felt he had been hounded by the press and betrayed by both sides of the legal profession.

While behind bars, Berry watched helplessly as Lonnie Mack had a hit with an instrumental version of "Memphis." Then, the Beach Boys took his instrumental score for "Sweet Little Sixteen," right down to the opening guitar riff, and turned it into the hit "Surfin' USA."

With time off for good behavior, Berry was released on his birthday, October 18, 1963. He soon found himself back in demand as the Beatles rerecorded several of his early hits including "Roll Over Beethoven." In May 1964, he made his first trip to England where he was greeted as a conquering hero. Back home, "Nadine," "No Particular Place to Go," "You Never Can Tell," and "Promised Land" were hits in 1964 and early 1965. Each of these songs had been composed in Springfield Prison. And then his career as a best selling recording artist came to an abrupt halt. He returned to England in January 1965 and appeared at the New York Folk Festival that June. The rest of the time, he was relegated to small clubs along America's byways.

After more than ten years, he left Chess Records in 1966 to record for Mercury. At the time, it looked like a good move. Mercury was a major recording company while Chess was still only a mid-sized independent operation. However, Berry was quickly lost in the maze of corporate politics and his stay at Mercury produced no hit singles or albums.

Through the end of the decade, Berry continued to alternate between tours of England and an occasional major appearance in the States or Canada. In May 1970, he returned to Chess Records. During a 1972 appearance at the Lanchester Arts Festival in England, an album was recorded "live," allegedly without his prior knowledge. From the material, "My Ding-A-Ling" was pulled to be issued as a single. The song had been around in one form or another for decades. The premise was simple, Berry sang a line using the phrase "my ding-a-ling" in a double-entendre context. The gleeful participation of the audience, combined with a relaxed atmosphere on the part of radio stations insofar as the lyrics were concerned, propelled the song to the top of the charts. "My Ding-A-Ling" was Berry's only Number One "pop" single, and the album from which it was taken, THE LONDON CHUCK BERRY SESSIONS, was the best selling album of his career. In the early days of 1973, "Reelin' and Rockin'," a "naughty" version of the song from the same London concert, became his last single to sell in appreciable numbers.

His second association with Chess was not a pleasant one for Berry. By this time, the company was a division of GRT and the business was being overseen by outsiders instead of its founders, Leonard and Phil Chess. At the same time, Berry was actively pursuing the past royalties due him from Chess. In the mid-1970s, GRT, a music conglomerate, went bankrupt and the Chess catalog was purchased by All Platinum, which also went bankrupt. The situation was very involved and presented "too much monkey business" to suit Berry. In 1979, he signed with Atco Records.

In the 1970s, America seemed to have forgiven Berry his past transgressions. He portrayed himself in the movie, "American Hot Wax," in

1978. A year later, he performed at the White House for President Carter. However, he was still fighting the American legal system. Barely a month after his presidential gig, he was sentenced to five months in jail for tax evasion. He served one hundred days.

The music-buying public was again quick to forgive him, and the 1980s saw Berry on the receiving end of numerous awards. In 1985, he accepted the Lifetime Achievement Award from the National Association of Recording Arts and Sciences during the Grammy Award Show. In 1986, he was among the first round of performers to be inducted into the Rock and Roll Hall of Fame. Later that year, Keith Richards, lead guitarist with the Rolling Stones and a longtime fan, put together a star-studded tribute to Berry in St. Louis to celebrate his sixtieth birthday. The show became the centerpiece in the documentary film "Hail, Hail Rock and Roll."

In 1988, Berry finally had his say with the publication of "Chuck Berry: The Autobiography." He had passed the manuscript around for nearly six years before Crown Publishers picked up the option. The book was remarkably candid, covering all aspects of his career, the good times as well as the bad.

The public had its first glimpse at the darker side of Chuck Berry in the early 1960s when he was tried and imprisoned. In 1972, other people were shocked when "My Ding-A-Ling" was released. Beginning in January 1988, Chuck Berry's private life was again on display. That January, a bench warrant was issued after he failed to appear in court on a charge of misdemeanor assault. In June, there was another bench warrant for failure to appear for booking. That same month, he was sued for $5 million in New York City by a woman who claimed he had struck her in the mouth. All of this was a preliminary action compared with the bombshell that was dropped in December 1989. In St. Louis, a female employee at Chuck Berry's Southern Air restaurant filed a suit claiming that he had secretly videotaped the ladies' rest room, tape recording more than two hundred women over the course of a year. Berry soon found himself facing a class action suit on behalf of all the women videotaped. About the same time, *High Society*, a soft-core adult magazine, published a series of photos of Berry with various women, all photographed in what appeared to have been hotel rooms, with everyone displaying full-frontal nudity.

On June 30, 1990, the Federal Drug Enforcement Agency raided Berry Park, apparently looking for evidence that Berry was trafficking in cocaine. The officers came up with sixty-two grams of marijuana and the videotapes allegedly showing the ladies' rest room. A month later, Berry surrendered to police on charges of possession of a controlled substance and child abuse—it turned out that three of the people on the videotapes were minors. Berry countersued St. Louis, claiming that the prosecutor was grandstanding as part of a campaign to win a close re-election bid. The child abuse charges were eventually dropped in November when Berry pleaded guilty to one count of misdemeanor marijuana possession. He was given a $5,000.00 fine and two years probation.

All of this would be a travesty if Berry had not already burned so many of his bridges as he traveled through his life. He was never cordial to those whom he did not know well. He could be a promoter's worst nightmare. He often performed in a perfunctory manner, giving fans a lackluster concert that bordered on unprofessional. More often than not, he acted as though the word "encore" was not in his vocabulary.

On the other hand, his accomplishments should not quickly be dismissed just because of the quirks in his personality. In the 1950s, along with a very small handful of rock 'n roll performers, including Little Richard and Fats Domino, Berry led the way in joining the white and black races when it came to music. He has been labeled the "poet laureate" or the "Shakespeare" of rock n' roll. Both titles are appropriate. More than any other rock 'n roll singer-songwriter of his era, Berry had a unique talent when it came to putting his thoughts into the form of a song and then transferring them onto a record. Each of his better songs was a complete picture of a slice of everyday life in middle America. While most of his songs were concerned with the joys of being a teenager, Berry's best work covered a wide range of universal subjects: love, money, fame, glory, loneliness, and rejection.

June 1958

JACKIE LEE COCHRAN
Jackie Lee Cochran could've been a contender. He had all the right qualities and a fair share of good breaks. Born February 5, 1941, in Dalton, Georgia, he grew up in Louisiana. In his early youth, he seemed to be mesmerized by the various musical styles indigenous to the area. He loved country, blues and Cajun tunes. More than just passive listening, Jackie wanted to perform. In May 1953, when he was fourteen, he traveled to Meridian, Mississippi, and wrangled an appearance on the "Jimmie Rodgers Memorial Day" show. By the mid-1950s, he was regularly performing rockabilly on the "Cowtown Jamboree" broadcast in Fort Worth, the "Big D Jamboree" in Dallas, and the "Louisiana Hayride" in Shreveport. In an attempt to land a recording contract, he traveled to Los Angeles and became a regular on Spade Cooley's television show. He was spotted by Decca Records, and in late 1956, he recorded "Ruby Pearl." It was his only release on the label. His youth and good looks led to a few cameo movie roles. He played a rock 'n roll singer in Marilyn Monroe's "Let's Make Love." He also appeared in the Disney film "Sancho." Through the late 1950s, he recorded for several small companies, including Sims ("Hip Shakin' Mama"), Spry ("Endless Love") and Jaguar ("I Wanna See You"). His 1958 recording of "I Want You," originally released on the Viv label, was picked up for reissue on ABC-Paramount. His song "Georgia Lee Brown" was featured in the movie "Exiles." By the late 1960s, he had virtually dropped out of show business when Ronnie Wiser rediscovered his older music and released three albums on his Rollin' Rock label. This led to his rise in popularity in England where he has a very large and loyal following. In 1985, taking time off from a triumphant tour of the United Kingdom, Cochran recorded some of his finest work.

JUN 1   The Irving Feld tour is denied a necessary permit to put on its "Big Show of 1958" in Washington, DC.
    Elvis Presley completes eight-weeks of basic training at Ft. Hood. After a two-week furlough in Memphis, he will return to Ft. Hood on June 16 to begin eight-weeks of advanced training as an armor crewman.
    Jimmie Rodgers makes his fourth appearance on television's the "Ed Sullivan Show."

JUN 2   En route home to St. Louis from his Topeka gig, Chuck Berry is arrested in St. Charles, Missouri, in the company of a French woman. It is alleged that he has molested the woman, a charge that both deny. A hearing is set for June 20, at which time Berry is charged with carrying a concealed weapon and an auto registration infraction. He is fined thirty dollars. During the hearing, the alleged molestation is not mentioned.

New Releases for the first week in June include "When" by the Kalin Twins on Decca; "Think It Over" by the Crickets on Brunswick; "Splish Splash" by Bobby Darin on Atco; Marvin Rainwater's "I Dig You Baby" on M-G-M; "Crazy Eyes For You" by Bobby Hamilton on Apt; The Dubs' "Be Sure" on Gone; "I Want You" by **Jackie Lee Cochran** on ABC-Paramount; Eddie Cochran's "Pretty Girl" on Liberty, "Ju-Judy" by the Casuals on Back Beat; and the reissue of Jimmy McCracklin's "I Need Your Loving" on Peacock.

JUN 4   Danny and the Juniors stop by the studios of "American Bandstand" to perform their hit "Rock and Roll Is Here to Stay."
    The Platters have been playing to sold-out houses around the world. Beginning today, they are booked for three performances in Casablanca, North Africa. In Casablanca, the group are greeted by 16,000 enthusiastic fans including the territorial governor.

JUN 6   The Playmates are slated for a two-week gig at Detroit's Cliche Club.

JUN 7   Paul Anka guests on Perry Como's television show on NBC-TV.
    On ABC-TV, "The Dick Clark Show" presents Jody Reynolds, Lee Andrews and the Hearts, and Tony Bennett.
    "High School Confidential" opens across the nation. The movie features a cameo singing performances by Jerry Lee Lewis who

also performs the title song.

EARLY JUNE

Mercury becomes the first major record company to discontinue the 78 r.p.m. record format.

New Releases for the second week in June include "Rama Lama Ding Dong" by the Edsels on Dub; "Hush Your Mouth" b/w "Dearest Darling" by Bo Diddley on Checker; Larry Williams' "Hootchy Koo" on Specialty; Thomas Wayne's "Tragedy" on Fernwood; "Drinking Wine" by Gene Simmons on Sun; "My Love Is a Charm" by the Shirelles on Decca; "I Got Fired" by the Chesterfields on Cub; and Boots Brown's "Cervesa" on RCA.

JUN 10 Back from England, Jerry Lee Lewis is booked into the Cafe de Paris in New York City. Much to Jerry Lee's dismay, the club will be without its famous "girl swimming in a champagne glass." The huge glass had recently shattered. The near-nude young lady inside received only minor cuts but went into shock from the experience.

Jimmie Rodgers makes his nightclub debut at Hollywood's Moulin Rouge.

JUN 11 Alan Freed receives yet another setback as a repercussion from the Boston riot. The New York Paramount Theater recently refused to allow Freed to hold his annual summer bash at their facility. Today, the Lowe's State Theater in the city, which Freed had booked for his July 4th rock 'n roll package, cancelled the date.

Jimmy Clanton appears on "American Bandstand."

JUN 13 The Apollo offers a strong lineup of rhythm and blues stars for the fans this week: the Coasters, Frankie Lymon, Lee Andrews and the Hearts, Robert and Johnny, Jerry Butler and the Impressions, the **Kodaks**, Ed Townsend, and the Storey Sisters.

In Washington, the Howard Theater's weekly revue offers the talents of Shirley and Lee, Huey Smith and the Clowns, and Buddy Johnson's orchestra with Ella Johnson.

JUN 14 On ABC-TV, "Dick Clark's Saturday Night" show features John D. Loudermilk singing "Yearbook." Also appearing are Frankie Avalon, the Royal Teens, and Toni Arden.

On NBC-TV, "The Perry Como Show" presents the Everly Brothers.

JUN 15 After continued poor attendance at his gig at the Cafe de Paris, Jerry Lee Lewis cancels the remainder of the two-week engagement.

Via a film clip made in Italy, the Platters perform "Twilight Time" on the "Ed Sullivan Show."

THE KODAKS

Jimmy Patrick's brother Charles was a member of the Monotones. Jimmy, himself, dreamed of singing with his own group. When the chance came, he joined with William Franklin, second tenor; Larry Davis, baritone; and William Miller, bass, to form a group named either the Supremes or the Kodoks. Whichever, they wanted to emulate Frankie Lymon's ultrahigh vocals with the Teenagers. To that end, they recruited fifteen-year old Pearl McKinnon. Then, just like Louis Lymon and the Teenchords, Pearl and the boys arrived at Bobby Robinson's record store looking to audition for the man who also owned Fury Records. In short order, Robinson had the group in the studio recording their first single "Teenager's Dream." When the record was issued, Robinson had used the name Kodaks on the label. Later singles also spelled the name Kodoks and Kodacs. Their second single, "Oh Gee Oh Gosh," is their best remembered recording. At this time, Davis and Franklin dropped out of the group for form the Sonics, and their places were filled by Richard Dixon and Harold Jenkins. Their final recording session produced their next two singles, "My Baby and Me" and "Runaround Baby," both released in 1958. Patrick was the next to leave the group, joining the Monotones. The Kodaks tried to continue as a quartet, but when Miller decided to leave, the group disbanded. Shortly after, Fury re-released "Teenager's Dream" as by Pearl and the Deltars. In 1959, the Kodaks re-formed with Jenkins, Miller, Renaldo Gamble, and Miller's wife, Jean. This group recorded one single each for the J&S and Wink labels before folding for good. Harold Jenkins joined Little Anthony and the Imperials. Pearl McKinnon took Frankie Lymon's place with the Teenagers in the early 1960s, sang with her own version of the Kodaks in the early 1970s, and with 2nd Verse in 1974.

MID-JUNE

SONNY BURGESS
If you thought the wild act on Sun Records was Elvis Presley, meet Sonny Burgess. On stage, he wore a flaming red suit and played a blazing red guitar. To top it off, he dyed his hair to match. Albert "Sonny" Burgess was born in 1931 in Newport, Arkansas. In 1955 after time in the Army, he formed the Pacers to perform country music. Two of the members went on to careers in music: Jack Nance (guitar, trumpet) traveled with the Jackson 5, and Russ Smith (drums) toured with Jerry Lee Lewis. As an Arkansas entertainer, it was natural that Burgess should gravitate to Memphis and Sun Records, the home to many locals, including Johnny Cash, another Arkansas native. Burgess arrived at Sun just after Elvis left for RCA Victor. Sun was desperately trying to come up with a replacement. Carl Perkins had "Blue Suede Shoes," then began a slow slide. Johnny Cash remained popular but he wasn't a rocker. Jerry Lee Lewis was still a year away from stardom. In early 1956, Sonny's first single was the torrid "Red Headed Woman" b/w "We Wanna Boogie." The mix was muddy and the band was raucous, just like they sounded in person. For the causal listener, this came across as drunken and rowdy. The record reportedly sold 100,000 copies although it never charted. It was almost a year before Burgess had a second session on Sun, and then "Restless" couldn't garner much airplay. More than a year passed before Burgess issued a pair of instrumentals, "Thunderbird" b/w "Itchy." By this time, Sun Records took so little notice of him that the names of the songs were reversed on the labels. Burgess moved on record for Memphis' Ara label where he issued a fine version of "Blues Stay Away from Me" in 1965. He was also on Arbur, Rolando, and Razorback. In the 1980s, he was welcomed by the Europeans. He still plays regularly around Little Rock, and is part of the popular Sun Session Band.

After Casablanca, locations visited by the Platters include Israel, Morocco, Germany, Holland, Monte Carlo, and Scandinavia. It is even reported that on their agenda includes the possibility of a performance in Moscow in late summer.

A rumor circulating through the music press has Elvis Presley signed to do four television appearances for Ed Sullivan in 1960, as soon as he has finished serving in the Army. (The performances never materialized.)

On tour at this time in New England are the Tune Weavers.

Jack Scott is making stops from New Orleans to Cleveland.

Patti McCabe, a member of the Poni-Tails, undergoes throat surgery in her hometown of Cleveland. The procedure is minor and she returns to work with the trio after a brief recuperation.

Fabian, Frankie Avalon's protege and Chancellor Records' stablemate, is currently on a trip to meet deejays in the East and Midwest.

JUN 16   Ricky Nelson performs at the Coliseum in Spokane. Tomorrow night he is booked to play Portland's Civic Auditorium (17).

New Releases for the third week in June include Elvis Presley's "Hard Headed Woman" b/w "Don't Ask Me Why" on RCA; Fats Domino's "Little Mary" on Imperial; "Right Behind You Baby" by Ray Smith on Sun; "Say You'll Be Mine" by the Aquatones on Fargo; "Tom Foolery" by the Monotones on Argo; "I Believe In You" by Robert and Johnny on Old Town; "There Stands My Love" by the Tune Weavers on Casa Grande; and "Nursery Rock" by Jan and Joe (Jones) on Vee-Jay. Also new this week is "I'm In Love" on Chancellor, the first release from Fabian, Philadelphia's latest teenager to bid for stardom.

JUN 19   Fabian is interviewed, but does not perform, on "American Bandstand."

Johnny Cash and **Sonny Burgess** open a West Coast road trip with a show in the Rolling Hills Ballroom, Riverside, California. The tour continues through California with performances in San Diego (20), Los Angeles (21-22), and Eureka (24). In Oregon, they play Klamath Falls (25), Coquille (26) and Portland (27). On June 28-29, Cash and Burgess appear in Seattle. Reports from the field indicate that each show is a major success. (See also JUL 1.)

Jimmie Rodgers opens for a week at the Casino Royal, 14th and H Streets, in Washington.

On this date, all members of the Del Vikings are finally out of the Air Force. Mercury Records announces that they are set to record a single and an album immediately with former lead singer Kripp Johnson. They are also scheduled for a series of personal appearances.

Ricky Nelson's show packs Vancouver's Exhibition Gardens tonight.

JUN 20   Tommy Leonetti begins a two-week run at the Muehlebach

Club in Kansas City.

The new show at the Howard Theater in Washington is headlined by Big Maybelle. Also appearing are Dion and the Belmonts, the **Dells**, and the Storey Sisters.

Frankie Avalon is booked for five shows in three days at the Civic Auditorium in Honolulu. Also on the bill of the "7th Show of Stars" are Teddy Randazzo, the Hi-Fives, the Six Teens, Robin Luke, and the Drifters.

JUN 21   In Atlantic City, Dick Clark has the first remote broadcast of his Saturday night television show. On the show, Danny and the Juniors sing "At The Hop." Other performers are Lou Monte, Janis Harper, and Bill Doggett, who plays "Blip Blop."

JUN 22   "The Ed Sullivan Show" offers at Tenth Anniversary filmed retrospective that includes a portion of Elvis Presley's previous appearances.

New Releases for the fourth week in June include Jerry Lee Lewis' "The Return of Jerry Lee" on Sun; "Poor Little Fool" by Ricky Nelson on Imperial; "Susie Darlin'" by Robin Luke on Dot; Jerry Byrne's "Lights Out" on Specialty; "You Cheated" by the Shields on Tender; Little Willie John's "Let's Rock While the Rockin's Good" on King; Glenn Glenn's "Laurie Lee" on Era; and Charlie Feathers' "Jungle Fever" on Kay. In addition, there are two releases from ABC-Paramount: "Born Too Late" by the Poni-Tails and "Midnight" by Paul Anka; two from Decca: "Ring-a My Phone" by Brenda Lee and "Girl On My Mind," a two-year old recording by Buddy Holly; and, finally, another version of the rollicking "Over and Over" by Thurston Harris on Aladdin.

JUN 26   "American Bandstand" features Chuck and Betty, the new duo from Decca Records.

JUN 27   At the Apollo Theater in New York, Roy Hamilton heads a show that includes the Clovers, Dion and the Belmonts, and Bobby Freeman.

JUN 28   This week's "Dick Clark Show" is headlined by Paul Anka, who is just back from a State Department-sponsored trip to the Soviet Union.

JUN 30   Alan Freed's new television show debuts in New York City. Making appearances are Chuck Berry and the Four Lads. The show is seen locally on WARD-TV from 5:00 to 6:00 p.m., Monday through Friday.

Fabian guests on "American Bandstand." As soon as he is through, he catches a flight to Albany, New York, to appear on...

"The Tower of Talent" awards show at Hughes Stadium in Albany. The benefit show grosses $10,000 while presenting the Everly Brothers, Jack Scott, Connie Francis, Fabian, the Lane

THE DELLS
If longevity counts, the Dells have certainly secured a permanent place in music history. They began in 1953 as students at Thornton High in Harvey, Illinois, near Chicago, and are still performing and recording into the 1990s. The original members were Johnny Funches, lead tenor; Marvin Junior, first tenor; Verne Allison, second tenor; Michael McGill, baritone; and Charles Barksdale, bass. After much rehearsal, the El Rays, as they called themselves, went to Chicago with hopes of recording for Chess Records. In May 1954, "Darling I Know" appeared on the Checker subsidiary. The single fared poorly and was the El Rays only release. The young men returned to Harvey and devoted a year to becoming more professional. In 1955, the group returned to Chicago and successfully auditioned for Vee-Jay Records. Their name was changed to the Dells for their first Vee-Jay release, "Tell the World." The year of rehearsal in Harvey had paid off in a cohesive, richly textured harmony. In January 1956, "Dreams of Contentment" was heard in areas outside of the Great Lakes. However, this newfound popularity was lost on the Dells. Seeing little future in performing, the group was on the verge of breaking up. Barksdale left to join the Moonglows, and he was replaced by Calvin Carter for what most thought would be the Dells' final session. In August 1956, "Oh, What a Nite" was released, and it became a huge R&B hit. With this dramatic increase in the Dells' popularity, Barksdale returned, and the Dells remained a unit until 1958. It was then that McGill was severely injured in an auto accident. The group had gone more than a year without a hit. While Vee-Jay continued to release singles by the Dells, the group was spent the next two years backing vocalists such as Dee Clark, Dinah Washington, and Jerry Butler.

Brothers, Rosemary June, Dakota Staton, Ersel Hickey, the Jive Bombers, the Kalin Twins, Annette, Johnny Janis, and Dickey Doo and the Don'ts.

LATE JUNE

Jimmie Rodgers opens for two weeks in the Venetian Room of the Fairmont Hotel in San Francisco.

Carl Perkins has an engagement in Myrtle Beach, as the South Carolina "Beach Music" scene begins to become an important East Coast venue.

The Upsetters, featuring pianist Lee Diamond, are backing Little Willie John on his current tour. The Upsetters previously worked with Little Richard.

THE TOP ROCK 'N ROLL RECORDS FOR JUNE 1958

1. Purple People Eater - Sheb Wooley
2. All I Have To Do Is Dream/Claudette - The Everly Brothers
3. Yakety Yak - The Coasters
4. Witch Doctor - David Seville
5. Secretly/Make Me A Miracle - Jimmie Rodgers
6. Jennie Lee - Jan and Arnie
7. Do You Want To Dance - Bobby Freeman
8. Endless Sleep - Jody Reynolds
9. Twilight Time - The Platters
10. Big Man - The Four Preps
11. Johnny B. Goode - Chuck Berry
12. Wear My Ring Around Your Neck - Elvis Presley
13. Oh Lonesome Me - Don Gibson
14. Rumble - Link Wray and His Ray Men
15. High School Confidential - Jerry Lee Lewis
16. For Your Love - Ed Townsend
17. Guess Things Happen That Way - Johnny Cash
18. What Am I Living For/Hang Up My Rock and Roll Shoes - Chuck Willis
19. No Chemise, Please - Gerry Granahan
20. Leroy/My True Love - Jack Scott
21. For Your Precious Love - The Impressions featuring Jerry Butler
22. El Rancho Rock - The Champs
23. You - The Aquatones
24. Oh My Soul/True Fine Mama - Little Richard
25. Don't Go Home - The Playmates
26. I Wonder Why - Dion and the Belmonts
27. Splish Splash - Bobby Darin
28. To Be Loved - Jackie Wilson
29. Let The Bells Keep Ringing/Crazy Love - Paul Anka
30. When - The Kalin Twins
31. (It's Been a Long Time) Pretty Baby - Gino and Gina
32. Rave On - Buddy Holly

33. I'm Sorry I Made You Cry - Connie Francis
34. Talk To Me, Talk To Me - Little Willie John
35. Willie and the Hand Jive - Johnny Otis
36. Hard Headed Woman - Elvis Presley
37. I Love You So - The Chantels
38. Tequila - The Champs
39. Try the Impossible - Lee Andrews and the Hearts
40. Just Married - Marty Robbins
41. Skinny Minnie - Bill Haley and His Comets
42. Dottie - Danny and the Juniors
43. Rebel Rouser - Duane Eddy
44. Flip Top Box/Nee Nee Na Na Na Na Nu Nu - Dicky Doo
    and the Don'ts
45. Bewildered - Mickey and Sylvia
46. Come What May - Clyde McPhatter
47. One Summer Night - The Danleers
48. You're Making a Mistake - The Platters
49. Moonlight Bay - The Drifters
50. Poor Little Fool - Ricky Nelson

Also on the "pop" charts:
Patricia - Perez Prado
Cha Hua Hua - The Pets

June 1958
ARTISTS OF THE MONTH

DAVID SEVILLE and SHEB WOOLEY

David Seville

On the surface, David Seville and Sheb Wooley would appear to have little in common other than having hit records with novelty songs. In truth, both men were driven professionally by the same force: to entertain people with humor.

Seville, whose real name was Ross Bagdasarian, was born on January 27, 1919, in Fresno, California. His parents were Armenian grape farmers; and his cousin was the famed playwright, William Saroyan. In 1939, while in New York appearing in Saroyan's play "The Time of Your Life," Bagdasarian teamed with Saroyan to compose the song "Come On-A My House" which was based on an old Armenian folk song.

In 1950, Saroyan used "Come On-A My House" in his Broadway play, "The Son." A year later, Rosemary Clooney's version of the song sold a million copies. In the meantime, Seville had served four years in the Air Force. He was stationed for a time in Seville, Spain, before returning to Fresno and the grape farm. Riding the coattails of the success of "Come On-A My House," Bagdasarian and his family moved to Los Angeles so he could pursue a career in music. At this time, the music business was beginning to shift from a dominant base in New York City to a division in operations between New York and Hollywood. In 1954,

273

Dean Martin recorded Bagdasarian's "Hey Brother, Pour The Wine," and the song did reasonably well. That same year, Bagdasarian released his own first single, "Lazy Lovers" b/w "One Finger Waltz" on Mercury, his only release on the label.

He landed a recording contract with Liberty Records in 1955. Soon, he was releasing humorous mini-hits as Alfi and Harry, including "The Trouble With Harry." This single, based on the movie of the same name, poked fun at other records. In 1956, Bagdasarian began using the name David Seville, a name partly recalled from his days in Spain. The most interesting single from this period was "Camel Rock," a whistling instrumental. The single's flip side, "Gotta Get To Your House," was an instrumental featuring a bouncy piano with whispered asides ("gotta get to your house," "gotta get to your eyes"). The intent of song became more confusing as the record progressed.

In the 1950s, Seville was able to parlay his moderate recording success into a brief film career. He had cameo roles in "Stalag 17," "Rear Window," "Viva Zapata," and "The Proud and the Profane," among others.

Seville's first real recording success was "Witch Doctor," which featured more of Seville's "singing" voice than his previous singles. In addition, Seville cleverly overdubbed his own voice with the sped-up voice of the witch doctor. Reportedly, it took Seville many days in the studio to complete the song. However, after Liberty executives heard it, they had copies on the street within twenty-four hours. The record sold more than a million copies during the early summer of 1958.

Seville issued two singles after "Witch Doctor." Neither was a hit, but each contained elements he would use again. Seville repeated the basic premise of "The Bird On My Head" often: the raspy, rinky-tink band; the cute, answering voice created by speeding up the tape recorder while slowly singing the lyrics; and the hapless character portrayed by Seville in a normal voice. "Judy" was another semi-instrumental with slightly humorous asides. This single presented a musical theme and an orchestration similar to the backing used on his next big hit.

Seville reasoned that a Christmas theme incorporating the same techniques he had used on "Witch Doctor" and "Bird On My Head" offered possibilities. Through the fall of 1958 he worked with various combinations of tape speed and vocal gimmicks. Finally, after four painstaking attempts, he came up with "The Christmas Song." Using the fast-tape device, he had created voices that reminded him of chipmunks. Seville wrote a brief, two-minute play about three chipmunks trying to sing a sweet Christmas song. In naming the chipmunks, he used the three heads of Liberty Records: Simon (Waronker), Theodore (Keep), and Alvin (Bonnett). The protagonist in the song was Alvin, a cantankerous, mischievous little imp of a chipmunk.

"The Chipmunk Song" became the fastest selling single in the history of records, up to that time. It sold three and a half million copies during the first five weeks it was in circulation, and more than seven million over the next few years. In part, the enormous acceptance of the Chipmunks must be attributed to Seville's expert technical production. Throughout the song, he carried on a four-part conversation with a tape recorder. He reacted with exasperation to Alvin's antics and created the credible illusion that the Chipmunks were real.

The characters of the Chipmunks also took on a life of their own. There were the expected follow-up releases, "Alvin's Harmonica," "Ragtime Cowboy Joe," and "Alvin for President." In addition, "The Chipmunk Song" was re-released year after year at Christmas time. In 1964, the Chipmunks even had a hit album when they sang songs by the Beatles.

After such an overwhelming success with a musical gimmick, many entertainers would have found themselves in a rut from which they could not escape. Not Seville. He enjoyed the characters he had created, and he was determined to breathe life into them after their days as recording artists were over. The Chipmunks were ready-made for a television series. They went to that medium in 1961 with "The Alvin Show" on CBS-TV. This was a time when the Jetsons, the Flintstones, and Yogi Bear each had a weekly television series. "The Alvin Show" ran in prime time until 1968. In 1983, the format was revamped to fill a slot in the Saturday morning array of children's cartoon shows.

Seville did not live to see his chipmunk creations renew their popularity. He died of a heart attack on February 5, 1972, at his home in Beverly Hills. In the early 1980s, the Chipmunks were revived by his son, Ross Bagdasarian, Jr. In this latest incarnation, they released four albums in the early 1980s. CHIPMUNK PUNK and CHIPMUNK ROCK featured "chipmunk" versions of some of the hits of the day, including "Betty Davis Eyes," "You May Be Right" and "Refugee." URBAN CHIPMUNK (a takeoff on the movie title "Urban Cowboy") had the Chipmunks singing country music. This was followed by THE CHIPMUNKS GO TO HOLLYWOOD. In 1992, they were back on the charts with ALVIN AND THE CHIPMUNKS IN LOW PLACES. This was another country compilation that featured vocal help from several top country singers including Billy Ray Cyrus, Charlie Daniels, Alan Jackson, Waylon Jennings, Aaron Tippin, and Tammy Wynette.

* * * * * * * *

Shelby "Sheb" Wooley was born April 10, 1921, in Erick, Oklahoma, just fourteen years after Indian Territory achieved statehood and took on its new name. Wooley was part Cherokee, and a skilled horseman who participated in rodeos as a teenager. At age eleven, he was drawn to music, trading a shotgun for a neighbor's guitar. His father played fiddle, and young Shelby proved to have a knack for songwriting. The younger Wooley formed a high school band calling themselves the Plainview Melody Boys. Soon, they had a radio program over KASA in Elk City.

Wooley was married by the time he was nineteen. To support his family during World War II, he found steady employment in a Long Beach, California, shipyard. After the War, Wooley decided to try to appear on the "Grand Ole Opry," so he and his family moved to Nashville in 1946. His first year in town was one of near starvation. He took what jobs were offered, including that of gardener. One of his clients was Eddy

Arnold, an up-and-coming singer at the time who offered encouragement.

Wooley's perseverance paid off, and he landed the 4:45 to 5:00 a.m. spot on WLAC-radio, one of Nashville's 50,000-watt stations. This led to a more lucrative, afternoon spot on WSM-radio, the home station for the "Grand Ole Opry."

In 1948, he became one of the first singers to record in Nashville when he laid down a few songs for Bullet Records, a new company founded by Jim Bullitt, a deejay on WSM. Wooley's first release was "Oklahoma Honky Tonk Gal" b/w "I Can Live On Without You."

He transferred his base of operations to Fort Worth in 1949, where he had another fifteen-minute radio show. Once again he formed a band, named the Calumet Indians after the show's advertising sponsor, Calumet Baking Powder. The Fort Worth show was leased to a dozen other radio stations and became popular throughout the Southwest. This insured continued bookings for the Calumet Indians. The increased popularity led to a recording contract with Bluebonnet Records. In turn, this led to his longtime association with M-G-M Records. At that time, M-G-M was having its first success in country music with Hank Williams.

Sheb Wooley

In 1950, Wooley moved to Hollywood. After a lean year, his natural abilities on horseback brought him to the attention of the movie companies. Over the next twenty years, he appeared in nearly fifty motion pictures, beginning with the Erroll Flynn opus "Rocky Mountain." His list of movie credits include some of the most prestigious of the period: "High Noon," "Rio Bravo," and "Giant."

He also continued writing songs for others. Hank Snow had a hit with "When Mexican Joe Met Jole Blon," and Teresa Brewer did well with "Too Young To Tango." Wooley's records for M-G-M remained firmly rooted in the country sounds of Tex Williams and Hank Thompson. He did have a minor "pop" hit with "Are You Satisfied" in 1955. The song briefly crossed over from country by using a female chorus and a moderately heavy beat from the drums and bass.

In 1958, Wooley composed "Purple People Eater," a spoof on the era of Sputnik and unidentified flying objects (UFOs). Wooley's funny lyrics were punctuated with short "quotes" from a squeaky-voiced spaceman. This effect was achieved by using the fast-tape technique pioneered by David Seville. The song became an immediate hit, quickly selling more than a million copies. Wooley recorded a seasonal follow-up, "Santa and the Purple People Eater," but its performance was lackluster.

J.P. Richardson, who would soon achieve fame as the Big Bopper, combined the characters in the recordings by Wooley and Seville to come up with "The Purple Eater Meets the Witch Doctor." Richardson's version appeared on the flip side of "Chantilly Lace" and was soon forgotten. Joe South, who would gain fame in 1969 and 1970 with "The Games People Play" and "Walk A Mile In My Shoes," had some success with Richardson's song on NRC.

In 1959, Wooley had another crossover hit with "Sweet Chile," a confused mixture of Cajun lyrics, a Ray Conniff-style chorus and a hurried delivery. That same year, he tried to use the "Purple People Eater" formula again in "Pigmy Love," but it received little attention. Wooley continued with his acting through this time, having landed a regular role as Pete Nolan in the television series "Rawhide." Wooley worked in the series from 1958 through 1963. In its early days, the show co-starred a young Clint Eastwood.

For several years, Wooley recorded singles that had potential, including "Pin Striped, Skin Tight, Purple Peddle Pushers" in 1961. A year later, he had one final hit single under his own name with the wild and wooly "That's My Pa." In 1963, he composed the theme song for the movie "Hootenanny Hoot" in which he had a cameo role.

About this time, Wooley's comedic personality manifested itself in a completely new character, the inebriated Ben Colder. As Colder, Wooley parodied many of the hit country songs from 1962 through 1968. He would take the original song's music and interpose his own rib-tickling lyrics. Some of his more successful spoofs were "Don't Go Near the Eskimos" (after Rex Allen's "Don't Go Near the Indians"), "Detroit City No. 2" (after the Bobby Bare song), "Still No. 2" (from Bill Anderson's crossover hit), "Almost Persuaded No. 2" (after the record by David Houston), and "Harper Valley P.T.A., Later That Same Day" (based on Jeannie C. Riley's smash). In all, Ben Colder issued nineteen albums of such material as well as appearing on many television shows. In 1964, Wooley received acclaim as the Country Music Association's Comedian of the Year. "Almost Persuaded No. 2" was even nominated for a 1966 Grammy.

Wooley's quirky songwriting and successful recording resume made him a natural for the original cast of "Hee Haw," the successful syndicated television series that began in 1969. Wooley also wrote the "Hee Haw" theme song.

After a few years of success on "Hee Haw," Wooley left the show to concentrate on writing and recording his songs as well as publishing movie scrips. He also founded his own Nashville recording studio, The Music Mill. After the Ben Colder fad cooled, Wooley remained with M-G-M, recording country songs under his own name with moderate success. In 1972, one of his last singles for the label was a version of Lloyd Price's hit "Personality." It proved to be a mismatch between the song's intent and Wooley's country delivery. In 1981, Wooley was recording for Songbird Records, a small Nashville Company. A single from that year, "Jackhammer Man," had a fine basic idea—a girl trying to kiss a man who works as a jackhammer operator—but the result fell short of the mark. He has remained a popular draw on the fair and club circuits throughout the years.

In an interview, Wooley summed up his philosophy of life: "Success lies in three things—dreams, hard work, and faith. You've got to dream the dreams, do the hard work, and have the faith. Success can't resist that kind of formula."

Wooley might have added that a person needs to keep their sense of humor. David Seville would have agreed with that.

July 1958

THE BIG BOPPER

Jay Perry Richardson was born in Sabine Pass, Texas, on October 24, 1930 (although early press releases said 1934 and 1935). Soon after, his family relocated to nearby Beaumont. After high school graduation, he served the Army. Returning to Beaumont, he attended Lamar College, married, and fathered a daughter. While in college, he began working as a deejay at KTRM. With the advent of rock 'n roll, his local popularity skyrocketed when he began billing himself as the Big Bopper. In May 1957, he broke a record for continuous broadcasting, staying on the air 122 hours and eight minutes. That same year, he began sending his songs to a Mercury Records talent scout. His first two singles, "Beggar to a King" and "Teenage Moon," both issued as by Jape Richardson, failed to create a stir. He composed a novelty tune combining two previous hits into "The Purple People Eater Meets the Witch Doctor." Unable to interest Mercury, he released his version on D Records as by the Big Bopper, backed by "Chantilly Lace," which parodied his radio persona. Joe South covered "The Purple People Eater Meets the Witch Doctor" for N.R.C Records of Atlanta, and had a mid-sized hit in July 1958. This encouraged Mercury to release the Big Bopper's record. Deejays began flipping the single and playing "Chantilly Lace," which sold a million copies. The second Big Bopper single, "The Big Bopper's Wedding" b/w "Little Red Riding Hood," was released in November and began selling well. In January 1959, he embarked on tour featuring Buddy Holly, Ritchie Valens, and Dion and the Belmonts. After crisscrossing the upper Midwest, the tour played Clear Lake, Iowa. Following the show, Holly, Valens and Richardson left from Mason City on a chartered plane. In a driving snow storm, the plane crashed shortly after takeoff, and all aboard were killed.

JUL 1   Johnny Cash's West Coast tour winds down with a one-night stand in Vancouver.

New Releases for the first week in July include two from Mercury: "One Summer Night" by the Danleers and "Chantilly Lace" by the **Big Bopper**; and two from Challenge: "How The Time Flies" by Jerry Wallace and "Three Months to Kill" by Huelyn Duvall. There are also two versions of "Early In The Morning:" by Buddy Holly on Coral and by the Rinky-Dinks on Atco. Other releases this week are "Beautiful Delilah" by Chuck Berry on Chess; "Stupid Cupid" by Connie Francis on M-G-M; "By the Light of the Silvery Moon" by Jimmy Bowen on Roulette; "Betty Lou Got a New Pair of Shoes" by Bobby Freeman on Josie; "The Freeze" by Tony and Joe on Dore; "Lean Jean" by Bill Haley and His Comets on Decca; the Fidelities' "Memories of You" on Baton; Gene Vincent's "Rocky Road Blues" on Capitol; "Chain of Love" by Bob and Earl on Class; and "Weekend" by the Kingsmen on East-West. Also out is a release from future superstar Kenny Rogers, "For You Alone" on Carlton. Finally, Joe South's NRC recording captures a double-shot of hot novelty action: "The Purple People Eater Meets The Witch Doctor."

JUL 2   "King Creole," Elvis Presley's fourth movie, begins its theatrical run.

JUL 4   Buddy Holly and the Crickets, sharing the stage with Tommy Allsup's Western Swing Band, begin a tour of the Upper Midwest with a show in Angola, Indiana. Other dates include Spring Valley, Illinois (5); Muskegon, Michigan (6); Waterloo (8), Decorah (9), and Delaware (10), Iowa; Duluth (11); and Wausau (12) and Rheinlander (13), Wisconsin.

Tommy Leonetti performs for two-weeks at the Cliche Club in Detroit.

The Applejacks return to Andy's Log Cabin in Philadelphia.

Headlining this Independence Day at the Howard Theater in Washington, and the rest of week, is Roy Hamilton who is ably assisted by the Clovers, Ketty Lester and Bobby Freeman.

JUL 5   Johnny Cash makes an appearance on Dick Clark's Saturday night show on ABC-TV. Also on the show are the Upbeats and Jan and Arnie performing "Jennie Lee."

On NBC-TV's "The Perry Como Show," Sheb Wooley performs "Purple People Eater."

Carl Perkins wraps up his stand at Myrtle Beach's Pavilion. He is off to Alaska for two weeks as the first rock 'n roller to visit the 49th state.

The Newport Jazz Festival, Newport, Rhode Island, offers a special "Blues in the Night" show featuring Joe Turner, Muddy Waters, Big Maybelle, Ray Charles, and Chuck Berry. Berry's rendition of "Sweet Little Sixteen" will become part of the 1960 documentary film "Jazz On A Summer's Day." The entire Ray Charles performance was recorded by Atlantic Records for album release as RAY CHARLES IN NEWPORT. Muddy Waters' appearance was likewise issued by Chess Records as MUDDY WATERS AT NEWPORT.

New Releases for the second week in July include "It's Only Make Believe" by Conway Twitty on M-G-M; Eddie Fontaine's "Nothin' Shakin'" on Sunbeam; "Win Your Love For Me" by Sam Cooke on Keen; "Harvey's Got a Girlfriend" by the Royal Teens on ABC-Paramount; "Levi Jacket" by Carl Perkins on Columbia; "Everlasting Love" by Barbara Pittman on Phillips International; the Flamingos' "Where Did Mary Go" on Decca; and two versions of "Prisoner's Song" the original by Warren Smith on Nasco and the cover by Joe Jones on Roulette.

JUL 12 **Joe South** guests on the "The Dick Clark Show" to plug his version of "The Purple People Eater Meets the Witch Doctor." Also appearing are David Seville, Jerry Butler and the Impressions, Jimmy Clanton, Don Gibson, and Lillian Briggs.

JUL 13 The Four Preps make a return engagement on CBS-TV's "Ed Sullivan Show."

JUL 14 The Four Mints, back from a successful tour of the clubs in Las Vegas, open in the Domino Lounge of the Imperial Hotel in their hometown of Atlanta.

New Releases for the third week in July include multiple releases from several record companies. There are two from M-G-M: "It's All In The Game" by Tommy Edwards and "You Thrill Me" by Mark Dinning; three from Roulette: "Are You Really Mine" by Jimmie Rodgers, "Somebody Touched Me" by Buddy Knox, and "My Broken Heart" by the Teenagers; two from End: "Tears On My Pillow" by the Imperials and "Money" by the Miracles; two from Epic: "Summertime, Summertime" by the Jamies and Ersel Hickey's "Goin' Down That Road;" two from Jamie: Sanford Clark's "Still As The Night" and "Look at Me" by the Sharps; In addition, there are two versions of "You Cheated"—the original by the Slades on Domino and a cover by the Del Vikings on Mercury. Other releases this week include Eddie Cochran's "Summertime Blues" on Liberty; Dale Hawkins' "La Doo Dah Dah" on Checker; "Pretty Baby" by the Addrisi Brothers on Brad; "Why Do I" by Lee Andrews and the Hearts on United Artists; Jo Ann Campbell's "I Really Really Love You" on Gone; Ray Peterson's "My Blue Eyed Baby" on RCA; and the Five Satins' "A Night

JOE SOUTH

Joe South was one of the musicians spawned by Atlanta's active rock 'n roll underground. Others included Jerry Reed and Ray Stevens. South was born in Atlanta, February 28, 1940. By his teens he was proficient on guitar and was playing in a country band. In 1956, Bill Lowery put together Stars Records to issue the original version of "Young Love" by the song's composer, Ric Cartey (Jerry Reed played in Cartey's band, the Jiva-Tones). Cartey's version of "Young Love" was vastly overshadowed by Sonny James and Tab Hunter, but the experience taught Lowery much about the business side of the recording industry. Two years later, he founded the National Recording Company (NRC Records), and his first release was Paul Peek's "Sweet Skinny Jenny," featuring South and Reed on guitar and Stevens on piano. Lowery then came across the Big Boppers' song "The Purple People Eater Meets the Witch Doctor." At the time, the Big Bopper's version was available only on the minuscule D label, so Lowery issued a version on NRC by Joe South. The record caught on from Texas to the Carolinas, but was quickly overtaken when the Big Bopper's version became available on Mercury Records. South released two more singles on NRC, "One Fool To Another" and "I'm Snowed." Neither sold in appreciable numbers. In 1961, he was recording for Fairlane Records, with three singles released, including "You're the Reason," another good seller in southern states. At the time, South was a deejay in Atlanta who was becoming known in the area for his songwriting. His "Untie Me" became the first hit for the Tams, and he played guitar on many of the Tams' sessions at Fame Studios in Muscle Shoals. His stay at Fairlane was followed by singles on Alwood, M-G-M, Apt and Columbia through 1967. In 1968, he signed with Capitol Records, beginning a productive, six-year association with the label.

To Remember" on Ember. Out this week is "The Gorilla" on Contender by Bert Convy, a former member of the Cheers and a popular television game show host beginning in the 1980s.

MID-JULY

Fans are turned away at the door as Paul Anka plays Atlantic City's Steel Pier.

It is announced that Alan Freed's new television show will be syndicated coast to coast by means of video tape. Thus far, artists who have stopped by Freed's daily show include Frankie Avalon, Clyde McPhatter, Danny and the Juniors, the Royal Teens, Jan and Arnie, Connie Francis, the Poni-Tails, Bobby Freeman, Gerry Granahan, Ed Townsend, the Monotones, the **Elegants**, the Kalin Twins, LaVern Baker, Jack Scott, the Chantels, and Dicky Doo and the Don'ts.

George Treadwell, the Drifters' manager and the owner of the group's name, fires all the personnel and replaces them with the members of the Five Crowns to fulfill contracted engagements for the next year. The Drifters will not enter the studio again until March 1959.

RCA Victor announces a four-track audio tape cartridge system to be introduced shortly.

JUL 18   In Wildwood, New Jersey, Sam Cooke begins a week at Club Bolero.

Bill Doggett and his combo layover for a two-week stay at the Flame Lounge in Detroit.

This week's offering at the Howard Theater in Washington stars Illinois Jacquet along with the Monotones and Jerry Butler and the Impressions.

In Honolulu at the Civic Auditorium, the "Eighth Show of Stars" features the Everly Brothers, Glenn Glenn, the Hollywood Flames, the Four Preps, Bobby Day, Bob and Earl, Robin Luke, and the Drifters.

JUL 19   Jerry Lee Lewis makes an appearance on KABC's "Country America" show in Los Angeles.

ABC-TV's Saturday night "Dick Clark Show" originates from Miami Beach. Guests include Duane Eddy, Bobby Darin, Jack Scott, and George Hamilton IV, who sings "I Know Where I'm Going."

Over on NBC-TV, Jimmie Rodgers stops by "The Perry Como Show."

In New York City, Alan Freed files a voluntary petition for bankruptcy citing liabilities of $51,000, mostly in cancelled bookings from his recent "Big Beat" tour. His assets are listed as zero.

JUL 21   On "American Bandstand," Dale Hawkins romps through "La-Do-Dada."

New Releases for the fourth week in July are "Bird Dog" b/w "Devoted

---

THE ELEGANTS

The Elegants hold the dubious distinction of being one of only four recording acts during the Golden Age of Rock 'n Roll to have their only charted record reach Number One. For a group to sell a million copies of their first single and have their second single not sell enough to brush the bottom of the charts is almost unheard of. The story begins in 1956, when Vito Picone (tenor) and Carmen Romano (baritone) were members of the Crescents from Staten Island. After a year without success, in January 1957, they joined three buddies to form another street corner group, the Elegants. With Picone, lead; Arthur Venosa, first tenor; Frank Fardogno (also spelled Tardogno), second tenor; Romano, baritone; and James Moschella, bass, the boys practiced for two months before making the rounds of talent shows, church socials, and the like. At St. Ann's Church in Staten Island, the Elegants were spotted by a woman who was a personal manager to other artists. She liked what she saw, and put the boys on a full rehearsal schedule for the next year. When she felt they were ready, she brought the boys to several record companies, but it still took three months before Hull Records offered them a session. Their only Hull release was "Little Boy Blue," and it dropped from sight quickly. The group rebounded by signing with Apt, a subsidiary of ABC-Paramount Records. Their first Apt release was "Little Star," a bastardization of Mozart's "Twinkle Little Star." The record tore up the charts, jumping to the top in a few weeks. "Please Believe Me" was released in September, and though the song was possibly even better than "Little Star," it languished on dealer's shelves. The group continued to release material: "Goodnight" on Apt and "Tiny Cloud" on ABC-Paramount. In 1960, they were briefly on United Artists. By this time the Elegants were only a summertime memory.

To You" by the Everly Brothers on Cadence; the Champs' "Chariot Rock" on Challenge; "No One Knows" by Dion and the Belmonts on Laurie; "Down the Aisle of Love" by the Quin-Tones on Hunt; Johnny Cash's "The Ways of a Woman in Love" on Sun; "Fire of Love" by Jody Reynolds on Demon; the Tune Rockers' "Green Mosquito" on United Artists; three from Atlantic: Ray Charles' "My Bonnie," Chuck Willis' "My Life," and the Bobbettes' "The Dream;" "Voodoo Eyes" by the Silhouettes on Ember; "Nervous" by Gene Summers on Jan; two on Mercury: "She Belongs to Me" by Gino and Gina and "Little Girl Step This Way" by **Narvel Felts**; "It's You I Love" by Mickey and Sylvia on Vik; "Ko Ko Joe" by Don and Dewey on Specialty; Don Deal's "A Chance Is All I Ask" on Era; Bill Craddock's "Lulu Lee" on Date; "If You Try" by the Chantels on End; Scott Engel's "Charley Bop" on Orbit; "This Is The End" by the Isley Brothers on Cindy; and three from Roulette: "One Day of the Year" by the Heartbeats, "She's So Fine" by the Cleftones, and "The Only Way To Love You" by Frankie Lymon. Finally, the novelty "Real Wild Child" by Ivan is released on Coral. Ivan is Jerry Allison of the Crickets.

JUL 24 Duane Eddy mimics to his recordings of "Moovin' 'N Groovin'" and "Rebel Rouser" on "American Bandstand."

JUL 25 Smiley Lewis performs for the hometown patrons at the High Hat in New Orleans for the next three days.
Washington's Howard Theater welcomes LaVern Baker, Bobby Darin, the Kodaks, Lee Andrews and the Hearts, and Solomon Burke for the week.

JUL 26 The Kalin Twins make an appearance on "The Perry Como Show" on NBC-TV.
"The Dick Clark Show" presents Tony and Joe singing "The Freeze" and Connie Francis singing "Carolina Moon." Also on tonight's bill are the Olympics and Bill Justis.

JUL 27 Sheb Wooley sings "Purple People Eater" on "The Ed Sullivan Show."

THE TOP ROCK 'N ROLL RECORDS FOR JULY 1958

1. Yakety Yak - The Coasters
2. Hard Headed Woman/Don't Ask Me Why - Elvis Presley
3. Poor Little Fool - Ricky Nelson
4. Purple People Eater - Sheb Wooley
5. Splish Splash - Bobby Darin
6. Rebel Rouser - Duane Eddy
7. Endless Sleep - Jody Reynolds
8. Secretly - Jimmie Rodgers
9. For Your Precious Love - The Impressions featuring Jerry Butler
10. All I Have To Do Is Dream - The Everly Brothers
11. Do You Want To Dance - Bobby Freeman

NARVEL FELTS
Albert Narvel Felts flirted with success for ten years before he found it. Born near Bernie, Missouri, on November 11, 1938, he was a teenager when he won his first talent show and landed a regular Saturday spot local radio. In the mid-1950s, he became a session musician for Sun Records in Memphis, appearing behind Charlie Rich and Harold Jenkins (Conway Twitty). He had a few sessions of his own, but his material was not released at the time. He was spotted by Mercury Records, and his first session, on May 13, 1957, produced ten songs, including his first single, "Kiss-A-Me, Baby." His third release was an instrumental, "Rocket Ride." The single was accidently played at the wrong speed by a deejay, and began to catch on as a "stroll" number. Mercury rerecorded the tune with Sil Austin's combo and re-released it under Felt's name as "Rocket Ride Stroll." Felts returned to Memphis and recorded three singles for Pink Records, a subsidiary of Hi Records. "Honey Love" peeked into the national charts in February 1960, and was Felt's only brush with success as a rock 'n roller. Later in 1960, he signed a two-year contract with M-G-M, but nothing was released. From 1962-65, he recorded for Starline, Sonic, Renay, ARA, and Hi. With little success, Felts seemingly disappeared until 1973, when he signed with Cinnamon Records. He immediately began a successful series of country hits, with his version of "Drift Away." When Cinnamon folded in 1975, Felts moved on to ABC/Dot, and had major country hits by rerecording such "oldies" as "Reconsider Baby," "Funny How the Time Slips Away," "My Prayer," "Lonely Teardrops," and "Everlasting Love." In the late 1970s, he was discovered by the rock fans in Europe, and he made a number of successful overseas trips. In the 1980s, he recorded for a number of labels, including Collage, KARI, GMC, Lobo, and Evergreen.

12. Guess Things Happen That Way - Johnny Cash
13. Willie and the Hand Jive - Johnny Otis
14. What Am I Living For - Chuck Willis
15. Witch Doctor - David Seville
16. Big Man - The Four Preps
17. Jennie Lee - Jan and Arnie
18. No Chemise, Please - Gerry Granahan
19. My True Love/Leroy - Jack Scott
20. One Summer Night - The Danleers
21. Just a Dream - Jimmy Clanton
22. When - The Kalin Twins
23. Oh Lonesome Me - Don Gibson
24. I Wonder Why - Dion and the Belmonts
25. Blue Blue Day - Don Gibson
26. Twilight Time - The Platters
27. For Your Love - Ed Townsend
28. High School Confidential - Jerry Lee Lewis
29. Dottie - Danny and the Juniors
30. Don't Go Home - The Playmates
31. Johnny B. Goode - Chuck Berry
32. Oh, My Soul - Little Richard
33. Rumble - Link Wray and His Ray Men
34. Little Mary - Fats Domino
35. Wear My Ring Around Your Neck - Elvis Presley
36. You're Making a Mistake - The Platters
37. Talk To Me, Talk To Me - Little Willie John
38. Gingerbread - Frankie Avalon
39. Little Star - The Elegants
40. El Rancho Rock - The Champs
41. (It's Been a Long Time) Pretty Baby - Gino and Gina
42. I Love You So - The Chantels
43. Born Too Late - The Poni-Tails
44. The Freeze - Tony and Joe
45. Western Movies - The Olympics
46. Think It Over - The Crickets
47. Stupid Cupid - Connie Francis
48. By the Light of the Silvery Moon - Jimmy Bowen
49. Early in the Morning - The Rinky-Dinks
50. Come What May - Clyde McPhatter

July 1958
ARTIST OF THE MONTH

RICKY NELSON

Ricky Nelson was the first rock star to be a true child of radio and television. In fact, he literally grew up with the eyes of the nation watching his every move.

His parents, Oswald George "Ozzie" Nelson and Harriet Hilliard (real name Peggy Sue Snyder), were popular entertainers during the 1930s. Ozzie fronted a dance band that had a Number One hit in 1935 with "And Then Some." Harriet was a movie actress, and became Ozzie's lead singer three years before she became his wife in 1935. Their marriage produced two children, both sons. As befit their transient life-style, David was born in Chicago on October 24, 1936, and Eric Hilliard ("Ricky") was born in Teaneck, New Jersey, on May 8, 1940. By the 1940s, the era of the big bands was changing. The best jazz virtuosos, among them Benny Goodman and Duke Ellington, were performing more frequently in concert settings as opposed to dance halls. Never a great instrumentalist, Ozzie continued to pursue a living in the old vaudeville fashion. Week after week he did one-nighters on the road while Harriet and the children remained in their rambling country home in Tenafly, New Jersey.

Ricky Nelson

The Nelsons, minus Ricky, moved to Hollywood in 1941 so that Ozzie could take a job as band leader for Red Skelton's radio program. Ricky stayed behind in Tenafly with his grandmother. The immediate success of Skelton's show permitted the Nelsons the chance to hunt for a permanent home. Just off Hollywood Boulevard, they found the house they would live in for the rest of their lives, a fourteen-room, two-story residence at 1822 Camino Palmero. In 1942, after they moved in, Ricky joined the family.

In 1944, Red Skelton left the radio show when the Army called, and Ozzie and Harriet were offered a chance to front a program on their own. This was a risky move, as Ozzie would be the first band leader to headline his own radio series. "The Adventures of Ozzie and Harriet" started slow but soon gathered momentum. The show was centered around the real personalities of the couple. Ozzie always seemed befuddled and out-of-sync with the happenings swirling around him. Harriet was the calm in the eye of the storm—with a little twinkle in her eye for good measure. The characters of David and Ricky were also present from the beginning of the show. During the first season, the youngsters were only mentioned in passing and were not part of the cast. When the time came to introduce the children, young actors were hired. By late 1948, David and Ricky were pressuring their parents to be allowed to play themselves. During this same time, the show moved first from CBS to NBC, and then to ABC.

On February 20, 1949, David and Ricky made their first appearance on "The Adventures of Ozzie and Harriet" in a program titled "Invitation to Dinner." Acquaintances have described David as down-to-earth, sincere, professional, quiet. Ricky is recalled as cocky, full of pranks, and insecure. Everyone agrees that between the two, Ricky was the natural-born entertainer.

In 1950, ABC offered the Nelsons a television show of their own based on the radio format. Ever the cautious businessman, Ozzie decided to first test the idea in the form of a low-budget movie. In 1951, "Here Come The Nelsons" played drive-ins and local theaters across the country. The movie earned moderate box office receipts but proved that the Nelsons were ready for their own television show.

"The Adventures of Ozzie and Harriet" moved to ABC-TV in the fall of 1952, occupying a Wednesday night slot. The show remained a television mainstay for fourteen seasons, through a staggering four hundred and thirty-five episodes.

During his early childhood, Ricky often suffered with asthma attacks, and he grew up thin and sickly. However, beginning with his television debut in 1952, Ricky grew from a scrawny, twelve-year old prankster—who's favorite line was "I don't mess around, boy!"—into a rakishly-charming young man by 1956. He also had a streak of self-effacing modesty—pounded into him by his parents over the years—that was his best offense. He had successfully navigated through Bancroft Junior High, where he was remembered as "quiet and well behaved." He enrolled in Hollywood High in 1954 where he was an average student. By this time, he was earning an annual salary of $100,000 from the television show.

In 1956, rock 'n roll was sweeping the country, as well as sweeping the old styles of music out of the way. Ricky was already a member of the Rooks, a clique at Hollywood High that reveled in causing trouble for authority figures. Ozzie and Harriet were as middle-of-the-road is it was possible to be and still be TV stars. Ricky resented their life-style and authority. In retaliation, he submersed himself into wild rock 'n roll music, the antithesis of the smooth sound of his father's big band. He tried to grow sideburns. He slicked his hair back with hair tonic. He wore shirts with the collars turned up. He tried to tattoo himself on the shoulder and wrist. Mostly, he listened to rock 'n roll music—loud.

However, he was too young and insecure to jump into the rock 'n roll movement as a performer. He had to be sidetracked into it. The story goes like this: Ricky was dating a beautiful teenager named Arlene, and his natural insecurity was about to eat him up. He was certain that Arlene would drop him any minute. After all, she was a year older than he. Their few dates together could be categorized as "cold." Not even lukewarm. On what Ricky was certain to be their last date, an Elvis song was playing on the car radio. Arlene swooned over Elvis. Ricky quickly blurted out that he was about to make his own record. Arlene responded with laughter.

On an upcoming episode of the family's TV show, Ricky did get a chance to impersonate Elvis in a skit about a costume party. The response was quick in coming. Ricky pleaded with Ozzie to help him make a record—Ozzie, after all, had been a recording star in his own right. Ozzie finally agreed, but first he called one of his many connections. Ricky found himself on stage as part of the entertainment at Knott's Berry Farm. Ozzie had decided that it was time for Ricky to try out his act. By all accounts, Ricky acquitted himself very well.

Next, Ozzie permitted Ricky to sing on the show. Ricky chose his favorite rock 'n roll number, Fats Domino's "I'm Walkin'." Again, the public's response was positive. A demo tape was made of the performance. The Nelson's talent agency, MCA, sent the tape out to more than twenty record labels. Each turned the aspiring rock 'n roller down flat. Then, Barny Kessel listened to the demo. Kessel was an acclaimed jazz guitarist and chief of artists and repertoire of the small Verve label. He had also been Ozzie's guitarist in the 1940s. Kessel realized that Ricky's image was already pre-sold through the weekly TV show. He reasoned that a little work on the vocals, some professional musical arrangements... Well, who knows? A deal was made for Ricky to have one three-hour recording session for Verve. At the end of that time, there were three songs completed: "I'm Walking," "A Teenager's Romance," and "You're My One and Only Love." It has been reported that the spelling of the title of Fats Domino's "I'm Walkin'" was changed at Ozzie's request to "I'm Walking." There would be no grammatical slang for Ozzie Nelson's son.

On April 10, 1957, Ricky had debuted "I'm Walking" on the TV show. Within a week, the single of "I'm Walking," backed with "A Teenager's Romance," was released by Verve. Through the summer, Ricky's version of "I'm Walking" chased Fats Domino's original up the charts. In midsummer, as "A Teenager's Romance" caught on, Ricky's record finally surpassed that of Domino. Verve was swamped with orders, and quickly fell behind in pressing new singles. They also fell behind in paying royalties, an unforgivable transgression in Ozzie's eyes.

Lew Chudd of Imperial, Fats Domino's label, was one of the first to notice Ricky. After all, Imperial held part of the publishing rights to "I'm Walkin'." Chudd approached Ozzie concerning Ricky's contract. When he learned of Ozzie's disenchantment with Verve and that Verve only had an agreement for the one session, Chudd and Ozzie struck a deal. Ricky would jump to Imperial with a five-year contract guaranteeing $50,000 a year against royalties. Verve retaliated by releasing "You're My One and Only Love" as a single with "Honey Rock," an instrumental by Kessel on the flip side. The three Verve songs also appeared as three-fourths of Ricky's first extended play release as well one-third of an album featuring Ricky.

The Verve single had just titillated the teen audience. It was obvious that Ricky's first Imperial single would be an instant smash. There were advance orders approaching a million copies even before Ricky stepped into the studio to record "Be Bop Baby" and "Have I Told You Lately That I Love You." A week later, millions of teens caught their first taste of the songs on the Nelson's television show. The single roared up the charts in the fall of 1957.

Ricky became increasingly dissatisfied with the musicians provided for his recording sessions. He felt that his generation and theirs were worlds apart. His decision to form his own band of younger players was solidified after a near-disastrous tour of the Midwest during which the promoter hired local musicians to back him. Ricky had always expressed an affinity for musicians from the South and Southwest. His favorite rock 'n roller was Carl Perkins, and he also admired Elvis, Dale Hawkins, and the two Buddys, Holly and Knox. After hearing a demo of "Red Hot" by Bob Luman, another Imperial recording artist, Ricky contacted Luman's bass player, James Kirkland, and guitarist, James Burton. After a brief workout with Ricky, they were hired to perform as Ricky's band on the television show. A short time later, Richie Frost was added on drums with Gene Garf on piano. Burton had been an original member of the Dale Hawkins' combo on "Susie-Q," before joining Luman in Los Angeles. Frost was a session drummer who had worked on the musical score for the Nelson's show.

While all this was happening, Ricky recorded and released his second Imperial single, "Stood up" and "Waitin' In School." His rocking style was becoming more professional with each new single, and "Stood Up" missed the top of the charts by a hair's breadth. The next single was the first to feature Ricky's new band. "Believe What You Say" had a full-blown, powerhouse sound, not unlike Dale Hawkins' better recordings. Burton's guitar work was full of fire and innovation while the remaining members of the combo more than held their own. Even Ricky's vocals, tentative up to this point, took on a sense of urgency. The flip side, "My Bucket's Got a Hole In It," a song originally performed by Hank Williams, was turned inside out, stripped bare and revved up like a Hollywood hot rod.

Now recording and performing with the band he had dreamed of, Ricky's career outside the family's TV show accelerated. He received credible reviews in 1959 when he co-starred in the John Wayne epic, "Rio Bravo." There was an instant sellout whenever one of his infrequent concerts was announced. His role in the television show expanded, not just to allow him to sing, but to allow him to act. He was receiving ten thousand fan letters each week, and was appearing as the hero in a monthly comic book. He raced cars and dated starlets. He was friends with Elvis, Gene Vincent, Eddie Cochran, and the Burnette brothers.

With "Poor Little Fool" he topped the charts for the first time. "Lonesome Town" proved he could handle slower material with sincerity. "Never Be Anything Else But You," "It's Late," "Just a Little Too Much," and "Sweeter That You," the four sides of the next two singles, gave him the creative freedom he so desperately desired.

(Rick Nelson's story will continue in the next volume of THE GOLDEN AGE OF AMERICAN ROCK 'N ROLL.)

August 1958

AUG 1   Johnny Cash leaves his three-year association with Sun Records and signs a long-term recording contract with Columbia Records. Hidden between the lines of the music-news reports is the desire by Cash to appeal to the broader "pop" audience. As though to finalize this change in his style, Cash moves his family from Memphis to Los Angeles.

    Charlie Gracie begins a one-week stand at Club Bolero in Wildwood, New Jersey.

    Tommy Ridgely plays the High Hat in New Orleans for this weekend and the next.

AUG 2   Bobby Darin appears on "The Dick Clark Show," singing "Early in the Morning."

New Releases for the first week in August include "Carol" by Chuck Berry on Chess; two from Brunswick: "We Have Love" by Jackie Wilson and "Is That All To The Ball" by Bill Riley; **Lee Allen**'s "Tic Toc" on Ember; "Holy Smoke Baby" by the Cadillacs on Josie; Ric Carty's "Scratching On My Screen" on NRC; "I Laughed So Hard I Cried" by the Rip-Chords on M.M.I; and "The Mess Around" by Richard Berry and the Lockettes on Flip.

AUG 5   On "American Bandstand," the Coasters perform their latest hit, "Yakety Yak."

AUG 6   This afternoon, Jackie Wilson plugs "We Have Love" on "American Bandstand." On the same program, the Royal Teens sing "Harvey's Got a Girlfriend." Even with this type of publicity, neither song made much of a dent in the national music charts.

AUG 7   Two vocal groups, the Poni-Tails and Dion and the Belmonts, are guests on "American Bandstand."

EARLY AUGUST

    Charlie Gracie leaves for England where he is scheduled to make a television appearance in London

AUG 9   George Hamilton IV makes another appearance on NBC-TV's "The Perry Como Show."

    "The Dick Clark Show" features Robin Luke singing "Susie Darlin'," along with Andy Williams, Ray Smith and Bobby Day.

LEE ALLEN

The sound that Lee Allen coaxed from his saxophone was important to the evolution of rock 'n roll. Allen was born July 2, 1926, in Pittsburgh, Kansas and he grew up in Denver. He was offered a music and athletic scholarship to Xavier College in New Orleans in 1943. Instead of finishing college, he joined Paul Gayten's combo. Beginning in the 1940s, Allen was featured on Gayten's recordings as well as those produced by Dave Bartholomew. Allen signed with Savoy in 1954 although only one single was released. Allen's record "Rockin' at Cosimo's" was released on Aladdin in 1956. The song's title was a reference to Cosimo Matassa, the wizard of J&M Studio, home of most of the important New Orleans R&B sessions. Allen's fame spread quickly, and he was in constant demand as a musician on sessions featuring Fats Domino, Little Richard, Huey Smith and the Clowns, Joe Turner, Ray Charles, Shirley and Lee, and Jimmy Clanton. In 1957, Allen became the New Orleans producer for New York's Herald/Ember Records. He recorded an instrumental riff he had written to close Fats Domino's shows. The number was released by Ember as "Walkin' With Mr. Lee," and it became a mid-sized hit in early 1958. Allen's follow-up singles, "Strollin' With Mr. Lee" and "Tic Toc," sold fewer copies but received considerable air play. There were two additional singles and an album on Ember before Allen's national popularity waned. However, he was even more in demand as a session musician, if that was possible. He toured with Fats Domino from 1961 to 1965. Then, for personal reasons, he took an aeronautics job in Los Angeles and confined his music to evening gigs. Ten years later he was back with Domino's show. In the late 1970s, the New Orleans label, Nola, released two albums by Allen. In the 1980s, he recorded and toured with the popular rockabilly band, the Blasters. He died of lung cancer on October 18, 1994, in Los Angeles.

THE DANLEERS
Like most "street-corner groups," the Danleers dreamed of success. When it came, it was enormous—and fleeting. John Lee and Jimmy Weston, both tenors, formed the Danleers as Brooklyn high school students. The remaining members were Willie Ephraim, second tenor; Nat McCune, baritone; and Roosevelt Mays, bass. They hired a manager with contacts to Amp-3 Records; and, for their first session, they recorded "One Summer Night." In a mix-up, the label of the Amp-3 single read "Dandleers," causing confusion with another group, the Danderliers. Amp-3 was distributed by Mercury, and when "One Summer Night" began to break, the single was re-released on Mercury. Into the fall of 1958, "One Summer Night" was a best seller. The Danleers were immediately booked for a series of personal appearances, including the Apollo and Howard theaters, and Alan Freed's Labor Day show at the Brooklyn Fox. Unfortunately, Mercury's promotion department was busy with the Platters, and the Danleers went the way of two other Mercury R&B groups, the Del-Vikings and the Penguins. By the end of 1958, the Danleers' wild ride was over. There were three more Mercury singles, including "I Really Love You," but none of them got off the ground. After leaving Mercury, the Danleers ceased to exist as a unit. Wanting to continue, Weston took another group, the Webtones, and named them the Danleers. This group recorded two singles for Epic in 1960, one for Everest, two for Smash 1964, and one final single for LeMans before dissolving. Weston and McCune tried a comeback in the 1970s, and this third group of Danleers (featuring Bill Carey, formerly with the Four Fellows) recorded a few tunes in 1974 before breaking up. In 1988, Weston gathered several original members to play the Westbury Music Festival. Jimmy Weston died June 10, 1993.

AUG 11   On "American Bandstand," Bobby Freeman plugs his latest releases, "Do You Want To Dance" and "Betty Lou's Got a New Pair of Shoes."
   The Drifters play a one-night stand at the Dew Drop Lounge in New Orleans.

New Releases for the second week in August include "Young School Girl" by Fats Domino on Imperial; Marvin Rainwater's "A Need For Love" on M-G-M; Duane Eddy's "Ramrod" on Jamie; "The End" by Earl Grant on Decca; "Someday (You'll Want Me To Want You)" by Jodie Sands on Chancellor; "Buddy" by Jackie Dee on Liberty; two from NRC: Joe South's "One Fool To Another" and Ray Stevens' "Cat Pants;" "Elevator Operator" by the Rays on XYZ; "Please Be My Love" by Janis and Her Boy Friends on RCA; "Little Baby" by Tommy Facenda on Nasco; and "You Ain't Sayin' Nothin'" by the Satellites on Class. Also new this week from Liberty is "Susie" by the soon-to-be country star, Willie Nelson.

AUG 14   In Memphis, Gladys Presley, Elvis' mother, dies unexpectedly. The Presleys had been living in Kileen, Texas, near Ft. Hood while Elvis was receiving his Army training when she became ill. She was taken by train to Memphis where she underwent treatment at Methodist Hospital for acute hepatitis.
   The Kingsmen rock through their instrumental, "Weekend," on "American Bandstand."
   Connie Francis embarks on a ten-day tour of the British Isles.

AUG 15   At his family home in Lubbock, Texas, Buddy Holly marries Maria Elena Santiago. They met when she was an employee at Southern Music in New York.
   New Orleans' Dew Drop welcomes Donnie Elbert for a one-night engagement.

MID-AUGUST
   Clyde McPhatter, the Coasters, Jerry Butler and the Impressions, and Sil Austin's combo are touring together.

AUG 16   Tonight's ABC-TV "The Dick Clark Show" is headlined by Frankie Avalon. Other guests include the Coasters, actor Patrick Wayne, and Mary Swan.
   Bo Diddley headlines the week-long revue at the Howard Theater in Washington. Also on the show are the **Danleers**, the Flamingos, the Pearls, and Arthur Prysock.

AUG 17   Jerry Lee Lewis performs at the Harrison Grove Country Music Park in Youngstown, New York.

AUG 18   B. B. King plays Chicago's Trianon Ballroom with Muddy Waters and Howling Wolf.

New Releases for the third week in August include "I Wish" by the Platters on Mercury; "Love Me" by the Impressions featuring Jerry Butler on Abner; "The Shadow Knows" by the Coasters on Atco; Dale Wright's "Please Don't Go" on Fraternity; Ruth Brown's "This Little Girl's Gone Rockin'" on Atlantic; "Nite Rock" by the Nite Rockers on RCA; Brook Benton's "Crazy In Love With You" on Vik; "Love Bug Bit Me" by the Lovers on Aladdin; "18-Year Old Blues" by Steve Carl and the Jags on Meteor; "The Whip" by the Originals on Jackpot; and "The Crawl" by the Fireflies on Roulette; and "The Ten Commandments of Love" by Harvey and the Moonglows on Chess.

AUG 22 Donnie Elbert returns to the Dew Drop Cafe in New Orleans for a full three-day stand. Also in town, Smiley Lewis plays the High Hat Club for three days.

Bobby Day, Thurston Harris, the Five Keys, Bob and Earl, the Satellites, and Bette McLaurin are featured this week at Washington's Howard Theater.

AUG 23 "The Dick Clark Show" on ABC-TV welcomes Dale Hawkins singing "La-Do-Dada." Also on tonight's show are Chuck Berry, Bobby Hendricks, Little Anthony and the Imperials, and Jerry Wallace.

"The Perry Como Show" features an appearance by Bobby Darin.

In North Carolina, the gross is $23,000 at the Charlotte Coliseum as Jerry Lee Lewis and Bill Haley and His Comets headline the show. Other artists on tonight's bill are LaVern Baker, Bobby Freeman, Dave "Baby" Cortez, the Pastels, the Gladiolas, and Lee Allen and his combo.

AUG 24 Dick Clark's Caravan show plays the Hollywood Bowl at 8:30 p.m. Featured artists are the Champs, Jan and Arnie, Sheb Wooley, **Ernie Freeman**'s combo, Jerry Wallace, Rod McKuen, the Blossoms, the Six Teens, and Jack Jones. Buddy Knox and Jimmy Bowen with the Rhythm Orchids were originally advertised to appear but did not—Knox was ill. The show grosses $29,000 from 11,800 fans.

Jo Ann Campbell opens the show for Johnny Mathis at Carter's Ballroom Amphitheatre in Washington, DC.

On television, the Teenagers reunite with Frankie Lymon once again to play the "Ed Sullivan Show."

New Releases for the fourth week in August include "Break Up" by Jerry Lee Lewis on Sun; "Baby Face" by Little Richard on Specialty; "Come On, Let's Go" by Ritchie Valens on Del-Fi; the Kingston Trio's "Tom Dooley" on Capitol; two from ABC-Paramount: Danny and the Juniors' "Crazy Cave" and the Ellis Brothers' "Sneaky Alligator;" "I'm So Young" by the Students on Checker; Terry Noland's "There's a Fungus Among Us" on Brunswick; two from King: Bill Doggett's "Hold It" and Little Willie John's "Tell It Like It Is;" Don Gibson's "Give Myself a

ERNIE FREEMAN
Ernie Freeman was a consummate professional studio musician with vision. He also had a recording career spanning twenty-five years under his own name. He was born about 1928 in Cleveland where he remained through college. He became a proficient jazz pianist. About 1952, he moved to Los Angeles. He found work as an arranger for Dinah Washington. In late 1955, Cash Records issued "Jivin' Around," a two-part instrumental that became a major juke box hit and a Top Ten R&B release. It featured another L. A. studio genius, Irving Ashby, on guitar. Freeman's band also did sessions for Cash including "Our Love" by Bobby Relf (Bobby Day). Freeman soon added Plas Johnson's sax and flute to his growing combo. His first album was a lone jazz release on Zephyr, JERRY LEIBER PRESENTS SCOOBY DOO. In 1956, he issued "Rockin' Around," the first of some two dozen singles on Imperial. "Jivin' Around" was redone in 1957, followed by "Dumplins," his first charted "pop" single. This was a cover of a release by Doc Bagby who had the slightly bigger hit. His next single, a cover of Bill Justis' "Raunchy," proved that cover versions needn't be pale imitations of the original. Freeman's "Raunchy" received a swinging reading by the combo, who played as though it were their own. There were several other minor hits for Freeman on Imperial: "Indian Love Call," "Theme from Dark at the Top of the Stairs" and an instrumental version of "The Twist." In 1962, he moved up the Imperial's parent company, Liberty, for three albums. Then it was on to Dunhill for an album in 1968. Freeman can be heard on countless records by hundreds of artists as diverse as Frank Sinatra, Simon and Garfunkel and Sandy Nelson. He even sneaked into rock stardom as B. Bumble and the Stingers on "Bumble Boogie." He retired to Hawaii in the late 1970s where he passed away in 1981.

Party" on RCA; Scott Engel's "Paper Doll" on Orbit; "Ific" by King Curtis on Atco; "The Right to Rock" by Trini Lopez on Volk; "Gee Whiz" by Bob and Earl on Class; Ronnie Self's "Petrified" on Columbia; and "You're the Girl" by Dave "Baby" Cortez on Clock.

AUG 26 Eddie Cochran returns to "American Bandstand" to sing "Summertime Blues."

AUG 27 At the Minnesota State Fair in Minneapolis, the Dick Clark "All Star Record Hop" plays to a less than capacity crowd after Clark cancels his appearance due to illness. Artists appearing tonight are Jack Scott, Jody Reynolds, Duane Eddy, Dale Hawkins, Eddie Cochran, and **Bobby Hendricks**. The troupe remains at the fair through August 29.

Ricky Nelson is booked for one show each night for the next three days at the Carter Baron Amphitheatre in Washington, DC. Gross receipts exceed $34,750.

The Playmates are at the Eden Roc in Miami Beach for an extended engagement.

AUG 28 Closing out their five-month tour of the world, the "Flying" Platters, as they are now referred to by the press, open at the Olympia in Paris for a twenty-one day stand.

AUG 29 Alan Freed's annual ten-day Labor Day revue, billed as the "Big Beat Show," opens at the Fox Theater in Brooklyn. Although scheduled to headline the last five days of the show, the Everly Brothers did not appear. Acts which did make it to the stage include Chuck Berry, Bill Haley and His Comets, the Elegants, the Danleers, the Kalin Twins, Larry Williams, Gino and Gina, Jimmy Clanton, Bobby Hamilton, Frankie Avalon, Jack Scott, the Poni-Tails, Jo Ann Campbell, Teddy Randazzo, the Olympics, Bobby Freeman and King Curtis. The run garnishes $200,000.

Wynona Carr and Tommy Ridgely entertain at the Masonic Hall in Algiers, Louisiana.

Little Caesar plays the High Hat Club in New Orleans for three days.

In Washington, the Howard Theater presents Ruth Brown, the Del Vikings, Robert and Johnny, and the Moonglows for the week.

AUG 30 "The Dick Clark Show" on ABC-TV welcomes Bill Haley and His Comets, the Poni-Tails, Jim Reeves and Eddie Cochran.

Ricky Nelson performs during the Labor Day weekend at the Steel Pier in Atlantic City. His three-day stand brings in $44,211, breaking Frank Sinatra's 1950 record of $41,000.

The Dew Drop in New Orleans presents Wynona Carr and Tommy Ridgely for a three-day engagement.

AUG 31 Ray Charles gives a concert and dance at the Labor Union Hall in New Orleans.

BOBBY HENDRICKS

Bobby Hendricks had a long and varied career in music. He was born in Columbus, Ohio, February 22, 1938 (or 1937). Even as a teenager, Hendricks' voice was a strong, clear tenor. In 1955, Hendricks replaced Irving Turner in the Swallows, one of R&B's earliest vocal groups. While Hendricks was a member, the Swallows did not record. In September 1956, he left the Swallows to work with ex-Drifter Bill Pinckney in the Flyers, which recorded one single for Atco, "My Only Desire." Pinckney's Flyers existed about a year before Pinckney returned to the Drifters, bringing along Hendricks who was hired to replace the recently drafted Johnny Moore. Hendricks' only session with the Drifters produced "Drip Drop" and "Suddenly There's a Valley." In June 1958, the Drifters had just completed an appearance at the Apollo Theater where they were sharing the stage with the Five Crowns when their manager fired the entire group, replacing them with the Five Crowns. (Several sources list Hendricks as a member of the Five Crowns as early as 1954, but this was not the case. Hendricks was among those dismissed.) Hendricks and guitarist Jimmy Oliver, an ex-Drifter, signed with Sue Records. Oliver had penned a tune titled "Itchy Twitchy Feeling" that they hoped to record. Reportedly using the Coasters as the backing group, Hendricks had a hit with his first solo effort. Hendricks had six more singles on Sue before he caught the public's ear again with "Psycho." It was his final Sue release. He then recorded three singles for Mercury, and one each for Cub, M-G-M, Williams, and United Artists. In the 1970s, he and Bill Pinckney teamed again as the Original Drifters. Hendricks' voice had an uncanny resemblance to that of Jackie Wilson. Perhaps it was too close, and the music buyers decided there was only one Jackie Wilson.

THE TOP ROCK 'N ROLL RECORDS FOR AUGUST 1958

1. Poor Little Fool - Ricky Nelson
2. My True Love/Leroy - Jack Scott
3. When - The Kalin Twins
4. Just a Dream - Jimmy Clanton
5. Splish Splash - Bobby Darin
6. Rebel Rouser - Duane Eddy
7. Little Star - The Elegants
8. Willie and the Hand Jive - Johnny Otis
9. Hard Headed Woman/Don't Ask Me Why - Elvis Presley
10. Gingerbread - Frankie Avalon
11. Born Too Late - The Poni-Tails
12. Yakety Yak - The Coasters
13. Western Movies - The Olympics
14. One Summer Night - The Danleers
15. Somebody Touched Me - Buddy Knox
16. For Your Precious Love - The Impressions featuring Jerry Butler
17. Think It Over - The Crickets
18. Chantilly Lace - The Big Bopper
19. Do You Want To Dance? - Bobby Freeman
20. Early In The Morning - The Rinky-Dinks
21. Bird Dog/Devoted To You - The Everly Brothers
22. Rock-In' Robin/Over and Over - Bobby Day
23. Guess Things Happen That Way - Johnny Cash
24. Blue, Blue Day - Don Gibson
25. What Am I Living For? - Chuck Willis
26. Early In The Morning - Buddy Holly
27. Stupid Cupid - Connie Francis
28. Are You Really Mine? - Jimmie Rodgers
29. Endless Sleep - Jody Reynolds
30. Susie Darlin' - Robin Luke
31. Itchy Twitchy Feeling - Bobby Hendricks
32. The Freeze - Tony and Joe
33. Summertime Blues - Eddie Cochran
34. Betty Lou's Got A New Pair of Shoes - Bobby Freeman
35. By The Light of the Silvery Moon - Jimmy Bowen
36. Win Your Love For Me - Sam Cooke
37. Tears On My Pillow - Little Anthony and the Imperials
38. She Was Only Seventeen - Marty Robbins
39. You Cheated - The Slades
40. Come What May - Clyde McPhatter
41. No Chemise, Please - Gerry Granahan
42. How The Time Flies - Jerry Wallace
43. Crazy Eyes For You - Bobby Hamilton
44. Hey Girl - Hey Boy - Oscar McLollie and Jeanette Baker
45. Lazy Summer Night - The Four Preps
46. Jennie Lee - Jan and Arnie
47. High School Confidential - Jerry Lee Lewis

48. Let's Go Steady for the Summer - The Three G's
49. Blue Boy - Jim Reeves
50. Summertime, Summertime - The Jamies

Also on the "pop" charts:
Nel Blu Dipinto Di Blu (Volare) - Domenico Modugno
That's How Much I Love You - Pat Boone
Fever - Peggy Lee
Everybody Loves a Lover - Doris Day

August 1958
ARTIST OF THE MONTH

JACK SCOTT

Jack Scott

Rock 'n roll was a music populated by singers who, more often than not, attempted to sound like someone else. Not Jack Scott. His rich baritone voice, his sense of musical timing, and his ability to write lyrics that could be turned into hit records, made Jack Scott unique. Even on the rocking numbers, his voice rarely strained the upper limits of his natural range. In a sense, Scott's self-assured baritone was the equivalent of Roy Orbison's luxurious tenor.

Jack Scott was born Jack Scafone (*) in Windsor, Ontario, on January 24, 1936 (*). The Scafone's were a large family—Jack was the oldest of seven children. The family moved from Windsor to nearby Detroit, settling in the suburb of Hazel Park when he was ten. Two years previous, he had received a guitar from his father, himself an accomplished musician. By the time he was sixteen, Jack and his brother, Jerry, had formed a high school band they called the Southern Drifters. Their country repertoire ran the gamut from Hank Williams—always a Scott favorite—to Roy Acuff and Carl Smith. Before long, the Southern Drifters were performing at local dances and amateur shows. They also gained enough of a reputation to appear frequently on various radio shows in the Detroit area. It was about this time that Jack changed his last name from Scafone to Scott to ease the pronunciation for radio deejays.

A local music entrepreneur, Carl Thom, owner of the largest record store in Hazel Park, liked Scott's style. Together, they decided to record a demonstration single featuring several of Scott's compositions. The disk featured a rockin' side, "Greaseball," backed with a ballad, "My True Love." "Greaseball," an early version of Scott's later "Leroy," was based on a friend who constantly found himself jailed for fighting, thus the line, "Leroy's back in jail again." In true fairy tale form, Scott's high school sweetheart was the inspiration for "My True Love."

The demo disk made it's way to an executive at Peer-Southern Music in New York who mentioned Scott's name to Jack Carlton, the chief of

---

(* Also spelled Scarfono. His date of birth was recently given as January 28, and his year of birth has appeared as 1938.)

artists and repertoire at ABC-Paramount Records. In early 1957, Carlton and ABC-Paramount were becoming very experienced at making quick decisions when it came to signing raw talent. Scott was immediately placed under contract and scheduled for a session at United Sound in Detroit in March. The musicians for Scott's first session were Stan Getz and the Tom Cats: guitarist Dave Rohiller, bassist Stan Getz (not the tenor sax artist of the same name), and drummer Dominic Scafone (Jack's cousin).

Scott's first single, "Baby She's Gone" b/w "You Can Bet Your Bottom Dollar," was released by ABC-Paramount in April 1957. He was back in the studio in September. Again, he used the Tom Cats to record "Two Timin' Woman" and "I Need Your Love." Also on hand for the first time were the Chantones handling the backing vocals.

"Two Timin' Woman," released in October, and "Baby She's Gone" were both done in a hot rockabilly style. "You Can Bet Your Bottom Dollar" and "I Need Your Love" featured a slower tempo. Both singles did well around Detroit, but neither broke nationally. The primary reason was that ABC-Paramount was expending most of its promotional budget on Paul Anka's early releases.

Jack Carlton and ABC-Paramount parted ways in early 1958, and Carlton started his own independent record label named Carlton Records. Among the first acts he signed was Jack Scott. Scott and the Chantones returned to United Sound in Detroit and recut "My True Love" and the slightly rewritten "Leroy." Lead guitar chores fell to Al Allen while George Kazakas played sax. Stan Getz continued to play bass and Dominic Scafone returned on drums.

The single was released in April 1958. By June, it was receiving nationwide airplay. At first, the action was on "Leroy." However, as "Leroy" began to fade, deejays turned the record over and "My True Love" actually became the bigger hit, taking the record over the million mark in sales. This single set the pattern for Scott's releases over the next few years: a powerful, uptempo number paired with an equally strong ballad. Unlike most rockabilly performers of the time, Scott used the saxophone break almost exclusively. The lead guitar and his own rhythm guitar were relegated to the background.

The Chantones deserve a special mention, too. The group was composed of Jack Grenier, Jim Nantais, Roy Lesperance, and Larry Desjarlais. They began performing in 1953 as the Teen Tones and would remain with Scott until 1962. Like the vocal backing performed behind Elvis by the Jordanaires, to which they are most often compared, the Chantones complemented Scott's rumbling vocals. They performed an airtight, four-part, wordless chant that was heavy on the lower sonic register.

In the late summer of 1958, Scott released "Geraldine" b/w "With Your Love." This time the ballad side caught on first and stayed the most popular. At the end of the year his new release was "My True Love" backed with "Save My Soul."

It looked like Scott was going to ride this wave of popularity for the foreseeable future when he received his draft notice from the Army. He was forced to be away from the music scene through the first half of

1959. Scott continued to record songs similar to those with which he had already been successful. As a result, record sales declined markedly for "I Never Felt Like This," "The Way I Walk," and "There Comes a Time." Not that there was anything wrong with the recordings, the lyrics, or Scott's style. It was more a matter of saturation on the part of the public.

On November 25, 1959, Scott left Carlton, signing with Top Rank Records in a deal that paid Carlton $30,000 with another $20,000 going to Scott to pay the royalties due him. Top Rank was the American subsidiary of Rank International, a British concern. Scott's popularity in the United Kingdom had remained high through the years, and Rank felt certain Scott's career could be revived. The night his contract was finalized, Scott was in the studio recording "What In The World's Come Over You." Within a week, Top Rank released the record. It quickly shot up the charts, eventually becoming Scott's second million selling single. The single, backed with the uptempo "Baby, Baby" differed little from those he had released on Carlton even though he was now recording at Bell Sound Studios, located at 53rd and Broadway in New York City. The Chantones were still there, along with a new rhythm section that still focused more on the sax than the guitars.

"Burning Bridges," in the spring of 1960, became another huge hit, while the flip side, "Oh, Little One" also did well. This single marked a slight change in the direction of Scott's music as "Burning Bridges" edged closer to contemporary country music than his previous recordings. While it didn't attract much attention in the country field, there was an indication that Scott was willing to try something different. As if to make that point, during his stay with Top Rank, Scott recorded an album titled I REMEMBER HANK WILLIAMS, as well as a gospel album THE SPIRIT MOVES ME.

After "Burning Bridges," Scott's recording career slowed again. "It Only Happened Yesterday," "Patsy," and "Is There Something On Your Mind" were all released during 1960 and none came close to the heights achieved with his first two Top Rank singles. Once again Scott's style remained the same, but the public's taste in music was moving to dance records and female vocal groups. There was the saturation factor, too, as Jack Carlton released two Scott singles in 1960 on his Guaranteed label, "What Am I Living For" and "Go Wild Little Sadie."

Top Rank, which had financial troubles as early as August 1960, finally folded in early 1961. At the time, Top Rank had been absorbed by EMI-England, the parent company of Capitol Records. Consequently, Scott's contract was moved to Capitol's Hollywood office. Here, he saw "A Little Feeling (Called Love)," "My Dream Came True," and "Steps 1 and 2" achieve only marginal success in 1961. His sound was now directed exclusively at the fans of country music, but country fans weren't having anything to do with Jack Scott. It is possible that he was being pigeonholed by the music industry as a result of his previous successes in the rock 'n roll field. In 1962 and 1963 Capitol issued Scott's records to a continued decline in sales before finally pulling the plug.

Scott was approached by Berry Gordy of Motown Records. Gordy wanted Scott for his new MoWest subsidiary. After mulling over Gordy's offer, Scott decided instead to accept an invitation from Groove Records, a subsidiary of RCA Victor. Scott had his first Groove session on October 23, 1963, in time to issue the Christmas single: "Jingle Bell Slide" b/w "There's Trouble Brewing." Generally, the singles on Groove were closer to rock 'n roll than anything he had recorded since Carlton. There were four more releases on Groove in 1964 before Scott moved up to the parent company. Now recording full-fledged country music and working with Chet Atkins as his producer, in 1965 Scott released three singles on RCA Victor. Unfortunately, not one of the Groove or RCA Victor singles created even a small ripple of excitement.

During the years 1966 to 1970, Scott's recording career was limited to one single each on ABC Paramount (again), Jubilee, and GRT. Finally, in January 1973, he was signed by Dot Records. After sixteen years of singing songs with a country twist, "Your Just Gettin' Better," Scott's second single for Dot, became his only incursion into the national country charts, appearing briefly in July 1974.

In 1975, he founded Ponie Records, his own independent label. Ponie was created to reissue Scott's older material, much of which had not been available for years. Scott was one of the few rock 'n roll artists to maintain control over his own catalog of music. He had the rights to almost everything he had recorded, including several interesting outtakes and unreleased songs. Most of his hits, with a few rarities, were issued by Ponie on an album in 1975. A year later, he had recorded enough new songs to fill a second album.

Scott continued to perform in clubs in and around Detroit, including a three-year stint at the Crazy Horse Lounge from 1972 to 1975. Like many other rock 'n rollers before him, he found the welcome mat waiting for his talents outside of the country. In the U.S., he was confined to small clubs, but overseas—in the England, France, Scandinavia, and Germany—he discovered he could still fill larger venues.

During his career, Jack Scott issued excellent rock 'n roll from 1957 through 1964, while his ballads retained a trace of country. His true country efforts most closely resemble those of Marty Robbins: straight from the heart, tightly composed, and well executed. The many fans who love Jack Scott deny that he has ever issued a bad recording.

September 1958

FRANKIE FORD
Frankie Ford's "Sea Cruise" stands as the ultimate example of New Orleans rhythm and blues. Francis Guzzo was born August 4, 1939, in the New Orleans suburb of Gretna. Voice lessons as a youth led, on September 18, 1952, to an appearance on Ted Mack's nationally televised "Original Amateur Hour." In high school, he joined a combo known as the Syncopators and later attended college on a music scholarship. In 1957, he came to the attention of a scout for Ace Records of Jackson, Mississippi. In short order, Ford was in J&M Studios recording "Cheatin' Woman." When the single was issued, Frankie was listed as the less ethnic "Frankie Ford" to help the single get airplay. For his tours, Ford put together a band featuring Mac Rebennack, later known as Dr. John. Their initial bookings were in the R&B theaters in the Northeast, as well as "American Bandstand." Returning to New Orleans, Ford found a pair of prerecorded music tracks waiting. The songs had been intended for Huey Smith and the Clowns. First he cut "Roberta," followed by "Sea Cruise." In the studio, Smith coached Ford, and played piano on the session. "Sea Cruise" was released in December 1958, and it remained a hit for four months. The following June, Ford, again with Smith's production, followed with "Alimony," which became a mid-sized hit, as did "Time After Time." In the meantime, Ford formed Spinet Records and had local success with "Chinese Bandits" by the Cheerleaders (a pseudonym for Huey Smith and the Clowns). Both Ford and Smith signed with Imperial Records in 1960, and of his six singles on the label, two were minor hits, "Seventeen" and a cover of Joe Jones' "You Talk Too Much." The Army draft effectively ended Ford's national popularity, although he recorded for half-dozen labels into the 1980s. He is still active on the New Orleans scene.

SEP 1   Remaining in New Orleans, Ray Charles performs at the Pontchartrain Park Baseball Stadium.
Even though he has yet to have a hit, **Frankie Ford** makes a guest appearance on "American Bandstand."

New Releases for the first week in September include "Need You" by Donnie Owens on Guyden; Clyde McPhatter's "A Lover's Question" on Atlantic; two from ABC-Paramount: "Just Young" by Paul Anka and "Open The Door" by the Royal Teens; Jack Scott's "With Your Love" b/w "Geraldine" on Carlton; two from Decca: "Forget Me Not" by the Kalin Twins and "Silly Willy" by Bobby Darin; "Mexican Hat Rock" by the Applejacks on Cameo; Glen Campbell's "I Wonder" on Ceneco; Mary Swan's "My Heart Belongs to You" on Swan; Joe Poovey's "Move Around" on Dixie; and Lord Rockingham XI's "Fried Onions" on London. The new novelty for the week is "The Blob" by the Five Blobs on Columbia. There is really only one "Blob," Bernie Nee, who overdubbed all the voices. The song was inspired by "The Blob," a film starring young Steve McQueen, which debuts September 15.

SEP 4   Jerry Butler and the Impressions perform "For Your Precious Love" on "American Bandstand."

SEP 5   Roy Brown brings his show to the High Hat Club in New Orleans for this weekend and the next. Also in town, Eddie Bo plays the Dew Drop Lounge for three days.

SEP 6   Marty Robbins guests on "The Big D Jamboree" in Dallas.
ABC-TV's "The Dick Clark Show" features Ruth Brown, Jack Scott, Willie Nelson, Tommy Edwards, and the Quin-Tones. Bobby Denton of Judd Records is also on the show to plug his new single, "Back To School."
Ray Charles and the Cookies perform at the Labor Union Hall in New Orleans.

EARLY SEPTEMBER
Bill Haley and His Comets set off on a Canadian tour encompassing the provinces of Nova Scotia and New Brunswick.
Danny and the Juniors are reportedly scheduled for a tour of Australia followed by a jaunt through Europe.
Bobby Darin is booked into Carmichael's in Birmingham, Alabama.
Attesting to the dramatic drop in his popularity, Jerry Lee Lewis is only able to draw four hundred fans to the 7,000-seat Nashville

Auditorium.

Chuck Berry, the Clovers, and Lloyd Price join forces as they take to the road for a series of one-night stands.

The Platters are guests of the Queen of Greece during a rare day off from their month-long engagement at the Olympia in Paris.

SEP 8   Paul Anka leaves on a three-week tour of the Far East. His first stop is Japan where he will perform for ten days at Tokyo's Kokusai Theater. From there, it's off to Osaka before returning for a concert in Tokyo's Koma Stadium. On his way back to the states he will play Hong Kong and Manila. (See also SEP 28.)

New Releases for the second week in September include **Johnny Tillotson**'s "Dreamy Eyes" on Cadence; "I Really Love You" by the Danleers on Mercury; Bobby Darin's "Queen of the Hop" on Atco; Jan and Arnie's "I Love Linda" in Arwin; "Leave Me Alone" by Dicky Doo and the Don'ts on Swan; Paul Peek's "Olds Mo Williams" on NRC; Gene Vincent's "Git It" on Capitol; "Pretty Girls Everywhere" by Eugene Church on Class; "The Blob" by the Zanies on Dore; Neil Sedaka's "Ring-A-Rockin'" on Guyden; Bobby Charles' "Since She's Gone" on Imperial; "Lily Lou" by Fabian on Chancellor; Troyce Key's "Baby Please Don't Go" on Warner Brothers; and Alvis Wayne's "Lay Your Head On My Shoulder" on Westport. Also new this week are several rockin' instrumentals: "What's Your Name?" by the Monorays on Nasco; "Poor Boy" by the Royaltones on Jubilee; "Bullwhip Rock" by the Cyclones on Trophy; and "King Cobra" by the Wild Tones on Tee Gee.

SEP 9   Dale Wright guests on "American Bandstand."

SEP 10   On "American Bandstand," Little Anthony and the Imperials sing "Tears on Your Pillow."

The Poni-Tails play a two-day stand at the Kentucky State Fair.

SEP 11   Back for a second guest shot, Dicky Doo and the Don'ts rock through "Nee Nee Na Na Na Na Nu Nu" on "American Bandstand."

SEP 12   It's jazz week at the Apollo Theater in Harlem, as the famed burlesque house welcomes Duke Ellington and his orchestra.

In Washington, the Howard Theater offers Lloyd Price, Little Anthony and the Imperials, the Five Satins, the Olympics, and the Videos for the week.

SEP 13   Fabian guests again on "The Dick Clark Show" this Saturday singing "Lilly Lou." Other artists appearing tonight are Johnny Nash, the Tune Rockers, and Somethin' Smith and the Redheads.

New Releases for the third week in September include Connie Francis' "Fallin'" on M-G-M; "Hideaway" by the Four Esquires on Paris; "It's So Easy" by the Crickets on Brunswick; Frankie Avalon's "I'll Wait For You"

JOHNNY TILLOTSON
Over a seven-year span, Johnny Tillotson had four Top Ten singles. Then, he faded into obscurity. He was born April 20, 1939 (or 1938), in Jacksonville, Florida. When he was nine, he was sent to care for his grandmother in the small town of Palatka. Here, influenced by Hank Williams' songs, he began singing on a local radio show. By his mid-teens, he was on a Jacksonville TV jamboree. In 1953, he had his own TV show. He began attending the University of Florida, majoring in journalism and playing dances at night. In a 1958 Nashville talent contest, he was discovered by Cadence Records. His first single, "Dreamy Eyes," was a sweet, teen-oriented ballad and a mid-sized hit. His next two releases, "True, True Happiness" and "Why Do I Love You So?" did even better. His fourth single, a pairing of the oldies "Earth Angel" and "Pledging My Love," did well. In the spring of 1960, "Poetry in Motion" became his only gold record. In 1961, "Jimmy's Girl" was topped by "Without You," another Top Ten hit. In 1961, "Dreamy Eyes" was re-released and did better than the first time. The next year, "It Keeps Right On A-Hurtin'" became his third Top Ten release, followed by "Send Me The Pillow You Dream On." He signed with M-G-M in 1963 after Cadence folded and picked up where he had left off when "Talk Back Trembling Lips" was a Top Ten hit. Each of his next seven M-G-M singles also sold in moderate numbers. By this time, every one of his Cadence and M-G-M singles had made the best seller charts. As 1966 dawned, he was poised to become a major country star. Yet he never had another hit record. He recorded for Amos (1969-70), Buddah (1971), Columbia (1973) and United Artists (1977). He turned to nightclubs for a while, then performed as an oldies act. By the late 1980s, he had all but disappeared.

on Chancellor; "To Know Him Is To Love Him" by the Teddy Bears on Dore; "Peaches and Cream" by Larry Williams on Specialty; Jerry Fuller's "The Door Is Open" on Lin; two from Old Town: "I'm Truly, Truly Yours" by Robert and Johnny and "Please Remember My Heart" by the Solitaires; Jimmy Bowen's "My Kind of Woman" on Roulette; Bobby Lee Trammell's "My Susie J, My Susie J" on Radio; "Night Theme" by the Three Souls on Argo; and Ray Peterson's "Dream Way" on RCA. Out this week is Larry Davis' "Texas Flood" on Duke, a song that was to have a major influence on Stevie Ray Vaughan.

MID-SEPTEMBER

Connie Francis returns to the states after her successful tour of Great Britain.

SEP 18 The Chantels are today's guest artist on "American Bandstand."
In Washington, DC, the Poni-Tails headline the burlesque revue at the Lotus Club, 14th Street and New York Avenue. They remain at the Lotus through September 23.

SEP 19 The Coasters headline a show packed with rhythm and blues acts at the Apollo Theater in New York. Also appearing are the Spaniels, the Danleers, the Olympics, Bobby Hendricks, the Quin-Tones, and Sil Austin's combo.
Private Elvis Presley and about a thousand other G.I.'s board a troop train at Ft. Hood bound for Brooklyn.
In Brooklyn, Johnny Nash entertains the crowd at the Club Elegante.

SEP 20 For four days, Wanda Jackson rocks the house at the Flame Lounge in Minneapolis.
The Big Bopper pays "The Dick Clark Show" a visit tonight. Also on the bill are Jill Corey, Betty Johnson, the Kalin Twins, the Shields, and Donnie Owens.
On NBC-TV, "The Perry Como Show" offers the talents of Tommy Sands.

SEP 22 At the Military Ocean Terminal in Brooklyn, Private Presley leaves the states on a troop ship bound for Germany, where he will be stationed at Ray Barracks, Friedburg, until March 1960.

New Releases for the fourth week in September include Ricky Nelson's "Lonesome Town" b/w "I Got A Feeling" on Imperial; two from Ace: Jimmy Clanton's "Letter to An Angel" and "I Sold My Heart to the Junkman" by the Silhouettes; "Willie Did The Cha Cha" by the Johnny Otis Show in Capitol; "Rockin' Mary" by the Champs on Challenge; "Our First Kiss" by the Aquatones on Fargo; "Do the Stop" by Joe Bennett and the Sparkletones on ABC-Paramount; "Walking Along" by the Solitaires on Argo; "My Greatest Love" by the Fidelities on Baton; **Esquirita**'s "Rockin' the Joint" on Capitol; Cozy Cole's two-part "Topsy" on Love; Johnny Burnette's "Kiss Me" on Freedom; Tommy Edwards' "Love Is All We Need"

ESQUIRITA

So you thought Little Richard was the wild man of rock 'n roll. Well, meet Esquirita. Eskew Reeder was born in Greenville, South Carolina. Throughout his career, he performed using various names, including Esquirita, S. Q Reeder, the Magnificent Malochi, and the King of Voola. He claimed he taught Little Richard how to play piano. He also said he was the inspiration for Richard's stage antics and wild hairstyle. It may even be Esquirita's photo on the cover of Little Richard's LP on Camden Records. He said that he composed the 1956 hit "Green Door" (officially listed as by Marvin Moore and Bob Davie). His first session was at Stellers Studio in Dallas, but the seven songs put on tape weren't released until 1987. In 1958, his name was associated with Gene Vincent. Through Vincent, he met Paul Peek, and Esquirita next showed up playing piano on one of rock 'n roll's wildest sessions, Peek's "Sweet Skinny Jenny" b/w "The Rock-A-Round." (Esquirita coauthored "The Rock-A-Round." See the sidebars for Paul Peek and Joe South for other information.) A man of such preposterous stature couldn't escape the recording companies for long. Through the urging of Gene Vincent, Esquirita signed with Capitol in 1958. Over the next year, he recorded twenty-eight songs. Only three singles, including "Rockin' the Joint" and "Laid Off," and one album were released by Capitol at the time. For the next ten years, he disappeared, retreating into the under belly of New Orleans. An occasional single on Minit or one of the other New Orleans labels would insure those who cared that he was still active. His name surfaced in 1970 as the co-composer of "Freedom Blues," "Dew Drop Inn" and the title song on Little Richard's album THE RILL THING. He was reportedly living in New York as a recluse. Eskew Reeder died of AIDS complications on October 23, 1986, in Harlem.

on M-G-M; "Mighty, Mighty Man" by Bobby Darin and the Rinky-Dinks on Atco; **Robin Luke**'s "My Girl" on Dot; Bobby Freeman's "Shame on You, Miss Johnson" on Josie; two from Apt: "Please Believe Me" by the Elegants and "How Come" by Bobby Hamilton; Little Walter's "Key to the Highway" on Checker; "Puppy Love" by Nino and the Ebb Tides on Tecorte; and the Six Teens' "Baby-O" on Flip. Also new this week are several rockabilly classics: Clyde Stacey's "You Want Love" on Bullseye; Sonny Burgess' "Thunderbird" on Sun; "Jodie" by Sammy Masters on 4-Star; Benny Barnes' "You Gotta Pay" on Starday; and Huelyn Duvall's "Friday Night on a Dollar Bill" on Challenge.

SEP 24   Johnny Tillotson sings both sides of his latest release, "Dreamy Eyes" and "Well I'm Your Man," on "American Bandstand." Also on in the spotlight during this afternoon's show is Wanda Jackson.

SEP 25   Tommy Edwards opens a week-long run at the Safari Club in Chicago.

SEP 26   Ruth Brown is top-billed at the Apollo this week. Appearing with Miss Brown are the Moonglows and the Kodaks.
The Coasters, the Danleers, the Dubs, and Wynona Carr entertain the crowd for the week at the Howard Theater in Washington.

SEP 27   "The Dick Clark Show" schedules a roster of three M-G-M Records artists: Conway Twitty, Connie Francis, and Joni James. Also on the bill are Gordon McRae, Bobby Freeman, and Valerie Carr.
Johnny Cash guests on the "Hometown Jamboree" television show in Los Angeles.
The Everly Brothers stop by NBC-TV's "Perry Como Show."

SEP 28   Paul Anka entertains an overflow crowd in Hong Kong. He will stop in Manila for a final concert before returning stateside.
On NBC-TV, Jimmie Rodgers is the guest of "The Steve Allen Show."

SEP 29   Jackie Dee and Her Dates headline the Teen-A-Rama in Terre Haute before she leaves on tour.

SEP 30   Starting on a new tour, Johnny Cash plays a one-night stand in Salt Lake City.

THE TOP ROCK 'N ROLL RECORDS FOR SEPTEMBER 1959

1. Bird Dog/Devoted To You - The Everly Brothers
2. Little Star - The Elegants
3. Just a Dream - Jimmy Clanton

ROBIN LUKE
Breaking into show biz in Honolulu is just about as far away from the "Great White Way" as one can get in America. Robin Luke was born March 19, 1942 in Los Angeles. His family moved to Hawaii when Robin was a child. He was taught guitar at an early age, and he spent his spare time composing songs that appealed to teens. He had a pleasant enough voice—for a sixteen-year old, and eventually he came to the attention of Bob Bertram of Bertram International Records. Bertram was Honolulu's jack-of-all-trades when it came to music. He was a deejay, promoter, agent, and studio operator as well as label owner. Bertram listened attentively to Luke as the boy ran through a dozen or so songs, then Bertram picked one that Robin had written for his younger sister. "Susie Darlin'" was recorded in Bertram's makeshift studio, using simple instrumentation: an muted guitar, muted percussion, muted vocal group. The rhythm had shades of Hawaii and Jamaica with a cha-cha thrown in for good measure. Luke's tender age was readily apparent in his delivery. Teenage girls had no doubt that the singer was one of their own. The record was a sensation in Hawaii and came to the attention of Dot Records, a company that was always on the lookout for fresh talent—and a ready-made hit. Through Bertram's hardheaded negotiations, he retained Luke's contract with International label while Dot released the same songs on their label. The catch was that Bertram's "territory" was limited to Hawaii, while Dot got the rest of the country. In the long run, it made little difference. Robin Luke only had the one hit in him. After "Susie Darlin'" peaked in the Top Ten, Luke never had another record that even dented the Top 100. After three more releases on International (all of which were issued on Dot) and an additional five singles only on Dot, Luke "retired" from show business at the age of nineteen.

4. Rock-In Robin/Over and Over - Bobby Day
5. My True Love/Leroy - Jack Scott
6. Born Too Late - The Poni-Tails
7. It's All In the Game - Tommy Edwards
8. Poor Little Fool - Ricky Nelson
9. Western Movies - The Olympics
10. Tears On My Pillow - Little Anthony and the Imperials
11. Gingerbread - Frankie Avalon
12. Are You Really Mine/The Wizard - Jimmie Rodgers
13. Susie Darlin' - Robin Luke
14. Summertime Blues - Eddie Cochran
15. Stupid Cupid - Connie Francis
16. Willie and the Hand Jive - Johnny Otis
17. Down the Aisle of Love - The Quin-Tones
18. Lazy Summer Night - The Four Preps
19. Rebel Rouser - Duane Eddy
20. When - The Kalin Twins
21. Somebody Touched Me - Buddy Knox
22. The Ways of a Woman In Love - Johnny Cash
23. Chantilly Lace - The Big Bopper
24. She Was Only Seventeen - Marty Robbins
25. How the Time Flies - Jerry Wallace
26. Win Your Love For Me - Sam Cooke
27. Summertime, Summertime - The Jamies
28. Carol - Chuck Berry
29. One Summer Night - The Danleers
30. Ramrod - Duane Eddy
31. Itchy Twitchy Feeling - Bobby Hendricks
32. No One Knows - Dion and the Belmonts
33. Splish Splash - Bobby Darin
34. You Cheated - The Shields
35. Green Mosquito - The Tune Rockers
36. Early in the Morning - The Rinky-Dinks
37. Betty Lou's Got a New Pair of Shoes - Bobby Freeman
38. Topsy II - Cozy Cole
39. Blue, Blue Day - Don Gibson
40. Hard Headed Woman - Elvis Presley
41. Cerveza - Boots Brown
42. Chariot Rock - The Champs
43. By The Light of the Silvery Moon - Jimmy Bowen
44. La-Do-Dada - Dale Hawkins
45. It's Only Make Believe - Conway Twitty
46. Ten Commandments of Love - Harvey and the Moonglows
47. Over the Weekend - The Playboys
48. Blue Ribbon Baby - Tommy Sands
49. Please Don't Do It - Dale Wright
50. Baby Face - Little Richard

Also on the "pop" charts:
Near You - Roger Williams

Tea For Two Cha-cha - Tommy Dorsey
The End - Earl Grant

September 1958
ARTIST OF THE MONTH

JIMMY CLANTON

Jimmy Clanton

The location of Baton Rouge, a short drive north of New Orleans, made it the perfect city in which to grow up if you loved rock 'n roll—and you didn't live in New Orleans. And, Jimmy Clanton loved rock 'n roll.

Clanton, born in Baton Rouge on September 2, 1940, came from a musical family. Both of his parents were proficient on various instruments. He remembers being influenced by the music of Fats Domino and Chuck Berry, but counts Ray Charles as his primary inspiration. By the time he was in his middle teens, Clanton was a proficient guitarist and leader of a local band of high school kids who billed themselves as the Dixie Cats when they played sock hops in school gymnasiums. There were other bands in the area, the Playboys with John Fred and the Night Trainers with Dick Holler. As band members drifted into and out of the various combos, eventually Holler and Clanton joined forces to form a band they called the Rockets. Holler played piano and Clanton played guitar. With other teens on bass, drums and tenor sax, the Rockets were one of the premier high school combos in Baton Rouge.

Like many other bands, the boys wanted desperately to know how they would sound on record. As New Orleans was only a short drive away; and, as the band-members were young and naive, they packed their gear into two cars and drove off on a weekday afternoon to make a record. Their destination was 525 Governor Nicholls Street, the address of J&M Recording Service owned and operated by Cosimo Matassa—"Coz" to his friends. J&M Studio was famous as the starting place for most of the hits coming out of New Orleans. The building had been a cold storage facility and it featured a large, bare-walled room that Coz used for his main studio because the sound inside was "alive."

The Rockets ventured into the front offices at J&M, asked the price of an hour's session, and paid their $25.00. Clanton recalls that the band wrapped up the two songs they had prepared and still had eight minutes of recording time remaining. The combo had not prepared any other material, but Clanton offered to sing a tune he had composed the night before, titled "Just a Dream." Eighteen-year old Clanton was overheard by Johnny Vincent, owner of Ace Records of Jackson, Mississippi, who happened to be in the studio. The result was a contract for Clanton with the Rockets as his backing band.

Vincent paid for the next session by the combo and issued a single "I Trusted You" b/w "That's You Baby." In south Louisiana, the record found a little attention, but in other areas it received no airplay. Clanton immediately became discouraged with Ace Records and sought out another label. Eventually, he recorded "Emma Lee" under the pseudonym Jimmie Dale for drew-Blan Records of Morgan City, Louisiana. This record is a fine example of Clanton's style, featuring a female chorus and stinging guitar break. The flip, "My Pride and Joy" is a harbinger of Clanton's future pop/R&B approach.

Vincent was convinced that Clanton's slightly off-key, nasal twang offered commercial potential. That is, if it could be coupled with a rhythm and blues backing that was softer than the style used by Fats Domino. For the next session, the Rockets stayed behind in Baton Rouge. Vincent and Matassa brought together top members of the New Orleans musical community including Allen Toussaint on piano and Malcom "Mac" Rebbenack on guitar, along with a female chorus thrown in to sweeten the offering. The result was a reworking of "Just a Dream" with writer's credit going to Clanton and Matassa. This time, the single captured the essence of the teen angst Clanton had penned into the lyrics, while the overall sound of the recording oozed New Orleans R&B.

"Just a Dream" was released in early spring, 1958. Sales were sluggish in the beginning. Vincent started blitzing the media trying to get some attention. Eventually, Clanton was booked to play the Uptown Theater in Philadelphia. He didn't realize that the performers and clientele at the Uptown were mostly black until he arrived for a rehearsal. The staff of the Uptown was also shocked. After all, Ace Records was well-known for its rhythm and blues artists. Who, then, was this pasty-faced white boy with the pompadour hairdo? Clanton later recalled that he was helped through the first show by the kindness of Clyde McPhatter and Thurston Harris.

Finally, in June, Clanton got the break he needed. He was booked for an afternoon appearance on ABC-TV's "American Bandstand." Within a month, "Just a Dream" started creeping up the national charts. On August 24, Clanton was working a Dick Clark show at the Hollywood Bowl. On August 29, he started a ten-day run with Alan Freed's "Big Beat Show" at the Fox Theater in Brooklyn. "Just a Dream" was reaching its peak in sales, taking it near the top of the charts. The record eventually sold almost two million copies.

In October, Clanton joined the "Biggest Show of Stars for '58" tour, appearing with Buddy Holly, Frankie Avalon, Bobby Darin, Dion, and Jack Scott. On a similar tour in February 1959, Buddy Holly was killed in a tragic plane crash. Clanton and Frankie Avalon were immediately enlisted to fill out the dates of that tour.

Clanton's follow-up to "Just a Dream" reportedly fared almost as well. "A Letter To An Angel" was credited to Clanton and Matassa, but it used a melody that was virtually identical to Johnny Ace's 1954 hit, "Pledging My Love." "A Letter To An Angel" was certified a million seller, though the music charts of the day have the record faltering before it reached the Top Twenty. The next release, "Ship on a Stormy Sea," featured a harder vocal over a more insistent melody-line. Vincent again declared that this single sold a million copies, but it never charted. A maudlin revision of "My Own True Love," the theme from "Gone With The Wind," fared better in the fall of 1959, at least according the music surveys.

Also in 1959, Clanton's association with Alan Freed reaped a huge reward. Jimmy was picked to play the lead in "Go, Johnny Go!" another in the series of the rock 'n roll films co-starring Freed and a host of musical talent. The difference with "Go, Johnny Go!" was that Clanton carried much of the story line by himself as well as handling some of the singing, including "Ship on a Stormy Sea." His acting was no better than could be expected. However, the movie was successful, in part because it also featured Ritchie Valens' only cameo film role as well as a speaking part for Chuck Berry. "Go, Johnny, Go" also had appearances by Jackie Wilson and Eddie Cochran who were at the beginning of their rise in popularity.

In 1959, just as it looked like things were going his way, Clanton was drafted into the Army. He served two years, coming out in 1961. Through this period, his recording dates had to be scheduled during his furloughs, and he was forced to limit his personal appearances to a handful of two-week leaves.

The romping "Go, Jimmy, Go," was a Top Ten hit for Clanton in early 1960. This was followed by a Neil Sedaka composition, "Another Sleepless Night," done in the mold of "Just a Dream." Then, for no apparent reason, the style of Clanton's recordings changed completely. "Come Back" and "What Am I Gonna Do" were teen "pop" through and through, with violins augmenting the syrupy female vocal group. The R&B backing was paired down to plinking piano triplets in an attempt to have Clanton compete in the market place with the same entertainers with which he had shared that tour bus a short time before: Frankie Avalon, Bobby Darin, and Dion. As such, Clanton became another pretty face singing "pop" for the masses. The result was that each new single stayed popular for a progressively shorter period of time. Now, Clanton was surviving on his apple-cheek good looks alone. He was still in demand on the caravan tours and holiday theater shows put together by Dick Clark, Alan Freed and others. And, his smiling face was featured prominently on magazines aimed at teenage girls.

In 1961, he was once again the star of a rock 'n roll movie, the quickly forgotten "Teenage Millionaire." Clanton's last big hit came in 1962 with "Venus in Blue Jeans" a mishmash of Latin rhythm, harps, and a brass band.

There were several more Ace releases, but none fared well. Clanton was paired with Mary Ann Mobley, the reigning Miss America, for the schmaltzy "Down the Aisle." He issued love songs with "Just a Moment (of Your Time)" and "Lucky In Love With You." Even a song penned by Neil Diamond, "I Care Enough (To Give The Very Best," couldn't be salvaged.

Clanton's recording contract with Ace expired and he switched to Phillips in late 1963, but the hits stopped after "Venus in Blue Jeans." Like many of the other American teen idols of the early 1960s, Clanton received a knockout-blow from the "British Invasion" of 1964. A year later he recorded a couple of singles for Mala, followed in 1967 by two singles for Imperial. In 1969, he recorded "Curly" for Laurie, a single that attracted enough attention to break into the top hits charts for a few weeks in November before fading from sight. In 1971, his career struck bottom when he recorded "The Coolest Hot Pants" for Spiral. It is, without doubt, his worst record. In 1976, there was a single of "Old Rock 'n Roller (Will It Happen Again)" for Starcrest, a Nashville label. Finally, in 1978, Starfire, a company owned by Rip Lay, a West Coast record dealer, put out "I Wanna Go Home" as a single.

During this time, Jimmy Clanton maintained his career in music by performing hundreds of one-night stands in every conceivable location. When the rock 'n roll revival swept the country in the 1969, he found he could work larger auditoriums. By the late 1970s, his professional life had settled into a routine divided between Philadelphia, Houston, Las Vegas, and Los Angeles. His "Jimmy Clanton Caravan" employed eleven people including his traveling band, road managers and sound men. He performed for thousands of fans six nights a week working the territory around one of his bases.

When he began recording, Jimmy Clanton exuded a youthful, cleancut appearance that the major record-merchandisers found irresistible. However, his background in Louisiana's rhythm and blues community imparted to his early singles a "down home" flavor and an musical honesty that was lacking with many of his rivals. Clanton did not ask to be a teen idol, he only wanted to be a performer. When he altered his style, it was under pressure exerted by various managers and record company executives—men looking to mold a hit-maker.

Truth be known, what Jimmy Clanton wanted most was to stand in the cold-storage room and sing in front of that wonderful horn section down at Cossimo's.

October 1958

OCT 2   Jerry Lee Lewis and Carl Perkins headline a Texas tour opening tonight in Lubbock. Other cities scheduled for a visit include Austin (3), San Antonio (4), Galveston (5), Houston (7), Amarillo (8), Fort Worth (9), and San Angelo (10).

"The Pat Boone Show" begins its second season on ABC-TV.

OCT 3   In Worcester, Massachusetts, the second edition of "The Biggest Show of Stars for 1958" kicks off an extended tour. Headliners are Buddy Holly and the Crickets, Clyde McPhatter, Frankie Avalon, the Coasters, Bobby Darin, Dion and the Belmonts, Jack Scott, the Danleers, the Jesters, Jimmy Clanton, **Bobby Freeman**, the Danleers, and Sil Austin's combo. Future dates include Providence, Rhode Island (4); Montreal (5), Peterborough (6), and Kitchener (7), Ontario; Toledo (8); Indianapolis (9); Columbus, Ohio (11); Pittsburgh's Syria Mosque Theater; Roanoke (15); Scranton (16); and Richmond.

Eddie Bo and Lee Diamond entertain patrons for three days at the High Hat Club in New Orleans. Diamond returns next weekend for three more days.

Mickey and Sylvia are guests of the Apollo Theater in New York this week.

The Copa Club in Newport, Kentucky, welcomes Dinah Washington for a weekend engagement.

In Washington, DC, the Clovers open a short engagement at Hy's Melody Inn.

Also in Washington, at the Howard Theater Jerry Butler and the Impressions, Ray Peterson, the Spaniels, the Quintones, Bobby Hendricks, and Doc Bagby's combo entertain for the week.

OCT 4   Duane Eddy and the Rebels perform on "The Dick Clark Show." Also appearing are Lou Monte and Kayli.

OCT 5   The Kalin Twins begin a four-week tour of England with a concert at Victoria Hall, Hanley, Stoke-on-Trent. Booked as the opening act for the Kalin Twins is a popular British club band making their concert-hall debut, Cliff Richard and the Drifters.

Bill Doggett performs for the Sunday night dance at the Labor Union Hall in New Orleans.

OCT 6   Sarah Vaughan opens for a week at the Casino Royal in Washington.

BOBBY FREEMAN
Bobby Freeman received something rare in the music business—a second chance. Born in San Francisco on June 13, 1940, he joined the Romancers at age fourteen. The group recorded two singles for Dootone and one for Bay Tone before falling apart. Bobby then founded the Vocaleers (not the group that recorded for Red Robin and Old Town). In 1958, while attempting to go solo, he brought a drummer into the studio to accompany him while he played piano and sang. The duo recorded four songs, including "Do You Want To Dance." The tape was loaned to a San Francisco deejay who played it for the owner of Jubilee Records, who happened to be in town on his honeymoon. The unfinished demo was quickly issued on Jubilee's Joz subsidiary as "Do You Want To Dance." The title was soon changed to "Do You Wanna Dance." It took two months for the record to catch on, but then it became a sensation. Freeman issued many other fine recordings on Joz (later changed to Josie), including "Shame, Shame, Shame" and "Ebb Tide." In 1960, his "I Do the) Shimmy, Shimmy" caught on with the dance crowd. He left Josie to record for Cameo, a label built on dance fads. With no immediate success, he moved on to King in 1961. His career stymied, he retreated to San Francisco and teamed up with a new producer, Sylvester Stewart (soon to become popular as Sly, of the Family Stone). They recorded "C'Mon and Swim," another dance song. It was Freeman's biggest hit since "Do You Wanna Dance." The follow-up, "S-W-I-M," faded quickly. After that, Freeman's popularity as a recording artist was over. There were still records released—on the Loma, Double Shot, Parkway, Touch, DHC, Avco, and Lakeside labels, but none mustered much attention. Back home, he worked at the notorious Condor Club, entertaining the crowds between the strip shows.

New Releases for the first week in October include Duane Eddy's "Cannonball" on Jamie; "So Far Away" by the Pastels on Argo; "Whoa Mabel" by Bill Haley and His Comets on Decca; "Try Me" by James Brown and the Famous Flames on Federal; "Gee Whiz" by the Twins on RCA; Buddy Ace's "Angel Boy" on Duke; and Young Jesse's "That's Enough for Me" on Atlantic. Also out this week is a re-release of the 1956 single "Sister Jenny" by Johnny Fuller on Imperial.

EARLY OCTOBER

Earl Grant is currently playing the Interlude Club in Los Angeles. He also has his own one-hour television program on KTLA-TV. In addition, he has been offered a cameo in the upcoming movie "Jamboree."

In Philadelphia, Kathy Linden gives birth to a son, William David Simonton.

OCT 9   Back for another appearance, Duane Eddy performs "Ramrod" on "American Bandstand."

OCT 10   "Jocko's Rocketship Revue" hits the Apollo for the week. The Upsetters back for a repeat performance, along with the Isley Brothers, the Chantels, Dee Clark, Little Anthony and the Imperials, and Little Willie John.

The Billy Williams Quartet lays over for a week at the Embers nightclub in Ft. Wayne.

Dinah Washington starts a three-week run at Roberts' Show Club in Chicago.

Jackie Wilson, the Heartbeats, and Oscar McLollie entertain at the Howard Theater in Washington for a week.

OCT 11   In the evening, "The Dick Clark Show" is broadcast live from the Southeastern Fair in Atlanta. Guests include Sam Cooke, Danny and the Juniors (singing "At the Hop"), Conway Twitty, the Applejacks, and Paul Peek. Earlier in the day, there was a matinee rehearsal at the same site. This was the first integrated show held at the Atlanta fairgrounds.

OCT 13   Sam Cooke returns to the Labor Union Hall for a show in New Orleans.

New Releases for the second week in October include Dale Hawkins' "A House, A Car, and a Wedding Ring" on Checker; "Beep Beep" by the Playmates on Roulette; Roy Orbison's "Sweet and Innocent" on RCA; "Wiggle, Wiggle" by the Accents on Brunswick; **Jimmy Scott**'s "Don't Be Misled" on King; "Please Wait My Love" by the Valiants on Keen; Jody Reynolds' "Closin' In" on Demon; Johnny Rivers' "You're The One" on Guyden; "The Creep" by Noble "Thin Man" Watts on Baton; Roddy Jackson's "Moose On The Loose" on Specialty; and Cliff Thomas' "Leave It To Me" on Phillips International.

JIMMY SCOTT

"Little" Jimmy Scott came by his nickname honestly—until he was forty, he stood just under five feet tall. Scott had a hereditary condition that caused him to stop growing for a while, then start again. Born July 17, 1925, in Cleveland, Scott began performing professionally at age seventeen. At age twenty, he was appearing at the Baby Grand Club in New York. He was hired as Lionel Hampton's vocalist in 1949 and remained with Hamp off and on for four years. His first records were cut with Hampton on Decca in 1950, and "Everybody's Somebody's Fool" became a minor hit. The same year he decided to issue some solo recordings on Roost Records. Over the course of two years, he issued a dozen Roost singles. He moved along to Coral and Brunswick, both subsidiaries of Decca, for a total of four records in 1952-53. After a two-year hiatus, he signed with Savoy in 1955 and moved on to King in 1956. After another break, he issued an album on Ray Charles' Tangerine label in 1962 and another LP on Atlantic in 1969. These two albums are considered to be the highlight of his career, although the work he did for Savoy and King was also outstanding. Jimmy Scott was a jazz balladeer, a singer of soulful tunes, a crooner. He doesn't really fit any particular mold. Early in life he learned to be himself and not copy anyone else's style. Scott admits that his influences were as varied as Paul Robeson, Duke Ellington and Louis Jordan. As he reached his 60th birthday, one might assume that he would be looking forward to retirement. Not Scott. In the 1990s, he underwent a revival as an entirely new audience discovered him. His new recordings on Sire received rave reviews from the critics.

OCT 15   The "Hellzapoppin' All Star Yock and Roll Show of 1959" starts a cross-country tour of eight cities through November 15. Humorists Olsen and Johnson represent the "yock" side, while the "roll" side is handled by Jerry Lee Lewis, Mickey and Sylvia, Dave "Baby" Cortez, the Applejacks, the Moonglows, and **Tommy Edwards**.

         The Clovers perform at the Dew Drop Cafe in New Orleans for an extended four-day stand.

MID-OCTOBER

    Dinah Washington is currently in Chicago playing nightly to a packed house at Robert's Show Club.

    Ray Charles is in the middle of an engagement at Philadelphia's Showboat.

OCT 17   Sarah Vaughan and Miles Davis' combo headline a jazz revue at New York's Apollo Theater this week.

         On CBS-TV's "Your Hit Parade," Tommy Edwards is the special guest singing "It's All In The Game" which is the number one hit for the week.

         Bobby Freeman guests on a record hop on WONE-TV in Dayton, OH.

OCT 18   On NBC-TV, Robin Luke makes a television appearance as a guest of "The Perry Como Show."

         On ABC-TV, "The Dick Clark Show" welcomes Neil Sedaka, Cozy Cole, the Elegants, Sonny James, and Julius LaRosa.

OCT 19   Jan and Arnie appear on "The Jack Benny Show" on CBS-TV.

New Releases for the third week in October include "One Night" b/w "I Got Stung" by Elvis Presley on RCA; Lloyd Price's "Stagger Lee" on ABC-Paramount; Chuck Berry's "Sweet Little Rock and Roll" on Chess; "Problems" by the Everly Brothers on Cadence; "Gotta Travel On" by Billy Grammer on Monument; two from End: "Lovers Never Say Goodbye" from the Flamingos and "So Much" by Little Anthony and the Imperials; Fats Domino's "Whole Lotta Lovin'" on Imperial; "Peek-A-Boo" by the Cadillacs on Josie; "C'Mon Everybody" by Eddie Cochran on Liberty; Buddy Holly's "Heartbeat" on Coral; Jackie Wilson's "Lonely Teardrops" on Brunswick; Sam Cooke's "Love You Most Of All" on Keen; Jerry Wallace's "Diamond Ring" on Challenge; Jesse Belvin's "Funny" on RCA; "Young and In Love" by the Crescendos on Nasco; two from King: "Poor Boy" by the Sugarcanes and "All My Love Belongs To You" by Little Willie John; "Here I Stand" by Wade Flemons on Vee-Jay; Buzz Clifford's "For Always" on Bow; and, finally, one from Savoy, **Little Anthony** (page 308 ➤) Goudine's "Must Be Falling In Love." A new single this week from Carlton is "Five Little Numbers" by Jack Scott's backing vocalists, the Chantones.

OCT 21   Freddy Bell and the Bell Boys open a five-day engagement at La Maina's in Philadelphia.

TOMMY EDWARDS

Tommy Edwards breached the gap between the singers of "pop" music and the buyers of rock 'n roll records. Older than his contemporary rockers (he was born in Richmond, Virginia, February 17, 1922, although his press releases claimed 1930), he was able to capitalize on the ballad side of rock. In fact, unknown to most of his fans, he had been popular years before his million selling "It's All in the Game." Edwards began his long career in show business at age nine. At one time, he had his own fifteen-minute radio show in Virginia. After college, he appeared in clubs throughout the East and Midwest. By 1950, he was devoting his energy to writing songs. His demonstration recording of his "All Over Again" brought him to the attention of M-G-M Records. In 1951, he had "pop" hits with "Morning Side of the Mountain" and an early version of "It's All in the Game." The flip side of "It's All in the Game" was "All Over Again," a both sides were popular in the R&B market. Edwards had no hits for the next seven years, although he continued recording for M-G-M. Some of his better efforts were "It Could Have Been Me" and "Pagin' Mr. Jackson." By 1958, M-G-M was about to drop Edwards from its roster when he rerecorded "It's All in the Game," using a rock 'n roll arrangement for the orchestral backing. The record immediately caught the public's ear and eventually racked up sales of more than three million copies, while remaining on the best seller charts for five months during the winter of 1958-59. Edwards followed with "Love Is All We Need" and "Please Mr. Sun," both Top Twenty hits in 1959. He was able to keep his records on the best seller lists through 1960, when "I Really Don't Want to Know" also charted in the Top Twenty. After that, the buyers turned their attention elsewhere. Edwards passed away on October 23, 1969, at his home near Richmond.

LITTLE ANTHONY & THE IMPERIALS
"Little" Anthony Gourdine (born January 8, 1941 in Brooklyn) was fifteen and a student at Boys High when he formed the Duponts, named after the chemical company. Other members were William Dockerty, tenor; William Delk, baritone; and William Bracey, bass. They released one single on Winley Records, "Must Be Falling in Love," in August 1956. The single was later reissued on Savoy Records (as by Little Anthony Gourdine and the Duponts) when Little Anthony was hot. The Duponts signed with Royal Roost Records in early 1957 for their only other release, "Prove It Tonight." After playing Alan Freed's Easter show, they dissolved, and Anthony joined the Chesters. This group featured Tracy Lord, tenor; Ernest Wright, tenor; Keith Williams, baritone; and Glouster "Nate" Rogers, bass. The Chesters had one single on Apollo Records, "The Fires Burn No More." At this time, Clarence Collins replaced Williams. Richard Barrett brought the group to George Goldner, who assigned them to his End label. During their first session, in May 1958, Ernest Wright was the featured vocalist as the group attempted "Two People in the World." At Barrett's suggestion, Anthony tried the high tenor part. The single, listed as by the Imperials, was released with "Tears on my Pillow" as the B-side. Deejays liked both songs, but "Tears on my Pillow" became the hit, and the group's only gold record. Alan Freed plugged the group as Little Anthony and the Imperials, and later pressings were changed accordingly. Next they chose to record "The Diary," a song by Neil Sedaka. No one was happy with the Imperials' version, and their second single was "So Much." Sedaka, himself, recorded "The Diary" and had a hit. Through the 1950s, the Imperials had hits with "Wishful Thinking," "A Prayer and a Juke Box," and "Shimmy, Shimmy, Ko-Ko-Bop."

OCT 22 Bo Diddley is the top-billed performer in the Apollo Theater's variety show this week. Opening acts are Thurston Harris, Dion and the Belmonts, the Shields, and Ella Johnson with Buddy Johnson's orchestra.
 Johnny Cash, Carl Perkins, and Sonny James are currently touring the middle of the county. Tonight, they stop in Denver. For the remainder of the week, dates include Colorado Springs (23), Tulsa (24), and St. Louis (25). (See also OCT 26.)

OCT 24 Currently on tour, LaVern Baker, Jackie Wilson, Bobby Day, and Lee Andrews and the Hearts play an engagement in Richmond tonight. Weekend shows include Washington (26), and Roanoke (27). Other cities scheduled through November 12 are Chattanooga and Knoxville; Bluefield, West Virginia; Portsmouth, Virginia; Raleigh, Asheville and Charlotte, North Carolina; Atlanta, Savannah, Macon, and Augusta, Georgia; and Columbia and Charleston, South Carolina.

OCT 25 Bobby Darin is booked for a two-day stand at the Erie Social Club in Philadelphia.
 On "The Dick Clark Show," tonight's performers are Frankie Avalon (singing "Gingerbread"), Don Gibson, Bobby Day, Robin Luke, and Buddy Holly and the Crickets.

OCT 26 In what must be ranked as the oddest booking listed herein, Tommy Sands is the star entertainer at the Huntsville (Texas) Prison Rodeo.
 The Johnny Cash road show continues with a performance in Oklahoma City. Other shows through the end of the month are San Angelo, TX (28); Houston (29); Corpus Christi (30); Mobile (31). (See also NOV 1.)

New Releases for the fourth week in October include two from ABC-Paramount: "Teen Commandments" from the combined talents of Paul Anka, George Hamilton IV, and Johnny Nash and "Seven Minutes in Heaven" by the Poni-Tails; "Philadelphia, U.S.A." by the Nu Tornados on Carlton; Jimmie Rodgers' "Bimbombey" on Roulette; "Rock House" by Ray Charles on Atlantic; "Sure of Love" by the Chantels on End; "Nature Boy" by the Shields on Dot; Charlie Rich's "Whirlwind" on Phillips International; "Well, I'll Be John Brown" by Huey Smith and the Clowns on Ace; "Nobody But You" by Dee Clark on Abner; and Jimmy Jones' "A Closer Walk" on Savoy. This week, the future country star Roy Clark has out "Please Mr. Mayor" on Debbie.

OCT 28 Buddy Holly and the Crickets stop by "American Bandstand" to sing "Think It Over," "Fool's Paradise," and "Heartbeat."

OCT 29 Larry Williams and his band top the bill at New York's Apollo Theater this week. Also in the spotlight are Lewis Lymon and the Teenchords, Baby Washington, the Pastels, and Ed Townsend.

"American Bandstand" hosts the Teddy Bears singing "To Know Him Is To Love Him."

Connie Francis begins an extended tour of Hawaii.

OCT 31   Joe Turner is currently playing the New Orleans area. Tonight he is in Thibodaux.

Roy Hamilton headlines this weeks revue at the Howard Theater in Washington. Also appearing are Shirley and Lee, Linda Hopkins, and the **Mello-Kings**.

LATE OCTOBER

The Applejacks are currently playing at the Lindenwold Inn in Philadelphia.

THE TOP ROCK 'N ROLL RECORDS FOR OCTOBER 1958

1. It's All in The Game - Tommy Edwards
2. Bird Dog/Devoted To You - The Everly Brothers
3. Rock-In Robin/Over and Over - Bobby Day
4. Tears On My Pillow - Little Anthony and the Imperials
5. Susie Darlin' - Robin Luke
6. Little Star - The Elegants
7. Chantilly Lace - The Big Bopper
8. Summertime Blues - Eddie Cochran
9. You Cheated - The Shields
10. Just a Dream - Jimmy Clanton
11. How The Time Flies - Jerry Wallace
12. Topsy II - Cozy Cole
13. It's Only Make Believe - Conway Twitty
14. Born Too Late - The Poni-Tails
15. No One Knows - Dion and the Belmonts
16. Carol - Chuck Berry
17. Down the Aisle of Love - The Quin-Tones
19. Mexican Hat Rock - The Applejacks
19. My True Love/Leroy - Jack Scott
20. Stupid Cupid - Connie Francis
21. Are You Really Mine - Jimmie Rodgers
22. Win Your Love For Me - Sam Cooke
23. Somebody Touched Me - Buddy Knox
24. La-Do-Dada - Dale Hawkins
25. Itchy Twitchy Feeling - Bobby Hendricks
26. Western Movies - The Olympics
27. Summertime, Summertime - The Jamies
28. To Know Him Is To Love Him - The Teddy Bears
29. Ten Commandments of Love - Harvey and the Moonglows
30. This Little Girls Gone Rockin' - Ruth Brown
31. Baby Face - Little Richard
32. I Wish - The Platters
33. Lazy Summer Night - The Four Preps

THE MELLO-KINGS
In the mid-1950s in Mount Vernon, a suburb of Buffalo, New York, Larry Esposita, Bob and Jerry Scholl, Neil Areana and Eddie Quinn formed a group called the Mellotones. After months of rehearsal, they began performing at school assemblies, teen canteens, parties and dances. Encouraged by the response, they traveled to New York City to audition for Herald Records. They chose Herald because this label, and its subsidiary Ember, had an enviable track record dating back to Faye Adams' "Shake a Hand" in 1953. The two labels had hits with "In the Still of the Night" by the Five Satins, "I Love You Madly" by Charlie and Ray, "Story Untold" by the Nutmegs, and "When We Dance" by the Turbans. The Mellotones were in good company. Their first session was produced by Dick Levister who had worked with most of the above groups. The result was "Tonite, Tonite," a thrilling close-harmony number. Unfortunately, as the record was being distributed to the New York deejays, word came from Gee Records that they had previously recorded a group with the same name. After a mad scramble, the company recalled all the Mellotones' singles and reissued "Tonite, Tonite" as by the Mello-Kings. The group began to make the rounds: "American Bandstand," a week at the Howard Theater in Philly followed by a week at the Apollo in New York. Interestingly, the song, which has become a standard oldie, never made the R&B charts and, although it was a "pop" hit for nearly three months, it never got close to the Top Forty. In early 1958, the Mello-Kings embarked on a tour with the Everly Brothers. In the meantime, their next singles failed to generate much in the way of sales. Herald issued a total of nine singles by the Mello-Kings up to 1961, at which time "Tonite, Tonite" once again entered the charts, albeit only briefly. It was too little, too late.

34. Hideaway - The Four Esquires
35. With Your Love - Jack Scott
36. I Got a Feeling - Ricky Nelson
37. Green Mosquito - The Tune Rockers
38. Forget Me Not - The Kalin Twins
39. Leave Me Alone - Dicky Doo and the Don'ts
40. Need You - Donnie Owens
41. Queen of the Hop - Bobby Darin
42. Real Wild Child - Ivan
43. Come On, Let's Go - Ritchie Valens
44. The Blob - The Five Blobs
45. Gingerbread - Frankie Avalon
46. Breakup - Jerry Lee Lewis
47. Nothin' Shakin' - Eddie Fontaine
48. When - The Kalin Twins
49. Poor Boy - The Royaltones
50. A Lover's Question - Clyde McPhatter

Also on the "pop" charts:
Tom Dooley - The Kingston Trio
For My Good Fortune - Pat Boone
Look Who's Blue - Don Gibson
The Day That The Rains Came - Jane Morgan
Treasure of Your Love - Eileen Rogers

October 1958
ARTISTS OF THE MONTH

BOBBY DAY and THE HOLLYWOOD FLAMES

Bobby Day

Bobby Day's pursuit of hits songs spanned three dozen years and two dozen different record labels. His records have been issued under a dozen artist's names including four variations of the Hollywood Four Flames. Add to this mix that Day often gave differing accounts of his lengthy career. Over the years, all of this led to a great deal of confusion as to just who was, or was not, Bobby Day.

James Robert Byrd was born on July 1, 1932, in Fort Worth, Texas. The date of his birth was something of a mystery. Often, it was given as 1934, but some sources list it as 1930. Byrd, in a 1988 interview, even said he was born in 1935.

The Byrd family moved to Los Angeles about the time Bobby graduated from high school. Again, the date of the move is in doubt. Byrd said it was 1947, which would make him about fifteen at the time. However, Byrd mentioned in the same 1988 interview that he came to Los Angeles to attend college.

In Los Angeles, he gravitated to the musical community that was developing around the various clubs catering to the rhythm and blues clientele. In 1949, a chance meeting of like-minded teenagers at a talent show at the Largo Theater led the formation of the Flames. Original members of the group included tenor David Ford, second tenor Willie Ray Rockwell, with Byrd covering both bass and baritone. After practicing as a trio for a short time, it was decided to expand to a quartet. Curley Dinkins was added as baritone so Byrd could concentrate on the bass lines.

Byrd enrolled in college, studying mathematics on a scholarship. However, his interest in music eventually drew him away from his studies. At this time, the group was discovered by Johnny Otis during one of the amateur nights at Otis' Barrelhouse Club. Through Otis' influence, Selective Records awarded them a one-shot recording contract. Their first single, issued in 1950 and listed as by the Flames, was "Please Tell Me Now" b/w "Young Girl." The record attracted enough attention in Los Angeles to bring the group to the attention of a larger company, Unique Records. During 1951, the group, now listed as the Hollywood Four Flames, issued three singles on Unique, "Dividend Blues," "Tabarin," and "Please Say I'm Wrong." "Tabarin" was a strong side, and as the version on Unique began receiving local airplay, it was reissued on the Fidelity label as by the Four Flames. This led to another single on Fidelity, "The Bounce." The group, again called the Hollywood Four Flames, was signed by Recorded In Hollywood, a label having success with Johnny Moore's Three Blazers. On Recorded In Hollywood, the group issued two singles in 1952, "I'll Always Be a Fool" and a rerecording of "Young Girl."

Through 1952, there was one single each from Specialty (the Four Flames) and Spin (the Flames). This was followed by a trio of singles on 7-11 by the Jets and the Flames. In 1953 and 1954, Aladdin released a total of four singles by the Flames, two when they accompanied Patty Anne (Mesner) and two without the female lead. On Lucky Records, billed as the Hollywood Flames, the group had four singles from late 1954 into early 1955. Then it was on to Swingtime for a single by the Hollywood Flames and one by the "?" (Question Marks). During 1954, the group also recorded for Money and Decca as the Hollywood Flames. While on Decca, "Tabarin" was rerecorded and issued as by the Tangiers.

During the two years following Decca, beginning in 1955, the recording career of the Hollywood Flames became even more confusing, if that is possible. There were lone releases on Flair (Bobby Relf and the Laurels), Hollywood (Hollywood Flames), Sage & Sand (a solo effort by Bobby Byrd), Modern (the Sounds), Specialty (the Ebbtides), Spark (Bobby Byrd and the Birdies), and Jamie (Robert Byrd). At the same time on Cash Records, there was a single by Bobby Byrd and the Birds. In addition, Byrd appeared on singles by the Turks and the Laurels. There were also many uncredited sessions as Byrd and the group backed other vocalists on various labels.

Over the course of the group's existence, up to 1957, several changes in personnel took place. Willie Ray Rockwell left in 1953 to sing with the Lamplighters, and he later died in an auto accident. Leon Hughes took his place. Hughes joined the Coasters in late 1955, and he was replaced by Gaynell Hodge, an early member of the Platters. In 1953, Curley

Dinkins also left, although he rejoined the group several times over the years. During those times when Dinkins was not available, Curtis Williams filled in until he started his own group, the Penguins. Clyde "The Thin Man" Tillis joined the group as a baritone/tenor. At the time the group was on Cash, Tillis had a solo effort on the label, "It Makes No Difference." In 1956, Hodge quit the group and his place was filled by Earl Nelson, Jr., a native of Lake Charles, Louisiana, who was born on September 8, 1928.

To complete this confusing scenario, in early 1957, Byrd was contemplating leaving the Hollywood Flames to go solo. His place was set to be filled by Bobby Relf, a member of various Los Angeles groups including the Laurels and the Voices on Cash, and the Crescendos on Atlantic. For the next twenty years, many music historians believed that Bobby Byrd and Bobby Relf were the same man.

Before Byrd officially left the Hollywood Flames, the group recorded a romping novelty that he had written titled "Buzz-Buzz-Buzz." As there were negotiations under way for Byrd's solo career, the single featured Earl Nelson on lead vocal. The group was between labels—a position in which they often found themselves. The single had been financed by John Dolphin, the owner of the Recorded In Hollywood, Money and Cash labels. Dolphin decided not to issue the record, and he sold the master to Lee Rupe, the ex-wife of Art Rupe, owner of Specialty Records. Miss Rupe was trying to launch her own new label, Ebb. In the fall of 1957, Ebb released "Buzz-Buzz-Buzz." After all their years of trying, "Buzz-Buzz-Buzz" was the first record by the Hollywood Flames to capture nationwide attention. Much to Byrd's chagrin, he discovered that he had lost half of the rights to the song, retaining only the lyricist's credit. Dolphin later admitted to owing Byrd more than six thousand dollars in back royalties, but he died before settling the debt.

According to Byrd, while this was happening, he was all set to start his solo career with Zephyr Records. To that end he had released a little piece of nonsense titled "Looby Doo" under his real name. Shortly thereafter, when he dropped by Zephyr's offices, the owner was out of town. Undaunted, Byrd walked down the hall to Class Records, a venture started by songwriter Leon Rene, father of band leader Googie Rene. The initial outcome of that meeting was that Byrd recorded "Come Seven" for Class. In order to avoid possible repercussions from Zephyr or Ebb Records, the Class single was credited to Bobby Day and the Satellites.

A short time later, Byrd penned "Little Bitty Pretty One." Rene thought the song showed potential. They quickly booked a studio and used the Hollywood Flames as the backing group. While Rene liked the song, he must not have been too sure of Bobby Day's sales potential, since he also covered his bets by alerting Aladdin Records to "Little Bitty Pretty One." Aladdin also acted in a hurry, and two versions of the song were on the street within days of each other. The bigger hit went to Thurston Harris on Aladdin on the strength of his appearance on "American Bandstand."

As quickly as he had tasted success, Bobby Day suffered defeat. His next four singles, issued over an eight-month period, failed to create a stir. Then one night, Leon Rene called Day to say that he had penned another novelty that he wanted Day to try. This song was "Rock-In Robin." As a flip side, the single featured a Day original, "Over and Over." Once again, Thurston Harris covered Day's song, only this time it was Day who had the last laugh. Bobby Day's version of "Over and Over" helped to propel "Rock-In Robin" to the upper level on all the major music charts. Riding the opening piccolo riff by Plas Johnson, "Rock-In Robin" caught the teenagers' attention and soon passed the million mark in sales.

Again, Day was unable to capitalize on his hit record with his next single, "Heavenly Angel." Thinking that the public wanted something similar to "Rock-In Robin," Day returned to "bird" songs with the similar-sounding "The Bluebird, the Buzzard & the Oriole." Plas Johnson even encored on piccolo. As might be expected, in chasing after another hit, the follow-up single was a little stale when compared to the freshness of "Rock-In Robin." By the summer of 1959, Day's recording career, insofar as having hit records was concerned, was over.

Nevertheless, Bobby Day continued to record profusely. He left Class in late 1959, moving on to another Leon Rene label, Rendezvous, for two years. At RCA Victor in 1963 and 1964, Day recorded in a variety of styles, including an overblown version of "Buzz-Buzz-Buzz."

Meanwhile, Day's name was associated with two singles that helped prolong the mystery of his recording activities. In 1958, while he was recording for Class, Bobby Day and Earl Nelson formed the duo Bob and Earl in an fruitless attempt to shake loose a hit. In 1963, "Harlem Shuffle" was a major hit for Bob and Earl. However, by this time "Bob" was Bobby Relf. Day was apparently mistaken when he later stated that "Bob" was actually soul singer Barry White. The second confusing single came in 1965, with Jackie Lee's "The Duck." Lee was really Earl Nelson, although many reviewers believed "Lee" was Day.

In 1967, Bobby Day returned from a tour of Australia and New Zealand where he picked up a marching anthem first done by the Bee Gees, and he recorded "Spicks and Specs" for Sure-Shot. Day also recorded for Highland as well as starting his own label, Byrdland, in the early 1970s. Through all this time, he was unable to come up with another hit on his own. Bobby Day passed away on July 27, 1990, after a long fight with cancer. He was survived by a wife, three children—one named Robin—and eight grandchildren.

The Hollywood Flames also issued many records over the years although none were nearly as popular as "Buzz-Buzz-Buzz." After Day left the group, the exact nature of the association between the group and Day remained hazy. The Hollywood Flames did back Day on most of his Class singles. On the other hand, it is probable that Day remained a part-time member of the Hollywood Flames during their stay at Ebb Records. It was the nature of the R&B groups around Los Angeles that membership in a specific unit was loose-knit. The Hollywood Flames left Ebb in 1959 and recorded one single for Chess before moving to Atco, which issued several Hollywood Flames records beginning later that year. There was one single on Vee-Jay in 1963, and a couple of releases on Symbol in 1965 and 1966, after which the group finally called it quits.

Both Bobby Day and the Hollywood Flames could take pride in their hits, as well as many of their misses. They brought a fresh sense of zeal to their recording sessions, and they were lucky enough to have had very long careers in a business they loved. Hit records may be one method to gauge an artist's popularity, but it cannot measure the sense of pride received each time a new record is released. Using that standard, Bobby Day and the Hollywood Flames were rewarded "over and over" again.

November 1958

NOV 1   The Johnny Cash tour continues with a packed house in Miami. Tomorrow night, he plays an engagement in Tampa.

    Ronnie Self rocks the house in Pittsburgh, Kansas.

    Continuing in the New Orleans area, Joe Turner plays a one-nighter at the Dew Drop Cafe. The next night he remains in New Orleans at the Autocrat Club before playing Plaquemine (3) and Baton Rouge (4).

    Bobby Darin, the Everly Brothers, the **Olympics**, and the Elegants appear on "The Dick Clark Show" on ABC-TV.

NOV 2   Earl Grant stops by "The Steve Allen Show" on NBC-TV.

NOV 3   Tommy Edwards starts a week at the Flame Club in Chicago.

New Releases for the first week in November include two from Mercury: "Smoke Gets In Your Eyes" by the Platters and "Little Red Riding Hood" by the Big Bopper; the Crests' "16 Candles" on Co-Ed; LaVern Baker's "I Cried A Tear" on Atlantic; Cozy Cole's "Caravan" on Grand Award; "Lucky Ladybug" by Billy and Lillie on Swan; "Sassy Fran" by Danny and the Juniors on ABC-Paramount; "I Got The Message" by the Shirelles on Decca; Thurston Harris' "Purple Stew" on Aladdin; "Manhattan Spiritual" by Reg Owen and his orchestra on Palette; and two versions of "Any Room In My Heart:" by Lee Andrews and the Hearts on United Artists and by Tony Bellus on Samson.

NOV 5   "American Bandstand" welcomes Tommy Mara to the show.

NOV 6   The Platters headline an extended engagement in the Flamingo Room of the Flamingo Hotel and Casino in Las Vegas. They remain at the hotel into December.

NOV 7   Bobby Darin begins two weeks at the Celebrity Room in Philadelphia.

    In Washington, the Shields, Thurston Harris, Ed Townsend, Damita Jo, and Redd Foxx entertain patrons all week at the Howard Theater.

EARLY NOVEMBER

    Back in Lubbock after their October tour, the members of the Crickets decide to remain at home while Buddy Holly will return to New York with his new wife. Holly relinquishes all rights to the

THE OLYMPICS

For a time, the Olympics rivaled the Coasters as rock 'n roll's court jesters. As a child, Walter Ward moved from Mississippi, where he had sung in a gospel group with his uncles, to Southern California. While a student at Centennial High in Compton, Ward formed the Challengers, with Eddie Lewis, first tenor; and Thomas Bush, bass. The trio expanded to a quintet with the addition of Charles Fizer and Melvin King. It is possible that this group recorded on the small Meladee label as Walter Ward and the Challengers. In 1956, they changed their name to reflect the Olympic games being held that year. It took two more years before they had a recording contract with Demon Records, a subsidiary of Liberty. With this much practice behind them, it's no wonder that their first Demon single was a Top Ten hit. "Western Movies" was a clever spoof on the many TV westerns of the day. The Olympics followed with "Dance with the Teacher," which barely made the charts, and "Chicken," which didn't. In July 1959, they shifted to Arvee Records, and issued "Private Eye," another TV-based song. The record languished for the remainder of the year. In early 1960, a deejay flipped it over and the B-side, "Hully Gully," took off. Through 1960, they issued "Big Boy Pete," "Shimmy Like Kate" and "Dance by the Light of the Moon." Each was a rousing get-out-on-the-dance-floor number that sold well and was a staple on radio for months. In 1961, the group's choice of material wavered. "Little Pedro" was followed by "Dooley," and then silence from the fans. Two years passed before "The Bounce," a Top Forty single issued on Tri-Disc. There were more singles on Loma and Mirwood into 1966. After breaking up for a time, the Olympics continue to perform into the 1990s, with Ward and Lewis joined by Kenny Sinclair (of the Six Teens) and William DeVose (of the Passions on Capitol).

Cricket's name and will to continue recording and performing as a solo artist.

NOV 8   Still in Kansas, Ronnie Self is booked for a one-nighter in Fort Scott.
Brenda Lee makes guests on ABC-TV's "Junior Jamboree."
Fats Domino, the Kalin Twins, Andy Williams, and Gordon McRae guest on "The Dick Clark Show."

NOV 9   Conway Twitty winds up his stand at Porky's in Fort Lauderdale.
Della Reese is welcomed back to "The Ed Sullivan Show" on CBS-TV.

NOV 10 Jimmie Rodgers begins a week-long run at the Latin Casino in Philadelphia. He will follow this gig with a week at Pittsburgh's Copa Club.
The RKO-Brunswick Theater in Brooklyn offers an evening's entertainment featuring the Fascinators, the Tranquils, the Deltairs, and the Tremaines.
In the early morning hours, Sam Cooke is injured in a serious auto accident in Marion, Arkansas. Cooke's chauffeur and valet, Ed Cunningham, is killed. Also critically injured is Cooke's close friend, Louis Rawls of the Pilgrim Travelers. Cooke was en route to Greenville, Mississippi, for yet another one-nighter.

New Releases for the second week in November include Jack Scott's "Goodbye Baby" on Carlton; the two-part "Turvy" by **Cozy Cole** on Love; "Donna" b/w "La Bamba" by Ritchie Valens on Del-Fi; two from Specialty: "She Knows How to Rock" by Little Richard and "You Know I Love You So" by Jerry Byrne; "You Gambled" by the Slades on Domino; two from RCA: Neil Sedaka's "The Diary" and Mickey and Sylvia's "Oh, Yeah! Uh-Huh;" Little Junior Parker's "Sweet Home Chicago" on Duke; "Ow-Wow" by the Midnighters on Federal; "Dance With the Teacher" by the Olympics on Demon; "Corrine Corrina" by Bill Haley and His Comets on Decca; "Flat Tire" by the Del Vikings on Mercury; "It's Too Bad You Had To Say Goodbye" by Little Joe and the Thrillers on Okeh; "Wolf" by the Four Mints on NRC; and Ersel Hickey's "You Never Can Tell" on Epic. In addition, there are four Christmas singles released this week, two of which are destined to become perennial classics: "The Chipmunk Song" by the Chipmunks with David Seville on Liberty; "Rockin' Around the Christmas Tree" by Brenda Lee on Decca; "Santa and the Purple People Eater" by Sheb Wooley on M-G-M; and "Green Christmas" by Stan Freberg on Capitol.

NOV 12 Conway Twitty makes a personal appearance in Savannah, Georgia.

NOV 14 A Memorial concert is held in Memphis for J. B. "Jay" Perkins, brother of Carl and a member of the Perkins band. The show is

COZY COLE
Drummers are a necessary ingredient for a good rock 'n roll record, yet few achieved the recognition they deserved. Fewer still issued records under their own name. In rock 'n roll in the 1950s, there was Sandy Nelson and Preston Epps (if one includes bongos). Jazz was more cognizant of a musician's talents, giving a special place for Gene Krupa, Louis Bellson and Buddy Rich. A man who bridged both types of music—and got his name in lights—was Cozy Cole. He was born William Randolph Cole, October 19, 1909, in East Orange, New Jersey. This would mean that by 1958, he was just shy of fifty years old—ancient in terms of rock 'n roll. He came from a musical family. Cole began his professional recording career with Jelly Roll Morton in 1930. He worked his way through a half-dozen bands, including those of Jimmie Lunceford, Stuff Smith and Benny Carter. He was with Cab Calloway from 1938 to 1942, where he was given numerous drum solos. In the 1940s, he recorded be-bop with Coleman Hawkins, Charlie Parker and Dizzy Gillespie. With Krupa, he founded a school for drummers. The Cozy Cole All Stars issued "Hound Dog Special," a lone single for M-G-M in 1954, a spin-off of Willie Mae Thornton's early rendition of "Hound Dog." In 1958, Cole's recording of an old Count Basie tune, "Topsy," on the Love label, became a rare crossover hit from mainstream jazz. The two-sided single was a true rarity for an instrumental in that both sides made the charts independently, a testament to Cole's inventiveness. Cole followed with a similar tune, "Turvy," which also made the charts. However,, in the space of six months, his day in the "pop" limelight was over. Cole happily returned to jazz. Recognized as a talented genius on percussion, Cole passed away in 1981.

headlined by Jerry Lee Lewis, and featured acts include Dickie Lee, **Thomas Wayne**, Curtis Gordon, the Collins Kids, Charlie Feathers, and various country artists. Jay died in October of a brain tumor. The show grossed $7,000, of which $4,750 was given to the widow after expenses and taxes had been deducted.

In Philadelphia, Eddie Cochran bowls over the studio audience at "American Bandstand" with his latest release "C'mon Everybody."

Paul Anka leaves the U.S. for a tour of Europe. (See NOV 21.)

In New Orleans, Gatemouth Brown and Eddie Bo split the bill at the Dew Drop Cafe for the next three days.

The Howard Theater in Washington presents Ray Charles, the Raelets, Dee Clark, Timmie Rogers, the Pastels, and the Cadillacs as part of this week's revue.

NOV 15 "The Dick Clark Show" welcomes the Nu Tornados to the Saturday night lineup. Also in the lineup are Dale Hawkins, the Teddy Bears, Clyde McPhatter, Polly Bergen, and Don Rondo.

Dicky Doo and the Don'ts, along with Mary Swan, start a two-day show at the Erie Social Club in Philadelphia.

Johnny Cash guests on "Hometown Party" in Los Angeles.

MID-NOVEMBER

Conway Twitty opens at the Safari Club in New Orleans.

The Diamonds are currently on a month-long tour of Australia.

NOV 17 Johnny Cash and the Collins Kids begin a week's tour with a show in Sweetwater, Texas. Other dates include Corpus Christi (18); Shreveport (19); Sheffield, Alabama (20).

New Releases for the third week in November include "My Happiness" by Connie Francis on M-G-M; Paul Anka's "(All of a Sudden) My Heart Sings" on ABC-Paramount; "Don't Pity Me" by Dion and the Belmonts on Laurie; Bobby Day's "The Bluebird, the Buzzard and the Oriole" on Class; "On My Mind" by the Darts on Apt; two from Capitol: Ray Stevens' "The Clown" and Cliff Richard's "Move It;" "That's Why I Cry" by Buddy Knox on Roulette; Dean Beard's "Keeper of the Key" on Challenge; and "Action Packed" by Ronnie Dee on Back Beat.

NOV 19 Duane Eddy, in what is becoming an almost monthly appearance, stops by "American Bandstand" to run through "Cannonball."

NOV 21 Bobby Darin opens another two week engagement at Brooklyn's Town and Country Club.

Paul Anka, starting his three-month tour of Europe, is welcomed by the Theater du Cirque Royal in Brussels, Belgium, for a two-week engagement. Other countries to be visited by Anka include Germany, Sweden, Norway, France, and Algeria. (See DEC 10.)

"American Bandstand" has Bobby Lord as the guest this afternoon.

THOMAS WAYNE

Thomas Wayne Perkins was born July 22, 1940, in Batesville, Mississippi. He was the brother of Luther Perkins, guitarist for Johnny Cash, and he mauy—or may not—have been related to Carl Perkins. At any rate, he dropped his last name to avoid professional confusion. After Carl, Johnny, Elvis, and Jerry Lee, made fortunes for themselves by recording in Memphis, Thomas Wayne could see no reason why he couldn't do the same. After all, in early 1958, every music entrepreneur was looking for the next Elvis. Wayne was in the right place with the right connections. His first sessions were produced by Scotty Moore, Elvis' guitarist, and they were recorded in the garage of the Fernwood Drive home owned by Ronald "Slim" Wallace. His first single, "You're the One That Done It," was issued on Wallace's small Fernwood label. In April 1958, when the record began to gather local momentum, it was leased to Mercury, but it failed to catch on nationally. For his second release, he recorded the plaintive ballad "Tragedy," which was in a similar vein as Jody Reynolds' "Endless Sleep," which was popular at the time. However, "Tragedy" failed to attract attention when issued in June 1958. Early the next year it began to sell, and it didn't stop until it was a gold record. His next single, "Eternally," brushed the bottom of the best seller lists before fading. Wayne released two more singles on Fernwood, including "The Girl Next Door Went A' Walking, a song he had written for Elvis. Wayne also recorded for Capehart, Phillips International and Santo. As the years passed, he became a respected songwriter and worked as a guitarist at Scotty Moore's Music City Recorders in Nashville. He founded his own Chalet Records, for which he also recorded. He was working as a recording engineer at Audio Recorders in Nashville when he died in an auto accident in Memphis, August 15, 1971.

BILL PARSONS
One can't begin to discuss Bill Parsons without also including Bobby Bare. Parsons was born September 8, 1934, in Crossville, Tennessee. He learned to play guitar by the age of eight, and he served as an entertainer in the Army's Special Services. Bobby Bare was born April 7, 1935, in Ironton, Ohio. He was raised in a musical family and joined his first country band as a teenager. He moved to Southern California at the age of eighteen. His talent brought him to Capitol Records, where he recorded briefly, and unsuccessfully. When he received his notice to report to the Army. He returned to Ohio in time to run into Parsons, whom he had known previously. The two musicians traveled to Cincinnati and rented a studio. With Parsons leading the studio band and Bare doing the singing, they recorded four numbers, including a novelty song based on Elvis Presley's recent Army induction. They men knew they were on to something, but Bare had to report to the Army. Parsons sold the completed tape to Fraternity Records, the best-known label in Cincinnati. When accepting the tapes, Fraternity notated the vocalist to be Parsons, an error that was repeated when "The All American Boy" was released in November 1958. By the time Bare heard the record, he was stationed at Fort Knox. Fraternity was reluctant to admit the error, and Parsons went out on personal appearances. There was one more Parsons single featuring Bare's vocal, "Educated Rock and Roll," but it lacked originality. In early 1960, Bobby Bare did record for Fraternity under his own name, issuing another Presley-inspired tune, "I'm Hangin' Up My Rifle." He went on to become a major country star. Among his more popular records are "500 Miles," "Detroit City," Miller's Cave" and Marie Laveau." Parsons recorded briefly for Starday Records in 1960 before dropping out of sight.

The Danleers return to the Howard Theater in Washington for the week. Also appearing are the Monotones, Robert and Johnny, and Charlie and Ray.

NOV 22   Jimmie Rodgers is the special guest on "The Perry Como Show" on NBC-TV.
On ABC-TV's "The Dick Clark Show," Jack Scott is a guest. Also appearing are the Poni-Tails, the Big Bopper, Cozy Cole, and the Cadillacs.

NOV 24   Della Reese brings her smooth vocal style to Mr. Kelly's in Chicago for a three-week run.
Dinah Washington opens a six-day run at Philadelphia's Showboat.
At the Lotus Club in Washington, the Playmates begin a week's stay.

New Releases for the fourth week in November include "The All American Boy" by **Bill Parsons** on Fraternity; "Tall Paul" by Annette on Disneyland; "I'm A Man" by Fabian on Chancellor; "Mathilda" by Cookie and the Cupcakes on Judd; "Rock-A-Conga" by the Applejacks on Cameo; Ray Charles' "The Right Time" on Atlantic; "I'll Sail My Ship Alone" by Jerry Lee Lewis on Sun; "Tomorrow" by Donnie Owens on Guyden; Conway Twitty's "Double Talk Baby" on Mercury; "Teasin'" by the Quaker City Boys on Swan; "Y-O-U" by Carl Perkins on Columbia; "The Gift of Love" by the Impressions featuring Jerry Butler on Abner; and Gene Vincent's "Be Bop Boogie Boy" on Capitol. There is also one standout among the Christmas singles released this week: Chuck Berry's "Merry Christmas, Baby" b/w "Run, Rudolph, Run."

NOV 26   "Ted Steele's Rockin' Bandstand" stageshow opens at the Brooklyn Paramount. This is the first such event for Steele, a New York deejay on WMCA radio. Headliners include Clyde McPhatter, Frankie Avalon, Lloyd Price, Connie Francis, the Big Bopper, Jimmy Clanton, Dickey Doo and the Don'ts, the Royaltones, the Kalin Twins, Jerry Butler and the Impressions, Cozy Cole, the Solitaires, Donnie Owens, and the Shields. The five-day run generates $73,500.

NOV 28   Bobby Helms stops by "American Bandstand."
Bobby Freeman, the Elegants, Baby Washington, the Silhouettes, and Willis Jackson's band entertain for the week at the Howard Theater in Washington.

NOV 29   The Nu Tornados perform as part of the halftime show at the annual Army-Navy football game at Philadelphia's Soldier's Field.
Conway Twitty guests on "The Perry Como Show" on NBC-TV.
Brenda Lee headlines a country and western jamboree in Wilmington, North Carolina.
"The Dick Clark Show" is arranged as a special twenty-ninth

birthday party for Clark. Guest hosts are Pat Boone, Bobby Darin, and **Sal Mineo**. Performers include Frankie Avalon and Connie Francis, who take time off from the Brooklyn show to appear, along with Danny and the Juniors, Eddie Cochran, and Little Anthony and the Imperials.

NOV 30   The Cincinnati Gardens plays host to a show featuring Jack Scott, Dale Wright, Eddie Cochran, Jackie Dee, Bill Parsons, and Neil Sedaka.

LATE NOVEMBER

Gene Vincent's career hits bottom. Unable to come up with a hit record, he and the Blue Caps split when he cannot pay the band three weeks in back salary. The musicians union in Los Angeles withdraws Vincent's union card. He eventually moves with his wife of six months to the Northwest where he will gig with local bands until mid-1959.

THE TOP ROCK 'N ROLL RECORDS FOR NOVEMBER 1958

1. It's Only Make Believe - Conway Twitty
2. It's All In The Game - Tommy Edwards
3. Topsy II - Cozy Cole
4. To Know Him Is To Love Him - The Teddy Bears
5. Chantilly Lace - Big Bopper
6. Rock-In Robin - Bobby Day
7. I Got A Feeling/Lonesome Town - Ricky Nelson
8. Queen Of The Hop - Bobby Darin
9. Forget Me Not - The Kalin Twins
10. Tears On My Pillow - Little Anthony and the Imperials
11. Mexican Hat Rock - The Applejacks
12. Susie Darlin' - Robin Luke
13. Bird Dog - The Everly Brothers
14. There Goes My Baby - The Drifters
15. A Lover's Question - Clyde McPhatter
16. Hideaway - The Four Esquires
17. Need You - Donnie Owens
18. Poor Boy - The Royaltones
19. You Cheated - The Shields
20. Beep Beep - The Playmates
21. Ten Commandments of Love - Harvey and the Moonglows
22. With Your Love - Jack Scott
23. I Got Stung/Such a Night - Elvis Presley
24. I'll Wait For You - Frankie Avalon
25. The Blob - The Five Blobs
26. Letter To an Angel/A Part of Me - Jimmy Clanton
27. No One Knows - Dion and the Belmonts
28. Fallin' - Connie Francis
29. Little Star - The Elegants

SAL MINEO

Several of the more popular rock 'n roll figures tried their hand at movie acting—Elvis, Alan Freed, Bill Haley, Jimmy Clanton, Fabian, Frankie Avalon, Annette, Bobby Rydell and Bobby Darin. A handful of actors attempted the reverse action: Tab Hunter, Ricky Nelson, Connie Stevens, Shelly Fabares, and Sal Mineo. In most cases the acting-singers seemed lost on screen while the singing-actors seemed lost when not in front of a camera. Mineo was a perfect example of the latter. He had Italian good looks, yet he looked more like a cherub than a Caruso. He began acting on Broadway at eleven in "The Rose Tattoo." Soon he appeared in "The King and I." In 1955, he began working in movies with roles in "Six Bridges to Cross," "The Private War of Major Benson" and "Rebel Without a Cause" starring James Dean. The next year, Mineo co-starred with Dean in "Giant." Receiving that much attention, it was natural that Mineo should try to increase his "teen idol" appeal. In 1957, he co-starred in "Rock Pretty Baby," a serious drama about rock 'n roll. He signed with Epic Records and recorded "Start Movin" using the same technique as Fabian: shove the vocal to the rear and cover up the mistakes with a morass of instrumentation. Epic clinched a Top Ten hit when it put picture sleeves of Mineo on each single. His next release, "Lasting Love" was a ballad, and barely slipped into the Top Forty. Mineo went back to uptempo tunes with "Party Time and "Little Pigeon," but his record sales slipped badly with each release. After four more singles into 1959, Mineo gave up singing for acting full time. In 1960, he co-starred in "Exodus" and was nominated for his second Academy Award. The first was for "Rebel Without a Cause." Mineo was murdered near his Hollywood apartment on February 12, 1976. His last film was the French movie, "Diplomatic Immunity" with Peter Falk in 1974.

30. Summertime Blues - Eddie Cochran
31. How the Time Flies - Jerry Wallace
32. Love Is All We Need - Tommy Edwards
33. Come On, Let's Go - Ritchie Valens
34. Cannonball - Duane Eddy
35. This Little Girl's Gone Rockin' - Ruth Brown
36. Problems - The Everly Brothers
37. Leave Me Alone - Dicky Doo and the Don'ts
38. Look Who's Blue/Give Myself A Party - Don Gibson
39. Bimbombey - Jimmie Rodgers
40. Baby Face - Little Richard
41. Win Your Love For Me - Sam Cooke
42. La-Do-Dada - Dale Hawkins
43. Sweet Little Rock and Roll - Chuck Berry
44. I Wish - The Platters
45. All Over Again - Johnny Cash
46. When I Grow Too Old To Dream - Ed Townsend
47. Blue Ribbon Baby - Tommy Sands
48. Almost In Your Arms - Johnny Nash
49. Whole Lotta Lovin' - Fats Domino
50. Smoke Gets In Your Eyes - The Platters

Also on the "pop" charts:
Call Me - Johnny Mathis

November 1958
ARTIST OF THE MONTH

CONWAY TWITTY

Conway Twitty

The Floyd Jenkins family settled in Friar's Point, a tiny Mississippi town nestled in a sweeping bend of the Mississippi River. According to a 1972 press release, Floyd was "a riverboat pilot who sailed the Mississippi River." Some might infer from this that Floyd's occupation was as glamorous as Mark Twain made it appear. Glamorous to everyone, that is, except those who actually worked the river in 1933. There was no bridge crossing the Mississippi at Friar's Point. The nearest bridge across the river was in Helena, thirty miles north of Friar's Point and about seventy miles south of Memphis. The actual job held by Floyd Jenkins was that of ferryman. He worked long days taking travelers from one side of the river to the other—day after day, year after year.

Harold Lloyd Jenkins was born into this family on September 1, 1933*. By the time he was ten, the family had moved up the river to Helena. There was little for an inquisitive child like Harold to do in Helena. Entertainment was where he found it. Harold had been given a

---

(* Twitty's birth date also listed as 1935.)

guitar by the time he was five, and he had practiced while riding on the ferry with his father. Shortly after moving to Helena, he was playing with the Arkansas Cotton Choppers. The Choppers big gig each week was Saturday afternoon at the local furniture store where they were hired to attract customers. Two years later, Harold was appearing on a local radio station in West Helena with an outfit called the Phillips County Ramblers.

Harold was acutely aware of the undercurrent of rhythm and blues music that permeated the area. He has attributed much of his early style to Rice Miller, famous as Sonny Boy Williamson, who also had a show on the same West Helena radio station. The Mississippi River was a highway for the music moving north from New Orleans and south from Chicago. Nearby were the rolling cotton plantations of the Arkansas hills and the Mississippi Delta. Each farm had a contingent of black field hands with their rich tradition of work songs, blues hollers, gospel harmonies and Saturday night dances. Like most people in the area, the Jenkins family held deep religious beliefs—at one time, Harold seriously considered entering the ministry. As he was trying to discover his own musical identity, he steeped himself in these varied musical influences.

Other than music, his only other diversion was sports, and he excelled in baseball. At that time, there were many semiprofessional teams across the country. After graduating from high school, Harold signed on with a minor league team in the Philadelphia Phillies' organization. He was ready to begin his career in baseball when he received his draft notice. He spent the next two years in the Army. During a tour of duty in Japan, he formed a country and western band, the Cimarrons, to play the various military installations around Tokyo.

Following his discharge in March 1956, Harold Jenkins returned to Helena. However, he could see there was no future for him in his hometown. His chance at a baseball career had passed him by, and the only route open for him was in music. It was 1956, and there was a major change brewing in the country's music business. In Helena, rhythm and blues music was readily available by way of the radio stations in nearby Memphis. At the time, Jenkins was earning a little money in the small clubs in the area. He had been aware for some time that there was a recording studio in Memphis that was having some success with the sessions it produced for performers such as B. B. King, Ike Turner, and Roscoe Gordon. The studio also had its own label, Sun Records, that was having minor hits with the new sound of Elvis Presley and Johnny Cash. When Sun Records had a million-selling single with Carl Perkins' "Blue Suede Shoes," this was all the motivation Harold Jenkins needed to make that seventy mile trip to Memphis to seek an audition.

Harold found he wasn't alone. There were dozens of hopeful musicians crowding the front offices of Sun Records, each hoping that Sam Phillips, the owner, would offer them a contract. Phillips' usual approach to this situation was to allow a brief audition and, maybe, a taping session. Then Phillips would send the performer home with directions to write a few more tunes and wait for a call before returning. Harold Jenkins was a little luckier than that. Over the course of eighteen months, he actually recorded about a dozen songs for Sun, but none were released at the time. While with Sun, he also wrote and recorded "Rockhouse." Jenkins' version was shelved. However, the song was recorded by Roy Orbison, although Sam Phillips took credit for writing the song when Orbison's single was released.

Discouraged, but not ready to give up just yet, Jenkins approached a Nashville representative of Mercury Records. By this time rock 'n roll was firmly established, but Mercury was still without a major rockabilly star. The company had issued records by Eddie Bond (another Sun Records hopeful) as well as a few Texas bands, but nothing had clicked. In the spring of 1957, Jenkins was granted a couple of Mercury-financed sessions. Mercury released two singles, "I Need Your Lovin'" and "Shake It Up Baby," to minimal fanfare. The singles merely aped Elvis' style without offering anything new or exciting. It was clear that Mercury had little idea how to produce a hit rock 'n roll single. Nevertheless, with records on the market, Harold found work playing the "Ozark Jubilee" in Springfield, Missouri. He also made a few brief tours, including one into Canada. When he returned home, however, his finances were running desperately low. Thankfully, Jenkins accepted a regular Friday night engagement in Pine Bluff, Arkansas, playing the Club Trio, owned by the popular country trio, the Browns. He was instantly successful, and he remained at the Club Trio for six months.

It has been a widely held belief that hard work and perseverance eventually pay off. Such was the case with Harold Jenkins. In the spring of 1958, M-G-M Records signed him to a short-term contract. At the time, M-G-M was another label without a major rock n' roll star. Elvis had just been booked into the Army for a two-year engagement. The executives at M-G-M decided against having Jenkins perform as a parody of Elvis, preferring, instead, to market him as an alternative to Elvis. However, this meant major changes in Jenkins' identity, and the first thing to go was his name. Harold Lloyd Jenkins wasn't catchy enough, even if he had been named after the silent film star. What was needed was something really different, exotic—a name that would grab the public's attention. Jenkins and Don Seat, his manager, came up with the new alias, pulling together the names of two small towns, Conway (Arkansas) and Twitty (Texas).

The first release on M-G-M for Conway Twitty was a song he had composed in only seven minutes while playing the Flamingo Lounge in Hamilton, Ontario. The structure of the song closely resembled the semi-religious "I Believe," a 1953 hit for Frankie Laine, which was also recorded by Elvis in 1957.

The production for "It's Only Make Believe" was restrained, yet it was expansive at the same time. Opening with Twitty's growling baritone, the ballad built dramatically to a whining crescendo before it reached the end of the first verse. It attained the same heights two more times before it was over. The lyrics didn't bare close scrutiny, being of the "moon-croon-June" variety—but after all, this was rock 'n roll. M-G-M, which had wanted an alternative to Elvis, got more than they bargained for. At first hearing, many people first thought the singer of "It's Only Make Believe" *was* Elvis. And, just like an Elvis single, "It's Only Make

Believe" quickly sold a million copies.

Like so many rockers before him, Twitty's follow-up singles couldn't match the popularity of his first hit. "The Story of My Love" played on the musical tricks in "It's Only Make Believe" but lacked the original song's conviction. "Hey Little Lucy! (Don'tcha Put No Lipstick On)" was simply a piece of weak material; the flip side, "When I'm Not With You," at least offered another dramatic reading. During the late summer of 1959, Twitty and Carl Mann chased each other up the charts with similar versions of "Mona Lisa." Carl Mann had taken the Nat King Cole ballad and injected a rolling boogie beat and a Tex-Mex guitar break. Twitty, having better vocal control than Mann, delivered a version more closely patterned on Cole's original. However, Mann's version outsold that of Twitty about two-to-one.

"Mona Lisa" set a pattern for Twitty's next release as he juiced up another standard, "Danny Boy." Without competition this time, he took the single into the Top Ten. Finally back on track, Twitty released "Lonely Blue Boy," a reworking of a song originally recorded by Elvis for the movie "King Creole." Elvis' version was titled "Danny" after the movie's lead character. It was decided not to use the song in the film, and Elvis' recording remained unreleased for more than twenty years. Twitty took much of Elvis' arrangement, deleted the line "Danny... oh, Danny is my name" and inserted "Lonely... oh, Lonely Blue Boy is my name." He also relied on his usual vocal pyrotechnics to inject the song with a harder edge. It became Twitty's second gold record.

In 1960, Twitty's dramatic vocal style came under attack from another ex-Sun recording artist, Roy Orbison. Orbison had the smoother voice, something that was in vogue at the time. The days of the hard-driving rockabilly performer were over. Twitty's first release in 1960 was a version of the Chuck Willis hit "What Am I Living For." It took the same path forged by "Lonely Blue Boy," while selling considerably fewer copies. The same held true for the next single, "Is A Blue Bird Blue."

Then came "What a Dream," the first attempt by Twitty to play on his country influences. The public didn't want anything to do with it, and it became his first flop on M-G-M. He tried to bounce back with a version of "Whole Lot of Shakin' Going On," but Twitty was never a true rock 'n roller and it showed. The B-side, "The Flame," was more interesting, presenting Twitty in the style of Frankie Laine. Then came Twitty's remake of "C'est Si Bon (It's So Good)" a song that had been done to a turn by Eartha Kitt in 1953. Twitty's version featured soaring violins and a bouncy beat, with Twitty trying in vain to sound like Jerry Lee Lewis.

By this time it was obvious that something was very wrong with the direction Conway Twitty's career was headed. It was not only that the music was uninspired, or, in the case of "C'est Si Bon," just plain strange. His choice of movie roles verged on the positively ludicrous. Beginning late in 1959, Twitty was featured in "Platinum High School," "Sex Kittens Go to College," and "College Confidential." Not a trio of films on which to base a future acting career.

The two singles following "C'est Si Bon" were among the better efforts from Twitty during this period. "The Next Kiss (Is The Last

Goodbye)" was built on a rhythmic foundation, while "Portrait of a Fool" featured one of Twitty's better vocal efforts. Neither fared well. The teenagers had pledged their allegiance to other singers.

In early 1962, Twitty left M-G-M without having another record company willing to take a chance on him. He moved to Oklahoma City and formed a band he called the Lonely Blue Boys. In Oklahoma City, he reverted completely to country music, refusing to perform his hit songs as part of his nightclub performance. For three years, he worked long, hard hours in cow-town roadhouses and juke-joint dives. Slowly, he built a new audience, adapting his stage act and songwriting skills to the new sounds of country music.

In 1965, Owen Bradley, one of Nashville's musical wizards, contacted Twitty. The result was a contract with Decca Records, a major player in the country music field. Twitty was also asked to syndicate a television show from Oklahoma City. "The Conway Twitty Show" allowed him to reach a completely new audience just as his first Decca singles were being released. Twitty moved to Nashville and joined the "Grand Ole Opry." He appeared on "Hee Haw" and "The Johnny Cash Show," and his records were selling again. From 1965 until the mid-1980s, most singles released by Twitty reached at least the Top Five on the country music charts, with more than thirty peaking at Number One.

Twitty's long-term success in country music allowed him the freedom to have fun with his life in ways barely hinted during his years as a rock 'n roll star. Aside from the normal investments in publishing companies and talent agencies, Twitty fulfilled a lifelong dream when he became part owner of the Nashville Sounds, a semipro baseball franchise in the New York Yankees' organization. In 1982, he also built a nine-acre amusement park in Hendersonville, on the outskirts of Nashville. Then he confounded everyone by placing his home right in the middle of Twitty City.

In the early morning hours of June 5, 1993, Twitty had just concluded an engagement at a dinner club in Branson, Missouri. He was returning to Twitty City. In his tour bus with him were his band and his second wife, Delores, whom he had married in 1987. During a rest stop in southwestern Missouri, an artery in his stomach burst. He was rushed to Cox Medical Center-South in nearby Springfield, but he died following emergency surgery. Conway Twitty was also survived by the four children he had fathered during the twenty-five years he spent with his first wife.

His sudden death was an even greater tragedy when his fans were reminded of the enormous successes of his early career. In his heart, Conway Twitty must have truly felt that his life was only make believe.

December 1958

New Releases for the first week in December include "Shirley" by **John Fred and the Playboys** on Montel; "Little Space Girl" by Jesse Lee Turner on Carlton; Jimmy Reed's "Odds and Ends" on Vee-Jay; Jimmy Bowen's "Always Faithful" on Roulette; two from Gone: Jo Ann Campbell's "Tall Boy" and the Isley Brothers' "The Drag;" and "I Want Somebody" by Harvey on Chess. Finally, this week sees the release of "Tear Down The House" by Morty Marker and the Impalas on Back Beat. Marker is Ronnie Dawson, who also records as Ronnie Dee.

DEC 3   The Nu Tornados guest on ABC-TV's "American Bandstand" this afternoon.
  The Playmates make an evening appearance on ABC-TV's "The Milton Berle Show."

DEC 5   The Apollo Theater in New York offers a jazz revue for patrons this week.
  In California, Ritchie Valens returns to his high school in Pacoima to entertain his local fans. The show is tape recorded for future release by Del-Fi Records.
  Cozy Cole, Lee Andrews and the Hearts, Lulu Reed, and the Fidelities entertain patrons at the Howard Theater this week in Washington.

DEC 6   The Chicago Opera House welcomes Frankie Avalon, the Everly Brothers, Connie Francis, and the Poni-Tails. The troupe is currently playing a series of one-nighters throughout the Midwest.
  Fabian sings "I'm a Man" on "The Dick Clark Show" on ABC-TV. Also appearing are Duane Eddy and Betty Johnson.

EARLY DECEMBER
  The Applejacks are currently playing the Bamboo Club in Clifton Heights, Pennsylvania.
  Conway Twitty is touring the Southwest until December 18.
  While at home in the Los Angeles area, Ritchie Valens films a cameo role for the upcoming picture "Go, Johnny Go!"

New Releases for the second week in December include "Oh! My Goodness" by the Kalin Twins on Decca; "The Real Thing" by the "5" Royales on King; Billy Graves' "The Shag" on Monument; Danny Lester's "Arlinda" on Blue Note; and "Gazachstahagen" by the Wild-Cats on United Artists.

JOHN FRED & PLAYBOYS

John Fred (last name Gourrier) was born in Baton Rouge on May 8, 1941 (also listed as 1945). As a teenager, he loved the music coming out of nearby New Orleans. In 1958, he formed the Playboys, an eight-piece ensemble of guitars, horns, and drums, that quickly became "the" band in the area. Their signature tune was a thumping R&B song titled "Shirley" that came to the attention of the only record label in town, Montel. A date was set for J&M Studio in New Orleans, but when it came time to cut the record, all of the Playboys except the sax player were left in Baton Rouge. The band on "Shirley" was the same studio ensemble, led by Lee Allen, that appeared on many other New Orleans hits. With Montel's limited distribution, it took three months before "Shirley" caught on. The Playboys began to tour, finally appearing on an Alan Freed show in New York, where "Shirley" was a local hit. "To Have and Hold" followed in May 1959, but it was only popular locally. There were two more singles released on Montel, but, by this time, John Fred was a student at Southeastern Louisiana College. After graduation in 1963, he re-formed the group and the band signed with Jewel Records, a major southern label. After two singles, they cut the ferocious "Boogie Children" for the N-Joy label of Monroe, Louisiana. It became a local hit and also appeared on Jewel. There were six more singles on Paula, Jewel's subsidiary, before the band had a gold record in 1967 with "Judy in Disguise," which combined their old R&B style with psychedelic and bubblegum overtones. Unfortunately, the band could not keep up the momentum. Their next single, "Hey, Hey Bunny" bounced around the bottom of the charts for a month. After a tour of England the Playboys retreated to Baton Rouge where they are active into the 1990s.

THE SKYLINERS
Until "Hey, Jude" by the Beatles, the Skyliners held the crown for the longest repetitive ending in popular music. In 1955, Jimmy Beaumont (born October 21, 1940 in Pittsburgh) joined the Crescents, which also featured Wally Lester and Jack Taylor. The group was attracting attention, but, through a combination of missed opportunities, failed to gain a record contract. In 1958, the three Crescents joined with Janet Vogel and Joe VerSharen of the El Rios to form a group with professional intentions. After months of rehearsals, they rented a studio and recorded a demo version of "Since I Don't Have You." The aforementioned ending, featuring the word "you" repeated thirteen times, proved to be a stumbling block when they approached various labels. The group finally landed a contract with Calico Records, a small local company. Christened the Skyliners, they agonized six weeks after "Since I Don't Have You" was released as deejays hesitated in spinning the record because they couldn't talk over the ending. The record did start to sell in Pittsburgh, and it was one of the first rock 'n roll hits to use a violin section. For their follow-up single, the Skyliners put together a complicated five-part harmony for "This I Swear." The group released four more singles on Calico before moving to Colpix in 1960, where their three singles failed to attract attention. Vogel and VerSharen retired from the group. The Skyliners had one release each on Cameo, Viscount and Atco by 1963. Beaumont was already recording solo by this time with singles on Colpix (1961), May (1962), Bang (1966) and Gallant (1967). The Skyliners added Sammy Morrow as lead tenor and issued three singles on Jubilee in 1965. Beaumont, Vogel, Lester and VerSharen reunited in 1970 with an album issued on Buddah. Vogel died on February 21, 1980. Beaumont continues to appear with a new group of Skyliners.

DEC 10 Paul Anka is booked into the Olympia in Paris for a month-long engagement. (See MID-JANUARY 1959.)

DEC 12 Fabian gets a chance to "sing" on "American Bandstand" as he plugs his hit, "I'm a Man."
Roy Brown, Amos Milburn and Charles Brown tear down the house at the High Hat Club in New Orleans. They are booked for several more weekends.
The Howard Theater offers the cool jazz sounds of Miles Davis, Jimmy Smith and Hoarce Silver for patrons this week in Washington.

DEC 13 "The Dick Clark Show" welcomes Fats Domino, Tommy Edwards, and June Valli.

DEC 15 JoAnn Campbell opens a week-long stand at the Lotus Lounge in Washington, DC.

New Releases for the third week in December include Dorsey Burnette's "Try" on Imperial; Frankie Ford's "Sea Cruise" on Ace; Little Willie John's "No Regrets" on King; "Beatnik" by the Champs on Challenge; Nino Tempo's "15 Girlfriends" on RCA; and Jimmy Darren's "There's No Such Thing" on Colpix.

DEC 18 Bobby Day performs "Rock-In Robin" and "The Bluebird, the Buzzard and the Oriole" on ABC-TV's "American Bandstand."
Bill Haley and His Comets return to the States following their ten-week tour of Europe.
Johnny Cash plays a one-night stand in Ottawa. The next night he guests on the "WJJL Jamboree in Niagara Falls, followed by ABC-TV's "The Dick Clark Show" (20).

DEC 20 "The Dick Clark Show" presents Johnny Cash, the Four Preps, Neil Sedaka, Dee Clark, and Lloyd Price.

DEC 21 On CBS-TV, "The Ed Sullivan Show" is visited by David Seville.

DEC 22 The Paris Sisters visit Vancouver, Washington, again for their annual two-week New Year's engagement at the Frontier Room.
The Four Esquires have an extended booking in Kansas City at the Hotel Meehlebach.

New Releases for the fourth week in December include Johnny Cash's "Don't Take Your Guns To Town" on Columbia; Brook Benton's "It's Just a Matter of Time" on Mercury; the Bell Notes' "I've Had It" on Time; "Since I Don't Have You" by the **Skyliners** on Calico; "Pink Shoe Laces" by Dodie Stevens on Crystalette; Brenda Lee's "Bill Bailey, Won't You Please Come Home" on Decca; the Midnighters' "Teardrops on Your Letter" b/w "The Twist" on King; Eddie Cash's "Doing All Right" on Peak; Dean Barlow's "True Love" on Beacon; Dwight Pullen's "By You By The

Bayou" on Sage; and Ben Joe Zeppa's "Shame On You" on Award.

DEC 23   LaVern Baker plays a two-day stand at the Orchid Room in St. Louis.

DEC 24   Alan Freed's "Christmas Rock 'N' Roll Spectacular" opens at the Lowe's State Theater in New York City. Performers include Frankie Avalon, Jimmy Clanton, Eddie Cochran, Jackie Wilson, Harvey and the Moonglows, the Flamingos, the Cadillacs, **Baby Washington**, the Crests, Chuck Berry, Bo Diddley, Jo Ann Campbell, Gino and Gina, Ed Townsend, the Nu Tornados, Dion and the Belmonts, and King Curtis. Johnny Ray is the headliner for the first five days, but his appeal to the teenagers is long since past and the Everly Brothers are rushed into the spotlight to close out the engagement. The eleven-day run grosses $200,000.

DEC 25   Marvin Rainwater begins a two-week run at the Flame Club in Minneapolis.

Opening a day early for the Christmas crowd, Washington's Howard Theater presents the Coasters, the Chantels, and Buddy and Ella Johnson for the week.

DEC 26   Cozy Cole opens a two-week jam session at Chicago's Preview Lounge.

Dicky Doo and the Don'ts are entertaining for the week at the Celebrity Room in Philadelphia.

Johnny Cash begins a five-day stand at the Showboat Casino in Las Vegas.

A teenager is stabbed following a Dick Clark appearance at a record hop at the Sunnybrook Ballroom in Pottstown, Pennsylvania. Clark has already left the area when the incident occurs, but it fuels the public's view that rock 'n roll is dangerous music.

DEC 27   On "The Dick Clark Show" on ABC-TV, tonight's guests are Jill Corey, Jimmy Clanton, the Crests, Ritchie Valens, and Jackie Wilson.

DEC 28   Della Reese is welcomed back to CBS-TV's "Ed Sullivan Show."

DEC 29   Tommy Edwards performs at Menuti's Lounge in Houston through New Year's Eve.

DEC 31   The Champs are back doing one-nighters following an auto accident that severely injured several members.

Johnny Cash starts a string of West Coast one-nighters in Compton, California.

Ray Charles helps New Orleans celebrate New Years' Eve with two performances at the Municipal Auditorium.

In Detroit, the Four Tops are part of the "Idlewild Revue" at the Flame Club for the New Year's Eve weekend.

BABY WASHINGTON

In 1954, Jeanette "Baby" Washington's long career in music was well under way. She was singing in clubs from Detroit's Flame Showbar to New Orleans' Dew Drop Inn to New York's Apollo Theater. At the same time, she was lead vocalist with the Hearts, a mixed male-female quartet (not related to Lee Andrews' group). Their first record, "Angel Baby," was issued by the Apollo label in 1953. Lack of sales doomed the group to only one release at the time. A year later, they issued "Lonely Nights," a torrid, shouter on Baton that reached the Top Ten on the R&B charts. Baton released four more singles into 1956, including "All My Love Belongs to You," "Until the Real Thing Comes Along" and "He Drives Me Crazy." The Hearts moved along to J&S Records, which had just had a major hit with "Over the Mountain" by Johnnie and Joe. First, Baby Washington had a solo release with "Every Day." The Hearts had the next J&S single, "Dancing In a Dream World." Baby Washington, with and without the Hearts, issued a total of 16 singles on J&S in 1957-58. By 1959, the group had broken up, but Baby Washington persevered. That year, she had R&B hits with "The Time" and "The Bells" on Neptune. Two years later, after "Nobody Cares" became her last Neptune hit, she signed with ABC-Paramount, staying only long enough to record two singles, including "My Time To Cry," before beginning a long association with Sue Records. From 1962's "Handful of Memories" to 1965's Top Ten R&B hit, "Only Those in Love," she was riding a wave of popularity. In 1969, she signed with Cotillion, issuing a total of four Cotillion singles including her last charted single, "I Don't Know." In 1979 she turned up on the AVI label for "I Can't Get Over Losing You."

THE TOP ROCK 'N ROLL RECORDS FOR DECEMBER 1958

1. To Know Him Is To Love Him - The Teddy Bears
2. Problems/Love of My Life - The Everly Brothers
3. One Night/I Got Stung - Elvis Presley
4. Beep Beep - The Playmates
5. A Lover's Question - Clyde McPhatter
6. Lonesome Town/I Got A Feeling - Ricky Nelson
7. It's Only Make Believe - Conway Twitty
8. Smoke Gets In Your Eyes - The Platters
9. Topsy II - Cozy Cole
10. Queen of the Hop - Bobby Darin
11. Bimbombey - Jimmie Rodgers
12. Love Is All We Need - Tommy Edwards
13. Whole Lotta Loving - Fats Domino
14. Cannonball - Duane Eddy
15. Chantilly Lace - Big Bopper
16. It's All In The Game - Tommy Edwards
17. I'll Wait For You - Frankie Avalon
18. Poor Boy - The Royaltones
19. Gotta Travel On - Billy Grammer
20. Need You - Donnie Owens
21. Lonely Teardrops - Jackie Wilson
22. Letter To An Angel - Jimmy Clanton
23. Walking Along - The Diamonds
24. Forget Me Not - The Kalin Twins
25. Philadelphia, U.S.A. - The Nu-Tornados
26. Hideaway - The Four Esquires
27. Donna - Ritchie Valens
28. Love You Most Of All - Sam Cooke
29. Teen Commandments - Paul Anka, George Hamilton IV and Johnny Nash
30. Turvy II - Cozy Cole
31. My Happiness - Connie Francis
33. Sweet Little Rock and Roll - Chuck Berry
33. Mexican Hat Rock - The Applejacks
34. 16 Candles - The Crests
35. Rock-In Robin - Bobby Day
36. Ten Commandments of Love - Harvey and the Moonglows
37. Peek-A-Boo - The Cadillacs
38. Nobody But You - Dee Clark
39. The Big Bopper's Wedding - The Big Bopper
40. Need Your Love - Bobby Freeman
41. C'Mon Everybody - Eddie Cochran
42. The Diary - Neil Sedaka
43. I Cried A Tear - LaVern Baker
44. Stagger Lee - Lloyd Price
45. Goodbye Baby - Jack Scott
46. Try Me - James Brown and the Famous Flames

47. Seven Minutes to Heaven - The Poni-Tails
48. Run, Rudolph, Run - Chuck Berry
49. Dreamy Eyes - Johnny Tillotson
50. Lucky Ladybug - Billy and Lillie

Also on the "pop" charts:
That Old Black Magic - Louis Prima and Keely Smith

December 1958
ARTIST OF THE MONTH

THE TEDDY BEARS

The Teddy Bears

In most histories of rock 'n roll, the Teddy Bears are relegated to a single line or two. After mentioning their million selling, Number One single, "To Know Him Is To Love Him," there usually follows a reference to this being the point at which Phil Spector got his start.

Harvey Phillip Spector was born December 26, 1940 in the Bronx, New York. His grandfather, a Russian Jew named Spektor, emigrated to the United States only to learn that his name had been changed to Spector as he passed through Ellis Island. The family has been described as lower middle class. Even beyond the tribulations implied by such a label, Phil suffered a traumatic childhood. His father, Benjamin, under severe strain because of his family's increasing indebtedness, committed suicide in 1949. In 1953, Bertha Spector uprooted Phil and his older sister, Shirley, and moved to Los Angeles in search of a better life. In the short term, the dream eluded her, and she took work as a seamstress.

As a teenager, Phil had difficulty fitting in to the sun-in-the-fun society in Los Angeles. He was short and on the skinny side. With his recessed chin, thin lips, and sad eyes, he looked forlorn. He had always been a loner, but he was willing to accept the responsibility of his own actions. His personality could best be described as blunt. He always took the direct approach whenever possible.

With little to interest him during high school, Phil was drawn like a magnet to music. He soon excelled on the guitar, piano, drums, bass, and French horn. He also gravitated to the increased activity in the local rhythm and blues scene. By the mid-1950s, Los Angeles was the West Coast center for the recording industry. There were dozens of small, independent record companies coming into the business each year. The larger Los Angeles labels—Imperial, Specialty, Aladdin, and Modern—had been churning out R&B hits for several years. Now, they were joined by new independent companies like Keen, Class, Challenge, and Liberty that had their eyes on rock 'n roll.

With this much action in town, it was inevitable that Phil would soon join the regular group of would-be musicians hanging around the studios. Here he met Jerry Leiber and Mike Stoller, two songwriters who were just beginning to have some success producing singles by the

Robins for their Spark label. The idea of two young men writing the songs, recording the sessions, as well as distributing their own records held tremendous appeal to Phil Spector.

On a trip back to the Bronx, Phil visited the grave of his father in the Beth David Cemetery at Elmont, Long Island. He was impressed enough with the inscription on the tombstone to make a note of it: "To know him was to love him." A short time later, back in Los Angeles, Spector took those words and wrote lyrics for them, coming up with a sweet, romantic ballad. Sitting in his bedroom, accompanying the song on his guitar, Phil knew it had the potential to be a hit.

After graduating from Fairfax High School in the spring of 1958, Spector began taking a course so he could become a court recorder. He soon realized that this was not the direction for him. Rekindling his hopes of breaking into the business of music, he booked a session at Gold Star Studios. At Gold Star, studio time cost $15.00 per hour plus an additional $6.00 for a reel of blank tape. Phil later said his first session cost him $40.00. His first obstacle as a record producer was to raise that forty dollars. As might be expected, his mother loaned him the first ten.

Phil next turned to Marshall Leib, a friend from Burroughs Junior High, who was now a nineteen-year old student at Los Angeles City College, majoring in business law and music. Leib was the physical opposite of Spector. Tall and tanned, Leib had been active in sports in high school and college. Leib and Spector only shared one trait, their love of rock 'n roll music. Marshall had some previous experience in the music business, having formed the Moondogs in 1958 with classmates Jimmy Smith and Elliott Inberger. (Smith would become famous using the moniker P.J. Proby, Taylor would be a founding member of Canned Heat, and Inberger worked with Frank Zappa's Mothers of Invention.) At Spector's urging, Leib kicked in the second ten dollars. ("Leib" has been the accepted spelling of Marshall's name for thirty-five years. The most recent biography on Spector, however, written with Marshall's cooperation, spells the name as "Lieb.")

Another student at Los Angeles City College, Harvey Goldstein, was talked into contributing another ten dollars. In exchange, he was promised he could sing bass in the budding group.

The final ten dollars came from a student at Fairfax High. In the summer of 1958, Annette Kleinbard was sixteen. A native of New Brunswick, New Jersey, she had a strong, emotional soprano voice of the glee club variety. Her only plans centered on studying psychology in college, and that was two years away. When approached to help Phil pay for his recording session, Annette quickly agreed, if she also could be included in the group. As it turned out, she had as much drive to make it in the world of music as Spector.

The first two-hour session was devoted to recording a Spector tune, "Don't You Worry My Little Pet." The song opened with a guitar line similar in style to those used by Buddy Holly on his songs. All four vocalists raced headlong through the mundane lyrics as though they were trying to beat that two-hour deadline. By using a little recording "magic," Spector played all the instruments on the single and acted as his own producer.

With the demonstration acetate disk in hand, Spector sought out Lew Bedell. Bedell was Spector's neighbor and the co-owner, with Herb Newsome, of Era Records. Era was a local "pop" label with Gogi Grant's "The Wayward Wind" as its biggest hit. Bedell and Newsome had started a second company, Dore Records, with the intention of issuing rock 'n roll music. Dore had been in business only a month or two before Spector arrived with his demo.

Spector and his three friends signed a four-song deal that offered what amounted to minimum royalties: one and one-half cents per copy sold to be split four ways. In the offices of Dore, they came up with a name for themselves: the Teddy Bears, after the hit song by Elvis Presley. They were also given a little more studio time to come up with an acceptable B-side. Spector's first choice was another of his compositions, "Wonderful, Loveable You." They used two more hours working on the song, but the final results did not satisfy Spector.

He decided to attempt a third session. This time, Goldstein was absent. For the first time, a drummer was added to help Spector with the instrumental backing. The drummer was Sandy Nelson, who would soon go on to have a successful career of his own. After they completed "Wonderful, Lovable You," and nearing the end of his allotted time at Gold Star, Spector coaxed Annette and Marshall into attempting "To Know Him Is To Love Him."

Annette sang the haunting lead while Phil and Marshall supplied the backing vocal. After they had an acceptable take, Spector ran the tape back, and they recorded additional backing vocals on a second tape deck while the original song was playing over the speakers in the studio. Leib later called this technique "stacking vocals." Considering the primitive methods used by Spector, the overall sound of "To Know Him Is To Love Him" is one of intimacy. There is also an openness and fullness to the song that is usually associated with more sophisticated production techniques.

When Dore mailed five hundred copies of the single to radio stations in early August 1958, the A-side was still "Don't You Know My Little Pet." The initial reaction was "ho-hum." Goldstein and Leib returned to their studies at college. For weeks, there was no sign of any sales. Then, in September, a deejay in Fargo, North Dakota, flipped the single over and played "To Know Him Is To Love Him." Shortly thereafter, an order came into the Dore offices from a distributor in Minneapolis requesting eighteen thousand copies. Bedell, Newsome and Spector thought that the order was either a bad joke or a misprint. They called the Minneapolis distributor who assured them it was neither a joke or a mistake. While he was on the line, the distributor even increased his order. On the basis of the news from Minneapolis, radio stations across the country started spinning the record. "To Know Him Is To Love Him" had finally found its audience.

The record was reviewed in the music press in the middle of September, and within a week it had jumped onto the national music charts. "American Bandstand" was on the line wanting to book the group for an appearance on October 29. This created a slight problem. "To Know Him Is To Love Him" featured only Phil, Annette, and Marshall. There was no invitation from "Bandstand" for Harvey Goldstein. At the time, it was widely believed that Goldstein was dropped from the group at Spector's insistence because he really couldn't sing the bass part. Goldstein sued Dore and the Teddy Bears. He settled out of court for a share of the royalties earned by the group over the next ten years.

The Teddy Bears appeared on "American Bandstand" that October without a hitch. "To Know Him Is To Love Him" went to the top of the charts, selling more than a million copies before Christmas. Late in 1958, "Wonderful Lovable You" became their second single from Dore. On January 3, they were guests on "The Perry Como Show," and they sang their big hit as well as the old standard "It's Only a Paper Moon." By this time, Spector had a falling out with Dore Records over royalties. It was the usual story of the small record company trying to capitalize on its first success, then being unable to get the wholesalers to pay for all the records that had been shipped. Spector claimed he was owed $20,000. Dore said it didn't have the money. Spector immediately made a deal for the Teddy Bears to sign with Imperial Records, and their first single for that label, "I Don't Need You Anymore" was on the shelves in mid-January.

Spector must have hated his time with Imperial. To begin with, his sessions were subject to internal corporate pressures. He was no longer in charge of the recording process, and the arrangements were overseen by Jimmie Haskell, a veteran A&R man. Imperial did not want him to use his beloved Goldstar Studios, sending him to Master Recorders, instead. Worse yet, the group was forced to record their material in stereo! Imperial didn't want any of the layers of stacked vocals he had used before. It was an experience Spector never forgot. The Teddy Bears only issued two singles and the one album on Imperial before Spector took his act elsewhere.

Spector had known Lester Sill for several years. Sill had started his own company, Trey Records, with Lee Hazlewood, who was Duane Eddy's producer. Sill coaxed Spector into the studio again in a final attempt to come up with hit records. By this time Annette Bard—she had dropped the "Klein-" when the group appeared on "American Bandstand"—began calling herself Carol Connors. Because of legal entanglements, the group could not use the name Teddy Bears, so the two Trey singles were issued by the Spectors Three. Neither sold in appreciable numbers. After this, Phil dismissed the other two and called it quits, insofar as being a record star was concerned.

Miss Kleinbard/Bard/Connors was involved in an auto accident in September 1959, but she recovered and soon attempted a solo singing career. Although she was not very well known, she did succeed in landing a contract with Columbia in 1961, followed by Era Records in 1962, and Mira Records in 1966, all under the name Carol Connors. She also recorded as Annette Bar, and was a member of the Bompers and the Storytellers. She had success as co-writer of "The Night the Lights Went Out in Georgia," a gold record for Vicki Lawrence in 1973 and a country hit in 1992 for Reba McEntire. She also co-wrote "Hey Little Cobra" for the Rip-Chords and "Gonna Fly Now" the theme from the first "Rocky" movie. She ahelped write the theme songs for "Sophie's Choice" and "Mr.

Mom." Over the years she has been nominated for two Academy Awards and four Emmys.

Marshall Leib became a Hollywood Argyle—singing "Alley-Oop" on tour only. He also played guitar on a couple of Duane Eddy sessions. He acted as music supervisor for a few low-budget movies in the 1970s, and he and Annette worked together on the score for the film "Tulips."

Phil Spector went on to be recognized as a genius when it came to record production. He had disliked almost everything associated with being "a recording star." He hated singing in public. He never liked large crowds. He didn't want all those people telling what he should do. Most of all, he disliked being away from the studio where he could be in charge.

And so, after a few more twists and turns in the path of his chosen profession, Phil Spector eventually returned to Gold Star Studios to make his "little symphonies for the kids."

> (More on Phil Spector will be found in the next volume of THE GOLDEN AGE OF ROCK 'N ROLL.)

reelin' & rockin'

THE GOLDEN AGE OF AMERICAN ROCK 'N ROLL

1959

1959
A Look Ahead

"See the girl with the red dress on;
she can do the Birdland all night long."
Ray Charles, 1959

    The big Grammy winner for 1959 is Bobby Darin's "Mack the Knife." It is voted Record of the Year, Darin is the Best New Artist, and Ahmet Ertegun (owner of Atlantic Records, for which Darin recorded the song) is given a Special National Trustees Award for Artist and Repertoire. The Grammy for Song of the Year is presented to "The Battle of New Orleans," a hit for Johnny Horton, who also wins Best Country and Western Performance. The Best Rhythm and Blues Performance is Dinah Washington's "What A Diff'rence a Day Makes."

    By the end of the year, a new word is added to the nation's vocabulary: payola. The exponential factor of "play for pay" finally reaches such proportions that a Senate Subcommittee begins to look into the practice in early November. The thrust of the Subcommittee's inquest is aimed at the deejays who took money and gifts from record companies in return for plugging records on their shows. The whole music industry is in a turmoil. Fearing the worst, one record company after another announces that it has given money to specific deejays. Twenty-five deejays and program directors are in immediate jeopardy of losing their careers. Among the more popular deejays who are snared in the scandal are Joe Niagara (WBIG, Philadelphia), Tom Clay (WJBK, Detroit), Murray "The K" Kaufman (WINS, New York), and Stan Richards (WILD, Boston). The top two deejays in the country, Alan Freed and Dick Clark are caught in the limelight. Freed's broadcast alliances quickly desert him and leave him to suffer the consequences. In the course of three days in late November, he is fired by both ABC-radio and WNEW-TV. Clark, with much more to lose—but with strong connections in and out of the record business—will come away almost unscathed. In an editorial, *Billboard* states, "The cancer of payola cannot be pinned on rock and roll." The journal notes that payola was rampant during vaudeville in the 1920s, and the big band era of the 1930s and 1940s. *Billboard* also notes that, over the years, payola has had very little to do with setting musical trends. The view from within the broadcast industry is voiced by John Sullivan of WNEW, who says, "I don't care if Frank Sinatra wants to give WNEW deejay Bill Williams a Cadillac because Williams would be playing Sinatra records already—thus such a gift wouldn't effect the music."

1959 also finds several of rock 'n roll's biggest stars in trouble with the law. The four male Platters are literally caught with their pants down during a vice raid, and Chuck Berry is arrested for violating the Mann Act forbidding the transporting of a woman across state lines for the purpose of prostitution. The Platters, who represent the more "pop" side of rock 'n roll, receive little more than a reprimand. Berry will wind up in prison.

Amid all of this furor, record sales bounce back from the low point in 1958, topping $400 million for the first time, with albums making up for an astounding $300 million of the total.

The trend of overhauling old material for the teen market continues unabated. Million sellers in 1959 included "Mack the Knife" (from 1956's "Three Penny Opera"), "Stagger Lee" (based on the folk song "The Ballad of Stack-O-Lee"), "Smoke Gets In Your Eyes" (1933), "Kansas City" (1952), "My Happiness" (1948), "(Now and Then There's) A Fool Such As I" (1952), "In the Mood" (1939), "Red River Rock" (based on "Red River Valley," a traditional folk song), "Guitar Boogie Shuffle" (based on "Guitar Boogie," 1942), and "Among My Souvenirs" (1927).

In our "female watch," Connie Francis is joined by a handful of other female vocalists, among them Annette, Dodie Stevens, two-thirds of the Fleetwoods, LaVern Baker, and Sarah Vaughan. However, the music business is still a year or more away from the mighty influx of women, either as solo artists or members of "girl groups."

Instrumentals, on the other hand, are bigger than ever. One of the sub-trends here is the use of novel sounds in the instrumentation. Dave "Baby" Cortez and Johnny and the Hurricanes feature an organ played in a "tooting" fashion. Santo and Johnny utilize a haunting, melodic approach with Santo's slack-string steel guitar on "Sleepwalk." For "Rebel Rouser," Duane Eddy adds bass strings to his electric guitar, giving it the deep-throated "twang" for which he is famous. Utilizing another of Duane Eddy's innovations, the vibrato bar, the Strangers' plodding "Caterpillar Crawl" comes across as an early form of swamp rock. The Storms, with "Tarantula," and Dick Dale, with "Miserlou," build on this sound, adding layers of echo in a predecessor of what will soon evolve into the "surf" instrumental. A surprising number of the more successful rock instrumentals in 1959 are patterned after Arthur Smith's "Guitar Boogie" (mentioned above). Besides "Guitar Boogie Shuffle" by the Virtues, there is "Woo-Hoo" by the Rock-A-Teens and "The Beat" by the Rockin' R's. The Fireballs, a guitar quartet recording in the same Clovis, New Mexico, studio utilized by Buddy Holly, begin their long career as prime purveyors of the Tex-Mex sound with "Torquay" and "Bulldog." Drummers are big, too, with Sandy Nelson having a hit with a regular trap set on "Teen Beat," and Preston Epps doing almost as well with a pair of bongos for "Bongo Rock." Adding one trend to another, Johnny and the Hurricanes take a series of old standards and come up with a string of hits by reforming the music into rock 'n roll for "Red River Rock," "Reville Rock," and "Beatnik Fly." Then there's Link Wray, who's crashing, thrashing cacophony titled "Rumble" single-handedly creates a backlash of criticism for its supposed theme of juvenile delinquency. It also leads to a sub-genre of rock called heavy metal.

For all of the music industry's efforts to package rock 'n roll into teen schmaltz, the style of rock music in 1959 is surprisingly diverse. The R&B solo act remains healthy in the person of Lloyd Price, Wilbert Harrison, Fats Domino, Jackie Wilson, Dee Clark, Chuck Berry, Bo Diddley, and Ray Charles. R&B groups, while in a marked decline, are represented by the Platters, Coasters, Falcons, Flamingos, and Fiestas. The rockers are led by Elvis, with Jack Scott and Ritchie Valens lending a helping hand. The Everly Brothers prove that country can rock as well as swing. Dion and the Belmonts, the Skyliners, the Crests, and the Mystics keep the vocal group doo-wop sound alive. Adding their own interesting sidelights are Skip and Flip, the Fireflies, and Travis and Bob. South Louisiana is represented by a group of previously unknown artists: Frankie Ford, Phil Phillips, Jivin' Gene and Rod Bernard. Still, the trend toward a softer rock sound is everywhere. In increasing numbers, teens are buying records by Perry Como, Dinah Washington, Andy Williams, Guy Mitchell, Della Reese, Sarah Vaughan, and Johnny Mathis. And, the teen idols, the Bobbys, Frankies, Jimmys, and Fabian, are hotter than ever.

NATIONAL NEWS

In November, before a Congressional Subcommittee hearing, Charles Van Doren admits to having been given the answers to the questions asked on the quiz show "Twenty-One," on which he won $129,000; the show was top-rated for two years... Castro's rebel army takes over Cuba... in the United States, 49 convicts are executed during the year... Hawaii becomes the nation's 50th state... the first weather satellite is placed into orbit by the Navy... the number of bowlers has doubled to more than 100 million in the past ten years... sales of musical instruments also doubled to $150 million... meanwhile, during the same period, consumption of vodka increased tenfold, to 9 million gallons, and nearly 600 tons of tranquilizers were prescribed... women wear leotards while men opt for the Ivy League look... Ford introduces the Falcon, a small car designed to counter the Volkswagen... the average car costs $1,180... Oscars are awarded to "Ben-Hur" for Best Picture, Director (William Wyler) and Actor (Charlton Heston) with Simone Signoret winning Best Actress honors for "Room at the Top"..."The Fabulous Fifties" wins an Emmy for Outstanding Achievement in the Field of Variety; Robert Stack is honored for his role in "The Untouchables;" Rod Serling also receives an Emmy for writing "Twilight Zone"... it is reported that 86% of all American households own a TV... Arthur Kornbert and Severo Ochoa share the Nobel Prize for medicine for their discovery of the biological synthesis of RNA and DNA... in baseball, Ernie Banks is voted the Most Valuable Player in the National League and the Cy Young Award as N.L. Rookie of the Year, both for the second straight year... it is also reported that the number Little Leagues reaches 5,700... the American Football League premiers with eight teams... Laos asks the United States for protection from North Vietnam... Sidney Poitier stars in "A Raisin in the Sun" on Broadway... Leon Uris' EXODUS sells the most copies of fiction while the best selling, nonfiction book is Pat Boone's 'TWIXT TWELVE AND TWENTY.

January 1959

JAN 1 Remaining in New Orleans, Ray Charles kicks off the New Year with a show at the Labor Union Hall. On succeeding nights, he will entertain at the Sugar Bowl Club in Thibodaux (2), the Branch Inn in Slidell (3), and the Harlem Gym in Metarie.

Also in New Orleans, Dave Bartholomew brings his band to the dance at the Club Riviera's Birdland Room.

JAN 3 Tonight's "Dick Clark Show" on ABC-TV welcomes Tab Hunter, the Nu Tornados, Billy and Lillie, and Al Alberts (of the Four Aces).

On "The Perry Como Show" on NBC-TV, the Teddy Bears make a rare appearance singing "To Know Him Is To Love Him."

JAN 4 "The Steve Allen Show" on NBC-TV presents Roy Hamilton.

New Releases for the first week in January include "Plain Jane" by Bobby Darin on Atco; "I Don't Need You Anymore" by the Teddy Bears on Imperial; "Sorry (I Ran All The Way Home)" by the **Impalas** on Cub; Conway Twitty's "The Story Of My Love" on M-G-M; Duane Eddy's "The Lonely One" on Jamie; the Fireballs' "Fireball" on Kapp; Link Wray's "Rawhide" on Epic; Billy Craddock's "Am I To Be The One" on Columbia; Gene Allison's "Reap What You Sow" on Vee-Jay; and "The Legend of Sleepy Hollow" by the Monotones on Argo.

JAN 7 Tommy Edwards is booked into the Orchid Room in Kansas City for the week.

EARLY JANUARY

Chuck Berry opens his own nightclub in his hometown of St. Louis. As a tribute to Dick Clark's influence on his career, the night spot is dubbed Club Bandstand.

JAN 9 Dion and the Belmonts sing "Don't Pity Me" on "American Bandstand."

Tommy Ridgely entertains for two days at the Birdland Room in New Orleans.

In Detroit, the Flame Show Bar welcomes Della Reese for a week-long stay.

Sarah Vaughan, James Moody's orchestra, and Redd Foxx entertain during the week at the Howard Theater in Washington.

JAN 10 Brenda Lee guests on ABC-TV's "Jubilee U.S.A."

Also on ABC-TV, "The Dick Clark Show" offers Annette, Dickey

THE IMPALAS
The Impalas had such promise. Three of the members, Anthony Carlucci (tenor), Lenny Renda (baritone), and Richie Wagner (baritone) were seniors in a Brooklyn high school in the fall of 1958. They decided to form a vocal group, and after auditioning various friends for the lead tenor spot, they enlisted fifteen-year old Joe Frazier, born September 5, 1943. (This Joe Frazier is not the heavyweight boxer.) The group took its name either from the Chevy Impala belonging to Lenny's dad, or from the animal—accounts vary. They rehearsed faithfully, and as their skills improved, the boys connected with Arthur Zwirn who had co-written a song for the group with "Gino" Giosassi (of Gino and Gina fame). Zwirn was able to obtain an audition for the Impalas with Alan Freed who, in turn, led them to M-G-M Records, which was struggling to launch Cub Records. The Impalas were one of the first acts signed. During the recording of "Sorry, I Ran All The Way Home," Frazier flubbed an opening cue and ad-libbed "uh oh." It stuck and became an integral part of the final record. The single was released in late 1958, but it failed to catch on. When Freed included the Impalas in his annual Easter show at the Brooklyn Fox, "Sorry" soon developed into a major national hit. In June, Cub released "Oh What A Fool" with advance orders of 100,000 copies. Following a quick start, the single faded after barely a month. There were three more singles on Cub, none of which generated much action. The original group broke up in 1961. Frazier continued on, recording a single in 1963 on 20th Century with a new group of Impalas. In the early 1980s, he was touring with another group of Impalas. Over the years, there were records on various labels—including Checker, Rite-On, Hamilton, and Sundown—by groups also calling themselves the Impalas. None were related to the quartet on Cub Records.

Doo and the Don'ts, Morton Downey, Jr., and LaVern Baker.

JAN 11   Huey Smith and the Clowns, backed by Robert Parker's band, entertain the patrons at the Birdland Room in New Orleans.

New Releases for the second week in January include "Charlie Brown" by the Coasters on Atco; Chuck Berry's "Anthony Boy" on Chess; Buddy Holly's "It Doesn't Matter Anymore" on Coral; "(I Wanna) Dance With The Teacher" by the Olympics on Demon; "Please" by the Wanderers on Cub; "She Say (Oom Dooby Doom)" by the Diamonds on Mercury; "Wishful Thinking" by Little Anthony and the Imperials on End; "Father Time" by the Poni-Tails on ABC Paramount; Bobby Hendricks' "It's Misery" on Sue; Robert and Johnny's "Give Me The Key To Your Heart" on Old Town; Charlie Gracie's "Hurry Up, Buttercup" on Coral; the Moonglows' "I'll Never Stop Wanting You" on Chess; Bobby Rydell's "Dream Age" on Veko; and Johnny Fuller's "Haunted House" on Specialty.

JAN 15   Guitarist Duane Eddy stops by "American Bandstand" to play his latest release, "The Lonely One."
      The Four Esquires begin a two-week booking at the Domino Lounge of the Imperial Hotel in Atlanta.

MID-JANUARY
Paul Anka is booked for a week in Antwerp to be followed by a return to Brussels for a week.
Bobby Darin performs for four days at the Honolulu Civic Auditorium before leaving to tour Australia. (See also JAN 31.)
Jerry Lee Lewis makes a court appearance in Memphis where he is charged with being behind $1,100 in alimony and child support payments to Jane Mitchum Lewis of Natchez, Mississippi.
Little Richard is scheduled to make a religious concert tour of Tennessee. Jordan Records announces that Richard has signed with them to record an album of gospel songs. (No album by Little Richard was ever issued on Jordan Records.)
Ricky Nelson wraps up filming "Rio Bravo" with John Wayne and Dean Martin. Exterior locations were shot at the permanent set in Old Tucson.

JAN 16   The revue at the Apollo Theater this week features Little Anthony and the Imperials, Jerry Butler and the Impressions, Wade Flemons, the Flamingos, the Quin-Tones, the **Crests**, and Doc Bagby's combo.
      The three top stars of Cadence Records, the Everly Brothers, the Chordettes, and Andy Williams, are in Europe making television appearances. Today and tomorrow they are in London where they appear on television's "Cool For Cats" and attend a reception in their honor at the Savoy Hotel. Other cities visited include Antwerp (18-19), Paris (20-21), Luxembourg (23), Hilversum (24), Copenhagen (25), Stockholm (26-27), and Berlin (29).
      Huey Smith and the Clowns return to the Birdland Room in

THE CRESTS
Johnny Mastrangelo was born on May 7, 1939, in the Lower East Side of Manhattan. Growing up, one of his influences was the Moonglows. When he met Tommy Gough, Jay Carter, and Harold Torres, they were just high school students who wanted to form a vocal group. They practiced nights in the Lexington Avenue subway station where the tiled surfaces created an impressive echo. One evening, a talent scout heard them and gave Johnny a business card for Al Brown of Joyce Records. Brown was excited with the group and signed them to a session. When their first release, "Sweetest One," was ready to be issued, they still needed a name, so with little thought, they came up with the Crests. About this time, Mastrangelo also changed his last name to Maestro. Neither of the two singles issued on Joyce sold well. The Crests did land a few personal appearances, including one in Hartford where they shared the bill with the Moonglows. The Crests soon moved to Co-Ed Records, another small company. Their first Co-Ed single, "Pretty Little Angel," went the same way as their previous records on Joyce. Then, as a second release, the Crests recorded "16 Candles." The record was an immediate hit, easily selling a million copies. Through 1959 and 1960, each of the Crests' singles made the charts, with "Six Nights a Week," "The Angels Listened In," "Step by Step," and "Trouble in Paradise" being the most successful. The group was in demand for television and stage appearances across the country. In 1961, the hits stopped coming. Maestro tried going solo in night clubs like New York's Copacabana, but he was too firmly entrenched in rock 'n roll to appeal to that clientele. The Crests, without Maestro, issued singles on Selma, Parkway, Coral and Musictone with no success. In 1968, he formed the Brooklyn Bridge, which had a major hit with "Worst That Could Happen."

New Orleans for a three-day gig.

Bill Doggett and the Moonglows are part of the revue at the Howard Theater in Washington this week.

JAN 17   Fabian makes an appearance on "The Dick Clark Show" on ABC-TV. Also on the show are Conway Twitty, Dion and the Belmonts, the Platters, and Johnny Olenn and the Blockbusters.

JAN 18   Johnny Cash is the special guest on "Jubilee U.S.A" on ABC-TV.

New Releases for the third week in January include "When the Saints Go Marching In" by Fats Domino on Imperial; "Moonlight Serenade" by the Rivieras on Co-Ed; "Bad Boy" by Larry Williams on Specialty; Roy Orbison's "Almost Eighteen" on RCA; "Tarantula" by the Storms on Sundown; "My Runaway Heart" by **Trini Lopez** on King; and "Embraceable You" by the Solitaires on Old Town.

JAN 22   Jimmie Rodgers is the subject of the "This Is Your Life" CBS-TV show. During the course of the show, he is presented with three gold records.

Sam Cooke performs at the Safari Club in New Orleans for two weeks.

JAN 23   Buddy Holly, Ritchie Valens and J. P. Richardson (the Big Bopper) are the headliners of "The Winter Dance Party" tour. Other performers riding the cramped bus through the upper Great Plains include Dion and the Belmonts and Frankie Sardo. Tonight's performance is at George Devine's Ballroom in Milwaukee. Other dates set through the end of the month include Kenosha, Wisconsin (24); Mankato, Minnesota (25); Eau Claire, Wisconsin (26); Montevideo (27); St. Paul (28); Davenport (29); Fort Dodge, Ohio (30); and Duluth (31).

Another package tour, "The Biggest Show of Stars for '59," takes to the road with a show in Columbus, Ohio. Featured performers are the Platters, Clyde McPhatter, Jimmy Clanton, Little Anthony and the Imperials, the Kalin Twins, the Crests, Duane Eddy, Bo Diddley, and the Cadillacs. Other shows through the end of the month include Indianapolis (24); Youngstown (25); Toronto (26); Kitchener, Ontario (27); Rochester (28); Scranton (29); Washington (30); and Norfolk (31). (See also FEB 2.)

The Flamingos, the Quin-Tones, Jerry Butler and the Impressions, Wade Flemons, and the Doc Bagby combo entertain for the week at the Howard Theater in Washington.

JAN 24   The Wild-Cats play their catchy instrumental "Gazachstahagen" and Bill Parsons performs "The All American Boy" on "The Dick Clark Show." Joni James fills out the roster.

Brenda Lee stops by Red Foley's NBC radio show to plug her latest recording, "Bill Bailey, Won't You Please Come Home."

TRINI LOPEZ
He might be termed the Latin Johnny Rivers or maybe Rivers should be called the Anglo Trini Lopez. Both are relics of the 1960's discotheque craze in L.A. Truth be known, Lopez began recording many years earlier, issuing some passable rock 'n roll before becoming too "pop" for rock. He was born Trinidad Lopez III on May 15, 1937. His hometown was Dallas and his Mexican-American parents were very poor. He learned about music from his father, a singer, dancer and actor on the local level. Trini fell in love with rock 'n roll after hearing Elvis and formed a six-piece band, the Big Beats. A short time later, he met Buddy Holly who took enough time with Lopez to point him toward Clovis, New Mexico, and Norman Petty's studio. Even though Trini was the Big Beat's singer, the session produced four instrumentals. Two of them were leased to Columbia Records in 1958, as "Clark's Expedition" became the first of nearly seventy singles for Lopez. He was hurt at losing his lead vocal status, and quit the group. Lopez formed another band and cut a second single, "The Right to Rock" for the local Volk label. Positive reaction to the record in Dallas brought Lopez to King Record of Cincinnati, where he recorded sixteen singles from 1959 to 1961, beginning with "Yes, You Do." Lopez' contract with King called for one master session each year in Cincinnati during which up to two dozen songs were waxed. He sang cover songs ("Since I Don't Have You") and he sang teen-oriented weepers ("Nobody Loves Me," "It Hurts to be in Love," and "Club for Broken Hearts"). He also sang jazzed up folk-type songs ("Here Comes Sally") in a style America would come to know very well, beginning in 1963 after he moved to California, became a sensation with the late high-tone party crowd, and recorded "If I Had a Hammer" for Reprise Records.

JAN 25 Johnny Cash and a group of country artists begin another outing with a show in Kansas City tonight. Other dates include Topeka (26); Sioux City (27); Scottsbluff (28); Lincoln (29); Omaha (30); and Wichita (31).

Dee Clark performs for the Sunday ball at the Blue Eagle Club in New Orleans.

New Releases for the fourth week in January include "So Fine" by the **Fiestas** on Old Town; Sam Cooke's "Everybody Likes To Cha Cha Cha" on RCA; Frankie Avalon's "Venus" on Chancellor; Frankie Lymon's "Up Jumped a Rabbit" on Roulette; Jerry Butler's "Lost" on Abner; "Shambalor" by Sheriff and the Revels on Vee-Jay; Ivan's "That'll Be Alright" on Coral; Sammy Turner's "Sweet Annie Laurie" on Big Top; and Eddie Bo's "Keep On Trying" on Ace. Also new this week is "Fried Eggs" by the Intruders on Fame, a regional hit for the Memphis label that would evolve into Stax Records.

JAN 27 The Playmates begin a two-week run at the Club Cliche in Detroit.

Cozy Cole opens in Miami Beach at the Rocking M.B. Lounge.

JAN 29 Jimmy Darren guests on "American Bandstand."

JAN 30 In Thibodaux, Louisiana, the Sugar Bowl Lounge welcomes Charles Brown and Amos Milburn. The duo continue to perform along the Gulf Coast, appearing in New Iberia (31), Braddock's Club in Opelousas (FEB 1), and the White Eagle Club in Gulfport (2).

Dinah Washington is featured for a week at the Flame in Detroit.

JAN 31 Bobby Darin headlines a week-long tour of Australia, with a show tonight in Newcastle. The remainder of the tour concentrates on Sydney and Melbourne. Other rockers in the package include Chuck Berry, George Hamilton IV, and Jo Ann Campbell.

Tommy Edwards is booked into the Rancho Don Carlos showroom in Winnipeg.

Shirley and Lee entertain at the Birdland Room of the Club Riviera in New Orleans.

On "The Dick Clark Show," Jack Scott is the special guest. Also appearing are Mitch Miller, Gordon McRae, the Applejacks, Earl Grant, and the Quaker City Boys.

Eddie Bond is featured on the regular, Saturday night "Louisiana Hayride" radio show, broadcast from Shreveport.

LATE JANUARY

Johnny Cash is currently doing a fortnight's worth of one-nighters throughout the South.

Wanda Jackson starts a ten-day tour of the Far East with shows in Japan.

THE FIESTAS

The Fiestas were a quartet from Newark, New Jersey, that featured Sam Ingalls (tenor), Eddie Morris (second tenor), Tommy Bullock, (baritone), Preston Lane (bass). The men had been singing as amateurs for a year when they pooled their money to make a demonstration record. The studio they chose belonged to Jim Gribble, a scout for various small record labels in New York City. After engineering the demo for the Fiestas, Gribble told the Fiestas that he thought they had enough potential to get a record company interested. The group was elated. After all, that was their reason for cutting the demo in the first place. Gribble approached several companies, but was turned down by executives who thought that they were not polished enough for the teenagers of the late 1950s. After all, the music of the Fiestas was strongly influenced by the gospel roots of the various members. Gribble wasn't easily dismayed, and eventually Old Town Records showed interest. A session was set and the group recorded "So Fine," a rolling, group harmony effort, with a thumping piano underpinning the sparse instrumentation. For his efforts, Jim Gribble accepted songwriter's credit for "So Fine." Then, in early May 1959, Johnny Otis sued Gribble and Old Town, claiming not to be the composer of "So Fine," but to have actually copyrighted the song in August 1955. Otis accepted a settlement two weeks later. "So Fine" remained very popular through the summer of 1959, especially along the Carolina coast and with Southern college students. The Fiestas proved to be a one-hit wonder. There were fifteen more singles released by Old Town through 1965, but only Broken Heart" in 1962 garnered any attention. The group, with various personnel changes also recorded for Vigor, RCA Victor, Respect and Chimneyville in the 1970s.

THE TOP ROCK 'N ROLL RECORDS FOR JANUARY 1959

1. Smoke Gets In Your Eyes - The Platters
2. To Know Him Is To Love Him - The Teddy Bears
3. One Night/I Got Stung - Elvis Presley
4. Problems - The Everly Brothers
5. My Happiness - Connie Francis
6. A Lover's Question - Clyde McPhatter
7. Gotta Travel On - Billy Grammer
8. Whole Lotta Lovin' - Fats Domino
9. Lonesome Town/I Got A Feeling - Ricky Nelson
10. Donna/La Bamba - Ritchie Valens
11. Beep Beep - The Playmates
12. 16 Candles - The Crests
13. Bimbombey - Jimmie Rodgers
14. Goodbye Baby - Jack Scott
15. It's Only Make Believe - Conway Twitty
16. Queen of the Hop - Bobby Darin
17. The Diary - Neil Sedaka
18. The All American Boy - Bill Parsons
19. Love You Most Of All - Sam Cooke
20. Philadelphia, U.S.A. - The Nu-Tornados
21. I'll Wait For You - Frankie Avalon
22. Stagger Lee - Lloyd Price
23. (All Of A Sudden) My Heart Sings - Paul Anka
24. Lucky Ladybug - Billy and Lillie
25. I Cried A Tear - LaVern Baker
26. Poor Boy - The Royaltones
27. Peek-A-Boo - The Cadillacs
28. Nobody But You - Dee Clark
29. C'Mon Everybody - Eddie Cochran
30. Rock-A-Conga - The Applejacks
31. Don't Pity Me - Dion and the Belmonts
32. Teasin' - The Quaker City Boys
33. Try Me - James Brown and the Famous Flames
34. Pledging My Love - Roy Hamilton
35. Wiggle, Wiggle - The Accents
36. Don't You Know, Yockomo - Huey Smith and the Clowns
37. The Bluebird, the Buzzard and the Oriole - Bobby Day
38. Little Space Girl - Jesse Lee Turner
39. Dreamy Eyes - Johnny Tillotson
40. Tall Paul - Annette
41. Pretty Girls Everywhere - Eugene Church
42. I'm A Man - Fabian
43. Gazachstahagen - The Wild Cats
44. Topsy II - Cozy Cole
45. Don't Take Your Guns To Town - Johnny Cash
46. It's Only the Beginning - The Kalin Twins
47. The Lonely One - Duane Eddy

48. Lovers Never Say Goodbye - The Flamingos
49. Jingle Bell Rock - Bobby Helms
50. Run, Rudolph, Run/Merry Christmas Baby - Chuck Berry

Also on the "pop" chart:
The Chipmunk Song - The Chipmunks
Little Drummer Boy - Harry Simeone Chorale
Manhattan Spiritual - Reg Owen and his Orchestra
Love Is All You Need - Tommy Edwards

January 1959
ARTIST OF THE MONTH

CONNIE FRANCIS

Connie Francis

For Connie Francis, it all started at an amusement park in Irvington, New Jersey, when, as a four-year old girl, she played "Anchors Aweigh" on the accordion. And, where it will end is anybody's guess.

Born on December 12, 1938, Concetta Rosa Maria Franconero began singing and performing as a small child. Music was a passion for her father, George, who made a living as a roofing contractor. He was a first-generation American whose own father had arrived in the United States from Italy in 1905. Of the few possessions Connie's grandfather brought with him, the most treasured were his musical instruments, a set of bagpipes, an ocarina, a sweet potato, and his beloved concertina.

The Franconero family settled on a small plot of land in Newark called "Little Italy." After George married his childhood sweetheart, they moved to Brooklyn. It was on a weekend visit back to Newark that Concetta was born. George was visibly upset with the arrival of his daughter as the family was struggling financially. It may have been this perceived disapproval that first nurtured Connie's love of music. She was doing it to please her father. She has admitted that she hated playing the accordion, but since it meant so much to her father, she became an accomplished player. In her autobiography, she gave her father complete credit for her success.

Once she took up music, she became the darling of the family. Connie had inherited her mother's fine singing voice, as well as the musical ability from her father's side of the family. She approached her music lessons with a single-mindedness rare in one so young. She practiced her accordion to the exclusion of most other youthful activities.

By the time she was ten, she was playing amateur shows and family gatherings. She was appearing on a local vaudeville show as a dancer as well as a singer and accordionist. She graduated to radio, appearing on the Horn and Hardart "Children's Hour," "The Ted Mack Amateur Hour," and "Tony Grant's Stars of Tomorrow." She performed on television for the first time as part of the "Paul Whiteman Show." When she was twelve, Arthur Godfrey invited her to sing on the special Christmas edition of his talent show. It was Godfrey who first suggested that Concetta Franconero might be a mouthful for an announcer, and maybe she should shorten it to Connie Francis.

In 1951, Connie became a regular member of the young cast of the popular New York television show "Star Time Kids." She remained with the show for four seasons. At the same time, she enrolled in Newark's Arts High School, a training ground for students aspiring to careers in art or music. At Arts High, Connie studied music theory and orchestration. In her Junior year, the family moved to Belleville, New Jersey. Connie enrolled in the local high school, finally getting the chance to live life as a regular teenager while remaining a member of "Star Time Kids." She joined the debating team and the glee club, as well as finding time to be coeditor of the school newspaper. She even took typing class and won a state sponsored contest.

At age fourteen, Connie began cutting demonstration records to promote the work of songwriters and music publishers. "Star Time Kids" went off the air in 1955, and Connie took to the road with her mother, appearing in supper clubs along the East Coast. This led to the first studio session of her own. She recorded four songs, and her manager sent them to most of the major record companies without getting a nibble. Finally, a demonstration tape crossed the desk of an executive at M-G-M Records. M-G-M was a company known for its soundtrack and original cast albums, and also as the label of Hank Williams, Sheb Wooley and Marvin Rainwater. Connie signed to M-G-M just before she graduated from Belleville High.

Her first record, "Freddy," attracted little attention in 1955. Connie received a scholarship to New York University to begin a pre-med course of study. The summer before classes were to begin, she took her first promotional swing through the Northeast and Midwest. She returned to find that NYU had recalled her scholarship, preferring to grant such an award to a more serious student. Connie accepted this slap in the face with her characteristic "I'll show you" attitude.

Becoming a success as a recording artist was proving to be much more difficult that attracting attention as a young female accordion player. Her second single featured a song co-written by another unknown, aspiring singer, Bobby Darin. Darin even sang backing vocals on "My First Real Love," but it didn't do much for the single's sales. However, meeting Bobby Darin did wonders for Connie's love life as well as her career.

Like many Catholic-Italian girls, Connie had been raised in a very strict environment. Her parents were loving and caring, but they feared the worst every time Connie would travel to New York alone. Their first meeting with the brash, self-assured Darin proved to be a disaster. Darin was ushered out of the Franconero home by Connie's father. Connie and Bobby still found occasions to be together and his talent and drive were an elixir for her own ambitions. At age seventeen, Connie was receiving a quick course in show business survival tactics.

M-G-M continued to release a new single by Connie every three months. And, like clockwork, each sputtered and disappeared. She was locked into a style that was better suited to someone older. The one "pop" star at M-G-M was Joni James, a beautiful young woman with an extraordinary voice. In part because M-G-M was dedicated to keeping Miss James on top of the music business, there was little time or money left over to promote Connie Francis.

During 1956, Connie continued to perform the supper club circuit, playing for the same small crowds month after month. Her expenses were costing more than her career took in. When her father lost the family's meager savings in a bad investment, they had to sell their home. Always in a rush, Bobby Darin asked Connie to marry him, and she begged off, ending her first romance. For Connie, this was a time of depression and soul searching.

It looked like everything in her world was sliding downhill, Then, she found a job working on a new rock 'n roll movie, "Rock, Rock, Rock." She had auditioned for an on-screen role in the film and had lost the job to a new actress, Tuesday Weld. When the movie producers discovered that Miss Weld couldn't sing a note, they went back to Connie and asked her to record the songs for Miss Weld to lip-sync. At the time, Connie felt like this was the unkindest cut of all. However, it did lead to similar work for Connie in the movie "The Sheriff of Fractured Jaw" when she sang the vocals for Jayne Mansfield.

Over the course of two years, she released a total of ten singles. One, "The Majesty of Love," was a duet with a rising country and western star, Marvin Rainwater. It has been reported that this single sold more than a million copies, but this is doubtful. At any rate, Connie Francis thought so little of the experience that she ignored it completely in her autobiography. She also failed to mention that, at this time, she was being billed as Johnny Ray's protege.

In late 1957, she was in the studio for what she felt would be her final M-G-M recording session. She was still recording songs aimed at an adult market. At the end of the session, with sixteen minutes of studio time remaining, she recorded "Who's Sorry Now" in a single take. "Who's Sorry Now" had first been a hit in 1923, and Connie only recorded it to appease her insistent father.

"Who's Sorry Now" was released in November 1957 to the usual lack of enthusiasm. Connie resigned her immediate future to studying medicine in college. Then on January 1, 1958, Dick Clark played the single on "American Bandstand." Connie was ecstatic. Still, nothing immediate happened. Clark was certain that the song had hit potential. On February 15, she was a guest on Clark's inaugural Saturday night television show. This was the boost Connie's career needed. "Who's Sorry Now," a single that had languished for months with no attention, finally caught the public's ear.

Overnight, everything changed for Connie Francis. When Jimmie Rodgers launched his own NBC-TV variety program on March 31, Connie was a regular guest on the show, singing a spotlight song in each show for the first six weeks. The bookings started rolling in, and not just for small supper clubs in out-of-the-way places. Her dates now were for the Casino Royal in Washington, the Chez Paree in Chicago, and Blinstrub's in Boston. She performed on "The Perry Como Show" on NBC-TV and

"The Ed Sullivan Show" on CBS-TV.

Her next few singles met a fate similar to that of other new rock 'n rollers. They did not approach the stratospheric heights of "Who's Sorry Now," which had gone on to sell a million copies. "I'm Sorry I Made You Cry" was a close copy of "Who's Sorry Now," but it probably sold less than half as many copies. "Heartaches" didn't sell enough to dent the charts. Then, overnight, the quality of the songs she was offered changed dramatically. Instead of ballads more suited for a middle-age woman, she was asked to sing songs directed at the teenage audience. In the summer of 1958, she released "Stupid Cupid," a song co-written by Neil Sedaka, an up-and-coming New York singer. "Stupid Cupid" sold more than a half-million copies and put her career on the fast-track once again.

In August 1958 she made her first overseas tour, a ten-day swing through the British Isles. After "Fallin'" failed to attract massive sales in the fall of 1958, M-G-M released "My Happiness" for the Christmas season. It was an old song from 1933 that Connie infused with emotion, and it sold even better than "Who's Sorry Now." By now the hits were flying off the M-G-M presses. In the summer of 1959, she had a million seller with "Lipstick On Your Collar." This song was backed with the equally popular "Frankie," a song dedicated to Frankie Avalon, with whom she had formed a mutual attachment after Bobby Darin. Then she dipped into her bag of old standards again, coming up with "Among My Souvenirs," a hit from 1927. Like the other "oldies," it too passed the million mark in sales. On November 18, 1959, during an appearance on "The Perry Como Show," at her father's insistence, she included the English translation of the Italian song "Mama" in her brief act. The response was tremendous. It was a major turning point in her career. In late November, she capped off an incredible two-years of success with a sold-out concert at New York's Carnegie Hall.

(The Connie Francis story will continue in the next volume of THE GOLDEN AGE OF AMERICAN ROCK 'N ROLL.)

February 1959

ROD BERNARD
Rod Bernard's recording career coincided with a resurgence of artists whose material was based loosely on the rhythms and vocal stylings of south Louisiana's Cajun subculture. Bernard was born August 12, 1940, in Opelusas, a small town near Ville Platte. Like other youngsters in the area, he showed an early interest in music. At the age of ten, he became a regular on the local radio station, KSLO. He had been discovered in a local talent contest, and when the radio station showed interest, he began to come by on Saturdays to sing and play his guitar. At seventeen, he was a staff announcer, nicknamed "Hot Rod." With a few other like-minded teens, including Bobby Charles and Johnnie Allen, he formed a combo to play rhythm and blues. The band was popular in the area, and Bernard had one single, "Linda Gail," issued on Carl Records, a minuscule local label. Bernard's reputation was strong enough to bring him to Jin Records, a new label founded with high expectations in Ville Platte. For his first release, Bernard chose to record "This Should Go On Forever," a number co-written by Karl King (Bernard Jolivette), vocalist with Guitar Gable (Gable Perrodin), a legend among the Louisiana blues community. "This Should Go On Forever" contained all of the trademarks of south Louisiana R&B: descending triplets, a horn section playing in unison, and a heavy, repetitive bass pattern. When the single began to attract attention, it was leased to Argo Records, a subsidiary of Chess, and it became a moderate hit. There was one other Argo single before Bernard switched to Mercury, where his first single, "One More Chance" attracted a little attention. He issued a total of six singles on Mercury into 1960, then moved to Hallway for another half dozen singles to 1964. He also recorded for Teardrop, Arbee and Crazy Cajun.' He also issued seven later singles on Jin.

FEB 1   Experiencing mechanical problems with the tour bus and below-freezing temperatures outside, "The Winter Dance Party" tour forges on through Wisconsin playing an afternoon show in Appleton and an evening performance in Green Bay.

FEB 2   Following the "Winter Dance Party" show at the Surf Ballroom in Clear Lake, Iowa, Buddy Holly decides to forego the tour bus for this night. He suggests booking an airplane for himself and his two new Crickets, Waylon Jennings and Tommy Allsup. Ritchie Valens and J. P. Richardson (The Big Bopper) successfully plead with the Crickets for their two seats. The trio travels to nearby Mason City and books a private plane to take them to Fargo, North Dakota, the nearest airport to their next destination, Moorhead, Iowa. Just after midnight, the plane takes off.
   In the South, "The Biggest Show of Stars for '59" continues to roll along, playing Winston-Salem tonight, Charlotte (3), Baltimore (4), Pittsburgh (5), Hershey (6), and Hartford (8). (See also MAR 5.)

New Releases for the first week in February include Lou Giordiano's "Stay Close To Me" on Brunswick, a record that would be long forgotten except that it was produced by Buddy Holly. Other new singles this week are **Rod Bernard**'s "This Should Go On Forever" on Mercury; Ricky Nelson's "It's Late" b/w "Never Be Anyone Else But You" on Imperial; Lloyd Price's "Where Were You (On Our Wedding Day)?" on ABC-Paramount; "Guitar Boogie Shuffle" by the Virtues on Hunt; "My Heart Is An Open Book" by Carl Dobkins, Jr. on Decca; "Leotards" by the Royal Teens on Mighty; "Margurita" by Chuck Rio and the Originals on Jackpot; "Because You're Young" by Jimmie Rodgers on Roulette; "But Not For Me" by the Flamingos on End; Billy Riley's "No Name Girl" on Sun; "See-Saw" by the Roylatones on Jubilee; "There Must Be A Reason" by James Brown and the Famous Flames on Federal; the Mello-Kings' "Chip Chip" on Herald; Troyce Key's "Ain't I Cried Enough" on Warner Brothers; and Jimmy McCracklin's "The Wobble" on Mercury. Finally, new this week is David Gates' "Swinging Baby Doll" on East-West. Gates would found the popular group Bread in 1970.

FEB 3   Early this morning it is reported that the light plane carrying Buddy Holly, Ritchie Valens, and the Big Bopper has failed to reach the airport in Moorhead. At 9:30 a.m., a search party discovers the wreckage just five miles from the Mason City airport. There are no survivors.
   Tonight at the Armory in Moorhead, Iowa, "The Winter Dance

Party" continues without three of its headliners. Recruited to fill in tonight are the Shadows, a group of newcomers from Fargo, North Dakota, led by sixteen-year old Bobby Velline, who would soon change his name to Bobby Vee. Reportedly, the group performed second on the bill, after Frankie Sardo and before Dion and the Belmonts. The Shadows perform "Bye Bye Love" and "Long Tall Sally."

FEB 4   In Sioux Falls, "The Winter Dance Party" reorganizes after its tragedy. Frankie Avalon and Jimmy Clanton are enlisted to complete the remainder of the shows while the Shadows remain as an opening act. Other dates for this tour include Des Moines (5); Cedar Rapids (6); Spring Valley, Illinois (7); and Chicago (8). (See also FEB 9.)

FEB 6   This afternoon's guest spot on "American Bandstand" is filled by the Poni-Tails.
This week, the Apollo Theater in New York offers a jazz revue headlined by Dakota Staton.
In New Orleans this weekend, Amos Milburn and Charles Brown entertain the Mardi Gras revelers at the Dew Drop Inn. Across town, **Eddie Bo** opens a three-day stand at the Club Riviera's Birdland Room.
Sarah Vaughan opens a three-day stand at Philadelphia's Red Hill Inn.
Ruth Brown, the Wanderers and Nappy Brown perform this week at the Howard Theater in Washington.

FEB 7   The funeral for Buddy Holly is held in Lubbock at the Tabernacle Baptist Church. Members of the Crickets and Phil Everly serve as pall bearers.
In San Fernando, California, Ritchie Valens is buried at the San Fernando Mission Cemetery.
The Nu Tornados open a two-day gig at the Erie Social Club in Philadelphia.
The Applejacks perform "Rock-A-Conga" on "The Dick Clark Show." Other artists appearing tonight are the Bell Notes, Brook Benton, and Thomas Wayne.
Connie Francis visits "The Parry Como Show" on NBC-TV.
Johnny Cash plays a one-night stand in White Plains, New York. Tomorrow night, he is a guest on "The Ed Sullivan Show."

FEB 9   Cozy Cole moves into Porky's Hideaway in Fort Lauderdale.
Carl Perkins begins a two-week stint in Toronto.
Suffering long nights on the same frigid bus that created the scenario leading to the deaths of Buddy Holly, Ritchie Valens, and J. P. Richardson, Frankie Avalon comes down with pneumonia and leaves the "Winter Dance Party" tour. To complete the last week of the tour, Paul Anka and Fabian are brought in as replacements. Tonight's show is in Waterloo, Iowa, with the remaining shows in

EDDIE BO

He was a musical workhorse. Born September 30, 1930, in New Orleans, Eddie Bocage's family was deeply rooted in the music of the region. He was influenced by his mother, a blues shouter named Iona Tucker Bocage. She also knew how to play the piano, and for Eddie's sake, she knew how to teach. In 1950, Eddie attended the Grunewald School of Music during the day and sat at Professor Longhair's side in the evening. Although he was a good student, he couldn't keep himself away from the nightclub scene. He loved jazz, but in New Orleans there was money to be made in the 1950s in R&B. In 1955, he made his first recordings for the Ace label of Jackson, Mississippi. As Little Bo, his "Baby" b/w "I'm So Glad" was the second Ace single. There were a couple more singles on Ace, but by this time Apollo, a New York label had scooped him up. Now billed as Eddie Bo, he issued five singles on Apollo during 1956-57. With little to show in the way of sales, he switched to Chess Records for "Every Day, Every Night," on Checker in 1957 and "Oh-Oh" on Chess in 1958. Back in New Orleans, he joined the Ric roster in 1959. It proved to be one of his longer recording associations. Throughout all this time, he and his band toured constantly, backing mainly female artists such as Etta James, Ruth Brown, Faye Adams, and the Teen Queens. In 1962, after several years with Ric, his recording of a local dance fad, "Check Mr. Popeye," was leased by Swan Records for East Coast distribution. It was as close as he came to a hit. Bo probably recorded for another dozen or so labels, including Rip, Cinderella At Last, Seven B and Capitol. He even had one single on his own label, Bo-Sound. While he never had a national hit, he played on hundred of sessions that sold millions. Today, he can be found holding down the piano stool at the Margaritaville Bar in the French Quarter.

Dubuque (10); Louisville (11); Canton (12); Youngstown (13); and Peoria (14). On February 15, the caravan finally struggles into Springfield, Illinois, for its final show at the Illinois State Armory.

New Releases for the second week in February include two from Checker: Bo Diddley's "I'm Sorry" and Dale Hawkins' "Class Cutter (Yeah, Yeah)"; **Marv Johnson**'s "Come To Me" on United Artists; "If I Didn't Care" by Connie Francis on M-G-M; "Come Softly To Me" by the Fleetwoods on Dolphin; Bobby Comstock's "Zig Zag" on Triumph; Neil Sedaka's "I Go Ape" on RCA; Robin Luke's "Strollin' Blues" on Dot; "I Got a Woman" by Bill Haley and His Comets on Decca; Bobby Rydell's "Makin' Time" on Cameo; "The Happy Organ" by Dave "Baby" Cortez on Clock; "I Can't Take It" by the Chantels on End; "Lulu" by Dave Burgess on Challenge; and Esquirita's "Laid Off" on Capitol.

FEB 10   Link Wray brings his raw-edged guitar style to "American Bandstand."

FEB 13   On "American Bandstand," the Skyliners sing "Since I Don't Have You."
　　　　This week's show at the Howard Theater in Washington has a jazz flavor as Dakota Staton and Ahmad Jamal entertain.

FEB 14   Charlie Gracie is booked into the Erie Social Club in Philadelphia for two days.
　　　　On television, "The Dick Clark Show" welcomes Frankie Avalon, Connie Francis, Duane Eddy, and the Kalin Twins.

FEB 16   Little Anthony and the Imperials bring their vocal harmonies to "American Bandstand."

New Releases for the third week in February include two from Specialty: Little Richard's "By the Light of the Silvery Moon" and "Big Boy Pete" by Don and Dewey; Eddie Cochran's "Teenage Heaven" on Liberty; Bobby Day's "That's All I Want" on Class; "Copy Cat" by the Cadillacs on Josie; two from Capitol: "Over the Rainbow" by Gene Vincent and His Blue Caps and "Livin' Lovin' Doll" by Cliff Richard and the Shadows; "Your Love" by the Olympics on Demon; Cozy Cole's "Topsy-Turvy" on Love; Jerry Fuller's "Lipstick and Rouge" on Lin; Warren Storm's "Troubles, Troubles" on Nasco; and two from Jesse Belvin: "Beware" on Tender and "Guess Who?" on RCA.

FEB 17   On "American Bandstand," the Rivieras drop by to entertain the fans with "Moonlight Serenade."
　　　　Clyde McPhatter begins an engagement at the Village Vanguard in New York City.

FEB 20   Fabian headlines a show at the Urline Arena in Washington, DC. Also appearing are the Crests, Linda Laurie, the Chantels, Dickey Doo and the Don'ts, and Jesse Lee Turner.

MARV JOHNSON

The success of Marv Johnson was directly attributable to the involvement of young Berry Gordy, a fledgling music entrepreneur from Detroit. Johnson was born October 15, 1938, in Detroit. By the time he attended Cass Technical High, he was a proficient pianist and had been coached in operatic voice by a neighbor. After graduation, as a member of the Junior Serenaders he joined a traveling carnival. When he returned to Detroit, he found work in a record store. Through this connection he came to the attention of Berry Gordy. In 1958, Johnson recorded "My Baby-O" for the small Kudo label. The session was reportedly produced by Gordy, who had just written and produced "Reet Petite" for Jackie Wilson. Johnson and Wilson had similar singing styles, an energetic combination of a gospel with operatic overtones. Johnson's next recording, "Come To Me," was the first release on Gordy's new Tamla label. There was some local action, and soon United Artists Records leased and reissued the song. Within a month, "Come To Me" was receiving national attention, remaining popular for almost four months. The follow-up, "I'm Coming Home" didn't fare as well, but Johnson's next two singles, "You've Got What It Takes" and "I Love the Way You Love" were both Top Ten hits. Into 1961, Johnson had several more medium-sized hits including "Move Two Mountains." His popularity brought him work with the rock 'n roll caravans and on TV variety shows. Unfortunately, he never achieved the widespread success of Jackie Wilson. Beginning in 1965, he recorded a few fine singles for Gordy Records, one of Berry Gordy's Motown companies. Even though his recording career was over, he remained on the Motown payroll as an executive. Marv Johnson died on May 16, 1993, in Columbia, South Carolina, of a stroke suffered backstage during the 40th anniversary concert for ex-Drifter Bill Pinckney.

Also in Washington, the Howard Theater offers LaVern Baker, Little Anthony and the Imperials, and Sarah McLawler for patrons this week.

The Platters sing "Smoke Gets in Your Eyes" and the soon-to-be-released "Enchanted" as their two spotlight offerings on "American Bandstand."

Ruth Brown is scheduled for a week's run at the Flame Show Bar in Detroit.

FEB 21   Joe Tex and Earl King have a two-day "Battle of the Blues" at the Dew Drop Lounge in New Orleans.

Richard Rome is a guest on "The Dick Clark Show." Also on tonight's lineup are Cathy Carr, the Diamonds, Billy Williams, and Tommy Leonetti.

New Releases for the fourth week in February include Jack Scott's "I Never Felt Like This" on Carlton; two from Sun: Jerry Lee Lewis' "Lovin' Up A Storm" and Johnny Cash's "Thanks A Lot;" "Robbin' the Cradle" by **Tony Bellus** on NRC; the Big Bopper's "Walking Through My Dreams" on Mercury; "Hey, Little Girl" by Thurston Harris on Aladdin; a reissue of "That's My Desire" by Bob and Earl on Class; "Tell Me So" by Sonny Til and the Orioles on Jubilee; and "Double Trouble" by Otis Rush on Cobra. New this week is "Ding Dong" on Milo, the first single from the 1970s hit-maker, Tony Orlando.

FEB 27   In Ferriday, Louisiana, Jerry Lee Lewis' wife, Myra, gives birth to their first child (his second), Steve Allen Lewis, named after the television entertainer who gave Jerry Lee his first national TV exposure. In 1962, three-year old Stevie drowned in the family's swimming pool.

In New Orleans, Earl King and Ted Taylor are booked at the Dew Drop Hotel and Cafe for three days. King and his combo will remain at the Dew Drop for the next few weeks.

Detroit's Flame Lounge books Etta James for the week.

Connie Francis begins an extended tour of England.

Lloyd Price headlines the revue at Washington's Howard Theater this week. Also appearing are the Crests, Marie Knight, and Jesse Lee Turner.

Duke Ellington and his orchestra entertain the fans at the Apollo Theater this week.

FEB 28   Bobby Freeman and Neil Sedaka are guests on "The Dick Clark Show" this Saturday night.

"The Perry Como Show" on NBC-TV features Paul Anka.

LATE FEBRUARY

Frankie Avalon and Jodie Sands, both Chancellor Records recording artists, leave the States for a brief tour of England where they will concentrate on television appearances.

Recently drafted, Jack Scott begins serving a two-year hitch in the

TONY BELLUS
Born Anthony Bellusci, on April 17, 1936, in Chicago, Tony Bellus was a rock and roll rarity. He played the accordion. As a high school student, Tony began writing songs that he submitted to local music publishers. Even with no professional experience, Tony began to attract attention. He enrolled in the Chicago Art Institute as a drama major. Like many aspiring thespians, he was short of cash, and he took a part-time job singing in a local club. His popularity grew so rapidly that he soon dropped out of the Institute. About 1958, he recorded one single, "Fancy Free," for the local Chi-Fi label. The record fared poorly, but Bellus (as he now billed himself) did not give up. He had written "Robbin' the Cradle," and his faith in the song led him to record a demonstration tape. Using other amateur musicians who happened to be in the studio that day, Bellus was able to come up with a suitable take. After the session, Bellus went to his regular night club gig, and when he mentioned from the stage that he had just recorded a song, he was approached by a scout for NRC Records of Atlanta. The scout returned to Atlanta with a raw mix of the song which Bill Lowrey of NRC released "as is." Lowrey promoted the record heavily, and by May it was garnering national attention. It went on to become the biggest hit the label ever had. Bellus was booked on tours with the other aspiring NRC rockers, including Ray Stevens, Jerry Reed and Joe South. Bellus never again had a national hit, although several of his six other NRC singles, including "Hey, Little Darlin'" were popular in areas where NRC had strong distribution. By 1960, NRC was in financial trouble. At the same time, Bellus was drafted into the Army. With no label backing him, and no personal appearances, his career stalled. Over the years, he has recorded for his own MMP label and Lowrey's 1-2-3 Records. Bellus continues to work the Chicago club scene today.

U.S. Army. He is stationed at Fort Knox, Kentucky.

THE TOP ROCK N' ROLL RECORD FOR FEBRUARY 1959

1. Donna/La Bamba - Ritchie Valens
2. Smoke Gets In Your Eyes - The Platters
3. 16 Candles - The Crests
4. Stagger Lee - Lloyd Price
5. My Happiness - Connie Francis
6. The All American Boy - Bill Parsons
7. Lonely Teardrops - Jackie Wilson
8. Gotta Travel On - Billy Grammer
9. Goodbye Baby - Jack Scott
10. A Lover's Question - Clyde McPhatter
11. (All Of a Sudden) My Heart Sings - Paul Anka
12. I Cried a Tear - LaVern Baker
13. The Diary - Neil Sedaka
14. Nobody But You - Dee Clark
15. Whole Lotta Lovin' - Fats Domino
16. Tall Paul - Annette
17. Lucky Ladybug - Billy and Lillie
18. Little Space Girl - Jesse Lee Turner
19. To Know Him Is To Love Him - The Teddy Bears
20. One Night - Elvis Presley
21. I'm A Man - Fabian
22. The Lonely One - Duane Eddy
23. Bimbombey - Jimmie Rodgers
24. Don't Take Your Guns To Town - Johnny Cash
25. Love You Most Of All - Sam Cooke
26. Don't Pity Me - Dion and the Belmonts
27. Pretty Girls Everywhere - Eugene Church
28. It's Only The Beginning - The Kalin Twins
29. She Say (Oom Dooby Doom) - The Diamonds
30. Try Me - James Brown and the Famous Flames
31. I've Had It - The Bell Notes
32. Charlie Brown - The Coasters
33. Lovers Never Say Goodbye - The Flamingos
34. Rock-A-Conga - The Applejacks
35. It's Just a Matter of Time - Brook Benton
36. Ambrose (Part 5) - Audrey
37. Tragedy - Thomas Wayne
38. Gazachstahagen - The Wild Cats
39. Plain Jane - Bobby Darin
40. The Story of My Love - Conway Twitty
41. The Shag - Billy Graves
42. Mathilda - Cookie and the Cupcakes
43. Wiggle, Wiggle - The Accents
44. Rawhide - Link Wray and His Ray Men
45. The Worryin' Kind - Tommy Sands

46. Teardrops Will Fall - Dickey Doo and the Don'ts
47. Venus - Frankie Avalon
48. Sea Cruise - Frankie Ford
49. Problems - The Everly Brothers
50. Jingle Bell Rock - Bobby Helms

Also on the "pop" charts:
The Hawaiian Wedding Song - Andy Williams
The Wedding - June Valli
May You Always - The McGuire Sisters
The Peter Gunn Theme - Ray Anthony and His Orchestra

February 1959
ARTIST OF THE MONTH

RITCHIE VALENS

Ritchie Valens was the first rock 'n roll singer of Mexican heritage to become influential on a national level. There had been many other Latin singers in the "pop" field, where orchestras and combos specializing in Latin rhythms had been popular for years. There were even Mexican-American rock 'n rollers before Ritchie Valens, but they did not capitalize on their ancestry.

The Joseph Steven Valenzuela family lived in San Fernando, a small hamlet in a valley north of Los Angeles. Steve was a tree surgeon by trade, but he also dabbled in mining operations and was a passable horse trainer. His youngest son, Richard Steven, was born on May 13, 1941, in Los Angeles at the County Osteopathic Hospital. At this time, Steve and his wife, Connie, were working in a munitions plant for the War effort.

In 1944, the parents divorced and Steve moved to nearby Pacoima while Connie and the four children stayed in San Fernando. This was a most difficult time for young Ritchie. Because the San Fernando home was small, he was shuttled off to live with a succession of aunts and uncles in various towns in the upper Los Angeles area. In 1951, Steve died and Connie moved to Pacoima, taking over her ex-husband's house which was large enough so she could gather her children again.

As a child, Ritchie grew up in much the same environment as the other children in the area. A Mexican-American family living in the San Fernando Valley faced many of the prejudices that were part of Hispanic life throughout southern California. However, the area was home to many family groups, Asians, blacks, and whites, as well as Hispanics.

Ritchie was an average student for whom music was his primary guiding force. He was influenced by the Mexican folk songs and the popular tunes sung by his relatives. However, his true love in music was the singing cowboy of the Saturday matinee movies. He also listened to country music played on the radio stations in the San Fernando Valley. Ritchie

Ritchie Valens

had only an average singing voice, but his relatives began teaching him to play guitar when he was about eleven.

At Pacoima Junior High, he appeared in several variety programs and played his guitar for his schoolmates during lunch breaks. As part of a woodworking project when he was thirteen, he assembled an electric guitar out of scrap lumber and secondhand electric parts. The lack of professional manufacturing techniques imparted to the instrument a raw, ragged sound that he liked.

By the time he entered San Fernando High School, he was performing with his guitar at school assemblies and after-school parties. In his junior year, he joined a group of like-minded rockers who called themselves the Silhouettes, after the song by the Rays. The band represented the ethnic population of the San Fernando area and featured members with Mexican, Japanese, and Afro-Cuban backgrounds. As the only rock 'n roll combo in the area, the Silhouettes quickly became local stars. At a January 1958 "rent party" held in the American Legion Hall in San Fernando, the band was tape recorded by a part time talent scout working for Bob Keane, a Los Angeles music entrepreneur and the owner of Keen Records. After listening to the tape, Keane decided he wanted to hear more of Ritchie.

It took five months of encouragement by his family and friends before Ritchie traveled to Los Angeles to audition for Keane. In May 1958, Keane's company, Keen Records, was in the middle of a string of hits with Sam Cooke. Keane was looking to expand his talent roster for a new venture, Del-Fi Records. Ritchie's audition went well enough for Keane to set up a formal recording session. Ritchie had many songs in the repertoire, but most of them were versions of other rock 'n roll hits. Keane wanted something fresh. Ritchie responded by playing an unnamed instrumental number on his guitar. Keane liked it enough to record it "as is," and he asked Ritchie to throw in some lyrics as he went along.

The resulting single, "Come On, Let's Go" b/w "Framed" was released locally during the early summer of 1958. On the record label, Richard Valenzuela's name was shortened to Ritchie Valens. The single began to receive attention almost immediately in Los Angeles. The popularity of "Come On, Let's Go" soon spread through the Southwest. In August, Del-Fi released the single nationally, and it eventually sold a half-million copies.

"Come On, Let's Go" was a thumping rock number opening with the instrumental riff Valens' had performed for Keane, played this time on his new Fender Stratocaster. Valens' voice was a strong tenor, delivered in a strained, nasal fashion. The guitar break in the middle of the song was rudimentary, and not as exciting as the vocal. "Framed" had been a minor hit for the Robins before they became the Coasters. The song was a talking blues with singing only during the chorus. The Robins' version had astutely used a deep bass vocal for the talking, and Valens' upper-register voice didn't do the song justice.

In October, Valens returned home after a short tour to face another recording session. Keane wanted a new single and material for a proposed album. Valens' second single took a completely different tact from

"Come On, Let's Go." "Donna" was a ballad written by Valens for his high school sweetheart. Rising above a muted vocal group and quiet arrangement from the combo, Valens' untrained tenor lent itself perfectly to the song's lyrics. The flip side, "La Bamba," was a reworking of a traditional Mexican folk song of the same name. Done in a straight-ahead rock 'n roll style, it had been one of the numbers that received the most attention when he was a member of the Silhouettes.

Ritchie's schedule was now full of appearances and recording sessions. In December, while he was home on a brief stopover, Valens returned to his junior high school for an afternoon assembly in the gymnasium. Keane fortunately recorded the event. At this time, Valens also filmed a cameo for the upcoming teen movie, "Go, Johnny Go!" In the film he sang "Ooh! My Head," which was a close cover of Little Richard's "Ooh! My Soul." Late in month, he returned to the East Coast to appear on "The Dick Clark Show" on December 27.

On January 23, 1959, Ritchie joined Buddy Holly, the Big Bopper, and Dion and the Belmonts for the "Winter Dance Party" tour of the Upper Midwest. As the first major storm of the season raged, the troupe moved from town to town, playing many of the communities in the area: Milwaukee, Kenosha, Mankato, Eau Claire, Montevideo, St. Paul, Davenport, Fort Dodge, Duluth, and Appleton.

At this time, Dion and the Belmonts were doing well with "Don't Pity Me." It was six months since the Big Bopper sold a million copies of "Chantilly Lace," and Buddy Holly's last hit was a brief run with "Heartbeat" in January 1959. However, Ritchie's single of "Donna" and "La Bamba" was rising rapidly toward the Top Ten, making him the most popular artist on the tour at that moment.

On February 2, 1959, the "Winter Dance Party" arrived in Clear Lake, Iowa, to play a dance that night at the Surf Ballroom. The heater of the converted bus on which the artists had been traveling had been malfunctioning for several days while the outside temperature hovered near zero. On the way to Clearlake, the bus had completely broken down, forcing a long delay. Buddy Holly voiced his displeasure with the traveling accommodations and arranged to fly to the next destination in a private airplane. He booked a four-seat Beechcraft Bonanza to take care of himself and his band members, Waylon Jennings and Tommy Allsup. However, J. P. Richardson (the Big Bopper) and Valens coerced the extra seats away from Jennings and Allsup. After the show at the Surf Ballroom, the three entertainers made their way to the local airport. Shortly after midnight, the plane took off for Fargo, North Dakota. It remained airborne only briefly and crashed into a pasture about a mile from the airport. All aboard were killed. Ritchie Valens was buried on February 7, in the San Fernando Mission Cemetery.

Valens had three singles under his name on the market at the time of his death. Besides "Donna" and "Come On, Let's Go," Del-Fi had also released "Fast Freight." This was an instantly-forgotten instrumental by an artist identified on the label as Arvee Allens, a semi-phonetic spelling of "R V-Alens." After his death, there were barely enough finished songs for RITCHIE VALENS, the album that Del-Fi released in March 1959. "That's My Little Suzie" and "Little Girl," the two singles after

"Donna," did not fare well. The album's sales stalled after six weeks. Nevertheless, Bob Keane continued to release singles by Valens through 1959. "Stay Beside Me" and "Cry, Cry, Cry" both sold poorly. A second album, RITCHIE, was comprised of completed songs and outtakes of material that Keane finished after Ritchie died. The tape from the December 1958 gymnasium concert was issued as RITCHIE VALENS IN CONCERT AT PACOIMA JR. HIGH. Over the years, there were also numerous compilations of Ritchie's material, including several greatest hits packages and a memorial album.

Ritchie Valens was only seventeen when he died. His long-lasting legacy was based primarily on the two songs "Donna" and "La Bamba." While he was popular with teenagers at the time of his death, his style of hard-rock music was being phased out in favor of teen-idols like Fabian and Frankie Avalon. Yet, his brief time in the spotlight created an image of the early Latino rocker that has persevered and inspired such luminaries as Los Lobos, Freddy Fender, The Midnighters, Trini Lopez, and Sunny and the Sunglows. "La Bamba" even became the model for the Isley Brothers' 1961 hit, "Twist and Shout." Valens also inspired artists as diverse as the Rascals, Bob Dylan and R.E.M. His untrained vocal and guitar style was the basis for the garage band revolution in the early 1960s. A mural depicting scenes from Ritchie's life was dedicated at Pacoima Junior High in 1985. In 1987, he was the subject of a very successful movie biography, "La Bamba." In 1990, he received a star on Hollywood's Walk of Fame.

One of the more interesting tributes to Ritchie Valens began in May 1959. Ritchie Valens "memorial dances" were held all over the Los Angeles area. These dances became a staple on the scene for several years. In 1961, a special New Years Eve memorial dance was held at the Long Beach Civic Auditorium. Entertaining that evening was an unknown "garage band" composed of three brothers, their cousin and a close friend. It was the first engagement for the Beach Boys. Such was the broad impact of Ritchie Valens' life and music.

March 1959

MAR 1   The Platters make another appearance on "The Ed Sullivan Show" on CBS-TV.

MAR 2   Tommy Leonetti opens a week-long stand at the Casino Royal in Washington, DC.

New Releases for the first week in March include "The Beat" by the Rockin' R's on Tempus; Jimmy Clanton's "A Ship on a Stormy Sea" on Ace; two from Jamie: Duane Eddy's "Yep!" and Sanford Clark's "Bad Luck;" Clyde McPhatter's "Lovey Dovey" on Atlantic; three from Brunswick: the Crickets' "Love's Made A Fool of You," Jackie Wilson's "That's Why," and Terry Noland's "Teen-Age Teardrops;" "Enchanted" by the Platters on Mercury; Paul Anka's "I Miss You So" on ABC-Paramount; Chuck Berry's "Almost Grown" on Chess; "Six Nights a Week" by the Crests on Co-Ed; "Tell Him No" by Travis and Bob on Sandy; Fabian's "Turn Me Loose" on Chancellor; "I Think I'm Gonna Kill Myself" by Buddy Knox on Roulette; "Little Boy" by the Tune Weavers on Casa Grande; "Nervous" by Jo Ann Campbell on Gone; "Hi, Hon" by the Blockbusters on Crystalette; and "At My Party" by **Paul Evans** on Atco. Finally, "Does Your Chewing Gum Lose It's Flavor (On the Bedpost Overnight?)" by Lonnie Donegan on Dot is released this week. It will nearly top the British charts in 1959, but will languish until 1961 before becoming a hit in the States.

MAR 3   Chuck Berry sings "Anthony Boy" and "Almost Grown" on "American Bandstand."

MAR 4   After ten months in the Boston court system, the most serious charge against Alan Freed, that of anarchy stemming from the riot following his production in Boston on May 3, 1959, is dropped. He still faces the misdemeanor charge of inciting a riot.

MAR 5   The latest caravan sent out by the Irving Feld Agency, "The Biggest Show of Stars for '59," continues across the country, playing tonight at the Syria Mosque in Pittsburgh. At this time, the acts include the Platters, Clyde McPhatter, Jimmy Clanton, Little Anthony and the Imperials, the Kalin Twins, the Crests, Duane Eddy, Bo Diddley, Johnny Olenn and the Blockbusters, Jesse Lee Turner, the Royal Teens, and the Buddy Johnson Orchestra. The tour will continue through states on the East Coast until March 22.
Frankie Avalon is a television guest of "The Pat Boone Show."

PAUL EVANS
Paul Evans was born March 5, 1938, in St. Albans, Queens, New York. After graduating from Andrew Jackson High, he enrolled in Columbia University to study engineering. He began performing at Basille's, a night club in Far Rockaway, on Long Island. With little musical experience, he decided to forego his formal education. He hung around Broadway's Brill Building, the home of New York's rock 'n roll business. In 1957, he signed with RCA, but when his first two singles failed to sell, he was released. He turned his attention to composing, having a major hit in "When" for the Kalin Twins on Decca Records. This led to Evans' own single on Decca in 1958. "I Think About You All the Time" was a hit in Canada, but it, and his two singles on Atco in 1959, couldn't generate national sales. In 1959, Jack Carlton, of Carlton Records, was looking to replace his biggest star, Jack Scott, who was about to jump to Top Rank Records. In his search, Carlton came across Evans. Their first collaboration, released on Carlton's Guaranteed label, was "Seven Little Girls (Sitting in the Back Seat)." Wrapped in an innocent delivery, "Seven Little Girls" presented a ribald picture of a teen named Fred who was being romantically overwhelmed by seven beauties in the back seat of his car. The song shot into the Top Ten in late 1959. Evans followed with "Midnight Special" and "Happy-Go-Lucky Me" in 1960, both of which were big sellers. By the end of the year, he had been drafted and his days as a recording star were over. He returned to songwriting, having hits for Elvis ("I Gotta Know"), Bobby Vinton ("Roses Are Red"), as well as Jackie Wilson, LaVern Baker, and Pat Boone, among others. He continued to record for some of the biggest labels of the day, Kapp, Epic, Columbia, Laurie, Dot, and Mercury. He has written advertising jingles for products ranging from Skippy peanut butter to Kent cigarettes.

ANNETTE

In 1959, Annette was every teenage boy's ideal girlfriend. At the time, she was sixteen, having been born Annette Funicello, October 22, 1942, in Utica, New York. Her family moved to California, where she was discovered at age twelve by Walt Disney while she was performing in a dance recital in Burbank. In 1955, Disney was preparing to launch "The Mickey Mouse Club," a new TV series aimed at preteens. The show became a legendary success, and she was it's biggest star. When "The Mickey Mouse Club" left the air in 1959, she began recording for Disney's various record labels, beginning with "Tall Paul" on Disneyland, and moving on to Vista Records for "Lonely Guitar," "First Name Initial," "O Dio Mio," and "Pineapple Princess." Each was a hit, and no one seemed to care that Annette couldn't carry a tune. She has commented on the situation, calling it a "running joke," and she credits her music arranger, Tutti Camarata, for double-tracking her voice to hide its weaknesses. After her recording star faded, Disney placed her in a series of "family" movies, beginning with "The Shaggy Dog." In the 1963, she co-starred with Frankie Avalon in "Beach Party," the first in a series of successful movies about teens having fun in the sun. In 1965, she married and became the mother of three children. During the 1970s, she was the spokeswoman for Skippy peanut butter. She married for a second time in 1986. A year later, she and Avalon reunited to make the popular movie "Back to the Beach." That same year, she was diagnosed with multiple sclerosis, a disease she continues to battle. In 1993, she launched her own line of perfume, Cello by Annette. She received her long overdue star on Hollywood's Walk of Fame in September 1993. Her autobiography was published in 1994.

MAR 6   In a rare television appearance, Fats Domino sings "Telling Lies" and "When the Saints Go Marching In" on "American Bandstand."

Bobby Darin and Dion and the Belmonts are making their way through the Midwest on a series of one-night stands through March 21.

In Washington, Tommy Edwards, the Cadillacs, and Baby Washington perform during the week at the Howard Theater.

MAR 7   Johnny Cash returns to the "Louisiana Hayride" in Shreveport for a special homecoming show.

The Coasters, Dale Hawkins, Paul Anka, and Jaye P. Morgan are the guests on "The Dick Clark Show."

EARLY MARCH

Connie Francis is currently in Britain playing concerts in Glasgow and Liverpool.

Clyde McPhatter leaves Atlantic Records after an association going back to 1953 when he formed the Drifters. He signs a contract with M-G-M reported to guarantee him $50,000 a year.

Paul Anka and the Platters have cameo appearances in the picture "Girls Town" (also released as "The Innocent and the Damned") starring Mamie Van Doren which is now in release.

MAR 8   Bobby "Blue" Bland and Little Junior Parker bring the blues to the Blue Eagle Club in New Orleans.

CBS-TV's "The Ed Sullivan Show" presents David Seville and the Chipmunks. The Chipmunks appear via filmed animation.

New Releases for the second week in March include "(Now and Then There's) A Fool Such As I" b/w "I Need Your Love Tonight" by Elvis Presley on RCA; "I Told Myself a Lie" by Clyde McPhatter on M-G-M; **Annette**'s "Jo-Jo The Dog-Faced Boy" on Vista; "That's My Little Susie" by Ritchie Valens on Del-Fi; "You're So Fine" by the Falcons on UnArt; "Please Don't Say No" by Billy Ward and His Dominos on Liberty; Johnny Otis' "Castin' My Spell" on Capitol; Carole King's "Baby Sittin'" on ABC-Paramount; "Tumbled Down" by Billy and Lillie on Swan; Bobby Lord's "Party Pooper" on Columbia; Marvin Rainwater's "Love Me Baby" on M-G-M; "Rock On" by Trini Lopez on King; "Going Out With the Tide" by Jivin' Gene on Mercury; Buddy Guy's "This Is the End" on Artistic; and future star Roger Miller has an early release with "Take It Like A Man" on Decca. Also out this week is the first musical tribute to the late Buddy Holly and Ritchie Valens, Ray Campi's "The Ballad of Donna and Peggy Sue" on D.

MAR 12   Fabian, singing "Turn Me Loose," makes another appearance on "American Bandstand."

MAR 13   Miles Davis headlines the jazz revue this week at New York's Apollo Theater.

Also in the New York area, Bobby Freeman plays the Boulevard Club in Queens.

Clyde McPhatter, the Coasters and Nina Simone entertain this week at Washington's Howard Theater.

MAR 14 The Everly Brothers stop by "The Perry Como Show" on NBC-TV.

In New Orleans, Dave Bartholomew's combo performs at the Club Riviera's Birdland Room for two days.

On "The Dick Clark Show," entertainment is provided by the Fleetwoods, Lou Monte, Art and Dotty Todd, and Sam Cooke.

New Releases for the third week in March include "Poor Jenny" b/w "Take a Message to Mary" by the Everly Brothers on Cadence; Spencer and Spencer's "Russian Bandstand" on Argo; "Lonely For You" by Gary Stites on Carlton; "Senorita, I Love You" by the Impressions on Abner; two from Decca: "Now and Then There's) A Fool Such As I" by Bill Haley and His Comets and "Cool" by the Kalin Twins; Billy Storm's "I've Come of Age" on Columbia; "Magic Mountain" by the Medallions on Dootone; Jody Reynolds' "Beulah Lee" on Demon; "Short Shortnin'" by Paul Peek on NRC; Johnny Rivers' "Your First and Last Love" on Dee Dee; and "Caramba!" by the Champs on Challenge. This week there is another tribute to the victims of the Iowa airplane crash earlier this month, "Three Stars" by Tommy Dee on Crest.

MAR 18 Brenda Lee begins a month-long run at the Olympia Theater in Paris.

"Rio Bravo," featuring Ricky Nelson, along with John Wayne and Dean Martin, opens today across the nation.

MAR 20 A local Philadelphian, Bobby Rydell, is interviewed on "American Bandstand."

Paul Anka begins a tour of Latin America. This is the fifth continent he has visited since breaking into show business only two years ago.

MAR 21 The Everly Brothers are booked for a return engagement on NBC-TV's "The Perry Como Show."

Annette, Jackie Wilson, Frankie Ford, **Link Wray**, and Tommy Leonetti guest on "The Dick Clark Show."

MAR 23 Frankie Ford rocks the "American Bandstand" crowd with "Sea Cruise."

New Releases for the fourth week of March include: "Kansas City" by Wilbert Harrison on Fury; two from Atlantic: Ray Charles' "That's Enough" and LaVern Baker's "I Waited Too Long;" "Dream Lover" by Bobby Darin on Atco; "A Teenager In Love" by Dion and the Belmonts on Laurie; two from Johnny Cash: "Frankie's Man Johnny" on Columbia and "Luther Played the Boogie" on Sun; two from Imperial: "You

LINK WRAY

Link Wray is credited with having more influence than his track record would indicate. Pete Townshend of the Who referred to him as "the king." Wray's been called the godfather of the guitar power chord and the father heavy metal rock. In fact, he may be all of this and more. Wray was born in rural Dunn, North Carolina, May 22, 1935. Both of Wray's parents were preachers in the Holiness Church. Link joined the Army straight out of high school and entertained on the Armed Forces Network in Germany. Returning home, he joined his brothers, Vernon and Doug, to form a combo. In 1956, as "Lucky" Wray and the Palomino Ranch Hands, they recorded the first of three country/rockabilly singles for Starday. Vernon (as Ray Vernon) led the band on four singles for Cameo in 1957-8. In 1959, an instrumental built around the stroll was picked up by Cadence Records, which was having huge success with the Everlys. "Rumble," with its crashing guitar chords set off a chain reaction as socially conscious groups petitioned to have the tune banned because of its perceived association with juvenile delinquency. Wray, who was not signed with Cadence, was quickly picked up by Epic Records, which channeled his energy into a series of less raucous instrumentals, including "Raw-Hide," "Comanche," and "Slinky." Doug Wray also recorded a single, "Goosebumps," for Epic in 1959. After a brief stop on Okeh, the Wrays recorded on several labels of their own, including Rumble, Atlas and Trans-Atlas labels. In 1963, Link showed up on Swan Records with his guitar back down in the gutter for "Jack the Ripper." He stayed with Swan until 1967. Thereafter, he recorded for a multitude of labels. It was apparent that he was unwilling to compromise his music to appeal to the masses. It was his attitude as much as his guitar skills that appealed to the punk rock crowd when they rediscovered Wray in the 1970s.

THE BELL NOTES

Groups that only had a hit or two and then disappeared are common in rock 'n roll. As teenagers from East Meadows on Long Island, New York, Carl Bonura (sax and vocals), Ray Ceroni (guitar and vocals), Larry Giambalvo (bass), Pete Kane (piano), and John Casey (drums) put together a hot combo to play high school sock hops. The guys were all tops in the looks department, and with their musical talent thrown in, they were the pride of East Meadows. The group was popular enough to be invited to appear on stage as part of Alan Freed's week-long Easter show at the New York Paramount in late March 1958 even though they had no recording contract. Several months later, a local deejay thought they could use a little professional boost, so he financed a recording session at a New York studio. The end result was "I've Had It." The recording was simple, direct, catchy—the type of record you could play over and over and not tire of it. The deejay, Alan Fredricks of New York's WADO, took the master tape to Time Records, a new entry in the rock 'n roll field. After one listen, the owner bought "I've Had It" as is. It was released the end of 1958, and by February it was being heard from coast to coast. Eventually, it peaked in the Top Ten. While the group never had another big hit, their remaining singles were well-received. "Old Spanish Town," released on Time in March 1959 and "Shortin' Bread," issued by Madison in 1960, both made the national charts. Along the way, Casey quit and his position on drums was taken by Russ Nagy, who, in 1972, was playing with a new group of Aquatones. In between their brief stays with Time and Madison, the Bell Notes issued one single on Autograph in 1960, "Little Girl In Blue." The group toured with Frankie Avalon and Duane Eddy in the summer of 1959 and appeared once on Dick Clark's Saturday night show.

Said Goodbye" by the Teddy Bears and "Record Hop Blues" by the Quarter Notes; "Kookie, Kookie, Lend Me Your Comb" by Edd Byrnes and Connie Stevens on Warner Brothers; two from Warwick: "Crossfire" by Johnny and the Hurricanes and "Laughing on the Outside" by the Harptones; "Just Keep It Up" by Dee Clark on Abner; "Endlessly" by Brook Benton on Mercury; "Old Spanish Town" by the **Bell Notes** on Time; Jimmy Heap's "Born To Love You" on D; "Five Long Years" by Little Junior Parker on Duke; Thurston Harris' "Bless Your Heart" on Aladdin; and "Charlie Brown Got Expelled" by Joe Tex on Ace.

MAR 25 Frankie Avalon, the Platters and Tommy Sands open their tour of Australia with a show in Sydney that grosses $24,000. The performers will return to the States on April 8.

"Lovers Never Say Goodbye" is the offering from the Flamingos on "American Bandstand."

MAR 26 Jerry Lee Lewis, in a never-say-die move, is off on a series of one-nighters.

MAR 27 Already a star as a Mouseketeer on "The Mickey Mouse Club," which is ABC-TV's afternoon lead-in to "American Bandstand," Annette guests on "Bandstand" singing "Tall Paul."

Alan Freed's annual ten-day Easter week pageant opens at the Brooklyn Fox Theater. Scheduled to appear are Fats Domino, Jackie Wilson, Bobby Day, Jimmy Clanton, Duane Eddy, Tommy Leonetti, Dale Hawkins, Larry Williams, Jo Ann Campbell, Sandy Stewart, the Impalas, Fabian, Thomas Wayne, the Mello-Kings, the Cadillacs, Bobby Freeman, the Skyliners, and King Curtis. The revue brings in $167,000.

Another version of "The Biggest Show of Stars for '59" sets sail. This package headlines Lloyd Price and features Clyde McPhatter, the Chantels, the Coasters, the Crests, Bo Diddley, LaVern Baker, Frankie Lymon, Wade Flemons, Bonny Hendricks, and Little Anthony and the Imperials. Tonight's show is in New York City. Other dates through the end of the month include Richmond (29); Charlotte (30; and Norfolk (31). (See also APR 1.)

Gloria Lynne opens her week-long engagement at the Flame Lounge in Detroit.

In Washington, Louis Jordan and Johnny "Guitar" Watson headline the weekly revue at the Howard Theater.

MAR 28 Headlining the "The Dick Clark Show" tonight is Lloyd Price. Other guests are Tab Hunter, Jimmy Clanton, James Darren, and the Chordettes.

The Kalin Twins, Bill Parsons, the Bell Notes, Jesse Lee Turner, and Link Wray begin a five-week tour of the Midwest. (See also APR 8.)

MAR 31 In New Orleans, Joe Tex plays a one night stand at the Dew Drop Cafe's "Gay Ball."

"The Jimmie Rodgers Show" debuts on NBC-TV at 8:30 p.m. This variety program features Connie Francis every week through June 9.

LATE MARCH

Ersel Hickey plays a special engagement in Charleston, West Virginia, entertaining 4,000 Boy Scouts and another 30,000 spectators at the annual Jamboree.

The instant success of Wilbert Harrison's "Kansas City" prompts a flood of versions by the end of the month. Little Willie Littlefield is rushed into the studio to cover his original Federal version of "K. C. Lovin'" from 1952. Others jumping on the bandwagon include Hank Ballard and the Midnighters on King, Rocky Olson on Chess, Rockin' Ronald and the Rebels on End, and Little Richard's "Kansas City/Hey-Hey-Hey-Hey" on Specialty, which he recorded in 1955.

THE TOP ROCK 'N ROLL RECORDS FOR MARCH 1959

1. Charlie Brown - The Coasters
2. Stagger Lee - Lloyd Price
3. Donna/La Bamba - Ritchie Valens
4. Venus - Frankie Avalon
5. I've Cried a Tear - LaVern Baker
6. I've Had It - The Bell Notes
7. 16 Candles - The Crests
8. It's Just a Matter of Time/Hurtin' Inside - Brook Benton
9. Tall Paul - Annette
10. The All American Boy - Bill Parsons
11. Tragedy - Thomas Wayne
12. Lonely Teardrops - Jackie Wilson
13. She Say (Oom Dooby Doom) - The Diamonds
14. Goodbye Baby - Jack Scott
15. My Happiness - Connie Francis
16. Smoke Gets In Your Eyes - The Platters
17. Never Be Anyone Else But You/It's Late - Ricky Nelson
18. (All of a Sudden) My Heart Sings - Paul Anka
19. Gotta Travel On - Billy Grammer
20. The Story of My Love - Conway Twitty
21. The Lonely One - Duane Eddy
22. Pink Shoelaces - Dodie Stevens
23. Sea Cruise - Frankie Ford
24. Rawhide - Link Wray and His Ray Men
25. It Doesn't Matter Anymore - Buddy Holly
26. Pretty Girls Everywhere - Eugene Church
27. First Anniversary - Cathy Carr
28. Don't Take Your Guns To Town - Johnny Cash
29. A Lover's Question - Clyde McPhatter
30. Little Space Girl - Jesse Lee Turner

31. Plain Jane - Bobby Darin
32. Mathilda - Cookie and the Cupcakes
33. Come Softly To Me - The Fleetwoods
34. When the Saints Go Marching In/Telling Lies - Fats Domino
35. Since I Don't Have You - The Skyliners
36. The Hanging Tree - Marty Robbins
37. Nobody But You - Dee Clark
38. Where Were You (On Our Wedding Day)? - Lloyd Price
39. If I Didn't Care - Connie Francis
40. Lovers Never Say Goodbye - The Flamingos
41. The Shag - Billy Graves
42. I'm Never Gonna Tell On You/Because They're Young - Jimmie Rodgers
43. Guitar Boogie Shuffle - The Virtues
44. Everybody Likes To Cha Cha Cha - Sam Cooke
45. This Should Go On Forever - Rod Bernard
46. I Go Ape - Neil Sedaka
47. Moonlight Serenade - The Rivieras
48. The Happy Organ - Dave "Baby" Cortez
49. Ballad of a Boy and a Girl - The Graduates
50. Teardrops on Your Letter - Hank Ballard and the Midnighters

Also on the "pop" charts:
Petite Fleur - The Chris Barber Jazz Band
Alvin's Harmonica - David Seville and the Chipmunks
Please Mr. Sun/The Morning Side of the Mountain - Tommy Edwards

---

March 1959
ARTIST OF THE MONTH

LLOYD PRICE
(Continued from Volume One of
THE GOLDEN AGE OF AMERICAN ROCK 'N ROLL.)

Lloyd Price

In 1952, "Lawdy, Miss Clawdy" by Lloyd Price became one of the biggest-selling singles of the early rock 'n roll era. Then the Army drafted Price in 1954 and sent him overseas. Back in the States in 1956, he found himself without a recording contract. On the strength of his name, he could still bring in large crowds to his concerts and dances across the country. However, without new records in the marketplace, even this would soon begin to fade.

The first move for Price was to transfer his base of operations from New Orleans to Washington, DC. In the Army, Price had fronted a large dance band that played swing music for the troops. This experience had given him the idea of combining the full sound of an orchestra with the rhythmic tempos of rhythm and blues to produce a new branch of the rock 'n roll. Price approached numerous record executives with his plan only to be turned away from every office. In 1956, the recording industry believed that rock 'n roll had to be performed by small combos because this was the sound that appealed to teenagers. There was no place in rock 'n roll for formal, intricate musical arrangements.

Thoroughly disgusted, Price turned to the only solution open to him. He founded his own record label. The Kent Recording Company, also known as K.R.C., began business in late 1956 with Price being the only artist "signed" to the label. On "Just Because," his first K.R.C. release, Price also played piano, wrote the song and produced the session.

"Just Because" was released in January 1957. The song opened with Price's distinctive shouting voice delivering the first line. The instrumental backing differed little from that used by Fats Domino: massed saxophones over a tight rhythm section. On the other hand, the flip side, "Why," offered a look at the Price's future. Taking a rolling shuffle and reducing the basic instrumental track to a pounding piano and rhythm, Price created a jump record with tension. All that was missing was a storyline. Lyrics such as "Please hear my plea, come on home to me, I'm so tired of being free" did little to hold the listener's interest.

Within days of its release, "Just Because" began to attract attention. On the East Coast, "Just Because" was doing very well in the areas around Washington, Baltimore and Philadelphia. These were locales where Price had continued to pack in the fans for his shows and getting his records into the shops in those cities was not a problem. K.R.C. soon ran into the same distribution problems that would befall so many other small record labels as the popularity of rock 'n roll increased. To break the record in a broader market Price needed help. In early February, he and ABC-Paramount Records reached an agreement allowing ABC-Paramount to re-release the K.R.C. master of "Just Because" b/w "Why." The deal was for one single and did not include Price's services as a recording artist.

With the help of ABC-Paramount, "Just Because" remained an active seller for more than four months, while Price took to the road to promote the latest release. He was very popular in the South, and his first bookings following the deal with ABC-Paramount brought him to Florida. Then he played the Apollo Theater in New York for a week in March. In April, he was touring the Midwest, and the next month he was crisscrossing the South again.

In the middle of June 1957, Price signed a distribution deal with Atlantic Records. The contract called for Price to issue records on his K.R.C. label while Atlantic would be the sole distributor.

Between his brief, two-week tours, Price returned to the studio to record material for new K.R.C. singles. In early July 1957, "Lonely Chair," backed by "The Chicken and the Bop" was K.R.C.'s second release. For more than two months, the single languished. Then in late September "Lonely Chair" caught a little airplay for one week before disappearing. During the year and a half that K.R.C. was distributed by Atlantic, K.R.C. also issued singles by the King Bees and Stella Johnson as well as three more singles by Price.

Atlantic allowed its deal with K.R.C. to expire from lack of interest in 1958. Price continued to release singles on K.R.C. As before, there were a few by himself as well by lesser-known talent, a total of five more in all. By this time, he was frustrated with the business of running a record company. He was ready to devote his full attention to being a performer.

He returned to ABC-Paramount in the fall of 1958, seeking a contract as a recording artist. ABC-Paramount agreed, and in late October, "Stagger Lee" became the first release under his new contract. After his recent string of unsuccessful singles, it took a while before "Stagger Lee" caught the public's fancy. When it finally did, in December 1958, the single shot to the top of the "pop" and R&B charts. It easily sold a million copies and went on to become the top R&B disk of 1959.

"Stagger Lee" used many of the ingredients Price had incorporated into "Just Because" and "Why." From a production standpoint, the primary change was the addition of a vocal group to back Price's shouting style. There was also a fullness—a "big band" sound. "Stagger Lee" was close to the idea of the swing band he had envisioned when he returned from the Army. Another change came with the song's lyrics. Finally, there was an interesting story. The song opened with two gamblers throwing dice in the park, and concluded with the losing gambler shooting the winner in a barroom. "Stagger Lee" first saw life as a folk song titled "The Ballad of Stak-O-Lee." A version of "Stack-O-Lee" had been an R&B hit in 1950 by Archibald (Leon Gross) on Imperial. Price and Harold Logan, his co-writer, cleaned up the lyrics, but there was still enough mayhem to ignite a campaign by the Legion of Decency. Accordingly, when "Stagger Lee" appeared on an album, it had been rerecorded and the lyrics had been significantly altered. Now, the two men were "arguing in the dark" instead of "gambling in the park." As might be expected, the homicide and the barroom were also tossed out of this version. This "clean" version remained the only version available for nearly twenty years.

As a follow-up to "Stagger Lee," "Where Were You (On Our Wedding Day)?" did a respectable business in the spring of 1959. It was followed by two more million-selling singles, "Personality" and "I'm Gonna Get Married." All three singles followed the format of "Stagger Lee" with one major exception. After the problems with the lyrical content of "Stagger Lee," each song was now aimed directly at the teen market.

Price remained with ABC-Paramount for several years, having hits with "Come Into My Heart," "Lady Luck," "No If's—No And's," and "Question." The songs varied little from the "Stagger Lee" formula: a bouncy, medium tempo made for dancing; a large R&B band; a vocal group; and Price's vocal sung at the top of his lungs. Eventually, the big band got bigger with the addition of brass and strings, but each recording was clearly recognizable as coming from Lloyd Price.

After 1960, his remaining releases for ABC-Paramount failed to attract much attention. Not that all of them were awful. "I Ain't Givin' Up Nothin'" was a fine attempt to attract the crowd that liked Dee Clark and Jackie Wilson, especially in the band's arrangement. "Under Your Spell Again" showed what a powerful R&B singer could do with a little country tune when he decided not to do it in a country style.

By 1962, Price was ready for another change. As he had done before, he started his own record label, Double-L. Working with Harold

Logan, who had remained his co-songwriter all this time, Price and his arranger, Sammy Lowe, experimented with traditional jazz arrangements in a big band setting. This tact was also used at this time by jazz organist Jimmy Smith and his arranger Oliver Nelson. An early Double-L single by Price was "Pistol Packin' Mama." The single featured a musical arrangement with a strong jazz flavor and a swinging undertone. Price's biggest hit on Double-L was a 1963 revival of the old standard, "Misty." Here, the band really had a chance to shine as it aped the musical style of the 1940s. The follow-up single, "Billie Boy" was a powerful, jazzed-up version of "Won't You Come Home, Bill Bailey." It was also the last of Price's singles to attract the public's attention. His final Double-L single was "Every Night," featuring a "boogaloo" rhythm. In keeping with the policy he began with K.R.C., Price also used Double-L to introduce new talent. It was on Double-L, in a series of heart breaking soul singles, that the nation got it's first glimpse of Wilson Pickett as a solo artist.

In 1964, Price became the first black artist to sign with Monument Records, of Hendersonville, Tennessee. Monument's claim to fame up to this time was Roy Orbison. Price's two singles on Monument, "I Love You" and "Amen," showed that the company had no idea how to produce his sessions. Both were an odd mixture of Floyd Cramer's honky-tonk piano and a gospel choir—with the big band, of course.

Price next joined Reprise Records, a company founded by Frank Sinatra. In 1968, Reprise was having a series of hits by Frank's daughter, Nancy. Price was reunited with Sammy Lowe for "I Won't Cry Anymore." The song featured Price against a smaller combo than usual, but still complete with the Double-L jazz overtones.

In 1968, Johnny Nash was having a second career with a Jamaican rhythm called reggae. He convinced Price to come over to JAD Records. However, Price's first JAD single, "Take All," was still in the big band R&B mode. With the help of JAD Records, Price started another record company, Turntable, as a division of JAD. On Turntable, he still wasn't singing true reggae, but the sessions were recorded in Jamaica. As his first Turntable singles, "I Understand" featured a rolling bass line and "The Truth" appeared on the album LLOYD PRICE IN REGGAE. In conjunction with the record company, Price also opened the Turntable nightclub in New York. In 1969, Price's longtime associate, Harold Logan, was murdered in the Turntable Club's offices.

Price moved on to Scepter Records in 1971 as that label was closing the books on their long association with Dionne Warwick. B. J. Thomas also had several big sellers on the label beginning in 1966. Price was asked to record "Hooked On a Feeling," Thomas' hit of 1968. The song was out of Price's vocal range and the backing instrumentation was too lush for Price's raw voice. Even using the recording studio at Muscle Shoals couldn't save it. The follow-up, "Natural Sinner," fared no better.

In 1972, Price recorded the theme song for the movie "The Legend of Nigger Charley," with the soundtrack being issued by Paramount Records. This was followed by two singles for GSF Records, "Sing A Song" and "Love Music." Both were derivative of the work being done at the time by Isaac Hayes. Finally, Price recorded "Feelin Good" for Ludix Productions. "Feelin' Good" was an inspirational number from the Broadway show "Roar of the Grease Paint." Price's version sounded as though a symphony orchestra was on the cut.

In the mid-1970s, Price preferred to make personal appearances and not chase the elusive riches of recording. His name still brought in crowds along the East Coast and through the South. By the 1980s, he was semiretired. In May 1991, he was coaxed to Hollywood to make a cameo appearance on the final episode of the hit television show, "Amen."

Price left his imprint on black students of music through a college fund he established in 1964. In 1974, he helped promote a music festival in Zaire, South Africa. The object of "Zaire '74" was to bring attention to the oppression and poverty of the region.

Lloyd Price has lived the dream he envisioned for himself at a very young age. He was a top-selling R&B performer in 1952 and again in 1958. He helped introduce jazz nuances to the R&B field with his K.R.C. and Double-L labels. He recorded for some of the largest independent companies in the business: ABC-Paramount, Monument, Reprise, and Scepter. In his wake, he left a large body of very fine material on which he imparted his indelible imprint.

April 1959

APR 1   Lloyd Price's version of "Biggest Show of Stars for '59" continues to pile up enormous revenues as it plays Winston-Salem tonight. Continuing through Appalachia, the tour plays Greenville (2); Raleigh (3); Augusta (4) and Birmingham (5).

Johnny Cash is booked for a one-night stand in Grand Rapids.

APR 3   Neil Sedaka sings both of his latest releases, "I Go Ape" and "The Diary," on "American Bandstand."

Bill Haley and His Comets and Marty Robbins take to the road with a show in Milwaukee. The next night they entertain in Green Bay. (See also APR 8.)

APR 4   Fabian drops by NBC-TV's "The Perry Como Show."

Edd "Kookie" Byrnes guests on "The Dick Clark Show" tonight. Also appearing are Jane Morgan, Dave "Baby" Cortez, and Travis and Bob.

APR 5   Aaron Neville entertains the crowd at New Orleans' Lincoln Beach Midway on Lake Pontchartrain.

The Fleetwoods and the Billy Williams Quartet visit "The Ed Sullivan Show" on CBS-TV.

APR 6   Cozy Cole takes over Pep's Lounge in Philadelphia through April 11.

In Detroit, Big Maybelle is featured at the Greystone Ballroom.

New Releases for the first week in April include Carl Mann's "Mona Lisa" on Phillips International; three from M-G-M: "Hey Little Lucy!" by Conway Twitty, Sheb Wooley's "Sweet Chile" and Mark Dinning's "A Life Of Love;" Jimmy Reed's "Take Out Some Insurance" on Vee-Jay; "I Know It's Hard But It's Fair" by the "5" Royales on King; "Blue Velvet" by the Velours on Cub; two from Columbia: Johnny Horton's "Battle of New Orleans" and **Billy Craddock**'s "Sweetie Pie;" "Gidget" by James Darren on Colpix; Bobby Vinton's "Always On My Mind" on Melody; Johnny Burnette's "Gumbo" on Freedom; "Velvet Waters" by the Megatrons on Accusticon; Jesse Belvin's "Little Darling" on Knight; Ersel Hickey's "Don't Be Afraid of Love" on Epic; "Baby Please Don't Go" by Jesse Lee Turner on Carlton; Herbie Alpert's "Sweet Georgia Brown" on Carol.

BILLY CRADDOCK

As a 135-pound halfback, Billy Craddock was nicknamed "Crash" by his high school teammates. He was born June 16, 1939, in Greensboro, North Carolina, into a family living far below the poverty level. Billy had nine brothers and sisters, three of whom died in infancy. For his own amusement, he sang country songs in the barn. When Billy turned eleven, Clarence, an older brother, gave him his first guitar. Ronald, another brother, and Billy formed a high school combo called the Four Rebels, which was a favorite at local talent shows. In 1957, they recorded "Smacky Mouth" for Sky Castle Records. The next year, Colonial Records released "Bird Doggin'," which brought Craddock to the attention of Columbia Records. He was placed on their Date subsidiary for "Lulu Lee," then switched to the parent company for "Am I To Be The One." With Elvis in Germany with the Army, record companies were searching through their talent rosters for someone to vie for the title of "king of rock 'n roll." Columbia picked Craddock as their entry, and began a massive, and very costly, advertising campaign in late 1959. The release of "Don't Destroy Me" was anticlimactic. No one could have lived up to that much advance publicity. Craddock had a total of seven singles on Columbia, none of which made an impression on young, American female teens. Interestingly, he had been a hit in Australia, where three of his singles reached the Top Ten. In 1960, he retired to Greensboro, where he continued to perform locally through the 1960s and had singles issued on the King, Chart and Mercury labels. In 1971, Craddock had a Number One country hit with his first Cartwheel release, "Knock Three Times." Other Cartwheel hits included "Ain't Nothin' Shakin'" and "Dream Lover." After ABC/Dot bought Cartwheel, and Craddock continued his string of country-rock hits with "Til the Water Stops Running" and "Rub It In."

JOHNNY CARROLL
John Lewis Carrell was born October 23, 1937, in Godley, Texas. His family were all proficient musicians, so it is no wonder that Johnny grew up loving music. At age eight, he earned enough to buy his own guitar. Two years later, he appeared on a local radio station. In high school, he and his combo won many local talent contests which brought them to the attention of J. G. Tiger, a Dallas studio owner, who took Johnny under his wing. Carroll's first singles were released on the WA label, which led to a contract with Decca. In 1956, at a Nashville session, he recorded "Rock N Roll Ruby," a single that did well in Texas. Carroll toured with Bill Haley and Clyde McPhatter. In 1957, he starred in a locally produced movie, "Rock, Baby, Rock It," in which he sang several of his better songs, including "Wild, Wild Women" and "Crazy, Crazy Lovin'." At this time, he and Tiger parted company after he accused his manager of keeping most of the money from his royalties and personal appearances. He switched to Phillips Intonation Records of Memphis for one single, "That's the Way I Love" in 1957. After a yearlong lull, in which he toured with Scotty Moore and Bill Black of Elvis' backup band, he was on Warner Brothers for "Bandstand Doll" and "Sugar" in 1959. Carroll was friends with Gene Vincent, and the members of their bands often played sessions and toured together. Through the 1960s, he remained in the Dallas-Fort Worth area, occasionally recording for one of Major Bill Smith's various labels. He stopped performing and became a club manager. When he was shot in the stomach, it was reported that he had died. Far from it. In the 1970s, he teamed with Rockin' Ronnie Weiser of Rollin' Rock Records for several hot rockabilly albums featuring both new and unreleased older material. In the 1980s, he toured England to wildly enthusiastic crowds.

APR 8   Frankie Avalon, Duane Eddy, Bill Parsons, the Bell Notes, and Jesse Lee Turner play an engagement in Milwaukee.

A Bill Haley/Marty Robbins tour stops in Norman, Oklahoma, tonight. Other tour dates include Houston (10-11); Sioux City (14); Omaha (15); Lincoln (16); Salina, Kansas (17); Wichita (18); Kansas City (19); Topeka (20); Clearwater, Minnesota (21); St. Paul (22); and Austin, Minnesota (23).

APR 10 Fats Domino performs at the Hotel Bradford in Boston. Also in town, Tommy Leonetti opens a two-day stand at the Sherry Biltmore Varsity Club.

In New Orleans, Sonny Boy Williamson entertains at the Club Riviera's Birdland Room. At Lincoln Beach, Joe Jones performs for the next three days.

APR 11 Frankie Avalon undertakes his own weekly ABC-radio show. Avalon's guest on his first show is Paul Anka.

Connie Francis opens an engagement at the Commodore Ballroom in Lowell, Massachusetts.

Entertainment on tonight's "Dick Clark Show" is provided by Marv Johnson, Rod Bernard, the Impalas, and Gail Davis, star of the "Annie Oakley" TV show.

APR 12 B. B. King swings through New Orleans with a one-night stand at the Blue Eagle Club.

Brook Benton drops by "The Ed Sullivan Show" on CBS-TV.

New Releases for the second week in April include "Personality" by Lloyd Price on ABC-Paramount; "Pointed Toe Shoes" by Carl Perkins on Columbia; "I Want To Go Home" by Charles Brown and Amos Milburn on Ace; "I Won't Cry" by Johnny Adams on Ric; **Johnny Carroll**'s "Bandstand Doll" on Warner Brothers; Mickey and Kitty's "Ooh-Sha-Lala" on Atlantic; "I Want You So Bad" by James Brown and the Famous Flames on Federal; Bobby "Blue" Bland's "I'm Not Ashamed" on Duke; Joe Hinton's "Pretty Little Mama" on Back Beat; Frankie Lymon's "What A Little Moonlight Can Do" on Roulette; Petula Clark's "Baby Lover" on Imperial; and Dolly Parton's "Puppy Love" on Goldband. "This Broken Heart" by the Sonics on Checker, released this week, is by an R&B group, not the garage band from Tacoma.

APR 14 Brook Benton appears on "The Ed Sullivan Show" on CBS-TV.

APR 15 Johnny Cash brings his own particular brand of country-rock to Australia for a brief tour, playing dates in Melbourne and Sydney.

MID-APRIL
Fats Domino is currently performing throughout Maine with shows at Lakeside, Worcester, and Portland.

APR 16   In New Orleans, Eddie Bo opens at the Lincoln Beach Midway for a three-day run. Also in town, at the Club Riviera, Smiley Lewis also starts a three-day gig.

APR 17   Dave "Baby" Cortez, the Fiestas, the Clovers, Ray Peterson, and Huet Smith and the Clowns entertain for the week at the Howard Theater in Washington.

APR 18   Bobby Darin drops by "The Perry Como Show" on NBC-TV.
Gary Stites makes his national television debut on ABC-TV's "The Dick Clark Show." Also appearing tonight are Fabian, Neil Sedaka and Roy Hamilton.

APR 19   The Blue Eagle in New Orleans offers the talents of Nappy Brown for patrons tonight.

APR 20   Jerry Lee Lewis opens a six-day tour of Australia. Co-starring with the wild man of rock 'n roll is Sammy Davis, Jr.
Bobby Darin opens for a week at Blinstraub's Club in Boston.

New Releases for the third week in April include "Lipstick On Your Collar" b/w "Frankie" by Connie Francis on M-G-M; Fats Domino's "I'm Ready" b/w "Margie" on Imperial; Thomas Wayne's "Eternally" on Fernwood; "Bongo Rock" by Preston Epps on Original Sound; Brenda Lee's "Let's Jump the Broomstick" on Decca; Ray Peterson's "The Wonder of You" on RCA; two from Mercury: "What a Diff'rence a Day Makes" by Dinah Washington and "It's The Truth, Ruth" by the Big Bopper; "Steal a Little Kiss" by Larry Williams on Specialty; Chubby Checker's "The Class" on Parkway; Bruce Channel's "Don't Leave Me" on Teenager; "Mad Gass" by the Royal Teens on Power; and two from King: "Teardrops Are Falling" by the Checkers and "Here Comes Sally" by Trini Lopez.

APR 21   Jesse Belvin vocalizes on "Guess Who" on "American Bandstand."

APR 24   The Teddy Bears make a return appearance on "American Bandstand" singing "Oh Why" and "I Don't Need You Anymore."

APR 22   The first American rock 'n roll package invades England. Featuring Conway Twitty, Dale Hawkins and the Poni-Tails, the tour is supported by England's own Cliff Richard. The brief tour will concentrate on major cities in England.
Dick Clark brings a revue to the Miami Beach Exhibition Hall. Featured performers are Connie Francis, the Diamonds, the Fleetwoods, Duane Eddy, Neil Sedaka, Steve Alaimo, Marv Johnson, Travis and Bob, and Jesse Belvin.
Fats Domino brings his rock 'n roll show to the Greystone Ballroom in Detroit.

RONNIE HAWKINS
Ronnie Hawkins was the original Arkansas rocker, and he became Canada's ambassador of rock. He was born January 10, 1935, in Huntsville, a hill town near Fayetteville. After living in St. Paul for a time, the family moved back to Fayetteville proper. Following a day's hard work, they found solace in their music. Ronnie looked up to his uncle Delmar, a semiprofessional musician who became Ronnie's mentor. Ronnie began performing in the 1940s, even sharing the stage once with Hank Williams. In 1952, as a high school student, he formed a band he called the Hawks and began opening for Roy Orbison and Conway Twitty when they came through the area. In 1957, he was drafted into the Army. When he was released, he went back to playing rock 'n roll in roadhouses in Arkansas and Texas with a band that featured drummer LeVon Helm. Ronnie's friendship with Twitty led to a long tour of Canada, where Twitty had been an early sensation. Ronnie followed suit, even recording his first single, "Hey Bo Diddley," on the Canadian Quality label. In early 1959, Roulette Records rushed him into a New York studio and released "Kansas City" as by Rockin' Ron and the Rebels on End Records. This was followed by "Forty Days" and "Mary Lou" under his own name on Roulette. Hawkins' musical style, developed through years in roadhouses in Arkansas and Canada was totally untamed. The singles sold well, but rock 'n roll was changing. Hawkins proved to be one of the last of the old-style rockers. He stayed on Roulette until 1963, then moved permanently to Canada. By this time, the members of his band included Robbie Robertson, Rick Danko and Richard Manuel, who, along with Helm, would back Bob Dylan's move to electric rock and later become The Band. Hawkins is still in Canada, living life and playing rock 'n roll like every night was 1959.

APR 24   Currently on tour, Wanda Jackson plays the next three nights in Milwaukee. Other dates to follow include Louisville on April 29.
        Bill Haley and His Comets take over the Million Dollar Ballroom in Milwaukee for two nights.
        Louis Jordan plays a one-night stand at the Flame Lounge in Detroit.
        In New Orleans, Joe Jones returns to the Lincoln Beach Midway for a three-day weekend.
        Frank Virtue and the Virtues set off on a mini-tour. Tonight, the group plays the Charlotte (NC) Coliseum. Tomorrow, they're at the Greenville (SC) Auditorium. They are booked at the Casino Royal in Washington, DC on April 27.
        Eugene Church, the Pearls, the Genies, and Marv Johnson are offered by the Howard Theater for Washington patrons this week.

APR 25   In Dallas, Ersel Hickey guests on "The Big D Jamboree."
        On television, Johnny Nash, Kathy Linden, Billy Grammer, and the Fleetwoods are in the spotlight on "The Dick Clark Show."

APR 26   Johnny Cash and the Everly Brothers are featured on "The Chevy Show" on NBC-TV.

APR 27   The Greystone Ballroom in Detroit welcomes LaVern Baker.

New Releases for the fourth week in April include "Forty Days" by **Ronnie Hawkins** and the Hawks on Roulette; Annette's "Lonely Guitar" on Vista; "Ain't That Lovin' You Baby" by Dale Hawkins on Checker; "Along Came Jones" by the Coasters on Atco; "Graduation's Here" by the Fleetwoods on Dolton; "Tallahassee Lassie" by Freddy Cannon on Swan; "I Only Have Eyes For You" by the Flamingos on End; Ruth Brown's "Jack O' Diamonds" on Atlantic; Bobby Freeman's "Mary Ann Thomas" on Josie; "Yes-Sir-ee" by Dodie Stevens on Crystalette; two from Mercury: a reissue of "You're The One That Done It" by Thomas Wayne and "Your Love" by the Danleers; and Curtis Johnson's "Baby, Baby" on Event. Also on Atlantic is "There Goes My Baby," the first release from the revamped Drifters.

APR 28   The instrumental group, the Rockin' R's, perform "The Beat" on "American Bandstand." Also on this afternoon's show, Chubby Checker sings his novelty song, "The Class."
        In Houma, Louisiana, Mrs. J. P. Richardson gives birth to the couple's only child, a son whom she names J. P. Richardson, Jr.

APR 29   The Everly Brothers, Marty Robbins and Wanda Jackson, along with numerous country and western stars, perform at the Kentucky Derby Festival in Louisville.

APR 30   Dee Clark sings "Just Keep It Up" on "American Bandstand."

LATE APRIL
   During their lengthy engagement, Billy Ward and His Dominoes break their own house-record at the Golden Horseshoe Hotel and Casino in Las Vegas.

THE TOP ROCK 'N ROLL RECORDS FOR APRIL 1959

1. Venus - Frankie Avalon
2. Come Softly To Me - The Fleetwoods
3. Pink Shoelaces - Dodie Stevens
4. It's Just A Matter of Time - Brook Benton
5. Never Be Anyone Else But You/It's Late - Ricky Nelson
6. Tragedy - Thomas Wayne
7. Charlie Brown - The Coasters
8. Guitar Boogie Shuffle - The Virtues
9. A Fool Such As I/I Need Your Love Tonight - Elvis Presley
10. Since I Don't Have You - The Skyliners
11. Sea Cruise - Frankie Ford
12. I've Had It - The Bell Notes
13. It Doesn't Matter Anymore - Buddy Holly
14. The Happy Organ - Dave "Baby" Cortez
15. This Should Go On Forever - Rod Bernard
16. Tell Him No - Travis and Bob
17. Where Were You (On Our Wedding Day)? - Lloyd Price
18. If I Didn't Care - Connie Francis
19. Donna - Ritchie Valens
20. Everybody Likes to Cha Cha Cha - Sam Cooke
21. Stagger Lee - Lloyd Price
22. Sorry, I Ran All The Way Home - The Impalas
23. I Cried A Tear - LaVern Baker
24. Turn Me Loose - Fabian
25. I'm Never Gonna Tell On You - Jimmie Rodgers
26. Enchanted - The Platters
27. Three Stars - Tommy Dee
28. I Go Ape - Neil Sedaka
29. The Hanging Tree - Marty Robbins
30. Take a Message To Mary/Poor Jenny - The Everly Brothers
31. Rawhide - Link Wray and His Ray Men
32. That's Why - Jackie Wilson
33. Moonlight Serenade - The Rivieras
34. Come Softly To Me - Ronnie Height
35. Class Cutter (Yeah, Yeah) - Dale Hawkins
36. As Time Goes By - Johnny Nash
37. Six Nights a Week - The Crests
38. Come To Me - Marv Johnson
39. Yep! - Duane Eddy
40. Almost Grown - Chuck Berry
41. The Beat - Rockin' R's
42. I Miss You So - Paul Anka

43. Tell Him No - Dean and Marc
44. So Fine - The Fiestas
45. Lovey Dovey - Clyde McPhatter
46 Mathilda - Cookie and the Cupcakes
47. Goodbye, Jimmy, Goodbye - Kathy Linden
48. That's My Little Susie - Ritchie Valens
49. Who's That Knockin' - The Genies
50. Star Love - The Playmates

Also:
Tijuana Jail - The Kingston Trio
No Other Arms - The Chordettes
Only You - Bill Pourcel's French Fiddles

April 1959
ARTIST OF THE MONTH

FRANKIE AVALON

Frankie Avalon

Frankie Avalon was the first, and most successful, of the teen idols from Philadelphia. He inherited his Italian charm and his rakish good looks. He could sing and he could play the trumpet. He also learned to act passably well. On top of that, he trained all of his life to be a star.

Francis Thomas Avallone was born on September 18, 1940*, to a family living in the south side of Philadelphia, a section of the city populated almost exclusively by Italian families. He was encouraged to perform by his parents from the time he was a child, beginning when he was tutored on the trumpet by his father, Nicholas. In the South Side was the CR Club, an extension of Palumbo's Restaurant. The CR Club was a private affair, open to families with precocious children, and the owner encouraged parents to bring their youngsters to entertain. It was in this setting that Frankie Avalon got his first taste of show business.

He soon progressed to amateur shows at the local theaters. On local Philadelphia television, his talent on the trumpet brought home the top prize in amateur contests. One week it would be a record player. Another week it might be a refrigerator.

In 1952, Frankie was an uninvited performer at a party held for Al Martino, another of Philadelphia's Italian singers. Martino had just signed a recording contract with Capitol Records, and he had invited his old neighborhood to share in his success. Frankie's boldness, as well as his skill on the trumpet, caught the eye of a New York talent scout who arranged for Frankie to appear on Jackie Gleason's CBS-TV show. This led to more performances on national television, including the shows of Ray Anthony and Paul Whiteman, over the course of several years. In March 1954, Frankie even had a single record released on the "X" label,

---

(*Year of birth has also been given as 1939.)

an instrumental titled "Trumpet Sorrento." By this time, Frankie was a teenager and the novelty of his act had worn off.

Between his television appearances and the record, Frankie found it difficult to return to his former life in South Philly. By the time he was twelve, he had joined Rocco and the Saints, a dance band that also featured another alumni of the CR Club, drummer Robert Ridarelli, who would soon bill himself as Bobby Rydell. The combo played wherever they could find a booking. This meant benefit appearances at parish bazaars, shows at the Sons of Italy Hall, weeknight sock hops in school gymnasiums, and weekend dances at teen clubs. No engagement was ignored. During the summer, Rocco and the Saints were regulars at Somers Point, a vacation resort on the New Jersey coast. This intense training would come to the aid of both Avalon and Rydell in the not-too-distant future.

In 1957, Philadelphia was the home of "Bandstand," a local television show that would soon become America's most popular afternoon program. Concurrent with the increased popularity of "American Bandstand" was a rise in the number of music entrepreneurs in Philadelphia. Among this new breed of businessman were two Italian songwriters and music publishers, Peter De Angelis and Robert Marcucci. With a loan from Marcucci's father, they founded Chancellor Records. De Angelis was very much aware of Frankie Avalon. His aunt had been Frankie's baby-sitter, and De Angelis often invited Frankie over to his home where the two rehearsed, Frankie on trumpet and De Angelis on saxophone.

Frankie was among the first to approach the new owners of Chancellor Records seeking an audition. With his talent and track record, he was signed almost immediately, and Marcucci and De Angelis became his managers. First, they tried Frankie on songs aimed directly at the teen audience. Frankie's first Chancellor single was "Cupid," backed by "Jivin' With the Saints," featuring the combo. This was followed by "Teacher's Pet" (not the same movie theme made popular by Doris Day in April 1958). Neither sold in appreciable numbers outside of Philadelphia. This did not deter Marcucci and De Angelis from wrangling a spot for Frankie and the band in the rock 'n roll film "Jamboree." In a cameo performance, Avalon and the Saints performed "Teacher's Pet." That September, Frankie also made a non-singing appearance on "American Bandstand," to talk with Dick Clark about his budding career.

On their third try for a hit single, Marcucci and De Angelis wanted Frankie to sing "De De Dinah," a song they had composed. The lyrics were teen fluff, and Frankie had difficulty singing the song believably. On one take Frankie even pinched his nose between his fingers while performing the song to show what a "stinker" it really was. Of course, it was the nasal version that was chosen by Chancellor to be issued in December 1957. A week before the single's national release, Frankie made his second appearance on "American Bandstand." With this push, "De De Dinah" soon sold a million copies. Frankie Avalon was on his way to becoming an "overnight" star.

The next three singles from Frankie continued along the same path blazed by his first releases. "You Excite Me," "Gingerbread," and "I'll Wait For You" were all packaged to appeal to teenage girls right down to

Frankie's bright smile on the picture sleeves. Sales for the singles varied from "Gingerbread," with nearly a million sold, to "You Excite Me," selling half as many.

On all of Avalon's early singles, De Angelis arranged the songs and conducted the studio musicians. From a production standpoint, he created a backing instrumental track designed to produce excitement by jamming notes and sound into every available niche. There were saxophones in abundance, drums with cymbals clashing, pianos, guitars, and bass. If he thought it was needed, De Angelis threw in backing vocals, handled at times by the Four Dates. The lyric content of these songs can be summed up in a verse from "Gingerbread" (one of the few songs by Avalon not written by Marcucci and De Angelis): "You're full-a sugar, you're full-a spice; you're kind-a naughty, but you're kind-a nice." The result was a synthetic, "whitewashed" rock 'n roll record. The sound was bouncy, and there was a happy message, but this was not music intended to have a lasting impact.

Just when it appeared that Avalon had exhausted this approach, Marcucci and De Angelis came up with "Venus," a song composed by Ed Marshall. With the musical arrangement for "Venus," De Angelis turned Avalon's career completely around. He forsook the rock 'n roll combo approach for an orchestra. Befitting the theme of the song, there was an ethereal sound created by a female vocal group, bells, and chimes over a soft cha-lypso beat. Gone were the saxophones and guitars, as well as any hint of Avalon holding his nose. On "Venus," he sang with as full a voice as his eighteen years could muster. The only ingredient that didn't change was the audience toward which the song was directed.

"Venus" was Avalon's biggest hit, selling more than a million copies in the spring of 1959. During the year, it was followed by three more million sellers in a row, "Bobby Sox to Stockings," "Just Ask Your Heart" and "Why." For two months during the late summer of 1959, at the time of his biggest success as a recording star, Frankie was booked on a exhausting tour of the fair circuit. He appeared at state and county fairs all along the East Coast, from Massachusetts to Kentucky. When he finally finished in September, he promised himself he'd never go back.

Over a two-year period, Avalon had seven songs in the Top Ten. Then, beginning in 1960, his recording career began a long, slow slide. During 1960, "Don't Throw Away All Those Teardrops," "Where Were You," "Togetherness," and "A Perfect Love" each failed to crack the Top Twenty. In 1961, his singles couldn't break into the Top Sixty.

As Avalon's record sales slipped, he turned his attention to Hollywood. In 1960, he had a co-starring role in "Guns of the Timberland" with Alan Ladd, and he was a member of the large cast in John Wayne's epic, "The Alamo." The next year, he lent his voice to the animated feature "Alakazam the Great." That same year, he had a minor part in the successful "Voyage to the Bottom of the Sea." He also co-starred with Robert Wagner in "Sail a Crooked Ship." True, he was appearing in feature films, but his acting career seemed stalled. It wasn't until 1963 that he had his first starring role in "Drums of Africa," a low-budget movie with no redeeming qualities.

In the early 1960s, the nationwide surfing craze was launched in

Los Angeles. Led by Jan and Dean and the Beach Boys, there were hundreds of other surfing bands hoping for a deal with a record company. Hollywood movie studios were not far behind. The movie companies had learned an important lesson in 1956 with the rise of rock 'n roll and the subsequent success of the "quickie" movies on the subject. As a result, the craze in Hollywood in the early 1960s was the beach movie. And, the leading stars of this genre were Frankie Avalon and Annette. In 1963, they appeared in the inaugural beach movie, "Beach Party." Avalon followed this with "Operation Bikini," a war film, not a beach movie. However, the trend was set. Hastily-produced movies followed in 1964 with "Bikini Beach" and "Muscle Beach Party." In 1965 it was "Beach Blanket Bingo," "How to Stuff a Wild Bikini," and "Dr. Goldfoot and the Bikini Machine." Also in 1965, Avalon left the beach for the mountains to star in "Ski Party." These movies shared common themes: fun in the sun, sweet romance, and dance music—performed by the film's stars as well as by such non-beach notables as James Brown, Stevie Wonder and the Kingsmen.

In 1966, Frankie and Annette joined Fabian, another of South Philly's teen idols, in "Fireball 500." Although the acting remained perfunctory, "Fireball 500" did feature remarkable footage of stock car racing. This film marked the end of Avalon's period as a singing movie star.

In 1965's "I'll Take Sweden" he co-starred with Bob Hope. Avalon was also in the 1969 Otto Preminger flop "Skidoo! Skidoo!" starring Jackie Gleason and Carol Channing. Other low-budget films in which Avalon starred or co-starred were 1962's "Panic in the Year Zero;" "The Castalian," a 1963 Spanish epic; and "Sergeant Deadhead" from 1965. Avalon also appeared in the long-forgotten gem, "The Million Eyes of Samuru."

After starring in "Horror House" (1970) and co-starring behind Billy Dee Williams in "The Take" (1974), Avalon remained in semi-retirement at his home in Los Angeles for most of the decade. He occasionally appeared in a television series, including a well-received guest shot on a "Love Boat" episode. He wasn't completely unproductive during this period, as he repeatedly became a father in a family that eventually boasted eight children.

Although his recording career did not produce any major hits after 1960 or any charted singles after 1962, Avalon continued to release both singles and albums on Chancellor though 1963. He moved on to United Artists in 1964 for a few singles and a pair of albums. Following United Artists, Avalon changed record labels almost annually. He was with Reprise in 1968, Amos in 1969, Metromedia in 1970 and Regalia in 1972. (At Reprise and Amos, Avalon was produced by Jimmy Bowen.) His last record to receive any attention was a disco version of "Venus" on De-Lite in 1976. Over the course of the year, De-Lite issued four additional singles by Avalon but nothing more happened. Even a De-Lite remake of Bobby Darin's "Splish Splash" in 1977 couldn't attract the record buyer's attention. Avalon's final recording was the single "You're the Miracle" on the Bobcat label in 1983.

He returned to movies in 1978 with a cameo role in the popular musical "Grease." In the film he played "Teen Angel" and sang "Beauty

School Dropout," a favorite song in a score filled with memorable tunes. In 1980, Hollywood turned the story of Frankie and Fabian and Bob Marcucci into "The Idolmaker." None of the principals appeared in the film although Marcucci acted as technical advisor. "The Idolmaker" concentrated on the crass commercialization that overwhelmed rock 'n roll in the late 1950s.

In the summer of 1985, Avalon joined Bobby Rydell and Frankie Avalon to tour the United States billed as "The Golden Boys of Bandstand." A fifty-city set of dates was arranged beginning July 6 in Dallas. Rehearsal performances the previous April at the Westbury Music Fair in Westbury, New York, were a huge success. Public Television's "On Stage at Wolf Trap" even aired a special in January 1986 that was built around their show at the Wolf Trap Farm Park as well as a retrospective of their individual careers. This success led to a reunion of Frankie and Annette in 1987's "Back to the Beach," a film parody of their earlier beach movies.

Today, Frankie Avalon lives the good life in the Los Angeles area. He reportedly invested much of his savings in the musical "Grease" and is now a millionaire. Avalon never stopped making personal appearances in nightclubs and concert theaters. Throughout the years, he often turned to Dick Clark for help with his career, and Clark always came through. In return, Avalon became a mainstay in many of the musical productions Clark produced for television. And, in spitre of his earlier promise to himself, he often worked with Clark's summer rock 'n roll tours of state fairs. Except this time, Frankie did it to return the love of his fans.

Staying true to form, in 1994, Frankie was the TV pitchman for the Sonic chain of drive-in hamburger joints.

May 1959

MAY 1   "American Bandstand" welcomes Freddy Cannon singing "Tallahassie Lassie."
    The Apollo Theater in Harlem features a gospel revue this week headlined by the Soul Stirrers.
    In Washington, the week-long Howard Theater revue features Bobby Day, Little Willie John, the Upsetters featuring Lee Diamond, and Big Jay McNeely.

MAY 2   Guests on "The Dick Clark Show" tonight are Connie Francis, Bobby Darin, Wilbert Harrison, the Crests, and the G-Notes.

MAY 3   Art Neville's Hawkettes perform at Lincoln Beach in New Orleans.

MAY 4   At Lake Tahoe, Bobby Darin begins a two-week run at Harrah's Casino in Stateline, Nevada.

New Releases for the first week in May include "Lonely Boy" by Paul Anka on ABC-Paramount; "It Was I" by **Skip and Flip** on Brent; "Straight Flush" by the Frantics on Dolton; "Dream Girl" by Robert and Johnny on Old Town; Stonewall Jackson's "Waterloo" on Columbia; "Wonderful, Loveable You" by the Teddy Bears on Imperial; "Cherrystone" by the Addrisi Brothers on Del-Fi; Bobby Rydell's "All I Want Is You" on Cameo; "I'm A Big Boy Now" by Bobby Hendricks on Sue; Bobby Lee Trammell's "Woe Is Me" on Warrior; Huelyn Duvall's "It's No Wonder" on Starfire; Charlie Gracie's "Angel of Love" on Coral; "Rock Around The Clock" by Jimmy DeKnight on Apt; and "Everlovin'" by Dave Burgess on Challenge.

MAY 5   The Crests sing "16 Candles" on "American Bandstand."
    The Royal Teens play Dick Lee's Musical Bar in Philadelphia for the next five days.

MAY 6   Cozy Cole opens at the Blue Note in Chicago.

MAY 7   Paul Anka guests on Pat Boone's ABC-TV show.

EARLY MAY
    Lloyd Price brings his big band into Pep's in Philadelphia. Also in town, Tommy Sands is playing the Latin Casino.
    Earl Grant is currently booked into Fack's II in San Francisco.

SKIP AND FLIP

Skip and Flip's "It Was I" was a fine record that launched two music careers. Flip produced such enduing hits as "The Monster Mash," "Alley Oop" and "Like Long Hair." Skip worked in one of rock's best loved bands. Gary Paxton was born in Coffeyville, Kansas, May 18, 1939. When he was twelve his family moved to Tucson. He formed his first band just prior to dropping out of high school. At seventeen, he created the Pledges, who recorded "Bermuda" for REV Records in 1957. The drummer for the Pledges was Clyde Battin, born February 2, 1934, in Gallipolis, Ohio. They went to Phoenix and recorded demos of two songs Paxton had written, which were sent off to the Bell Notes who were successful at the time. Paxton moved to Washington state where he played bass behind a young Buck Owens in Seattle and picked fruit around Eugene. In the meantime, the demo ended up at Time Records (the Bell Notes' label) and owner Bobby Shad put it out "It Was I" on his Brent subsidiary as by Skip and Flip (the name of Shad's poodles). The record caught on, and Battin was contacted to go on tour. When Paxton could not be located, Chuck Mendall became "Flip." Mendall was a deejay from nearby Mesa and a student at the University of Arizona. It was two months after the release of "It Was I" before Paxton heard his song on a radio. He immediately returned to Tucson and took his rightful place as Flip. "It Was I" remained a hit for four months and the duo followed with "Fancy Nancy" (the other demo song) and "Cherry Pie," a remake of Marvin and Johnny's 1954 recording. Skip and Flip disbanded in late 1959. Paxton became a major figure behind the rock music scenes in Hollywood. He also had many singles under his own name, but not one was even a minor hit. Skip Battin was drummer with the Byrds beginning in 1969 and the original bassist with the New Riders of the Purple Sage.

FLOYD ROBINSON
At heart, Floyd Robinson was a country artist, and his style was reminiscent of that of George Hamilton IV. But, he also possessed a humorous streak. Robinson was a Nashville native, born about 1937. By the time he was twelve, he was appearing as an amateur with the Eagle Rangers Band, a combo which he had founded. In high school, he and his combo had secured a fifteen-minute program on WSM radio, Nashville's powerhouse station and the broadcasting home of the "Grand Ole Opry." Shortly thereafter, Robinson was playing guitar with Little Jimmie Dickens. By this time, Robinson considered himself on track to become a professional songwriter. He was submitting songs to various publishing houses. It was a novelty, "Little Space Girl," that caught the ear of Jesse Lee Turner, becoming a medium-sized hit in early 1959. In turn, the song brought Robinson to the attention of RCA Victor Records, and he was contracted to record his own songs. Another novelty, "My Girl," was chosen as his premier single, but it was the flip side, "Makin' Love," that cause the furor. The song's title, by itself, could have sold quite a few records in 1959. For a singer to express his outspoken desire to be "makin' love" was almost unheard of. The song relied on Robinson's quiet, unhurried delivery to sell its message without becoming blatant, and the ploy worked. Through the summer of 1959, "Makin' Love" sold well enough to bounce around the Top Twenty. Robinson followed with a remake of "Tonight You Belong To Me," Patience and Prudence's 1956 smash. The single failed to catch the public's ear. Of note, the B-side was "Let It Be Me" which would be a best seller for the Everly Brothers in 1960. With no hits, Robinson's recording career took a nose-dive, although continued to have singles issued by RCA, Jamie (where he engineered sessions for Duane Eddy), Dot, Groove and United Artists into 1966.

MAY 8   New York's Apollo Theater presents Pearl Bailey and drummer Louis Bellson's band for the week.

MAY 9   Ronnie Hawkins and the Hawks perform on "The Dick Clark Show" on ABC-TV. Also guesting on the show are Paul Anka, Jesse Belvin, the Skyliners, and Johnny Horton.
  In England, Conway Twitty performs on the "Oh, Boy!" television show. He will repeat a week later, on May 16.
  Danny and the Juniors play the Erie Social Club in Philadelphia for the next three days.

MAY 10 Conway Twitty turns up at the Cannes Film Festival.

MAY 11 Annette makes a rare television appearance outside of her daily role on "The Mickey Mouse Club," as she guests on "Make Room For Father" with Danny Thomas.
  Fats Domino opens at Sciolla's Club in Philadelphia.
  Paul Anka begins a tour of England with a performance in Birmingham's Hippodrome. He plans to remain in England through June 14.
  Sandy Stewart entertains guests at the Celebrity Room in Philadelphia for the next two weeks.
  Roy Hamilton opens for a week at Washington's Casino Royal.

New Releases for the second week in May include "Here Comes Summer" by Jerry Keller on Kapp; Frankie Avalon's "Bobby Sox To Stockings" b/w "A Boy Without a Girl" on Chancellor; "Ring-A-Ling-A-Lario" by Jimmie Rodgers on Roulette; three from RCA: **Floyd Robinson**'s "Makin' Love," Neil Sedaka's "You Gotta Learn Your Rhythm and Blues" and "Chili Beans" by Boots Brown; "A Prayer and a Juke Box" by Little Anthony and the Imperials on End; Bobby Day's "Gotta New Girl" on Class; "Merry-Go-Round" by Eddie Holland on United Artists; "Steel Guitar Rag" by the Dynatones on Bomarc; Wayne Cochran's "The Coo" on Scottie; "Rockin' In The Jungle" by the Eternals on Hollywood; "Nameless" by the Rockin R's on Tempus; Groovy Joe Poovey's "Eight To The Bar" on Dixie; and "Would You Believe It (I've Got A Cold)?" by Huey Smith and the Clowns on Ace. Also new is Waylon Jenning's first release, "Jole Blon" on Brunswick another Buddy Holly production.

MAY 13 The Falcons' pre-soul stylings grace "American Bandstand" today.

MAY 14 Earl Grant stops at the El Dorado Club in Houston for two weeks.

MAY 15 Organist Dave "Baby" Cortez swings through "The Happy Organ" on "American Bandstand."
  At the Howard Theater in Washington, Wilbert Harrison headlines the revue that features the Chantels, Valerie Carr, and Joe Medlin.

MID-MAY
LaVern Baker is currently entertaining at Pep's in Philadelphia.

MAY 16   "The Dick Clark Show" presents Jimmie Rodgers, Chico Holiday and LaVern Baker.

MAY 17   Bill Doggett plays a one-night stand at the Longshore Club in San Francisco. Tomorrow, he opens a two-day gig at the 53 Club in Oakland.
　　　Joe Jones return to Lincoln Beach in New Orleans for a one-night stand.

MAY 18   Jesse Lee Turner performs his novelty recording "Little Space Girl" on "American Bandstand."
　　　Detroit's own Jackie Wilson headlines at the Greystone Ballroom. Shortly thereafter, he's off to Hollywood.

New Releases for the third week in May include "Hushabye" by the **Mystics** on Laurie; Duane Eddy's "Forty Miles of Bad Road" on Jamie; Bo Diddley's "Crackin' Up" on Checker; "Tall Cool One" by the Wailers on Golden Crest; Sam Cooke's "Only Sixteen" on RCA; "The Whistling Organ" by Dave "Baby" Cortez' on Clock; "Flower of Love" by the Crests on Co-Ed; Marvin Rainwater's "Half-Breed" on M-G-M; Clyde McPhatter's "Since You've Been Gone" on Atlantic; "Say Yeah" by Maurice Williams on Selwin; and Jerry Byrne's "Raining" on Specialty. New this week is Roland James' "Guitarsville" on Judd. His real last name is Janes, and he is the guitarist on most of Jerry Lee Lewis' sessions.

MAY 19   Wanda Jackson, just returned from a tour of the Orient, opens for two weeks at the Showboat Hotel and Casino in Las Vegas.

MAY 20   Sciolla's Club in Philadelphia welcomes Connie Francis for a week's stay.
　　　The Playmates open for a week at Washington's Casino Royal.
　　　The Platters are forced to delay by two weeks their tour of England due to Zola Taylor's illness. They were originally scheduled to play Leed's on this date.

MAY 22   In Cleveland, Jimmie Rodgers plays a benefit for fellow Roulette recording artist, Vince Wayne, who died recently of a stroke while performing at a local high school hop. Wayne had only one release on Roulette, "Fare Thee Well" in April 1958, before his untimely death.
　　　Sam Cooke opens a special two-week engagement at the Flame Show Bar and Lounge in Detroit.
　　　Marvin Rainwater plays a two-day engagement in Houston.
　　　Dave "Baby" Cortez headlines the week-long revue at the Apollo. Also featured are the Heartbeats, Bo Diddley, the Fiestas, Bobby Day, and the Cadillacs.
　　　In New Orleans, Roy Brown starts the first of several week-

THE MYSTICS
The Mystics might be dismissed as just another doo-wop group of Italian heritage from the New York area, like Dion and the Belmonts and the Elegants. Their biggest hit wasn't even a Number One single. But, oh what a record! In 1959, the Mystics were Phil Craolici, lead tenor, guitar and piano; his brother, Albee, 2nd tenor; Bob Ferrante, 1st tenor; George Galfo, 2nd tenor; and Allie Contrera, bass. They tried to get an audition, but record labels in New York were awash with similar unknown groups. They were asked the same question, "Can you leave a demo?" They saved their money and went to a Manhattan recording studio for this purpose. While there, they were overheard by an agent who signed them and introduced them to Laurie Records, the label of Dion and the Belmonts. Their first single, "Hushabye," had the same feel as a Dion release: a rolling rhythm, tight harmony, a teenager's point of view. The record sold by the box-load along the East Coast but failed to generate massive sales further west. Their second release, "Don't Take the Stars," barely dented the Top 100. By the end of 1959, their dreams of becoming a hit recording group were fading. They left Laurie in 1960, although the label continued to release singles into 1961, issuing a total of six Mystics singles. An interesting sidelight: their third single on Laurie, "All Through the Night," featured a young singer billed as Jerry Landis. This was future superstar Paul Simon. In 1960 they turned up on King as the Hitones ("Fool, Fool, Fool"), followed by two forgettable singles as the Mystics, "The Hoppy Hop" and "The Jumping Bean." The Hitones also had records released on Fonsca ("Just For You," "I Don't Know Why") and Shytone. These were issued in 1961 but may have been recorded before "Hushabye."

end engagements at the Pimlico Club. He has just completed a tour of the Midwest and East Coast. Also in town, Johnny Adams starts a three-day engagement at Lincoln Beach.

The Howard Theater in Washington presents Pearl Bailey with Louis Bellson's orchestra for the next two weeks.

MAY 23 On tonight's "Dick Clark Show," Frankie Avalon performs "Venus" and Chubby Checker sings "The Class."

MAY 24 Fabian makes a guest appearance on "The Ed Sullivan Show" on CBS-TV. Also appearing on tonight's show is Billy Storm.

Ray Charles appears tonight at the Labor Union Hall in New Orleans.

MAY 25 Tommy Edwards opens a one-week stand at the Key Club in Minneapolis.

While appearing at the Flame Lounge in Detroit, Sam Cooke does double duty tonight, performing at the Ford Auditorium with Sarah Vaughan and the Duke Ellington orchestra.

New Releases for the fourth week in May include Fabian's "Tiger" on Chancellor; two from Mercury: "Remember When?" by the Platters and "Sea of Love" by **Phil Phillips** and the Twilites; "There Is Something On Your Mind" by Big Jay McNeely on Swingin'; Jackie Wilson's "I'll Be Satisfied" on Brunswick; Chuck Berry's "Back In The U.S.A." b/w "Memphis, Tennessee;" Jack Scott's "The Way I Walk" on Carlton; Ritchie Valens' "We Belong Together" on Del-Fi; "Summertime" by the Slades on Domino; Rod Bernard's "Life Is a Mystery" on Argo; "I'll Do The Same For You" by Johnny Otis on Capitol; Jesse Belvin's "It Could Have Been Worse" on RCA; "That Old Black Magic" by the Clovers on United Artists; "Sweet Sugar Lips" by the Kalin Twins on Decca; "To Have and To Hold" by John Fred and the Playboys on Montel; Johnny Nash's "And the Angels Sing" on ABC-Paramount; "Shufflin' Along" by the Virtues on Hunt; and "Teen-Age Vision" by Travis and Bob on Sandy.

MAY 27 Minneapolis' Flame Club welcomes Marvin Rainwater for four days.

Sarah Vaughan and the Jimmy Smith Trio entertain theatergoers at New York's Apollo Theater this week.

MAY 28 In a driving downpour at Atlanta's outdoor Herndon Stadium the show goes on with Roy Hamilton, Ray Charles, Jimmy Reed, the Drifters, Ruth Brown, the Fiestas Johnny Adams, Huey Smith and the Clowns, B.B. King and Buddy Johnson's orchestra featuring Ella Johnson. The show, celebrating WAOK radio's Fifth Anniversary, is repeated tomorrow night.

Frank Virtue and the Virtues play a two-day gig at Old Orchard Beach, Maine.

MAY 30 This Saturday night's "Dick Clark Show" is headlined by the

---

PHIL PHILLIPS

Like Rod Bernard, Phil Phillips was a product of south Louisiana's Cajun country. John Phillip Baptiste was born March 14, 1931, near Lake Charles. By 1959, he had served a tour in the Navy as an enlisted man and was back in Lake Charles working as a hotel bell hop. In earlier days, he had been a member of the Gateways Quartet, a group popular enough in the area to have their own radio program on a Lake Charles station. Baptiste wrote songs, accompanying himself on guitar and dreamed of being a recording star. Then, in 1959, the musical flood gates of south Louisiana seemed to open, and artists like Cookie and the Cupcakes, Rod Bernard, and Jivin' Gene were having national hits. Goldband, a local record company owned by George Khoury, was in the middle of the action. The studio at Goldband was being used by many artists looking for their break, and this is where Baptiste turned to record a love song he had written for his girl friend. "Sea of Love" had a moody, rolling rhythm befitting its subject matter. The song, released as by Phil Phillips, came out first on Khoury Records, a subsidiary of Goldband. When it caused a local stir, the master tape was marketed to Mercury Records, the company that was then releasing Rod Bernard's singles. "Sea of Love," with all of its rough edges showing, took two months before it started to become popular on a national level. Once it did, it rose steadily, reaching the upper levels of the record charts by September. It missed the coveted Number One spot only because Santo and Johnny's "Sleepwalk" wouldn't budge. Although there were several more Mercury releases, Philips never had another national hit, although his singles sold very well in Louisiana. "Sea of Love" was recorded for a new audience in 1982 by Del Shannon and in 1984 by the Honeydrippers. At this time, Baptiste is working in Jennings, Louisiana, as a deejay.

Four Preps. Also featured on the show are Annette, **Billy Storm** and Duane Eddy.

Returning to the New Orleans area, Ray Charles entertains tonight at the Sugar Bowl Lounge in Thibodaux. He moves to Baton Rouge on June 1.

Brenda Lee drops by "Jubilee U.S.A." on CBS-TV.

MAY 31 "The Ed Sullivan Show" welcomes Bobby Darin.

LATE MAY

The Four Mints are currently back in their hometown of Atlanta playing the Imperial Hotel's Domino Lounge.

It is reported in the music press that Carl Perkins is en route to Hollywood to work on a movie with a Hawaiian theme. The film, titled "Hawaiian Boy," disappeared without a trace.

THE TOP ROCK 'N ROLL RECORDS FOR MAY 1959

1. The Happy Organ - Dave "Baby" Cortez
2. Sorry, I Ran All The Way Home - The Impalas
3. (Now and Then There's) A Fool Such As I/I Need Your Love Tonight - Elvis Presley
4. Come Softly To Me - The Fleetwoods
5. Pink Shoelaces - Dodie Stevens
6. Guitar Boogie Shuffle - The Virtues
7. Kansas City - Wilbert Harrison
8. Turn Me Loose - Fabian
9. Kookie, Kookie, Lend Me Your Comb - Edd "Kookie" Byrnes and Connie Stevens
10. Tell Him No - Travis and Bob
11. Enchanted - The Platters
12. Three Stars - Tommy Dee
13. That's Why - Jackie Wilson
14. Take A Message To Mary/Poor Jenny - The Everly Brothers
15. Since I Don't Have You - The Skyliners
16. Dream Lover - Bobby Darin
17. So Fine - The Fiestas
18. Goodbye, Jimmy, Goodbye - Kathy Linden
19. Six Nights a Week - The Crests
20. Endlessly/So Close - Brook Benton
21. Venus - Frankie Avalon
22. Come To Me - Marv Johnson
23. Guess Who - Jesse Belvin
24. Almost Grown - Chuck Berry
25. Personality - Lloyd Price
26. Never Be Anyone Else But You/It's Too Late - Ricky Nelson
27. This Should Go On Forever - Rod Bernard
28. Sea Cruise - Frankie Ford

BILLY STORM AND THE VALIANTS
"A rose by any other name..." Billy Storm's career is difficult to trace because of the many stage names he used. Born William Jones in Dayton on June 29, 1938, Billy dreamed of playing professional basketball. When his athletic prowess didn't pan out, he turned to music. To that end, the moved to the West Coast and enrolled in the Los Angeles City College, majoring in music. He joined the local R&B movement, becoming a member of the Sabers for one single each on Cal-West ("Always, Forever") and the Chavelles on Vita ("Valley of Love"). In both groups, he was joined by Chester Pipkin, who had sung with the Squires on Vita and the Bluejays on Now Dig This, and Sheridan "Rip" Spencer. The trio decided to form yet another group, the Valiants with the addition of Bruce Corfield of the Chavelles. In late 1957, they landed a contract with the newly formed Keen Records, the label of Sam Cooke's early "pop" success. "This Is The Night," their first Keen release, featured Storm's incredibly high tenor. The record caught the public's ear and even cracked the "pop" charts for nearly two months. There were two more Keen singles, along with one record each on Keen's subsidiaries Andex and Ensign. Storm signed as a solo act with Columbia in 1959, and his first release, "I've Come of Age," was a big "pop" hit, staying on the charts for more than three months. The song was an odd mix of syrupy strings, heavenly choir and twangy guitar, with Storm's tenor in the Sam Cooke mold. At the same time, Valiants issued "Let Me Ride on Joy in 1950 then became the Untouchables for one single on Madison ("Goodnight, Sweetheart, Goodnight") and Liberty ("You're on Top"). Storm didn't have another hit, and moved from Columbia to Disney's Vista label for a half-dozen forgettable singles with more violins and puppy love.

29. I've Come of Age - Billy Storm
30. It's Just a Matter of Time - Brook Benton
31. Lonely For You - Gary Stites
32. I Miss You So - Paul Anka
33. Everybody Likes to Cha Cha Cha - Sam Cooke
34. It Doesn't Matter Anymore - Buddy Holly
35. Yep! - Duane Eddy
36. As Time Goes By - Johnny Nash
37. You're So Fine - The Falcons
38. Just Keep It Up - Dee Clark
39. I Waited Too Long - LaVern Baker
40. Crossfire - Johnny and the Hurricanes
41. Tell Him No - Dean and Marc
42. The Morning Side of the Mountain - Tommy Sands
43. That's My Little Susie - Ritchie Valens
44. Lovey Dovey - Clyde McPhatter
45. I'm Ready/Margie - Fats Domino
46. Castin' My Spell - The Johnny Otis Show
47. I Think I'm Gonna Kill Myself - Buddy Knox
48. My Heart Is An Open Book - Carl Dobkins, Jr.
49. Tallahassee Lassie - Freddy Cannon
50. Robbin' the Cradle - Tony Bellus

Also on the "pop" charts:
The Battle of New Orleans - Johnny Horton
Quiet Village - Martin Denny
Bonaparte's Retreat/The Kissin' Tree - Billy Grammer

May 1959
ARTIST OF THE MONTH

DAVE "BABY" CORTEZ

Dave "Baby" Cortez

Today, Dave Cortez, like Bobby Day, is usually remembered for one release. And, like Day, Dave Cortez had a long and, at times, successful recording career both before and after his hit.

David Cortez Clowney was born August 13, 1938*. He grew up in Detroit where he attended North Western High School. He showed musical aptitude at an early age and was guided toward the piano by his father. Young David took lessons on the piano for ten years, honing his skills as accompanist for the local church choir. He was also developing into a fine vocalist. In his teens, Dave switched from piano to organ as a result of his association with the church. However, it was his love of singing that first led him into the recording studio.

The Dave "Baby" Cortez story really begins in 1952 with the Val-

---

(*Cortez' year of birth also frequently reported to be 1939.)

entines, a street-corner group from the Washington Heights section of New York City. Carl Hogan, a fine baritone, had drifted in and out of various aggregations until he was asked by Mickey Francis to join an amateur group that called themselves the Dreamers. The Dreamers consisted of Francis (first tenor), Raymond "Pops" Briggs (tenor and the brother of Lillian Briggs), and Ronnie Bright (bass). In style, the Dreamers emulated the successful groups of the day, especially the Clovers and the Velvets.

Also living in Washington Heights was Richard Barrett, an aspiring songwriter who had recently moved from Philadelphia. What Barrett lacked in personal finances, he more than made up for in self-motivation. In 1954, shortly after he met the Dreamers, Barrett took over the lead spot, while Francis moved to second tenor. At Barrett's suggestion, the Dreamers changed their name to the Valentines. They also performed on one of the Apollo Theater's amateur night shows. This led a mid-sized hit for the Valentines with "Tonight Kathleen" for Old Town.

In 1955, the Valentines went through a series of personnel changes. First to go was Carl Hogan who left to form the Miracles, a group that issued one single on Fury but was not the group that recorded for Motown. Hogan's place in the Valentines was filled by Donald Raysor of the Velvets.

Also in 1955, David Clowney and several friends formed the Pearls. A member of the group was Bobby Spencer who had formerly recorded with the Crickets on Jay-Dee and had been associated with the Chords shortly after they recorded "Sh-Boom." The lead singer for the Pearls was Howard Guyden. The group secured a short-term contract with Atlantic Records that resulted in two singles on Atco, "Shadows of Love" and "Bells of Love." Neither single was successful, and the Pearls disbanded. Spencer continued his musical odyssey by joining the Cadillacs where he remained a mainstay for more than fifteen years.

During the first week of November 1955, as the Pearls' "Shadows of Love" was being issued by Atco, the Valentines' "Lily Maebelle" became their first release on Rama. By this time, Eddy Edghill had succeeded Don Raysor. With the success of "Lily Maebelle," the Valentines were invited to appear on Alan Freed's Christmas revue at the Academy of Music in New York City.

In early 1956, as it looked like the Valentines were on the road to fame and fortune, Ray Briggs left the group. He was replaced by Dave Clowney. During Clowney's stay with the Valentines, they continued to have minor hits with "The Woo Woo Train," "I'll Never Let You Go," "Nature's Creation," and "Don't Say Goodnight," all on Rama. Failing to find his fortune with the Miracles, Hogan returned to the Valentines, replacing Edghill. By 1957, the group was recording sporadically and performing even less. In 1958, the Valentines disbanded for good. Hogan went on to be a successful songwriter with "Don't Say Goodnight" by the Dubs and "So Long" by Little Anthony and the Imperials among his many credits. Ronnie Bright later recorded for Co-Ed with the Schoolmates and sang bass on Johnny Cymbal's 1963 hit, "Mr. Bass Man." Richard Barrett remained with Rama Records, becoming one of the most successful independent record producers over the next half-dozen years.

His list of hit records included those by Frankie Lymon and the Teenagers, Little Anthony and the Imperials, and the Chantels.

Dave Clowney remained with the Valentines less than a year, returning to the Pearls in late 1956 after they landed a contract with Onyx Records. Unfortunately, the Pearls still could not come up with a record that sold even moderately, even though they had five singles on Onyx. As a sign of things to come, however, the Dave Clowney Band released an instrumental in 1956 titled "Movin' and Groovin'" on Ember Records.

In late 1957, after the Pearls disbanded, Clowney had a brief association with Okeh, a subsidiary of Columbia Records. Under the name Baby Cortez, his only Okeh release was a vocal effort, "Honey Baby" b/w "You Give Me Heebie Jeebies." The A-side was straight-ahead, medium-tempo rock 'n roll that featured piano triplets, a guitar break, and a thumping rhythm. The flip, although it sought an association with the classic rave-up by Little Richard, lacked the original's punch or drive.

Cortez must have realized that he couldn't earn a living on his vocal talent alone. Relying on his years of piano and organ lessons, he found employment as a studio musician in New York. He became a favorite pianist for the sessions produced for George Goldner's labels, including End, Gone and Roulette. Among the artists he worked with were the Chantels and Little Anthony and the Imperials. At the same time, in early 1958, "Hoot Owl" was released by Paris Records with the label listing Dave Clowney again.

In 1958, his previous association with Ember Records brought him to Clock Records, a brand new label. Clock Records was initially distributed by Ember. Cortez seemed to have difficulty deciding which direction his recording career should take. Consequently, he recorded in a variety of styles, singing ripe ballads in the style of Jesse Belvin or Jerry Butler, while playing organ instrumentals like a madman. His first Clock release in August 1958 was a vocal, "You're the Girl." In February 1959, his next Clock single featured a tear-jerker, "Love Me As I Love You," that was too close to the style of "For Your Precious Love" to muster any airplay. Deejays soon flipped the record over and started playing the B-side, an instrumental with a bouncy melody and an organ lead. The tune was perfect for closing out a radio show at the top of the hour. Appropriately enough, the song was titled "The Happy Organ." It opened with an ascending piano glissando (probably played by Cortez) that lead directly to the sprightly main theme performed by Cortez in a staccato fashion on the organ. This theme was so simple it could have easily been based on a children's nursery rhyme. The organ verse was repeated several times before an out-of-place, hard-rock guitar bridge led back to the organ once again. Beating all odds, "The Happy Organ" caught on quickly and became the Number One record in the country by May 1959.

Cortez' follow-up single was "The Whistling Organ." This tune was a virtual copy of "The Happy Organ." It opened with another piano figure; the organ played a bright, but simple, melody; the guitar bridge was out of character; and the tune ended with the organ. Being so close to "The Happy Organ" in format and style, "The Whistling Organ" could only maintain its marginal popularity for a couple of months.

By late summer, Clock's distribution deal with Ember had fallen through. In stepped RCA Victor to issue the album DAVE "BABY CORTEZ AND HIS HAPPY ORGAN, released in September 1959. Clock Records had approached RCA Victor with a unique offer. Since RCA was successful with the merchandising of albums, Cortez' LP release would be handled through RCA. In return, Clock, which had proven capable of distributing singles, would be allowed to issue some of the lesser RCA artists' single releases. The plan stopped almost as soon as it was set in motion when the various legal departments called a halt to this unorthodox arrangement. Clock later issued the album on its own label, but not before RCA sold thousands of copies.

After two single releases, Dave "Baby" Cortez' solo career came to a sudden halt. This was the year of the rock 'n roll instrumental, and few artists or groups lasted beyond the sophomore slump. Clock was able to parlay the two singles into three album releases during 1960-61. Meanwhile, Clock's distribution was handled first by Independent Distributors before Clock became a subsidiary of Mercury Records.

Over the same period, there were more than a half-dozen singles released by Cortez on Clock after "The Whistling Organ." Most were instrumentals aimed at the dance crowd such as "The Piano Shuffle," "Organ Shout" and "Come On and Stomp." Not one could garner enough radio airplay to sustain sales. Without a hit, Cortez retreated to New York and session work again. While he patiently waited for another chance at a hit single, he recorded "The Madison Shuffle" an instrumental that appeared on the flip side of Buster Brown's "John Henry" on Fire Records in 1960.

In the summer of 1962, Cortez found the elusive formula for another instrumental hit with "Rinky Dink." It was originally issued on the small Julia label but was picked up by Chess Record when it started to attract attention. On organ again, Cortez used a four-chord instrumental pattern built over a halting, cha-cha beat as punctuation throughout the verse with the organ carrying the melody during the bridge. There were only brief interjections from a sax and guitar to break the cha-cha rhythm. Remarkably, with so little to recommend it, the single became a Top Ten hit. Falling back on the pattern of his previous success, the second Chess single was "Happy Weekend." As with "The Whistling Organ," it remained a minor hit for most of two months. Late in 1962, while Cortez was signed to an exclusive contract with Chess, a single titled "Fiesta" on Emit Records created a minor stir. "Fiesta" was apparently something left over from an earlier session. Cortez had three more singles on Chess into 1963, but each failed to attract any radio play.

After Chess, Cortez recorded for a seemingly endless succession of labels. There was a two-sided, repetitious, up-tempo instrumental for the Winley label titled "Scotty" in 1963. In 1964, he was back with Okeh Records for "Popping Popcorn," a stomping, semi-instrumental that featured a big band and gospel-styled vocals from a female group. The flip side, "The Question (Do You Love Me)" tried to be an emotional soul ballad but the production was marred as it switched gears into a high-stepping gospel shout midway through before returning to the slower style at the close.

In 1965, Cortez signed with George Goldner's Roulette label. Roulette issued three albums and a few singles through 1967. One single, "Count Down," briefly caught the public's fancy in June 1966. Then it was on to Speed Records as Dave Cortez and the Moon People issued "Happy Soul (w/a Hook)," an instrumental featuring minimal organ from Cortez combined with a wah-wah guitar and a funky bass line. On Sound Pak Records, Dave Cortez and We The People released "(Do It) The Funky Dance." This time Cortez' organ was relegated to background work behind We The People's vocal harmonies, even though he received top billing. In 1973, All-Platinum Records issued Dave "Baby" Cortez' final single, "Hell Street Junction" which was an imitation of Sly and the Family Stone's "Life."

Dave Cortez was one of those instrumental artists who tweaked the music buyer's ear briefly and then faded into obscurity. His talent on piano and organ insured that he could always earn a living, generously supplemented by the royalties of the hit tunes he had composed.

June 1959

JUN 1   On "American Bandstand," Dion and the Belmonts lip-sync their way through "Teenager In Love."

Bobby Darin opens for the week at the Casino Royal in Washington, DC.

New Releases for the first week in June include "Oh What a Fool" by the Impalas on Cub; "I Love an Angel" by **Little Bill** and the Bluenotes on Dolton; Marv Johnson's "I'm Comin' Home" on United Artists; "What Is Love?" by the Playmates on Roulette; Bob Beckham's "Just As Much As Ever" on Decca; "Don't Go Away" by the Teddy Bears on Imperial; "See You In September" by the Tempos on Climax; "Baby Talk" by Jan and Dean on Dore; Wilbert Harrison's "Baby, Don't You Know" on Savoy; "Summer's Gone" by Richard Barrett with the Chantels on End; Whitey Pullen's "Let's All Go Wild Tonight" on Sage; "Rollin' Home" by Louis Brooks and the Hi-Toppers on Nasco; and a reissue of "The Chosen Few" by Dion and the Timberlanes on Jubilee. Also out this week is "Goose Bumps" on Epic, a record by Link Wray's brother, Doug Wray.

JUN 3   At the Charlotte (NC) Coliseum, Jerry Lee Lewis headlines a big revue. Featured performers include Sam Cooke, Jackie Wilson, the Midnighters, the Falcons, Jesse Belvin, Marv Johnson, Baby Washington, the Pips, and Johnny "Guitar" Watson. (See also JUN 9.)

On "American Bandstand," Preston Epps plays his instrumental hit "Bongo Rock."

JUN 4   "American Bandstand" welcomes the instrumental combo Johnny and the Hurricanes who perform "Crossfire" and introduce a new number, "Red River Rock."

Bobby Freeman plays the Hacienda Club in Fresno, California.

JUN 5   The Skyliners, the Shirelles, Joe Turner, the Heartbeats, and Bobby Hendricks rock the house all week at the Howard Theater in Washington.

JUN 6   Dale Hawkins makes another appearance on "The Dick Clark Show" tonight. Also appearing are Dave "Baby" Cortez and Vic Damone.

JUN 7   Bill Haley and His Comets rock the house at the Buck Lake Ranch in Angola, Indiana.

LITTLE BILL
Bill Engelhart, born in 1940 in Brainero, Minnesota, is an unlikely choice for a rock 'n roll legend. At age six, polio left his legs almost useless and forced him to motivate using arm-braces. By his teens his family was living in Tacoma and Bill was attending a vocational high school learning a trade. He turned inward, relying on music to soothe his physical anguish. He became proficient on the guitar and organ. In 1956, he joined the Bluenotes, a combo that, by 1958, included Buck Ormsby, bass; Tom Geving, tenor sax; Lassie Aanes, drums; Frank Dutra, tenor sax; Buck Mann, baritone sax; and Robin Roberts, vocals. The Bluenotes were one of the few local bands using a full horn section with which they duplicated the best R&B of the day. They paid for a session at a Seattle studio, and toward the end, with time remaining, they recorded an impromptu version of "I Love an Angel." The studio owner contacted Dolton Records, Seattle's only viable label, and soon the Bluenotes were rerecording "I Love an Angel," in a style that came straight from Louisiana. The record was released as by Little Bill and the Bluenotes although the band never referred to itself as such. It quickly topped the local charts and made a respectable showing nationally. Dissension among the group over Engelhart's billing forced Ormsby and Roberts out, and the Bluenotes ceased to exist. In 1960, Little Bill had a regional hit with "Sweet Cucumber" on Topaz. A year later, he recorded a version of Richard Berry's 1957 classic "Louie Louie," which was covered by Rockin' Robin Roberts. This was two years before the hit version by the Kingsmen, another band from the area. Engelhart worked in various bands for the next ten years, traveling from Alaska to California. Back in Seattle since 1978, he continues to front popular club bands, while recording an occasional album of excellent rhythm and blues.

Roy Brown performs during the afternoon for Lincoln Beachcombers on Lake Pontchartrain in New Orleans.

New Releases for the second week in June include two from Atlantic: the two-part "What'd I Say" by Ray Charles and "Just One Kiss" by Chuck Willis; two versions of "Sugaree": by Rusty York on Chess and by Hank Ballard and the Midnighters on King; two from Challenge: "Primrose Lane" by Jerry Wallace and "Little Lover" by Dean Beard; Rosco Gordon's "No More Doggin'" on Vee-Jay; Link Wray's "Comanche" on Epic; Little Richard's "Shake a Hand" on Specialty; Jackie Lee's "Happy Vacation" on Swan; Warren Storm's "I've Got My Heart In My Hand" on Nasco; and Jerry Butler's "Rainbow Valley" on Abner.

JUN 9   Bobby Darin begins a month-long engagement at the Sahara Hotel and Casino in Las Vegas. He backs George Burns, who is making his debut nightclub engagement in Las Vegas.

Sam Cooke headlines a revue at the Coliseum Arena in New Orleans. Also on the bill are Jackie Wilson, Marv Johnson, the Falcons, the Midnighters, Jesse Belvin, Baby Washington, Johnny "Guitar" Watson, and Sil Austin's combo.

JUN 11   The **Wailers** visit "American Bandstand" to perform "Tall Cool One."

JUN 12   The "Record Stars on Parade" show at Chicago's Tivoli Theater features Dave "Baby" Cortez, the Virtues, and the Moonglows.

Saxophonist Red Prysock rocks his way through a gig at La Maina's Musical Bar in Philadelphia.

New Orleans' Dew Drop Cafe welcomes Amos Milburn for the first of two weekend engagements.

JUN 13   Preston Epps performs "Bongo Rock" and Dee Clark sings "Just Keep It Up" on tonight's "Dick Clark Show." Also on hand are Carl Dobkins, Jr. and Mark Damon.

Dinah Washington is in London for television appearances.

JUN 14   Brook Benton guests on "The Ed Sullivan Show" on CBS-TV.

The Applejacks featuring Dave Appell are booked for a week into the Steel Pier in Atlantic City.

Lloyd Price performs for a "Welcome Home Dance" at the Rosenwald Gym in New Orleans.

JUN 15   Clyde McPhatter opens at Blinstrub's in Boston.

Ray Charles entertains fun-lovers on the Delaware River boat ride with a production titled "Opus in Jazz."

In Detroit, B. B. King and Wilbert Harrison bring their blues show to the Elk's Auditorium.

New Releases for the third week in June include Ricky Nelson' "Sweeter That You" b/w "Just a Little Too Much" on Imperial; Bobby Rydell's

THE WAILERS

Like Bill Engelhart, the Wailers have a long history as one of Tacoma's early rock 'n roll bands. When Buck Ormsby and Rockin Robin Roberts left Little Bill and the Bluenotes in 1959, they joined the Wailers. At the time, the group also included John Greek lead guitar; Richard Dangel, guitar; Mark Marush, sax; Kent Morrill, piano and vocals; and Mike Burke, drums. The combo had first formed in October 1958 when they met at a jam session. Their first single, released on the local Golden Crest label, was an impressive instrumental, "Tall Cool One." The single featured a jazz-influenced opening which was followed by a pounding, sax-led middle section, with each portion alternating until the record fades. In an era of instrumental combos, the Wailers were able to ride "Tall Cool One" into the national charts. The follow-up single, "Mau Mau" b/w "Dirty Robber" also found a national audience. There were several more singles on Golden Crest in 1960, before the group began recording for their own Etiquette label. The first Etiquette release found the Wailers backing Rockin' Robin Roberts on his version of "Louie, Louie" in 1961. Very shortly thereafter, the combo issued "Mashi," another instrumental with an offbeat musical style. Over the next few years, both Golden Crest and Etiquette released singles by the group. In 1964, when "Tall Cool One" became a national hit once again, "Mashi" was leased to Imperial Records for re-release. By this time, the group's sound was being identified with the surf music fad. Years later, the Wailers were hailed as the first punk band, with "Dirty Robber" and "Out of Our Tree" being touted as classics. The Wailers also recorded in an R&B style for United Artists, Viva and Bell into 1968. The Wailers, and their cohorts the Sonics, paved the way for the many bands from the Seattle area who revived the flagging music scene in the early 1990s.

"Kissin' Time" on Cameo; Frankie Ford's "Alimony" on Ace; Robin Luke's "Five Minutes More" on Dot; "Miami" by **Eugene Church** on Class; "Leave My Kitten Alone" by Little Willie John on King; "Helpless" by the Solitaires on Old Town; "Bells, Bells, Bells" by Billy and Lillie on Swan; "Shakey" by Bill Haley and His Comets on Decca; "High School Yearbook" by Ray Stevens on NRC; Billy Riley's "Got The Water Boiling" on Sun; "Honeydripper" by King Curtis on Atco; "Let Your Conscience Be Your Guide" by Sonny Boy on Checker; Herbie Alpert's "Hully Gully" on Andex; and Buck Rogers' "Crazy Baby" on Montel.

MID-JUNE

Johnny Cash and Skeets McDonnald are playing one-nighters in New Mexico.

The Mystics are on a short promotional tour of the Midwest.

Bobby Darin inaugurates his own label, Addison Records. He will work as artist and repertoire director for the company but will continue to record for Atco.

Suffering from ulcers, Jack Scott is discharged from the U.S. Army after five months.

The Everly Brothers' current tour of Australia, especially the cities of Sydney and Melbourne, is very successful. Also along to entertain are actor/singers Tab Hunter and Sal Mineo.

Angelo D'Aleo, tenor with Dion and the Belmonts, joins the U. S. Navy for a six-month tour of duty. The vocal group continues to perform as a trio.

Jimmie Rodgers is booked for a few days at Ottawa's Chaudiere nitery.

JUN 16 Bobby Freeman opens a three-week stand at the Cloisters in Chicago.

JUN 17 In an appeal for funds for handicapped children, Fabian and Frankie Avalon make a non-singing personal appearance at 13th and Market Street in their hometown of Philadelphia.

JUN 18 Bobby Freeman makes a quick round trip from Chicago to Philadelphia to make an afternoon appearance on "American Bandstand" singing "Mary Ann Thomas."

Johnny Cash, just back from a tour of Alaska, performs as part of the annual Jimmie Rodgers Day celebration in Meridian, Mississippi.

Roy Brown returns to Lincoln Beach in New Orleans. He will perform nightly, except Mondays, for the next several weeks.

JUN 19 Della Reese is this week's entertainment at the Flame Show Bar in Detroit.

LaVern Baker takes the spotlight at Washington's Howard Theater this week. Sharing the bill are the Falcons, the Impalas, Ray Peterson, and Little Joe and the Thrillers.

JUN 20 The Mystics make their television debut on "The Dick Clark

EUGENE CHURCH

The professional recording career of Eugene Church reads like a who's who roster of mid-1950s Los Angeles. Born in Dallas (some sources list St. Louis) on January 23, 1938, he moved to L. A. as a child. In 1955, his cousin, Mel Williams, who was a regular with the Johnny Otis revue, invited him to attend a recording session for the Sheiks. So loose were the "rules" at the time in L. A. that Church found himself singing backup with Williams, Jesse Belvin and Harold Lewis on the Sheiks' "So Fine," released on Federal. That night, Church and Belvin formed a lifelong friendship. In 1956, their next venture was "Girl of my Dreams" on Modern, featuring the duet as the Cliques. After one more Cliques single, Church had a lone release on Specialty, "Open Up Your Heart," that listed him as the soloist, although the record also featured Belvin with Gaynell and Alex Hodge of the Turks. He then recorded as the Saxons on Contender with one release, "Rock & Roll Show." The song is quite similar to his biggest hit, "Pretty Girls Everywhere" on Class, recorded as by Eugene Church and the Fellows. Membership in the Fellows was as loose-knit as all of his previous groups. Among those who passed through the group were both Hodges, Tommy "Buster" Williams, Richard Berry (famous as the composer of "Louis, Louie"), and Belvin. "Pretty Girls Everywhere" rambunctious tune that was a Top Forty "pop" hit and a Top Ten R&B hit during the opening months of 1959. On its strength, the follow-up single, "Miami," did almost as well. Church remained with Class into 1960. Then he went to Class' sister label, Rendezvous, for one single before going to King for five singles into 1963. With no hits in four years, Church returned to Dallas and retired from music. He became ill in the early 1990s and died on April 16, 1993.

JOHNNY PRESTON
"Running Bear" is one of the least-likely songs to have been a rock 'n roll Number One million seller. John Preston Courville was born in Port Arthur, Texas, on August 18, 1939. In high school he formed an R&B group, the Shades, (with Johnny Wilson and Kearny Rivette) to play local teen dances. However, a career in music was the furthest thing from his mind as he enrolled in Lamar University in nearby Beaumont. He was set on a business degree. He kept the Shades together, and one evening while playing a club in Beaumont, he was approached by J. P. Richardson (The Big Bopper) and Bill Hall of TFC-Hall and Hallway Records. Richardson had yet to record "Chantilly Lace," and was the afternoon deejay on KTRM in Beaumont. He had recorded for the D label, and was negotiating a contract with Mercury for release of his local hit, "Chantilly Lace." Once on Mercury, Richardson made a pitch for Preston (as he now called himself). Preston's first session produced nothing usable, so Richardson offered him a new composition, "Running Bear." The Bopper did not live to see his song come to fruition in Preston's rendition. Released in June, then delayed until August because of legal matters arising from the Bopper's death, the song went nowhere until late fall when it broke in St. Louis. A bouncy ditty about "Little White Dove" and the love of her life, "Running Bear," complete with Indian "ugh's" (reportedly sung by the Bopper & George Jones!) defied all logic and became a best seller. Preston followed with "Cradle of Love," "Feel So Fine," "Leave My Kitten Alone," and "Free Me" over the course of the next two years. As his sales declined, he switched to Hallway and TCF-Hall, and he issued a total of five singles between the two. In the 1960s, Preston moved from label to label: ABC, Imperial, 20th Century-Fox.

Show." Also appearing tonight are Sam Cooke, James Darren, Stonewall Jackson, Julius LaRosa, and Tony Bellus, singing "Robbin' the Cradle."

Brenda Lee guests once again on television's "Jubilee U.S.A."

Johnny Cash takes to the road with a show in El Paso. He plays Albuquerque tomorrow night.

JUN 21   Fabian makes his another appearance on the eleventh anniversary special edition of CBS-TV's "The Ed Sullivan Show."

Carl Perkins entertains the crown in a one-nighter in Houston.

JUN 22   Sam Cooke opens for a week at the Casino Royal in Washington, DC.

New Releases for the fourth week in June include five from Mercury: Brook Benton's "Thank You Pretty Baby," "Riffin' With Red" by Red Prysock, "Running Bear" by **Johnny Preston**, "Pink Petticoats" by the Big Bopper, and Sarah Vaughan's "Broken Hearted Melody." Other releases through the end of June are "Linda Lu" by Ray Sharpe on Jamie; two from RCA: Elvis Presley's "A Big Hunk O' Love" b/w "My Wish Came True" and the Browns' "The Three Bells;" Gary Stites' "Hey Little Girl" on Carlton; James Darren's "Angel Face" on Colpix; Mitchell Torok's "Caribbean" on Guyden; Jimmy Clanton's "My Own True Love" on Ace; "Sleep Walk" by Santo and Johnny on Canadian-American; "Night Train" by the Champs on Challenge; "The Ballad of Billy Joe" by Jerry Lee Lewis on Sun; two from Johnny Cash: "I Forgot To Remember To Forget" on Sun and "Five Feet High and Rising" on Columbia; two from M-G-M: Conway Twitty's "Mona Lisa" and Clyde McPhatter's "Twice As Nice;" "Right Now" by Gene Vincent and His Blue Caps on Capitol; "In The Mood" by the Ernie Fields Orchestra on Rendezvous; "Lifeguard Man" by Dale Hawkins on Checker; Kathy Linden's "You Don't Know Girls" on Felsted; two from Fraternity: Dale Wright's "Forget It" and "Too Much In Love" by Bill Parsons; "Little Bitty Johnny" by Travis and Bob on Sandy; Jerry Reed's "Soldier's Joy" on NRC; "Where'd She Go" by Johnnie and Joe on J & S; "Until Then" by Cookie and the Cupcakes on Judd; Ray Vernon's "Sugar Plum" on Liberty; and "Play The Game Fair" by the Shields on Tender.

JUN 23   At Coney Island's Moonlight Gardens in Cincinnati, the first in a series of Tuesday-night shows aimed at the teen audience features Gary Stites, Freddy Cannon, Johnny and the Hurricanes, Carl Dobkins, Jr., the Mystics, and Frankie Ford.

"The Jimmie Rodgers Show" on NBC-TV offers the talents of Kathy Linden.

JUN 24   Billy Williams performs at the Starlight Roof of the Chase Hotel in St. Louis.

JUN 26   The Everly Brothers and many country stars perform in Portland as part of the city's Centennial celebration. The shows run through July 5.

Johnny Cash, along with Lorrie Collins and the Big Beats, gives a show in Salem, Oregon. Other dates include the Portland Centennial (27); and Eureka, California (28). Lorrie is half of the Collins Kids team.

In New York, the Apollo Theater welcomes another "Dr. Jive's Rhythm and Blues Show." Headlining is Brook Benton. He is supported by Nappy Brown, the Shirelles, **Wilbert Harrison**, the Imperials, and Shirley and Lee.

In Washington, the Roy Hamilton "Summer Starlite Revue" begins a week-long run at the Howard Theater. The only other R&B acts on the bill is the Solitaires.

JUN 27 In Bridgeport, Connecticut, Connie Francis and Tommy Leonetti entertain at the Eleventh Annual P. T. Barnum Festival.

Paul Anka, Jack Scott, Dee Clark, Jerry Keller, and the Tassels entertain tonight on "The Dick Clark Show."

JUN 28 Frankie Avalon and Lloyd Price are the guests on CBS-TV's "The Ed Sullivan Show."

Dick Clark's first one-hour ABC-TV special, "The Record Years," features performances from pop and jazz entertainers. Representing rock 'n roll are Fats Domino and Fabian. The Trendex service gives the show a 50.6 share and a 24.8 rating. (A share is a percentage of the sets actually turned on at the time; a rating is a percentages of the total number of sets in the country.)

JUN 29 "American Bandstand" plays host to Sam Cooke who performs "Everybody Likes to Cha Cha Cha."

In Washington, Billy Storm begins a one-week stand at the Casino Royal.

JUN 30 The Drifters sing "There Goes My Baby" on "American Bandstand."

Della Reese opens at the Desert Inn in Las Vegas.

In Cincinnati, Fabian performs at the weekly teen dance at Coney Island's Moonlight Gardens.

LATE JUNE

Little Richard, back in Hollywood after a gospel music tour, announces that he will record spiritual songs for Gone/End Records.

In Boston, a municipal judge postpones indefinitely any further hearings on charges filed against Alan Freed as a result of the May 3, 1958, riot.

WILBERT HARRISON
Before the age of synthesizers and overdubbing, Wilbert Harrison was the only "one-man band" to have a Number One hit. Born in Charlotte, North Carolina, January 6, 1929, he was thirty when he first tasted success. He began recording in Miami in 1953 for Rockin' Records then moved to Newark, New Jersey. In 1954, he recorded "Don't Drop It" for Savoy Records, where he remained for the next five years (during which time he never had a hit). In 1959, he approached Savoy about re-recording "K. C. Lovin'," a song that had been a best seller for Little Willie Littlefield in 1953. Savoy declined; Harrison sought out Bobby Robinson, who teamed Harrison with guitarist Jimmy Spruill (who would soon work on Elmore James' sessions for Robinson). The result was a cohesive, jumping version that Robinson released in March 1959 on his own Fury label as "Kansas City." As Robinson said later, the record broke "like a thunder storm." In April, Savoy sued Fury, claiming an exclusive contract with Harrison dated November 1954. The next month, Fury was sued by the Armo Music for copyright infringement of "K. C. Lovin'," which had been composed by Jerry Leiber and Mike Stoller. None of this legal wrangling slowed the sales of "Kansas City." It went all the way to Number One. The main casualty was Harrison. The lawsuits stopped Fury from releasing new material for six months, and he was unable to come up with a hit in nine more releases with the label. In 1970, long after Harrison had retreated from the music scene, Sue Records issued his "Let's Work Together," a strange semi-blues featuring Harrison as a one-man band, playing guitar, drums, harmonica and piano. The single sold very well—considering. After that, Harrison did vanish. Not so "Kansas City." Over the decades, the song became a staple for bar bands around the world, including the Beatles. Harrison died of a stroke, October 26, 1994.

THE TOP ROCK 'N ROLL RECORDS FOR JUNE 1959

1. Dream Lover - Bobby Darin
2. Personality - Lloyd Price
3. Kansas City - Wilbert Harrison
4. Teenager In Love - Dion and the Belmonts
5. The Happy Organ - Dave "Baby" Cortez
6. Kookie, Kookie, Lend Me Your Comb - Edd "Kookie" Byrnes and Connie Stevens
7. Tallahassee Lassie - Freddy Cannon
8. Sorry, I Ran All The Way Home - The Impalas
9. So Fine - The Fiestas
10. Turn Me Loose - Fabian
11. Endlessly/So Close - Brook Benton
12. Lipstick on Your Collar/Frankie - Connie Francis
13. Along Came Jones - The Coasters
14. Goodbye, Jimmy, Goodbye - Kathy Linden
15. I'm Ready - Fats Domino
16. Lonely Boy - Paul Anka
17. (Now and Then There's) A Fool Such As I/I Need Your Love Tonight -Elvis Presley
18. Pink Shoelaces - Dodie Stevens
19. Bobby Sox to Stockings/A Boy Without a Girl - Frankie Avalon
20. Guitar Boogie Shuffle - The Virtues
21. Just Keep It Up - Dee Clark
22. Bongo Rock - Preston Epps
23. Take a Message To Mary/Poor Jenny - The Everly Brothers
24. Crossfire - Johnny and the Hurricanes
27. My Heart Is An Open Book - Carl Dobkins, Jr.
26. Lonely For You - Gary Stites
27. That's Why - Jackie Wilson
28. Guess Who - Jesse Belvin
29. You're So Fine - The Falcons
30. I've Come of Age - Billy Storm
31. I Only Have Eyes For You - The Flamingos
32. The Class - Chubby Checker
33. Tell Him No - Travis and Bob
34. The Wonder of You - Ray Peterson
35. Graduation's Here - The Fleetwoods
36. Almost Grown - Chuck Berry
37. Come To Me - Marv Johnson
38. Come Softly To Me - The Fleetwoods
39. Tall Cool One - The Wailers
40. Three Stars - Tommy Dee
41. Hushabye - The Mystics
42. Since I Don't Have You - The Skyliners
43. Rockin' Crickets - The Wild Cats
44. Ring-A-Ling-A-Lario - Jimmie Rodgers
45. What A Diff'rence A Day Makes - Dinah Washington

46. Six Nights a Week - The Crests
47. This I Swear - The Skyliners
48. Robbin' The Cradle - Tony Bellus
49. Old Spanish Town - The Bell Notes
50. Mona Lisa - Carl Mann

Also on the "pop" charts:
Waterloo - Stonewall Jackson
Little Dipper - Mickey Mozart Quintet
My Melancholy Baby - Tommy Edwards

June 1959
ARTIST OF THE MONTH

BOBBY DARIN

Bobby Darin

Bobby Darin was one of the premier song stylists of the late 1950s. His astounding career continued almost unabated through the 1960s. Still, with Bobby Darin there was always that sense of "what might have been."

Those who knew him best recall his boundless energy. He was a human dynamo. Others thought he was overly brash—a genuine pain in the butt. Both sides agree that it never occurred to him that he might not become a big star.

Robert Walden Cassotto was born May 19, 1936, in a low-income Bronx neighborhood in upper New York City. He never knew his Italian father, who died a few months before Bobby was born. His mother was from England where she had been a professional entertainer for many years. After her husband's death, she was forced to raise Bobby and his sister, Nina, on welfare payments. As a child, Bobby was sickly and often did not receive the medical attention he needed. At age eight, he suffered with rheumatic fever and the disease left him with a weakened heart, a condition that remained with him the rest of his life.

By the time he attended the Bronx High School of Science, Bobby was already an accomplished musician. However, he was too impatient to stick with one instrument until he completely mastered it. He quicklypicked pick up enough technique to play drums, then switched to guitar. In this manner, he also learned to play piano, bass and vibraphone. At age fifteen, he was playing drums in a local band that also included Walter Raim on piano.

After high school, Bobby entered Hunter College on a scholarship. His association with higher education lasted only a year. He spent his time away from classes prowling Times Square looking for a way to get into show business. He was torn between wanting to be an actor and a musician. Consequently, he alternated between trying to get auditions

---

(*The year of birth is also given as 1937.)

for stage shows and hounding music publishers with his songs. In both cases, he met with little positive reaction. As he became more familiar with the ground rules required to become a successful performer, he decided to change his last name from the ethnic Cassotto to the more generic Darin. In his usual style, once he had decided to make the change, he quickly chose his new name out of a telephone book, picking the first one that sounded usable.

Darin's combo was playing small clubs. At the same time, he was singing jingles and making demonstration records for other songwriters when he could find the work. His tenacity eventually brought him a personal manager who secured a one-year contract for Darin with Decca Records in 1956. Two years earlier, Decca had signed one of rock 'n roll's biggest acts, Bill Haley and His Comets. However, Decca was also one of the world's largest record companies, and this sluggish corporation was unable to capitalize on its past success when it came to this new form of music. Not that Decca didn't try. The company signed dozens of aspiring singers during the years following "Rock Around the Clock."

Bobby Darin was a prime example of Decca's misdirection. Instead of harnessing Darin's exuberance, they placed him in a restrained musical setting and had him sing "pop" fluff such as "Silly Willy," "Blue-Eyed Mermaid," and a cover version of "Rock Island Line." Darin was confused and frustrated. When he happened to meet Connie Francis, he found another artist who felt the same way. She was having difficulty finding her niche with M-G-M Records.

Darin's instincts about rock 'n roll were clear, and he followed those instincts to Atlantic Records, the home of Ray Charles, Joe Turner, Clyde McPhatter, LaVern Baker, the Drifters, Coasters, and the Clovers. Atlantic signed Darin to a one-year contract and placed him with their Atco subsidiary. Darin was assigned duties as an arranger and songwriter, and secondarily as a recording artist. Even before his first single on Atco was released, Darin's "Love Me Right" was recorded by LaVern Baker. Much to Darin's obvious chagrin, his first three singles for Atco lacked a real knockout punch. "I Found a Million Dollar Baby," "Don't Call My Name," and "Just In Case You Change Your Mind" each sank quietly from view shortly after its release.

Darin was disheartened. He was only weeks away from the one-year deadline on his Atco contract and had one final single set for release. He knew that he had the right material for a teen-oriented hit. In June 1958, Darin had approached Brunswick Records, one of Decca's subsidiaries, with a thumping rocker titled "Early in the Morning." Brunswick was impressed, but because he was still under contract to Atco, "Early in the Morning" was issued as by the Ding Dongs. There was an immediate reaction from New York deejays to the record; and, in short order, Atco discovered the deception. Brunswick was forced to turn over the master tape to Atco, which released the Darin single as by the Rinky Dinks. Brunswick, now fully convinced that the song had the potential to be a hit, had Buddy Holly cover it. Both versions of "Early in the Morning" came out the first week of July. After two television appearances on "The Dick Clark Show" and one on "The Perry Como Show," the Darin version went on the edge out the Holly version in sales, however both were only moderate hits.

While all of this was happening, also in early June, Atco released the final single under Darin's contract. The song was another up-tempo tune that Darin had recorded the previous April. "Splish Splash" was a novelty rocker that mentioned other hit records of the day like "Good Golly, Miss Molly," "Movin' and Groovin'" and "Peggy Sue." The song had reportedly been composed in ten minutes, and it sounded like it. And, as soon as it hit the streets, it quickly sold a million copies.

After "Splish Splash," there were two similar rock 'n roll singles from Darin including "Queen of the Hop" (another million-seller recorded during the "Splish Splash" session) and "Plain Jane." Between the two, Atco released a holdover from the earlier Rinky Dinks' session, "Mighty Mighty Man." This one was so bad it could have ended the career of a lesser performer. But, not Bobby Darin.

During the December 1958 sessions that produced "Plain Jane," Darin also recorded an album's worth of songs with a brass-heavy big band. For some time, Bobby had envisioned himself as the heir to Frank Sinatra's crown as a masterful jazz singer. Using arrangements by Richard Wess, Darin belted out swinging versions of old standards like "Beyond the Sea," as well as a version of the theme from the hit musical "The Three Penny Opera." However, Darin was in the middle of a string of rock 'n roll hits, so the release of the album was shelved for several months.

"Dream Lover" was released in March 1959. The song was built upon a Latin dance rhythm, a shuffle beat nicknamed "cha-lypso." The tune represented a subtle change in Darin's choice of music, away from songs with a simplistic rock 'n roll structure and toward songs designed to appeal to a more mature audience. The ploy worked, and "Dream Lover" became his third million-selling single.

Darin's big band album, THAT'S ALL, was finally released in the late spring. To nearly everyone's surprise, the theme song from "The Three Penny Opera" began getting airplay on radio stations almost immediately. The song had been an instrumental hit in 1956 for several artists under the title "Moritat." Louis Armstrong had even had a Top Twenty vocal version of the song in 1956 under the name "Mack the Knife." Darin's rendition leaned heavily on the stylized vocal inflections developed Sinatra. Interestingly, Sinatra's music career had peaked with "Witchcraft" in early 1958, and he wouldn't have another top hit single until 1966.

"Mack the Knife" defied all the preconceived notions for having a hit record in 1959. Except those devised by Bobby Darin. He was making music in the form that he felt he was best suited. The single sold two million copies and topped the record charts for months. "Mack the Knife" received the Grammy Award as Record of the Year. Darin was voted the Best New Artist—after three years of trying.

By the end of 1959, Bobby Darin was sitting on top of the musical world. He had gone from playing state fairs during the late summer to headlining at the finest supper clubs including the Chez Paree in Chicago and Sciolla's in Philadelphia by Christmas. He packed them in to the showroom at the Sands in Las Vegas, and he seemed to be on television at least once a week. He had made more than enough money to buy a home in New Jersey on Lake Hiawatha, about thirty miles west of the Bronx.

Darin, everyone said, was "in a groove."

(Bobby Darin's story will continue in the next volume of THE GOLDEN AGE OF AMERICAN ROCK 'N ROLL.)

July 1959

JUL 1   Jimmy Clanton stops by "American Bandstand" to plug "My Own True Love."

           In Albany, New York, the "Tower of Talent" show brings in Frankie Avalon, Connie Francis, Gary Stites, Kathy Linden, the Impalas, the Playmates, Annette, and Jerry Keller.

           The Everly Brothers appear at the International Frontier Fair in Detroit.

JUL 3   Brook Benton, the Crests, Wade Flemons, and Beverly Ann Gibson entertain patrons at the Howard Theater this week in Washington.

           The Apollo Theater in New York presents the Coasters and the Falcons for the first night of a week-long engagement.

           Big Jay McNeeley is in the New Orleans area. Tonight he performs at the Masonic Hall in Algiers. On July 4, he entertains at the Blue Eagle Club in the Crescent City. On July 5, he remains in New Orleans for a show at the Labor Union Hall.

           This afternoon on "American Bandstand," Ray Peterson sings "The Wonder of You."

JUL 4   On this Independence Day, Johnny Cash performs in Honolulu for two days as part of the yearlong celebration as Hawaii anticipates becoming the nation's 50th state on August 21.

           In New Orleans, Tommy Ridgely and his orchestra, along with Roy Brown, perform at Lincoln Beach for the holiday.

           On television, Tommy Sands, the Playmates, Jackie Lee, and Clyde McPhatter are spotlighted on "The Dick Clark Show."

JUL 7   This Tuesday in Cincinnati, it's Jack Scott and Dale Wright who are in the spotlight at Coney Island's Moonlight Gardens.

New Releases for the first week in July include Fats Domino's "I Want To Walk You Home" b/w "I'm Gonna Be A Wheel Someday" on Imperial; LaVern Baker's "So High, So Low" on Atlantic; "Red River Rock" by Johnny and the Hurricanes on Warwick; "(Baby) Hully Gully" by the Olympics on Arvee; Paul Peek's "Waikiki Beach" on NRC; "That's Right" by the Bell Notes on Time; Johnny Tillotson's "True, True Happiness" on Cadence; "Boogie Bear" by Boyd Bennett and His Rockets on Mercury; Charlie Rich's "Rebound" on Phillips International; "I've Been There" by Tommy Edwards on M-G-M; Jo Ann Campbell's "Beachcomber" on Gone; **Doug Sahm**'s "Crazy Daisey" on Warrior; "I Like Girls" by Nervous Norvous on Embee; Dean Hawley's "New Fad" on Dore; and "Always

DOUG SAHM
Douglas Wayne Sahm has had enough careers for half a dozen musicians. His style of music is diverse enough to allow him to record with Junior Parker, Bob Dylan and Flaco Jiminez. He was born November 6, 1941 (or 1942), in San Antonio, Texas. By the time he was six, he had learned to play almost any instrument with strings. By age eleven, he was statewide sensation on steel guitar and a veteran of two years on the Mutual Radio Network. He had already played the "Louisiana Hayride" and the "Big D Jamboree." Back home, he was a regular performer in San Antonio's premier C&W club, The Barn. In 1955, as Little Doug, he recorded his first single, "A Real American Joe," for Sarg Records of nearby Luling, Texas. The single led to Sahm being asked to join the "Grand Ole Opry." He turned down the invitation to stay in junior high. By 1959, he had fallen under the dual spell of rock 'n roll and R&B when he released his second single, "Crazy Daisey" on Warrior. As local sales increased it was also released by Satin Records. Since then, Sahm has had dozens of records released on a myriad of labels, most of which were local and Texan. In the early days, these included Harlem, Cobra, Renner, Swingin', and Personality. Sahm recorded for Major Bill Smith's Soft label and Huey P. Meaux's Pacemaker. In 1964, he formed the Sir Douglas Quintet in answer to the English rock invasion and began recording for Tribe Records, another Meaux enterprise distributed by London Records. His first Tribe release "She's About a Mover," was a fine example of Sahm's ability to combine rock influences with Tex-Mex border rhythms. Continued success has always eluded Sahm. Of his next six releases, only "The Rains Came" was a hit. This was followed by another year of "lost" singles. In 1968, Sahm and the Quintet moved to the northern California coast. A year later, they paid tribute to the area in their last big hit, "Mendocino."

My Darling" by the Cadillacs on Josie. New this week also is Chan Romero's "The Hippy Hippy Shake" on Del-Fi. Romero, from Billings, Montana, auditioned for Del-Fi by playing a tape during a long distance telephone call. His version of "The Hippy Hippy Shake" fared poorly, but, in 1964, it was a big hit for the Swinging Blues Jeans, proving that fine songs never go out of style.

JUL 9   Faron Young appears on "American Bandstand."

Jul 10 Gospel is the mainstay this week at New York's Apollo Theater, with the Swan Silvertones headlining.
    The latest rock 'n roll movie, "Go, Johnny Go!" opens nationwide.
    Dee Clark, the Drifters, the Quin-Tones, the Isley Brothers, and Lulu Reed perform at the Howard Theater in Washington this week.

JUL 11 In England, the Poni-Tails make the first of three weekly guest television shots on "Drumbeat," a teen rock 'n roll show. They will return on July 18 and 25.
    "The Dick Clark Show" greets Anita Bryant, Dick Caruso, the Flamingos, and Connie Francis, who sings "Lipstick on Your Collar."

JUL 13 In Hollywood, Fabian begins production on his first motion picture, "Hound Dog Man."

JUL 14 In Cincinnati, Frankie Avalon headlines the Tuesday-night teen dance at Coney Island's Moonlight Gardens.

New Releases for the second week in July include "Breaking Up Is Hard To Do" by Jivin' Gene on Mercury; a reissue of "Nite Owl" by Tony Allen on Specialty; two from Warner Brothers: "Like I Love You" by Edd Byrnes and "Class of '59" by Bob Luman; "I'm Alright" by Little Anthony and the Imperials on End; "Clouds" by the Spacemen on Alton; Bobby Day's "Ain't Gonna Cry No More" on Class; Johnny Burnette's "Sweet Baby Doll" on Freedom; "Down By The River" by Wade Flemons on Vee-Jay; "Good, Good Lovin'" by James Brown and the Famous Flames on Federal; "Our Anniversary" by the Fiestas on Old Town; **Carole King**'s "Short Mort" on RCA; "I'm Confessin'" by the Chantels on Gone; and "The F.B.I. Story" by Rudy Grazell and the Thunderbirds on Award.

JUL 15 Connie Francis opens a four-day stand at the Bolero Club in Wildwood, New Jersey.
    Duane Eddy brings his "twangy guitar" to "American Bandstand" to perform "Forty Miles of Bad Road" and "The Quiet Three."

JUL 16 ABC-TV broadcasts "Oh Boy!" a teen-oriented British show. The guests include Cliff Richard and the Shadows, Lord Rockingham IV, and the John Barry Seven.

CAROLE KING

As a teenager, Carole King began composing songs for a group of friends who had formed a quartet called the Co-Signs. She was born Carol Klein, February 9, 1942, in Brooklyn. In high school, her boyfriend was Neil Sedaka. She graduated at age sixteen and entered Queens College where she met Gerry Goffin, who would become her husband. She was already recording by this time, having released "The Right Girl" on ABC-Paramount in May 1958. Carole had a half dozen singles before she had a national hit in 1962 with "It Might as Well Rain Until September" on the Dimension label, which she and Goffin had founded. By then, she was writing the music to Goffin's lyrics. Working out of the Brill Building on Broadway in New York City, the duo composed classic songs aimed directly at teens. In 1961, they had two Number One hits, the Shirelles' "Will You Still Love Me Tomorrow" and Bobby Vee's "Take Good Care of My Baby." On Dimension in 1962, they wrote, produced and released another Number One hit, Little Eva's "Loco-Motion." That same year they wrote "Up on the Roof, a Top Ten hit for the Drifters. In 1963, "One Fine Day" by the Chiffons reached Number One. Their music wasn't limited to American artists. In 1964, "I'm Into Something Good" was the first American hit for Herman's Hermits, and in 1965, "Don't Bring Me Down" was a best seller for the Animals. As music changed, so did the composing style of Goffin and King. In 1967, Aretha Franklin had a Top Ten record with "(You Make Me Feel Like) A Natural Woman." A year later, King and Goffin divorced. Many thought this would be the end of her musical career. However, in 1971 she began recording in earnest. Her first single on Ode Records, "It's Too Late," went to Number One and the album from which it came, TAPESTRY, sold 13 million copies and remained on the charts for and astounding six years.

Dale Wright make a personal appearance at the Bartholomew County Fair in Columbus, Indiana.

JUL 17   Roy Hamilton headlines the revue at the Apollo Theater in New York. Also on the bill are the Solitaires.

Lee Allen rocks the house at the Dew Drop Cafe in New Orleans for the next two weekends.

JUL 18   Kathy Linden, Chuck Berry, Bobby Rydell, Gary Stites, and Skip and Flip drop by "The Dick Clark Show" this evening.

JUL 19   Bill Doggett is booked for a matinee performance at the Flame Lounge in Detroit. His reception is so overwhelming that he is held over for a full week.

JUL 20   In Washington, DC, Connie Francis opens at the Casino Royal.

JUL 21   In Cincinnati, Coney Island's Moonlight Gardens offers the talents of the Addrisi Brothers, Skip and Flip, Carl Mann, Jo Ann Campbell, Jerry Keller, and Dicky Doo and the Don'ts.

Cozy Cole opens at the Metropole Cafe in New York.

New Releases for the third week in July include Lloyd Price's "I'm Gonna Get Married" on ABC-Paramount; "The Angels Listened In" by the Crests on Co-Ed; Eddie Cochran's "Somethin' Else" on Liberty; "The Shape I'm In" by Johnny Restivo on RCA; "I Ain't Never" by the Four Preps on Capitol; Jerry Fuller's "Betty, My Angel" on Challenge; "Virtue's Boogie Woogie" by the Virtues on Hunt; "Bad Girl" by the Miracles on Chess; "Dirty Robber" by the Wailers on Golden Crest; and "Hully Gully" by the Turks on Class. Also out this week is Jimmy Gilmer's "Look Alive" on Decca. Gilmer joined the Fireballs in 1961, and together they had several hits, including the Number One "Sugar Shack" in 1963.

JUL 23   The Everly Brothers are currently on tour. Tonight, they play Salt Lake City. Tomorrow its Casper, Wyoming.

JUL 24   Paul Anka opens a lengthy run in Knokke, Belgium. Sharing the spotlight is England's Petula Clark.

The Howard Theater in Washington offers a week-long jazz revue featuring Al Hibbler, Eddie "Lockjaw" Davis, and James Moody.

JUL 25   Eddie Cochran plays a one-nighter at the Shadow Lake Ballroom near Seattle.

Carl Mann performs "Mona Lisa" and the Falcons sing "You're So Fine" on tonight's "Dick Clark Show." Also appearing are Annette, Stonewall Jackson, and Eddie and Betty.

JUL 26   Chuck Berry's show brings in 1,300 fans to Nashville's Hippodrome.

CARL MANN

In 1959, Carl Mann and Conway Twitty were matched in a race up the music charts with virtually identical versions of a Nat King Cole song. Two more different young men it would be hard to imagine. At the time, Twitty was twenty-eight, married, ex-Army, and a veteran of the rock 'n roll circuit since 1955. He had tasted the sweet euphoria that comes with a Number One record ("It's Only Make Believe") and the frustration when the follow-up singles don't sell as well. Carl Mann was a sixteen-year old with only his aptitude as a pianist for credentials. He was born August 24, 1942, in Huntingdon, Tennessee. He formed his first band when he was twelve, and, as befits a combo trying to entertain in a rural setting, they played in many styles. Mann started on guitar, and it wasn't until the group's pianist quit that switched to piano. In 1959, Carl was in Jackson, Tennessee, playing in a band led by Eddie Bush. They were discovered by Carl Perkins' drummer who arranged an audition with Sun Records in Memphis. Sun had seen better days. Sun's stars had left for major record labels. Jerry Lee Lewis remained, but his records were banned in many areas. It would appear that what Sun Records didn't need was another piano-playing rocker. Mann's first single was a rollicking send-up of "Mona Lisa" which was issued on the Phillips International subsidiary. Twitty got wind of "Mona Lisa" and duplicated the arrangement. However, Mann's record was already attracting attention. In the late summer of 1959, the two singles leapfrogged up the charts. In the end, they sold about the same number of copies, and neither was as big as it might have been without the other's competition. Twitty went on to much greener pastures. Mann recorded jive versions of other standards including "Pretend," "Some Enchanted Evening" and "South of the Border," but his time in the spotlight had passed.

THE FIREBALLS

"Tex-Mex" was hot in 1959. Fueled by Buddy Knox, Buddy Holly, and the Champs, the mix of stinging guitar (usually a Fender) and Latin rhythms was a sure-fire crowd pleaser. The Fireballs were an instrumental combo with occasional vocals. The boys had just graduated from high school in Raton, New Mexico, where they were locally popular. In January 1959, they released "Fireball" on Kapp. The single sold well enough to bring them to Top Rank, a new record company with ties to England (where Holly and Knox were huge). The Fireballs used the same studio in Clovis, NM, as Knox and Holly. Top Rank allowed the band to indulge their Tex-Mex roots to the fullest. The Fireballs were George Tomsco, lead guitar; Stan Lark, bass; Dan Trammell, guitar; and Eric Budd, drums. Chuck Tharp was listed as vocalist, but had little to do. Their first Rank release, "Torquay," came in late summer 1959. It was bumpy and jumpy, like the singles being released by the Champs. It made the Top 40. "Bulldog," featuring an intricate rhythm line on guitar, cracked the Top 25. When it looked like the Fireballs were going to have a huge hit, the "pop" audience turned fickle. "Foot Patter" and "Vaquero" languished. The next two Top Rank releases did even worse. The group switched to the small Lucky label in an attempt to recapture the magic. Their only Lucky release, "Long, Long Ponitail," wasn't so lucky. The song was leased to Jaro Records, but still went nowhere. The combo moved on to Warwick Records, after Johnny and the Hurricanes departed. Their first release, Holly's sweet "True Love Ways," did nothing for the band. Three singles later, they had a minor hit with "Quite a Party." The group then recorded for 7 Arts and Hamilton before finally landing with Dot, where they again found success. (More on the Fireballs and their new singer, Jimmy Gilmer, in *The Golden Age of Rock 'n Roll*, Vol. 3.)

JUL 28   This Tuesday, Tommy Sands is the featured performer at the teen show at Coney Island's Moonlight Gardens in Cincinnati.

New Releases for the fourth week in July include "Just To Be With You" by the Passions on Audicon; "Caterpillar Crawl" by the Strangers on Titan; "Torquay" by the **Fireballs** on Top Rank; "'Til I Kissed You" by the Everly Brothers on Cadence; "Mary Lou" by Ronnie Hawkins and the Hawks on Roulette; "Love Potion No. 9" by the Clovers on United Artists; Buddy Holly's "Peggy Sue Got Married" on Coral; "Fog Cutter" by the Frantics on Dolton; "Joey's Song" by Bill Haley and His Comets on Decca; Sam Cooke's "Summertime" on Keen; "Little Johnny Green" by Bobby Hendricks on Sue; "A Door That Is Open" by Kripp Johnson on Mercury; and the Addrisi Brothers' "Saving My Kisses" on Del-Fi.

JUL 29   Trying for a second hit, Frankie Ford performs "Alimony" on "American Bandstand."
            At the Hippodrome in Nashville, Clyde McPhatter, Bo Diddley, the Crests, and Chubby Checker perform for the appreciative crowd.
            Bobby Freeman starts a week at the Flame in Detroit.

JUL 31   LaVern Baker opens at the Copa Club in Newport, Kentucky, for a three day stint.
            Carl Perkins and Brenda Lee share the spotlight at the county fair in Urbana, Illinois.
            The Pacific Paradise Ballroom in Honolulu welcomes Conway Twitty.

THE TOP ROCK 'N ROLL RECORDS FOR JULY 1959

1. Lonely Boy - Paul Anka
2. Personality - Lloyd Price
3. Lipstick On Your Collar/Frankie - Connie Francis
4. Dream Lover - Bobby Darin
5. Tallahassee Lassie - Freddy Cannon
6. Tiger - Fabian
7. Bobby Sox To Stockings/A Boy Without a Girl - Frankie Avalon
8. My Heart Is An Open Book - Carl Dobkins, Jr.
9. I Only Have Eyes For You - The Flamingos
10. Bongo Rock - Preston Epps
11. You're So Fine - The Falcons
12. Forty Miles of Bad Road/The Quiet Three - Duane Eddy
13. Hushabye - The Mystics
14. Just Keep It Up - Dee Clark
15. What A Diff'rence A Day Makes - Dinah Washington
16. There Goes My Baby - The Drifters
17. The Wonder Of You - Ray Peterson
18. This I Swear - The Skyliners
19. Lavender Blue - Sammy Turner
20. Along Came Jones - The Coasters

21. Robbin' The Cradle - Tony Bellus
22. Only Sixteen - Sam Cooke
23. I'll Be Satisfied - Jackie Wilson
24. Kansas City - Wilbert Harrison
25. Just A Little Too Much/Sweeter Than You - Ricky Nelson
26. Teenager In Love - Dion and the Belmonts
27. A Big Hunk O' Love/My Wish Came True - Elvis Presley
28. Back In The U.S.A. - Chuck Berry
29. Mona Lisa - Carl Mann
30. Remember When - The Platters
31. Since You've Been Gone - Clyde McPhatter
32. So Fine - The Fiestas
33. Ring-A-Ling-A-Lario/Wonderful You - Jimmie Rodgers
34. Crossfire - Johnny and the Hurricanes
35. There Is Something On Your Mind - Big Jay McNeely
36. I'm Ready - Fats Domino
37. Tall Cool One - The Wailers
38. Kookie, Kookie, Lend Me Your Comb - Edd "Kookie" Byrnes and Connie Stevens
39. Here Comes Summer - Jerry Keller
40. Forty Days - Ronnie Hawkins
41. What'd I Say - Ray Charles
42. I've Come Of Age - Billy Storm
43. It Was I - Skip and Flip
44. Sea of Love - Phil Phillips
45. Endlessly - Brook Benton
46. Lonely For You - Gary Stites
47. Velvet Waters - The Megatrons
48. Goodbye, Jimmy, Goodbye - Kathy Linden
49. The Way I Walk - Jack Scott
50. The Whistling Organ - Dave "Baby" Cortez

Also on the "pop" charts:
M.T.A. - Kingston Trio
Twixt Twelve and Twenty - Pat Boone

July 1959
ARTIST OF THE MONTH

FABIAN

In the hyperbole of teen-oriented magazines he was "The Fabulous Fabe." To the news media, he was rock 'n roll's answer to Hollywood's blonde bombshell. One critic even called him "the worst pop star in the world." Just how did such a nice guy end up with so much of the world's attention and criticism heaped on him?

Fabian was born Fabiano Antonio Forte on February 6, 1943. He

Fabian

grew up in Philadelphia's South Side, within blocks of the homes of Frankie Avalon and Bobby Rydell. He attended South Philly High and belonged to the same boys club as Avalon and Rydell. However, unlike those two Italian-Americans, Fabian had no desire to express himself musically.

As he was growing up, his family called him Tony, the diminutive variation of his middle name. By the age of ten, he was working as a janitor's assistant in their apartment building. When he was fourteen, his father, a Philadelphia police officer, suffered a heart attack. For months afterward, Fabian was forced to work extra jobs to help the family meet its financial obligations.

He tried out for a few sports teams in junior high school. He also auditioned for the school glee club. Unfortunately, his athletic prowess and his musical ability were equally dismal. However, he did have a God-given attribute that required no talent whatever. Even as a young teenager, Fabian's face was strikingly handsome. From the top of his light brown hair to the tip of his aristocratic jaw, from his deep blue eyes to his pouting lower lip, Fabian had the looks "to die for." According to Dick Clark, who ought to know, Fabian had "it."

The success of Frankie Avalon in 1958 led Bob Marcucci and Peter De Angelis on a talent search through the South Philly neighborhoods. At Avalon's suggestion, they looked up the Forte family, and discovered Fabian sitting on the front stoop. Legend has it that he was crying over the health of his father and the plight of his family. Without hesitation, Marcucci approached the fifteen-year old boy and asked him if he'd ever thought of being a rock 'n roll star. No matter what his future critics might think about him, Fabian was never anyone's fool. He was quoted as saying of his abrupt introduction to show business, "I only wanted to make some money... I was only in it for my family..."

In the hands of Marcucci and De Angelis, Fabian was given a complete make-over. He was dressed in new clothes, especially V-neck sweaters that were used to accentuate his facial features. His hair was piled high in a beautifully sculptured pompadour. His occasional bouts with acne were covered with pancake makeup. After his first, disastrous recording session, he enrolled with a vocal coach in hopes that he could develop a passable singing voice.

In June 1958, Fabian's first release on Chancellor Records was "I'm In Love" b/w "Shivers." The single's production mirrored the early releases by Frankie Avalon with one major exception. Behind Fabian's non-singing vocal was a prepubescent-sounding female vocal group. To promote the single's release, Fabian was sent on a short trip through the Midwest and East Coast to visit with deejays. On June 19, he even stopped by "American Bandstand." He was not asked to lip-sync his new record. All he had to do was look cute and answer a few easy questions from Dick Clark. The reaction to Fabian by the young females in the audience was pandemonium. As a result, on June 30, he made a second non-singing appearance on "Bandstand." That same evening he made his first personal appearance in Albany, New York.

All of this promotion brought Fabian's name and face to the American teenagers, but it could still not make "I'm In Love" into a hit. It also did little for his second single, "Lily Lou" b/w "Be My Steady Date," when it was released in September. Both sides of the record sounded like discarded remnants from one of Frankie Avalon's first sessions a year earlier, right down to the nasal vocal.

In November, "I'm a Man" was Fabian's third release. For two months, right through the Christmas season, it looked as though the single would suffer the same fate as his previous two. Then, through the magic of "American Bandstand," teens finally fell for Fabian's image. He appeared on the show on December 6. Six days later, he was back on "Bandstand." This time, he was finally allowed to mimic singing while his record played in the studio. Finally, after a January 17 appearance, "I'm a Man" began selling in moderate numbers. It didn't come close to the million mark in sales; but, considering Fabian's past track record, it was a hit.

In rock 'n roll, many acts are unable to build upon their first hit record. Marcucci and De Angelis were determined that this would not happen with Fabian. They had invested much time and money to insure that Fabian became a teen singing star. When "I'm a Man" started to sell, they reasoned that promoting an older image of Fabian was the route to success. As a result, the follow-up to "I'm a Man" was "Turn Me Loose." Gone was the whining vocal, replaced by a self-assured, growling baritone. Also missing was the female vocal group, their place having been filled by the Four Dates, the same group used behind Avalon's earliest successes. The next single, "Tiger," relied even more strongly on promoting Fabian as a dangerous date for the teenage female fan. It became his only gold record.

Fabian was still was a long way from being considered a serious vocalist. Dick Clark accurately accessed the situation this way: "Fabian got the screams though he couldn't sing a note." De Angeles, who acted as arranger on all of Fabian's early sessions, mixed the backing instrumental and vocal group tracks in thick layers to cover much of Fabian's singing. The net result was more of an impression that Fabian was singing rather than an actual voice to be critically dissected.

With his good looks and a few hit records, Fabian became one of the favorite images for the newly created teen-magazine industry. Throughout 1959 and 1960, his face seemed to be on every cover. Often, the stories inside the magazine offered little real insight, and could as easily have been written about Frankie, Freddy, Bobby, or Jimmy. Typical of the coverage were the "Win a Date with Fabian" contests aimed at swooning teenage girls.

Fabian was also a marketable product in the eyes of Hollywood's film producers. His first movie in 1959, the period piece "Hound Dog Man," also offered him his first starring role. The plot was thin, but he had a chance to sing the title song as well as three more tunes. In "Hound Dog Man," Fabian's acting was stilted, as might be expected, but he proved that he had drawing power with teenagers. He went on to co-star in "High Time" with Bing Crosby and "North to Alaska" with John Wayne (both in 1960). In 1961, he co-starred with Tommy Sands in the soon-forgotten romantic comedy, "Love in a Goldfish Bowl."

He was named "Most Promising Vocalist" in a 1959 poll. However, after having a Top Ten hit with "Hound Dog Man" in late 1959, what was left of his brief career disappeared by the end of 1960 as his singles of "This Friendly World," "String Along" and "Kissin' and Twistin'" each did less business than the one before. Shortly thereafter, he deserted the recording industry, leaving it to others with more talent.

He transferred his base of operations to Los Angeles, eventually living in the Toluca Lake area. It was his first time away from home and he was not yet twenty years old. He was frequently seen cruising around town in his flashy new Jaguar. He attended every party in the area, and it was reported that he had started drinking heavily and was smoking marijuana.

If there was no success for him in records, it looked as though he might find a lasting career in Hollywood. In 1962, he had a supporting roles in the comedies "Mr. Hobbs Takes a Vacation" with James Stewart and "Five Weeks in a Balloon" with Red Buttons. That same year, he appeared in "The Lion Walks Among Us," an episode of the television series "Bus Stop." His portrayal of a psychotic killer in "Bus Stop" may have been the high point of his acting career.

He began taking acting lessons in an attempt to garner better roles. He had a minor part in "The Longest Day," an epic war movie in 1963. In 1964, he followed Frankie Avalon into beach movies with his own starring vehicle, "Ride the Wild Surf." Fabian joined Frankie and Annette for "Fireball 500" in 1966. Then he became stuck in the genre of car movies, starring in "Thunder Alley" with Annette in 1967, "The Wild Racers" in 1968, and "The Devil's 8" in 1969.

Through the years, Fabian also co-starred in "Dear Brigitte" with James Stewart (1965) and "Ten Little Indians" with Hugh O'Brien and "Dr. Goldfoot and the Girl Bombs" with Vincent Price, both in 1966. He starred as a teacher in "Maryjane" in 1968 and had the title role of the gangster in "A Bullet for Pretty Boy" in 1970. In addition, he appeared in episodes of various television series and made-for-TV movies into the 1970s.

For Fabian, the 1970s were the worst of times. He was married with two children, and he was supporting his parents. He attempted a singing comeback when the rock 'n roll revival hit early in the decade. In New York, he was so frightened on stage that he couldn't sing. The movie roles had dwindled to forgettable roles in "Lovin' Man" (1972) and "Little Laura and Big John" (1973).

In an attempt to revive his flagging career, he posed for a controversial semi-nude layout in the September 1973 issue of *Playgirl* magazine. He was sued for assaulting his wife, Katie, and his mother-in-law. After he was divorced, he fell behind in child support payments. He subsisted on acting roles in the dismal "Disco Fever" (1979) and the later-day rock 'n roll epic "Get Crazy" (1983). His fitful movie career stalled after he starred as a drug-using wanderer in "Soul Hustler" in 1986. His continued failure to find substantial success led to long periods of psychoanalysis. Eventually, he was able to come to terms with himself as an individual.

Fabian has had plenty of time to look back over his days in the limelight. It's no wonder that for many years his attitude toward his past was one of nostalgia mixed with a generous helping of bitterness. "I was molded to fit a certain ideal," he has stated. When Johnny Horton was chosen to sing the theme song for "North to Alaska," Fabian realized early on that he was not being taken seriously as a performer. He often referred to his image as "plastic," something to be bought and sold with little care for the person who was Fabian. For that, he has regrets.

Like Frankie Avalon, Fabian continued his association with Dick Clark long after his status as a hit-maker was over. Through the 1980s, Fabian often headlined Clark's traveling revues, acting more as emcee that as aging teen idol. In the summer of 1985, he joined Avalon and Bobby Rydell for the popular "Boys of Bandstand" tour.

By the late 1980s, Fabian had settled into the business side of Hollywood, becoming a producer of films and events. The new-found stability in his life allowed time for another marriage. In 1993, he was music producer for the critically acclaimed Time-Warner television series "The Real West."

Having dispensed with his devils, the future looks brighter for Fabian now than at any time since 1958 when the girls were screaming and his records were all hits and Hollywood offered a pot of gold at the end of his rainbow.

August 1959

CLIFF RICHARD
Cliff Richard was the first English rocker to make a name for himself in America. He wouldn't be the last. He was born Harry Roger Webb, October 14, 1940, in Lucknow, India. In 1948, his family moved back to England, eventually settling in a London suburb. He joined the Quintones, a skiffle group, while attending secondary school. In 1957, he worked at a lamp factory by day while playing the local pubs at night. Within a year, he had formed a rock 'n roll band called Harry Webb and the Drifters. After months on the club circuit, the name was changed to Cliff Richard and the Drifters. A July 1958 talent show in London led to EMI Records and Richard's first single, "Move It." Although the Drifters were credited on the label, studio musicians were hired to play on Richard's first three records. He opened for the Kalin Twins on their tour of England and became a regular on UK television's "Oh Boy!" In six months, Richard was the toast of England as "Move It" peaked near the top of the English charts. In 1959, he released "High Class Baby," "Livin' Lovin' Doll," "Mean Streak," "Living Doll," and "Traveling Light." Each was a best seller in England, with "Living Doll" also becoming a mid-sized hit in America. That same year, he co-starred in two movies, "Serious Charge" and "Expresso Bongo." In the meantime, the Drifters changed their name to the Shadows to avoid confusion with the American R&B group. In January 1960, Richard toured America with Frankie Avalon. For years, Cliff Richard was the English equivalent of the American teen idol, although he would not have another charted single in America until 1963's "Lucky Lips." In 1976, with a push from Elton John's Rocket Records, his career finally caught fire in America. Over the next four years, he had Top Ten hits with "Devil Woman," "We Don't Talk Anymore" and "Dreaming."

AUG 1   Wanda Jackson performs on "The New Dominion Barn Dance" broadcast from Richmond, Virginia.
  Frankie Avalon is on the county fair circuit. Tonight he opens in Harrison, Delaware.
  Bill Haley and His Comets stop by "The Dick Clark Show" tonight. Also appearing are Lou Monte, Jackie Wilson, Santo and Johnny, and Jimmy Clanton, who sings "My Own True Love."

AUG 2   Ricky Nelson plays a two-day gig at the Indiana State Fair.
  The Platters make their third guest appearance on "The Ed Sullivan Show" singing "Remember When," "Dance With Me Henry" and "Darktown Strutter's Ball."

AUG 3   At Detroit's Windsor Arena, Count Basie and Joe Williams headline a show that also features LaVern Baker, Marv Johnson, the Miracles, Bobby Day, and Eddie Holland.

New Releases for the first week in August include two from Atco: Bobby Darin's "Mack the Knife" and "Poison Ivy" by the Coasters; two from Atlantic: "Papa Daddy" by Ruth Brown and "Got You On My Mind" by Joe Turner; "Hey Little Girl" by Dee Clark on Abner; Freddy Cannon's "Okefenokee" on Swan; Sanford Clark's "Run, Boy, Run" on Jamie; "Living Doll" by **Cliff Richard** and the Shadows on ABC-Paramount; two from Duke: "Is It Real" by Bobby "Blue" Bland and "Blue Letter" by Little Junior Parker; "I'm Grateful" by Trini Lopez on King; and Kenny Rankin's "I Cry By Night" on Decca. Also new this week is "Suzie Baby" by Bobby Vee and the Shadows on Liberty. The single had originally been issued on Soma, a local Minneapolis label.

AUG 3   Johnny Cash plays the Macon County Fair in Decatur, Ilinois.

AUG 4   Bobby Rydell offers "Kissin' Time" on "American Bandstand."
  Dick Clark and Frankie Avalon start a three-day personal appearance in Detroit.
  The Lincoln Beach Midway in New Orleans welcomes Clyde McPhatter, Bo Diddley, the Crests, and Chubby Checker for one big show.

AUG 5   Annette makes her second appearance on "American Bandstand" singing "Lonely Guitar."

AUG 6   On "American Bandstand," Eugene Church makes a rare television appearance singing "Miami."

AUG 7   The Coasters lead the bill at the Howard Theater in Washington for the week. Included on the show are Milt Buckner, Tiny Topsy and the Jesse Powell combo.
    Skip and Flip sing "It Was I" on "American Bandstand." Also, Dave "Baby" Cortez stops by the studio to perform "Whistling Organ" for the fans.
    Della Reese is playing the Regal Theater in Chicago this week.
    In Detroit, Dinah Washington moves into the Flame Show Bar for a week.

EARLY AUGUST

Huey Smith and the Clowns are on a tour of the West Indies though the month.

Johnny Cash, who recently made a cameo appearance on an episode of "Maverick" on television, is contracted to sing the title song of the new television series "The Rebel" starring Nick Adams that will debut on ABC-TV on October 4. Cash will also make a few guest appearances on the show.

Bobby Darin appears at the Playboy Jazz Fest in Chicago.

Bill Haley and His Comets leave for Germany and Italy where they will perform for a month. During their stay, they are scheduled to appear in two rock 'n roll films for the European market.

AUG 8   Headlining tonight at the Asbury Park (NJ) Convention Center is Connie Francis.
    "The Dick Clark Show" is broadcast from Hollywood tonight and for the remainder of August as Clark films "Because They're Young." Tonight's guest performers are Freddy Cannon, LuAnn Simms, Sammy Turner, the Tempos, and Thomas Wayne.

AUG 9   Conway Twitty plays a club date in Columbus, Indiana.
    Atlantic City's Steel Pier plays host to Frank Virtue and the **Virtues**.
    Ray Charles and his Raelets play the Labor Union Hall in New Orleans. He remains in the area, performing in Baton Rouge at the Temple Roof Club (10) before returning to New Orleans for a big show at the Municipal Auditorium (11).

AUG 10   The four male members of the Platters are arrested in Cincinnati and charged with "aiding and abetting prostitution" and "lewdness" after a raid by police on their hotel room. According to news reports, there were four nineteen-year old women in the Platters' rooms, three of them white. The case languished in the municipal court four months until December 2, when the men were acquitted of the morals charge.

New Releases for the second week in August include "You're Gonna

THE VIRTUES
Frank Virtuoso (who billed himself professionally as Frank Virtue) formed his first combo in 1947 in his hometown of Philadelphia. For the two years prior to that, he had endured a tour in the Navy where he had been stationed with Arthur Smith, the composer of what may be the best known guitar instrumental of all time (in its various incarnations), "Guitar Boogie." Back in Philly, he put together the Virtuoso Trio, with his brother Frank on Bass and Jimmy Bruno on guitar. The little combo played around town, building a local following. By 1959, with the advent of rock n' roll, Virtue added a drummer (Joe Vespe) and sax (John Renner). Virtue had always liked the Smith number., and in 1959, the combo, now calling itself the Virtues, juiced it up and released it as "Guitar Boogie Shuffle" on Hunt Records, an ABC-Paramount subsidiary. The single sold a million copies and led to similar rock instrumentals based on the tune: "Woo-Hoo" and "The Beat." The Virtues followed with "Flippin' In," a sax-led number with no guitar lead. The single caught the public by surprise, and sold poorly. The band attempted various other turns, "Pickin' the Stroll," "Virtue's Boogie Woogie" and "Blues in the Cellar" before Hunt closed its doors. In 1960, they had one single on Highland, "Happy Guitar." The Virtues surfaced on Sure Records in 1962 for a one-up single with the incompatible name "Guitar Boogie Shuffle Twist," which dented the Top 100. After that, the Virtues disbanded. Frank continued on using the combos' name and studio musicians on "Guitar Boogie Shuffle '65" on the Fayette label, and "Guitar on the Wild Side" on his own Virtue label in 1969. He also produced several hits, the biggest of which was Eddie Holman's "Hey There Lonely Girl" in 1969-70.

Miss Me" by Connie Francis on M-G-M; a pair from RCA: "Come and Get It" by Ray Peterson and the two-part "Shout" by the **Isley Brothers**; "You Were Mine" by the Fireflies on Ribbon; Frankie Avalon's "Just Ask Your Heart" on Chancellor; "Love Walked In" by the Flamingos on End; Paul Anka's "Put Your Head On My Shoulder" on ABC-Paramount; "Mr. Blue" by the Fleetwoods on Dolton; Carl Perkins' "One Ticket To Loneliness" on Columbia; "Mystery Train" by Vernon Taylor on Sun; "Marie" by the Fidelities on Sir; "My Baby's Got Soul" by Larry Williams on Chess; "The Storm" by Jody Reynolds on Demon; "If You're Looking" by Donnie Brooks on Era; Sandy Nelson's "Teen Beat" on Original Sound; and "Where Did My Baby Go?" by Bobby Freeman on Josie. Released this week is Jackie Shannon's "Troubles" on P.J. The single would be reissued on Dot within the next two weeks.

AUG 11   Frankie Avalon plays a county fair in Louisville.
         In Cincinnati, Conway Twitty, Rusty York, and Jackie Shannon play the Tuesday night teen show at Coney Island's Moonlight Gardens.

AUG 12   Connie Francis opens a three-day run in Ottawa.
         On "American Bandstand," LaVern Baker makes one of her infrequent television appearances singing "So High, So Low."
         San Francisco's Facks II offers the talents of Roy Hamilton for patrons this week.

AUG 13   Terri Stevens guests on "American Bandstand" this afternoon.

AUG 14   On a one-nighter tour through the middle of the country, Carl Perkins plays Dyersburg, Tennessee, tonight. Tomorrow he is in Centralia, Illinois.
         The Howard Theater in Washington offers the talents of Eartha Kitt for the next two weeks.

AUG 15   Johnny Cash performs in Terre Haute.
         Frankie Avalon stars at yet another county fair, this time in Redding, Pennsylvania.
         "The Dick Clark Show" welcomes Tommy Edwards, Jack Scott, Rusty York, Johnny and the Hurricanes, the Browns, and Carl Mann.

MID-AUGUST

In California, Ray Charles performs at the Oakland Auditorium.
Doc Bagby is in the middle of a long engagement at the Cadillac Sho-Bar in New York.

AUG 16   Tarheel Slim and Little Ann star at the Blue Eagle Lounge in New Orleans.
         In Hamilton, Ohio, the Spatz Show Bar welcomes the Cadillacs for a five-day run.

ISLEY BROTHERS

Listening to "Shout" by the Isley Brothers, it is a simple matter to imagine the three brothers singing in a gospel choir. In fact, it was in a church in their home town of Cincinnati that O'Kelly (born December 25, 1937), Rudolph (born April 1, 1939) and Ronald Isley (born May 21, 1941) got their start. With a younger brother, Vernon, they began as a quartet, singing in churches in the upper Midwest. Unfortunately, Vernon was killed in 1954 in a bicycle accident. After this tragedy, the other three brothers stopped singing for a time, but their family soon persuaded them to continue. Within two years, they had fallen under the spell of R&B music, and the trio moved to New York in 1956. Their gospel training had turned them into a credible performing act, and between jobs washing dishes, they found gigs at the bottom of the bill on the theater circuit that included the Apollo in New York and the Howard in Washington. They recorded a one-off single, "Angels Cried" for the Teenage label in 1957, but the record sank without a trace. Undaunted at this failure, in 1958, the Isleys recorded one single for Cindy and two more for Gone Records, all with no success. It was their live act that paid the bills. In 1959, awhile playing the Howard Theater, a scout for RCA Victor Records saw the group and immediately arranged for a recording session. Their first single, "Turn Me On," followed their previous recording efforts into oblivion. However, for a second release, the brothers convinced RCA to allow them to record a song they had written as a showstopper. The result was "Shout." It became an instant classic, although the single was not a major hit at the time. The Isleys continued to record for RCA for a year with no more hits. In fact, it wasn't until 1962, and "Twist and Shout" (another instant classic), that they were back on the charts. But, this was just the beginning. The Isley Brothers went on to become legends.

AUG 17   Ronnie Hawkins and the Hawks finally make their "American Bandstand" debut performing "Forty Days" and "Mary Lou."
Ray Charles and his orchestra entertain the patrons at the Greystone Ballroom in Detroit.

New Releases for the third week in August include "Seven Little Girls (Sitting In The Back Seat)" by Paul Evans on Guaranteed; "If You Don't Want My Lovin'" by Carl Dobkins, Jr. on Decca; "Come On And Get Me" by Fabian on Chancellor; two from Mercury: "Wish It Were Me" by the Platters and "Mary's Place" by Bing Day; Jackie Wilson's "You Better Know It" on Brunswick; **Ray Smith**'s "Rockin' Little Angel" on Judd; "Loveable" by Jerry Keller on Kapp; "Boys Do Cry" by Joe Bennett and the Sparkletones on ABC-Paramount; "Say Man" by Bo Diddley on Checker; "Nowhere To Go" by Johnny Adams on Ric; two from Capitol: "Believe Me" by the Royal Teens and "Baby Just You" by the Johnny Otis Show; "St. Louis Blues" by Mickey and Kitty on Atlantic; "Cute Little Ways" by Hank Ballard and the Midnighters on King; "To Keep Our Love" by Cleve Duncan (former lead singer with the Penguins) on Dootone; and Little Richard's first gospel single, "Troubles of the World" on End. Also out this week is Barry Mann's "All The Things You Are" on JDS. Mann, who was primarily a songwriter, had his biggest hit single in 1961 with "Who Put the Bomp" on ABC-Paramount. Finally, "Don't Knock Elvis" by Felton Jarvis is released on Viva. In the 1960s, Jarvis would become one of the regular co-producers of Elvis' sessions.

AUG 18   Connie Francis embarks on a ten-day whirlwind tour of England, France, and Germany. While in England, she records three albums for future release.

AUG 19   The county fair in Brockton, Massachusetts, welcomes Frankie Avalon. Other fairs visited by Avalon this month include Trenton, New Jersey (22-23); and Ashland, Kentucky (25).

AUG 20   Carl Perkins is in Oklahoma City for a four-day run.

AUG 21   Jerry Lee Lewis plays an 8:00 p.m. outdoor date at the Holiday Drive-In Theater in Burnet, Texas.

AUG 22   Edd Byrnes is a guest at the Chicagoland Music Festival.
Lee Dorsey opens at the Dew Drop Cafe in New Orleans for the first of three weekend dates.
Fabian, Bobby Darin, Dodie Stevens, and Mitchell Torok entertain tonight on "The Dick Clark Show."

New Releases for the fourth week in August include two from M-G-M: "Danny Boy" by Conway Twitty and "Anna Belle" by Jerry Landis; "Woo-Hoo" by the Rock-A-Teens on Doran; "Sandy" by Larry Hall on Hot; Duane Eddy's "Some Kind-A Earthquake" on Jamie; Jimmie Rodgers' "Tucumcari" on Roulette; "It Happened Today" by the Skyliners on Calico; "A Lover's Prayer" by Dion and the Belmonts on Laurie; "Chapel of

RAY SMITH
Raymond Eugene Smith was born October 31, 1934, in rural Melber, Kentucky. His father was an itinerant sharecropper with a deep love of music. After years of moving from farm to farm, about 1944, the family settled in Lone Oak, near Paducah. Ray began working early in life, eventually quitting school at the age of fourteen. In 1952, he joined the Air Force and began singing in public for the first time. Back in Paducah in 1956, he formed the Rock and Roll Boys. Over the next two years, they performed in clubs and on radio from Kentucky to Arkansas. In May 1958, he signed with Sam Phillips' Sun Records of Memphis, and his first session was produced by an otherwise unknown Memphis jazz pianist, Charlie Rich, who also wrote all four songs recorded. For Smith's first single, Sun released "Right Behind You Baby" b/w "So Young." Smith had four more singles on Sun, then in 1959, he began recording for Judd Records, a Memphis label owned by Sam Phillip's brother, Judd. His first Judd release, "Rockin' Little Angel," proved to be the biggest hit of his career. He remained with Judd for three more singles, then began a recording odyssey that led to more than a dozen labels over the next eight years, including Infinity, Warner Brothers, Vee Jay, Smash, and Tollie. In 1972, he signed with Cinnamon, an up-and-coming country label that would have success with another ex-rocker, Narvel Felts. "A Tilted Cup of Love," Smith's first Cinnamon release, did well in the C&W market, but he was unable to capitalize on it. Like many other American rock 'n rollers in the late 1970s, he found a new market outside of the United States. As early as 1975, his records had been regularly released in Canada. In 1978, he began touring in the United Kingdom, Holland and Germany to enthusiastic receptions. On November 29, 1979, to the shock of his family and fans, Ray Smith committed suicide in Burlington, Ontario.

Dreams" by the Dubs on Gone; "Poco Loco" by Gene and Eunice on Case; "Big Town" by Ronnie Self on Decca; Sammy Salvo's "Afraid" on Imperial; "Sky High" by the Champs on Challenge; "You're A Big Girl Now" by the Bell Notes on Time; two from RCA: "Don't You Know" by Della Reese and "Oh, Carol" by Neil Sedaka; Johnny Thunder's "Horror Show" on Epic; "Everyday" by **Johnny Rivers** on Cub; Dorsey Burnette's "Lonely Train" on Imperial; T.V. Slim's "Flat Foot Sam Met Jim Dandy" on Speed; and Bobby Vinton's "First Impression" on Alpine. New this week also is "Storm Warning" by Mac Rebennack on Rex. Rebennack, a mainstay in the New Orleans studio scene, is more famous under his pseudonym Dr. John.

AUG 25   Brenda Lee and Carl Perkins play the Clinton County Fair in Wilmington, Ohio.

In Cincinnati, he Poni-Tails perform at Coney Island's Moonlight Gardens.

AUG 26   Carl Dobkins, Jr. begins a five-day run in Hawaii.

AUG 28   Johnny Cash makes a one-night stand in Montecello, Illinois.

Ricky Nelson begins a two-day stand at the Steel Pier in Atlantic City.

Johnny Nash and Eartha Kitt share the spotlight at the Apollo Theater in New York.

AUG 29   While in Meridian, Mississippi, for a one-night stand at a fraternity party, Chuck Berry is accused of trying to date a white girl. According to press reports, he is run out of town. According to Berry's autobiography, he spent the night in a jail cell under police protection and was charged $700.00 for disturbing the peace.

Tab Hunter, Connie Stevens, Johnny Horton, and the Diamonds guest on "The Dick Clark Show."

AUG 30   Brenda Lee and Carl Perkins close their current round of shows with a performance in Detroit. Miss Lee is set to immediately leave the U. S. to begin a three-week series of shows in Rio de Janeiro.

Jack Scott and Anita Bryant perform as part of a Dick Clark show at the Hollywood Bowl. Also on the bill are Connie Francis and Jackie Shannon (formerly Jackie Dee and soon to be Jackie DeShannon). Attendance is pegged at 20,000.

LATE AUGUST

Buck Ram, producer of the Platters, embarks on a tour of Europe with twenty acts. Their first stop is Italy where they are set for a long sting of one-nighters.

JOHNNY RIVERS

In 1964, Johnny Rivers was battling a hoard of British rock groups for the top positions on the American music charts. Playing nightclub versions of 1950s hits, such as "Memphis," "Maybelline" and "Mountain of Love," Rivers was able to hold his own. He was born John Ramistella in New York City, on November 7, 1942. When he was a small child, his family moved to Baton Rouge, Louisiana, where young Johnny fell in love with R&B music. He formed his first rock 'n roll band before he was in high school, and in 1957, John Ramistella and the Spades recorded "Hey, Little Girl" for Suede Records of Natchez, Mississippi. It was the beginning of a seven-year search for a hit record by a young man with incredible persistence. Each school vacation found him back in New York, visiting relatives and breaking into show business. He was introduced to Alan Freed, who was able to wrangle a recording session with Gone Records. Rechristened Johnny Rivers, his only Gone single, "Baby Come Back," was issued in March 1958. In October of that year, Philadelphia's Guyden Records released "You're the One." In March 1959, the small Dee Dee label released "Your First and Last Love." This was followed by "Don't Bug Me Baby" on Riveraire, possibly his own company. "Everyday" was the first of two singles on Cub, the second being "Answer Me My Love" in 1960. That same year, he moved to Los Angeles where Louis Prima helped him with his night club act. The years 1961-62 saw "Call Me" on Era, followed by three singles on Chancellor, "Knock Three Times," "Blue Skies" and "To Be Loved." Two singles on Capitol in 1962-63 followed: "Long Black Veil" and "If You Want It, I've Got It." Coral Records issued "Your First and Last Love" in 1963. By then, Johnny Rivers was the headliner at Hollywood's Whiskey A-Go-Go, playing sets filled with rock 'n roll oldies.

THE TOP ROCK 'N ROLL RECORDS FOR AUGUST 1959

1. A Big Hunk O' Love/My Wish Came True - Elvis Presley
2. My Heart Is An Open Book - Carl Dobkins, Jr.
3. Lonely Boy - Paul Anka
4. There Goes My Baby - The Drifters
5. Lavender Blue - Sammy Turner
6. Tiger - Fabian
7. What A Diff'rence A Day Makes - Dinah Washington
8. Forty Miles of Bad Road - Duane Eddy
9. What'd I Say (part 1-2) - Ray Charles
10. Just A Little Too Much/Sweeter Than You - Ricky Nelson
11. Sea Of Love - Phil Phillips
12. It Was I - Skip and Flip
13. Here Comes Summer - Jerry Keller
14. Lipstick On Your Collar/Frankie - Connie Francis
15. What Is Love - The Playmates
16. Thank You Pretty Baby - Brook Benton
17. Robbin' The Cradle - Tony Bellus
18. I'll Be Satisfied - Jackie Wilson
19. Mona Lisa - Carl Mann
20. Kissin' Time - Bobby Rydell
21. See You In September - The Tempos
22. The Way I Walk - Jack Scott
23. I'm Gonna Be A Wheel Someday/I Want To Walk You Home
    - Fats Domino
24. Makin' Love - Floyd Robinson
25. Broken-Hearted Melody - Sarah Vaughan
26. Since You've Been Gone - Clyde McPhatter
27. Baby Talk - Jan and Dean
28. I Only Have Eyes For You - The Flamingos
29. Personality - Lloyd Price
30. Sleep Walk - Santo and Johnny
31. Red River Rock - Johnny and the Hurricanes
32. A Boy Without a Girl/Bobby Sox To Stockings - Frankie Avalon
33. You're So Fine - The Falcons
34. Mona Lisa - Conway Twitty
35. Hushabye - The Mystics
36. My Own True Love - Jimmy Clanton
37. Lonely Guitar - Annette
38. There Is Something On Your Mind - Big Jay McNeely
39. I'm Gonna Get Married - Lloyd Price
40. Dream Lover - Bobby Darin
41. The Wonder Of You - Ray Peterson
42. This I Swear - The Skyliners
43. Tallahassee Lassie - Freddy Cannon
44. Bongo Rock - Preston Epps
45. So High, So Low - LaVern Baker

46. Linda Lou - Ray Sharpe
47. Remember When - The Platters
48. Only Sixteen - Sam Cooke
49. Just Keep It Up - Dee Clark
50. Leave My Kitten Alone - Little Willie John

Also on the "pop" charts:
The Three Bells - The Browns
Tennessee Stud - Eddy Arnold
Caribbean - Mitchell Torok
I Loves You Porgy - Nina Simone

August 1959
ARTIST OF THE MONTH

CARL DOBKINS, JR.

Carl Dobkins, Jr.

He had a sweet, country voice reminiscent of George Hamilton IV. Like so many other stars during the heyday of American rock 'n roll, Carl Dobkins, Jr. had one big hit, one minor hit, a couple of non-hits, and he disappeared from public view within a year, although he continued to make records for another ten.

Carl was born in January, 1941, and he grew up in Cincinnati. His parents were musically inclined, and both played guitar, so it was natural that Carl would learn to play from them. His first instrument was a ukulele with a plastic attachment across the frets so he could play chords by pushing buttons. It wasn't long before his curiosity got the better of him, and he tore apart the attachment in an attempt to discover how it worked. He soon learned to play chords on his own. Later, he also took up the banjo.

While Carl was attending Hughes High in Cincinnati, he was performing on local television's "Sunday Swing Dance Club." He also had a part-time job in a bakery. When he had accumulated a week's wages, he took his guitar to a small recording studio to cut a demonstration acetate so he could hear how he sounded. The two songs he sang that day were his own compositions, "Take Hold Of My Hand" and "That's Why I'm Asking."

Gil Shepherd was a Cincinnati deejay who was locally famous for doing live remote broadcasts out of the back of his converted Volkswagen bus. Carl showed up at one of Shepherd's promotions with his acetate and convinced the deejay to give one of the songs some airplay. Shepherd was impressed enough to become Dobkins' manager.

Late in 1957, through Shepherd's aggressive tactics, Carl and his acetate were shown to Harry Carlson, owner of Fraternity Records. Fraternity, up to that time, was known for Jimmy Dorsey's "So Rare" and Cathy Carr's "Ivory Tower." Carlson liked the unassuming quality of "Take Hold of My Hand," and he released the single early in 1958.

The single received some attention in Cincinnati, mostly due to Shepherd's radio broadcast. In due course, Dobkins was approached by Harry Silverstein, a representative for Decca Records. In March, 1958, Dobkins' first Decca single was released. "If You Don't Want My Lovin'" b/w "Love Is Everything" was an interesting coupling that sounded like a cross between Jimmy Clanton and Ricky Nelson. The single did not generate much beyond regional sales, and it looked as though Decca was ready to let Carl's brief contract expire.

At this time, a song co-written by Hal David caught the attention of Jimmy Dean, a country and western deejay from Washington, DC. Dean was just beginning to make a name for himself with his daytime show on CBS-TV. He recorded "My Heart Is An Open Book" and his single was released by Columbia Records in October 1958. Like many of Dean's records at that time, this one fared only moderately.

Dobkins was in Nashville looking for songs to record for a second single. He was booked for a session at Owen Bradley's studio and had eliminated a long list of possible material. A representative of a Nashville music publisher convinced Bradley and Dobkins to try singing "My Heart Is an Open Book." Bradley was much more convinced about the song's potential than Dobkins. Nevertheless, a single was recorded and eventually released in February 1959.

For two months, it looked as though Dobkins' assessment of "My Heart Is An Open Book" would prove to be true. The record languished on dealer's shelves. Dobkins and Gil Shepherd tried every angle to get the song played on radio stations throughout the South and Midwest with a complete lack of success. Finally, Shepherd contacted a station representative in Detroit who shed some light on their predicament. Dobkins was perceived to be a "hillbilly" artist. Just why this happened is anyone's guess. Maybe it was his association with Decca Records, a major company in Nashville. Maybe it was that "Junior" tag on his name.

Shepherd convinced the executive at the Detroit radio station to allow Dobkins to play a record hop at a local armory. The deejay that night was Tom Clay, a very influential radio personality. Clay's appearance drew more than six thousand teenagers, and Dobkins' appeared, doing his best to lip-sync "My Heart Is An Open Book."

Within two weeks, the record started to break in Detroit and Toronto. Then it spread to upper Ohio, especially around Cleveland. Dobkins was also a hit in Charleston, West Virginia.

"My Heart Is An Open Book" remained a national hit for most of the next six months. The song was gentle and polite. It presented an attitude that was completely non-threatening, something that obviously appealed to the preteen crowd. This was a song of puppy love, not passionate lust. It had a bouncy beat with a saccharine "tootle-ooo" vocal backing from the Anita Kerr Singers. The sparse instrumentation was provided by an acoustic guitar, a muted electric guitar, and a bass. Even the drums were played with brushes. To Dobkins' credit, his voice, while displaying his youth, also had an inner strength enhanced by his years of experience.

His first major appearance as a rock 'n roll star was a hometown booking at the popular Coney Island amusement area on June 23.

Dobkins performed at the Moonlight Gardens Ballroom as part of a series of Tuesday shows for teenagers. Sharing the bill with Dobkins that night were Gary Stites, Freddy Cannon, Johnny and the Hurricanes, the Mystics, and Frankie Ford. Dobkins recalled that this package toured for several weeks, playing the small towns in Iowa, Wisconsin and Illinois.

Decca re-released "If You Don't Want My Lovin'" in August, but even with a million copies of "My Heart Is An Open Book" on the market, this "new" single received little attention the second time around. That same month, Dobkins began a five-day tour of Hawaii, stopping in San Francisco for personal appearances on the return trip.

Dobkins arrived back in Cincinnati just in time to enter the Ohio National Guard for a six-month of duty that included two months of basic training at Fort Knox, Kentucky. The timing of Dobkins' military service could not have been worse. With the slow sales of "If You Don't Want My Lovin'," the only means of promoting himself was through tours. Confined to Fort Knox through most of October and November, he watched from the sidelines as his chance to become a recording star slipped away.

In mid-November, as he was finishing basic training, "Lucky Devil" was released as a single. Aimed directly at preteens, the single sold a half-million copies in early 1960. The follow-up single, "Exclusively Yours," sold about half of that.

In 1961, as his own career was reaching bottom, Carl decided to branch out into artist management in Cincinnati. He knew of the Casinos, a group of high school students from Dobkins' alma mater. Led by Gene Hughes and J. T. Sears, the group had a polished stage act but no recording contract. Under Dobkins' tutelage, the Casinos signed with a small company, Name Records. The group had only local success then, but in 1964, they had a major hit with "Then You Can Tell Me Goodbye" on Fraternity. By this time, however, Dobkins' association with the group was over.

After "Exclusively Yours," Dobkins' brief run as a national recording star was also over. Decca continued to put out singles, a total of five more through mid-1962. In 1963 Dobkins had one single on Atco, "If Teardrops Were Diamonds." By this time, he sounded less like Jimmy Clanton and more like Bobby Goldsboro. In 1965, he had another single on Colpix.

His roots were in Cincinnati, and there he remained. He married in September 1960, and he fathered two daughters. He eventually moved to the suburbs, settling in Evendale. Dobkins continued to perform occasionally in New Year's Eve shows and similar events. In 1969, the small Chalet label released two of his singles including a newly recorded version of "My Heart Is An Open Book." He also recorded a third version of his biggest hit in 1977 that was released on a single and on compilation albums by Gusto/Starday Records.

In the 1980s, Carl Dobkins, Jr. was the shipping and receiving supervisor for the local General Electric warehouse.

September 1959

SEP 1 In Cincinnati, Bobby Darin wows the crowd Coney Island's Moonlight Gardens.

Billy and Lillie entertain at the Bambou Club in Chicago. They will remain at the Bambou for four weeks. (See also SEP 4.)

The New Orleans Municipal Auditorium welcomes a big revue headlined by Dee Clark. Also sharing the spotlight are Ruth Brown, the Drifters, Rosco Gordon, the Shirelles, Wilbert Harrison, Preston Epps, **Johnny "Guitar" Watson**, Jerry Butler, Jimmy McCracklin, and Doc Bagby's combo.

SEP 2 The Everly Brothers begin a four-day run in Sacramento at the California State Fair.

At the Carter Baron Amphitheater in Washington, DC, Fabian and Duane Eddy headline a special two-day version of "The Biggest Show of Stars for '59." Also appearing are Annette, Clyde McPhatter, Ray Peterson, Gary Stites, the Kalin Twins, the Clovers, and George Hamilton IV.

SEP 3 Carl Dobkins, Jr. is in the San Francisco area doing personal appearances.

SEP 4 For the long Labor Day weekend, the Michigan State Fair in Detroit headlines a show put together by Dick Clark for a four-day stand. Talent on the bill includes Frankie Avalon, the Coasters, LaVern Baker, Billy and Lillie, Jack Scott, Anita Bryant, Freddy Cannon, Bobby Rydell, Rusty York, Skip and Flip, Jan and Dean, Santo and Johnny, and Duane Eddy. The record breaking attendance is pegged at 58,296, twenty-percent higher than the nearest event.

With Paul Anka replacing Frankie Avalon and Duane Eddy, "The Biggest Show of Stars for '59" remains at the Carter Baron Amphitheater in Washington for another four days.

In New York, Alan Freed offers another "Big Beat" revue at the Brooklyn Fox, Flatbush and Nevins Avenues.

At the Central Washington State Fair in Marshfield, Buddy Knox and Jimmy Bowen and the Rhythm Orchids entertain the crowd.

Currently on tour, the Falcons entertain their fans in Vista Park, Maryland. Tomorrow, the group plays a two-day stand at the Sunset Lake Resort in Portsmouth, Virginia.

Jimmie Rodgers is at the Steel Pier in Atlantic City for the three-day weekend.

JOHNNY WATSON

Johnny "Guitar" Watson is an enigma in the Los Angeles blues community—a man less remembered for any specific achievement than for his legend. He was born on February 3, 1935, in Houston, Texas. His family moved to Los Angeles when he was a young boy. Johnny was soon swept up in the blues music that seemed to be happening on every street corner. He was proficient on a variety of instruments, including piano, tenor saxophone and guitar. When he was eighteen, he joined Chuck Higgins, whose band frequently performed in the area's ballrooms, especially the 5-4 and the Savoy. Higgins landed a recording contract with Combo Records, and his first release was "Pachuco Hop," a popular record with the budding Chicano population. The B-side of the single, "Motor Head Baby," featured John Watson on vocals. Over the next few years, Higgins released a half-dozen singles on Combo while, at the same time, having singles released on Specialty, Lucky, Dootone and Aladdin. Watson's first solo single, "Highway 60," was issued in 1953 on the Federal label, which billed him as Young John Watson. There were three more Federal singles that year, including a version of "Motor Head Baby." In 1954, Federal issued "Half Pint of Whiskey" and "Gettin' Drunk." Watson toured with the biggest names of the day, including Muddy Waters, Charles Brown, Roy Brown, and Etta James. In 1955, he was on R.P.M. Records, which issued a half dozen singles by Johnny "Guitar" Watson over the next two years, including a cover of Earl King's "Those Lonely Lonely Nights." In 1957, he had another regional hit with "Gangster of Love" on Keen Records. It was not until 1962, with "Cuttin' In" on King Records, that Watson had a record on the R&B charts. In 1967, he was signed to Okeh label which teamed him with Larry Williams. Their duet of "Mercy, Mercy, Mercy" was a mid-sized hit.

Jazz is on the bill for the Howard Theater in Washington with the Jimmy Smith Trio, Betty Carter and Oscar Peterson.

SEP 5   "The Dick Clark Show" is broadcast from the Michigan State Fair tonight. Guests include Anita Bryant, Frankie Avalon, Jan and Dean, and Duane Eddy.

SEP 6   Bobby Darin and Frankie Avalon appear on "The Ed Sullivan Show" on CBS-TV.

Connie Francis, just returned from England, stops by the California State Fair for a four-day engagement.

Little Richard begins his first gospel tour in Dayton, Ohio.

SEP 7   Johnny Cash brings his traveling show to the crowd at Buck's Lake Resort in Angola, Indiana.

Dinah Washington opens a six-day run at Pep's Musical Bar in Philadelphia.

Ernie Kado performs at Russell's Drive-In in New Orleans. Kado, whose name was Ernest Kador, Jr., had his biggest hit in 1961 with their Number One "Mother In Law" using the name Ernie K-Doe.

New Releases for the first week in September include "There Comes A Time" by Jack Scott on Carlton; "You Got What It Takes" by Marv Johnson on United Artists; "Enchanted Sea" by the **Islanders** on Mayflower; Clyde McPhatter's "You Went Back On Your Word" on Atlantic; Chuck Berry's "Childhood Sweetheart" on Chess; "Piano Shuffle" by Dave "Baby" Cortez on Clock; "Liza Jane" by Dale Hawkins on Checker; "I'll Be Seeing You" by the Poni-Tails on ABC-Paramount; "Heartaches By The Number" by Guy Mitchell on Columbia; Jesse Belvin's "Give Me Love" on RCA; "Oh, Yeah" by Travis and Bob on Sandy; Jerry Butler's "Couldn't Get To Sleep" on Abner; Charlie Gracie's "Oh-Well-A" on Coral; and Johnny Olenn's "Devil Darling" on Personality.

EARLY SEPTEMBER

Following an outbreak of teen violence in New York City, including the knifing deaths of two boys, WCBS bans all versions of "Mack the Knife."

SEP 8   Della Reese brings her smooth vocal stylings to the Riptide Club in Brooklyn for six days.

On its last broadcast of the season, NBC-TV's "The Jimmie Rodgers Show" is visited by Johnny Cash, Cathy Carr and the Playmates.

SEP 9   LaVern Baker brings her show to the Spatz Show Bar in Hamilton, Ohio, for five nights.

SEP 11   Johnny Cash headlines the talent offered today and tomorrow by the New York State Fair in Syracuse.

THE ISLANDERS

There was other music being heard across the land in the late 1950s besides rock 'n roll—there was also something called "Exotica." Martin Denny, a club pianist with no future, threw in some bird calls on a recording session and came with the multimillion selling "Quiet Village." Suddenly, everyone was doing it. (Record label executives were nothing if not copycats.) Warren Nadel was a dentist in the Bronx. He was also an aspiring songwriter from the Bronx with enough good looks to issue five obscure records in 1957 on the Dale label and one on Mayflower in 1958 using the stage name "Randy Starr." He even toured with Charlie Gracie and appeared on "American Bandstand." In 1958, Starr became acquainted with Frank Metis, an accordionist from Nuremberg, Germany, who was studying at the Schillinger School of Musical Composition. Metis had worked with jazz pianists Dave Brubeck and George Shearing as a writer-arranger. He also met Eddie Layton, an accomplished organist The three men put together the Islanders, a studio-only group, to record exotic instrumentals issued by Mayflower Records. Their first, "The Enchanted Sea," opened with the sound of waves, a fog horn and buoy bell. Over a piano playing triplets, Starr whistled the opening verse, followed by Metis on accordion on the second verse. There was a guitar, vocal chorus, and more special effects before the single faded. It was pleasant and refreshing, and it skipped up the charts, landing in the Top Twenty late in 1959. The follow-up single, "Tornado," didn't attempt to capture the essence of the tropics the way "Enchanted Sea" had done. It also failed to sell as many copies. The Islanders issued three more singles, all in 1960 before disbanding. Starr went on to record more obscure singles, compose songs for Elvis, and form the New Christy Minstrels.

Frankie Avalon performs at the Kentucky State Fair for four days.

The Apollo Theater in New York offers a "Jazz at the Philharmonic" week for patrons. Featured performers are Ella Fitzgerald, Oscar Peterson, Sonny Stitt, Roy Eldridge, and Terry Gibbs.

Earl Bostic is at La Maina's in Philadelphia for three days.

Big Maybelle, **Arthur Prysock** and the Four Tops entertain this week's crowd at the Flame in Detroit.

SEP 12   The Everly Brothers play a two-day engagement at the West Texas State Fair in Abilene.

Paul Anka, Roberta Shaw, Bobby Rydell, and the Fleetwoods appear on "The Dick Clark Show."

SEP 13   At his rented home in Bad Nauheim, Germany, Elvis Presley meets Priscilla Beaulieu, the fourteen-year old daughter of an Air Force Captain stationed at nearby Wiesbaden Air Force Base. He is immediately smitten by this young beauty.

SEP 14   Ray Peterson starts a week-long engagement at the Mardi Gras Club in Baltimore.

Clyde McPhatter entertains the fans at Blinstrub's in Boston for the week.

Della Reese opens for a week at the Chaudiere Club in Brooklyn.

Still on the fair circuit, Johnny Cash stops for two days at the Tennessee Valley Fair in Knoxville. Following the show, Cash leaves the U. S. for England and Germany.

Bobby Darin plays a two-day engagement at the Santa Clara County Fair in San Jose, California.

Conway Twitty opens a week-long gig at the Smart Spot in Haddenfield, New Jersey.

New Releases for the second week in September include "Handy Man" by Jimmy Jones on Cub; two from Mercury: Dinah Washington's "Unforgettable" and Rod Bernard's "One More Chance;" "Don't Destroy Me" by Crash Craddock on Columbia; Bobby Rydell's "We Got Love" on Cameo; Annette's "First Name Initial" on Vista; Bobby Comstock's "Tennessee Waltz" on Blaze; "So Tenderly" by the Mystics on Laurie; "Fancy Nancy" by Skip and Flip on Brent; a reissue of Carl Mann's "Rockin' Love" on Phillips International; "Unchained Melody" by Bobby Day on Class; "Young Girls" by Marvin Rainwater on M-G-M; "Teenage Misery" by **Jesse Lee Turner** (page 420 ➤) on Fraternity; "Baby Open Your Heart" by the Dells on Vee-Jay; and Jimmy Reed's "I Wanna Be Loved" on Abner.

SEP 15   Making another appearance on "American Bandstand," Duane Eddy performs "Some Kind-A Earthquake."

At the Redding (PA) County Fair, Fabian replaces Frankie Avalon for a two-day engagement. Following this booking, Fabian leaves the States for a one-week tour of Australia.

ARTHUR PRYSOCK

In 1959, Arthur Prysock was billed as "America's newest baritone sensation." In fact, Prysock had been singing professionally for almost twenty years. He was born January 2, 1925, in Greensboro, North Carolina. His family lived for a time in Spartanburg, South Carolina, where, following high school graduation he drove a delivery truck was a short order cook. At the outbreak of World War II, the Prysock family moved to Hartford, Connecticut, and Arthur found work in an aircraft factory. At night, he performed at the Flamingo Club where he fronted Harold Holt's combo. If he idolized any other recording artist it was Buddy Johnson's Walk 'em Rhythm Band. In 1943, when Johnson was playing Hartford, Prysock got the chance to audition for the male vocalist spot. He was hired and left immediately on a yearlong tour. In October 1944, Prysock's first recording session with the Buddy Johnson band on Decca Records produced the hit "They All Say I'm the Biggest Fool." Other Johnson hits featuring Prysock's vocals were "I Wonder Where Our Love Has Gone" and "Because." In 1952, Johnson was considering jumping from Decca to Mercury Records. Prysock felt that this would be a good time make a break. He remained with Decca for a time, having a 1952 hit in the R&B market with "I Didn't Sleep a Wink Last Night." He and Eckstine went head-to-head in the period just before rock 'n roll swept the land, with Eckstine eventually having the bigger career. Prysock worked night clubs and television and bided his time as a recording artist. Finally, in 1960, he hit with "The Very Thought of You" on Old Town, followed in 1962 by "One More Time." In 1965, "It's Too Late, Baby, Too Late" was his first hit in both the R&B and "pop" markets. "When Love Is New" in 1976 was his last charted single. More recently, his voice has been heard singing the praises of Lowenbrau beer.

The Flamingos entertain the crowd at the Ebony Club in Houston.

MID-SEPTEMBER
Brook Benton is currently at Robert's Show Club in Chicago.
Mark Dinning is performing at the Club Peachtree in Atlanta.

SEP 16   Barry Mann drops by "American Bandstand" this afternoon.
The West Texas State Fair in Abilene welcomes Bobby Darin for two days.

SEP 18   Following the cancellation of the original tour of "The Dick Clark Caravan" in late May as a result of the repercussions generated by rock 'n roll's bad press in Boston, the first "Dick Clark Caravan" sets off on the road on a mammoth series of forty-four one-night stands extending through October 31 with no days off. Scheduled performers initially include Paul Anka, Duane Eddy, Lloyd Price, LaVern Baker, Annette, the Coasters, the Skyliners, and Bobby Rydell. The Drifters and Phil Phillips join the roadshow during it's first week out. Cities on the first leg of the itinerary include Syracuse, Montreal, Toronto, Rochester, Richmond, and Norfolk. (See also SEP 27.)
Teddy Randazzo plays the Club Safari in College Point, Queens, New York.
Ricky Nelson entertains today at the Santa Clara County Fair in San Jose.
Hank Ballard and the Midnighters lead the show at the Howard Theater in Washington for the week. Also appearing are Sammy Turner, Valerie Carr and Sam Hawkins.
The Apollo Theater offers a gospel caravan for theatergoers this week.

SEP 19   Jerry Wallace, Carl Dobkins, Jr., and Ronnie Hawkins and the Hawks perform on tonight's "Dick Clark Show."

SEP 20   Johnny Cash performs in Frankfurt as part of his European tour.
The Poni-Tails are scheduled to play a date in Brockton, Massachusetts.

New Releases for the third week in September include "Dance With Me" by the Drifters on Atlantic; Brook Benton's "So Many Ways" on Mercury; Brenda Lee's "Sweet Nothin's" on Decca; two from Tony Bellus: "Young Girls" and "Hey Little Darlin'" both on NRC; Sam Cooke's "There I've Said It Again" on Keen; "Taste of the Blues" by Buddy Knox on Roulette; "Tu-Ber-Cu-Lucas and the Sinus Flu" by Huey Smith and the Clowns on Ace; "Little Queenie" by Jerry Lee Lewis on Sun; "Midnight Stroll" by the Revels on Norgolde; "High School U.S.A." by Tommy Facenda on Atlantic; Donnie Brooks' "White Orchid" on Era; Roy Orbison's "Paper Boy" on Monument; "Doing the Ronde" by the Shirelles on Scep-

JESSE LEE TURNER
Jesse Lee Turner's career zoomed into orbit, then flamed out like a shooting star. His few recordings owe a big debt to Elvis Presley. Turner, who was from Bowling, Texas, was probably first impressed with the future "king of rock 'n roll" in the period beginning in late 1954 when Elvis swept back and forth across Texas, playing one roadhouse after another. Turner was also impressed with Jack Scott, and it was on Carlton Records, Scott's label, that Turner's first and biggest record was released. The late 1950s were a time when aliens from outer space, chipmunks and witch doctors populated the record grooves. When singer/songwriter Floyd Robinson penned "Little Space Girl" it appeared to be likely hit material. (Robinson had the good sense not to record it himself.) Jack Carlton, of Carlton Records, took an option on the song and placed it with his latest acquisition, Jesse Lee Turner. Turner did his best with the material, and the single sold a respectable number of copies. However, those teens who flipped the record over and played "Shake, Baby, Shake" knew immediately where Turner's musical loyalty lay. "Little Space Girl," featuring the chipmunk-like voice of Paul Belin, a Texas deejay, was released in December 1958, and by January it was a national hit. Turner never had another although he tried. "Baby Please Don't Go," issued in April 1959, was his only other Carlton single. Turner had one recording session for Fraternity Records that resulted in "Teenage Age Misery," released in September 1959. Turner next turned up on Top Rank in 1960, shortly after Jack Scott arrived there from Carlton. His lone Top Rank single, "Do I Worry? (Yes I Do)" had potential but got lost in the shuffle. Turner attempted to recover with "The Little Space Girl's Father" on Imperial in 1960. In 1963, he tried "The Voice Changing Song" and the "Ballad of Billie Sol Estes" on GNP, but his career had been over for years.

ter; "To A Young Lover" by the Tassels on Madison; and "Turnabout Heart" by Jodie Sands on Thor.

SEP 22 Frankie Avalon and Fabian split the bill at the New Jersey State Fair for two days.
   Wanda Jackson begins a three-week stand at the Showboat Hotel in Las Vegas.

SEP 23 The Clovers appear on "American Bandstand" to sing "Love Potion No. 9."
   Steve Gibson and His Red Caps open at Sciolla's in Philadelphia.

SEP 24 "American Bandstand" presents Paul Evans today.

SEP 25 Ray Charles headlines a jazz revue at the Howard Theater in Washington this week. Also appearing on stage are Art Blakely and Sonny Stitt.
   The instrumental combo the **Rock-A-Teens** perform "Woo-Hoo" on ABC-TV's "American Bandstand."
   The Poni-Tails open in Ashland, Oregon.
   Sam Cooke performs this week at the Apollo Theater in New York.

SEP 26 Chuck Berry duck-walks across the stage tonight at the Armory in Paterson, New Jersey.
   Fabian returns to Cincinnati to play the Castle Farm Club. Only 205 teens show up and the gate is reported to be $1167.50. The promoter claims to have spent $2,300 on the show.
   On television, "The Dick Clark Show" offers Dion and the Belmonts, Dee Clark, and Skip and Flip.

SEP 27 Brook Benton makes his third appearance on "The Ed Sullivan Show."
   Carl Dobkins, Jr. enters the National Guard for six months of duty. He will be stationed at Fort Knox, Kentucky.
   The Flamingos and Professor Longhair are booked into the Aristocrat Club in New Orleans.
   Off on his first tour, Billy "Crash" Craddock entertains his fans in Cincinnati for two days. Craddock also plays Cleveland on September 29-30. (See also OCT 1.)
   Connie Francis is a guest on "The Chevy Show" on NBC-TV tonight.

SEP 28 Currently crisscrossing Canada, Carl Perkins rocks the Casino Theater in Toronto for the next two weeks.
   "The Dick Clark Caravan" continues to pile up exceptional revenues as it plays Raleigh tonight. Other dates in the near future include Greenville (29); and Charlotte (30). (See also OCT 1.)
   Bobby Darin opens for a week's run at the Casino Royal in

THE ROCK-A-TEENS
"Woo-Hoo" was the only hit for the Rock-A-Teens. It sounded like a band demo, the type of composition that would be put together to show off the musical talents of the various members. "Woo-Hoo" featured electric guitar, drums (including cow bell), and acoustic rhythm guitar. There was also a "vocalist" singing "woo-hoo" during those periods when no instrumentalist was taking the lead. In addition, the backing instruments included bass and sax. The Rock-A-Teens were from Richmond, Virginia, and consisted of Vic Mizelle, Bill Cook, Bill Smith, Paul Evans, Bob Walke, and Eddie Robinson. As "Woo-Hoo" clearly shows, the group was well-rounded and talented. In 1959, George McGraw, the owner of McGraw's Record Shop in Salem, a Richmond suburb, took over management of the Rock-A-Teens. The combo cut "Woo-Hoo" in the back room of the record store, and McGraw had a few hundred pressed on the Doran label. Teenagers who knew of the band quickly bought the available copies. McGraw dutifully relayed this information to Roulette Records, a label that was always on the lookout for raw talent. "Woo-Hoo" was leased to Roulette, which issued the single in August 1959. It took two months before it began to find national attention, and then, through the end of the year, it was one of the hottest instrumentals on the market. "Twangy," the follow-up single on Roulette, came out in December, but it sold poorly. The Rock-A-Teens had no other single releases. They did, however, release an album that clearly shows the band to be a tight rockabilly unit with lead vocals by Vic Mizelle. In addition, the album pays tribute to two Virginia rockers: "Lotta Boppin'" owes its sound to Gene Vincent and "Janis Will Rock," is dedicated to Janis Martin. In 1960, Bill Smith surfaced on Chess Records with the Billy Smith Combo for two instrumental singles, "Heartbreak Hotel" and "Raunchy."

Washington, DC.
Cozy Cole opens at the Colonial Tavern in Toronto.

New Releases for the fourth week in September include "Every Little Thing I Do" by Dion and the Belmonts on Laurie; **Sammy Turner's** "Always" on Big Top; Jerry Fuller's "Tennessee Waltz" on Challenge; "The Big Hurt" by Toni Fisher on Signet; "There's a Girl" by Jan and Dean on Dore; "The Cross Roads of Love" by the Tempos on Climax; "Why Don't You Believe Me" by the Kalin Twins on Decca; "Shadows" by the Five Satins on Ember; two from Ron: Robert Parker's "All Night Long" and Professor Longhair's "If I Only Knew;" "Give Me Love" by Larry Williams on Specialty; "Love Me Completely" by the Harptones on Warwick; Baby Washington's "Baby Work Out" on Neptune; "Starry Eyed" by Gary Stites on Carlton; "It's Love" by the Addrisi Brothers on Del-Fi; "Playing Hard To Get" by Danny and the Juniors on ABC-Paramount; "Unemployment" by Harvey and the Moonglows on Chess; "Hawaiian War Chant" by the Dynatones on Bomarc; and Piano Red's "This Old World" on Jax. Also new this week is "Teach Me Tiger" by April Stevens on Imperial. Miss Stevens teamed with her brother Nino Tempo (their real last name was LoTempio) for the Number One hit "Deep Purple" in 1963.

SEP 30 The Everly Brothers are special guests on the season premier of "The Perry Como Show" on NBC-TV as the show moves from Saturday to Wednesday nights.

LATE SEPTEMBER
Johnny Cash performs on Britain's "Boy Meats Girls" television program.

SAMMY TURNER

He possessed a wavering tenor and he came along when songs from the pre-rock era were popular. He wasn't a rocker, by any stretch of the imagination, but he wasn't pure "pop," either. His handsome good looks made him a popular on stage, and he bridged the doo-wop of the 1950s and the soul of the 1960s. Samuel Black was born June 2, 1932, in Paterson, New Jersey. He began performing with the Twisters (no relation to the dance craze of 1960). With hundreds of record companies coexisting in Manhattan, vocal groups could be found on every street corner within the New York area. For one to be picked for an audition required hard work and good luck. The Twisters had both. Using Turner's lead vocal, they refined their sound, until they were the hit every time they sang. This brought Big Top Records, a new entry in the rock 'n roll record business. The company had yet to steal Johnny and the Hurricanes away from Warwick or sign Del Shannon. They were eager for talented performers, and they uncovered a gem in Sammy Turner. His first release was "Sweet Annie Laurie," sung in a fairly straight delivery. It never really had a chance. Next, "Lavender Blue," was also resurrected from another era. Here, Turner's voice took wing, reaching incredible heights then dropping back to a baritone. The backing featured violins with back-beat. The Twisters (if they are on the record at all) were relegated to a muted heavenly choir. The record came very close to going gold, and Turner had a second hit with a similar treatment of "Always," another "old" oldie. However, "Paradise," the next single, just grazed the Top 100. Turner never came close to having another hit. He left Big Top in 1961 after eleven singles. In the 1960s, he recorded for Verve, 20th Century-Fox, and Motown (reviving "Only You"). In 1978, his last singles were issued on Casablanca's Millennium label.

THE TOP ROCK 'N ROLL RECORDS FOR SEPTEMBER 1959

1. Sleep Walk - Santo and Johnny
2. Sea Of Love - Phil Phillips
3. I'm Gonna Get Married - Lloyd Price
4. Red River Rock - Johnny and the Hurricanes
5. ('Til) I Kissed You - The Everly Brothers
6. Broken-Hearted Melody - Sarah Vaughan
7. I Want To Walk You Home/I'm Gonna Be A Wheel Someday - Fats Domino
8. Lavender Blue - Sammy Turner
9. What'd I Say (part 1-2) - Ray Charles
10. Kissin' Time - Bobby Rydell
11. Baby Talk - Jan and Dean
12. There Goes My Baby - Drifters
13. It Was I - Skip & Flip
14. Thank You Pretty Baby - Brook Benton
15. A Big Hunk O' Love/My Wish Came True - Elvis Presley
16. Mack The Knife - Bobby Darin

17. What A Diff'rence A Day Makes - Dinah Washington
18. Makin' Love - Floyd Robinson
19. Poison Ivy - The Coasters
20. Primrose Lane - Jerry Wallace
21. My Own True Love - Jimmy Clanton
22. Robbin' The Cradle - Tony Bellus
23. Put Your Head On My Shoulder - Paul Anka
24. Hey, Little Girl - Dee Clark
25. Just Ask Your Heart - Frankie Avalon
26. Mona Lisa - Conway Twitty
27. The Mummy - Bob McFadden & Dor
28. The Angels Listened In - The Crests
29. I Got Stripes - Johnny Cash
30. Mary Lou - Ronnie Hawkins
31. You're Gonna Miss Me - Connie Francis
32. Mr. Blue - The Fleetwoods
33. Teen Beat - Sandy Nelson
34. My Heart Is An Open Book - Carl Dobkins, Jr.
35. Like I Love You - Edd Byrnes
36. What Is Love - The Playmates
37. Here Comes Summer - Jerry Keller
38. Somethin' Else - Eddie Cochran
39. Okefenokee - Freddy Cannon
40. Linda Lu - Ray Sharpe
41. See You In September - The Tempos
42. True, True Happiness - Johnny Tillotson
43. Forty Miles of Bad Road - Duane Eddy
44. Lonely Boy - Paul Anka
45. Suzie Baby - Bobby Vee and the Shadows
46. The Shape I'm In - Johnny Restivo
47. Poco Loco - Gene and Eunice
48. You Were Mine - The Fireflies
49. Leave My Kitten Alone - Little Willie John
50. You Better Know It - Jackie Wilson

Also on the "pop" charts:
Morgen - Ivo Robic
High Hopes - Frank Sinatra
I Ain't Never - Webb Pierce
The Battle of Kookamonga - Homer and Jethro
I've Been There - Tommy Edwards

September 1959
ARTISTS OF THE MONTH

SANTO AND JOHNNY
JOHNNY AND THE HURRICANES

Santo & Johnny

By mid-1959, a new "fad " had overtaken rock 'n roll. Hot guitar and saxophone instrumentals were competing with male teen idols for the largest share of the record and radio markets. The first hit rock n' roll instrumental was Bill Doggett's "Honky Tonk" in late 1956. It took more than a year before there was a second big rock n' roll instrumental, "Raunchy," a hit for Bill Justis, Eddie Platt and Ernie Freeman. By mid-1958, the Champs and Duane Eddy were beginning careers that would bring each a long streak of instrumental hits.

Riding the coat tails of Doggett, Justis, Eddy and the Champs came dozens of artists and combos, most of them relegated to one minor hit record. Among the more successful were the Applejacks ("Mexican Hat Rock"), Link Wray ("Rumble"), the Royaltones ("Poor Boy"), the Gone All-Stars ("7-11"), the Kingsmen ("Weekend"), Lee Allen ("Walking With Mr. Lee"), Dave "Baby" Cortez ("The Happy Organ"), Ernie Fields ("In The Mood"), Sandy Nelson ("Teen Beat"), the Virtues ("Guitar Boogie Shuffle"), Preston Epps ("Bongo Rock"), the Rock-A-Teens ("Woo-Hoo"), the Wailers ("Tall Cool One"), the Fireballs ("Torquay"), Chet Atkins ("Boo Boo Stick Beat"), the Hot-Toddys ("Rockin' Crickets"), the Rockin' R's ("The Beat"), the Wildcats ("Gazachstahagen"), the Intruders ("Fried Eggs"), the Quarter Notes ("Record Hop Blues"), and the Frantics ("Straight Flush"). And, those were just the individuals and groups with a "hit" record through the end of 1959.

Two of the more unique instrumental groups from the late 1950s, each of which also had a long-lasting impact, were Santo and Johnny and Johnny and the Hurricanes.

Santo and Johnny's biggest hit was "Sleep Walk," a medium-tempo, moody and infectious number featuring Santo's swirling melody line played on a Hawaiian steel guitar. Santo and Johnny Farina were brothers, with Santo born October 24, 1937, and Johnny born April 30, 1941. As boys, they were raised in Brooklyn. While not considered a hotbed of country music, in actuality, the northeastern portion of the United States had been home to lovers of country fans since the 1940s. Santo Farina recalled that he listened frequently to the "Home Town Frolics," a country radio show. Through that association, he came to love the sound of the steel guitar by the time he was ten years old. Shortly thereafter, Santo visited the neighborhood music store and convinced the owner to modify an acoustic guitar to allow him to play it like a steel. Thus, Santo became the shop owner's first steel guitar pupil.

Santo was mesmerized with the sounds he could produce on his new guitar, and he practiced the looping melody lines day and night. Within two years, he was performing for amateur shows on a new Gibson six-string steel guitar that he held in his lap and played while seated. Soon after, he acquired a steel guitar teacher who had learned the art in Hawaii.

In 1952, at the age of fourteen, Santo formed an instrumental trio with a guitarist and drummer. By this time, he was composing songs as well as playing his own renditions of the hits of the day. He also included a few Hawaiian standards when the group performed at local dances and parties. With the money he made from performing, Santo purchased another steel guitar. This one had three necks, each with eight strings. As he no longer had an instructor, he experimented with various adjustments of the two additional strings until he came up with tunings that appealed to his musical sensibilities. It was then that Santo began to teach his younger brother, Johnny, to play accompaniment on a standard electric guitar. Johnny proved to be a quick-learner, and the Farina Brothers began to gather fans from Brooklyn to Long Island.

As their popularity grew on a local level, the duo recorded a couple of demonstration tapes. It fell to Johnny to make the rounds of the New York record companies. Eventually, the brothers came to the attention of a music publishing company and they signed a song writer's contract. This led to a recording deal with a new company, Canadian-American Records. Their first release was "Sleep Walk," a song composed by Santo and Johnny with help from their mother, Anna. After ten years of trying, Santo was prepared for success. The brothers were immediately booked on coast-to-coast tours and television shows. Their first album also was a hit as was their second single, "Teardrop."

Their fame spread to other countries and the boys were booked on tours of Australia, Mexico and Europe. In the United States, their record sales began to wane by the end of 1960. They had a resurgence of stateside popularity in 1964 with an album of songs made famous by the Beatles. Santo and Johnny remained with Canadian-American, releasing a total of nine albums, before the company folded in 1965. In 1966, Santo and Johnny were briefly associated with United Artists Records before joining Imperial Records in 1967 on the strength of their international sales. Unfortunately, in 1968, Imperial also closed shop shortly after the release of Santo and Johnny's fourth album.

By this time, Santo and Johnny had an established reputation worldwide, except in the United States. They continued to record, mostly for Italian labels, issuing albums filled with James Bond movie themes, Hawaiian songs, old standards, country music, light classics, and rock 'n roll hits. In 1976, the duo finally broke up, with Santo continuing to record internationally.

Santo's biggest success—after "Sleep Walk"—came from an unexpected direction. His album, SANTO, on the Italian PA/USA label, was chosen as theme music for the Jazzercise company. This was a very lucrative association for Santo. Two movie themes recorded by Santo also became hits in Italy: "My Rifle, My Pony, and Me" (from "Rio Bravo") and the "Indiana Jones" theme. By the mid-1980s, Santo had settled on Long Island where he continued to perform locally.

If Santo and Johnny captured the listener's imagination with soaring melodies and unique, steel guitar ballads, Johnny and the Hurricanes captured the listener's dancing feet with a powerhouse sound built upon layers of organ, saxophone and guitar.

The Hurricanes began as an Ohio combo formed in 1957 by a group of students from Toledo's Rossford Catholic High. The acknowledged leader of the group was saxophonist Johnny Paris, born John Pocisk, 1940, in Walbridge, Ohio. Paris grew up listening to jazz greats like Charlie Parker until Bill Haley became a popular using a combination sax/guitar backing. Enlisting Dave Yorko on guitar and Paul Tesluk on accordion, Paris formed the Orbits, a band that saw action playing on a few locally released recordings behind Mack Vickery, an otherwise obscure rockabilly singer.

Tesluk soon moved up to a Hammond chord organ, and Lionel "Butch" Mattice joined in on bass. The drummer for the group changed regularly. Originally, it was Tony Kaye. Later drummers included Don Staczek, Lynn Bruce (from Detroit) and William "Little Bo" Savitch who had played with the Royaltones.

The members of the Orbits had a common bond in music. When they first decided to form a dance band, none of the members wanted to sing. The boys also shied away from soft, weepy ballads. They just wanted to blow through hot tunes that kept the dancers in a whirling-dervish atmosphere. The band was a sensation with the weekend crowd of teens at Pearson Park in Toledo.

In 1958, they felt that they had enough experience playing sock hops and high school dances, so the Orbits traveled to Detroit to be interviewed by Harry Balk and Irving Micahnik of Artists, Inc., a management agency that had handled Little Willie John and was currently having a hit with the instrumental "Poor Boy" by the Royaltones. This led to a long-term managerial contract and subsequently to engagements outside the Toledo area. In early 1959, the combo, now calling themselves Johnny and the Hurricanes, signed with Micahnik and Balk's Twirl Records, and their first release was "Crossfire," a blazing blend of thumping electric guitar and growling saxophone punctuated with hand-claps. When the single began to receive regional airplay, the group's recording contract was leased to Warwick Records, a subsidiary of United Telefilm.

Johnny & The Hurricanes

The record caught on immediately and was a medium-sized hit across the country through the summer of 1959. The group's first, brief tour began in June in Cincinnati at Coney Island's Moonlight Gardens. Along with the Hurricanes were several other newcomers, Carl Dobkins, Jr., Frankie Ford and Freddy Cannon. For about ten days, this package gave shows around the Cincinnati area.

As a follow-up to "Crossfire," Johnny and the Hurricanes altered their sound, rewriting "Red River Valley," the traditional cowboy song, into "Red River Rock." The song opened with the single-note melody snapped out by Paul Tesluk on the organ. The sound was that of a pan flute gone berserk. The arrangement was pinned underneath by the guitar, bass and drums in a rolling boogie-beat. Beginning with the second verse, Johnny's snarling sax joined the melee. There was a hot guitar solo midway through the song and two repetitions of the organ-sax verse before the song faded out just short of two minutes and fifteen seconds. "Red River Rock" was irresistible. The sound of Johnny and the Hurricanes, for all of its various components, was very clean, with each instrument clearly heard. This would be a trademark for most of the Hurricanes' recordings. "Red River Rock" sold a million copies and was followed by two singles with a similar theme and production: "Reville Rock" (based on the "reveille" bugle call) and "Beatnik Fly" (patterned after the folk song "Blue Tail Fly").

After a year with Warwick, Johnny and the Hurricanes jumped to Big Top Records in the summer of 1960. (Material recorded by the Hurricanes continued to be released by Warwick as uncredited B-sides of three singles by another instrumental group, the Craftsmen.) Such a move might have signaled a change in musical direction for the group, yet none was evident. The first Big Top single was a remake of "Down Yonder" with the trademark organ lead and roaring saxophone. The group followed with "Rocking Goose" (a rare original piece), "Revival" (an adaptation of "When the Saints Go Marching In"), and "You Are My Sunshine."

Most of the material performed by Johnny and the Hurricanes was credited to "T. King and I. Mack," a pseudonym for Balk and Micahnik. None of the Hurricanes received acknowledgment or royalties, for songwriting, though most of the musical arrangements were worked out within the group.

Johnny and the Hurricanes remained a viable record-selling band for another year. However, the continued use of such similar record production, combined with the gimmick of performing an old tune with a rock 'n roll beat, resulted in fewer record sales with each release as the novelty wore off. By early 1961, when "Ja-Da" barely dented the musical charts, Johnny and the Hurricanes dropped out of the musical mainstream. Nevertheless, the group continued recording for Big Top, issuing eight additional singles.

Big Top Records quickly rebounded with a new artist, Del Shannon, who was also managed by Balk and Micahnik. In fact, it was rumored that Shannon was backed by the Hurricanes on several of his recording sessions at Big Top, but this was not so. (On Amy Records, Shannon's album of Hank Williams songs credited the Hurricanes for the instrumental backing, but the group actually performing was the Royaltones.)

After a tour of Britain in 1963, Johnny and the Hurricanes moved on to Jeff Records for one single, then to the Atilla label for five more. In 1965, they ended their recording career with two singles for Mala Records. By this time, only Paris of the original Hurricanes remained. Paris, in his frequent trips overseas, found new fans in Europe. He extended his career with sojourns to Germany and England while remaining based in Toledo where he managed a talent agency and played weekend gigs.

"Red River Rock" became one of the most popular of all the "oldies." The instantly recognizable opening by Paul Tesluk on the Hammond chord organ still could fill the dance floor in a heartbeat. And, if the deejay threw in "Sleep Walk" for a change of pace, you had a one-two punch that defined the unique parameters of the rock 'n roll instrumental sound in the late 1950s.

October 1959

DODIE STEVENS
Dodie Stevens has done it all. She had a huge hit at thirteen. She made the transition to ballad singer. She even recorded an Elvis "answer" record. Born Geraldine Ann Pasquale in Chicago on February 17, 1946, her family moved to Temple City, California, when she was two. By the time she was six, she was performing regularly in local shows. At age eight, she appeared on Art Linkletter's "House Party" to plug her first single, "Merry Go, Merry Go Round," released as by Geri Pace on the Goldstar label. In the mid-1950s, she appeared frequently on Frankie Laine's national TV program. In 1957, she was noticed by the owner of Crystalette Records, but it took more than a year to find material suited to her age. Her first Crystalette release, under the name Dodie Stevens, was "Pink Shoe Laces." The song was sweet and innocent, as befits a young teenager, and was an immediate hit with the preteen crowd easily selling a million copies. Crystalette couldn't control such massive distribution, so the single was shipped by Dot Records. Her follow-up single on Crystalette, "Yes-Sir-Ee," failed to catch on, and Dodie moved on to record for Dot. Unfortunately, Dot was also unable to find material suited for a thirteen-year old, and she was relegated to adult ballads. In 1960, she recorded "Yes, I'm Lonesome Tonight," an answer to Elvis' megahit, "Are You Lonesome Tonight?" It was Dodie's last record to sell in appreciable numbers. After Dot failed to turn her into a country singer, she left the label. Over the next few years, she recorded for Imperial, Dolton and World Pacific as both Dodie and Geraldine Stevens. She rebelled against her parents, marrying when at sixteen and dropping out of school. At age twenty, divorced and with a baby, she began a successful professional comeback, as a background singer for Mac Davis, Sergio Mendes, and many others. Today, she is managed by Dick Clark Productions.

OCT 1 The Poni-Tails plug "I'll Be Seeing You" on "American Bandstand."
Leaving the States for a tour of Australia are the Champs, Jimmie Rodgers, and **Dodie Stevens**.
Frankie Avalon plays the county fair in Shelby, North Carolina.
Billy "Crash" Craddock continues his tour of the Midwest with a three-day stand in Detroit followed by a two-day engagement in Chicago (4-5).
Fabian makes a guest appearance on television's "The Pat Boone Show."
"The Dick Clark Caravan" rolls along through the South, playing tonight in Columbia, SC. Other dates include Charleston, West Virginia (2) and Louisville (3). In Cincinnati (5), the show brings in $8,300 after the promoter spent $2,000 in promotion. (See also OCT 6.)

OCT 2 Sam Cooke takes the spotlight at the Flame Show Bar in Detroit for a week.
Brook Benton headlines his own caravan at it sets off on a ten-week, fifty-city jaunt. Other acts on the bill include Ruth Brown and the Falcons. Tonight's show is in Richmond. Other dates include Forestville (7) and Street, Maryland (9); Youngstown (10); Cleveland (11); and Raleigh (12).

OCT 3 Carl Perkins guests on "The Red Foley Show" on NBC radio.
In Dallas, at the "Big D Jamboree," Johnny Cash is the guest.
Connie Francis, Dale Hawkins, Paul Evans, the Playmates, and Darrell Howe guest on "The Dick Clark Show."

OCT 4 Dick Clark kicks off another ABC-TV venture, the weekly "World of Talent" broadcast at 10:30 p.m. Over the brief course of the program, no rock 'n roll artists appear.

New Releases for the first week in October include "Be My Guest" by Fats Domino on Imperial; "Reville Rock" by Johnny and the Hurricanes on Warwick; LaVern Baker's "Tiny Tim" on Atlantic; "First Love" by the Playmates on Roulette; "(New In) The Ways of Love" by Tommy Edwards on M-G-M; Sarah Vaughan's "Smooth Operator" on Mercury; "That Was Me" by the Fiestas on Old Town; Little Richard's "Whole Lotta Shakin'" on Specialty; "Look In My Eyes" by the Jaguars on Original Sound; and two versions of "The Hunch": by Paul Gayten on Anna and by Bobby

Peterson on V-Tone. Also new this week is Ral Donner's "Tell Me Why" on Scottie. Donner, whose voice closely resembled that of Elvis Presley, will have a Top Ten hit in 1961 with "You Don't Know What You've Got" on Gone. Finally, Joe Stampley's "Glenda" is released on Imperial. Stampley had a mid-sized country career in the 1970s and was lead vocalist on the Uniques' "Not Too Long Ago" on Paula in 1965.

OCT 6   Dinah Washington winds up an extended engagement at New York's Village Vanguard.

Bobby Darin opens at the Sands Hotel and Casino in Las Vegas for three weeks.

"The Dick Clark Caravan" moves through Ohio as it plays Canton tonight. Other dates in the near future include Lorain (7); Columbus (8); Toledo (9); and Grand Rapids, Michigan (10). (See also OCT 20.)

OCT 7   Wynonie Harris moves into the Club 20 Grand in Detroit for a week.

EARLY OCTOBER

Ronnie Hawkins and the Hawks are currently playing gigs across their home country of Canada.

Also in Canada, Ersel Hickey is booked into the Brown Derby in Toronto.

Huey Smith and the Clowns are playing one-nighters through the South.

Shirley and Lee are also on the road, playing dates in Florida and Louisiana.

Jackie Wilson is scheduled to perform at the Flamingo Hotel in Las Vegas with actress Betty Grable. At Miss Grable's insistence, Wilson is forced off the bill. It is reported that she feared his rising popularity.

OCT 8   Billy "Crash" Craddock visits Los Angeles for a three-day engagement.

OCT 9   Tommy Sands participates in a salute to Red Skelton on CBS-TV.

The Playmates join the Sammy Davis, Jr. revue at the Apollo Theater this week.

OCT 10   Brenda Lee, just back from a tour of Brazil, is forced to cancel her scheduled television appearance on "Jubilee U.S.A." She is hospitalized for a week with a thyroid deficiency.

"The Dick Clark Show" features Eddie Cochran, Sammy Turner, Teddy Randazzo, the **Fireflies** and the Isley Brothers.

OCT 12   On "American Bandstand," the Tempos offer "See You In September."

THE FIREFLIES

The Fireflies were a rarity in the music business at this time, a quartet with each member doing double duty as an instrumentalist. Their saga began as Lee Reynolds was going to an audition. He played bass and sang 2nd tenor, and was from Knoxville, Tennessee. He had migrated to New York and worked at the airport while awaiting his "big break." Also at the audition were Vinnie Rodgers, guitar, and Gerry Granahan, vocals. When they discovered that the audition was for a group, the three joined forces and got the gig. This led to "The Crawl," a twangy, guitar instrumental on Roulette by the Fireflys [sic] in 1958. Granahan was part owner of the Ribbon label. Paul Giacalone, from Brooklyn's Eastern District High who also played drums, brought in a new composition, "You Were Mine." He and Granahan finished writing it and called in Ritchie Adams, guitar and baritone and a graduate of Bishop Loughlin High in Brooklyn, to sing lead on what was considered to be a demo. As the demo made the rounds it was obvious it had hit potential, and Granahan released it on Ribbon as by the Fireflies. When calls came in for a group to perform on shows—Adams, Reynolds and Giacalone brought in Johnny Viscelli, sax from Clifton, New Jersey, and Carl Girasoli, guitarist with Dickey Doo and the Don'ts, to fill out the sound. Adams hated performing live so Granahan took over lead on tours. He even sang lead on the record's B-side, "Stella Got a Fella." "You Were Mine" just missed the Top Twenty nationally. The follow-up, "I Can't Say Goodbye" just barely crept into the Top 100. There was one more Ribbon release before the Fireflies went on to Canadian-American for "Marianne" in 1960. Two years later, they were on Tarus for four singles and an album over a space of six years. Granahan became very successful in many areas of show business; Reynolds died in the late 1980s.

RAY SHARPE

Ray Sharpe was born February 8, 1938, in Fort Worth, Texas. He seldom strayed far from his hometown, and he remains a Fort Worth legend today. He grew up in a large, poor family in a small home on East Leuda. From an early age, Ray loved country music, and his early influences were the blue yodeler, Jimmie Rodgers, and Bob Wills. He worked as a janitor's helper to earn enough money to buy his first guitar. From then on, he and his guitar were inseparable. When he was fifteen, the family moved to an area surrounded by beer joints, and Ray learned firsthand of the power of live music. He played guitar and sang in high school talent shows. After school, he sneaked into local bars to listen to the blues men. Before he was asked to come on stage and play. He formed a band called the Blues Wailers and his popularity increased. While playing the Penguin Club, he was discovered by Darrell Glenn, the original singer of "Crying in the Chapel." Glenn asked the Blues Wailers to back him in an upcoming recording session. After Glenn was finished, there was still time remaining, so Sharpe recorded two numbers, an instrumental and "That's the Way I Feel," a song with Coasters' overtones. Sharpe's tapes were sent to producers along with Glenn's, and Lee Hazlewood of Phoenix showed interest. Sharpe was brought to Phoenix for a session that featured guitarist Al Casey. He rerecorded "That's the Way I Feel" which was released on Hamilton, a subsidiary of Dot Records, in September 1958. Hazlewood was producing Duane Eddy for Jamie Records, and Sharpe was invited back to Phoenix to record for Jamie in January 1959. Sharpe played lead guitar this time, backed by Eddy and Casey, with Jim Horn on sax. The result was "Linda Lu," a rock 'n roll classic. He never had another hit, but he issued excellent records for Trey, Gregmark, Park Central, Garex, Atco, Monument, A&M, and Flying High.

New Releases for the second week in October include "I'm Movin' On" by Ray Charles on Atlantic; two from ABC-Paramount: Lloyd Price's "Come Into My Heart" and "Early In The Evening" by the Dubs; **Ray Sharpe**'s "T. A. Blues" on Jamie; three from RCA: Ray Peterson's "Goodnight My Love," "Scarlet Ribbons" by the Browns, and Don Gibson's version of "I'm Movin' On;" the two-part "Smokie" by Bill Black's Combo on Hi; Edd Byrnes' "Kookie's Love Song" on Warner Brothers; Ray Stevens' "My Heart Cries For You" on NRC; "Take This Heart" by Phil Phillips on Mercury; "Stay Beside Me" by Ritchie Valens on Del-Fi; "Whispering Winds" by the Megatrons on Audiocon; Little Willie John's "Let Them Talk" on King; and Lee Allen's "Cat Walk" on Ember.

OCT 13   Dion and the Belmonts are currently playing a series of one-night stands across the Upper Midwest. Tonight's show is in Sioux Falls, South Dakota; Other dates include Clear Lake, Iowa (14); Omaha (15); Cedar Rapids (16); Moline, Illinois (17); and Green Bay (18).

OCT 14   Santo and Johnny make a rare television appearance on "The Perry Como Show on NBC.

OCT 15   As the county fair circuit concludes, Frankie Avalon plays his last one for 1959, in Raleigh, North Carolina, through October 17.

MID-OCTOBER

Dion DiMucci, leader of Dion and the Belmonts, is ordered by his doctor to take a leave of absence from touring. The Belmonts cancel a cross-country tour scheduled for late this month.

Larry Williams is currently on tour through the South.

The Everly Brothers return from a tour of Canada in time to set off on another round of dates with a show in Mobile, Alabama. Rumors are flying that the group is negotiating an end to their contract with Cadence Records. Mentioned as possible candidates as their future label are RCA Victor and Warner Brothers.

In Chicago, Sam Cooke marries his high school sweetheart, Barbara Campbell.

OCT 16   Sam Cooke begins three days at the Copacabana in New York City.

At the Apollo Theater, Pearl Bailey and hubby, drummer Louis Bellson, perform for a week.

The Howard Theater in Washington presents a jazz week featuring Miles Davis, Red Garland, and Dakota Staton.

"Midnight Stroll" is the instrumental offering from the Revels on "American Bandstand."

OCT 17   Connie Francis is off on another tour outside of the United States, this time to Australia.

The Tempos headline a show in Newburgh, New York.

Wanda Jackson makes a guest appearance on CBS-TV's "Jubilee U.S.A."

In England, Sammy Turner guests on the television show "Boy Meets Girls."

"The Dick Clark Show" presents Kitty Kallen, the Spacemen, and the **Passions**.

OCT 18   Ray Charles holds forth at the Masonic Auditorium in Detroit.

OCT 19   Bill Doggett and his combo appear at the Key Club in Minneapolis.

New Releases for the third week in October include Fabian's "Hound Dog Man" b/w "This Friendly World" on Chancellor; Bobby Bare's "I'm Hangin' Up My Rifle" on Fraternity; Charlie Ryan's "Hot Rod Lincoln" on 4-Star; Sandy Nelson's "Drum Party" on Imperial; "Bye Everybody" by the Impalas on Cub; Eddie Holland's "Everybody's Going" on United Artists; two from King: "Dream On" by the Five Keys and "My Sugar Sugar" by the "5" Royales; Bob Luman's "Buttercup" on Warner Brothers; and Adam Wade's "Tell Her For Me" on Co-Ed. Also out this week is the instrumental "Stampede" by the Scarlets on Price. The single will be reissued on Dot within a few weeks.

OCT 20   Diving through the Southwest, "The Dick Clark Caravan" plays Dallas tonight. Succeeding days find the troupe in Houston (21); San Antonio (22); and Oklahoma City (23). (See also OCT 27.)

OCT 23   Johnny Cash guests on NBC-TV's "The Bell Telephone Hour." He will remain in New York City for two more days playing local club dates.

Connie Francis opens at the Chez Paree in Chicago.

Baby Washington, Bobby Freeman, the Miracles, and Gene and Eunice hit the boards at the Howard Theater in Washington this week.

OCT 24   Tommy Edwards begins three days at the El Rancho Club in Winnipeg.

On ABC-TV, "The Dick Clark Show" offers Jan and Dean, the Royal Teens and Jack Scott for viewers.

OCT 25   Brook Benton headlines the show at New Orleans' Municipal Auditorium. Also on the bill are Ruth Brown, the Falcons and the Pips.

OCT 26   Marv Johnson stops the show on "American Bandstand" with his rendition of "You've Got What It Takes."

New Releases for the fourth week in October include two from M-G-M: "Among My Souvenirs" by Connie Francis and "Let's Try Again" by Clyde McPhatter; Jackie Wilson's "Talk That Talk" on Brunswick; "Tear Drop"

THE PASSIONS
The last year of the 1950s was a good one for Brooklyn vocal groups. Both the Mystics and the Crests had big hits that year. So did the Passions. The members of the Passions were Jimmy Gallagher, lead tenor; Tony Armato, tenor; Albee Galione, second tenor; and Vince Acerno, baritone. In 1959, all of the members were seventeen except Armato, who was eighteen. Three of the Passions had previously sung with other local street-corner groups. Gallagher had been part of the Runarounds. Armato had belonged to the Overons, which also had two future members of the Mystics. Galione had recorded one single with the Four Evers on Columbia. The success of the Mystics' "Hushabye" in the summer of 1959 led Jim Gribble to the group, and he quickly signed them to a managerial agreement. They were soon contracted to Audicon Records. For their first release, the group recorded "Just To Be With You," a new song written by Carole King and Paul Simon, who were students at Queens College at the time. "Just To Be With You" was released in July 1959. Remarkably, it took three months before it caught the public's ear. Even when it did, it was not the national hit one might have predicted. It took another fifteen years before it was considered a 1950s standard, becoming a staple on oldies radio stations. Reportedly, it sold a half million copies, as did the follow-up single, "I Only Want You," which was built upon the tune "Life Is But a Dream," but with a much faster tempo. At this time, Acerno was replaced by Lou Rotondo who had sung with the Del-Rays. For their third single, the Passions reached back into the roots of R&B music, reviving the Cadillacs "Gloria." The Passions recorded two more singles for Audicon before leaving the label in 1960. During the next three years, they recorded one single each for Octavia, Jubilee, Diamond and ABC-Paramount, but none sold well.

LARRY HALL

Like so many artists with big hits in the late 1950s, Larry Hall tasted success only once. He was born June 30, 1942 (or 1941), in Cincinnati. His hometown had been a hotbed of rock 'n roll activity for almost ten years, but Hall had only flirted with the fringes of Cincinnati's music scene. It wasn't until 1959, when he was a senior in high school, with graduation straight ahead, that he decided to become a singing star. Following this whim, he contacted the owner of Ever Green Records, a local label. Just how Hall ended up with "Sandy," a song composed by Terry Fell, a respected C&W singer and songwriter at the time, is not known. At any rate, he recorded "Sandy" in a rollin' ramblin' style. Not too much was thought of the song, and it was coupled with "Lovin' Tree," a quasi-folk song, which was designated the A-side of the single. Before the record had much of a chance, Ever Green folded, and the songs were leased to the Hot label. By this time it was obvious that "Lovin' Tree" had little potential to be a hit. Hot began promoting the flip side, and was doing well with "Sandy." However, when a national audience discovered the song, Hot was swamped with orders. In August 1959, both Hall and "Sandy" ended up on Strand Records of New York. "Sandy" was a hit through the end of 1959 and into 1960. Hall tried his best to come up with a second hit, but his material defeated him. His second Strand single was "A Girl Like You." It had cute lyrics by a young Burt Bacharach, but Hall's voice was not up to the Latin rhythm of the melody. His third single, "I'll Stay Single," wasn't much better. Just the title of his fourth release, "Kool Luv," notified everyone that Larry Hall's recording career was over just after it began. He stayed with Strand into 1961, issuing two more singles on the label. Later, he also recorded for the Gold Leaf label before he disappeared completely.

by Santo and Johnny on Canadian-American; "El Paso" by Marty Robbins on Columbia; "Shimmy, Shimmy, Ko-Ko-Bop" by Little Anthony and the Imperials on End; Freddy Cannon's "Way Down Yonder in New Orleans" on Swan; two from King: "Nobody Listens to a Teenager" by Trini Lopez and "I Could Love You" by Hank Ballard and the Midnighters; "Heavenly Blues" by King Curtis on Atco; Bobby Freeman's "Ebb Tide" on Josie; "The Evening Star" by the Jamies on United Artists; "Wouldn't It Be Wonderful" by the Four Esquires on Paris; and "Shotgun" by the Playboys on Ric. Finally, this weeks sees the release of Frankie Valley's "Please Take a Chance" on Decca. Valley, whose real last name is Castelluccio, will use the spelling Valli as lead vocalist with the Four Lovers and the Four Seasons.

OCT 27 Dave "Baby" Cortez is currently working the tour circuit in the Southeast. Tonight he plays Durham, North Carolina. Other dates include Spartanburg (28); Jackson, Tennessee (29); Nashville (30); and Winston-Salem (31). (See also NOV 1.)
"The Dick Clark Caravan" cuts back through the nation's midsection playing Omaha tonight, as well as Minneapolis (28); Des Moines (29); Peoria (30); and finally ending its successful run with a show in Milwaukee (31).
Teddy Randazzo performs at the Club Elegante in Brooklyn through November 1.

OCT 28 New York's Copacabana rolls out the red carpet for Dinah Washington as she starts a week-long engagement.

OCT 30 Carl Perkins plays a two-day stand in Tulsa.
"American Bandstand" welcomes the Revels to the show as they perform "Midnight Stroll."

OCT 31 Over the next ten days, Wanda Jackson runs through a quick tour of Kansas, Iowa, Nebraska, and Missouri.
Larry Hall guests on "The Dick Clark Show" along with Carl Mann, the Revels, the Crests, and Santo and Johnny.
Fabian's first movie, "Hound Dog Man," opens nationally.

THE TOP ROCK 'N ROLL RECORDS FOR OCTOBER 1959

1. Mack The Knife - Bobby Darin
2. Put Your Head On My Shoulder - Paul Anka
3. Sleep Walk - Santo and Johnny
4. ('Til) I Kissed You - The Everly Brothers
5. Teen Beat - Sandy Nelson
6. Mr. Blue - The Fleetwoods
7. I'm Gonna Get Married - Lloyd Price
8. Poison Ivy - The Coasters
9. Red River Rock - Johnny and the Hurricanes
10. Just Ask Your Heart - Frankie Avalon

11. Primrose Lane - Jerry Wallace
12. Broken-Hearted Melody - Sarah Vaughan
13. Sea Of Love - Phil Phillips
14. Hey Little Girl - Dee Clark
15. I Want To Walk You Home/I'm Gonna Be A Wheel Someday
    - Fats Domino
16. Makin' Love - Floyd Robinson
17. The Angels Listened In - The Crests
18. Say Man - Bo Diddley
19. Mary Lou - Ronnie Hawkins
20. You Were Mine - The Fireflies
21. (7 Little Girls) Sittin' In the Back Seat - Paul Evans
22. You're Gonna Miss Me - Connie Francis
23. You Better Know It - Jackie Wilson
24. Just As Much As Ever - Bob Beckham
25. Danny Boy - Conway Twitty
26. Tucumcari - Jimmie Rodgers
27. In The Mood - Ernie Fields
28. Every Little Thing I Do - Dion and the Belmonts
29. Where - The Platters
30. Woo-Hoo - The Rock-A-Teens
31. Love Potion #9 - The Clovers
32. Torquay - The Fireballs
33. Baby Talk - Jan and Dean
34. Shout (part 1-2)- The Isley Brothers
35. Boo Boo Stick Beat - Chet Atkins
36. The Enchanted Sea - The Islanders
37. Kissin' Time - Bobby Rydell
37. Lavender Blue - Sammy Turner
39. Come On And Get Me - Fabian
40. Some Kind-a Earthquake - Duane Eddy
41. What'd I Say (part 1-2) - Ray Charles
42. I'm a Hog For You - The Coasters
43. My Own True Love - Jimmy Clanton
44. Okefenokee - Freddy Cannon
45. There Goes My Baby - The Drifters
46. It Was I - Skip and Flip
47. Plenty Good Lovin' - Connie Francis
48. Oh Carol - Neil Sedaka
49. We Got Love - Bobby Rydell
50. Two Fools - Frankie Avalon

Also on the "pop" charts:
Don't You Know - Della Reese
Lonely Street - Andy Williams
Battle Hymn of the Republic - The Mormon Tabernacle Choir
Deck of Cards - Wink Martindale
Worried Man - The Kingston Trio

October 1959
ARTIST OF THE MONTH

PAUL ANKA

Paul Anka

Considering the close ties between the United States and Canada, both economically and culturally, it is interesting how few Canadian rock 'n rollers could make the big break into the United States music markets in the 1950s. Before Paul Anka, the number of Canadian rock 'n rollers could be counted on the fingers of one hand. The Diamonds were the best known group, although their style certainly was not pure rock n' roll by any stretch of the imagination. During the 1950s, Jack Scott was the biggest solo rock 'n roll artist from Canada, other than Anka, although Scott had moved to Detroit long before he started performing.

Anka was born in Ottawa, Ontario, on July 30, 1941. His father, Andrew, was a restaurateur whose clients included many of the members of the Canadian Parliament. Paul was diminutive in size but his build was stocky. He drove himself to excel in sports, but his real love from early childhood was always music. By the age of eleven, he was a regular act in the nightclubs across the Ottawa River in Gatineau and Hull in the province of Quebec. He also appeared as far away as Glouscester, Massachusetts. His performance at this time consisted mainly of impersonations of the "pop" vocalists of the day.

At Fisher Park High School, he was part of the vocal trio calling themselves the Bobby Soxers. They became locally popular and often opened shows for better-known groups such as the Four Aces and the Rover Boys. It was then that Anka began composing songs based on his personal experiences. He was also taking lessons on piano and guitar. At age fifteen, Anka auditioned for local television shows without success. Disappointed, he decided to spend part of 1956 visiting Los Angeles, where he stayed with an uncle who worked at the local Civic Playhouse.

On a brief trip to Las Vegas in 1956, Paul Anka and his uncle attended the show at the New Frontier Hotel. Third on the bill that night was Elvis Presley. Anka passed a note backstage, asking to speak with Elvis, who readily obliged. The two maintained their friendship for the next twenty years.

Anka's uncle became interested in young Paul's music and arranged for the industry contacts Paul needed. On a whim, the two made an appointment with Modern Records where they were introduced to Ernie Freeman, band leader and artists and repertoire director for the label. Freeman was impressed with Anka and invited him to come to his home to rehearse. Soon, Paul was in the Modern studios recording a couple of songs he had just completed, "I Confess" and "Blau-Wile Deveest Fontaine." Backing vocals on the release were performed by one of the resident groups at Modern, the Cadets—who also recorded as the Jacks. The record received little attention upon its release, selling a reported three-thousand copies. Anka later recalled that it was being played in Buffalo and the Canadian provinces when he returned home in September.

Just imagine. Here he was, just barely fifteen and with his first record on the market. However, Paul Anka considered this a natural progression, and he was disappointed when his first release was only a minor hit in Canada. More than ever, he was determined to make the "big time." He felt certain that the key to his success was through his songwriting. To that end, he began pouring his heart out on paper, writing reams of couplets and adding musical accompaniment.

In early 1957, with no further action on "I Confess," and no offer to return to Los Angeles for a follow-up single, Anka started making plans to attend college and was considering careers in law or news reporting.

During the Easter vacation from high school, he convinced his parents to allow him to travel to New York in the company of the Rover Boys, a Canadian quartet. The Rover Boys took Anka along when they met with Don Costa, the director of artists and repertoire for ABC-Paramount Records, the label for whom the Rover Boys recorded. Initially, Costa was more impressed with young Paul's sheaf of completed songs than with his singing ability. Paul's father was summoned to New York, and a contract was signed. Under Costa's direction, Paul was sent to voice coaches and he received schooling in song composition. Within a month, ABC-Paramount was ready to record Paul's composition of "Diana" backed with "Don't Gamble With Love."

"Diana" was an anguished plea from a young teenage boy who was crying for love from an older teenage girl. The musical accompaniment was based on a popular Latin rhythm called "cha-lypso," a modified cha-cha done to a calypso beat. The cha-lypso had been invented a few months earlier, when teenagers needed a special step so they could dance to Mickey and Sylvia's "Love Is Strange." The cha-lypso would show up again in 1959 when Bobby Darin released "Dream Lover." The enormity of the popularity of "Diana" as a song can be measured by the more than three-hundred recordings of "Diana" issued in sixteen countries between 1957 and 1963. Worldwide, Anka's own version reportedly sold more than nine million copies.

One of the first people to recognize that "Diana" had the makings of a hit record was Irving Feld. He was the owner of a chain of record stores in the Northeast as well as the entrepreneur who financed the rock 'n roll caravan dubbed the "Biggest Show of Stars." Feld wasted no time in securing Anka for his fall tour. By the time the "Biggest Show of Stars for '57" took to the road, on September 6, "Diana" was already riding the top of the record charts, and Anka's second single, "I Love You Baby," was set for release.

For Paul Anka, the next three years must have been a blur. "You Are My Destiny," his third ABC-Paramount single, reached the Top Ten in early 1958. Then Anka's career began a yearlong decline. There were new singles every two or three months. Where "Crazy Love" and "(All of a Sudden) My Heart Sings" cracked the Top Twenty, "Midnight," "Just Young" and "I Miss You So" did not fare as well.

By early 1959, it appeared to many observers that Paul Anka's success with "Diana" might just be a onetime stroke of good fortune. Then, Anka was chosen to play a role in a low-budget movie, "Girl's Town." In the film, he sang another song pleading for love. It was titled

"Lonely Boy," and it became one of his biggest hits. The songwriting may have been dramatic and the music symphonic in its presentation, but it was just what teens wanted. The single leapt to the top of the record charts. It was followed, in rapid succession, by "Put Your Head On My Shoulder, "It's Time To Cry," "Puppy Love," and "My Home Town," all Top Ten hits.

Anka was in demand around the world. He appeared at the London Palladium as well as other English venues in November 1957 and toured Australia the following January with Buddy Holly. In 1960, he performed in South Africa. He later had a gold record in Italy for "Ogni Volta," a song he first introduced at the 1964 San Remo Song Festival.

After Anka turned eighteen, he began adapting his image and style to appeal to the adult customers of the better supper clubs around the country. In 1959, he debuted at the Sahara Hotel in Las Vegas. A year later, he became the youngest performer to headline the revue at the Copacabana. As a result, his popularity among teenage record-buyers began to falter again. After "My Home Town," Anka still had good-sized hits with "Summer's Gone," "The Story of My Love," "Tonight My Love, Tonight," and "Dance On Little Girl." However, his singles were having difficulty breaking into the upper echelon of record sales. Anka's film role in "Girl's Town" led to appearances in "Look In Any Window" (1961) and "The Longest Day" (1962), and he wrote the theme songs for each.

In 1962, in an attempt to shore up his record sales as well as reach a broader audience, Anka switched record labels and signed with RCA Victor. His first few singles for the new label sold well, and he had hits with "Love Me Warm and Tender" and "A Steel Guitar and a Glass of Wine." There were also failures such as "I'm Coming Home" and "Hello Jim." During the five years after 1963, Anka didn't place a single on the charts. By 1971, he was ready to leave RCA Victor, signing this time with Buddah Records, a new label that he felt was more in tune with the current record-buying audience. There were a handful of singles on Buddah, but Anka's songwriting style was out of vogue. He went a couple of years without a record contract. Then, in 1974, he released another misguided effort on Fame Records, a company widely respected for its intense soul sound.

Later in 1974, Anka signed with United Artists Records, a company known at this time for its middle-of-the-road music, and at onetime home to Don Costa. Remarkably, Anka's first release for the label, "(You're) Having My Baby" went straight up the charts to Number One. The song's point of view generated feedback from the budding feminist movement and Anka obliged them by performing the song on stage as "(You're) Having Our Baby." Over the course of two years, Anka's comeback continued with "One Man Woman/One Woman Man," "I Don't Like To Sleep Alone," and "Times Of Your Life." His songs were no longer directed toward teens but at the newly discovered "adult contemporary" market.

As mentioned earlier, in the late 1950s, Anka concentrated his live performances on venues catering to adults. By the 1970s, his show was built around a blend of big-band standards, his own hits, and the songs he had composed for others.

Paul Anka is credited with writing twelve songs that became gold records. Most were recorded by himself. However, among Anka's many successes as a songwriter, his greatest triumph was "My Way," a deft blending of his own lyrics with a melody by French composers Claude Francois and Jacques Revaux. "My Way" became the signature piece for Frank Sinatra, but it was also recorded by hundreds of other artists including Elvis Presley and Anka, himself. Anka also composed "It Doesn't Matter Anymore," released by Buddy Holly just before Holly's tragic death. "She's A Lady" was a million-seller for Tom Jones in 1971. Anka has also written songs for Wayne Newton, Engelbert Humperdink, and Sammy Davis, Jr. It was Anka's theme music that introduced Johnny Carson and "The Tonight Show" to television audiences every weeknight beginning in 1962. In addition, in 1972, Donny Osmond had hits with "Puppy Love" and "Lonely Boy." In the late 1970s, Kodak revived "The Times of Your Life" for a successful advertising campaign. Unknown to many, Paul Anka produced the 1969 album and single of "Oh, Happy Day" by the Edwin Hawkins Singers.

Today, Paul Anka is a multimillionaire, due to his nightclub successes, his record and songwriting royalties, and his wise investments including two music publishing houses. He maintains a lifestyle that includes a personal jet, a large ranch on the California coast near Monterey and a home in Las Vegas. In 1991, he purchased a percentage of the Ottawa Senators hockey team.

In August 1990, Paul Anka officially became a citizen of the United States. In a strange way, this act seems somewhat out of place. More than most other entertainers, Paul Anka is truly a man of the world.

November 1959

JERRY KELLER
Jerry Keller never aspired to be a rock 'n roller. He just wanted to sing. Keller was born on June 20, 1937, in Fort Smith, Arkansas. His family moved to Tulsa when he was seven. During high school, he joined a vocal group calling themselves the Lads of Note. He and the Lads of Note had their own fifteen-minute radio show on KACK, where Keller was a deejay, as well as appearing on local television. After graduation in 1955, he set his sights on a college degree. To help pay his tuition, he began singing with a local orchestra headed by Jack Dalton. Encouraged by friends and family, but frustrated by his inability to grow professionally in Tulsa, he moved to New York City in 1956. If Keller was unhappy with Tulsa, he must have been distraught with the Big Apple. For more than a year, he could not find work as a singer and, in desperation, took a clerking position. He auditioned for singing jobs while taking voice lessons and writing songs. Eventually, he was hired to record demos of songs written by others. After church one Sunday, he ran into Pat Boone, who was attending Columbia University while maintaining a rigorous recording and personal appearance schedule. Boone was helpful in leading Keller to a competent manager. Keller signed a contract with Kapp Records, a subsidiary of Capitol. His first release was "Here Comes Summer," an upbeat song that he had composed. The timing was perfect, as the single was released in mid-May 1959. It was just the song disc jockeys needed to perk up their summer programming. The record remained a best seller until fall. Then, for years it was revived briefly each spring to help usher in summer again. Keller's popularity faded quickly. He left Kapp after a few more releases. In 1961, he had two singles on Capitol, after which he recorded for Coral, Reprise, and RCA. All along, he continued to write songs, including "Turn Down Day," a best seller in 1966 for Cyrkle.

NOV 1   Paul Anka pays a visit to CBS-TV's "The Ed Sullivan Show." Immediately following the show, he leaves for Paris where he will open a four-week stay at the Olympia Theater on November 4.
   Continuing with his southern tour, Dave "Baby" Cortez plays Atlanta tonight as well as Charleston (2); Greenville (3); Charlotte (5); Macon (6); Columbia (7); Birmingham (7); and Chattanooga (9).

New Releases for the first week in November include Paul Anka's "It's Time To Cry" on ABC-Paramount; two from Imperial: Ricky Nelson's "I Wanna Be Loved" and "Someday" by the Paris Sisters; "Why?" by Frankie Avalon on Chancellor; Jimmy Clanton's "Go, Jimmy, Go" on Ace; four from RCA: "If I Had a Girl" by Rod Lauren; "Tonight You Belong To Me" by Floyd Robinson, Johnny Restivo's "Our Wedding Day," and "He'll Have to Go" by Jim Reeves; "Darling Lorraine" by the Knockouts on Shad; Bo Diddley's "Say Man, Back Again" on Checker; "A Year Ago Tonight" by the Crests on Co-Ed; "Harlem Nocturne" by the Viscounts on Madison; Jimmy McCracklin's "The Georgia Slop" on Mercury; Robin Luke's "Walkin' In The Moonlight" on Dot; Bonnie Guitar's "Candy Apple Red" on Dolton; "Mediterranean Moon" by the Rays on XYZ; **Jerry Keller**'s "There Are No Such Things" on Kapp; "The Sheik of Araby" by Johnny and the Rebels on Roulette; and "White Buckskin Sneakers and Checker-Board Socks" by the Bell Notes on Time. Finally, Fernwood releases "Beg Your Pardon" by Dewey Phillips, the Memphis deejay who introduced Elvis Presley to the world on July 10, 1954.

NOV 3   Wanda Jackson is playing one-nighters across the Great Plains. Tonight she's in Sioux City, followed by Topeka (4); Omaha (5); Lincoln (6); Wichita (7); and Kansas City (8).

NOV 4   The Copa Club in Newport, Kentucky, welcomes Bill Doggett and his combo for a five day run.
   In France, Paul Anka begins a four-week stay at the Olympia Theater in Paris.
   Fabian is touring the Pacific Northwest with Floyd Robinson, playing Seattle tonight, as well as Portland (7) and Spokane (8).

NOV 5   Fats Domino entertains the crowd in Raleigh, North Carolina, tonight. Future dates include Durham (6); Charlottesville, Virginia (7); and Nashville (9).

NOV 6   Freddy Cannon offers "Okefenokee" and "Way Down Yonder in New Orleans" on "American Bandstand."

    Carl Perkins is currently on tour in Colorado. Tonight he entertains in Denver, followed by Montrose (7) and Fort Collins (8).

    The Apollo Theater offers the talents of Clyde McPhatter, LaVern Baker, and Santo and Johnny for patrons this week.

    Bill Haley and His Comets perform at the Lindenwold Inn in Philadelphia.

    Pearl Bailey and Louis Bellson entertain the crowd this week at Washington's Howard Theater.

NOV 7   Annette, Bobby Rydell, the Skyliners, and the Nutty Squirrels entertain the TV audience tonight on "The Dick Clark Show."

EARLY NOVEMBER

- The Platters are the headliners at the grand opening of the Versailles Del Prado Hotel in Mexico City.
- The Fiestas are currently touring through the South.
- Rod Lauren's new RCA Victor release is the subject of a massive advertising campaign in which 25,000 copies of the single in its "day-glo pink" picture sleeve are given away to dealers.
- Marvin Rainwater is working his way through a sixteen-day tour of Canada.
- Minnesota Mining and Manufacturing (3-M), the leader in blank recording tape, introduces its own version of the tape cartridge to compete with RCA. The biggest difference is that the 3-M tape will travel at 1-7/8" per second while the RCA tape travels at 3-3/4" per second. Introduction of the RCA cartridge has been less than successful due to manufacturing "bugs" in the playback units. Neither of these formats became successful, and it remained for the designer of the Lear Jet to devise the 8-track system in the 1960s before tape cartridges flourished.
- Earl Bostic is currently at the El Rancho Club in Philadelphia. Also in town, Roy Hamilton is currently performing at the Celebrity Room.
- Connie Francis is currently performing at the Chez Paree in Chicago.

NOV 8   Lee Allen brings his instrumental combo to the Sunday ball at the Labor Union Hall in New Orleans.

NOV 9   Annette makes another appearance on "American Bandstand," this time singing "First Name Initial."

    Louis Jordan starts a week-long engagement at the Showboat in Philadelphia.

New Releases for the second week in November include "Lucky Devil" by Carl Dobkins, Jr. on Decca; "Honey Hush" by Joe Turner on Atlantic; two from Mercury: "What Does It Matter" by the Platters and "Naughty Rock & Roll" by Boyd Bennett; **Eddie Cochran**'s "Hallelujah, I Love

EDDIE COCHRAN (PT. 2)
During the height of his popularity, Eddie Cochran was constantly in demand as a guitarist. While recording for Crest Records in 1956, he played on Bo Davis' Crest single, "Let's Coast Awhile." That year he also backed Memphis rocker Lee Denson's "New Shoes" on Vik and Ray Stanley's two singles on Zephyr. In 1957, he worked on Bob Denton's session that produced "Sick and Tired." In 1958, the year of "Summertime Blues" and "C'Mon Everybody," he played on Skeets McDonald's hottest record, "You Oughta See Grandma Rock" on Capitol. That same year he taught Paul Peek the guitar intro for "Sweet Skinny Jenny." He also sang backing vocals on Gene Vincent's recording sessions in 1958. Cochran's frequent collaborator, Jerry Capehart, recorded "I Hates Rabbits" as Jerry Neal (with Cochran on guitar) which was issued on Dot. Cochran was lead guitarist on Troyce Key's "Drown In My Tears" on Warner Brothers. He played on "Should I" by Mike Clifford issued on Liberty in 1959. That same year, he produced and played on the sessions for his own band, the Kelly Four, on Silver. Also on Silver, Cochran did the same in 1960 for Jewel and Eddie (Jewel Akens of "The Birds and The Bees" and Eddie Daniels). "Strollin' Guitar" by the Kelly Four, which also appeared as the flip side of "Opportunity" by Jewel and Eddie, is an instrumental featuring Eddie on guitar. Also in 1960, he performed on "My Tattle Tale" on Guaranteed Records by the Galaxies. A 1961 Crest single by the Gee Cee's (Glen Campbell), "Annie Had a Party," featured Cochran. This must have been one of his final sessions. In the early morning of April 17, 1960, Cochran, his fiancee Sharon Sheeley, his manager Patrick Thompkins, and Gene Vincent were speeding toward London's airport when their taxi blew a tire and careened into a lamp post. Eddie was taken to St. Martin's Hospital. He died within a matter of hours.

Her So" on Liberty; **Mark Dinning**'s "Teen Angel" on M-G-M; Jimmy Reed's "Baby What You Want Me To Do" on Vee-Jay; "Don't Sweat It Baby" by the Four Seasons on Alanna; "Dynamite" by Cliff Richard on ABC-Paramount; "Jack of All Trades" by Eugene Church on Class; "This Heart of Mine" by the Falcons on Chess; and Sanford Clark's "I Can't Help It" on Jamie. Also out this week is a solo single from the lead vocalist with the Five Satins and the Scarlets: Rudy West's "As Sure As I Live" on King.

NOV 10   Fats Domino makes a rare appearance on "American Bandstand" to sing "Be My Guest."

NOV 11   Lloyd Price is the featured artist at the Copacabana in New York City.
　　　　Bobby Darin guests on "The Louis Jordan Timex Special" on NBC-TV.

NOV 13   The Chicago Music Fair runs for the next ten days. Rock 'n roll talent offered on various days includes Fabian, Jimmie Rodgers, the Platters, and Lloyd Price.
　　　　The weekly revue at the Apollo Theater in New York features the Crests.
　　　　In Detroit, Bill Doggett returns to the Flame Lounge for a week.

NOV 14   Tommy Edwards takes the stage at the Erie Social Club in Philadelphia.
　　　　Fabian, Sam Cooke, Jimmy Clanton, and Johnny and the Hurricanes are guests on "The Dick Clark Show."

NOV 15   Johnny Cash, the Collins Kids, and Carl Perkins crisscross the nation's breadbasket, playing in Jefferson City, Missouri, tonight. Other scheduled dates include Delorah, Iowa (16); Sioux Falls (17); Ottumwa, Iowa (18); Topeka (19); Ft. Worth (20), and Austin (21). Cash takes ill in Ottumwa and is hospitalized with acute appendicitis. Johnny Horton fills in for Cash on the remaining dates.
　　　　Earl Grant appears on "The Ed Sullivan Show" on CBS-TV.

MID-NOVEMBER

Bill Haley and His Comets leave on an extended tour of South America.

The Drifters are currently on an exhausting tour through the South which extends until early December.

Johnny and the Hurricanes are playing dates in North Carolina.

ABC-Paramount Records announces the signing of Ray Charles to its growing roster of rhythm and blues acts. Charles has been with Atlantic Records since June 1952 and recently has matured dramatically as a recording and performing artist. Atlantic is unable to match the three-year contract offered by ABC-Paramount which includes Charles' ownership of his own recordings

MARK DINNING
He didn't create the "death rock" song, as he has been credited. Jody Reynolds' "Endless Sleep" probably deserves that dubious accolade. However, Mark Dinning's mega-hit, "Teen Angel," infused the category with graphic images not heard since "Transfusion." He was born in 1933 in Grant County, Oklahoma, the youngest son in a family that boasted nine children. His father was an evangelistic singer in the Church of Christ. The family's baby sitter was Clara Ann Fowler, who became famous as Patti Page. Three of his siblings were the popular country trio, the Dinning Sisters, who had a million seller with "Buttons and Bows" for Capitol Records in 1948. His brother. Ace, also had a combo. With this much musical activity in the family, it's no wonder young Mark decided early in life to pursue his own career in music. Mark married right out of high school and had a baby the next year. He was drafted into the Army in 1954. He was stationed in the Mojave Desert where he entertained the lonesome troops for two years. On his discharge, he headed straight for Nashville. With his connections and fine voice, he soon landed a contract with M-G-M Records as a country artist. In 1957, "Shameful Ways" was his first single. It flopped. He next tried a teen-oriented ditty, "School Fool," with the same results. Over the course of two years, M-G-M issued six singles by Dinning that sold miserably. Then, his sister Jean wrote "Teen Angel." With lyrics describing the death of a young woman trapped in a car that his smashed by a locomotive, it took a while for the public to catch on. When it did, "Teen Angel" shot to the top of the charts. Three of his next ten releases on M-G-M made the Top 100 into 1963. The song kept Mark worked club dates for years. He died suddenly on March 21, 1986, following a show in Jefferson, Missouri, his home at the time.

and the establishing of his own Tangerine publishing company.

Jack Scott leaves the Carlton label for a lucrative deal with Top Rank Records which pays him a lump sum of $50,000.

In a similar move, RCA Victor Records makes an guaranteed offer of $100,000 per year to Sam Cooke if he will not renew his contract with Keen Records and sign with RCA. After six-weeks of thoughtful consideration, Cooke will accept RCA's offer on January 23, 1960.

(As a point of reference, almost exactly four years earlier, Elvis Presley's recording contract had been purchased from Sun Records by RCA Victor for only $35,000.)

Danny and the Juniors are currently the house entertainment at the Celebrity Room in Philadelphia.

NOV 16   Bobby Darin begins a one-week stand at Sciolla's in Philadelphia.

Dinah Washington plays a week at the Club 20 Grand in Detroit.

In Washington, the Casino Royal presents Earl Grant for the week.

New Releases for the third week in November include "Run, Red, Run" by the Coasters on Atco; Dee Clark's "How About That" on Abner; Sam Cooke's "Happy In Love" on Specialty; Rosco Gordon's "Just a Little Bit" on Vee-Jay; Lowell Fulson's "It Took A Long Time" on Checker; "Don't Hold It Against Me" by **Joe Tex** on Ace; "I Really Do" by the Spectors Three on Trey; and Johnny Tillotson's "Never Let Me Go" on Cadence.

NOV 17   Through the magic of videotape, Bobby Darin is the guest on NBC-TV's "Lincoln-Mercury Startime" show, "George Burns in the Big Time," an hour-long broadcast at 9:30 p.m.

NOV 18   "The Biggest Show of Stars for '59" arrives at the Municipal Auditorium in New Orleans. Jackie Wilson headlines a show that features Little Willie John, Eugene Church, Frankie Lymon, Baby Washington, Gene and Eunice, the Five Keys, Bobby Lewis, and Sil Austin and his band.

Connie Francis makes a guest appearance on "The Perry Como Show" on NBC-TV. She introduces her version of "Mama," a song from an album she recorded while in England.

Steve Gibson and His Red Caps open at the New Frontier Hotel in Las Vegas for six weeks.

Red Prysock is welcomed to the El Rancho Club in Philadelphia.

NOV 20   This week, Clyde McPhatter is playing to a full house nightly at the Howard Theater in Washington. Also appearing are the Crests and the Clovers.

Louis Jordan and the Tympany Five start a two-week run at the Key Club in Minneapolis.

JOE TEX
Joe Tex would compete with James Brown for the title of "Soul Brother Number One." Then he would give it up for the church. And, like many others, he would be done too soon. He was born August 8, 1933, in Baytown, Texas. His early singing lessons came as a member of the church choir. At eighteen, he won an amateur contest with the grand prize being a trip to New York City and a spot on the Apollo Theater's weekly talent show. He won, not once, but four weeks in a row. Back in Baytown, he continued to sing gospel on Sundays, but nights would find him entertaining in East Texas clubs. His fame spread slowly, eventually reaching Jackson, Mississippi, and Ace Records. In 1958, Tex recorded "Cut It Out," the first his half dozen singles for Ace. In 1960, he signed with Anna Records, a fledgling Detroit label. The owner, Berry Gordy, was recording just about anything that walked into his office, hoping for a hit. Any of the three Anna singles by Tex could have been a best seller. In fact, James Brown had a hit with his cover of Tex's third Anna release, "Baby, You're Right." Gordy was busy promoting his new group, the Miracles, and most Anna artists shuffled aside. Tex moved on to Checker Records, which released "You Can Keep Her" in 1963. (Two other singles, including a reissue of "Baby, You're Right," would be released by Checker in 1964-65.) At this point, Joe Tex could be forgiven for feeling disappointed. Nevertheless, he continued on. In 1964 he landed a deal with Dial Records, a label distributed by Atlantic. His first Dial release, "Hold On To What You've Got," was a huge hit. Over the next five years, Tex had one R&B hit after another. In 1972, after a three year hiatus from the charts, his "I Gotcha" was his biggest selling single. Soon after, he left show business for three years to concentrate on religion. He died on August 13, 1982, of a heart attack suffered at his home in Navasota, Texas.

441

SANDY NELSON
Sander L. "Sandy" Nelson was born December 1, 1938, in Santa Monica, California. As a teenager he took lessons on a variety of instruments—piano, vibraphone, guitar, and drums. Influenced by legendary percussionist Earl Palmer, Nelson concentrated on drums. He played with jazz combos until he met Kip Tyler, a local legend who had recorded the soundtrack for "Rock, Pretty Baby." Tyler had had two singles on Challenge, and his band included Larry Knechtel (guitar—a future member of Bread), Steve Douglas (sax—Duane Eddy sessions) and Bruce Johnston (piano—Beach Boys). Through Johnston, Nelson met Phil Spector and played on "To Know Him Is To Love Him." When drummer Cozy Cole hit with "Topsy" in 1958, Nelson was encouraged. In the summer of 1959, Preston Epps had a best selling single with "Bongo Rock" on Original Sound Records, a label owned by L. A. deejay Art Laboe. Laboe helmed the Starla label, for which Kip Tyler recorded "Let's Monkey Around." At that session, Nelson approached Laboe with a demo of a drum instrumental. The subsequent session featured backing by Johnston on piano, with guitar by Richie Podolor (who later recorded on Imperial as Richie Allen). "Teen Beat," issued on Original Sound, was an immediate sensation. With this million-seller on his resume, Nelson found himself playing on hits by Kathy Young, the Hollywood Argyles, Mel Carter, Johnny Crawford, Ron Holden, and Little Caesar among others. His own recording career fizzled for two years following "Teen Beat." Nelson, who was not under contract to Original Sound, signed with Imperial. It took four singles before "Let There Be Drums" earned him a second gold record in late 1961. In 1963, a motorcycle accident resulted in the loss of part of his right leg. He came back a better drummer and remained with Imperial until 1969.

Crash Craddock begins a southern tour with the "Holiday House Party" that will take him from North Carolina through Virginia and Tennessee to Florida.

In Texas, Johnny Cash performs tonight in Corpus Christi. Tomorrow finds the trouper in Austin.

The Roxy in Philadelphia offers the dynamic Dynatones for patrons this week.

Jocko's "Rocketship Revue" takes over the Apollo Theater for a week. Featured performers are the Five Satins, the Isley Brothers, Little Anthony and the Imperials, and the Flamingos.

NOV 21   Brenda Lee guests on a fifteen-minute portion of NBC radio's "Monitor" which is hosted by Red Foley.

Freddy Cannon, Frankie Laine, the Browns, and Billy Storm are featured on "The Dick Clark Show."

NOV 22   Connie Francis headlines the show at the Carnegie Theater in New York City.

The second edition of "The Dick Clark Caravan" sets off for thirty-eight days with Frankie Avalon at the helm.

NOV 23   Connie Francis opens a one-week engagement at the Faisan Bleu in Montreal.

Pep's Lounge in Philadelphia welcomes the Bill Doggett Combo for a week's stay.

New Releases for the fourth week in November include Roy Orbison's "Uptown" on Monument; two from Top Rank: Jack Scott's "What In The World's Come Over You" and "Bulldog" by the Fireballs; Duane Eddy's "Bonnie Came Back" on Jamie; Johnny Burnette's "Settin' The Woods On Fire" on Liberty; "Gonna See My Baby" by the Addrisi Brothers on Del-Fi; "I Can't Say Goodbye" by the Fireflies on Ribbon; Crash Craddock's "I Want That" on Columbia; "Look At Little Sister" by Hank Ballard and the Midnighters on King; "Hill Stomp" by the Strangers on Titan; "Down By The Station" by the Four Preps on Capitol; Ronnie Hawkins' "Southern Love" on Roulette; "Wild Cat" by Gene Vincent and His Blue Caps on Capitol; Larry Williams' "Get Ready" on Chess; "I Was Such a Fool" by the Flamingos on End; and Chubby Checker's "Samson and Delilah" on Parkway. Also new this week is Dee Dee Ford's "Good Morning Blues" on Todd. Miss Ford teamed with Don Gardner for a few hits in 1962, the biggest of which was "I Need Your Loving" on Fire.

NOV 24   **Sandy Nelson** packs his drum kit off to Hawaii for dates through November 30. Appearing with Nelson is Jimmy Clanton.

NOV 25   In Newport, Kentucky, the welcome mat is out for the LaVern Baker show which is booked for the next five days.

Alan Freed completes a two-day marathon with Senate investigators who are probing the widening payola scandal. Freed has recently been fired from his deejay jobs with WABC radio and WNEW-TV.

NOV 26   The Coasters bring their brand of musical comedy to "American Bandstand," singing "What About Us."

Connie Francis is the Cinderella Queen in Macys' Thanksgiving Day Parade in New York.

NOV 27   Clyde McPhatter appears at the Town Hall in Brooklyn through December 3.

The Dew Drop Cafe and Hotel in New Orleans welcomes Joe Tex for a three-day stand.

Della Reese entertains the crowd at Fack's II in San Francisco this week.

The Five Satins headline the revue at the Howard Theater in Washington this week. Also on the show are the Dubs, the Cadillacs and the Fireflies.

NOV 28   This Saturday night's guests on "The Dick Clark Show" are Frankie Avalon, Lloyd Price, Rod Lauren, Gary Stites, and the Am-Par's. Also on hand is Bobby Freeman, who will appear on "American Bandstand" on the Monday, November 30.

Tommy Sands is special guest artist with the Rochester (NY) Civic Symphony Orchestra.

Conway Twitty plays the Shadow Lake Resort near Seattle. He is in the middle of a tour of the Pacific Northwest that began on November 25.

Chuck Berry entertains at the Youth Hall at the New Mexico State Fair Grounds in Albuquerque.

Bill Haley and His Comets appear at the Erie Social Club in Philadelphia.

NOV 29   **Marty Robbins** does double duty at the State Fair Grounds in Nashville. In the afternoon, he races his modified stock car and at night he performs for the fans.

At the Second Annual Grammy Awards ceremony, Bobby Darin's "Mack The Knife" wins Record of the Year, and Darin is named Best New Artist. In addition, Ahmet Ertegun, owner of Atlantic Records and producer of "Mack the Knife" is honored with the Special Trustees Award for Artists and Repertoire Contribution. The Rhythm and Blues Performance of the year goes to Dinah Washington for "What a Diff'rence a Day Makes."

In New Orleans, Ray Charles pulls out all the stops during his show at the Coliseum Arena.

NOV 30   Lloyd Price brings his band to Sciola's Club in Philadelphia. Also in town, the Flamingos begin a six-day stay at Pep's.

LATE NOVEMBER

Charlie Gracie is currently appearing at the Capri in Philadelphia.

MARTY ROBBINS

Marty Robbins is not known as a rock 'n roll artist, but in the 1950s he tasted the forbidden fruit while searching for a hit. Martin Robinson and a twin sister were born September 26, 1925 in Glendale, Arizona. When they were twelve the family moved to Phoenix. At seventeen, he joined the Navy, where he learned to play guitar and entertain. Back in Phoenix, he occasionally sat in with a country band. He formed the K-Bar Cowboys and landed a spot on KYTL radio in nearby Mesa. In 1952 he signed a contract with Columbia Records. His first single, "Tomorrow You'll Be Gone," was okay. Not bad, but nothing out of the ordinary. He released twelve more just like it into late 1954. Then, after hearing Elvis' first single, Marty recorded his own version of "That's All Right." It had more of a country feel than Elvis', but it was a long way from the blues of Big Boy Crudup. Best of all, it was a medium-size hit. In mid-1955, he toured with Elvis. About this time, he covered Chuck Berry's "Maybellene," which was a lot hotter than "That's All Right." In short order, he issued a series of rockers: "Pretty Mama," "Mean Mama Blues" and "Tennessee Toddy." In the fall of 1956, he issued the record that put him over the top: "Singing the Blues." The song ran neck-and-neck with another version by Guy Mitchell. Marty won hands down with the country and rock fans. This was followed by Robbins' wicked version of "Long Tall Sally," followed by "Respectfully Miss Brooks" and another huge hit, "A White Sport Coat (and a Pink Carnation)." He eased back on the throttle after that. He sensed that he was getting to far away from his roots. Thereafter, he issued songs for a more adult audience, while still singing in a style that appealed to teenagers. (More on Marty Robbins in volume three of *The Golden Age of American Rock 'n Roll*.)

THE TOP ROCK 'N ROLL RECORDS FOR NOVEMBER 1959

1. Mack The Knife - Bobby Darin
2. Mr. Blue - The Fleetwoods
3. Put Your Head On My Shoulder - Paul Anka
4. Teen Beat - Sandy Nelson
5. Primrose Lane - Jerry Wallace
6. (7 Little Girls) Sittin' In The Back Seat - Paul Evans
7. In The Mood - Ernie Fields
8. So Many Ways - Brook Benton
9. Just Ask Your Heart - Frankie Avalon
10. Danny Boy - Conway Twitty
11. Oh, Carol - Neil Sedaka
12. Poison Ivy - The Coasters
13. We Got Love - Bobby Rydell
14. You Were Mine - Fireflies
15. ('Til) I Kissed You - The Everly Brothers
16. The Enchanted Sea - The Islanders
17. Unforgettable - Dinah Washington
18. Woo-Hoo - The Rock-A-Teens
19. Dance With Me/(If You Cry) True Love, True Love - The Drifters
20. Say Man - Bo Diddley
21. Love Potion #9 - The Clovers
22. Living Doll - Cliff Richard
23. Be My Guest/I've Been Around - Fats Domino
24. Just As Much As Ever - Bob Beckham
25. High School U.S.A. - Tommy Facenda
26. Hey Little Girl - Dee Clark
27. Believe Me - The Royal Teens
28. Torquay - The Fireballs
29. The Angels Listened In - The Crests
30. Joey's Song - Bill Haley and His Comets
31. Poco Loco - Gene and Eunice
32. Come Into My Heart - Lloyd Price
33. Mary Lou - Ronnie Hawkins
34. Clouds - The Spacemen
35. Always - Sammy Turner
36. Reville Rock - Johnny and the Hurricanes
37. Tennessee Waltz - Bobby Comstock
38. Pretend - Carl Mann
39. Sleep Walk - Santo and Johnny
40. You Got What It Takes - Marv Johnson
41. Midnight Stroll - The Revels
42. Red River Rock - Johnny and the Hurricanes
43. I'm Gonna Get Married - Lloyd Price
44. First Name Initial - Annette
45. I Dig Girls - Bobby Rydell
46. Some Kind-a Earthquake - Duane Eddy
47. The Big Hurt - Toni Fisher

48. Shout (part 1-2) - The Isley Brothers
49. The Hunch - Bobby Peterson
50. Sea of Love - Phil Phillips

Also on the "pop" charts:
Scarlet Ribbons - The Browns
Heartaches By The Number - Guy Mitchell
Misty - Johnny Mathis

November 1959
ARTISTS OF THE MONTH

THE FLEETWOODS

The Fleetwoods

By 1959, in the brief span of four years, the world of music had changed to the point where the Fleetwoods could be considered a rock 'n roll act.

In 1958, Barbara Laine Ellis (born February 20, 1940) and Gretchen Diane Christopher (born February 29, 1940) wanted to form a singing group in their hometown of Olympia, Washington, to entertain at school functions during their senior year. At first, they auditioned other coeds in an attempt to come up with a trio or a quartet, but none of the applicants qualified. Then Barbara and Gretchen decided to work as a duo with instrumental accompaniment. They enlisted Gary Robert Troxel (born November 28, 1939), from nearby Centralia, to play trumpet.

The girls' harmonizing was fine, but Gary's trumpet was out of place. Instead, a suggestion was made to have Gary wordlessly vocalize the trumpet part. Thus, by accident, was born the unique sound of the Fleetwoods—who were known at that time as Two Girls and a Guy. Around their hometown of Olympia, the trio gained immediate popularity when they performed their quiet versions of rock 'n roll hits such as "Goodnight My Love," "Confidential," and "Runaround."

Up to that time, the Pacific Northwest had been largely ignored as a producer of hit rock 'n roll records. To the music industry's way of thinking, "pop" hits came from New York, Los Angeles, Philadelphia, Memphis, or New Orleans. Still, in the area between Portland and Seattle, there was a sizable teen audience that was hungry for entertainment. Concerts and dances by the biggest names in rock n' roll music such as Fats Domino, Little Richard and Ritchie Valens were regular sellouts. Even Elvis made a swing through the area in August and September 1957.

The local success of Two Girls and a Guy did not go unnoticed in Seattle. Country and western songstress Bonnie Guitar was preparing to launch her own Dolphin Record label and was looking for a musical group with teen appeal. Miss Guitar had put out the word that she was auditioning recording acts. A talent scout in Olympia sent in a tape of a version of a song co-written by Two Girls and a Guy titled, "Come Softly."

Miss Guitar was impressed enough to contact the group and invite them to come to Seattle for an audition. The trio ran through a couple of rock 'n roll standards before Miss Guitar asked if would try "Come Softly." It was a simple tune in which the male and female lead voices alternated in counterpoint. In short order, the group found themselves in the studio.

Retitled "Come Softly To Me," the song opened with Gary's tenor voice lightly singing a cappella the non-words "dom-doobie-do" as he runs through one chorus of the melody. For the next two verses, Gary continues while Barbara and Gretchen join in with variations of the repeated phrase "come softly darling." Finally, a full minute into the song, Gary sings the actual verse. The girls and Gary alternate leads for two verses before Gary returns to the "dom-doobie-do" as the song does a slow fade.

"Come Softly To Me" obviously defies easy categorization. Certainly it is among the quietest of all rock 'n roll recordings, possessing a definite folk style that is enhanced by the muted acoustical guitar accompaniment by Miss Guitar. The three voices have an angelic quality. This is not classic rock 'n roll in any sense of the term. However, because the song was aimed to appeal to teenagers, neither is it purely "pop."

The group had recorded a fine piece of material. Now, they needed a less-cumbersome name than Two Girls and a Guy. The name Fleetwoods was proposed—either from the Fleetwood model Cadillac or from the Fleetwood telephone exchange in Olympia. Whichever, it stuck, and the group was ready for stardom.

In mid-February 1959, "Come Softly To Me" became the first release on Dolphin Records. However, a month later, because there was already a company named Dolphin, a lawsuit brought a halt to production as the tune was breaking in the Northwest. In addition, Miss Guitar lacked the resources to press and distribute the large orders she was beginning to receive. For many first-time releases, this would have been a one-two knockout punch. However, Bonnie Guitar was quick-witted. She and Liberty Records of Los Angeles came up with a mutual arrangement where Liberty temporarily released "Come Softly To Me" on its label before there was any serious loss of momentum. Miss Guitar also altered her company's name to Dolton Records, and later releases appeared with the new logo.

With Liberty's help, and with all obstacles out of the way, "Come Softly To Me" started to sell in even larger quantities. The Fleetwoods made their first national television appearance on March 14 on "The Dick Clark Show," and they were on "The Ed Sullivan Show" on April 5. By this time, teenagers across the country were eager for their copy of the record. "Come Softly To Me" sped up the charts, leaping into the Top Twenty in two weeks, and on to Number One by mid-April.

As "Come Softly To Me" sat comfortably atop the record charts, "Graduation's Here" was released as the Fleetwoods' second single. It lacked the premium qualities of "Come Softly To Me," but it sold moderately well nevertheless, remaining a favorite of teens through the summer. Meanwhile, the Fleetwoods stayed in the Northwest, playing club dates. Their only major excursion outside this area had taken place the previous March-April, with the television appearance on the Ed Sullivan show, two of Dick Clark's Saturday night shows, and a Clark-sponsored Miami concert.

After two successful singles, coming up with new material was a problem. The trio had composed "Come Softly To Me" and "Graduation's Here," but they did not consider themselves songwriters. They relied on material from others for most of their stage act, but they needed something unique for their third release. They found what they were looking for in "Mr. Blue." Released in August, the song was an immediate million-seller, staying near the top of the charts through the end of 1959.

As a follow-up to "Mr. Blue," "Outside My Window" was as skillfully crafted, but it did not fare as well. Unfortunately, just when they should have been on the road promoting their latest release, Gary was called into the Navy. He was assigned to a destroyer that was alternately stationed at San Diego and at Alameda near Oakland. The only recourse for the two Fleetwood females was to meet Troxel in Hollywood for recording sessions during his brief periods of shore leave. This arrangement lasted into 1962.

A direct result of this complication in their normal working relationship was that the previous high quality of their recorded work started to falter. With the new constrictions, they could not spend the considerable amount time normally required for each session. They were pushed to attempt to rework material to suit the expectations of their fans. On close inspection, it is clear that the critical balance of voices within the group had changed. The gentle instrumental backing had also given way to pianos and full orchestras on occasion. On "Runaround," their summer hit of 1960, the new change is the style of Fleetwoods is readily apparent. In addition, "Runaround" was the first single released by the Fleetwoods to have been a previous hit for another artist, the Three Chuckles in 1954.

After the poor showing of "The Last One To Know" and "Confidential" (a hit for Sonny Knight in 1956), the Fleetwoods returned to the Top Ten position on the charts with "Tragedy" (a hit for Thomas Wayne in early 1959). By now, the Fleetwoods sounded more like a solo effort by Troxel with the female voices assigned to singing harmony in a background role.

If the Fleetwoods lost sight of the unique vocal harmony that had made them best selling entertainers, they were still selling many singles and albums. This came in the face of changes within the rock 'n roll music business. Every week brought new girl groups, early soul records, and the latest dance fads—not to mention an avalanche of male teen idols. After "Tragedy," the Fleetwoods released "(He's) The Great Imposter" and "Lovers By Night, Strangers By Day." Each sold more than 200,000 copies. However, between those records were "Billy Old Buddy" and "Sure Is Lonesome Downtown," which sold poorly .

The Fleetwoods' last charted single came during the summer of 1963 with "Goodnight My Love," which had been a 1956 hit for Jesse Belvin. The group continued releasing singles on Dolton—eight more over the next two years. However, with the coming of the Beatles and the British Invasion there was little demand for a trio singing sweet harmony. Their recording contract was allowed to expire.

One of the vocal groups most directly influenced by the Fleetwoods' male-female vocal relationship was the folk trio of Peter, Paul and Mary. In late 1962, as the Fleetwoods' popularity reached a low ebb, Peter, Paul and Mary started their long reign as one of folk music's most popular groups.

After their six-year fling at success, the Fleetwoods went their separate ways. The group reformed briefly in the early 1970s to meet the demand for oldies acts. By the late 1970s, Gary was working at a plywood plant near the Canadian border. Barbara (Ellis) Pizzutello managed a mobile home location in Ontario, California. Gretchen (Christopher) Matzen continued to perform solo on occasion while becoming a housewife and instructor of modern dance. In 1982, Gretchen (now divorced) and Gary were working the oldies circuit with a new partner, Cheryl Huggins. Gary was in and out of the group for a time, while Gretchen trained replacements. By 1984, when the Fleetwoods were booked for a week at a large club in Canada, Gretchen was the only remaining original member. Gigs for the Fleetwoods came in spurts: a week at Expo '86, an evening in Seattle. In the 1990s, the Fleetwoods consisted of Gretchen, Karen Cohn and Gene Howard. On the strength of their past hits, they performed across the country, from the Southern California Exposition to Madison Square Garden in New York City.

December 1959

DEC 1   Chuck Berry entertains the crowd in El Paso. Following the show, he meets a young, fourteen-year old Apache woman and agrees to bring her to St. Louis to work as the hat-check stand in his Bandstand Club. (See also DEC 21.)

DEC 2   Jackie Wilson is the special guest of the Copa Club In Newport, KY, for the next five days.
Connie Francis guests on Sid Caesar's CBS-TV special.

DEC 3   The Drifters sing a pair of songs on "American Bandstand."

DEC 4   Bobby Darin opens a three-week run at the Chez Paree in Chicago.

DEC 5   Jimmy Clanton appears at the Youth Hall at the State Fair Grounds in Albuquerque.
Gene Vincent arrives at London's Heathrow Airport to an enthusiastic welcome from his British fans. The following night, he performs at Tooting Granada, London. He is scheduled to remain in England several weeks.
On ABC-TV, "The Dick Clark Show" welcomes Neil Sedaka, Connie Francis, Paul Anka, Marv Johnson, and Ralph DeMarco.

DEC 7   Cozy Cole opens at Baker's Keyboard Lounge in Detroit.

New Releases for the first week in December include "Where Or When" by Dion and the Belmonts on Laurie; the two-part "(Do the) Mashed Potatoes" by Nat Kendricks and the Swans on Dade; "Slouchie" by Bill Justis on Play Me; two from RCA: Nino Tempo's "When You Were Sweet Sixteen" and "Respectable" by the Isley Brothers; Bobby Day's "My Blue Heaven" on Class; "Every Day, Every Way" by the Hollywood Flames on Atco; "Since I Made You Cry" by the **Rivieras** on Co-Ed; Ernie K-Doe's "Where There's A Will There's A Way" on Minit; and Paul Peek's "Hurtin' Inside" on NRC.

EARLY DECEMBER
Conway Twitty is in Hollywood filming "Platinum High School."

DEC 9   Connie Francis performs for her fans at Sciolla's in Philadelphia.
On NBC-TV's "The Perry Como Show," Tommy Sands makes another guest appearance.

THE RIVIERAS
For a moment in the late 1950s, the popularity of the Rivieras rivaled that of their labelmates, the Crests. In 1952, as a high school student in Hackensack, New Jersey, Homer Dunn formed a vocal group called the Bob-O-Links. The young men rehearsed for months, finally entering the Wednesday amateur show at the Apollo Theater in nearby New York. They didn't win the grand prize, but they were noticed by a scout for Okeh Records. The Bob-O-Links had one recording session, from which "Trying" was issued as a promo record. When there was no interest, plans for a regular release were scrapped. In 1954, after several members were drafted, the group fell apart. Dunn married and moved to Englewood, New Jersey. His neighbor, Charlie Allen sang bass in the Sentimentals. The two of them formed a new vocal group with Roland Cook and Andy Jones. As the Four Arts, they worked the area for two years, singing in a "pop" style. In 1957, they changed the name to the El Rivieras, and the volume of work increased. In January 1958, the group was discovered by the manager of the Ames Brothers, one of America's most popular groups. They were introduced to George Paxton, a music publisher who had just started Coed Records. "Count Every Star" by the Rivieras (as they were renamed) was the third release on the label, behind the Crests and the Booktones. The record was a summertime hit along the East Coast in 1958. As their next single, "Moonlight Serenade," was beginning to gain momentum, Tommy Leonetti released a cover version, and the Rivieras watched helplessly as Leonetti was booked on the bigger shows. Still, the Rivieras had the bigger version. The third single by the Rivieras was "Our Love" b/w "Midnight Flyer." Once again, they saw their thunder stolen from them as "Midnight Flyer" was covered by Nat King Cole. The Rivieras released a total of nine singles on Coed before breaking up in 1961.

Little Jimmy Scott opens a two-week stand at the Club 20 Grand in Detroit.

DEC 10   Rod Lauren is making the rounds of radio deejays through the Midwest. Today he's in Cincinnati. A day or two later he will be in Chicago.

DEC 12   In London, Gene Vincent appears in the weekly television production of "Boy Meets Girls." Vincent will also appear on the show December 19 and 26. As a result of Vincent's overwhelming reception, the show's producer, Jack Good, persuades Vincent to remain in England indefinitely.

Johnny Cash is back on the road following his appendectomy last month. Tonight he appears in Moorehead, Minnesota.

Tonight's "Dick Clark Show" presents Tommy Facenda, Bobby Comstock and the Counts, and actress Gloria DeHaven.

DEC 13   Johnny Cash, Marvin Rainwater, and Carl Mann team up to pull in more than 10,000 fans for three shows in Des Moines. This date was also postponed from the previous month due to Cash's illness.

On television tonight, Brook Benton and David Seville and the Chipmunks appear on "The Ed Sullivan Show" on CBS-TV.

New Releases for the second week of December include "Don't Mess With My Man" by **Irma Thomas** on Ron; two from Roulette: "Waltzing Mathilda" by Jimmie Rodgers and "Twangy" by the Rock-A-Teens; "Hot Dog" by Dale Hawkins on Checker; Frankie Ford's "Time After Time" on Ace; "Too Much Tequila" by the Champs on Challenge; Solomon Burke's "It's All Right" on Singular; "Dave's Special" by Dave "Baby" Cortez on Clock; and "Let the Good Times Roll" by Ray Charles on Atlantic. This week sees the release of Conway Twitty's "Lonely Blue Boy" on M-G-M. The song was originally titled "Danny," and was intended to be the title song from Elvis Presley's movie "King Creole," which was based on the Harold Stone novel, "A Stone for Danny Fisher." Elvis had even recorded a version, but the song was not used, nor was it released until 1978.

MID-DECEMBER

Chuck Berry is swinging through the South on a tour of one-nighters.
Between appearances on the "Boy Meets Girls" TV show in England, Gene Vincent is currently performing throughout Germany.

DEC 16   Mark Dinning stops the show with "Teen Angel" on "American Bandstand."

At the Apollo Theater this week, Little Willie John is the headliner. Also on the bill are the Drifters and James Brown and the Famous Flames.

DEC 18   Jesse Lee Turner is a hit in Nashville at the Marine Corps Armory with a Toys For Tots show.

IRMA THOMAS

Irma Thomas may have been the best of the New Orleans female vocalists, but she was almost forgotten. Born Irma Lee on February 18, 1941, in Pontchatoula, Louisiana, she left school in the eighth grade, married and became pregnant. She eventually worked as a waitress at New Orleans' Pimlico Club. There she met Tommy Ridgley, a New Orleans' hot R&B entrepreneur. When she began winning the Pimlico's weekly talent night, the owner forced her to quit her job as a waitress. Ridgely immediately hired her as his band's lead singer and introduced her to local Ron Records. Her first session produced "(You Can Have My Husband, But) Don't Mess With My Man," one of the most popular pieces for female singers in all R&B music. The record was a hit with R&B buyers, but failed to attract crossover sales. She had two sessions for Ron, also recording "Got a Good Man," before she signed with Minit Records, a New Orleans label distributed by Imperial. There she was produced by Allen Toussaint, and her hits included "It's Raining," "Ruler of my Heart," and "Done Got Over It." Incredibly, none of these records found a national audience. Minit was absorbed by Imperial and, beginning in early 1964, her recordings began to have a more polished feel. Her first Imperial release, "Wish Someone Would Care," was her first record to reach outside the R&B community. She continued to have hits on Imperial, including "Anyone Who Knows What Love Is," "Times Have Changed" and "He's My Guy." One Imperial release, "Time Is On My Side," was also covered by the Rolling Stones in 1964. On Chess in 1968, but recording in Muscle Shoals, Alabama, her version of Otis Redding's "Good To Me" was her final hit record. She has continued to perform, with records issued by Roker, Fungus, RCA and Maison de Soul. Recently, her albums on Rounder have found a new audience for "The Soul Queen of New Orleans."

DEC 19   Guest performers on tonight's "Dick Clark Show" are Anita Bryant, Jackie Wilson, the Four Preps, Bill Black's Combo, Toni Fisher, and humorist Sam Levinson.

Conway Twitty entertains at the State Fair Grounds in Albuquerque.

DEC 20   Rusty York closes a two-week engagement at the Showboat Club in Vincennes, Indiana.

DEC 21   As a consequence of having hiring the fourteen-year old young woman in El Paso on December 1, Chuck Berry is arrested in St. Louis for violating the Mann Act forbidding the transportation of a female across state lines for prostitution. Berry is subsequently convicted and sentenced to five years in prison and fined $5,000. The original verdict is thrown out because of racial comments from the presiding judge. In 1962, Berry will be retried and sentenced to three years in the Indiana Federal Penitentiary.

New Releases for the third week in December include three from Decca: "Skokiaan" by Bill Haley and His Comets, Bobby Darin's "Ring Them Bells," and Bob Beckham's "Crazy Arms." Other releases this week are "Let It Be Me" by the Everly Brothers on Cadence; and "Dangerous Woman" by Little Junior Parker on Duke.

DEC 22   Making his fourth appearance on "American Bandstand" in a year, Duane Eddy rips through "Bonnie Came Back."

Paul Anka makes a guest shot on "The Arthur Murray Dance Party."

DEC 23   Connie Francis opens her Christmas engagement at the Deauville Hotel in Miami.

DEC 25   The Alan Freed "Big Beat Show," opening for the holiday at the Brooklyn Fox, is headlined by Jackie Wilson and Bobby Rydell. Other performers on the bill are Santo and Johnny, the Skyliners, Bo Diddley, Teddy Randazzo, the Passions, the Isley Brothers, Johnny Restivo, **Tommy Facenda**, Crash Craddock, Linda Laurie, the Wheels, and Alan Freed's eighteen-piece band with Sam "The Man" Taylor.

Christmas in Detroit at the Club 20 Grand brings entertainment from Marv Johnson, the Miracles, Faye Adams, John Lee Hooker, and the Royal Jokers.

The Howard Theater in Washington welcomes Sammy Turner, the Falcons, the Spaniels, Joe Medlin, the Pearls, and Dean and Jean as this week's entertainment.

DEC 26   Brook Benton, Jimmy Clanton, Freddy Cannon, Carl Dobkins, Jr., and Ray Peterson make up the all-male cast of tonight's "Dick Clark Show."

TOMMY FACENDA
Tommy Facenda was born November 10, 1939, in Portsmouth, Virginia. In school, he excelled in sports, including football, basketball, boxing. He was distantly related to Dickie Harrell, the staff drummer on "Country Showtime," a weekly radio broadcast on WCMS in Norfolk. Through Harrell, he met Gene Vincent before he recorded "Be-Bop-A-Lulu." In early 1957, when Vincent was returning to performing after being hospitalized following an auto accident, Facenda joined his band to sing backing vocals and provide hand-claps. Working in Vincent's band was always a "temporary" engagement and, in about a year, Tommy was out of a job. He was able to convert his training into a onetime record, "Little Baby" on Nashville's Nasco label. Back in Virginia, he turned to Frank Guida, a record store owner who was just starting LeGrand Records. Guida had an idea for a novelty record, and he was looking for the right vocalist. The song was built around the names of forty-five Virginia high schools, with only a "Bo Diddley" beat, a sax bridge, and minimal lyrics to hold it together. The backing vocal group on the LeGrand version of "High School U.S.A." included Gary Anderson, who would soon have hits on LeGrand under the name Gary "U.S." Bonds. When the record was played in Norfolk, it created an enormous reaction. Guida couldn't handle the demand and turned to Atlantic Records to help with distribution. Atlantic wanted versions for the rest of the country, and they wanted Bobby Darin to record them. Guida stood by Facenda, and Atlantic gave in. Atlantic did insist on rerecording the instrumental and backing vocal tracks, this time without Gary Bonds. Tommy did twenty-eight different versions of "High School U.S.A." covering most of the major cities or regions of the country. It was a hit into early 1960. His only other record was the quickly forgotten "Bubba Ditty" on Atlantic.

HAROLD DORMAN

"One-hit wonders." Rock 'n roll spawned more than its share. At the very essence of a rock 'n roll hit is its freshness. Just when it seems that everything has been done before and the copycats are driving a good idea into the ground—along comes an unknown artist who has spent weeks—maybe even months or years—perfecting his one song. Such was the case with Harold Dorman. He offered a last gasp to a dying sound. Considering the length of this recording career, he is as unknown as a bestselling recording artist can get. Prior to "Mountain of Love," he had no other records. After "Mountain of Love," he no other hits. He recorded for Memphis' Rita label, a co-op between Billy Lee Riley (one of Sun's torrid rockers) and Roland Janes (Jerry Lee Lewis' guitarist). The original demos of "Mountain of Love" were issued without the violin section backing Dorman. The song was a rolling, medium-tempo number with Dorman's southern voice singing the lyrics in a plaintive manner. When it began to break, Rita sold distribution rights to N.R.C. Someone at Rita or N.R.C. must have felt that in its original state, "Mountain of Love" wouldn't appeal to the same teenage girls who swooned over the Frankies, the Jimmys, and the Bobbys. So the strings played a four-beat figure usually reserved for the piano. The song almost peeked into the Top Twenty on the "pop" charts in early 1960 and did a lot better in the R&B field, reaching #7. Dorman's next single, "River of Tears," tried to capture the geographic magic but flopped. (It was reissued on the Tince label.) "Moved to Kansas City" was his final Rita release (it was reissued on Top Rank). There were three singles on Sun Records, where he was backed by Scotty Moore (Elvis' guitarist) and Ace Cannon (the sax wizard), but by this time, Sun was a mere shadow of its former self. Dorman faded back into obscurity. He passed away in 1988.

DEC 28   On the West Coast, Jimmy Clanton begins a brief one-nighter tour running through January 2, 1960.

Big Maybelle performs at Pep's Lounge in Philadelphia through New Year's Eve.

New Releases for the fourth week in December include Chuck Berry's "Let It Rock" on Chess; "Midnight Special" by Paul Evans on Guaranteed; "Are You From Dixie?" by Joe Bennett and the Sparkletones on ABC-Paramount; Jan and Dean's "Clementine" on Dore; "Mumblin' Mosie" by the Johnny Otis Show on Capitol; LaVern Baker's "Shake a Hand" on Atlantic; **Harold Dorman**'s "Mountain of Love" on Rita; "Providing" by Phil Phillips on Mercury; Robin Luke's "Bad Boy" on Dot; "Wabash Cannonball" by Dicky Doo and the Don'ts on Swan; two from Little Jimmy Scott: "What Good Would It Be" on Savoy and "I'm Afraid The Masquerade Is Over" on Jamie; and two from King: Bruce Channel's "Slow Down Baby" and "Sweet Thing" by Trini Lopez. Finally, Specialty released "Wearin' Black" by Don Christy, a pseudonym for Salvatore "Sonny" Bono.

DEC 31   The Champs close out the year with a show at the Youth Hall of the New Mexico State Fair Grounds in Albuquerque.

Wanda Jackson spends the three-day New Year's holiday performing in Alameda, California.

Jo Ann Campbell opens at the Club Safari in Long Island for the New Year's weekend.

Steve Gibson and His Red Caps are at Larry Potter's Club in Hollywood.

Not surprisingly, the last day of the decade finds the Platters with bags packed as they embark on their third world tour.

THE TOP ROCK 'N ROLL RECORDS FOR DECEMBER 1959

1. Mack The Knife - Bobby Darin
2. Mr. Blue - The Fleetwoods
3. In The Mood - Ernie Fields
4. We Got Love - Bobby Rydell
5. So Many Ways - Brook Benton
6. The Big Hurt - Toni Fisher
7. Be My Guest/I've Been Around - Fats Domino
8. Oh, Carol - Neil Sedaka
9. Danny Boy - Conway Twitty
10. It's Time To Cry - Paul Anka
11. Hound Dog Man/Friendly World - Fabian
12. Why - Frankie Avalon
13. (7 Little Girls) Sitting in the Back Seat - Paul Evans
14. Dance With Me/(If You Cry) True Love, True Love - The Drifters
15. Put Your Head On My Shoulder - Paul Anka
16. Always - Sammy Turner
17. Come Into My Heart/Wont'cha Come Home - Lloyd Price

18. Way Down Yonder in New Orleans - Freddy Cannon
19. Reville Rock - Johnny and the Hurricanes
20. Among My Souvenirs - Connie Francis
21. I Wanna Be Loved/Mighty Good - Ricky Nelson
22. Primrose Lane - Jerry Wallace
23. Believe Me - Royal Teens
24. You Got What It Takes - Marv Johnson
25. Just As Much As Ever - Bob Beckham
26. First Name Initial - Annette
27. Sandy - Larry Hall
28. Woo-Hoo - The Rock-A-Teens
29. Running Bear - Johnny Preston
30. Teardrop - Santo and Johnny
31. Love Potion #9 - The Clovers
32. You Were Mine - The Fireflies
33. The Enchanted Sea - The Islanders
34. I'm Movin' On - Ray Charles
35. High School U.S.A. - Tommy Facenda
36. Midnight Stroll - The Revels
37. Teen Beat - Sandy Nelson
38. Clouds - The Spacemen
39. Living Doll - Cliff Richard
40. Smokie, Part 2 - Bill Black's Combo
41. Talk That Talk - Jackie Wilson
42. Joey's Song - Bill Haley and His Comets
43. Torquay - The Fireballs
44. Goodnight My Love - Ray Peterson
45. Tiny Tim - LaVern Baker
46. A Year Ago Tonight - The Crests
47. Go, Jimmy, Go - Jimmy Clanton
48. What About Us - The Coasters
49. One More Chance - Rod Bernard
50. How About That - Dee Clark

Also on the "pop" charts:
El Paso - Marty Robbins
Unforgettable - Dinah Washington
Smooth Operator - Sarah Vaughan
Uh! Oh! - The Nutty Squirrels
Pretty Blue Eyes - Steve Lawrence

December 1959
ARTIST OF THE MONTH

BOBBY RYDELL

Bobby Rydell

Bobby Rydell's professional life was caught in the crossroads between the rock 'n rollers and the teen idols. Bobby Darin and Frankie Avalon wanted to swing like Sinatra, and they quickly turned their backs on their rock 'n roll past. Freddy Cannon and Fabian remained rockers, as neither had the voice to approach Sinatra.

Robert Louis Ridarelli was born on April 26, 1942*. He grew up in the same deeply entrenched Italian neighborhood of South Philadelphia as Frankie Avalon, Fabian, and James Darren. Bobby's father took an interest in his musical education from the start. While other children were busy listening to the latest hits of the day, Bobby's father took him to listen the last remaining big bands working the various Philly clubs. It was a musical legacy he never forgot.

He started taking lessons on the drum kit as a child of five. Three years later, he was an accomplished cabaret performer, playing drums and doing imitations. At the age of nine, he was a regular on Paul Whiteman's television show that was broadcast from Philadelphia. It was Whiteman—a show business veteran from as far back as the 1920s—who suggested that the Ridarelli name might be a bit too ethnic. Whiteman suggested changing it to the more acceptable Rydell.

By the time Bobby entered his teenage years, he was playing drums in a popular dance band called Rocco and the Saints, that also featured Frankie Avalon on trumpet. The group was constantly in demand, playing—among other venues—many USO shows at the various veteran's hospitals in Philadelphia and Valley Forge. When Bobby was fourteen, Rocco and the Saints began their annual summer bookings in the seaside resorts around Atlantic City. Bobby did not confine himself to drums, however. He also excelled on guitar and bass, and he was a natural comedian.

Rocco and the Saints were managed by Frankie Day, bass player with Billy Duke and the Dukes. Day became interested in Rydell as a solo act. With the approval of Bobby's father, Day started taking Bobby to different record company offices—RCA Victor, Capitol, Columbia—mainly in the New York area. For several years, Day was unsuccessful in landing a recording contract for Rydell although Rocco and the Saints had backed Frankie Avalon's first sessions on the Chancellor label of Philadelphia.

Then, in late 1958, Bobby recorded a teen-oriented ditty titled "Fatty Fatty" b/w "Dream Age" for the minuscule Veko Records in Baltimore. The release caused barely a ripple of concern, and the promoters quickly vanished with the master tapes, leaving Bobby's father with the bill for the sessions. "Fatty Fatty," with inane lyrics repeating endlessly "fatty fatty, boom ba-latty" may be among the worst records ever recorded, exceeded only by the "moon-June-croon" style of "Dream Age." Rydell

---

(* Some biographies give Rydell's birthdate as 1940.)

later called both songs "absolutely horrible." Needless to say, the single disappeared with barely a trace. Later, after Rydell had a few hits, "Fatty Fatty" b/w "Happy Happy" appeared on the Venise label, apparently issued by the original promoters.

Almost as a last resort, Frankie Day approached the offices of Cameo Records of Philadelphia. The owner of the company was Bernie Lowe. He had been Rydell's vocal coach when Bobby was ten. In January 1959, Rydell signed a recording contract with Lowe, and his first Cameo single was on the streets in early February. However, that first release, "Please Don't Be Mad" b/w "Makin' Time," fared little better than "Fatty Fatty." Lowe secured a guest shot for Rydell on "American Bandstand." Bobby was only interviewed and didn't sing, but he did get a chance to plug "Please Don't Be Mad."

In May 1959, Rydell had a second single released by Cameo, "All I Want Is You." Again, there was little action on the record. "American Bandstand" didn't even offer an invitation this time. Rydell was getting discouraged. His old friend, Frankie Avalon, had been making hit records for over a year, and "Venus" was one of the biggest hits in 1959. Even Fabian, who told everyone who would listen that he couldn't sing a note, had been having hit records since the first of the year. So, why not Bobby Rydell?

Rydell had almost resigned himself to being a second-rate drummer in a second-rate combo. Then Bernie Lowe came up with a little song called "Kissin' Time." Almost as soon as it was released in mid-June, the record caught on in Philadelphia. The same thing happened in Detroit and Boston. Then Dick Clark started to play "Kissin' Time" on "American Bandstand," and it went over the top. Within three weeks after its release, "Kissin' Time" was a national hit. Bobby had just turned seventeen, and he and Rocco and the Saints were booked for another summer in Wildwood, on the New Jersey coast.

With "Kissin' Time" climbing the charts, Rydell returned to "American Bandstand" in August. This time he was asked to sing (actually lip-sync) his latest hit. The next month, Cameo released "We Got Love," and it became a solid follow-up single.

In September 1959, Rydell was part of a Labor Day extravaganza put on by Dick Clark at the Michigan State Fair Grounds. This led to his appearance on Dick Clark's first touring rock 'n roll caravan that took to the road on September 18, booked for forty-four shows through the end of October. By then, "We Got Love" had gone gold to become his first Top Ten record. For the Christmas vacation, Rydell shared top billing with Jackie Wilson at Alan Freed's "Big Beat Show" at the Brooklyn Fox.

"Wild One" was released early in 1960, and it became Rydell's biggest selling single, easily passing the million mark. By this time, both sides of his singles were regularly appearing on the charts. "Swinging School" b/w "Ding-A-Ling" became his springtime hit and third million seller. For the summer, Rydell reached back into a previously unsuccessful recording session to pull out "Volare." The song had already sold a million copies in 1958 for both Domenico Modugno (as "Nel Blu Dipinto Di Blu") and Dean Martin. The session that produced "Volare" had been scheduled to record songs in a big band style to help introduce Rydell to a more mature audience. Except for "Volare" and one or two other songs, the project was scrapped. Still, "Volare" might have remained on the shelf if the song wasn't a favorite of Rydell's mother. Rydell's version was issued in early summer 1960 and went gold like those before it, becoming his biggest-selling single.

For the next three years, while other male singing idols saw their careers extinguished by the many changes in rock 'n roll music, Rydell had an almost continuous string of records that sold more than a half-million copies each. Several, including "Good Time Baby," "I've Got Bonnie," "I'll Never Dance Again," "The Cha-Cha-Cha," and "Wildwood Days," even cracked the Top Twenty barrier. In late 1963, "Forget Him" almost topped the sales charts, easily selling a million singles.

Unlike so many other singing stars, Rydell did not immediately jump into the movies. When he did decide to take a role, it was in the 1963 film version of the Broadway hit musical "Bye, Bye Birdie." Although the story had to do with a rock 'n roll singer, Rydell was cast with Ann-Margret as a pair of high school sweethearts. Rydell's only other film appearance was in the quickly forgotten "That Lady From Peking."

In early 1964, as "Forget Him" was fading from popularity, the first wave of singles by the Beatles and other English rock groups was racing up the American charts, clogging the top positions and dominating radio airtime. Overnight, rock 'n roll music changed forever. Avalon, Darin, Nelson, and many others including Bobby Rydell, found themselves completely shut off from the hit-making machinery of the record business.

Rydell was able to place only a few more records on the charts in 1964, including a version of a Lennon-McCartney song, "A World Without Love." According to Rydell, his manager had arranged for him to have exclusive rights to the American release of the song. However, McCartney was also dating Peter Asher's sister, and the song ended up being recorded by Peter and Gordon. While Rydell was waiting for Cameo to release his single, the version by Peter and Gordon beat him to the marketplace by a week. Peter and Gordon's version went gold—Rydell's sputtered and stalled.

Rydell was so upset with this turn of events that he left Cameo Records and signed with Capitol—the American label of the Beatles, as well as Peter and Gordon. At Capitol, Rydell found himself assigned to producers who wanted him to sing country or soul music. When Rydell finally did get a piece of material that he felt he could make his own, such as the ballad version of Paul Anka's "Diana," he found Capitol's financial resources diverted to other artists and projects.

His career problems were compounded when he received his draft notice from the Army. Faced with two years on active duty, Bobby tried to get out of military service as "hardship case." He wrote to the draft board that he employed his father and was the sole means of support for his grandparents who lived with him. His attempts were futile. As a last resort, he joined a local Philadelphia National Guard unit. As a result, his career was interrupted for only six months of basic training in 1964.

Rydell remained with Capitol for three years. In 1969, he moved on to Reprise, a record company founded by Frank Sinatra, whom Rydell openly admired. However, there were strange happenings for Rydell at Reprise. His first single was "Lovin' Things" b/w "It's Getting Better." Rydell discovered that his record was receiving no promotional effort from Reprise. Then, "Lovin' Things" was covered by the Grassroots, and "It's Getting Better" was recorded by Mama Cass, and each become a mid-sized hit. Rydell's next Reprise single was "The River Is Wide." Again, he found his single languishing while a version by the Grassroots went up the charts. Finally, after three singles, he threw in the towel.

In 1970, he signed with RCA Victor, but only one single was released. "It Must Be Love" was written by members of Jaggerz, who had a hit with "The Rapper" in 1970. The B-side, "Chapel on the Hill," was composed by Teddy Randazzo.

In the late 1960s, Rydell tried to get his career moving again by joining the rock 'n roll revival shows at Madison Square Garden. He even worked the same show that encouraged a disgusted Rick Nelson to compose "Garden Party." Bobby didn't have a personal problem with being labeled an oldies act—so long as he could continue to entertain with other types of material. He had broken house records at the Copacabana in New York as early as 1961. By the 1970s, he was a popular draw at the chain of nightclubs run by Hugh Hefner's Playboy empire. He also worked the Hyatt Regency and Waldorf hotel chains and made appearances at the Disney theme parks.

Rydell recorded for Perception Records in 1974, with two singles issued, but nothing became of them. His last fling with the record business came in 1976 when he recorded three singles for the Pickwick label, including a disco version of "Sway." It failed to catch on Stateside, but a 12" pressing on the Alta label was the Number One disco record in Canada for a time.

In the late 1970s, he was considering a career move that would take him into the "pop" direction already forged by Barry Manilow. He appeared in a summer stock touring company of "Bye Bye Birdie," playing the part of the father this time out. He also appeared in a pilot for comedy-variety television show titled "One More Time" that was to be produced by the Osmond clan.

In the summer of 1985, he joined Frankie Avalon and Fabian on the successful "Boys of Bandstand" tour. For the next ten years, Rydell stayed busy performing in a big band style in various clubs across the country. He has been seen frequently on the various Dick Clark television specials recalling the early days of rock 'n roll.

Those who are close to him say that Bobby Rydell was never one to be bowled over by the fame he achieved. When asked why this is so, Rydell always gives credit to his family roots. As far back as he can remember, his mother, father, and grandparents all lived under the same roof. When the South Philly apartment of his parents became too crowded, the whole clan moved to the Philadelphia suburbs. When last heard from, Bobby Rydell was still there, with his parents, his wife, and two children.

reelin' & rockin'

The Golden Age of American Rock 'n Roll

Appendixes & Bibliography

Appendix A
ADDRESSES OF ROCK 'N ROLL RECORD COMPANIES, 1956-1959

Aardell
6130 Selma Avenue
Hollywood, CA

Abbott
Box 38
Malibu, CA

ABC-Paramount (a division of Am-Par)
1501 Broadway
New York, NY

Abner
7507 Newburgh Road
Evansville, IN
(March 1956; after November 1957 see Vee-Jay)

Ace
1650 Broadway
New York, NY

Ace
227 Culbertson Avenue
Jackson, MS

Addit
1107 Broadway
New York, NY

AFO
712 North Claiborne Avenue
New Orleans, LA

AFS
P. O. Box 66
Miami, FL

Aladdin
451 North Canyon Drive
5352 W. Pico Blvd. (by 1958)
Beverly Hills, CA

Allstar
1908 Leeland Avenue
Houston, TX

Amber
Box 1484
Dallas, TX

Amp-3
527 Lexington Avenue
(November 1957)
701 Seventh Avenue
(March 1958)
New York, NY

Amusing
1674 Broadway
New York, NY

Andex see Keen

Angel Tone Records
271 West 125th Street
New York, NY

Antler
511 Fifth Avenue
New York, NY

Apache
375 Bridge Street
Brooklyn, NY

Apollo
457 West 45th Street
New York, NY

Apt see ABC-Paramount

Argo
750 East 49th Street
Chicago, IL (1956)
(Chess sub'y by Nov. '56)

Arlen
Philadelphia, PA

Atco see Atlantic

Athens
c/o WLAC Radio
Nashville, TN

Atlantic
234 West 56th Street
(in 1956)
157 West 57th Street
(in May 1956)
New York, NY

Atlas
270 West 125th Street
New York, NY

Atco
235 West 56th Street
(January 1956)
157 West 57th Street
(May 1956)
271 West 125th Street
(March 1957)
New York, NY

461

Atlas
271 West 125th Street
New York, NY

Audition see Four Star

Avenue
1697 Broadway
New York, NY

Back Beat see Duke

Bally
203 N. Wabash
Chicago, IL

Bart
548 Woodward Avenue
Detroit, MI

Baton
108 West 44th Street
New York, NY

Beam
1726 Popular
Abilene, TX

Bee
19273 Warrington
Detroit, MI

Bee
664 Schuylkill Avenue
Reading, PA

Beech
1650 Broadway
New York, NY

Bingo
1715 Chestnut Street
Philadelphia, PA

Blue Chip
3323 Viking Road
Lennox, MA

Blue Moon
Route 4
Seminole, TX

Blue Note
47 West 63rd Street
New York, NY

Bobby
801 North Parkdale Drive
Tyler, TX

Bonnie
6000 Sunset Boulevard
Hollywood, CA

Bow
1650 Broadway
New York, NY

Bramble
6410 Madison Road
Cincinnati, OH

Brunswick see Decca

Bullet
421 Broad Street
Nashville, TN

Bullseye
1650 Broadway
New York, NY

Cadence
40 East 49th Street
New York, NY

Cameo
1721 East Tulpehocken Street
Suite 904, 1405 Locust Street
   (in March 1958)
Philadelphia, PA

Candlelight
Box 231
Manhasset, NY

Canton
P. O. Box 1694
Fort Worth, TX

Capitol
Sunset & Vine
   (January 1956)
Hollywood & Vine
   (March 1956)
Hollywood, CA

Caprock
Box 1051
Big Springs, TX

Carlton
157 West 57th Street
New York, NY

Carnation
62 Todd Street
Huntington, NY

Cascade
238 East 26th Street
New York, NY

Cash
2601 South Crenshaw
Los Angeles, CA

Cat see Atlantic

Challenge
6920 Sunset Boulevard
Hollywood, CA

Chancellor
206 South 13th Street
Philadelphia, PA

Charm
1650 Broadway
New York, NY

Chart
1214 South West 8th Street
1880 Coral Gate Drive
   (by 1958)
Miami, FL

Chase
255 West 144th Street
New York, NY

Checker see Chess

Chess
750 East 59th Street
    (January 1956)
4750 S. Cottage Grove Avenue
    (June 1956)
2120 South Michigan Avenue
    (November 1957)
Chicago, IL

Chic
Thomasville, GA

Chock
701 Seventh Avenue
New York, NY

Cholly
2620 Dalton Avenue
Los Angeles, CA

Chord
1650 Broadway
New York, NY

Christy
15520 El Gato Lane
Los Gatos, CA

Class
1107 El Centro
Hollywood, CA

Club
1650 Broadway
New York, NY

Co-Ed
12 West 117th Street
    (February 1957)
1619 Broadway
    (1959)
New York, NY

Cobra
2854 West Roosevelt
Chicago, IL

Colonial
504 West Franklin
Chapel Hill, NC

Columbia
799 Seventh Avenue
New York, NY

Combo
1107 El Centro Avenue
Hollywood, CA

Comet
2905 San Jacinto
Beaumont, TX

Comet see Corvet

Continental
500 Fifth Avenue
New York, NY

Cool
Harrison, NJ

Coral see Decca

Cornel
1674 Broadway
New York, NY

Corvet
Box 118
Atlanta, GA

Cosmic
331 West Franklin Avenue
Cleveland, OH

Coxx
P. O. Box 164
Manchester, CN

Crest
1248 South Berendo
Los Angeles, CA (1956)

9109 Sunset Boulevard
Hollywood, CA

Crown see Modern

Cub see M-G-M

Dale
607 5th Avenue
New York, NY

Dana
315 West 47th Street
New York, NY

Dash
8070 Lankershim
North Hollywod, CA

Dawn
39 West 60th Street
New York, NY

Deb
Nashville, TN

Debut
331 West 51st Street
New York, NY

Decca
50 West 57th Street
New York, NY

Dee Jay
P. O. Box 99
Valley View, TX

Del-Fi
Studio City, CA

Del-Ray
11 Center Street
Harrington, DE

DeLuxe see King

Demon
2821 West View Street
Los Angeles, CA

Dig see Aladdin

Disneyland
2400 West Alameda Avenue
   (February 1957)
500 South Buena Vista Street
   (March 1958)
Burbank, CA

Dixie
236 North College Street
Charlotte, NC

Dixie
Madison, TN
   (see Hollywood)

Dolton (formerly Dolphin)
708 Sixth Avenue
Seattle, WA
   (1958; in 1959 see Liberty)

Domino
Austin, TX

Domme
1650 Broadway
New York, NY

Dooto
9512 South Central Avenue
Los Angeles, CA

Dot
c/o Randy's Record Shop
Gallatin, TN
   (1956)
Sunset & Vine
Hollywood, CA
   (1958)

Double Dee
20 East Jackson Boulevard
Chicago, IL

Dove
25 Broad Street
New York, NY

Drew-Blan
P. O. Box 444
Morgan City, LA

Dub
Club Road & Kavanaugh
Little Rock, AR

Duke
2809 Erastus Street
Houston, TX

Duplex
115 West College
Fayetteville, TN

Dynamic
1674 Broadway
New York, NY

Eagle
7407-1/2 Melrose Avenue
Los Angeles, CA

East West see Atlantic

Ebb
4523 South Western Avenue
Los Angeles, CA

Ebony
1417 South 13th Street
Abilene, TX

Echo
583 Rosemont Avenue
Cincinnati, OH
   (January 1956)
713 Yankee Road
Middletown, OH
   (March 1956)

Eclipse
1650 Broadway
New York, NY

Ekko
4949 Hollywood Boulevard
Hollywood, CA

Ember see Herald

Emerald
501 Gettle Building
Fort Wayne, IN

End see Tico, Roulette

Epic see Columbia

Essex
3208 South 84th Street
Philadelphia, PA

Event
P. O. Box 432
Hudson, NY

Excell
1354 Wright Street
Los Angeles, CA

Excello see Nashboro

Fable
2608 Sunset Boulevard
Los Angeles, CA

Fabor
Box 38
Malibu, CA

Falcon
7507 Newburgh Road
Evansville, IN
   (1956; after November
   1957 see Vee-Jay)

Falcon
P. O. Box
McAllen, TX

Fantasy
654 Natoma Street
San Francisco, CA

Fargo
P. O. Box 656
Lindbrook, NY
   (late 1957)

224 West 49th Street
   (March 1958)
New York, NY

Fascination
253 Waverly Avenue
Highland Park, MI

Fashion
Box 926
Claris, NM

Federal see King

Felsted
539 West 25th Street
New York, NY

Fidelity see Rocket

Flair see Modern

Flair-X
1650 Broadway
New York, NY

Flash
623 East Vernon Avenue
Los Angeles, CA

Flip
618 South Ridgely Drive
Los Angeles, CA

Flip see Sun

Foremost
12th & Walnut Street
Kansas City, MO

Fortune
11629 Linwood
   (January 1956)
3942 Third Avenue
   (August 1957)
Detroit, MI

Four Star
305 South Fair Oaks
Pasadena, CA

Fox
Box 142
Abilene, TX

Fox
15836 Plymouth Road
Detroit, MI

Fran
428 Conrad Street
Louisville, KY

Fraternity
413 Race Street
Cincinnati, OH

Friendly
812 Ninth Street, N.W.
Moultrie, GA

Fury
271 West 125th Street
New York, NY

Future
6407 North 6th Street
Philadelphia, PA

Future
1164 South Glenstone
Springfield, MO

Gale
48 West 48th Street
New York, NY

Gallo
782 Eighth Avenue
New York, NY

Gametime
1650 Broadway
New York, NY

Gee see Tico, Roulette

Gilt Edge see Four Star

Glory
17 Hastings Street
West Roxbury, MA

Glory
2 West 47th Street
   (January 1956)
157 West 57th Street
   (August 1957)
New York, NY

Golden Crest
220 Broadway
Huntington Station, NY

Golden Rod
P. O. Box 115
Scottsville, KY

Golden West
Plaza Building
Sacramento, CA

Gone
1650 Broadway
New York, NY

Grand
109 West 49th Street
New York, NY

Groove see RCA Victor

Guest
Box 75, West Farms Station
New York, NY

Gulf
1906 LeLand
Houston, TX

Herald
1697 Broadway
New York, NY

Hi
306 Poplar
Memphis, TN

Hickory
2410 Franklin Avenue
Nashville, TN

Hi-Class
298 9th Street
San Francisco, CA

Hilite
173 Washington Avenue
Barre, VT

Hillcrest
6309 Hillcrest
Dallas, TX

Hip
6087 Sunset Boulevard
Hollywood, CA

Holiday
2294 8th Avenue
New York, NY

Hollywood
P. O. Box 115
Madison, TN

Hull
1595 Broadway
New York, NY

Hunt see ABC-Paramount

Hut
340 Beale Street
Memphis, TN

Imperial
6425 Hollywood Boulevard
Los Angeles, CA

Indio
P. O. Box 8271
Emeryville, CA

Irma
1483 23rd Avenue
Oakland, CA

Island
14409 Thames Avenue
Cleveland, OH

Ivy
1697 Broadway
New York, NY

J & S
1651 Washington Avenue
 (February 1957)
1075 Tiffany Street
 (March 1958)
Bronx, NY

J.O.B. see after Jiffy

Jaguar
1650 Broadway
New York, NY

Jalo
5000 Vins Street
Charleston, SC

Jamie
1330 West Girard Avenue
Philadelphia, PA

Jan
271 Meadows Building
Dallas, TX

Jay
82 Bradford Road
Watertown, MA

Jay Dee
441 West 49th Street
New York, NY

Jet
5621 Washington Avenue
Houston, TX

Jet
5234 East 69th Street
Indianapolis, IN

Jewel
Springfield Road
Roanoke, VA

Jiffy
c/o KBYR Radio
Anchorage, AK

J.O.B.
1121 West 59th Street
Chicago, IL

Joco
406 South Division Street
Northfield, MN

Johnson
111 East 4th Street
Cincinnati, OH

Josie (formerly JOZ) see
 Jubilee

Joy
P. O. Box 1461
Durham, NC

Joy
401 East Randall
Beeville, TX

Jubilee
1650 Broadway
1721 Broadway
 (March 1958)
315 West 47th Street
 (late 1958)
New York, NY

Judd see NRC

Juno
154-02 119th Avenue
Queens, NY

Kady
2002 N. Los Palmos Avenue
Hollywood, CA

Kaiser
2450 North 32nd Street
Philadelphia, PA

Kandy
457 State Street
Hammond, IN

Kapp see Capitol

Kay-Y
P. O. Box 43
Chester, PA

Keen
1606 Argyle
Hollywood, CA
    (March 1957)
8479 Higuera Street
Culver City, CA
    (March 1958)

Ken
261 Melville Street
Rochester, NY

Kerry
301 East 55th Street
New York, NY

Key
Box 46128
Hollywood, CA

King
1540 Brewster Avenue
Cincinnati, OH

Klick
944 Chapel Street
New Haven, CN

Kobb
2nd & Porter Streets
Taylor, TX

K-Pep
San Angelo, TX

K.R.C. see Atlantic

Lamp see Aladdin

Lance
15 West 84th Street
New York, NY

Lark
6708 Jackson Avenue
Hammond, IN

Las Vegas
1570 East 6th Street
Stockton, CA

LaSalle
218 West 47th Street
New York, NY

Lee
1343 Walnut Street
Cincinnati, OH

Legend
310 Fort Hood Road
Kileen, TX

Liberty
6920 Sunset Boulevard
1556 North La Brea
    (December 1957)
449 South Beverly Drive
    (March 1958)
Hollywood, CA

Liberty Bell
P. O. Box 7176
Phoenix, AZ

Lin
Gainesville, TX

London
530 West 25th Street
New York, NY

Longhorn
1650 Broadway
New York, NY

Lu
600 North Davis Street
Jackson, TN

Lyric
112 West Ninth Street
Los Angeles, CA

M.A.D.
1207 East 53rd Street
Chicago, IL

M-G-M
701 Seventh Avenue
New York, NY

Madison
New York, NY

Magnolia
219-1/2 Auburn Avenue
Atlanta, GA

Manhattan
1650 Broadway
New York, NY

Mardi-Gras
424 West 49th Street
New York, NY

Mark
700 Lafayette Street
Utica, NY

Mar-Vel
Box 841
Hammond, IN

Masquerade
Box 487
Temple, AZ

Masquerade
1619 Broadway
New York, NY

Mayflower
359 Warren Street
Flint, MI

Maze
Hollywood, CA

Mecca
298 9th Street
San Francisco, CA

Mel-O-Tone
701 Polk
Houston, TX

Mercury
745 Fifth Avenue
   (Janaury 1956)
35 East Wacker Drive
   (March 1956)
Chicago, IL

Meteor
1914 Chelsea Avenue
Memphis, TN

Middle-Tone
2903 2nd Avenue
Los Angeles, CA

Modern
9317 West Washington
Culver City, CA

Monogram
1650 Broadway
New York, NY

Moon
630 Fifth Avenue
New York, NY

Moonglow
72-10 Fourth Avenue
Woodside, NY

Montel
Baton Rouge, LA

Murray
271 West 125th Street
New York, NY

Music City
1815 Alcatraz Avenue
Berkeley, CA

Music City
1035 Chestnut Street
Philadelphia, PA

N.R.C. see after Novelty

Nasco see Nashboro

Nashboro
177 3rd Avenue, North
Nashville, TN

National Recording Co.
   (NRC)
1224 Spring Street, NW
Atlanta, GA

Neil
220 West 42nd Street
New York, NY

Nina
312 West 51st Street
New York, NY

Nocturne
368 North Street
New Rochelle, NY

Norgran see Aladdin

Novelty
Box 422
Emeryville, CA

N.R.C. (National Record Co.)
1224 Fernwood Circle, NE
Atlanta, GA

Nu-Clear
P. O. Box 1281
Columbus, GA

O-Dell see Herald

OJ
1018 North Watkins Avenue
Memphis, TN

Okeh see Columbia

Old Town
701 Seventh Avenue
New York, NY

Opportunity
2854 Hudson Boulevard
Jersey City, NJ

Orbit
Box 4432
Miami Beach, FL

Orbit
7603 Sunset Boulevard
Los Angeles, CA

Original Sound
8510 Sunset Boulevard
Hollywood, CA

Paradise
701 Seventh Avenue
New York, NY

Paris
1619 Broadway
New York, NY

Parkway see Cameo

Parrot
32 North State Street
Chicago, IL

Patio
520 Royal
New Orleans, LA

Peacock see Duke

Pearl
802 Arlington Road
Covington, KY

Peek-A-Boo
13 Highland Avenue
Newark, NJ

Pep
9652 Winchell Street
Rivera, CA

Phillips International see
Sun

Pop
2746 Country Club, Road
Philadelphia, PA

Pop
54 Third Street
North Arlington, NJ

Porter
4236 North Central
   (March 1957)
512 West Stella Lane
   (March 1958)
Phoenix, AZ

Prep
(see Capitol)

President
1619 Broadway
New York, NY

PRO
2232 Vista De Mar Plaza
Hollywood, CA

Queen
Box 1095
Snyder, TX

R.P.M. see Modern

Rainbow
767 Tenth Avenue
New York, NY

Rama see Tico, Roulette

Razor Back
817 Chevy Place
Muskogee, OK

RCA Victor
155 East 24th Street
New York, NY

Real
1486 North Fair Oaks
Pasadena, CA

Record Releasing Corp.
1590 Crossroads of the Old
   World
   (February 1957)
Hollywood, CA
1744 North Berendo
   (March 1958)
Los Angeles, CA

Recorte
414 West 44th Street
New York, NY

Regency
Toronto, ONT

Reknown
803 South Cedar Street
Durham, NC

Rendezvous
1310 South New Hampshire
Los Angeles, CA

Republic
714 Allison
Nashville, TN

Request
443 West 49th Street
New York, NY

Rev
3703 North 7th Street
Phoenix, AZ

Rex
New Orleans, LA

Rim
226 West 53rd Street
New York, NY

   (1956)
1293 Dean Street
Brooklyn, NY
   (1958)

Rita
Perth Amboy, NJ

Robbins
319 Seventh Avenue, North
Nashville, TN

Robin
11628 San Vincente Blvd.
West Los Angeles, CA

Robin
5015 Irving Street
Philadelphia, PA

ROC
1650 Broadway
New York, NY

Rock
1704 South 12th Street
Waco, TX

Rocket
420-A Broadway
Nashville, TN

Roman
1650 Broadway
New York, NY

Ron
New Orleans, LA

Roost
625 Tenth Avenue
   (January 1956)
664 Tenth Avenue
   (March 1958)
New York, NY

Rose
Stillwater, OK

Rose
120 West 86th Street
New York, NY

Roulette
659 10th Avenue
New York, NY

Ruby
1285 Parkamo Avenue
Hamilton, OH

Rustic
831 South Wabash Avenue
Chicago, IL

Safari
701 Seventh Avenue
New York, NY

Saga
2016 North Berwick
Indianapolis, IN

Sage & Sand
5653-1/2 Hollywood Boulevard
Hollywood, CA

Sandy
c/o WKAB Radio
Mobile, AL

Sarg
311 Davis Street
Luling, TX

Satellite
344 West 88th Street
New York, NY

Savoy
58 Market Street
Newark, NJ

Score see Aladdin

Security
1706 East Ninth Street
Mount Pleasant, TX

Selma
197-13 McLuaghlin
Jamaica, NY

7-11 see Aladdin

Signal
762 Tenth Avenue
New York, NY

Silver
292 South La Cienega Blvd.
Beverly Hills, CA
   (before 1958)
9109 Sunset Boulevard
Hollywood, CA
   (about 1958)

Sims
7502 Denny Avenue
Sun Valley, CA

Skippy
Box 4121
Dallas, TX

Sky Castle
P. O. Box 114
Greensboro, NC

Smash
146 Seventh Avenue, North
Nashville, TN

Solid Gold
359 Burgess Avenue
Indianapolis, IN

Solo
6119 Selma Avenue
Hollywood, CA

Soma
29 Glenwood Avenue
Minneapolis, MN

Southland
New Orleans, LA

Spade
P. O. Box 7205
Houston, TX

Spark
8567 Melrose Avenue
Hollywood, CA

Specialty
8508 Sunset Boulevard
Hollywood, CA

Star
1615 Bennett Avenue
Chattanooga, TN

Star
1429 Hawthorne Street
Pittsburgh, PA

Star X
19600 Rogge Avenue
Detroit, MI

Starday
Box 1689
Beaumont, TX

Stardisc
10337 East Beach
Bellflower, CA

Starfire
1651 North Cosmo Street
Hollywood, CA

Star-Hi
9913 Waller Road
Tacoma, WA

Starla
1107 North El Centro
Los Angeles, CA

Stars, Inc.
P. O. Box 1027
Atlanta, GA

States see United

Sue
271 West 125th Street
New York, NY

Suede
P. O. Box 94
Natchez, MS

Sun
706 Union Avenue
Memphis, TN

Sundown
9308 East Whittier Blvd.
   (March 1957)
9115 Union Street
   (March 1958)
Pico, CA

Supreme
117 West 46th Street
New York, NY

Surf
618 South Glenwood Place
Burbank, CA

Tally
P. O. Box 742
Miami, FL

Tampa
2638 West Pico
Los Angeles, CA

Tara
1902-1/2 Leeland
Houston, TX

Target
1650 Broadway
New York, NY

Teenerama
1650 Broadway
New York, NY

Tender see Dot

Terp
1001 Garden Highway
North Sacramento, CA

Tico
220 West 42nd Street
   (in 1956)
659 10th Avenue
New York, NY
   (by 1958)

Tide
2146 West View Street
Los Angeles, CA

Tiger
82 Walraven Drive
West Inglewood, NJ

Tilt
5019 Willow Glen Drive
Houston, TX

Time
Box 1231
Dallas, TX

Tip Top
3409 West Leigh Street
Richmond, VA

Titan
Hollywood, CA

TNT
1422 West Poplar
San Antonio, TX

Todd
101 West 55th Street
New York, NY

Tone
601 East 18th Street
Bakersfield, CA

Trend
119 West 57th Street
New York, NY

Triple D
c/o KDDD Radio
Dumas, TX

Tune
123 East Alabama Street
Florence, AL

Tuxedo
132 Nassau Street
New York, NY

Unicorn
79 Commonwealth Avenue
Boston, MA

United
5052 Cottage Grove Avenue
Chicago, IL

United Artists
c/o United Artists Pictures
Hollywood, CA

Vanity
259 21st Avenue
Patterson, NJ

Vee-Jay
2129 South Michigan Avenue
Chicago, IL

Vellez
P. O. Box 248
Lomita, CA

Verne
1724 Madison Avenue
New York, NY

Verve see Aladdin

Vik see RCA Victor

Vim
1427 Landon Avenue
Jacksonville, FL

Vin see Ace (Jackson, MS)

VIP
157 West 57th Street
New York, NY

Viv
7342 11th Place
Phoenix, AZ

Viva
Miami, FL

Warner Brothers
c/o Warner Brothers Pictures
Hollywood, CA

Warrior
Pleasanton, TX

Warwick (a division of United Telefilms)

Wayside
5131 John C. Lodge Street
Detroit, MI

Web
155 West 46th Street
New York, NY

Westport
3814 Washington
Kansas City, MO

Whippet
8584 Sunset Boulevard
Hollywood, CA

Whirlin' Disc
315 West 47th Street
New York, NY

White Rock
Box 7724
Dallas, TX

Wilco
Hollywood, CA

Wing see Mercury

Winley
205 West 84th Street
New York, NY

"X" see RCA Victor

X Tra
32 St. Nicholas Avenue
New York, NY

XYZ
160 East 87th Street
New York, NY

York
52 East Queen Street
Hampton, VA

Zip
P. O. Box 412
Pasadena, TX

Zipp
Corlot Building
10 South Main Street
Akron, OH

Appendix B
SELECTED NEW YORK RECORD LABELS ARRANGED BY STREET ADDRESS

1619 BROADWAY
- Co-Ed
- Masquerade
- Paris
- President

1650 BROADWAY
- Ace
- Beech
- Bow
- Bullseye
- Charm
- Chord
- Club
- Domme
- Eclipse
- Flair-X
- Gametime
- Gone
- Jaguar
- Josie
- Jubilee
- Longhorn
- Manhattan
- Monogram
- ROC
- Roman
- Target
- Teenerama

1674 BROADWAY
- Amusing
- Cornel
- Dynamic

1697 BROADWAY
- Avenue
- Ember
- Herald
- Ivy

155 EAST 24TH STREET
- Groove
- RCA Victor
- Vik
- "X"

220 WEST 42ND STREET
- Gee
- Neil
- Rama

315 WEST 47TH STREET
- Dana
- Whirlin' Disc

50 WEST 57TH STREET
- Brunswick
- Coral
- Decca

271 WEST 125TH STREET
- Angeltone
- Atlas
- Fury
- Murray
- Sue

745 FIFTH AVENUE
- Mercury
- Wing

701 SEVENTH AVENUE
- Amp-3
- Chock
- Old Town
- Paradise
- Safari

799 SEVENTH AVENUE
- Columbia
- Okeh

Bibliography

In addition to the many references listed in the bibliography to *SHAKE, RATTLE & ROLL*, the following books, magazines, and newspapers were of significant value while working on *REELIN' & ROCKIN'*:

BOOKS

B.M.I. Editors. BMI: *Meet the Artist*. New York: Broadcast Music, 1957.

Bashe, Phillip. *Travelin' Man: The Complete Biography of Rick Nelson*. New York: Hyperion, 1992.

Berry, Chuck. *Chuck Berry: The Autobiography*. New York: Simon & Schuster, 1987.

Bronson, Fred. *The Billboard Book of Number One Hits*. New York: Billboard, 1988.

Broven, John. *South to Louisiana: The Music of the Bayous*. Gretna, LA: Pelican, 1987.

Busnar, Gene. *It's Only Rock 'N' Roll*. New York: Wanderer, 1979.

Clark, Alan. *Eddie Cochran: Never To Be Forgotten*. West Covina, CA: National Rock 'N Roll Archives, 1991.

Clark, Dick. *Rock, Roll & Remember*. New York: Thomas Y. Crowell, 1976.

Cottrill, Les. *45's Label Lists*. Vol. 1-4. No info.

Cross, Wilbur and Michael Kosser. *The Conway Twitty Story*. New York: Dolphin, 1986.

Ehrenstein, David and Bill Reed. *Rock on Film*. New York: Delilah, 1982.

Elson, Howard and John Brunton. *Whatever Happened to...?* New York: Proteus, 1981.

Escott, Colin and Martin Hawkins. *Sun Records: A Brief History of the Legendary Record Label*. New York: Quick Fox, 1980.

Francis, Connie. *Who's Sorry Now?* New York: St. Martin's, 1984.

Gillette, Charlie. *Making Tracks*. St. Albans, U.K.: Granada, 1975.

Greig, Charlotte. *Will You Still Love Me Tomorrow?* London: Virago, 1989.

Gribin, Dr. Anthony and Dr. Matthew M. Schiff. *Doo-Wop: The Forgotten Third of Rock 'n Roll*. Iola, WI: Krause, 1992.

Guralnick, Peter. *Lost Highway*. New York: Vintage, 1979.

Hannush, Jeff. *I Hear You Knockin': The Sound of New Orleans Rhythm and Blues*. Ville Platte, LA: Swallow, 1985.

Hawkins, Ronnie and Peter Goddard. *Ronnie Hawkins: Last of the Good Ol' Boys*. Toronto: Stoddart, 1989.

Hill, Randall C. *Collectible Rock Records*. Orlando, FL: House of Collectibles, 1979.

Jancik, Wayne. *One-Hit Wonders*. New York: Billboard, 1990.

Karpp, Phyllis. *Ike's Boys: The Story of the Everly Brothers*. Ann Arbor, MI: Pierian Press, 1988.

Kiersch, Edward. *Where Are You Now, Bo Diddley?* New York: Dolphin, 1986.

Laufenberg, Frank and Hugh Gregory. *Rock and Pop Day by Day*. London: Blandford, 1992.

McColm, Bruce and Doug Payne. *Where Have They Gone*. New York: Tempo, 1979.

Mendheim, Beverly. *Ritchie Valens: The First Latino Rocker*. Tempe, AZ: Bilingual, 1976.

Millar, Bill. *The Coasters*. London: Star, 1974.

Nite, Norm N. *Rock On: The Solid Gold Years*. New York: Thomas Y. Crowell, 1974.

Norman, Philip. *The Road Goes On Forever*. New York: Fireside, 1982.

Oliver, Paul. *Blues Off the Record*. Turnbridge Wells, Kent, U.K.: Baton, 1984.

Osborne, Jerry and Bruce Hamilton. *Blues/Rhythm & Blues/Soul*. Phoenix: O'Sullivan Woodside, 1980.

—. *55 Years of Recorded Country/Western Music*. Phoenix. O'Sullivan Woodside, 1976.

—. *Record Albums Price Guide*. Phoenix: O'Sullivan Woodside, 1982.

—. *Rock Rock & Roll 45s*. Phoenix: O'Sullivan Woodside, 1983.

Pollock, Bruce. *When Rock Was Young*. New York: Holt, Reinhart, Winston, 1981.

Redmond, Mike and Fernando L. Gonzales. *Disco-File: The Discographical Catalog of American Rock & Roll and Rhythm & Blues Vocal Groups*. No other info.

Rees, Dafydd and Luke Crampton. *Rock, Movers & Shakers*. New York: Billboard, 1991.

Ribowsky, Mark. *He's a Rebel*. New York: Dutton, 1989.

Shore, Michael with Dick Clark. *The History of American Bandstand*. New York: Ballantine, 1985.

Stambler, Irwin. *The Encyclopedia of Pop, Rock and Soul*. New York: St. Martin's, 1977.

Stambler, Irwin and Gruen Landon. *The Encyclopedia of Folk, Country and Western Music*. New York: St. Martin's, 1984.

Toches, Nick. *Country: The Biggest Music in America*. New York: Delta, 1977.

—. *The Unsung Heroes of Rock 'n' Roll*. New York: Harmony, 1991.

Umphred, Neal. *Goldmine's Price Guide to Collectible Albums*. Iola, WI: Krause, 1993.

—. *Goldmine's Rock 'n Roll 45RPM Record Price Guide*. Iola, WI: Krause, 1992.

Uslan, Michael and Bruce Solomon. *The First 25 Years of Rock & Roll*. New York: Greenwich, 1981.

Ward, Ed, Geoffrey Stokes and Ken Tucker. *Rock of Ages: The Rolling Stone History of Rock & Roll*. New York: Rolling Stone, 1986.

Whitburn, Joel. *Pop Annual, 1955-1977*. Menomonee Falls, WI: Record Research, 1978.

—. *Top Pop Records, 1955-1982*. Menomonee Falls, WI: Record Research, 1983.

—. *Top Rhythm and Blues Records, 1949-1971*. Menomonee Falls, WI: Record Research, 1977.

I also referred to *Shake, Rattle & Roll* more frequently than the casual reader might imagine.

MAGAZINES

Bim Bam Boom
Blue Suede News
Blues and Rhythm
Big Town Review
Country Sounds
DISCoveries
50s Revisited
Goldmine
Music World
New Kommotion (U.K.)
Not Fade Away (U.K.)
Now Dig This (U.K.)
R&B magazine
Record Auction Monthly
Record Collectors Journal
Record Collector's Monthly
Record Digest
Record Exchanger
Record Finder
Record Profile Magazine
Record Spinner
Remember Then
Stormy Weather
Variety
Who Put The Bomp
Yesterday's Memories

NEWSPAPERS

Atlanta Journal-Constitution
Billboard
Cashbox
Los Angeles Sentinel
Louisiana Weekly (New Orleans)
Michigan Chronicle (Detroit)
Oakland Tribune
Sacramento Bee
Sacramento Union
San Francisco Chronicle
Washington (DC) *Post* and *Times Herald*
Variety

reelin' & rockin'

The Golden Age of American Rock 'n Roll

Indexes

Performer Index

In order to make the contents of this book more easily accessible, a method of citation based on references to specific dates or features of the book has been employed, rather than using more general references to page numbers.

KEY TO CITATIONS

By day: 1/15/56 = January 15, 1956
By week: F/1/58 = First week of January 1958
(F = first week;
S = second week;
T = third week;
Fo = fourth week)

A

Ace, Buddy 10/7/56, 12/15/56, 5/12/57, F/10/58
Ace, Johnny F/1/56, T/7/56
Accents S/10/58
Adams, Faye 1/20/56, 3/11/56, 4/13/56, 6/29/56, 8/24/56, M/10/56, 3/13/57, 4/26/57, 6/14/57, 6/28/57, 7/5/57, L/8/57, 5/23/58, 12/25/59
Adams, Johnny S/4/59, 5/22/59, 5/28/59, T/8/59
Adams, Marie M/9/57, T/9/57, 4/6/58
Adams, Nick E/8/59
Addrisi Brothers T/7/58, F/5/59, 7/21/59, Fo/7/59, Fo/9/59, Fo/11/59
Alaimo, Steve 4/22/59
Alberts, Al 1/3/59
Alice Jean and the Mondellos T/5/57
Allen, Lee T/9/56, T/11/57, 2/7/58, 3/16/58, F/8/58, 8/23/58, 7/17/59, S/10/59, 11/8/59
Allen, Tony S/7/59
Allison, Gene Fo/4/56, 2/21/58, F/1/59
Allison, Joe S/3/58
Allsup, Tommy 7/3/58, 2/2/59
Alpert, Herbie F/4/59, T/6/59
Ambers T/3/58
Am-Par's 11/28/59
Andrews, Lee and the Hearts Fo/5/56, 2/2/57, F/7/57, 8/2/57, 8/9/57, 8/16/57, 8/30/57, 10/11/57, Fo/10/57, 11/28/57, 12/25/57, 2/14/58, 2/21/58, F/4/58, 5/8/58, 6/7/58, 6/13/58, T/7/58, 7/25/58, 10/24/58, F/11/58, 12/5/58
Angels T/10/56
Anka, Paul T/9/56, Fo/5/57, 7/1/57, 8/8/57, 8/16/57, 9/6/57, T/9/57, 9/18/57, 10/10/57, 11/1/57, 11/3/57, 11/4/57, 12/7/57, T/12/57, 12/17/57, 12/25/57, 1/8/58, 1/27/58, 1/30/58, 2/1/58, 2/9/58, M/2/58, 3/1/57, T/3/58, 4/5/58, 4/6/58, 5/12/58, 6/7/58, Fo/6/58, 6/28/58, M/7/58, Fo/7/58, F/9/58, 9/8/58, 9/28/58, Fo/10/58, 11/14/58, T/11/58, 11/21/58, 12/10/58, M/1/59, 2/9/59, 2/28/59, F/3/59, 3/7/59, E/3/59, 3/20/59, 4/11/59, F/5/59, 5/7/59, 5/9/59, 5/11/59, 6/28/59, 7/24/59, S/8/59, 9/4/59, 9/12/59, 9/18/59, 11/1/59, F/11/59, 11/4/59, 12/5/59, 12/22/59
Annette (Funicello) 6/30/58, Fo/11/58, 1/10/59, S/3/59, 3/21/59, 3/27/59, Fo/4/59, 5/11/59, 5/30/59, 7/1/59, 7/25/59, 8/5/59, 9/2/59, S/9/59, 9/18/59, 11/7/599,
Appell, Dave (See Applejacks)
Applejacks F/4/56, 12/9/57, 3/28/58, 7/3/58, F/9/58, 10/11/58, 10/15/58, L/10/58, Fo/11/58, E/12/58, 1/31/59, 2/7/59, 6/14/59
Aquatones F/3/58, 4/19/58, T/6/58, Fo/9/58
Arden, Toni 6/14/58
Arthur, Charlene 9/9/56
Atkins, Chet 8/6/57
Austin, Sil 6/8/56, 1/28/57, 3/15/57, 4/21/57, 5/17/57, 10/18/57, 9/19/58, 10/3/58, 6/9/59, 11/18/59
Autry, Gene L/4/57, E/8/57
Avalon, Frankie Fo/5/57, F/9/57, 9/18/57, 11/12/57, 12/12/57, T/12/57, F/3/58, 3/8/58, 3/15/58, 3/28/58, 6/14/58, M/6/58, 6/20/58, M/7/58, 8/16/58, 8/29/58, T/9/58, 10/3/58, 10/25/58, 11/26/58, 11/29/58, 12/6/58, 12/24/58, Fo/1/59, 2/4/59, 2/9/59, 2/14/59, L/2/59, 3/5/59, 3/25/59, 4/8/59, 4/11/59, S/5/59, 5/23/59, 6/17/59, 6/28/59, 7/1/59, 7/14/59, 8/1/59, 8/4/59, S/8/59, 8/11/59, 8/15/59, 8/19/59, 9/4/59, 9/5/59, 9/6/59, 9/11/59, 9/15/59, 9/22/59, 10/1/59, 10/15/59, F/11/59, 11/22/59, 11/28/59
Avons T/7/56

B

Bagby, Doc 10/3/58, 1/16/59, 1/23/59, M/8/59, 9/1/59
Bailey, Pearl 1/13/56, 10/26/56, 11/16/56, 3/7/58, 5/8/58, 5/22/59, 10/16/59, 11/6/59
Baker, LaVern 1/11/56, Fo/1/56, 2/1/56, 2/6/56, 2/18/56, T/2/56, T/4/56, 4/20/56, 6/21/56, 6/29/56, 6/30/56, 7/30/56, 8/6/56, Fo/8/56, 8/31/56, 9/9/56, 9/26/56, F/11/56, 12/5/56, 1/3/57, 1/8/57, 2/15/57, 3/28/57, 4/10/57, T/4/57, 5/11/57, 5/24/57, 6/7/57, 6/12/57, 7/1/57, Fo/7/57, 9/6/57, 9/26/57, L/9/57, 10/10/57, Fo/10/57, 11/1/57, 1/10/58, 1/17/58, 1/20/58, T/2/58, 2/28/58, 4/6/58, M/7/58, 7/25/58, 8/23/58, 10/24/58, F/11/58, 12/23/58, 1/10/59, 2/20/59, Fo/3/59, 3/27/59, 4/27/59, M/5/59, 5/16/59, 6/19/59, F/7/59, 7/31/59, 8/3/59, 8/12/59, 9/4/59, 9/9/59, 9/18/59, F/10/59, 11/6/59, 11/25/59, Fo/12/59
Baker, Mickey (See also Mickey and Sylvia) 6/29/56
Ballard, Hank (See Midnighters)
Bare, Bobby Fo/7/57, T/10/59
Barlow, Dean 3/30/56, F/9/57, Fo/12/58
Barnes, Benny Fo/9/58
Barnes, Billy 10/11/57
Barry, Dave Fo/7/56
Barry, John 7/16/59
Barrett, Richard F/6/59
Bartholomew, Dave 3/15/57, 7/10/57, 1/1/59, 3/14/59
Bascomb, "Handsome" Jim F/3/58
Bash, Otto F/7/56
Basie, Count 1/6/56, 3/11/56, 5/12/56, 5/28/56, 6/29/56, 10/29/56, 5/9/58, 8/3/59
Beard, Dean Fo/4/57, Fo/10/57, T/11/58, S/6/59
Beasley, Jimmy 7/19/56, Fo/7/56
Beaulieu, Priscilla 9/13/59
Beavers S/4/58
Beckham, Bob F/6/59, T/12/59
Bell, Freddy and the Bell Boys 3/14/56, T/3/56, F/7/56, 5/5/57, F/5/57, 12/21/57, 4/20/58, 10/21/58
Bell Notes 3/28/58, Fo/12/58, 2/7/59, Fo/3/59, 3/28/59, 4/8/59, F/7/59, Fo/8/59, F/11/59
Bellson, Louis 10/26/56, 11/16/56, 5/8/59, 5/22/59, 10/16/59, 11/6/59
Bellus, Tony F/11/58, Fo/2/59, 6/20/59, T/9/59
Belvin, Jesse Fo/10/56, 12/21/56, 1/4/57, 1/18/57, M/2/57, Fo/9/57, T/10/58, T/2/59, F/4/59, 4/21/59, 4/22/59, 5/8/59, Fo/5/59, 6/3/59, 6/9/59, F/9/59
Bennett, Boyd and His Rockets T/1/56, Fo/2/56, T/10/56, F/7/59, S/11/59
Bennett, Joe and the Sparkletones T/7/57, 9/20/57, 10/27/57, F/11/57, 11/5/57, F/2/58, 3/9/58, Fo/5/58, Fo/9/58, T/8/59, Fo/12/59
Bennett, Tony 6/7/58
Benton, Brook Fo/1/56, 3/30/56, Fo/7/56, Fo/1/57, L/9/57, T/8/58, Fo/12/58, 2/7/59, Fo/3/59, 4/12/59, 4/14/59, 6/14/59, Fo/6/59, 6/26/59, 7/3/59, M/9/59, T/9/59, 9/27/59, 10/2/59, 10/25/59, 12/13/59, 12/26/59

479

Bergen, Polly 11/15/58
Bernard, Rod F/2/59, 4/11/59, Fo/5/59, S/9/59
Berry, Chuck 1/3/56, T/1/56, 2/1/56, 2/10/56, 2/12/56, 4/2/56, S/5/56, 6/18/56, 6/29/56, 7/2/56, 7/22/56, 8/6/56, F/9/56, 9/21/56, 9/28/56, 10/20/56, M/11/56, Fo/11/56, 12/5/56, 2/1/57, 2/8/57, 2/15/57, S/3/57, 3/19/57, 3/28/57, 4/10/57, 6/7/57, 6/12/57, 6/21/57, Fo/6/57, 7/1/57, M/8/57, 9/6/57, 9/26/57, L/9/57, 10/10/57, S/10/57, 11/1/57, 11/8/57, 12/25/57, Fo/1/58, 2/21/58, 2/22/58, 3/7/56, 3/28/58, F/4/58, 5/17/58, L/5/58, 6/2/58, 6/30/58, F/7/58, 7/5/58, F/8/58, 8/23/58, 8/29/58, E/9/58, Fo/10/58, Fo/11/58, 12/24/58, E/1/59, S/1/59, 1/31/59, F/3/59, 3/3/59, Fo/5/59, 7/18/59, 7/26/59, 8/29/59, F/9/59, 9/26/59, 11/28/59, 12/1/59, M/12/59, 12/21/59, Fo/12/59
Berry, Richard 4/6/56, 4/20/56, Fo/6/56, F/4/57, F/8/58
Big Bopper (See also Richardson, J. P.) F/7/58, 9/20/58, F/11/58, 11/22/58, 11/26/58, 1/23/59, 2/2/59, 2/3/58, 2/9/59, Fo/2/59, T/4/59, Fo/6/59
Big Maybelle (Smith) 2/3/56, 4/2/56, 4/27/56, T/5/56, 8/24/56, 12/7/56, 2/22/57, 3/8/57, 7/21/57, 8/30/57, 11/8/57, 3/7/58, 6/20/58, 7/5/58, 4/6/59, 9/11/59, 12/28/59
Bill Black's Combo S/10/59, 12/19/59
Billy and Lillie T/12/57, 2/22/58, 3/24/58, Fo/3/58, 3/28/58, 5/17/58, F/11/58, T/12/58, 1/3/59, S/3/59, T/6/59, F/8/59
Birdsong, Larry 7/9/56, 1/20/57, 3/22/57, 4/28/57
Black, Bill 9/21/57
Blackwell, Otis M/6/57
Blakey, Art 9/25/59
Bland, Billy Fo/5/56, 6/29/56
Bland, Bobby "Blue" 8/26/56, 10/7/56, 12/15/56, M/3/57, S/3/57, 4/22/57, Fo/7/57, 5/25/58, 3/8/59, S/4/59, F/8/59
Blockbusters (R&B) 8/3/56, 12/4/56
Blockbusters (See also New Blockbusters or Olenn, Johnny) F/3/59
Blossoms 8/24/58
Bo, Eddie 6/1/56, 6/8/56, 4/18/58, 9/5/58, 10/3/58, 11/14/58, Fo/1/59, 2/6/59, 4/16/59
Bob and Earl Fo/9/57, F/7/58, 7/18/58, 8/22/58, Fo/8/58, Fo/2/59
Bobbettes L/2/57, Fo/5/57, 6/28/57, 8/16/57, 9/2/57, 9/6/57, 9/18/57, 9/26/57, F/11/57, 12/6/57, 5/9/58, Fo/7/58
Bond, Eddie Fo/4/56, 5/28/56, 6/2/56, 1/31/59
Bond, Luther and the Emeralds Fo/9/56
Bonn, Skeeter S/1/56
Bonnie Lou (Sally Carson) S/3/56
Bono, Sonny E/8/57
Boone, Nick (See Todd, Nick)
Boone, Pat S/1/56, T/3/56, 4/20/57, Fo/4/57, L/8/57, F/10/57, 2/6/58, 2/15/58, 10/1/58, 11/29/58
Bop Chords 6/29/56, 2/2/57
Bostic, Earl 2/10/56, 4/12/56, 4/27/56, 10/4/57, 10/11/57, 9/11/59, E/11/59
Bowen, Jimmy T/12/56, L/1/57, 2/22/57, 3/15/57, 4/7/57, T/4/57, 4/19/57, M/6/57, Fo/7/57, 8/11/57, 8/19/57, 9/6/57, S/9/57, 9/18/57, 10/10/57, 11/1/57, 11/12/57, 4/18/58, F/7/58, 8/24/58, T/9/58, F/12/58, 9/4/59
Bowman, Priscilla 2/3/56, 2/10/56
Bowties Fo/11/56
Bradley, Owen T/1/58
Bragg, Johnny and the Marigolds T/9/56
Brewer, Teresa 3/1/58
Briggs, Lillian 1/13/56, 7/12/58
Brooks, Billy T/2/56
Brooks, Donnie S/8/59, T/9/59
Brooks, Louis and the Hi-Toppers
Brown, Billy Fo/10/57, 1/8/58, T/1/58, Fo/5/58
Brown, Boots S/6/58, S/5/59
Brown, Charles 2/3/56, 2/17/56, 3/2/56, S/3/56, E/3/56, 3/14/56, E/4/56, 9/29/56, T/10/56, 2/15/57, 12/12/58, 1/30/59, 2/6/59, S/4/59
Brown, Clarence "Gatemouth" 4/20/56, 6/21/56, 11/8/56, 12/2/56, 2/1/57, 3/15/57, 6/9/57, 6/11/57, 11/14/58
Brown, Clifford 1/20/56
Brown, James and the Famous Flames Fo/2/56, T/5/56, 6/24/56, S/8/56, T/10/56, F/1/57, S/7/57, S/11/57, F/2/58, F/10/58, F/2/59, S/4/59, S/7/59, 12/16/59
Brown, Nappy 2/3/56, Fo/11/56, 2/22/57, 3/8/57, 3/15/57, Fo/3/57, 5/17/57, 7/28/57, 8/23/57, 10/28/57, 2/6/59, 4/19/59, 6/26/59
Brown, Roy E/1/57, S/2/57, 3/15/57, T/4/57, 6/14/57, 6/28/57, 7/5/57, 10/28/57, 9/5/58, 12/12/58, 5/22/59, 6/7/59, 6/18/59, 7/4/59
Brown, Ruth 1/13/56, M/1/56, 1/20/56, 3/2/56, 3/11/56, 3/23/56, 4/1/56, E/4/56, 4/22/56, 5/25/56, 6/29/56, 8/27/56, 9/28/56, F/11/56, 12/28/56, T/1/57, 2/22/57, 3/15/57, 4/15/57, 6/7/57, 6/15/57, 7/10/57, S/9/57, 11/15/57, 11/22/57, T/8/58, 8/29/58, 9/6/58, 9/26/58, 2/6/59, 2/20/59, Fo/4/59, 5/28/59, F/8/59, 9/1/59, 10/25/59
Browns Fo/6/59, 8/15/59, S/10/59, 11/21/59
Brunson, Frankie 11/30/56, E/1/57
Bryan, Wes F/12/57
Bryant, Anita 7/11/59, 8/30/59, 9/4/59, 9/5/59, 12/19/59
Buchanan, Bill Fo/5/58
Buchanan and Ancel T/10/57
Buchanan and Goodman S/7/56, M/8/56, E/10/56, 11/13/56, Fo/2/57, Fo/6/57
Buckner, Milt 8/7/59
Burgess, Dave L/4/57, T/1/58, S/2/59, F/5/59
Burgess, Sonny 8/20/56, 5/16/58, 6/19/58, Fo/9/58
Burke, Solomon F/9/56, 1/6/57, 6/21/57, S/3/58, 7/25/58, S/12/59
Burks, Clifford 10/11/57
Burnette, Dorsey Fo/2/57, T/12/58, F/4/59, Fo/8/59
Burnette, Johnny (solo) Fo/10/58, S/7/59, Fo/11/59
Burnette, Johnny and the Rock 'n Roll Trio E/4/56, T/5/56, 6/21/56, Fo/7/56, 8/6/56, 9/9/56, S/10/56, 12/5/56, Fo/12/56, T/5/57, Fo/8/57, F/12/57
Burns, George 6/9/59, 11/17/59
Butler, Jerry (solo; see also Impressions featuring...) Fo/1/59, S/6/59, 9/1/59, F/9/59
Byrd, Bobby T/4/57

Byrne, Jerry Fo/6/58, S/11/58, T/5/59
Byrnes, Edd "Kookie" Fo/3/59, 4/4/59, S/7/59, 8/22/59, S/10/59

C

Cadets S/6/56, T/9/56, 9/28/56, 10/19/56, 10/29/56, F/11/56
Cadillacs 1/27/56, 2/10/56, 4/1/56, E/4/56, 4/22/56, 5/25/56, 6/1/56, F/6/56, 6/8/56, 6/29/56, 6/30/56, 8/20/56, 11/16/56, 1/11/57, S/2/57, 2/22/57, 3/15/57, Fo/5/57, 7/1/57, 8/2/57, 8/9/57, 8/16/57, 8/23/57, 10/18/57, 12/20/57, 4/13/58, F/8/58, T/10/58, 11/14/58, 11/22/58, 12/24/58, 1/23/59, T/2/59, 3/6/59, 3/27/59, 5/22/59, F/7/59, 8/16/59, 11/27/59
Calloway, Cab 5/18/56, 6/29/56, 4/17/57
Calvaes Fo/9/56, 3/2/57
Campbell, Choker 1/20/56, 2/17/56, 5/25/56, 5/31/57, 2/7/58
Campbell, Glen F/9/58
Campbell, Jo Ann 11/30/56, S/1/57, 4/19/57, F/5/57, 6/7/57, 8/16/57, 8/23/57, 8/30/57, 10/20/57, Fo/11/57, 12/25/57, 1/10/58, Fo/1/58, 3/28/58, S/4/58, T/7/58, 8/24/58, 8/29/58, F/12/58, 12/15/58, 12/24/58, 1/31/59, F/3/59, 3/27/59, F/7/59, 7/21/59, 12/31/59
Campi, Ray Fo/2/57, S/8/57, S/3/59
Cannon, Freddy Fo/4/59, 5/1/59, 6/23/59, F/8/59, 8/8/59, 9/4/59, Fo/10/59, 11/6/59, 11/21/59, 12/26/59
Capehart, Jerry 3/10/56
Capris 2/4/57
Cardinals 1/1/56, Fo/3/56, F/8/56, 10/5/56, 11/9/56, T/1/57, 3/8/57
Carl, Steve and the Jags T/8/58
Carr, Cathy 4/15/56, 7/2/56, 7/22/56, 10/27/56, 3/15/57, 2/21/59, 9/8/59
Carr, Valerie 9/27/58, 5/15/59, 9/18/59
Carr, Wynona 5/18/56, 11/28/57, 8/29/58, 8/30/58, 9/26/58
Carroll, Diahann 3/14/56
Carroll, Johnny 8/31/57, 12/7/57, S/4/59
Carson, Martha 5/4/57
Carter, Betty 9/4/59
Carty, Ric F/8/58
Caruso, Dick 7/11/59
Cavello, Jimmy and the House Rockers 10/19/56, 12/7/56
Casey, Al S/12/56, Fo/4/57, F/12/57
Cash, Eddie Fo/12/58, 6/20/59
Cash, Johnny 2/3/56, 4/21/56, 5/28/56, 6/2/56, 7/7/56, 8/12/56, 8/18/56, 8/26/56, 9/9/56, 10/14/56, 12/4/56, 1/19/57, 2/8/57, 3/24/57, 3/31/57, 4/6/57, 4/7/57, 4/13/57, 4/20/57, 5/1/57, 5/13/57, 5/18/57, 5/21/57, 5/23/57, 5/25/57, 5/29/57, 6/1/57, 6/9/57, 6/12/57, 6/15/57, 8/31/57, E/9/57, 10/16/57, 10/18/57, 11/26/57, 12/1/57, F/1/58, 1/13/58, 1/14/58, 1/21/58, 3/8/58, 3/14/58, 3/29/58, 4/18/58, 4/28/58, E/5/58, 5/10/58, 5/14/58, 5/16/58, Fo/5/58, 6/19/58, 7/1/58, 7/5/58, Fo/7/58, 8/1/58, 9/27/58, 9/30/58, 10/22/58, 10/26/58, 11/1/58, 11/15/58, 11/17/58, 12/18/58, 12/20/58, Fo/12/58, 12/26/58, 12/31/58, 1/18/59, 1/25/59, 2/7/59, Fo/2/59, 3/7/59, Fo/3/59, 4/1/59 , 4/15/59, 4/26/59, M/6/59, 6/18/59, Fo/6/59, 6/26/59, 7/4/59, 8/3/59, E/9/59, 8/15/59, 8/28/59, 9/7/59, 9/8/59, 9/11/59, 9/14/59, 9/20/59, L/9/59, 10/3/59, 10/23/

59, 11/15/59, 11/20/59, 12/12/59, 12/13/59
Castelles S/6/56
Casuals Fo/11/57, 1/18/57, 2/19/58, 3/28/58, 4/18/58, F/6/58
Cellos F/4/57, 4/19/57, 7/5/57, 7/26/57, M/9/57
Chaffin, Ernie S/2/57
Champs Fo/1/58, Fo/4/58, 5/7/58, 5/8/58, Fo/7/58, 8/24/58, Fo/9/58, T/12/58, 12/31/58, T/3/59, Fo/6/59, Fo/8/59, 10/1/59, S/12/59, 12/31/59
Channel, Bruce T/4/59, Fo/12/59
Channels T/8/56, 8/24/56, 10/12/56, Fo/1/57, 2/2/57, 2/8/57, 2/22/57, 3/1/57, T/5/57, 7/5/57, 11/1/57, 11/8/57, F/1/58
Chantels 10/18/57, Fo/11/57, 1/3/58, 1/10/58, 2/21/58, Fo/2/58, 3/1/58, 3/28/58, S/5/58, M/7/58, Fo/7/58, 9/18/58, 10/10/58, Fo/10/58, 12/25/58, S/2/59, 2/20/59, 3/27/59, 5/15/59, F/6/59, S/7/59
Chanticleers S/3/58
Chantones T/10/58
Charles, Bobby 1/27/56, 2/17/56, S/3/56, T/6/56, 7/2/56, 7/22/56, S/1/57, 2/22/57, S/9/58
Charles, Ray 1/6/56, 1/16/56, Fo/1/56, 2/1/56, 2/11/56, E/4/56, S/5/56, 6/30/56, S/9/56, 9/17/56, 11/17/56, 12/23/56, S/1/57, 1/28/57, T/5/57, 8/23/57, F/9/57, 10/28/57, 11/27/57, 11/28/57, F/1/58, 3/8/58, Fo/3/58, 5/16/58, Fo/7/58, 8/30/58, 9/1/58, 9/6/58, M/10/58, Fo/10/58, 11/14/58, Fo/11/58, 12/31/58, 1/9/59, Fo/2/59, 5/24/59, 5/28/59, 5/30/59, S/6/59, 6/15/59, 8/9/59, M/8/59, 8/17/59, 9/25/59, S/10/59, 10/18/59, M/11/59, 11/29/59, S/12/59
Charlie and Ray 1/13/56, F/3/56, 3/30/56, 8/24/56, 1/11/57, 1/25/57, T/5/57, 6/28/57, 7/19/57, 10/18/57, 12/25/57, 11/21/58
Charmers T/10/56
Charms (See Williams, Otis and His...)
Charts T/6/57 , 6/28/57, 8/30/57, 9/13/57
Checker, Chubby T/4/59, 4/28/59, 5/23/59, 7/29/59, 8/4/59, Fo/11/59
Checkers T/4/59
Cheers T/2/56
Chenier, Clifton S/1/56, 5/25/56
Chesterfields S/6/58
Chimes 5/18/56
Chipmunks featuring David Seville S/11/58, 3/8/59, 12/13/59
Chips S/10/56, 11/16/56, 2/2/57
Chordettes 8/5/57, S/2/58, 2/22/58, 1/16/59, 3/28/59
Christy, Don Fo/12/59
Chuck and Betty 6/26/58
Chuck and Bill F/6/57
Chuckles (See Three Chuckles)
Church, Eugene S/9/58, 4/24/59, T/6/59, 8/6/59, S/11/59, 11/18/59
Clanton, Jimmy S/10/57, 6/11/58, 7/12/58, 8/29/58, Fo/9/58, 11/26/58, 12/24/58, 12/27/58, 1/23/59, 2/4/59, F/3/59, 3/5/59, 3/27/59, 3/28/59, 7/1/59, 8/1/59, F/11/59, 11/14/59, 11/24/59, 12/5/59, 12/26/59, 12/28/59
Clark, Dee S/6/57, S/10/57, E/11/57, 2/21/58, 10/10/58, Fo/10/58, 11/14/58, 12/20/58, 1/25/59, Fo/3/59, 4/30/59, 6/13/59, 6/27/59, 7/10/59, F/8/59, 8/4/59, 9/1/59, 9/26/59, T/11/59

Clark, Dick 8/5/57, 2/15/58, 5/30/58, 6/21/58, 8/24/58, 8/27/58, 12/26/58, 4/22/59, 9/4/59, 9/18/59, 9/28/59, 10/1/59, 10/4/59, 10/6/59, 10/20/59, 10/27/59, 11/22/59
Clark, Petula S/4/59, 7/24/59
Clark, Roy Fo/10/58
Clark, Sanford Fo/6/56, T/11/56, T/1/57, 3/14/57, 3/23/57, Fo/3/57, 4/13/57, T/5/57, F/10/57, 12/28/57, T/7/58, F/3/58, F/8/59, S/11/59
Clay, Joe F/5/56, T/7/56
Cleftones 1/27/56, 3/30/56, Fo/3/56, 4/20/56, 6/8/56, T/6/56, 6/21/56, 7/2/56, 7/22/56, 8/29/56, 9/14/56, 10/5/56, 10/27/56, Fo/1/57, 2/1/57, 2/22/57, 5/10/57, 5/17/57, 8/23/57, 8/30/57, F/9/57, Fo/7/58
Clifford, Buzz T/10/58
Cliques Fo/3/56, 5/4/56, F/8/56
Clovers F/1/56, 1/16/56, 1/23/56, 1/27/56, 2/24/56, 3/12/56, 4/1/56, 4/22/56, 5/11/56, S/5/56, 5/25/56, 8/24/56, 9/28/56, 10/20/56, M/11/56, 12/7/56, 12/28/56, 1/20/57, 3/8/57, S/3/22/57, 4/19/57, 5/4/57, 8/4/57, 9/6/57, S/9/57, 10/18/57, 12/25/57, 4/11/58, 6/27/58, 7/3/58, E/9/58, 10/3/58, 10/15/58, 4/17/59, Fo/5/59, Fo/7/59, 9/2/59, 9/23/59, 11/20/59
Clowney, David (See Cortez, Dave "Baby")
Coasters E/2/56, T/2/56, 4/20/56, 5/11/56, S/6/56, 7/28/56, 9/28/56, 11/8/56, T/3/57, 4/26/57, 5/17/57, 6/7/57, 6/14/57, Fo/6/57, 7/10/57, 7/26/57, S/8/57, M/9/57, 10/18/57, F/11/57, 11/15/57, F/2/58, F/5/58, 6/13/58, 8/5/58, 8/16/58, T/8/58, 9/19/58, 9/26/58, 10/3/58, 12/25/58, S/1/59, 3/7/59, 3/13/59, 3/27/59, Fo/4/59, 7/3/59, F/8/59, 8/7/59, 9/4/59, 9/18/59, T/11/59, 11/26/59
Cobb, Arnett 11/1/57
Cochran, Eddie E/1/56, 3/10/56, E/5/56, 12/25/56, Fo/2/57, M/4/57, F/5/57, 6/21/57, F/7/57, L/8/57, 10/8/57, 10/12/57, 11/1/57, Fo/11/57, 1/8/58, S/1/58, 1/29/58, 4/28/58, F/6/58, T/7/58, 8/26/58, 8/27/58, 8/30/58, T/10/58, 11/14/58, 11/29/58, 12/24/58, T/2/59, T/7/59, 7/25/59, 10/10/59, S/11/59
Cochran, Hank E/1/56, E/5/56
Cochran, Jackie Lee F/2/57, F/6/58
Cochran, Wayne S/5/59
Cochran Brothers (See also Cochran, Eddie and Cochran, Hank) F/6/56
Cogan, Shaye 8/30/57
Cole, Ann 2/10/56, 4/1/56, 11/16/56, 11/23/56, 2/15/57, M/3/57, 6/28/57, 7/19/57, 8/16/57, 10/11/57
Cole, Cozy Fo/9/58, 10/18/58, F/11/58, S/11/58, 11/22/58, 11/26/58, 12/5/58, 12/26/58, 1/27/59, 2/9/59, T/2/59, 4/6/59, 5/6/59, 7/21/59, 9/28/59, 12/7/59
Cole, Nat King 3/11/56, 6/29/56, 2/1/57
Cole, Sonny F/5/57
Collegians T/1/58
Collins, Lorrie 6/26/59
Collins Kids S/10/56, T/1/57, F/5/57, F/10/57, 11/14/58, 11/17/58, 11/15/59
Colts 1/6/56, 2/3/56, S/2/56, 2/17/56, 4/20/56, 5/19/56, T/5/56, 6/8/56, F/1/58
Comstock, Bobby S/2/59, S/9/59, 12/12/59
Coney Island Kids T/8/56
Convy, Bert T/7/58

Cook, Dale (See Cooke, Sam)
Cooke, Sam F/3/57, F/9/57, S/11/57, Fo/11/57, 12/1/57, 12/6/57, 12/12/57, 1/14/58, 1/17/58, 1/20/57, 1/29/58, 2/7/58, S/2/58, 2/19/58, 2/20/58, 3/2/58, 3/6/58, 4/6/584/6/58, F/5/58, S/7/58, 7/18/58, 10/11/58, 10/13/58, T/10/58, 11/10/58, 1/22/59, Fo/1/59, 3/14/59, T/5/59, 5/22/59, 5/25/59, 6/3/59, 6/9/59, 6/20/59, 6/22/59, 6/29/59, Fo/7/59, T/9/59, 9/25/59, 10/2/59, M/10/59, 10/16/59, 11/14/59, M/11/59, T/11/59
Cookie and the Cupcakes Fo/11/58, Fo/6/59
Cookies Fo/1/56, 6/1/56, 6/29/56, 1/11/57, 7/19/57, 5/16/58, 9/6/58
Cooley, Eddie and the Dimples T/9/56, 11/1/56, 12/21/56, 2/15/57
Corey, Jill 9/20/58, 12/27/58
Cortez, Dave "Baby" S/11/56, Fo/2/58, 8/23/58, Fo/8/58, 10/15/58, S/2/59, 4/4/59, 4/17/59, 5/15/59, T/5/59, 5/22/59, 6/6/59, 6/12/59, 8/7/59, F/9/59, 10/27/59, 11/1/59, S/12/59
Counts F/2/56
Covay, Don 7/30/56
Craddock, Billy "Crash" T/11/57, Fo/7/58, F/1/59, F/4/59, S/9/59, 9/27/59, 10/1/59, 10/8/59, 11/20/59, Fo/11/59, 12/25/59
Crayton, Pee Wee M/2/56, E/4/56, M/5/56, 5/25/56, 7/20/56, 10/27/56, 12/25/57
Crescendos (on Atlantic) T/9/56
Crescendos (on Nasco) S/11/57, 1/14/58, 1/24/58, 3/2/58, S/3/58, 4/6/58, T/10/58
Crests F/11/58, 12/24/58, 12/27/58, 1/16/59, 1/23/59, 2/20/59, 2/27/59, F/3/59, 3/5/59, 3/27/59, 5/2/59, F/5/59, T/5/59, 7/3/59, T/7/59, 7/29/59, 8/4/59, 10/31/59, F/11/59, 11/13/59, 11/20/59
Crewe, Bob 2/18/56, S/11/57
Crickets (Without Buddy Holly; see also Holly, Buddy and the... or Ivan) E/11/58, 2/7/59
Crowns (See also Maye, Arthur Lee and the...)
Cuff Links F/12/56, T/2/58
Cunningham, Ed 11/10/58
Cupp, Pat T/9/56
Curtis, King (See King Curtis)
Curtis, Mac M/4/56, F/5/56, F/12/56, 12/21/56, Fo/6/57, T/1/58, F/3/58
Curtis, Sonny Fo/4/58
Cyclones S/9/58

D

Dale, Dick Fo/5/58
D'Aleo, Angelo (See Dion and the Belmonts)
Damon, Mark 6/13/59
Damone, Vic 6/6/59
Danleers F/7/58, 8/16/58, 8/29/58, S/9/58, 9/19/58, 9/26/58, 10/3/58, 11/21/58, Fo/4/59
Danny and the Juniors F/11/57, 12/1/57, 12/25/57, 1/8/58, Fo/1/58, 2/15/58, M/2/58, 5/12/58, S/5/58, 5/16/58, 6/4/58, 6/21/58, M/7/58, Fo/8/58, E/9/58, 10/11/58, F/11/58, 11/29/58, 5/9/59, Fo/9/59, M/11/59
Daps Fo/2/56
Darin, Bobby Fo/3/56, 4/15/56, T/5/56, Fo/9/56, S/6/57, 7/25/57, 10/18/57, S/11/57, 12/17/57, F/2/58, F/6/58, 7/19/58, 7/25/58, 8/

481

2/58, 8/23/58, F/9/58, E/9/58, S/9/58, Fo/9/58, 10/3/58, 10/25/58, 11/1/58, 11/7/58, 11/21/58, 11/29/58, F/1/59, M/1/59, 1/31/59, 3/6/59, Fo/3/59, 4/18/59, 4/20/59, 5/2/59, 5/4/59, 5/31/59, 6/1/59, 6/9/59, M/6/59, F/8/59, E/8/59, 8/22/59, 9/1/59, 9/6/59, 9/14/59, 9/16/59, 9/28/59, 10/6/59, 11/12/59, 11/16/59, 11/17/59, 11/29/59, 12/4/59, T/12/59

Darnell, Ravon F/8/56
Darren, James T/12/58, 1/29/59, 3/28/59, F/4/59, 6/20/59, Fo/6/59
Darts T/11/58
Davis, Eddie "Lockjaw" 7/24/59
Davis, Gail 4/11/59
Davis, Larry T/9/58
Davis, Link F/5/56
Davis, Miles 10/17/58, 12/12/58, 3/13/59, 10/16/59
Davis, Sammy Jr. 4/11/58, 4/20/59, 10/9/59
Day, Bing Fo/2/58, T/8/59
Day, Bobby (See also Byrd, Bobby and Relf, Bobby) F/3/57, T/8/57, 11/8/57, Fo/11/57, T/3/58, M/4/58, 7/18/58, 8/9/58, 8/22/58, 10/24/58, 10/25/58, T/11/58, 12/18/58, T/2/59, 3/27/59, 5/1/59, S/5/59, 5/22/59, S/7/59, 8/3/59, S/9/59, F/12/59
Day, Margie 4/19/57, 9/27/57
Deal, Don F/7/57, T/11/57, Fo/7/58
Dean, Bobby Fo/10/57
Dean and Jean 12/25/59
Debutantes 11/1/56
Dee, Jackie (Jackie DeShannon; see also Shannon, Jackie) 7/1/57, 7/3/57, S/8/58, 9/29/58, 11/30/58
Dee, Jimmy F/11/57, 12/1/57
Dee, Johnny F/2/57, Fo/5/57
Dee, Ronnie T/11/58
Dee, Tommy T/3/59
DeHaven, Gloria 12/12/59
DeKnight, Jimmy F/5/59
Del Vikings (See also Dell-Vikings) S/6/57, 8/30/57, L/8/57, T/9/57, 10/4/57, 10/11/57, 11/22/57, F/12/57, 12/6/57, 1/15/58, S/2/58, 2/22/58, 6/19/58, T/7/58, S/11/58
Delegates S/9/56
Dell, Jimmy T/3/58
Dell-Vikings (See also Del Vikings) S/1/57, F/2/57, 3/15/57, 4/19/57, 5/4/57, E/5/57, F/9/57
Dells F/2/56, S/8/56, 10/12/56, 11/1/56, 11/16/56, 12/21/56, S/2/57, 4/19/57, Fo/4/57, S/6/57, Fo/6/57, 8/23/57, Fo/10/57, 11/8/57, 2/7/58, 2/21/58, 4/4/58, 6/20/58, S/9/58
Delroys S/7/57, 8/16/57
Delta Rhythm Boys 6/29/56
Deltairs 11/10/58
DeMarco, Ralph 12/5/59
Denton, Bobby 9/6/58'
DeShannon, Jackie (See Dee, Jackie or Shannon, Jackie)
Diablos (See Strong, Nolan and the...)
Diamond, Lee (See also Upsetters) 10/3/58
Diamonds 9/8/56, 1/17/57, Fo/2/57, 4/13/57, 4/19/57, Fo/5/57, 6/2/57, 7/7/57, 8/30/57, L/8/57, 10/31/57, 11/1/57, 11/28/57, F/12/57, 12/5/57, 2/22/58, 2/24/58, 3/1/58, 3/22/58, M/11/58, S/1/59, 2/21/59, 4/22/59, 8/29/59
Diddley, Bo 2/1/56, S/2/56, 3/14/56, 3/30/56, E/4/56, 4/20/56, 5/19/56, 6/24/56, Fo/6/56, 8/24/56, F/10/56, 10/19/56, 10/29/56, 11/16/56, 12/25/56, 12/28/56, 3/13/57, 3/22/57, Fo/3/57, 4/19/57, 5/31/57, 6/14/57, 7/10/57, 8/30/57, 10/28/57, Fo/11/57, 1/3/58, E/1/58, 4/13/58, S/6/58, 8/16/58, 10/22/58, 12/24/58, 1/23/59, S/2/59, 3/5/59, 3/27/59, T/5/59, 5/22/59, 7/29/59, 8/4/59, T/8/59, F/11/59, 12/25/59
Dillard, Varetta 10/4/57, 2/7/58
Dimples 2/15/57
DiMucci, Dion (See also Dion and the Belmonts and Dion and the Timberlanes) M/10/59
Dinning, Mark Fo/9/57, T/7/58, F/4/59, M/9/59, S/11/59, 12/16/59
Dion and the Belmonts (See also DiMucci, Dion) 4/16/58, F/5/58, 5/24/58, 6/20/58, 6/27/58, Fo/7/58, 8/7/58, 10/3/58, 10/22/58, T/11/58, 12/24/58, 1/9/59, 1/17/59, 1/23/59, 2/3/59, 3/6/59, Fo/3/59, 6/1/59, F/6/59, M/6/59, Fo/8/59, 9/26/59, 10/13/59, F/12/59
Dion and the Timberlanes T/6/57
Dixon, Floyd 1/16/56, F/2/57
Dixon, Willie Fo/11/56
Dobkins, Carl Jr. Fo/5/58, F/2/59, 6/13/59, 6/23/59, T/8/59, 8/26/59, 9/3/59, 9/19/59, 9/27/59, S/11/59, 12/26/59
Dr. Jive (See Smalls, Tommy)
Dodds, Malcom and the Tunedrops T/4/57, 10/4/57, F/10/57, 3/7/58
Dodo, Joe T/3/58
Doggett, Bill 2/10/56, 4/12/56, S/7/56, 7/13/56, M/10/56, F/11/56, T/1/57, 2/15/57, 5/21/57, 7/19/57, 10/28/57, 11/19/57, 3/14/58, 6/21/58, 7/18/58, Fo/8/58, 10/5/58, 1/16/59, 5/17/59, 7/19/59, 10/19/59, 11/4/59, 11/13/59, 11/23/59
Doggett, Ray T/4/57
Domino, Fats S/1/56, M/1/56, L/1/56, T/3/56, 4/1/56, E/4/56, 4/8/56, 4/22/56, 5/6/56, 6/15/56, F/7/56, 7/7/56, 7/20/56, 7/28/56, 7/29/56, 8/29/56, 9/2/56, M/9/56, T/9/56, 9/24/56, 10/12/56, M/11/56, 11/18/56, F/12/56, 12/25/56, L/1/57, 2/2/57, 2/5/57, 2/15/57, M/2/57, Fo/2/57, 2/26/57, M/3/57, 3/28/57, 4/10/57, Fo/4/57, 5/18/58, 5/25/57, 6/1/57, 6/9/57, M/6/57, 6/17/57, T/7/57, 7/23/57, 7/26/57, L/7/57, 8/9/57, 8/16/57, 8/30/57, L/8/57, 9/6/57, Fo/9/57, 9/26/57, 10/10/57, 11/1/57, 11/12/57, Fo/11/57, 12/25/57, 1/11/58, 1/23/58, F/2/58, 2/22/58, 3/29/58, 4/4/58, F/4/58, 5/16/58, Fo/6/58, S/8/58, T/10/58, 11/8/58, 12/13/58, T/1/59, 3/6/59, 3/27/59, 4/10/59, M/4/59, T/4/59, 4/22/59, 5/11/59, 6/28/59, F/7/59, F/10/59, 11/5/59, 11/10/59
Dominoes (See Ward, Billy and His...)
Don and Dewey Fo/3/57, T/8/57, F/10/57, 11/28/57, F/12/57, Fo/7/58, T/2/59
Don Juans 4/21/57
Donegan, Lonnie 6/21/56, F/3/59
Donner, Ral F/10/59
Doo, Dickey and the Don'ts Fo/12/57, 1/13/58, 3/15/58, 3/28/58, F/4/58, 5/10/58, 6/30/57, M/7/58, F/9/58, 9/11/58, 11/15/58, 11/26/58, 12/26/58, 1/10/59, 2/20/59, 7/21/59, Fo/12/59

Dorman, Harold Fo/12/59
Dorsey, Jimmy Fo/2/57, 6/12/57
Dorsey, Lee 8/22/59
Downey, Morton Jr. L/3/58, 1/10/59
Dreamers 7/28/56
Drifters 2/1/56, 2/10/56, 3/9/56, 3/14/56, Fo/3/56, 4/20/56, 5/19/56, T/7/56, 8/31/56, 10/27/56, T/1/57, 2/22/57, T/5/57, 5/27/57, E/6/57, 6/14/57, 7/10/57, 9/6/57, 9/26/57, 10/10/57, 11/1/57, 2/7/58, 2/19/58, 4/4/58, 6/20/58, M/7/58, 7/18/58, 8/11/58, T/4/59, 5/28/59, 6/30/59, 7/10/59, 9/1/59, 9/18/59, T/9/59, M/11/59, 12/3/59, 12/16/59
Drifters, Cliff Richard and the (See Richard, Cliff)
Dubs Fo/4/57, 8/30/57, 10/18/57, 11/1/57, 12/25/57, 1/10/57, 1/20/58, 2/7/58, 2/19/58, 3/14/58, F/6/58, 9/26/58, Fo/8/59, S/10/59, 11/27/59
Duncan, Cleve T/8/59
Duponts T/8/56, 2/22/57
Dupree, Champion Jack 1/20/56, T/2/56, Fo/6/56, E/1/57, Fo/2/57, Fo/5/57, S/11/57
Duvall, Huelyn F/4/58, F/7/58, Fo/9/58, F/5/59
Dynatones S/5/59, Fo/9/5209,

E

Echoes T/1/57
Eddie and Betty 7/25/59
Eddy, Duane Fo/2/58, Fo/5/58, 7/19/58, 7/24/58, S/8/58, 8/27/58, 10/4/58, F/10/58, 10/9/58, 11/19/58, 12/6/58, F/1/59, 1/15/59, 1/23/59, 2/14/59, F/3/59, 3/5/59, 3/27/59, 4/8/59, 4/22/59, T/5/59, 5/30/59, 7/15/59, Fo/8/59, 9/2/59, 9/4/59, 9/5/59, 9/15/59, 9/18/59, Fo/11/59, 12/22/59
Edsels S/6/58
Edwards, Chuck M/3/57
Edwards, Jimmy Fo/10/57, 1/8/58, T/2/58
Edwards, Tommy 4/8/58, T/7/58, 9/6/58, Fo/9/58, 9/25/58, 10/15/58, 10/17/58, 11/3/58, 12/13/58, 12/28/58, 1/7/59, 1/31/59, 3/6/59, 5/25/59, F/7/59, 8/15/59, F/10/59, 10/24/59, 11/14/59
El Capris S/2/56
El Dorados F/1/56, 1/11/56, 2/13/56, L/2/56, 3/9/56, F/4/56, S/7/56, 8/17/56, Fo/10/56, 11/1/56, 11/30/56, 2/22/57
El Vinos E/1/57
Elbert, Donnie F/4/57, 6/28/57, 8/4/57, T/9/57, 11/1/57, 1/10/58, 1/17/58, S/2/58, 2/21/58, 8/15/58, 8/22/58
Eldridge, Roy 9/11/59
Elegants M/7/58, 8/29/58, Fo/9/58, 10/18/58, 11/1/58, 11/28/58
Ellington, Duke 9/12/58, 2/27/57, 5/25/59
Ellis Brothers Fo/8/58
Emeralds (See Bond, Luther and the...)
Empires Fo/1/56, T/6/56, Fo/1/57
Endsley, Melvin F/7/57
Engel, Scott Fo/7/58 Fo/8/58
Epps, Preston T/4/59, 6/3/59, 6/13/59, 9/1/59
Ertegun, Ahmet 11/29/59
Esquires (See also Four Esquires) 11/19/56, L/12/56
Esquirita Fo/9/58, S/2/59
Eternals S/5/59

Evans, Paul T/5/57, S/8/57, F/3/59, T/8/59, 9/24/59, 10/3/58, Fo/12/59
Everly, Phil 2/7/59
Everly Brothers S/2/56, S/4/57, 6/21/57, Fo/6/57, 6/30/57, 7/1/57, 7/12/57, 8/4/57, Fo/8/57, 9/6/57, 9/13/57, 10/6/57, 10/10/57, 11/1/57, 12/7/57, 12/25/57, 1/5/58, 1/8/58, S/1/58, 2/20/58, 2/25/58, 3/9/58, 4/5/58, 4/6/58, F/4/58, 4/27/58, 6/14/58, 6/30/58, 7/18/58, Fo/7/58, 8/29/58, 9/27/58, Fo/10/58, 11/1/58, 12/6/58, 12/14/58, 1/16/59, 3/14/59, T/3/59, 3/21/59, 4/26/59, 4/29/59, M/6/59, 6/26/59, 7/1/59, 7/23/59, Fo/7/59, 9/2/59, 9/12/59, 9/30/59, M/10/59, T/12/59

F

Fabian M/6/58, T/6/58, 6/19/58, 6/30/58, S/9/58, 9/13/58, Fo/11/58, 12/6/58, 12/12/58, 1/17/59, 2/9/59, 2/20/59, F/3/59, 3/12/59, 3/27/59, 4/4/59, 4/18/59, 5/24/59, Fo/5/59, 6/17/59, 6/21/59, 6/28/59, 6/30/59, 7/13/59, T/8/59, 8/22/59, 9/2/59, 9/15/59, 9/22/59, 9/26/59, 10/1/59, T/10/59, 10/31/59, 11/4/59, 11/14/59
Facenda, Tommy S/8/58, T/9/59, 12/12/59, 12/25/59
Fairburn, Werly S/10/56
Faire, Johnny Fo/11/57
Falcons Fo/8/56, M/9/56, 11/3/56, 2/8/57, Fo/11/57, S/3/59, 5/13/59, 6/3/59, 6/9/59, 6/19/59, 7/3/59, 7/25/59, 9/4/59, 10/25/59, S/11/59, 12/25/59
Farrell, Billy S/2/58
Fascinators 11/10/58
Feathers, Charlie S/12/56, S/3/57, 7/13/57, Fo/6/58, 11/14/58
Fell, Terry 3/10/56, S/11/56
Felts, Narvel Fo/6/57, T/9/57, T/1/58, Fo/7/58
Fi Tones 2/2/57, 3/30/56
Fidelities Fo/2/58, F/7/58, Fo/9/58, 12/5/58, S/8/59
Fields, Ernie Fo/6/59
Fiestas Fo/1/59, 4/17/59, 5/22/59, 5/28/59, S/7/59, F/10/59, E/11/59
Fireballs F/1/59, Fo/7/59, Fo/11/59
Fireflies T/8/58, S/8/59, 10/10/59, Fo/11/59, 11/27/59
Fisher, Sonny F/6/56
Fisher, Toni Fo/9/59, 12/19/59
Fitzgerald, Ella 2/3/56, 9/11/59
Five Blind Boys of Mississippi 6/22/56
Five Blobs F/9/58
Five Crowns M/7/58
Five Dollars M/3/56, 4/21/57
Five Keys 1/13/56, Fo/1/56, 2/1/56, 2/18/56, F/4/56, E/4/56, 5/25/56, F/6/56, 7/13/56, T/8/56, 8/24/56, 9/24/56, M/10/56, Fo/11/56, 2/15/57, 6/7/57, T/6/57, S/8/57, 8/30/57, 10/25/57, F/11/57, 11/15/57, 8/22/58, T/10/58, 11/18/59
"5" Royales Fo/3/57, T/5/57, F/10/57, T/12/57, 4/13/58, S/12/58, F/4/59, T/10/59
Five Satins Fo/5/56, 8/24/56, T/10/56, 11/23/56, 11/30/56, M/1/57, S/3/57, Fo/5/57, 6/14/57, 7/10/57, 7/26/57, 8/30/57, M/9/57, F/10/57, 10/18/57, 10/21/57, 10/25/57, 11/15/57, 11/28/57, 1/10/58, T/7/58, 9/12/58, Fo/9/59, 11/20/59, 11/27/59

Flairs Fo/4/56, 6/1/56, T/9/56, 9/28/56, 10/20/56, M/11/56
Flamingos F/1/56, 1/27/56, 2/10/56, 2/17/56, 3/30/56, 4/20/56, F/5/56, 5/19/56, 6/29/56, 8/6/56, F/10/56, 10/12/56, Fo/11/56, 2/22/57, 6/21/57, 9/21/57, 4/4/58, S/7/58, 8/16/58, T/10/58, 12/24/58, 1/16/59, 1/23/59, 3/25/59, Fo/4/59, 7/11/59, S/8/59, 9/15/59, 9/27/59, 11/20/59, Fo/11/59
Fleetwoods S/2/59, 3/14/59, 4/5/59, 4/22/59, 4/25/59, Fo/4/59, S/8/59, 9/12/59
Flemons, Wade T/10/58, 1/16/59, 1/23/59, 3/27/59, 7/3/59, S/7/59
Flowers, Phil Fo/8/56
Foley, Red 7/8/58
Fontaine, Eddie 4/22/56, T/8/56, 9/14/57, S/7/58
Ford, Dee Dee Fo/11/59
Ford, Frankie 9/1/58, T/12/58, 3/21/59, 3/23/59, T/6/59, 6/23/59, 7/29/59, S/12/59
Four Aces 3/16/56, 4/15/56, 4/19/58
Four Dates 3/1/58
4 Deuces T/2/56
Four Esquires (See also Esquires) F/10/57, 12/11/57, 12/23/57, 12/25/57, Fo/1/58, 2/20/58, 3/29/58, T/9/58, 12/22/58, 1/15/59, Fo/10/59
Four Fellows F/8/56
Four Jokers S/6/56
Four Lads 12/6/57, 3/29/58, 6/30/58
Four Lovers (See also Four Seasons) T/4/56, F/9/56, T/12/56, F/2/57
Four Mints F/4/58, 7/14/58, S/11/58, L/5/59
Four Preps T/11/57, 3/23/58, 4/12/58, T/4/58, 5/7/58, 7/13/58, 7/18/58, 12/20/58, 5/30/59, T/7/59, Fo/11/59, 12/19/59
Four Seasons (See also Four Lovers or Vally, Frankie) S/11/59
Four Tops S/5/56, 2/1/57, 9/6/57, 12/31/58, 9/11/59
Four Tunes Fo/1/56, 1/27/56
Foxx, Redd 1/9/59
Francis, Connie S/3/56, M/4/56, 6/16/56, Fo/9/56, S/11/56, 12/5/56, Fo/2/57, Fo/5/57, 6/10/57, 7/12/57, 7/26/57, S/9/57, T/11/57, 1/23/58, 2/15/58, 3/22/58, 4/14/58, S/4/58, 4/26/58, 5/11/58, 6/30/58, F/7/58, M/7/58, 7/26/58, 8/14/58, T/9/58, M/9/58, 9/27/58, 10/29/58, T/11/58, 11/26/58, 11/29/58, 12/6/58, 2/7/59, S/2/59, 2/14/59, 2/27/59, E/3/59, 3/31/59, 4/11/59, T/4/59, 4/22/59, 5/2/59, 5/20/59, 6/27/59, 7/1/59, 7/11/59, 7/15/59, 7/20/59, 8/8/59, S/8/59, 8/12/59, 8/18/59, 8/30/59, 9/6/59, 9/27/59, 10/3/59, 10/17/59, 10/23/59, Fo/10/59, E/11/59, 11/18/59, 11/22/59, 11/23/59, 11/26/59, 12/2/59, 12/5/59, 12/9/59, 12/23/59
Franklin, Aretha 3/17/57
Franklin, Rev. C.L. 3/17/57
Frantics F/5/59, Fo/7/59
Freberg, Stan S/11/58
Fred, John and the Playboys (see also Playboys) F/12/58, Fo/5/59
Freed, Alan 1/7/56, 2/25/56, 3/14/56, 3/23/56, 3/30/56, S/4/56, 4/14/56, 4/15/56, 5/12/56, 6/30/56, 6/8/56, F/12/56, 12/21/56, 2/22/57, 4/6/57, 4/19/57, L/4/57, 5/4/57, 5/11/57, 7/12/57, M/8/57, 8/30/57, L/8/57, L/9/57, 10/20/57, 12/25/57, 3/28/58, 3/30/58, 4/1/58, 4/25/58, 5/3/58, 5/10/58, 5/16/58, 6/11/58, 6/30/58, M/7/58, 7/19/58, 8/29/58, 12/24/58, 3/4/59, 3/27/59, L/6/59, 9/4/59, 11/25/59, 12/25/59

Freeman, Bobby T/3/58, 6/27/58, F/7/58, 7/3/58, M/7/58, 8/11/58, 8/23/58, 8/29/58, Fo/9/58, 9/27/58, 10/17/58, 11/28/58, 2/28/59, 3/13/59, 3/27/59, Fo/4/59, 6/4/59, Fo/6/59, 6/16/59, 6/18/59, 7/29/59, S/8/59, 10/23/59, Fo/10/59, 11/28/59
Freeman, Ernie T/1/56, 2/18/56, 3/14/56, 4/6/56, 7/28/56, 8/10/56, S/8/57, 10/18/57, T/10/57, 11/15/57, 2/7/58, 2/19/58, 8/24/58
Frizzell, Lefty E/5/56
Fuller, Jerry T/9/58, T/2/59, T/7/59, Fo/9/59
Fuller, Johnny Fo/2/56, F/10/58, S/1/59
Fulson, Lowell E/2/56, 5/4/56, 5/18/56, 10/18/57, T/11/59

G

Gailard, Slim 10/4/57
Garland, Red 10/16/59
Garnett, Gale L/11/57
Gates, David F/2/59
Gaylarks T/5/57
Gayten, Paul F/10/59
G-Clefs 9/21/56, 10/27/56, S/11/56, 11/30/56, 12/21/56, L/12/56, 2/22/57, Fo/2/57, 3/1/57, 4/19/57, 5/17/57, 8/23/57
Gene and Eunice 1/6/56, 11/16/56, 12/7/56, 2/22/57, 5/3/57, 6/3/57, Fo/7/57, 7/26/57, Fo/8/59, 10/23/59, 11/18/59
Genies 4/24/59
Getz, Stan M/4/58
Gibbs, Georgia 1/3/57, 3/1/57
Gibbs, Terry 9/11/59
Gibson, Beverly Ann 7/3/59
Gibson, Don Fo/12/57, 3/29/58, 5/16/58, 7/12/58, Fo/8/58, 10/25/58, S/10/59
Gibson, Steve and His Red Caps 1/23/56, 10/1/56, 10/12/56, 6/17/57, 5/16/58, 9/23/59, 11/18/59, 12/31/59
Gillespie, Dizzy 6/22/56
Gilley, Mickey T/2/58
Gilmer, Jimmy T/7/59
Gino and Gina Fo/7/58, 8/29/58, 12/24/58
Giordiano, Lou F/2/59
Gladiolas F/2/57, T/5/57, 8/23/58
Glenn, Glenn S/2/58, Fo/6/58, 7/18/58
G-Notes 5/2/59
Gone All Stars Fo/11/57
Goodman, Benny 3/23/56
Gordon, Curtis 11/14/58
Gordon, Rosco E/9/57, S/6/59, 9/1/59, T/11/59
Gourdine, Little Anthony (See also Little Anthony and the Imperials) T/10/58
Grable, Betty M/10/59
Gracie, Charlie T/1/57, 3/10/57, 3/25/57, T/4/57, 4/19/57, 5/11/57, M/6/57, 6/21/57, L/6/57, S/7/57, 8/5/57, 9/4/57, T/10/57, 11/12/57, 12/13/57, 3/15/58, E/4/58, S/5/58, 8/1/58, E/8/58, S/1/59, 2/14/59, F/5/59, F/9/59, L/11/59
Grammer, Billy T/10/58, 4/25/59
Granahan, Gerry Fo/4/58, M/7/58
Grant, Earl S/8/58, E/10/58, 11/2/58, 1/31/59, E/5/59, 5/13/59, 11/15/59, 11/16/59

483

Graves, Billy S/12/58
Grazell, Rudy "Tutti" F/11/56, T/6/57, Fo/5/58, S/7/59
Green, Rudy E/1/57
Green, Vernon (See also Medallions) 4/20/56, T/3/59
Greer, Big John 7/6/56, 5/17/57, 7/28/57
Guitar, Bonnie 12/6/57, F/11/59
Guitar Gable F/8/56
Guitar Slim 2/17/56, E/4/56, 8/24/56, 9/24/56, 11/23/56, 5/18/58
Gum Drops Fo/9/56
Gunter, Shirley and the Queens 4/11/56, 6/1/56, 7/28/56, 9/28/56, 10/20/56
Guy, Buddy S/3/59

H

Haley, Bill and His Comets 1/7/56, 1/27/56, 2/1/56, M/2/56, F/3/56, 3/14/56, T/3/56, 4/20/56, 5/19/56, Fo/5/56, 6/3/56, 6/5/56, 6/16/56, T/7/56, 8/6/56, 8/25/56, 9/12/56, 9/25/56, 9/28/56, S/10/56, 10/11/56, 10/14/56, 10/20/56, M/11/56, Fo/11/56, 1/8/57, 1/31/57, 2/6/57, Fo/2/57, L/2/57, 4/26/57, 4/28/57, 5/9/57, 5/11/57, T/5/57, 6/2/57, 6/17/57, 6/27/57, 6/29/57, 7/5/57, Fo/7/57, 8/2/57, E/8/57, 8/30/57, L/8/57, E/9/57, 9/30/57, S/10/57, 10/25/57, 11/15/57, 11/27/57, 12/7/57, T/12/57, 2/20/58, Fo/2/58, 2/25/58, 3/22/58, 4/6/58, 4/9/58, M/4/58, F/7/58, 8/23/58, 8/29/58, 8/30/58, E/9/58, F/10/58, S/11/58, 12/18/58, S/2/59, T/3/59, 4/3/59, 4/8/59, 4/24/59, 6/7/59, T/6/59, Fo/7/59, 8/1/59, E/8/59, 11/6/59, M/11/59, 11/28/59, T/12/59
Hall, Larry Fo/8/59, 10/31/59
Hall, Rene F/12/57
Hall, Tom T. 3/10/56
Hamilton, Bobby F/6/58, 8/29/58, Fo/9/58
Hamilton, George IV F/7/56, 12/21/56, 3/14/57, 3/15/57, L/6/57, 7/8/57, Fo/10/57, 1/24/58, 2/1/58, 7/19/58, 8/9/58, Fo/10/58, 1/31/59, 9/2/59
Hamilton, Roy 2/1/56, 2/10/56, 2/24/56, 4/13/56, 5/4/56, 6/6/56, 9/7/56, 8/4/57, 9/27/57, 10/11/57, 11/28/57, F/12/57, 1/10/58, 1/20/58, M/2/58, 4/6/58, 4/11/58, 5/1/58, 5/8/58, 6/27/58, 7/3/58, 10/31/58, 1/4/59, 4/18/59, 5/11/59, 5/28/59, 6/26/59, 7/17/59, 8/12/59
Hamilton Sisters 7/6/56
Hampton, Lionel 3/11/56, 6/29/56, 2/1/57, 6/29/57
Hardesty, Herb M/1/56
Harper, Janie 6/21/58
Harpo, Slim S/7/57
Harptones 2/3/56, E/2/56, S/4/56, Fo/8/56, 8/29/56, 9/14/56, 10/19/56, 3/8/57, 4/19/57, 8/30/57, Fo/3/59, Fo/9/59
Harrison, Wilbert Fo/3/59, 5/2/59, 5/15/59, F/6/59, 6/15/59, 6/26/59, 9/1/59
Harvey and the Moonglows (See also Moonglows) T/8/58, F/12/58, 12/24/58, Fo/9/59
Harris, Ray Fo/7/57
Harris, Thurston T/9/57, 10/10/57, 10/18/57, 11/28/57, F/12/57, 12/25/57, 1/10/58, 1/20/58, 2/7/58, 2/19/58, Fo/3/58, 4/11/58, 5/2/58, Fo/6/58, 8/22/58, 10/22/58, F/11/58, 11/7/58, Fo/2/59, Fo/3/59
Harris, Tony F/5/57, F/11/57
Harris, Wynonie 7/21/57, 10/7/59
Harrison, Wilbert Fo/8/56
Hartman, Johnny 7/10/57
Hawkettes 7/26/56, M/3/57, 9/20/57
Hawkins, Dale T/6/56, Fo/4/57, 8/7/57, 10/11/57, S/10/57, F/4/58, 4/12/58, T/7/58, 7/21/58, 8/23/58, 8/27/58, S/10/58, 11/15/58, S/2/59, 3/7/59, 3/27/59, 4/22/59, Fo/4/59, 6/6/59, Fo/6/59, F/9/59, 10/3/59, S/12/59
Hawkins, Erskine 2/10/56, 10/5/56, 11/9/56
Hawkins, Ronnie Fo/4/59, 5/9/59, Fo/7/59, 8/17/59, 9/19/59, M/10/59, Fo/11/59
Hawkins, Sam 9/18/59
Hawkins, Screamin' Jay 2/1/56, 2/10/56, 2/14/56, M/4/56, 6/1/56, Fo/10/56, 11/1/56, 11/16/56, 12/21/56, 1/18/57, 2/22/57, 3/22/57, F/4/57, 4/19/57, 5/4/57, 7/1/57, 8/4/57, 9/20/57, 11/8/57, 11/28/57, 1/31/58, 3/28/58
Heap, Jimmy Fo/3/59
Heartbeats 1/20/56, 2/10/56, 2/13/56, Fo/2/56, 3/14/56, S/10/56, 12/7/56, 12/21/56, 1/4/57, 1/18/57, 2/8/57, 4/19/57, 5/24/57, 6/7/57, 6/28/57, 11/1/57, 12/25/57, S/1/58, T/2/58, 2/21/58, 3/7/58, 5/16/58, Fo/7/58, 5/22/59, 6/5/59
Heartbreakers 6/22/56, 11/16/56, 4/19/57, 6/14/57
Hearts (on Baton) Fo/8/56
Hearts (See Andrews, Lee and the...)
Heartsman, Johnny T/5/57, 6/7/57
Helms, Bobby F/6/56, 5/25/57, 6/22/57, T/8/57, 12/1/57, 12/16/57, 5/24/58, 11/28/58
Henderson, Douglas "Jocko" 1/4/57, 1/20/57
Hendricks, Bobby E/6/57, 8/23/58, 8/27/58, 9/19/58, 10/3/58, S/1/59, 3/27/59, F/5/59, 6/5/59, Fo/7/59
Henry, Clarence "Frogman" T/10/56, 1/4/57, 1/18/57, Fo/2/57, 5/10/57, S/8/57, L/8/57, 9/20/57
Herrera, Little Julian Fo/9/56
Hibbler, Al 1/11/56, 1/19/56, 3/30/56, 5/11/56, 7/2/56, 7/22/56, 12/28/56, 3/15/57, 1/3/58, 5/10/58, 7/24/58
Hickey, Ersel 2/14/58, T/2/58, 5/3/58, 6/30/58, T/7/58, S/11/58, L/3/59, F/4/59, 4/25/59, M/10/59
Hi-Fives 6/20/58
Higgins, Chuck 3/30/56, 6/30/56
Hightower, Donna 1/20/56, 2/17/56
Hinton, Joe S/4/59
Hi-Toppers (See Louis Brooks and the...)
Holiday, Billie 5/11/56, 5/17/57, 11/27/57
Holiday, Chico 5/16/59
Holland, Eddie S/5/59, 8/3/59, T/10/59
Holliday, Jay T/9/57
Holly, Buddy and the Crickets (see also Crickets or Ivan) 1/26/56, S/4/56, T/12/56, F/6/57, T/6/57, 8/2/57, 8/9/57, S/8/57, 8/16/57, 8/23/57, 8/26/57, 8/30/57, 9/6/57, 9/18/57, Fo/9/57, 10/10/57, Fo/10/57, 11/1/57, 12/1/57, 12/25/57, F/1/58, 1/8/58, 1/26/58, 1/27/58, Fo/1/58, 1/30/58, 2/1/58, 2/20/58, 2/25/58, 2/27/58, 3/1/57, 3/2/58, 3/27/58, 3/28/58, T/4/58, F/6/58, Fo/6/58, F/7/58, 7/3/58, 8/15/58, T/9/58, 10/3/58, T/10/58, 10/25/58, 10/28/58, E/11/58, S/1/59, 1/23/59, 2/2/59, 2/3/59, 2/7/59, 2/9/59, F/3/59, Fo/7/59
Hollywood Flames F/10/57, 11/15/57, 1/7/58, 1/8/58, 1/31/58, F/2/58, 2/26/58, 7/18/58, F/12/59
Hooker, John Lee T/1/56, M/2/56, 12/1/56, 7/4/57, 7/12/57, 12/25/59
Hopkins, Linda 2/17/56, 3/15/57, 11/8/57, 10/31/58
Horton, Johnny 8/12/56, 8/18/56, 8/26/56, 9/9/56, 2/8/57, F/4/59, 5/9/59, 8/29/59, 11/15/59
Houston, Joe 1/27/56, 4/27/56, 5/22/56, 6/16/56
Howe, Darrell 10/3/59
Huey and Jerry F/5/58
Hunter, Ivory Joe Fo/1/56, 2/18/56, 3/23/56, 5/11/56, 12/25/56, T/3/57, 5/11/57, 5/13/57, M/5/57
Hunter, Tab T/12/56, 6/21/57, 1/3/59, 3/28/59, M/6/59, 8/29/59
Hurricanes S/1/56, F/3/56, 10/19/56, Fo/2/57
Huskey, Ferlin 5/19/56, 4/7/57, 5/25/57, 5/29/57, L/9/57

I

Impalas F/1/59, 3/27/59, 4/11/59, F/6/59, 6/19/59,, T/10/59
Imperials (See Little Anthony and the...)
Impressions T/3/59
Impressions featuring Jerry Butler Fo/5/58, 6/13/58, 7/12/58, 7/18/58, T/8/58, 9/4/58, 10/3/58, Fo/11/58, 11/26/58, 1/16/59, 1/23/59
Intruders Fo/1/59
Islanders F/9/59
Isley Brothers 5/11/56, Fo/5/57, F/3/58, 5/9/58, Fo/7/58, 10/10/58, F/12/58, 7/10/59, S/8/59, 10/10/59, 11/20/59, F/12/59, 12/25/59
Ivan (See also, Holly, Buddy and the Crickets) Fo/7/58, Fo/1/59

J

Jacks S/4/56
Jackson, Al 10/5/56
Jackson, Bullmoose 3/22/57, L/8/57
Jackson, Roddy S/10/58
Jackson, Stonewall F/5/59, 6/20/59, 7/25/59
Jackson, Wanda S/11/56, 11/17/56, S/2/57, 4/20/57, 5/1/57, 5/13/57, 5/23/57, 5/25/57, Fo/7/57, 8/17/57, Fo/11/57, 11/30/57, 3/15/58, Fo/3/58, 9/20/58, 9/24/58, 4/24/59, 4/29/59, 5/19/59, 8/1/59, 9/22/59, 10/17/59, 10/31/59, 11/3/59, 12/31/59
Jackson, Willis "Gatortail" M/1/56, 4/27/56, 5/16/58, 11/28/58
Jacquet, Illinois 1/27/56, 2/3/56, 4/20/56, 7/2/56, 12/28/56, 7/18/58
Jaguars Fo/11/56, F/10/59
Jamal, Ahmad 2/13/59
James, Etta 1/16/56, 1/23/56, Fo/2/56, 3/9/56, 3/14/56, 3/30/56, Fo/8/56, M/10/56, 11/23/56, 12/7/56, 3/1/57, 2/27/59
James, Joni 3/29/58, 9/27/58, 1/24/59
James, Roland T/5/59
James, Sonny 9/9/56, F/12/56, 1/20/57, 3/14/57, 4/20/57, 5/13/57, 5/23/57, 5/25/57, 5/29/

57, 6/22/57, 7/8/57, E/4/58, 4/18/58, 10/18/58, 10/22/58
Jamies T/7/58, Fo/10/59
Jan and Arnie Fo/4/58, 5/10/58, 7/5/58, M/7/58, 8/24/58, S/9/58, 10/19/58
Jan and Dean F/6/59, 9/4/59, 9/5/59, Fo/9/59, 10/24/59, Fo/12/59
Jan and Joe T/6/58
Janis, Johnny 4/26/57, T/7/57, 6/30/58
Janis and Her Boyfriends (See also Martin, Janis) S/8/58
Jarvis, Felton T/8/59
Jay, Johnny S/11/57
Jay Netts S/12/56
Jayhawks S/5/56, 6/29/56, 7/30/56, S/9/56, T/5/57
Jenkins, Gus F/11/56
Jennings, Waylon 2/2/59, S/5/59
Jesters 6/28/57
Jewels 2/18/56
Jive Bombers S/12/56, 3/22/57, 4/19/57, 6/14/57, E/9/57, 6/30/58
Jive-A-Tones F/12/57
Jivers F/3/57
Jivin' Gene (Bourgeois) S/3/59, S/7/59
Jo, Damita (See also Gibson, Steve) 11/7/58
Jodimars F/3/56, 3/30/56, Fo/5/56, L/6/56, Fo/11/56, S/2/57, E/1/58, 2/25/58
John, Little Willie 1/20/56, F/3/56, 3/12/56, 4/1/56, 4/22/56, Fo/4/56, 5/21/56, 6/24/56, 6/29/56, Fo/8/56, 9/24/56, T/10/56, T/12/56, 12/25/56, 1/28/57, 2/1/57, 4/19/57, 4/26/57, 5/17/57, 11/1/57, 11/8/57, Fo/1/58, 3/14/58, 4/13/58, Fo/6/58, L/6/58, Fo/8/58, 10/10/58, T/10/58, T/12/58, 5/1/59, T/6/59, S/10/59, 11/18/59, 12/16/59
Johnnie and Joe F/11/56, 2/2/57, F/3/57, 4/26/57, 5/24/57, 6/7/57, 7/1/57, 7/12/57, Fo/7/57, 8/4/57, 8/23/57, F/9/57, 9/6/57, 9/18/57, 9/26/57, Fo/6/59
Johnny and the Hurricanes Fo/3/59, 6/4/59, 6/23/59, F/7/59, 8/15/59, F/10/59, 11/14/59, M/11/59
Johnny and the Rebels F/11/59
Johnson, Betty 3/22/58, 5/17/58, 9/20/58, 12/6/58
Johnson, Bubber 1/6/56, 2/10/56, 4/19/57
Johnson, Buddy and Ella 2/5/56, M/2/56, 4/20/56, 9/21/56, 9/28/56, 10/20/56, 2/1/57, 2/8/57, 4/19/57, 5/17/57, 8/4/57, 8/30/57, 3/2/58, 6/13/58, 10/22/58, 12/5/58, 3/5/59, 5/28/59
Johnson, Curtis Fo/4/59
Johnson, Kripp (See also Del Vikings) Fo/11/57, 6/14/58, Fo/7/59
Johnson, Marv S/2/59, 4/11/59, 4/22/59, 4/24/59, F/6/59, 6/3/59, 6/9/59, 8/3/59, F/9/59, 10/26/59, 12/5/59, 12/25/59
Jones, Jack 8/24/58
Jones, Jimmy Fo/10/58, S/9/59
Jones, Joe 2/10/56, 6/11/56, F/10/56, S/4/58, S/7/58, 4/10/59, 4/24/59, 5/17/59
Jordan, Louis 1/1/56, 3/10/56, 3/30/56, 5/30/56, 6/1/56, 8/3/56, 8/17/56, 9/14/56, 3/15/57, 4/19/57, 4/26/57, F/5/57, 6/8/57, 9/8/57, 4/18/58, 4/25/58, 3/27/59, 4/24/59, 11/9/59, 11/12/59, 11/20/59
Jordanaires 5/6/58
Joy, Benny S/2/58, Fo/5/58

Julian, Don (See Meadowlarks)
June, Rosemary 6/30/58
Justis, Bill S/10/57, 2/22/58, F/5/58, 7/26/58, F/12/59

K

Kado, Ernie (See also Ernie K-Doe) 9/7/59
Kalin Twins Fo/1/58, F/6/58, 6/30/58, M/7/58, 7/26/58, 8/29/58, F/9/58, 9/20/58, 10/5/58, 11/8/58, 11/26/58, S/12/58, 1/23/59, 2/14/59, 3/5/59, T/3/59, 3/28/59, Fo/5/59, 9/2/59, Fo/9/59
Kallen, Kitty 10/17/59
Kaye, Sammy 3/23/56
Kayli 10/4/58
K-Doe, Ernie (see also Kado, Ernie) F/12/59
Keller, Jerry S/5/59, 6/27/59, 7/1/59, 7/21/59, T/8/59, F/11/59
Kendricks, Nat F/12/59
Kenner, Chris S/2/56, T/6/57
Key, Troyce S/9/58, F/2/59
King, B.B. S/1/56, M/1/56, 2/17/56, Fo/2/56, F/5/56, 5/28/56, Fo/7/56, 7/28/56, 10/21/56, Fo/10/56, 11/30/56, E/12/56, S/3/57, T/4/57, 5/19/57, 6/7/57, Fo/7/57, 9/8/57, 11/8/57, 8/18/58, 4/12/59, 5/28/59, 6/15/59
King, Carole F/5/58, S/3/59, S/7/59
King, Earl 1/20/56, 4/20/56, 2/21/59, 2/27/59
King, Sid and His Five Strings F/5/56, Fo/10/56
King Curtis (Ousley) F/7/56, 2/22/57, Fo/3/57, Fo/8/58, 8/29/58, 12/24/58, 3/27/59, T/6/59, Fo/10/59
Kings F/7/57
Kingsmen F/7/58, 8/14/58
Kingston Trio M/4/58
Kirby, George 1/6/56, 9/14/56
Kitt, Eartha 8/14/59
Knight, Gladys and the Pips (See Pips)
Knight, Marie 10/19/56, 2/27/59
Knight, Sonny F/8/56, Fo/10/56, Fo/6/57, S/8/57, 11/28/57
Knockouts F/11/59
Knox, Buddy T/12/56, L/1/57, 2/22/57, 3/15/57, 4/7/57, T/4/57, 4/18/57, 4/19/57, M/6/57, 7/12/57, S/8/57, 8/11/57, 9/6/57, 9/18/57, 10/10/57, 11/1/57, 11/12/57, T/12/57, 1/7/58, E/4/58, 4/18/58, T/7/58, 8/24/58, T/11/58, F/3/59, 9/4/59, T/9/59
Kodaks 6/13/58, 7/25/58, 9/26/58
Kool Gents T/6/56
Kuf-Linx Fo/12/57

L

Landis, Jerry Fo/8/59
Lane Brothers F/6/57, 8/6/57, 1/16/58, S/4/58, 6/30/58
Laine, Frankie 11/21/59
Larks 3/11/56
Larktones T/3/58
LaRosa, Julius 10/18/58, 6/20/59
Lauren, Rod F/11/59, 11/28/59, 12/10/59
Laurie Annie T/1/57, 3/15/57, 4/19/57, 7/17/57, 7/28/57, 8/4/57, 10/28/57
Laurie, Linda 2/20/59, 12/25/59
Lawrence, Syd S/8/56
Leaders 3/2/56

Lee, Brenda F/28/56, T/9/56, F/11/56, 11/17/56, 1/5/57, T/1/57, 2/2/57, 2/24/57, 3/30/57, T/5/57, 7/8/57, L/7/57, S/8/57, 12/13/57, Fo/6/58, 11/8/58, S/11/58, 11/29/58, Fo/12/58, 1/10/59, 1/24/59, 3/18/59, T/4/59, 5/30/59, 6/20/59, 7/31/59, 8/25/59, 8/30/59, T/9/59, 10/10/59, 11/21/59
Lee, Dickie Fo/6/57, T/11/57, 11/14/58
Lee, Jackie 2/14/57, M/6/57, S/6/59, 4
Leonetti, Tommy T/3/56, 2/7/56, 6/19/57, 6/20/58, 7/3/58, 2/21/59, 3/2/59, 3/21/59, 3/27/59, 4/10/59, 6/27/59
Lesley, Alis 9/28/56, 1/24/57, 2/14/57
Lester, Danny S/12/58
Lester, Ketty 7/3/58
Levinson, Sam 12/19/59
Lewis, Bobby 11/18/59
Lewis, Bobby "Mumbles" F/3/56, 4/2/56, 6/21/56, 12/25/56
Lewis, Jerry Lee 12/4/56, S/12/56, 12/14/56, 2/23/57, 3/24/57, 3/30/57, 3/31/57, 4/7/57, 4/20/57, 5/1/57, 5/13/57, T/5/57, 5/23/57, 5/25/57, 6/12/57, M/6/57, 6/22/57, 7/28/57, 8/2/57, 8/5/57, 8/11/57, 8/19/57, 8/22/57, 9/27/57, 10/11/57, 10/18/57, 11/3/57, 11/4/57, F/11/57, 11/12/57, 12/6/57, 12/17/57, 12/25/57, 1/8/58, 1/25/58, 1/27/58, 1/30/58, 2/1/58, S/2/58, 2/15/58, 2/20/58, 2/25/58, 3/8/58, 3/18/58, 3/28/58, Fo/5/58, 5/22/58, 5/28/58, 6/7/58, 6/10/58, 6/15/58, Fo/6/58, 7/19/58, 8/17/58, 8/23/58, Fo/8/58, E/9/58, 10/1/58, 10/15/58, 11/14/58, Fo/11/58, M/1/59, Fo/2/59, 2/27/59, 3/26/59, 4/20/59, 6/3/59, Fo/6/59, 8/21/59, T/9/59
Lewis, Joe 1/6/57
Lewis, Nolan 1/20/56
Lewis, Smiley 1/20/56, S/2/56, T/4/56, 6/7/56, T/8/56, S/11/56, Fo/3/57, 6/14/57, 7/10/57, S/11/57, 7/25/58, 8/22/58, 4/16/59
Linden, Kathy S/9/57, F/2/58, F/5/58, 5/24/58, E/10/58, 5/25/59, Fo/6/59, 6/23/59, 7/18/59
Little Anthony and the Imperials (See also Gourdine, Little Anthony) T/7/58, 8/23/58, 9/10/58, 9/12/58, 10/10/58, T/10/58, 11/29/58, S/1/59, 1/16/59, 1/23/59, 2/16/59, 2/20/59, 3/5/59, 3/27/59, S/5/59, 6/26/59, S/7/59, Fo/10/59, 11/20/59
Little Bill and the Bluenotes F/6/59
Little Caesar 9/29/58
Little Esther (Phillips) T/5/56, 4/12/57, 5/17/57
Little Joe and the Thrillers 2/22/57, S/7/57, 8/30/57, 10/11/57, 10/18/57, F/11/57, 12/25/57, 1/10/58, 1/17/58, 1/20/58, 2/21/58, F/3/58, 5/2/58, S/11/58, 6/19/59
Little Norman Fo/6/57
Little Richard 2/17/56, T/2/56, 3/9/56, S/3/56, 4/1/56, 4/22/56, 5/11/56, S/6/56, 7/6/56, 7/16/56, 7/17/56, 7/29/56, E/8/56, 9/2/56, 9/14/56, F/10/56, M/10/56, T/11/56, 12/23/56, 12/25/56, 1/11/57, 1/25/57, Fo/2/57, 4/15/57, Fo/4/57, T/5/57, M/6/57, M/7/57, L/7/57, F/9/57, M/9/57, L/9/57, 10/8/57, 10/12/57, 10/18/57, 10/20/57, 11/3/57, E/11/57, S/1/58, 1/27/58, 3/14/58, Fo/5/58, Fo/8/58, S/11/58, M/1/59, T/2/59, S/6/59, L/6/59, T/8/59, 9/6/59, F/10/59
Little Walter E/2/56, Fo/2/56, 9/10/56, 12/

22/56, S/8/57, Fo/9/58
London, Laurie F/2/58
Long Tall Marvin (Phillips) S/6/56
Lopez, Trini T/1/59, S/3/59, T/4/59, F/8/59, Fo/10/59, Fo/12/59
Lord, Bobby 5/25/57, Fo/5/57, 5/29/57, 6/11/57, 11/21/58, S/3/59
Lord Rockingham XI F/9/58, 7/16/59
Lorenz, George "Hound Dog" 10/18/57
Loudermilk, John D. S/4/58, 6/14/58
Lovenotes F/5/57
Lovers Fo/4/57, 9/20/57, 10/11/57, T/8/58
Lowe, Jim T/8/56
Luke, Robin 6/20/58, Fo/6/58, 7/18/58, 8/9/58, Fo/9/58, 10/18/58, 10/25/58, S/2/59, T/6/59, F/11/59, Fo/12/59
Luman, Bob T/7/57, T/10/57, S/1/58, S/7/59, T/10/59
Lymon, Frankie (solo) 9/6/57, Fo/9/57, 9/26/57, 10/10/57, 11/1/57, S/11/57, 11/28/57,, T/1/58, 3/28/58, 5/17/58, 6/23/58, Fo/7/58, Fo/1/59, S/4/59, 11/18/59
Lymon, Frankie and the Teenagers (See also Teenagers) F/2/56, 2/18/56, 2/24/56, 3/30/56, F/4/56, 4/12/56, 4/20/56, 5/19/56, 6/8/56, 6/21/56, Fo/6/56, 7/2/56, 7/22/56, 8/6/56, 8/29/56, 9/9/56, 9/14/56, T/9/56, 9/28/56, 10/20/56, M/11/56, T/11/56, 12/5/56, S/2/57, 2/22/57, 3/1/57, 4/1/57, F/4/57, 4/26/57, 5/6/57, 5/13/57, 5/19/57, 6/6/57, 7/1/57, F/7/57, L/9/57, 12/22/57, 1/24/58, 5/25/58, 8/24/58
Lymon, Lewis and the Teenchords 2/8/57, 2/22/57, 4/19/57, 5/10/57, M/6/57, 7/1/57, L/8/57, 11/12/57, 1/17/58, 10/29/58
Lynne, Gloria Fo/2/56, 5/4/56, 11/9/56, 3/27/59

M

Mack, Warner T/10/57
Magnificents S/5/56, 9/28/56, 3/2/57
Mann, Barry T/8/59, 9/16/59
Mann, Carl Fo/3/57, F/4/59, 7/21/59, 7/25/59, 8/15/59, S/9/59, 10/31/59, 12/13/59
Mann, Gloria 2/13/56, L/6/57
Mara, Tommy 11/5/58
Marchan, Bobby 7/6/56, S/3/57, 4/19/57, 5/17/57, 8/4/57, 9/20/57
Marigolds (See Bragg, Johnny and the...)
Mark IV 2/22/58, 3/8/58
Marker, Morty F/12/57
Marquees S/9/57
Martin, Dean M/1/59, 3/18/59
Martin, Freddy 4/23/56
Martin, Janis (See also Janis and Her Boyfriends) M/2/56, Fo/4/56, F/6/56, 3/23/57
Martin, Vince and the Tarriers 2/15/57
Marty T/8/56
Marvin and Johnny Fo/1/56, 3/11/56, 5/11/56, 5/18/56
Masters, Sammy T/5/56, Fo/9/58
(Will) Maston Trio (See Davis, Sammy Jr.)
Mathis, Johnny 6/7/57, 9/21/57, 8/24/58
Maye, Arthur Lee and the Crowns S/4/56
McCabe, Patti (See Poni-Tails)
McCracklin, Jimmy F/2/56, S/8/56, F/6/57, T/1/58, 4/5/58, T/4/58, F/6/58, F/2/59, 9/1/59, F/11/59

McDevitt, Charles and Skiffle Group 6/30/56, 7/12/57
McDonald, Skeets M/6/59
McFadden, Ruth 10/12/56
McGriff, Edna 3/22/57, 8/2/57
McKuen, Rod 8/24/58
McLaurin, Bette 8/22/58
McLawler, Sarah 2/20/59
McLollie, Oscar 2/3/56, 5/4/56, 7/28/56, 10/10/58
McNeeley, Big Jay E/5/56, 8/24/56, 9/24/56, M/10/56, 5/1/59, Fo/5/59, 7/3/59
McPhatter, Clyde M/1/56, T/3/56, 4/19/56, 4/20/56, 5/19/56, 6/8/56, 7/28/56, 7/30/56, 8/6/56, 8/17/56, 8/31/56, S/9/56, 9/28/56, 10/20/56, 12/7/56, 1/4/57, 1/18/57, 2/15/57, Fo/3/57, 5/17/57, 7/1/57, F/7/57, 8/2/57, 8/9/57, 8/16/57, 9/6/57, 9/26/57, L/9/57, 10/10/57, 11/1/57, 12/6/57, 1/31/58, 3/16/58, 4/6/58, F/4/58, M/7/58, M/8/15, F/9/58, 10/3/58, 11/15/58, 11/26/58, 1/23/59, 2/17/59, F/3/59, 3/5/59, E/3/59, S/3/59, 3/13/59, 3/27/59, T/5/59, 6/15/59, Fo/6/59, 7/4/59, 7/29/59, 8/4/59, 9/2/59, F/9/59, 9/14/59, Fo/10/59, 11/6/59, 11/20/59, 11/27/59
McRae, Gordon 9/27/58, 11/8/58, 1/31/59
McShann, Jay 2/3/56, 2/10/56
McVoy, Carl F/12/57, 5/17/58
Meadowlarks S/6/56, F/10/57
Medallions 3/30/56, 4/20/56, 7/28/56, Fo/2/57
Medlin, Joe 5/15/59, 12/25/59
Megatrons F/4/59, S/10/59
Mello-Kings 9/3/57, 9/20/57, 10/4/57, 1/8/58, F/4/58, F/2/59, 3/27/59
Mello-Tones M/10/56, T/4/57
Mickey and Kitty S/4/59, T/8/59
Mickey and Sylvia 2/10/56, 3/14/56, 4/20/56, 5/11/56, S/8/56, 9/14/56, T/11/56, 1/4/57, E/1/57, 2/16/57, 2/22/57, 3/1/57, 3/18/57, T/3/57, 3/22/57, 4/19/57, M/5/57, T/6/57, 8/16/57, T/8/57, 8/30/57, 9/13/57, 10/28/57, 12/9/57, 4/4/58, 5/8/58, 5/12/58, Fo/7/58, 10/3/58, 10/15/58, S/11/58
Midnighters S/1/56, 1/13/56, S/3/56, S/5/56, 5/18/56, Fo/10/56, Fo/12/56, F/4/57, Fo/5/57, 4/13/58, S/11/58, Fo/12/58, 6/3/59, S/6/59, 6/9/59, T/8/59, 9/18/59, Fo/10/59, Fo/11/59
Milburn, Amos 3/9/56, 3/11/56, 3/14/56, 3/30/56, 6/1/56, 6/8/56, 6/29/56, F/9/56, 3/22/57, 4/26/57, 8/23/57, 12/12/58, 1/30/59, 2/6/59, S/4/59, 6/12/59
Miller, Clint Fo/11/57
Miller, Mitch 1/31/59
Miller, Roger S/3/59
Milton, Roy 1/13/56, 4/6/56, 4/27/56, 5/11/56, 9/28/56, 10/19/56, 1/20/57
Mineo, Sal Fo/4/57, 5/4/57, T/7/57, 9/18/57, F/10/57, 12/8/57, F/1/58, 4/27/58, 11/29/58, M/6/59
Mints F/1/56
Miracles Fo/2/58, T/7/58, T/7/59, 8/3/59, 10/23/59, 12/25/59
Mitchell, Bobby and the Toppers S/2/56, M/3/57, 3/15/57, 9/30/57, F/12/57, 3/14/58
Mitchell, Freddie 12/21/56
Mitchell, Guy 12/25/56, 5/4/57, F/9/59

Mondellos (See Alice Jean and the...)
Monorays S/9/58
Monotones F/2/58, 4/6/58, T/6/58, M/7/58, 7/18/58, 11/21/58, F/1/59
Monte, Lou S/10/56, 4/12/58, 6/21/58, 10/4/58, 3/14/59, 8/1/59
Montrel, Roy Fo/9/56
Moody, James 12/7/56, 1/9/59, 7/24/59
Moonbeams M/9/57, 4/6/58
Moonglows (See also Harvey and the...) 1/20/56, E/2/56, S/3/56, 3/30/56, 2/17/56, 5/4/56, 5/18/56, 6/22/56, T/7/56, 8/6/56, 9/26/56, M/10/56, Fo/11/56, 12/21/56, 2/15/57, Fo/2/57, 5/31/57, S/6/57, 7/1/57, 8/2/57, E/8/57, 8/30/57, S/9/57, L/9/57, 10/20/57, 10/25/57, 8/29/58, 9/26/58, 10/15/58, S/1/59, 6/12/59
Moore, Johnny (of Drifters) E/6/57
Moore, Scotty 9/21/57
Morgan, Jane 4/4/59
Morgan, Jaye P. 3/7/59
Morris, Joe 1/23/56
Moss, Roy T/4/56
Mullican, Moon S/3/56
Myles, Big Boy 6/28/56, 9/30/57
Myles, Billy F/10/57, 11/28/57, 1/26/58
Mystics T/5/59, M/6/59, 6/20/59, 6/23/59, S/9/59

N

Nash, Johnny S/10/56, M/10/57, 5/24/58, 9/13/58, 9/19/58, Fo/10/58, 4/25/59, Fo/5/59, 8/28/59
Native Boys F/4/56
Nee, Bernie Fo/12/57
Nelson, Ricky S/4/57, 4/10/57, 6/1/57, S/8/57, E/8/57, S/9/57, M/9/57, 11/27/57, F/12/57, F/3/58, 3/15/58, 6/16/58, 6/19/58, Fo/6/58, 8/27/58, 8/30/58, Fo/9/58, M/1/59, F/2/59, 3/18/59, T/6/59, 8/2/59, 8/28/59, 9/18/59, F/11/59
Nelson, Sandy S/8/59, T/10/59, 11/24/59
Nelson, Willie S/8/58, 9/6/58
Nervous Norvous S/5/56, T/7/56, F/7/59
Neville, Aaron 4/5/59
Neville, Art Fo/12/56, 3/15/57, 9/20/57, 5/3/59
New Blockbusters (See also Olenn, Johnny) F/12/56
Newman, Ted F/9/57
Night Hawks F/12/57
Nino and the Ebb Tides Fo/10/58
Nite Rockers T/8/58
Nitecaps F/4/56, 6/21/56, 12/25/56, E/1/57
Noland, Terry F/6/57, S/11/57, 12/25/57, F/2/58, Fo/5/58, Fo/8/58, F/3/59
Nu Tornados Fo/10/58, 11/15/58, 11/29/58, 12/3/58, 12/24/58, 1/3/59, 2/7/59
Nutmegs S/6/56, 4/19/57
Nutty Squirrels 11/7/59

O

O. C. Allstars S/3/58
Oakes, Bob and the Sultans Fo/4/56
Offitt, Lillian 10/18/57
O'Keefe, Johnny S/5/58
Olenn, Johnny 12/25/56, 1/17/59, 3/5/59, F/9/59

Olsen and Johnson 10/15/58
Olympics 7/26/58, 8/29/58, 9/12/58, 9/19/58, S/11/58, T/2/59, F/7/59
Orbison, Roy M/5/56, 5/28/56, 6/2/56, 6/30/56, 7/25/56, 8/12/56, 8/18/56, 8/26/56, 9/9/56, 9/10/56, 10/14/56, 11/15/56, S/4/57, 6/15/57, 4/27/58, 5/16/58, S/10/58, 11/1/58, S/1/59, T/1/59, T/9/59, Fo/11/59
Orbits S/1/57
Originals (See Rio, Chuck and the...)
Orioles 1/27/56, 3/16/56, T/6/56, 6/24/56, 4/17/57, L/8/57, 9/13/57, Fo/2/59
Orlando, Tony Fo/2/59
Otis, Johnny M/1/56, 8/19/56, 10/14/56, T/11/56, M/9/57, 4/6/58, F/4/58, Fo/9/58, S/3/59, Fo/5/59, T/8/59, Fo/12/59
Overbea, Danny 2/3/56, 2/10/56
Owen, Reg F/11/58
Owens, Donnie F/9/58, 9/20/58, Fo/11/58, 11/26/58

P

Page, Patti 9/18/57
Palmer, Clarence Fo/6/57
Palmer, Earl T/5/57
Paragons T/3/57, 4/19/57, 8/23/57
Paris Sisters S/1/56, T/1/56, 3/10/58, M/4/58, 12/22/58, F/11/59
Parker, Little Junior 8/26/56, 10/7/56, 12/15/56, S/1/57, M/3/57, 4/22/57, 5/12/57, 8/18/57, Fo/4/58, 5/25/58, S/11/58, 3/8/59, Fo/3/59, F/8/59, F/8/59, T/12/59
Parker, Robert 7/10/57, 11/11/59, Fo/9/59
Parris, Fred and the Scarlets S/2/58
Parsons, Bill Fo/11/58, 11/30/58, 1/24/59, 3/28/59, 4/8/59, Fo/6/59
Parton, Dolly S/4/59
Passions Fo/7/59, 10/17/59, 12/25/59
Pastels F/1/56, Fo/11/57, F/1/58, 2/7/58, 2/21/58, F/3/58, 3/14/58, 3/28/58, 8/23/58, F/10/58, 10/29/58, 11/14/58
Patience and Prudence S/7/56
Paul Bunny 12/25/56
Pearls 10/12/56, 4/19/57, 5/10/57, 6/7/57, 8/16/58, 4/24/59, 12/25/59
Peek, Paul S/3/58, S/9/58, 10/11/58, T/3/59, F/7/59, F/12/59
Penguins S/2/56, M/2/56, 4/4/56, F/5/56, 7/30/56, M/8/56, 8/29/56, 9/3/56, 12/4/56, Fo/1/57, F/4/57, Fo/12/57
Perkins, Carl 1/28/56, 2/3/56, F/2/56, 2/18/56, 3/17/56, 3/21/56, 4/21/56, 5/5/56, 5/19/56, 5/26/56, 5/28/56, F/6/56, 7/2/56, 7/22/56, M/8/56, F/9/56, 9/26/56, 9/29/56, 10/13/56, 10/27/56, 11/10/56, 11/15/56, 12/4/56, 12/14/56, 2/2/57, S/2/57, 3/14/57, 3/31/57, 4/6/57, 4/7/57, 4/20/57, 5/1/57, 5/21/57, 6/15/57, 8/5/57, 8/30/57, 9/1/57, 9/28/57, 11/12/57, 11/19/57, 11/26/57, 12/1/57, 12/28/57, F/1/58, 1/15/58, M/2/58, S/3/58, 3/14/58, E/4/58, 4/19/58, 4/27/58, 5/3/58, 5/6/58, L/6/58, 7/5/58, S/7/58, 10/1/58, 10/22/58, 11/14/58, Fo/11/58, 2/9/59, S/4/59, L/5/59, 6/21/59, 7/31/59, S/8/59, 8/14/59, 8/20/59, 8/25/59, 8/30/59, 9/28/59, 10/3/59, 10/30/59, 11/6/59, 11/15/59
Perkins, Jay 3/21/56, E/4/58, 11/14/58
Perkins, Roy T/2/58

Peterson, Bobby F/10/59
Peterson, Oscar 9/4/59, 9/11/59
Peterson, Ray 12/8/57, Fo/5/58, T/7/58, T/9/58, 10/3/58, 4/17/59, T/4/59, 7/3/59, S/8/59, 9/2/59, 9/14/59, S/10/59, 12/26/59
Pets F/5/58
Petty, Norman Fo/10/57
Phillips, Dewey F/11/59
Phillips, Esther (See Little Esther)
Phillips, Marvin (See Long Tall Marvin & Marvin and Johnny)
Phillips, Phil Fo/5/59, 9/18/59, S/10/59, Fo/12/59
Phillips, Sam M/5/56
Piano Red T/1/56, E/1/57, Fo/3/57, Fo/9/59
Picks S/1/58
Pinckney, Bill F/5/58
Pipes T/8/56
Pips 6/3/59, 10/25/59
Pittman, Barbara S/10/56, S/7/58
Planets 6/15/57
Platt, Eddie Fo/1/58, 3/1/58
Platters F/1/56, 1/18/56, 2/1/56, 2/11/56, 2/18/56, F/3/56, 3/14/56, 3/30/56, 4/7/56, 4/20/56, 5/19/56, F/6/56, 6/16/56, 6/24/56, 6/30/56, 8/3/56, 8/12/56, S/9/56, 9/21/56, 9/28/56, 10/11/56, 10/20/56, M/11/56, Fo/11/56, 12/4/56, 12/25/56, 1/28/57, 1/29/57, 2/22/57, Fo/2/57, M/3/57, 3/26/57, 4/29/57, F/5/57, 6/10/57, 6/14/57, M/7/57, E/8/57, Fo/8/57, L/10/57, 11/3/57, 12/8/57, F/1/58, 2/10/58, 3/8/58, 3/14/58, 4/19/58, 5/1/58, 5/9/58, M/5/58, Fo/5/58, 6/4/58, 6/15/58, M/6/58, T/8/58, 8/28/58, E/9/58, F/11/58, 11/6/58, 1/17/59, 1/23/59, 2/20/59, 3/1/59, 3/5/59, E/3/59, 3/25/59, 5/20/59, Fo/5/59, 8/2/59, 8/10/59, T/8/59, L/8/59, E/11/59, S/11/59, 11/13/59, 12/31/59
Playboys (See also John Fred and the...) Fo/10/59
Playmates Fo/3/57, M/7/57, F/12/57, 2/7/58, 4/6/58, 5/24/58, 6/6/58, 8/28/58, S/10/58, 11/24/58, 12/3/58, 1/27/59, 5/20/59, F/6/59, 7/1/59, 7/4/59, 9/8/59, 10/3/59, F/10/59, 10/9/59
Poni-Tails T/1/57, M/8/57, F/9/57, M/6/58, Fo/6/58, M/7/58, 8/7/58, 8/29/58, 8/30/58, 9/10/58, 9/18/58, Fo/10/58, 11/22/58, 12/6/58, S/1/59, 2/6/59, 4/22/59, 7/11/59, 8/29/59, F/9/59, 9/20/59, 9/25/59, 10/1/59
Poovey, "Groovy" Joe 7/13/57, 8/31/57, 10/5/57, 11/23/57, 12/7/57, F/9/58, S/5/59
Portuguese Joe F/11/57
Powell, Jesse 2/13/56, 8/7/59
Premiers (See also Stevens, Julie and the...) Fo/3/56
Presley, Elvis 1/10/56, 1/14/56, Fo/1/56, 1/28/56, 2/5/56, 2/20/56, L/2/56, 3/14/56, 3/17/56, T/3/56, 4/1/56, 4/3/56, 4/8/56, 4/23/56, L/4/56, F/5/56, 5/13/56, 6/5/56, 6/22/56, 7/1/56, 7/2/56, S/7/56, 8/3/56, 8/22/56, 9/9/56, 9/26/56, 10/11/56, 10/28/56, 11/16/56, 11/22/56, 12/4/56, 1/6/57, F/1/57, 1/19/57, T/3/57, 3/28/57, 4/1/57, F/6/57, Fo/6/57, E/7/57, 7/9/57, 8/30/57, 9/1/57, T/9/57, 9/21/57, 9/27/57, 10/17/57, 10/26/57, 10/28/57, 11/9/57, 12/19/57, Fo/12/57, 3/15/58, 3/24/58, 3/28/58, F/4/58, 6/1/58, M/6/58, T/6/58, 6/22/58, 7/2/58, 8/14/58, 9/19/58, 9/22/58,

T/10/58, S/3/59, Fo/6/59, 9/13/59
Presley, Gladys 8/14/58
Preston, Johnny Fo/6/59
Pretenders 6/8/56, T/6/56, 6/21/56, T/3/57
Price, Lloyd 1/1/56, 2/10/56, S/2/56, 4/13/56, 5/11/56, T/5/56, 9/14/56, Fo/1/57, E/2/57, L/2/57, 3/8/58, 3/22/57, 4/21/57, Fo/4/57, 5/5/57, F/7/57, M/8/57, S/10/57, 3/14/58, Fo/5/58, E/9/58, 9/12/58, 11/26/58, 12/20/58, F/2/59, 2/27/59, 3/27/59, 3/28/59, 4/1/59, S/4/59, E/5/59, 6/14/59, 6/28/59, T/7/59, 9/18/59, S/10/59, 11/12/59, 11/13/59, 11/28/59, 11/30/59
Professor Longhair 6/9/57, 9/30/57, 5/9/58, 9/27/59, Fo/9/59
Prysock, Arthur 2/17/56, 3/30/56, 4/2/56, 10/29/56, 12/25/56, 3/22/58, 8/16/58, 9/11/59
Prysock, Red 2/1/56, M/2/56, 2/17/56, Fo/3/56, 4/20/56, 5/19/56, S/8/56, 10/29/56, F/11/56, Fo/2/57, 4/26/57, 5/24/57, 6/7/57, 5/9/58, 6/12/59, Fo/6/59, 11/18/59
Pullen, Dwight Fo/2/58, Fo/12/58
Pullen, Whitey F/6/59

Q

Quails 9/27/57
Quaker City Boys Fo/11/58, 1/31/59
Quarter Notes Fo/3/59
Quarternotes T/12/57
Queens (See Gunter, Shirley and the...)
Quin-Tones 4/4/58, Fo/7/58, 9/6/58, 9/19/58, 10/3/58, 1/16/59, 1/23/59, 7/10/59

R

Raeletes 11/14/58, 8/9/59
Rainbows 7/30/56, 8/24/56, 12/28/56
Rainwater, Marvin F/1/56, Fo/1/57, Fo/6/57, 7/14/57, S/9/57, E/4/58, 4/20/58, F/6/58, S/8/58, 12/25/58, S/3/59, T/5/59, 5/22/59, 5/27/59, S/9/59, E/11/59, 12/13/59
Ram, Buck E/8/57, 8/L/9/59/59
Ram Rocks Fo/5/58
Rambo, Gene 7/13/57, 8/31/57, 10/5/57, 11/23/57, 12/7/57
Randall, Tony 4/26/58
Randazzo, Teddy 12/5/56, 12/21/56, 7/1/57, L/9/57, 10/20/57, 6/20/58, 8/29/58, 9/18/59, 10/10/59, 10/27/59, 12/25/59
Rankin, Kenny F/8/59
Ravens 2/3/56, 2/10/56, 3/9/56, L/6/56, F/8/56, 7/5/57
Rawls, Louis 11/10/58
Ray, Johnnie 2/15/58, 12/24/58
Rays F/5/57, 9/26/57, 11/28/57, 12/1/57, 12/6/57, 12/25/57, 1/8/58, 1/31/58, 3/23/58, F/4/58, S/8/58, F/11/59
Rebennack, Mac Fo/8/59
Reed, Jerry T/5/57, 4/18/58, Fo/6/59
Reed, Jimmy F/1/56, L/2/56, 3/9/56, T/7/56, S/11/56, 2/3/57, 2/22/57, Fo/2/57, 2/28/57, 5/17/57, F/6/57, 10/6/57, F/1/58, Fo/3/58, 4/6/58, S/4/58, F/12/58, F/4/59, 5/28/59, S/9/59, S/11/59
Reed, Lulu 6/1/57, 7/26/57, 12/5/58, 7/10/59
Reese, Della 1/27/56, 3/16/56, 4/20/56, 7/2/56, 7/22/56, L/9/56, 11/9/56, 11/17/56, 12/7/56, 12/25/56, 4/19/57, 6/21/57, 7/1/57, T/7/57, 8/30/57, 9/6/57, L/11/57, M/2/58, M/

487

2/58, 3/30/58, 5/2/58, 11/9/58, 11/24/58, 12/28/58, 1/9/59, 6/19/59, 6/30/59, 8/7/59, Fo/8/59, 9/8/59, 9/14/59, 11/27/59
Reeves, Glenn Fo/9/56, F/3/58
Reeves, Jim 8/30/58, F/11/59
Relf, Bobby Fo/11/56
Rene, Googie M/4/58
Restivo, Johnny T/7/59, F/11/59, 12/25/59
Revels T/9/59, 10/16/59, 10/30/59, 10/31/59
Reynolds, Jody T/3/58, 5/9/58, 6/7/58, Fo/7/58, 8/27/58, S/10/58, T/3/59, S/8/59
Rhythm Rockers (See Atkins, Chet)
Rich, Charlie Fo/10/58, F/7/59
Richard, Cliff 10/5/58, T/11/58, T/2/59, 4/22/59, 7/16/59, F/8/59, S/11/59
Richardson, J. P. "Jape" (See also Big Bopper) M/9/57, Fo/10/57, 4/28/59
Richardson, Mrs. J. P. 4/28/59
Ridgely, Tommy 4/12/57, 6/9/57, Fo/6/57, 8/1/58, 8/29/58, 8/30/58, 1/9/59, 7/4/59
Riley, Billy Lee Fo/2/57, 3/24/57, 4/7/57, F/8/58, F/2/59, T/6/59
Rinky-Dinks F/7/58
Rio, Chuck and the Originals T/8/58, F/2/59
Rip-Chords F/8/58
Rivers, Johnny Fo/3/58, S/10/58, T/3/59, Fo/8/59
Rivieras T/1/59, 2/17/59, F/12/59
Rob-Roys T/8/57
Robbins, Marty T/3/56, T/6/56, 2/8/57, F/3/57, Fo/6/57, T/7/57, F/10/57, 5/17/58, 9/6/58, 4/8/59, 4/29/59, Fo/10/59, 11/29/59
Robert and Johnny S/4/56, 6/29/56, 10/12/56, F/11/56, 11/16/56, S/3/57, F/2/58, 2/7/58, 4/12/58, 5/16/58, 6/13/58, T/6/58, 8/29/58, T/9/58, 11/21/58, S/1/59, F/5/59
Robins 1/11/56, S/3/56, 5/11/56, 5/12/56, T/6/56, M/10/56, Fo/3/57, S/4/57
Robinson, Floyd S/5/59, F/11/59
Rock-A-Teens Fo/8/59, 9/25/59, S/12/59
Rockin' R's F/3/59, 4/28/59, S/5/59
Rodgers, Jimmie S/8/57, 8/25/57, 8/30/57, 9/8/57, 9/10/57, T/10/57, 10/31/57, 11/3/57, 12/30/57, 1/8/58, S/1/58, 2/20/58, 2/25/58, 4/6/58, 4/16/58, T/4/58, 5/3/58, 5/8/58, 6/1/58, 6/10/58, 6/19/58, L/6/58, T/7/58, 7/19/58, 9/28/58, Fo/9/58, 11/10/58, 11/22/58, 1/22/59, F/2/59, 3/31/59, 5/16/59, 5/22/59, M/6/59, Fo/8/59, 9/4/59, 9/8/59, 10/1/59, 11/13/59, S/12/59
Rogers, Buck T/6/59
Rogers, Jimmy (blues) 3/2/57
Rogers, Kenny F/7/58
Rogers, Timmie 11/14/58
Rome, Richard 2/21/59
Romero, Chan F/7/59
Rover Boys Fo/2/56, T/4/56, 4/30/56, 6/21/56, 10/21/57
Rogers, Eileen 10/27/56
Rondo, Don 11/15/58
Ronnie and the Rockin' Kings Fo/5/58
Royal Jokers 1/27/56, 5/28/56, 6/21/56, E/8/56, Fo/9/56, 12/25/56, 2/4/57, 5/29/57, 7/12/57, 12/25/59
Royal Teens F/1/58, 2/4/58, 2/15/58, M/2/58, 2/25/58, 4/6/58, Fo/4/58, 5/12/58, 6/14/58, S/7/58, M/7/58, 8/6/58, F/9/58, F/2/59, 3/5/59, T/4/59, 5/5/59, T/8/59, 10/24/59

Royaltones 3/30/56, S/9/58, 11/26/58, F/2/59
Rush, Otis 10/27/56, 3/2/57, 8/2/57, 8/9/57, 8/16/57, Fo/2/59
Ryan, Charlie T/10/59
Rydell, Bobby S/1/59, S/2/59, 3/20/59, F/5/59, T/6/59, 7/18/59, 8/4/59, 9/4/59, 9/12/59, S/9/59, 9/18/59, 11/7/59, 12/25/59

S

Sad Sacks S/4/58
Sahm, Doug F/7/59
Salvo, Sammy Fo/8/59
Sands, Jodie M/6/57, 7/1/57, 9/1/57, S/11/57, 11/12/57, 1/27/58, 1/30/58, 2/1/58, S/8/58, L/2/59, T/9/59
Sands, Tommy Fo/3/57, Fo/4/57, 5/16/57, 5/19/57, Fo/12/57, 4/23/58, 9/20/58, 10/26/58, 3/25/59, E/5/59, 7/4/59, 7/28/59, 10/9/59, 11/28/59, 12/9/59
Santiago, Maria Elena 8/15/58
Santo and Johnny Fo/6/59, 8/1/59, 9/4/59, 10/14/59, Fo/10/59, 10/31/59, 11/6/59, 12/25/59
Sardo, Frankie 1/23/59, 2/3/59
Satellites (See also Day, Bobby) S/8/58, 8/22/58
Saunders, Little Butchie F/8/56, T/11/56
Scarlets (See Parris, Fred and the...)
Schoolboys 3/30/56, 6/29/56, 11/16/56, Fo/11/56, 1/25/57, 2/15/57, F/4/57, 6/14/57, 7/10/57, 8/16/57, T/8/57
Scott, Billy T/11/57
Scott, Jack T/4/57, 4/26/57, Fo/10/57, E/4/58, S/4/58, 5/16/58, M/6/58, 6/30/58, M/7/58, 7/19/58, 8/27/58, 8/29/58, F/9/58, 9/6/58, 10/3/58, S/11/58, 11/22/58, 11/30/58, 1/31/59, Fo/2/59, L/2/59, Fo/5/59, M/6/59, 6/27/59, 7/7/59, 8/15/59, 8/30/59, 9/4/59, F/9/59, 10/24/59, Fo/11/59, 11/25/59
Scott, Little Jimmy 7/6/56, Fo/8/56, 5/10/57, S/10/58, 12/9/59, Fo/12/59
Sedaka, Neil Fo/11/57, S/9/58, 10/18/58, S/11/58, 11/30/58, 12/20/58, S/2/59, 2/28/59, 4/3/59, 4/18/59, 4/22/59, S/5/59, Fo/8/59, 12/5/59
Self, Ronnie T/6/56, F/4/57, 5/21/57, Fo/8/57, E/12/57, Fo/1/58, F/5/58, Fo/8/58, 11/1/58, 11/8/58, Fo/8/59
Sensations T/3/56, 4/13/56, 6/21/57, 6/28/57
Serenaders 9/27/56
Seville, David (See also Chipmunks featuring...) T/3/58, 4/12/58, 4/19/58, 7/12/58, 12/21/58, 12/13/59
Shadows (See either Richard, Cliff or Vee, Bobby)
Shannon, Jackie (Jackie DeShannon; see also Dee, Jackie) S/8/59, 8/11/59, 8/30/59
Sharpe, Ray Fo/6/59, S/10/59
Sharps T/3/57, T/7/58
Shaw, Ricky Fo/7/57
Shaw, Roberta 9/12/59
Shells 8/23/57
Shepherd Sisters 9/26/56, 10/18/57, 10/28/57, 12/25/57, 1/8/58
Sheriff and the Revels Fo/1/59
Shields Fo/6/58, 9/20/58, 10/22/58, Fo/10/58, 11/7/58, 11/26/58, Fo/6/59
Shirelles F/2/58, 3/7/58, 4/5/58, 4/25/58, S/6/58, F/11/58, 6/5/59, 6/26/59, 9/1/59, T/9/59
Shirley and Lee 1/11/56, 2/1/56, 2/10/56, 6/11/56, T/6/56, 7/2/56, 7/22/56, 8/9/56, 8/12/56, 9/21/56, 9/28/56, 10/1/56, 10/20/56, Fo/10/56, M/11/56, 12/21/56, 1/6/57, F/2/57, 2/17/57, T/5/57, 5/17/57, 6/16/57, Fo/7/57, 6/13/58, 1/31/59, 6/26/59, M/10/59
Show Brothers M/4/58
Silhouettes F/1/58, 1/10/58, 1/17/58, 2/7/58, 2/19/58, 3/8/58, S/3/58, 3/16/58, 4/6/58, Fo/7/58, Fo/9/58, 11/28/58
Silva-Tones S/10/57
Silver, Horace 12/12/58
Simmons, Gene S/6/58
Simms, LuAnn 8/8/59
Simone, Nina 3/13/59
Six Teens S/4/56, 7/28/56, F/9/56, S/1/57, Fo/4/57, T/9/57, 6/20/58, 8/24/58, Fo/9/58
Skip and Flip F/5/59, 7/18/59, 7/21/59, 8/7/59, 9/4/59, S/9/59, 9/26/59
Skyliners Fo/12/58, 2/13/59, 3/27/59, 5/9/59, 6/5/59, Fo/8/59, 9/18/59, 12/25/59
Slades F/12/57, T/7/58, S/11/58, Fo/5/59
Smalls, Tommy 3/30/56, 8/24/56
Smith, Betty M/4/58
Smith, Huey and the Clowns (See also Huey and Jerry) S/9/56, 5/17/57, S/6/57, 6/16/57, 8/4/57, 8/30/57, 9/20/57, 9/30/57, S/10/57, T/1/58, 3/15/58, 4/6/58, 4/18/58, 5/9/58, 6/13/58, Fo/10/58, 1/11/59, 1/16/59, 4/17/59, S/5/59, 5/28/59, E/8/59, T/9/59, M/10/59
Smith, Jimmy 12/12/58, 5/27/59, 9/4/59
Smith, Ray T/6/58, 8/9/58, T/8/59
Smith, Ocie (O.C. Smith) 1/11/57, 3/8/57, 7/19/57, 8/30/57, 9/13/57, 12/25/57
Smith, Somethin' and the Redheads 4/26/58, 9/13/58
Smith, Warren S/4/56, 5/28/56, 6/2/56, 7/25/56, F/10/56, 11/15/56, 12/14/56, T/5/57, Fo/1/58, S/7/58
Solitaires 3/30/56, S/4/56, Fo/7/56, 10/12/56, 11/1/56, Fo/1/57, 3/8/57, 4/19/57, 5/17/57, T/9/58, Fo/9/58, 11/26/58, T/1/59, T/6/59, 6/26/59, 7/17/59
Sonics S/4/59
Sonny Boy (See also Williamson, Sonny Boy) T/6/59
Sophomores F/5/56, S/3/57, F/12/57
Soul Stirrers 5/1/59
Sounds S/2/56
South, Joe F/7/58, 7/12/58, S/8/58
Spacemen S/7/59, 10/17/59
Spaniels Fo/2/56, L/2/56, F/5/56, 7/2/56, S/7/56, 7/22/56, S/12/56, 2/1/57, 2/8/57, 2/22/57, Fo/4/57, 6/21/57, 8/4/57, 9/6/57, 9/18/57, Fo/9/57, 9/26/57, 11/28/57, 12/6/57, 3/14/58, 4/4/58, 9/19/58, 10/3/58, 12/25/59
Sparks, Milton (See Delroys)
Sparrows F/10/56
Spencer and Spencer T/3/59
Spectors Three T/11/59
Spiders 1/14/56, 2/10/56, S/6/56, 3/15/57
Squires Fo/4/56
Stacey, Clyde Fo/9/58
Stampley, Joe F/10/59
Stanley, Ray S/10/57
Starkes, Doc and the Nite Riders L/6/56, Fo/2/58

Starr, Andy F/2/57
Starr, Frankie S/1/56
Starr, Randy T/7/57
Staton, Dakota 1/27/56, 6/30/58, 2/6/59, 2/13/59, 10/16/59
Steele, Ted 11/26/58
Steele, Tommy Fo/4/57
Stevens, April Fo/9/59
Stevens, Connie Fo/3/59, 8/29/59
Stevens, Dodie Fo/12/58, Fo/4/59, 8/22/59, 10/1/59
Stevens, Julie and the Premiers T/8/56
Stevens, Ray T/6/57, Fo/10/57, F/5/58, S/8/58, T/11/58, T/6/59, S/10/59
Stevens, Terri 8/13/59
Stewart, Billy S/6/56
Stewart, Sandy 3/27/59, 5/11/59
Stites, Gary T/3/59, 4/18/59, Fo/6/59, 6/23/59, 7/1/59, 7/18/59, 9/2/59, Fo/9/59, 11/28/59
Stitt, Sonny 9/11/59, 9/25/59
Storey, Dean S/5/58
Storey Sisters S/1/58, 4/6/58, 6/13/58, 6/20/58
Storm, Billy T/3/59, 5/24/59, 5/30/59, 6/29/59, 11/21/59
Storm, Warren T/2/59, S/6/59
Storms T/1/59
Strangers Fo/7/59, Fo/11/59
Strikes T/3/57
Strong, Nolan and the Diablos 1/27/56, 2/6/56, 4/2/56, 9/27/56, 11/10/56, 4/21/57
Students Fo/8/58
Sugarcanes T/10/58
Suggs, Brad Fo/6/56
Sullivan, Niki T/4/58
Summers, Gene Fo/2/58, Fo/7/58
Sunnyland Slim 3/2/57
Supremes Fo/7/56
Suzuki, Pay 5/10/58
Swallows Fo/5/58
Swan, Mary 8/16/58, F/9/58, 11/15/58
Swan, Jimmy S/4/56
Swan Silvertones 7/10/59
Sweethearts 1/27/56

T

T.V. Slim T/7/57, Fo/8/59
Tall, Tom and the Tom Cats Fo/3/58
Tan, Roy Fo/6/57
Tarheel Slim and Little Ann 8/16/59
Tarriers (See Martin, Vince and the...)
Tassels 6/27/59, T/9/59
Taylor, Burt M/12/57
Taylor, Johnny F/6/56
Taylor, Sam "The Man" 2/13/56, F/3/56, 3/30/56, 9/9/56, 3/15/57, 5/4/57, 12/25/59
Taylor, Ted 2/27/59
Taylor, Vernon S/8/59
Techniques T/10/57
Teddy Bears T/9/58, 10/29/58, 11/15/58, 1/3/59, F/1/59, Fo/3/59, 4/21/59, F/5/59, F/6/59
Teen Queens F/1/56, 2/18/56, 3/30/56, T/4/56, 4/20/56, 5/19/56, T/6/56, 7/28/56, Fo/8/56, T/10/57
Teen Tones S/2/58
Teenagers (See also Lymon, Frankie and the...) Fo/11/57, 12/25/57, T/7/58

Tempo, Nino T/12/58, F/12/59
Tempos F/6/59, 8/8/59, Fo/9/59, 10/12/59, 10/17/59
Terry, Al S/10/56
Tex, Joe 2/3/56, 2/10/56, Fo/2/56, S/4/56, Fo/10/56, 3/15/57, S/1/58, 2/21/59, Fo/3/59, 3/31/59, T/11/59, 11/27/59
Therrien, Joe Jr. Fo/7/57
Thomas, Cliff S/10/58
Thomas, Danny 5/11/59
Thomas, Irma S/12/59
Thompson, Sonny 6/1/56, F/1/57, 7/26/57
Thornton, Willie Mae "Big Mama" S/8/56, M/9/57
Three Chuckles T/2/56, 4/4/56, S/10/56, 12/5/56, 12/25/56
Three Friends Fo/10/56, 12/21/56
Three Souls T/9/58
Three Tons of Joy M/9/57, 4/6/58
Thunder, Johnny
Til, Sonny and the Orioles (See Orioles)
Tillis, Mel F/7/57
Tillotson, Johnny S/9/58, 9/24/58, F/7/59, T/11/59
Tiny Topsy 8/7/59
Todd, Art and Dotty 5/11/58, 5/17/58, 3/14/59
Todd, Nick L/8/57, S/9/57, 12/6/57, 2/6/58
Tokens T/5/56
Tom and Jerry T/11/57, 11/22/57, F/3/58
Tony and Joe F/7/58, 7/26/58
Toppers (See Mitchell, Bobby and the...)
Torok, Mitchell Fo/6/59, 8/22/59
Tousan, A. (See Toussaint, Allen)
Toussaint, Allen T/3/58, 4/19/58
Townsend, Ed Fo/2/58, 3/28/58, 6/13/58, M/7/58, 10/29/58, 11/7/58, 12/24/58
Trammell, Bobby Lee S/1/58, F/4/58, T/9/58, F/5/59
Tranquils 11/10/58
Travis and Bob F/3/59, 4/4/59, 4/22/59, Fo/5/59, Fo/6/59, F/9/59
Treadwell, George M/7/58
Tremaines 11/10/58
Treniers L/6/56
Tune Rockers Fo/7/58
Tune Weavers F/6/57, S/8/57, Fo/8/57, 9/11/57, 10/11/57, F/11/57, 11/28/57, 1/8/58, 5/2/58, S/16/58, M/6/58, T/6/58, F/3/59
Tunedrops (See Dodds, Malcom and the...)
Turbans 1/20/56, 4/1/56, E/4/56, 4/22/56, F/5/56, 5/25/56, 9/26/56, 10/5/56, Fo/1/57, 3/13/57, 8/23/57, 2/21/58, 5/16/58
Turks Fo/2/56, 5/11/56, 7/28/56, T/7/59
Turner, Jesse Lee F/12/58, 2/20/59, 2/27/59, 3/5/59, 3/28/59, F/4/59, 4/8/59, 5/18/59, S/9/59, 12/17/59
Turner, Joe 1/16/56, 1/23/56, 1/23/56, 2/1/56, E/2/56, 3/11/56, T/3/56, 4/20/56, F/5/56, 5/19/56, T/7/56, 7/26/56, 8/13/56, 8/29/56, 9/24/56, 9/26/56, M/10/56, 11/23/56, T/12/56, 1/8/57, 2/22/57, 2/24/57, S/3/57, 5/20/57, 5/31/57, F/6/57, 7/1/57, F/9/57, 10/28/57, Fo/11/57, F/4/58, 7/5/58, 10/31/58, 11/1/58, 6/5/59, F/8/59, S/11/59
Turner, Sammy Fo/1/59, 8/8/59, 9/18/59, Fo/9/59, 10/10/59, 10/17/59, 12/25/59
Turner, Titus 10/12/56, 9/17/57
Twilighters S/12/56

Twin Tones 12/25/57, 3/28/58
Twins F/10/58
Twitty, Conway Fo/3/57, S/7/57, S/7/58, 9/27/58, 10/11/58, 11/9/58, 11/12/58, M/11/58, Fo/11/58, 11/29/58, E/12/58, F/1/59, 1/17/59, F/4/59, 4/22/59, 5/9/59, 5/10/59, Fo/6/59, 7/31/59, 8/9/59, 8/11/59, Fo/8/59, 9/14/59, 11/28/59, E/12/59, S/12/59, 12/19/59
Tyler, Big "T" Fo/6/57

U

Upbeats 7/5/58
Upsetters 6/28/56, E/11/57, 3/14/58, 4/13/58, L/6/58, 5/1/59

V

Valens, Ritchie Fo/8/58, S/11/58, 12/5/58, E/12/58, 12/27/58, 1/23/59, 2/2/59, 2/3/59, 2/7/59, 2/9/59, S/3/59, Fo/5/59, S/10/59
Valentines 6/8/56, Fo/6/56, 9/14/56, F/10/56, 1/11/57, 2/8/57
Valiants F/11/57, S/10/58
Valli, Frankie (See Vally, Frankie)
Valli, June 5/4/57, 12/13/58
Vally, Frankie (Frankie Valli) Fo/10/59
Van Doren, Mamie E/3/59
Vaughan, Sarah 3/11/56, 4/27/56, 6/29/56, 2/1/57, 6/57/57, 1/20/58, 2/25/58, 10/6/58, 10/17/58, 1/9/59, 2/6/59, 5/25/59, 5/27/59, Fo/6/59, F/10/59
Vaughn, Billy T/10/57
Valentines 2/10/56, T/2/56, 8/24/56
Vee, Bobby 2/3/59, 2/4/59, F/8/59
Veline, Bobby and the Shadows (See Vee, Bobby)
Velours 10/12/56, 6/28/57, 7/19/57, 8/16/57, 10/28/57, 3/28/58, F/4/59
Velvetones S/4/57, 6/15/57, Fo/8/57
Velvets 2/4/57, 3/7/58
Vernon, Ray S/6/57, Fo/6/59
Videos 9/12/58
Vincent, Gene L/4/56, Fo/5/56, 6/4/56, 7/28/56, E/9/56, 9/17/56, Fo/9/56, 9/28/56, E/12/56, 12/25/56, 3/14/57, Fo/3/57, M/4/57, 5/21/57, 5/23/57, 5/25/57, 5/29/57, 6/11/57, F/7/57, M/7/57, 8/12/57, 9/7/57, M/9/57, 10/8/57, 10/12/57, T/10/57, 10/26/57, M/11/57, 11/17/57, 12/7/57, 12/14/57, 12/16/57, E/1/58, S/1/58, 2/7/58, M/3/58, 3/29/58, T/4/58, 4/28/58, F/7/58, S/9/58, Fo/11/58, L/11/58, T/2/59, Fo/6/59, Fo/11/59, 12/5/59, 12/12/59, M/12/59
Vinson, Eddie "Cleanhead" 5/3/57, 6/3/57, 10/11/57
Vinton, Bobby F/4/59, Fo/8/59
Virtue, Frank (See Virtues)
Virtues F/2/59, 4/24/59, Fo/5/59, 5/28/59, 6/12/59, T/7/59, 8/9/59
Viscounts F/11/59
Voxpoppers 3/29/58

W

Wade, Adam T/10/59
Wailers T/5/59, 6/11/59, T/7/59
Walker, T-Bone 2/3/56, 2/17/56, 3/12/56, 3/30/56, 4/27/56, 7/20/56, 7/5/57, 9/6/57, L/1/58
Wallace, Jerry T/1/56, L/4/57, F/6/57, Fo/2/

58, F/7/58, 8/23/58, 8/24/58, T/10/58, S/6/59, 9/19/59
Wanderers 10/19/56, S/1/59, 2/6/59
Ward, Billy and His Dominoes S/5/56, F/6/56, 9/1/56, 9/24/56, F/10/56, T/12/56, E/4/57, T/5/57, S/8/57, T/8/57, L/8/57, 9/15/57, 9/18/57, 10/18/57, F/12/57, F/3/58, Fo/4/58, S/3/59, L/4/59
Washington, Baby 10/29/58, 11/28/58, 12/24/58, 3/6/59, 6/3/59, 6/9/59, Fo/9/59, 10/23/59, 11/18/59
Washington, Dinah 1/27/56, 3/12/56, 5/4/56, 5/18/56, 8/21/56, 9/7/56, 9/21/56, 9/24/56, 1/28/57, 2/18/57, 6/3/57, 9/13/57, 5/16/58, 10/3/58, 10/10/58, M/10/58, 11/24/58, 1/30/59, T/4/59, 6/13/59, 8/7/59, 9/7/59, S/9/59, 10/6/59, 10/28/59, 11/16/59, 11/29/59
Waters, Muddy E/3/56, F/8/56, S/3/57, 7/5/58, 8/18/58
Watson, Johnny "Guitar" 3/14/56, 6/21/56, 9/28/56, 10/18/57, 3/27/59, 6/3/59, 6/9/59, 9/1/59
Watts, Noble "Thin Man" 7/21/57, S/8/57, L/8/57, Fo/10/57, Fo/1/58, 2/21/58, S/10/58
Wayne, Alvis S/9/58
Wayne, John M/1/59, 3/18/59
Wayne, Patrick 8/16/58
Wayne, Thomas F/4/58, S/6/58, 11/14/58, 2/7/59, 3/27/59, T/4/59, Fo/4/59, 8/8/59
Wayne, Vince 5/22/59
Weld, Tuesday 12/5/56
West, Rudy S/11/59
West, Sonny S/2/58
Wheeler, Onie 6/12/57
Wheels S/4/56, 7/6/56, 10/19/56, 12/25/59
Whiskey, Nancy (See McDevitt, Charles)
White, Kitty 5/12/56
Whiteman, Paul 3/23/56

Wild Cats S/12/58, 1/24/59
Wild Tones S/9/58
Will Maston Trio (See Davis, Sammy Jr.)
Williams, Andre M/3/56, 11/10/56, 1/25/57, 3/2/57, 4/19/57, S/8/57
Williams, Andy 3/15/58, 8/9/58, 11/8/58, 1/16/59
Williams, Billy 10/26/56, T/5/57, 7/12/57, 8/5/57, 8/16/57, 10/19/57, 11/22/57, 3/7/58, 10/10/58, 2/21/59, 4/5/59, 6/24/59
Williams, Cootie 5/3/57, 6/3/57
Williams, Joe 1/6/56, 5/28/56, 10/29/56, 5/9/58, 8/3/59
Williams, Larry Fo/2/57, T/5/57, 8/30/57, 9/20/57, F/10/57, 10/28/57, Fo/2/58, 3/28/58, S/6/58, 8/29/58, T/9/58, 10/29/58, T/1/59, 3/27/59, T/4/59, S/8/59, Fo/9/59, M/10/59, Fo/11/59
Williams, Maurice T/5/59
Williams, Mel M/9/57, 4/6/58
Williams, Otis and His Charms 1/14/56, 1/20/56, 2/17/56, 3/9/56, 4/2/56, 4/15/56, 5/4/56, Fo/5/56, 6/27/56, Fo/8/56, 11/18/56, 3/15/57, 5/10/57, T/5/57, 8/16/57, 9/13/57
Williams, Paul 5/25/56, 10/10/57
Williams, Tony (See also Platters) T/7/57
Williamson, Sonny Boy (See also Sonny Boy) T/1/56, 4/10/59
Willis, Chuck 1/14/56, F/2/56, E/3/56, E/4/56, S/5/56, Fo/10/56, 2/22/57, T/3/57, 5/26/57, 7/19/57, Fo/7/57, 10/23/57, Fo/11/57, 12/25/57, 2/15/58, F/4/58, Fo/7/58, S/6/59
Willis, Rod S/6/57
Willows T/2/56, 3/30/56, 4/27/56, Fo/6/56
Wills, Oscar T/7/57
Wilson, Jackie 2/15/57, 5/17/57, 6/14/57, L/8/57, F/9/57, 9/13/57, 10/4/57, 11/15/57, 11/22/57, 11/28/57, 12/25/57, T/1/58, 2/26/58, Fo/5/58, F/8/58, 8/6/58, T/9/58, 10/10/58, T/10/58, 10/24/58, 12/24/58, 12/27/58, F/3/59, 3/21/59, 3/27/59, 5/18/59, Fo/5/59, 6/3/59, 6/9/59, 8/1/59, T/8/59, Fo/10/59, 11/18/59, 12/2/59, 12/19/59, 12/25/59
Witherspoon, Jimmy 3/14/56, 3/30/56, 8/23/57
Wolf, Howlin' S/2/56, F/2/57, 4/21/57, 6/16/57, 8/18/58
Wood, Anita 7/9/57
Wooley, Sheb S/5/58, 7/5/58, 7/28/58, 8/24/58, S/11/58, F/4/59
Wray, Doug F/6/59
Wray, Link and His Ray Men F/4/58, 5/10/58, F/1/59, 2/10/59, 3/21/59, 3/28/59, S/6/59
Wray, Lucky F/4/57
Wright, Billy 2/16/57, 5/30/58
Wright, Dale 1/20/58, S/4/58, T/8/58, 9/9/58, 11/30/58, Fo/6/59, 7/7/59, 7/16/59
Wyatt, Aubrey (See Jodimars)

Y

York, Rusty S/6/59, 8/11/59, 8/15/59, 9/4/59, 12/20/59
Young, Faron 8/12/56, 8/18/56, 8/26/56, 9/9/56, 7/9/59
Young, Jesse (Obe) 4/20/56, S/9/56, 9/21/56, F/10/58
Youngsters F/6/56, Fo/11/56

Z

Zacherle, John T/2/58, 3/1/58
Zanies S/9/58
Zeppa, Ben Joe Fo/12/58

Song Title Index

In order to make the contents of this book more easily accessible, a method of citation based on references to specific dates or features of the book has been employed, rather than using more general references to page numbers.

KEY TO CITATIONS

By day: 1/15/56 = January 15, 1956
By week: F/1/58 = First week of January 1958
(F = first week;
S = second week;
T = third week;
Fo = fourth week)

A

"ABC's of Love, The"—Teenagers T/9/56
"Action Packed"—Ronnie Dee T/11/58
"Affection"—Gloria Lynn F/2/56
"Afraid"—Sammy Salvo Fo/8/59
"After the Hop"—Bill Pinkney F/5/58
"Ain't Gonna Cry No More"—Bobby Day S/7/59
"Ain't Got No Home"—Clarence Henry T/10/56
"Ain't He Sweet"—Sensations T/3/56
"Ain't I Cried Enough"—Troyce Key F/2/59
"Ain't I'm a Dog"—Ronnie Self Fo/8/57
"Ain't That Love"—Ray Charles S/1/57
"Ain't That Love"—Brenda Lee S/8/57
"Ain't That Lovin' You Baby"—Dale Hawkins Fo/4/59
"Ain't That Loving You Baby"—Jimmy Reed F/1/56
"Aladdin's Lamp"—Flairs T/9/56
"Alimony"—Frankie Ford T/6/59
"All Alone"—Charmers T/10/56
"All American Boy, The"—Bill Parsons Fo/11/58
"All I Have To Do Is Dream"—Everly Brothers F/4/58
"All I Want Is You"—Bobby Rydell F/5/59
"All My Love Belongs To You"—Little Willie John T/10/58

"All Night Long"—Bob Luman T/7/57
"All Night Long"—Robert Parker Fo/9/59
"All of a Sudden My Heart Sings"—Robins Fo/3/57
"(All of a Sudden) My Heart Sings"—Paul Anka T/11/58
"All of My Life"—Sam Cooke F/5/58
"All Shook Up"—Elvis Presley T/3/57
"All The Things You Are"—Barry Mann T/8/59
"Almost Eighteen"—Roy Orbison T/1/59
"Almost Grown"—Chuck Berry F/3/59
"Along Came Jones"—Coasters Fo/4/59
"Altar of Love"—Channels F/1/58
"Always"—Sammy Turner Fo/9/59
"Always and Forever"—Four Esquires Fo/1/58
"Always Faithful"—Jimmy Bowen F/12/58
"Always My Darling"—Cadillacs F/7/59
"Always On My Mind"—Bobby Vinton F/4/59
"Am I To Be The One"—Billy Craddock F/1/59
"Among My Souvenirs"—Connie Francis Fo/10/59
"And That Reminds Me"—Della Reese T/7/57
"And the Angels Sing"—Johnny Nash Fo/5/59
"Angel Boy"—Buddy Ace F/10/58
"Angel Face"—James Darren Fo/6/59
"Angel of Love"—Charlie Gracie F/5/59
"Angel of My Life"—Richard Berry Fo/6/56
"Angels Cried"—Isley Brothers Fo/5/57
"Angels Listened In, The"—Crests T/7/59
"Anna Belle"—Jerry Landis Fo/8/59
"Answer to the Flying Saucer - U.F.O"—Syd Lawrence S/8/56
"Anthony Boy"—Chuck Berry S/1/59
"Any Little Thing"—Paul Evans S/5/59
"Any Room In My Heart"—Lee Andrews F/11/58
"Any Room In My Heart"—Tony Bellus F/11/58
"A-1 In My Heart"—Spiders S/6/56
"Ape Call"—Nervous Norvous T/7/56
"Apple Cider"—Doc Starkes Fo/2/58
"April Love"—Pat Boone F/10/57
"Are You Ever Coming Back?"—Little Willie John F/3/56
"Are You From Dixie?"—Joe Bennett & Sparkletones Fo/12/59
"Are You Really Mine"—Jimmie Rodgers T/7/58

"Arlinda"—Danny Lester S/12/58
"Arrow of Love"—Six Teens Fo/4/57
"As Long As I Live"—Jackie Wilson T/5/58
"As Sure As I Live"—Rudy West S/11/59
"At My Party"—Paul Evans F/3/59
"At The Hop"—Danny & the Juniors F/11/57
"A-Tisket A-Tasket"—Joe Jones S/4/58

B

"Baby"—Premiers Fo/3/56
"Baby"—Slades S/12/57
"Baby Baby"—Dale Hawkins S/10/57
"Baby Baby"—Curtis Johnson Fo/4/59
"Baby Baby"—Teenagers T/11/56
"Baby Blue"—Gene Vincent T/4/58
"Baby Come Along With Me"—Spaniels S/7/56
"Baby Come Back"—Johnny Rivers Fo/3/58
"Baby Come Home"—Robert & Johnny S/3/57
"Baby Doll"—Joe Allison S/3/58
"Baby Don't You Know"—Wilbert Harrison F/6/59
"Baby Face"—Little Richard Fo/8/58
"(Baby) Hully Gully"—Olympics F/7/59
"Baby Just You"—Johnny Otis T/8/59
"Baby Lover"—Petula Clark S/4/59
"Baby Loves Him"—Wanda Jackson S/2/57
"Baby Mine"—Teen Queens T/4/56
"Baby Open Your Heart"—Dells S/9/59
"Baby Please Come Home"—Lloyd Price Fo/4/57
"Baby Please Don't Go"—Troyce Key S/9/58
"Baby Please Don't Go"—Jesse Lee Turner F/4/59
"Baby She's Gone"—Jack Scott T/4/57
"Baby Sittin'"—Carole King S/3/59
"Baby Talk"—Jan & Dean F/6/59
"Baby What You Want Me To Do"—Jimmy Reed S/11/59
"Baby Work Out"—Baby Washington Fo/9/59
"Baby-O"—Six Teens Fo/9/58
"Back In The U.S.A."—Chuck Berry Fo/5/59
"Bad Boy"—Jive Bombers S/12/56
"Bad Boy"—Robin Luke Fo/12/59
"Bad Boy"—Larry Williams T/1/59
"Bad Girl"—Miracles T/7/59
"Bad Luck"—Sanford Clark F/3/59
"Bad Luck"—B.B. King Fo/7/56
"Bad Luck Blues"—Smiley Lewis S/11/57

491

"Bad Motorcycle"—Storey Sisters S/1/58
"Ballad of a Teenage Queen"—Johnny Cash F/1/58
"Ballad of Billy Joe, The"—Kerry Lee Lewis Fo/6/59
"Ballad of Donna and Peggy Sue, The"—Ray Campi S/3/59
"Banana Boat Story, The"—Buchanan & Goodman T/2/57
"Bandstand Doll"—Johnny Carroll S/4/59
"Barefoot Girl"—Playmates Fo/3/57
"Battle of New Orleans"—Johnny Horton F/4/59
"Be Bop Boogie Boy"—Gene Vincent Fo/11/58
"Be Lovey Dovey"—Four Lovers F/9/56
"Be My Guest"—Fats Domino F/10/59
"Be My Lovin' Baby"—Penguins Fo/12/57
"Be Sure"—Dubs F/6/58
"Beachcomber"—Jo Ann Campbell F/7/59
"Beat, The"—Rockin' R's F/3/59
"Beating of My Heart, The"—Moonglows S/9/57
"Beatnik"—Champs T/12/58
"Beautiful Delilah"—Chuck Berry F/7/58
"Be-Bop Baby"—Ricky Nelson S/9/57
"Be-Bop-A-Lulu"—Gene Vincent Fo/5/56
"Because You're Young"—Jimmie Rodgers F/2/59
"Been So Long"—Pastels (Mascot) Fo/11/57
"Been So Long"—Pastels (Argo) F/1/58
"Beep Beep"—Playmates S/10/58
"Beep-Beep-Beep"—Bobby Day Fo/11/57
"Beg Your Pardon"—Dewey Phillips F/11/59
"Beggar to a King"—Jape Richardson Fo/10/57
"Begging Begging"—James Brown F/2/58
"Believe Me"—Royal Teens T/8/59
"Believe What You Say"—Ricky Nelson F/3/58
"Bells Bells Bells"—Billy & Lillie T/6/59
"Bermuda Shorts"—Delroys S/7/57
"Bertha Lou"—Johnny Faire Fo/11/57
"Bertha Lou"—Clint Miller Fo/11/57
"Better You Should Whip-a-me"—Dean Storey S/5/58
"Betty and Dupree"—Chuck Willis Fo/11/57
"Betty Lou Got a New Pair of Shoes"—Bobby Freeman F/7/58
"Betty My Angel"—Jerry Fuller T/7/59
"Beulah Lee"—Jody Reynolds T/3/59
"Beware"—Jesse Belvin T/2/59
"B-I-Bickey-Bi Bo Bo Go"—Gene Vincent Fo/3/57
"Big Beat, The"—Fats Domino Fo/11/57
"Big Blon' Baby"—Ronnie Self F/5/58
"Big Boy Pete"—Don & Dewey T/2/59
"Big Fool"—Ronnie Self F/4/57
"Big Guitar, The"—Owen Bradley T/1/58
"Big Hurt, The"—Toni Fisher Fo/9/59
"Big Leg Emma"—Jack Dupree Fo/6/56
"Big Man"—Four Preps T/4/58
"Big Name Button"—Royal Teens Fo/4/58
"Big Town"—Ronnie Self Fo/8/59
"Bill Bailey Won't You Please Come Home"—Brenda Lee Fo/12/58

"Billy"—Kathy Linden F/2/58
"Billy's Blues"—Billy Stewart S/6/56
"Bim Bam Boom"—El Dorados Fo/10/56
"Bimbombey"—Jimmie Rodgers Fo/10/58
"Bird Dog"—Everly Brothers Fo/7/58
"Bird Doggin'"—Bill Craddock T/11/57
"Black Slacks"—Joe Bennett & Sparkletones T/7/57
"Blanche"—Three Friends Fo/10/56
"Blast Off"—Noble Watts Fo/1/58
"Bless Your Heart"—Thurston Harris Fo/3/59
"Blob, The"—Five Blobs F/9/58
"Blob, The"—Zanies S/9/58
"Blue Days Black Nights"—Buddy Holly S/4/56
"Blue Eyed Mermaid"—Bobby Darin T/5/56
"Blue Jean Baby"—Jerry Wallace F/6/57
"Blue Letter"—Little Junior Parker F/8/59
"Blue Monday"—Fats Domino F/12/56
"Blue Mood"—Julie Stevens T/8/56
"Blue Moon"—Meadowlarks F/10/57
"Blue Suede Shoes"—Boyd Bennett F/2/56
"Blue Suede Shoes"—Carl Perkins F/2/56
"Blue Suede Shoes"—Sam "The Man" Taylor F/3/56
"Blue Velvet"—Velours F/4/59
"Blueberry Hill"—Fats Domino T/9/56
"Bluebird of Happiness"—Hearts Fo/5/56
"Bluebird the Buzzard and the Oriole, The"—Bobby Day T/11/58
"Bluebirds Over the Mountain"—Ersel Hickey T/2/58
"Bluejean Bop"—Gene Vincent Fo/9/56
"Bo Weevil"—Fats Domino S/1/56
"Bobby Sox To Stockings"—Frankie Avalon S/5/59
"Bongo Rock"—Preston Epps T/4/59
"Bonnie Came Back"—Duane Eddy Fo/11/59
"Bony Moronie"—Larry Williams F/10/57
"Booger Red"—Sid King F/5/56
"Boogie Bear"—Boyd Bennett F/7/59
"Book of Love"—Monotones F/2/58
"Boom Boom Out Goes the Light"—Little Walter S/8/57
"Bop Baby Bop"—Brad Suggs Fo/6/56
"Bop-A-Lena"—Ronnie Self Fo/1/58
"Boppin' in a Sack"—Lane Brothers S/4/58
"Boppin' The Blues"—Carl Perkins F/6/56
"Boppin' With Sonny"—Sonny Boy Williamson T/1/56
"Born To Love You"—Jimmy Heap Fo/3/59
"Born Too Late"—Poni-Tails Fo/6/58
"Bottles To The Baby"—Charlie Feathers S/12/56
"Boy Without a Girl, A"—Frankie Avalon S/5/59
"Boys Do Cry"—Joe Bennett & Sparkletones T/8/59
"Break Up"—Jerry Lee Lewis Fo/8/58
"Breaking Up Is Hard To Do"—Jivin' Gene S/7/59
"Breath of Air"—Squires Fo/4/56
"Breathless"—Jerry Lee Lewis S/2/58

"Bring Me Love"—Brook Benton F/1/56
"Broken Hearted Melody"—Sarah Vaughan Fo/6/59
"Brown-eyed Handsome Man"—Chuck Berry F/9/56
"Buddy"—Jackie Dee S/8/58
"Bulldog"—Fireballs Fo/11/59
"Bullwhip Rock"—Cyclones S/9/58
"Busy Body Rock"—Mints F/1/56
"But Not For Me"—Flamingos F/2/59
"Buttercup"—Bob Luman T/10/59
"Butterfingers"—Tommy Steele Fo/4/57
"Butterfly"—Charlie Gracie T/1/57
"Buzz Buzz Buzz"—Hollywood Flames F/10/57
"By the Light of the Silvery Moon"—Jimmy Bowen F/7/58
"By the Light of the Silvery Moon"—Little Richard T/2/59
"By You By The Bayou"—Dwight Pullen Fo/12/58
"Bye Bye Love"—Everly Brothers S/4/57
"Bye Everybody"—Impalas T/10/59

C

"C. C. Rider"—Chuck Willis T/3/57
"Call Me Shorty"—Mickey Gilley T/2/58
"Can't Wait"—Del Vikings S/2/58
"Can't We Be Sweethearts"—Cleftones T/6/56
"Candy"—Big Maybelle T/5/56
"Candy Apple Red"—Bonnie Guitar F/11/59
"Cannonball"—Duane Eddy F/10/58
"Caramba!"—Champs T/3/59
"Caravan"—Cozy Cole F/11/58
"Caribbean"—Mitchell Torok Fo/6/59
"Carol"—Chuck Berry F/8/58
"Carol"—Schoolboys T/8/57
"Castin' My Spell"—Johnny Otis S/3/59
"Casual Look, A"—Six Teens S/4/56
"Cat Pants"—Ray Stevens S/8/58
"Cat Walk"—Lee Allen S/10/59
"Caterpillar"—Ray Campi Fo/2/57
"Caterpillar Crawl"—Strangers Fo/7/59
"Caught"—Paul Evans F/8/57
"'Cause You're Mine"—G-Clefs S/11/56
"Caveman"—Terry Fell S/11/56
"Cervesa"—Boots Brown S/6/58
"Cha-Hua-Hua"—Pets F/5/58
"Chain of Love"—Bob & Earl F/7/58
"Chance Is All I Ask, A"—Don Deal Fo/7/58
"Chantilly Lace"—Big Bopper F/7/58
"Chapel of Dreams"—Dubs Fo/8/59
"Charades"—Sophomores S/12/57
"Chariot Rock"—Champs Fo/7/58
"Charley Bop"—Scott Engel Fo/7/58
"Charlie Brown"—Coasters S/1/59
"Charlie Brown Got Expelled"—Joe Tex Fo/3/59
"Charm Bracelet"—Bob Crewe S/11/57
"Cheat, A"—Sanford Clark T/11/56
"Cheat, A"—Sanford Clark (reissue) F/10/57
"Cherry"—Clarence Palmer Fo/6/57
"Cherry Lips"—Robins S/3/56
"Cherrystone"—Addrisi Brothers F/5/59
"Chickee Wah-Wah"—Bobby Marchan S/3/57

"Chicken"—Cheers   T/2/56
"Chicken Baby Chicken"—Tony Harris   F/5/57
"Chicken Hop"—Billy Bland   Fo/5/56
"Chicken Shack"—Amos Milburn   F/9/56
"Childhood Sweetheart"—Chuck Berry   F/9/59
"Chili Beans"—Boots Brown   S/5/59
"Chip Chip"—Mello-Kings   F/2/59
"Chipmunk Song, The"—Chipmunks & David Seville   S/11/58
"Chosen Few, The"—Dion & Timberlanes   T/6/57
"Chosen Few, The"—Dion & Timberlanes (reissue)   F/6/59
"Church Bells Are Ringing"—Willows   T/2/56
"Class Cutter (Yeah Yeah)"—Dale Hawkins   S/2/59
"Class of '59"Bob Luman   S/7/59
"Class, The"—Chubby Checker   T/4/59
"Claudette"—Everly Brothers   F/4/58
"Clementine"—Jan & Dean   F/12/59
"Click-Clack"—Dickey Doo   Fo/12/57
"Close Your Eyes"—Pretenders   T/3/57
"Closer Walk, A"—Jimmy Jones   Fo/10/58
"Closer You Are, The"—Channels   T/8/56
"Closin' In"—Jody Reynolds   S/10/58
"Cloud 99"—Jodimars   S/2/57
"Clouds"—Spacemen   S/7/59
"Clown, The"—Ray Stevens   T/11/58
"C'Mon Everybody"—Eddie Cochran   T/10/58
"Comanche"—Link Wray   S/6/59
"Come Along With Me"—Del Vikings   T/9/57
"Come and Get It"—Ray Peterson   S/8/59
"Come Go With Me"—Dell-Vikings (Fee-Bee)   S/1/57
"Come Go With Me"—Dell-Vikings (Dot)   F/2/57
"Come Into My Heart"—Lloyd Price   S/10/59
"Come On"—Sharps   T/3/57
"Come On and Get It"—Midnighters   Fo/10/56
"Come On and Get Me"—Fabian   T/8/59
"Come On Baby"—Jo Ann Campbell   S/1/57
"Come On Home"—Chuck Willis   F/2/56
"Come On Let's Go"—Ritchie Valens   Fo/8/58
"Come Seven"—Bobby Day   F/3/57
"Come Softly To Me"—Fleetwoods   S/2/59
"Come To Me"—Marv Johnson   S/2/59
"Come What May"—Clyde McPhatter   F/4/58
"Confessin' My Dream"—Wilbert Harrison   Fo/8/56
"Confidential"—Charles Brown   T/10/56
"Confidential"—Sonny Knight (Vita)   F/8/56
"Confidential"—Sonny Knight (Dot)   Fo/10/56
"Congo Mambo"—Guitar Gable   F/8/56
"Convention, The"—Delegates   S/9/56
"Coo, The"—Wayne Cochran   S/5/59
"Cool"—Kalin Twins   T/3/59

"Cool Baby"—Charlie Gracie   T/10/57
"Cool It Baby"—Jimmy Dell   T/3/57
"Cool It Baby"—Eddie Fontaine   T/8/56
"Cool Love"—Wanda Jackson   Fo/7/57
"Cool Shake"—Del Vikings   S/6/57
"Cops and Robbers"—Bo Diddley   F/10/56
"Copy Cat"—Cadillacs   T/2/59
"Corrido Rock"—Handsome" Jim Bascomb   F/3/58
"Corrine Corrina"—Bill Haley   S/11/58
"Corrine Corrina"—Ray Moss   T/4/56
"Corrine Corrina"—Joe Turner   T/3/56
"Corrine Corrina"—Joe Turner (1941)   F/5/56
"Cotton Pickin' Rocker"—Joe Bennett & Sparkletones   F/2/58
"Couldn't Get To Sleep"—Jerry Butler   F/9/59
"Country Boy Rock"—Lloyd Price   T/5/56
"Crackin' Up"—Bo Diddley   T/5/59
"Crash the Party"—Benny Joy   T/5/59
"Crawl, The"—Fireflies   T/8/58
"Crazy Arms"—Bob Beckham   T/12/59
"Crazy Arms"—Jerry Lee Lewis   S/12/56
"Crazy Baby"—Buck Rogers   T/6/59
"Crazy Cave"—Danny & Juniors   Fo/8/58
"Crazy Daisy"—Doug Sahm   F/7/59
"Crazy Dream"—Terry Noland   Fo/5/58
"Crazy Eyes For You"—Bobby Hamilton   F/6/58
"Crazy Girl"—Charlie Gracie   S/1/58
"Crazy In Love With You"—Brook Benton   T/8/58
"Crazy Love"—Paul Anka   T/3/58
"Creature, The"—Buchanan and Ancel   T/10/57
"Creep, The"—Noble Watts   S/10/58
"Cross Over"—Jimmy Bowen   S/9/57
"Cross Roads of Love, The"—Tempos   Fo/9/59
"Crossfire"—Johnny & Hurricanes   Fo/3/59
"Cry Baby Cry"—Narvel Felts   T/9/59
"Cupid"—Frankie Avalon   Fo/5/57
"Cute Little Ways"—Midnighters   T/8/59

D

"Dance to the Bop"—Gene Vincent   T/10/57
"Dance With Me"—Drifters   T/9/59
"Dance With Me"—Dale Wright   S/4/58
"Dance With the Teacher"—Olympics   S/11/58
"Dancing the Bop"—Jodimars   F/3/56
"Dangerous Woman"—Little Junior Parker   T/12/59
"Danny Boy"—Conway Twitty   Fo/8/59
"Dark Is the Night"—B.B. King   F/5/56
"Darling How Long"—Heartbeats   F/2/56
"Darling It's Wonderful"—Lovers   Fo/4/57
"Darling Lorraine"—Knockouts   F/11/59
"Darling Please Forgive Me"—Screamin' Jay Hawkins   F/4/57
"Dave's Special"—Dave "Baby" Cortez   S/12/59
"Dealer of Dreams"—Penguins   F/5/56
"Dear Heart"—Spaniels   F/5/56
"Dearest Darling"—Bo Diddley   S/6/58

"Dearest One"—Dean Barlow   F/9/57
"Dede Dinah"—Frankie Avalon   T/12/57
"Dedicated to the One I Love"—5 Royales   T/12/57
"Deep Purple"—Billy Ward   S/8/57
"Dem Low-Down Blues"—Marvin Rainwater   F/1/56
"Desire"—Charts   T/6/57
"Devil Darling"—Johnny Olenn   F/9/59
"Devil Doll"—Roy Orbison   S/4/57
"Devil or Angel"—Clovers   F/1/56
"Devoted To You"—Everly Brothers   Fo/7/58
"Diamond Ring"—Jerry Wallace   T/10/58
"Diana"—Paul Anka   Fo/5/57
"Diary, The"—Neil Sedaka   S/11/58
"Did We Have A Party"—Billy Brown   Fo/10/57
"Diddy Wah Diddy"—Bo Diddley   S/2/56
"Ding Dong"—Freddie Bell   T/3/56
"Ding Dong"—Echoes   T/1/57
"Ding Dong"—Tony Orlando   Fo/2/59
"Dinner with Drac"—John Zacherle   T/2/58
"Directly From My Heart"—Little Richard   T/2/56
"Dirty Robber"—Wailers   T/7/59
"Dirty Woman"—Jack Dupree   Fo/2/57
"Dixie Fried"—Carl Perkins   F/9/56
"Dizzy Miss Lizzy"—Larry Williams   Fo/2/58
"Do Anything"—Five Keys   F/11/57
"Do Something for Me"—Little Willie John   Fo/8/56
"(Do the) Mashed Potatoes"—Nat Kendricks   F/12/59
"Do the Stop"—Joe Bennett & Sparkletones   Fo/9/58
"Do What You Did"—Thurston Harris   F/12/57
"Do You Wanna Dance"—Bobby Freeman   T/3/58
"Does Your Chewing Gum Lose It's Flavor (On the Bedpost Overnight?)"—Lonnie Donegan   F/3/59
"Doing All Right"—Eddie Cash   Fo/12/58
"Doing the Ronde"—Shirelles   T/9/59
"Don't"—Elvis Presley   Fo/12/57
"Don't Ask Me To Be Lonely"—Dubs   Fo/4/57
"Don't Ask Me Why"—Elvis Presley   T/6/58
"Don't Be Afraid of Love"—Ersel Hickey   F/4/59
"Don't Be Cruel"—Elvis Presley   T/7/56
"Don't Be Misled"—Jimmy Scott   S/10/58
"Don't Blame It On Me"—Fats Domino   S/1/56
"Don't Cry"—Solomon Burke   S/3/58
"Don't Destroy Me"—Crash Craddock   S/9/59
"Don't Feel Sorry For Me"—Jimmy Beasley   Fo/7/56
"Don't Go Away"—Teddy Bears   F/6/59
"Don't Go No Further"—Muddy Waters   F/8/56
"Don't Go To Strangers"—Orioles   F/1/56
"Don't Hold It Against Me"—Joe Tex   T/11/59

493

"Don't Knock Elvis"—Felton Jarvis T/8/59
"Don't Knock The Rock"—Bill Haley Fo/11/56
"Don't Leave Me"—Bruce Channel T/4/59
"Don't Let Go"—Roy Hamilton F/12/57
"Don't Let Her Pin That Charge on Me"—Chris Kenner S/2/56
"Don't Mess With My Man"—Irma Thomas S/12/59
"Don't Mind Dying"—Jayhawks S/9/56
"Don't Pity Me"—Dion & Belmonts T/11/58
"Don't Say Goodbye"—Moonglows T/2/57
"Don't Sweat It Baby"—Four Seasons S/11/59
"Don't Take Your Guns To Town"—Johnny Cash Fo/12/58
"Don't Tell Anybody"—Paris Sisters T/1/58
"Don't Touch My Gal"—Empires T/6/56
"Don't Treat Me This Way"—Gene & Eunice Fo/7/57
"Don't You Know"—Della Reese Fo/8/59
"Don't You Know I Love You"—Bobby Charles S/3/56
"Don't You Know I Love You So"—Fats Domino F/2/58
"Doncha' Think It's Time"—Elvis Presley F/4/58
"Donna"—Ritchie Valens S/11/58
"Door Is Open, The"—Jerry Fuller T/9/58
"Door That Is Open, A"—Kripp Johnson Fo/7/59
"Dottie"—Danny & Juniors S/5/58
"Double Date"—Randy Starr T/7/57
"Double Talk Baby"—Conway Twitty Fo/11/58
"Double Trouble"—Otis Rush Fo/2/59
"Down and Out"—Daps F/2/56
"Down By The River"—Wade Flemons S/7/59
"Down By The Station"—Four Preps Fo/11/59
"Down in Mexico"—Coasters T/2/56
"Down in the Alley"—Clovers S/9/57
"Down the Aisle of Love"—Quin-Tones Fo/7/58
"Down Through the Years"—Guitar Slim S/6/56
"Down Yonder We Go Ballin'"—Smiley Lewis T/8/56
"Drag Strip Baby"—Little Norman Fo/6/57
"Drag, The"—Isley Brothers F/12/58
"Dream, The"—Bobbettes Fo/7/58
"Dream Age"—Bobby Rydell S/1/59
"Dream Girl"—Robert & Johnny F/5/59
"Dream Lover"—Bobby Darin F/3/59
"Dream On"—Five Keys T/10/59
"Dream Way"—Ray Peterson T/9/58
"Dreams of Contentment"—Dells F/2/56
"Dreamy Eyes"—Johnny Tillotson S/9/58
"Dreamy Eyes"—Youngsters Fo/11/56
"Drinking Wine"—Gene Simmons S/6/58
"Drinking Wine Spo-Dee-O-Dee"—Johnny Burnette Fo/8/57
"Drive In"—Sonny Thompson F/1/57
"Drive-In Show"—Eddie Cochran F/7/57

"Drop Top"—Roy Perkins T/2/58
"Drown In My Own Tears"—Ray Charles F/1/56
"Drum Party"—Sandy Nelson T/10/59
"Ducktail"—Joe Clay F/5/56
"Dumplin's"—Ernie Freeman S/8/57
"Dynamite"—Brenda Lee S/5/57
"Dynamite"—Cliff Richard S/11/59

E

"Eager Beaver Baby"—Johnny Burnette S/5/57
"Early In The Evening"—Dubs S/10/59
"Early In The Morning"—Buddy Holly F/7/58
"Early In The Morning"—Rinky-Dinks F/7/58
"Easy Going"—Noble Watts S/8/57
"Ebb Tide"—Bobby Freeman Fo/10/59
"Echoes Keep Calling Me, The"—Little Joe F/11/57
"Eddie My Love"—Teen Queens F/1/56
"Eight To The Bar"—Groovy Joe Poovey S/5/59
"Eighteen"—Connie Francis Fo/5/57
"18-Year Old Blues"—Steve Carl T/8/58
"El Paso"—Marty Robbins Fo/10/59
"El Rancho Rock"—Champs Fo/4/58
"Elevator Operator"—Rays S/8/58
"Ellie Mae"—Louis Jordan F/5/57
"Elvis Blues, The"—Otto Bash F/7/56
"Elvis Presley for President"—Lou Monte S/10/56
"Embraceable You"—Solitaires T/1/59
"Empty Arms"—Ivory Joe Hunter T/3/57
"Enchanted"—Platters F/3/59
"Enchanted Sea"—Islanders F/9/59
"End, The"—Earl Grant S/8/58
"End of the Road"—Jerry Lee Lewis S/12/56
"Endless Sleep"—Jody Reynolds T/3/58
"Endlessly"—Brook Benton Fo/3/59
"Eternally"—Twilighters S/12/56
"Eternally"—Thomas Wayne T/4/59
"Evening Star, The"—Jamies Fo/10/58
"Ever Since I Can Remember"—Bowties Fo/11/56
"Ever Since That Night"—Jimmy Bowen Fo/7/57
"Everlasting Love"—Barbara Pittman S/7/58
"Everlovin'"—Dave Burgess F/5/59
"Evermore"—Billy Ward T/12/56
"Every Day Every Way"—Hollywood Flames F/12/59
"Every Little Thing I Do"—Dion & Belmonts Fo/9/59
"Every Night (I Pray)"—Chantels Fo/2/58
"Every Night About This Time"—Sophomores F/5/56
"Every Time I Hear That Mellow Saxophone"—Roy Montrell Fo/9/56
"Everybody Likes To Cha Cha Cha"—Sam Cooke Fo/1/59
"Everybody Loves Me"—Sophomores S/3/57
"Everybody Rock"—Jimmy McCracklin T/4/58

"Everybody Rock & Roll"—Isley Brothers F/3/58
"Everybody Stroll"—O.C. Allstars S/3/58
"Everybody's Been Rockin' My Baby"—Rod Willis S/6/57
"Everybody's Going"—Eddie Holland T/10/59
"Everybody's Movin'"—Glenn Glenn S/2/58
"Everybody's Wailin'"—Huey Smith & Clowns S/9/56
"Everyday"—Johnny Rivers Fo/8/59
"Everyone Needs Someone"—Connie Francis Fo/9/56
"Everyone's Laughing"—Spaniels Fo/4/57
"Evil Angel"—Ray Vernon S/6/57

F

"F.B.I. Story, The"—Rudy Grayzell S/7/59
"Fabulous"—Charlie Gracie T/4/57
"Face of an Angel"—Five Keys F/8/57
"Fallen Out of Love"—Three Chuckles S/10/56
"Fallen Tear, A"—El Dorados S/7/56
"Fallin'"—Connie Francis T/9/58
"False Love"—Spaniels F/2/56
"Fancy Nancy"—Skip & Flip S/9/59
"Farther Up the Road"—Bobby "Blue" Bland Fo/7/57
"Father Time"—Poni-Tails S/1/59
"Fee-Fee-Fi-Fo-Fum"—LaVern Baker T/4/56
"Feelin' Happy"—Joe Turner T/12/56
"Feelin' Low"—Ernie Chaffin S/2/57
"Fever"—Little Willie John Fo/4/56
"15 Girlfriends"—Nino Tempo T/12/58
"Fine Girl"—Calvaes Fo/9/56
"Fine Little Girl"—Solitaires S/4/56
"Fire Engine Baby"—Jive-A-Tones S/12/57
"Fire of Love"—Jody Reynolds Fo/7/58
"Fireball"—Fireballs F/1/59
"First Impression"—Bobby Vinton Fo/8/59
"First Love"—Playmates F/10/59
"First Name Initial"—Annette S/9/59
"Five Feet High and Rising"—Johnny Cash Fo/6/59
"500 Miles To Go"—Heartbeats S/1/58
"Five Little Numbers"—Chantones T/10/58
"Five Long Years"—Little Junior Parker Fo/3/59
"Five Minutes More"—Robin Luke T/6/59
"Five More Steps"—Ray Stevens Fo/10/57
"Flat Foot Sam Met Jim Dandy"—T.V. Slim Fo/8/59
"Flat Tire"—Del Vikings S/11/58
"Flat-Foot Sam"—T.V. Slim T/7/57
"Flat-Foot Sam"—Oscar Wills T/7/57
"Flip-Flop"—Teenagers F/11/57
"Flirt, The"—Shirley & Lee Fo/7/57
"Florence"—Paragons T/3/57
"Flower of Love"—Crests T/5/59
"Flying Saucer, The"—Buchanan & Goodman S/7/56
"Flying Saucer the 2nd"—Buchanan & Goodman Fo/6/57

"Flying Saucers Rock and Roll"—Billy Lee Riley   T/2/57
"Fog Cutter"—Frantics   Fo/7/59
"Fool In Love, A"—Robins   S/4/57
"Fool, The"—Sanford Clark   Fo/6/56
"Fools Fall In Love"—Drifters   T/1/57
"Fools Rush In"—Malcom Dodds   F/10/57
"For Always"—Buzz Clifford   T/10/58
"For You Alone"—Kenny Rogers   F/7/58
"For Your Love"—Ed Townsend   Fo/2/58
"For Your Precious Love"—Impressions   T/5/58
"Forget It"—Dale Wright   Fo/6/59
"Forget Me Not"—Kalin Twins   F/9/58
"40 Cups of Coffee"—Bill Haley   Fo/2/57
"Forty Days"—Ronnie Hawkins   Fo/4/59
"Forty Miles of Bad Road"—Duane Eddy   T/5/59
"14 Boy Friends"—Dee Clark   S/10/57
"Frankie"—Connie Francis   T/4/59
"Frankie's Man Johnny"—Johnny Cash   Fo/3/59
"Freeze, The"—Tony & Joe   F/7/58
"Friday Night on a Dollar Bill"—Huelyn Duvall   Fo/9/58
"Fried Eggs"—Intruders   Fo/1/59
"Fried Onions"—Lord Rockingham XI   F/9/58
"From the Bottom of My Heart"—Clovers   S/9/56
"Fruit Boots"—Red Prysock   Fo/3/56
"Fujiyama Mama"—Wanda Jackson   Fo/11/57
"Funny"—Jesse Belvin   T/10/58
"Funny Thing"—Jo Ann Campbell   F/5/57

G

"Gazachstahagen"—Wildcats   S/12/58
"Gee Golly"—Coasters   F/2/58
"Gee Whiz"—Bob & Earl   Fo/8/58
"Gee Whiz"—Twins   F/10/58
"Georgia Slop, The"—Jimmy McCracklin   F/11/59
"Geraldine"—Jack Scott   F/9/58
"Get a Job"—Silhouettes   F/1/58
"Get on the Right Track"—Ray Charles   S/5/57
"Get on the Right Track"—Joe Clay   T/7/56
"Get Ready"—Larry Williams   Fo/11/59
"Get Up Get Up"—LaVern Baker   F/1/56
"Gidget"—James Darren   F/4/58
"Gift of Love, The"—Impressions   Fo/11/58
"Girl Can't Help It, The"—Little Richard   T/11/56
"Girl In My Dreams"—Cliques   Fo/3/56
"Girl On My Mind"—Buddy Holly   Fo/6/58
"Git It"—Gene Vincent   S/9/58
"Give Me Love"—Jesse Belvin   F/9/59
"Give Me Love"—Larry Williams   Fo/9/59
"Give Me The Key To Your Heart"—Robert & Johnny   S/1/59
"Give Myself a Party"—Don Gibson   Fo/8/58
"Glad All Over"—Carl Perkins   F/1/58
"Gleam in Your Eyes, The"—Channels   Fo/1/57
"Glenda"—Joe Stampley   F/10/59

"Gloria"—Dee Clark   S/6/57
"Gloria"—Arthur Lee Maye   S/4/56
"Glory of Love, The"—Angels   T/10/56
"Glory of Love, The"—Sanford Clark   Fo/3/57
"Glory of Love, The"—Velvetones   S/4/57
"Go Away Don't Bother Me"—Collins Kids   T/1/57
"Go Jimmy Go"—Jimmy Clanton   F/11/59
"Go On To School"—Jimmy Reed   S/4/58
"Goin' Down That Road"—Ersel Hickey   T/7/58
"Goin' Steady"—Tommy Sands   Fo/4/57
"Going Out With the Tide"—Jivin' Gene   S/3/59
"Gonna Find Me A Bluebird"—Marvin Rainwater   Fo/1/57
"Gonna See My Baby"—Addrisi Brothers   Fo/11/59
"Good and Bad"—Jerry Wallace   Fo/2/58
"Good Golly Miss Molly"—Little Richard   S/1/58
"Good Good Lovin'"—James Brown   S/7/59
"Good Lovin'"—Dickie Lee   T/11/57
"Good Morning Blues"—Dee Dee Ford   Fo/11/59
"Good-bye My Love"—Gene Allison   Fo/4/56
"Goodbye Baby"—Jack Scott   S/11/58
"Goodnight My Love"—Jesse Belvin   Fo/10/56
"Goodnight My Love"—Ray Peterson   S/10/59
"Goody Goody"—Teenagers   F/7/57
"Goose Bumps"—Doug Wray   F/6/59
"Gorilla, The"—Bery Convy   F/7/58
"Got a Job"—Miracles   Fo/2/58
"Got My Mojo Working"—Muddy Waters   S/3/57
"Got The Water Boiling"—Billy Riley   T/6/59
"Got You On My Mind"—Joe Turner   F/8/59
"Gotta New Girl"—Bobby Day   S/5/59
"Gotta Travel On"—Billy Grammer   T/10/58
"Graduation Day"—Rover Boys   T/4/56
"Graduation's Here"—Fleetwoods   Fo/4/59
"Great Balls of Fire"—Jerry Lee Lewis   F/11/57
"Greatest Builder, The"—Bobby Darin   Fo/9/56
"Greatest Magic of All, The"—Jerry Wallace   T/1/56
"Green Christmas"—Stan Freeberg   S/11/58
"Green Door"—Jim Lowe   T/8/56
"Green Mosquito"—Tune Rockers   Fo/7/58
"Greenback Dollar Watch and Chain"—Ray Harris   Fo/7/57
"Groovy"—Joe Dodo   T/3/58
"Guess Things Happen That Way"—Johnny Cash   T/5/58
"Guess Who?"—Jesse Belvin   T/2/59
"Guided Missiles"—Cuff Links   F/12/56
"Guitar Boogie Shuffle"—Virtues   F/2/59
"Guitar Man"—Al Casey   Fo/4/57
"Guitarsville"—Roland James   T/5/59
"Gumbo"—Johnny Burnette   F/4/59

"Gypsy Boogie"—Teen Tones   S/2/58

H

"Half-Breed"—Marvin Rainwater   T/5/59
"Hallelujah I Love Her So"—Ray Charles   S/5/56
"Hallelujah I Love Her So"—Eddie Cochran   S/11/59
"Handy Man"—Jimmy Jones   S/9/59
"Hang Up My Rock and Roll Shoes"—Chuck Willis   F/4/58
"Happiness"—Billy & Lillie   Fo/3/58
"Happy Am I"—Four Lovers   T/12/56
"Happy and Gay"—Castelles   S/6/56
"Happy Baby"—A. Tousan   T/3/58
"Happy Happy Birthday Baby"—Tune Weavers (Casa Grande)   F/6/58
"Happy Happy Birthday Baby"—Tune Weavers (Checker)   F/8/57
"Happy In Love"—Sam Cooke   T/11/59
"Happy Organ, The"—Dave "Baby" Cortez   S/2/59
"Happy Vacation"—Jackie Lee   S/6/59
"Hard Headed Woman"—Elvis Presley   T/6/58
"Hard Times (The Slop)"—Noble Watts   Fo/10/57
"Harlem Nocturne"—Viscounts   F/11/59
"Harvey's Got a Girlfriend"—Royal Teens   S/7/58
"Haunted House"—Johnny Fuller   S/1/59
"Have I Sinned"—Donnie Elbert   T/9/57
"Have Mercy Mr. Percy"—Long Tall Marvin   S/6/56
"Hawaiian War Chant"—Dynatones   Fo/9/59
"He Drives Me Crazy"—Hearts   Fo/8/56
"He Loves You Baby"—Luther Bond   Fo/9/56
"He'll Have to Go"—Jim Reeves   F/11/59
"He's Got the Whole World in His Hands"—Laurie London   F/2/58
"Head Snappin'"—Red Prysock   Fo/2/57
"Heading for the Poorhouse"—Silhouettes   S/3/58
"Heartaches By The Number"—Guy Mitchell   F/9/59
"Heartbeat"—Buddy Holly   T/10/58
"Heartbreak Hotel"—Elvis Presley   F/1/56
"Heavenly Blues"—King Curtis   Fo/10/59
"Heebie Jeebies"—Little Richard   F/10/56
"Hello Little Girl"—Lloyd Price   S/10/57
"Helpless"—Platters   F/1/58
"Helpless"—Solitaires   T/6/59
"Henrietta"—Jimmy Dee   F/11/57
"Here Comes Sally"—Trini Lopez   T/4/59
"Here Comes Summer"—Jerry Keller   S/5/59
"Here I Stand"—Wade Flemmons   T/10/58
"Hey Babe"—Cleftones   F/9/57
"Hey Baby Baby"—Jimmy Swan   S/4/56
"Hey Bo Diddley"—Bo Diddley   Fo/3/57
"Hey Little Darlin'"—Tony Bellus   T/9/59
"Hey Little Girl"—Dee Clark   F/8/59
"Hey Little Girl"—Thurston Harris   Fo/2/59
"Hey Little Girl"—Gary Stites   Fo/6/59
"Hey! Little Girl"—Techniques   T/10/57

"Hey Little Lucy!"—Conway Twitty F/4/59
"Hey Little Nell"—Four Mints F/4/58
"Hey Little School Girl"—Marquees S/9/57
"Hey Schoolgirl"—Tom & Jerry T/11/57
"Hi Hon"—Blockbusters F/3/59
"Hideaway"—Four Esquires T/9/58
"High Blood Pressure"—Huey Smith T/1/58
"High School Confidential"—Jerry Lee Lewis T/5/58
"High School U.S.A."—Tommy Facenda T/9/59
"High School Yearbook"—Ray Stevens T/6/59
"High Voltage"—Bobby Lord Fo/5/57
"Hill Stomp"—Strangers Fo/11/59
"Hippy Hippy Shake, The"—Chan Romero F/7/59
"Hit Git and Split"—Young Jesse S/9/56
"Hold It"—Bill Doggett Fo/8/58
"Hold My Baby's Hand"—James Brown S/8/56
"Holy Smoke Baby"—Cadillacs F/8/58
"Honest I Do"—Jimmy Reed S/9/57
"Honey Bop"—Wanda Jackson Fo/3/58
"Honey Chile"—Phil Flowers Fo/8/56
"Honey Hush"—Joe Turner S/11/59
"Honey Where You Going?"—Jimmy Reed Fo/2/57
"Honeycomb"—Jimmie Rodgers F/8/57
"Honeydripper"—King Curtis T/6/59
"Honky Tonk"—Bill Doggett S/7/56
"Hoot Owl"—Dave Clowney Fo/2/58
"Hootchy Koo"—Larry Williams S/6/58
"Hop Skip and Jump"—Collins Kids F/5/57
"Horror Show"—Johnny Thunder Fo/8/59
"Hot Dog"—Dale Hawkins S/12/59
"Hot Dog Buddy Buddy"—Bill Haley Fo/5/56
"Hot Dog! That Made Him Mad"—Wanda Jackson S/11/56
"Hot Rock"—Ram Rocks Fo/5/58
"Hot Rod Lincoln"—Charlie Ryan T/10/59
"Hot Rod Queen"—Roy Tan Fo/6/57
"Hound Dog"—Elvis Presley S/7/56
"Hound Dog"—Willie Mae Thornton S/8/56
"Hound Dog Man"—Fabian T/10/59
"House A Car and a Wedding Ring, A"—Dale Hawkins S/10/58
"How About That"—Dee Clark T/11/59
"How Come"—Bobby Hamilton Fo/9/58
"How Do I Love You"—B.B. King S/3/57
"How Long How Long Blues"—Billy Ward S/5/56
"How Many Times"—Lloyd Price Fo/2/58
"How Soon?"—Jacks F/2/56
"How The Time Flies"—Jerry Wallace F/7/58
"Hoy Hoy"—Collins Kids F/1/58
"Hula Love"—Buddy Knox F/8/57
"Hully Gully"—Herbie Alpert T/6/59
"Hully Gully"—Turks T/7/59
"Humdinger"—Huelyn Duvall F/4/58
"Humpty Dumpty Heart"—LaVern Baker Fo/7/57
"Hunch, The"—Paul Gayten F/10/59
"Hunch, The"—Bobby Peterson F/10/59
"Hurry Up Buttercup"—Charlie Gracie S/1/59
"Hurtin' Inside"—Paul Peek F/12/59
"Hush Your Mouth"—Bo Diddley S/6/58
"Hushabye"—Mystics T/5/59
"Hypnotized"—Drifters S/5/57

I

"I Ain't Never"—Four Preps T/7/59
"I Am Old Enough"—Schoolboys F/4/57
"I Beg of You"—Elvis Presley Fo/12/57
"I Believe In You"—Robert & Johnny T/6/58
"I Can't Help It"—Sanford Clark S/11/59
"I Can't Help It"—Burt Taylor—M/12/57
"I Can't Love You Enough"—LaVern Baker Fo/8/56
"I Can't Say Goodbye"—Fireflies Fo/11/59
"I Can't Take It"—Chantels S/2/59
"I Can't Wait"—Ray Stanley S/10/57
"I Confess"—Paul Anka T/9/56
"I Could Love You"—Midnighters Fo/10/59
"I Cried A Tear"—LaVern Baker F/11/58
"I Cry By Night"—Kenny Rankin F/8/59
"I Dig You Baby"—Marvin Rainwater F/6/58
"I Don't Know"—James Brown T/5/56
"I Don't Need You Anymore"—Teddy Bears F/1/59
"I Dreamt I Dwelt in Heaven"—Five Keys F/4/56
"I Drempt I Was Elvis"—Sonny Cole F/5/57
"I Feel Good"—Shirley & Lee Fo/10/56
"I Forgot To Remember To Forget"—Johnny Cash Fo/6/59
"I Found a Job"—Heartbeats T/2/58
"I Found a Love"—Clarence Henry F/8/57
"I Found a Million Dollar Baby"—Bobby Darin S/6/57
"I Found My Love"—Velvetones Fo/8/57
"I Go Ape"—Neil Sedaka S/2/59
"I Got a Baby"—Gene Vincent S/1/58
"I Got a Feeling"—Ricky Nelson Fo/9/58
"I Got a Woman"—Bill Haley S/2/59
"I Got Fired"—Chesterfields S/6/58
"I Got Loaded"—Cadets T/9/56
"I Got Stung"—Elvis Presley T/10/58
"I Got The Message"—Shirelles F/11/58
"I Gotta Get Myself a Woman"—Drifters T/7/56
"I Just Go Wild Over Rock and Roll"—Bobby Dean Fo/10/57
"I Just Got Lucky"—Orioles T/6/56
"I Know It's Hard But It's Fair"—5 Royales F/4/59
"I Laughed So Hard I Cried"—Rip-Chords F/8/58
"I Like Girls"—Nervous Norvous F/7/59
"I Love an Angel"—Little Bil & Bluenotes F/6/59
"I Love Linda"—Jan & Arnie S/9/58
"I Love My Baby"—Tokens T/5/56
"I Love You Baby"—Paul Anka T/9/57
"I Love You Baby"—Jimmy Reed T/7/56
"I Love You Darling"—Valentines T/2/56
"(I Love You) For Sentimental Reasons"—Sam Cooke Fo/11/57
"I Love You Madly"—Charlie & Ray S/5/57
"I Love You So"—Chantels S/5/58
"I Met Him on a Sunday"—Shirelles F/2/58
"I Miss You"—Teen Queens T/10/57
"I Miss You So"—Paul Anka F/3/59
"I Need a Girl"—Joe Turner F/9/57
"I Need a Man"—Barbara Pittman S/10/56
"I Need Someone"—Pat Boone T/3/56
"I Need Your Love Tonight"—Elvis Presley S/3/59
"I Need Your Lovin'"—Conway Twitty Fo/3/57
"I Need Your Loving"—Jimmy McCracklin F/6/58
"I Never Felt Like This"—Jack Scott Fo/2/59
"I Never Had a Sweetheart"—Connie Francis S/11/56
"I Only Have Eyes For You"—Flamingos Fo/4/59
"I Promise To Remember"—Teenagers Fo/6/56
"I Put A Spell On You"—Screamin' Jay Hawkins Fo/10/56
"I Really Do"—Spectors Three T/11/59
"I Really Love You"—Danleers S/9/58
"I Really Really Love You"—Jo Ann Campbell T/7/58
"I Remember Dear"—Tune Weavers Fo/11/57
"I Sit In My Window"—Four Fellows F/8/56
"I Smell Trouble"—Bobby "Blue" Bland S/3/57
"I Sold My Heart to the Junkman"—Silhouettes Fo/9/58
"I Think I'm Gonna Kill Myself"—Buddy Knox F/3/59
"I Think of You"—Rudy Grazell Fo/5/58
"I Told Myself a Lie"—Clyde McPhatter S/3/59
"I Trusted You"—Jimmy Clanton S/10/57
"I Waited Too Long"—LaVern Baker Fo/3/59
"I Wanna Be Loved"—Jimmy Reed S/9/59
"I Wanna Be Loved"—Ricky Nelson F/11/59
"(I Wanna) Dance With The Teacher"—Olympics S/1/59
"I Wanna Holler"—Butchie Saunders T/11/56
"I Want Somebody"—Harvey F/12/58
"I Want That"—Crash Craddock Fo/11/59
"I Want To Go Home"—Charles Brown & Amos Milburn S/4/59
"I Want To Walk You Home"—Fats Domino F/7/59
"I Want You"—Jackie Lee Cochran F/6/58
"I Want You I Need You I Love You"—Elvis Presley F/5/56
"I Want You So Bad"—James Brown S/4/59
"I Want You to Be My Girl"—Teenagers F/4/56

"I Want You to Know"—Fats Domino   Fo/11/57
"I Was Such a Fool"—Flamingos   Fo/11/59
"I Wish"—Platters   T/8/58
"I Won't Cry"—Johnny Adams   S/4/59
"I Won't Make You Cry Anymore"—Cardinals   F/8/56
"I Won't Plead No More"—James Brown   T/10/56
"I Wonder"—Glen Campbell   F/9/58
"I Wonder Why"—Dion & Belmonts   F/5/58
"Idol with the Golden Head"—Coasters   S/8/57
"If I Didn't Care"—Connie Francis   S/2/59
"If I Had a Girl"—Rod Lauren   F/11/59
"If I Had Me A Woman"—Mac Curtis   F/5/56
"If I Only Knew"—Professor Longhair   Fo/9/59
"If You Can't Rock Me"—Strikes   T/3/57
"If You Don't Want My Lovin'"—Carl Dobkins Jr.   T/8/59
"If You Only Knew"—Little Jimmy Scott   Fo/8/56
"If You Try"—Chantels   Fo/7/58
"If You're Looking"—Donnie Brooks   S/8/59
"Ific"—King Curtis   Fo/8/58
"I'll Always Be In Love With You"—Hurricanes   Fo/2/57
"I'll Be Forever Loving You"—El Dorados   F/1/56
"I'll Be Home"—Flamingos   F/1/56
"I'll Be Satisfied"—Jackie Wilson   Fo/5/59
"I'll Be Seeing You"—Poni-Tails   F/9/59
"I'll Be Spinning"—Cadets   F/11/56
"I'll Be Spinning"—Johnnie & Joe   F/11/56
"I'll Come Running Back to You"—Sam Cooke   T/11/57
"I'll Do The Same For You"—Johnny Otis   Fo/5/59
"I'll Never Let You Go"—Valentines   Fo/6/56
"I'll Never Stop Wanting You"—Moonglows   S/1/59
"I'll Sail My Ship Alone"—Jerry Lee Lewis   Fo/11/58
"I'll Wait For You"—Frankie Avalon   T/9/58
"I'm a Big Boy Now"—Bobby Hendricks   F/5/59
"I'm a Country Boy"—Clarence Henry   Fo/2/57
"I'm a Fool"—Turks   F/2/56
"I'm a Fool About Your Love"—Werly Fairburn   S/10/56
"I'm a King Bee"—Slim Harpo   S/7/57
"I'm a Man"—Fabian   Fo/11/58
"I'm Afraid The Masquerade Is Over"—Little Jimmy Scott   F/12/59
"I'm Alright"—Little Anthony   S/7/59
"I'm Ashamed of Myself"—Floyd Dixon   F/2/57
"I'm Comin' Home"—Marv Johnson   F/6/59
"I'm Confessin'"—Chantels   S/7/59
"I'm Gonna Be A Wheel Someday"—Fats Domino   F/7/59

"I'm Gonna Be A Wheel Someday"—Bobby Mitchell   S/12/57
"I'm Gonna Get Married"—Lloyd Price   T/7/59
"I'm Gonna Lasso Santa Claus"—Brenda Lee   F/11/56
"I'm Gonna Shake this Shack Tonight"—Sid King   Fo/10/56
"I'm Gonna Sit Right Down and Write Myself a Letter"—Billy Williams   S/5/57
"I'm Grateful"—Trini Lopez   F/8/59
"I'm Hangin' Up My Rifle"—Bobby Bare   T/10/59
"I'm In Love"—Fabian   T/6/58
"I'm In Love Again"—Fats Domino   T/3/56
"I'm In Love With a Girl"—Cliques   F/8/56
"I'm Movin' On"—Ray Charles   S/10/59
"I'm Movin' On"—Don Gibson   S/10/59
"I'm Nobody's Angel"—Turbans   F/5/59
"I'm Not Afraid"—Bobby Relf   Fo/11/56
"I'm Not Ashamed"—Bobby "Blue" Bland   S/4/59
"I'm Out to Getcha"—Thurston Harris   Fo/3/58
"I'm Ready"—Fats Domino   T/4/59
"I'm Sending an S.O.S."—Avons   T/7/59
"I'm So Young"—Students   Fo/8/58
"I'm Sorry"—Bo Diddley   S/2/59
"I'm Sorry"—Platters   Fo/2/57
"I'm Sorry I Made You Cry"—Connie Francis   S/4/58
"I'm Spinning"—Dell-Vikings   F/9/57
"I'm Stickin' With You"—Jimmy Bowen   T/12/56
"I'm the One"—Jimmy McCracklin   F/6/57
"I'm Truly Truly Yours"—Robert & Johnny   T/9/58
"I'm Walkin'"—Fats Domino   T/2/57
"I'm Walking"—Ricky Nelson   S/4/57
"In Paradise"—Cookies   F/1/56
"In the Doorway Crying"—Midnighters   F/4/57
"In the Mood"—Ernie Fields   Fo/6/59
"In the Still of the Night"—Five Satins   Fo/5/56
"Ina-Dell"—Ravon Darnell   F/8/56
"Is It Real"—Bobby "Blue" Bland   F/8/59
"Is That All To The Ball"—Billy Riley   F/8/58
"Is Your Love For Real"—Midnighters   Fo/5/57
"It Ain't Me"—Ray Campi   S/8/57
"It Could Have Been Worse"—Jesse Belvin   Fo/5/59
"It Doesn't Matter Anymore"—Buddy Holly   S/1/59
"It Happened Today"—Skyliners   Fo/8/59
"It Hurts the One You Loves You"—Ray Doggett   T/4/57
"It Hurts To Be In Love"—Annie Laurie   T/1/57
"It Took A Long Time"—Lowell Fulson   T/11/59
"It Was I"—Skip & Flip   F/5/59
"It Was There"—Johnnie & Joe   F/9/57
"It's a Groove"—Five Keys   T/4/57
"It's All In The Game"—Tommy Edwards   T/7/58

"It's All Over"—Niki Sullivan   T/4/58
"It's All Right"—Solomon Burke   S/12/59
"It's All Right"—Jimmy McCracklin   F/2/56
"It's Just a Matter of Time"—Brook Benton   Fo/12/58
"It's Just My Luck to be 15"—Poni-Tails   F/9/57
"It's Late"—Ricky Nelson   F/2/59
"It's Love"—Addrisi Brothers   Fo/9/59
"It's Misery"—Bobby Hendricks   S/1/59
"It's No Wonder"—Huelyn Duvall   F/5/59
"It's Only Make Believe"—Conway Twitty   S/7/58
"It's So Easy"—Crickets   T/9/58
"It's The Truth Ruth"—Big Bopper   T/4/59
"It's Time To Cry"—Paul Anka   F/11/59
"It's Too Bad You Had To Say Goodbye"—Little Joe   S/11/58
"It's Too Late"—Chuck Willis   S/5/56
"It's You I Love"—Mickey & Sylvia   Fo/7/58
"I've Been There"—Tommy Edwards   F/7/59
"I've Come of Age"—Billy Storm   T/3/59
"I've Got Love If You Want It"—Warren Smith   Fo/1/58
"I've Got My Heart In My Hand"—Warren Storn   S/6/59
"I've Got to Have You Baby"—Pretenders   T/6/56
"I've Had It"—Bell Notes   Fo/12/58
"Ivory Tower"—Charms   S/3/56

J

"Jack O' Diamonds"—Ruth Brown   Fo/4/59
"Jack of All Trades"—Eugene Church   S/11/59
"Jailbait"—Andre Williams   F/8/57
"Jailhouse Rock"—Elvis Presley   T/9/57
"Jambalya"—Brenda Lee   T/9/56
"Jeannie Jeannie Jeannie"—Eddie Cochran   S/1/58
"Jennie Lee"—Jan & Arnie   Fo/4/58
"Jennie Lee"—Billy Ward   Fo/4/58
"Jenny Jenny"—Little Richard   T/5/57
"Jig-Ga-Lee-Ga"—Rudy Grazell   F/11/56
"Jim Dandy"—LaVern Baker   F/11/56
"Jim Dandy Got Married"—LaVern Baker   T/4/57
"Jitterbug Mary"—Del Vikings   S/6/57
"Jo-Ann"—Playmates   F/12/57
"Jodie"—Sammy Masters   Fo/9/58
"Joey's Song"—Bill Haley   Fo/7/59
"Johnny B. Goode"—Chuck Berry   F/4/58
"Johnny's House Party"—Johnny Heartsman   S/5/57
"Johnny's House Party"—Earl Palmer   S/5/57
"Jo-Jo The Dog-Faced Boy"—Annette   S/3/59
"Joker, The"—Billy Myles   F/10/57
"Jole Blon"—Waylon Jennings   S/5/59
"Juanita"—Chuck Willis   Fo/10/56
"Juice"—Al Casey   S/12/56
"Ju-Judy"—Casuals   F/6/58
"Juke Box Man"—Mel Tillis   F/7/57

"Jump for Joy"—Joe Turner F/4/58
"Jump with You Baby"—B.B. King S/1/56
"Jungle Fever"—Charlie Feathers Fo/6/58
"Jungle Hop"—Don & Dewey Fo/3/57
"Jungle Magic"—Dorsey Burnette T/2/57
"Just a Little Bit"—Roscoe Gordon T/11/59
"Just a Little Lovin'"—Don & Dewey S/12/57
"Just a Little Too Much"—Ricky Nelson T/6/59
"Just a Lonely Clown"—Huey Smith S/10/57
"Just As Much As Ever"—Bob Beckham F/6/59
"Just Ask Your Heart"—Frankie Avalon S/8/59
"Just Because"—Lloyd Price Fo/1/57
"Just Because"—Larry Williams T/2/57
"Just For You and Me"—Joe Tex S/1/58
"Just In Case You Change Your Mind"—Bobby Darin F/2/58
"Just Keep It Up"—Dee Clark Fo/3/59
"Just One Kiss"—Midnighters S/6/59
"Just To Be With You"—Passions Fo/7/59
"Just To Hold My Hand"—Clyde McPhatter Fo/3/57
"Just Young"—Paul Anka F/9/58

K

"Kansas City"—Wilbert Harrison Fo/3/59
"Keep A Knockin'"—Little Richard F/9/57
"Keep A-Lovin' Me"—Everly Brothers S/2/56
"Keep A-Movin' Me Baby"—Melvin Endsley F/7/57
"Keep On Trying"—Eddie Bo Fo/1/59
"Keeper of the Key"—Dean Beard T/11/58
"Key to the Highway"—Little Walter Fo/9/58
"Key to the Kingdom"—Nutmegs S/6/56
"King Cobra"—Wild Tones S/9/58
"King Kong"—Big "T" Tyler Fo/6/57
"King's Rock"—King Curtis Fo/3/57
"Kiss From Your Lips, A"—Flamingos F/5/56
"Kiss Me"—Johnny Burnette Fo/9/58
"Kiss Me Baby"—Four Tops S/5/56
"Kiss-a Me Baby"—Narvel Felts Fo/6/57
"Kisses Sweeter Than Wine"—Jimmie Rodgers T/10/57
"Kissin' Time"—Robby Rydell T/6/59
"Kneel and Pray"—Ravens F/8/56
"Ko Ko Joe"—Don & Dewey Fo/7/58
"Kookie Kookie Lend Me Your Comb"—Edd Byrnes & Connie Stevens Fo/3/59
"Kookie's Love Song"—Edd Byrnes S/10/59

L

"La Bamba"—Ritchie Valens S/11/58
"La Dee Dah"—Billy and Lillie T/12/57
"La Doo Dah Dah"—Dale Hawkins T/7/58
"Laid Off"—Esquirita S/2/59
"Lasting Love"—Sal Mineo T/7/57
"Later Baby"—Johnny Janis T/7/57
"Laughing on the Outside"—Harptones Fo/3/59
"Laura Lee"—Bobby Charles T/10/56
"Laurie Lee"—Glenn Glenn Fo/6/58
"Lay Your Head On My Shoulder"—Alvis Wayne S/9/58
"Lean Jean"—Bill Haley F/7/58
"Leave It To Me"—Cliff Thomas S/10/58
"Leave Me Alone"—Dicky Doo S/9/58
"Leave My Kitten Alone"—Little Willie John T/6/59
"Leave My Woman Alone"—Ray Charles S/9/56
"Leavin' It All Up to You"—Don & Dewey F/10/57
"Leaving It up To You"—Don & Dewey T/8/57
"Legend of Sleepy Hollow, The"—Monotones F/1/59
"Lend Me Your Comb"—Bernie Nee Fo/12/57
"Leotards"—Royal Teens F/2/59
"Leroy"—Jack Scott S/4/58
"Let It Be Me"—Everly Brothers T/12/59
"Let It Rock"—Chuck Berry Fo/12/59
"Let the Four Winds Blow"—Roy Brown T/4/57
"Let the Good Times Roll"—Ray Charles S/12/56
"Let the Good Times Roll"—Shirley & Lee T/6/56
"Let Them Talk"—Little Willie John S/10/59
"Let Your Conscience Be Your Guide"—Sonny Boy T/6/59
"Let's All Go Wild Tonight"—Whitey Pullen F/6/59
"Let's Do the Boogie"—B.B. King F/2/56
"Let's Get Together"—Gene & Eunice Fo/5/56
"Let's Get Wild"—Rudy Grazell T/6/57
"Let's Jump the Broomstick"—Brenda Lee T/4/59
"Let's Make It"—James Brown F/1/57
"Let's Rock While the Rockin's Good"—Little Willie John Fo/6/58
"Let's Start All Over Again"—Tony Williams T/7/57
"Let's Try Again"—Clyde McPhatter Fo/10/59
"Letter, The"—Larktones T/3/58
"Letter, The"—Medallions T/2/57
"Letter to An Angel"—Jimmy Clanton Fo/9/58
"Levi Jacket"—Carl Perkins S/7/58
"Life Is a Mystery"—Rod Bernard Fo/5/59
"Life Of Love, A"—Mark Dinning F/4/59
"Lifeguard Man"—Dale Hawkins Fo/6/59
"Lights Out"—Jerry Byrne Fo/6/58
"Like I Love You"—Edd Byrnes S/7/59
"Like You Bug Me"—Quarternotes T/12/57
"Lily Lou"—Fabian S/9/58
"Linda"—Empires Fo/1/57
"Lindy Lou"—Little Butchie Saunders F/8/56
"Linda Lu"—Ray Sharpe Fo/6/59
"Lipstick and Rouge"—Jerry Fuller T/2/59
"Lipstick On Your Collar"—Connie Francis T/4/59
"Lipstick Powder and Paint"—Joe Turner T/7/56
"Listen to Me"—Buddy Holly Fo/1/58
"Little Baby"—Tommy Facenda S/8/58
"Little Bird, A"—Hollywood Flames F/2/58
"Little Bit of Loving, A"—Little Willie John T/12/56
"Little Bitty Johnny"—Travis & Bob Fo/6/59
"Little Bitty Pretty One"—Bobby Day T/8/57
"Little Bitty Pretty One"—Thurston Harris T/9/57
"Little Boy"—Tune Weavers F/3/59
"Little By Little"—Nappy Brown Fo/11/56
"Little Chick-ee-Wah-Wah"—Huey & Jerry F/5/58
"Little Chick-ee-Wah-Wah"—Ray Stevens F/5/58
"Little Darlin'"—Diamonds T/2/57
"Little Darlin'"—Gladiolas F/2/57
"Little Darling"—Jesse Belvin F/4/59
"Little Fool"—Charlie & Ray F/3/56
"Little Girl"—Frankie Lymon S/11/57
"Little Girl of Mine"—Cleftones Fo/3/56
"Little Girl Step This Way"—Narvel Felts Fo/7/58
"Little Johnny Green"—Bobby Hendricks Fo/7/59
"Little Lover"—Dean Beard S/6/59
"Little Mary"—Fats Domino T/6/58
"Little Miss Bobby Sox"—Bonnie Lou S/3/56
"Little Miss Ruby"—Jordanaires—5/6/58
"Little Pig"—Dale Hawkins F/4/58
"Little Pigeon"—Sal Mineo F/1/58
"Little Queenie"—Jerry Lee Lewis T/9/59
"Little Red Riding Hood"—Big Bopper F/11/58
"Little Space Girl"—Jesse Lee Turner F/12/58
"Little Turtle Dove"—Bobby Day T/3/58
"Livin' Lovin' Doll"—Cliff Richard T/2/59
"Living Doll"—Cliff Richard F/8/59
"Living End, The"—Bobby Bare Fo/7/57
"Liza Jane"—Dale Hawkins F/9/59
"Lollipop"—Chordettes S/2/58
"Lonely Avenue"—Ray Charles S/9/56
"Lonely Blue Boy"—Conway Twitty S/12/59
"Lonely Boy"—Paul Anka F/5/59
"Lonely Chair"—Lloyd Price F/7/57
"Lonely For You"—Gary Stites T/3/59
"Lonely Guitar"—Annette Fo/4/59
"Lonely Island"—Sam Cooke S/2/58
"Lonely One, The"—Duane Eddy F/1/59
"Lonely Teardrops"—Jackie Wilson T/10/58
"Lonely Train"—Dorsey Burnette Fo/8/59
"Lonesome Love"—Wes Bryan F/12/57
"Lonesome Town"—Ricky Nelson Fo/9/58
"Lonesome Train"—Johnny Burnette Fo/12/56
"Long Gone Daddy"—Pat Cupp T/9/56
"Long Tall Sally"—Pat Boone T/3/56
"Long Tall Sally"—Little Richard S/3/56
"Long Tall Sally"—Marty Robbins T/3/56

"Long Lonely Nights"—Hearts F/7/57
"Long Lonely Nights"—Kings F/7/57
"Long Lonely Nights"—Little Julian Herrera Fo/9/56
"Long Lonely Nights"—Clyde McPhatter F/7/57
"Looby Doo"—Bobby Byrd T/4/57
"Look Alive"—Jimmy Gilmer T/7/59
"Look At Little Sister"—Midnighters Fo/11/59
"Look at Me"—Terry Noland F/2/58
"Look at Me"—Sharps T/7/58
"Look In My Eyes"—Jaguars F/10/59
"Lost"—Jerry Butler Fo/1/59
"Lotta Lovin'"—Gene Vincent F/7/57
"Louie Louie"—Richard Berry F/4/57
"Lovable"—Dale Cook F/3/57
"Love Bird"—Charlie Gracie S/5/58
"Love Bug Bit Me"—Lovers T/8/58
"Love Bug Crawl"—Jimmy Edwards Fo/10/57
"Love Charms"—Sanford Clark T/5/57
"Love Is A Treasure"—Mickey & Sylvia T/8/57
"Love Is All We Need"—Tommy Edwards Fo/9/58
"Love Is Everything"—Carl Dobkins Jr. Fo/5/58
"Love Is Strange"—Mickey & Sylvia T/11/56
"Love Letters In The Sand"—Pat Boone Fo/4/57
"Love Love Love"—Clovers S/5/56
"Love Made Me Your Fool"—Brook Benton Fo/7/56
"Love Me"—Buddy Holly S/4/56
"Love Me"—Impressions T/8/58
"Love Me Baby"—Marvin Rainwater S/3/59
"Love Me Completely"—Harptones Fo/9/59
"Love Me Forever"—Four Esquires F/10/57
"Love Me Tender"—Sparrows F/10/56
"Love Potion No. 9"—Clovers Fo/7/59
"Love Roller Coaster"—Joe Turner F/6/57
"Love the Life I Live"—Pipes T/8/56
"Love Walked In"—Flamingos S/8/59
"Love Will Make You Fail In School"—Mickey & Sylvia T/6/57
"Love You Most Of All"—Sam Cooke T/10/58
"Loveable"—Jerry Keller T/8/59
"Lover Boy"—Paris Sisters S/1/56
"Lovers Never Say Goodbye"—Flamingos T/10/58
"Lover's Prayer, A"—Dion & Belmonts Fo/8/59
"Lover's Prayer, A"—Medallions F/10/57
"Lover's Question, A"—Clyde McPhatter F/9/58
"Love's Made A Fool of You"—Crickets F/3/59
"Lovesick Blues"—Sonny Knight Fo/6/57
"Lovey Dovey"—Clyde McPhatter F/3/59
"Lovin' Up A Storm"—Jerry Lee Lewis Fo/2/59
"Loving You"—Elvis Presley F/6/57
"Lucille"—Little Richard Fo/2/57

"Lucky Devil"—Carl Dobkins Jr. S/11/59
"Lucky Ladybug"—Billy & Lillie F/11/58
"Lucky Lips"—Ruth Brown T/1/57
"Lulu"—Dave Burgess S/2/59
"Lulu Lee"—Bill Craddock Fo/7/58
"Luther Played the Boogie"—Johnny Cash Fo/3/59

M

"Ma He's Making Eyes At Me"—Marie Adams T/9/57
"Mack the Knife"—Bobby Darin F/8/59
"Mad Gass"—Royal Teens T/4/59
"Magic Mountain"—Medallions T/3/59
"Magic Touch, The"—Platters F/3/56
"Majesty of Love, The"—Marvin Rainwater & Connie Francis S/9/57
"Make Up Your Mind Baby"—Bob Luman S/1/58
"Makin' Love"—Floyd Robinson S/5/59
"Makin' Time"—Bobby Rydell S/2/59
"Mambo Chillun"—John Lee Hooker T/1/56
"Manhattan Spiritual"—Reg Owens F/11/58
"Margie"—Fats Domino T/4/59
"Margurita"—Chuck Rio & Originals F/2/59
"Marie"—Fidelities S/8/59
"Marty on Planet Mars"—Marty T/8/56
"Mary Ann Thomas"—Bobby Freeman Fo/4/59
"Mary Lou"—Ronnie Hawkins Fo/7/59
"Mary Mary Lou"—Bill Haley T/12/57
"Mary's Place"—Bing Day T/8/59
"Matchbox"—Carl Perkins S/2/57
"Mathilda"—Cookie & Cupcakes Fo/11/58
"Maybe"—Chantels Fo/11/57
"Maybe Baby"—Crickets Fo/1/58
"Maybe I'm Right"—Little Richard Fo/4/57
"Maybe It's All For The Best"—Hurricanes S/1/56
"Maybelle"—Dave Burgess T/1/58
"Me and My Mule"—Jack Dupree T/2/56
"Mean When I'm Mad"—Eddie Cochran F/5/57
"Mediterranean Moon"—Rays F/11/59
"Meet Me in the Alley Sally"—Billy Brown T/1/58
"Memories of You"—Fidelities F/7/58
"Memphis Tennessee"—Chuck Berry Fo/5/59
"Merry Christmas Baby"—Chuck Berry Fo/11/58
"Merry-Go-Rock"—Robins T/6/56
"Merry-Go-Round"—Eddie Holland S/5/59
"Mess Around, The"—Richard Berry F/8/58
"Message of Love"—Orbits S/1/57
"Mexican Hat Rock"—Applejacks F/9/58
"Miami"—Eugene Church T/6/59
"Midnight"—Paul Anka Fo/6/58
"Midnight"—Jodimars Fo/11/56
"Midnight Creeper, The"—Johnny Otis T/11/56
"Midnight Special"—Paul Evans Fo/12/59

"Midnight Stroll"—Revels T/9/59
"Midnight Train"—Johnny Burnette Fo/7/56
"Mighty Mighty Man"—Bobby Darin Fo/9/58
"Miss You"—Bill Haley Fo/7/57
"Missy Ann"—Mac Curtis F/3/58
"Mixed Up Rhythm and Blues"—Johnny Taylor F/6/56
"Modern Don Juan"—Buddy Holly T/12/56
"Mona Lisa"—Carl Mann F/4/59
"Mona Lisa"—Conway Twitty Fo/6/59
"Money"—Miracles T/7/58
"Moonbeams"—Picks S/1/58
"Moondreams"—Norman Petty Fo/10/57
"Moonlight Serenade"—Rivieras T/1/59
"Moose On The Loose"—Roddy Jackson S/10/58
"Mountain of Love"—Harold Dorman Fo/12/59
"Move Around"—Joe Poovey F/9/58
"Move It"—Cliff Richard T/11/58
"Movin' and Groovin'"—David Clowney S/11/56
"Movin' and Groovin'"—Duane Eddy Fo/2/58
"Movin' On"—King Curtis F/7/56
"Mr. Blue"—Fleetwoods S/8/59
"Mr. Lee"—Bobbettes Fo/5/57
"Mumbles Blues"—Bobby Lewis F/3/56
"Mumblin' Mosie"—Johnny Otis Fo/12/59
"Must Be Falling In Love"—Little Anthony T/10/58
"My Angel"—Willows Fo/6/56
"My Baby's Got Soul"—Larry Williams S/8/59
"My Biggest Mistake"—Joe Tex F/2/56
"My Blind Date"—Don Deal T/11/57
"My Blue Eyed Baby"—Ray Peterson T/7/58
"My Blue Heaven"—Bobby Day F/12/59
"My Blue Heaven"—Fats Domino T/3/56
"My Bonnie"—Ray Charles Fo/7/58
"My Brand of Blues"—Marvin Rainwater Fo/6/57
"My Broken Heart"—Teenagers T/7/58
"My Bucket's Got a Hole in It"—Ricky Nelson F/3/58
"My Confession of Love"—Donnie Elbert S/2/58
"My Dream"—Platters F/5/57
"My First Real Love"—Connie Francis S/3/56
"My Girl"—Robin Luke Fo/9/58
"My Girl"—Frankie Lymon Fo/9/57
"My Girl Friend"—Cadillacs Fo/5/57
"My Greatest Love"—Fidelities Fo/9/58
"My Happiness"—Connie Francis T/11/58
"My Happiness Forever"—LaVern Baker T/2/56
"My Heart Belongs to You"—Mary Swan F/9/58
"My Heart Cries For You"—Ray Stevens S/10/59
"My Heart Is An Open Book"—Carl Dobkins Jr. F/2/59
"My Heart's Desire"—Wheels S/4/56
"My Honey"—Jimmy Edwards T/2/58

"My Kind of Woman"—Jimmy Bowen T/9/58
"My Life"—Chuck Willis Fo/7/58
"My Life"—Howlin' Wolf F/2/57
"My Love Is a Charm"—Shirelles S/6/58
"My Own True Love"—Jimmy Clanton Fo/6/59
"My Prayer"—Platters F/6/56
"My Runaway Heart"—Trini Lopez T/1/59
"My Special Angel"—Bobby Helms T/8/57
"My Steady Girl"—Rays F/5/57
"My Story of Love"—Valentines F/10/56
"My Sugar Sugar"—5" Royales T/10/59
"My Surprise"—Six Teens T/9/57
"My Susie J My Susie J"—Bobby Lee Trammell T/9/58
"My True Love"—Jack Scott S/4/58
"My Wish Came True"—Elvis Presley Fo/6/59
"Mystery of You, The"—Platters Fo/8/57
"Mystery Train"—Vernon Taylor S/8/59

N

"Nameless"—Rockin' R's S/5/59
"Natural Born Lover"—Gum Drops Fo/9/56
"Nature Boy"—Shields Fo/10/58
"Naughty Rock & Roll"—Boyd Bennett S/11/59
"Near You"—Cardinals T/1/57
"Nee Nee Na Na Na Na Nu Nu"—Dicky Doo F/4/58
"Need For Love, A"—Marvin Rainwater S/8/58
"Need You"—Donnie Owens F/9/58
"Nervous"—Jo Ann Campbell F/3/59
"Nervous"—Gene Summers Fo/7/58
"Never Be Anyone Else But You"—Ricky Nelson F/2/59
"Never Let Me Go"—Johnny Tillotson T/11/59
"Never Let You Go"—Ambers T/3/58
"Never No More"—Colts T/5/56
"New Fad"—Dean Hawley F/7/59
"(New In) The Ways of Love"—Tommy Edwards F/10/59
"Next"—Billy Brown Fo/5/58
"Next Time You See Me"—Little Junior Parker S/1/57
"Night Theme"—Three Souls T/9/58
"Night To Remember, A"—Five Satins T/7/58
"Night Train"—Champs Fo/6/59
"Nite Owl"—Tony Allen (reissue) S/7/59
"Nite Rock"—Nite Rockers T/8/58
"No Chemise Please"—Gerry Granahan Fo/4/58
"No Money Down"—Chuck Berry T/1/56
"No More Doggin'"—Roscoe Gordon S/6/59
"No Name Girl"—Billy Riley F/2/59
"No Other One"—Connie Francis Fo/2/57
"No Regrets"—Little Willie John T/12/58
"Nobody But You"—Dee Clark Fo/10/58
"Nobody Listens to a Teenager"—Trini Lopez Fo/10/59
"Nobody's Woman"—Charlie Feathers S/3/57
"Nothin' Shakin'"—Eddie Fontaine S/7/58
"(Now and Then There's) A Fool Such As I"—Bill Haley T/3/59
"(Now and Then There's) A Fool Such As I"—Elvis Presley S/3/59
"Now That It's Over"—Falcons Fo/11/57
"Now That You're Gone"—El Dorados F/4/56
"Nowhere To Go"—Johnny Adams T/8/59
"Number One"—Etta James F/2/56
"Nursery Rock"—Jan & Joe T/6/58

O

"Odds and Ends"—Jimmy Reed F/12/58
"Off Shore"—Cardinals Fo/3/56
"Oh Baby Doll"—Chuck Berry Fo/6/57
"Oh Boy!"—Crickets Fo/10/57
"Oh Carol"—Neil Sedaka Fo/8/59
"Oh Happy Day"—Five Satins S/3/57
"Oh Julie"—Crescendos S/11/57
"Oh Lonesome Me"—Don Gibson Fo/12/57
"Oh! My Goodness"—Kalin Twins S/12/58
"Oh What a Fool"—Impalas F/6/59
"Oh What a Nite"—Dells S/8/56
"Oh Yeah"—Travis & Bob F/9/59
"Oh Yeah! Uh-Huh"—Mickey & Sylvia S/11/58
"Oh-Oh I'm Falling In Love Again"—Jimmie Rodgers S/1/58
"Oh-Well-A"—Charlie Gracie F/9/59
"Okefenokee"—Freddy Cannon F/8/59
"Ol Man River"—Tune Weavers Fo/11/57
"Old Spanish Town"—Bell Notes Fo/3/59
"Old Time Rock and Roll"—Champion Jack Dupree Fo/5/57
"Olds Mo Williams"—Paul Peek S/9/58
"On My Mind"—Darts T/11/58
"On My Word of Honor"—B.B. King Fo/10/56
"On My Word of Honor"—Platters Fo/11/56
"One Day of the Year"—Heartbeats Fo/7/58
"One Fool To Another"—Joe South S/8/58
"100 Years From Today"—Mondellos S/5/57
"One in a Million"—Platters Fo/11/56
"One Kiss Led To Another"—Coasters S/6/56
"One More Chance"—Rod Bernard S/9/59
"One More Time"—Andy Starr F/2/57
"One Night"—Smiley Lewis S/2/56
"One Night"—Elvis Presley T/10/58
"One Night Only"—Charms Fo/5/56
"One Step At a Time"—Brenda Lee T/1/57
"One Summer Night"—Danleers F/7/58
"One Ticket To Loneliness"—Carl Perkins S/8/59
"Only Jim"—Six Teens S/1/57
"Only Sixteen"—Sam Cooke T/5/59
"Only Way To Love You, The"—Frankie Lymon Fo/7/58
"Ooby Dooby"—Sid King F/5/56
"Ooby Dooby"—Janis Martin F/6/56
"Ooh Baby Baby"—Midnighters Fo/12/56
"Ooh! My Soul"—Little Richard T/5/58
"Ooh-Marie"—Dick Dale Fo/5/58
"Ooh-Sha-Lala"—Mickey & Kitty S/4/59
"Ooo Baby"—Sanford Clark T/1/57
"Oooo-Whee Baby"—Art Neville Fo/12/56
"Open The Door"—Royal Teens F/9/58
"Open Up the Back Door"—Midnighters S/3/56
"Our Anniversary"—Fiestas S/7/59
"Our Anniversary"—Five Satins F/10/57
"Our First Kiss"—Aquatones Fo/9/58
"Our Love"—Ernie Freeman T/1/56
"Our Song"—Tom & Jerry F/3/58
"Our Wedding Day"—Johnny Restivo F/11/59
"Out In The Cold Again"—Teenagers F/4/57
"Out of Sight Out of Mind"—Five Keys T/8/56
"Out of this World with Flying Saucers"—Dave Barry Fo/7/56
"Over and Over"—Thurston Harris Fo/6/58
"Over and Over Again"—Moonglows Fo/11/56
"Over The Mountain Across the Sea"—Johnnie & Joe F/3/57
"Over the Rainbow"—Gene Vincent T/2/59
"Ow-Wow"—Midnighters S/11/58

P

"Papa Daddy"—Ruth Brown F/8/59
"Paper Boy"—Roy Orbison T/9/59
"Paper Castles"—Teenagers S/2/57
"Paper Doll"—Scott Engel Fo/8/58
"Party"—Collins Kids F/10/57
"Party Doll"—Roy Brown S/2/57
"Party Doll"—Buddy Knox T/12/56
"Party Party"—Dean Beard Fo/10/57
"Party Pooper"—Bobby Lord S/3/59
"Party Time"—Sal Mineo F/10/57
"Patty Baby"—Terry Noland S/11/57
"Peace and Love"—Five Keys F/6/56
"Peaches and Cream"—Larry Williams T/9/58
"Peanuts"—Little Joe S/7/57
"Peek-A-Boo"—Cadillacs T/10/58
"Peggy Sue"—Buddy Holly Fo/9/57
"Peggy Sue Got Married"—Buddy Holly Fo/7/59
"Penny Loafers and Bobby Socks"—Joe Bennett & Sparkletones F/11/57
"Personality"—Lloyd Price S/4/59
"Petrified"—Ronnie Self Fo/8/58
"Philadelphia U.S.A."—Nu Tornados Fo/10/58
"Piano Shuffle"—Dave "Baby" Cortez F/9/59
"Pink and Black"—Sonny Fisher F/6/56
"Pink Cadillac"—Sammy Masters T/5/56
"Pink Peddle Pushers"—Carl Perkins S/3/58
"Pink Petticoats"—Big Bopper Fo/6/59
"Pink Shoe Laces"—Dodie Stevens Fo/12/58
"Plain Jane"—Bobby Darin F/1/59
"Play The Game Fair"—Shields Fo/6/59
"Playing For Keeps"—Elvis Presley F/1/57
"Playing Hard To Get"—Danny & Juniors Fo/9/59

"Plaything"—Ted Newman F/9/57
"Plaything"—Nick Todd S/9/57
"Please"—Wanderers S/1/59
"Please Be My Love"—Janis & Boyfriends S/8/58
"Please Believe Me"—Elegants Fo/9/58
"Please Don't Drive Me Away"—Charles Brown S/3/56
"Please Don't Go"—Dale Wright T/8/58
"Please Don't Say No"—Billy Ward S/3/59
"Please Love a Fool"—Meadowlarks S/6/56
"Please Mr. Mayor"—Roy Clark Fo/10/58
"Please Please Please"—James Brown F/2/56
"Please Remember My Heart"—Solitaires T/9/58
"Please Send Me Someone to Love"—Moonglows S/6/57
"Please Take a Chance"—Frankie Vally Fo/10/59
"Please Wait My Love"—Valiants S/10/58
"Pledge of Love"—Penguins F/4/57
"Pneumonia"—Joe Tex Fo/10/56
"Poco Loco"—Gene & Eunice Fo/8/59
"Pointed Toe Shoes"—Carl Perkins S/4/59
"Poison Ivy"—Coasters F/8/59
"Ponitail Partner"—Bing Day Fo/2/58
"Poor Boy"—Royaltones S/9/58
"Poor Boy"—Sugarcanes T/10/58
"Poor Jenny"—Everly Brothers T/3/59
"Poor Little Fool"—Ricky Nelson Fo/6/58
"Prayer and a Juke Box, A"—Little Anthony S/5/59
"Pretty Baby"—Addrisi Brothers T/7/58
"Pretty Baby"—Bobby Darin S/11/57
"Pretty Bad Blues"—Ronnie Self T/6/56
"Pretty Girl"—Nappy Brown Fo/3/57
"Pretty Girl"—Eddie Cochran F/6/58
"Pretty Girls Everywhere"—Eugene Church S/9/58
"Pretty Little Mama"—Joe Hinton S/4/59
"Primrose Lane"—Jerry Wallace S/6/59
"Priscilla"—Eddie Cooley T/9/56
"Prisoner's Song"—Joe Jones S/7/58
"Prisoner's Song"—Warren Smith S/7/58
"Problems"—Everly Brothers T/10/58
"Providing"—Phil Phillips Fo/12/59
"Puppy Love"—Nino & Ebb Tides Fo/9/58
"Puppy Love"—Dolly Parton S/4/59
"Purple People Eater"—Sheb Wooley S/5/58
"Purple People Eater Meets The Witch Doctor, The"—Joe South F/7/58
"Purple Stew"—Thurston Harris F/11/58
"Put Your Arms Around Me"—Pastels F/1/56
"Put Your Arms Around Me Honey"—Bobby Charles S/1/57
"Put Your Head On My Shoulder"—Paul Anka S/8/59

Q

"Queen of the Hop"—Bobby Darin S/9/58
"Quit My Baby"—B.B. King Fo/6/57

R

"Rags to Riches"—Rays F/4/58
"Rainbow Valley"—Jerry Butler S/6/59
"Raining"—Jerry Byrne T/5/59
"Raining in My Heart"—Hurricanes F/3/56
"Rakin' and Scrapin'"—Dean Beard Fo/4/57
"Ram Bunk Shush"—Bill Doggett T/1/57
"Rama Lama Ding Dong"—Edsels S/6/58
"Ramrod"—Duane Eddy S/8/58
"Rang Tang Ding Dong (I'm a Japanese Sandman)"—Cellos F/4/57
"Rattle My Bones"—Jodimars Fo/5/56
"Raunchy"—Ernie Freeman T/10/57
"Raunchy"—Bill Justis S/10/57
"Raunchy"—Billy Vaughn T/10/57
"Rave On"—Buddy Holly F/4/58
"Rave On!"—Sonny West S/2/58
"Rawhide"—Link Wray F/1/59
"Ray Pearl"—Jivers F/3/57
"Real Thing, The"—5" Royales S/12/58
"Real Wild Child"—Ivan Fo/7/58
"Real Wild Child"—Johnny O'Keefe S/5/58
"Reap What You Sow"—Gene Allison F/1/59
"Rebel Rouser"—Duane Eddy Fo/5/58
"Rebound"—Charlie Rich F/7/59
"Record Hop Blues"—Quarter Notes Fo/3/59
"Red Hot"—Bob Luman T/10/57
"Red River Rock"—Johnny & Hurricanes F/7/59
"Red Sails in the Sunset"—Joe Turner S/3/57
"Red Top"—Teen Queens Fo/8/56
"Reet Petite"—Jackie Wilson F/9/57
"Remember When?"—Platters Fo/5/59
"Respectable"—Isley Brothers F/12/59
"Respectfully Miss Brooks"—Marty Robbins T/6/56
"Return of Jerry Lee, The"—Jerry Lee Lewis Fo/6/58
"Reville Rock"—Johnny & Hurricanes F/10/59
"Riffin' With Red"—Red Prysock Fo/6/59
"Right Around the Corner"—Boyd Bennett T/1/56
"Right Behind You Baby"—Ray Smith T/6/58
"Right Girl, The"—Carole King F/5/58
"Right Now"—Gene Vincent Fo/6/59
"Right Now Right Now"—Alan Freed S/4/56
"Right Time, The"—Ray Charles Fo/11/58
"Right to Rock, The"—Trini Lopez Fo/8/58
"Ring Them Bells"—Bobby Darin T/12/59
"Ring-A-Ling-A-Lario"—Jimmie Rodgers S/5/59
"Ring-A My Phone"—Brenda Lee Fo/6/58
"Ring-A-Ding"—Tommy Sands Fo/3/57
"Ring-A-Rockin'"—Neil Sedaka S/9/58
"Rip It Up"—Bill Haley T/7/56
"Rip It Up"—Little Richard S/6/56
"Robbin' the Cradle"—Tony Bellus Fo/2/59

"R-O-C-K"—Bill Haley T/3/56
"Rock All Nite"—Shirley & Lee S/5/57
"Rock and Roll Guitar"—New Blockbusters F/12/56
"Rock and Roll Is Here to Stay"—Danny & Juniors Fo/1/58
"Rock and Roll Music"—Chuck Berry S/10/57
"Rock and Roll Party"—Red Prysock S/8/56
"Rock and Roll Polka"—Collins Kids S/10/56
"Rock and Roll Story, The"—Applejacks F/4/56
"Rock Around The Clock"—Jimmy DeKnight F/5/59
"Rock Around With Ollie Vee"—Buddy Holly S/8/57
"Rock Billy Boogie"—Johnny Burnette S/12/57
"Rock House"—Ray Charles Fo/10/58
"Rock House"—Roy Orbison S/10/56
"Rock Island Line"—Bobby Darin Fo/3/56
"Rock 'N Roll Call"—Four Tunes F/1/56
"Rock 'N' Roll Ruby"—Warren Smith S/4/56
"Rock On"—Trini Lopez S/3/59
"Rock the Joint"—Bill Haley S/10/57
"Rock Your Little Baby to Sleep"—Buddy Knox T/4/57
"Rock-A-Billy Walk, The"—Hank and Frank F/5/57
"Rock-A-Boogie Lou"—Glenn Reeves F/3/58
"Rock-A-Bye Baby"—Skeeter Bonn S/1/56
"Rock-A-Chicka"—Warner Mack T/10/57
"Rock-A-Conga"—Applejacks Fo/11/58
"Rocket Ride"—Narvel Felts T/1/58
"Rockin' Around the Christmas Tree"—Brenda Lee S/11/58
"Rockin' Country Style"—Glenn Reeves Fo/9/56
"Rockin' Daddy"—Eddie Bond Fo/4/56
"Rockin' in Baghdad"—Jerry Reed T/5/57
"Rockin' in the Jungle"—Eternals S/5/59
"Rockin' Is My Business"—Freddy Bell F/5/57
"Rockin' Little Angel"—Ray Smith T/8/59
"Rockin' Love"—Carl Mann Fo/3/57
"Rockin' Love"—Carl Mann (reissue) S/9/59
"Rockin' Mary"—Champs Fo/9/58
"Rockin' Pneumonia and the Boogie Woogie Flu"—Huey Smith S/6/57
"Rockin' the Joint"—Eqquitita Fo/9/58
"Rockin' Up a Storm"—Boyd Bennett T/10/56
"Rocky Road Blues"—Gene Vincent F/7/58
"Roll Over Beethoven"—Chuck Berry S/5/56
"Rollin' Home"—Louis Brooks & Hi-Toppers F/6/59
"Rompin' and Stompin'"—Freddy Bell F/7/56
"Roses Are Blooming"—Silva-Tones S/10/57
"Rosie Lee"—Malcom Dodds T/4/57

"Rosie Lee"—Mello-Tones T/4/57
"Rough House Blues"—Al Terry S/10/56
"Rubber Biscuit"—Chips S/10/56
"Ruby Baby"—Drifters Fo/3/56
"Ruby Pearl"—Jackie Lee Cochran F/2/57
"Rudy's Rock"—Bill Haley S/10/56
"Rumble"—Link Wray F/4/58
"Run Boy Run"—Sanford Clark F/8/59
"Run Red Run"—Coasters T/11/59
"Run Rudolph Run"—Chuck Berry Fo/11/58
"Run Run Little Joe"—Gladiolas S/5/57
"Running Bear"—Johnny Preston Fo/6/59
"Russian Bandstand"—Spencer & Spencer T/3/59

S

"Sack Dress"—Beavers S/4/58
"Sack Dresses"—Sad Sacks S/4/58
"Sam"—George Hamilton IV F/7/56
"Samson and Delilah"—Chubby Checker Fo/11/59
"Sandy"—Larry Hall Fo/8/59
"Santa and the Purple People Eater"—Sheb Wooley S/11/58
"Sassy Fran"—Danny & Juniors F/11/58
"Saving My Kisses"—Addrisi Brothers Fo/7/59
"Say! Boss Man"—Bo Diddley Fo/11/57
"Say It"—5" Royales F/10/57
"Say Man"—Bo Diddley T/8/59
"Say Man Back Again"—Bo Diddley F/11/59
"Say So"—Mac Curtis Fo/6/57
"Say Yeah"—Maurice Williams T/5/59
"Say You'll Be Mine"—Aquatones T/6/58
"Scarlet Ribbons"—Browns S/10/59
"School Day"—Chuck Berry S/3/57
"School Fool"—Mark Dinning Fo/9/57
"School Girl"—Crescendos S/3/58
"School of Rock and Roll"—Gene Summers Fo/2/58
"Scratching On My Screen"—Ric Carty F/8/58
"Scroungie"—Bill Justis F/5/58
"Sea Cruise"—Frankie Ford T/12/58
"Sea of Love"—Phil Phillips Fo/5/59
"Searchin'"—Coasters T/3/57
"Secretly"—Jimmie Rodgers T/4/58
"See You In September"—Tempos F/6/59
"See You Soon Baboon"—Dale Hawkins T/6/56
"See-Saw"—Moonglows T/7/56
"See-Saw"—Royaltones F/2/59
"Send Me Flowers"—Six Teens F/9/56
"Senorita I Love You"—Impressions T/3/59
"September Song"—Billy Ward S/12/57
"Settin' The Woods On Fire"—Johnny Burnette Fo/11/59
"7-11"—Gone All Stars Fo/11/57
"Seven Little Girls (Sitting In The Back Seat)"—Paul Evans T/8/59
"Seven Minutes in Heaven"—Poni-Tails Fo/10/58
"Seven Nights to Rock"—Moon Mullican S/3/56
"Shadow Knows, The"—Coasters T/8/58

"Shadows"—Five Satins Fo/9/59
"Shag, The"—Billy Graves S/12/58
"Shake a Hand"—LaVern Baker Fo/12/59
"Shake a Hand"—Four Lovers F/2/57
"Shake a Hand"—Little Richard S/6/59
"Shake Baby Shake"—Champion Jack Dupree S/11/57
"Shake It Up"—Conway Twitty S/7/57
"Shakey"—Bill Haley T/6/59
"Shambalor"—Sheriff & Revels Fo/1/59
"Shame On You"—Ben Joe Zeppa Fo/12/58
"Shame On You Miss Johnson"—Bobby Freeman Fo/9/58
"Shame Shame Shame"—Smiley Lewis S/11/56
"Shape I'm In"—Johnny Restivo T/7/59
"Shattered Dreams"—Youngsters F/6/56
"She Belongs to Me"—Gino & Gina Fo/7/58
"She Knocks Me Out"—Piano Red T/1/56
"She Knows How to Rock"—Little Richard S/11/58
"She Loves to Rock"—Flairs Fo/4/56
"She Say (Oom Dooby Doom)"—Diamonds S/1/59
"She's Gone Gone"—Penguins S/2/56
"She's Got It"—Little Richard F/10/56
"She's Got Me Hook Line and Sinker"—Smiley Lewis T/4/56
"She's Mine"—Joe Tex S/4/56
"She's Mine All Mine"—Royal Jokers Fo/9/56
"She's So Fine"—Cleftones Fo/7/58
"Sheik of Araby, The"—Johnny & Rebels F/11/59
"Shimmy"—Marigolds T/9/56
"(Shimmy Shimmy) Ko Ko Wop"—El Capris S/2/56
"Shimmy Shimmy Ko-Ko-Bop"—Little Anthony Fo/10/59
"Ship on a Stormy Sea, A"—Jimmy Clanton F/3/59
"Shirley"—John Fred & Playboys F/12/58
"Shirley"—Schoolboys Fo/11/56
"Shirley Lee"—Bobby Lee Trammell S/1/58
"Short Fat Fanny"—Larry Williams T/5/57
"Short Mort"—Carole King S/7/59
"Short Shortnin'"—Paul Peek T/3/59
"Short Shorts"—Royal Teens F/1/58
"Short Walk"—Sonny Knight S/8/57
"Shotgun"—Playboys Fo/10/59
"Shout"—Isley Brothers S/8/59
"Show Me"—Ruth Brown S/9/57
"Showtime"—Neil Sedaka Fo/11/57
"Shufflin' Along"—Virtues Fo/5/59
"Sick and Tired"—Fats Domino F/4/58
"Sick and Tired"—Chris Kenner T/6/57
"Silly Willy"—Bobby Darin F/9/58
"Silver Bracelet"—Ray Stevens T/6/57
"Since I Don't Have You"—Skyliners Fo/12/58
"Since I Made You Cry"—Rivieras F/12/59
"Since She's Gone"—Bobby Charles S/9/58
"Since You've Been Gone"—Clyde McPhatter T/5/59

"Sing Boy Sing"—Tommy Sands Fo/12/57
"Sister Jenny"—Johnny Fuller Fo/2/56
"Sister Jenny"—Johnny Fuller (reissue) F/10/58
"Sister Sookey"—Turbans F/2/56
"Sittin' in the Balcony"—Eddie Cochran T/2/57
"Sittin' in the Balcony"—Johnny Dee F/2/57
"Six Nights a Week"—Crests F/3/59
"16 Candles"—Crests F/11/58
"Sixteen Chicks"—Link Davis F/5/56
"16 Teens"—Rover Boys F/2/56
"Skinny Minnie"—Bill Haley Fo/2/58
"Skokiaan"—Bill Haley T/12/59
"Sky High"—Champs Fo/8/59
"Sleep Walk"—Santo & Johnny Fo/6/59
"Slouchie"—Bill Justis F/12/59
"Slow Down"—Larry Williams Fo/2/58
"Slow Down Baby"—Bruce Channel Fo/12/59
"Slow Walk"—Bill Doggett F/11/56
"Smoke Gets In Your Eyes"—Platters F/11/58
"Smokestack Lightning"—Howlin' Wolf S/2/56
"Smokie"—Bill Black's Combo S/10/59
"Smooth Operator"—Ruth Brown F/11/56
"Smooth Operator"—Sarah Vaughan F/10/59
"Sneaky Alligator"—Ellis Brothers Fo/8/58
"So Far Away"—Pastels F/10/58
"So Fine"—Fiestas Fo/1/59
"So High So Low"—LaVern Baker F/7/59
"So Lonely"—Johnny Ace F/1/56
"So Long"—Fats Domino F/7/56
"So Long I'm Gone"—Warren Smith S/5/57
"So Many Ways"—Brook Benton T/9/59
"So Much"—Little Anthony T/10/58
"So Rare"—Jimmy Dorsey T/2/57
"So Tenderly"—Mystics S/9/59
"So Tough"—Casuals Fo/11/57
"So Tough"—Cuff Links T/2/58
"So Tough"—Kuf-Linx Fo/12/57
"Soldier of Fortune"—Drifters T/7/56
"Soldier's Joy"—Jerry Reed Fo/6/59
"Solitude"—Billy Ward F/3/58
"Some Kind-A Earthquake"—Duane Eddy Fo/8/59
"Somebody Touched Me"—Buddy Knox T/7/58
"Someday"—Paris Sisters F/11/59
"Someday (You'll Want Me To Want You)"—Jodie Sands S/8/58
"Somethin' Else"—Eddie Cochran T/7/59
"Song of the Dreamer"—Billy Brooks T/2/56
"Sorry (I Ran All The Way Home)"—Impalas F/1/59
"Southern Love"—Ronnie Hawkins Fo/11/59
"Speedy"—Bobbettes F/11/57
"Splish Splash"—Bobby Darin F/6/58
"Squeeze Box Boogie"—Clifton Chenier S/1/56
"St. Louis Blues"—LaVern Baker Fo/10/57

"St. Louis Blues"—Mickey & Kitty T/8/59
"St. Theresa of the Roses"—Billy Ward F/6/56
"Stack-a-Records"—Tom Tall Fo/3/58
"Stagger Lee"—Lloyd Price T/10/58
"Stampede"—Scarlets T/10/59
"Stardust"—Billy Ward T/5/57
"Starry Eyed"—Gary Stites Fo/9/59
"Start Movin'"—Sal Mineo Fo/4/57
"Stay Beside Me"—Ritchie Valens S/10/59
"Stay Close To Me"—Lou Giordiano F/2/59
"Stay True Baby"—Dickie Lee Fo/6/57
"Steady With Betty"—Benny Joy S/2/58
"Steal a Little Kiss"—Larry Williams T/4/59
"Steel Guitar Rag"—Dynatones S/5/59
"Still As The Night"—Sanford Clark T/7/58
"Still I Love You So"—Johnny Ace T/7/56
"Stood Up"—Ricky Nelson F/12/57
"Storm, The"—Jody Reynolds S/8/59
"Storm Warning"—Mac Rebennack Fo/8/59
"Story of Love, The"—Five Keys F/1/56
"Story of My Life, The"—Marty Robbins F/10/57
"Story Of My Love, The"—Conway Twitty F/1/59
"Straight Flush"—Frantics F/5/59
"Stranded in the Jungle"—Cadets S/6/56
"Stranded in the Jungle"—Jayhawks S/5/56
"Strange Love"—Native Boys F/4/56
"Stroll, The"—Diamonds F/12/57
"Strollin' Blues"—Robin Luke S/2/59
"Stupid Cupid"—Connie Francis F/7/58
"Substitute"—LaVern Baker T/2/58
"Such a Mess"—Lloyd Price Fo/5/58
"Suffering with the Blues"—Little Willie John T/10/56
"Sugar Doll"—Johnny Jay S/11/57
"Sugar Plum"—Ray Vernon Fo/6/59
"Sugar Sugar"—Cadillacs S/2/57
"Sugaree"—Rusty York S/6/59
"Summer's Gone"—Richard Barrett & Chantels F/6/59
"Summertime"—Sam Cooke Fo/7/59
"Summertime"—Slades Fo/5/59
"Summertime Blues"—Eddie Cochran T/7/58
"Summertime Summertime"—Jamies T/7/58
"Sun Is Shining, The"—Jimmy Reed F/6/57
"Sunglasses After Dark"—Dwight Pullen Fo/2/58
"Sure of Love"—Chantels Fo/10/58
"Susie"—Willie Nelson S/8/58
"Susie Darlin'"—Robin Luke Fo/6/58
"Susie-Q"—Dale Hawkins Fo/4/57
"Susie's House"—John D. Loudermilk S/4/58
"Suzie Baby"—Bobby Vee F/8/59
"Swanee River Rock"—Ray Charles F/9/57
"Sweet and Innocent"—Roy Orbison S/10/58

"Sweet Annie Laurie"—Sammy Turner Fo/1/59
"Sweet Baby Doll"—Johnny Burnette S/7/59
"Sweet Chile"—Sheb Wooley F/4/59
"Sweet Dreams"—Crescendos T/9/56
"Sweet Georgia Brown"—Herbie Alpert F/4/59
"Sweet Georgia Brown"—Coasters F/11/57
"Sweet Home Chicago"—Little Junior Parker S/11/58
"Sweet Little Rock and Roller"—Chuck Berry T/10/58
"Sweet Little Sixteen"—Chuck Berry Fo/1/58
"Sweet Mama Do Right"—Midnighters S/1/56
"Sweet Nothin's"—Brenda Lee T/9/59
"Sweet Sixteen"—Colts S/2/56
"Sweet Sixteen"—Sounds S/2/56
"Sweet Skinny Jenny"—Paul Peek S/3/58
"Sweet Sugar Lips"—Kalin Twins Fo/5/59
"Sweet Thing"—Trini Lopez Fo/12/59
"Sweeter Than You"—Ricky Nelson T/6/59
"Sweetie Pie"—Billy Cradock F/4/59
"Swingin' Daddy"—Jimmy Bowen T/12/57
"Swinging Baby Doll"—David Gates F/2/59
"Symbol of Love"—G-Clefs T/2/57

T

"T. A. Blues"—Ray Sharpe S/10/59
"Tail Light"—Ray Peterson Fo/5/58
"Take a Message to Mary"—Everly Brothers T/3/59
"Take It Easy Greasy"—Bobby Charles T/6/56
"Take It Like A Man"—Roger Miller S/3/59
"Take Out Some Insurance"—Jimmy Reed F/4/59
"Take This Heart"—Phil Phillips S/10/59
"Talk That Talk"—Jackie Wilson Fo/10/59
"Talk To Me Talk To Me"—Little Willie John Fo/1/58
"Talkin' 'Bout You"—Ray Charles F/1/58
"Tall Boy"—Jo Ann Campbell F/12/58
"Tall Cool One"—Wailers T/5/59
"Tall Paul"—Annette Fo/11/58
"Tallahassee Lassie"—Creddy Cannon Fo/4/59
"Tarantula"—Storms T/1/59
"Taste of the Blues"—Buddy Knox T/9/59
"Teach Me Tiger"—April Stevens Fo/9/59
"Teacher's Pet"—Frankie Avalon F/9/57
"Tear Down The House"—Morty Marker F/12/58
"Tear Drop"—Santo & Johnny Fo/10/59
"Tear Fell, A"—Ivory Joe Hunter F/1/56
"Tear It Up"—Johnny Burnette T/5/56
"Teardrops"—Lee Andrews Fo/10/57
"Teardrops Are Falling"—Checkers T/4/59
"Teardrops on Your Letter"—Midnighters Fo/12/58

"Tears On My Pillow"—Little Anthony T/7/58
"Teasin'"—Quaker City Boys Fo/11/58
"Teddy Bear"—Elvis Presley F/6/57
"Teen Age Letter"—Joe Turner Fo/11/57
"Teen Age Marriage"—Ricky Shaw Fo/7/57
"Teen Angel"—Mark Dinning S/11/59
"Teen Beat"—Sandy Nelson S/8/59
"Teen Commandments"—Paul Anka George Hamilton IV and Johnny Nash Fo/10/58
"Teenage Cutie"—Lucky Wray F/4/57
"Teenage Dream"—Marty Robbins T/7/57
"Teenage Heaven"—Eddie Cochran T/2/59
"Teenage Misery"—Jesse Lee Turner S/9/59
"Teenage Queen"—Johnny Dee Fo/5/57
"Teenage Riot"—Portugese Joe F/11/57
"Teenage Rock"—Red Prysock F/11/56
"Teen-Age Teardrops"—Terry Noland F/3/59
"Teen-Age Vision"—Travis & Bob Fo/5/59
"Teenager In Love, A"—Dion & Belmonts Fo/3/59
"Teenager Sings the Blues, A"—Johnny Nash S/10/56
"Tell Her For Me"—Adam Wade T/10/59
"Tell Him No"—Travis & Bob F/3/59
"Tell It Like It Is"—Little Willie John Fo/8/58
"Tell Me"—Three Chuckles T/2/56
"Tell Me Pretty Baby"—Empires F/1/56
"Tell Me So"—Orioles Fo/2/59
"Tell Me Why"—Ral Donner F/10/59
"Tell Me Why"—Rob-Roys T/8/57
"Tell the World"—Platters F/1/56
"Ten Commandments of Love, The"—Harvey & Moonglows T/8/58
"Ten Little Women"—Terry Noland F/6/57
"Tennessee Rock 'n' Roll"—Bobby Helms F/6/56
"Tennessee Waltz"—Bobby Constock S/9/59
"Tennessee Waltz"—Jerry Fuller Fo/9/59
"Tequila"—Champs Fo/1/58
"Tequila"—Eddie Platt Fo/1/58
"Texas Flood"—Larry Davis T/9/58
"Thank You Pretty Baby"—Brook Benton Fo/6/59
"Thanks A Lot"—Johnny Cash Fo/2/59
"That Ain't Nothin' But Right"—Mac Curtis F/12/56
"That Dood It"—James Brown S/11/57
"That Old Black Magic"—Clovers Fo/5/59
"That Train Has Gone"—Chuck Willis Fo/7/57
"That Was Me"—Fiestas F/10/59
"That'll Be Alright"—Ivan Fo/1/59
"That'll Be the Day"—Buddy Holly (Decca) S/8/57
"That'll Be the Day"—Crickets F/6/57
"That's All I Want"—Bobby Day T/2/59
"That's Enough"—Ray Charles Fo/3/59
"That's Enough for Me"—Young Jesse F/10/58
"That's My Desire"—Bob & Earl Fo/9/57

"That's My Desire"—Bob & Earl (reissue) Fo/2/59
"That's My Little Susie"—Ritchie Valens S/3/59
"That's Right"—Bells Notes F/7/59
"That's The Way It Goes"—Harptones Fo/8/56
"That's The Way the Big Ball Bounces"—Frankie Starr S/1/56
"That's What I Wanna Do"—Shirley and Lee F/2/57
"That's What I'll Do"—Shirley & Lee F/2/56
"That's Why"—Jackie Wilson F/3/59
"That's Why I Cry"—Buddy Knox T/11/58
"There Are No Such Things"—Jerry Fuller F/11/59
"There Comes A Time"—Jack Scott F/9/59
"There Goes My Baby"—Drifters Fo/4/59
"There Goes My Heart"—Johnnie & Joe Fo/7/57
"There Is Something On Your Mind"—Big Jay McNeely Fo/5/59
"There I've Said It Again"—Sam Cooke T/9/59
"There Must Be A Reason"—James Brown F/2/59
"There Oughta Be a Law"—Mickey & Sylvia T/3/57
"There Stands My Love"—Tune Weavers T/6/58
"There's a Fungus Among Us"—Terry Noland Fo/8/58
"There's a Girl"—Jan & Dean Fo/9/59
"There's No Such Thing"—Jimmy Darrne T/12/58
"Thing, The"—Bill Buchanan Fo/5/58
"Things I Love, The"—Fidelities Fo/2/58
"Think"—5 Royales T/5/57
"Think It Over"—Crickets F/6/58
"Thirty Days"—Clyde McPhatter S/9/56
"Thirty-Second Lover"—5" Royales Fo/3/57
"This Broken Heart"—Sonics S/4/59
"This Day"—Falcons Fo/8/56
"This Friendly World"—Fabian T/10/59
"This Heart of Mine"—Falcons S/11/59
"This I Promise You"—Five Keys T/6/57
"This Is the End"—Buddy Guy S/3/59
"This Is The End"—Isley Brothers Fo/7/58
"This Is The Night"—Kool Gents T/6/56
"This Is the Nite"—Valiants F/11/57
"This Little Girl of Mine"—Everly Brothers S/1/58
"This Little Girl's Gone Rockin'"—Ruth Brown T/8/58
"This Old World"—Piano Red Fo/9/59
"This Should Go On Forever"—Rod Bernard F/2/59
"Thousand Miles Away, A"—Heartbeats S/10/56
"Three Bells, The"—Browns Fo/6/59
"Three Months to Kill"—Huelyn Duvall F/7/58
"Three Stars"—Tommy Dee T/3/59
"Thumb Thumb"—Frankie Lymon T/1/58
"Thunderbird"—Sonny Burgess Fo/9/58
"Tic Toc"—Lee Allen F/8/58
"Tiger"—Fabian Fo/5/59

"'Til I Kissed You"—Everly Brothers Fo/7/59
"Time After Time"—Frankie Ford S/12/59
"Time Makes You Change"—Dells Fo/10/57
"Tiny Tim"—LaVern Baker F/10/59
"Tired and Sleepy"—Cochran Brothers F/6/56
"To A Young Lover"—Tassels T/9/59
"To Be Loved"—Jackie Wilson T/1/58
"To Each His Own"—Billy Ward T/8/57
"To Have and To Hold"—John Fred & Playboys Fo/5/59
"To Keep Our Love"—Cleve Duncan T/8/59
"To Keep Your Love"—Chanticleers S/3/58
"To Know Him Is To Love Him"—Teddy Bears T/9/58
"To Our Love"—Counts F/2/56
"To the Aisle"—Five Satins Fo/5/57
"Tom Dooley"—Kingston Trio Fo/8/58
"Tom Foolery"—Monotones T/6/58
"Tomorrow"—Donnie Owens Fo/11/59
"Tonight"—Supremes Fo/7/56
"Tonight You Belong to Me"—Patience & Prudence S/7/56
"Tonight You Belong To Me"—Floyd Robinson F/11/59
"Too Much"—Elvis Presley F/1/57
"Too Much In Love"—Bill Parsons Fo/6/59
"Too Much Monkey Business"—Chuck Berry F/9/56
"Too Much Tequila"—Champs S/12/59
"Topsy"—Cozy Cole Fo/9/58
"Topsy-Turvy"—Cozy Cole T/2/59
"Tore Up Over You"—Midnighters S/5/56
"Torquay"—Fireballs Fo/7/59
"Touch of Love, The"—Kathy Linden S/9/57
"Tough Lover"—Etta James Fo/8/56
"Tough Mama"—Nitecaps F/4/56
"Tragedy"—Thomas Wayne S/6/58
"Train Kept A-Rollin'"—Johnny Burnette S/10/56
"Train To Paradise"—Robert & Johnny S/4/56
"Transfusion"—Four Jokers S/6/56
"Transfusion"—Nervous Norvus S/5/56
"Treasure of Love"—Clyde McPhatter T/4/56
"Tricky"—Gus Jenkins F/11/56
"Troubles"—Jackie Shannon S/8/59
"Troubles of the World"—Little Richard T/8/59
"Troubles Troubles"—Warren Storm T/2/59
"Troubles Troubles Troubles"—B.B. King T/4/57
"True Love"—Dean Barlow Fo/12/58
"True True Happiness"—Johnny Tillotson F/7/59
"Try"—Dorsey Burnette T/12/58
"Try Me"—James Brown F/10/58
"Try Rock and Roll"—Bobby Mitchell S/2/56
"Try The Impossible"—Lee Andrews F/4/58
"Tu-Ber-Cu-Lucas and the Sinus Flu"—Huey Smith T/9/59
"Tucumcari"—Jimmie Rodgers Fo/8/59
"Tumbled Down"—Billy & Lillie S/3/59
"Turn Me Loose"—Fabian F/3/59
"Turnabout Heart"—Jodie Sands T/9/59
"Turvy"—Cozy Cole S/11/58
"Tutti Frutti"—Pat Boone F/1/56
"Twangy"—Rock-A-Teens S/12/59
"Twenty Flight Rock"—Eddie Cochran Fo/11/57
"29 Ways"—Willie Dixon Fo/11/56
"26 Miles"—Four Preps T/11/57
"Twice As Nice"—Clyde McPhatter Fo/6/59
"Twist, The"—Midnighters Fo/12/58
"Twitchy"—Rene Hall S/12/57
"Two Timin' Woman"—Jack Scott Fo/10/57

U

"Ubangi Stomp"—Warren Smith F/10/56
"Uh-Uh Honey"—Lane Brothers F/6/57
"Unchained Melody"—Bobby Day S/9/59
"Unemployment"—Harvey & Moonglows Fo/9/59
"Unfaithful Diane"—Don Deal F/7/57
"Unforgettable"—Dinah Washington S/9/59
"United"—Charms T/5/57
"United"—Lovenotes F/5/57
"Until the Day I Die"—Teen Queens T/6/56
"Until Then"—Cookie & Cupcakes Fo/6/59
"Up Jumped a Rabbit"—Frankie Lymon Fo/1/59
"Up on the Mountain"—Magnificents S/5/56
"Uptown"—Roy Orbison Fo/11/59

V

"Valerie"—Mello-Kings F/4/58
"Valley of Love"—Turbans Fo/1/57
"Valley of Tears"—Fats Domino Fo/4/57
"Velvet Waters"—Megatrons F/4/59
"Venus"—Frankie Avalon Fo/1/59
"Virtue's Boogie Woogie"—Virtues T/7/59
"Voice, The"—Fred Paris S/2/58
"Voodoo Eyes"—Silhouettes Fo/7/58
"Vow, The"—Flamingos F/10/56

W

"Wabash Cannonball"—Dicky Doo & Don'ts Fo/12/59
"Waikiki Beach"—Paul Peek F/7/59
"Wait a Minute"—Jo Ann Campbell Fo/11/57
"Wait and See"—Fats Domino Fo/9/57
"Waitin' In School"—Ricky Nelson F/12/57
"Wake Up Little Susie"—Everly Brothers Fo/8/57
"Walk, The"—Jimmy McCracklin T/1/58
"Walkin' in a Dream"—Solomon Burke F/9/56
"Walkin' In The Moonlight"—Robin Luke F/11/59
"Walkin' To School"—Kalin Twins Fo/1/58

"Walking Along"—Solitaires (Old Town) Fo/1/57
"Walking Along"—Solitaires (Argo) Fo/9/58
"Walking in the Rain"—Mickey & Sylvia S/8/56
"Walking Through My Dreams"—Big Bopper Fo/2/59
"Walking with Mr. Lee"—Lee Allen T/11/57
"Wall, The"—Brook Benton Fo/1/57
"Waltzing Mathilda"—Jimmie Rodgers S/12/59
"Wanderin' Eyes"—Charlie Gracie S/7/57
"Wang Dang Do"—Jay Holliday T/9/57
"Warm Up To Me Baby"—Jimmy Bowen T/4/57
"Watch Your Step"—Chuck & Bill F/6/57
"Waterloo"—Stonewall Jackson F/5/59
"Way Down Yonder in New Orleans"—Freddy Cannon Fo/10/59
"Way I Love You, The"—Jodie Sands S/11/57
"Way I Walk, The"—Jack Scott Fo/5/59
"Way You Look Tonight, The"—Jaguars Fo/11/56
"Ways of a Woman in Love, The"—Johnny Cash Fo/7/58
"We Belong Together"—Robert & Johnny F/2/58
"We Belong Together"—Ritchie Valens Fo/5/59
"We Go Together"—Moonglows S/3/56
"We Got Love"—Bobby Rydell S/9/59
"We Have Love"—Jackie Wilson F/8/58
"We Want a Rock and Roll President"—Coney Island Kids T/8/56
"We Want to Rock"—Swallows Fo/5/58
"Wear My Ring Around Your Neck"—Elvis Presley F/4/58
"Wearin' Black"—Don Christy Fo/12/59
"Weekend"—Kingsmen F/7/58
"Well I'll Be John Brown"—Huey Smith Fo/10/58
"We've Had It"—Joe Bennett & Sparkletones Fo/5/58
"What a Diff'rence a Day Makes"—Dinah Washington T/4/59
"What a Little Moonlight Can Do"—Frankie Lymon S/4/59
"What Am I Living For"—Chuck Willis F/4/58
"What Can I Do"—Donnie Elbert F/4/57
"What Do You Do?"—Channels T/5/57
"What Does It Matter"—Platters S/11/59
"What Goes On?"—Five Keys F/1/56
"What Good Would It Be"—Little Jimmy Scott Fo/12/59
"What In The World's Come Over You"—Jack Scott Fo/11/59
"What Is Love?"—Playmates F/6/59
"What Is Your Decision?"—Harptones S/4/56
"What Made Maggie Run"—Dell-Vikings Fo/4/57
"What You Want"—Mac Curtis T/1/58
"What'cha Gonna Do?"—Tommy Ridgely Fo/6/57
"What'd I Say"—Ray Charles S/6/59

"What's Happened to Your Halo!"—Little Joe F/3/58
"What's the Reason I'm Not Pleasin' You"—Fats Doino F/12/56
"What's Your Name?"—Monorays S/9/58
"When"—Kalin Twins F/6/58
"When I Get You Back"—Tony Harris F/11/57
"When I See You"—Fats Domino T/7/57
"When My Dreamboat Comes Home"—Fats Domino F/7/56
"When the Saints Go Marching In"—Fats Domino T/1/59
"When You Were Sweet Sixteen"—Nino Tempo F/12/59
"Where Did Mary Go"—Flamingos S/7/58
"Where Did My Baby Go?"—Bobby Freeman S/8/59
"Where Or When"—Dion & Belmonts F/12/59
"Where There's A Will There's A Way"—Ernie K-Doe F/12/59
"Where Were You (On Our Wedding Day)?"—Lloyd Price F/2/59
"Where'd She Go"—Johnnie & Joe Fo/6/59
"Whip, The"—Originals T/8/58
"Whirlwind"—Charms Fo/8/56
"Whirlwind"—Charlie Rich Fo/10/58
"Whispering Bells"—Dell-Vikings S/6/57
"Whispering Winds"—Megatrons S/10/59
"Whistling Organ, The"—Dave "Baby" Cortez T/5/59
"White Buckskin Sneakers and Checker-Board Socks"—Bell Notes F/11/59
"White Orchid"—Donnie Brooks T/9/59
"White Sport Coat (And a Pink Carnation), A"—Marty Robbins F/3/57
"Who?"—Little Walter F/2/56
"Who Do You Love"—Bo Diddley Fo/6/56
"Whoa Mabel"—Bill Haley F/10/58
"Whole Lot of Shakin' Going On"—Jerry Lee Lewis T/5/57
"Whole Lotta Lovin'"—Fats Domino T/10/58
"Whole Lotta Shakin'"—Little Richard F/10/59
"Who's Sorry Now"—Connie Francis T/11/57
"Why?"—Frankie Avalon F/11/59
"Why Did I Fall In Love"—Jacks S/4/56
"Why Do Fools Fall In Love"—Teenagers F/2/56
"Why Do I"—Lee Andrews T/7/58
"Why Do You Have To Go"—Dells S/2/57
"Why Do You Love Me Like You Do?"—Cleftones Fo/1/57
"Why Don't They Understand"—George Hamilton IV Fo/10/57
"Why Don't You Believe Me"—Kalin Twins Fo/9/59
"Why Oh Why"—Kathy Linden F/5/58
"Wiggle Wiggle"—Accents S/10/58
"Wild Cat"—Gene Vincent Fo/11/59
"Wild Fire"—Piano Red Fo/3/57
"Will You Be Mine"—Penguins Fo/1/57
"Will You Remember?"—Billy Ward F/10/56

"Will You William?"—Janis Martin Fo/4/56
"Willa Mae"—Al Casey S/12/57
"Willie and the Hand Jive"—Johnny Otis Fo/4/58
"Willie Did The Cha Cha"—Johnny Otis Fo/9/58
"Win Your Love For Me"—Sam Cooke S/7/58
"Window Shopping"—Ray Vernon F/5/58
"Wisdom of a Fool"—Five Keys Fo/11/56
"Wish It Were Me"—Platters T/8/59
"Wishful Thinking"—Little Anthony S/1/59
"Witch Doctor"—David Seville T/3/58
"With Your Love"—Jack Scott F/9/58
"Wobble, The"—Jimmy McCracklin F/2/59
"Woe Is Me"—Bobby Lee Trammell F/5/59
"Woe Is Me"—Cadillacs F/6/56
"Woke Up This Morning"—Kripp Johnson Fo/11/57
"Wolf"—Four Mints S/11/58
"Wonder of You, The"—Pat Peterson T/4/59
"Wonderful Girl"—Five Satins T/10/56
"Wonderful Loveable You"—Teddy Bears F/5/59
"Wonderful Wonderful One"—Marvin & Johnny F/1/56
"Wondering"—Little Junior Parker Fo/4/58
"Woo Ho Ho"—Lloyd Price S/2/56
"Woo-Hoo"—Rock-A-Teens Fo/8/59
"Words of Love"—Diamonds Fo/5/57
"Words of Love"—Buddy Holly T/6/57
"Would I Be Crying?"—Flamingos Fo/11/56
"Would You Believe It (I've Got A Cold)?"—Huey Smith S/5/59
"Wouldn't It Be Wonderful"—Four Esquires Fo/10/59
"W-P-L-J"—4 Deuces T/2/56
"Wrong"—Tommy Leonetti T/3/56
"Wrong Again"—Sonny Curtis Fo/4/58

Y

"Yakety Yak"—Coasters F/5/58
"Yeah Yeah"—Billy Farrell S/2/58
"Year Ago Tonight, A"—Crests F/11/59
"Yep!"—Duane Eddy F/3/59
"Yes Indeed"—Ray Charles Fo/3/58
"Yes-Sir-ee"—Dodie Stevens Fo/4/59
"You"—Aquatones F/3/58
"Y-O-U"—Carl Perkins Fo/11/58
"You Ain't Sayin' Nothin'"—Satellites S/8/58
"You Are My Destiny"—Paul Anka T/12/57
"You Are My One Desire"—Buddy Holly F/1/58
"You Are My Sunshine"—Smiley Lewis Fo/3/57
"You Are My Sunshine"—Carl McVoy F/12/57
"You Better Know It"—Jackie Wilson T/8/59
"You Can Bet Your Life"—Little Esther T/5/56

"You Can't Catch Me"—Chuck Berry Fo/11/56
"You Cheated"—Del Vikings T/7/58
"You Cheated"—Shields Fo/6/58
"You Cheated"—Slades T/7/58
"You Done Me Wrong"—Joe Jones F/10/56
"You Don't Know Girls"—Kathy Linden Fo/6/59
"You Excite Me"—Frankie Avalon F/3/58
"You Gambled"—Slades S/11/58
"You Gave Me Peace of Mind"—Spaniels S/12/56
"You Got Me Cryin'"—Jimmy Reed Fo/3/58
"You Got What It Takes"—Marv Johnson F/9/59
"You Gotta Learn Your Rhythm and Blues"—Neil Sedaka S/5/59
"You Gotta Pay"—Benny Barnes Fo/9/58
"You Gotta Rock and Roll"—Bob Oakes Fo/4/56
"You Hit the Wrong Note Billy Goat"—Bill Haley S/5/57
"You Know (I Can't Live Without You)"—Ronnie & Rockin' Kings T/5/58
"You Know I Love You So"—Jerry Byrne S/11/58
"You Mostest Girl"—Bobby Lee Trammell F/4/58
"You Must Be Falling In Love"—Duponts T/8/56
"You Never Can Tell"—Ersel Hickey S/11/58
"You Said Goodbye"—Teddy Bears Fo/3/59
"You Send Me"—Jesse Belvin Fo/9/57
"You Send Me"—Sam Cooke F/9/57
"You Thrill Me"—Mark Dinning T/7/58
"You Want Love"—Clyde Stacey Fo/9/58
"You Went Back On Your Word"—Clyde McPhatter F/9/59
"You Were Mine"—Fireflies S/8/59
"You'll Never Know"—Platters S/9/56
"Young and In Love"—Crescendos T/10/58
"Young Blood"—Coasters T/3/57
"Young Girls"—Tony Bellus T/9/59
"Young Girls"—Marvin Rainwater S/9/59
"Young Love"—Tab Hunter T/12/56
"Young Love"—Sonny James F/12/56
"Young School Girl"—Fats Domino S/8/58
"You-oo"—Jo Ann Campbell S/4/58
"Your Book of Life"—Del Vikings F/12/57
"Your First and Last Love"—Johnny Rivers T/3/59
"Your Love"—Danleers Fo/4/59
"Your Love"—Olympics T/2/59
"Your True Love"—Carl Perkins S/2/57
"Your Wild Heart"—Poni-Tails T/1/57
"You're A Big Girl Now"—Bell Notes Fo/8/59
"You're Driving Me Mad"—Jo Ann Campbell Fo/1/58
"You're Gonna Cry"—Spaniels Fo/9/57
"You're Gonna Miss Me"—Connie Francis S/8/59
"You're Long Gone"—Joe Therrien Jr. Fo/7/57
"You're Making a Mistake"—Platters Fo/5/58
"You're Mine"—Robert & Johnny F/11/56
"You're Mine You're Mine"—James Brown S/7/57
"You're My Baby"—Night Hawks S/12/57
"You're My One and Only Love"—Ricky Nelson F/8/57
"You're So Fine"—Falcons S/3/59
"You're Something Else"—Jimmy Reed F/1/58
"You're the Apple of My Eye"—Four Lovers T/4/56
"You're the Girl"—Dave "Baby" Cortez Fo/8/58
"You're the Greatest"—Billy Scott T/11/57
"You're the One"—Jimmy McCracklin S/8/56
"You're the One"—Johnny Rivers S/10/58
"You're the One That Done It"—Thomas Wayne F/4/58
"You're The One That Done It"—Thomas Wayne (reissue) Fo/4/59
"You've Got Me Dizzy"—Jimmy Reed S/11/56
"You've Sinned"—Solitaires Fo/7/56

Z

"Zig Zag"—Bobby Constock S/2/59
"Zoom Zoom Zoom"—Collegians T/1/58

About the Author

After fourteen years in business, Lee Cotten closed his unique record store, Golden Oldies, in October 1986. He spent the next three years writing. Lee's *The Elvis Catalog*, published by Doubleday in August 1987, remains the only book dealing with the life of the singer that is authorized by the Elvis Presley estate. *Shake, Rattle & Roll*, published in March 1989 by Popular Culture Ink, also found a waiting audience. Then, in the summer of 1989, Lee went to work for a large West Coast chain of record stores in store management. In early 1993, frustrated and disillusioned by the corporate world, he returned to writing full time. Lee continues to live in Sacramento with his wife. His two children are now in college. In 1995, High Sierra Books published *Did Elvis Sing In Your Hometown?*, Lee's masterwork on Elvis' 1950s' performances (which includes over a hundred that were previously undocumented in the Elvis literature). In the immediate future, as well as beginning work on the final volume in the series on the Golden Age of American Rock 'n Roll, Lee is currently working on an update of *All Shook Up*, another of his successful books on Elvis Presley, for Popular Culture Ink.